ENGINEER DEPARTMENT, (U. S. ARMY.)

REPORT

OF

EXPLORATIONS

ACROSS THE

GREAT BASIN OF THE TERRITORY OF UTAH

FOR A

DIRECT WAGON-ROUTE FROM CAMP FLOYD TO GENOA, IN CARSON VALLEY,

IN 1859,

BY

CAPTAIN J. H. SIMPSON,

CORPS OF TOPOGRAPHICAL ENGINEERS, U. S. ARMY,

[NOW COLONEL OF ENGINEERS, BVT. BRIG. GEN., U. S. A.]

MADE

BY AUTHORITY OF THE SECRETARY OF WAR, AND UNDER INSTRUCTIONS FROM BVT. BRIG. GEN. A. S. JOHNSTON, U. S. ARMY, COMMANDING THE DEPARTMENT OF UTAH.

WASHINGTON:
GOVERNMENT PRINTING OFFICE.
1876.

OFFICE OF THE CHIEF OF ENGINEERS,
Washington, D. C., May 17, 1875.

SIR: I have the honor to submit herewith a report by Captain (now Colonel and Brevet Brigadier-General) James H. Simpson, of his Explorations in the Great Basin of Utah in 1859, with a view of recommending that it be printed.

It contains much valuable information concerning the geography, topography, geology, meteorology, zoölogy, ethnology, history, and statistics of the country through which Captain Simpson explored a route from Camp Floyd, in the vicinity of Salt Lake City, to Carson City, Nev., which was afterward known as "Simpson's route."

This was an *original* route, *i. e.*, it had not been before explored, and as it shortened the distance from the East to San Francisco more than two hundred and fifty (250) miles, it was at once adopted by the overland mail, the pony-express and the telegraph.

The report also contains a description of an exploration for a wagon-road from the valley of the Timpanogos River, over the Uintah Mountains, to the Green River, and a translation from the Spanish of the narrative of Padre Escalante of his remarkable journey from Santa Fé to Utah Lake and return by way of Oraybe (one of the villages of the Moquis), Zuñi, and Acoma, in 1776–'77.

A large part of the country traversed by Captain Simpson has not been described by any subsequent explorer; and as his report was not printed, owing to the late war coming on about the time it was completed, the valuable information it contains is not available for the use of the Government or the public.

I would therefore respectfully recommend that it be printed at the Government Printing-Office, and that 1,500 copies be furnished on the usual requisition.

By direction of Brigadier-General Humphreys, and in his absence.

Very respectfully, your obedient servant,

GEORGE H. ELLIOT,
Major of Engineers.

Hon. WM. W. BELKNAP,
Secretary of War.

Approved:
By order of the Secretary of War.

H. T. CROSBY,
Chief Clerk.

WAR DEPARTMENT, *May* 19, 1875.

TABLE OF CONTENTS.

APPENDIX K.

APPENDIX L.

APPENDIX M.

APPENDIX N.

APPENDIX O.

APPENDIX P.

APPENDIX Q.

APPENDIX R.

MAPS AND ILLUSTRATIONS.

ERRATA.

Page 6, line 5, for 5 read 385.
Page 29, bottom line, for *Rivers* read *River*.
Page 30, line 12, for *Lynogris* read *Linosyris*.
Page 31, line 8, for *Lynogris* read *Linosyris*.
Page 31, line 14, for *Epledra peduculata* read *Ephedra pedunculata*.
Page 42, line 43, for *Sangrede Christs* read *Sangre de Cristo*.
Page 45, line 25, for *lynosyris* read *linosyris*.
Page 52, line 37, for *aremost* read *are most*.
Page 55, number of page, for 5 read 55.
Page 69, line 18, for *Greator* read *Creator*.
Page 76, line 38, for *reveillé* read *reveille*.
Page 84, line 21, for *morphôsedst, ratified* read *morphosed, stratified*.
Page 95, line 19, for *Putman* read *Putnam*.
Page 110, line 36, for *Won-a-ho-pe* read *Won-a-ho-no-pe*.
Page 118, line 10, for *amp* read *Camp*.
Page 141, line 15, for *would add* read *I would add*.
Page 159, lines 2 and 6, for *Putman* read *Putnam*.
Page 162, line 5, for *Putman* read *Putnam*.
Page 163, line 15, for *Putman* read *Putnam*.
Page 164, in table, line 25, for *akaline* read *alkaline*.
Page 171, in table, line 8, for *hand* read *had*.
Page 181, line 29, for *rec ords* read *records*.
Page 192, in table, for *Fahredheit* read *Fahrenheit*.
Page 197, line 31, for *recurs* read *occurs*.
Page 211, in table, line 6, for *Bar River* read *Bear River*.
Page 234, lines 4, 5, and 21, for *Zuni* read *Zuñi*.
Page 248, line 2, for *prevalance* read *prevalence*.
Page 281, line 2, for *fragillis* read *fragilis*.
Page 309, line 9, for *cious* read *ceous*.
Page 321, line 26, for *Artimisia* read *Artemisia*.
Page 332, line 13, for *ashe* read *ashes*.
Page 414, line 34, for *thymology* read *etymology*.
Page 439, line 40, for *Bigelw* read *Bigelow*.
Page 498, line 41, first column, for *purpurens* read *purpureus*.

Page 499, line 3, second column, for 429 read 423; line 26, for *Phractocephalis* read *Phractocephalus;* line 6, from below, for *Potamocattus* read *Potamocottus*.

Page 501, line 31, first column, for *Escalanté* read *Escalante;* line 24, from below, second column, strike out *Kern, R* . . . . 483.

Page 502, line 26, for *Ute, Pete,* read *Ute Pete*.

Page 504, line 16, first column, for 294 read 295; line 18, for *Wan-a-ho-nupe* read *Won-a-ho-no-pe*.

Page 506, line 3, second column, for 996 read 296; line 26, second column, for 239 9, 251 read 239, 249, 251.

Page 507, line 7, first column, for *Bacevellia* read *Bakevellia;* line 20, first column, for *Campeloma* read *Campelona;* line 3, from bottom, for *Ventricosa* read *ventricosa;* line 9, from bottom, second column, for *Myatellinordes* read *Mya tellinoides*.

Page 508, line 20, first column, for *Phillophora* read *Phyllopora;* line 3, second column, for *Mensebachianus* read *Meusebachianus*.

Page 509, line 13, first column, for 371 read 271.

Page 510, line 27, first column, for *To-si-withes* read *To-si-witches;* line 29, first column, for 460 read 459; line 7, second column, for *Boupland* read *Bonpland;* line 19, from bottom, for *Utah* 3, 6 . . . read *Utah* 4, 6 . . .

Page 511, line 14, first column, for 121 read 120; line 13, from bottom, first column, for 272 read 262.

Page 513, top line, second column, for 254, 25 read 254, 257; line 4, second column, for *attitude* read *altitude*.

Page 516, between lines 15 and 16, first column, insert *Kern* . . . . 483; line 27, second column, for *Won-a-ho-un-pe* read *Won-a-ho-no-pe*.

Page 518, line 9, first column, for *Thornburg* read *Thornberg;* line 20, second column, for 184, 189, etc., read 142, 184, 189, etc.

LETTER OF TRANSMITTAL.

WASHINGTON, *February* 5, 1861.

SIR: Under date of December 28, 1858, I had the honor to submit to the headquarters of the Department of Utah a map and report of my explorations and opening, under instructions from Bvt. Brig. Gen. A. S. Johnston, commanding the department, of a new wagon-route from Camp Floyd to Fort Bridger, Utah, by the way of Timpanogos River Cañon and White Clay Creek, and of my explorations west of Camp Floyd, as far as Short Cut Pass, preparatory to more extended explorations during the ensuing year for a direct wagon-route from that post to Carson Valley.*

I have now the honor to submit a report and map of my explorations and opening, in 1859, of two new wagon-routes across the Great Basin of Utah, from Camp Floyd to Carson Valley, by means of which the traveling distance from Camp Floyd to San Francisco, when compared with the old Humboldt River route, has been shortened, in the case of my more northern route, 283 miles, and in the case of my more southern route, 254 miles.

The orders of the Hon. John B. Floyd, Secretary of War, sanctioning the explorations, and the instructions of General Johnston, commanding the Department of Utah, directing the movement, will be found inserted in their proper place in the sequel.

The report will be found also to include the exploration, by direction of General Johnston, of a new pass from the valley of the Timpanogos River over the Uintah range of mountains into the Green River Valley, by means of which, it is believed, a wagon-route can be obtained thence to Denver City, in Kansas, and thus, by this route, in connection with my route across the Great Basin, a more direct route be obtained across the continent to San Francisco than any which at the present time exists.

The above are the most notable results of the expedition, but embraced in the report will be found information respecting the history, geography, topography, geology, meteorology, botany, zoölogy, ethnology, and statistics of the country traversed, which will not be without interest, as I trust, to the scientific as well as popular mind.

All these subjects are indicated in the Table of Contents, and under each head, in the report, will be found presented the discussions, descriptions, pictorial sketches,

* This report forms Senate Ex. Doc. No. 40, 35th Cong., 2d Sess.

diagrams, and tables necessary to an elucidation and comprehension of the various topics growing out of the explorations.

To my assistants, Lieuts. J. L. Kirby Smith and H. S. Putnam, of the Corps of Topographical Engineers; Mr. Henry Engelmann, geologist, meteorologist, and botanical collector; Mr. Charles S. McCarthy, taxidermist; Messrs. Edward Iagiello and William Lee, chronometer-keepers and meteorological assistants; and Mr. H. V. A. Von Beckh, artist, I hereby tender my thankful acknowledgments for faithful and efficient services rendered. The work performed by each will appear generally in the sequel, to which I refer for proof of the useful character and merit of their respective labors.

Lieutenants Smith and Putnam having, under my instructions, had an opportunity to practice for more than a month with the sextant, astronomical transit, unifilar magnetometer, and dip-circle, at Fort Leavenworth, before the Utah forces destined for Utah in the spring of 1858 took up the line of march for that Territory, and practicing with these instruments again on the march to Utah, they became so dexterous in their use as to make it unnecessary for me to have anything more than a general supervision over their observations subsequently across the Great Basin. To Lieutenant Smith, therefore, were intrusted the daily observations with the sextant for latitude and longitude, and to Lieutenant Putnam the occasional observations with the transit of moon and moon-culminating stars for longitude, and with the magnetometer and inclinometer, or dip-circle, for the intensity, declination, and dip of the magnetic needle.

In the "lunars" for longitude both would assist me, three sextants being used, they taking the altitude and I the angular distance, and all at the same instant of time. The other duties performed by these gentlemen will appear noted in the mention made in the journal of the organization at Camp Floyd of the expedition.

The very valuable contributions to my report by Mr. Henry Engelmann, in respect to the geology and meteorology, and by Mr. F. B. Meek, of the paleontology of the country, from Fort Leavenworth to the Sierra Nevada, and especially of that hitherto *terra incognita* in these respects, the Great Basin of Utah, I feel assured, will be readily acknowledged by all who take an interest in such subjects.

To Mr. Von Beckh I am indebted for the original sketches of scenery, and to Mr. John J. Young, of this city, for the very handsome manner in which they have been elaborated and perfected in the office for my report. I carried out with me a photographic apparatus, carefully supplied with the necessary chemicals by Mr. E. Anthony, of New York, and a couple of gentlemen accompanied me as photographers; but although they took a large number of views, some of which have been the originals from which a few accompanying my journals have been derived, yet, as a general thing, the project proved a failure. Indeed, I am informed that in several of the Government expeditions a photographic apparatus has been an accompaniment, and that in every instance, and even with operators of undoubted skill, the enterprise has been attended with failure. The cause lies in some degree in the difficulty, in the field, at short notice, of having the preparations perfect enough to insure good pictures, but chiefly in the fact that the camera is not adapted to distant scenery. For objects very close at hand, which of course correspondingly contracts the field of vision, and for single portraits of persons and small groups, it does very well; but as, on exploring expeditions, the chief *desideratum* is to daguerreotype extensive mountain-chains and other notable objects having considerable extent, the camera has to be correspondingly distant to take in the whole field, and the consequence is a want of sharpness of outline, and in many instances, on account of the focal distance not being the same for every object within the field of view, a blurred effect, as well as distortion of parts. In my judgment, the camera is not adapted to explorations in the field, and a good artist, who can sketch readily and accurately, is much to be preferred.

The contributions of Dr. George Engelmann upon the botany, Professor Spencer F. Baird on the ornithology, and of Mr. Theodore Gill on the ichthyology of the country traversed by the expedition, will also command attention, on account of the well-earned reputation of these gentlemen in their several special branches of scientific inquiry.

I must also draw attention to the contribution of Dr. Garland Hurt, in respect to the statistics and resources of Eastern Utah and the history and present condition of the Indian tribes inhabiting the Territory of Utah. The residence of this gentleman for several years in Utah as Indian agent, and his well-known intelligence and probity, give his statements a value which I am pleased here to acknowledge.

I must also express my thanks to Maj. Frederick Dodge, the General Government agent of the Washoe and Pi-Ute Indians, for information in relation to these Indians and the vocabularies of their languages, to be found appended to my report. The courteous treatment of my party by this gentleman on our arrival at Genoa, in Carson Valley, and afterward, was a cordial which can never be forgotten.

I also present my grateful acknowledgments to Mr. Edward M. Kern for his very valuable journal of his exploration of the Humboldt River, Carson Lake, and Owen's River and Lake in 1845, under Capt. John C. Frémont, Corps Topographical Engineers, now for the first time given to the public. The fact that this exploration under the authority of the War Department was the original source of the information and maps which we have of this particular portion of our country, gives it a peculiar value which all must acknowledge.

I would also draw attention to the map, synopsis, and extracts from the diary of Father Escalante's journey from Santa Fé to Utah Lake, and thence back to Santa Fé, by way of the Moqui country and the Indian *pueblos* of Zuñi and Acoma, in 1776–'77, by Mr. Philip Harry, of the Bureau of Topographical Engineers. Mr. Harry, at my solicitation, has done good service in the cause of geographical history, in translating the manuscript of this Spanish Franciscan monk, and now for the first time presenting extracts from it to the public, with a sketch plotted by him from this father's notes. The manuscript was kindly placed at my disposal for the purpose stated by Col. Peter Force, of this city, whose well-stocked library has before been drawn upon by officers of our corps for information in relation to the early history of our country. In the introduction to my report, it will be noticed that, before giving a general description of the physical characteristics of the Great Basin, I have gone fully into the history of all the explorations that have been made in it from the time of Escalante to the present period, which I trust will not prove unacceptable to all who take an interest in such researches.

I must also express my acknowledgments of cheerful service rendered by my assistant in the office, Lieut. Charles R. Collins, Corps Topographical Engineers, and Mr. J. R. P. Mechlin, of this city, in the aid they have given in the computation of scientific data and the draughting of the maps and profiles which accompany my report.

I should also fail in my obligations did I not bring to the notice of the War Department the very valuable assistance I received in the prosecution of my duties in the field from Lieut. Alexander Murry, Tenth Infantry, the commander of the escort accompanying the expedition. Lieutenant Murry is an officer of great energy, and zealous in the promotion of the best interests of the service; and it is a gratification to me to present him thus honorably to the consideration of the Government.

I have the honor to be, sir, very respectfully, your obedient servant,

J. H. Simpson,

Captain Corps Topographical Engineers, United States Army.

Col. J. J. Abert,

Chief Corps Topographical Engineers.

EXPLORATIONS ACROSS THE GREAT BASIN OF UTAH.

INTRODUCTION

TO

REPORT AND JOURNAL.

INTRODUCTION.

HISTORY OF THE EXPLORATIONS WITHIN THE GREAT BASIN OF THE TERRITORY OF UTAH, FROM THE TIME OF FATHER ESCALANTE, IN 1776, TO THE PRESENT PERIOD, AND A GENERAL DESCRIPTION OF THE COUNTRY.

The country known since the date of the explorations of Frémont, in 1843 and 1844, and by his appellation, as the Great Basin, has been, since the days of Fathers Sylvester Velez Escalante, and Francisco Atanacio Dominguez, in 1776, one of great interest.[a] This interest has grown out of the circumstance of its reported inaccessibility from extended deserts, its occupancy by Indians of an exceedingly low type, and the laudable curiosity, which prevails in the minds of men, to know the physical characteristics of a country which has so long remained a *terra incognita*.

This Great Basin has a triangular shape, nearly that of a right-angled triangle, the mountains to the north of the Humboldt River and of Great Salt Lake constituting the northern limit or border, and forming one leg of the triangle; the Sierra Nevada, or western limit, the other equal leg; and the Wahsatch range at the eastern, and (in continuation) the short mountain ranges and plateau country to the north of and not far distant from the Santa Fé and Los Angeles caravan or Spanish trail route to the southeast, the hypothenuse. These limits are embraced approximately within the 111th and 120th degrees of west longitude from Greenwich, and the 34th and 43d of north latitude, or within a limit of nine degrees of longitude and nine of latitude.

The earliest records we have of any examination of any portion of this Basin is derived from the journal of Father Escalante, descriptive of the travels of himself and party in 1776–'77, from Santa Fé to Lake Utah (by him called *Laguna de nuestra Señora de la merced de Timpanogotyes*, and also Lake Timpanogo), and thence to Oraybe, one of the villages of the *Moquis*, and back to Santa Fé. A manuscript of

(*a*) Humboldt, in his "New Spain," translated by John Black, vol. 1, second edition, London, 1814, chap. II, p. 22, says: "These regions," referring to those between the Colorado and Lake Timpanogos (Utah Lake), "abounding in rock-salt, were examined in 1777 by two travelers, full of zeal and intrepidity, monks of the order of Saint Francis, Father Escalante and Father Antonio Velez." According to the manuscript narrative of these travels by Father Escalante, referred to subsequently in this report, and which I have consulted, I find that Friar Francisco Atanacio Dominguez, and not Velez, was associated with Escalante in these explorations, and that no such person as Velez accompanied the expedition. It is something singular, however, that Escalante's name was Silvester *Velez* Escalante. Can it be that Humboldt has fallen into the error of making two distinct persons out of this father's name, and of omitting that of Dominguez altogether? Or did a monk by name Antonio Velez explore this same region separately from the others and in the same year? I notice, also, that Humboldt dates Escalante's journey A. D. 1777. The manuscript shows that it was commenced July 29, 1776, and terminated in January, 1777.

this journey in the Spanish language is to be found in the rare and valuable library of Col. Peter Force, city of Washington, to which, agreeably to his well-known liberality, I have had ready access, and from which has been extracted for this report the valuable summary to be found, marked Appendix R, and for which I am indebted to the zealous co-operation of Mr. Philip Harry of the Bureau of Topographical Engineers. There will also be found in Mr. Harry's paper an extract from the manuscript, descriptive of Lake Utah and its valley, which Escalante explored as far north, doubtless, as the Timpanogos River (by him called the Rio San Antonio de Padua), and an allusion to the outlet of Lake Utah into a large body of salt water farther north, without question Great Salt Lake.

The destination of Escalante, his journal shows, was Monterey, on the Pacific coast; but being forced, doubtless by the desert immediately west of Lake Utah, to take the so-called southern or Los Angeles route, which Bonneville's party in 1834 and Frémont in 1844 followed, and finding that, while making a great deal of southing, he had made but little progress toward Monterey, his provisions giving out, and he fearing the approach of winter, with some difficulty he prevailed upon his party to abandon the idea of reaching Monterey, and to return to Santa Fé by the way of the villages of the Moquis and of Zuñi. (See the map of his route, Plate I, Appendix R.)

The next authentic record which shows that any portion of the Great Basin system was explored at an early date is to be found on the map entitled *Appendiente al Diario que formo el P. F. Pedro Font del Viaye que hizo á Monterey y Puerto de San Francisco, y del Viaye que hizo el P. Garces al Moqui*, "*P. F. Petrus Font fecit Tubutana anno* 1777;" which may be freely translated as follows: "A supplement to the diary of Father F. Pedro Font's journey to Monterey and San Francisco, and of Father Garces's to Moqui, executed by P. F. Petrus Font, at Tubutana, in the year 1777."[b]

According to this map, it appears that Father Garces traveled as early as 1777 (Humboldt says in 1773)[c] from the mission of San Gabriel, near the Pacific coast, in California, to Oraybe, one of the villages of the Moquis, and that his route was along the Rio de los Matires (evidently, from its position, the Mojave). Frémont and others supposed that the Mojave was a tributary of the Colorado, and therefore did not belong to the Great Basin system; but this idea was exploded by Lieutenant William-

(*b*) A copy of this map is in the Bureau of Topographical Engineers, it having been furnished by Capt. E. O. C. Ord, Third Artillery, from an original one in the archives of California, and is quite interesting as showing the large number of Spanish settlements in Middle Sonora at the time of the travels of Fathers Font and Garces, and the exact routes explored by them.

According to Humboldt, Father Garces was the principal personage in these explorations, and to Father Font were intrusted the observations for latitude. Greenhow, in his Oregon and California, 4th ed., p. 114, speaking of the journals of Friars Escalante and Dominguez, and of Friars Garces and Font, says, "They are still preserved in manuscript in Mexico, where they have been consulted by Humboldt and other travelers, but they are, from all accounts, of no value." In regard to the journal of Escalante, Mr. Greenhow's criticism is unjust, for not only is this journal written in a plain, unpretending, direct manner, but it abounds in excellent and apparently just observations and facts; and it is wonderful that the courses and distances given by him from Utah Lake back to Santa Fé, by way of Oraybe and Zuñi, should plot so correctly, and should agree so well as they do with our present maps. And in regard to the journal of Friars Garces and Font, Humboldt, in speaking of the *Chronica* from which he derives his information respecting the travels of these monks, expressly states that "it forms a large folio volume of 600 pages, and is well-deserving of an extract being made from it." He goes on to say: "It contains very accurate geographical notions as to the Indian tribes inhabiting California, Sonora, the Moqui, Nabojoa, and the banks of the Gila." (See note, Humboldt's New Spain, vol. II, p. 253.)

(*c*) See his New Spain, vol. II, page 268.

son, Topographical Engineers, in 1853,[d] and afterward by Lieutenant Parke, Topographical Engineers, in 1855,[e] both of whom fully determined that this stream sank, and that intervening it and the Colorado was a ridge which separated these waters.

In this connection, it may be interesting to observe that Humboldt, speaking of the delay on the part of the Spaniards, notwithstanding their enterprising spirit, in opening communications between New Mexico and California, holds the following language:

"The letter post still (at the date of his researches in 1803–'04) goes from this port (San Diego) along the northwest coast to San Francisco. This last establishment, the most northern of all the Spanish possessions of the new continent, is almost under the same parallel with the small town of Taos, in New Mexico. It is not more than 300 leagues distant from it, and though Father Escalante, in his apostolical excursions in 1777, advanced along the western bank of the river Zaguananas toward the mountains *de los Guacaros*, no traveler has yet come from New Mexico to the coast of New California. This fact must appear remarkable to those who know, from the history of the conquest of America, the spirit of enterprise and the wonderful courage with which the Spaniards were animated in the sixteenth century. Hernan Cortez landed for the first time on the coast of Mexico, in the district of Chalchinhcuecan, in 1519, and in the space of four years had already constructed vessels on the coast of the South Sea, at Zacatula and Tehuantepec.

"In 1537, Alvar Nuñez Cabeza de Vaca appeared, with two of his companions, worn out with fatigue, naked, and covered with wounds, on the coast of Caliacan, opposite the peninsula of California. He had landed with Panfilo Narvaez in Florida, and after two years' excursions, wandering over all Louisiana and the northern part of Mexico, he arrived at the shore of the great ocean in Sonora. This space which Nuñez went over is almost as great as that of the route followed by Captain Lewis from the banks of the Mississippi to Nootka and the mouth of the river Columbia.[f] When we consider the bold undertakings of the first Spanish conquerors in Mexico, Peru, and on the Amazon River, we are astonished to find that for two centuries the same nation could not find a road by land in New Spain from Taos to the port of Monterey."[g]

Humboldt here was undoubtedly in error. The map of Father Font, before referred to, shows that as early as 1777 Father Garces traveled from the mission of San Gabriel, near the Pacific coast, to Oraybe, one of the villages of the Moquis, in New Mexico, and the inscription on the rock "*El Moro*," near Zuñi, in New Mexico, an account and transcript of which I give in my "Journal of a military reconnaissance from Santa Fé to the Navajo country in 1849,"[h] show that there was as early as 1716 a communication opened with the Moquis from Santa Fé. The inscription is as follows: "In the year 1716, upon the 26th day of August, passed by this place

(*d*) Pacific Railroad Reports, vol. V, pages 33 and 34.

(*e*) Pacific Railroad Reports, vol. VII, page 3.

(*f*) "This wonderful journey of Captain Lewis was undertaken under the auspices of Mr. Jefferson, who by this important service rendered to science has added new claims on the gratitude of the savans of all nations." (Note by Humboldt.)

(*g*) Humboldt's New Spain, vol. ii, pp. 289–290.

(*h*) See Sen. Ex. Doc. 64, 31st Cong., 1 sess., p. 123, or same published by Lippincott, Grambo & Co., 1852, p. 104.

Don Felix Martinez, governor and captain-general of this kingdom, for the purpose of reducing and uniting Moquis—" (a couple of words here not decipherable). The manuscript of Father Escalante's journal before referred to also shows that there was a well-known road from Oraybe, *via* Zuñi, to Santa Fé, and which his party followed. These facts show that at least as early as 1777, and most probably as early as 1773 (the date according to Humboldt of Garces's journey to Oraybe), there was a communication all the way from Santa Fé, and without doubt from Taos, *via* Moqui, to San Gabriel; and, as Father Font's map shows, even all the way to Monterey and the bay of San Francisco.

The next published account of the earliest discoveries of any portion of the Great Basin of Utah, which has aided me very much in my historical investigations, I find, in the most excellent memoir of Lieut. Gouverneur K. Warren, Corps Topographical Engineers, United States Army, exhibiting the data and authorities from which was compiled the map of the United States territory between the Mississippi River and the Pacific Ocean, intended to illustrate the reports upon the Pacific Railroad explorations. In this memoir, which shows great labor and research, is a letter to Lieutenant Warren from Mr. Robert Campbell, a well-known gentleman of Saint Louis, who has been connected with the fur-trade in the tramontane region of the West. In this letter Mr. Campbell gives verbatim the statement of Mr. James Bridger,[i] corroborated by Mr. Samuel Tolleck, both Indian traders, to the effect that he (Bridger) was the first discoverer of Great Salt Lake, in the winters of 1824 and 1825.[k]

(*i*) Lieutenant Warren's Memoir, vol. xi, Pacific Railroad Reports, p. 35.

(*k*) Mr. Bridger further states, in Mr. Campbell's letter, that "in the spring of 1826 four men went in skin boats around it to discover if any streams containing beaver were to be found emptying into it, but returned with indifferent success." Washington Irving, in his "Bonneville's Adventures," revised edition of 1849, page 186, says: "Captain Sublette, in one of his early expeditions across the mountains, is said to have sent four men in a skin canoe to explore the lake, who professed to have navigated all round it, but to have suffered excessively from thirst, the water of the lake being extremely salt, and there being no fresh streams running into it."

Captain Bonneville doubts this report, or that the men accomplished the circumnavigation, "because," he says, "the lake receives several large streams from the mountains which bound it to the east."

It would thus appear that Sublette, in all probability, was the person who sent out the four men referred to by Bridger, in a skin canoe, to explore the lake; and, though Bonneville doubts the report of the occurrence, yet the testimony of Bridger is corroborative of it, and the circumstance of its being an actual fact that there are no streams coming into the lake on its west shore, along its whole length, and Captain Stansbury, as he says, in his survey of the lake in 1850 (see his report, page 103), "having frequently found it necessary to make a voyage of fifty miles to obtain a supply even for a few days," certainly account for the thirst of Sublette's party. It may be true that Sublette's party did not discover the fresh-water streams running into the lake from the south and east which Bonneville speaks of; but this only shows that they did not explore the lake *thoroughly*, not that they did not explore it at all. In this connection, however, I think it proper to insert the following communication of a Mr. W. Marshall Anderson, taken from the National Intelligencer, which, it will be perceived, claims for both Messrs. Ashley and Provost the credit of prior discovery of Great Salt Lake to either Bridger or Bonneville:

"'WHO DISCOVERED SALT LAKE?

"'Among the 'thousand and one' articles of freight and baggage which went down to the bay by the steamer Queen City yesterday, were two old flint-lock, smooth-bore rifles of the real old 'Kaintuck' stripe. They were brought on board by a man who looked as weather-beaten, flinty-locked, and hard-stocked as themselves. Being curious to learn their history, and who it was that possessed them, we made a few inquiries, and the owner, being mellowed by the genial influences of the corn-vintage, communicated the following facts: His name was Seth Grant, a Scotchman by birth, who came to America at an early age, in the year 1819, and joined the American Fur Company. In 1826 he accompanied Bridger—the founder of Fort Bridger—and his partner, Colonel Vasquez, to the then unknown wilds of the West, far beyond the headwaters of the Platte or Yellowstone. It was on one of these fur-seeking, marauding expeditions that the Frenchman, Colonel Vasquez, while out on an excursion, discovered the Great Salt Lake of Utah. The immense extent of the lake, with its mountains and islands, so deceived Vasquez and his party that they reported to their fellows that they had discovered an arm of the Pacific Ocean, and so, indeed, it seemed, for it was years before the error was

The next authentic account of any discoveries within the Great Basin I find given in "Bonneville's Adventures," by Washington Irving. Colonel Bonneville, it would appear, was the first explorer to cross, in 1832, the Rocky Mountains into the valley of Green River, *with wagons*.[1] To quote from Irving:

"On the 24th July, 1833, by his (Captain Bonneville's) orders, a brigade of 40 men set out from Green River Valley to explore the Great Salt Lake. They were to make the complete circuit of it, trapping on all the small streams which should fall in their way, and to keep journals and make charts calculated to impart a knowledge of the lake and the surrounding country. All the resources of Captain Bonneville had been taxed to fit out this favorite expedition. The country lying to the southwest of the mountains, and ranging down to California, was as yet almost unknown; being out of the buffalo range, it was untraversed by the trapper, who preferred those parts of the wilderness where the roaming herds of that species of animal gave him comparatively an abundant and luxurious life. Still, it was said the deer, the elk, and the big horn were to be found there, so that, with a little diligence and economy, there was

corrected. The two rifles in possession of Mr. Grant were a portion of the arms of the original party, and bore the marks of having seen long and honorable service. Mr. Grant values them highly, and being on his way back to his own native land, intends taking them as trophies, to be hung up with the tartans and claymores of his countrymen.'—*Sacramento Standard.*

"SEVEN OAKS, *February* 16, 1860.

"*Messrs. Editors of the National Intelligencer:*

"Allow me to call your attention to the above paragraph, credited to the Sacramento Standard. The writer, on the authority of a Mr. Seth Grant, says that my old friend Vasquez, of the Rocky Mountains, was the discoverer of the Great Salt Lake, of Utah. The honor could not possibly have been bestowed upon a worthier man. Can this geographical fact be now ascertained and settled beyond dispute? Was Colonel Vasquez the discoverer of that remarkable body of water? My answer is, no. I not only doubt, but I emphatically deny, that statement. A little more than a quarter of a century ago I heard the very subject of the priority of its discovery debated by old mountaineers, almost in the vicinity of the lake itself. To furnish better proof than unassisted memory, I send you the following extract from a letter written by me in 1837, at the request of the venerable Skinner, and published in the 8th volume of the American Turf Register:

"'Here, for a time, I will end my description of the animals of the boundless prairies, and here, too, I will end this hasty letter, after protesting, solemnly protesting, against an act of injustice done to a numerous, brave, and adventurous class of our western citizens, by our much admired Irving, or by Captain Bonneville through him. In the name of Sublette, Fitzpatrick, Fontinelle, Deippes, Bridger, and Campbell, I protest against the name 'Lake Bonneville,' given by the author of 'Astoria' and the 'Rocky Mountains' to that great inland sea, the 'Urimiah' of our continent. In the name of Ashley, who had described this lake eighteen or twenty years before Captain Bonneville ever crossed the mountains, I protest against that name. What justice, what honor can there be, in claiming the right of naming that 'wonder of the western waters' after Bonneville, when it had been found, circumambulated, and trapped on as early as 1820 by Provost? This lake was once called 'Ashley,' and with much more propriety, high and respected as is the authority of Irving. '*Fiat justitia.*'"

"The above was written at the time indicated, from my journal-notes, taken down in the presence of the interlocutors in 1834. Provost was then 'no more.' Neither praise nor censure could reach him. His survivors and brothers in the hardships and hazards of mountain life gave to him alone the credit of having discovered and made known the existence and whereabouts of that inland sea. Notwithstanding the positive assertion of Seth Grant, 'made under the genial influence of the corn-vintage,' I deny its truth. I will not pursue the subject further than to add that only eight years had elapsed since Vasquez and his companions had come upon 'that arm of the Pacific Ocean,' and yet he, then present, made no claim, and his associates, and equals, of both the American and Rocky Mountain Fur Companies, with whom he was the general favorite, did not assign him even a secondary honor.

"Confidently appealing to my surviving friends and acquaintances of the mountains for correction or confirmation, I assure you, gentlemen, of the reverential esteem of

"W. MARSHALL ANDERSON."

(*l*) "Captain Bonneville now considered himself as having fairly passed the crest of the Rocky Mountains, and felt some degree of exultation in being the first individual that had crossed, north of the settled provinces of Mexico, from the waters of the Atlantic to those of the Pacific, with wagons. Mr. William Sublette, the enterprising leader of the Rocky Mountain Fur Company, had two or three years previously reached the valley of the Wind River, which lies on the northeast of the mountains, but had proceeded with them no farther." (Bonneville's Adventures, rev. ed., p. 61.)

no danger of lacking food. As a precaution, however, the party halted on Bear River, and hunted for a few days, until they had laid in a supply of dried buffalo meat and venison; they then passed by the headwaters of the Cassie River, and soon found themselves launched on an immense sandy desert. Southwardly, on their left, they beheld the Great Salt Lake, spread out like a sea, but they found no stream running into it. A desert extended around them, and stretched to the southwest as far as the eye could reach, rivaling the deserts of Asia and Africa in sterility. There was neither tree nor herbage, nor spring, nor pool, nor running stream, nothing but parched wastes of sand where horse and rider were in danger of perishing.

"Their sufferings at length became so great that they abandoned their intended course, and made toward a range of snowy mountains, brightening in the north, where they hoped to find water. After a time they came upon a small stream, leading directly toward these mountains. Having quenched their burning thirst, and refreshed themselves and their weary horses for a time, they kept along this stream, which gradually increased in size, being fed by numerous brooks. After approaching the mountains it took a sweep toward the southwest, and the travelers still kept along it, trapping beaver as they went, on the flesh of which they subsisted for the present, husbanding their dried meat for future necessities.

"The stream on which they had thus fallen is called by some Mary's River, but is more generally known as Ogden's River, from Mr. Peter Ogden, an enterprising and intrepid leader of the Hudson's Bay Company, who first explored it."[m] * *

"The trappers continued down Ogden's River, until they ascertained that it lost itself in a great swampy lake, to which there was no apparent discharge. They then struck directly westward across the great chain of California mountains intervening between these interior plains and the shores of the Pacific.[n]

"For three and twenty days they were entangled among these mountains, the peaks and ridges of which are in many places covered with perpetual snow. Their passes and defiles present the wildest scenery, partaking of the sublime rather than the beautiful, and abounding with frightful precipices. The sufferings of the travelers among these savage mountains were extreme; for a part of the time they were nearly starved. At length they made their way through these, and came down upon the plains of New California, a fertile region extending along the coast, with magnificent forests, verdant savannas, and prairies that look like stately parks. Here they found deer and other game in abundance, and indemnified themselves for past famine. They now turned toward the south, and, passing numerous small bands of natives posted upon various streams, arrived at the Spanish village and post of Monterey."[o]

It would thus seem that Walker and his party failed in exploring around the west portion of the Great Salt Lake on account of the desert in that region, and were forced to take a route along the northern section of the Great Basin to California; and it is

(*m*) Since the explorations of Frémont in 1845-'46, this river has been known altogether by emigrants and others as the Humboldt River, the name Frémont gave it.

(*n*) Irving is here in error. Walker did not go directly *westward* from the Swamp (sink) of the Ogden's River (the Humboldt) across the great chain of California mountains (the Sierra Nevada), but striking southwardly, continued down along their *east* side for nearly 5° of latitude before he crossed them, near their southern termination, by a pass since known as Walker's Pass. I get this information from Mr. E. M. Kern, the assistant of Frémont, who ten years subsequently was guided by Walker over this very route. (See Kern's Journal, Appendix Q.)

(*o*) Bonneville's Adventures, pp. 326-328.

represented by Irving that on their return they turned the Sierra Nevada at its southern extremity. This being the case, it is likely they took the Spanish trail route, which Frémont, ten years after, in 1844, followed, and on which, at Vegas de Santa Clara, he was overtaken by this same Joseph Walker, in charge of a trading-party.

The next authentic account we have of any explorations of the Great Basin is from the report by Colonel Frémont of his expedition, in 1843–'44, to Oregon and California, through the South Pass, where, on the 6th September, of the former year, he attained the summit of a butte near the mouth of Weber River, whence he saw, for the first time, the waters of Great Salt Lake.[p]

Forming an encampment near the mouth of the Weber, he remained in the vicinity a few days to make some observations and take a hasty sketch of the lake.

Subsequently, in continuation of his expedition, he explored in the following winter from Fort Vancouver along the east base of the Sierra Nevada, or along what may be called the northwestern edge of the Great Basin, as far as the vicinity of Johnson's Pass, where he crossed the Sierra to the valley of the Sacramento. On his return east in the spring of 1844 he turned the Sierra Nevada at its southern extremity, got upon the Spanish trail along the Mojave River in the Great Basin, crossed the Rio Virgin and other tributaries of the Colorado, and, near Las Vegas de Santa Clara, again entered the Great Basin, and explored it along its southern and eastern edge up to the eastern portion of Lake Utah, where he left it and crossed the dividing ridge into the valley of Green River.

Colonel Frémont's report shows that in this expedition he had not seen, or did not care to give heed to, the previously published history and map of the explorations of Bonneville; for, had he done so, he would probably not have been led into the error to which he attributed a great deal of his hardships, of constantly looking for the hypothetical river of Buenaventura, which, as he supposed, taking its rise in the Rocky Mountains, emptied itself into the bay of San Francisco, and upon which he expected to winter. His language is as follows:

"In our journey across the desert, Mary's Lake" [most probably the sink of the Humboldt, formerly called Mary's River] "and the famous Buenaventura River were two points on which I relied to recruit the animals and repose the party. Forming, agreeably to the best map in my possession, a connected water-line from the Rocky Mountains to the Pacific Ocean, I felt no other anxiety than to pass safely across the intervening desert to the banks of the Buenaventura, where, in the softer climate of a more southern latitude, our horses might find grass to sustain them and ourselves be sheltered from the rigors of winter and from the inhospitable desert."[q]

Touching this question, Colonel Bonneville, in a letter to Lieutenant Warren on the subject of his explorations in and west of the Rocky Mountains, uses the following language; and as it bears upon the fact as to whom should be accorded the credit of the discovery of the Great Basin, I think proper to make an extract from it. I find the letter in Lieutenant Warren's Memoir of Explorations, page 33:

"GILA RIVER, N. MEX., *August* 24, 1857.

"DEAR SIR: I thank you for your desire to do me justice as regards my map and

(*p*) Frémont's Report, House Cong. Doc. No. 166, p. 151, published in 1845.
(*q*) Frémont's report for 1843–'44, p. 205; see also pp. 196, 214, 219, 221, 226, 255.

explorations in the Rocky Mountains. I started for the mountains in July, 1832. * * * I left the mountains in July, 1836, and reached Fort Leavenworth, Mo., the 6th of August following. During all this time I kept good account of the courses and distances, with occasional observations with my quadrant and Dolland's reflecting telescope. * * * I plotted my work, found it proved, and made it into three parts: one a map of the waters running east to the Missouri State line; a second of the mountain region itself; and a third, which appears to be the one you have sent me, of the waters running west. On the maps you send I recognize my names of rivers, of Indian tribes, observations, Mary's or Maria's River, running southwest, ending in a long chain of flat lakes, never before on any map, and the record of the battle between my party and the Indians, when twenty-five were killed. This party clambered over the California range, were lost in it for twenty days, and entered the open locality to the west, not far from Monterey, where they wintered. In the spring they went south from Monterey, and turned the southern point of the California range, to enter the Great Western Basin. On all the maps of those days the Great Salt Lake had two great outlets to the Pacific Ocean; one of these was the Buenaventura River, which was supposed to head there;[r] the name of the other I do not recollect. It was from my explorations and those of my party alone that it was ascertained that this lake had no outlet; that the California range *basined* all the waters of its eastern slope without further outlet; that the Buenaventura and all other California streams drained only the western slope. It was for this reason that Mr. W. Irving named the Salt Lake after me; and he believed I was fairly entitled to it. * * * * *

"Yours, &c.,

"B. L. E. BONNEVILLE,
"*Colonel Third Infantry.*

"Lieut. G. K. WARREN,
"*Topographical Engineers.*"

It would appear from Colonel Frémont's report that it was a favorite purpose of his, on his return from California, to *cross* the Great Basin *directly*, instead of turning it at its southern extremity. He is speaking of what occurred as he was turning the southern end of the Sierra Nevada, by the Tah-e-chay-pah Pass, to get on the Spanish trail. "In the evening a Christian Indian rode into the camp, well dressed, with long spurs and a *sombrero*, and speaking Spanish fluently. It was an unexpected apparition and a strange and pleasant sight in the desolate gorge of a mountain—an Indian

(*r*) Colonel Bonneville is here probably in error. On Finley's map of North America (Philadelphia, 1826), given by Lieutenant Warren in his Memoir, p. 30, and which purports to include all "the recent geographical discoveries" up to the date stated, the Buenaventura is represented not as one of the outlets of Great Salt Lake into the Pacific, but as the outlet of Lake Salado, doubtless the Lake Sevier of our present maps. The two rivers which are represented on this map as disemboguing from the Great Salt Lake into the Pacific are the Rio Los Mongos and Rio Timpanogos. The fact of Father Escalante in 1776 giving the name of Buenaventura to a river (evidently from the plotting of his notes, Green River) which on Humboldt's map is represented as flowing westwardly into Lake Salado (Sevier) from the Rocky Mountains, the western limits of which he has left undetermined, points, I think, to the origin of the Rio Buenaventura, and of its subsequent hypothetical extension from Lake Sevier to the Bay of San Francisco. It is due, however, to the accuracy of Escalante to say that he expressly states in his journal that from the manner the Indians spoke of the Sevier River, which he followed and which he calls the Santa Ysabel, he was led to the idea that it and the Buenaventura were the same stream; though he could not really think so, for the reason that there was not enough water in the Sevier. He, however, represents that the Santa Ysabel, after emptying into a lake, flows out of it westwardly, and this may have given rise to the idea that it continued to the Pacific.

face, Spanish costume, jingling spurs, and horse equipped after the Spanish manner. He informed me that he belonged to one of the Spanish missions to the south, distant two or three days' ride, and that he had obtained from the priests leave to spend a few days with his relations in the Sierra. Having seen us enter the *pass*,[s] he had come down to visit us. He appeared familiarly acquainted with the country, and gave me definite and clear information in regard to the desert-region east of the mountains. I had entered the pass with a strong disposition to vary my route, and *to travel directly across toward* the Great Salt Lake, in the view of obtaining some acquaintance with the interior of the Great Basin, while pursuing a direct course for the frontier; but his representation, which described it as an arid and barren desert, that had repulsed by its sterility all the attempts of the Indians to penetrate it, determined me for the present to relinquish the plan, and, agreeably to his advice, after crossing the Sierra, to continue our intended route along its eastern base to the Spanish trail." [t]

Thus, like Father Escalante and Walker, Frémont was foiled of directly crossing the Great Basin, on account of its reported arid nature, and evaded it by keeping along its southern edge.

The next authentic account we have of any explorations within the Great Basin is to be found in the pamphlet entitled "Geographical Memoir upon Upper California, in illustration of his map of Oregon and California, by John Charles Frémont, addressed to the Senate of the United States." [u] This memoir and the accompanying map show that Colonel Frémont entered the Great Basin by way of the Timpanogos River,[v] followed down the valley of Utah Lake and its outlet, the Jordan River, to its mouth in Great Salt Lake; turned this lake at its southern extremity; passed westwardly by Pilot's Peak to Whitton's Spring; and thence his party was divided, Mr. E. M. Kern, with Joseph Walker as guide, striking northwestwardly for the Humboldt (Mary's) River, following it down to its sink, and thence striking southwestwardly, and passing along the east shore of Carson Lake, to Walker's River; and Colonel Frémont, with Carson and Godey as guides, and a portion of the party, striking southwestwardly more directly across the Great Basin to near Walker's Lake, where the parties again met. Here separating again, Mr. Kern, guided by Walker, proceeded southwardly to the head of and along Owen's River and Lake, and thence to Walker's Pass of the Sierra Nevada, where he left the basin and crossed the Sierra into the valley of Lake Tulare

(*s*) Frémont (pp. 248 and 270 of his Report) calls this *Walker's* Pass, but Mr. E. M. Kern, one of his assistants at the time, informs me that Walker's true pass was about half a degree to the north of this, and was the pass through which Walker, the discoverer of it, led him in 1845. The pass through which Frémont went was the Tah-e-chay-pah Pass. (See Kern's Journal, Appendix Q; also Lieutenant Williamson's Report Pacific R. R. R., vol. v, pp. 17 and 19.) I notice, however, that Frémont in his letter to the editor of the National Intelligencer, dated June 13, 1854, speaks of both these passes as Walker's, which is the fact so far as that Walker passed into the valley of the San Joaquin by the more northern one, in 1833, and the next year out of it by the other, the Tah-e-chay-pah. (See note *o*.) The charge of error upon Frémont has arisen, doubtless, from the circumstance that he did not in his report of 1843 and 1844 speak of both the passes, but refers to but one, and that not usually denominated Walker's Pass.

(*t*) Frémont's Report, p. 254..

(*u*) Senate Miscellaneous Doc. No. 148, 30th Cong., 1st Sess.

(*v*) Frémont's map represents that he passed from the Duchesne's Fork, up Morin's Fork, and thence across the divide to the Timpanogos. This was a physical impossibility, for Morin's Fork, or White Clay Creek, as it is now called, is a tributary of the Weber, and instead of running into Duchesne's Fork, and being thus a tributary of the Colorado, is, on the contrary, a branch tributary of the Great Salt Lake. In other words, Duchesne's Fork and Morin's Fork are on opposite sides of the divide (the Uintah range), and, therefore, could not *both* be followed up from the Colorado side.

and the Rio San Joaquin. Frémont, on the contrary, traveled northwardly to Carson River, where he crossed it at the same point as in his preceding exploration; and thence to Salmon Trout Creek, up which he traveled and crossed the Sierra Nevada, in latitude 39° 17′ 12″ N., or 38.2 miles north of his pass of 1844.

For a very interesting account of Mr. Kern's branch expedition above alluded to, I refer to his journal, (Appendix Q,) now for the first time given to the public, and which he has kindly submitted to me for this purpose; and as it goes into the particulars of his exploration of the country along the Humboldt River, Carson, Walker's, and Owen's Lakes, the plat of which furnished the basis for Colonel Frémont's map accompanying his memoir, but a detailed report of which the latter has never given, I consider it a valuable addition to the knowledge of the Great Basin, and take this opportunity of thanking Mr. Kern for it.[w]

The geographical memoir of Frémont, as already stated, does not enter into the particulars of his exploration of 1845 and 1846, but only gives a general view of the Great Basin. This view is graphic, and in the main, so far as my observations extended, just, and corrects some errors into which, from imperfect data, he had fallen in his previous explorations. The idea which he had entertained of the Basin's being made up of a *system of small lakes and rivers, scattered over a flat country*,[x] was found to be entirely untrue, and, on the contrary, that the *mountain* structure predominated.[a] The long stretch of mountain range, however, which on his map is represented as being the continuation westwardly of the Wahsatch range, and as separating the waters of the Great Basin from those of the Colorado, is evidently hypothetical.[b]

(*w*) Mr. Kern, it seems, got on the Humboldt, on a then *old California emigrant wagon-road*, which followed the Humboldt down to its sink, and then crosses over to the Carson River and, following up its valley, crosses the Sierra Nevada at the head of the South Fork of the American River. This is the route which Hastings and many others who preceded Frémont traveled over with wagons, and which emigrants have since continued to take. Kern followed this well-beaten road to near Carson Lake, where he left it. I get this information from him personally, and besides, he speaks of this "emigrant wagon-trail" (as he calls it) in his journal. I have endeavored to find out who first tracked this road; but all I can learn in addition to what Mr. Kern has informed me is the following, which I extract from "*The Annals of San Francisco*," published by Appleton & Co., 1855, pp. 85, 86:

"So early as 1837, several societies were formed in the American States to promote emigration to Oregon and California. In the following years, and particularly in 1843, 1844, 1845, and 1846, many thousand emigrants journeyed across the Rocky and Snowy Mountains, enduring much suffering by the way, to settle in California and the adjacent territory of Oregon."

I have thus been particular in this matter for the reason that in Frémont's memoir it is not made clear that such a road did exist at the time of his exploration, and that his expedition followed it. And I would here remark that it is to be regretted that officers having charge of exploring expeditions do not always report when they are following *old wagon-roads*, so that a full history of the route may be given. Had this been done, a great deal of injustice which has been exercised to other officers since the explorations of Frémont would have been spared, and more liberal and just reports made.

Since penning the foregoing, Mr. Kern has courteously furnished me with the following extract from a letter dated San Francisco, November 3, 1860, from Maj. J. R. Snyder:

"Dr. Townshend and party brought wagons as far as Truckee Lake in 1844. I am not confident that he succeeded in getting them over the mountains. Moses Shellenberger remained all winter at the lake with the property, and I think in the spring they had assistance to bring everything to the fort.

"Our party in 1845 brought wagons through the Johnson's Pass to the headwaters of Bear River, and so on through the Sacramento Valley, without interruption. This was, probably, the first party that came directly through. There was no trail or the sign of any where we passed, from the Oregon road, over the Goose Creek Mountains, to the head of Mary's (Humboldt) River."

(*x*) Frémont's Report, p. 235.

(*a*) Frémont's Memoir, p. 7.

(*b*) On Frémont's map illustrating his explorations of 1845 and 1846, and which he says in his Memoir, p. 3, was prepared under his directions, it is represented that this extensive chain of mountains was "seen from elevated points on his northern exploring line." I think the colonel must have labored here under a misapprehension, for I passed more

This view, however, in no way militates against the theory and fact of the Great Basin system as one distinct from the valley of the Colorado; because, as is to be seen in many instances in the basin itself, a very slight rim or rise of ground may be the divide between distinct sub-basin systems.

The next authentic account, in the order of dates, we have of explorations within the Great Basin, is to be found in the report by Capt. Howard Stansbury, Topographical Engineers, of his "*Exploration and Survey of the Valley of the Great Salt Lake of Utah in* 1849," published by order of Congress. This report I cannot but regard, in a geographical point of view, as of great value. I have had occasion, in many instances, in my reconnaissances west of the Rocky Mountains and in the region of the Great Salt Lake, to test the accuracy of Captain Stansbury's work; and it has been a gratification to me to find that his report and map have represented the country so correctly and have been of so much service to me. To him and his assistant, the lamented Captain Gunnison, Topographical Engineers, the public is indebted for a thorough triangular survey of the Great Salt Lake; and to them is the credit due of a complete exploration of the lake, around its entire limits, a feat which Joseph Walker, by Colonel Bonneville's directions, attempted, as before stated, sixteen years previously; but which, on account of the desert lying on its west and the consequent want of fresh water, he failed to execute. Stansbury, however, extended his explorations into the Great Basin only as far as Pilot Knob, a prominent landmark sixty-four miles in a due west direction from Great Salt Lake.

The next authentic account of explorations in the Great Basin is that by Capt. E. G. Beckwith, Third Artillery, the assistant of Captain Gunnison in his expedition for the survey of a railroad-route near the 41st parallel, and who took charge of the expedition after the massacre of Gunnison and a portion of his party by Indians, on Sevier River, on the 26th October, 1853. The party entered the Great Basin from the valley of Green River by the Wahsatch Pass and a creek he calls Salt Creek, a branch of the Sevier;[c] and thence they returned to the usually-traveled route from Los Angeles, and proceeded, by the way of Nephi, Payson, Provo, &c., to Great Salt Lake City.

In the ensuing year, 1854, Captain Beckwith explored some of the tributaries of Great Salt Lake and Utah Lake, issuing from the Wahsatch and Uinta Mountains, and, passing by the southern end of Great Salt Lake, he struck generally a north-of-

than a degree nearer to these mountains than he did, and I saw nothing of them. Besides, I notice in his letter to the editor of National Intelligencer, dated June 13, 1854, constituting Mis. Doc. House of Reps. No. 8, 33d Cong., 2d Sess., that he passed right along where he has located this extensive range, and yet he says nothing to *confirm* his previous report. On the contrary, his language in reference to this portion of his route is: "We found the country a high table-land, bristling with mountains, often in short, isolated blocks, and sometimes accumulated into considerable ranges with numerous open and low passes." I have, therefore, no doubt that the representation of this long chain of mountains on the maps of Utah, by Colton, Monk, and Mitchell, is a fiction, and should be discontinued.

(*c*) Messrs. Beale and Heap passed over nearly this same route in 1853, in advance of Captain Gunnison's party, and after reaching Vegas de Santa Clara, took the Spanish trail route to California. (See Heap's Journal, published by Lippincott, Grambo & Co., 1854.) This journal gives a statement of Rev. J. W. Brier, in which he represents that he and a small party found their way, in the fall of 1849, from Vegas de Santa Clara, in a tortuous and, in general, a southwestwardly course, across the southwest corner of the Great Basin to Walker's Pass.

Colonel Frémont, also, subsequently, during the winter of 1853–'54, followed very nearly the route of Captain Gunnison to Grand River, and thence to Parowan and Cedar City on the Spanish trail. Thence his course was directly west, over the Great Basin to the Sierra Nevada, which, on account of snow, he was obliged to cross over by Walker's Pass, some sixty to eighty miles to the southward. (See Frémont's letter to editor National Intelligencer, of June 13, 1854, constituting House Mis. Doc. No. 8, 2d Sess. 33d Cong.)

west course across the Great Basin to the Humboldt Pass of the Humboldt range; thence southwestwardly in Ruby Valley to the Hasting's Road Pass of this same range; and thence northwestwardly across the mountains to the south of the Humboldt, to Lassen's Meadows, on the Humboldt River. Thence his course was westwardly through the valley of the Mud Lake to the Madelin Pass of the east range of the Sierra Nevada, where he left the Great Basin.[d] It will be noticed that up to this time this was the most direct exploration which had been made across the Great Basin from Great Salt Lake City; but yet it was too far north and too tortuous to be of great value as offering a *direct* wagon-route to Placerville, Sacramento, and San Francisco. Besides, as a wagon-route to Lassen's Meadows I believe it has never been used, on account of its roughness, west of the South Fork of the Humboldt.

The next report we have of an attempt being made to cross the Great Basin directly from Great Salt Lake City toward Walker's Lake, for the purpose of avoiding the great detour by the Humboldt River, and getting the shortest route to San Francisco, is to be found in the report of Capt. Rufus Ingalls, United States Army, to the Quartermaster-General, dated August 25, 1855, giving an account of the movements of Colonel Steptoe's command to and from Great Salt Lake City. His language on this point is as follows:

"The wagon-routes across the continent are so very rough in mountainous regions, and always quite circuitous, particularly from Great Salt Lake City to the Bay of San Francisco, that Colonel Steptoe took measures to have the country lying directly west explored for a more nearly air-line road. Two Mormons were engaged as principal explorers, and directed to explore from the south end of the Great Salt Lake on the Beckwith route, or near to it, to Carson Valley. This party left the lake in September, and returned the following November. It proved quite an expensive trip, owing, in my present opinion, to the tricky character of the Mormons. They made a most flattering report. They said they had discovered a wagon-road along which a command could move with ease, &c., saving 150 or 200 miles. The colonel had not seen Lieutenant Beckwith's report, nor had he any other information than that given by his exploring party; but being deeply sensible of the importance to the Territory of Utah and the overland emigrants of laying out and opening a more direct and practicable road than the crooked ones now traveled, he determined to take his command and the large wagon-train over this new route.

"As spring approached, however, the chief Mormon who had agreed to act as guide became rather restive, and evinced an unwillingness to go, which caused the colonel to distrust him, and shook his confidence in the report he had made of the road. As a matter of security another party was organized, under 'Porter Rockwell,' a Mormon, but a man of strong mind and independent spirit, a capital guide and fearless prairie man. He went out as far as the great desert tracts lying southwest of the lake, and very nearly on a level with it, and found that at *that season* they could not be passed over, 'unless with wings,' and returned. It proved fortunate that we did not undertake the march with O. B. Huntington as guide. The march would have been disastrous; though Rockwell and others are of the opinion that, by going on a

(d) P. R. R. R., vol. ii.

line some thirty miles farther south, along the foot of mountains seen in that direction, a fine road can be laid out, avoiding, in a great degree, the desert. I believe such to be the case myself. I am clearly of the opinion that a suitable officer could, by a proper reconnaissance, lay out a road passing by 'Rush Valley,' turning southward and going by New River, Walker's Lake, into Carson Valley, and save 200 miles distance.

"This route having been declared impracticable, the colonel decided to pass around the north end of the lake, and thence by the Humboldt to Carson Valley."[e]

It thus seems that Colonel Steptoe was deterred from attempting a direct route across the Great Basin toward San Francisco by the reports which he had received, and took the old roundabout road by way of the Humboldt River.[f]

I have now, as I believe, exhausted the subject of the explorations in and around the Great Basin up to the time of my reporting for duty with the army under General A. S. Johnston in Utah. This history shows that, up to this period, a direct road toward San Francisco, from Great Salt Lake or Camp Floyd across the Great Basin, had never been thoroughly attempted, but that in every instance, from fear of encountering reported deserts, explorers had shrunk back from the task. It was universally believed in Utah that, at this period, not even a Mormon had ventured to cross the Basin in this direct manner toward Carson or Walker's Lake, though their settlements in Carson Valley made such a route so desirable.

Some individuals, more venturous than others, had made a less circuitous bend than the old route by the Humboldt River, but yet a direct journey across not one had effected.

It was this failure on the part of others to accomplish this desirable exploration, as well as the possible advantages of a new and short road to San Francisco, which stimulated me to submit, through General Johnston, a project of exploration to the War Department, which had in view the accomplishment of this very enterprise, and thus, if possible, the opening of a wagon-road which would be of benefit to the Army and country. This project of exploration is inserted in the first page of my journal, and to it do I refer for particulars. Suffice it here to remark, it was approved by General Johnston, and met with the sanction of the Secretary of War, Hon. John B. Floyd, and upon the authority of the latter the expedition was ordered, and received the thorough outfit it did at the hands of the former.

The result of the expedition has been the opening of a wagon-route which, starting from Camp Floyd, branches 28 miles distant into two generally parallel routes, which come together again at a distance from Camp Floyd of 286 miles, and thence are generally coincident the rest of the way to Genoa, at the east foot of the Sierra Nevada. The distance from Salt Lake City to Genoa, by my more northern or outward route, and the cuts-off which I made on my return, is 571 miles, and from Camp

(e) See Appendix A, Quartermaster-General's Report, accompanying Secretary of War's Annual Report, 1855, vol. i, part ii, constituting Ex. Doc. No. 1, House of Reps., p. 156, 34th Cong., 1st Sess.

(f) Mr. John Kirk, superintendent of a road-making party, under instructions from the Interior Department, passed over the road from Honey Lake, by way of the Humboldt River, to the City of Rocks. His assistant engineer, Mr. Francis N. Bishop, in his report refers to the reports of Frémont and Beckwith for information respecting the country traversed. (See Report upon Pacific Wagon Roads, by Albert H. Campbell, General Superintendent, Ex. Doc. No. 108, H. R., 35th Cong., 2d Sess., pp. 36, 38.)

Floyd to Genoa 531 miles. By the old Humboldt route, according to the itinerary in Captain Marcy's "Prairie Traveler," the distance from Salt Lake City to Reese's Ranch, Genoa, is 774 miles; and as Camp Floyd is 40 miles from Great Salt Lake City, the distance from Camp Floyd to Genoa, by this route, is 814 miles. That is, my more northern route from Salt Lake City to Genoa is 203 miles shorter than the old Humboldt River route, and from Camp Floyd 283 miles shorter.[g] By my return, a more southern route, the distance from Genoa to Camp Floyd is 560 miles, or 29 miles longer than my outward route; but while longer, in grade, grass, and extent of cultivable soil, it is better. Both these new routes have been since traveled by emigrants and droves of cattle, and continue to be traveled by them, and upon the more northern is now running the mail and pony express. The Placerville and Saint Joseph Telegraph Company are now also extending their wires along it, and have already reached, as I am informed, Fort Churchill, at the bend of Carson River eastwardly from San Francisco,[h] and from Saint Joseph, Mo., westward, the telegraph is in operation as far as Fort Kearney, on the Platte River. The easy connection of my inward or southern route from Chapin's Spring with Captain Gunnison's along the Sevier River and Grand River will also be apparent, as well as the great advantage of the new wagon-road pass I explored at the head of Coal Creek, a tributary of the Timpanogos River, for the extension of my routes over the Uintah Mountains, and by the way of Duchesne's Fork, White River, and the Middle Park of the Rocky Mountains to Denver City in Kansas; and thence to Saint Joseph or Leavenworth City. The map herewith, on which will be seen these routes, and the topography of the country traversed, and to which, in reading the journal, constant reference should be had, has been projected upon the polyconic method on a scale of $\frac{1}{1,000,000}$, and the meridians and parallels of latitude laid down agreeably to data obtained from the tables arranged by Mr. J. E Hilgard, and published in the annual report of Professor A. D. Bache, Superintendent of the United States Coast Survey, for 1856.

(*g*) It will be noticed that in my project of explorations to the War Department, of January 6, 1859, I stated that I hoped to shorten the old route from Camp Floyd, 260 miles. The actual shortening has been 283 miles.

(*h*) In the above I say nothing about the comparative advantages between my routes and the old Humboldt route, except that to those emigrants *who go by the way of Salt Lake City or Camp Floyd,* there is no question that my route are far preferable, being 203 miles shorter in the first case and 283 in the second, and doubtless as good in respect to hardness, water, and grass, and a great deal better as regards wood. To enable the emigrant, however, as he reads my journal, to institute some sort of comparison between the routes, I give below some extracts from the reports of different Government officials in respect to the character of the old route along the Humboldt River, and inform him, at the same time, that while on my routes at either end there is some desert country to go over, yet that besides the alkaline water, grass, and mire, which emigrants on the old road have to contend with along the Humboldt, they have to cross, in the case of their taking hence the Carson River route, a desert of 45 miles and another of 26; and in the case of the Honey Lake route, also a desert of about 60 miles where there is a scarcity of water and grass. I would also state that the distance from the Missouri River, *via* South Pass, Great Salt Lake City, and my shortest route across the basin, is 41 miles shorter than that by Landers's "Cut-off" and the Carson River route, to San Francisco, and 55 miles shorter than by his "cut-off" and the Honey Lake road.

Lieutenant Beckwith, vol. ii, P. R. R. Reports, speaking of the Humboldt River, June 4, 1854, at Lassen's Meadows, uses the following language:

"We moved camp 6.80 miles down the river to a point selected for crossing it, where it has no bottom-land upon it. These low lands being very much overflowed at this season, and miry, are entirely impassable for horses or cattle; and many arriving here in a weak condition, are annually lost by emigrants from becoming mired. But one of the chief causes of the loss of cattle by emigrants upon this stream is allowing them to eat the grass in the river-bottom, which is extremely unwholesome. The more experienced stock-drovers to California send their cattle back from the river to feed on the nutritious grass of the hills; but as these are frequently distant from the road and from water, it is only by experience that men learn its importance."

And Maj. I. Lynde, Seventh Infantry, in his report to General A. S. Johnston, of October 24, 1859, states that he

For the particulars of each day's travel across the Great Basin, as well as a minute description of the country traversed, I refer to my journal. But as a previous general account always renders an examination into particulars more satisfactory, it may not be unacceptable to say something in this regard.

The first thing which will strike one, on looking at the map, will be the *great number of mountain ranges* which the routes cross in the Great Basin; and this will appear to him the more remarkable, as the idea has been generally entertained, since the explorations of Frémont in 1843 and 1844 (though, as before remarked, he corrected the error in his succeeding expedition), that this Great Basin was a *flat country, scattered over with a system of small lakes and rivers*, and destitute of mountains. The fact, on the contrary, is that it is the most mountainous region, considering its extent, we have probably within the limits of our domain; and so far from being scattered over with a system of small lakes and rivers, which seem to imply a considerable number of this kind of water area, it has but a limited number of lakes, and they almost entirely confined to the bases of the great Sierra which bound the Basin.

These lakes are, proceeding from north to south and along the circumference of the Great Basin, Great Salt Lake, Lake Utah, Sevier Lake, and Small Salt Lake, on the eastern side of the Basin; and on the western, proceeding from south to north, Soda Lake, Owen's Lake, Walker's Lake, the two Carson Lakes, Humboldt Lake, Pyramid Lake, the Mud Lakes, and Lake Abert. Beside these, there are Franklin Lake and Goshoot Lake, which are to be seen to the east of the East Humboldt range.

These constitute all the lakes that have been discovered in the Great Basin, and they are all without outlet. Great Salt Lake is 70 miles long and from 20 to 30 broad. Pyramid Lake and Walker's Lake, the next largest, are both 30 miles long by 10 wide. All the others are smaller. Pyramid Lake, Walker's Lake, and Utah Lake, which are

reached Gravelly Ford, on the Humboldt, 12th July, and found "the mosquitoes and flies very troublesome to the men and animals, and the water very much impregnated with alkali." He proceeded thence down the river 118 miles, and says, "the greater part of this distance the valley, which does not average more than three-fourths of a mile in width, was covered with water, and deep sloughs running parallel to the river render it impossible to reach the main stream except at long intervals. The water in these sloughs was so much impregnated with alkali as to render it dangerous for the animals to drink it, and the mosquitoes and flies were worse than I ever saw them before." (See doc. accompanying Secretary of War's Report, of 1860. See also the testimony of my guide, Mr. John Reese, on this point, in my journal, under date of June 12.)

It seems from Mr. Albert H. Campbell's report to the Secretary of the Interior, of February 19, 1859, that Mr. John Kirk, the superintendent of the Humboldt division of the wagon-road, "was instructed to select a road from Honey Lake Valley to City of Rocks, avoiding as much as possible the Humboldt, leaving it to the south," the reason assigned being "the alleged deleterious character of the waters of the river, and its destructive effects upon cattle and horses, which rendered it advisable to avoid it as much as possible." It appears, however, from reading Mr. Kirk's report, that he failed in finding any better route, and besides, speaks most encouragingly of the quality of the water and grass along the Humboldt. His language is: "It is believed that the experience of this season will correct the current opinion in relation to the pernicious qualities of the water of the river and the grass upon its bank. Except at the lake and its vicinity, we found the water good and the grass superior, both in quantity and quality. From the examinations already made, it is evident that the greatest difficulty in the road is between the west bend of the Humboldt and California." He does not say why, but probably it is on account of the desert.

I give the above statements, and it is for the reader to draw his own inference in respect to the character of the water and grass generally along the Humboldt toward its lower end and westward toward the Sierra Nevada. I mention these objections to this route, not to condemn it—for if emigrants do not go by the way of Salt Lake City or Camp Floyd, it may possibly be the most advantageous route—but only that, as already remarked while reading my journal, they may be enabled to institute for themselves some sort of comparison and arrive at some definite conclusion in the matter; for, after all, in the selection which emigrants make of any of the routes across the continent, they will always find that it will be a selection of that which is comparatively better and not that which is absolutely good. Every one of them, they will find, have some portion of exceptional desert country to be traversed.

fresh-water lakes, abound in fine, large trout, and Carson Lake in fish of a smaller kind. Great Salt Lake, according to Stansbury, contains 20 per cent. of pure salt.[i]

The principal rivers, which, on account of their width and depth, require bridging or ferry, in their flush state, during the time of melting-snow, are the Bear, Weber, Roseaux or Malade, Jordan, Timpanogos, Spanish Fork, and Sevier Rivers, which have their sources in the Wahsatch Mountains, on the east side of the Basin, and flow into the lakes near the base of these mountains; the Mojave, Owen's, Walker's, Carson, and Truckee, or Salmon Trout Rivers, which have their sources in the Sierra Nevada, and flow into lakes at their base and sink; and the Humboldt River, which flows from east to south of west along the northern portion of the Basin and sinks. The largest of these is probably the Humboldt, about 300 miles long; and the next, Bear River, 250 miles long. The others range from about 40 to 120 miles in length. These streams vary from 50 to about 150 feet in width, and from 2 to about 15 in depth, depending upon the season and locality.

All the other streams are of small extent; and taking their rise in the many mountain ranges with which the Basin is traversed (generally from north to south), they seldom flow beyond their bases, where, in the alluvion, they sink. These streams are generally so small that you can jump across them, and seldom require bridging. The large as well as the small streams mentioned, when not brackish, not unfrequently contain trout.

The trend of the mountain ranges is almost invariably north and south, the limits of variation being between the true and magnetic north. The mountains rise quite abruptly from the plain, and from bases varying in breadth from a few miles to about twelve. These mountain ranges are so frequent and close together as to make the area between them more like valleys than plains, and the roads cross them on the average every 10 or 15 miles. In length they equal the ranges. Longitudinally they are nearly level, the inclination in portions not being perceptible; sometimes tending northward and sometimes southward, and, not unfrequently, they are made up of minor valleys, separated by small ridges or rims. In cross-section they are slightly concave.

The most massive and lofty mountains, commencing at Camp Floyd and proceeding westward, are the Oquirr, Guyot, Goshoot or Tots-arr, Un-go-we-ah, Mon-tim, Humboldt, We-ah-bah, Pe-ĕr-re-ah, and Se-day-e ranges. Of these, the Tots-arr, Un-go-we-ah, Humboldt, Pe-er-re-ah, and Se-day-e are the most massive and lofty, snow appearing in patches upon their loftiest portions the whole year round. The lengths of the ranges in some instances our explorations enabled us to determine were at least 120 miles, and they there extended into unknown regions beyond the field of our explorations. These ranges attain, in the case of Union Peak, the highest point of the Tots-arr or Goshoot range, an altitude above the plain of from 5,000 to 6,000 feet, or of from 10,000 to 11,000 feet above the sea. In the case of the Oquirr range, the highest point, Camp Floyd Peak, according to Lieutenant Putnam's measurement, by theodolite, was found to be 4,214 feet above Camp Floyd: and as this locality, by barometric measurement, is 4,860 feet above the sea, the peak referred to is 9,074 feet above the sea. The highest pass was on our return-route and through the Un-go-we-ah

(*i*) Stansbury's report, "Salt Lake," pp. 418, 419.

range. By barometric measurement it was 8,140 feet above the sea. The passes are all, with but little difficulty, surmountable by wagons; but their grades, given in Appendix F, and also on the profiles of the routes, Appendix E, will show, I think, that as railroad routes they are impracticable, except (in comparison with other probably attainable routes) at an inadmissible cost.

The chief agricultural characteristic of the country traversed is desert, the exceptions being as follows: On my more northern route, in the case of the large valleys between the mountain ranges, going westward from Camp Floyd: Rush Valley, Pleasant Valley (the valley of Fish or Deep Creek, not on the route, but in vicinity of Pleasant Valley), Ruby Valley, Walker's Valley, and Carson Valley—all these are cultivable in limited portions; and on my return route, going eastward from Genoa, Carson Valley (common to outward routes), Steptoe Valley, Antelope Valley, and Crosman Valley. The elevation of all these valleys above the sea varies from 3,840 feet, the lowest depression of Carson Valley, to 6,146 feet, the altitude of Steptoe Valley. For a particular description of these and their capabilities, I refer to my journal at the proper dates. Carson Valley has already shown its capacity to grow the small cereals and garden vegetables; and, I doubt not, the other valleys named, though higher in altitude, will be found sufficiently warm to mature the growth of the more hardy cereals, plants, and roots. It will be noticed, by reference to the journal, that my return or more southern route, though 27 miles longer than my outward, with the cut-off made on my return, is much the best, in respect to cultivable valleys and grass, and also timber. The other exceptions to the desert character of the Basin are the small, narrow valleys and ravines of the mountain streams, which, taking their rise high up in the mountains, course down to the plains or main valleys and sink. These valleys, though rich, are generally too high in altitude, and therefore too cold for arable purposes, but are of great value in furnishing, in great abundance, the small mountain bunch-grass, which has fattening qualities almost, if not quite, equal to oats.

Another exception to the universal characteristic of desert is the abundance of the dwarf cedar, which is to be seen on almost every one of the mountain ridges, and which high up in the mountains is not unfrequently intermingled with the pine, piñon balsam, quaking ash, and mountain mahogany. The abundance of this cedar, as well as occasional supply of other kinds of timber, will make either of my routes, independent of their being the shortest across the Great Basin, particularly in connection with a direct route from Camp Floyd to Denver City by way of the Timpanogos River and Duchesne's Fork, decidedly the most practicable for the overland telegraph.

The portions of the country traversed which may be called unmitigatingly desert are, on my more northern route:—the region between Simpson's Springs, in the Champlin Mountains, and the Sulphur Springs, at the east base of the Tots-arr or Goshoot range, a distance of 80 miles, (albeit the grass and water at Fish Springs and water at Devil's Hole intervene to make the greatest distance between water and grass 48½ miles and between water 43 miles); between the west base of the Se-day-e Mountains and Carson Lake, a distance of 50 miles; (this is also mitigated by the grass and water got by digging at Middle Gate, and at Sulphur Spring,) and between Carson Lake and Walker's Rivers, a distance of 21 miles. On my return, or more southern route, between Carson River and Carson Lake, a distance of 23 miles, and between the Perry range and the Champlin Mountains, a distance of 103 miles, though Chapin's Springs and Tyler Spring, with their limited pasture-grounds and the good Indian Spring, with its small supply of water but abundance of grass and cedar, within this interval, alleviate, in a very material degree, this last stretch, and take it out of the category of continuous unmitigated desert. (See itineraries, Appendixes A and B, for particulars and directions.)

The most abundant plant in the Great Basin is the *artemisia*, or wild sage, and as it is seen almost everywhere in the valleys and on the mountains, it gives its peculiar bronze color to the general face of nature. Sometimes this all-prevailing color is modified by the more vivid green of the *Sarcobatus vermicularis*, or greasewood; sometimes by the yellowish light-green of the *Lynogris*, or rabbit-bush, both of which are found interspersed not infrequently among the *artemisia* and on the mountains, not infrequently by the dark color of the scrub cedar, and occasionally of the pine and balsam. This plant, the *artemisia*, I have seen covering probably as much as nine-tenths of the whole country intervening the east base of the Rocky Mountains (longitude 104°) and the east base of the Sierra Nevada (longitude 119° 40′), or over a breadth of more than 800 miles, beyond which, east or west, it does not grow. In the aggregate it constitutes no inconsiderable hinderance to the progress of teams over untracked virgin regions. In height it is ordinarily about 2½ feet, though I have seen it in one locality as high as 8 feet. Near the ground its trunk usually ranges in diameter from 3 to 6 inches, though I have seen it, when very luxuriant, nearly a foot. It is quite brash in fiber, and therefore easily trampled down, and the light soil admits of its being readily plucked up by the roots. On this account, and because of its rich resinous properties, it makes a very quick and acceptable fuel, and, indeed, in the main valleys and plains, where there is scarcely ever any timber, it constitutes the chief resource in this particular. It also constitutes an easy and ever available means to the Digger Indians of making for themselves circular inclosures or barriers of about four feet in height against the wind, and which, summer and winter, are their only habitations. It is also used by them to make their long line of fences, on which they hang, vertically, their nets across the paths of the rabbits, and in this way catch them. It emits, particularly when brushed by your person or trampled upon, a very strong, pungent odor, resembling both camphor and turpentine, and the atmosphere is almost constantly charged with its aroma. Indeed, the idea is ever uppermost that on account of this property it will eventually be found of value in the *materia medica* and mechanic arts. It seems to thrive best in an arid, dry climate, and its presence is a sure indication of the desert character of the soil and of its utter worthlessness for purposes of agriculture.[1]

The *Sarcobatus vermicularis*, or greasewood, is the next most abundant plant, and, like the *artemisia*, is found co-extensive with the country lying between the Rocky Mountains and the Sierra Nevada. It is sometimes found alone, but more frequently scattered among the *artemisia*, and, like it, on account of its rich carbonaceous qualities, is a very common fuel on the plains. Its height, ordinarily, is 3 to 4 feet. It

(*l*) See scientific description of this shrub, by Dr. Geo. Engelmann, Appendix M.

seems to flourish best in a rather moist, argillaceous soil. On account of its thorny spines it is a very considerable hinderance to men and beasts wherever it has to be encountered. The wood, when dry, is very hard, and on this account is used by the Digger Indians to generate fire, in the primitive mode, by the friction of two pieces, as described under date of June 3. Its spines are also used by the Indians to barb their arrows.[m]

A third plant, which, probably, is about as abundant as the greasewood, and is co-extensive with it and the *artemisia*, is the *Lynogris*, or rabbit-bush, sketched in journal under date of May 2. In height it is generally 2½ to 5 feet, and, like the greasewood, commingles with the *artemisia*.

The rabbit is mostly found where it prevails.[m]

Another tolerably common plant, which, however, does not show itself to any considerable extent until you reach the western portion of the Great Basin, is the *Epledra peduculata*, a sketch of which is seen in journal, under date of May 27.[m]

A fourth plant, or, as it may be called, a tree, which I have never seen anywhere else than in the mountains of the Great Basin, is what the Mormons call the mountain mahogany. It is found in scattered groves, usually near the summit of the mountain-passes, and, at a distance, looks like the apple-tree, its leaf resembling somewhat that of the live-oak. It is somewhat scrubby in appearance, ramifying in several branches from the ground, and not unfrequently attains a height of from 15 to 20 feet, and an aggregate diameter, across its branches, in the tree, of 15 to 20 feet. Its wood is very hard, and is used for cogs, journals, gudgeons, &c. It is not seen in considerable quantities. (See sketch in journal, under date of May 12.)[m]

The chief complexion of the face of the country is, I have already remarked, a sort of bronze color, caused by the all-prevailing *artemisia*, which has in the map a color of this kind. Another characteristic which occasionally obtains is the white alkaline effloresence which margins, in portions, some of the streams, such as Meadow Creek, Steptoe Creek, Reese's River, Walker's River, and which sometimes characterizes whole valleys, such as White and Alkali valleys. These streams and valleys, when seen in the distance, have all the appearance of being draped in virgin snow. The alkali, however, does not appear to affect the taste of the water of the streams mentioned, though that of the wells dug in the alkaline valleys were nauseously unpalatable. This saline efflorescence is a sure poison to vegetation, and hopelessly worthless is any soil where it is seen. It is the fact, too, (and it is one of great importance in this Territory), that soils which have been originally quite productive under cultivation have, by that very process, gradually become more and more alkaline, until at length, on account of their unproductiveness from this cause, they have of necessity been abandoned. This has been the history of many a field in Great Salt Lake and Utah Valleys, and I am inclined to the belief that it will be the history of the greater portion of the cultivable land of the Territory. These soils, particularly of the valleys, on account of the streams within them having no outlets, are more or less impreg-

(*m*) See scientific description, by Dr. Geo. Engelmann, Appendix M.

nated with the salts which are brought down by the rains from the mountains, and these salts, it would seem, are gradually evolved to the surface by the process of tillage. Indeed, the truth seems to be that not only is the cultivable portion of the Territory a very inconsiderable fraction of the whole area, but even this portion is destined, in all probability, by tillage to become more and more contracted. The abandoned ruins of cities in New Mexico point, most indubitably, with their present surrounding desert wastes, to a like deterioration of soil, and such is likely to be the fate of the present cultivable portion of Utah.[o] The great staple is wheat, of which, in the valley of Great Salt Lake, I have been informed as many as seventy-five bushels have been raised to the acre. This, however, is rare. Forty bushels are more common. Oats and barley thrive; corn is raised in some of the warmer valleys, but the high altitude of the valleys generally makes the climate too cold for this cereal. Potatoes, garden vegetables, and berries do well. The peach, apricot, and melon also mature, and the apple is raised in Great Salt Lake Valley. It must be borne in mind, however, that in order to raise anything in this Territory, the land, in addition to the usual tillage, has to be irrigated. The kind of fencing used, on account of the difficulty of obtaining suitable rails, is the mud or adobe wall, which, in consequence of degradation from rains, requires extensive repairs every spring.

In regard to the resources of the Territory, agricultural, manufacturing, and personal, I refer the reader to the interesting paper from Dr. Garland Hurt, constituting Appendix N. To this should be added the arable capabilities of the valley of Green River, in the eastern portion of the Territory; of Crosman, Antelope, and Steptoe Valleys, on my more southern route; and of Walker's and Carson's Valleys, in the western portions of the Territory.

In regard to the pastoral capabilities of the Territory, I may say that they abound in a number of valleys, and on the mountains generally, the chief difficulty being the preservation of stock in the winter, which, on account of the rigor of the climate, except in the lowest and warmest valleys, or under artificial shelter, cannot endure till spring. The Government and Government contractors have in the aggregate lost, I may say, thousands of heads from this cause since the entry of the Army into the Territory in the fall of 1857.

In relation to the propriety of the term "Great Basin," as applied to this region of country, I may remark that if by it the notion is entertained that this great area is chiefly of a hydrographic character, that is filled with lakes and rivers, the idea is erroneous. Erroneous will also be the idea that, because it is called a basin, it must, as a whole, present a generally concave surface. The truth is, this is only a basin so far as that the few lakes and streams that are found within it sink within it, and have no outlet to the sea.

It may also be considered as made up of several minor or subsidiary basins, and, regarding them in succession, not in the order of magnitude, we have—

1st. Lake Sevier Basin, elevation of lowest point above the sea slightly less than 4,690 feet.

2d. Great Salt Lake Basin, elevation of lowest point above the sea, 4,170 feet.

(o) See my report of Navajo expedition, Sen. Ex. Doc. No. 64, 31st Cong., 1st sess., pp. 74 and 106.

3d. Humboldt River Basin, elevation of lowest point above the sea, near Lassen's Meadows, according to Beckwith, 4,147 feet.

4th. Carson River Basin, elevation of lowest point above the sea, at Carson Lake, 3,840 feet.

5th. Walker's River Basin, elevation of lowest point above the sea, 7 miles above Walker's Lake, 4,072 feet.

(Walker's Lake Basin estimated at about same as Carson, 3,840 feet.)

6th. Owen's Lake Basin, altitude unknown.

7th. Mojave River Basin, estimation of lowest point above the sea (Williamson), 1,111 feet.

All these valleys or sub-basins, it will be noticed, are along the outskirts of the Great Basin, just within its circumference; and as the valleys of the great central area have an average altitude of about 5,500 feet, which is, for much the larger portion of the area, about 1,500 feet higher than said basins, and for the Mojave portion over 4,000 feet higher, it will at once be apparent that, as a whole, the Basin should be conceived as an elevated central region extended over much the greater portion of the Basin, and in proximity to the circumference, sloping toward the sub-basins bordering the circumference. When this idea is entertained, and this extended central portion is in addition conceived of as being traversed by high and extensive ranges of mountains, on an average about 15 miles apart, ranging north and south, and correspondingly corrugated with intermediate valleys of commensurate lengths, and the mind conceives at the same time that the order of depression of the basins is from Lake Sevier, where it is least, around successively by Great Salt Lake, Humboldt River Valley, Carson Lake, Walker's Lake, to the valley of the Mojave, where it is much the greatest, a very good mental daguerreotype can be had of the Great Basin inside of its inclosing mountains. From this description I think it will be obvious that, while the so-called Great Basin is in some small degree a basin of lakes and streams, it is pre-eminently a basin of mountains and valleys.

In regard to the geological character of the mountains within the Great Basin, I would remark that, from Camp Floyd west, as far as about Kobah Valley, those of carboniferous origin much predominate; though over the desert proper, between Simpson's Springs and the Tots-arr range, the igneous are the characteristic; and near the Humboldt range those of Devonian age obtain. From Kobah Valley to the Sierra Nevada the ranges are almost exclusively of igneous origin, and present few indications of stratified rocks. The knowledge, geologically, of this extensive *terra incognita*, now for the first time given to the public in the reports of my assistant, Mr. Engelmann, and Mr. Meek, the paleontologist, is an interesting result of the expedition, and will go far to fill up the gap that remained to complete the geological profile of our country from the Atlantic to the Pacific, on the line of our explorations. These reports, it will be noticed, do not only discuss the geology and paleontology of the Great Basin, but of the whole route through from Fort Leavenworth to the Sierra Nevada, and to no two geologists, probably, could the work have been better assigned, since Mr. Engelmann was the geologist of Lieutenant Bryan's expedition to the Rocky Mountains in 1856, and of my expedition all the way from Fort Leavenworth to Sierra Nevada and back; and Mr. Meek's well-earned reputation as a paleontologist will certainly engage for him the attention of the scientific world. As these reports are very thorough, and include many facts of great interest to the geologist, I respectfully ask for them the perusal which their importance in reference to so great an extent of country demand.

In regard to the Indians, for a particular description of their persons and habits, I refer the reader to my journal, with its illustrations, and to the journal of Mr. Kern (Appendix Q); also the communication of Dr. Garland Hurt (Appendix O), whose residence in Utah for several years as Indian agent and well-known intelligence and character for truth and patriotism render his essay of great value. I would also refer to the communication of Maj. Frederick Dodge, Indian agent, incorporated in my journal of June 12, for information respecting the Pi-Utes and the Wa-shoes inhabiting Western Utah and Eastern California.

The Sho-sho-nees are divided by Dr. Hurt into the Snakes, Bannacks, To-si-witches, Go-sha-Utes, and Cum-um-pahs, though he afterward classes the two latter divisions as hybrid races between the Sho-sho-nees and Utahs, and this last I think the best classification.[p]

The Snakes are fierce and warlike in their habits and inhabit the country bordering on Snake River, Bear River, Green River, and as far east as Wind River. They are well supplied with horses and fire-arms, and subsist principally by hunting. They are the enemies of the Crows and Blackfeet on account of the buffalo having disappeared from their country west of the Rocky Mountains and their being obliged from necessity to hunt them as trespassers on the territory of these tribes east of the mountains. They have also been at war with the Utes for several generations. They, however, profess friendship for the whites, and it is their boast that, under their chief, *Wash-i-kee*, the blood of the white man has never stained their soil. It is certain, however, that small parties of this band, living in Box Elder County, in the Territory, with some Bannack Indians from Oregon, robbed, during the season of 1859, three parties of emigrants on the emigration road to the north and east of Great Salt Lake, and killed ten or twelve of their number.[q]

The Bannacks inhabit the southern borders of Oregon along the old Humboldt

(*p*) Dr. I. Forney, superintendent of Indian affairs in Utah, classes and numbers the various tribes and bands of Indians in Utah as follows:

Sho-sho-nees, or Snakes	4,500
Bannacks	500
Uinta Utes	1,000
Spanish Fork and San Pete farms	900
Pah-Vants (Utes)	700
Pey-utes (South)	2,200
Pey-utes (West)	6,000
Elk Mountain Utes	2,000
Wa-sho of Honey Lake	700
	18,500

The Sho-sho-nees claim the northeastern portion of the Territory for about four hundred miles west, and from one hundred to one hundred and twenty-five miles south from the Oregon line. The Utes claim the balance of the Territory. (See Pres. Mes. and Doc., 1859–'60, part 1, p. 733.)

(*q*) See report of General Johnston to headquarters of the Army, of November 2, 1859; Supt. I. Forney's letter to Major Porter, of September 22; and Maj. I. Lynde's report to General Johnston, of October 24, accompanying Annual Report of Secretary of War for 1859.

River emigrant-road, and have the reputation of infesting the emigration along that portion of the route, and of being of a very thievish, treacherous character.

The To-sa-witches, or White Knives, inhabit the region along the Humboldt River, and, according to Dr. Hurt, have the character of being very treacherous. We met them ranging in small parties between the Un-go-we-ah Range and Cooper's Range, on our more northern route. The Ute tribe Dr. Hurt divides into the Pah-Utes, Tamp-Pah-Utes, Cheveriches, Pah-vants, San Pitches, and Py-eeds.

The Utahs proper inhabit the waters of Green River south of Green River Mountains, the Grand River and its tributaries, and as far south as the Navajo Country. They also claim the country bordering on Utah Lake and as far south as the Sevier Lake as theirs. They are a brave race, and subist principally by hunting. The buffalo having left their country and gone east over the Rocky Mountains, their hunting this game in the country of the Arrapahoes and Cheyennes brings them in continual conflict. Dr. Hurt says it is his opinion, from a familiar acquaintance with them, that there is not a braver tribe to be found among the aborigines of America than the Utahs; none warmer in their attachments, less relenting in their hatred, or more capable of treachery. Their present chief is *Arrapene*, Indian name Sin-ne-roach,[r] the successor of the renowned *Wacca*, sometimes erroneously called Walker. Some of the weaker bands both of the Snakes and Utahs are almost continually in a state of starvation, and are compelled to resort almost exclusively to small animals, roots, grass, seed, and insects for subsistence. The General Government has opened farms for these Indians in the valleys of the Spanish Fork and San Pete.

The Pah-vants occupy the Corn Creek, Paravan and Beaver Valleys, and the valley of the Sevier. On Corn Creek they have a farm under the supervision of the General Government. It was a portion of this tribe that massacred Captain Gunnison and a portion of his party. Their chief is Kan-nash.

The Pi-eeds live adjoining the Pah-vants down to the Santa Clara, and are represented as the most timid and dejected of all the Utah bands. They barter their children to the Utes proper for a few trinkets or bits of clothing, by whom they are again sold to the Navajos for blankets, &c. They indulge in a rude kind of agriculture, which they probably derived from the old Spanish jesuits. Their productions are corn, beans, and squashes. The Mountain Meadow massacre is ascribed by the Mormons to them, but, as Dr. Hurt justly remarks, "any one at all acquainted with them must perceive at once how utterly absurd and impossible it is for such a report to be true". Indeed the report of Mr. I. Forney, the superintendent of Indians in Utah, of September 29, 1859, fixes the stigma of this horrible outrage on the Mormons.[s] Their chiefs are Quanarrah and Tatsigobbets.

The Goshoots Dr. Hurt classes, as I have remarked, among the Sho-sho-nees; but, according to Mr. George W. Bean, my guide in the fall of 1858, and who has

(*r*) This chief, according to the newspapers, has recently died.

(*s*) The Commissioner of Indian Affairs, A. B. Greenwood, in his report of November 26, 1859, to Secretary of the Interior, says, in relation to this matter:

"Many of the numerous depredations upon the immigrants have doubtless been committed by them in consequence of their destitute and desperate condition. They have, at times, been compelled either to steal or starve; but there is reason to apprehend that in their forays they have often been only the tools of lawless whites residing in the

lived in Utah for the last ten or twelve years, and been frequently employed as interpreter among the Indians, they are an offshoot from the Ute Indians, and are the offspring of a disaffected portion of this tribe, that left their nation about two generations ago, under their leader or chief *Go-ship*, and hence their name Go-ship-Utes, since contracted into Go-shutes. I am disposed, too, to believe that they are thus derived from the fact that I noticed among them several Utes who, while claiming that they belonged to the Utes proper, yet had intermarried with and were living among them.

These Goshoots are few in number, not more than probably 200 or 300, and reside principally in the grassy valleys west of Great Salt Lake, along and in the vicinity of my roads as far as the Un-go-we-ah range. They are of the very lowest type of mankind, and illustrate very forcibly the truth which the great physicist of our country, Prof. Arnold Guyot, of Princeton College, has brought out so significantly in his admirable work, "Earth and Man," to wit: "*That the contour, relief, and relative position of the crust of the earth is intimately connected with the development of man.*" These Indians live in a barren and, in winter, on account of its altitude, a cold climate, and the consequence is that they are obliged to live entirely on rabbits, rats, lizards, snakes, insects, rushes, roots, grass-seeds, &c. They are more filthy than beasts, and live in habitations which, summer and winter, are nothing more than circular inclosures about three feet high, made of the *artemisia* or sage-bush or branches of the cedar, thrown around in the circumference of a circle, and which serve only to break off the wind. As the thermometer in the winter must at times be as low as zero, and there must fall a good deal of snow, it will readily be perceived that they must suffer a great deal. Anything like an inclosed lodge or wick-e-up of any sort I did not see among them. Their dress, summer and winter, is a rabbit skin tunic or cape, which comes down to just below the knee, and seldom have they leggins or moccasins.[t]

Territory. In some of the worst outrages of this kind, involving the lives as well as the property of our emigrants, the latter are known to have participated. That this was the case in the atrocious and dreadful massacre at 'Mountain Meadow,' in September, 1857, the facts stated in the report of the superintendent, in regard to that occurrence, leave no room for doubt. The lives of from one hundred and fifteen to one hundred and twenty peaceable emigrants, of all ages and both sexes, were inhumanly and brutally sacrificed on that occasion, some young children only being spared." (See "Message and Doc., 1859–'60, pp. 386 and 737–740.")

(*t*) WASHINGTON, *June* 14, 1860.

DEAR SIR: Permit me to bring to your knowledge as a fact, which it is pleasing to me to inform you, that I have in my exploration across the continent given to a very conspicuous range of mountains over which I passed the name of your worthy self, by which I feel that I not more honor a distinguished votary of physical science than I do honor to myself. Surely one who has spoken so modestly, so adoringly, so well of nature as the handiwork of the great I AM and has shown that she and history are but the counterparts of each other, both illustrating and developing the Great Intelligent First Cause and His goodness in thus "arranging all things for the education of man and the realization of the plans of His mercy," deserves this small tribute of respect and praise; and I bestow it, as I have said, feeling that I not more do honor to a great physicist than I honor myself.

The range of mountains which, on my forthcoming map, I have given the name of Guyot range, is a very conspicuous one, trending north and south, and stretching from the southern shore of Great Salt Lake well on toward the Sevier River. It lies about thirty-five miles west of the valley of the Jordan and of Lake Utah. The pass through it which my routes to California from Camp Floyd take is a fine one, and I have, with his permission, called it after General A. S. Johnston, the distinguished officer of the Army who has recently been in command of the forces in Utah. Its altitude above the sea is 6,227 feet. That of the highest peaks of the range is probably about 2,000 feet higher.

My maps, profiles, and report are nearly finished, but not sufficiently so to be presented to Congress for publication at its present session.

I inclose a paper read before the Academy of Natural Sciences of Philadelphia, anticipatory of my more elaborate report in reference to the paleontological collection of my expedition. This may soon be followed up with a publication

Between the Cooper range and the Pe-er-re-ah range we found along our routes a number of the Digger tribe, who said that they were of Sho-sho-nee origin, but had no chief. They live scatteredly, and, like the Go-shoot, are of a low type, and live and dress in the same way. Like them, their bow, arrow, ratsticks, traps, and nets are their principal instruments of subsistence. They place great value on a pair of moccasins, as they are of great service in enabling them to tramp through the sharp sage bush. They appear to be very few in number, and, like the Go-shoots, are to be little feared by an emigrant party, who are at all on their guard, against theft and treachery.

The Py-utes (according to Major Dodge) number between 6,000 and 7,000 souls. They inhabit Western Utah from Oregon to New Mexico, their locations being generally in the vicinity of the principal rivers and lakes of the Great Basin, viz: Humboldt, Carson, Walker, Truckee, Owen's, Pyramid, and Mono. They resemble in appearance, manner, and customs the Delawares on our Missouri frontier, and with judicious management and assistance from Government would in three years equal them in agriculture. Their chief is Wan-muc-ca (The Giver), and it was a portion of this tribe under this chief who have been engaged recently in the massacre in Western Utah. Their language resembles in some of its words the Sho-sho-nee (see Appendix J), yet it differs so much from it that my guide, Ute Pete, who spoke both Ute and

by the same society of some extracts from my report, which will be more particularly descriptive of the new species of fossils which were found.

My report I think, among other things, will illustrate, in the low type of man to be found in the Indians of the "Great Basin" of our continent, called "Root Diggers," how intimately connected with the contour, relief, and relative position of the crust of the earth is the development of the human race, and will add one more to the many facts which you have given in your "Earth and Man" of this important geographical truth.

Permit me to subscribe myself, very respectfully and truly, yours,

J. H. SIMPSON,
Captain Topographical Engineers.

To Prof. ARNOLD GUYOT, LL.D.,
Princeton, N. J.

PRINCETON, N. J., *June* 20, 1860.

DEAR SIR: I have the honor to acknowledge the receipt of your most acceptable letter, and I thank you very heartily for the kind feeling expressed in it. Guyot range of mountains will recall to my mind more than a lofty mountain chain; it will tell me of the sympathy that truths dear to me, because fruitful of much good and enjoyment for me and for many others, have found with you. Believe me, dear sir, when I say that I feel particularly gratified to find a man of your busy profession and of your attainments so well acquainted with, and so appreciative of, the views so briefly exposed in the little volume to which you allude in so kind terms. Common convictions and a common faith on such grand topics are a bond of union among men which cannot easily be broken. So I shall now feel when thinking of you.

I have read with great interest the geological notice of Messrs. Meek and Englemann on your geological discoveries. The presence of all the great geological formations, from the Silurian and Devonian up to the Tertiary, in the Great Basin, and also the circumstance of the Paleozoic rocks constituting the chief formations west of the Salt Lake, are data which throw much light on the geological history of this country.

I shall look with eagerness to your coming report for more light still on these regions so long unknown; and I am very glad that you did not forget the study of the poor human beings who were the first tenants of these wildernesses. and of the influence that the niggard nature amidst which their lot is cast had on shaping their present condition.

I remain, my dear sir, with great regard and very truly, yours,

A. GUYOT.

To Capt. J. H. SIMPSON,
Topographical Engineers, United States Army.

Sho-sho-nee, could not understand them.[u] This tribe is frequently confounded with the Pah-Utes, with which they show only a distant affinity.

The Washoes, according to Major Dodge, "number about 900 souls, and inhabit the country along the eastern slope of the Sierra Nevada, from Honey Lake on the north to the Rio Clara, the west branch of the Walker's River, a distance of 150 miles. They are not inclined to agricultural pursuits nor any other advancement toward civilization. They are destitute of all the necessaries to make life even desirable. There is not one horse, pony, or mule in the nation. They are peaceable, but indolent. In the summer they wander around the shores of Lake Bigler, in the Sierra Nevada, principally subsisting on the fish found in it. In the winter they lay about in the *artemisia* of their different localities, subsisting on a little grass-seed." The Indian vocabulary (Appendix J) will show that they are a distinct tribe, and in no way assimilated with the Utes, Sho-sho-nees, or Py-Utes.

The Indians living along or in the vicinity of my routes are, as above stated, starting from Camp Floyd, first, the Go-shoots, as far as the Un-go-we-ah range; second, the Humboldt Indians, from the Un-go-we-ah range to Cooper's range; third, the Diggers or Pah-Utes, who are of Sho-sho-nee origin, from Cooper's range to the Pe-er-re-ah range; fourth, the Pi-Utes, from the Pe-er-re-ah range to the Sierra Nevada; and, fifth, the Washoes, at the base of the Sierra Nevada. All these Indians, as they seldom carry any weapons but the bow and arrow, will be found perfectly harmless to parties of emigrants who are tolerably well armed and sufficiently on the alert not to invite attacks or theft. In our case, as a general thing, it was as much as we could do to get them to visit us at all, their fright was so great. Indeed, never do emigrants meet with any difficulty from Indians passing over the plains, when they observe but ordinary vigilance and care.[v]

(*u.*) Mr. J. Forney, superintendent of Indians in Utah, in his report of September 29, 1859, to the Secretary of the Interior (Mess. and Doc., 1859-'60, p. 732), speaking of these Indians, says, "the Utah-Pah-Vant and Py-Ute, although they are designated by several different names, yet all have emanated from one nation or tribe and speak the same language." My vocabulary (in Appendix J) will show that in this last particular he is incorrect; at least so far as the Py-Utes are concerned.

(*v.*) Major Lynde, in his report to General Johnston, of October 24, 1859, giving an account of his expedition against the Indians who had committed some massacres on the old Humboldt River road, makes the following remarks in relation to the carelessness of emigrants he met in respect to proper vigilance against Indian surprises and attacks:

"Every train that has been attacked acknowledge that they were perfectly unprepared for defense. The Indians watch the trains from the hills, and if they see a train well-armed and watchful, they do not molest it. I have seen many trains on the road during the summer which had plenty of arms, but they were carried in the wagons, and in many cases without being loaded. The emigrants would laugh at me when I told them of the necessity of always having their arms ready for instant use." (See report of Secretary of War, 1859, p. 241.)

EXPLORATIONS ACROSS THE GREAT BASIN OF UTAH.

REPORT AND JOURNAL.

REPORT AND JOURNAL.

On the 6th of January, 1859, at Camp Floyd, Utah Territory, I had the honor to submit, through General A. S. Johnston, commanding the Department of Utah, to the War Department, for its approval, the following project of exploration:

OFFICE OF TOPOGRAPHICAL ENGINEERS, DEPARTMENT OF UTAH,
Camp Floyd, Utah Territory, January 6, 1859.

SIR: Agreeably to instructions from the headquarters of this department, as you are aware, a new route has been opened from Fort Bridger to this post, by the way of Timpanogos River Valley, which, in connection with Lieutenant Bryan's route, or even by the old South Pass road, makes an excellent link in the chain of routes from the States to this post. There has also been explored, by direction of the commanding general, and is now in use by the United States as a postal route, a route west of this post across the Great Salt Lake Desert, which has been extended by the mail company all the way to the Humboldt, and which they report as promising a hard wagon-road, with a sufficiency of fuel, water, and grass. These improvements in the old route have already been of great service to the Army and country, but it is believed that still greater can be made. It is believed that a direct route from this post to Carson Valley, in Utah, can be obtained, which would avoid the detour by the Humboldt to the right, and that by the Las Vegas and Los Angeles route to the left, and that it could be obtained so as to make the distance hence to San Francisco less than 800 miles; that is, that a route could be found in this direction 260 miles shorter than the Humboldt River route and 390 miles shorter than the Los Angeles route. To make this plain, I respectfully refer you to the accompanying extract from my report of December 28 to these headquarters, giving a detailed account of reconnaissances recently made by me under the order of the commanding general.

In this connection I would respectfully state that it is believed, also, that a still shorter and better route may be obtained from Camp Floyd to Fort Leavenworth than by either the South Pass or Lieutenant Bryan's route. I refer now to a route hence to the headwaters of the Arkansas and thence via Bent's Fort to Fort Leavenworth. This route, it will be noticed by reference to the map recently compiled in the office of explorations and surveys, promises to be at least as short as either of the others, and might prove considerably better as a wagon-route. The routes passed over by Frémont, so far as his published report informs me, as well as that of Captain Gunnison, which is too far south, I should suppose, would be impracticable for the object in view; but still it is believed that more information than when they crossed over the country is now obtainable, and it is not at all improbable that Colonel Loring, who has recently returned to Santa Fé by a new route, and has reported his trip as successful, may be enabled to give important information in the matter.* I would, therefore, respectfully report, as a project of reconnaissance for the present year, to be commenced as soon as the season will permit, an exploration hence to Carson Valley, there to connect properly with a known route; a return exploration thence to this post for a further improvement of the route; the party to be here refitted and to explore a new route hence to Fort Leavenworth by way of the sources of the Arkansas and Bent's Fort; the report and maps to be made up in Washington. I would require an assistant, which might be Lieutenant Putnam, Topographical Engineers, as he is junior to Lieut. J. L. K. Smith, and in order to the facilitation of the survey, and the insurance of its success, an escort such as the commanding general might deem advisable.

I respectfully submit this project to the consideration of the commanding general, in order, if it is approved, it may be referred, through the Bureau of the Topographical Engineers, to the Hon. Secretary of War for his sanction.

I am, sir, very respectfully, your obedient servant,

J. H. SIMPSON,
Captain Corps of Topographical Engineers.

Bvt. Maj. FITZ JOHN PORTER,
Assistant Adjutant-General.

*At the time of writing the above it was believed that Colonel Loring had returned to Santa Fé by a new route, but I find on looking at the map of his route, since received, that he took mainly Captain Gunnison's route of 1853.

The project was approved by General Johnston and met with the sanction of the Secretary of War, as follows:

BUREAU OF TOPOGRAPHICAL ENGINEERS,
Washington, February 17, 1859.

SIR: Your letter of 6th ultimo, inclosing a project of exploration for the present year, approved by the commanding general of the department, having been submitted to the Hon. Secretary of War, has been returned with the following indorsement:

"WAR DEPARTMENT, *February* 16, 1859.

"Approved.

"J. B. FLOYD,
"*Secretary of War.*"

Respectfully, sir, your obedient servant,

I. C. WOODRUFF,
Captain Topographical Engineers, Assistant to Bureau, in Charge.

Capt. J. H. SIMPSON,
Corps Topographical Engineers, Camp Floyd, Utah Territory.

In accordance with the foregoing authority, the following orders were issued from the headquarters of the Department of Utah:

HEADQUARTERS DEPARTMENT OF UTAH,
Camp Floyd, Utah Territory, April 26, 1859.

SIR: Under authority from the Secretary of War, bearing date December 18, 1858, and February 16, 1859, Brigadier-General Johnston directs you to renew, as soon as the season will permit, the exploration commenced under his instructions of 15th October ultimo, and which was brought to a close by the rapid approach of winter; and also to arrange for an examination of the country hence to the Arkansas, in accordance with your project of January 6, 1859.

The general directs me to address you as follows, as a recapitulation of the duties assigned to you:

First. To explore south of the Great Desert, in order to ascertain the practicability and economy of locating and working, for military purposes and for general traveling, a wagon-road hence to Carson Valley, and there to connect with a known route across the Sierra Nevada; returning, to explore for an improvement in that route, or, should that not be feasible, for an improvement in the new route from the Humboldt to this post.

Second. To examine for a new route hence to Fort Leavenworth by the way of the sources of the Arkansas and Bent's Fort.

In connection with obtaining geological and botanical information of the country, your attention is specially called to determining the quality and extent of the grass, building-materials, and fuel at positions suitable for the location of a military post, it being understood by suitable positions those in or near the Indian country, having, in addition to easy access to and control over the avenues of communication, the three essentials, fuel, water, and grass.

It is desirable, from its military importance, to procure information of the number and size of the Indian tribes through which you will pass, the extent of the country of each, their mode of living, carrying on war, how armed, &c

On your return to this camp, while waiting the refitting of your party, you will, as connected with your second expedition, make an examination to the sources of White River, (western branch of Green River,) passing up both the Timpanogos and Spanish Forks.

Whichever route, Colonel Loring's trail through San Pete Valley or one of the above, indicates most favorably for making a short and feasible road, that one will be taken to White River, whence Colonel Loring's trail will be followed and improved to and up Grand River, and thence through the Cochatope Pass to Fort Garland, Sangrede Christo Pass, down the Huerfano, to the Arkansas, &c., to Fort Leavenworth.

Should you find it advisable to examine from the Cochatope Pass or its vicinity direct to the Arkansas, you are authorized to do so; but if a route in that direction be not economically practicable, you will return and renew the examination of the route above indicated.

From Fort Leavenworth, with the assistants necessary to make up your work, you will repair to Washington and report to the Adjutant-General.

To enable you to perform these duties, you will take with you all your party, civil and military, and be furnished with an escort on your first expedition of one officer and twenty men (ten mounted) and a guide and interpreter. A new escort will be provided on your return to this camp.

The commanding general wishes a report of your progress and success from time to time, as occasion may offer. Should there be any change in your instructions, they will be found at Genoa or on your return to this camp.

I am, sir, very respectfully, your obedient servant,

F. J. PORTER,
Assistant Adjutant-General.

To Capt. JAMES H. SIMPSON,
Topographical Engineers, Camp Floyd, Utah Territory.

HEADQUARTERS DEPARTMENT OF UTAH,
Camp Floyd, Utah Territory, April 25, 1859.

SPECIAL ORDERS, No. 31.

An escort of one officer and twenty men (ten mounted and ten foot) from Camp Floyd will be furnished Capt. James H. Simpson, Topographical Engineers, charged, under the authority of the Secretary of War, with an exploration for military purposes of the country hence direct to Carson Valley.

The officer will furnish such aid and assistance to Captain Simpson as will facilitate his operations, and will act as assistant quartermaster and commissary to the command.

A medical officer will be assigned to the command.

By order of Bvt. Brig. Gen. A. S. Johnston.

F. J. PORTER,
Assistant Adjutant-General.

HEADQUARTERS CAMP FLOYD, *April* 26, 1859.

SPECIAL ORDERS, No. 110.

Pursuant to Special Orders No. 31, from the headquarters of the Department of Utah, dated on the 25th instant, the following party is detailed to accompany Captain Simpson, Topographical Engineers, who has been ordered on a tour of exploration for military purposes, as an escort to and from Carson Valley, Utah Territory:

Second Lieut. Alexander Murry, one sergeant and one corporal, and eight privates, Tenth Infantry; two non-commissioned officers and eight privates, well mounted, Second Dragoons.

Lieutenant Murry will consult with Captain Simpson immediately in regard to their transportation and supplies for the party. Seventy rounds of ammunition will be taken.

Assistant Surgeon Joseph C. Bailey will accompany the expedition.

By order of Bvt. Col. C. F. Smith:

CLARENCE E. BENNETT,
Second Lieutenant and Adjutant Tenth Infantry, Post Adjutant.

Pursuant to the foregoing, the following orders were issued by me to my party:

[Orders No. 1]

OFFICE TOPOGRAPHICAL ENGINEERS, DEPARTMENT OF UTAH,
Camp Floyd, Utah Territory, April 29, 1859.

Agreeably to orders emanating from this department of April 25 and 26, the topographical engineer party under the command of the undersigned will leave the post early on the morning of the 2d proximo, for the purpose of exploring a new route to California.

To Lieut. J. L. K. Smith, topographical engineers, is assigned the duty of taking sextant observations for latitude and time or longitude. These observations will be made at every camp, and those on the sun will be preferred. Equal altitudes of the sun every twenty-four hours will be made, either when practicable on the same day, or, which will generally be the case, in the afternoon of one day and, when the sun is at corresponding altitudes, the next morning. Observations on east and west stars will be made when, on account of unfavorable weather, the sun cannot be observed.*

To Lieut. H. S. Putnam, topographical engineers, is assigned the duty of making the proper magnetic observations for dip, intensity, and declination of the needle. In addition to those for declination with the magnetometer, which will be taken at least within every fifty miles, he will also observe on Polaris for the same purpose, the epoch being when it is at either of its culminations or greatest eastern or western elongation, when the reading of the needle of the theodolite or compass will be noted.

To Lieutenant Putnam is also assigned the duty of observing with the astronomical transit, at the proper epochs, the moon and moon-culminating stars for longitude. Observations for lunar distances, and altitudes will be also observed for the same purpose, the three sextants being used at the same time by as many observers.

To Lieutenant Putnam is further assigned the duty of surveying the route by noting, in a proper manner, the bearings and distances of the various deflections of the route and of the topographical features of the country within the limits of vision. These notes will be plotted every evening, and thus our exact position from day to day shown.

Lieutenant Putnam will further keep up an itinerary of the route, according to the prescribed form with which he will be furnished, the distance to be measured by two odometers to provide against error.

To Mr. Henry Engelmann, geologist, is assigned the duty of observing the country passed through geologically and botanically, specimens in each department being collected for this purpose and properly labeled and packed away.

Mr. Engelmann will also take charge of the barometrical and meteorological observations, the object being to obtain an exact profile of the route as well as a knowledge of the climate and its relation to the physical aspects of the region traversed.

Messrs. Edward Jagiello and William Lee will assist the above-named officers in the required observations in the mode which may be found most expedient.

---

* These last observations were most resorted to on the expedition on account of being generally practicable.

To Mr. Charles McCarthy is assigned the duty of taxidermist and collector of specimens illustrative of the animal and insect world. In order to this, he will be assiduous in the collection of the necessary proportion of specimens, and in their being properly prepared for preservation and transportation.

To Mr. H. V. A. Von Beckh is assigned the duty of sketching the country in a manner to illustrate its common as well as peculiar characteristics.

The escort, under the orders from the Department of Utah, will be commanded by Lieut. Alexander Murry, Tenth Infantry, who has also been charged with the duties of quartermaster and commissary, and directed to see that the expedition is supplied with everything in these departments, according to the requisitions which have been approved by the proper authority.

Lieut. J. L. K. Smith will act as ordnance officer, and will obtain from the Ordnance Department the necessary arms and ammunition for the party.

The expedition we are about to enter upon being an important one, it is expected by the officer commanding that each and every officer, soldier, and citizen engaged in it will do his utmost to secure its success.

J. H. SIMPSON,
Captain Corps Topographical Engineers, in Charge of Expedition.

Camp Floyd, May 2, 1859.—Longitude, 112° 8′ 7″; latitude, 40° 13′ 18″; elevation above the sea, 4,860 feet; magnetic variation, 17° 10′ 8″ E. The topographical party under my command left this post at a quarter of 8 a. m., to explore the country intervening this locality and Carson River, at the east foot of the Sierra Nevada, for a new and direct route to California.

My orders of the 29th ultimo show who my assistants are, and their several vocations. The employés of the party number nine persons, and make the total number of the topographical party, inclusive of assistants, one guide, two Mexican packers, and two Indians of the Ute tribe, twenty-two.

The escort is composed agreeably to post orders No. 110, above given, and aggregates, rank and file, twenty-two persons.

We have with us twelve six-mule quartermaster-wagons, for the transportation of supplies, three more loaded with forage, for the first five or six days, and one six-mule and one four-mule ambulance, for the conveyance of the instruments. We are rationed for three months, six commissary beeves being driven on foot. The wagons were all parked yesterday for inspection preparatory to being turned over to us by the depot quartermaster, and what parts were found defective supplied by others. The number of teamsters is fourteen, exclusive of the three belonging to the forage-wagons, which are to return to Camp Floyd, and Mr. Henry Sailing is the wagon-master. We have also with us one wheelwright, one blacksmith, and four herders, making the aggregate number of the topographical party, escort, and quartermaster's employés sixty-four. Included in the number is a commissary sergeant (Miller, Tenth Infantry), and Private Thatcher, Tenth Infantry, hospital steward and acting bugler.

The topographical party and teamsters are provided each with a navy-revolver. Of course, the military escort has its proper arms.

Our instruments are, three sextants, three artificial horizons, one astronomical transit, four chronometers (one large box and three pocket), two cistern-barometers, one magnetic dip-circle, or inclinometer, and one magnetometer. This last is the instrument which Dr. Kane had with him on his polar expedition, and has all the dingy, worn appearance which such an expedition would naturally cause. We have also a number of Schmalkalder, or prismatic, and pocket compasses.

The route we take is that I explored last fall on my return from Short Cut Pass, of Colonel Thomas' range, a report and map of which have already been rendered and, by order of Congress, published.* Our course lay slightly south of west, up a scarcely perceptible ascent, out from Cedar Valley to Camp Floyd Pass (altitude, 5,234 feet above the sea), 3 miles distant from Camp Floyd; through this broad champaign pass 3 miles, and thence, nearly southwest, 12.2 miles, to Meadow Creek, in Rush Valley, where we encamped. Journey, 18.2 miles. Road good.

Finding that the California mail party, after threading Camp Floyd Pass, had missed my route of last fall, and had unnecessarily made too great a detour to the northward, I struck directly across to Meadow Creek with the wagons, and thus marked out a short cut which would shorten the road a mile or two.

For the conformation of Cedar Valley, in which Camp Floyd is situated, and of Rush Valley, in which we are encamped, and of the mountains limiting them, see map herewith.

These valleys are slightly concave in cross-section east and west, Cedar Valley averaging a breadth of 8 miles and Rush Valley a breadth of 13 miles, and lie longitudinally north and south, Cedar Valley, for a length of 30 miles, and Rush Valley, for a length of 40 miles, and give evidence, from the appearances of water-lines along the base of the mountains, that they were once submerged, and doubtless a part of the Great Salt Lake. The whole of Cedar Valley has been reserved by the General Government for military purposes, and at the northern portion of Rush Valley, is the small military reserve laid out by directions of Lieutenant-Colonel Steptoe in 1855.

The soil is argillo-calcareo-arenaceous in character, has a sort of buff color, and quickly absorbs the rains, which seldom fall in this region except in the fall, winter, and spring. The vegetable growth is principally the *artemisia tridentata*, or wild sage, with the *sarcobatus vermicularis*, or greasewood, and the *lynosyris*, or rabbit-bush, intermingled.

These valleys are very sparsely watered, and though the soil in itself has all the elements of fertility, yet for want of the necessary moisture, for agricultural purposes, except in a small number of areas containing but a few acres which can be irrigated, it is utterly worthless. The cultivable portions in Cedar Valley are at Cedar Fort, a Mormon settlement, 5 miles north of Camp Floyd, and at Camp Floyd, and in Rush Valley, at Johnson's Settlement, on Clover Creek, in the northwestern portion of the valley, where there are about 200 acres of good farming land. Not a tree is to be seen anywhere in either of the valleys, though scrub-cedar and pine crown the mountain-heights. There is quite an abundance of good grass upon the bases of the mountains and in the cañons, and in some places it is to be found in patches in the valley. It is also found along Meadow Creek, in Rush Valley, and along other short streams in the southwestern portion of this valley. Indeed, both in the southwestern and northern portions of this valley there is a great deal of excellent grass, and the Government herds of beef-cattle and mules were wintered at these points during the past winter. The pasture on Meadow Creek is slightly alkaline.

The mountains limiting the valley are at points quite formidable, the Oquirrh range dividing Cedar and Rush Valleys discovering along its crest in midsummer

* Sen. Ex. Doc. No. 40, 35th Cong., 2d sess.

shreds of snow which the sun has not been able to dissipate. The highest point of this range, which I call Camp Floyd Peak, on account of its proximity to the post of that name, is 4,214 feet above the camp, or 9,074 feet above the sea. The formation of these mountains is made up of highly siliceous altered limestones, slate-rock, and altered sandstones (quartzite) of the Carboniferous period, the slaty, calcareous rocks predominating.

The roads in these valleys are good and lead out in various directions into the adjoining valleys.

The weather has been pleasantly warm. For exact state of it to-day and succeeding days, see meteorological diary, Appendix U.

May 3, *Camp No.* 1, *on Meadow Creek.*—Elevation above the sea, 5,205 feet. The bugle sounded reveille at daybreak. Thermometer at 5 a. m., 39°. Moved at 6 a. m. Follow up Meadow Creek a mile, and then cross just above old adobe corral. Crossing only tolerable. This stream, which is of gentle current, is so narrow that you can jump across it, and is but a few inches in depth. It runs northerly about ten miles and sinks. About a half mile above the crossing the mail company has a station, at present consisting of a Sibley tent, and a cedar-picket corral for stock is being made. From this station our course lay nearly southwest, seven miles to east, foot of General Johnston's Pass, which I discovered last fall, and which I called after the general commanding the Department of Utah. The mountain range, which is quite a formidable one, I call after Prof. Arnold Guyot, LL. D., the distinguished physicist and professor in the college of New Jersey.

In about a mile more, by a good grade, you reach the top of the pass (altitude above the sea, 6,237 feet), and thence, in three-quarters of a mile, by a steep descent, which, for a portion of the way, teams going east would have to double up, you attain to a spot where is a patch of grass, and where we encamped. There is a small spring near us, on the north side of the pass, which, however, our animals soon drank dry, and which doubtless is dry during the summer. Road to-day good. Journey, 9.9 miles, reaching camp a little after meridian.

The Ute Indian, brother of Arrapene, chief of the tribe, who accompanied us as guide, reporting himself too sick to go on with the party, I permitted him to return to Camp Floyd. Saw two antelope, a couple of sage hens, and McCarthy shot a curlew, from which he took, perfectly formed in the shell, an egg as large as a chicken's. The California mail-stage passed us on its way to Camp Floyd. Cho-kup, chief of the Ruby Valley band of Sho-sho-nees, was a passenger, on his way to see the Indian agent. He is the best-looking Indian I have seen in the Territory.

Near our camp, Russell, Major & Waddel have a herd-camp. The herds find excellent and abundant pasture on both sides of this range of mountains, a few miles to the south, in Rush and also in Porter Valley. Water also abundant at these points.

The summits of the highest mountains have still their wintry garb of snow upon them. Last winter was an unusually severe one, and the consequence is that the spring has been backward, and the grass is yet quite short and tender; though on the mountain slopes and in the gorges it is sufficiently advanced for grazing.

May 4, *Camp No.* 2, *three-quarters of a mile below summit of General Johnston's Pass.*—

Elevation above the sea, 5,816 feet. This morning at daylight we found that a driving snow-storm had set in from the west and about six inches of snow had fallen. The Sibley tent occupied by some of the assistants had become prostrated, under the combined effects of the snow and wind, and when I saw it its occupants were still under it. Lieutenant Murry reports the spring full again this morning. Thermometer at 5½ a. m., 32½°.

Moved camp at 10 minutes after 7 a. m., our course being westwardly down General Johnston's Pass into Skull Valley (altitude, 4,850 feet above the sea), and thence southwestwardly, in a somewhat tortuous direction to avoid a low mountain, to a spring which I discovered last fall, and which I called, in my last report, Pleasant Spring, but which now, I find, goes by the name of Simpson's Spring. This spring is on the base and north side of some mountains, which I call after Captain Stephen Champlin, of the United States Navy.

Journey, 16.2 miles. Road good.

We are now on the southern side of the Great Salt Lake Desert, which extends, with an occasional interruption from small isolated mountains, all the way to the most northern portion of the Great Salt Lake, a distance of over 100 miles. The whole scene is that of a somber, dreary waste, where neither man nor beast can live for want of the necessary food and water, and over which a bird is scarcely ever seen to fly. The surface is singularly flat, a very slight downward grade, however, being observable northwardly toward the lake. The soil is argillo-calcareo-arenaceous, and produces only a small growth of *artemisia* and greasewood. As you approach Great Salt Lake the ground becomes more level and low, and the valley presents the appearance of a mud-flat, which, in some localities, is covered with an incrustation of common salt, and over which it would be hazardous for wagons to cross. Captain Stansbury, in his report of March 10, 1852, very justly remarks that "these plains are but little elevated above the present level of the lake, and have, beyond question, at one time, formed part of it." Indeed, the water lines indicate, as in Rush and Cedar Valleys, that the whole desert has at one time been submerged, and constituted a part of the Great Salt Lake. Captain Beckwith, in his report of November 25, 1854, speaking of the portion of the desert over which he passed, to the northward of our route, says: "Five miles from Granite Mountain we left the dry soil on which we terminated our march last evening, and passing over a narrow ridge of sand, entered upon a desert of stiff mud, as level as a sheet of water, which we found great difficulty in crossing with our wagons, for 17.66 miles. For this entire distance there is not a sign of green vegetation, and only here and there a dry stalk of *artemisia*, where it has been transported by the wind. The lightest sheet of effloresced salt covered the moist earth at intervals, and the track of a single antelope or wolf could be seen crossing the desert for miles, by the line of dark mud thrown up by its feet, so level, soft, and white was the plain; and the whole scene was as barren, desolate, and dreary as can be imagined." While such was the character of the country where Captain Beckwith passed, I would remark that at the southern portion of the desert, where our route lay, the plain or valley is sufficiently high to be dry and affords a good road.

The Champlin Mountains, at the foot of which we are encamped, are composed of porphyritic and other igneous rocks, which have tilted up and much altered the stratified rocks around them, to wit, sand-rocks, siliceous limestones, and being quite high, and giving rise to springs and short running streams on their west, south, and east sides, and covered as they are with cedar and, in many places, grass, they formed a very valuable topographical feature in the line of travel over the Great Desert, as will be seen more fully in my notes of my return route. The other mountains to the north and southwest are to be seen looking dark and dreary, and indicate by their scorched, vitreous, and, in some portions, ashy hue, that they have been subjected to igneous action. Not a tree is to be seen upon them, nor a patch of green vegetation of any kind. They are fit monuments of the desolation which reigns over the whole desert.

The spring where we are encamped furnishes but a scant supply of water, which, however, the mail company, which has a station here, has collected in a reservoir formed by a dam across the ravine. The accommodations of the company are at present a Sibley tent, set upon a circular stone wall. There is an abundance of grass in the vicinity and cedar on the heights, but not conveniently near.

We found our guide, Mr. Reese, here, agreeably to appointment. I had sent him in advance of the party six days to examine the country to the south and southwest of this spring to see if the Short Cut Pass, which is objectionable on account of its high grade, 20 miles to the southwest, through Colonel Thomas's range, could not be avoided. He informed me that he has been fully 35 miles in the direction stated, and is convinced that for 60 miles there can no water be found. He has been up a cañon ten miles to the south of Simpson's Spring, in Champlin Mountains, where there is plenty of grass and water; but to go to this water now would be out of our way. It is possible, however, that on our return from Carson Valley it would be expedient for us to go directly from Short Cut Pass to the cañon referred to, and, by thus being able to get into Porter Valley, get into Rush Valley toward its south extremity, and thus reach Camp Floyd by a route which might furnish more water and grass than by our present route.

Skull Valley, which is a part of the Great Salt Lake Desert, and which we have crossed to-day, Mr. George W. Bean, my guide over this route last fall, says, derives its name from the number of skulls which have been found in it, and which have arisen from the custom of the Goshoot Indians burying their dead in springs, which they sink with stones or keep down with sticks. He says he has actually seen the Ute Indians bury their dead in this way near the town of Provo, where he resides.

May 5, Camp No. 3, Simpson's Spring.—Longitude, 112° 47′ 18″; latitude, 40° 1′ 55″; magnetic variation, 15° 30′ E.; altitude above the sea, 4,850 feet. Morning bright. Thermometer, at 5 a. m., 40°. Guide left us at half past 5, with two men and one pack-mule, to explore a pass about five miles to the northward of "Short Cut Pass," in the range beyond us, and thus, if possible, cut off a bend of the mail-route beyond "Short Cut." He is to join us to-morrow at the next watering-place. My instructions contemplated my keeping south of my old route from Simpson's Spring; but the guide finding no water in that direction, I am forced on my old route. I may be able, however, on my return, to keep more south.

My party moved at quarter to six. Course nearly southwest, across desert (altitude above the sea, 4,370 feet), thinly covered with short *artemisia*, or sage, to "Short Cut Pass," altitude above the sea, 5,347 feet, in a mountain range, which I call Colonel Thomas' range, after Lieut. Col. Lorenzo Thomas, assistant adjutant-general of the Army. Through this pass Chorpenning & Company, the mail-contractors, have made a road, but it is so crooked and steep as to scarcely permit our wagons to get up it. In other respects, road to-day good.

Encamp 1.3 miles west of summit of pass, where there is little or no grass, and no water. Journey, 23.2 miles.

At foot of pass we find a couple of men of the mail-party living in a tent. They are employed in improving the road through the pass, and digging for water. They have been digging for two weeks in different places in the vicinity, and as yet have found none. At the well, near this tent, they had got down ten feet, and came to hard rock. The dip of the rocks being decidedly to the other or west side of the range, it is more probable, if water can be found at all by digging, which I very much doubt, it would be found in that quarter. My idea has been all along that it will be found useless to dig for water in these deserts, except where there are springs, and that when water is found, it will be entirely due to them, and not to a general sub-stratum of water. At Camp Floyd, near the spring, there are several wells of water, which have been dug; but about six miles south of the post, in the valley, where General Johnston had several dug, and where there are no signs of springs, not a drop of water could be found, though the earth was penetrated to a depth of forty feet.

I examined a pass about one-half a mile to the north of Short Cut Pass, which is of good grade, and which, if the same amount of labor had been bestowed upon it as upon Short Cut Pass, would have furnished a far better road. I recommended to the mail-party a change, even now, of the road to this new pass.

A half-gallon of water per man for night and morning has been distributed to the different messes, and one-third of a gallon of water and half a ration of forage to each animal.

The solitary mountains and mountain-ranges in the desert, as I have before remarked, are of igneous origin, entirely denuded of vegetation, and look in some instances as if they have been blasted by fire. Such is the case with Colonel Thomas' range, in the pass of which we are encamped. More particularly speaking, this range is a combination of stratified and trachytic rocks, partly semi-fused stratified rocks.

May 6, Camp No. 4, Short Cut Pass.—1.3 miles west of summit; altitude above the sea, 5,005 feet. The grass at this camp being very scant, and it being important to reach water as soon as possible, the expedition, under charge of Lieutenant Murry, left at twelve midnight on its onward march, myself remaining behind with a small party to look at the country by daylight. I with my party moved at twenty-five minutes after five.

My exploration of last fall only extended from Camp Floyd as far as Short Cut Pass. Thence it is my intention to follow Chorpenning's extension of my route to Hasting's Pass, in the Humboldt Mountains, a distance of 166 miles, and at that point diverge from it more southwardly; Beckwith's, as well as Chorpenning & Company's, striking off to the Humboldt too far northwardly. All this while I shall keep the guide with a party to the south of me, examining the country in that direction along a line generally parallel to that I shall follow, so that on my return I shall, if possible, be able to open a route farther to the south, and thus obtain a better and shorter route to California.

The road we are following for one mile continues down the pass north of west, and then turns more southwardly, Thomas' range flanking us on our left, or to the east, and the desert on our right. In 6 miles you enter Cedar Valley, made by Thomas' range on your left, and a short range on your right. Threading this, in 3 miles you emerge from it, and cross a valley 9 miles wide, which, on your right, is a salt-spring marsh and boggy, and therefore forces the road to the south, as indicated on the maps. This valley crossed, the road takes a sharp turn to the right, and, running northwestwardly, skirts a range of highly-altered calcareous and slaty rocks on your left, and in 1.5 miles passes by Devil's Hole, and in 5.5 miles more reaches Fish Springs, where Lieutenant Murry and command are encamped. Whole journey, 25.3 miles. Road, though not what may be called bad, yet in some places sandy, and in others stony; soil, areno-calcareo-argillaceous, the wild sage and greasewood characterizing it; not a tree visible, except a few dwarf cedars in Cedar Valley; mountain formations metamorphic, as already stated; general dip of strata north of west, and partly decided.

The Devil's Hole is a natural well, about 15 feet in diameter, and measures 25.5 feet in depth. A whitish clay efflorescence incrusts the sides, and the water is slightly saline in taste, the horses drinking it pretty freely. In color it is greenish. The surface of the water is 10 feet below that of the ground, and therefore can be reached only with the pail.

There is a mail-station at these springs, where we are encamped. At present the only shelter is a thatched shed. The mail-agent reports that it is perfectly impracticable to shorten the route by striking directly across the valley to this station, on account of the alkaline flat, which will scarcely allow animals with packs to cross. The springs are large and copious, very clear, the bottom presenting a whitish appearance, with a hue of green. An innumerable quantity of fish are to be seen sporting in the water. We have caught some specimens. They are about 6 inches long, have darkish, speckled scales, and seem to be a kind of chub. They are very inferior for the table. The water is slightly brackish and lukewarm, but when allowed to cool is palatable.

Rained slightly in showers to-day. Grass in scant quantities along the road in places; to be found in tolerable quantity on side of a mountain near camp.

May 7, Camp No. 5, Fish Springs.—Elevation above the sea, 4,289 feet. Thermometer at 5 a. m., 40°.25. The guide did not return until this morning. He corroborates the statement of the mail-agent in respect to the impossibility of crossing the valley directly to the east of this camp, he having been obliged to unpack his animals to get over the marsh. Since yesterday morning he has traveled about 60 miles, having been incessantly going all night. He could find no water in pass to the south of Devil's Hole. A Ute Indian at the mail-station says, however, there is water there, and I have therefore instructed the guide to take the Indian with him and examine the region again in that direction. If water is found there, I shall change the road accordingly on my return from Carson Valley.

Took up march at 6¼ o'clock. In 3.5 miles pass Warm Spring and a mail-station. Soon after starting it commenced to rain, which softened the road at the outset so much as to cause the wagons, 6 miles from Fish Springs, to stall occasionally in a distance of one-quarter of a mile. Detained an hour on this account. At this point the road doubles the point of the range along which we have been traveling, and continues on the plain of the desert toward the Go-shoot or Tots-arrh Mountains, meaning high mountain range. After making a journey of 29.7 miles, and coming for the first time to grass, the mules beginning to give out, we were obliged about sundown to encamp without water, except that in our kegs. I however found water 2.5 miles ahead, to which we will move to-morrow. The journey to-day has been a hard one, on account of the sandy and, in some places, boggy character of the soil. The country passed over is as desert a region as I ever beheld, scarcely a spear of grass visible, and in some areas not even the characteristics of an arid soil, greasewood, or sage. In some places the ground is perfectly bare of everything, and is as smooth and polished as a varnished floor. The first grass we have met with is that in which we are encamped.

The Go-shoot or Tots-arrh Mountains have been nearly all day long directly ahead of us, and appear very high. The peaks are covered with snow, and some 70 miles quartering to the left from our camp may be seen a towering one, which I call Union Peak, on account of its presenting itself in a doubled and connected form.* The geological character of the range is sedimentary, intermingled with quartz-rock

Our teams, considering the hard winter they have just passed through at Camp Floyd and the short forage upon which, of necessity, they have been fed, have thus far done remarkably well.

May 8, *Camp No.* 6, *Great Salt Lake Desert.*—Altitude above the sea, 4,593 feet. Bugle sounded reveille at 4. Morning bright and clear. Thermometer at 4½ a. m., 33°.75. Moved at half past five. In one mile, pass on our left an alkaline spring. Water not drinkable. In 1.2 miles more, come to a sulphur spring, where there is an abundance of water and grass, and where we encamped. It being Sunday, and the animals and party requiring rest, we have only made this short march of 2.5 miles to get to feed and water. The water, though sulphurous, is quite palatable to man and beast.

The shrill whistle of the curlew and the harsh croaking of the sand-hill crane indicate that we are in a better region than that we have been passing over for a few days back. The view from this camp, in contrast with that we have witnessed since we left General Johnston's Pass, is quite refreshing. Grass can be seen for a considerable stretch in the valley to the south of our camp, and the mountains, among them the Granite and Go-shoot Mountains, hemming us in at distant points, make up an agreeable landscape.

Just before dinner a Parvan (Ute) Indian (Black Hawk) came into camp. This is

(*) This peak was again seen on our return route, July 20, and still, in its recesses, it was covered with snow.

the first Indian we have seen on our route. His squaw is a Go-shoot woman, and he lives among that people. Gave him his dinner and some tobacco. Had a sketch of him taken. He wears his hair tied up at the temples and behind; carries a buckskin pouch and powder-horn; a bow and quiver swung on his right side; wears a pink checked American shirt, buckskin leggins and moccasins, and a blanket around his loins; an old black silk handkerchief is tied about his neck. He has one huge iron spur on his right heel, and rides a sorrel pony. His height is 5 feet 7½ inches; has a stout square frame; age, probably, 35; carries a rifle. His bow is 3 feet long, and is made of sheep's horn; arrow, 25 inches long, feathered, and barbed with iron. His countenance is ordinarily sardonic, but lights up in conversation, and shows as much intelligence as Indians do ordinarily.

This evening, just at dark, two six-mule teams, belonging to the mail company, came in from Ruby Valley, and, after watering, continued on to Fish Springs. Took them five days to make the trip, they lying over one day. Report the road worked through to Ruby Valley, and the mail-stage is to run the next trip as far as the station in that valley from Camp Floyd. Heretofore it has run only as far as Simpson's Spring; from that point to the Humboldt River the mail has been carried on pack-mules.

May 9, *Camp No.* 7, *Sulphur Spring.*—Longitude, 113° 46′ 19″; latitude, 39° 40′ 36″. Altitude above the sea, 4,633 feet. The forage brought by the three teams from Camp Floyd being about expended, they left this morning on their return to the post. Morning bright and clear. Thermometer at 5 a. m., 37°.25. Resumed march at 25 minutes of 6, and shaped our course south of west for a wide pass through the Go-shoot Mountains, which we commence ascending in 4.5 miles. In 6 miles more you reach the east summit (altitude above the sea, 6,903 feet), by a tolerable grade, and thence, in 2.5 miles, descend, by a good grade, to Pleasant Valley, where we find an abundance of grass and plenty of water. A mile more brought us to the spring, the copious source of the stream which runs eastwardly through the valley into a large valley, which I call Crosman Valley, after Lieut. Col. George H. Crosman, deputy quartermaster-general and chief of the quartermaster's department in the Military Department of Utah. This stream (Pleasant Valley Creek) has a width of 12 feet, is 5 feet in depth, of sandy bottom, and has a rapid current. The water is of a very pure, wholesome character. Near the spring we encamp, after a march of 13.4 miles. At this point is a mail-station, a log house. The mail company has done a great deal of work in the pass we have just come through, in removing rocks, filling up gullies, and making side cuts.

We have to-day seen a number of Go-shoot Indians. They are most wretched-looking creatures, certainly the most wretched I have ever seen, and I have seen great numbers in various portions of our country. Both men and women wear a cape made of strips of rabbit-skins, twisted and dried, and then tied together with strings, and drawn around the neck by a cord. This cape extends to just below the hip, and is but a scant protection to the body. They seldom wear leggins or moccasins, and the women appear not to be conscious of any impropriety in exposing their persons down to the waist. Children at the breast are perfectly naked, and this at a time when overcoats were required by us. The men wear their hair cut square in front, just above the eyes, and it is allowed to extend in streamers at the temples. The women let their hair grow at random. They live on rats, lizards, snakes, insects, grass-seed, and roots, and their largest game is the rabbit, it being seldom that they kill an antelope.

I learn from Mr. Faust, the mail-agent at this point, that there are only about 200 Go-shoots all told of every age. They use, generally, the bow and arrow, there being only one gun to about 25 men. He represents them as of a thievish disposition, the mail company having lost by them about 12 head of cattle and as many mules. They steal them for food.

The farm the Government has opened for them is on Deep Creek, 25 miles west of north from this station. The Indian agent is Mr. Jarvis. Mr. Faust represents the valley of Deep Creek (by Beckwith called Fish Creek, by others I-van-pah), as quite large and fertile. The creek is narrow and so deep (from 6 to 12 feet) as to drown animals, and 1,500 acres of good land can be profitably irrigated by it. Captain Beckwith, in speaking of this valley, says: "The valley is here several miles wide, and the stream lined with grass, which is not all, however, of superior quality. Many of the small settlements of Utah are not so well supplied with the requisites for successful cultivation as those found on this stream." Mr. Faust also represents that there is a large quantity of fine timber (pine, fir, and cedar) in the vicinity, and, doubtless, building-stone.

Just at sunset I walked out with Mr. Faust to see some of these Go-shoots at home. We found, about 1.5 miles from camp, one of their habitations, which consisted only of some cedar branches disposed around in the periphery of a circle, about 10 feet in diameter, and in such a manner as to break off, to the height of about 4 feet, wind from the prevailing direction. In this inclosure were a number of men, women, and children. Rabbit-skins were the clothing generally, the poor infant at the breast having nothing on it. In the center was a camp-kettle suspended to a three-legged crotch or tripod. In it they were boiling the meat we had given them. An old woman superintended the cooking, and at the same time was engaged in dressing an antelope-skin. When the soup was done, the fingers of each of the inmates were stuck into the only dish, and sucked. While this was going on, an Indian came in from his day's hunt. His largest game was the rat, of which he had a number stuck around under the string of his waist. These were soon put by the old woman on the fire, and the hair scorched; this done, she rubbed off the crisped hair with a pine-knot, and then, thrusting her finger into the paunch of the animal, pulled out the entrails. From these, pressing out the offal, she threw the animal, entrails and all, into the pot.

The rats are caught by a dead-fall made of a heavy stone, and supported by a kind of figure 4, made as it ordinarily is for a trap, except that, instead of a piece of wood, a string is used, tied, and provided with a short button, which, being brought around the upright, is delicately held in position by a spear of dried grass or delicate piece of wood, which, pressing against the button, rests at the other end against the ground or stone. Traps like these are placed over the holes of the rats, and they, coming in contact with the long or lower piece of the figure 4, bring the stone upon them. They are also speared in their holes by a stick turned up slightly at the end and pointed, and with another, of a spade-form at the end, the earth is dug away until the animal is reached and possessed.

The Go-shoots, as well as the Diggers, constantly carry about with them these instruments of death, which, with the bow and arrow and net, constitute their chief means for the capture of game. Hanging on the brush about their "kant," as they call their habitations, I noticed one of these nets. It was well made, of excellent twine fabricated of a species of flax which grows in certain localities in this region, is 3 feet wide, and of a very considerable length. With this kind of net they catch the rabbit. A fence or barrier, made of the wild sage-bush plucked up by the roots, or cedar branches, is laid across the paths of the rabbits, and on this fence the net is hung vertically, and in its meshes the rabbit is caught.

The fear of capture causes these people to live generally some distance from the water, which they bring to their "kant" in a sort of jug made of willow tightly platted together and smeared with fir-gum. They also make their bowls and seed and root baskets in the same way—a species of manufacture quite common among all the Indian tribes, and which, in 1849, I saw in the greatest perfection among the Navajos and Pueblo Indians of New Mexico.*

I noticed a species of the food they eat, and which is made from seeds and roots which they get in the bottoms. I tasted it, but it looking precisely like a cake of cattle-ordure, and having anything but an agreeable taste, I soon disgorged it.

The Go-shoots, according to Mr. Bean, my guide of last fall, who has lived in this country for the last ten years, and professes to be well acquainted with the various tribes inhabiting the Territory, are an offshoot from the Ute Indians, and left their tribe about two generations ago, with their leader or chief, Goship, a disaffected leader. Their proper name, therefore, is probably Goship-Utes, which has become contracted into Go-shoots. Their language is a sort of gibberish, made up of the Ute and Sho-sho-nee dialects. It is said they are little esteemed by the original tribe, though I find occasionally a Ute Indian among them married to one of their people. They have until recently recognized no chief. Now, at the instigation of the Government, they have elected one, but as yet do not know how to respect him. It was amusing to see how the women slyly tucked under their rabbit-skins the hickory (checked) shirts we gave them, their whole demeanor representing that they are a suspicious, secretive set.

We found the guide, Mr. Reese, at our present camping-ground. He found the water at the places represented by the Indian he took with him from Camp No. 5, but farther south than he had gone. Paid the Indian in tobacco and a couple of hickory shirts.

May 10, *Camp No.* 8; *Pleasant Valley.*—Altitude above the sea, 6,150 feet. Ice formed in the bucket last night. Thermometer at 5 a. m., 33°.75. The guide, with Ute Indian Pete and two other men, left us this morning to continue an examination of the country to the south of and parallel to our route. They are to continue on, if possible, in that direction, and join us in Ruby Valley.

Pleasant Valley, which is very narrow, contains grass all along it, but no water

* See my report of Navajo expedition, Sen. Ex. Doc. No. 64, 31st Cong., 1st sess., p. 118.

above the spring where we encamped last night, except occasionally. The mountains are covered with cedars, and also contain pine and fir large enough for building purposes, and stone. Below the spring there is a very limited amount of cultivable land, which might be irrigated. This is the first cultivable land we have seen since we left Camp Floyd. The universal scene has been an arid, light argillo-arenaceous soil in the valleys, and the *artemisia* more or less everywhere. From Pleasant Valley to Camp No. 8, the road, which has a general direction north of west, traverses in 8.5 miles two or three steep but short hills, which, however, did not require the teams to be doubled, to the west summit of the Tots-arrh range (altitude above the sea, 7,150 feet), and thence 4 miles to camp. The mail company have done on this portion of the route some little work, but not enough to make the road what it should be. The road as made does not follow the direct pack-route, but makes quite a detour to the right or north. The mail-man, who has piloted us from the last camp, says a road, however, could be made by the pack-mule route, which would save several miles. The difficulty is a very steep declivity into Antelope Valley.

The formation of the Tots-arrh range, in which Pleasant Valley lies, is made up of slaty and calcareous rocks, mostly highly altered, and on the south side of the valley are seen granite rocks and quartzite. On the west side, near our present camp (No. 9), impure limestones and sandstones abound, pointing to the Carboniferous formation. The soil of the valleys correspond.

The Go-shoots that came to our camp in Pleasant Valley have followed us to our present camp, and have been regaling themselves with the entrails and refuse of a beef we have killed.

Two of our party went in advance to shoot antelope in Antelope Valley, in which we are informed they are frequently visible; they have returned, however, unsuccessful. Journey, to-day, 12.5 miles.

In this country, where grass is scattered as it is in the case of the bunch-grass, or scarce, it is necessary, in order to keep up the condition of the animals, to herd them. For this purpose we have four herders, three of whom are Mexicans and one an American. One of these drives the herd during the day, the others sleeping in the wagons, and at night the last mentioned take care of them. We have, therefore, brought with us only a few lariats for the horses, which, however, are seldom used except as guys to our wagons along side-hills, and to close up the gaps between the wagons when corralled for stock-catching in the morning. At Camp Floyd and other places in Utah, there are a number of Mexicans who prove valuable as herders. Besides being capital for looking up stray animals, they are generally expert in throwing the lasso.

May 11, *Camp No.* 9, *east slope of Antelope Valley.*—Altitude above the sea, 6,658 feet. Ice formed again last night. Thermometer, at 4½ o'clock this morning, 22°. Atmosphere sharp but clear. Moved at 25 minutes of 6. Course, south of west across Antelope and Shell Valleys. Just after leaving camp we have a fine distant view of the mountains hemming in the Antelope Valley at the west and north. After getting across the valley you can see to the east of south, glittering with snow, the high peak of the Go-shoot, or Tots-arrh range (Union Peak), some 60 miles off. This valley runs north and south, is flatly and smoothly concave, and about 12 miles wide; is bounded on the east by the Tots-arrh or Go-shoot range; on the west by the Un-go-we-ah, or Pine Timber range, which are next to the Tots-arrh in height; at the north distantly it appears to be hemmed in by mountains, and at the south is uninterrupted in view. Altitude above the sea, 5,690 feet. The soil is a sandy gravel on the benches, in the bottom argillaceous and covered with short sage. In the vicinity where we cross it there are no indications of water or grass, but some 50 miles to the south of us, to the north of our return-route, there is water and an abundance of grass. After crossing Antelope Valley, you ascend a rather low range of mountains, composed of slaty, stratified rocks, by a tolerable grade, and get into a shallow valley, called Shell Valley on account of its being covered with shale. Crossing this you descend over a formation of dioritic rocks, in 2 miles, by a good grade, into Spring Valley, where there is an extensive bottom of alkaline grass and of spring water, and where we encamp early in the afternoon. Journey, 19 miles; road generally good.

This is a narrow valley, running north and south, and lies between the Un-go-we-ah range on the west and a low minor range on the east. It is called Spring Valley, from the number of springs which make a chain of small shallow lakes or ponds in the direction of its length. The grass in it is abundant, but coarse and alkaline. Better grass can be found in the ravines and on the bench on the west side of the valley. The alkaline nature of the soil makes it unfit for cultivation. The formation of the valley, which is of a highly metamorphosed character, is composed, probably, of semi-fused stratified rocks.

Found some Root-Diggers here, one a very old woman, bent over with infirmities, very short in stature, and the most lean, wretched-looking object it has ever been my lot to see. Had her likeness taken.

These Indians appear worse in condition than the meanest of the animal creation. Their garment is only a rabbit-skin cape, like those already described, and the children go naked. It is refreshing, however, in all their degradation, to see the mother studiously careful of her little one, by causing it to nestle under her rabbit-skin mantle.

At first they were afraid to come near us, but bread having been given to the old woman, by signs and words she made the others in the distance understand that they had nothing to fear, and prompted them to accompany her to camp to get something to eat. Notwithstanding the old woman looked as if she was famished, it was very touching to see her deal out her bread, first to the little child at her side, and then, only after the others had come up and got their share, to take the small balance for herself. At camp, the feast we gave them made them fairly laugh for joy.

Near our camp I visited one of their dens or wick-e-ups. Like that already described, it was an inclosure, 3 feet high, of cedar-brush. The offal around, and in a few feet of it, was so offensive as to cause my stomach to retch, and cause a hasty retreat. Mr. Bean told me the truth when he spoke of the immense piles of *fæces* voided by these Indians, about their habitations, caused doubtless by the vegetable, innutritious character of the food.

These Digger Indians certainly demand the care and beneficence of the Government, and it is a satisfaction to know that an Indian agent has been sent among them to teach them the arts of civilized life. Sure I am, if the discontented among our people could only see these poor creatures in their want and wretchedness, they could not repine at their lot.

I noticed the women carrying on their backs monstrous willow baskets filled with a sort of carrot root, which they dig in the marsh, and the cacti, both of which they use for food. The stature of these Indians, both male and female, is under size. After dark a number came in; but it is a rule with us not to permit them to remain all night in camp, and they were told that though they could not remain with us, they could come in the morning. Their joyous conversation shows that they believe they have got among good friends.

May 12, *Camp No.* 10, *Spring Valley.*—Altitude above the sea 6,133 feet. Thermometer at 4½ o'clock this morning, 22°. Had quite a cold night; fires still desirable in the morning; water in the valley frozen over. Ever since we left Camp Floyd snow has covered the high mountains. The grass in the valley is yet but a few inches long. On the sides of the mountain, however, where it is to be found, it is sufficiently long for grazing. This valley, doubtless on account of its altitude, is a cold one.

In consequence of some of our mules straying away, which, however, were found, we did not get off till 20 minutes after 6. Our Go-shoot friends were in camp again just before starting, and were a little impudent, so much so as to cause me to give some significant evidences of displeasure. Our course lay west of north for about 3 miles, when we turned up a ravine south of west, along a rapid mountain-stream (Spring Creek), which we followed for 3.5 miles, when we left it, and continuing up a branch ravine, in 2 miles, by a good wagon-road grade, attained the summit of the Un-go-we-ah range (7,530 feet above the sea), whence could be seen lying immediately to the west of us Steptoe Valley. Descending the west slope of the mountain, which is somewhat steep, about 2 miles more, along a pure, mountain-gushing stream, which I call after Lieutenant Marmaduke, of the Seventh Infantry, brought us to the mail-station on the east side of Steptoe Valley, in the vicinity of which we encamped after a journey of 11.1 miles among good grass, water, and fuel.

The road crossed the stream, which I call Spring Creek, on the east slope of the range, several times. These crossings, which are short, boggy pitches, the mail company has not properly fixed, and the consequence was we were detained two hours by the breaking up of a tongue. This stream is 4 feet wide and 1 foot deep, and there is an abundance of grass in the ravine all along, from about 1.5 miles above its entrance into Spring Valley. It therefore furnishes a better camping place than Spring Valley. Gooseberry bushes grow along the creek, and cedars abound on the side-hill, and cedars, pines, and what the Mormons call *mountain mahogany* in the pass. This tree (the *Cercocarpus ledifolius*) grows generally at the summit of the passes. It is somewhat scrubby in appearance, ramifying in several branches from the ground, and in form resembles the apple-tree. Its greatest height is about 20 feet, and the aggregate breadth of its branches 20 feet. Its wood is very hard, and is used for cogs, journals, gudgeons, &c. A minute description of it by Dr. Engelmann will be found in Appendix M.

In this ravine we met a couple of men belonging to the mail-station where we are encamped, one of them named Lott Huntingdon, who says he has charge of the mail company's operations from Pleasant Valley to the Humboldt River. They were in search of mules, which they reported as having been run off by the Indians last night. They were sure of it because they had tracked them. Fortunately we had fallen in with the mules, and they had joined our herd. It was also in this ravine where I saw a deserted wick-e-up, in which Mr. Lee found a charred human skull—whether the result of cannibalism, sacrifice, or accident, we do not know.

The ravine in which we are encamped is also well grassed, and there are others of the same character in the vicinity.

The Un-go-we-ah Mountain-range, which we have just crossed, is composed of porphyritic rocks and altered stratified rocks (quartzite, slaty rocks, and siliceous limestones), heaved up to the summit.

Called at the mail-station. I find the mail company's road-party, consisting of eight men, have worked the road no farther than this camp. From this point onward we will have to open the road ourselves. They report a stream in the bottom of Steptoe Valley, six miles distant, which we will have to cross, and cannot do without bridging. Breadth 25 feet. They have been hauling logs to the spot for the purpose, and have nearly all that will be required. They promise to haul the remainder to-morrow, so as to enable us to build the bridge. The mail accommodations at this station are a shed and tent.

May 13, *Camp No.* 11, *east slope of Steptoe Valley.*—Altitude above the sea, 6,600 feet. Last evening it commenced blowing very hard, and this morning we have a cold, driving snow-storm from the east. Thermometer, at 5.45 a. m., 34°.25. Lieutenant Murry and myself left, with a small party of soldiers and teamsters, to make the bridge in Steptoe Valley, referred to yesterday, the balance remaining in camp. By noon the bridge was finished except a few logs, which the mail company promised to haul and put on. Lieutenant Murry deserves credit for his energy in this work. It snowed and rained at times during the day, till in the afternoon the clouds broke away, and the sun came out bright. The wind was high all day.

Mr. Huntingdon has been in this region during the past winter, and says there were six feet of snow in the upper portion of the cañon, in which the mail-station is, and two feet at the station. The mail party also inform us that Mr. Egan, the principal agent of Chorpenning & Company, tried twice to get south from Ruby Valley, toward Genoa, in Carson Valley, but was once defeated by the snow, and once business in Salt Lake City diverted him. It is from this point, near the southern extremity of Ruby Valley, Hasting's Pass, where we reach it, that I contemplate striking off southwestwardly from the route we are following, and shall attempt to get through with our wagons to Genoa in that direction.

The mail from Camp Floyd passed this afternoon, on mule-back, to California, and the carrier reported two stages at Pleasant Valley Station, just through from Salt Lake City.

May 14, *Camp No.* 11, *east slope of Steptoe Valley.*—Weather still cold. Thermometer, at 5 a. m., 28°.25. The animals have been in good grass at this camp, and have recuperated by the day's halt. Moved at 5.30 o'clock. Course westwardly, directly across Steptoe Valley to Egan Cañon. This valley, trending about north and south, is bound by the Un-go-we-ah Mountains on the east, and the Montim* Mountains on the west, and is open at either end as far as the eye can reach. Its breadth is about twelve miles, and, like all the wide valleys we have crossed, is flatly concave in cross-sections. At the benches the soil is gravelly. In the bottom it is areno-calcareo-argillaceous, and on the west side of the valley, in wet weather, must bog a great deal. Greasewood is the characteristic; ordinary height, 3 to 4 feet. (See minute description of this shrub by Dr. Engelmann, in Appendix M). Along the axis of the valley a stream runs northwardly, which, at the present time, is twenty-five to fifty feet wide; bottom miry; depth, in places, three feet; current moderate. It is said to dry up in the summer. Curlew, ducks, and other aquatic birds frequent it. There is a considerable margin of salt grass along it, which would be poisonous to animals, though the water does not taste alkaline. This is a poor, arid valley, perfectly useless for cultivation where we cross it; but farther south, where I crossed it on my return, as my report will show, there is a great deal of good, available pastural and cultivable soil. Altitude above the sea, 5,816 feet. Small streams, however, of pure water course down from the mountains and sink generally before reaching the middle of the valley; and on the mountain-sides and in the ravines is to be found a great deal of grass.

On account of the marshy approach to the bridge we constructed yesterday over this creek, we were detained three-quarters of an hour. Several of the wagons were taken over by hand. At noon, 6.8 miles from bridge, we reached the mouth of Egan Cañon, down which a fine, rapid stream runs, and on which we encamp. Grass on the side of the mountain. Journey 13.3 miles. Road good to the bridge; and from there, a part of the way, the soil is light and porous, and cuts up easily. After reaching camp-ground, I examined, with Lieutenant Murry, Egan Cañon, which had been reported as requiring considerable work to enable the wagons to pass, but find little will be necessary. We have had to-day with us, from Steptoe Valley, one of the mail company's men, who joined us at my request and by direction of Mr. Egan.

This afternoon the astronomical transit was set up for observations of the transit of the moon and moon-culminating stars. We were successful in the evening with our observations. Also observed as usual for time (or longitude) and latitude. Also took four sets of lunar observations for longitude with sextants and artificial horizons, two sets being on each side of the moon. Lieutenant Smith observed for double altitudes of the stars; Lieutenant Putnam, for double altitude of the moon; and I, for lunar distances, Mr. Lee noting audibly the time. The observations, being simultaneous, are regarded as quite satisfactory. I would ask, "Are you all ready?" If so, each would reply, "Ready!" I would then say, "Count!" While Mr. Lee was counting, Lieutenant Smith would be keeping up the superposition of the reflected and direct image of the star in the artificial horizon; Lieutenant Putnam, the tangential contact of the reflected and direct image of the bright limb of the moon, also in an artificial horizon; and I, the tangency of the star and bright limb of the moon directly. At the proper instant, I would call out the time, and if the other observers would respond, "All right!" to

* The meaning of this word I have not been able to ascertain.

my query, the angles of time were recorded. We got through at midnight. Also, determined the magnetic variation at this camp, by observations on Polaris.

The survey of the day is plotted after getting into camp, and thus, as we proceed, we have daily a correct view of our position. All of our notes, astronomical and barometerical and itinerary, are also perfected. The four chronometers are also daily, at the same hour, compared, and a record kept of the daily difference of each with the large box-chronometer. Find longitude of this camp (No. 12) to be 114° 58′ 15″; latitude, 39° 51′ 46″; altitude, 5,986 feet; magnetic variation, 16° 47′ E.

The dews in this region are scarcely perceptible, and my flannel, I notice, is generally highly charged with electricity.

May 15, *Camp No.* 12, *mouth of Egan Cañon.*—Extremely cold this morning. Thermometer at sunrise, 26°. Air pure, sun bright, and the wind strong from the west. Moved at quarter to 6. The pioneer party went ahead, in order to prepare the road. Our course is westward, up Egan Cañon, by an easy ascent, to Round Valley, about 2.5 miles, thence six miles across Round Valley, and by a ravine which required some work, to the summit of the Montim range (elevation above the sea, 7,135 feet), and thence 9.5 miles across Butte Valley, to the vicinity of a small well on the west side of the valley.

Egan Cañon we found quite narrow, and somewhat remarkable on account of the rocks which wall it in on either side. These rocks are tremendously massive, and rise sheer to a height in one place of about 1,000 feet. They are a compact quartz granite, of a grayish color, which becomes embrowned by exposure, and is intermingled with altered slate. Small veins of pure white quartz are seen traversing it very conspicuously. The general character of the range (Montim) is granitic at the base in some places, but mostly tilted and highly-altered stratified rocks, quartzite, slates, &c. Higher up, siliceous limestones, and, on the west side, porphyritic rocks. The ravines and heights abound with cedar, and thick *artemisia* characterizes the valleys. Just after crossing Round Valley we passed through a sort of cedar and sage-brush fence, which must have been about .75 of a mile long, and put up by the Indians. Its purpose, doubtless, was to catch rabbits by the suspension upon it of a net, in the mode explained before, and their attempting to run through it.

The Montim Range, between Steptoe and Butte Valley, is the boundary between the Go-shoot and Sho-sho-nee tribes of Indians; the latter ranging to the west of the line.

Round Valley, which is about 4 miles wide and 16 miles long, abounds in grass.

Butte Valley ranges north and south, and at the north appears to be uninterrupted except by low hills; at the south it is closed in by a cross-range some 30 miles off. It is about 8 miles wide, and takes its name from the buttes or table-hills in it. Soil of the usual yellowish color, and of a dry argillo-arenaceous character, good for nothing but to sustain the *artemisia.* (Altitude above the sea, 6,148 feet). The range of mountains limiting it on its west side are low, and, though covered with cedar, present but little indications of water. Those at the south end, from their height and snow, give better indications. The Humboldt range has appeared ahead of us to-day, looming up above the range limiting Butte Valley on the west, and is covered with snow. It is the most imposing range I have seen since leaving the Wahsatch Mountains, and is to be seen stretching far to the northward.

Our day's travel has been 18.1 miles, and, as it was quite warm in the afternoon, we found it very fatiguing crossing Butte Valley. Road generally good. Met five Sho-sho-nees on the road, clothed in rabbit-skins, like the Go-shoots, but all had leggings. We are encamped at the foot of a dark brown, isolated, porphyritic rock, near the summit of which is a small dug well, 10 feet deep and 2 feet wide. The water in this well can only get here on the principle of the siphon bringing it from some distant source. At present it is only 2½ feet deep in the well, and is barely sufficient for culinary purposes. The grass is about 1.5 miles to the northeast of the spring, on the side of the hill, and does not appear abundant. The dearth of water on the route to-day makes it important, if for no other reason, that the route should be changed farther to the south. (Subsequent to this date, in the summer, this point had to be abandoned by the mail company as a station on account of the well drying up. I have learned, however, that they have since found water in the vicinity, probably about 2 miles to the southeast, where a Sho-sho-nee told us there was water.)

The mail company has three traveling agents between Salt Lake City and the Humboldt River—Howard Egan, superintending agent; Ball Robert, district agent between Salt Lake City and Pleasant Valley; and Lott Huntingdon, the agent for the district between Pleasant Valley and the Humboldt. Then they have an agent called station agent, and from three to seven persons at each station, one being the mail-carrier. The number of mules varies at these stations from 8 to 15. The mail during this winter was carried on a pack-mule, which was sometimes led and sometimes driven. The required rate of travel (which was accomplished) was 60 miles in every twenty-four hours, changing every 20 to 30 miles. The superintending agent is said to get from $200 to $250 per month, the district agent $100, the station agent from $50 to $75, and the hands from $25 to $50, according to worth.

One of the mail company informs me that along the route from this station to the Humboldt they had last winter to subsist themselves on mule and coyote (wolf) meat. Their stock was transferred from the old road so late last fall as to have caused the death of one man, who died from cold on his last trip over the Goose Creek Mountains, and they were consequently ill supplied with provisions on the new route. During the winter the stock had a little grain, but subsisted principally on grass. The snow on the divide between Butte and Steptoe Valleys was from 2 to 4 feet deep; in some places in the mountains as much as 10 feet; in Butte Valley about 18 inches.

It is reported by some of the mail company that there is a cave, about three days' travel to the south of Steptoe Valley, into which persons have traveled a mile; some say as many as 3 miles, when they came to a precipice which prevented their going farther. They rolled rocks down, and the lapse of time before striking the bottom showed the depth to have been very great. There is said to be a number of rooms, in one of which is a beautiful spring. It was found by some persons who came from Fillmore City and traveled west. The location of the cave is not given, however, with any precision, and it is not in my power, for want of time, to certify, myself, to the truth of the report. (I may as well say here, however, that on our return route, which was 25 or 30 miles to the south of this, although we saw some small caves, we saw none of the extent described.)

May 16, *Camp No.* 13, *west slope of Butte Valley.*—Altitude 6,523 feet. First mild morning we have had. Thermometer at 5 a. m., 32°. Moved at 20 minutes of 6. Course continues a little north of west. In 2 miles reach summit of divide between Butte and Long Valleys (altitude above the sea 6,670 feet), by a very gradual ascent, and 2.5 miles more, by an easy descent, reach Long Valley. This valley, which lies, like those we have crossed, from south to north, is shut in by a pretty high mountain at its north end, from 10 to 15 miles off, showing passes in that quarter; and the south end appears closed, some 25 or 30 miles off, by a cross-range, also exhibiting passes through it. Elevation above the sea, 6,195 feet. Crossing this dry valley, which is 2.7 miles wide, 3.1 miles more up a tolerable grade brings you to the summit of a low range, running north and south, dividing Long from Ruby Valley, about one mile below which, on the west slope, we encamp, at a spring just discovered by Lott Huntingdon, of the mail party, and which therefore I have called after him. It is a good camping-place, and grass and fuel are convenient. Journey to-day, 12 miles. Road good.

Siliceous limestones were seen in the range dividing Butte and Long Valleys; and in the range bordering this last valley, on its east and west sides, are light-yellowish, earthy limestones, full of fossils of the Carboniferous range; also compact light-gray limestone, some siliceous and slaty rocks, &c. Igneous rocks, of a basaltic appearance (brown porphyry), are found near the limestones in the vicinity of Huntingdon Spring. Soil of valleys accordingly.

Cedar and pine characterize the *Sylva* of the mountains, and the *Artemisia tridentata*, or wild sage, a certain index of sterility, the valleys. The latter has impeded our wagons a great deal to-day, and has been seen almost everywhere from Fort Laramie as far as we have come, and was afterward found to characterize the country even to the east foot of the Sierra Nevada.

A high snow-mountain has appeared some 30 miles off to the south of us, which will doubtless be of service in furnishing water on our return trip in that quarter. Several antelope have been seen for the first time since we left Camp Floyd.

About an hour after we went into camp the guide and party came in. It will be recollected that he parted from us at Pleasant Valley, Camp No. 8, May 10. He reports that in consequence of his getting out of provisions, and the Indian he had picked up as guide knowing nothing of the country farther west, he struck north for our trail, and met it at the bridge in Steptoe Valley. Thence he followed our track. He represents that he has found a route generally parallel to the one we are on, and some 30 miles to the south, which is practicable for wagons, and furnishes water and grass at intervals of 15 to 20 miles. Indeed, a good portion of the way is an old wagon-road, which, according to Lott Huntingdon, was used by a party of emigrants who attempted to make their way from Fillmore to California and perished. (On our return trip, however, we got on this road, and were told by the Indians that it had been made by the Mormons the spring previous, and was, without question, that which they made when they fled before the approach of the troops, and when it was reported they had gone to Silver Mountains.)

Got a number of the Sho-sho-nee words through Ute Pete from a Sho-sho-nee, by name Tar-a-ke-gan. It is to be regretted that the necessity of sending Pete always with the guide, so as to enable him to get information from the Indians in relation to the country south of us, makes it impossible for me to have that converse with the Indians I meet which I would like in order to obtain a knowledge of their manners, customs, &c. But to get a good wagon-road, if possible, to the south of us, is of the first importance, and therefore the guide cannot dispense with his services. Besides, though young, he is a capital *voyageur*, and well acquainted with signs of water, grass, &c.; and already in this respect the chief guide has found him invaluable. I can never forget the kindness of Dr. Hurt in recommending him to me.

May 17, *Camp No.* 14, *Huntingdon's Spring, east slope of Ruby Valley.*—Altitude above the sea, 7,190 feet. The guide leaves us again this morning with a Sho-sho-nee Indian, Tar-a-ke-gan, to go south, and continue his examination of the country south and west, and will join us at our first camp after leaving Ruby Valley. Pete and two others of the party accompany him.

Thermometer at 5 a. m., 44°. Move at quarter to 6, and, shortly after attaining summit of Too-muntz range (7,283 feet above the sea,) pass down a cañon, which I call Murry's Cañon, after Lieut. Alexander Murry, the commanding officer of the escort. The rocks are more calcareous and slaty than those we passed yesterday, and are of yellowish color. Some little work done in the cañon, to allow the wagons to get along. In 3.9 miles we reach the mouth of the cañon, and immediately cross Ruby Valley, requiring 5.3 miles more of travel to mail-station in the valley, where we encamp at 9.30 a. m. Journey, 9.2 miles. Road good.

At our camp is a spring which sends out a small stream of pure water, flowing along the valley northwardly. Ruby Valley is well supplied farther north with streams from the Humboldt Mountains, which limit it on its west side; and some 25 or 30 miles north of us, in the valley, is said to be a large lake, which doubtless is Beckwith's Lake Franklin.

This valley, like all those we have crossed, has a dirty-yellowish, forbidding appearance; is covered with *artemisia*, and very level, and has a thirsty appearance, though doubtless farther north it is more inviting. It is said to extend north as far as the Humboldt River, a distance of 60 to 70 miles, and has a great deal of cultivable soil in that direction, which is capable of irrigation. At the south, about 10 miles from our camp, it is hemmed in by the mountains, which close in from the east and west sides, showing, however, a pass through to the valley lying to the south. The breadth of the valley where we cross it is about 9 miles.

Mr. Jarvis, the Indian agent, has commenced, I am informed, an Indian farm in this valley, about 40 miles to the north of our camp, for the Sho-sho-nees. An abundance of grass, water, cedar, and pine is found in the mountains on either side of the valley, particularly in the Humboldt range skirting it on the west, and it is represented as being quite a warm valley. The snow last winter is represented as not having been more than one-half foot deep in it. In Hasting's Pass, which leads through the Humboldt range into the valley of the south fork of the Humboldt, the snow was 4 feet deep.

Large numbers of Sho-sho-nees winter in Ruby Valley, on account of its being warmer than the other valleys around. One of the mail party represents that as many as 1,500 must have staid here last winter. At the present time they are scattered, for purposes of hunting. They are a fine-looking tribe of Indians, and all those I have seen have good countenances. They have generally nothing but the brush-barrier or inclosed fence, summer and winter, like the Go-shoots, to protect them from the weather, though some of them erect pole-lodges. Mr. Huntingdon thinks that one-third of them carry guns; the rest carry the bow and quiver. They have committed no depredations lately, though last year they attempted to steal some horses from some emigrants.

A great deal of game, such as antelope and aquatic fowl, is said to abound in this region, and deer and mountain-sheep are also seen. Ruby Valley takes its name from the circumstance, so I am informed, of rubies having been picked up in it on the west side, a few miles north of the mail-station. However this may be, it is very certain we could not find any, and the probabilities are that it is no more a ruby valley than the others we have crossed. The mail-station at this point is at present a mere shed. Pine-log houses are at present being put up.

The Humboldt Mountains, white with snow, have for the last two days been seen at times, and have looked grand and massive. Their Indian name is Tac-a-roy, meaning snow-mountains. They are certainly the most formidable mountains we have seen since we left Camp Floyd, and are composed of siliceous limestones, quartzite, coarse sandstones, &c.

May 18, *Camp No.* 15, *Ruby Valley.*—Altitude, 5,953 feet. The mules ran against the cords of the barometer-tent early this morning and prostrated it, carrying with it the two barometer, swhich were suspended from the tripod. Fortunately, only one was affected by the accident, a little air getting into the tube, which can be easily remedied.

Thermometer at 4.45 a. m., 38°. Moved at 5½ o'clock. Struck immediately for Hasting's Pass, lying southwest from mail-station, the foot of which we reach in 2.5 miles, and the summit by a remarkably easy ascent in 3.3 miles more. This pass leads through the Humboldt range from Ruby Valley into the valley of the South Fork of the Humboldt, which some call Huntingdon's Creek. For the first time we in this pass get into Beckwith's, here coincident with Hasting's, road, both of which at the present time are very indistinct. Descending from the summit, by the finest kind of grade, in about 4 miles we leave Beckwith's and Hasting's roads, which go, the former northwestwardly to join the old road along the Humboldt, 10 miles above Lassen's Meadows, the latter northwardly to join the same road at the mouth of the South Fork of the Humboldt; while we strike southwestwardly, over an unknown country, toward the most northern bend of Walker's River, my object being to cut off the great detour which the other roads make in going all around by the Humboldt River and sink, to reach Genoa in Carson Valley. We also now leave Chorpenning's or Mail Company's extension of my route from Hasting's Pass, it also turning northward, and joining the old road near Gravelly Ford, which they follow by way of the sink of the Humboldt and Ragtown, on Carson River, to Genoa. Frémont, I notice by the Topographical

Bureau map, has traveled over a portion of the country to the southwest of us, but as he has never submitted a detailed report of this reconnaissance, and his track is no longer visible, and it goes too far south for our purposes, his exploration is of no service to us in our progress. From this point, therefore, to where we expect to strike the old road on Carson River, we will have to be guided entirely by the country as it unfolds itself. This Hasting's Pass, the summit of which is 6,580 feet above the sea, is the finest, on account of its breadth and easy grade, of any we have threaded, except Camp Floyd Pass. The twittering of the birds we found here also more resonant and delightful than in any other locality. There is a bird in the mountains a little larger than the jay, and of a deeper blue color, that utters an impudent screaming note, and seems to become particularly saucy in proportion as we approach it. It is, however, quite wild, and it is difficult to approach near enough to shoot it.

It was in this pass that Messrs. Duncan and Lufkin overtook us on their way from Salt Lake City to Genoa. They had left the city two weeks previously, and Mr. Duncan, who has traveled the old route by the City of Rocks, says he thinks the one he is now on is the best. They follow from this point the mail-route, toward the main Humboldt. I was much pleased with the little two-horse wagon they had with them. It was very light, and was hung at the middle on two springs, placed longitudinally; and they say they have carried 1,000 pounds in it over the Sierra Nevada. I should think it a capital wagon for rapid traveling over the plains. It was built at Concord, N. H.

After reaching the west foot of Hasting's Pass, in the valley of the South Fork of the Humboldt, we struck for a pass in the next western range, which we could see lying to the southwest of us, about 9 miles off, and which looked favorable for admission into the next valley. In 4 miles we struck the South Fork of the Humboldt, a rapid stream, stony bottom, 6 feet wide, ½ foot deep, course northwardly. We follow up this creek for about a mile, and then leaving it, in about 2 miles, come to a small mountain-stream flowing over a stony bottom, where we encamp at 1 o'clock. Grass along the stream, and plenty higher up on the slopes of the mountains. Sage plentiful. Journey 17.6 miles. Road good, though the high sage-brush, as usual, impeded us a little. This our heavy train, however, breaks down, and makes a very passable road for those who may follow us.

The valley of the South Fork of the Humboldt, which takes its rise near and to the northwest of our camp, is a very open one, both north and south; a slight rise some 15 miles off toward its south end, showing a rim in that direction. Its soil is a yellowish areno-argillaceous earth, which is capable, to a limited extent, of being irrigated by the stream running through it. As usual the *artemisia* covers the valley, and in this locality is quite rank in growth. Altitude of valley above the sea 5,640 feet.

A Sho-sho-nee Indian and his squaw, with her child strapped on her back, followed us to camp. Both seem kind-hearted and have good countenances. The child is a perfect picture of a fat, well-conditioned boy, and has a very pleasing expression of countenance. He is perfectly naked, and around his neck has several strings of wampum. The squaw is naked from her head to her loins, and is not in the slightest disconcerted by the gaze of spectators.

Mr. Reese, the guide, came into camp this evening, and reports plenty of water and grass, and a good country for a road parallel to our route, and south of us from the point he visited south of Camp 14 to the valley we are now in, but sees no way of getting through the range of mountains lying west of us, except by the pass near us, which we are aiming at. If so, the contemplated southern parallel route would be at this point too far north, and we should not gain in distance over the route we have come. I trust, however, we will yet find that we can continue our more southern route westwardly without deviating so much from the proper direction. I think I can see indications of a pass which will make the thing practicable. This proved to be the fact on our return.

We have had thunder and some little lightning this afternoon and evening, but only a few drops of rain.

May 19, *Camp No.* 16, *Valley of South Fork of the Humboldt.*—Altitude above the sea, 6,028 feet. Thermometer at 4.30 a. m., 38°.25. Morning bright and pleasant. Raised camp at 25 minutes of 6, and directed our course west of south to pass of the mountain-range directly west of us. In 2 miles cross a small rapid mountain-rill. These streams may not run in the summer and fall, but their sources, which are springs at the base of the mountains, are doubtless perennial. Wild parsnips, said to be poisonous to man and beast, abound here. Grease, or whisky and gunpowder, are said to be the antidote. Pass places where the Indians have dammed up the rills to cause them to flood the habitations or holes of badgers, gophers, rats, &c., and thus they secure them for their flesh and skins.

In two more miles we commence ascending the pass, which on the east side is quite steep, all the teams doubling but the leading one, and ropes being used to keep the wagons from upsetting. Some side-hill cutting done; train detained 2½ hours on that account. A road, however, of good grade can be made up the pass; (and since we traveled over it I have been informed that the mail company, which has transposed its stock on my route from Ruby Valley, has made a road here.) Probably south side of pass will furnish best grade. Altitude of summit of pass above the sea, 7,300 feet.

From this summit we obtain a most extensive view of distant mountains. Toward the east may be seen four distinct ranges, some of them covered with snow. These are the ranges we have been crossing for several days back. Toward the west, bounding a valley running north and south, and over which lies our course, may be seen a range, and back of it one or two more; the highest covered with snow. The valley referred to is quite white toward the north with a saline efflorescence, and bearing about due west and lying in it is a small lake, into which apparently runs a good-sized stream.

I visited a high promontory near the pass to reconnoiter for a pass through the next range lying immediately to our west. Determined to try the one bearing magnetically S. 40° W. as being the most favorable in direction. There is another bearing directly west, but it would be too far to the north. Directed guide to proceed to the pass in advance, and send back, first, a report about grass and water, at east foot of the pass for to-morrow's camp; and, subsequently, another in respect to the practicability of the pass. My plan has been to keep the guide well in advance, and to have him send or bring back reports from time to time, so as to have as little detention as possible, and get the best route.

Descending from pass by an easy grade down the west slope of the range, albeit in places slightly sidling, in 3 miles and at quarter to 1 p. m., encamped in splendid and abundant grass, near the small stream which comes down the pass. Day's travel 7.1 miles; road good except at points as stated, and which can be remedied.

Several Sho-sho-nees joined us on our route. One of them amused the party very much by his awkward attempts to mount a mule, and, when he got on, his rabbit-skin dress frightened the animal so much as to cause him to run off with his nondescript load, much to the merriment of the men. They wear their skin capes summer and winter, and on such a hot day as this I should suppose the warmth of it would be insupportable. I notice that before they venture to join us they take a good look at us from distant prominent points.

The merry sound of the blacksmith's anvil and forge, and the hammer of the wheelwright, after we got into camp, reminds me constantly of the very efficient manner, thanks to General Johnston, commanding the Department of Utah, in which I have been fitted out by the Quartermaster's Department. The army wagons are, however, of such superior character as very seldom to require repairs. On the march of the Utah forces from Fort Leavenworth these wagons were the admiration of every one, so strongly were they made, and so suitable in weight and capacity. I doubt if any army in any country can show anything superior. The portable forge, however, of which no expedition like ours should be destitute, we found indispensable for the preparation of the shoes for the animals, and other purposes.

Among the Sho-sho-nees who have visited our camp is Cho-kup, the chief of the Humboldt River band of the Sho-sho-nees. It is to be regretted, as I have before remarked, that I am obliged to let Indian Pete, the interpreter, go with my guide ahead, in order to talk with the Indians they may meet. I am thus deprived of the advantages of the information I might otherwise obtain from this chief respecting his tribe. I have had a sketch of him taken. He is a very respectful, intelligent, well-behaved Indian, and seems to have gained the approbation of the California Mail Company. In age I should suppose he was about thirty-five years. He is dressed in buckskin pants, a check under, and a woolen over shirt; has a handkerchief tied around his neck, wears shoes, and has a yellowish felt hat. His air is that of a man who, while knowing his own powers, is capable of scanning those of others. He showed me a letter of Mr. Chorpenning, recommending him as a good Indian, &c. This, together with my intercourse with him, has induced me, from motives of policy as well as justice, to give him the following paper:

"Camp No. 17, Cho-kup's Pass,
"*May* 19, 1859.

"To all whom it may concern:

"This is to inform persons that the bearer of this paper is Cho-kup, chief of the Sho-sho-nees south of the Humboldt River, and as he is represented, and from my intercourse with him, I believe him, to be a friend of the white man, and a good, respectable, and well-behaved Indian, I bespeak for him and his people the kind treatment at the hands of the travelers through their country that their recent good conduct entitle them to, and which, if they continue to receive, will insure all who may pass through their country safety to their persons and property.

"J. H. SIMPSON,
"*Captain Topographical Engineers.*"

I have made it a point to treat the Indians I meet kindly, making them small presents, which I trust will not be without their use in securing their friendly feeling and conduct. A great many of the difficulties our country has had with the Indians, according to my observation and experience, have grown out of the bad treatment they have received at the hands of insolent and cowardly men, who, not gifted with the bravery which is perfectly consistent with a kind and generous heart, have, when they thought they could do it with impunity, maltreated them; the consequence resulting that the very next body of whites they have met have not unfrequently been made to suffer the penalties which in this way they are almost always sure to inflict indiscriminately on parties, whether they deserve it or not.

The mountain range which we have just crossed, and near the foot of which we are encamped, is called the We-a-bah Mountains, or the mountains, as Ute Pete says, of the fluttering or night bird. It is composed of sandstones, siliceous conglomerates, and, distant from the road, of bluish-gray limestone. The general name for mountain, among the Sho-sho-nees, seems to be Toy-ap. The pass we have come through I call after the chief, Cho-kup's Pass.

May 20, *Camp No.* 17, *west slope of Cho-kup's Pass.*—Altitude above the sea, 6,018 feet. The dragoon I sent out with the guide returned last night at 10 o'clock, and reports water and grass 15 miles off, in the direction of pass, through the next range, ahead. Thermometer at 4.30 a. m., 38°.75. Moved at 5.30 o'clock. In 1 mile reach foot of pass in Pah-hun-nupe, or Water Valley. This valley apparently closed at south end, say 25 miles off; at north end, some 30 miles off; low passes apparently at either end. The indications are that this valley can be passed through over to a more southern, southeastern, or southwestern valley by practicable passes, a fact of significance on our return route. Sand-hill cranes, curlew, and other marsh birds abound in the valley, and antelope are seen in the distance. Six and eight-tenths miles farther brings us to a large spring, in marsh, where we water. Plenty of grass about it, though not of best quality. This valley is in some portions argillaceous and in some arenaceous. The latter glitter with small crystals of quartz, of very pure character, which we amuse ourselves in picking up, and facetiously call California diamonds. The appellation, doubtless, as veritable as the epithet of ruby, which seems to belong to the precious stones said to have been found in Ruby Valley. A great deal of alkaline marsh, and water in small lakes, north of route. Altitude of valley above the sea, 5,660 feet.

In 5.6 miles more reach a large spring on west side of valley, at foot of mountain range, where we encamp in pure salt grass, which the animals eat with avidity. It is, however, not abundant. Bunch-grass can be found in cañon back of camp.

Road to-day good, though it might cut up early in the spring. Higher ground, however, exists below or south of the road, over which, in this case, the wagons could travel. Day's travel, 13.3 miles.

The damaged barometer cleaned and refitted with fresh mercury by Mr. Engelmann. At sunset ascended high peak, back or west of camp, to view the pass we have been aiming at. It looks favorable. From this peak had a most magnificent view of the mountains in every quarter of the horizon—the Humboldt range, to the east of north, showing its white snowy summits far above the intervening ones. These distant views have, at least on my mind, a decidedly moral and religious effect; and I cannot but believe that they are not less productive of emotions of value in this respect than they are of use in accustoming the mind to large conceptions, and thus giving it power and capacity. The mysterious property of nature to develop the whole man, including the mind, soul, and body, is a subject which I think has not received the attention from philosophers which its importance demands; and though Professor Arnold Guyot, of Princeton, has written a most capital work on the theme, "Earth and Man", yet a great deal remains to be done to bring the matter to the profit of the world at large, which, it seems to me, a wise and beneficent Greator has ordained should be gathered from the contemplation and proper use of his works.

But then the question arises, Do we rise from the contemplation of nature to nature's God, and therefore to a realization of the amplitude and reach to which our minds are capable, by our own unaided spirit; or is it by the superinduced Spirit of the Almighty Himself, which we have received, it may be, on account of His only Son? But these speculations may be considered as foreign to the necessary rigor of an official report; and I, therefore, will indulge in them no further than to say that, according to my notions, the latter I believe to be the true theory.*

---

* I must confess that in all the works of Baron Humboldt with which I am conversant, I have never seen anything to indicate that he ever arose in his conceptions of nature to the ultimate idea which, to my mind, they are intended to disclose, to wit, the power and goodness of the Creator, and thus to produce within us the ability and delight of adoring Him " of whom, and through whom, and to whom are all things," (Romans xi, 36.) In his *Cosmos* the utmost he says upon the subject is contained in this sentence: " The earnest and solemn thoughts awakened by a communion with nature intuitively arise from a presentiment of the order and harmony pervading the whole universe, and from the contrast we draw between the narrow limits of our own existence and the image of infinity revealed on every side, whether we look upward to the starry vault of heaven, scan the far-stretching plain before us, or seek to trace the dim horizon across the vast expanse of ocean." Now, here, the height of his conception is an idea of infinity, in connection with the order and harmony of the universe, but he sees or acknowledges nothing of an *Infinite Mind*, which has created and still upholds all things, and seems to be utterly unconscious of that *moral* and *spiritual microcosm*, which to some persons is mirrored in their souls when they contemplate nature in her grandest and most beautiful forms. Indeed, to my mind, his application of the word *Cosmos* to "*the universal all*," (Το Παν,) and yet non-recognition of Him " in whom we live and move and have our being," and " by whom the world and all things therein were made," is as sensible as it would be for a physician to talk of the faculties and functions of the human body, and yet ignore entirely the sentient, reasoning soul, the seat of its life and the controller of its actions.

January 29, 1861.—Since writing the foregoing, I have read Professor Guyot's interesting address of February 16, 1860, to the American Geographical and Statistical Society, on Carl Ritter, the world-renowned author, as he terms him, of the classical "Erdkunde, &c., or the science of the globe in its relations to nature and to the history of mankind.' From this address I learn that the crowning excellence of this great physicist was his Christian belief and character, through which he was enabled to see nature purely and describe her graciously as the work of an all-wise and benevolent Creator, who has so harmonized all things, both in the world of matter and spirit, as by their beautiful adaptation, and relation to disclose the infinitude of Him who is the beginning and end, the alpha and omega, of all things.

The spirit in which Ritter studied nature is well shown by the motto which he placed at the bottom of the portrait presented to him by the students of the University of Berlin, through a committee, of which Mr. Guyot was one,

On descending to camp, found Pete had come in from the guide's party, and he reports all right ahead for 18 miles, to a point where there is grass and water, and where I expect to camp to-morrow. It seems the guide took a pass a little to the north of the one I saw from the high promontory of Cho-kup's Pass yesterday; but Pete, in returning to camp, went through the one I referred to, and found it not only more direct but easier. Our observations place this camp (No. 18) in longitude 115° 56′ 52″, latitude 39° 49′ 43″.

May 21, *Camp No.* 18, *west side of Pah-hun-nupe Valley.*—Elevation above the sea, 5,692 feet. Morning bright. Thermometer at 4½ o'clock a. m., 32°. Raised camp at 5.25 a. m. Keep up the Pah-hun-nupe Valley, or south, two miles; then turn to the right up toward the pass of west range bounding the valley; two miles more commence ascending pass. Notice a couple of bush-fences or barriers converging to a narrow pass, and a large hole in this last portion. Pete says they are to guide deer near the hole, in which the Indian hides himself, and shoots them as they pass with bow and arrows at night, a fire being used as a lure. Notice a plant of small leaf, and taste of the turnip. In five miles more, by a very gradual ascent, reach second highest

---

as follows: "Our earth is a star among the stars; and should not we, who are on it, prepare ourselves by it for the contemplation of the universe and its Author?"

Professor Guyot, in speaking of the special peculiarities of Ritter and Humboldt, in his address, discourses as follows:

"The picture that I have just attempted of Ritter's ideas, method, and labors sufficiently defines, if I err not, the part performed in geographical science by that faithful and gifted scholar, from that achieved by Humboldt. Humboldt seeks to determine the general laws of the physical world. Ritter seizes them as applied, and in their concrete and actual connection in every given country and in the whole globe, and considers nature in its totality as an element in the development of mankind, from which alone these natural forms and influences receive their true and final significance.

"At the moment these faithful guides leave us to ourselves, when their voice will utter no more words of wisdom, it may be well for us to ask ourselves how far they led us in the high-road of science, and what is the task which is still before us. Humboldt, with a surpassing richness of knowledge, attempted to give us a connected picture of the totality of the physical universe; but admirable as is the Cosmos, after having read its eloquent pages, we pause and involuntarily ask for the final object of the Creator in building up that marvelous structure; we ask for a tie which connects it with Him, at least that portion of the creation in which we dwell; for a voice which rises from it as a word of praise and we find it not. Far from me even the idea of casting a blame upon the great and good philosopher. I am fully aware that his plan was purposely limited to the material world which is his theme. I only wish to remark that we cannot stop there.

"It is, indeed, a universal law of all that exists, as I have elsewhere said, not to have in itself either the reason or the entire aim of its existence. Every order of facts, like every individual being, forms but a portion of a greater organization, the plan and idea of which go infinitely beyond it, and in which it is destined to play a part. The reason of its existence, therefore, is not in itself, but out of it; not below, but above it. The explanation of the beautiful but often mysterious arrangements of the physical globe is to be found not in it, but in the higher moral and intellectual sphere of man, for whom they were made, in order to be there the means of accomplishing a more exalted end than their mere material existence. The key which opens for us the mysteries of the evolutions of history, is to be sought in that future perfect economy which is its end, and toward which, under God's guidance, human progress is advancing with a steady step. A science of the globe which excludes the spirit world represented by man, is a beautiful body without a soul. Ritter, as I trust I have abundantly shown, put a soul into that body. This will make his memory live forever in the grateful remembrance of all lovers of true science.

"Let us, therefore, continue in the footsteps of these masters in science. Humboldt furnished the means, Ritter marks the goal. Like Humboldt, let us study nature in a truth-loving and devoted spirit, and with combined forces perfect that edifice which he has already reared so high. Like Ritter, let us, with scrupulous care and a pure mind, pursue in all parts of our earthly domain the investigation of these wondrous harmonies of nature and history of which he has traced the great outlines. With the lofty ideal which was before his mind, let us try to realize his conception, which still needs a further growth to unfold all its beauty; and we shall have a right to look with hope toward a future science and a future cosmos, which will be the full and adequate expression of the wisdom and goodness displayed in God's plan of the material and moral creation, which will satisfy all the legitimate craving of the human mind for knowledge, and which, by its very utterance, shall be, according to Ritter's own words, man's song of praise and of adoration to the divine Author of the universe."

summit of pass, whence can be seen, to the south and southwest, a low ridge trending apparently northwest and southeast, and, still farther, two other ranges, generally parallel to the other, and their highest portions covered with snow. Bearing, magnetically, south 5° west, probably some 25 or 30 miles off, is quite a conspicuous peak of one of the more distant ranges. Ever since we left Camp Floyd we have only crossed valleys and mountain-ranges, generally running north and south, to see others lying to the west of us, running in the same direction, and which we have in turn crossed. This system continues to prevail.

The pass we have come through, a most excellent one for a wagon-road, the only steep portion being for about 100 yards at the summit. Altitude above the sea, 6,757 feet. Cedar abounds in it and on the adjacent side-hills. Immediately to our north is a conical peak, which, as we found afterward, in our journey westward, continued for days a most notable landmark, and which I call Cooper's Peak, after Adjutant-General Cooper of the Army.

In 6 miles from summit, by an easy grade, at a quarter to 1 o'clock, reach the She-o-wi-te, or Willow Creek, where we encamp. The short, steep hill which we passed down just before reaching camp, may be turned at the south by making a short detour. She-o-wi-te Creek, a fine one, 4 feet wide, 1 foot deep, and quite rapid. It sinks about 1 mile below camp. Grass along it and on side-hills. Journey, 14.9 miles. Road good, except short hill referred to, which can be avoided. Passing generally over ridges and benches, the soil has been, in some places, arenaceous, in other, argillo-arenaceous, and, in most, gravelly. The rocks have been granular, crystalline, magnesian limestone of a light-gray color, near Camp No. 18, and, as we advanced, subcrystalline compact limestones, altered slates, quartzite, and other highly metamorphosed rocks have prevailed, indicating the proximity of igneous rocks.

The valley in which we are encamped differs from any we have seen. Heretofore they have ranged north and south, and averaged a breadth of probably only one-fourth their length. This one, however, has no particular form, and, while branching out laterally in different directions, shows a form as long as it is broad. The Digger Indians that have come into our camp call it Ko-bah, or Face Valley, a very good name.

There are three of these Indians, who appear to be grandfather, son, and grandson. They confirm the names of valleys and mountains as given by Cho-kup. I inquired of them the number of their kind of people. To this I could only get the answer there were very few of them. One of them is an old man of at least sixty years, and he as well as the others represent that they have always lived in this valley, and, never having gone far from it, cannot tell us of the water and mountains beyond their limited range. They say they have no chief, though they speak the Sho-sho-nee language; are clothed with the rabbit-skin cape, similar to the Go-shoots, and represent that they wear no leggings, even in the winter. This is scarcely credible, cold as the winter must be in this region, but it seems to be a fact. They are very talkative and lively. Eat rats, lizards, grass-seeds, &c., like the Go-shoots. The guide says he saw them, after throwing the rats in the fire, and thus roasting them, eat them, entrails and all, the children in particular being very fond of the juices, which they would lick in with their tongues and push into their mouths with their fingers. The old man represents that a number of his people died last winter from starvation and cold.

We found one of the guide's party here. The guide and another man are still out toward the southwest looking for a pass in that direction.

Five of the men within the last two or three days have reported themselves sick. The disease the doctor pronounces a species of intermittent fever.

This afternoon, just before sundown, Lieutenant Murry and myself took a stroll up the creek to view a wick-e-up of the Diggers that have visited our camp. It had been reported to be but about from one-eighth to one-fourth of a mile above our camp; but, with all the search we could give for about a mile up, we could see nothing of it. Returning on the other side of the creek, we at last got sight of it, it being only distinguished from the sage-bushes around it by the circular form given to its development, it being made of these bushes in their still growing state, and some few loose ones thrown in. To our surprise the inmates were gone. This we conceived strange, as they had come into our camp immediately on our arrival, and seemed to be very confident of protection and safety. What makes the matter more strange, it appears that in going off they shot an arrow into one of our beeves, which looks as if they had become offended at something. The wound, however, was but slight, and has done the animal no material damage.

May 22, *Camp No.* 19, *She-o-wi-te, or Willow Creek.*—Altitude above the sea, 6,414 feet. Thermometer at 7 a. m., 59°. Morning beautiful. Whole command allowed to sleep longer than usual, on account of our laying over to recruit our animals and observe the Sabbath. The guide came in last night about 11 o'clock, having traveled from daylight to that hour. He thinks he must have traveled 60 miles. Reports water to the west of south and also to the southwest of us, and our ability to get through the mountains in that direction. Assistant Surgeon Baily reports three more men on the sick-list with same complaint as already stated. This makes eight of the command unfit for duty. This day's rest, it is hoped, may be of service to them.

Learned this morning the cause of the conduct of the Indians yesterday, in leaving so hastily their wick-e-up, and shooting an arrow into one of our beeves. It seems the cook of my mess, as he says, jokingly pointed very significantly to the revolver about his waist, as a means to keep the dirty fellows from hovering, with their uncombed *lively* hair, over his viands; and the effect was just as he might have expected, an immediate scampering of them and their families from the vicinity, with some considerable hate in their bosoms, which was evinced in their flight by their putting an arrow into one of our beeves. I regret this act of thoughtlessness on the part of the cook exceedingly, both on account of its giving us a bad name among the Indians whom they may meet, and because it has deprived us of the information I was in hopes of deriving from them. I have given orders to the effect that if the like indiscreet act should be committed again the perpetrator would be held to a strict account for it, and should be punished to the extent of his crime. As I have before stated, my policy with the Indians has always been one, so far as it could be, of peace and good-will toward them; and I have never found anything but good resulting from it.

This morning I read service in front of my tent, and was glad to see a number present. This evening, before sundown, I ascended, with Messrs. Jagiello and McCarthy, the high peak to the northeast of our camp, for the purpose of viewing the surrounding country. The peak is probably about 1,500 feet above our camp. After some very considerable exertion, which, immediately after dinner, I found not so very easy, we attained the summit. On every hand could be seen high mountains; to the northeast, some 60 miles off, the Humboldt range; to the east the We-a-bah range we crossed, on the 19th; to the south, some isolated mountains, and to the west several ranges, the most distant ones covered with snow, and ranging apparently north and south. This Kobah Valley is the most extensive one we have seen, and, like the Great Salt Lake Desert, seems once to have been a lake. It seems to be filled with mountains, more or less extended, and running in a variety of directions, though generally north and south, and the valley extends around the points of these mountains, and, in some instances, runs off to an indefinite distance. Streams run from the sides of the mountains, toward the valleys, but sink in the alluvion at their base. They are generally grassed, particularly up in the cañons or ravines.

May 23, *Camp No.* 19, *She-o-wi-te, or Willow Creek.*—Morning cloudy and lowering. Thermometer at 5.30 a. m., 49°. The guide reports two passes, one north of west, and the other west of south. Neither is in the most direct line of approach to our ultimate point, but the latter is much the nearer of the two, and therefore we take it, bearing off, however, still more southwardly in order to certainly reach water within a reasonable distance. (We found, however, the next day that we could have taken a more direct course, (southwest,) as laid down on the map, and have saved about 10 miles. Wagons should take this latter course, which they will find practicable.)

Eight miles from camp ran a short distance parallel to a small stream, which sinks. Willows along it. Grass scant and alkaline. About 4 miles farther cross a wash or creek running southeast, the bed of which is 12 feet wide, and which at times must void a great deal of water, though at present it only exists in pools. Bunch-grass along it, but too alkaline for use. Two miles farther, pass, on our right, about a mile off, a mound, in which are some warm springs, one of them so warm as scarcely to admit the hand. The mound is the product of the springs, and is a calcareous tufa. Three and a half miles more brought us to a small spring, which I call after Private Shelton, of the dragoons, who found it, and who, besides being a soldier in appearance, is no less so in the thorough manner in which he executes the orders which are given him. No grass of any account about the spring, and not a sufficient quantity of water for the animals. They are consequently driven about 1.5 miles to the mountain slopes. Day's travel, 17.5 miles. Road good. Soil argillaceous and covered with sage and greasewood.

In cleaning out the spring, where we have encamped, the bones of a human being were found far-gone in decomposition. This is corroborative of the statement of my guide, last fall, that the Indians of this region bury their dead frequently in springs. It may be imagined that those who had drunk of the water did not feel very comfortable after the discovery. Fortunately for my mess the cook had used the water from the kegs which had been filled at the last camp. We were thus freed from the consciousness of having done an unpleasant thing. (On my return route, we found numerous springs in this valley to the north of, and not far from, our present camp.) Two more men on sick-list. All improving, except Clarke.

May 24, *Camp. No.* 20, *Shelton's Spring.*—Altitude above the sea, 5,993 feet. Thermometer at 5 a. m., 41°. Pete came in this morning, having traveled all night to pilot us to the next camping-place. In consequence of our having made a longer march yesterday than the guide thought we should, our to-day's travel will be only about 7 miles. Our course lay south of west, through a pass at the foot of Antelope Mountain, and continues over the foot-hills on the north side of the same, to a rushing stream, 3 feet wide and 1 deep, where, at 9.15 a. m., among the foot-hills, we encamp, in good grass and abundant cedar timber. This stream, which the Diggers call Wonst-in-dam-me (Antelope) Creek, coming from a high mountain, is doubtless constant, and, indeed, the Indians so represent it. The mountain from which it flows is magnificently serrated, and can well be distinguished by this peculiarity and its many cones. Several other streams course down its sides and sink in the valley after running a mile or two. Abundant grass can be found along the streams high up and on the cañon.

These mountains are of a different kind from those we have crossed since leaving Short-Cut Pass. The latter have been mostly of a sedimentary character, tilted as far as the We-a-bah range, generally to the west. Since then they have tilted toward the east. These rocks have in many instances been altered by heat, but not sufficiently so to come strictly under the classification of metamorphic rocks. Those we have passed through to-day, however, are decidedly igneous, though stratified rocks, some of them semifused and metamorphosed, have also been seen.

To-day on the route passes could be seen in the mountain-range to the east of us, which may be useful on our return. Colonel Cooper's Peak, on account of its cone-like shape and isolated position, has been all day a very conspicuous object. Journey 7 miles. Road hilly, but good. Some beautiful cacti, of hemispherical shape and covered with buds, seen to-day. Another man reported sick.

The weather for the past two days has been very bracing, and the effects of it are an alacrity in the men to their work, a general hilarity of conversation, and sports of different kinds in camp. This morning, after reaching camp, my assistants and myself have been practicing with the lasso or lariat. The Mexican herders with us and Indian Pete are so expert at it and useful in capturing two or three of our mules, which could not be otherwise caught, as to make us feel the value of the accomplishment.

In this country, where the bunch-grass prevails, the animals of a train should never be picketed, but be allowed to rove freely for grass, under the guidance and control of the herders. All of our animals are free from halters or lariats, and in the morning, when they are driven into camp, the teamsters have no difficulty in catching each his own mules. If you have wagons enough, however, it saves time to drive them into a corral made of them and connecting-ropes.

Our little camp, made up of four wall-tents, three Sibley's, and three common tents, with our twelve covered wagons and two spring or instrument wagons, with all the appurtenances of living men and animals, constitute quite a picturesque scene.

May 25, *Camp No.* 21, *Wons-in-dam-me, or Antelope, Creek.*—Altitude above the sea, 6,595 feet. Longitude, 116° 39′ 12″; latitude, 39° 29′ 13″. Thermometer at 4½ a. m., 22°. Ice in the buckets this morning. Sky clear and bright. Course westwardly, over a shoot or branch of Kobah Valley. In 4.3 miles cross Saw-wid Creek, a rapid stream, 3 feet wide and 1 deep, which comes from the Antelope Mountains, on our left, and sinks 500 yards below our crossing. Fine grass upon it toward the mountains. This branch of Kobah Valley, partially shut in at the south by a low range 8 miles off, but shows passes to the southwest and also to the southeast. Colonel Cooper's Peak still conspicuous. Many signs of sage-hen and antelope in this valley. A herd of the latter seen. At 12 m. reach foot of range, on west side of valley, after a journey of 13.7 miles, and encamp on a small creek, which I call Clarke's Creek, after John Clarke, one of the men, and upon which, and in the cañons higher up in the mountains, is plenty of grass. Road good, except the difficulty of breaking down the stubby sage-bush. The sage we have daily to break through with our wagons ranges from 3 to 8 inches at butt. It can be seen from this that the constant recurrence of this kind of hinderance in the aggregate amounts to a great deal. Soil argillaceous. *Artemisia* the characteristic. Altitude of Kobah Valley above the sea, 6,210 feet.

The mountain-range immediately to our west is called by the Indians the *Pah-re-ah*, or Water Mountain, on account of the many streams which flow down its sides into Kobah Valley, and on them is to be seen an abundance of grass. As I have before remarked, this stream, or one to the north of it, can and ought to be struck directly by wagons from Camp No. 19, and thus some 10 miles saved. (See map.)

Some fifteen or twenty Diggers have come into camp. From these I have been enabled to get the names of some of the mountains and streams. They are the most lively, jocose Indians I have seen. Say two rats make a meal. Like rabbits better than rats, and antelope better than either, but cannot get the latter. Have no guns; use bow and arrow. They occasionally amuse us very much in their attempts to ride our mules, which are, however, so much frightened at their rabbit-skin dress as to cause them to run off with them. One of them from this cause caught to-day a tumble.

I have worn my great-coat all the morning, and at times found it not warm enough. The guide returned at 2 o'clock, and reports a good camp 15 to 18 miles ahead of us, at the east foot of the second range to the west of us.

May 26, *Camp No.* 22.—Altitude above the sea, 6,373 feet. Up to this morning fifteen persons, nearly one-fourth of the command, have reported sick. A portion, however, have been returned to duty. Morning fine, but cool. Thermometer at 5 a. m., 29°. Night sensibly colder than any we have had, caused, doubtless, by the vicinity of the snow mountains, the Pe-er-re-ah range, to the west of us. Our morning departure very exhilarating. The crack of the whip, the "gee! get up!" of the teamsters, the merry laugh, the sudden shout from the exuberance of spirits, the clinking of armor, the long array of civil, military, and economic *personnel*, in due order, moving with hope to our destined end, coupled with the bright, bracing morning, and, at times, twittering of birds, make our morning departure from camp very pleasing.

Skirt the foot of the Pah-re-ah Mountains; course, southwardly; the pass immediately back or west of camp, which would shorten the route considerably, not being practicable for wagons, though pack-animals can use it. In 2 miles commence turning gradually westward, and in 2 miles farther, up an easy wagon-grade, reach summit of pass. Altitude above the sea, 6,440 feet. From this pass the Pe-er-re-ah (meaning Big or High) Mountain appears directly before us, some 12 miles off, trending north and south. These mountains in solidity put you in mind of the Humboldt Mountains. They have been conspicuous for several days back.

The road down the west side of the Pah-re-ah range is carried on the ridge of the spur, which furnishes a passable grade, though that down the cañon is not bad, and is entirely practicable for wagons without work, though a little sidling.

The first rattlesnake I have seen on the route I passed within a foot or two of my horse. The taxidermist, Mr. McCarthy, secured him with his fingers by the neck, much to the astonishment of the men near.

After reaching, in 7 miles from summit of pass, the valley called Won-a-ho-nupe, we turned northwest diagonally across it to the pass, through the Pe-er-re-ah Mountains. In 10 miles from summit of pass, through the Pah-re-ah range, we came to a rapid creek (Won-a-ho-nupe), 8 or 10 feet wide, 1½ deep, and running southwardly between steep sand-banks, 15 feet high. In 4 miles more cross this stream at mouth of cañon, and encamp one-fourth of a mile above on the stream, in good grass and where cedar abounds. Journey, 18.2 miles. Road generally to-day very good; over the Pah-re-ah range a large portion of it rocky from the loose igneous rocks scattered over the ground. Notice ranging along the west slope of the Pah-re-ah range a number of columns of stone, doubtless put by the Indians as landmarks to guide them over this trackless region.

Won-a-ho-nupe Valley is from 9 to 12 miles wide. Soil areno-argillaceous, and is very thinly covered with *artemisia.* At the south it appears uninterrupted; at the north is closed by a low range, a few miles above where we enter the pass of the Pe-er-re-ah range, admitting, however, a road of easy grade into the next valley. Altitude of valley above the sea, 5,443 feet.

A number of antelope seen. Notice under a cedar near our camp a very large willow basket of conical shape, which would contain probably a bushel and a half. Concealed under the same cedar were a number of rolls of willow peeling nicely tied together; also faggots or bundles of peeled willow—the stock in trade of some industrious Digger. Directed they should not be disturbed.

May 27, *Camp No.* 23, *Won-a-ho-nupe Cañon.*—Altitude above the sea, 5,870 feet. Thermometer at 5 a. m., 37°. One herder reported sick. This makes sixteen on sick-list from commencement. The bugle having become bent, and therefore not serviceable, reveillé not as prompt as usual. Morning bright. Leave at 6.10 a. m. Course westwardly up the cañon. This cañon quite luxuriant with willow and grass, the latter appearing in places quite green. The *Ephedra pedunculata* also begins to be quite common. The stream in the cañon is quite pure, and I think there must be trout in it. The road is winding through the cañon, but of easy grade, the only bad places being the frequent crossings of the creek, which occasionally are somewhat boggy. At these places, and on some short ascents and descents, the men have been required to do some excavation and embankment. At 11 o'clock, after a journey of 4.9 miles, we come to a small lake and the cañon expands into a sort of park about 4 by 3 miles in area. The landscape here quite pretty and very unique for this country. After giving orders to go into camp upon this lake, I continued up the main stream expecting in about a mile to reach the summit. After riding 7 miles I had not reached the source of the stream, and the indications were that it came from a snow peak ahead, which was still quite 5 miles off. This stream comes from northwest by west magnetically, and is quite rapid, and continued quite copious as far as I went up it. There is a great deal of meadow along it, and bunch-grass on the sides of the mountains; the grade, as far as I went, was easy. It leading me, however, too far north, I returned to camp with the hope of a more direct pass being found more westwardly.

An old Digger has visited our camp and represents that we are the first white persons he has ever seen. He says there is a large number of Indians living around, but they had run away from fear of us. I asked him why he had not been afraid. He said he was so old that it was of no consequence if he did die. I told him to say to them that we would be always glad to see them, and whenever they saw white men always to approach them in a friendly way, and they would not be hurt. He has been around eating at the different messes, and at length had so gorged himself as to be unable to eat more until he had disgorged, when he went around again to renew the pleasure. I showed him my watch, the works of which he looked upon with a great deal of wonder. He said he would believe what I told him about the magnetic telegraph the next time he was told it. He is at least sixty years old, and says he never had a chief. I asked him if his country was a good one. He said it was. He liked it a good deal better than any other. I asked him why. Because, he said, it had a great many rats. I asked him if they ever quarreled about their rat country. He said they did. So it would appear that civilized nations are not the only people who go to war about their domains.

The guide and party left us this morning, and are to be absent two or three days in researches ahead. Pete returned this evening from this party and reports our pass to-morrow to be the one directly west from camp, as I had concluded from this afternoon's reconnaissance.

The lake we are on is several acres in extent. Ducks frequent it. The grass about it and along the creek is quite luxuriant, and expands in places into meadows of considerable area. Cedar is found on the heights. Should it ever become necessary to establish a post, say near the east entrance of Won-a-ho-nupe Cañon, the grass, water, and timber of this mountain-range would be amply sufficient, and fine granite building-stone could be found in the cañon.

The party has given my name to this lake, park, and pass; and also to the creek, but as it has been my rule to preserve the Indian names, whenever I can ascertain them, and Won-a-ho-nupe is the name of the creek, I shall continue so to call it.

For the past two days the ground has been so resplendent with flakes of mica of a golden hue as to constantly remind you how rich it would be in gold were the shining particles veritably such.

May 28, *Camp No.* 24, *Simpson's Park, Pe-er-re-ah range.*—Longitude, 116° 49′; latitude, 39° 30′ 32″. Altitude above the sea, 6,355 feet. Thermometer at 5 a. m., 30°. Morning somewhat cloudy. Renewed journey at 10 minutes to 6 a. m. Leave valley of Won-a-ho-nupe Creek and strike west for Simpson's Pass, which we reach by a very easy ascent in 4.7 miles; altitude above the sea, 7,104 feet. The grass in the pass very abundant and of the finest character. This fine mountain bunch-grass fattens and strengthens our animals like oats. The pass at summit is as much as a mile wide, and both backward and forward the views are beautiful. The mountains near our camp of May 25 are seen very conspicuously back of us; and ahead of us, limiting Reese Valley, which we are approaching, is a low range trending generally north and south, and beyond them a very high range covered with snow, called by the Indians the Se-day-e or Lookout Mountains. The Pe-er-re-ah Mountains, which we are now about to leave, are composed, up Won-a-ho-nupe Cañon, of quartzite, altered slates, and granite rocks; and near Simpson's Park the rocks are highly metamorphosed, semifused and stratified. At the pass they are granitic.

Descending from the summit of Simpson's Pass, west side, by not a very steep but sandy grade, and along a short sidling place, near foot of ravine, (which our wagons passed by use of ropes to upper side, but which will require some slight side-excavation when the route is improved,) in 2.8 miles reach Reese Valley, which, in 3.7 miles more, we traverse to Reese River; this we cross by ford, and in 2.6 miles more up the river, or southwardly, reach our camping ground. Fuel should be brought. Day's travel, 13.8 miles. Road generally good. The ravine on west side of Simpson's Pass is filled with a thorn-bush in full bloom, 2 to 3 feet high; blossoms like those of the crab-apple.

The valley in which we are encamped, as well as its creek, I call after Mr. Reese, our guide, who, with two other men, discovered it some years since in their peregrinations between Salt Lake City and Carson Valley. They gave it the name of New River; but as Mr. Reese has been of considerable service, and discovers very laudable zeal in examining the country ahead in our explorations, I have thought it is but just to call the river and valley after him. The Indian name of the river is Pang-que-o-whop-pe, or Fish Creek. Mr. Reese is now, for the first time, on ground he has been once over, but confesses it has been so long ago it does not appear familiar to him.

Reese River is 10 feet wide, 1½ deep; current moderate; water good, though of a slight milky color from sediment; runs northwardly, and is the largest stream we have seen this side of the Jordan. Trout weighing 2½ pounds are found in it. The grass along it is luxuriant, but in many places alkaline. It is best and very abundant farther up the stream, and extends as far as the eye can reach.

Reese Valley is from 10 to 15 miles wide; at the north appears uninterrupted; at the south seems to be bounded by a range of mountains 30 miles off. Next to Spring Valley, it is the whitest with alkaline efflorescence we have seen. Soil argillo-arenaceous and covered with the wild sage and greasewood. It is quite well watered, and several streams well grassed can be seen tending to it from the west slope of the Pe-er-re-ah range. Altitude above the sea, by barometric measurement, 5,530 feet.

Sanchez returned from guide's party this afternoon, and reports next camp about 22.5 miles off.

May 29, *Camp No.* 25, *Reese River.*—Altitude above the sea, 5,563 feet. Magnetic variation, 16° 10′ E. Thermometer at 4.50 a. m., 22°.5. Intended spending the Sabbath here, but the grass not being of the best kind, think it best to move. Morning lovely, though cool. The mules more and more difficult to catch up; attribute it to the improved condition, caused by the nutritious properties of the mountain bunch-grass. Moved at 5 minutes to 6 a. m. Course southwestwardly, to a depression or pass of the low range bounding Reese Valley on its west side, which we reach by an easy grade in 13.5 miles. Altitude above the sea, 6,483 feet. This pass is remarkable on account of the igneous, reddish rocks about it, several of them appearing in the form of peaks, domes, and knobs. These are semifused, stratified, and porphyritic rocks. Notice a very small spring to the left of the road, just before reaching summit. The recent foot-prints of Indians leading to it show that they cannot be far from us. The water is doubtless not constant.

From summit of pass see another valley to the west of us, ranging generally north and south, and bounded by the Se-day-e or Lookout range, on its west side In 2 miles from summit reach west foot of pass in valley by a tolerable descent, and without difficulty.

This valley is exceedingly forbidding in appearance. To the south the bottom is an extended clay flat, perfectly divested of vegetation, terminating toward the south in a small lake. In the distance it all looked so much like a sheet of water that I sent a dragoon ahead to examine it; but, with my spy-glass, seeing him gallop over it, I concluded it was passable; so gave the word forward. I struck magnetically S. 60° W., to the green spot across the valley Sanchez pointed out as our camp-ground, and on going to it passed over a portion of the clay flat referred to. In its checkered and smooth state it put me in mind of a polished tesselated floor. Clouds of dust, like smoke, could be seen eddying over it in different directions. In 5.8 miles from foot of pass, at 3½ p. m., after a journey of 21.2 miles, come to a creek, where we encamp in tolerable grass. The creek is 5 feet wide, 2 deep, and, running with considerable rapidity, spreads out in many rills, and sinks in the lake referred to. Abundant grass can be found at the mouth of the cañon of this stream. Both the stream and cañon I call after my assistant, Lieut. J. L. Kirby Smith.

This valley, which I call after Capt. I. C. Woodruff, Corps Topographical Engineers, is 10 to 15 miles wide, and closed partially at the north by a pretty high mountain, some 12 miles off, and at the south by a range which seems to admit of egress at the southeast and also the southwest angle. Its altitude above the sea is 6,000 feet. Road to-day in Reese Valley, for 2 miles from camp, heavy; remainder good, except a little rough going down from the pass in the valley, on account of some gullies. A couple of wolves noticed in the vicinity of camp, the first we have seen.

May 30, *Camp No.* 26, *Smith's Creek, Woodruff Valley.*—Elevation above the sea, 5,960 feet. Thermometer at sunrise, 35°. Our guide told Sanchez before leaving him day before yesterday that he would meet us at this camp last evening. This he has not done; and as he is alone, contrary to my orders, which require him always to come in with the last man of his party, I am not gratified, though doubtless his zeal has led him to this unauthorized venture. We have therefore remained in camp to-day on his account. Meantime I sent out Pete, Payte, and Sanchez to examine the pass directly to our west, up Smith's Creek, and they have returned and report it impracticable for wagons without a great deal of bridging and other work. (The diary of my return route will show, however, that on our return we got through this pass without any great difficulty; and though some work is necessary to make the road through it what it should be, yet in grade it was far better, though 4 miles farther, than by the way of the pass to the south of it, which we took in our outward route.)

Payte and party report they saw Diggers in the mountains to the west of us to-day, but that they fled as soon as they were perceived. They found one little fellow, about four years of age, hid behind a sage-bush, but as soon as their backs were turned the youngster put off as fast as his legs would carry him.

On our return we ascertained that the Pe-er-re-ah range, which we crossed on the 28th, is the boundary between the Sho-sho-nee Diggers (or what has been called, as I think erroneously, the Pah-utes) and the Pi-utes, as the Un-go-we-ah range seems to be the boundary between the Sho-sho-nee Diggers and the Go-shoots. Why the Pah-utes should have been thus called I am at a loss to comprehend, for their language is Sho-sho-nee, and not Ute, and, therefore, they are more certainly a people derived from, or cognate with, that tribe than the Ute. I also notice that the Pi-utes and Pah-utes are designated on the maps as one and the same people. This is also a mistake, and doubtless has arisen from similarity of their names. They are all, however, more or less Diggers; that is, they live on roots, rats, lizards, insects, grass-seeds, &c.

May 31, *Camp No.* 26, *Smith's Creek.*—Thermometer at 5.20 a. m., 29°. Mr. Reese, the guide, not returning last night, I have thought it expedient to send out Payte to explore to the south and west, giving him special instructions in the premises, so that in case any accident may have happened to Mr. Reese we may at once move forward to his rescue. Pete and Sanchez and two dragoons accompany him. He is to keep me advised daily of the proper places to encamp ahead. The party take three days' provisions. One of the party returned at 1 o'clock, and reported grass and water 10 miles ahead, in a southwest direction, and a pass near, which looked favorably for crossing the Se-day-e range.

June 1, *Camp No.* 26, *Smith's Creek.*—Thermometer at 5.25 a. m., 30°. Mr. Reese has not yet made his appearance. I feel quite anxious about him, as he is entirely alone. He has hitherto been very prompt in fulfilling his engagements, riding sometimes late at night, and, on one occasion, all night, to effect it. I therefore have sent out Mr. McCarthy and two dragoons to track him, and at the same time have ordered the whole party forward to the water and grass reported yesterday. This is in the direction in which he told Sanchez he would cross the next, or Se-day-e, Mountain.

Just after commencing the march, I noticed apparently an old, decrepit-looking man approaching the train from the west side, and supporting himself by a couple of crutches or sticks. At first I took him for a Digger Indian. On more close scrutiny, however, I found it to be Mr. Reese, our guide, who, as soon as we reached him, sank down exhausted into a sage-bush. His clothes were nearly torn off him, and altogether he presented a most pitiable aspect. As soon as he could collect his mind he informed us that the day before yesterday, when on the other or west side of the Se-day-e Mountains, about 17 miles off, his mule gave out, and that he has ever since been on foot, trudging over the mountains to find us. He had no clothing except what he had on his back, and as he had lost his matches he could make no fire, though the night was quite cold. He had lost his haversack of provisions, and the consequence was that he had had nothing to eat. Some Digger Indians he met kindly offered him three fat rats, but as they had been roasted with entrails and offal unremoved, he said he did not feel hungry enough to accept their generous hospitality. We were exceedingly glad to see him, and had him supplied with something to eat, after which he went to sleep in one of the wagons. Finding him safe, I sent a dragoon to notify Mr. McCarthy and party of the fact, and direct their return.

Our course to-day has been magnetically S. 25° W., between the base of the Se-day-e range on our right and the clay flat and small lake of Woodruff Valley on our left. In 1.6 miles from camp cross a fine rapid stream, 5 feet wide, 2 deep, bottom somewhat soft, which I called after Mr. Engelmann, the geologist of my party. It expends itself in the lake. Two and a half miles farther cross another small stream running in the same direction, and after a day's march of 10.2 miles come to a swift creek running east from the mountains, which I call after Lieutenant Putnam, Topographical Engineers, one of my assistants. It is 6 feet wide, 2 deep, and of gravelly bottom. After running 5 or 6 miles it expends itself in the small lake before referred to. Willows line it. Soil of Woodruff Valley argillaceous, benches gravelly. The *artemisia* the characteristic. Cedars cover the mountains near.

Payte with party returned to camp just after we had pitched our tents, and reports a pass 10 miles south of this, which he thinks, without considerable work, impracticable, and says it looks very steep on the other side. There is, however, a practicable pass 20 miles south of us, but as after we get through it, according to him, we will have to go 20 miles more before we can get water, I have determined to go and look myself for a pass, Lieutenant Murry, Mr. Jagiello, Payte, and Pete accompanying me.

8.30 *o'clock p. m.*—Just returned from a reconnaissance of a pass, the foot of which is 2 miles southwest from camp. Started from camp at 2.30, returned at 8.30, just after tattoo; distance traveled about 24 miles. Found the pass on the east side of the mountain quite steep, and that on the west side quite rough, on account of the rocks and of the stream which passes down it. Think, however, it practicable, with some labor, and shall therefore attempt it to-morrow.

Lieutenant Putnam reports the cañon of Putnam's Creek, north of west from camp, for 2½ miles so narrow as to make it perfectly impracticable for wagons without a great deal of excavation, revetting, and blasting.

June 2, *Camp No.* 27, *Putnam's Creek.*—Longitude, 117° 27′ 34″; latitude, 39° 14′ 13″. Elevation above the sea, 6,325 feet. Thermometer at 5 a. m., 48°. Moved at 5 minutes of 6 a. m. Course southwestwardly to the base of the Se-day-e Mountain, and then generally westwardly through what I call the Gibraltar (or south) Pass, examined by me yesterday. The teams reached summit of pass, 5 miles from last camp, at 10 o'clock, without doubling. The only exceedingly steep place is about three-fourths of a mile up, where the ravine is left and a minor ridge surmounted to get over into the south branch of Putnam's Creek. The ascent of this minor ridge is steep, and the descent on the west side still more so. To accomplish the latter without accident we had to lock and rough-shoe the wheels. A good grade is possible, with the labor of some twenty men one day, on left side of track. Two and one-half miles thence up Putnam's Creek by a good grade brought us to summit of pass, 7,741 feet above the sea, and 3.7 miles more down Gibraltar Creek (a small stream) to a point in the cañon, where, at half past 4, we encamped. The road on the west side of the pass is very rough, on account of its frequent crossings of Gibraltar Creek and large, loose rocks scattered around, but by bridging the creek and removing the rocks—no very great work—it could be made good. Met with two upsets, and the breaking of a wagon-tongue, hound, and coupling in this cañon.

On right of cañon, descending from summit, some stupendous granitic and porphyritic rocks, probably 500 feet above the valley, are noticeable. Journey 8.7 miles. I continued 7 miles farther down the cañon to examine it, returning about 9 o'clock p. m., and finding the command uneasy about me, as I was alone. The guide, Mr. Reese, found his mule where he had left him the other day, saddle and everything safe.

The cañons of this mountain abound in pure water and splendid grass. The mountain-mahogany is also seen. Cedar and pines are also found, as they have been in nearly every range since we left the Great Salt Lake Desert. These cedars branch immediately from the ground, are 12 or 15 feet high, and present in the mass a rotund form. The pines are generally on the summits of the ridges, and are generally not more than 25 or 30 feet, though some attain a height of 50.

The rocks of the Se-day-e Mountain are porphyritic and trachytic, also semifused stratified rocks. West of summit they are white granite, lower down red and brown porphyritic rocks.

June 3, *Camp No.* 28, *Gibraltar Creek.*—Thermometer at 5.10 a. m., 48°. Morning pleasantly cool, and as usual clear. Mr. Reese, with Pete, Sanchez, and two dragoons, left this morning to be absent for several days, probably four or five, to examine the country in advance, and keep me advised daily of route and camping-places. Raised camp at 6.15, and continued down Gibraltar Cañon. For about a mile it continued rough from isolated rocks; after this no difficulty. Creek sinks 1.7 miles below camp. Five and a half miles farther strike a small creek and a spring, which might be called an extension or re-appearance of Gibraltar Creek, though strictly it is a continuation of its more northern branch, which comes in from the mountain at this point. Half a mile farther pass through a gap or gate between some stupendous rocks of a dark-gray and brown porphyritic character, which form a range of narrow breadth perpendicular to our course. This defile from the cañon to the valley I call the Gate of Gibraltar. It is about 50 yards wide, and of champaign character. From this gate, following the course of Gibraltar Creek (very small) in a southwest direction, we cross in 7.2 miles a valley or plain, and arrive at a second gate or gap in a low range, running north and south, where, at 4 p. m., we encamp near the sink of Gibraltar Creek. A limited amount of grass is found at the gap; more in vicinity on west side. The mountain range which crosses here is perfectly devoid of timber. Road to-day rough, the first 2 miles down Gibraltar Cañon, and subsequently somewhat soft on account of the pulverulent character of the soil of the valley to the west of the Se-day-e range. This valley, along the route, is quite a desert one, scattering greasewood and the wild sage being the principal growth.

On reaching our camping-place, which I call the Middle Gate, saw a naked Indian stretched out on the rocks at an angle of about 20 degrees. He was so much of the color of the rocks as to escape our notice for some time. On being aroused he looked a little astonished to see so many armed men about him, but soon felt assured of safety by their kind treatment. He seemed particularly pleased when he saw the long string of wagons coming in, and laughed outright for joy. I counted twenty-seven rats and one lizard lying about him, which he had killed for food. He had with him his appliances for making fire. They consisted simply of a piece of hard greasewood, about 2 feet long, and of the size or smaller than your little finger in cross-section. This was rounded at the but. Then a second flat piece of the same kind of wood, 6 inches long by 1 broad and ½ thick. This second piece had a number of semi-spherical cavities on one of its faces. With this piece laid on the ground, the cavities uppermost, he placed the other stick between the palms of his hands, and with one end of the latter in a cavity, and holding the stick in a vertical position, he would roll it rapidly forward and back, till the friction would cause the tinder, which he had placed against the foot of the stick in the cavity, to ignite. In this way I saw him produce fire in a few seconds.

After sundown a Pi-ute Indian, the first we have met, came into camp, habited in a new hickory (coarse check) shirt, doubtless of the stock I gave the guide this morning, as presents to the Indians for information and guidance to water and grass. The shirt is most probably the credentials of his office as guide to us to-morrow, besides, his gestures (Pete is away and we therefore cannot talk to him) seem to indicate the same thing. In addition, the guide has sent no dragoon back, as directed, and this seems to confirm our suspicions that he has been sent to us as a guide. Dr Baily reports only one person on the sick-list, Mr. Jagiello. The day has been oppressively hot, and everything indicates that, from the Se-day-e range, we have descended to a lower level of altitude than we have experienced at any time along the route. The mountains, too, appear lower, and are entirely free from snow; the general face of the country is very arid and forbidding. The men had hard work to pitch our tents on account of the high wind and dust.

June 4, *Camp No.* 29, *Middle Gate.*—Elevation above the sea, 4,665 feet. For the first time it was so warm last night that I slept under a single comforter. Heretofore I could scarcely make myself warm enough with all the bed-clothing I could muster. Thermometer at 5 a. m., 38°. Morning clear and pleasant. Moved at 6. Our new Indian guide cut an amusing figure in attempting to mount his mule. He rides by clinging to the pommel of the saddle. Immediately after passing through Middle Gate, strike southwestwardly over a pulverulent prairie to a third gate, which we reach in 3½ miles, and which I call the West Gate. It is also a gap in a low range of mountains running north and south. After threading this defile, pass over another thirsty-looking, marly prairie, surrounded by low, ashy-looking mountains, with passes between. In 5 miles get across this valley, and attain summit of a low ridge, whence we descend to another shallow valley, altitude above the sea 4,090 feet, which I call

Dry Flat Valley, on account of the whitish clay flat we cross, and which is as smooth and as hard as a floor. Indeed, the glare from it was almost blinding. Twenty miles from camp we attain the summit of the range dividing Dry from a valley I call Alkaline Valley, on account of its general whitish alkaline appearance from saline efflorescence. Descending this ridge 1.7 miles, and turning northwardly and skirting it for 2.7 miles, we come to our camp-ground, where the guide party, which is in advance of us, has dug a number of small wells.

The water is found in an efflorescent sand-flat, and lies 3 feet below the surface. In some of the holes it is strongly alkaline; in others just tolerable. The addition of vinegar improves it very much. It is, however, difficult to keep up a supply of water on account of the sand tumbling in. The grass in the vicinity is very alkaline and scant, and altogether this is a miserable camping-place, the worst we have had. Fuel, rabbit-bush, a miserable substitute for the sage or greasewood.

The wagons reached camp at half past 4. Journey, 24.5 miles. Road pretty good. Country very arid and desert. Mountains in the distance perfectly devoid of timber, and of a thirsty, ashy hue, except the last range we crossed, which is of a dark-brown appearance, approaching black, and therefore called Black Mountains. The rocks at our morning's camp, Middle Gate, are porphyritic; westward of these as far as the Black Mountains, first quartzite, and then highly altered stratified rock, siliceous limestones, slates, dolomite. The Black Mountains are made up of partly strongly-metamorphosedst, ratified rocks and partly igneous and scoriaceous, lava-like rocks traversed by quartz-veins.

The day has been very hot, and we have all felt very thirsty; not knowing when we started that water would be so far off, we had not taken the precaution which we should have done to have our water-kegs filled at Gibraltar Cañon. Our great thirst over these desert plains is no doubt owing to the dry condition of the atmosphere, which favors the rapid dessication or drying up of the humors of the body.

On the route, one of the dragoons returned from the guide's party with a note from Mr. Reese, informing me of the locality of to-night's camp, and giving the unpalatable news that the water was not good, the grass poor, and that we were within 12 miles of the north end of Walker's Lake, where we would encamp to-morrow. The consequence is, that as the point I have been aiming at is the north bend of Walker's River, and not the Lake, we are a great deal too far to the south, and must therefore make the necessary corresponding northing. This error could only have occurred on the supposition of Walker's Lake being wrongly placed on the Topographical Bureau map, for I feel confident that the latitudes which I have worked out, and upon which we have based our southing, have been correct. If Mr. Reese had not assured me that he had been over this portion of the country before, I should doubt the truth of his representations; but, relying on the accuracy of his observations, we are obliged to change our course from our present camp in a northwest direction in order to reach in the most direct way the north bend of Walker's River.

June 5, Camp No. 30, *Alkaline Valley.*—Altitude above the sea, 3,900 feet. Thermometer at 3.30 a. m., 48°. Up at half past 3 a. m., but in consequence of mules straying off to get grass and water, the train did not move until 5. Course north of west, along west foot of Black Mountains, to the north end of what turned out to be Carson instead of Walker's Lake. The guide, therefore, at fault, and neither the Topographical Bureau map nor my calculations wrong. As the map will indicate, it will be perceived that before I made the turn to the northwest, pursuant to the representation of our whereabouts by our guide, my course was direct for the bend of Walker's River, the locality aimed at from the commencement of the expedition at Camp Floyd. The consequence is that we have lost about 12 miles by our guide's errors, and will have to retrogade, for a distance, our steps.

The road to-day has been along the east edge of Alkaline Valley, and the west foot of the Black Mountains. In the valley it has been heavy, and on the benches, on account of the basaltic rocks, rough. The valley, which is almost everywhere white with saline incrustation, is about 16 miles long and 8 broad, and in wet weather must cut up a great deal. The mountains inclosing it are low, and give indications of passes in almost every direction. Not a sign of a tree is to be seen on any of them. The Sierra Nevada, seen for the first time to the west of us, some 60 or 70 miles off, is covered with snow. Journey, 16.6 miles. Teams got in at 12 meridian. O the luxury of good sweet water to a thoroughly thirsty traveler! How little do we value the daily common bounties of Providence! For the past few days a draught of pure cold water has been prized at its true value; and it is only the real absence of our comforts that causes us to estimate them at their full value.

We are encamped at the head of the outlet from Carson Lake into the sink of Carson, where our only fuel is dry rush. This outlet is about 50 feet wide and 3 or 4 feet deep, and voids the lake rapidly into its sink, which is some 10 or 15 miles to the northeast of us. The water is of a rather whitish, milky cast, and though not very lively, is yet quite good. The Carson River to the northwest, where it empties into the lake, can be seen quite distinctly, marked out by its line of green cottonwoods.

The name of the river and lake was given by Colonel Frémont, in compliment to Kit Carson, one of his celebrated guides.

The alluvial bottom about Carson Lake is quite extensive and rich, as the luxuriant growth of rushes shows, and could, I think, be easily irrigated. The only drawback to its being unexceptionable for cultivation in every part is its being somewhat alkaline in places, particularly toward its southern portion. Curlew, pelican, and ducks, and other aquatic birds frequent the locality, and the lake is filled with fish. A number of Pi-utes, some two dozen, live near our camp, and I notice they have piles of fish lying about drying, principally chubs and mullet. They catch them with a seine. Their habitation consists of flimsy sheds, made of rushes, which screen them from the sun and wind. They present a better appearance than the Diggers we have seen, both in respect to clothing and features. Indeed, they act as if they had been in contact with civilization, and had to some degree been improved by it. The decoy-ducks they use on the lake to attract the live ducks are perfect in form and fabric, and I have obtained a couple for the Smithsonian Institution.

This valley of Carson Lake presents at sunset a very pretty landscape. It lies very level, and on every side, at a considerable distance, with intervals between, are very pretty blue mountains lying along the horizon, giving variety to the picture. The air this afternoon has been also very soft and balmy, having a tranquilizing effect on the senses and inducing one to drink in with delight what lies before him.

Pete, whom I found at camp, and had sent out to bring in the rest of the guide's party, returned at 6 p. m., bringing with him the infantry soldier, Sanchez, and the pack-mule. He missed the track of Mr. Reese, who will be in to-night, probably, or to-morrow. The Pi-ute with the check shirt accompanied us all the way to our present camp. In mounting his mule, he invariably would protrude his legs through and between his arms while resting his hands on the saddle, and in one instance, in his attempt to mount in this way, awkwardly tumbled off on the other side.

June 6, Camp No. 31, north end of Carson Lake.—Longitude, 118° 30′ 01″; latitude, 39° 23′ 37″; altitude above the sea, 3,840 feet; thermometer at 4.45 a. m., 43½°. Mr. Reese returned during the night. The Indians in camp early this morning, with fish to barter in exchange for old clothing, powder, &c. Seem to be pretty keen in a trade about small things; but in larger matters—as, for instance, the barter of a child—one of the Indians said he would sell his, a lad of about 8 years of age, for a jackknife. They seem to be perfectly beside themselves at the idea of a train of wagons passing through their settlement. Nothing of the kind has ever occurred before. They laugh and jabber like so many parrots, and it has been difficult to get any distinct notions from them about the country in advance of us.

We retrograde to-day in our course, southerly direction, and skirt the east shore of Carson Lake. Air balmy and throwing a blue veil over the near and distant mountains. The snowy peaks of the Sierra Nevada seen on our right; the water of Carson Lake beautifully blue; lake margined with rushes; the shores are covered with muscle-shells; pelicans and other aquatic fowl a characteristic. Upper half, that is, north half, of east margin of Carson Lake very slightly alkaline. South half, east margin, white with alkali. Indeed, as I proceed I find that the margin of the lake generally, as far as I can see, looks alkaline. In 9.7 miles leave the lake at its southern end, and, passing over and through some sand-hills, in 5.7 miles come to a small spring of calcareous water, where there is no grass. Here there has been a number of these springs, and the locality for a very considerable area is nothing but calcareous tufa, formed by the springs, which are all closed but one. Three miles more brought us through some heavy sand-drifts to a very small spring of miserable mineral-water, so nauseous as not to permit me to take even a swallow. No grass in vicinity. After proceeding a few miles further, in consequence of the day being very warm and the sand-hills heavy, halted at 3 o'clock, and turned out the animals to graze upon the little grass which exists in bunches around. At 5 start again, and, still ascending to crest of dividing ridge between Walker's Lake Valley and Saleratus Valley, in 9.4 miles reach summit, 4,595 feet above the sea. Just before doing so, Lieutenant Murry sent word that some of the mules were giving out, and he was afraid he would be obliged to halt. I sent word back to him to try and hold on till he could reach the summit, and after that there would be no difficulty. He managed, by exchanging some of the mules, to get the wagons all up to the top of the divide, but it was midnight before we reached Walker's River, 6.9 miles distant, and as the night was quite dark, we considered ourselves very fortunate that we got along without accident. Some of the party were so fagged out on reaching the camp-ground as to immediately roll themselves in their blankets on the ground and go to sleep. We find ourselves on (for this country) a noble river, but will have to await daylight to disclose its features; perceive, however, we are amid good grass and timber and have an abundance of water. Journey to-day a hard one. Country wretchedly sandy and barren, mountainous or hilly. Distance, 31.2 miles. The guide has been a Pi-Ute Indian, hired at Carson Lake. The formations along the route have been trachytic, scoriatic rocks and volcanic tufas. In the pass, just before attaining summit of divide, noticed some hieroglyphics on detached bowlders.

June 7, *Camp No.* 32, *Walker's River.*—Altitude above the sea, 4,072 feet; thermometer at 7.30 a. m., 69°. In consequence of getting into camp so late last evening, and the teams requiring rest, we lay over at this point till this afternoon. The river we are encamped on (Walker's) is the largest I have yet seen this side of Green River; is about one hundred yards wide and from six to ten feet deep at its present stage, which seems to be high. It flows quite strongly toward Walker's Lake, in which it sinks. Its color is very much like that of the Missouri (a rather dirty yellow), and in taste is quite soft and palatable. Its banks, which are vertical, are about four feet above the surface of the water. The name Walker, applied to this river and to the lake into which it flows, first appears on Frémont's map of 1848, and was doubtless given by him in honor of Mr. Joseph Walker, the leader of the party sent by Colonel Bonneville, in 1835, to explore Great Salt Lake, and who subsequently, on his way to Monterey, Cal., passed by this river. Walker, after this, in 1845, was Frémont's guide along this same river and lake.

I have sent Mr. Reese ahead with a few men to construct a raft to enable the party to cross Carson River when we shall reach it. After attending to this, he is to proceed on to Genoa and bring back our mail. Some Pi-Utes from Walker's Lake have come into camp to sell or trade salmon-trout, caught in the lake. The largest they have weighs about 20 pounds. These Indians talk a little English and dress, some of them, like white people. In condition they are superior to those we have seen.

Raise camp at 3 p. m. Sun scorching hot. Course northwestwardly along the left or north bank of the river, being forced occasionally by the river from the bottom to the sand-bench. River-bottom from one-fourth to one-half mile wide. Soil, a dark loam, very rich. Grass quite abundant and of good quality. Cottonwoods (sparsely) and willows (abundantly) fringe the river. The river-bottom could be readily and copiously irrigated and made very productive. A range of low mountains run parallel to the river on north, and another also on south side, each about eight or ten miles distant. Not a tree or shrub is to be seen on them. The contrast between the perfectly barren, sandy, thirsty-looking country to be seen on every side and the valley of Walker's River, fringed with green cottonwoods and willows, very refreshing. After marching ten miles, at 7 o'clock encamped again on the river. Road good except on banks of valley, where it was sandy. Pete came in from guide's party, and reports bend of Walker's River six miles ahead, where I expect to camp to-morrow.

June 8, *Camp No.* 33, *Walker's River.*—Longitude, 118° 49′ 00″; latitude, 39° 07′

38″; altitude above the sea, 4,200 feet; thermometer at 4.45 a. m., 53°. Morning, as usual since we crossed the Se-day-e Mountains, oppressively warm immediately after sunrise. Moved at twenty minutes after 5. Continue 6.3 miles up valley of Walker's River, as far as the North Bend, and, at 8 a. m., encamp in tolerable grass. Road good, except the sandy portion wherever we left the bed of the river. Characteristics of country same as yesterday.

June 9, *Camp No.* 34, *North Bend of Walker's River.*—Elevation above the sea, 4,288 feet; thermometer at 4.25 a. m., 52°. Morning clear and pleasant. The Mexican, Sanchez, did not come in last night from guide's party to show us the road to next camp. We shall, however, push ahead, a Pi-Ute with us offering himself as guide. Our course lies northwestwardly to Carson River. Just after leaving camp, Sanchez met us and presented a letter from the guide, as follows:

"PLEASANT GROVE, CARSON RIVER, *June* 8, 1859.

"Captain SIMPSON:

"SIR: All is right. Mr. Miller will build a raft that will take the wagons over, for $30. The logs have to be hauled some three miles. The people here feel pleased that you and your party are so near. It is now 12 o'clock, and I am ready to start for Genoa. I shall be back before you arrive, to ferry on the raft. Mr. Miller says he will have it done to-morrow night.

"Yours,

"J. REESE."

Six miles from camp we pass some hot and cold springs to left of road in valley. Thermometer rose to 165° when immersed in one of the hot springs. One of them is ten by twenty-five feet, and quite a stream flows from it. The water boils up at different points, and while it is of a sort of blue color in the body, along the margin it is a reddish-yellow color, doubtless caused by iron. The blue color is probably due to the sulphur it contains. It is the hottest spring I have seen, not excepting those near Salt Lake City. The valley, ever since we left our camp of this morning, has been exceedingly alkaline. Leaving the valley of Walker's River and striking for Carson River, we cross the point of a low mountain—ascent and descent good—and in three and one-half miles more get into an old wagon-road, which we follow. One mile more brings us to a cañon, which we thread, and in which we find a considerable patch of grass and rushes. In this cañon, on left side, fourteen miles from last camp, embowered among wild roses and willows, is a small spring of good, cool water, about which there is a little grass; a plenty of the latter one-half mile south. Two miles farther, pass over the steepest and roughest hill, or spur, we have seen. We would like to continue down the valley until we strike Carson River, and then turn up its valley to the left, and thus avoid this spur, but the height of the water prevents. At this hill we were detained two and one-half hours. All the teams had to double to get up, except Payte's, which seems thus far to carry off the meed of power and good management. Three miles more along and up Carson River upon its bank brought us to a good spot on the river, where we encamp in good grass.

Carson River at our camp about 100 yards wide, quite swift; depth, from ten to fifteen feet; color, somewhat whitish or clayey. The river-bottom is about one-fourth of a miles wide, very rich, and can be readily irrigated. At this time the banks are full, and in places overflowing; large cottonwoods, solitary and in groves, along it. Mosquitoes, for the first time in our exploration, troubled us on Carson Lake, and we have had them, much to our annoyance, ever since. The country to-day, between Walker's River and Carson River, miserably arid and worthless for agricultural purposes. No timber; greasewood the principal plant, and the largest I have seen six feet high and as many across its branches. Journey, 19 miles. Road good, except steep hill three miles back. Have noticed this side, or west, of Se-day-e Mountains, the dove. Trap, vesicular, and trachytic rocks; also metamorphic strata characterize the region between Walker and Carson Rivers. We are now in the gold-region.

June 10, *Camp No.* 35, *Carson River.*—Altitude above the sea, 4,200 feet. The mosquitoes were so troublesome last night on the river-bottom that some of the men went on the bluff and slept. Last remaining ox of six we brought with us from Camp Floyd shows, by his constantly bellowing, his sense of his loneliness. The others have been killed for beef. Thermometer at 4.35 a. m., 58°. Morning pleasant and clear. Moved at quarter of 5. Continue westward along south side of Carson River as far as opposite Pleasant Grove, where at 8 o'clock a. m. we arrive. Find the raft ready, made of cottonwood-trees of an old log-house belonging to Mr. Miller, the agent of the California Mail Company at this station, and which he has pulled down for the purpose. This point a good one for ferry or ford; banks on either side low and firm. By 5½ p. m. the wagons and property were rafted across safely, except one wagon, which unfortunately capsized, causing the loss of some $31 belonging to the driver, Payte, (as he said,) and some clothing, also three sets of harness. What I however grieve the most about is, that a portion of our *herbarium* has got soaking-wet. The mules were driven across. The men have worked hard and have been constantly in the water, and obliged frequently to swim. It was amusing to see the cook, Storer, throw away the coffee-pot he was bringing over on the raft, when it capsized, and plunge for his life into the stream. Fortunately, he, as well as the other fellow on the raft, could swim, and therefore there was no loss of persons. It was, however, very provoking to hear the teamster discover his *morale*, by the vociferation which he made just as he jumped from the raft: "Let her go; I am safe." This was the more so, as the fellow had been a great brag; but, like all such, his courage, as well as honesty, failed him just at the moment of trial and when it was really needed.

Journey to-day, 9 miles. Road in places stony. A mountain-range skirts the river on north side of river. Its geological character is probably metamorphic. Along the road the rocks have been porphyritic, trachytic, and vesicular.

We have now at Pleasant Grove, for the first time, got into the old Humboldt River and Carson Valley emigrant-road. The California Mail Company have a station here, under the charge of Mr. Miller, who occupies quite a good, weather-boarded house. The grove of cottonwoods near it give the place its name.

June 11, *Camp No.* 36, *Pleasant Grove.*—Elevation above the sea, 4,288 feet. Moved at quarter to 7. Immediately follow up the valley of Carson River, on its north side, the old emigrant-road, which is as well beaten as any in the States; our course, west of south; mountain-range continues parallel to road on north side, three miles off, and on south side of river there is another, five miles off. Notice along the road three claim-shanties, and some ditching for mining purposes.

After proceeding 7.4 miles from camp, come to China Town, on Carson River; elevation above the sea, 4,360 feet. This is a mining town of twelve houses, and contains about fifty Chinese. Including all engaged in mining in a vicinity of six miles, the population is about one hundred and fifty. Can clear at these diggings, called the Gold Cañon Flat Diggings, when there is water, from $5 to $8 per day per man. These diggings have been worked since 1852. The material is taken out of the ravine, or *arroya*, which is composed of sand and cobblestones, and the gold sifted from it by a "rocker" or "cradle." Quality of the gold-dust, $13 to the ounce.

There are some new diggings seven miles northwest from this place up Gold Cañon, which were commenced last April, and which yield an average of $15 per day to the hand, with the cradle. Two men have been known, with one rocker, to make in one day $155; quality, $12½ to the ounce. (It is in this vicinity that the late splendid discovery of silver-ore, called the Washoe mines, has been made.) The great difficulty is the want of water, and on this account the mines are worked only in winter. There is a talk of tapping Carson River high up, or Bigler Lake, and thus supplying the mines with water. A rocker is a simple cradle with a sieve, through which the material passes on water being thrown upon it and it is rocked. The "long tom" is one or more long troughs connected, and a sieve at the end and a lower receiver. In this trough the material and water are introduced and the gold collected all along, the finest on the lowest platform or receiver.

China Town has two stores, one recently kept by E. Sam, a Chinese, who was drowned the other day in attempting to ford Carson River on horseback, and the other by Keller & Cohen. I am indebted to Mr. Long, who is at present in charge of E. Sam's store, for the above information in relation to the mines of this region, and he has given me the prices of commodities, as follows: Sugar, 3 pounds for $1; coffee, 3 pounds for $1; beef, 17 and 18 cents per pound; bacon, 37½ cents per pound; potatoes, 8 cents per pound; flour, 16 cents; shoes, ordinary kind, $3; boots, (pegged,) $6 to $10; hickory shirts, $1.25; barley, 10 cents per pound; oats, 10 cents per pound; whisky, $3 per gallon. The timber they use is pine, and it is hauled twenty-five miles from Washoe Valley; cost at mill, $20 per thousand; at China Town, $40.

Mr. Long conducted me to a room where a couple of the principal Chinamen were smoking opium. They were reclining, facing each other, on a kind of platform, their head supported by a stool or bench. Between them was a lamp burning. They had a pipe of about two feet long, the bowl of it being two-thirds of the distance from the mouth-end. One or the other keeps the bowl, charged with opium, constantly applied to the lamp, and, drawing hard, passes the smoke through the nose and mouth. Mr. Long says $8 worth of opium will last two persons about six months. It stupefies, rather than enlivens, and, when indulged in excessively, perfectly paralyzes the energies.

He also showed me a room in which there were six of these fellows gambling. They have a large number of pieces, like dominos, and counters, and take a great deal of interest in the game; run through it with the greatest dexterity and rapidity. They are represented as being very fond of gambling when they have nothing else to do, and not unfrequently lose all their earnings in this way.

These Chinamen have the characteristic look of their nation, the tawny color and peculiar eyes; shave the hair clear around to the top of the head, giving a peculiar effect to the forehead, and let the balance fall behind in a tail or plait. Their foreheads are retreating; eyes, hazel; wear wide pants and ordinary hickory (check) shirts. There are no women at this place.

To proceed with route. At China Town we bear off somewhat from Carson River, one mile bringing us to forks of road; right leads to Johnstown, 1.5 miles off in Gold Cañon. Six miles farther up, in a branch of Gold Cañon, are the new rich gold-diggings referred to above. All along this emigrant-route, ever since we struck it, the bones of oxen attest the effects of the old Humboldt route, on account of poisonous water and grass along the Humboldt and desert, in destroying stock.

Four miles from China Town, cedars 15 to 20 feet high appear on either side of the road on the mountains and in the valley—the first we have seen since leaving the Se-day-e Mountains. Seven and one-half miles farther brings us to Carson City, in Eagle Valley, at the east foot of the Sierra Nevada, where, at 5 p. m., we encamp. The Sierra Nevada has appeared ahead of us to-day, towering high, covered with snow, and looking fine, covered as it is with tall pines from base to summit—a spectacle we have not seen before on the trip.

Carson City has about a dozen small frame houses; two stores—Major Ormsby proprietor of one. Eagle Valley, in which it is situated, is of small extent but very fertile. A small stream courses through it, a large portion of which is expended in irrigation. The location is a good one, on account of its proximity to the new diggings in Gold Cañon, (said to be the richest yet discovered,) about 7 miles off, and its commercial relations with Honey Lake and other valleys to the north. I am informed that this same system of fertile valleys lying between spurs from the Sierra Nevada, on its east side, continues for a very considerable distance both to the north and south of this valley. Road to-day, except over a couple of sloughs of narrow width, good. Journey, 19 miles. Spent a very agreeable evening at Major Ormsby's,* where I, for the first time since I left Camp Floyd, encountered the society of ladies. Mr. Crane, the former delegate to Washington in behalf of the claims of that section of country to a new Territory (Nevada), to be taken off from the western portion of Utah, was present.

June 12, *Camp No.* 37, *Carson City*, *Eagle Valley.*—Altitude above the sea, 4,587 feet. This morning at sunrise an overcoat not unpleasantly warm. Thermometer at 5 a. m., 44°. This camp-ground beautiful; the prospect the most pleasing and Eastern-States-like of any I have seen. It reminds me of a pastoral landscape of the lower Delaware, below Trenton. This is the first morning there has been dew on the grass sufficient to show on your boots.

Par parenthese.—Mr. Reese, who has repeatedly been over the old route by way of Humboldt River, says it is objectionable, on account of high water in the spring overflowing the valley and forcing the road on the bluffs, which are very sandy. This

* This gentleman, I notice by the papers, has since been killed by the Pi-Utes, against whom he was operating with a party of citizens.

high water affects the road for about 150 miles along the Humboldt and Thousand Spring Valley. It is also objectionable on account of the bad water (alkaline) and alkaline grass, which extends along the lower part of the Humboldt for 75 miles, and on account of the desert between the sink of the Humboldt and the sink of Carson, and the scarcity of feed from Ragtown, on Carson River, to Big Bend of Carson, about 30 miles. Twenty-five per cent. of stock, he assures me, on the average, has been lost annually on the route from these causes. The Goose Creek and Bear River Mountains make it also useless in the winter, on account of snow, and the distance is greater than by my route. He also represents that all along the Humboldt, that is, for a distance of over 300 miles, there is no timber but small willows; none in Thousand Spring Valley, and none on Goose Creek. Poor prospect this for the magnetic telegraph. Whereas on this our outward route, except between the Champlin Mountains and the Go-shoot range (86 miles), and between the Se-day-e Mountains and Carson Lake (56 miles), the mountain-ranges are covered with pine, piñon, balsam, quaking ash, and mountain mahogany, all of which make the telegraph a feasible project, the maximum haul of the poles, except at the points stated, being not over 10 miles.*

Leave Carson City at quarter past 5. Course southwardly, continuing on the old emigrant-road between the base of the Sierra Nevada and Carson River. In 3¼ miles cross Clear Creek, a beautiful stream running from the Sierra Nevada into Carson River. Nearly all these streams from the Sierra Nevada are so copious as to be ample for mill purposes, and the pines near (yellow and white or sugar) average probably 4 feet through, and sometimes attain, Mr. Reese assures me, a diameter of 10 and a height of 150 feet. Near Clear Creek approach again Carson River, and continue along it about 10 miles to Genoa. Noticed along the road the gallows on which the vigilance committee hung "Lucky Bill," last June or July, a reported horse-thief and murderer. Was astonished that the relic of such a season of popular agitation and excitement should be left to be harped upon by every passer-by. Notice, also, several farms along the road, a very common mode of fencing being the laying of single trunks of large pines in a line between the fields. The cattle look very fat, and sleek; hogs in like excellent condition. These latter are said to thrive on the roots of the tuilla or rush. The butter of this valley is of a rich gold color, and is said to command a higher price than the California butter.

This valley is good for the small cereals. Wheat and barley do well. Corn has been raised, but the birds and frosts generally destroy the crops; very little oats have been raised. A few peaches have been produced, but as yet no apples. Grapes have never been tried. All garden-vegetables, as also the strawberry, raspberry, and gooseberry, thrive. Potatoes are raised, but the cultivation of the sweet-potato has been a failure, and I am informed that they cannot be raised in California. The soil is generally irrigated. As a pastoral region it is superb. Cattle on the hoof command 10 cents per pound. Barley brings about $3 per bushel. The trade heretofore has consisted principally in exchanging goods with emigrants for their stock.

Reached Genoa at half past 9 a. m. Journey, 12.9 miles; road good. Just as we

* My return route in respect to timber generally along the route, and particularly on the deserts at either extreme, was found still better adapted to the telegraph.

For additional information in relation to the Humboldt River route, see Introduction, page 22.

entered town, were saluted by the citizens with thirteen guns and the running up of the national flag, in honor of the party's having successfully accomplished the object of the exploration—the opening of a new and short road across the Great Basin from Camp Floyd, and thus facilitating the mails and emigration. Encamped among some giant pines at the foot of the Sierra Nevada, just upon the southern edge of the town, and on a gushing stream of pure water which courses down from the mountain. Our position is so high on the base of the mountain that we can overlook a large portion of the valley; and a beautiful one it is, fenced off, as it appears, into inclosures, and dotted with cattle. The sheen of the river (Carson), in its present high stage, discovers its course along the valley.

Genoa, at the present time, has 28 dwelling-houses, 2 stores, 2 hotels, 1 printing establishment, and 1 electric-telegraph office. There are also in it and vicinity 2 grist-mills, 4 saw-mills, and 1 under way. Population, between 150 and 200. The town was commenced in 1855. It is now in connection, by electric telegraph, with San Francisco, 260 miles distant,* and, three days before we reached this place, our arrival at Walker's River had been announced in the papers of the Golden City. Indeed, we had no sooner arrived than I received a telegraphic dispatch from Col. Fred. A. Bee, the president of the Placerville and Saint Joseph's Overland Telegraph, inquiring about my route for the proposed telegraph across the continent. Replied that as I was going immediately to San Francisco, through Placerville, I would be happy to talk with him on the subject when I should meet him.

The Indian agent, Maj. Fred. Dodge, has called upon me, and extended all the civilities of a courteous and refined gentleman. He is the agent of the Pi-Ute and Washo tribes of Indians living in this region, and has politely furnished me with the following information in regard to them, which I give in his own language:

"The Pi-Ute nation number from 6,000 to 7,000 souls. They inhabit Western Utah from Oregon to New Mexico. They are divided into bands of about 200 strong each, commanded by a subchief. The head-chief of the nation is Wan-a-muc-a (the giver). The largest portion of the nation is generally to be found in the vicinity of the principal rivers and lakes of the Great Basin, viz, Humboldt, Carson, Walker, Truckee, Owen's, Pyramid, and Mono. The Pi-Utes resemble, in appearance, manner, and customs, the Delawares on our Missouri frontier, and with judicious management and assistance from the General Government, they would equal in three years their brother Delawares in agricultural or other advancements made by them toward civilization. The Pi-Utes are poor, but honestly inclined. They are also the most interesting and docile Indians on the continent.

"The Wa-sho nation number about 900 souls, and inhabit the country along the eastern slope of the Sierra Nevada from Honey Lake on the north to Clara River, a branch of Walker's, on the south, a distance of 150 miles. They are divided into three bands of about 300 each, commanded by three head-chiefs. Deer Dick's band is on the north, in the vicinity of Honey Lake and Long Valley; Captain Jim's band is in

* The telegraph has since been carried (as has been before remarked in Introduction) eastwardly beyond this point on my route as far as Fort Churchill, at the bend of Carson River, and it is the intention to continue it all the way to Great Salt Lake City, and, indeed, to the Platte River, which has already been reached at Fort Kearney from the east.

the center of the nation, and occupies the valleys of Steamboat, Wa-sho, Eagle, and Carson. Pas-sonke's band lives and claims Little Valley and the valleys on the head-waters of the Rio Clara. The Washos are not inclined to agricultural pursuits, nor any other advancement toward civilization. They are destitute of all necessaries to make life even desirable. There is not one horse, pony, or mule in the nation. They are peaceable, but indolent. In the summer these houseless wanderers stay around the shores of Lake Bigler, in the Sierra Nevada. In the winter they lie about in the *artemisia* (wild sage) of their different localities, subsisting on a little grass-seed." *

The vocabularies of these tribes of Indians, for which I am also indebted to the major, will be found in Appendix P.

Besides Major Dodge, other gentlemen of the place have called on us, all of whom express themselves very much gratified at the success of our expedition, and tender us all the hospitality in their power. Major Dodge is going to-morrow to Placerville, with one of the head-chiefs of the Pi-Utes, Won-a-muc-a the younger, and two braves, and has extended to me an invitation to accompany him. It is necessary for me to go to San Francisco, on account of the party, and I therefore have gladly accepted the invitation, and will take advantage of the facilities which he offers.

Now that we have reached the termination of explorations westward, it may be well to briefly state the fruits of it. For the first 64 miles west from Camp Floyd, as far as Short Cut Pass, the route we have come was that I explored and established in October, 1858; thence to Hasting's Pass, 70 miles, it was Chorpenning, the California mail-contractor's extension of my route, made by him subsequently to my exploration in the winter of 1858–'59. To Hasting's Pass, Chorpenning's extension was pretty direct toward Genoa, but from that point, on account of his agent, Mr. Egan, failing, as I was informed, to get through in a southwest direction to Carson Lake, he was forced to take a northwardly course, and join the Humboldt route at Gravelly Ford, thus making a great detour in that direction. Finding Chorpenning's continuation of my route of last fall wrong from Hasting's Pass, I struck southwestwardly from that point for the north bend of Walker's River, and was rewarded in getting a route which most favorably compares with the old route from Camp Floyd (via City of Rocks and Humboldt River, and with Chorpenning's route), as follows:

From Great Salt Lake City to Genoa, by City of Rocks, Humboldt River, and Carson River, as given me by my guide, Mr. Reese, who has been several times over the route, and says it was measured by some foreigner	813	miles.
Great Salt Lake City to Camp Floyd	40	"
Total from Camp Floyd to Genoa by old Humboldt River road	853	"
Camp Floyd to Genoa by Chorpenning's route, via Hasting's Pass and Humboldt River and Carson River, 64 + 170 + 455	689	"
Camp Floyd to Genoa, by my route	565	"

* For other information in relation to the Indians of Utah Territory than is contained in my Journal and Introduction, see Appendix O.

Difference in favor of my route over the old City of Rocks and Humboldt River route	288 miles.
Difference in favor of my route over Chorpenning's, or the present mail route	124 "

Thus we have got a route over which we have conducted our 14 wagons without any great difficulty, and which, except at the extreme ends (over Great Salt Lake Desert and over the desert just to the east of Carson Lake), furnishes an abundance of scrub cedar on the mountain-ranges, which will require a maximum haul of only about 10 miles, to supply the telegraphic lines with the necessary poles (if they will answer by splicing) for the support of the wire. Over the deserts referred to the maximum haul would be, on the Salt Lake Desert, about 50 miles; on the Carson Lake Desert, about 25 miles. The route, also, is quite well supplied with the best of grass and water, except over the deserts mentioned. (The sequel will show that I shortened the route still further on my return to Camp Floyd; and, also, on my more southern route, reduced the haul of cedars for telegraphic purposes over the Salt Lake Desert to 15 or 20 miles*).

June 13, *Camp No.* 38, *Genoa.*—Longitude, 119° 40′ 30″; latitude, 38° 59′ 33″; magnetic variation, 16° 40′ E.; elevation above the sea, 4,824 feet; thermometer at 6 a. m., 54°.50. After giving directions to Lieutenants Smith and Putman to keep up the astronomical observations, and Lieutenant Putnam to make an examination of the old road as well as the Daggett trail over the first range of the Sierra Nevada into Lake Valley, leave the party in the charge of Lieutenant Murry, and start for San Francisco, 260 miles distant, via Placerville and Sacramento, at 8 a. m., with Major Dodge. Expect to be absent about 12 days, during which our animals and party will be able to recruit. Besides the three Pi-Utes mentioned yesterday, the Major has with him his interpreter, Dick, a lad about 15 years of age, and as bright a boy as I have seen for a long while. The major takes a great deal of interest in him, and looks after his welfare as if he were his own son. We all go mounted and take one pack-mule, the mule I ride, as well as a share of the pack-mule, having been kindly tendered to me by the major.

Our course lay for a short distance up Carson Valley, or southwardly on old road. In 1.5 miles from Genoa, pass Warm Springs, at foot of Sierra Nevada; 1.5 miles farther brought us to the Daggett trail, which we take over the east range of the Sierra Nevada to Lake Valley; the traveled wagon-road which we have left continu-

* The distance from Great Salt Lake City to Genoa on old Humboldt River route, as given above, may be incorrect, and I suspect it is so; but, in the absence of anything official at the time, I could find nothing more reliable. Since my return to Washington, I find that Captain Marcy, in his "Prairie Traveler," lays down the distance from Salt Lake City to Reese's ranch (now Genoa) by this route as 774 miles. The case will then stand thus, regarding the cuts-off I made on my return to Camp Floyd:

From Salt Lake City to Genoa, according to Marcy	774 miles.
From Camp Floyd to Salt Lake City (Simpson)	40 "
From Camp Floyd to Genoa by old Humboldt River road, then	814 "
From Camp Floyd to Genoa, by my more northern route and "cuts-off"	531 "
Difference in favor of my shortest route over old Humboldt route from Camp Floyd	283 "
Difference in favor of my shortest route from Salt Lake City	203 "
Difference in favor of my route over Chorpenning's	158 "

ing along the foot of the Sierra Nevada, on its east side, from 18 to 20 miles, before turning to the west to cross the range. Find the trail up to Daggett Pass quite steep. It runs along the side-hill, and at times is dangerous. It is possible, however, that a better grade might be got along the ravine for a road. In about 3.5 miles from foot of the Sierra reach summit of pass, 7,180 feet above the sea, and lying about 4 miles to the northwest of us could be seen Lake Bigler, beautifully embosomed in the Sierra.* Descending by a tolerable grade, 2.5 miles farther brought us to Lake Valley, lying between the east and west ranges of the Sierra, which we thread in the direction of its length about 12.5 miles southwardly to mail-station, which we reach at half-past 1, and where we dine. Distance from Genoa, 21.5 miles.

The ride this morning the most charming I have had for a long while. Lake Valley is like a beautiful park, studded with large, stately pines. The glades between the trees are beautifully green, and the whole is enlivened by a pure, babbling mountain-stream, the most southern and principal branch of the Truckee, coursing along northwardly to its expansion, Lake Bigler. The pines of various kinds are very large, and attain a height of probably from 100 to 150 feet. Their diameter is not unfrequently as much as 8 feet, and they sometimes attain the dimension of 10 feet. Just before we reached the mail-station, noticed a splendid waterfall or cascade, a tributary of the Truckee, tumbling into the valley from the west range. Saw in the valley a large herd of cattle and hogs, all looking finely. Indeed, I never have seen more sleek, saucy-looking cattle anywhere.

At the mail-station met Mr. T. A. Thompson, the celebrated Norwegian, who carried the mail across the Sierra Nevada, on snow-shoes, from about the middle of last April to fore part of May. He represents the snow to have been, in places where he had to go, 10 feet deep. One of the hands at the mail-station told me that in the spring the snow at one time was as high as the top of the window (pointing to it), that is about 8 feet. This between the two ranges in Lake Valley. Thompson says that the first wagon went over the road across the mountains about 20th of May, the snow preventing it before.

After dinner proceeded on journey. Just after leaving mail-station, commence ascending, by a side cut, the west range of the Sierra Nevada, and directly under the spray of the falling cataract mentioned before, which comes down from a height of several hundred feet, and rushes directly over the road. In about 2 miles from foot, attain summit of range, or Johnston's Pass (altitude above the sea, 7,222 feet). Grade of road good until near top, where it is rather steep. This grade is the commencement of a road which the people of El Dorado and Sacramento Counties, of California, at the expense of some $50,000, have made from Lake Valley across the west range of the Sierra Nevada; and quite well has the work been laid out and executed. I am told the superintending engineer was Mr. Sherman Day, of San José, Cal., who bears the reputation of being quite accomplished in his profession.

As soon as we attained the summit of the range, Mr. Thompson took us to a point where we obtained a fine view of Lake Bigler. After reaching summit, soon find

* Frémont, in his report of 1845 and 1846, calls this sheet of water *Mountain Lake;* on his map of 1848 he calls it *Lake Bonpland.* It now is known by the name of *Lake Bigler,* and according to the report of Mr. George H. Goddard, of California, "it is a noble sheet of water, from 15 to 20 miles in length by 6 or 7 in width."

yourself passing along the north side of the South Fork of the American River, and a more roaring, rushing, cataract mountain-stream I never beheld. Indeed, the views along this stream, and at the Slippery Ford, are superbly magnificent. The mountains at Slippery Ford, 6 miles from Johnston's Pass, are a mass of granite from bottom to top. Major Dodge and myself would ever and anon stop to contemplate and discourse upon the beauty of the prospect. Indeed, my ride to-day can never be effaced from my mind.

Mr. Thompson showed me stumps, or broken-off trees, that he looked down upon last winter and spring when he carried the mail across the mountains on snow-shoes. This corroborates his statement that the depth was as much as 10 feet. He said he found a man in Lake Valley, last winter, that for 12 days had remained at one spot, not able to move on account of his feet having become frozen. All this time he lived on a little flour.

At half-past 5 reach Barry's, where we stop for the night; by the way we have come (Daggett's trail) 33 miles from Genoa. Judge Child, of Genoa, and Mr. Thompson, also put up here. The soil, after crossing first range of the Sierra, is generally of a reddish hue, and is a sort of arenaceous loam. The valley of the South Fork of the American below Slippery Ford is called Strawberry Valley, on account of its being prolific of this fruit.

Mr. Thompson showed me how he walked on his snow-shoes last winter. They are smooth pieces of board from 6 to 8 feet long, 6 inches broad at forepart, 4 at middle, and less at ends, the forepart slightly turned up like a sleigh-runner. A little in front of the middle portion a strap or thong is nailed across, in which he slips his toes, then there is a cleat nailed across, against which the heel of his shoe strikes or pushes. He then gently lifts the shoe, and at the same time pushing it along with his foot, causes himself to slide first with one shoe and then with the other. He has at the same time a stick against which, as he goes down hill, he supports himself, and which he uses also as a break. He says he has a standing bet with any one that, let him select his ground along a side-hill, he will travel a mile a minute; that he sometimes passes over precipices of 10 feet, and would land at a distance of 20 feet, and still stand upright. When a child in Norway he used, with other boys, to practice this kind of leap, and thus made himself an expert.

I notice that the telegraph-line along the road over the mountains is, in many instances, supported by living trees as posts. Also noticed a number of coils of wire lying along the road, which are intended to be used in extending it from Genoa toward Camp Floyd and Great Salt Lake City.

June 14, *Barry's, on South Fork of American River, Sierra Nevada.*—Bunks erected for travelers at this stopping-place, and blankets and comforters for bed-clothes. The luxury of sheets not yet gone into. House of split clapboards, and quite rude, but yet a fair mountain-house in a new country, and table quite good.

Renewed journey at 10 minutes before 6. Met a four-horse comfortable-looking stage going over to Genoa, to run between that place and the new gold-mines on the Rio Ida, the East Fork of Walker's River, 90 miles from Genoa. These placers were discovered in the fall of 1858, and are pronounced very rich. The gold is said to be worth $18 per ounce, it being mostly shot-gold, and not in the dust. Two miles from Barry's a side cut of excellent grade commences, which continues for 25 miles, and is a piece of road which would do credit to any of our older States. Its defects are in not being sufficiently wide for teams of more than two draught animals to turn (except with the greatest care) its sometimes sharp angles, and in places it does not admit of teams passing each other. These defects should be rectified. Ten miles from Barry's reach Boswell's, a very good log-house, and place of refreshment and lodging. Seventeen miles more, at 11½ o'clock, reach Peter Burdie's, where we dine and feed animals.

Leave at 25 minutes of 2. One and a half miles from Burdie's, cross South Fork of American River to south side by bridge, and do not see it again till we reach Sacramento. To this point (the bridge) we have been traveling from summit of Johnston's Pass along north side of this river, which at times we could see as much as 1,000 feet below us, and always raging, rushing, and making a din, out of which we have not been since we got on it. As yesterday, until about 5 miles back, the granite has shown itself in magnificent proportions.

As soon as we cross the American Fork we emerged from the mountainous region, and the country became more open and rolling. Farms, farm-houses, and improvements generally, increase as you approach Placerville, and the fences, fruit-trees (principally peach), wheat, potatoes, gardens, domestic pigeons, reddish Maryland color of the soil, and large umbrageous oaks, which become more frequent, intermingling with the pines, make you almost think you are east of the Rocky Mountains in an old settled country. Indeed, until my present exploration, I have had no proper idea either of the Sierra Nevada or of the country at its western base. The transit from the arid plains east of the Sierra Nevada to the quick teeming country lying on its western slope is most singularly marked and sudden, and shows how much, irrespective of latitude, the laws of climate and production are dependent upon physical circumstances and features of country.

Pass a tavern called Sportsman Hall, 6.5 miles from bridge over South Fork of American, and 12 miles more brought us, about sundown, to Placerville, a mining-town on a small tributary of the South Fork of the American, 79.5 miles by Daggett's trail from Genoa. This town is built principally upon one street, and is divided into what is called upper and lower town. The latter is the business portion, and has a great number of stores; some pretty white cottages, with roses clambering up the porticoes, and gardens filled with vegetables and fruit-trees, being visible. Pits seen everywhere, where they have been digging for gold, and the little stream coursing through the town is red with the sediment, which has been the result of gold-washings. The streets, I notice, are filled with people, and the hotels are full, caused by the assemblage of a convention for the nomination of county officers. Thanks, however, to the kindness and forethought of friends, a room has been reserved for Major Dodge and myself at the Carey House. Population of town about 3,500, and of township, 10,000. Was called on by several influential men of the place, who congratulated us upon the success of our expedition in getting across the Great Basin and shortening the central overland mail-route so much. Col. Fred. A. Bee, the president of the central overland, called the Placerville and Saint Joseph Telegraph Company, was particularly gratified, and remarked to me that I might consider my route as adopted for the line. I told him to wait till I could report from Camp Floyd the results of our exploration for a shorter return-route before he decided, for I believed I could get a still better one, which would be from 30 to 50 miles shorter.

June 15, *Placerville.*—Remain here to-day to perfect arrangements about sending a few supplies over the Sierra Nevada to party at Genoa. Require some extra wagon-tongues and couplings, and think it well to provide ourselves with a little forage and a few other things to meet contingencies.

Visited steam-crushing quartz-mill in the city for the extraction of the gold. It has 20 vertical iron tamps, about 2 inches in diameter, placed in upright frames, and so fixed with projecting shoulders that a horizontal shaft, turning on its axis and provided also with projections, lifts the tamps, and their own weight is such that they fall heavily and tamp or crush the quartz, which is placed in a box at their feet. A stream of water is constantly passing through the box, and carries the *débris* and gold over an inclined apron, on which are arranged, horizontally, slats or riffles, which catch the gold as it passes. The quartz is conveyed to the mill from the mine, near, in cars, which run on a railway from a shaft or tunnel which at the present time has penetrated the bluff horizontally about 200 yards, and is about 40 yards below the superior surface of the ground. I entered the shaft and saw the miners at work getting out the masses of quartz. It is singular that in any of the quartz I saw I could not, with the eye, detect the slightest speck of gold; and yet I am told the investment in the business is a good one.

Visited, with Major Dodge, Colonel Bee and lady, and were regaled with fresh strawberries from their garden, and brandied peaches, which were the first foretaste I had had of the fine rich fruits for which this region is famous. The colonel has a pretty cottage residence, tastefully adorned with flowers and fruit-trees, and conspicuous in his garden is a windmill, by which the water is raised from a well and so conducted by small canals as to irrigate the soil. The windmill, I notice, is quite a common feature in the landscape of this country, and has become so on account of the necessity of irrigating the soil to make it productive, to which purpose it is applied.

Ordered a bill of supplies to be transported to Genoa, at 7 cents per pound. The usual charge, I am told, is about 5 cents, but in order to insure their being carried over immediately, I am obliged to pay 7 cents. One cent per pound is to be forfeited if not delivered by the 22d instant. The cause of this heavy charge for transportation is the steep, rocky character of the portion of the road over the east range of the Sierra Nevada, between Lake Valley and Carson Valley, which I shall examine on my return to Genoa, and on which the Californians have expended no labor, for the reason, doubtless, that it lies mostly, if not entirely, in Utah.

June 16, *Placerville.*—Left with Major Dodge for Folsom, 28 miles distant, at 6 a. m., Pi-Ute interpreter Dick in company. Conveyance the finest kind of stages, and drawn by large, strong, well set up, stylish horses. Fare to Sacramento, $6. Breakfast at Duroc's. At Folsom took railroad-cars for Sacramento, the capital of the State, 23 miles distant, which we reached about 1. Country between Placerville and Folsom beautifully rolling; between Folsom and Sacramento, very level. It is generally cultivated, and beautifully rich with grain, which is being harvested, and the neat board fences and houses everywhere attest the rapid growth of the State and the enterprising character of the people. The pine is seldom seen after you leave Placerville, and from Folsom west the oak is almost entirely the native tree. They are very large and umbrageous, and being interspersed in a park-like way, give a beautiful aspect to the landscape. The ugly stumps of the recently-cleared lands in our older States are nowhere to be seen.

At Sacramento there were nine steamers, great and small, lying at the wharves. The Eclipse, in which we took passage at 2 o'clock for San Francisco, is like our Mississippi boats, and as handsome, comfortable, and neat as the best of them. Fare to San Francisco, $5, and $1 additional for dinner. Distance, 120 miles. Had but little time to glance at the city, but saw enough to convince me of its business thrift. Hope to see more of it on my return. Saw Mr. Upson, editor of the Union, who expressed himself as delighted with the success of our expedition across the Great Basin.

The Sacramento is a noble stream, probably about 200 yards wide. Its color quite red, like all the streams I have seen this side of the foot of the Sierra Nevada, caused, I am informed, by the universal use of the water for washing gold out of the soil, which is of a red color. At the present time the river is from 4 to 6 feet below the top of its banks, and at times is said to overflow them. Indeed, in order to protect the city of Sacramento from inundation, a levee has been made all around it. The country between Sacramento and the bay of San Francisco lies very low and level, as far as the eye can reach, and everywhere looks rich and productive. Windmills for purposes of irrigation are a prominent characteristic. As you approach San Francisco the land assumes a higher and bolder aspect, and the mainland, as well as the islands, become remarkable on account of their peculiarly bold and convex shape from the water up; and the brownish-red colored oats, at this season of the year, occasionally relieved by dark patches of timber, give a very unique character to the landscape. Touched at Benicia, where there is a military post, and had a chat with Maj. George P. Andrews and Lieut. Job J. Chandler, Second Artillery, who, seeing me in military attire, introduced themselves. Reached San Francisco at a quarter after 9 in the evening, and put up at the International Hotel.

June 18, *San Francisco.*—Intending to leave to-morrow on my return to Genoa, have only time to see friends. Find, however, the place exceedingly city-like. Has many fine, substantial houses. The streets, especially Montgomery street, are full of people. Everything seems to be done on the high-pressure principle. Rents, I am informed, are still very high. Visited the market and saw a splendid exhibition of vegetables. They have the largest strawberries here I have ever seen. Notice the egg of a wild water-fowl, which is found on the islands and exposed for sale. Called on a number of old friends, principally officers of the Army. Was invited to take a ride about the city and suburbs, but had not the time. The cool breeze from the Pacific, generally in the afternoon, makes winter-clothing agreeable even in the depth of summer. Messrs. McCrellish & Woodward, of the Alta-California, are anxious that I should allow Mr. Walter Lowry, their city commercial correspondent, and who is an invalid, to accompany us on our return to the States. He is desirous to see his friends and relatives once more in that quarter, and thinks that a trip across the plains will restore him to health. In consequence of the rough character of the country, I have demurred until I could see him personally at Placerville.

June 19, *San Francisco.*—Having transacted all my business, at 4 p. m. Major Dodge and myself took passage on board the steamer for Sacramento, on our return to Genoa, $7.50 fare for passage and half of state-room. I leave with a great deal of regret, feeling that my visit has been so short as scarcely to have permitted me to see anything; but duty requires me to join my party without delay. The harbor of San Francisco, which we now see by daylight, is doubtless one of the boldest in the world. The grand characteristics are its commodiousness, and, as I have before stated, bold, convex character of its islets and headlands, and the peculiar brown or russet color of the face of the country, caused by the all-prevailing wild oats in their present ripe condition.

June 19, *Sacramento.*—Reached this city in the night. Put up at Saint George Hotel, General C. J. Hutchinson proprietor and landlord. In the morning Major Dodge and myself went to Episcopal church with Mrs. Hutchinson and another lady, the general having politely extended to us seats in his carriage. The whole style of the services and the sermon, as well as of the church, carried me back to the happy occasion, when, with my own family and friends, I had, more than a year previous, been enabled to join them in these sacred duties.

Among the gentlemen who have called upon me and showed us a great deal of attention is Mr. James R. Hardenburgh, an old schoolmate and fellow-townsman of mine, from New Brunswick, N. J. We had not met for 28 years, and, of course, the pleasure was correspondingly enhanced. I must also acknowledge the kind tender of services of Mr. M. S. Brocklebank, the brother-in-law of Governor Weller, who made himself known to me, and treated me very civilly. The city is full of strangers, drawn here by the State convention, which is about to meet, to nominate candidates for State offices. Among the distinguished is Governor Denver, whom I last saw at Fort Leavenworth, just before I left for Utah, in the spring of 1858. This city is very well built, considering its age; has a number of fine dwellings, and the country around it is remarkably rich and productive.

June 20, *Sacramento.*—Took cars for Folsom at 7, and arrived at Placerville at 2. Settled with Mr. Richardson for supplies, which have been forwarded to Genoa according to agreement. Was introduced by Colonel Bee to Mr. Walter Lowry, the correspondent of the Alta-California, the gentleman Mr. McCrellish, of San Francisco, spoke to me about. Saw at once his feeble state of health would not permit him to endure a journey across the continent, and tried to dissuade him from accompanying us. He will, however, not heed my advice; and my hope is that, if he finds the journey across the Sierra Nevada too fatiguing, he will yet give up the idea of continuing on with us from Genoa.

June 21, *Placerville.*—Left at 9½ o'clock, with Major Dodge, Mr. Walter Lowry, and Mr. Van Duyck, for Genoa, retracing as far as Lake Valley our old route. Our conveyance is an ambulance, which the major has had made at this place. Our driver is the famous Norwegian, Thompson, of whom I have before spoken; Pi-Ute Dick is also along. Stopped for the night at Peter Burdie's, 20 miles from Placerville.

June 22, *Peter Burdie's, Sierra Nevada.*—Left at 5 a. m., and reached Yankee's, or mail-station, in Lake Valley, 40 miles from Burdie's, and staid all night. I notice that, after leaving the 25-mile side-hill grade, before spoken of, and before reaching Johnston's Pass, the road is very rocky, and in many places steep, and, like the portions mentioned under date of June 14, should be improved.

June 23, *mail-station, Lake Valley, Sierra Nevada.*—Elevation above the sea, 6,311 feet. In order to get over to Genoa as early as possible, left Major Dodge at station, and took passage in the mail-stage, leaving at 3 a. m. Passengers, a lady and child and two men, with myself. Driver a famous whip, but who, unfortunately, had all night long been carousing with some others at the station, and was quite drunk when he started. He seemed, however, to be sober enough to ask me to sit with him outside, and, as I thought, that I might take the lines if there should be occasion. Had scarcely left, before, on account of the darkness of the night, the mules got out of the road, and came near breaking the stage by passing between two stumps. Being on the box, I was enabled to draw up the team in time, not, however, without the loss of a whipple-tree. The next obstacle was the bridge, from the farther half of which the puncheon flooring had been removed by some mischievous persons during the night, and piled up on the bank.* I got off, and, with the assistance of one of the passengers, who was, like the driver, a little boosy, replaced the flooring, a space of about 2 feet being left on the farther side, on account of a deficiency of material. Nothing daunted, however, the driver rushed over, and fortunately gained the opposite bank without accident. After this, in ascending the acclivity from Lake Valley to summit of Luther's Pass, 5 miles from mail-station, had a very serious time. All hands out to enable him to get up the hill. Driver so drunk as not to know what to do, and yet as obstinate as a mule; slashes the animals all around, but yet in such a way as not to make them work together; the consequence is a dead halt. Was glad of it, for the reason that if he could have got to the summit before he became sober he would have dashed us all to pieces in his descent on the other side. At last, just before reaching summit, the stage upset and broke the tongue. Luckily, at my suggestion, all were out at the time. Here was a dilemma. I helped to get the stage out of the road. The driver then took his mules and went down to the next house on the road, for a wagon. About an hour after, Major Dodge appeared with his ambulance, and kindly took the lady and myself in with him, and left Mr. Van Duyck and Dick to follow in the stage. In about 4 miles, met driver returning with a wagon, a good deal sobered and subdued. At about 9 o'clock reach Woodford's, at the mouth of Carson River Cañon, where we stopped and got breakfast.

The road from Lake Valley to mouth of Carson Cañon, where the fork debouches from the mountains into the valley of Carson River, a distance of 12 or 13 miles, *is the worst portion of the whole road over the Sierra Nevada.* The ascent from Lake Valley

* The breaking of the whipple-tree I consider providential and a blessing, since without its occurrence we would all have been upset in the creek, and our lives lost or bones broken. The carousing at the mail-station and the taking up of half the bridge was, as I think, all done by the parties who instigated it to rob the mail, Indian agent, and myself, who, it was doubtless well known, had gold on account of the expedition.

to summit of Luther's Pass is very steep, and the road is filled with tremendous rocks, which should have been removed. It is astonishing, considering this is a portion of the great emigration route over the continent, that Congress has not done something toward ameliorating it. There is no portion of my route from Camp Floyd, though the greater portion of it is entirely new, so bad as this. If a road can at all be got over the Daggett trail, which is probable, it ought, by all means, to be done, both on the score of distance and quality of road. At least $30,000 should be appropriated for the portion between Carson Valley and Johnston's Pass, and $10,000 for the portion to the west of said pass. Several bridges to be built across fork of Carson River in cañon. Reached Genoa at 4 p. m. Road from mouth of Carson Cañon good. Distance, 19 miles. Total journey from mail-station in Lake Valley, 31 miles. Lieutenant Murry reports that matters have been going on well during my absence. The good citizens paid my party the compliment of a public ball last evening, which, they informed me, passed off much to the satisfaction of every one. In consequence of Major Dodge and myself having been delayed on the route longer than we had anticipated, we were deprived of the privilege of being present. Paid off several of the party and settled outstanding accounts.

RETURN TO CAMP FLOYD.

June 24, *Genoa, Camp No.* 1.—Thermometer at 4.50 a. m., 65°. Concluded settlement of accounts, and at 7 a. m. we took up our march on our return to Camp Floyd. Mr. Lowry will not listen to any advice in opposition to his accompanying us, and I, therefore, think it my duty to acquiesce, though I feel morally certain that he cannot survive the trip. Mr. Reese, though a citizen of Genoa, returns with us as guide, and I have sent him, Ute Pete, and two other persons in advance, to provide for improvement of route, by taking a short cut from bend of Carson to south side of Carson Lake, and to explore for passage through the mountain-range to the east of the sink of Carson. Having been politely invited to dine at Mr. Dorsey's, who lives 7 miles from Genoa, on our road, Lieutenant Murry, Mr. Lowry, Mr. Smith, of Genoa, Mr. Lee, and myself stopped for a few hours, and were kindly entertained by him and his lady. Mr. and Mrs. Noteware, kind neighbors of the family, were present. Train reached Carson City early in the afternoon, and party encamped. We reached it about dark. Journey, 13.8 miles. Route the same as traveled on outward journey. In the evening were visited by Major Ormsby and lady, and other persons, who take a kind interest in the success of our expedition.

June 25, *Camp No.* 2, *Carson City.*—Had the first cool night I have experienced for some time. Consequence, a refreshing sleep. Moved at 5 a. m. In 11.7 miles reach Chinatown, about 9.30 a. m. Altitude above the sea, 4,360 feet. Here leave our old road, and immediately cross Carson River by ford, and take route along river on south side. Depth of water, 3.5 feet. Wagons barely escaped receiving water in them. One forage-wagon capsized. All the rest got over without difficulty. By 11 all across. Five miles from ford, after crossing some bad sloughs, which may be obviated by taking higher ground, reach camping-place for the night. Journey, 17.2 miles.

June 26, *Camp No.* 3, *Carson Valley.*—Elevation above the sea, 4,300; thermometer at 5 a. m., 49°. Mosquitoes during the night terrible. Moved at 5 a. m. Continued along an old road on south side of Carson River for 2 miles, where we join, opposite Pleasant Grove, our old outward track, and continued on same 12.6 miles to east foot of ugly hill referred to June 9, which we found we could not, as we hoped, evade by passing between it and the river. Going east, however, the hill is not bad. The difficulty, as before stated, is in the ascent from the east side. After attaining valley on east side of hill, we left our outward track and old road, and turned to the left down the valley to within a few hundred yards of Carson River, and then go over another spur, and in about a mile get into valley of Carson River again, which we follow down 2 miles, and at 1.15 o'clock encamp on the river bank. Journey, 18.2 miles. Our experience shows that the road from Pleasant Grove on north side of river better to Chinatown than that on south side. It is a characteristic of this valley that the miry, rich soil prevents your approaching the stream except at a few points, and these are the best camp grounds. Cottonwoods and willows line the banks. The mules fattened up wonderfully at Genoa, and they are now in prime condition. One of the guide's party came into camp this afternoon, to show us our route to-morrow.

June 27, *Camp No.* 4, *Carson River.*—Elevation above the sea, 4,154 feet; thermometer at 4.30 a. m., 52½°. Resumed march at 5. Continued down valley of Carson River eastwardly about 2 miles, when we leave it and strike for south end of Carson Lake. Low mountains, perfectly destitute of timber, and of a brownish-reddish hue, range on either side and parallel to the river. Eight miles farther commence ascending a sandy ravine of slight grade, and in 3 miles attain summit of a low range 4,460 feet above the sea, from which, looking back, Carson River can be seen, well marked by the trees which line its banks. At intervals of 2.5 and 1.7 miles cross other low ridges, the last tolerably steep on east side; and 7½ miles farther, at half past 5, reach south end of Carson Lake, where we encamp. Journey, 25.1 miles. Road first 10 miles good, next 12 miles sandy and heavy, last 3 miles over margin of lake and good. Fine grass and rushes where we are encamped. Fuel should be brought.

June 28, *Camp No.* 5, *south end of Carson Lake.*—Elevation above the sea, 3,840 feet; night refreshingly cool; thermometer at 4.58 a. m., 55°. Moved at 5 minutes after 5. Continue along shore of Carson Lake, at foot of point of low range or spur, being sometimes, on account of marsh, forced on first bench; and, after crossing an alkali flat, 7.5 miles from last camp, join our outward route, which we follow along the lake shore 4.5 miles farther and encamp. Journey, 12.2 miles. Road good. It was my intention to proceed farther along the lake, but Wilson Lambert, of the guide's party, meeting us here, and informing me that Mr. Reese had not, as was hoped, been able to find a practicable route for wagons through the mountain-range immediately to the east of the sink or more northern lake of Carson River, I am obliged to give up the idea of shortening my route in that direction, and to strike eastwardly and cut off the angle or cusp, caused on my outward route by the mistake of my guide, mentioned in my journal of June 5. There is an Indian trail, it appears, east from the sink of Carson, which is practicable for pack animals, but it would require considerable work to make it so for wagons. The next camp-ground, according to guide, is 7 to 9 miles from here, and is represented as being alkaline, and the supply of water a small spring. The guide, it seems, supposed we could not reach this spring till to-morrow, and intended sending back a man, the day after, to report the camp beyond. The result is that as our animals will fare best where we are, I have ordered a halt, and the command, as stated, to go into encampment.

I have noticed the pelican to-day floating on the lake and looming so large as to look like a small sail-boat. Our old road along the lake is at present overflowed by the water of the lake, and this when Carson River, which feeds it, has declined several feet. This shows that the lake does not sink and evaporate as fast as the water flows in. The best grass is to the north of our camp, to which we have driven our herd. Fuel should be brought.

June 29, *Camp No.* 6, *east side of Carson Lake.*—Elevation above the sea, 3,840 feet; thermometer at 6 a. m., 70°. In consequence of laying over at this camp for the benefit of the water and feed, and not wishing to tarry any longer than necessary at our next, where the water and grass are said to be very scant, and the latter alkaline, we did not move till 2 o'clock. At 11 o'clock a Mr. Ward, of Placerville, and three other persons, joined us, in order to accompany us on our route and thus have the benefit of our protection.

The nearest direction for the road would be from south end of Carson Lake directly across eastwardly to Alkaline Valley, but though there is a low pass to admit of a pack-route, Mr. Reese has reported it too full of sand to allow the passage of wagons.

We cross a low rocky ridge, 1 mile to the east of camp, and gradually bear to the right, and pass east of south along west edge of Alkaline Valley. Five and a half miles from camp come to grassy bottom, where there is some tolerable grass, and water probably within a foot of the surface. To the west of this place in the flat is a very small warm spring of pretty good water. The efflorescence around it is not alkali, but pure salt. This being the case, the probabilities are that by digging wells in the vicinity where there are indications of water, good water might be obtained. Two and a half miles farther brought us to a spring 6 feet long, 2 deep, and 1½ wide, which is sulphurous, but not unpalatable. There is a small patch of rushes in the vicinity, but no grass. This was the locality intended by our guide as our camping-ground for the night, but the water and grass proving insufficient we only water the animals scantily and then push on, believing it better to get to the best grass and water as soon as possible, though in order to do so we shall have to travel all night.

Leave spring at 17 minutes after 5, and in 7.5 miles after crossing Alkaline Valley, join our outward route, near point of mountain, not far from our old camp, No. 30. Here we halt to take some coffee and feed the draught mules with some of the forage we have brought with us. The Alkaline Valley where we crossed it will evidently be impassable from mire in wet weather. In this case, persons coming from Carson Lake, should cross the valley about 7 miles north of dug-holes, and then cross on tolerably hard and high ground.

Leave at half past 11 p. m. Night pleasantly cool. Just before daylight felt oppressively sleepy, and every once in a while, though riding in the saddle, would catch myself dozing. One of my assistants passed me at daybreak, at a gallop, as I thought to quickly arrive at our next camping-ground, but I had not continued far before I found him stretched out on the ground, fast asleep, holding his mule. Proceeding on in advance of train, I arrived at old camp (No. 29), Middle Gate, 23.4 miles from halting place of last evening, at 7 a. m. June 30; but unfortunately found the water, which was running before, was now to be got only by digging, and that scantily. The train did not get in till 10. We shall turn out our mules to graze and let them drink what water they can in the dug wells. Meantime, get breakfast. Found Pete at this point, and Mr. Reese came in subsequently on his return from a reconnaissance still farther ahead.

It should be remarked that there is not the slightest doubt that water in abundance could be got at this point (Middle Gate) by sinking suitable wells. Indeed, it exists now in springs in an *arroyo* near, and we got it in another easily accessible place by digging not more than two feet deep. There is plenty of rock at hand to wall the wells. I think it very probable, also, that in "West Gate," 3.5 miles west of this, water may be obtained by digging. Indeed, the indications are decided, also, that in the moist places in the Alkaline Valley we passed over yesterday afternoon, where there is no alkaline efflorescence, water could be got in sufficient quantity, and that it possibly would be good. I have already noted that while portions of the desert are alkaline, some portions discover pure salt on the surface, and others none of any kind. There are several families of Pi-Utes at this Middle Gate, collecting grass-seed, which they separate from the husks by first rubbing the heads lightly under stones and then winnow, by throwing it up in the wind. Afterward they convert it into a flour by rubbing it by the hand between stones. I notice they use a variety of seeds in making flour These Indians have come from Carson Lake, and appear to be industrious and able-bodied. I doubt not their present life is such as to make them facile subjects of husbandry and civilization generally. Indeed, I have been assured that some of them do hire themselves out as laborers in California for considerable periods of time—as long as a year at a time—and that they have been found faithful and to work well.

Resumed march at half past 1. In 1.75 miles cross an *arroyo* where the water yesterday, according to Mr. Reese, was running, but now exists in small pools. A small spring about two feet deep and one wide has been found to the right of this point, about three-quarters of a mile. There is no grass about it. Water not unpalatably sulphurous, but too scant for anything of a party. After crossing an *arroyo*, or creek, immediately leave old road, and bearing off to the left or northwardly, pass up valley, bounded by the Se-day-e Mountains on our right and a range of high mountains on our left. Distance between crests probably fifteen to twenty miles. Trees for first time since leaving Carson Valley appear on the Se-day-e Mountains, and also on the range to our left toward its north portion Grass and water are visible in the ravines of the Se-day-e Mountains.

Ten miles from Middle Gate reach, near base of Se-day-e Mountain, a small running brook of icy-cold, pure water, which I call Cold Spring, and which, after running a few hundred yards, sinks. A more refreshing drink than I obtained from this brook, after the parched, wearisome travel of last night, I believe I never had. The men all seemed equally eager for the cold draught, and were equally delighted. But we have felt most for the poor animals, which have had but about a pailful apiece since yesterday afternoon. They are so fagged, that they failed to get up with the wagons to the stream, and we are forced, therefore, to go into camp a mile from the water. The animals are driven to the water, and find an abundance of grass at the head of the creek.

Mr. McCarthy reports water in the mountains to our left, or west of us; also says he found the water running at Gibraltar Gate. Journey, since 2 p. m. yesterday, 49.9 miles; road good.

July 1, *Camp No.* 7, *Cold Spring.*—Elevation above the sea, 5,570 feet; thermometer at 6.30 a. m., 72°. All hands had a most refreshing sleep last night, and it is astonishing what a restorative pure cold water is. At 9 a. m. Mr. Thompson, the Norwegian, before spoken of, arrived and brought our mail from Genoa. He left the latter place on the 27th ultimo, and came by the way of Ragtown, on Carson River, crossing over thence to south side of Carson Lake, where he got into our road.

Mr. Reese, Pete, and four other men, including two soldiers, left about 10 o'clock to examine the country for the purpose of connecting our present route with the new proposed route, south of Ruby Valley. This examination will involve an extent of travel ahead of from 130 to 150 miles.

Party and train decamped at 1 p. m., and continue northwardly up valley. After proceeding 11 miles come to rapid stream of pure water, 2 feet wide, ¾ deep, flowing from the Se-day-e Range. On this we encamp. Willows fringe it, and grass is to be found higher up in the cañon. I call the stream after one of my assistants, Mr. Edward Jagiello, a Polish gentleman; his surname being difficult of pronunciation, I have preferred his Christian name as the appellation. Road, to-day, stony, on account of being on bench; farther down in the valley it would be smooth.

Opposite our camp, in the range of mountains lying to the west of us, is a deep pass, in which can be plainly seen an extensive bottom of grass, and a creek running down from it into the valley in which we have been traveling. This creek, and the valley into which it flows, I propose calling after Major Frederick Dodge, the Indian agent of the Pi-Utes and Washos, who was so courteous to my party, and myself, at Genoa. The pass referred to, at the head of this creek, Mr. Reese has examined sufficiently to assure me that a good wagon-road can be got through it without a great deal of expense; and, as he pronounces, after examination, the corresponding pass in the next western range, lying nearest and east of the sink, or north lake of Carson, capable of being also made practicable without a very great deal of labor, a wagon-road could be made direct from Dodge Valley through to the North Carson Lake, which would reduce the intervals between water to 15 miles.

He also reports that cedars are to be found on the mountain-ranges at this interval. This, then, would be also the route for the telegraph. The road might keep to the north or south of North Carson Lake, as might be deemed expedient, and the bend of Carson River could be cut off from its crossing near north end of South Carson Lake, to a point higher up, so as to make the interval between grass and water 15 to 25 miles, as might be found best. This route, as I have already noted, the guide says is now perfectly practicable for pack animals and stock, and is a most capital one for feed and water. It will at once, then, be seen that in the improvement of the route, at any future period, the change referred to should by all means be made. The Indians represent that the snow falls in Dodge Valley as much as 2 feet deep, and that in some winters there is scarcely any. They say that generally there is very little snow from Genoa to the Se-day-e Mountains.

July 2, *Camp No.* 8, *Edward Creek, Dodge Valley.*—Longitude, 117° 31′ 42″; latitude, 39° 28′ 56″; altitude above the sea, 5,486 feet; thermometer at 6 a. m., 71°. Private Collamer returned from the guide's party at sunrise, and reports that he rode till 12 midnight, then took 2 hours sleep, and his mule having given out, he came the rest of the way to camp on foot. He therefore is our guide to-day.

Mr. Thompson left us at half past 7 for Genoa, and intends going by the way of North Carson Lake.* We at the same time decamp, our course being southeast up the cañon of Edward Creek, the purpose being to cross the Se-day-e range. After traveling 7 miles, at half past 1, go into camp in superior grass, and on the babbling Edward Creek, three-fourths of a mile short of summit of pass. The road up the cañon is good and of excellent grade. A few patches of snow seen on the highest ridges of the Se-day-e Mountains. The piñon is almost the only *sylva* of the mountains. Willows, aspens, and cottonwood line the creek. It is quite refreshing to men and animals to again toil in the cañons, where nature has been more lavish of the essentials of a good emigrant route, to wit, wood, water, and grass.

July 3, *Camp No.* 9, *Edward Creek Cañon.*—Se-day-e Mountains. Elevation above the sea, 7,022 feet; thermometer at 7 a. m., 76°. Remain in camp to-day, on account of its being Sunday, and the animals require the good mountain-grass which we have here in great abundance. Lieutenants Murry and Putnam and Mr. McCarthy went this morning through the pass at the head of Edward Creek to Woodruff Valley, and report but little work to get through with the wagons.

July 4, *Camp No.* 9, *Edward Creek Cañon.*—Thermometer at 4.45 a. m., 62°.50. Move at 5.15 o'clock. Continue three-fourths of a mile up cañon to summit of pass, 7,260 feet above the sea, and then turning eastwardly, in 1.5 miles, by branch ravine, reach Kirby Smith's Creek, the cañon of which we follow down, 3.25 miles, to where

---

* Mr. Thompson, on his return to Carson Valley, at my request, addressed me the following letter on the practicability of a more direct route than mine from Edward Creek to Carson Valley:

"CARSON VALLEY, *July* 28, 1859.

"Captain SIMPSON:

"SIR: I have the honor to report to you my exploration on my return trip from your camp, on the 2d of July.

"I crossed Dodge Valley, and took up a cañon about half-way from Dodge Creek to the low gap on the right. This cañon is well adapted to a wagon-road; it is about 200 yards wide, and bunch-grass stands 2 feet high and very thick. I crossed over this range, but the cañon on the other side is very steep and difficult to go down. Then I came into another valley similar to Dodge Valley, but there is no stream that reaches into the valley. I crossed over this valley, and another high range of mountains, and came to the 'Forty-mile Desert,' on the old Humboldt route, and struck the road 17 miles from Ragtown.

"I did not see any route north of yours that is practicable, and I think yours is the only route in that vicinity that can be made passable.

"Respectfully, yours,

"J. A. THOMPSON."

This letter seems to militate against the report of my guide, Mr. Reese, on this subject, as given above (July 1), but it doubtless is on account of Mr. Thompson having gone to the north of the sink of Carson, and, therefore, much farther north than *he* did.

it debouches into Woodruff Valley, and, continuing along creek 3.3 miles farther, encamp on it. About 2 miles from summit of pass is a rock projecting from north side toward the stream, which made it necessary for us to go behind and over the rock on its north side; though by twice bridging the stream, which is 8 feet wide and 1 deep, a road of unexceptionable grade could be made in the bottom of the creek. Trains going east, like ours, could easily take our route, but going west, to do so they would be obliged to double up a steep ascent for about 100 feet. About 2 miles farther down the cañon there was another bad place where the teams had to double to ascend from the bottom of the creek to the top of the bank, and from which they again immediately descended to the creek. A very little labor, however, would be required to carry the road along the bottom at this point.

Road to-day near summit of pass, east side, for 1.5 miles, very rough from rocks which ought to be removed, and requiring improvement at points along creek, as above. Journey, 8.5 miles. On rough portion of road broke tongue of large ambulance, a coupling-pole of one of the wagons, and a wheel of small ambulance.

There is a great deal of grass in Smith's Cañon and the adjoining ravines, and some little clover in the former; but the south pass, or that of our outward route, is still better in respect to pasture. The distance, also, is about 4 miles in favor of the more southern route, but in grade the more northern is much the best. I think it also probable, on account of the bottom of Smith's Creek being moist and, therefore, miry *early in the season*, that until about the middle of June the route through the southern pass would be preferable for wagons; after that, however, the most northern route will be found the best. The truth is, both branches of the route should be made perfectly practicable when the road is perfected, so that either can be taken at any time.

The rocks along the Se-day-e Mountains to Edward Creek and through the pass to Woodruff Valley are porphyritic, of a brown color.

Just after getting into camp, rain began to fall, the first we have had for several weeks. A rainbow also appeared Indians report deepest snow in winter in pass we have come through to be 2.5 feet.

July 5, *Camp No.* 10, *Smith's Creek.*—Woodruff Valley. Elevation above the sea, 6,070 feet; thermometer at 4.45 a. m., 48°. The rain of yesterday, though slight, seems to have purified and refreshed the air. Decamped at 20 minutes after 5. Course north of east, directly toward our old pass between Woodruff and Reese Valleys. In 3.7 miles get into our outward route, and follow it till near Reese's River, where we leave it to the left, and encamp on river, about 2 miles above old Camp No. 25. This river takes its rise about 5 miles above or to the south of our camp, in some pure, cold springs in the valley, and also receives accession from streams from the Pe-er-re-ah Mountains, on the east side of the valley. Saw fine meadows for stock about the springs. Speckled trout weighing from 1½ to 2½ pounds caught in Reese's River. McCarthy brought in a large mess of ducks. Several Pi-Utes followed us yesterday and to-day—two armed with rifles. For further particulars of this valley and to-day's route see report of outward route. Day's travel, 20.8 miles. I would remark that there is an excellent pass from Woodruff to Reese's Valley, to the south of that we used, which would furnish a cut-off from either pass through the Se-day-e range to that of the Pe-er-re-ah range south of the Simpson Pass; which, if the latter is practicable, would cut off the great bend in the road between Woodruff Valley and Won-a-ho-no-pe Valley. There are indications of a pass in this direction in the Pe-er-re-ah range, but we had not time to examine it.

July 6, *Camp No.* 11, *Reese River.*—Elevation above the sea, 5,630 feet; thermometer at 4.40 a. m., 42°. Noticed, going west on our outward route, a great increment of temperature on west side of Se-day-e Mountains, and now since we have crossed to its east side, the thermometer has become correspondingly depressed. Move at 5 a. m. Morning bright as it almost invariably has been. The twittering of the birds, particularly of the meadow-lark, very cheerful. The contrast between the desert to the west of the Se-day-e Mountains, and the valleys and mountains east of it, very marked; the former being of the most forbidding cast, and the latter quite smiling and pleasant.

About a mile below camp cross Reese's River; ford, miry; not near so good as that used on outward route. In 5 miles more join outward route and continue on it through Simpson's Pass and park in the Pe-er-re-ah Mountains to about a mile below the lake, where we encamp in the cañon on Won-a-ho-no-pe Creek. Journey, 16.5 miles. The lake in Simpson's Park we find has fallen considerably since we passed by it before, it at present being only about 2 feet deep, and Won-a-ho-no-pe Creek, which before was a running stream a number of miles above our camp, at this time first gives indications of its existence at the camp. The grass in Reese Valley, through the cañons we have passed to-day, as well as everywhere nearly on the mountains, very abundant; more so than when we passed before. Hundreds of acres of good hay may be cut in Simpson's Park.

Some seventeen Indians have come into our present camp, two of them riding horses. They are Diggers, and speak the Sho-sho-nee language. One of them, who speaks a little English, says the Pi-Utes are to the west of them. These mountains, then (the Pe-er-re-ah range), are the dividing boundary between the Pi-Utes and the Diggers proper. The talk I had with the old Indian I met here before seems to have had the effect of removing the fears of the Indians to come into camp. Some patches of snow visible on the highest portions of the Pe-er-re-ah range, and the probabilities are that it is to be found in spots the year round. The Indians represent the snow in the pass to be in the winter about 15 inches.

Messrs. Lee and McCarthy brought in from Reese River ten brook trout, some weighing 2½ pounds, and represent that just after we left camp this morning there was a very heavy fall of rain in that quarter.

July 7, *Camp No.* 12, *Won-a-ho-pe Creek Cañon.*—Elevation above the sea, 6,285 feet. The guide, Mr. Reese, came into camp at daylight this morning, and reports the route I directed him to examine ahead favorable. The remaining portion of his party are some 75 miles in advance, continuing the examination of the country. Thermometer, at 5.40 a. m., 47°. Decamped at 6.15 o'clock. Continue down the Won-a-ho-no-pe Cañon. A good deal of work necessary in this cañon to make the road good. At present it is miry in places; occasionally for short distances sidling; and in some places, of short extent, rocky. Side-hill cutting generally easy. Currants, red and black, abound in the cañon. Grass abundant; some clover. Piñon abundant on sides of mountain. After journeying 4.8 miles, at 9 a. m. encamp at spring near mouth of cañon and sink of creek. Make only this short march so as to be enabled to reach Wons-in-dam-me Creek to-morrow. Some rain to-day, with thunder.

July 8, *Camp No.* 13, *mouth of Won-a-ho-no-pe Cañon.*—Elevation above the sea, 5,811 feet. Thermometer at 5 a. m., 58°. Leave outward track, and, taking a short cut, join it again in 3.1 miles. Continue on it 1.3 miles, and then leaving it and taking another short cut through a good pass in the Pah-re-ah range, join it again in 18 miles, within 1.3 miles of our old Camp 21, on Wons-in-dam-me Creek, where we again encamp. Journey, 25.4 miles. In consequence of nearly all the road being new, and a great deal of it passing through heavy sage, we did not get into camp till about 6 in the afternoon. Road now, however, on account of having been tracked, good. The Saw-wid Creek, 4.3 miles, and another, 6.8 miles, back from where we are encamped, and which we crossed to-day, are both running streams along the road, and furnish an abundance of pasture up in their cañons. These can be beneficially used by emigrants, who, in that case, should pass on the south side of the small sugar-loaf about 2.5 miles to the southwest of camp, and encamp at the mouth of the cañon.

Some eight or ten Diggers have followed us to camp, each carrying his two rat-sticks. Several of them are entirely naked, except the breech-cloth. Quite a heavy shower of rain has been falling, but, although it came down cold and chilly, these Indians seemed to take it as if it was not an extraordinary occurrence. One of the Indians, who was improperly frightened away at our camp on She-u-wi-te Creek (see journal of May 21 and 22) by my cook, has been again met, and by kind treatment has become reconciled. Indeed, he has performed for us excellent service as a guide, and we have therefore rewarded him with some presents.

July 9, *Camp No.* 14, *Wons-in-dam-me (or Antelope) Creek.*—Elevation above the sea, 6,595 feet. Thermometer at 5 a. m., 53½°. Morning cloudy. Small ambulance, a wheel of which was broken the other day, taken apart and packed in one of the wagons. Moved at 7. Just before leaving, the Indians (some twenty) amused us with a specimen of one of their dances, all entering into it with a great deal of zest, and shouting with the utmost delight. The appearance of so many white men and wagons in their country is quite an epoch in their lives, and they are correspondingly elated.

After proceeding on outward route 1.6 miles, we diverge to left slightly around some foot-hills, and in 5.1 miles come to a couple of springs, which I call Twin Springs. Bearing east of north, half a mile from these springs are half a dozen springs, which I call Barr Springs, after Sergeant Barr, of the Dragoons, who discovered them. These springs, with the grass about them and in their vicinity, would probably suffice for a considerable party. Two miles further we cross our old road, and leave it, not to get into it again, probably, until near Camp Floyd. One mile further reach a spring, which I call Fountain Spring, on account of its welling up like a fountain. Here is an abundance of water of good quality, but the grass is scant and alkaline. There are, however, two or three acres of rush-grass about it, which would answer for a small party. The pools are tinged with red, probably from ferruginous causes. Six and three-tenths miles further across the valley (Ko-bah) we come to a creek, which, on account of the color of the water, I call Clay Creek. The water exists in holes, but is pronounced constant by the Indians. There is a great deal of grass on different portions of it. Train got into camp at half past 2. Ko-bah Valley, such as described in outward route. Journey 16.1 miles. Road good.

Showers all around us to-day, with thunder and lightning, and this evening the rain fell in torrents, and the lightning and thunder were severe. Another beautiful rainbow just before sundown, the third I have seen in the past week. Mr. Reese informs me that these rains at this season are a great anomaly. The ordinary rainy season in Carson Valley is from the last of October to some time in May; and sometimes they have a little rain in June. Mr. Lowry says that in California thunder and lightning are scarcely known. I call the isolated mount just to the west of north of our camp after this last-mentioned gentleman.

As we have probably left our westward route, not to join it again until near Camp Floyd, it is proper here to note that up to the last junction of the two routes, 7.4 miles back from our present camp, we have shortened our outward route, by the short cuts we have made, 21.8 miles; and if the short cut across Ko-bah Valley, noted by the dotted line, which is practicable, is taken, the outward route has been shortened fully 30 miles.

July 10, *Camp No.* 15, *Clay Creek, Ko-bah Valley.*—Longitude 116° 05′ 45″; latitude 39° 33′ 24″; elevation above the sea, 5,998 feet; thermometer, at 5.20 a. m., 51°. First clear, sunny morning we have had for several days. Intending to travel only about 5 miles to reach a better camp-ground, we did not move till half past 6. The rain of last evening, copious as it was, has made but little impression on the soil, so porous and absorbent is it. Immediately at camp, cross Clay Creek by an excellent crossing, and traveling in a northeasterly direction, a range of mountains lying off to our right about 2 miles, in 5.2 miles reach some fine springs (three or four in number), which I call after Mr. William Lee, one of my assistants. These springs are in a narrow grassy outshoot of Ko-bah Valley, and the pasture in the vicinity being abundant, is a favorable place to encamp.

At these springs we found Wilson Lambert and Stevenson, two of the guide party, encamped, drying their clothes. They report that they have been 45 miles ahead, and in consequence of their mules giving out, were not able to join us yesterday. The prospect ahead, according to them, is unfavorable. There is water about 10 miles ahead, and thence about 9 miles beyond, but they both represent the We-a-bah range of mountains, over which the route would lie, impracticable for wagons. Ute Pete, they say, left their party three days since to go to the mail-station on our outward route, in Butte Valley, for the purpose of procuring the Indian who had shown the water before, and has not since been heard from. Here there is apparently a baulk. The guides persist in representing the mountain range ahead impracticable, and it would seem that I am after all forced to join my old route, and go through Cho-kup's Pass, which, on account of its steepness, is not so good as I could like. To strike off from these springs would make the turn in the road too abrupt. I have, therefore, ordered the party to return immediately to our old camp ground of last night, on Clay Creek, so as to make the divergence to old road as slight as possible. Train reached old camp at 15 minutes to 11 p. m.

After returning to camp, I called Stevenson again, and had another talk with him and Mr. Reese about the prospect ahead. He (Stevenson) is not so decided about the new pass in the We-a-bah Mountains being so impracticable as he this morning represented it. I have, therefore, some little hope that we may yet, by a more thorough examination, get through the mountains ahead of us, without being forced to take our old road through Cho-kup's Pass. I have accordingly ordered Mr. Reese, Stevenson, Lambert, and Private Collamer, with two pack-animals and 10 days' provisions, to go again forward and make a more thorough and conclusive examination of the passes. If a practicable pass is found Collamer is immediately to return and report the fact. Rain to-day again around us, and a few drops upon us.

July 11, *Camp No.* 15, *Clay Creek.*—Remained stationary to-day, waiting report from guide's party. The first clear day we have had in 8 days. Took advantage of it to keep up our accustomed astronomical observations. Observed east and west stars for time, Polaris for latitude, and took a double set of lunars, using stars on each side of the moon for the purpose of eliminating errors.

July 12, *Clay Creek.*—Private Collamer came in just after 12 o'clock, (midnight,) and reported, to our joy, a practicable pass in the range ahead of us, on the proposed course of our new return-route. The pass had been found by Ute Pete, who, though he had been four days and three nights without food, except roots, yet had been the instrument of finding us a pass, and thus enabling us to keep on our course. It appears that on his arrival at the mail-station, in Butte Valley, he found it abandoned on account of the spring failing at that point, and the consequence was that he not only failed in seeing the Indian he was in search of, but was disappointed in getting anything to eat.

All hands up at daybreak, but in consequence of the mules having been herded at a considerable distance, we did not get off till 25 minutes of 6. Thermometer, at 4.15 a. m., $42\frac{1}{2}°$. Retrace our steps to Lee's Springs, 5.2 miles, and turning to the right around the point of some low rolling hills, and threading a narrow valley thickly clothed with different kinds of grass of luxuriant growth, in 2.5 miles get into a plain cañon or pass of Colonel Cooper's range, which, in 1.5 miles, leads us into Pah-hun-nu-pe Valley. The rocks of this cañon are quite fine, on account of their abrupt height and well-defined stratification and dip, the latter being about 40° to the northeast. In consequence of the number of swallows which build their nests in its walls, I call it Swallow Cañon. Cedars crown its heights. Leaving this cañon we cross Pah-hun-nu-pe Valley, (elevation above the sea, 5,820 feet,) the cross range of mountains closing it at the south being about 5 miles distant, and the passes through it appearing practicable. To the southwest the ravines in this range are clothed with grass, and water appears to be coursing down them. Six miles from mouth of Swallow Cañon brings us to the sink of a fine creek, which comes from the pass through the We-a-bah Mountains to which we are tending, which creek I call after Mr. Charles S. McCarthy, the indefatigable taxidermist of the party. We turn southwestwardly up along this creek, and in 2.1 miles, at 1.15, reach a locality where, amid excellent and superabundant hill and bottom grass and good wood fuel, we encamp. The stream at this point is 3 feet wide and 1 deep, and flows with a rapid current in a tolerable deep bed.

Road, to-day, excellent; journey, 17.3 miles; soil, for first 3 miles in Kobah Valley, a rich grass or meadow bottom; in Pah-hun-nu-pe Valley it is argillo-arenaceous, in places gravelly; sage the characteristic; cedars cover the mountains. The grass extends up the hills of the We-a-bah range as far as the eye can reach. Indeed, the valley of McCarthy's Creek furnishes the best exhibition of mountain and bottom grass I have seen. It is almost inexhaustible. Large quantities of bottom-grass could be cut for winter. Cedar fuel, convenient, as also good limestone in lower portion of McCarthy's Cañon, and a whitish tufa in lower portion, good for building purposes, available. This tufa so soft as to be easily sawed into blocks of suitable size, and so light as to be easily transported. Indeed, there are all the requisites in this valley of a good dragoon post, which, on account of the altitude, should be kept as low down the creek as possible.

The formation of the mountains to the south of Clay Creek are an altered impure limestone, probably of the Carboniferous period, also altered sandstones.

July 13, *Camp No.* 16, *McCarthy's Creek, We-a-bah Mountains.*—Elevation above the sea, 6,184 feet; thermometer, at 4.30 a. m., 54°. Decamped at 5 minutes of 5. Continue up McCarthy's Creek, the grass continuing along and on the neighboring heights in the greatest abundance and luxuriance. The flowers in the valley, as we approach the summit, are of various colors, and very beautiful. Some aspens and wild currants are also seen. The creek continues to within a mile of summit, which is 6.2 miles from last camp. Pass rocky near summit; grade all the way up very good. Some few patches of snow visible on highest portion of range. Elevation of summit of pass above the sea, 7,270 feet.

Went to higher point on right of pass to get an extensive view. To northeast, east, and southeast could see the country for probably 60 miles, chopped up with mountain ranges, running generally north and south, exhibiting passes between them. The valley immediately to the east of us shows a clay flat, denuded of vegetation, and looking arid. Cedars abound in the mountains nearly everywhere.

We find the descent from pass to valley, east side of We-a-bah range, steeper than we have just come up, on west side, but still not objectionable, though a little sidling. About a mile from summit strike a small, swift mountain stream, 3 feet wide, $\frac{1}{4}$ deep, which we follow down into the main valley, which I call after Maj. Don Carlos Buell, assistant adjutant general. The stream I call after Capt. Thomas H. Neill, Fifth Infantry. Grass continues abundant in the cañon of this stream. At mouth of cañon, about 1.25 miles from summit, turn northwardly up west side of Buell Valley through an extensive grove of cedars, and in 7.9 miles reach a small stream, which I call Bluff Creek, on account of the imposing bluffs of the cañon, through which it debouches from the We-a-bah range into the valley. We encamp on this creek at quarter of 1 o'clock, after a journey of 15.5 miles. Road good, except for short distances in pass on west side, where it is rough on account of rocks. There is an abundance of grass in Buell Valley, not far from camp. The stream upon which we are encamped, like all others in this great basin, sinks a short distance from its debouchment into the valley. There is another and larger stream, about three-fourths of a mile to our north, running down from the mountains into Buell Valley.

On our way to-day we met Stevenson, of guide-party, who had been left behind by guide-party with a broken-down mule. About 3 o'clock Mr. Reese came in and reported water and grass ahead of us about 30 miles. Pete and Lambert are still ahead looking up points of route. The pass immediately to the west of us, by Bluff Creek, has been examined to McCarthy's Creek, and found to be only an indifferent pack-route. An Indian trail passes this way.

The formations along McCarthy's Creek are limestones so much fused as to come very nearly under the head of igneous rocks. At the summit of the pass siliceous conglomerates obtain, and they continue down to the east foot. Near our present camp limestones, partly pure, and partly subcrystalline, and partly impure and slaty, crop out, and by some fossils found in them are recognized as belonging to the Devonian age, rocks of which age have not been known before to exist west of the Missouri only to a very limited extent.

July 14, *Camp No.* 17, *Bluff Creek.*—Elevation above the sea, 5,998 feet; thermometer at 4.30 a. m. 56°.50. Raised camp at 10 minutes of 5. Strike eastwardly across Buell Valley. This valley, apparently limitless at north, open in places at south. In 6.4 miles reach a point in mid-valley, where I put a ☞ pointing to mouth of Neill's Cañon, as follows:

TO GOOD CAMP AND ROAD, 8 MILES. ☞ (A short cut.)

By this cut-off about 6 miles can be saved. Proceeding 6.7 miles farther, we commence going up pass over a low ridge, dividing Buell Valley from the adjoining valley lying east of it, which I call Phelps Valley, after Capt. John W. Phelps, Fourth Artillery. In 1.8 miles reach summit (6,523 feet above the sea) by a gentle grade, and in 1 mile east foot, also by an easy descent. Then striking northeastwardly, 8.1 miles across Phelps Valley, brings us to the west foot of the Too-muntz range of mountains, dividing Phelps Valley from Butte Valley. Ascending this range 8.3 miles, by an excellent grade through a winding cañon, we attained the summit of the pass, a quarter of a mile below which, on east side, we encamp, at the foot of a conspicuous bluff called by the Indians, on account of its dark basaltic color, Black Head, or Too-muntz Mountain. Here is an icy-cold spring, and about half a mile farther down, or to the east, a small stream to which we drive our stock. Good grass in vicinity. The spring I call Summit Spring. Elevation of summit of pass above the sea, 7,103 feet.

Buell Valley, in spots, is entirely denuded of vegetation, and presents the appearance of a clay flat; elsewhere it is covered with small *artemisia* and rabbit-bush. Phelps Valley appears closed by a cross-range at south, about 6 miles off; at north, the range closing it is about 15 miles off. Soil argillo-arenaceous. Small sage the characteristic. Small cedars in the passes of the ranges we have crossed to-day. The journey has been 32.4 miles, too long a day's travel, but necessary to get to water. Road good. Train reached camp at 8.30 p. m.

July 15, *Camp No.* 18, *Summit Spring, Too-muntz range.*—Longitude, 115° 12′ 14″;

latitude, 39° 32′ 53″; elevation above the sea, 7,057 feet; thermometer at 9.30 a. m. 72°. The guide and Stevenson left this morning early to find water, if possible, about 10 miles ahead, and if they return in time, we are to move that distance to-day. Mr. Engelmann and myself left at 8.30 o'clock to make some observations from some high points to the south of camp. After a hard struggle attain top of bluff (Black Head) and get views of country from 60 to 100 miles around. West of north, far distant, where are the high snow-clad summits of what, doubtless, is the Humboldt range. To the west the We-a-bah range appeared quite near, though quite 30 miles off. To the southwest could be seen, evidently, the Antelope range, at the foot of which we encamped July 8, seven days ago. To the south, for 60 miles, mountain-range after mountain-range appeared running in every variety of direction; and to the east, some 30 miles off, a number of parallel ranges trending generally north and south. Between the east and west ranges there seems to have been an upheave of igneous rocks breaking the sedimentary rocks and causing the irregularity of trend of the ranges, and this seems also to have been the case to the south of us. These rocks are of a brown porphyritic character. To the north of our camp the formations are the same yellowish limestones of Carboniferous age which were before found on both sides of Long Valley. As far as the eye can reach to the south of us the mountains are covered with cedars, which is almost a sure indication that water and grass also exist in that region. Got back to camp at half past 11. At about 5 the guide, Pete, and Stevenson, returned to camp, and reported water 12 miles ahead, and also 3 miles beyond that.

July 16, *Camp No.* 18, *Summit Spring, Too-muntz Mountain range.*—Thermometer at 4.40 a. m. 53°. Move at 5, and continue eastwardly down cañon to Butte Valley. In 1 mile from camp pass a fine gushing spring, which issues from foot of bluff, and gives rise to the small stream referred to before, which, after running a third of a mile, sinks. This spring, creek, and cañon I call after Pete, the Ute Indian, who has been of so much service to us in our explorations. The bottom-grass along it, as also the bunch-grass in the vicinity, is abundant.

The grasses I have noticed along the route at different times and in different localities are as follows: First, the very fine mountain-grass, the fruit of which is very small and pretty. This grass attains a height of 1½ to 2 feet. Second, the slightly coarser mountain-grass, existing, like the other, in bunches, but showing larger fruit. This attains a height of about two feet. These two kinds are found chiefly on the mountain benches and slopes and in the ravines. Third, the rye or wheat grass. Fourth, the large high bunch-grass which is principally found on benches along streams, and attains a height of from 3 to 4 feet. Fifth, the sage-grass, very seldom seen, but found among the *artemisia*, or wild sage; and which grows about 1½ feet high. Its fruit resembles, in the husk, the wild wheat. Sixth, the desert-grass, small, fine, and presenting a glossy kind of blossom or fruit. Its height is about 8 inches. The animals prefer the mountain-grass or the first two kinds to all others, and these abound generally on both our routes.

In three-quarters of a mile from Pete's Spring reach mouth of cañon by gentle descent, and 10.9 miles more cross Butte Valley, (6,268 feet above the sea,) with low range of mountains, 5 miles off, limiting it at the south, and strike a stream of pure cold water which I call after Dr. Garland Hurt, the late accomplished Indian agent for the Ute Indians. The stream is tolerably rapid, 3 feet wide, ½ foot deep, and sinks ½ mile below mouth of cañon. Willows line it, and pi on is found on the heights. Currants grow in the cañon. Ascending the cañon by a good grade, albeit in some places a little sidling and rocky, 3.2 miles brought us to the summit of the pass of the Mon-tim range dividing Butte and Steptoe valleys; elevation of summit above the sea, 7,398 feet. Descending the eastern slope by a winding cañon of pretty steep grade for 200 or 300 yards, near summit, 3 miles more in a south direction brought us to a spring, where we encamped. At this spring we have made several excavations, which can be multiplied to any desirable extent, as the spring is running, and the excavations will fill up with water. The guide also reports four more springs within the compass of half a mile from camp. I have therefore called this cañon Spring Cañon. Grass abounds about the camp. Mon-tim range, in which we are encamped, is covered with tall trees, like the fir, which would supply poles for the telegraph for a long distance. The mountain mahogany also exists near our camp in larger quantities than I have before seen it. Brown porphyry characterizes, geologically, Hurt's Cañon; while the main portion of the Mon-tim range consists, like those farther north, of compact calcareous rocks and some few sandstones. Road, to-day, generally hard and good. Journey, 19.1 miles.

July 17, *Camp No.* 19, *Spring Cañon.*—Elevation above the sea, 6,828 feet; thermometer at 5 a. m., 43°. The air this morning very chilly. Decamped at 25 minutes of 6; continued in an east of south direction down Spring Cañon, the grade of which, except near summit, is exceedingly slight. This cañon gradually opens to 2.5 miles wide as you descend to Steptoe Valley, and the cedar on either side is almost inexhaustible. There is grass everywhere in the cañon and on the mountain-slopes, though it is not near so flourishing and thick as that in McCarthy's Cañon. Springs also common in it. On the north side of the ca on the mountains are very bold and precipitous. There is an old beaten trail down this cañon, about the largest we have seen on the trip. The Indians say it is the trail of the To-sa-witch band of the Sho-sho-nees, living about the Humboldt River, who yearly take this route, to trade horses with the Pahvant Indians about Fillmore. These horses they probably get from the Bannacks, to the north of them.

Just at outlet of Spring Cañon into Steptoe Valley, 8 2 miles from camp on north side of cañon, there is a spur from the north wall or mountain of the cañon, through which there is a gap, gate, or cañon, which, for sublimity, on account of its confining walls, equals, probably, anything we have seen on the route. The walls are composed of a siliceous limestone, interstratified with shale, and are nearly vertical. There are several caves, niches, and benches to be seen high up in the wall. The bottom of the cañon is quite springy and covered with a luxuriant grass. Fine grass also exists in the vicinity. I call the place the Gate of Hercules, on account of its stupendous walls. The echo in it is very fine, and our fire-arms have startled a great number of swallows and hawks. The road leaves this gate to the left about 0.5 mile, and 1.7 miles further down Spring Cañon brings us to Steptoe Valley, which we follow, on its western side, for 4 miles, in a southeasterly direction, and encamp on a noble creek, which I call after Lieut. Alexander Murry, the energetic officer in command of the escort of my party. This stream heads some 12 miles off in the mountain range, is rapid, and, after running in a northeasterly direction, sinks 2 miles below camp. At this camp it is from 6 to 10 feet wide and about 1 deep; bottom gravelly and rocky. The grass in the vicinity of our camp, along the bottom of the creek, in the valley, and in the mountains, is exceedingly abundant. Currants are found on the creek. Road, to-day, good; soil, argillo-arenaceous; the wild sage and rabbit-bush the characteristics of the valleys, cedars and firs the mountains. It is very possible that a cut-off may be made from the mouth of Neill's Creek to the mouth of Stevenson Cañon, when the road is perfected; and the intervening country should be examined for the purpose.

July 18, *amp No.* 20, *Murry's Creek, Steptoe Valley.*—Elevation above the sea, 6,193 feet; thermometer, at 5 a. m., 46°. Moved at 20 minutes after 5; course, southeastwardly, across Steptoe Valley. Two miles and eight-tenths from camp get into and follow a wagon-road, which, an Indian who lives in this valley says, was made by the Mormons in the spring of last year. He represents that they came into Steptoe Valley from the east; had about 50 wagons, and after proceeding north of our camp some 8 or 12 miles, turned into a cañon of the Un-go-we-ah range, whence they turned back and retraced their old route to the settlements. I have no doubt that this was the route taken by the Mormons at the time it was reported they were flying from our troops last spring, and were going to Silver Mountains. This is the route that Lott Huntingdon, a Mormon mail-agent at Ruby Valley, reported to me as one which had been traveled by some emigrants in an attempt to reach California from Fillmore, and that nothing more had ever been heard from them! (Mr. Bean, August 10, informed me that he, Bean, was one of the guides to the Mormons, on the occasion referred to above, and that they had 14 horse and mule teams, and about 30 ox teams, and that they returned because they did not like the country.)

About a mile from where we struck the Mormon road, we cross a fine creek, which I call after Capt. Carter L. Stevenson, of the Fifth Regiment of Infantry. This stream comes from the Un-go-we-ah range, and, after getting into Steptoe Valley, runs northwardly in it for 3 or 4 miles below where we crossed it, and sinks. It is 5 feet wide, 1½ deep, of rocky bottom, rapid current, of milky hue, its taste good, and would be serviceable in irrigating the rich bottom along it. Indeed Steptoe Valley in this locality exhibits a very extensive bottom of luxuriant grass, intermingled with clover, and if not too cold (it is 6,146 feet above the sea, or 1,286 feet above Camp Floyd), as both Murry Creek and Stevenson Creek could be used in its irrigation, it would furnish an excellent location for a post or Government farm. An abundance of hay could be cut for the winter, and possibly the cereals (except corn), as well as garden vegetables, would thrive. The fort or post could be located on either Murry or Stevenson Creek, though the former, probably, on account of its being on the west side of the valley, and therefore the freest from snow in the winter, would be preferable as a site. The Indian living here says the snow in the valley is only generally about six inches deep, and some winters there is none at all. It never lasts long. In Spring Cañon Pass of Mon-tim range, it is about 2 feet deep. Should the Government ever locate a post here, the military reserve should be bounded by the highest crests of the Mon-tim range, limiting Steptoe Valley on the west; by the highest crests of the Un-go-we-ah range, limiting said valley on the east; and by an east and west line across said valley from crest to crest, 10 miles north of post; and by an east and west line across said valley from crest to crest, 20 miles south of post. The reserve should be thus large to embrace the necessary pasture and timber. Good building-stone can be got from the mountains, and tall pines or fir from the same source. If preferable, adobes could be used instead of stone. The Indian referred to reports another stream as large as Murry's Creek, to the south of our camp, and which also flows from the Mon-tim range.

After crossing Stevenson Creek we left the Mormon road (which goes around by the way of the mouth of the cañon, through which the creek flows,) and cut across some short and rather steep hills, crossing the river again 7.5 miles from last crossing, up in the cañon, and joining again and following the Mormon road up the cañon from this point. The stream at this last crossing was so miry as to make it necessary to take the teams over by hand. In one-half mile we crossed it twice again. At the last crossing the road, instead of passing where it does, through a narrow miry cañon, should keep straight ahead and turn the hill of rocks about 200 yards higher up.

This cañon discovers some splendid rocks of the most massive character, some of them being isolated and looking like castles. In one instance, on right side of cañon, high up, I noticed a very pretty arch, through which I could see the blue sky. There is a great deal of fine-grained colored limestone here, which, I should think, might be classed among the marbles. A great deal of it is diversified with white streaks coursing through it.

A mile and a quarter from where we last struck Stevenson's Creek, we again leave it and take up a branch ravine, which we follow for 2 miles, and encamp at a fine spring, the source of the branch, among good luxuriant grass and timber.

This Stevenson's Cañon requires four good bridges of spans, from 12 to 20 feet, to make the road passable, and in two places, where the bottom is miry for about 100 yards, the road should be excavated along the side-hills. In point of grade the cañon is excellent, and abounds in grass, cedar, pine, mountain mahogany, and aspen timber. Road good, except at points noted. Journey 14.5 miles. In consequence of bad crossings, train did not reach camp till 4 p. m.

July 19, *Camp No.* 21, *Stevenson's Cañon, Un-go-we-ah range.*—Elevation above the sea, 7,443 feet. Thermometer at 4.40 a. m., 52°. Sent out guide-party early this morning, with particular instructions to send back a man daily to inform me of the country ahead. We are approaching, doubtless, the most difficult portion of our route, and I feel anxious that there shall be no *faux pas.* The party goes out with ten days' provisions, and, besides the usual persons (Reese, Stevenson, and Lambert), I have ordered three soldiers to accompany them. Pete also accompanies them for a distance, and then is to push on with all dispatch with my report to General Johnston, at Camp Floyd.

Main party moved at 5.45. Course eastwardly up branch of Stevenson's Cañon, 1.7 miles to summit of Un-go-we-ah or Pine range, and thence down a cañon I call after Capt. Henry Little, Seventh Infantry, 7.4 miles to its debouchment into Antelope Valley. Thence 6.6 miles, or about two-thirds of the way across Antelope Valley, to some springs, which, by being opened, may be made to serve a large command. We encamp at these springs at 2.15 The road near the pass of the Un-go-we-ah range, on west side, has two or three short, steep, as well as sidling places, which require grading. The general ascent, however, of the cañon from where we struck it is good. The mountain mahogany is found in it. On the top of the pass I noticed four dug holes, evidently places in which the Mormons had *cached* some of their property when they passed here in the spring of 1858, but which now were empty. The distant view, from this summit, of mountain ranges, peaks, and valleys, lying to the southeast, very beautiful. The descent immediately at summit, on east side, tolerably steep, but good the rest of the way down to Antelope Valley. A couple of fine peaks are visible on right of cañon; also other notable rocks, some of them being fine massive exhibitions of a species of veined limestone. These rocks contain small caves. A spring and fine grass are reported by Sergeant Barr, 1.5 miles down the cañon and a quarter of a mile to right, in a branch cañon, and another spring about 3 miles down the cañon to the right, also in a branch cañon. Cedar and pine abound in the mountain range. As you descend Little's Cañon to Antelope Valley, the Go-shoot, or Tots-arrh, range looms up toweringly in front of you, the most conspicuous portion being Union Peak. Antelope Valley, in which we are encamped, exhibits a much better soil in this portion of it than where we crossed it on our outward route. To the north, commencing about three-quarters of a mile from our camp, a bottom of good grass (a great deal of it red-top), 2 or 3 miles wide, extends for a distance of 8 or 10 miles northwardly, and probably further, and intermingled with it are extensive groves of tall cedars, which thus far on our routes, existing, as these groves do, in the *bottom* of the valley, is quite an anomaly. Birds frequent these groves, and make the air resonant with their music. The scenery, too, is quite pretty. This valley is 5,633 feet above the sea, and therefore 513 feet lower than Steptoe Valley where we last crossed it. It is not, however, so well watered as the latter, neither is the grass so luxuriant. There are, however, some fine cold springs which we will pass to-morrow, about 2 miles up Turnley's Cañon, and 8 miles to the northeast of this camp, which might be useful were a fort established in this valley. Adobes could be made or building-stone (limestone) got from the mountain. Road to-day generally good. Journey 15.7 miles. A little rain just before sunset.

The Un-go-we-ah Mountains, in the neighborhood of our route, are composed of calcareous rocks, mostly an impure limestone, with some slaty and other strata. Near the summit the rocks are porphyritic.

July 20, *Camp No.* 22, *Springs, Antelope Valley.*—Longitude, 114° 26′ 52″; latitude, 39° 06′ 09″. Elevation above the sea, 5,633 feet. Thermometer at 4.40 a. m., 54°. Weather quite mild at sunrise and during the night. Decamped at 20 minutes past 5. Course east of north, 5.8 miles up Antelope Valley, to mouth of cañon, which I call after Capt. P. T. Turnley, assistant quartermaster at Camp Floyd, and which leads us to the pass over the Go-shoot or Tots-arrh range. Our road turns up this cañon southeastwardly, and 2.2 miles from mouth we find some fine copious cold springs, which I call also after Captain Turnley. Grass and wood-fuel found in vicinity. Persons traveling our route will find a road to the north of ours, and more direct from near the mouth of Little's Cañon to the mouth of Turnley's Cañon, which will cut off several miles. In that case they will make their encampment at these springs, and not where we did in Antelope Valley. Proceeding up Turnley's Cañon 1.8 miles by a remarkably easy grade, the cañon being amply wide, we reach summit of pass of the Go-shoot or Tots-arrh range (7,060 feet above the sea), whence we had toward the east a fine view of some distant mountains, Union Peak of the Tots-arrh range to the east of the summit towering far above every other height, and showing a great deal of snow and apparently depending icicles in its recesses. Indeed, I think this peak the highest we have seen on either of our routes. Descending from pass on east side, by a cañon of very easy inclination, in 7.2 miles reach a fine spring of flowing water, where we encamp. This cañon I call Red Cañon, on account of its red-colored rocks. The spring is called by the Indians Un-go-pah, or Red Spring. Plenty of grass exists near and in vicinity, and I notice also some springs to the south side of us, in the cañon, about 2 miles off. Union Peak, which lies some 10 or 15 miles to the west of south of us, the Indians call Too-bur-rit; but I cannot learn its meaning. The mountain range is covered with cedar, piñon, and fir. Road to-day very good. Journey 17.1 miles. Train got into camp at 12.45. Met Private Marpool, of guide's party, before reaching camp. He had returned from the guide's party to conduct us to our present camp. Pete we found at this camp. His mule had given out on account of sore feet, and he was waiting our arrival to have him shod. Private Nune also came into camp from guide's party to conduct us to our camp-ground to-morrow. Pete has been supplied with a fresh mule, and at 3 p. m. he started again on his way to Camp Floyd, the bearer of my report of progress. An elk was seen for the first time yesterday in Stevenson's Cañon, and one to-day in Red Cañon; also, a mountain sheep for the first time.

The Tots-arrh range, on west side, is composed of altered limestone and quartzite. The limestone forms the mountains on both sides of summit of pass. On east side, along the road, was noticed a great deal of calcareous conglomerate; also, quartzite and impure limestones.

July 21, *Camp No.* 23, *Un-go-pah or Red Springs.*—Elevation above the sea, 5,927 feet. Sergeant Miller and Corporal Duvall came in during the night with the beef which was found missing when we reached Camp 21. This is the only beef remaining, and is one of those we took from Camp Floyd, and he has improved ever since we left that post. Thermometer at 5 a. m., 61½°. Resumed journey at 25 minutes after 4. Course eastwardly. Continue to descend Red Cañon to valley on east side of Tots-arrh range, which valley I call after Deputy Quartermaster-General George H. Crosman, stationed at headquarters Department of Utah. The road we are following, and have been since we left Steptoe Valley, is the Mormon road referred to July 18. The indications are that some fifty wagons have been over it. The tracks of the cattle are still visible, and the dung yet remains on the road. About 3 miles from camp we leave the road, to cut off a bend of it. About 2.5 miles farther cross a dry branch just below its sink. Cottonwood at crossing. Five and a half miles farther brings us to a rush spring of tolerable water, which, by excavation, could be made to serve a pretty large command. There is a great deal of grass about it, and in the vicinity. Three and a half miles farther we join and follow again the Mormon road. Half a mile farther we come to creek, 3 feet wide, 1 deep, which comes from the south, and sinks a quarter of a mile below camp. In places it is lined with rushes and willows. On this creek, which I call also after Colonel Crosman, we encamp at half past 12, amid abundance of grass. This valley, which, like nearly all the others, lies north and south, is 12 to 15 miles wide, and is partially closed at either end by high mountains, some 25 or 30 miles off. Its elevation above the sea is 4,920 feet. It has a great deal of grass in it, in localities, and is at these places supplied with springs, which are either copious or can be made sufficiently so. Small greasewood the characteristic. Road to-day generally very good, sometimes cutting up from alkali. Soil generally gravelly. Journey, 14.8 miles.

July 22, *Camp No.* 24, *Crosman Creek.*—Elevation above the sea, 4,920 feet. Thermometer, at 5 a. m., 65°. Cloudy this morning at sunrise, and a few drops of rain. The mules during the night gave indications of a stampede. At first supposed it might have been caused by some Indians, who acted as if they were angry last evening because they were not permitted to remain in camp after dark; but as such indications are not unusual, it was probably due to other causes. The guard, however, was visited and admonished to observe vigilance, &c.

Moved at 5, and continue on Mormon road. Course, northwardly in valley for 10.2 miles, when we come to a number of small springs, which I call after Lieut. Peter W. L. Plympton, Seventh Infantry. These springs at present do not afford a great deal of water, for the reason of there being no proper excavations, but a great sufficiency could be easily obtained in this way. The soldier who last joined us at Un-go-pah Springs was directed by the guide to conduct us to a spring 12 miles distant from our last camp, but as these are only 10 miles distant, and the soldier has not been to the place, we continued on in the hope of seeing the springs referred to within about a couple of miles and camping at it. It proved, however, that at this distance there were no springs, so that I was lured on in the hope of finding them a little farther on. At 13, 14, and 15 miles from camp we saw none, and then, according to the notes of the guide, which he had shown me, feeling confident that they were beyond, in striking distance, I continued on till, at quarter to 5 o'clock, we had traveled 30.1 miles, when we were obliged to encamp near some puddles of water, which had been made by the rain, just before we reached the spot. The misfortune is, too, that there is no grass in the vicinity, but the barley we purchased at Placerville now comes into requisition, and we shall thus be enabled to get through the night.

After reaching, as above stated, Plympton's Springs, our route lay eastwardly 6.7 miles to foot of pass, across a low, thirsty mountain-ridge, which I call Perry Range; thence 3.1 miles by a good grade, up a broad cañon to summit, the rocks on the left side being buttress or bluff-like; and thence, by gentle descent 10.1 miles to camp. The ridge we have passed over is composed of highly altered silico-calcareous rocks, and is almost entirely bare of trees. From the summit of the pass, 5,657 feet above the sea, could be seen, some 25 or 30 miles off, on east side of range of mountains, quite remarkable on account of its well-defined stratification and the resemblance of portions of its outline to domes, minarets, houses, and other structures. On this account I call it the House range. Between it and the ridge forming our point of view is a very extensive valley, very generally white with alkaline efflorescence, and I have therefore called it White Valley. It is some 25 miles wide, and partially closed north and south by low ranges, about 15 miles off. Soil, areno-argillaceous. Small greasewood the characteristic. It is in the middle of this valley we have encamped, and on account of the guides having neglected to send back a man, as he was wont, according to orders, to point to me a camp of *which he was personally cognizant*, the party is in its present uncomfortable situation.

July 23, *Camp No.* 25, *White Valley.*—Elevation above the sea, 4,406 feet; thermometer at 5 a. m., 60°. Koenig, the dragoon, did not come in from the guide party in the night, as was anticipated. I do not understand the guide's movements. It was enjoined upon him over and over again to send us a man back daily, to guide the party with certainty to water and grass, and he has still Pete, Lambert, Stevenson, and Private Koenig with him. It will be hazarding too much to persist in going forward at a venture, though Sanchez, who was with the guide when he examined to the northeast of the House range, on our outward trip, says there is water on the *east* side of the House Mountains. The route to the water, however, is not known to be practicable, and it would consume nearly the whole day to have it examined, and in the meantime the animals are without grass and water, and we cannot afford to give them another feed of forage, it being necessary for the desert stretch, which we may possibly have to pass before reaching Rush Valley. I have, therefore, determined to fall back to Plympton's Springs, where we can get grass and water, and await there the arrival of some one from the guide's party.

Leave at 7 a. m., and retrace our steps to Plympton's Springs, where, at 2, we encamp. Journey, 18.7 miles. At 5 p. m. had a very severe hail and rain storm, the severest I have experienced since I have been in this region; hail as big as marbles, and rain so copious as to flood the tents; thunder and lightning the accompaniments. In these high regions the thunder and lightning, however, are infrequent, and not severe.

July 24, *Camp No.* 26, *Plympton's Springs.*—Elevation above the sea, 4,814 feet; thermometer, at 6.30 a. m., 62°. Private Koenig of guide party has not yet returned. Begin to feel very uneasy, and have, therefore, directed Sergeant Barr, Private Collamer, and Sanchez, the Mexican, to examine the country beyond where we encamped night before last, in White Valley, and see if we can get our wagons to the water reported by Sanchez as lying to the east of House range. Should they meet Koenig, and all is right, they are to continue on to the water, and Koenig is to return and report. Should they not meet him, then Sanchez is to return by the pass to the north of the reputed water, and report the facts. The teamsters and men, meantime, are engaged in cutting grass to take along with us over the desert. Some little rain this afternoon.

July 25, *Camp No.* 26, *Plympton's Springs.*—Thermometer at 5.15 a. m., 51°. Sergeant Barr came in at 11 last night, having ridden 40 miles, and reports that 2 miles beyond our rain-puddle camp (No. 25) he found a note from the guide to me stuck in a cleft-stick near a rush pond, informing me that the Indian with him says there are water and grass 10 miles beyond that locality. This mode of guiding me by notes stuck up, depending upon the contingency of my reaching or getting them, is a new feature introduced by the guide since I have approached the desert, and is entirely unauthorized. It is true that he sent word by Private Nune, the last man he sent in, that I could continue to follow the Mormon road, and that if anything was wrong he would send a man back to notify me. But this is placing me entirely at his mercy, and this I do not choose to sanction. I must know what lies before me. The sergeant alone came back. Collamer and Sanchez continued on to examine the water and grass ahead, and are to return to us at Rush Pond, where the note was found. I have concluded, therefore, to again move forward.

Started at 5.45 and retraced our track to our old camp-ground, No. 25. A mile and a half farther brought us, at 1 o'clock, to the Rush Pond reported yesterday by Sergeant Barr. Journey, 20.3 miles. The rain yesterday in this valley must have been very heavy. The sage-brush has been torn up by the roots and carried as if by a flood down an *arroyo* and lodged on either side clear over its banks. Not finding either Collamer or Sanchez here as I expected, and noticing with my reconnoitering glass two persons coming toward us from the cañon ahead of us, out of the House range, I have ordered a halt till they could come up, and make their report. At 2.30 they arrived, and proved to be Koenig and Sanchez. Koenig reporting water and grass 15 miles ahead, and it being impossible for us to make the distance to advantage to-day, we go into camp where we are, at the Rush Pond. A rather poor camp, but the rushes will prove sufficient for our animals, and the water is sufficiently abundant.

Koenig has come in all tattered and torn. He has been two days without food, and all on account of the guides neglecting to send a man back to report every camp instead of sticking up notes which I might not, and did not, at the proper time, get. His horse giving out, he was obliged to walk a great deal on foot. Collamer and Sanchez happily met him this morning in the cañon ahead, waiting for us, and relieved him of his troubles. Collamer let him have his mule, and remains ahead of us till we can overtake him to-morrow.

Showers of rain around this afternoon, with slight thunder and lightning. There is a spring to the north of our camp, so Sanchez reports, some 5 miles off, near a small mound, or hill, but no grass; he found it when examining the country on our outward route.

July 26, *Camp No.* 27, *Rush Pond, White Valley.*—Longitude, 113° 31′ 54″; latitude, 39° 19′ 37″; altitude above the sea, 4,350 feet; thermometer at 5 a. m., 56°. Decamped at 5.30 o'clock. Continue on old Mormon road, north of east to mouth of cañon, leading to pass through House range. To get to it, cross an alkali flat, 3 miles wide, which, in wet weather, must cut up very much. It can be avoided, doubtless, by bearing around more southwardly. After crossing flat, pass through a mile of sand knolls, where the pulling is difficult. Reach foot of cañon, 8 miles from camp, and 4.1 miles further, by a good grade, except near summit, where for about 100 yards it is rather steep, we reach the culminating point of pass. Elevation above the sea, 6,674 feet. The bluffs at the entrance of this cañon are tremendously high and massive; that on the right very high, probably 1,500 feet, and like a dome. Call the cañon, therefore, Dome Cañon. Excellent and tolerably abundant grass in this cañon, but no water. Cedars and a few firs on slopes of cañon. The walls of the cañon full of small caves, and as usual showing a great deal of the resinous, pitchy substance, that seemingly oozes out of the rock; but it may be the dung of birds or of small animals. The formation of the mountain range is made up of highly altered limestones and some altered sandstones, &c.

Ascended a high point to right of pass to get an extensive view. To the south, some 20 miles off, lies a lake of sky-blue color, apparently some 10 or 15 miles long, and less broad. This is doubtless Sevier Lake, the sink of Sevier River, on which Captain Gunnison and party were massacred in 1853, and to which he was tending for the purpose of examining it when the catastrophe occurred. The valley lying to the north of this lake exhibits one extended low, flat, desert plain, showing many spots of a whitish alkaline character. Coursing from south to north across it, at its eastern portion, some 20 miles off, is a low range of mountains, its north end terminating directly east of my point of view. Far beyond can be seen a continuous range of mountains, running north and south, which doubtless is the formidable Wahsatch range. The prospect of palatable water directly east is poor indeed.

After descending from summit on east side, about two miles, met Collamer, who conducted us up a cañon to the left about half a mile, when we came to a fine cold spring of good water, where, at 12.45, we encamp. Road to-day excellent, except across alkaline portion of the White Valley as stated. Animals driven to the creek, up the cañon about a mile from camp, where there is a considerable quantity of fine grass and a growth of pines. Journey 14.5 miles. This spring, creek, and cañon I call after Lieut. Gurden Chapin, Seventh Infantry.

Met the guide, Mr. Reese, at this camp ground. He arrived here yesterday afternoon without food. Reports water and grass 15 miles ahead. The rest of the party, Pete, Lambert, and Stephenson, are awaiting us at that locality; their animals all broken down from sore feet. They had been two days without water. The guide had been unsuccessful in finding the water pointed out in the distance on our outward route by the red-shirted Indian (Black Hawk's brother) in the Short-Cut Pass range, although they were engaged two days looking for it. This was the water which was to shorten the distance between water on the desert to 35 miles.

Persons following us may suppose that, from Rush Pond, we might have come more directly to our present camp, by the pass just to the north of us, in the House range; but besides White Valley not being practicable, on account of alkaline mire in that direction, the pass referred to is not practicable for wagons. This pass was examined by the guide-party on our outward route.

The old ox which remained of those we took from Camp Floyd, on our way out, was slaughtered for beef this evening, and not without considerable regret. He had traveled with us the whole way, and we felt reluctant at parting with him even for beef.

July 27, *Camp No.* 28, *Chapin's Spring.*—Elevation above the sea, 6,530 feet. Thermometer at 5 a. m., 67°. For the last 2 nights the weather has been quite warm. Marched at 20 minutes past 5. Retraced our steps one-fourth of a mile to old Mormon road, and then leave it and cut off an unnecessary detour, by winding in the cañon to the left. Three and a half miles further get into it again, in Sevier Valley, and after following it a few yards, leave it entirely, we turning to the left around a southeast spur of the House range, and the Mormon road continuing in an easterly direction to Fillmore and crossing the Sevier, it is said, at the Government bridge on the main southern road to Los Angeles. It is from the point of mountain at this locality that the view of Sevier Lake has been taken. A low mountain range bounds the lake on its south shore; but on its north, the valley goes down to it without any intervening hill or ridge, and it looks traversable by wagons in every direction. Continuing around along the east base of House range our route, after proceeding northwardly up the valley about 11 miles, turns to the left up a cañon a quarter of a mile, where we reached some good springs, and at 12 meridian, encamped. In this vicinity there are other springs, and about half a mile further up toward the mountain, there is a small creek, 4 feet wide, 1 deep, which, after running a short distance, sinks. The springs' creek, and cañon I call after Lieut. Charles H. Tyler, Second Dragoons. To this creek, along which there is an abundance of grass, we drive our mules.

At this camp we found Pete, Lambert, and Stevenson of guide's party, all broken down, on account of animals giving out. At 6 p. m. I dispatched Pete, Stevenson, and Sanchez about 75 miles ahead, to look up pass into Rush Valley, suitable for this, our return, route. Pete is to continue on to Camp Floyd with my report and letters, and bring back the mail.

In Tyler's Cañon, a short distance to the north of our camp, is an artificial corral or inclosure made of rocks, and capable of holding about 50 horses. It is represented as being the place were Tintic, an Indian chief, a year or two ago concealed a lot of stolen horses.

Journey to-day 15.5 miles. Road stony along east base of House range, otherwise good.

July 28, Camp No. 29, Tyler's Spring.—Elevation above the sea, 5,992 feet. Thermometer at 6 a. m., 72°. Remained in camp till 2.30 p. m. for the purpose of recruiting the animals, preparatory to crossing the desert, and traveling all night. Take a course northwardly for about 15.6 miles up a branch or arm of Sevier Lake Valley, where we, about 11 o'clock, stopped to take supper and bait the animals with some grass we had brought with us. From this point we bore off northeastwardly to a pass through Colonel Lorenzo Thomas's range, 3 miles, by an easy grade, bringing us to the summit, 5,520 feet above the sea. Descending on east side by a good grade, 2.2 miles more, we halted, at 3 o'clock in the morning, to take breakfast, and feed the animals with barley. There being no moon, and it being cloudy, it was somewhat difficult for us to find our way through the pass; but, by the use of a lantern ahead as a guide to the foremost wagons, we were enabled to get along better than I expected.

At 4.15 a. m., July 29, we left our place of bivouac, and in 2 miles reached second summit of range, 5,330 feet above the sea, whence, bearing magnetically north 25 E., could be seen the Champlin Mountains, for the water in which we were aiming. It was in the region of this summit, southward, that the red-shirted Ute Indian had, from a distance, pointed out the locality of a spring; but, as I have already in my journal stated, although the guide-party had spent two days in looking for it, they had not been able to find it. The consequence is that we are obliged to push on farther for a good camp-ground. The route we have come from Tyler's Springs, evidently a crooked one, in Colonel Thomas range; and besides, it makes too great a detour to the north. The true route should evidently pass the range 4 or 5 miles to the south of us, and the indications are, there would be no difficulty. The guide, though he has examined these passes twice, has bungled a great deal to-day. At half past 9 a. m., being about 5 miles in advance of column, hurrying on alone over the desert to the east of Thomas range to examine a pass ahead, I heard a halloa from some one in rear, whom I found to be Mr. McCarthy. He brought me the intelligence that Stevenson had returned and reported a small spring and some grass to the right of the route we were pursuing, and about 6 miles from the train; also another spring, or rather a couple of springs, 6 miles beyond that again, in the mountains. In consequence of this, I immediately sent word to Lieutenant Murry to divert the train to the first mentioned spring, going there also myself. I found, however, at the locality two trifling springs of no value, the water even by digging not being sufficient for half a dozen men. Besides, it had a very poor taste.

These springs proving of no value, after resting the mules and putting in fresh ones for those broken down, we attempted to reach with our wagons the springs reported by Stevenson, 6 miles farther on. The teams, however, were too much fagged out to accomplish it, and the consequence was that late in the afternoon, after proceeding 3 miles, we were obliged to halt and encamp for the night in a locality near some triple peaks, where there was neither grass nor water. At about sundown the mules were driven to the water and grass supposed to be 3 miles distant, in two herds; Mr. Reese and Privates Shelton and Schwartz with the first, and Private Kennedy, Lambert, and one of the Mexican herders ("the old man") with the other. We have been traveling since yesterday at half-past 2, or for about 30 hours; the weather has been warm, and the mules have had no water. The consequence is that all are fagged out, and we feel that we must reach water soon, or the expedition become demoralized and we fail of getting through to Camp Floyd across the Great Salt Lake Desert by a new return-route, as I had hoped. My dependence, however, is in a higher power, and as He has never yet failed to help me in the straits of life through which I have passed, I am still encouraged to believe that He will yet conduct us safely through our trials and difficulties.

Country to-day and yesterday unusually arid and forbidding. Colonel Thomas' range a combination of trachytic and dioritic igneous rocks and some metamorphosed stratified rocks. Journey from Tyler's Springs 36.9 miles. Road good except the last 3 miles, which have been unnecessarily bad and hilly on account of our not having taken a route from the springs slightly farther to the left over the mountains than we have come. We had, this afternoon, a very copious shower of rain. Stevenson, as soon as he had pointed out to one of our men the next spring, left us to join the guide-party ahead.

July 30, *Camp No.* 30, *near Triple Peaks.*—Elevation above the sea, 5,750 feet; thermometer at 6 a. m., 62°. About 9 a. m. Kennedy came in and reported that the drove of animals he went with last evening did not reach water till this morning. Found the water-hole entirely insufficient without being dug out. Mr. Reese had left in the morning to find the other water-hole. Sent out Sergeant Miller with some shovels to enlarge spring. At 12 meridian the herd Kennedy had been with came in, and the report is that the portion Reese was with had strayed away and could not be found, my horse, which I had let him have last night, of the number. The mules which have been brought in are all put to the wagons, leaving one without a team, which of necessity we are obliged for the present to leave behind. We strike our course northeastwardly to one of the springs we hoped to reach yesterday. The animals look sorry enough, and if they do not get water soon, must perish. On our way we were met by Mr. Reese with the remaining animals. He reports he found the other spring through the happy circumstance of meeting a crippled Indian, who showed it to him, just at the time he was despairing of finding it. It is about a mile to the northwest of the first spring. After proceeding in a general northern direction 5.6 miles, or 2.6 miles farther than Stevenson said it would be, we came to one of the springs and encamped. Greatly to our disappointment I found it affording but a very small quantity of water; scarcely enough for cooking purposes. Every effort was made, however, by cleaning out the cavity, to collect the water with the greatest possible economy; but after all we could do we could only water the animals by successive bucketfuls, and that at intervals of several minutes. At this rate it was evident the animals would die before we could satisfy them. I then visited, with Lieutenants Putnam and Murry, the other spring, about a mile to the northwest, and found scarcely a pint of water in it. Prospect of watering the mules gloomy enough! Notice, bearing magnetically N. 20 E., probably 12 miles off, in the Champlin Mountains, what appears to be a creek and plenty of grass. As soon as possible send all the mules except the weakest, which can be watered here, to said creek, under care of four dragoons and eight teamsters, Mr. Reese and the old crippled Indian we have found here going along as guides. This Indian has his hip out of joint, but was perfectly willing and anxious to go if we would put him on a mule. He was therefore bodily lifted up and placed on the mule, and he went off very cheerfully. The spring which he showed us, and near which he has his wick-e-up, I call the Good Indian Spring, after this Good Samaritan Indian. Certainly such disinterestedness as he has shown deserves at least this small tribute. The anxiety he displayed in his gestures and language to get our animals to water, in our present strait, has been remarkable, and looks like a signal interposition of Providence for our relief. The greater portion of the mules have been without water since about noon day before yesterday, that is 54 hours, and they will not get any till they reach the creek, 12 miles distant, which will take four hours more. It was pitiable to-day to see them huddling together at the spring and eager to stick their noses in it, and yet of necessity forced away with the whip. Some of them were so dry as to eat the moist mud. The weather has been excessively warm, and this has added to the thirst. O, the value of water, and how little it is prized when it is to be had in abundance! These trips across our desert plains make it very plain why such value, in the days of Abraham, Isaac, and Jacob, was placed on wells.

The mountains in which we are encamped I call after Major Irvin McDowell, assistant adjutant-general. It contains an abundance of the finest kind of grass, and is covered with cedars. Its geological formation is igneous. The springs near us are represented by the good Indian as having been made by some horse-thieves (white men) about a year and a half ago.

Our route to-day was across a divide about a mile from last camp, and then down a cañon, to within a mile of Sevier Lake Desert on southeast side of these mountains, and then up a ravine across the crest again of the mountain to the north slope of cañon, leading down to Salt Lake Desert, or Sevier Lake Desert, as the dividing rim is scarcely perceptible. Road good. Journey, 5.6 miles.

This evening, about 9 o'clock, we had a shower of rain, accompanied with pretty severe thunder and lightning. The party driving the herd to water has a dark night of it.

July 31, *Camp No.* 31, *Good Indian Spring.*—Longitude, 113° 56′ 36″; latitude, 39° 46′ 09″; elevation above the sea, 5,771 feet; thermometer at 6.30 a. m., 78°. We have been enabled to water, during the night and this morning, the weak mules that have been left behind of the herd that was driven off yesterday evening. Some of them drank as many as 9 bucketfuls, and yet stuck around the spring until they were driven away. One of them, Sergeant Barr informs me, actually drank, in the course of a couple of hours, as many as 14 bucketfuls before he was satisfied. The truth is, on these dry deserts the whole system of man and beast becomes so arid and depleted, on account of the dry and, therefore, evaporating power of the air upon the fluids of the body, as to require not only a sufficiency of water to satisfy the ordinary demands of thirst, but to supply the dessication of the whole system from this cause.

The wagon which was left at our last camp was brought in to-day. Several of the mules, in their anxiety to get water, got mired in the mud-spring, and had to be hauled out. At 1 p. m. Stevenson, Sanchez, and the son of the good Indian, who had been their guide, came in, and reported they reached the south end of Rush Valley yesterday at 12 m., where Pete left them for Camp Floyd. Stevenson reports in the direction of our route ahead of us water and grass at convenient distances, and the pass across the Guyot range, to the more southern portion of Rush Valley, practicable.

Mr. Reese returned this afternoon, and reports that the herd last night, during the thunder-storm, and in the darkness of the night, in a thick grove of cedars, got separated, and, while the strong animals, under him and the good Indian, pushed forward and reached the water about 14 miles distant, the weak ones had lagged behind and had gone in another direction to find water. He thinks they will be joined together again to-day and be driven back to-morrow.

At 7 p. m. the good old Indian, crippled as he is, came in and discovered by his words and gestures that though he was very much fatigued, yet he had a good heart toward us. He made signs to us to show that his helplessness was such as to make it necessary for him to be lifted bodily from his horse. He was taken off and carried to near the cook fire, and I had a supper prepared for him. All hands feel grateful to him for his extraordinary kindness to us. He had permitted his son, who was his only support and protector, to go away with the guide-party for several days, and now he had done us the signal service, crippled as he was, to conduct our mules to water, and thus possibly save them from perishing and us from failing in this portion of our route. Of course we all felt grateful, and testified it by some presents to him and his son. The fine Spanish knife I gave him he seemed to particularly prize Believing that "Wolf's Schnapps" would prove acceptable to him as a restorative, I handed him some, but he immediately smelt of it and replied, "*No bueno*" (no good), at the same time rubbing his hip, thus indicating that he wished it to be applied there. It was so applied, much to his satisfaction. His only mode of locomotion is on his haunches and hands, just as I have seen children who could not walk propel themselves forward. Of course this mode of progression bore heavily on his hands, which were very liable to be cut by the rocks and rough sage-brush over which he was required to make his way, and he expressed a wish that a pair of gloves might be given him to protect them, which was done. In his case it was gloves that were considered highly valuable for purpose of locomotion through sage-brush; but in the case of the Go-shoot and Digger Indians generally, it is moccasins, which, on account of the great difficulty of entrapping or killing any larger animal than the rabbit, they cannot easily command. Our sympathy for the poor cripple has been such as to suggest a pair of crutches for him, and Mr. Jagiello has manufactured a pair. He is pleased with the present, but makes no attempt to use them. He is treated so much like a king that he looks upon us occasionally with a look of wonder, and seems to ask himself, "Is this attention indeed real?" and then breaks out into a laugh, in which is intermingled as much of astonishment as joy. At his request, I have permitted him to sleep in camp, the only strange Indian to whom this privilege has been granted on the trip.

August 1, *Camp No.* 31, *Good Indian Spring.*—Thermometer at 6 a. m., 66°. The old, crippled Indian is named *Quah-not.* I had him helped up this morning, and the crutches put under him, but, alas! find he cannot stand on either leg. We had thought it was only one leg that was affected, but it appears now that he is paralyzed from his loins down, and this is the reason why he has not availed himself of the crutches. His son's name is Ah-pon.

9 *a. m.*—The mules which were sent to water night before last are momentarily expected, but we think it best to get the mules we have with us to the next water as soon as possible, since the spring where we are is so small that, without the use of troughs to collect and economize the water, but few animals can be watered satisfactorily. The civil portion of my party, with three wagons, therefore, move forward, leaving the balance to follow us as soon as the other mules arrive. Pass down cañon, in a northwardly direction, through a thick grove of cedars, over a rolling country, skirting McDowell Mountains to our right, and in about seven miles reach a desert valley or plain running southeastwardly from Great Salt Lake Valley into Sevier Valley. In about two miles more, reach west foot of bench of Champlin Mountains, and encamp at half past 2 within about two miles of good and abundant water and grass in cañon of the mountains, to which the mules are driven. Journey 9.2 miles; road good. About an hour after getting into camp, Sergeant Miller passed us with the remaining portion of the herd on his way to our old camp. It appears that the herd which became separated night before last only got together this morning. The spring, creek, and cañon near our camp I call after Assistant Surgeon Thomas H. Williams, United States Army

The sunset from our camp this evening superb. The amber hue of the sky, the purple and roseate clouds in the west, and the variegated colors of the clouds in other parts of the heavens, make up a fine view.

About dark, Pete came in with a large mail from Camp Floyd, having first visited our old camp at Good Indian Spring. It was pleasant to see so large a bundle of letters and papers for me; but, alas! the black-edged envelopes of many of them showed that, since the last mail, the insatiable destroyer had been at work.

August 2, *Camp No.* 32, *Williams's Spring.*—Elevation above the sea, 4,558 feet. Thermometer at 6 a. m., 66°. At half past 2 this morning, Lieutenant Murry, with the other portion of our party, joined us. At 5 a. m., after getting breakfast, the whole party moved forward; general course eastwardly, around the southwest base of Champlin Mountains. The rim or dividing line between the Great Salt Lake Desert and Sevier Lake Desert is so slight as to be scarcely perceptible. The Champlin Mountains to our left are abundantly clothed, in the ravines, with grass, and running springs are to be seen in the same localities. Cedars are also abundant. At half past 12 we reach a creek flowing from the Champlin Mountains, upon which we encamp. This creek is four feet wide and a few inches deep; bottom, gravelly; banks four feet high. Grass in abundance on side-hills near camp. I call it after Maj. Henry Prince, paymaster United States Army. The road to-day, in places, stony and rough, and occasionally hilly, on account of ravines. Soil of main valley, areno-argillaceous; benches of mountains, gravelly and stony. The animals have been scarcely able to get the wagons to camp, so much have they suffered for the past few days on account of the absence of water and incessant traveling.

August 3, *Camp No.* 33, *Prince's Creek.*—Elevation above the sea, 5,411 feet. Thermometer at 5.30 a. m., 68½°. Start at quarter to 6, in advance of party for Camp Floyd, Pete accompanying. Continue up Prince Creek for half a mile, and then leave it to left, and pass up a branch cañon, filled with cedars, one-half mile more, to summit of pass. These cañons are of good grade. From summit of pass, by pretty good descent, get into a valley, which I call after Maj. Fitz John Porter, assistant adjutant-general. This is a fine grass valley, and is well supplied with water. It is an excellent valley for stock, both summer and winter. The grove of cedars in it, in which the cattle could take shelter during driving storms in the winter, is quite extensive and thick. I notice that Russell & Co. have a herd of cattle feeding in this and the southern portion of Skull Valley, to the north of it. Proceeding northwardly through this valley, in 2.3 miles cross Porter's Creek; 2.7 miles more brings us to the slight rim or divide between Skull Valley and Porter Valley, and 3.2 miles more to a spring, which I call after Assistant Surgeon Charles Brewer, United States Army. Turning northeast, or to the right, in 2.3 miles you reach, by a pretty good ascent, the summit of the Guyot range, by what I call Oak Pass, about 5 miles south of General Johnston's Pass. This pass leads, across the Guyot range of mountains, to Rush Valley. Chief obstacle to a road in this pass is the oak brush, which, for wagons, will have to be cut away for about half a mile, and the road will have to run in the bottom of the cañon, where it is very narrow, and, in some places, stony. A road, however, can be got through by filling the gully in some places, and enlarging in others. The descent into

Rush Valley from summit, for about sixty yards, is pretty steep; balance easy. Some little filling up of bottom of cañon and at crossings necessary, and a little cutting of oak bushes. Two miles from summit reach east foot of pass in Rush Valley. The southern and southwestern portion of this valley for 8 or 10 miles in every direction is covered with beautiful and luxuriant grass, and so are the bases of the mountains. There are some springs to the south of the pass in the valley. From east foot of pass strike northeastwardly across Rush Valley for Camp Floyd Pass, in 6.7 miles crossing Meadow Creek, a flowing stream, 4 feet wide and 6 inches deep, and along which are good camping places; in about 18 miles more attaining summit of Camp Floyd Pass, and in about three miles more, at 7.15 p. m., reaching Camp Floyd. Road to-day, except as stated, through Oak Pass, good. Journey 44.5 miles. Reported to General Johnston in person same evening.

August 4, *Camp Floyd.*—At my suggestion, by direction of General Johnston, two men, with Pete as guide, and two pack-animals, were sent out this morning to my party. They take four days' provisions for the command, and some sharp hatchets to cut away the oak brush in Oak Pass of the Guyot range. The following orders have been issued:

[Special Orders No. 64.]

HEADQUARTERS DEPARTMENT OF UTAH,
Camp Floyd, Utah, August 4, 1859.

1. The infantry portion of the escort to the topographical exploring party under Capt. James H. Simpson will be replaced by one non-commissioned officer and ten privates from the same arm of service at Camp Floyd. This detachment will be formed from those men of the command whose term of service will expire in or about the month of November.

The detachment from Company A, Second Dragoons, will continue to form part of the escort, and join the company at Fort Kearney.

Second Lieut. Alexander Murry, Tenth Infantry, will continue in command of the escort, and furnish all assistance necessary to enable Captain Simpson to perform the duties with which he is charged.

2. The command will reorganize immediately on its return to Camp Floyd, and prepare to march on the 9th instant, rationed for twenty-two days, five-sevenths of the meat-ration on the hoof.

3. The proper staff department will provide the necessary transportation and supplies.

4. Captain Simpson will dispatch a subaltern of his party over the last 100 miles of his new route, with minute instructions to straighten the portion west of Rush Valley, and establish guide-marks upon it.

A detail of one non-commissioned officer and ten dragoons, rationed for twelve days, will escort this officer. This detachment will be immediately prepared, and held ready to march on the arrival of the surveying party.

The depot quartermaster will provide the necessary transportation and material for making stakes, and also for water-troughs at a particular point which Captain Simpson will designate.

By order of Bvt. Brig. Gen. A. S. Johnston.

F. J. PORTER,
Assistant Adjutant General.

August 5, *Camp Floyd.*—Topographical party, with escort under Lieutenant Murry, reached this post this afternoon. It seems that Pete was too late in reaching Lieutenant Murry with the hatchets, the party having got through the difficult portion of Oak Pass before they met. The road through the pass has not been made as practicable for wagons as I had intended, but, in consequence of the General Johnston Pass, 5 miles farther north, being wider and therefore not so liable to obstruction by snow in the winter, and it not lengthening the route a great deal, probably my return route should have come into Rush Valley by this pass. In order to make this connection with my outward route, Lieutenant Smith has received from me, by direction of General Johnston, verbal orders to this effect, and also the following instructions in relation to the shortening the route between Tyler's Springs and William's Spring, and establishing water-troughs at the Marmaduke Spring:

CAMP FLOYD, UTAH, *August* 5, 1859.

SIR: You will to-morrow proceed to Camp No. 32, near William's Spring, on our return-route from Genoa, for the purpose of straightening the road thence to Tyler's Spring, making the Marmaduke, or, as it has been called, the Big Horn Spring, a point of the road. The distance to Marmaduke Spring from Camp No. 32 is believed to be not more than 25 miles, and, by passing through the cañon most convenient to the spring, it is conjectured the distance from it to Tyler's Spring will be about 16 miles.

You will take with you suitable stakes and guide-boards for marking out the road, as also a number of wooden troughs for the purpose of collecting and economizing the water of the Marmaduke Spring for the benefit of emigrants and other travelers. These troughs will be disposed of in the best way for the object in view, and established as firmly as may be required.

You will be escorted by a detachment of one non-commissioned officer and ten dragoons.

Messrs. Reese and Stevenson, who are acquainted with the localities, will accompany you as guides.

Fifteen days' provisions will be carried, and the deputy quartermaster has been directed from headquarters to furnish you with the necessary transportation. He will also furnish you with the troughs, stakes, and tools which will be required.

On accomplishing this duty you will return with all dispatch to this post, and after turning over your escort and quartermaster's property, join the topographical party, which will be encamped at Round Prairie, on the Timpanogos River, *en route* for Fort Leavenworth.

I am, sir, very respectfully, your obedient servant,

J. H. SIMPSON,
Captain Corps Topographical Engineers.

Lieut. J. L. K. SMITH,
Corps Topographical Engineers.

There were also issued to-day the following orders, by which it will be perceived that my instructions of April 26, before given, are so far modified as to cause me to make a reconnaissance for a practicable pass from the Timpanogos Valley, through the Uintah Mountains to Green Valley, and then return to Fort Leavenworth, via Fort Bridger:

HEADQUARTERS DEPARTMENT OF UTAH,
Camp Floyd, Utah, August 5, 1859.

SIR: As, by the time you will be able to leave this camp, the season will be too far advanced to proceed to Fort Leavenworth by the headwaters of the Arkansas, and with safety make any important explorations beyond the Wahsatch range of mountains, the commanding general directs the following modifications of your instructions of the 26th April:

That, as soon as you reorganize your party and train to adapt them to your future duties, you proceed to Round Prairie, on the Timpanogos River, whence, after establishing camp in a suitable position for recruiting your animals, you will ascertain the practicability of opening a wagon-road to Green River, through the valley of the Uintah River; then, discharging those of your guide-party no longer needed, and sending, by the guide, to the commanding general a report of the result of the examinations, you will continue to Fort Leavenworth *via* Fort Bridger, and carry out your former orders.

There is reason to believe that you will, by this examination, connect this portion of the country with the valley of White River (on east branch of Green), ascending which a practicable road can easily be made and connected, if necessary, with the trail of Colonel Loring and Captain Gunnison; but, on account of the imminent danger of being caught in the snows which fall early in the season in the elevated passes of the Rocky Mountains near the Parks, the commanding general will not risk sending you that way.

Moreover, as from the plateau of the South Park an eastern outlet for wagons has not yet been discovered, he thinks it more advisable to attempt, by special explorations up the branches of the South Platte and Arkansas, to unite by a practicable road the eastern with the western slope of the Rocky Mountains, and will suggest this course to the Secretary of War.

I am, sir, very respectfully, your obedient servant,

F. J. PORTER,
Assistant Adjutant General.

Capt. J. H. SIMPSON,
In charge of Surveying Party of Topographical Engineers.

August 6, *Camp Floyd.*—Lieutenant Smith and party left this morning, pursuant to instructions of yesterday. A party of California emigrants, with seven wagons, take, also, my return-route. I have furnished them with an itinerary. Balance of my party engaged in preparations to leave this post, in prosecution of instructions from headquarters given above.

August 7, *Camp Floyd.*—An emigrant train of about thirty wagons passed through to-day, taking my more southern route to California. Supplied them with an itinerary.

August 8, *Camp Floyd.*—Gave Dr. Hobbs, agent of Russell & Co., an itinerary of my inward route. He intends to send immediately over it a thousand head of cattle to California.

Lieutenant Murry, by virtue of the following orders, is relieved from the command of the escort of my party:

[Special Orders No. 67.]

HEADQUARTERS DEPARTMENT OF UTAH,
Camp Floyd, Utah, August 8, 1859.

Second Lieut. Alexander Murry, Tenth Infantry, being an important witness for the United States in a case before the United States district court now in session in Salt Lake City, is relieved from the operation of paragraph 1, Special Orders No. 64, from these headquarters, and, so soon as he turns over the property for which he is responsible, will report to the commanding officer of Camp Floyd.

Captain Simpson will immediately appoint an officer of his party to relieve Lieutenant Murry of his responsibilities. The senior non-commissioned officer of the escort will report to Captain Simpson for duty.

By order of Bvt. Brig. Gen. A. S. Johnston.

F. J. PORTER,
Assistant Adjutant General.

In accordance with the foregoing orders, Lieutenant Putnam has been assigned the duties of quartermaster and commissary, as follows:

OFFICE TOPOGRAPHICAL ENGINEERS, DEPARTMENT OF UTAH,
Camp Floyd, Utah, August 8, 1859.

SIR: Lieut. Alexander Murry, Tenth Infantry, having been released from the command of the escort which has been directed to accompany the Topographical Engineer party to Fort Leavenworth, and therefore of the duties of acting assistant quartermaster and of acting assistant commissary, you will act in these capacities.

Very respectfully, your obedient servant,

J. H. SIMPSON,
Captain Topographical Engineers.

Lieut. H. S. PUTNAM,
Corps Topographical Engineers.

August 9.—Left Camp Floyd at 12 m., in prosecution of orders of August 5, from headquarters Department of Utah, given above. Party and escort consist, all told, of 54 persons.

Have with us 8 quartermaster's wagons, 1 large spring wagon, 1 light ambulance, and 98 animals. Took the usually traveled road to the bridge over the Jordan; thence through the towns of Lehi, American Fork settlement, Battle Creek settlement, and valley of Timpanogos River to Round Prairie, where, August 10, we encamped. Distance from Camp Floyd 50 miles. For description of these places and the Timpanogos Valley, I extract, as follows, from my report of the route I explored and opened from Camp Floyd to Fort Bridger, under instructions from General Johnston, commanding the Department of Utah, last fall. This report is to be found in Senate Ex. Doc. No. 40, 35th Congress.

"DESCRIPTION OF THE PORTION OF THE ROUTE FROM CAMP FLOYD TO THE MOUTH OF THE TIMPANOGOS RIVER CAÑON, A DISTANCE OF 29.25 MILES.

"The route from Camp Floyd pursues a course east of north for about 9 miles, when it passes over a low ridge, and, gradually turning more eastwardly, leaves Cedar Valley, and gets into the valley of Jordan River, which river it crosses in 5 miles, by a toll-bridge sixty feet long; and thence, continuing its course eastwardly along, and 2 miles from, the foot of Utah Lake, in 2.75 miles reaches Lehi City; thence, turning gradually southwardly, and slightly diverging eastwardly from a parallelism to the shore of Utah Lake, which it leaves to the right at about an average distance of 3.5

miles, and skirting the Wahsatch Mountains on your left, in 3 miles it passes through American Fork settlement (Lake City on the maps); in 3.25 miles more Battle Creek (Pleasant Grove on the map); and in 6.25 miles, reaches the mouth of Timpanogos River Cañon, which it crosses by a good ford. Whole distance from Camp Floyd 29.25 miles.

"The road to this point, except occasionally where irrigating ditches cross it, is excellent, the only hills being those 9 miles out from Camp Floyd. The soil of Cedar Valley, as also that of Utah Valley, which is generally of a yellowish color, is of an areno-argillaceous character, superposed on sand, and the consequence is that, although containing all the elements of fertility, the rains are not of themselves copious and constant enough to keep it sufficiently moist to sustain vegetation. Where the land, therefore, cannot be irrigated, which is the case in Cedar Valley, except in two or three localities of small area, the soil, for agricultural purposes, is utterly worthless. Along the road, however, in Utah Valley, in the neighborhood of the towns named, there are extensive fields, which, on account of the irrigation they receive, are quite productive. The irrigation is made possible by the availability of the mountain streams, Dry Fork, American Fork, and Battle Creek; the waters of which are distributed in acequias or ditches, from which the fertilizing element is carried over the soil in numerous rills. The first two streams are tributary to Lake Utah, and Battle Creek loses itself in the soil before reaching the lake. It is something notable that a large number of the fields have been abandoned from the soil becoming saline by use; and it is quite possible that from this cause a large portion of it will, in time, be rendered worthless. Indeed, while the country in the Territory, as a whole, presents a very insignificant fraction of cultivable soil, that which can be cultivated experience shows is likely to become barren from use.

"The great staple is wheat, of which Mr. Bullock assures me as many as seventy-five bushels have been raised to the acre. This, however, is rare; forty bushels are more common, and generally not more than twenty. Oats and barley do well. Corn does not mature sufficiently, on account of the early frosts of autumn, and therefore but little is planted. Potatoes and garden vegetables generally grow quite luxuriantly. Fruits like the melon, peach, and apricot mature tolerably well, and the apple also grows here, but as yet I have seen none to assure me that they at all equal those which can be raised in the States. It is also to be borne in mind, in the cultivation of the cereals, vegetables, and fruits, that frequent irrigation is necessary; and to this, of course, is superadded all the other labor of tillage, which makes the aggregate of work necessary to make the soil produce to any advantage, excessive. The fields are generally inclosed by mud walls, which not unfrequently give evidences of dilapidation.

"The ordinary tract of land owned and cultivated by a single hand is twenty acres, though larger tracts are owned and cultivated by those who can afford to buy more and command the necessary labor. There is grass along the route, except on the Jordan, and no wood. The fuel which is used by the inhabitants of the towns named is brought from the cañons in the mountains at a very great expense. Forage and fuel, however, are purchasable by the Government.

"Lehi City is a walled town, containing probably 100 houses and 1,000 inhabitants. The houses are of *adobes* (sun-dried bricks), and in some instances of logs. The appearance of the town is rather indifferent, and indicates no great thrift."

"American Fork settlement (Lake City) has some 50 houses and probably some 500 inhabitants. The houses are generally adobe, quite small, and of but one story, all indicating a poor and shiftless population."

"Battle Creek settlement contains probably 60 houses, all small, mean-looking adobe huts, and the population is about 600. A very common mode of building in these towns is to take the earth from the foundation of the building to make the adobes, and thus have one story below and one above ground. The generality of the houses is far below in character what obtains among the poorest of our population in the States. The roofs are generally of mud, and give frequent evidences of tumbling in; and the doors and windows all indicate penury and an inattention to cleanliness."

"Provo is a city in the valley of Lake Utah, about 5 miles south of the Timpanogos Cañon. It derives its name, according to Mr. Bullock, from a Frenchman of that name from Saint Louis, who was the first white man that ever came from Fort Bridger by way of the Timpanogos Valley.* The Timpanogos River has been, therefore, known among the inhabitants as the Provo River, and hence the origin of the name of the town near. It is much better built than the towns I have described. The guide who lives there, says it contains about 400 houses and probably 600 families, 7 to a family, or about 4,200 inhabitants in the whole town; to me rather a large estimate. It, like the other towns I have seen in Utah, is built principally of adobes; the houses, however, being generally small. Each town has a large building, which they call the tabernacle, and which is devoted to religious and secular purposes; the theater, I noticed, being held in one of them. The main street of Provo is probably eight rods wide, the others six. This town, like all the others I have described, is laid out in regular squares. They are all inhabited by farmers, who cultivate the land contiguous to the town, and the yards are filled with the implements of husbandry, stacks of wheat and hay; and in the evening, during harvest, there is to be seen a constant succession of wagons, filled with the produce of the field, and cattle driven in for security. The inhabitants send out their cattle in herds to pasture, the herdsman passing in the morning from one end of the town to the other, and as he does so, sounding his horn as a signal for the owners to turn their stock into the general herd. The charge is about two cents per animal per day."

"FROM THE MOUTH OF TIMPANOGOS CAÑON TO THE TOP OF THE DIVIDE BETWEEN THE TIMPANOGOS AND SILVER CREEK, 31.5 MILES.†

"The Timpanogos River is a splendid dashing mountain-stream of pure water of a width ranging in places from 30 to 100 feet, and generally about 2 feet deep. Large trout are found in it. Its bottom is rocky. Its sources are in the Uintah Mountains, from which it flows for about half its length (which probably is 60 miles) in a westerly

* The name of this person was probably Pro-vost (pronounced Provo), and is doubtless the same referred to in Mr. Anderson's letter, inserted in note (E) of Introduction.

† For an interesting account of the Timpanogos River Valley, Weber River Valley, and White River Valley, see Captain Beckwith's report of his reconnaissance between Great Salt Lake City and Green River, in the spring of 1854. (Pacific Railroad Reports, vol. ii.)

direction, and then, breaking through the Wahsatch Mountains, in a southwest direction for the balance of the way (30 miles) into Utah Lake. The road, after crossing the river by ford at the mouth of the cañon, takes up its valley, which is deeply cañoned for about 7 miles above its debouchment into Utah Lake Valley. The rocks on either side, commensurate with the cañon, especially on the south, are magnificent, and, encroaching as they do very nearly on the stream, show themselves in their full proportions. Those on the south side have their escarpments very nearly vertical, while those on the north are girted at their base by terraces of narrow breadth. About 4 miles up the cañon, on its south side, may be seen a beautiful perennial waterfall of from 800 to 1,000 feet in height, and, coming as it does from such an altitude, and apparently fed by nothing, it is an object of a great deal of interest. I have called it on the map Beautiful Cascade. Through this cañon, and 5 miles farther, say for a distance of 12 miles from its mouth, there is at present a road which the people of the Territory constructed last spring and summer. Previous to the opening of this road, persons could pass only upon horseback along an Indian trail; the rocky promontories or points of the confining walls, as well as the narrowness of the cañon, effectually obstructing wheel-carriages. A company of citizens, however, have, by dint of great labor, cut through these promontories, made deep excavations along the steep, and in many instances rocky, side-hills, and have built up revetted embankments; the consequence of which is they have an excellent mountain-road, and one that does them a great deal of credit. The width of the roadway, however, in many places and for considerable distances, is not sufficient for teams to pass each other, and the turns are sometimes so short that heavy six-yoke ox-teams are liable, except the driver use the greatest care, to capsize into the stream below. The drainage of the mountain streams and rills from the upper side of the road is defective, and the consequence is that pools of water have been allowed to collect in the road, and the road at these places made boggy. With these defects obviated the road would be as good as is to be found anywhere. It was constructed by the inhabitants to open the communication to Round Prairie (an expansion of Timpanogos Valley, 14 miles above the mouth of the cañon), and to enable the people of Provo to carry away the wood found along the river and in the side cañons. About 1 mile above the mouth of the cañon the road crosses the Timpanogos by an excellent bridge, 60 feet long. The tolls upon the road are here collected, and, as it is of interest to know the rates, I here insert a notice which I saw stuck up on the post of the toll-gate:

Rates of toll on the Provo Cañon road.

For one cord of wood or timber hauled out	$1 00
For one pair of horses, mules, and carriage	50
For one horse, mule, and rider	10
Cattle, horses, or mules, driven up or down, for each head	05
Sheep and hogs	03
For each load of brick or hay	1 00

The above is a correct list of rates of toll as fixed by the county court. And all persons are hereby notified and instructed that no one will be permitted to travel the road without an order from Bishop E. H. Blackburn, and the gatekeeper will take due notice of the above instructions, and govern himself accordingly.

Done by order of the county court of Utah County:

E. H. Blackburn,
General Agent.

"In this connection I think it proper to say that no permission was asked by me to go through the cañon, and no objections were made; and this I believe has been the experience of all the Government and contractor's trains which have passed over the route.

"To resume my account of the route. Four miles from the mouth of the cañon is the first sufficiently wide place for a small command to encamp, and here will be found plenty of grass. Two miles farther is the first sufficiently wide place for ox-teams to corral, and grass also exists here in abundance. Indeed, from this point as far as the road extends along the Timpanogos, a distance of 23 miles, at short distances can be found most excellent camping-places for the largest commands and trains. The river is well timbered from the mouth of the cañon up, and there is every other requisite needed.

"As I have before remarked, the turnpike extends from the mouth of the cañon for a distance of 12 miles. Thence the route continues along the Timpanogos, crossing it about a mile above Wall's ranch, and through Round Prairie for a distance of 10 miles, when it enters another cañon, or, rather, narrow valley, 4 miles long, where the river is in places obstructed for about 3 miles by beaver-dams and where the road for a few hundred yards is rather soft. This cañon gone through and the line crossed again, the route leaves the main Timpanogos and, passing along a small tributary, in 4.5 miles commences going up the divide between the Timpanogos and Silver Creek, and in a distance of 1.5 miles, with a pretty fair grade and on rather a stony slope, reaches the summit. The principal timber on the creek is the oak, cottonwood, box-elder, sugar-maple, birch, and willow. Pine and the fir-tree are to be seen on the mountains. Currants, red and black; the sweet sarvisberry, and a blue berry like the small winter grape, and which the Mormons call the mountain grape, are found in considerable quantities in the valley.

"In Round Prairie, near where Rattlesnake Creek debouches from the mountains, on the north side of the valley, are to be seen a number of hot springs, the highest point the thermometer indicating in any one of them being 109°.50. These springs, which are of great depth, well up from the surface, and, running over, deposit a residuum or tufa, which accumulates about their mouths and forms tumuli, in one instance of about 60 feet in height and 200 feet in diameter at base. These tumuli are hemispherical in some instances, and in others conical, and after attaining a certain height the water ceases to flow, and the walls begin to disintegrate and tumble down, and are eventually lost in the general level of the country.

"For several miles the substratum, for a depth in some places of 60 feet, as far as could be discovered, was composed entirely of this calcareous rock, and there is no doubt it is entirely due to an origin of the same sort. Rattlesnakes abound about these springs, and in a warm summer's day you cannot tread near some of them without hearing their sharp rattle. Traces of coal are to be seen in the lower cañon, near its mouth, and the guide informs me that he has picked up specimens in the creek, which, on that account, has been called Coal Creek. The Timpanogos Valley is remarkably well watered, and the traveler will be greatly pleased, particularly on a hot summer's day, with the many cold, gushing, pure streams which he will cross, all flowing into the Timpanogos.

"The grass, particularly in Round Prairie, where there is a great deal of meadow land, is abundant, and I know no place where stock could be better fed, sheltered, and watered during summer and winter. Already have stock-grazers gone into this valley and secured a considerable quantity of hay for the winter. The soil is, a great deal of it, of excellent character, and, as it is capable of being easily irrigated, I doubt not it will prove very productive."

I would add to the foregoing that Mr. Wall, who has a ranch at the lower portion of Round Prairie, informs me that, on the night of the 7th August last, a frost killed all the vines, corn, and vegetables he had planted as an experiment to see if they would mature in this valley. The spring wheat and oats were not injured, though the former is backward. He is confident that fall wheat, oats, barley, and rye will mature. Has 1,000 head of sheep and 2,000 head of cattle grazing in the valley. It is a singular circumstance that, higher up the valley, in Round Prairie, at Heber City, the frost has not proved near so destructive, it having as yet done little or no damage. The elevation of Round Prairie above the sea is 5,571 feet. Longitude, 111° 25′ 56″; latitude, 40° 29′ 25″.

August 12, *Camp on Torbert's Creek, Round Prairie.*—Elevation above the sea, 5,786 feet. Thermometer at 5.30 a. m., 43°. Having established my main camp at this point, I leave this morning to examine pass over Uinta range into Green River Valley, agreeably to orders of General Johnston of August 5th. Take with me one of my assistants, Mr. Henry Engelmann, (geologist and meteorologist,) ten dragoons, Mr. James Gammell, as guide, Ute Pete, Clark, and Dougherty, in all sixteen persons, with three pack-mules. After being engaged nine days in this reconnaissance, I returned to the main camp August 19, and reported the next day, as follows, to General Johnston:

"CAMP, TORBERT CREEK, ROUND PRAIRIE,
TIMPÁNOGOS VALLEY, UTAH TERRITORY, *August* 20, 1859.

"SIR: Agreeably to the orders of the commanding general of the 5th instant, I left Camp Floyd with my party on the 9th, reorganized for its return to the States, and prepared to make, on its arrival at this camp, the examination required in said orders, of the country intervening this and the Uinta Valley for the ascertainment of the practicability of a wagon-road hence to Green River.

"I arrived here on the 11th; started on the explóration referred to the next day, and returned last evening. My course was about northeast 4.5 miles to mouth of Coal Creek Cañon; thence, magnetically south 65° east, up the cañon of Coal Creek about twelve miles, to summit of divide of the Uinta Mountains; elevation above the sea, 9,680 feet; thence down the valley of Potts's Fork,* generally north 70° east, 24 miles, to its junction with Du Chesne's Fork of the Uinta River; elevation above the sea, 6,814 feet; and thence, generally south 70° east, down the valley of the Du Chesne 39 miles, to its junction with the Uinta River. Longitude, 110° 20′ 33″; latitude, 40° 09′ 50″. Elevation above the sea, 5,345 feet. Whole distance from mouth of Coal Creek Cañon to the Uinta River, 75 miles. Here my examination ended, on

* This fork is a branch of Du Chesne's Fork, and I have called it after the lamented Lieut. E. Kane Potts, Seventh Infantry, who died at Camp Floyd April 23, 1859. He was a bright young officer, and greatly beloved by his brother officers and the soldiers.

account of the dragoon-horses of the escort, all except one, giving out, and, of neces sity, having been left behind, 10 miles. Their crippled condition was produced by the extraordinarily rough, steep, and stony character of the reconnaissance from Round Prairie over the Uinta Mountains as far as the Du Chesne. It is gratifying to report that I found the pass of the Uinta range, by the way of Coal Creek Cañon and Potts's Fork of the Du Chesne, the route I explored, a most excellent one. The grade from Round Prairie to the summit of the Uinta range is quite good, and thence down to the Du Chesne's Fork and to the Uinta still better. The route, however, is at present far from being practicable for wagons, and not even is it practicable for pack-mules without the very greatest tax upon man and animals; the most difficult and laborious reconnaissance I ever have made being from Round Prairie to the Fork of the Du Chesne, rendered so by willow, aspen, and fir thickets, and by steep and rocky precipices and ridges. It is not to be wondered that Mr. Gammell, the guide, in his previous examination of the route, was obliged to leave his horse on account of its crippled condition, and came near losing another.

"The principal work required for the passage of wagons will be the removal of the fallen and standing timber, and willows in the bottom of Coal Creek Cañon, from its mouth to within about a couple of miles of the summit of the pass, say for about 9 miles; the removal of the willows in Potts's Fork, from about 3 miles from the summit all the way down, about 21 miles, to the fork of the Du Chesne, and the causewaying of the miry places in the bottom of this creek, caused principally by beaver-dams. In the valley of the Du Chesne there will be required about 6 miles of not very heavy cutting through cottonwood and brush, and some grading, to pass over several tolerably deep gullies.

"My examination of Coal Creek Cañon and Valley extended to the exploration of three parallel routes which presented themselves, to wit, the swale or vale under the mountain ridge to the north side of the creek; the swale under the mountain ridge to the south side of the creek; and the bottom of the creek or cañon itself. The last, or that in the bottom of the creek, will require more work than the swale on the south side; but when done will make the best grade and road. The next best route, and requiring, perhaps, the least work, is the swale on the south side of the creek.

"My examination also extended to the three branches or cañons from the summit of the Uinta Pass, leading into the cañon of Potts's Fork. The best are the middle and most northern; either of which may be taken.

"I have already stated that my exploration, of necessity, stopped short of Green River, having terminated at the junction of the Du Chesne's Fork with the Uinta River. I consider, however, the reconnaissance conclusive as to the ascertainment of a pass from the valley of the Timpanogos to the Uinta River; and from the plateau or table character of the country, thence east to Green River, which could be very well seen, the practicability of the valley of the Uinta where I struck it, and the assurance of the guide, whose report of the route, as far as I have gone, except as to distance, I have found correct in every particular, that the valley of the Uinta grew still wider and better for a road in proportion as it approached Green River, I have not the slightest doubt that a good wagon road can be made all the way from Round Prairie to Green River, and that the principal work required will be that which I have already specified.

"I consider the discovery of this pass, in connection with the Timpanogos route through the Wahsatch range, a most fortunate one, and doubt not it will end in the formation of a wagon-route all the way through the Rocky Mountains, which will greatly ameliorate the present traveled routes, and be of great service in the extension of my lately explored route from California eastward by way of Denver City to the States.

"I am preparing to leave for Fort Leavenworth to-morrow morning.

"I am, major, very respectfully, your obedient servant,

"J. H. Simpson,
"*Captain Corps Topographical Engineers.*

"Major F. J. Porter,
"*Assistant Adjutant General, Camp Floyd, Utah Territory.*"

would add to the foregoing that the route, as far as the Uinta River, is quite well wooded: on Coal Creek Cañon with cottonwoods and fir trees; on Potts' Creek with the fir, and on the Du Chesne with the cottonwood and dwarf cedar. I would also remark that the valley of the Du Chesne, which varies from a quarter to two miles wide, is a great deal of it cultivable, and as it lies well for irrigation is well watered, and probably warm enough for crops. I doubt not when it shall have been made accessible by a good wagon-road it will rapidly fill up with population. The valley of the Uinta, Mr. Gammell represents as also being very fine, all the way to Green River, being covered with groves of large cottonwood, beautiful grass, and so lying as to be easily irrigated. It is, besides, accounted as one of the warmest valleys in the Territory. He says it is from one to ten miles wide. Both the Du Chesne Fork and the Uinta River, where they meet, are about 50 feet wide, and from one to three feet deep. The former is said to contain trout and white-fish, the white-fish weighing from 10 to 25 pounds. The valleys of these rivers are deeply seated between inclosing heights, varying from 200 to 500 feet. The formation of the rocks is like that of White Clay Creek, whitish sandstones alternating with sandstone shales.

Besides the value of the discovery of this pass, in connection with the extension of my routes, and the establishment of the magnetic telegraph from California directly eastward, through the Rocky Mountains, via Denver City, or some other Pike's Peak country town, to the States, and thus shortening the present postal route from Camp Floyd to Saint Joseph from 60 to 100 miles, the construction of the road will be of great value in opening an avenue of trade between the Mormon settlements and the Pike's Peak country, by which the produce of the former may be conveyed to the latter, much to the benefit of the miners.

It will be also noticed that a link of about 100 miles, between the mouth of Du Chesne's Fork and Gunnison's route, along the Grand River, which the guide says is practicable, will open a route to the headwaters of the Arkansas, and to Santa Fé from Camp Floyd; which will be much shorter, and, doubtless, in other respects much preferable to the present roundabout route, by the way of Salt Creek and the Sevier Valley.

Pete says the Indians call the Uinta the Pow-up. He does not know its meaning. The Du Chesne, which they call the Kopes-se-parge, or Smoky Fork, according to them, is a tributary of the Ke-air-re-gan, which comes from the northeast into the Du Chesne, about 13 miles above its junction with the Uinta, and carries its name all the way to the Uinta. The two streams, at their junction, are about the same in size. The bull-berry is very abundant in the valley of the Du Chesne, and as the bear is very fond of them, the signs of these animals are very fresh and frequent. I have noticed also the prairie dog; the location being the most western limit of these animals I have observed. The branch of the Uinta, called on the maps Lake Fork, the Indians call Whi-tum-bitch, or Yellow Rock Creek. I have inquired of Pete the meaning of Uinta. He thinks it may possibly have come from the word U-umph, which means, a sort of pine common to the Uinta range.

On my return to main camp, August 19, found Lieutenants Murry and Smith had just arrived and joined the party. The former has joined the expedition again, agreeably to the following orders:

[Special Orders No. 72.]

HEADQUARTERS DEPARTMENT OF UTAH,
Camp Floyd, Utah, August 17, 1859.

Second Lieut. Alexander Murry, Tenth Infantry, will join and take command of the escort to the exploring party under Captain Simpson, Topographical Engineers.

The depot quartermaster will provide the necessary transportation for Lieutenant Murry and Lieut. J. L. Kirby Smith, Topographical Engineers, and his party, now at this post.

By order of Bvt. Brig. Gen. A. S. Johnston:

F. J. PORTER,
Assistant Adjutant-General.

August 20, *Camp, Torbert's Creek, Round Prairie.*—Thermometer at 7 a. m., 65°. I have received, to-day, from Lieutenant Smith the following report, in fulfillment of my instructions, given to him at Camp Floyd, August 5:

CAMP ROUND PRAIRIE, UTAH, *August* 20, 1859.

CAPTAIN: I have the honor to submit the following report of the fulfillment of your instructions to me, dated Camp Floyd, Utah Territory, August 5, 1859, a copy of which is herewith inclosed. In obedience to those instructions I left Camp Floyd on the 6th instant, reaching Meadow Creek, in Rush Valley, the same evening. I was provided with four large troughs, destined to collect the water of Marmaduke Spring, and with the tools and material for erecting guide-boards to mark the new and direct trail. On the morning of the 7th I moved west, through Johnston's Pass, to its west foot. Here, as directed by you, I left the beaten road, and, turning to the left, moved up a ravine which leads into Johnston's Pass from the south, and furnishes a path thence into the ravine of Brewer's Spring and Creek. The distance by the odometer from the point where I left Johnston's Pass to the point where I struck the ravine of Brewer's Creek is eight miles and four-tenths. The trail over this portion of the route is tolerably direct, but it is somewhat hilly in its southern half, crossing a number of ravines, which presented themselves at right angles and could not be turned without too great a detour. From the point where I struck the ravine of Brewer's Creek I moved up that ravine to your recent return-trail from California, a distance of three miles. I encamped near here on the 7th; Mr. Reese, the guide, whom I had sent forward in the morning to examine a supposed pass through the Champlin Mountains, returned at night and reported it impracticable for wagons.

On the 8th I proceeded by your trail to the point three miles from William's Spring, alluded to in your letter of instructions as camp "No. 32." On the morning of the 9th three mules from one of the teams were found to be missing, and the day was passed in an unsuccessful attempt to find them. Leaving Stephenson, one of the guides, with my mule, to continue the search for the lost animals, I moved on at nightfall for Marmaduke or Big Horn Spring. I followed your trail for about a mile and a half, and then diverged from it to the right. Our road now lay through the range of hills in which Indian Spring is situated, and was necessarily somewhat tortuous, though its general direction was nearly correct. I halted when the moon set (about midnight), and continued the march on the morning of the 10th. We soon emerged from the hills and moved west of south across the valley west of Good Indian Spring, reaching Marmaduke Spring about 3 p. m. We found here, by digging, sufficient water for our immediate wants, but the holes soon ceased to fill up, and the water gave out entirely before night. It seemed evident to me, on examination of the locality, that the supposed spring at this point was nothing more than a reservoir of rain-water, retained in a natural basin of rocks and protected from evaporation by the sand which fills the basin. I found the distance from the camp near William's Spring to this point to be 24.4 miles, verifying nearly your previous estimate.

On the 11th I proceeded to Tyler's Spring by the most direct route possible, finding a good pass through the mountain west of Big Horn Spring. I improved Tyler's Spring by digging several new reservoirs there, and on the 12th commenced my return. I adopted a pass through the mountain west of Big Horn Spring, a little north of the pass I used going out, and preferable to it in some respects. Being forced to abandon Big Horn Spring as a camping or watering place, it seemed necessary to make the Good Indian Spring a point of the route, and I decided to carry the troughs thither. I sent Mr. Reese forward, accordingly, to ascertain the best route to Indian Spring. He found a very direct eligible route thither, and we reached that point on the morning of the 13th instant. The distance from Tyler's Spring to Good Indian Spring, by the trail I followed, is 35 miles. I remained at the latter spring during the 13th and 14th, placing the troughs and perfecting their arrangement as far as possible. On the night of the 14th Stephenson arrived, with the lost mules.

I left Good Indian Spring on the 15th, following your trail to within two and a half miles of Camp No. 32, near William's Spring. Here I diverged to the right, striking your trail again about two miles this side of the camp near William's Spring, cutting off between one and two miles of the distance from Indian Spring to Prince's Creek, and reducing that distance to 16 miles. I adopted no further changes in the route I pursued going out, from Prince's Creek to Camp Floyd, which post I reached on the 17th instant. Wherever the trail I adopted intersected or diverged from any other wagon-trail, the route to Carson's Valley was indicated by a guide-board, and if the other fork was a trail which I had abandoned, it was ditched across and further obstructed by sage or cedar brush.

A party of emigrants, with six wagons, overtook me going out, near William's Spring, and followed my outward trail to Tyler's Spring. Returning I met upon the proper trail five other parties, having in all, I should think, about thirty wagons, and one herd of cattle numbering a thousand head. I gave them all such information as they required about the route ahead of them, and have no doubt they followed the trail I recommended to Tyler's Spring, making that the most marked and best beaten road.

In compliance with your instructions I have added to your itinerary of the route from Genoa to Tyler's Spring my notes of the route from that point to Camp Floyd.

I am, sir, very respectfully, your obedient servant,

J. L. KIRBY SMITH,
Second Lieutenant Topographical Engineers.

Capt. J. H. SIMPSON,
Corps of Topographical Engineers.

The day spent in reporting by letter to General Johnston result of expedition to Uinta Valley (report given above), and preparing for return to Fort Leavenworth, via Fort Bridger.

August 21, *Camp Torbert's Creek, Round Prairie.*—Whole party decamped this morning, on its return to the States. Course up the valley of the Timpanogos. Having reached the point where the road leaves the main branch of the Timpanogos, we encamped. Journey 14 miles. Since my exploration of this valley last fall a small settlement called Heber City, containing ten families, has sprung up in Round Prairie. The frost, two weeks since, nipped the potatoes here, but did not permanently injure them; they are still growing finely, and already some are eatable and have been sold in our camp.

Lieutenant Swaine and family arrived, on their way to Camp Floyd, this afternoon, and have encamped near us.

August 22, *Camp, bend of Timpanogos River.*—Longitude, 111° 26′ 03″ ; latitude, 40° 36′ 15″ ; thermometer at 8.30 a. m., 64°. Wishing to see if my route to Fort Bridger from Camp Floyd, via Timpanogos, Weber, and White Clay Creek Valleys, opened last fall, can be shortened, I have directed Lieutenant Murry to proceed with the main party and wagon-train, independently of me, to Fort Bridger, by that route, and I take a party of seven persons, including my assistant, Mr. Englemann, with two pack-animals, for the purpose of exploring a more direct route by the way of Kamas Prairie, the east fork of the Weber and one of its tributaries, across to the head of White Clay Creek, or Bear River.

I reached Fort Bridger with my party August 26, and find that Lieutenant Murry with the train and main party had reached there the day before. As my report to

General Johnston of the results of my side reconnaissance is sufficiently explicit, I insert an extract from it below instead of the journal. I refer the reader to my published report, before adverted to, to be found in Senate Executive Document No. 40, Thirty-fifth Congress, Second session, for a detailed account of my route of last fall, pursued by Lieutenant Murry, as also of Kamas Prairie, and other portions of country contiguous. I met Lieutenant-Colonel Chapman, Fifth Infantry, with a battalion of recruits and train of wagons, on my route between the Muddy and Sulphur Creeks, and he expressed himself as being very much pleased, as far as he had gone on it from Fort Bridger.

FORT BRIDGER, UTAH,
August 27, 1859.

MAJOR: I have the honor to report that, wishing to improve if possible my route of last fall from Camp Floyd to Fort Bridger, by avoiding the worst portion of it, White Clay Creek, in whole or in part, I left the main portion of my party *en route*, in Timpanogos Valley, for Fort Bridger, August 22, and with an escort of four dragoons, three civil employés, and a couple of guides, who professed, each, to know different portions of the country, proceeded to make the exploration requisite for the purpose. Our provisions and necessary equipage were carried on two pack-mules.

I found a feasible wagon-route as follows:

Leave my old route at a point in Timpanogos Valley, in sight of where the road commences to ascend the steep portion of the divide between the Timpanogos and Silver Creeks, that is, about a mile below the foot of the ascent; from this point pass up on the top of a low spur, with good and regular grade, to near summit; and thence, by taking advantage of the swales or vales of the divide, pass along their sides to the summit of the divide, 2.5 miles from the branch of the Timpanogos you have left; elevation above the sea, 6,955 feet; thence taking down a ravine of good grade (general direction east), which widens gradually into a fine, wide vale, full of grass, in 3 miles you reach Kamas Prairie, 6,244 feet above the sea; thence in a course very nearly direct to the mouth of the cañon of the east branch of Weber (bearing slightly to the right of it), in about 7.25 miles, you cross Kamas Prairie over very good ground, and reach the east fork of Weber, which you ford; thence pass up the cañon of this fork of Weber 8.5 miles, about a mile of it through thick aspen timber, the balance, principally in the bottom, covered with willows, which, however, are not large; thence you leave the Weber and turn to the left up a rather narrow cañon, which I call Clarke's Cañon, after Captain Clarke of the Subsistence Department, where some cutting would be necessary through aspen and willows thickets, and two or three small points of hills should be taken off with the pick and shovel; 4.5 miles up this cañon, with tolerable grade, brings you to the summit of the pass of the high range between the Weber and the heads of White Clay Creek; elevation of summit above the sea, 8,953 feet; thence, turning gradually to the right, skirt closely for 9.25 miles the high ridge of the mountain range, keeping just below it and crossing through aspen thickets, a number of the heads of the tributaries of White Clay Creek, you are brought over a very steeply-rolling and rich country to the main branch of White Clay Creek; thence, in 3.5 miles, down this main branch, with good grade, you connect at the lower end of the upper cañon of White Clay Creek with my wagon-road of last fall. This is one connection. Another would be, not to go down entirely to the old road, but, passing down the branch only about a mile, to cross it and, turning by a heavy side-cut for about 100 yards up a high ridge on the right, strike over so as to join the old road about 8 or 9 miles above the point of junction with old road above mentioned. The first connection would shorten the present Timpanogos route about 7 miles; the second about 12.

The first route could be opened by any command equal to a company in twenty days between Fort Bridger and Camp Floyd. The second would require a day or two longer.

In respect to the character of the route it would be shorter as stated than my old route, and the bottom of the Weber, though moist and principally covered with willows, would furnish a drier road than White Clay Creek bottom; but the objections to it are that, though the grass along it might prove sufficient, yet for 9 miles along the north side of the range, between the Weber and White Clay Creek, the road would be exceedingly hilly, and, as the soil is very rich, would cut up considerably until it could become packed by use. Another objection is that, on this high mountain range, the road could not be used early in the spring or late in the fall, on account of snow.

Taking the advantages and disadvantages together, and the fact that during dry weather my road of last fall down the valley of White Clay Creek is as good a one in every respect, almost, as needs be, as all who will travel over it at such times, I think, will testify; and that when the country is wet the newly proposed route would be almost, if not quite, as exceptionable on that account as the old, and the trains would in preference take the old Echo Cañon route as far as the Weber, and then turn up the Weber to join my Timpanogos route; it is scarcely, I think, expedient that the route I have just explored should be opened, at least by the troops.

Lieutenant Murry and Lieutanant Putnam report that they had not the slightest difficulty in getting the train of my party over my White Clay Creek route, and the fact that the traveling time from Camp Floyd to Fort Bridger was only 8.5 days, and that in every instance they got into camp before 6 in the afternoon, are evidences in favor of the route.

There is a slough, however, about one-fourth of a mile to the east of the main branch of Bear River which should be corduroyed or causewayed with logs without delay. Ten men, with two wagons and sharp axes, might do it on the ground in two days. This done, in ordinary dry weather the road will be a very good one, and by some considerable outlay in causewaying in places in the bottom of White Clay Creek it could be made a good road at all times.

I regret to say that in my reconnaissance I lost a dragoon horse and one mule, which could not be turned back to camp, in a thick aspen thicket after dark. Every exertion was made to recover them, I stopping a day for the purpose, but with no avail. The guides have promised, if possible, on their return to find them, and one of them to take them into Camp Floyd, as well as a pack-saddle I was obliged to leave. The names of these guides are Charles E. Colton and Hiram Oakes. They live at Heber City in Round Prairie, and either of them, if called upon, would show the route I have described.

It might be best, instead of taking up the bottom of the Clarke's Cañon from the

Weber to the Uinta Divide, to run the road up, and on top of, the ridge on either side of the cañon, as might be found expedient.

I expect to leave for Fort Leavenworth Monday morning, the 29th instant.

I am, major, very respectfully, your obedient servant,

J. H. SIMPSON,
Captain Corps Topographical Engineers.

Major F. J. PORTER,
Assistant Adjutant-General, Camp Floyd, Utah.

August 27, *Fort Bridger.*—Longitude, 110° 23′ 47″; latitude, 41° 20′ 23″; altitude above the sea, 6,656 feet; thermometer at 5.30 a. m., 37°.5. Replenishing supplies and preparing for a move on the 29th.

August 28, *Fort Bridger.*—Lieutenant-Colonel Canby, the commanding officer of this post, informs me that oats, spring wheat, barley, potatoes, and turnips, grow well in this locality; beets tolerably well. The sutler, Judge Carter, has a farm at Camp Supply, 12 miles higher up, on Smith's Creek, where agriculture does better than at this point, owing, as it is supposed, to the winds in that direction keeping off the frost. The season this summer, however, has been much better than usual, more rain having fallen than was ever known before.

Colonel Canby has had a saw-mill put up by the soldiers, made up of the parts of two mills, which saws 4,000 feet per day, and the cost per 1,000 feet does not exceed $10.

To-day a train of about 100 hand-carts passed the fort, drawn by Mormon men and women, all having a sort of harness suitable for the work. I did not see it, but the officers who did pronounced it a most lamentable sight.

August 29, *Fort Bridger.*—My party left this morning, in prosecution of its march eastward to Leavenworth, via South Pass. Arrived at Fort Laramie September 17, Fort Kearney October 3, and Fort Leavenworth October 15. As this route has been so frequently reported on by others it will be unnecessary for me to say anything in relation to it.

I think it proper, however, to record the singular meteorological phenomenon, which I witnessed on the Big Sandy, on the night of the 1st of September, and I do it by inserting the letter I addressed to Professor Henry, Secretary of the Smithsonian Institution, on the subject.

"CAMP NO. 33, NORTH FORK OF PLATTE RIVER,
"SIX HUNDRED AND NINETY-TWO MILES FROM CAMP FLOYD,
"EN ROUTE TO FORT LEAVENWORTH, *September* 23, 1859.

"DEAR SIR: Although keeping a meteorological diary in my reconnaissance, which may eventually be brought to your notice, yet it has occurred to me that the remarkable phenomenon I witnessed on the night of the 1st of September instant, on the Big Sandy, a branch of Green River, in latitude about 42° north, and longitude 109° 50′ west of Greenwich, ought to be brought to your attention at once, so that it may be used in any comparison you might wish to make of like phenomenon which might have been noticed before or at the same period in other portions of the globe.

"I had retired to bed and gone to sleep, when waking up and perceiving it quite light and no one stirring in camp, I began to think that the cooks had not been called by the guard, and that we were likely to have a late start for the day. Taking up my watch, which was lying on the table near me, I could distinctly read on its metallic face the time of the night, and, to my surprise, found it was only 11 o'clock. Before I went to bed, about 9 o'clock, the moon had set, and I recollected that it was with some difficulty I had been able to discern the figures of a couple of my assistants who were taking astronomical observations, though they were not far from me. These facts were curious, and I leaped to the front of my tent to clear up the matter. As soon as I looked out the anomaly was explained. About two-thirds of the whole southern celestial concave was one sheet of beautiful roseate light.

"For a while the light continued in a state of repose, the most concentrated portion forming a belt, and extending from a point on the horizon a few degrees north of east (about 10) clear across the heavens to a point on the horizon about due west. From this belt the light, with its roseate hue, was diffused southwardly all over the heavens, with marked distinctness, down to the arc of a circle, the angle of whose plane with the horizon was about 10 degrees.

"For a period, as stated, the phase of the phenomenon appeared constant; it then changed gradually, alternately varying to a less or greater intensity, the rosy light still remaining diffused. At length, however, the light assumed a more intense form and shot up in whitish coruscations from the base or lower limit of the illuminated portion to the apex or crown, which was about 20° to the south of the zenith; the appearance of the concave all this while being that of an illuminated globe divided into an innumerable number of meridians, and the vanishing-point or apparent pole the apex referred to.

"At the time of the phenomenon, I observed the magnetic needle, but could not perceive that it was sensibly affected by it. It being, however, only a pocket one, it could not, of course, be capable of expressing any but very large perturbations.

"The phenomenon was so extraordinary and beautiful that I called up my assistants to observe it. It then appeared that one of them (Mr. Jagiello) had observed it at 10 o'clock, and, as it disappeared about 12, it must have lasted about 2 hours.

"The aurora borealis, as seen north of the zenith, is a phenomenon of frequent occurrence; but a southern illumination, like that I have described, I have never before seen, and I leave it to those who are familiar with such subjects to explain the cause.*

"I am, very respectfully, your obedient servant,

"J. H. SIMPSON,

"*Captain Corps Topographical Engineers.*

"Professor JOSEPH HENRY, LL. D.,

"*Secretary of Smithsonian Institution, Washington, D. C.*"

---

* I have received the following reply to this letter from Professor Henry:

"SMITHSONIAN INSTITUTION, WASHINGTON, D. C., *October* 25, 1859.

"DEAR SIR: I write to thank you for your very interesting letter relative to the aurora borealis of the 1st of September, which is important, particularly on account of its locality and the precision with which you have described the phenomena.

"The information of the corona in your locality is an interesting fact, and, in connection with the other observations of a similar kind in other places, will furnish the data for settling some points of importance in the theory of this

I cannot, however, conclude my report without expressing my acknowledgments to Maj. Hannibal Day, Second Regiment Infantry, the officer commanding at Fort Laramie, for his very courteous and acceptable treatment of the party while we were encamped near his post. It was in the cemetery of this post we buried Mr. Walter Lowry, the gentleman who had joined us at Genoa (see journal of June 20 and 24), and who accompanied us, with the expectation that the trip would be of benefit to his health, and that he would be enabled to reach his friends in Philadelphia. His disease was of a pulmonary character, and although at the outset of the journey he rallied a little and was enabled to ride for an hour or two on horseback, before he reached Camp Floyd he found himself incapable of this, and was necessitated to confine himself to the carriage, to which he had eventually to be carried bodily. Major Day kindly permitted him to be cared for at the hospital, and Assistant Surgeon Johns rendered him all the medical aid he required. He survived, however, only one day after he reached the post. It is a pleasure to me to record the disinterested kindness of the sutlers of the post, Messrs. Ward and Fitzhugh, in disposing of the effects of the deceased, forwarding the proceeds to his friends, and placing, at my request, a memorial of him upon his grave. The deceased had for several years been connected with the papers in San Francisco, as commercial editor, and was highly esteemed by those who knew him.

On the 19th October, having shipped at Fort Leavenworth for Washington our instruments, geological, botanical, and other specimens, illustrative of the country we had explored, and discharged all the party except my assistants I left for the purpose of repairing to the seat of Government and reporting to the Adjutant-General.

All of which is very respectfully submitted.

J. H. SIMPSON,
Captain Corps of Topographical Engineers, U. S. Army.

To Col. J. J. ABERT,
Chief Corps Topographical Engineers.

---

meteor. I presume the magnetic needle which you observed was a short one, supported on a point, and, therefore, no action, except one of very unusual intensity, could be observed. The needles generally used for this purpose are those suspended by a single fiber of silk, and the deviations observed by the reflection of the divisions of a scale into the axis of a telescope. Theoretically, however, the action of the aurora on the needle ought to be very uncertain, since if the aurora be an electric discharge to the earth, no action on the needle could be anticipated when this discharge took place with equal intensity east and west of the needle. If, however, the action was much more powerful to the west than to the east, a slight deviation in one direction or the other ought to be observed.

"We are very anxious to obtain the result of your meteorological observations. They will not only be interesting in themselves when published as a part of your report, but particularly so to us, in studying the phenomena of the progress of atmospheric disturbances. You are almost in the very region of the great laboratory of American storms, and every observation you may record in regard to the weather may prove of special interest.

"Very respectfully, yours,

"JOSEPH HENRY.

"To Capt. J. H. SIMPSON."

[I would remark, in relation to the above letter, in respect to the importance of having a proper needle for the discovery of slight perturbations from terrestrial or other causes, that we had with us a unifilar magnetometer, the same which Dr. Kane had on his last Arctic expedition, and which could be converted into a declinometer; but on account of the unseasonable and unexpected occurrence of the phenomena referred to, and although we observed results from it on other occasions, which are given in my report, we did not make use of it on this.]

EXPLORATIONS ACROSS THE GREAT BASIN OF UTAH.

APPENDIXES A, B, AND C.

ITINERARIES OF WAGON-ROUTES.

APPENDIX A.

ITINERARY OF THE MORE NORTHERN OR OUTWARD WAGON-ROUTE FROM CAMP FLOYD, UTAH, TO GENOA, IN CARSON VALLEY.

Localities.	Captain Simpson's camps.	Intermediate distances.	Total miles from Camp Floyd.	Fuel.	Water.	Grass.
Meadow Creek, mail station	C.	18.2	18.2	G. W.	W.	G.
General Johnston's Pass, Guyot range, three-fourths of a mile below summit, on west side; springs to right and left of road; but little water, and probably not constant	C.	9.9	28.1	W.	W.	G.
Simpson Spring, mail station: Water not abundant; fill water-kegs for crossing the desert, which commences here	C.	16.2	44.3	G. W.	W.	G.
Devil's Hole: Water quite brackish; animals can only be watered by bucket		43.1	87.4			
Fish Spring, mail station: Water brackish, but palatable when cool; grass saline	C.	5.4	92.8	G. W.	W.	G.
Warm Spring		3.4	96.2	G. W.	W.	G.
Sulphur Spring: Water in abundance, and palatable; grass also abundant	C.	28.8	125.5	Wil. and S.	W.	G.
Fine Spring, Pleasant Valley, Goshoot range, mail station	C.	13.4	138.4	W.	W.	G.
East side of Antelope Valley	C.	12.5	150.9	W.	W.	G.
Spring Valley: Best grass on west bench of valley	C.	19	169.9	G. W.	W.	G.
Mouth of Spring Creek		3.5		W.	W.	G.
Spring Creek: Grass and wood along creek for 3½ miles above this point		1.0		W.	W.	G.
Summit of pass of Un-go-we-ah range		4.5				
Shell Creek, east side of Steptoe Valley, mail station	C.	2.1	181.0	W.	W.	G.
Steptoe Creek: Dry in summer		6.5				
Mouth of Egan Cañon, in Montim range: Grass on side-hills	C.	6.8	194.3	W.	W.	G.
West side of Butte Valley: Water very scant; grass 1½ miles northeast from water-hole. It is probable that since Captain Simpson's explorations the mail station at this point has been changed to another and better locality in vicinity	C.	18.1	212.4	W.	W.	G.
Spring in Too-muntz range	C.	12	224.4	W.	W.	G.
Spring in Ruby Valley, mail station: Grass on west side of valley	C.	9.2	233.6	G. W.	W.	G.
South Fork of Humboldt		14.4			W.	
Small mountain stream, west side of valley of South Fork of Humboldt; grass toward the mountains	C.	3.3	251.3	G. W.	W.	G.
Summit of Cho-kups Pass, of We-ah-bah range		4.0				
West slope of We-ah-bah range	C.	3.0	258.3	S.	W.	G.
Spring in Pah-hun-nupe Valley		7.8	266.1	S.	W.	G.
Sulphur Spring, west side of Pah-hun-nupe Valley: Marsh grass; a better bunch grass in cañon northwest of spring	C.	5.5	271.6	G. W.	W.	G.
Summit of Cooper's range		8.9				
She-u-wi-te or Willow Creek, in Ko-bah Valley: Some ten miles saved by taking a southwest direction from this camp, as indicated on map, to water; west slope of Pah-rea Mountain	C.	6.0	286.5	S.	W.	G.
Junction with Captain Simpson's return route: Take right hand		16.5	303.0			
Twin Spring: Sergeant Barr's Springs, half mile west; little grass		2 0	305.0	S.	W.	G.
Junction of routes		5.0				
Wons-in-dam-me or Antelope Creek: Abundance of wood, water, and grass	C.	1.5	311.5	W.	W.	G.
Fork of road: Take left hand		1.3				
Saw-wid Creek: Water running one mile above; grass in cañon		3.0		S.	W.	G.
Dry Creek: Water running above road; grass in cañon		2.5		S.	W.	G.
Summit of Pah-rea range		7.1				
Junction of roads		5.5				
Fork of roads: Take left hand		2.4				
Mouth of Won-a-ho-no-pe Cañon	C.	3.1	336.4	W.	W.	G.
Simpson's Park: Abundance of water and grass	C.	5.5	341.9	W.	W.	G.
Summit of Pe-er-re-ah, or High Mountain range		5.0	346.9			
Fork of roads: Take left hand		4.5				
Reese's River: Contains trout; fuel to be brought		5.0	356.4		W.	G.
Forks of road: Take right hand; (left hand 4 miles shorter, but more rugged over the Se-day-e Mountain range. This last best early in the season for trains going west, and always best for herds; water and grass at intervals of 2½, 10, 3, 3, 3, 7, 8; total, 36½ miles to junction with more northern road)		17.8	374.2			
Kirby Smith's Creek, Woodruff Valley: Some grass along creek; abundant within the cañon of same creek	C.	3.5	377.7	G. W.	W.	G.
Mouth of Kirby Smith's Creek Cañon		3.2	380.9	W.	W.	G.
Road leaves Smith's Creek		3.0	383.9	W.	W.	G.
Summit of Pass of Se-day-e Mountains		1.3	385.2			
Edward Creek	C.	.5	385.7	W.	W.	G.
Leave Edward Creek, in Dodge Valley	C.	7.0	392.7	S.	W.	G

APPENDIX A.—*Itinerary of the more northern or outward wagon-route from Camp Floyd, &c.*—Cont'd.

Localities.	Captain Simpson's camps.	Intermediate distances.	Total miles from Camp Floyd.	Fuel.	Water.	Grass.
Cold Spring: From this point, as far as Carson Lake, water and grass very scarce; water-keg should be filled at this point to cross desert	C.	11.2	403.9	S.	W.	G.
Cross small branch and join the other road; water sometimes running; sometimes stagnant in holes in small quantities	......	9	412.9	S.	W.	......
Gibraltar Creek, Middle Gate: Early in the season water running; at other times got by digging; at these times only sufficient for small parties; grass in vicinity, but scarce	C.	1.8	414.7	S.	W.	G.
Forks of road: Take left hand	......	23.5	438.2	......	......	......
Sulphur Spring: Little or no grass; water very scant	......	7.8	446	......	......	......
Carson Lake: Take road going south along the lake; rushes, but grass scarce; fuel brought; grass 5 miles north on lake	C.	9	455	R.	W.	R.
Forks of road: Take right hand	......	4.5	459.5	......	......	......
Leave Carson Lake: Fuel brought	C.	7.5	467	......	W.	G.
Carson River: Wood, water, and grass from this point up along river	C.	23.2	490.2	W.	W.	G.
Opposite Pleasant Grove: Cross Carson River here and join old Humboldt River road; can keep on along south side of River and cross at China Town	C.	18	508.2	W.	W.	G.
The river at Pleasant Grove and China Town only fordable late in the season	......	7.5	515.7	W.	W.	G.
Carson City, Eagle Valley	C.	11.8	527.5	S.	W.	G.
Genoa, (or regarding the cut-off indicated between Shu-wi-te Creek and the Pah-re-ah range, which saves about 10 miles, the total distance from Camp Floyd to Genoa, by Captain Simpson's more northern route, is 531 miles)	C.	13.8	541.3	W.	W.	G.

NOTE.—The distances were measured by an odometer. C. stands for camp; W. for wood; G. W. for greasewood; S. for sage; Wil. for willow; W. for water; G. for grass; and R. for rushes.

This itinerary has been prepared for emigrants; the cuts-off made by Captain S. on his return route to Camp Floyd being regarded. From She-u-wi-te Creek, west, therefore, it does not in every instance give the day's journey as indicated in journal.

In order to cross the desert between Simpson Spring and Fish Spring, and between Cold Spring and Carson Lake, with comfort, water-kegs should be provided for the persons of the party, and at least two grain-feeds for the draught-animals, one for each desert.

APPENDIX B.

ITINERARY OF MORE SOUTHERN OR RETURN WAGON-ROUTE FROM GENOA, IN CARSON VALLEY, OVER THE GREAT BASIN, TO CAMP FLOYD, UTAH.

Localities.	Captain Simpson's camps.	Intermediate distances.	Total miles from Genoa.	Fuel.	Water.	Grass.
Genoa	C.	......	......	W.	Wat.	G.
Carson City, Eagle Valley	C.	13. 8	13. 8	S.	Wat.	G.
China Town: Cross Carson River here early in the season by ferry or raft; later, by ford, or can cross at Pleasant Grove, 11¾ miles lower down, by same means	......	12. 1	25. 9	W.	Wat.	G.
Carson River, south side	C.	5. 1	31. 0	W.	Wat.	G.
Opposite Pleasant Grove, Carson River	......	2. 0	33. 0	W.	Wat.	G.
Carson River	C.	16. 2	49. 2	W.	Wat.	G.
Road leaves Carson River	......	1. 9	......	......	......	......
And goes over several sandy ridges to Carson Lake; fuel should be brought	C.	23. 1	74. 2	R.	Wat.	G.
Carson Lake: Fuel should be brought; rushes for feed; grass 5 miles farther north; water-kegs should be filled for crossing the desert, which commences here	C.	12. 2	86. 4	R.	Wat.	R.
Sulphur Spring, Alkali Valley: Barely sufficient for small party; little or no grass	......	9. 0	......	......	......	......
Junction with route: Take right-hand	......	7. 7	......	......	......	......
Middle Gate: Early in the season water running; later, to be got by digging; poor camping-place; grass in vicinity, but scarce; fuel should be brought	......	23. 2	......	......	Wat.	G.
Cross small branch: Water in holes; take left-hand road; (right hand 4 miles shorter, but more rugged over the Se-day-e Mountains, and a very steep hill to ascend near summit. This last road always best for herds; abundance of water and grass can be found on it at intervals of 8, 7, 3, 3, 3, 10, and 2½, total 36½ miles, to junction with more northern road in Woodruff Valley)	......	1. 8	......	......	......	......
Cold Spring: Excellent water and grass	C.	8. 2	136. 3	S.	Wat.	G.
Edward Creek, Dodge Valley: Fine grass 2 miles farther up the cañon	C.	11. 2	147. 5	S.	Wat.	G.
Edward Creek and cañon	C.	7. 0	154. 5	W.	Wat.	G.
Summit of pass of Se-day-e range	......	6	......	......	......	......
Kirby Smith Creek	C.	7. 9	163. 0	S.	Wat.	G.
Junction of routes	......	3. 7	......	......	......	......
Reese's River: Contains trout	C.	17. 1	183. 8	Wil.	Wat.	G.
Summit of pass of Pe-er-re-ah range	......	10. 7	......	......	......	......
Simpson Lake	......	4. 8	......	W.	Wat.	G.
Won-a-ho-nu-pe River	C.	1. 0	200. 3	W.	Wat.	G.
Spring, Won-a-ho-nu-pe River: Take right-hand road	C.	4. 8	205. 1	S.	Wat.	G.
Junction of roads	......	3. 8	......	......	......	......
Fork of roads: Take right hand	......	2. 6	......	......	......	......
Summit of pass of Pah-re-ah range	......	4. 6	......	......	......	......
Cross Dry Creek: Water running half mile above; grass in cañon	......	7. 4	......	S.	Wat.	G.
Cross Saw-wid Creek; water running 1 mile above; grass in cañon	......	2. 8	......	S.	Wat.	G.
Wons-in-dam-me, or Antelope Creek	C.	4. 6	230. 5	W.	Wat.	G.
Fork of roads: Take left hand	......	1. 6	......	......	......	......
Twin Springs: Barr Springs half mile north; grass sufficient for small parties in vicinity	......	5. 1	......	S.	Wat.	G.
Road crosses outward route	......	2. 0	......	......	......	......
Fountain Springs: About two acres of rush-grass	......	1. 1	......	S.	Wat.	......
Clay Creek: Plenty of grass above and below	C.	6. 3	246. 6	S.	Wat.	G.
Lee's Springs	......	5. 2	......	S.	Wat.	G.
Sink of McCarthy's Creek	......	10. 0	......	S.	Wat.	G.
McCarthy's Creek: Abundance of grass, wood, and water	C.	2. 1	263. 9	W.	Wat.	G.
Road leaves McCarthy's Creek	......	4. 4	......	......	......	......
Summit of We-a-bah range	......	1. 8	......	......	......	......
Leave Neill's Creek and take left-hand road (though, by striking across the valley (Buell's) in a northeastwardly direction, and joining the road in probably 6 miles, in mid-valley, you shorten the distance about 8 miles. The distance to Summit Spring very little farther, by this route, from Neill's Creek, than from Bluff Creek)	......	1. 4	......	W.	Wat.	G.
Bluff Creek	C.	7. 9	279. 4	S.	Wat.	G.
Summit Spring, one-fourth of a mile east side of summit of pass of Too-muntz range	C.	32. 4	311. 8	W.	Wat.	G.
Ute Pete Spring and Creek	......	1. 0	......	......	......	......
Dr. Hurts' Creek and Cañon	......	11. 9	......	......	......	......
Summit of pass of mountain-range	......	3. 2	......	......	......	......
Spring, Spring Cañon: Several springs in vicinity, and grass	C.	3. 0	330. 9	W.	Wat.	G.
Gate of Hercules, and spring, one-fourth of a mile left of road	......	8. 2	......	......	......	......
Lieutenant Murry's Creek, Steptoe Valley: abundance of grass and water	C.	5. 8	344. 9	S.	Wat.	G.
Captain Stevenson's Creek: Abundance of grass and water	......	3. 6	......	S.	Wat.	G.
Captain Stevenson's Creek	......	7. 5	......	W.	Wat.	G.
Spring, Stevenson Cañon	C.	3. 4	359. 4	W.	Wat.	G.

Itinerary of more southern or return route from Genoa, &c.—Continued.

Localities.	Captain Simpson's camps.	Intermediate distances.	Total miles from Genoa.	Fuel.	Water.	Grass.
Summit of pass of Un-go-we-ah or Perry range (some springs and grass about 1½ miles east of summit, to right of road, in branch of Captain Little's Cañon)	......	1.7	......	......	......	......
Near mouth of Little's Cañon: The left-hand road goes direct to Turnley's Spring, and is the shortest	......	7.4	......	......	......	......
Springs, Antelope Valley: Grass and cedars abundant half mile north	C.	6.6	375.1	S.	Wat.	G.
Turnley's Spring	......	8.1	......	W.	Wat.	G.
Summit of pass of Totts-arr or Goshoot range	......	1.8	......	......	......	......
Un-go-pah, or Red Springs: Union Peak opposite	C.	7.2	392.2	Wil.	Wat.	G.
Rush Spring (small), Crosman Valley	......	10.9	......	G. W.	Wat.	G.
Crosman Creek, 3 feet wide, 1 deep; grass and water abundant	C.	3.9	407.0	Wil.	Wat.	G.
Plympton's Springs: Several in compass of half a mile, plenty of grass	C.	10.2	417.2	G. W.	Wat.	G.
Rush Pond: little or no grass; a few rushes	C.	21.3	438.5	......	Wat.	......
Summit of pass of House range	......	12.2	......	......	......	......
Chapin's Springs: Grass not abundant	C.	2.4	453.1	W.	Wat.	G.
Tyler's Springs: Grass limited; water-kegs should be filled here to cross desert	C.	15.5	468.6	W.	Wat.	G.
Summit of pass of Thomas' range	......	17.0	......	......	......	......
Good Indian Spring, McDowell Mountains: A very small spring here; water-trough fixed for the collection and preservation of the water; grass and wood abundant	C.	18.0	503.6	W.	Wat.	G.
Prince's Creek, Champlin Mountains	C.	16.0	519.6	W.	Wat.	G.
Porter Creek, Porter Valley: Wood, water, and grass abundant	......	3.5	523.1	W.	Wat.	G.
Brewer's Spring: Wood, water, and grass abundant	C.	5.5	528.6	W.	Wat.	G.
Junction with outward route, in General Johnston's Pass of the Guyot range	C.	11.3	539.9	W.	......	G.
Meadow Creek	C.	10.0	549.9	G. W.	Wat.	G.
Camp Floyd: Grass and wood in Oquirr Mountains, 3 miles off	C.	18.2	568.1	......	Wat.	

NOTE.—The distances were measured by an odometer. C. stands for camp; W. for wood; G. W. for greasewood; S. for sage (*Artemesia*); Wil. for willows; Wat. for water; G. for grass; and R. for rushes.

In order to cross the desert, between Carson Lake and Cold Spring, and between Tyler's Spring and Prince's Creek, water-kegs should be provided for the persons of the party, and at least two grain-feeds for the draught-animals, one for each desert.

APPENDIX C.

ITINERARY OF A WAGON-ROUTE FROM FORT BRIDGER TO CAMP FLOYD.

Localities.	Intermediate distances.	Total miles from Fort Bridger.	Fuel.	Water.	Grass.
Fort Bridger	....	....	W.	Wat.	G.
Cañon Black's Fork	6	6	W.	Wat.	G.
Muddy Creek	7¼	13¼	W.	Wat.	G.
Last water in ravine	5½	18¾	S.	Wat.	G.
East Branch, Sulphur Creek	5¾	24½	S.	Wat.	G.
West Branch, Sulphur Creek	3½	28	Wil.	....	G.
East Branch, Bear River	5¼	33¼	W.	Wat.	G.
West or Main Branch of Bear River	3	36¼	W.	Wat.	G.
First Camp on White Clay Creek	9¾	46	W.	Wat.	G.
Foot of upper cañon: good camps in localities down to mouth of White Clay Creek	5¼	51¼	Wil.	Wat.	G.
Junction of White Clay Creek with Weber River and old Parley's Park road; turn up the Weber	19¼	70½	W.	Wat.	G.
Good camps up the Weber to point where you leave it to cross divide between it and Silver Creek	12	82½	W.	Wat.	G.
Silver Creek: Turn up the creek	6	88½	S.	Wat.	G.
Leave Silver Creek	3¾	92¼	S.	Wat.	G.
First camp on Timpanogos River	6	98¼	W.	Wat.	G.
Good camps at intervals to commencement of cañon	21	119¼	W.	Wat.	G.
Beautiful cascade	2¼	121½	W.	Wat.	......
Toll-bridge over Timpanogos	3¼	124¾	....	....	......
Mouth of Timpanogos Cañon	1	125¾	W.	Wat.	......
Battle Creek (Pleasant Grove): Fuel should be brought; forage purchasable	6¼	132	....	Wat.	......
American Fork (Lake City): Fuel should be brought; forage purchasable	3¼	135¼	....	Wat.	......
Lehi: Fuel should be brought; forage purchasable	3	138¼	....	Wat.	......
Toll-bridge over Jordan: Fuel should be brought	2¾	141	....	Wat.	G.
Camp Floyd: Fuel and grass in the mountains, 2½ miles off	14	155	....	Wat.	......

NOTE.—The distances were measured by an odometer. W. stands for wood; S. for sage; Wat. for water; Wil. for willows; and G. for grass.

APPENDIX D.

ASTRONOMICAL OBSERVATIONS

AND

GEOGRAPHICAL POSITIONS.

APPENDIX D.

ASTRONOMICAL OBSERVATIONS AND GEOGRAPHICAL POSITIONS OF THE MOST IMPORTANT POINTS.

The subjoined letters of Lieut. H. S. Putman, Topographical Engineers, and of Mr. D. G. Major, with the Table of Geographical Positions, give all needful information in respect to this portion of the expedition. The sextant observations were chiefly made by my assistant, Lieut. J. L. K. Smith, Topographical Engineers; the transit observations by Lieut. H. S. Putman, and those for lunar distance by both these officers and myself, the altitude of the moon and star, as well as the angular distance, being taken at the same instant of time.

The chief fact noticeable in the results is the disagreement between our longitudes and those of Colonel Frémont at Great Salt Lake City, the north bend of Walker's River, and at Genoa, the western termination of our routes, where our explorations have been either coincident or so closely approximate as to enable us to institute a comparison.

In Frémont's second expedition (1843–'44) he makes the longitude of the summit of Frémont Island, in Great Salt Lake, west of Greenwich 112° 21′ 05″. According to Stansbury's rigid triangular survey of Great Salt Lake, Salt Lake City is east of this summit 25′ 39″. This makes the longitude of Salt Lake City, as derived from Frémont's observations in second expedition, 111° 55′ 26″.

In Frémont's report of this expedition he remarks that "in this exploration, it became evident that the longitudes established during the campaign of 1842 were collectively thrown too far to the westward." He therefore abandons his determinations of his first expeditions, and assumes as correct those of his second. In his third expedition (of 1845–'46) he does not compare his longitudes with those of his previous expeditions; but, instituting a comparison myself, I find the result as follows: In this third expedition he makes one set of transit observations October 20, 1845, of the moon and moon-culminating stars, at the present site of Great Salt Lake City, and determines its longitude to be 112° 06′ 08″. That is, he makes the longitude of Salt Lake City in this expedition 10′ 42″ greater than in his second; or, in other words, moves collectively his positions back again westwardly 10′ 42″.

Now our observations of the transit of the moon and moon-culminating stars at Camp Floyd, consisting of five complete sets, made during two lunations, in the months of March and April, 1858, give a resulting longitude for this post of 112° 08′ 07″. Chronometrically, I found Great Salt Lake City east of Camp Floyd, 13′ 07″. This gives a resulting longitude for Great Salt Lake City, according to our observations, of 111° 55′ 00″, differing from Frémont's, in his second expedition, only 26″, and from his determinations in his third expedition, 11′ 08″. This result, I think, is corroborative of the accuracy of his longitude, as determined in his second expedition, and of our own.*

Again, Frémont makes the longitude of the most northern bend of Walker's River, in his third expedition, 119° 05′ 23″. We make the longitude of this same bend, by observations of east and west stars and lunar distances, 118° 56′ 00″, differing from his 09′ 23″, but as our station appears to have been about 2′ farther west than his, the disagreement between us amounts to about 11′ 23″.†

Thus far it will be noticed our disagreements have been 11′ 08″ at Salt Lake City, and 11′ 23″ at the most northern bend of Walker; but from this point westward, within a measured distance, by odometer, of only 60 miles along our route, and a difference of longitude of only 46′ 50″, our longitudes become suddenly so variant, as at the junction of the east and west branches of Carson River, at the base of the Sierra Nevada, to make us differ as much as 21′ 30″. Supposing, possibly, that I might have been in error, I have examined my map and notes critically upon this point, and feel confident that this suddenly enlarged discrepancy is not due to any errors we have committed. Besides, what makes me more disposed to think that the error does not lie with us is that Mr. George H. Goddard, the civil engineer who was intrusted by the State of California, in 1855, with the determination of the eastern boundary of that State, makes the longitude of Genoa 119° 48′ 25″,‡ or 7′ 55″ greater than mine, while Frémont's of this point, so far as it can be determined from its proximity to the junction of the east and west forks of Carson River, laid down on his map of his expedition of 1845–'46, is 21′ 30″ greater.

I have been thus particular in giving the points of difference between Frémont's longitudes and my own, from the circumstance that they have been hitherto regarded as correct, and succeeding explorers have referred their longitudes chronometrically to them as standards.

Before dismissing this subject, I cannot but bring to the attention of the Bureau the great importance of sending into the field, and of officers intrusted with expeditions of securing, the very best chronometers and astronomical instruments which can be purchased. A hundred dollars or more on a chronometer or other field-instrument may insure results which may be reliable and permanent; whereas a false economy which would be content with anything less will frequently jeopard the results of the whole expedition, and cause the expenditure of thousands of dollars, as well as the opportunity of gaining correct geographical knowledge, to have been entirely nugatory.

I would also state that the very best possible way we found of carrying our chronometers (four in number) was to place them in a soft-cushioned box prepared for the purpose, and to strap the box on the middle seat of an easy ambulance or spring-wagon. Our box-chronometer we allowed to play freely in the gimbals, only placing

*My latitude of Great Salt Lake City differs from Frémont's 10″; from Stansbury's, 3″.

† Our latitude of this bend agrees within 26″.

‡ Mr. Goddard appears to have been supplied with all the requisite astronomical instruments to insure good results. See Annual Report of Surveyor-General of California, 1855, pp. 92–124.

on the face of the chronometer a sufficient quantity of curled hair to restrict its oscillations within proper limits within the box and prevent its turning over.

I would here remark that according to my experience good chronometers can, with care, as above directed, be carried in our field-expeditions and very fair results be obtained from them, the precaution, however, being taken to determine the longitude absolutely at proper intervals,* as tests and checks of the work.

The astronomical observations which we took for time, or longitude and latitude, are so numerous as to make it inexpedient to incumber the report with them, but as they have been filed in the Bureau of Topographical Engineers, they are available for reference. I think it proper, however, to present below some of the forms we used for the entering of astronomical data; as they may be of service to future explorers.

As every hint of practical value is of use to explorers in the field I would suggest that in taking the altitudes of the sun with the sextant, I have found that to set the instrument, say every 20′ of arc, and wait for the contact or separation of the images,

---

* I notice that Lieutenant Warren, in his memoir of explorations (Pacific Railroad Reports, vol. xi, 399), in comparing my longitudes on my exploration to the Navajo country from Santa Fé, in 1849, with those of Captain Whipple, of 1853 prefers those of Captain Whipple, for the reason that mine, as I stated in my report, were chronometric, and based upon the longitude of Santa Fé (106° 2′ 30′), as determined by Major Emory. This is all very well, for the reason that Captain Whipple determined his longitudes absolutely; but when the difference between us, 13′, is said "to be not greater than is liable to the method employed, viz, chronometric differences by chronometers transported over rough and mountainous country," he does me, doubtless unintentionally, an act of injustice; assigns an erroneous reason for the difference, and, according to my experience, makes the errors, liable from the cause assigned, very much greater than there is any necessity for. The truth is, the difference between Captain Whipple and myself arose not from the chronometers having been transported *over a rough country*, but because Major Emory had placed the longitude of Santa Fé too far to the westward; and hence, as mine were based on his, they were carried correspondingly 13′ too far to the westward, as was determined by Captain Whipple.

All this is corroborated by the fact that Capt. J. N. Macomb, topographical engineers, as his letter will show, by an observation of an occultation of the star B. A. C., 4984, August 5, 1859, has determined the longitude of Santa Fé to be 105° 47′ 14″.25 west from Greenwich; or 15′ 15″.75 to the eastward of that given by Emory.

WASHINGTON, D. C., *October* 22, 1860.

DEAR SIR: At your request I give you the result of my observations for longitude upon my recent exploration west of the Rio Bravo del Norte. At my camp upon the Rio Florido (a tributary of Rio Las Animas, which empties into the San Juan), I observed an occultation of B. A. C. 4984, on August 5, 1859, from which the longitude of 107° 46′ 30″ was obtained, and from this I deduced the longitude of Santa Fé by the use of a sidereal chronometer. My result for Santa Fé is 105° 47′ 14″.25.

I remain, very respectfully, yours, &c.,

J. N. MACOMB,
Captain Topographical Engineers, in Charge of San Juan Expedition, &c.

Capt. J. H. SIMPSON,
Topographical Engineers, U. S. A., in Charge of Explorations in Utah, &c.

I would also state that Lieutenant Warren has fallen into an error in respect to the real difference between my longitude of Fort Defiance and Captain Whipple's. He makes the difference 16′, whereas the real difference is 13′ 30″; thus:

My longitude of Camp No. 21, west mouth of Canoncito Bonito, as laid down in Appendix E of my report of Navajo expedition	109° 15′ 30″
Fort Defiance, east of this locality	3 00″
Longitude of Fort Defiance, according to my observations	109° 12′ 30″
Captain Whipple, longitude Fort Defiance, according to Lieutenant Warren	108° 59′ 00″
True difference	13′ 30″

Besides, in his table of comparative longitudes (doubtless a clerical error), he has entered Whipple's longitude of Ojos del Pescado, as 108° 14′ 18″. This makes a difference between my longitude of this place (108° 41′ 45″), and Whipple's, of as much as 27′ 27″. By reference, however, to Whipple's Table of Astronomical Positions, I find that the longitude of Inscription Rock has been placed down incorrectly, as that of Ojos del Pescado, and that the true longitude of the latter is 108° 27′ 54″, or differing from mine 13′ 51′.

has the advantage of securing uniformity of result, an avoidance of error in the hasty reading of the instrument and record of the angles, and a general satisfaction in the observations. Of course in the case of only occasional glimpses of the sun on account of intervening clouds this mode should not be practiced.

Lieutenant Putman submits results of observations for latitude and longitude.

WASHINGTON, D. C., *March* 1, 1860.

SIR: The subjoined table gives the geographical positions for the most important points on the new routes between Fort Bridger and Genoa, Utah.

It will be observed that the longitude of Camp Floyd, and consequently chronometrically, that of Great Salt Lake City, has been decreased about 11′ from that given by Colonel Frémont. This change, however, has been made only when a careful series of observations on the moon and moon-culminating stars warranted the alteration. These observations, consisting of five complete sets, were made during two lunations (in the months of March and April, 1859), and a mean of all the results, which did not differ essentially, was taken as the true longitude.

The longitude of Genoa is determined from a single set of observations of the same kind as the foregoing; the age of the moon and other circumstances, made it impossible to take as full a series as was desirable. Between Camp Floyd and Genoa other observations on the moon and moon-culminating stars, and of lunar distance were made for absolute determinations of longitude.

Equal altitudes of the sun, or double altitudes of "east and west stars," were taken at intervals which, with the known error and rate of the chronometer, affords the means for arriving at the longitude of intermediate points.

Latitude has been computed from double altitudes of the sun or Polaris at nearly every camp on the route.

The computations for latitude and time have been made by myself, assisted by Lieut. C. H. Collins, Topographical Engineers, and Mr. J. R. P. Mechlin; each computation being made by two persons to guard against mistakes. The longitudes by the moon and moon-culminating stars, and by lunar distances, have been computed by Mr. D. G. Major of Washington.

The instruments employed in the field were:

1st. A portable transit, made by Würdemann; focal length, two feet. After reaching Camp Floyd, the spider-lines of the reticle were found broken; they were replaced by such substitutes as could be obtained there, and it is believed the results are worthy of full confidence.

2d. One box, mean solar, chronometer by Parkinson and Frodsham, London, No. 1821, and two pocket chronometers, one, No. 221, by Frodsham, and one No. 8189, by A. P. Walsh, London. Of these, No. 1821 was used in most cases, and a proof of its reliability is to be found in the correspondence between the longitude as given by it, and that determined absolutely.

For instance, at the North Bend of Walker's River, the chronometer gives longitude 118° 56′ 08″ west from Greenwich, and an observation on the moon, Alpha Virginis, and Alpha Leonis, gives 118° 56′ 00″. Again at Clay Creek, the chronometer gives 116° 09′ 13″, while by lunar distances it is 116° 05′ 45″, a difference not great when it is remembered that the chronometer has been transported over 800 miles, and most of the way through a rough country, where there was no road.

3d. Two sextants made by Gamby (Paris), and one by Würdemann. All of these were used, simultaneously, by as many observers, in taking an observation for longitude by lunar distances.

The one marked "No. 1," was used by Lieutenant Smith, in all the observations made for time and latitude, and the results obtained from it were very satisfactory. In some cases a set of six pairs of equal altitudes of the sun would be taken, and on computing each pair separately, the greatest difference between any two errors, thus found, would seldom exceed a small fraction of a second; a proof of the extreme nicety of the observation.

I am, captain, very respectfully, your obedient servant,

H. S. Putman,
Lieutenant Topographical Engineers.

Capt. J. H. Simpson,
Corps Topographical Engineers.

Mr. Major submits results of calculations for longitude.

Washington, D. C., *February* 6, 1860.

Dear Sir: I have the honor herewith to inclose the essential calculations, and final results of the series of astronomical observations for longitude.

The transit work requires no explanation; the usual method of discussion having been adopted, so far as the data afforded.

The lunar distances have been computed by the improved method of Chauvenet, Astronomical Journal, vol. 2, also American Ephemeris, vol. 1. The places of the moon and stars, also other data, are taken from the American Ephemeris, with but one or two instances from the British Nautical Almanac.

I have to express regret that this work has been delayed, owing to an accident, by which the former calculations were destroyed. The inclosed results differ (in most cases very slightly), from those previously deduced on account of using these last as close approximations in the reductions.

Yours very truly,

D. G. Major.

Captain Simpson,
Topographical Engineers, U. S. A.

Table showing the geographical positions of the most important places between Camp Floyd and Genoa, Utah, on Capt. J. H. Simpson's outward route.

Place.	No. of camp.	North latitude. ° ′ ″	Longitude west from Greenwich. ° ′ ″
Camp Floyd		40 13 18	(c) 112 08 07
Meadow Creek	1	40 11 27	
Simpson's Spring	3	40 01 55	112 47 18
In the Desert	4	39 51 33	
Fish Spring	5	39 50 54	
In the Desert, (Sulphur Spring)	7	39 40 36	113 46 19
Pleasant Valley	8	39 41 12	
Antelope Valley	9	39 46 36	
Spring Valley	10	39 46 38	
Steptoe Valley	11	39 47 27	
Egan Cañon	12	39 51 46	(c) 114 58 15
Butte Valley	13	39 55 42	
Huntington Spring, east slope of Ruby Valley	14	40 00 29	
South Fork Humboldt River	16	39 55 39	
Pah-hun-nupe Valley	18	39 49 43	115 56 52
She-u-wi-te Creek	19	39 44 34	
Shelton Spring	20	39 29 56	
Clarke Creek	22	39 29 13	116 39 12
Won-a-ho-no-pe Creek	23	39 27 21	
Simpson's Park Creek	24	39 30 32	116 49 00
Reese River	25	39 29 29	
Smith Creek	26	39 20 28	
Putnam Creek	27	39 14 13	117 27 34
Gibralter Cañon	28	39 13 42	
Alkaline Springs	30	39 17 06	
Carson Lake	31	39 23 37	118 30 01
Walker's River	33	39 07 38	(d) 118 49 00
North Bend Walker's River	34	39 08 39	(d) 118 56 00
Carson City	37	39 09 24	
Genoa	38	38 59 33	(c) 119 40 30

Table showing the geographical positions of the most important points between Genoa and Fort Bridger, Utah, on Capt. J. H. Simpson's return route.

Place.	No. of camp.	North latitude. ° ′ ″	Longitude west from Greenwich. ° ′ ″
Carson River	4	39 16 18	
Carson Lake	5	39 16 47	
Cold Creek	7	39 23 06	
Edward Creek	8	39 28 56	117 31 42
Near summit of Se-day-e Mountain, (west side)	9	39 23 40	
Clay Creek	15	39 33 24	(d) 116 05 45
McCarthy Creek	16	39 32 51	
Huff Creek	17	39 32 21	
Summit Spring	18	39 32 53	115 12 14
Spring Cañon	19	39 27 02	
Murry Creek	20	39 15 30	
Spring in Antelope Valley	22	39 06 09	114 26 52
Uan-go-pah or Red Spring	23	39 05 21	
Crosman Spring	24	39 06 41	
Plympton Spring	26	39 15 56	
Rush Pond	27	39 19 37	113 31 54
Chapin Spring	28	39 20 09	
Tyler Spring	29	39 24 19	
Good Indian Spring	31	39 46 09	112 56 36
Prince Creek	33	39 52 24	
Brewer Spring	34	39 58 58	
Meadow Creek	35	40 05 41	
Torbert Creek, Round Prairie		40 29 25	111 25 56
Timpanogos River, (Bend of)		40 36 15	111 26 03
Weber River, (Crossing)		40 52 44	111 24 49
Near summit of Uintah Mountains, (side reconnaissance)		40 27 24	
Mouth of Duchesne Fork, (side reconnaissance)		40 09 50	110 20 33
Fort Bridger		41 20 23	110 23 47

NOTE.—The camps on the return route are numbered from Genoa, the camp at that place being No. 38 of the outward or No. 1 of the return route.

Longitudes marked *c* have been computed from observed lunar culminations; those *d* from lunar distances. All others are chronometric.

The longitude of Great Salt Lake City, chronometrically referred to the meridian of Camp Floyd, is 111° 55′ 00″. The latitude is 40° 46′ 03″ north.

[Form used.]

Comparison of chronometers, Camp Floyd, Utah, Tuesday, March 1, 1859.

Box chronometer No. 1821.			Pocket chronometer No. 221.			Difference.		
h.	*m.*	*s.*	*h.*	*m.*	*s.*	*h.*	*m.*	*s.*
9	29	45	9	30	20	00	00	35
9	30	15	9	30	50	00	00	35
9	30	35	9	31	10	00	00	35
			Pocket chronometer No. 8189.					
9	31	44	9	35	50	00	04	06
9	32	04	9	36	10	00	04	06
9	32	44	9	36	50	00	04	06
			Pocket chronometer No. 8212.					
9	33	41	9	33	50	00	00	09
9	34	11	9	34	20	00	00	09
9	34	31	9	34	40	00	00	09

[Form used.]

Comparison of chronometers and daily rates.

Date.	No. of Camp.	Station.	No. of chronometer.	Reading of chronometer.	Difference.	Chronometer, fast (+) or slow (−) of mean time.	Chronometer, fast (+) or slow (−) of sidereal time.	+ fast or − slow of mean time.	+ fast or − slow of sidereal time.
1859.				*h. m. s.*	*h. m. s.*	*h. m. s.*	*h. m. s.*	*m. s.*	*m. s.*
Mar. 1		Camp Floyd, Utah Territory	1821	9 30 15		− 0 01 20.14	− 10 37 39.17		
1		do	221	9 30 50	00 00 35	− 0 00 45.14	− 10 37 4.17		
1		do	1821	9 32 04					
1		do	8189	9 36 10	00 04 06	+ 0 02 45.86	− 10 33 33.17		
1		do	1821	9 34 11					
1		do	8212	9 34 20	00 00 09	− 0 01 11.14			
10		do	1821	12 29 08		− 0 01 44.86	− 11 13 32.6	− 00 02.75	− 03 59.22
10		do	221	12 30 00	00 00 52	− 0 00 52.86	− 11 12 40.6	− 00 00.86	− 03 57.38
10		do	1821	12 30 11					
10		do	8189	12 35 25	00 05 14	+ 0 03 29.14	− 11 08 18.60	+ 00 04.81	
10		do	1821	12 31 28					
10		do	8212	12 31 05	00 00 23	− 0 02 07.86	− 11 13 09.6	− 00 04.68	

[Form used.]

Equal altitudes of sun's upper limb.—Camp Floyd, Utah, Thursday, March 3, 1859.—*Sextant No.* 5, *Würdemann box chronometer No.* 1821.—*Capt. J. H. Simpson, observer.*

A. M.						P. M.		
h.	*m.*	*s.*	°	′	″	*h.*	*m.*	*s.*
8	52	38	49	40	00	3	29	26
8	54	11	50	10	00	3	27	50
8	55	47	50	40	00	3	26	12
8	57	21	51	10	00	3	24	38
8	58	57	51	40	00	3	23	03
9	00	35	52	10	00	3	21	27
9	02	15	52	40	00	3	19	49
9	03	48	53	10	00	3	18	13
9	05	28	53	40	00	3	16	35
9	07	08	54	10	00	3	14	56
9	08	43	54	40	00	3	13	20

Index error.			Difference.	Mean.	Grand mean.	Atmosphere.
		′ ″	′ ″	′ ″	′ ″	
Bef. obs	On arc	34 40				A. M.
do	Off arc	30 10	− 4 30			Bar. 25, 423.
Aft. obs	On arc	34 50				Alt. ther. 56°.
do	Off arc	30 00	− 4 50			Det. ther. 30°.
A. M	Sum		− 9 20	− 2 20		
					− 2 15	
Bef. obs	On arc	35 00				
do	Off arc	30 40	− 4 20			P. M.
Aft. obs	On arc	35 00				Bar. 25, 320.
do	Off arc	30 40	− 4 20	− 2 10		Alt. ther. 61½°.
P. M	Sum		− 8 40	− 4 30		Det. ther. 47°.

[Form used.]

Astronomical observations with transit—Camp Floyd, Utah Territory.

Date.	Name of object.	Times of transit over the wires.							Illuminated end of axis.	Reading of level.				Observer.
										X end east.		X end west.		
		I.	II.	III.	IV.	V.	VI.	VII.		E.	W.	E.	W.	
1859.		*m. s.*	*m. s.*	*m. s.*	*h. m. s.*	*m. s.*	*m. s.*	*m. s.*						
Mar. 13	Sirius	11 11	11 32.5	11 56	7 12 17.8	12 39	13 02	13 24	......	590	550	590	550	
Mar. 13	Delta geminorum..	....	44 12	....	7 45 00	45 23	45 46.5	....	......	590	550	590	550	
Mar. 13	Moon's W. limb ..	54 17	54 41.5	55 06.5	7 55 31	55 53	56 19	56 43	......	590	550	590	550	
Mar. 13	Beta geminorum...	8 44	9 06	9 31	8 9 56	10 18	10 43	11 07.5	......	590	550	590	550	

EXPLORATIONS ACROSS THE GREAT BASIN OF UTAH.

APPENDIX E.

BAROMETRICAL AND METEOROLOGICAL OBSERVATIONS

AND

COMPUTATION OF ALTITUDE THEREFROM,

BY

HENRY ENGELMANN,
GEOLOGIST AND METEOROLOGIST OF THE EXPEDITION.

APPENDIX E.

REPORT ON THE BAROMETRICAL AND METEOROLOGICAL OBSERVATIONS AND ON THE COMPUTATION OF THE ALTITUDES THEREFROM, BY HENRY ENGELMANN, GEOLOGIST AND METEOROLOGIST OF THE EXPEDITION.

WASHINGTON, D. C., *December* 5, 1860.

SIR: I herewith submit to you my report on the barometrical and meteorological observations taken during the explorations under your command in Kansas, Nebraska, and Utah Territories, 1858 and 1859; and on the computation of the altitudes from the same, upon which the profiles are based, of the routes traveled by parties under your command between Fort Bridger, Utah, and the Sierra Nevada.

The observations cover a large area, and besides their value for the computation of altitudes, of which only those points west of Fort Bridger have been calculated, they afford an insight into the climatical conditions of the most elevated central portion of the North American continent. By their large number I have been enabled to deduce most striking results in regard to the fluctuations of the temperature and of the moisture of the atmosphere in the so-called Great Basin of Utah, which has an extremely continental climate, the like of which is only known to exist in the center of the vast continent of Asia, and also of several points in the plains, east of the Rocky Mountains, the climate of which, although not quite as arid as that of the Basin, still differs very materially from that of the intermediate valley of the Mississippi River and of the Eastern States, and presents insurmountable obstacles to the successful occupation of by far the largest portion of that region by any other than a nomadic population, the main interest of which cannot be agriculture. From the records of the observations given in full, much more interesting facts may be derived by their comparison with contemporaneous observations at other points, but my time has been too much limited to follow up the subject farther than I have done.

I avail myself of this opportunity to acknowledge the valuable assistance rendered me during the prosecution of the surveys, by Capt. J. W. Phelps, Fourth Artillery, U. S. A., (now resigned,) at Camp Floyd, and by Messrs. Edward Jagiello and William Lee, who assisted me along the route. For the communication of some of the meteorological records, which I have made use of in the computations, I am indebted to the Medical Department of the Army. I am also under obligation to Prof. A. D. Bache, Superintendent of the United States Coast Survey, for some observations at San Francisco, Cal., and for liberal access to the library of the Smithsonian Institution, and other facilities offered to me by the distinguished Secretary of the Institution, Prof. Joseph Henry.

I am, sir, your obedient servant,

HENRY ENGELMANN.

Capt. J. H. SIMPSON,
Topographical Engineers, U. S. A.,
In charge of Exploring Expedition.

INSTRUMENTS.

On starting from Fort Leavenworth, we were provided with three cistern barometers, Nos. 1062, 1237, and 1279, made by James Green, of New York, with scales graduated down to 20 inches, and with verniers reading to thousandths of an inch. These instruments, as improved now by Mr. Green, were again found to be admirably adapted to the wants of exploring expeditions, when they are transported over many hundreds of miles of rough mountain roads, and exposed to all accidents contingent to their daily use on the road and in camp. One of their principal advantages is the readiness with which they may be repaired in the field when damaged by long use or broken by accidents, which will happen to the most careful observer. Against such emergencies we were provided with several glass tubes, pure mercury, and other requisites. A portable tripod was furnished by Mr. Green with the instruments, and found very useful, indeed, indispensable. The immovable support which it gives can often not be obtained otherwise in the field, and adds to the correctness of the observations and to the preservation of the instruments.

We were also provided with aneroid barometers, which, however, were not used, as no reliable results could be expected from them at the elevation and in the climate where we might have needed them most. Besides these, we had a number of thermometers and a rain-gauge.

OBSERVATIONS.

Regular observations of the barometer, dry and wet bulb thermometers, cloudiness of the sky, direction and force of the wind, quantity of rain, &c., were kept up from the time of the arrival of the party at Fort Leavenworth, Kans., in May, 1858, to our return there in October, 1859. As it was desirable to obtain observations for as long a period as possible at each successive camp, and from the warmest to the coldest time of the day, the first observation was made soon after reaching a camp, and the last one shortly before leaving it again, conforming, as much as possible, to the hours of 6 a. m., 9 a. m., 12 m., 3 p. m., 6 p. m., and 9 p. m., which were fixed upon as the regular hours for observations when in camp. In the mountain regions, during the explorations between Camp Floyd, Utah, and Fort Bridger, Utah, and between Camp Floyd and Carson Valley, Utah, numerous observations were made on the road, with a view to the construction of the profile. Besides, a very large number of hourly observations were most carefully made at every point where a protracted stay offered an opportunity, in order to obtain data for the determination of the daily variation of the atmospheric pressure, the temperature, the elastic force and weight of vapor, and the relative humidity of the different districts.

REDUCTION OF THE OBSERVATIONS.

The first step, in preparing the records for discussion and computation, is the reduction of the observed readings of the barometer to what which they would have been had the temperature of the mercury been uniformly 32° Fahrenheit; for which purpose I made use of the tables of Prof. A. Guyot, of Princeton, published by the Smithsonian Institution.

INSTRUMENTAL ERRORS.

Next, the correction for instrumental error was applied. Before the barometers left the hands of the maker their scales were adjusted, so that they read precisely with the Smithsonian standard. Their comparative reading and the change which they had undergone was then tested by a long series of observations, made at Fort Leavenworth, under the direction of Capt. J. W. Abert, Topographical Engineers, which were repeated at Fort Kearney by myself, and afterward in every stationary camp, and as often as it appeared desirable. On the march we generally made use of only one barometer, to keep the others perfect for future service and comparison.

It will be sufficient here to give the errors as they were found at different times, without giving all the details regarding the determination and origin of their changes.

Table of zero-errors of the barometers.

Date.	Barometers.		
	1062	1279	1237
Found during May, 1858, (in inches English)	− 0. 002	+ 0. 002	− 0. 002
End of June, 1858, (from most reliable observers)	0. 000	0. 000	− 0. 004
End of July, 1858	0. 000	0. 000	− 0. 005
After August 20, 1858, (1062 had been cleaned)	− 0. 014	0. 000	− 0. 005
After September 2, 1858	− 0. 014	− 0. 005	− 0. 005
After September 16, 1858	− 0. 020	− 0. 008	− 0. 005
In January, 1859. (A new tube had been inserted in 1062)	− 0. 042	(*)	− 0. 006
In January, 1859, (1279 hand been refitted)	− 0. 042	(*)	+ 0. 005
In April, 1859	− 0. 042	(*)	0. 000
From June 1 to 21, 1859	− 0. 055	(*)	0. 000
After June 21. (A new tube had been inserted in 1279)	....	(*)	0. 015
From August 28, 1859, to end	....	− 0. 008	....

* Kept at Fort Bridger.

I wish to call the attention of observers who might meet with similar circumstances to the fact that, in determining these zero errors, I found a very valuable check in Part C, Table XXVII, of the second edition of the above-named Smithsonian Tables, which gives the depression of the mercurial column due to capillary action, with the internal diameter of the tube, and the height of the meniscus as arguments, reduced to English measure from a table of Delcros. The use of it may be seen from the following example: In January, 1859, at Camp Floyd, I had to replace the original tube of barometer No. 1062, which had been broken, by a new one. The inner diameter of the latter was 0.16 inch, while that of the former had been 0.20 inch. Having performed the operation with all possible care, I waited some days, in order to give the instrument time to obtain its normal conditions. I then compared it with the other, and found its zero-error equal to 0.042 inch. The meniscus of No. 1062 was now 0.024 inch high, which corresponds, according to the table, to a depression of 0.064 inch. To correct for the capillary attraction of the old and wider tube, the maker had shortened the scale 0.028 inch, as indicated by a mark on the brass tube. The apparent error, after the insertion of the new tube, ought, therefore, to have been 0.064 minus 0.028, equal to 0.036 inch. That the direct comparison gave it a little larger, 0.042, may be accounted for by my inability to measure the inner diameter of the tube to a fraction, as the beautifully clear sound of the instrument (produced when the mercury struck the closed end of the tube) indicated that the vacuum was perfect. The result certainly was very satisfactory. It proved that the zero-errors of the instruments had been recorded correctly, or very nearly so. I might, then, have shortened the scale, as the maker would have done in a similar case, being satisfied that this zero-error was not the consequence of a fault of the instrument, but of the increased capillary depression in the narrower tube. I preferred, however, to leave the scale unchanged.

In one case an accident happened to the two instruments, which, at the time, were the only ones in my possession. Some of the mules got entangled in the cords of the tent, and, pulling it down, threw the tripod, with both barometers, to the ground. Air entered the vacuum of No. 1062, and rendered it temporarily unserviceable. A bubble of air also entered the tube of No. 1279, but left it again on turning the instrument, which, from all appearances, had not suffered any permanent damage. The sound of the tube seemed to indicate that the vacuum was still perfect. After the tube of No. 1062 had been refilled, with all possible precaution, I found the result of calculation closely corresponding with the result of the direct comparison of the instruments, and in this way I was again re-assured that No. 1279 had not suffered from the accident, an assurance which I could not well have arrived at in any other way. These examples show how useful it is to keep account of the width of the tubes, the height of the meniscus, the clearness of the sound, and other observations in regard to the condition of the instruments.

The thermometers—the attached as well as the detached ones—also did not perfectly agree with each other. I therefore tested their graduation by direct experiments, from which I calculated a table of corrections. The readings of the thermometer, as found in the records, were thus corrected whenever it was found necessary.

METHOD OF COMPUTATION.

I could scarcely hesitate in the selection of the method for computing the altitudes, since the one developed according to the requirements of the case during the computation of the profiles of the Pacific Railroad surveys, and discussed by Lieut. Henry L. Abbot, Topographical Engineers, in Vol. VI of the Reports (to which I refer for particulars), gives results which may be regarded as absolutely correct, as demonstrated by Lieutenant Abbot, if suitable corrections can be obtained; and under less favorable circumstances, the results are at least more generally reliable than those obtained in any other way. By the introduction of the corrections for horary and abnormal oscillations of the barometric column, if such can be obtained from points of similar climatical features, not too far distant, nor differing too much in altitude from the point the altitude of which is to be determined, all causes of error are eliminated the more the nearer these conditions are fulfilled, including the effects of the

Horary Oscillations of the Barometric Column.

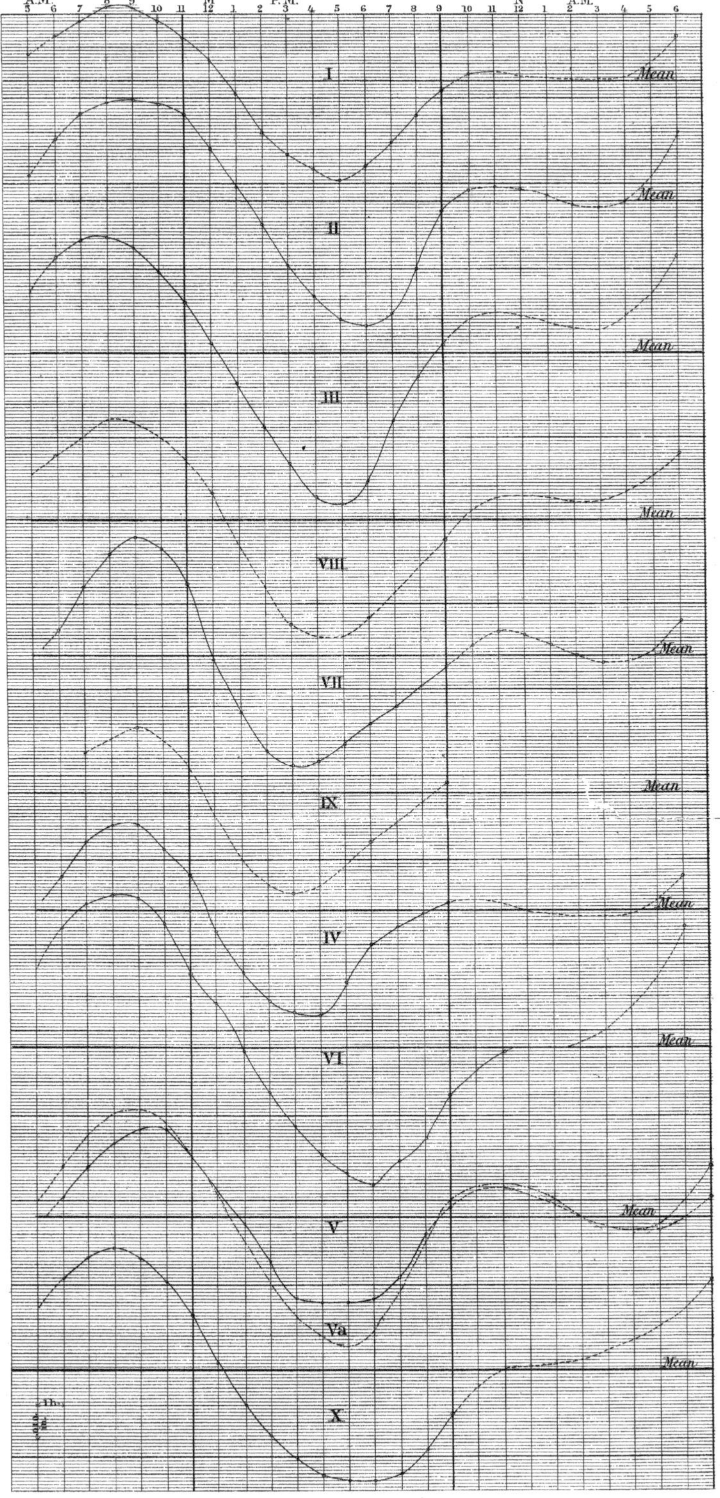

aqueous vapor in the atmosphere upon its pressure, which we cannot bring into calculation in any other way with a reasonable hope of success. This constitutes one of the most prominent advantages of the new method. Those formulæ in which the atmospheric moisture appears as a separate element are open to a great many objections, and in their application we meet with obstacles which we are not now prepared to overcome. The most prominent among them is our want of accurate knowledge of the laws of the distribution and transmission of moisture through the atmosphere, and the great variability of its amount in different strata of the air, depending partly on altogether local influences, which may not extend beyond the lowest strata of the atmosphere. Only under particularly favorable circumstances these formulæ can be expected exceptionally to give very favorable results.

The new method required the use of a mean reading of the barometer and thermometer at the fixed station, and the corrections which are applied give an approximation to the mean reading of the barometer at the station the altitude of which is to be determined. If this mean was really obtained, then the mean temperature of the place would give the correct result; but as the corrections fail to be perfect, the introduction of the mean temperature of the respective day or days seems generally to give the best results.

CORRECTIONS FOR THE HORARY OSCILLATIONS OF THE MERCURIAL COLUMN.

The horary oscillations differ according to the latitude, climate, and altitude of the stations, and the seasons of the year. Their values for the regions traversed by us were not known. I determined them, therefore, for as many points as it could be done. Hourly observations were made for the purpose, mostly during 16 hours of each day, and kept up for several days or weeks. From these the variations were deduced, with the aid of diagrams and interpolations, as described by Lieutenant Abbot. The following table exhibits the results obtained, which are also graphically illustrated by the curves on Plate A, on an enlarged scale. The full black lines in those diagrams connect the computed hourly means, while the dotted lines, like the values put in brackets in the following table, are not actually determined by observations:

A.—*Corrections for the horary oscillation of the barometric pressure.*

[In inches (English) of the mercurial column.]

Hours.	I.	II.	III.	IV.	V.	V *a.*	VI.	VII.	VIII.	IX.	X.
5 a. m	[—.008]	[—.007]	[—.018]	[—.000]	[—.000]	[—.004]	[—.023]	....	[—.014]	....	[—.018]
6 a. m	—.013	—.018	—.028	—.010	—.006	—.015	—.035	—.013*	—.019	....	—.027
7 a. m	—.018	—.026	—.033	—.020	—.015	—.026	—.042	—.020	[—.026]	—.012	—.033
8 a. m	—.022	—.029	—.034	—.026	—.022	—.031	—.045	—.030	[—.030]	....	—.036
9 a. m	—.022	—.029	—.031	—.025	—.026	—.032	—.044	—.035	—.028	—.024	—.033
10 a. m	—.018	—.028	—.024	—.018	—.026	—.028	—.036	—.032	[—.025]	....	—.026
11 a. m	—.013	—.025	—.014	—.010	—.019	—.019	—.022	—.021	[—.019]	....	—.016
12 m	—.006	—.015	—.003	+.006	—.008	—.007	—.008	+.001	—.008	+.007	—.002
1 p. m	+.004	—.004	+.009	+.018	+.002	+.007	+.006	+.017	[+.007]	....	+.010
2 p. m	+.015	+.007	+.022	+.027	+.013	+.018	+.018	+.028	[+.021]	....	+.019
3 p. m	+.021	+.019	+.033	+.030	+.024	+.029	+.028	+.032	+.031	+.030	+.026
4 p. m	+.025	+.028	+.043	+.031	+.025	+.035	+.036	+.031	[+.034]	....	+.031
5 p. m	+.029	+.035	+.045	+.021	+.025—	+.038	+.042	+.026	[+.034]	....	+.032
6 p. m	+.025	+.037	+.039	+.010	+.024	+.033	+.046	+.020	+.029	+.015	+.032
7 p. m	+.018	+.034	+.020	+.005	+.018	+.020	+.038	+.015	[+.021]	....	+.030
8 p. m	+.010	+.020	+.007	+.001	+.005	+.006	+.027	+.009	[+.013]	....	+.023
9 p. m	+.003	+.003	—.003	—.002	—.003	—.005	+.014	+.003	+.006	—.003	+.012
10 p. m	....	—.003	....	....	....	—.008	....	....	....	....	....

*6.30 a. m.

No. I was deduced from 23 days' hourly observations taken at Fort Leavenworth, Kans., from May 3 to 26, 1858, at an elevation of near 900 feet above the level of the sea. The mean temperature during that time was 59° Fahrenheit, the weather rainy and stormy. The hourly variations were often obliterated by the abnormal changes, and the amplitude of the diagram is, therefore, comparatively small; it corresponds very nearly with that for the same month at Philadelphia.

No. II was deduced from observations taken at Fort Kearney, Nebr., from June 19 to July 1, 1858, at an elevation of 2,200 feet above the level of the sea. The mean temperature was 77°.5, the weather mostly fine, with the exception of some rains and high winds. Great abnormal variations took place during this interval, but I found that they did not change much the mean result. Therefore I eliminated only one very irregular day, and calculated the table from the remaining 11 days, after correcting a few obvious irregularities. The values thus obtained are very satisfactory.

No. III was deduced from 4 days' observations taken at Fort Laramie, Nebr., from July 30 to August 1, 1858, at an elevation of about 4,470 feet above the level of the sea, and with a mean temperature of 67°. The weather was rather favorable. The diagram has a marked sweeping shape.

No. IV was deduced from observations taken at Fort Bridger, Utah, from September 28 to October 7, 1858, at an elevation of 6,656 feet above the level of the sea. The weather turned out so stormy, and the variations so irregular, that I had to reject all observations made after the first 2 days, which have a mean temperature of 57°.

No. V was deduced from observations taken at Camp Floyd, Utah, at an elevation of 4,860 feet above the level of the sea, from April 4 to 23, 1859. The mean air temperature was 42°, and the weather mostly cloudy, stormy, and rainy. The amplitude is, therefore, rather small.

No. V *a*. A more graceful diagram and of larger amplitude was obtained from only the first 3 days of No. V, from April 5 to 8, 1859, with a mean temperature of 41° and fine weather.

No. VI was deduced from 3 days' observations taken at Camp Floyd, Utah, from August 6 to 9, 1859. The mean temperature was about 70°, and the weather clear and favorable, with the exception of some high winds.

No. VII was deduced from 10 days' hourly observations taken at Camp Floyd, Utah, from October 30 to November 9, 1858. The mean temperature was about 35°, the weather fine, and no great abnormal variations took place. These results are, therefore, of superior value. The diagram shows a bold, sweeping shape.

No. VIII was deduced from 22 days' tri-hourly observations at Camp Floyd, Utah, taken by Capt. J. W. Phelps, Fourth Artillery, from September 22 to October 13, 1858. The mean temperature was 57°, the weather partly stormy. The values for the intermediate hours were found by plotting the calculated ones, and combining them by a curve, which seemed best to correspond to the other diagrams.

No. IX was deduced from tri-hourly observations taken at Camp Floyd, Utah, from November 3 to 29, 1858. The mean temperature was 35°, the weather mostly calm and clear, but some great abnormal variations took place, and some snow fell. The amplitude is, therefore, smaller than in No. VII.

No. X was deduced from observations at Genoa, Carson Valley, Utah, at an elevation of 4,824 feet above the level of the sea, taken from June 12 to June 23, 1859. The mean temperature was 76°.3, and the weather fine; but the condition of the atmospheric pressure was not as uniformly regular as might have been desired. The diagram has, therefore, a less marked shape and amplitude than one might expect, but it must be remembered that the situation of Genoa is a peculiar one, on the margin of the arid interior, not far from extensive deserts, but also close to the foot of the Sierra Nevada, with its snow-clad summits, its abundance of water, and luxuriant vegetation.

I also tried to obtain the barometric variations in Woodruff Valley, one of the desert valleys of the interior of the Basin, at an elevation of nearly 6,000 feet above the level of the sea, at the end of May, 1859. The mean temperature there was then 53° Fahrenheit. But as a barometric storm occurred in these days, I did not obtain satisfactory results. I can only state that the barometer seems to oscillate very little between sunrise and noon, that then it sinks for some hours and begins to rise again rather abruptly toward sunset. The peculiarity of this change is due to the influence of the aqueous vapor, or rather to the extraordinarily small amount of aqueous vapor in that region, as will appear from the discussion of that subject below, while we might expect a large amplitude on account of the large daily oscillation of the temperature.

These tables of oscillations were made use of for correcting the observations, either directly or by combining them so as to answer the purpose more satisfactorily. Most of the camping-places along our routes in Utah did not require very large corrections, partly on account of their high altitudes, which mostly varied between 5,500 and 7,000 feet above the level of the sea, partly on account of the reason stated above. The largest corrections were needed in the neighborhood of Carson Lake, and at some other low points with high temperatures; but in no instance were the oscillations found nearly as large as those observed by Lieutenant Abbot at a much lower elevation with higher temperature, in August, at Fort Reading, in the Sacramento Valley, or those obtained farther south, in New Mexico.*

CORRECTION FOR THE ABNORMAL VARIATIONS OF THE ATMOSPHERIC PRESSURE.

The amount of this variation differs much according to the climatical character and elevation of the stations. There was no meteorological station in the interior of Utah, in the climatical zone of our survey, besides that at Camp Floyd, where barometric observations were taken under direction of the medical department of the Army. Although we went several hundred miles from that place and passed high ranges of mountains, I considered it safe to apply the corrections indicated by the changes of the barometer at Camp Floyd, as it is a well-established fact that the variations extend over hundreds of miles of the same zone with little change. Although we were part of the

* I am compelled to confine myself merely to allude here to the change of the amplitudes, in value and time, in the different months and localities, and to the more gradual or abrupt increase or decrease of pressure which is graphically represented in the diagrams; nor can I discuss the varying influence of the elastic force of vapor in the atmosphere upon the oscillations of the barometer at the different hours of the day, and in the different seasons of the year. These interesting questions must be left to future investigation. They are by far not so easily solved as it would appear from a superficial examination.

time nearer to San Francisco, I preferred to base the corrections throughout on Camp Floyd, because the climate of San Francisco is one of periodical changes, while that of the interior is non-periodic, and because San Francisco is several thousand feet lower than the Basin. The difference of the monthly mean readings of the barometer from the yearly mean has not been found analogous in both districts, although many of the great variations of the atmospheric pressure will undoubtedly be felt simultaneously in the interior of Utah and on the Pacific coast.

The diagram of the observations at Camp Floyd, corrected for the horary oscillations, showed in general a satisfactory agreement with the corresponding diagrams of the single camps, and even for the most western point reached by us; for as regards the city of Genoa, in Carson Valley, Utah, these diagrams agree better with each other than those for Genoa and San Francisco. Local storms and rains in the single mountain ranges affect the parallelism of the diagrams in some instances; but the differences produced in that way are probably not considerable, and partly, at least, are counterbalanced by the corresponding changes in temperature, &c.*

Between the abnormal variations of the barometers at Camp Floyd and Fort Bridger I also found a most remarkable coincidence, and nearly simultaneous changes, when I plotted the diagrams of corresponding observations, made very carefully at these points in September and October, 1858.

CORRECTION OF THE OBSERVED AIR-TEMPERATURES.

The method of computation requires the introduction of the mean temperatures of the days, instead of the observed temperatures. To find the mean temperature more accurately, and make the correction more systematic, I have deduced the following tables from observations made in connection with the hourly observations of the barometer for determining the horary oscillations of the mercurial column. These interesting tables show the mean difference of the temperature of each hour from the mean temperature of the day for different stations and seasons. The curves on plate B represent these variations graphically. The marks * indicate the times of sunrise and sunset.

As no observations had been made during the hours of night, the mean temperature of the twenty-four hours was calculated under the supposition that the temperature decreases regularly from 9 p. m. to near sunrise, which, in the highly elevated regions, comes very near the truth.

* Long after the computation of the altitudes had been finished, I took up the study of the hygrometrical observations, the leading results of which will be found in the latter portion of this report. They impressed me still more with the necessity of selecting, as a lower or fixed station, a point which actually presents the same climatical features as the station the altitude of which is to be determined. I found, besides, that when the local storms occur, the hygrometrical observations will enable an experienced meteorologist to apply some discretionary corrections and to judge better the comparative accuracy of the results of different computations; although I still repudiate the introduction of the force of vapor into the hypsometric formulæ. By them he is also enabled better to judge which one of the various tables of horary oscillations is best adapted to the single observations.

Hourly Variation of Temperature

at different stations and seasons.

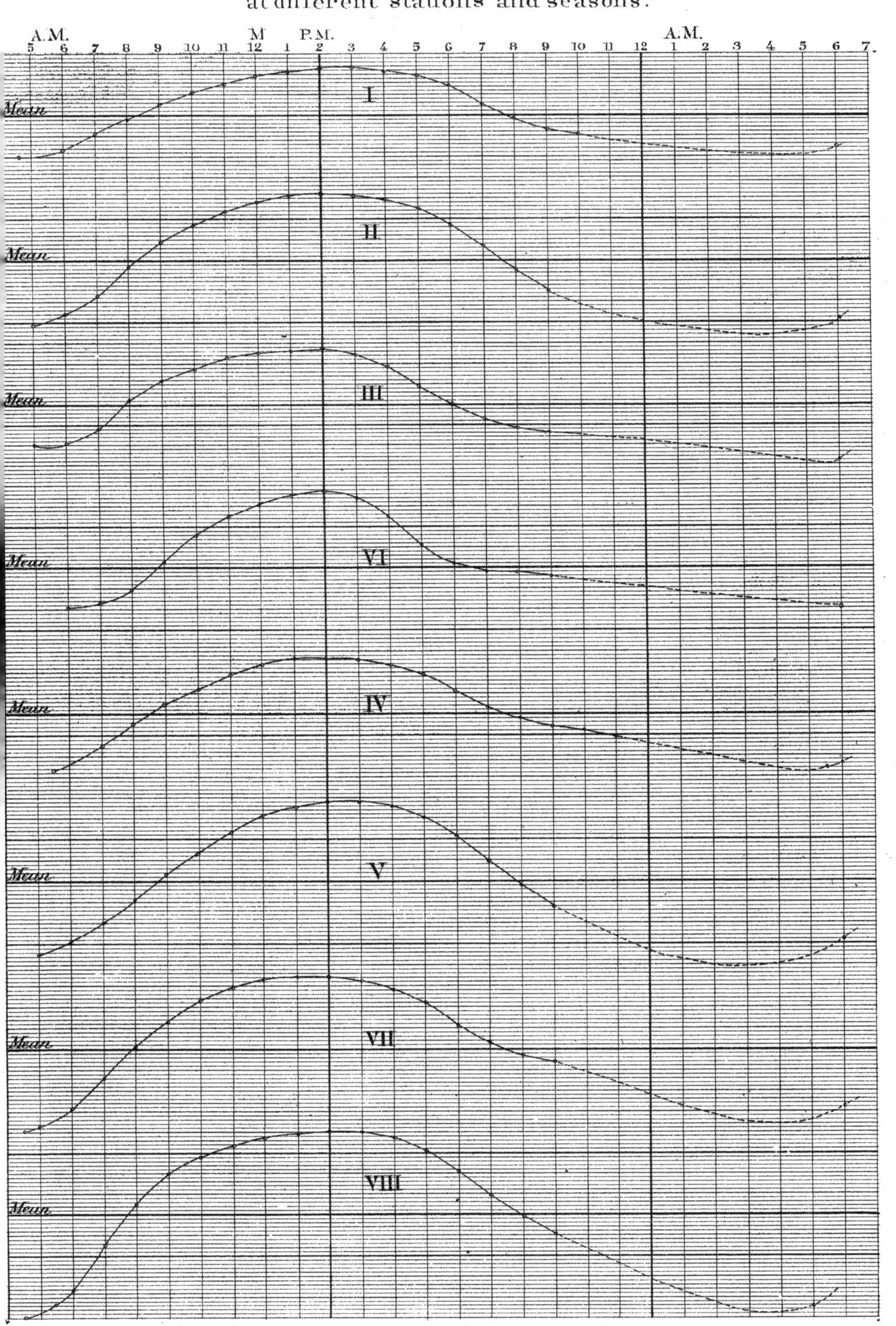

B.—*Corrections for horary oscillation of temperature, in degrees, Fahrenheit.*

Hours.	I.	II.	III.	IV.	V.	VI.	VII.	VIII.
5 a. m	[+ 9.8]	[+15.2]	....	+13.0*	+17.5	....	[+19.0]	+22.0*
6 a. m	+ 8.0	+13.8	+10.0	+11.7	+14.5	+ 9.5†	+14.0]	[+18.0]
7 a. m	+ 4.8	+ 8.2	+ 5.7	+ 7.0	+10.0	+ 9.2	+ 7.0	[+ 8.0]
8 a. m	+ 1.5	+ 1.7	− 1.7	+ 2.3	+ 4.5	+ 5.5	− 0.5	[− 3.0]
9 a. m	− 2.0	− 4.5	− 6.0	− 2.0	− 1.0	− 0.5	− 6.5	−10.0
10 a. m	− 5.2	− 8.7	− 9.0	− 6.3	− 6.5	− 7.0	−11.0	[−14.0]
11 a. m	− 7.5	−11.7	−11.0	− 9.5	−11.5	−12.0	−14.0	[−16.0]
12 m	− 9.2	−13.7	−13.0	−11.5	−15.5	−15.0	−16.0	−18.0
1 p. m	−10.5	−15.2	−13.5	−13.0	−18.0	−17.0	−17.0	[−19.0]
2 p. m	−11.2	−16.0	−13.5	−13.5	−18.5	−18.5	−17.0	[−20.0]
3 p. m	−11.2	−15.5	−12.0	−13.0	−18.5	−17.0	−16.0	−20.0
4 p. m	−10.5	−14.5	− 9.0	−11.7	−18.0	−13.0	−14.3	[−18.5]
5 p. m	− 9.5	−12.5	− 4.7	− 9.7	−15.0	− 6.0	−11.0	[−15.5]
6 p. m	− 7.0	− 9.0	0.0	− 5.7	−11.0	− 1.0	− 5.0	−11.0
7 p. m	− 2.3	− 4.0	+ 3.3	− 1.0	− 5.0	0.0	− 1.5	[− 4.5]
8 p. m	+ 1.3	+ 3.0	+ 5.3	+ 1.3	+ 1.5	+ 1.0	+ 1.0	[+ 1.0]
9 p. m	+ 3.3	+ 7.0	+ 6.3	+ 3.0	+ 5.5	+ 2.0	+ 3.2	+ 4.7

* 5.30 a. m. † 6.30 a. m.

No. I was deduced from 9 days' observations at Fort Kearney, Nebr., taken between June 19 and July 1, 1858, at an elevation of 2,200 feet above the level of the sea. Three more days' observations were rejected on account of great irregularities, in consequence of rain. The mean temperature was 77°.5; the weather mostly fine.

No. II was deduced from 4 days' observations taken at Fort Laramie, Nebr., from July 30 to August 3, 1858, at an elevation of 4,470 feet, with a mean temperature of 67°, and favorable weather.

No. III was deduced from 6 days' observations at Fort Bridger, Utah, taken from September 28 to October 4, at an elevation above the sea of 6,656 feet, with a mean temperature of 53°. The weather was mostly fair, partly cloudy and rainy. Some more days' observations had to be rejected on account of a snow-storm.

No. IV was deduced from observations taken at Camp Floyd, Utah, from April 4 to 23, 1859, at an elevation above the level of the sea of 4,860 feet, with a mean temperature of 42°. The weather was partly clear, but mostly cloudy, even with some snow and rain. The diagrams of the single days are very irregular, but as the observations had been taken so long, it was not considered necessary to eliminate the irregularities. The mean variations, which are given in the table, include them all.

No. V was deduced from 3 days' observations taken at Camp Floyd, Utah, from August 6 to 9, 1859, with a mean temperature of 69°.5, and clear, favorable weather.

No. VI was deduced from observations taken at Camp Floyd from October 30 to November 10, 1858, with a mean temperature of 35°. The weather was calm and clear, and the diagram presents, therefore, sharply marked features.

No. VII was deduced from observations taken at Genoa, Carson Valley, Utah, at an elevation of 4,824 feet above the level of the sea, from June 12 to 23, 1859. The mean temperature was 76°.3, the weather fine and clear. The shape of this diagram, with its early maximum, may be due partly to local causes incident to the peculiar situation of the camp.

No. VIII was deduced from 2 days' tri-hourly observations in Woodruff Valley, one of the desert valleys of the interior of Utah Territory, at an elevation of 5,940 feet above the level of the sea, taken end of May, 1859, with a mean temperature of 53°, and clear weather.*

* A diagram of still more marked shape was obtained from 2 days' observations at Camp Floyd, in the middle of September. It has the excessive amplitude of 48°.3 Fahrenheit. More will be said of it below.

It is scarcely necessary to remark that, in the application of these corrections, proper discretion is required on the part of the computer, and that the tables are merely intended to help him. While the variations are smaller on a clouded and rainy day, not favorable for radiation, they are larger on a clear day, and much depends upon local circumstances, and the direction and force of the winds, &c. When the successive camps and minor stations are in the same valley, or do not differ much in altitude and physical relations, the mean temperatures may be determined with great precision; but where the altitude and relative position of the stations vary much, as they did on our survey in Utah, from low, arid valleys or scorched slopes to narrow cañons or high mountain summits, it is very difficult to determine the mean temperature of the day from one or a few observations, the more so because the hour of the maximum temperature also changes according to the relative situation of the stations.

SELECTION OF A FIXED STATION.

After all these corrections had been applied, the observations were ready for computation. The tables of Prof. A. Guyot, based on La Place's formula, were used for this purpose. Next the question arose what should be taken as the lower or fixed station for the calculation of the altitudes in Utah. As most of them are considerably high, between 5,000 and 8,000 feet, the air-temperature appears as an important element in the computation. A difference of 1 degree in the temperature changes the result 1 foot for every 900 feet of the height. By taking the sea-level as the lower station, with a comparatively high mean temperature, this element appears to exercise an unduly great influence on the result, after all the corrections have been applied, which, if fully answering the purpose, would require the mean temperature of the year to be used, not the one, generally much higher, of the day of the observation.

Camp Floyd was an elevated inland station, for which the mean reading of the barometer and thermometer could be ascertained, and the altitude of which could, therefore, be determined satisfactorily. By taking Camp Floyd as the lower station, I decreased in a great measure the influence of the temperature in the computations, and all errors arising from that source. The altitudes of all places not very far from Camp Floyd were certainly obtained much more correctly in this way, and I believe also most of the others; at least I obtained by this method results which agreed very satisfactorily in several cases when observations, taken at different times, controlled each other, while the use of the sea-level as the lower station would mostly have given greater discrepancies.

It might be urged that, in case the altitude of Camp Floyd was not correctly determined, this error would be propagated by assuming it as the fixed station. The error in the altitude might originate from various causes: Firstly. The values assumed as mean readings of barometer and thermometer at the level of the sea might not be those best adapted for the special purpose; then the computer would introduce the same causes of error into the other calculations, and the results would be obtained even more uniform on assuming an intermediate station for references. Secondly. The mean reading of barometer and thermometer, as given for Camp Floyd, might not be absolutely correct. This error cannot be great. If the values did not correspond to the station of Camp Floyd, they would correspond to an imaginary one a few feet higher or lower. The altitude computed for Camp Floyd would then be that of this imaginary station, and the other altitudes would not be affected by that error at all, but would be obtained correctly. Lastly. It might be doubted whether the altitude of a station far inland, with a peculiar climate, could be determined correctly, even from the yearly mean reading of the barometer and thermometer, and that thus the elevation computed for Camp Floyd might be incorrect. Errors arising from that source would certainly be much greater if minor inland stations were directly compared with the sea-level, than if they were computed with reference to a station with their own climatical features, the altitude of which had been determined from a whole year's observations. If not correct, the elevation would then at least be obtained more relatively correct among themselves. The introduction of the corrections for horary and abnormal variations has done a great deal toward eliminating errors from that source, but as these corrections cannot possibly be found to suit each single observation, I consider it the best policy to decrease the liability of errors in the results of calculation by decreasing the altitude between the upper and lower stations; in other words, by assuming Camp Floyd as the lower station instead of the level of the sea.

The lowest portion of the route is lower than Camp Floyd, and I hesitated to make use of that station as the fixed one. Still, I considered it better to retain uniformity in the computations. The different values obtained for the altitude of Genoa, in Carson Valley, by the different modes of computation, will show the advantages of the method followed by me. Twelve days' careful observations had been taken there, and minor errors were thus eliminated. The diagrams of the abnormal variations of the barometers at Genoa and Camp Floyd, as well as their mean readings for those days, correspond well together, as I have stated above, and the temperature at the time was very high at both points. If the altitude of Camp Floyd had been calculated from these observations only, by whatever method, it would have been found very near equal to that of Genoa computed in the same way. By my method this was obtained. I found Genoa 4,824 feet high, while Camp Floyd is 4,860 feet high. I then computed the altitude with reference to the mean reading at the level of the sea, and the abnormal oscillation observed at Camp Floyd. I found it 5,004 feet, which is much too high, because in this case, where the corrections give a nearly exact compensation, the mean temperature of the year only would give a good result, while the high temperature of these days, in connection with the great difference of level between the upper and lower stations, raises the result unduly. Again, I computed the altitude with reference to observations during the same days at San Francisco, thus introducing the very large abnormal oscillation of the barometer in the middle of June at that place, which, I felt satisfied, was larger than the correction required for Genoa, but which might have been compensated by the high degree of temperature. Thus I obtained the altitude, only 4,633 feet (as near as I could get it without some corrections, the values of which were unknown to me). It will be seen that the mean of these two extreme results, 5,004 and 4,633, happens to be 4,818, very near what my method gives. This example shows forcibly what I consider as the advantage of computing from a fixed station, which does not differ too much in altitude from those which shall be determined, namely, that extremes of error are thus avoided, although in single instances other methods may give better results. In calculating the profile of a country, quite different rules must be followed from those best answering for the computation of the altitude of a single mountain.

The altitudes of points on the roads between Camp Floyd and Fort Bridger, Utah, were computed before the yearly mean readings at Camp Floyd had been determined. I had, therefore, to make use of the corresponding readings of the barometer at both stations, which answers the same purpose, and of the mean temperature of the days. But as the temperature, during the season of these surveys, was generally moderate, and the difference of the altitude of the upper and lower stations mostly not very considerable, the obtained values must be nearly correct. The altitude of Fort Bridger, determined in that way, agrees perfectly with that obtained from a large mean. Some of these observations could not be referred to simultaneous observations at Camp Floyd or Fort Bridger, and I had to compare them with such obtained on the same days at other camps, the altitudes of which had been determined before, or even with camps of the preceding and following days. Although this method is very objectionable as a general thing, I consider the results in this case as more reliable because the circumstances were uncommonly favorable; and especially the corrections for the daily variations of the barometer gave such complete compensation that the plot of the barometric readings of the single stations could be filled up satisfactorily for the intervening hours. Of the different values thus obtained for a point, the means were taken, which probably give a close approximation to the real altitudes.

ALTITUDE OF CAMP FLOYD.

The determination of the mean reading of the barometer and thermometer at Camp Floyd was a matter of considerable importance to me, because I wanted to make use of them, and the altitude of the station computed from them, as a basis for most of the other computations, as I have stated above. At our station observations had been regularly taken during the 6 months from November, 1858, to April, 1859; partly hourly, 16 a day; partly 6 every day, and partly at the hours of 7 a. m., 2 p. m., and 9 p. m., every day. The mean of these was calculated with due reference to the different number of observations, and the necessary corrections were applied. This mean was found to be 25.129 inches at 32° of the mercury. The results of observations during the next 6 months, from May to October, 1859, regularly taken at the hospital at Camp Floyd, at the hours of 7 a. m., 2 p. m., and 9 p. m., were kindly furnished by the medical department. Their mean, reduced to our standard and station, is 25.150 inches. The mean for the whole year is, therefore, 25.140 inches, English, at 32° of the mercury.

The mean temperature of the year was deduced from 6 months' observations at our station; 3 months' observations by Asst. Surg. Thomas H. Williams, medical director of the Department of Utah, and 3 months' observations at the hospital, under direction of Asst. Surg. J. Moore, U. S. A. It is 47° Fahrenheit.

I assumed 30.050 inches as the mean reading of the barometer, the mercury reduced to 32° Fahrenheit, and 54° as mean air temperature at the level of the sea, best adapted for the computation of the altitude of Camp Floyd and points of a similar geographical position. It is the mean of the values corresponding to the Pacific coast in the neighborhood of San Francisco, and to the Atlantic coast near the 40th parallel of latitude. I thus obtained the altitude of Camp Floyd as 4,867 feet. To test the correctness of this result, I computed the elevation of Fort Bridger from a mean of 8 months' observations, taken there from January to August, 1859, under direction of Asst. Surg. R. Bartholow, and, later, of Asst. Surg. K. Ryland, U. S. A. This mean, corrected for the zero error of the instrument, is 23.513 inches, and 42° air temperature, which values probably represent very nearly the mean of the year. I thus found the altitude 6,688 feet—1,791 more than that of Camp Floyd, while the mean difference of elevation between both points, determined in various ways, from very careful simultaneous observations, and from large means, is 1,796 feet. These results agree very satisfactorily, and speak for the correctness of the observations and method. Taking into consideration, moreover, the height of the instruments above the ground, we may assume as well established the altitude of Camp Floyd (parade ground, near headquarters) as 4,860 feet, and of Fort Bridger (parade ground), as 6,656 feet. In these computations, as in the other, the elastic force of the aqueous vapor has not been taken into consideration, but La Place's formula has been made use of, for the reasons stated above.

GENERAL REMARKS IN REGARD TO CAMP FLOYD AND THE UTAH BASIN.

The reading of the barometer at Camp Floyd varied considerably during the different months. The highest monthly mean was observed in January; the lowest in February. A higher atmospheric pressure seems to prevail in the fall and first part of winter; a lower one in the spring and part of summer; but as the observations have not all been made with the same degree of accuracy, and cover too limited a time, it would be unsafe to draw definite conclusions from them. The subjoined table contains the monthly means, the authorities for which I have stated above (namely, myself, Dr. Williams, and Dr. Moore). It also contains the quantities of rain and melted snow at Camp Floyd, taken, from 1858 to 1859, from the rec ords of the Medi cal Department of the Army, and at Salt Lake City, from March, 1857, to February, 1858, upon the authority of a Mr. W. W. Phelps, a citizen of that place.

Month.	Barometric pressure.			Temperature.			Rain and melted snow, in inches.			
							Observer, Dr. Moore.		Observer, Mr. W. W. Phelps.	
	Year.	Inches, English.	Observer.	Year.	Degrees, Fahrenheit.	Observer.	Year.	Camp Floyd.	Year.	Salt Lake City.
November	1858...	25.208	E.	1858...	34.0	E.	1858...	0.50	1857...	2.80
December	1858...	25.106	E.	1858...	22.0	E.	1858...	0.30	1857...	5.40
January	1859...	25.297	E.	1859...	16.2	E.	1859...	0.35	1858...	0.30
February	1859...	25.031	E.	1859...	29.9	E.	1859...	1.14	1858...	1.37
March	1859...	25.069	E.	1859...	31.9	E.	1859...	0.28	1858...	0.39
April	1859...	25.062	E.	1859...	43.6	E.	1859...	0.40	1858...	0.19
May	1859...	25.082	M.	1859...	54.7	W.	1859...	0.40	1858...	0.83
June	1859...	25.122	M.	1859...	74.7	W.	1859...	0.03	1858...	1.01
July	1859...	25.175	M.	1859...	75.0	W.	1859...	2.28	1858...	0.64
August	1859...	25.133	M.	1859...	72.1	M.	1859...	0.18	1858...	0.85
September	1859...	25.173	M.	1859...	58.4	M.	1859...	1.72	1857...	0.57
October	1859...	25.213	M.	1859...	50.7	M.	1859...	0.00	1857...	1.10
Mean	1 year	25.140	......	....	47.0	......	Total	7.58	Total	15.45

The heaviest precipitation of rain takes place during the fall and winter, but generally every month has some rain, and the climate of Utah does in that respect by no means exhibit the periodicity of the climate of California, and of more southern latitudes.

During the summer months the showers seldom continued any length of time, and frequently only a few drops fell. The precipitation is most copious near high mountains, not only for the same causes which in all countries favor the precipitation of moisture on high mountains, but also, it appears, because the clouds and drops of rain, while sinking through the parched lower strata of the atmosphere, are partly again dissolved into vapor, and thus become less before reaching the bottom of the valleys, unless the rain should happen to be heavy. This is the contrary of what takes place in moister climates, where the quantity of rain frequently increases with every foot of its descent through the air, which is saturated with moisture.

In June we had no rain in the field, but in July numerous short showers occurred, which, in the aggregate, amounted, however, only to 2 inches of rain. At Camp Floyd 2.28 inches were measured in July. I am unable to determine whether the difference in the amount of precipitation between Camp Floyd and Salt Lake City, as exhibited by the above table, is mainly due to the irregularity of the distribution of rain and snow in the different years, or to other causes, although I have no doubt but that the fall of rain and snow is more abundant at Salt Lake City, which is situated at the very foot of the high and wide range of the Wahsatch Mountains, near the most elevated summits of which considerable banks of snow remain unmelted all the year round, although they cannot be said to reach the limit of perpetual snow, and the moister atmosphere of which is indicated by a different vegetation than farther off these mountains near Camp Floyd, and in the other open valleys. In 1857, six feet of snow fell near Salt Lake City; certainly much more than is likely ever to fall at Camp Floyd during a single winter.

Dew falls very rarely in the vast desert valleys and on most of the mountain ranges of Western Utah, in the so-called Great Basin. The scarcity of grass in the valleys, which are mostly covered with a thin growth of *Artemisia* and other desert plants, combined with the great dryness of the atmosphere, which is indicated by the small amount of rain, is not favorable to its formation. On our whole march from Camp Floyd to the Sierra Nevada and back, during May, June, July, and part of August, that is, from the time when it was still snowing occasionally to the time when the greatest heat of the summer was over, we observed dew only on three mornings, and then it was confined to a border of grass of only a few feet in width along the banks of creeks. In Section V of the Geological Report, I have shown that the cause of this great deficiency of moisture is a consequence of the geographical situation and hypsographical character of the country.

The remarkable dryness of the atmosphere influences also its electric condition. We know that dry air is a non-conductor of electricity, while moist air is a conductor. The electricity which is constantly developed in various ways, is, under ordinary circumstances, mostly at once conducted to the earth or diffused in the moist air. In the comparatively moist climate of Western Europe, in Germany, for example, electricity can therefore always be detected in the air by delicate instruments, while even in the Mississippi Valley, in the drier climate of the summer months, frequently not the slightest trace of it is indicated by the same instruments, as I am informed by Dr. Ad. Wislizenus, of Saint Louis, who has lately commenced an interesting series of experiments upon this subject. In the arid climate of Utah the air conducts the electricity still less, and even the parched pulverulent soil appears to become a non-conductor. Thus the electricity is accumulated where it is developed. Not only do woolen clothes, buffalo-robes, and all sorts of peltry, and even the saddle-blankets on the horses become highly charged, but the glass on wood-cased pocket-compasses becomes so electric that the needle adheres to the glass and persistently refuses to work, and the equilibrium cannot be restored by merely touching the glass with the hand. Where thus every part of the instruments, and the body and clothing of the observer are apt to be electric, and the soil and air are non-conductors, all the delicate magnetic observations become exceedingly difficult to take.

I cannot conclude these remarks without mentioning a phenomenon familiar to all the settlers along the foot of the Wahsatch range. During certain seasons, regularly every evening soon after sunset, a wind rises, blowing from the summit of the mountains down the cañons, toward the wide longitudinal valleys at their base. It is by them called cañon-wind, and finds its explanation in the circumstance that in the evening when the other winds generally lull, the radiation of heat of the bare dry soil of the valleys, and consequently the upward movement of the heated air continues for several hours, and the equilibrium is restored by the afflux of colder air from the mountain summits by the channels of the narrow side-valleys, in which the temperature is depressed by the evaporation of their streams, which makes a great deal of heat latent. This phenomenon bears resemblance to the land and sea breezes on the coast.

Another phenomenon of frequent occurrence near Camp Floyd are whirlwinds, which for months may be seen nearly daily traversing Cedar Valley in its longitudinal direction from north to south. They have no great diameter, but considerable height, and may readily be followed with the eye by the high cylindrical column of dust which they raise. When they passed our barometrical station, I observed several times that the mercurial column fell momentarily, and then rose again to its former height; all within the few seconds occupied by the passage of the whirl. I never observed, instrumentally, the quantity of this fall, but it cannot have been less than 0.1 inch, and perhaps it was much larger. The fall of the barometer is partly caused by the upward movement, and thus diminished pressure of the air, of which the height of the column of dust affords a proof, but I explain it principally by the fact that the whirl, being formed by a body of air in violent motion, does not exercise the pressure corresponding to a similar column of air at rest or comparative rest outside the whirl. This is in strict conformity to the laws of pneumatics, and analogous to the laws of the difference of the static and dynamic pressure of fluids. A third cause is to be found in the circumstance that the progressing whirl, imparting its rapid rotary motion to bodies of air before comparatively at rest, tears them off from the main body of the air, which is unable to join in that motion so rapidly as not to exhibit a slight expansion and consequent diminution of the pressure. The causes of the frequent occurrence, and of the regular development of this interesting phenomenon, may be found in the great width and length of the valleys, which are free from any obstruction; in the large quantity of heat radiated from their sparsely-covered and dry soil; in the powerful fluctuations of the atmosphere, caused by the difference of temperature between the bottom of the valleys and the upper regions of the air, and the great amplitude of the daily oscillations of the temperature. Near Camp Floyd, in Cedar Valley, they may be caused directly by the distribution and configuration of the mountains at the northern end of the valley. The winds from the north and northwest, after sweeping over the immense unbroken level of the Salt Lake Valley, when they approach Cedar Valley, are divided into two branches by the mountains which separate Tuilla Valley from the valley of Jordan River. The western branch meets, at the southern end of Tuilla Valley, with the mountain mass of Floyd's Peak, and partly continues into Rush Valley, partly is diverted to the southeast and enters the northwestern extremity of Cedar Valley, across a depression in the O-quirrh Mountains. The eastern branch enters Cedar Valley by various depressions in the much less elevated so-called Traverse Mountains. These different currents, when meeting again, appear to form the whirls whenever the accessory circumstances are favorable.

HYGROMETRICAL CONDITIONS OF THE ATMOSPHERE.

I have already spoken of the smallness of the amount of rain, snow, and dew which falls in Central and Western Utah. Before discussing this subject farther, I will introduce some general remarks for the benefit of the scientific reader.

The formation of vapor in the air is especially dependent upon two conditions, namely, upon the temperature and upon the presence of water. With an unlimited supply of moisture, vapor will be found in proportion to the height of the temperature; but with equal degrees of temperature, more vapor will be formed in districts which abound in water than in those which do not. Hence it follows that the absolute quantity of vapor in the air, other circumstances being the same, is less in the interior of continents than on the seashore. As more vapor is diffused through the air at a high temperature, and as with an increasing heat the water evaporates more and more from the surface of large masses of water and from the moist ground, the quantity of water contained in the form of vapor in the lowest stratum of the air by which we are surrounded will diminish and increase in the course of the day. In climates of moderate humidity, such as Western Europe, the quantity of vapor in the air is generally increased as the temperature rises with the rising of the sun. This, however, only lasts till about 9 a. m., when the ground becomes dryer, and an ascending current of air, occasioned by the strong heating of the surface of the ground, carries the vapor on high, so that the weight of water contained in the lower strata of the air diminishes, although the formation of vapor continues. This diminution continues till toward 4 p. m.; then the quantity of water of the lower strata of the air again increases, because the upwardly-directed current of air ceases to carry away the vapor formed. This increase lasts, however, only until toward 9 p. m., because the decreasing temperature puts a limit to the further formation of vapor. In winter, when the action of the sun is less intense, the state of the case is different. Then there is generally only one maximum of the quantity of water in the air at about 2 p. m., and only the minimum at the time of sunrise. The weight of vapor in the air is, besides, smaller in winter, on account of the lower temperature.

The ratio between the quantity of aqueous vapor which air of a certain temperature is able to dissolve and the quantity which it actually contains, its relative humidity or degree of saturation, is subject to similar changes during the day. The relative humidity is generally smallest about the time of the afternoon minimum of the weight of vapor in the air, and greatest near the hour of the lowest temperature, about or before sunrise. Air of high relative humidity is called damp—it is the reverse of dry air—in which latter moistened objects become rapidly dry. In damp air a further decrease of temperature occasions a precipitation of moisture. Thus dew is formed. It is, however, by no means necessary to the formation of dew that the temperature of the air should sink below the point at which it would be saturated by the vapor present; on the contrary, then, not dew but rain would fall. Dew forms only on objects which, by stronger eradication of heat, become cooled below the temperature of the surrounding air. This difference may amount to from 7 to 25 degrees Fahrenheit.

The same quantity of vapor contained in a certain volume of air exercises a different pressure upon the inclosing vessel, according to its temperature. This tension, or elastic force, can be measured by the barometric column, and the indications of the barometer are partly due to the pressure of the air itself, partly to the pressure of the aqueous vapor diffused through it. The elastic force of vapor in the lowest stratum of the atmosphere also varies during the day with the changing temperature and quantity of weight of vapor in the air.

As the hygrometrical conditions and laws of the atmosphere are still imperfectly known, it is presumed that the remarkable results obtained by this expedition will be acceptable to the friends of meteorology. They throw some light on the climatical conditions of a district which in this, as in most other respects, differs vastly from the Eastern States of the Union. From our observations we cannot deduce complete laws, because the observations could not be continued for long periods at one station, but have mostly been taken for short times only, at numerous different points; but further explorations may complete the results. The observations have been executed with as much care as was possible under the circumstances, and the uniformity of the results, of which the following tables and diagrams afford a proof, appears highly satisfactory and testifies to their relative correctness. Still I do not hesitate to declare that the obstacles in the way of obtaining absolutely correct results, very great at fixed observatories, as those best know who have studied most fully these matters, can scarcely be obviated in the field, where the most simple arrangements can only be used to advantage.

The observations were taken with an August's hygrometer. The dry and wet bulb thermometers were suspended in the shade of the instrument wagon, generally 6 or 7 feet from the ground. I missed very much a suitable casing which would have better secured the observations against vitiating outside influences. The indications of a Mason's hygrometer in which a wide glass tube, closed on top, and fastened between the two thermometers, contained the water for moistening the wet bulb, were found to be very slow, and therefore inaccurate at times when the temperatures changed rapidly; besides, the instrument proved inconvenient for use in the field, and was badly constructed, the two thermometers not reading conformably, and thus making corrections necessary in the records.

The following tables, C and D, exhibit the mean daily oscillation of the elastic force of vapor, and of the relative humidity of the air, at certain stations and seasons, as deduced from our observations. They are graphically represented in the plates, C and D. The full black lines of the diagrams connect the values obtained for each successive hour by direct calculation. Where dotted lines run alongside of the full lines they illustrate the actual result of calculation, inclusive of all irregularities, while then the full lines represent the values which I am led to consider as the means unimpaired by the abnormal oscillations produced by irregular rains, high winds, and similar casualties. In the tables C and D, the values are given only for the hours during which observations have been taken. In other subsequent tables I have given the values obtained for the hours of the night, by interpolation, which are also graphically represented on the diagrams by dotted lines. They were obtained by drawing, in the diagrams of the oscillations of temperature, of the force of vapor, and of the relative humidity, separately and independently of each other, the curves for the hours of the night, such as they appeared to be, required under the circumstances. Then I calculated from two of the thus-obtained values the third, and represented it also on the diagrams. If the discrepancy between the first and second values was beyond the limits of the differences found to exist between the means of the computations of the single observations and the values computed from the means of these observations at the actually observed hours, then I critically examined the diagrams and changed them accordingly, until all the requirements appeared to be fulfilled. I am confident that they will be found to agree very closely with the results of observations which in future may be made in this line. In computing, I have made use of the meteorological and physical tables prepared for the Smithsonian Institution by Prof. A. Guyot, second edition, particularly of Tables B, VI, VII, IX, and X, which are deduced from Regnault's formula and the values obtained by him in his famous investigations on the vapor, instituted by order of the French government. In many instances I could not make use of the tables directly, because they do not extend to the quite abnormal extremes which my observations exhibit. I then had to apply directly the formula. The results of all the single computations will be found in the records of meteorological observations accompanying the report. The means in the following tables, C and D, were calculated without making the slightest discretionary corrections in the single observations, because I consider it impossible correctly to estimate the abnormal influences exercised upon the values by irregular changes of wind and weather, and that it is best to leave them to be balanced against each other.

C.—*Table of daily oscillations of the force of vapor, in inches (English), of the mercurial column.*

Hour.	I.	II.		III.	IV.		V.	VI.	VII.		VIII.
		Observed.	Cor-rected.		Observed.	Cor-rected.			Observed.	Cor-rected.	
6 a. m	0. 609	0. 332	0. 332	0. 100	0. 144	0. 144	0. 270	0. 118	0. 289		5.20 a. m. 0. 125
7 a. m	. 614	. 353	. 346		. 158	. 157	. 280		. 300		
8 a. m	. 627	. 349	. 357		. 169	. 170	. 290		. 317		
9 a. m	. 654	. 362	. 366	. 057	. 180	. 182	. 297	. 172	. 323		. 115
10 a. m	. 679	. 370	. 370		. 190	. 190	. 294		. 303		
11 a. m	. 690	. 364	. 364		. 173	. 181	. 288		. 275		
12 m	. 680	. 329	. 336	. 103	. 177	. 172	. 282	. 097	. 224		. 106
1 p. m	. 670	. 340	. 330		. 159	. 164	. 273		. 181		
2 p. m	. 637	. 322	. 327		. 160	. 156	. 258		. 202		
3 p. m	. 622	. 348	. 336	. 086	. 151	. 150	. 230	. 048	. 240		. 064
4 p. m	. 612	. 353	. 348		. 143	. 146	. 196		. 246		
5 p. m	. 605	. 339	. 361		. 154	. 142	. 162		. 243		
6 p. m	. 602	. 385	. 372	. 104	. 138	. 139	. 140	. 057	. 240	0. 235	. 041
7 p. m	. 611	. 357	. 368		. 138	. 138	. 172		. 229	. 223	
8 p. m	. 617	. 342	. 360		. 143	. 143	. 175		. 203		
9 p. m	. 625	. 363	. 351	. 086	. 153	. 152	. 185	. 102	. 193		. 057
10 p. m	. 625										

D.—*Table of daily oscillations of the relative humidity. Saturation* = 100.

Hour.	I.	II.		III.		IV.	V.		VI.	VII.		VIII.
		Observed.	Cor-rected.	Observed.	Cor-rected.		Observed.	Cor-rected.		Observed.	Cor-rected.	
6 a. m	81. 3	75. 2	75. 0	37. 0	37. 0	76. 0	64. 0		41. 5	51. 8		5.20 a. m. 59. 0
7 a. m	75. 0	66. 5	66. 5		25. 5	69. 5	57. 0			42. 7		
8 a. m	70. 4	51. 5	56. 0		16. 5	63. 0	49. 0			34. 7		
9 a. m	66. 6	49. 5	49. 5	9. 0	11. 5	57. 0	41. 0		21. 5	29. 2		22. 0
10 a. m	62. 3	44. 7	44. 0		10. 0	51. 0	30. 0			23. 0		
11 a. m	57. 8	38. 2	38. 0		9. 5	43. 0	25. 0			18. 7		
12 m	52. 0	31. 2	33. 5	11. 5	9. 0	39. 0	21. 0		7. 5	15. 2		14. 0
1 p. m	49. 3	31. 0	31. 0		9. 5	37. 0	19. 0			11. 4		
2 p. m	46. 7	30. 0	30. 0		10. 0	35. 0	22. 0	17. 0		13. 4		
3 p. m	45. 9	33. 7	31. 5	10. 7	10. 7	34. 0	16. 3	16. 0	3. 5	15. 6		7. 7
4 p. m	45. 2	33. 2	33. 0		12. 7	35. 0	15. 3	15. 0		17. 7		
5 p. m	47. 7	34. 5	36. 0		14. 7	37. 0	17. 7	14. 0		18. 6		
6 p. m	50. 2	43. 2	40. 0	16. 7	16. 7	40. 0	14. 0	14. 5	7. 0	22. 2	20. 0	5. 3
7 p. m	60. 3	46. 2	46. 0		18. 8	46. 0	22. 0	19. 0		23. 7	21. 0	
8 p. m	68. 4	56. 2	56. 0		20. 9	52. 0	25. 3	25. 0		21. 9	22. 0	
9 p. m	74. 6	66. 2	66. 0	23. 0	23. 0	60. 0	33. 0	33. 0	22. 5	23. 8		15. 0
10 p. m	78. 9											

No. I C and D was deduced from 11 days' observations at Fort Kearney, Nebraska, from June 19 to 30, 1858, at an elevation of 2,200 feet above the level of the sea.

The mean temperature was 77°.5 Fahrenheit. The mean force of vapor was 0.628 inch; the relative humidity, 68.4, and the mean weight of vapor in one cubic foot of air, 6.75 grains troy. (See Table E.) No. I C and D corresponds to No. I B, and very nearly also to No. II A, which may be considered as forming together one set. It rained on five occasions altogether during 28 hours, but the aggregate quantity of rain was only 1.40 inches. Dew was observed on 3 mornings. Of the 12 nights which this mean includes sheet-lightning was observed on 7, which on one occasion terminated in a thunder-storm, of which there were two. The cloudiness of the sky between the hours of 6 a. m. and 10 p. m. averaged 3.66, the whole sky being 10, and, including the hours of the night by interpolation, 3.35. The clouds were mostly cirro-cumuli, or cirro-stratus, except when it rained. The 190 hourly observations of the wind during that time, between 5 a. m. and 10 p. m., give the following results, the strength being expressed by the numbers from 0 to 10:

	Per cent.	Av. force.		Per cent.	Av. force.
South wind	32.1	4.8	Northeast wind	1.1	1.5
South-southeast wind	30.0	4.4	North-northeast wind	1.1	1.5
Southeast wind	12.6	3.7	North wind	0.5	1.0
East-southeast wind	4.7	1.8	Southwest wind	0.5	5.0
East wind	2.1	2.0	South-southwest wind	2.1	5.0
East-northeast wind	2.1	1.7	Calmness	11.1	0.0

From north-northwest and west-southwest no wind occurred during this time. The average force of the wind, including the calms, was 3.65, exclusive of the night. The only slight discretionary correction of the obtained mean values was made in C at 5 p. m. and 6 p. m., as indicated in the diagram, where an evident irregularity occurred, probably caused by some abnormal change in the atmosphere, rain-storm, or the like.

No. II C and D was deduced from 4 days' observations taken at Fort Laramie, Nebr., from July 30 to August 3, 1858, at an elevation of about 4,470 feet above the level of the sea. The mean temperature of these days was 67°.0 Fahrenheit; the mean force of vapor was 0.344; the relative humidity, 57.0; the mean weight of vapor in 1 cubic foot of air, 3.78 grains troy. Nos. II C and D correspond to No. II B and No. II A; they form altogether one set. It had thundered, and rained a few drops, shortly before the first observation was taken, and it rained twice afterward, for a few moments; but the average quantity of rain was scarcely 0.01 inch. Dew was observed every morning near the river. On 2 of the evenings sheet-lightning was observed, and once distant thunder. Thunder-storms are numerous in that neighborhood and season. The cloudiness of the sky between the hours of 6 a. m. and 9 p. m. averaged 4.62, and, including interpolations for the night, 4.37, the clouds being mostly cumuli. This increased cloudiness compared with Fort Kearney, while the relative humidity is, on the contrary, less, is a consequence of the neighborhood of the highly-elevated summits of the Rocky Mountains, the lower temperature and comparative moistness of which favors the formation of clouds, which, however, dissolve again when they sink into the lower regions of the air. Of the 64 observations of the wind during these 4 days, between 6 a. m. and 9 p. m.—

24 showed easterly winds, including N. E. and S. E., with average force of 2.4.
14 showed westerly winds, including N. W. and S. W., with average force of 3.0.
13 showed northerly winds, including N. N. W. and N. N. E., with average force of 2.0.
3 showed southerly winds, including S. S. E. and S. S. W., with average force of 2.0.
10 showed perfect calmness.

The average force of wind, including the calms, was 2.0. The wind shifted continually, and this, in connection with the peculiar situation of Fort Laramie, at the foot of the high range of the Rocky Mountains, and bordering on the vast arid plains, in consequence of which the shifting wind at once brings currents of air of a quite different temperature and degree of moisture, makes the observed values of No. II C and D somewhat irregular, which irregularity is increased by the influence of the two thunder-storms. Some discretionary corrections have, therefore, been required.

No. III C and D was deduced from tri-hourly observations, taken at Fort Bridger, Utah, from September 2 to September 5, 1858, at an elevation of 6,616 feet above the level of the sea. The mean temperature during these days was 59°.0 Fahrenheit; the mean force of vapor only 0.088 inch; the relative humidity, 21.6; and the mean weight of vapor in 1 cubic foot of air, 0.98 grain troy. Nos. I C and D do not exactly correspond to No. III B and No. IV A, which were taken a fortnight later, under somewhat different circumstances. Neither rain nor dew fell, but a few hours after the close of the observations a rain-storm set in, which gradually brought on snow. The cloudiness of the sky between the hours of 6 a. m. and 9 p. m. averaged 2.33, mostly cirri, and, including the hours of the night, by interpolation, 1.75. Western winds were prevailing, with an average force of 4, coming from the arid regions of the Great Basin. A very slight discretionary correction has only been made in No. III D.

No. IV C and D was deduced from 19 days' observations taken at Camp Floyd, Utah, from April 4 to April 23, 1859, at an elevation of 4,860 feet above the level of the sea. The mean temperature was 42°.0 Fahrenheit; the mean force of vapor, 0.155 inch; the relative humidity, 57.0; and the mean weight of vapor in 1 cubic foot of air, 1.68 grains troy. No. IV C and D correspond to No. IV B, and very nearly also to No. V A, which together form one set. During the time of these observations it snowed on nine occasions and rained on one, in an aggregate 22 hours, of which 10 hours were on the 9th, the remainder on the 10th, 11th, 12th, and 13th. The whole precipitation probably did not exceed 0.5 inch of water. The cloudiness of the sky between the hours of 6 a. m. and 9 p. m. averaged 5.37, and, including the hours of night, by interpolation, 5.16. The clouds were mostly cumuli. During 18 hours out of 100 the sky was cloudless. This rather large cloudiness has its cause in the altitude of the surrounding mountain ranges, which were still extensively covered with snow, while the temperature in the deserts to the west was already high and the evaporation strong. The 312 hourly observations of the wind during that time, between 6 a. m. and 9 p. m., give the following results:

North, north-northeast, and northeast winds, 33.3 per cent., with an average force of 2 8.
South and southeast winds, 12.8 per cent., with an average force of 3.4.
Southwest and west-southwest winds, 9.3 per cent., with an average force of 4.0.
West and west-northwest winds, 8.3 per cent., with an average force of 2.0.
Northwest and north-northwest winds, 6.1 per cent., with an average force of 1.8.
East, east-southeast, and southeast winds, 10.3 per cent., with an average force of 2.3
Perfect calmness, 19.9 per cent.

This table of winds will be better understood and appreciated if I mention that the north and northeast winds pass longitudinally over Cedar Valley, the valley in which Camp Floyd is situated, coming over low hills from the Salt Lake Valley. The south and south-southeast winds, and the southwest and west-southwest winds, the strongest winds, pass also more or less longitudinally over the valley, the former from the valleys at the base of the Wahsatch range; the latter over low mountains, from the vast deserts in the direction of Sevier Lake. The west and west-northwest winds pass across the valley, entering it from Rush Valley. They acquire less force because they are intercepted, in their forward and backward direction, by high ranges of mountains. For the same reason the eastern winds are not very strong. The northwest and north-northwest winds are still less numerous and weaker, because they find still more obstructions. The average force of wind, including the calms, was 2.27, and, including the hours of the night, by interpolation, probably 1.84. We may account for this comparatively small force by the circumstance that the valley is surrounded by high mountain ranges which break the force of the currents in the lower strata of the atmosphere. Some very strong squalls were felt, however, lasting for several hours.

In No. IV D not the least corrections have been found necessary; but in No. IV C some small corrections have been required, in consequence of the unsettled state of the weather.

No. V C and D was deduced from 3 days' observations taken at Camp Floyd, Utah, from August 6 to August 9, 1859. The mean temperature of these days was 69°.5 Fahrenheit; the mean force of vapor was 0.238 inch; the mean relative humidity, 38.0, and the mean weight of vapor in 1 cubic foot of air, 2.59 grains troy. No. V C and D correspond to No. V B, and very nearly to No. VI A, which may be considered as forming together one set. No rain nor dew fell. The cloudiness of the sky between the hours of 6 a. m. and 9 p. m. averaged only 0.56, but if we make interpolations for the hours, probably to 0.62. The average force of the wind, including the calms, between 6 a. m. and 9 p. m. was 1.7; fully one-half of the observations showed northerly winds, with an average force of 2.5; 23 per cent. were calms, and the remainder southerly and westerly winds. No. V C did not require the slightest corrections, but for No. V D a few slight corrections appeared to be desirable, and have been indicated.

No. VI C and D was deduced from 3 days' hourly observations taken at Camp Floyd, from September 15 to 18. The mean temperature was 64°.7 Fahrenheit; the mean force of vapor was 0.103 inch; the mean relative humidity was 21.9; the mean weight of vapor in one cubic foot of air, 2.67 grains troy. Nos. VII C and D correspond to No. VII B and No. X A, with which they form one set. The weather was fine; no rain nor thunder-storms occurred. No dew was observed at camp, but was formed most likely on the meadows below. The cloudiness of the sky between the hours of 6 a. m. and 9 p. m. averaged 1.6; and including interpolations for the night, probably 1 3. The clouds were mostly cumulo-cirri and some cumulo-stratus; over half of the time the sky was perfectly cloudless. The average force of the wind between 6 a. m. and 9 p. m. was 1.6 including the calms, which lasted 18.5 per cent. of the time; 23.8 per cent. were north and northeast winds, passing up the valley with an average force of 1.7; 38.5 per cent. were south and southwest winds, blowing down the valley with an average force of 2.1; 11.3 per cent. were west and northwest winds, passing down a narrow cañon in the Sierra Nevada with a force of 2.4; only 7.9 per cent. were east winds, passing up that cañon with an average force of 1.1.

The computed values of No. VII D appeared to require a slight correction at the hours of 6 and 7 p. m., and then No. VII C was changed slightly to make it correspond better to D; but it is very likely that the uncorrected values are preferable, the apparent irregularity being caused by the peculiar situation of the station.

No. VIII C and D was deduced from 3 days' tri-hourly observations taken from May 29 to June 2, 1859, in Woodruff Valley, one of the arid deserts of the interior of Utah, at an elevation of about 6,000 feet above the level of the sea. The mean temperature of these days was 55°.0 Fahrenheit; the mean force of vapor was only 0.093 inch; the mean relative humidity was 29.1, and the mean weight of vapor in one cubic foot of air was 1.08 grains troy. Nos. VIII C and D correspond very nearly, although not exactly, to No. VIII B. They give the unaltered means of the computed values. The cloudiness of the sky averaged 1.4, or, including interpolations for the night, 1.3. The force of the wind averaged 2.4, while its direction changed between north, south, and west.

After having thus stated the particulars in regard to each of the above tables I will give a more comprehensive view of the results, and have for that purpose arranged the Table E. It is based upon the Tables B, C, and D, but contains interpolations for all the hours when no direct observations have been taken, and corresponds mostly to the same diagrams. The columns for temperature, force of vapor, and relative humidity contain the means of direct observations, or of computations from the single observations. The columns headed force of vapor at saturation, and weight of vapor at saturation, are deduced from the columns of temperature with the aid of Regnault's tables. The columns headed weight of vapor in one cubic foot of air, are deduced from the mean values of temperature and relative humidity. Their values would probably have been slightly different if the weight of vapor could have been deduced for each single observation, as it has been done with the force of vapor and relative humidity, but that would have required more time than I had at my disposition. The column headed means contains the means of the values for the single hours as given in the tables.

E.—*Table of the hourly oscillations of temperature and hygrometric conditions.*

	Hours.																								
	o	1 a. m.	2 a. m.	3 a. m.	4 a. m.	5 a. m.	6 a. m.	7 a. m.	8 a. m.	9 a. m.	10 a. m.	11 a. m.	12 m.	1 p. m.	2 p. m.	3 p. m.	4 p. m.	5 p. m.	6 p. m.	7 p. m.	8 p. m.	9 p. m.	10 p. m.	11 p. m.	Means.
Fort Kearney, Utah, in June.																									
Temperature, degrees Fahrenheit	70.5	69.7	69.0	68.3	67.7	67.7	69.5	72.7	76.0	79.5	82.7	85.0	86.7	88.0	88.7	88.7	88.0	87.0	84.5	79.8	76.2	74.2	72.8	71.5	77.5
Force of vapor in inches, English, of mercury	.620	.617	.614	.610	.607	.606	.609	.614	.627	.654	.679	.690	.680	.670	.637	.622	.612	.605	.602	.611	.617	.625	.625	.623	0.628
Force of vapor at saturation	.745	.725	.708	.692	.671	.678	.721	.803	.897	1.006	1.117	1.203	1.270	1.323	1.353	1.353	1.340	1.282	1.184	1.016	.903	.845	.806	.771	0.975
Relative humidity, per cent	85.3	87.7	89.0	89.5	89.0	86.0	81.3	75.0	70.4	66.0	62.3	57.8	52.0	49.3	46.7	45.9	45.2	47.7	50.2	60.3	68.4	74.6	78.9	82.5	68.4
Weight of vapor in 1 cubic foot of air at saturation, grains troy	8.12	7.92	7.74	7.57	7.42	7.42	7.86	8.71	9.67	10.73	11.90	12.76	13.43	13.96	14.25	14.25	13.96	13.55	12.57	10.55	9.73	9.14	8.74	8.39	10.43
Weight of vapor in 1 cubic foot of air in grains troy	6.93	6.94	6.89	6.77	6.60	6.38	6.39	6.54	6.81	7.18	7.41	7.37	6.98	6.88	6.61	6.49	6.31	6.46	6.31	6.36	6.66	6.82	6.90	6.92	6.75
Fort Laramie, Nebr., first days of August.																									
Temperature, degrees Fahredheit	55.0	54.0	53.3	52.7	52.0	51.8	53.2	58.8	65.3	71.5	75.7	78.7	80.7	82.2	83.0	82.5	81.5	79.5	76.0	71.0	64.0	60.0	57.7	56.2	67.0
Force of vapor, inches, English, of mercury	.331	.326	.323	.321	.320	.322	.332	.346	.357	.366	.370	.364	.336	.330	.327	.336	.348	.361	.372	.368	.360	.351	.343	.336	0.344
Force of vapor at saturation	.433	.418	.407	.398	.388	.385	.406	.496	.624	.774	.888	.980	1.047	1.099	1.128	1.110	1.074	1.006	.897	.758	.596	.518	.477	.452	0.698
Relative humidity, per cent	78.2	80.0	81.0	82.0	83.0	84.0	75.0	66.5	56.0	49.5	44.0	38.0	33.5	31.0	30.0	31.5	33.0	36.0	40.0	46.0	56.0	66.0	72.0	75.8	57.0
Weight of vapor at saturation	4.86	4.70	4.58	4.49	4.38	4.35	4.57	5.53	6.86	8.39	9.58	10.52	11.19	11.71	12.00	11.82	11.47	10.78	9.67	8.25	6.57	5.76	5.33	5.06	7.60
Weight of vapor in 1 cubic foot, grains	3.80	3.76	3.71	3.68	3.64	3.66	3.43	3.68	3.84	4.15	4.22	4.00	3.75	3.63	3.60	3.72	3.78	3.88	3.87	3.80	3.68	3.80	3.84	3.86	3.78
Camp Floyd, Utah, in April.																									
Temperature, degrees Fahrenheit	35.0	33.8	32.5	31.2	30.0	29.0	30.3	35.0	39.7	44.0	48.3	51.5	53.5	55.0	55.5	55.0	53.7	51.7	47.7	43.0	40.7	39.0	37.6	36.3	42.0
Force of vapor, inches	.155	.151	.147	.143	.141	.139	.144	.157	.170	.182	.190	.181	.172	.164	.156	.150	.146	.142	.139	.138	.143	.152	.156	.157	0.155
Force of vapor at saturation	.204	.194	.185	.175	.167	.160	.169	.204	.245	.288	.339	.381	.410	.433	.441	.433	.413	.384	.331	.277	.254	.23[illegible]	.226	.214	0.282
Relative humidity, per cent	73.0	75.0	76.5	77.3	77.7	78.0	76.0	69.5	63.0	57.0	51.0	43.0	39.0	37.0	35.0	34.0	35.0	37.0	40.0	46.0	52.0	60.0	66.0	70.0	57.0
Weight of vapor at saturation	2.38	2.27	2.17	2.06	1.97	1.89	1.99	2.38	2.83	3.31	3.85	4.31	4.62	4.86	4.94	4.86	4.68	4.34	3.77	3.19	2.93	2.76	2.62	2.50	3.23
Weight of vapor, grains	1.74	1.71	1.66	1.59	1.53	1.48	1.51	1.65	1.78	1.88	1.96	1.85	1.80	1.80	1.73	1.65	1.63	1.61	1.51	1.47	1.53	1.66	1.73	1.75	1.68
Camp Floyd. Utah, first part of August.																									
Temperature, degrees Fahrenheit	57.6	56.1	54.5	53.2	52.5	52.0	55.0	59.5	65.0	70.5	76.0	81.0	85.0	87.5	88.0	88.0	87.5	84.5	80.5	74.5	68.0	64.0	61.2	59.2	69.5
Force of vapor, inches	.228	.240	.251	.258	.262	.266	.270	.280	.290	.297	.294	.288	.282	.273	.258	.230	.196	.162	.140	.172	.175	.185	.200	.215	0.238
Force of vapor at saturation	.476	.451	.425	.406	.395	.388	.433	.509	.617	.745	.897	1.057	1.203	1.303	1.323	1.323	1.303	1.184	1.040	.853	.685	.596	.540	.503	0.777
Relative humidity, per cent	51.0	56.0	60.0	64.0	67.0	68.0	64.0	57.0	49.0	41.0	30.0	25.0	21.0	19.0	17.0	16.0	15.0	14.0	14.5	19.0	25.0	33.0	40.0	46.0	38.0
Weight of vapor at saturation	5.31	5.04	4.78	4.57	4.46	4.38	4.86	5.66	6.79	8.12	9.67	11.29	12.76	13.75	13.96	13.96	13.75	12.57	11.12	9.23	7.49	6.57	5.99	5.60	8.40
Weight of vapor, grains	2.71	2.83	2.87	2.92	2.99	2.98	3.11	3.23	3.33	3.33	2.90	2.82	2.68	2.61	2.37	2.23	2.06	1.76	1.61	1.75	1.87	2.17	2.40	2.58	2.59
Camp Floyd, Utah, middle of September.																									
Temperature, degrees Fahrenheit	50.0	48.0	46.0	44.5	43.0	42.5	43.0	50.5	62.0	73.0	81.0	85.5	88.5	90.5	90.8	89.0	85.5	79.5	71.5	64.8	60.4	57.0	54.8	52.2	64.7
Force of vapor in inches, English, of mercury	.113	.114	.114	.114	.114	.114	.118	.140	.160	.172	.152	.123	.097	.096	.060	.048	.043	.044	.057	.077	.092	.102	.109	.112	0.103
Force of vapor at saturation	.361	.335	.311	.294	.277	.272	.277	.367	.556	.811	1.057	1.222	1.344	1.432	1.446	1.366	1.222	1.006	.771	.613	.523	.465	.430	.391	0.715
Relative humidity, per cent	32.3	35.0	37.2	39.5	41.0	42.0	41.5	36.0	28.0	21.5	16.5	12.0	7.5	5.0	4.0	3.5	3.5	4.5	7.0	12.0	18.0	22.5	26.0	29.0	21.9
Weight of vapor in 1 cubic foot of air, at saturation, grains troy	4.09	3.81	3.55	3.37	3.19	3.13	3.19	4.16	6.15	8.80	11.29	12.95	14.17	15.03	15.16	14.38	12.95	10.78	8.39	6.75	5.83	5.20	4.83	4.41	7.69
Weight of vapor in 1 cubic foot of air, grains	1.32	1.33	1.32	1.33	1.31	1.32	1.32	1.50	1.72	1.80	1.86	1.55	1.06	0.75	0.61	0.50	0.45	0.49	0.59	0.81	1.05	1.17	1.26	1.28	1.[illegible]6
Genoa, Carson Valley, Nevada, in June.																									
Temperature, degrees Fahrenheit	66.2	63.9	61.5	59.3	57.1	57.3	62.3	69.3	76.8	82.8	87.3	90.3	92.3	93.3	93.3	92.3	90.6	87.3	81.3	77.8	75.3	73.1	70.9	68.5	76.3
Force of vapor, inches, English	.222	.240	.255	.266	.273	.280	.289	.300	.317	.323	.303	.275	.224	.181	.202	.240	.246	.243	.235	.223	.203	.193	.193	.[illegible]05	0.248
Force of vapor at saturation	.644	.594	.546	.505	.467	.470	.562	.716	.921	1.121	1.294	1.423	1.515	1.563	1.563	1.515	1.436	1.294	1.067	.95[illegible]	.876	.814	.756	.696	0.971
Relative humidity, per cent	35.0	41.0	47.8	54.0	61.0	60.0	57.8	42.7	34.7	29.2	23.0	18.7	15.2	11.4	13.4	15.6	17.7	18.6	20.0	21.0	22.0	23.8	26.5	30.0	30.6
Weight of vapor at saturation	7.07	6.55	6.05	5.62	5.22	5.26	6.22	7.81	9.92	11.93	13.67	14.94	15.85	16.32	16.32	15.85	15.08	13.67	11.40	10.23	9.46	8.82	8.23	7.62	10.38
Weight of vapor	2.47	2.69	2.89	3.04	3.18	3.15	3.22	3.34	3.44	3.48	3.14	2.79	2.41	1.86	2.19	2.47	2.67	2.54	2.28	2.15	2.08	2.10	2.18	2.28	2.67

Woodruff Valley, Utah, end of May.

Temperature, degrees Fahrenheit	41.7	38.6	35.8	33.1	31.4	31.8	36.0	45.0	57.0	63.6	67.0	69.5	71.7	73.7	75.5	76.4	75.0	71.5	66.5	60.0	55.0	51.0	48.1	44.8	55.0
Force of vapor, inches, English	.108	.117	.123	.127	.129	.129	.125	.122	.119	.115	.112	.109	.106	.093	.078	.064	.053	.045	.041	.038	.041	.057	.078	.095	0.093
Force of vapor at saturation	.264	.234	.210	.189	.177	.180	.212	.299	.465	.588	.662	.721	.776	.831	.882	.909	.868	.771	.650	.518	.433	.374	.336	.297	0.494
Relative humidity, per cent	41.0	50.0	59.0	67.0	73.0	72.0	59.0	43.0	31.0	22.0	18.5	16.0	14.0	11.9	9.8	7.7	6.9	6.1	5.3	6.0	9.0	15.0	23.0	32.0	29.1
Weight of vapor at saturation	3.04	2.72	2.45	2.22	2.08	2.11	2.47	3.43	5.20	6.49	7.25	7.86	8.44	9.00	9.52	9.79	9.37	8.39	7.14	5.76	4.86	4.23	3.82	3.40	5.46
Weight of vapor	1.25	1.36	1.45	1.48	1.52	1.52	1.46	1.47	1.61	1.43	1.34	1.26	1.18	1.07	0.93	0.75	0.65	0.51	0.38	0.35	0.44	0.64	0.88	1.09	1.08

For comparison with and better appreciation of Table E, I subjoin Table F, which shows the daily oscillation of temperature, force of vapor, relative humidity, and weight of vapor at Philadelphia, for the same months for which such data have been presented in E. I have compiled it from the summary of results of the hourly meteorological observations taken at the Girard College, Philadelphia, in 1842, 1843, 1844, and first half of 1845, by Prof. A. D. Bache, as published by order of Congress. From these tables I have compiled directly the values for temperature and force of vapor, and from these I have deduced the values for relative humidity and weight of vapor. For the additional computations, which I had thus to make, I made use of the tables based upon the results obtained at the Greenwich observatory, which differ a little, and are not quite as reliable as those of Regnault, because the original computations of the force of vapor had been based upon these English values, and the application of the French tables on my part would have vitiated the results.

F.—*Table of the hourly oscillations of temperature and hygrometric conditions, at Philadelphia.*

	Hours.																								
	0	1 a. m.	2 a. m.	3 a. m.	4 a. m.	5 a. m.	6 a. m.	7 a. m.	8 a. m.	9 a. m.	10 a. m.	11 a. m.	12 m.	1 p. m.	2 p. m.	3 p. m.	4 p. m.	5 p. m.	6 p. m.	7 p. m.	8 p. m.	9 p. m.	10 p. m.	11 p. m.	Means.
January.																									
Temperature, degrees Fahrenheit	31.2	30.6	30.4	30.1	29.9	29.6	29.3	29.1	29.5	30.9	32.6	34.1	35.4	36.6	37.3	37.4	37.1	35.6	34.7	33.8	33.1	32.5	31.9	31.4	32.7
Force of vapor, inches, English, mercury	.169	.165	.165	.163	.164	.162	.159	.159	.159	.161	.165	.168	.170	.174	.178	.180	.179	.181	.181	.179	.175	.173	.170	.169	0.170
Force of vapor at saturation	.194	.190	.188	.186	.185	.183	.181	.180	.182	.192	.204	.215	.225	.235	.240	.241	.239	.227	.219	.213	.207	.203	.198	.195	0.205
Relative humidity per cent	87	87	88	88	89	89	88	88	87	84	81	78	76	74	74	75	75	80	83	84	85	85	86	87	83.2
Weight of vapor in 1 cubic foot of air at saturation, grains troy	2.31	2.26	2.24	2.22	2.20	2.18	2.16	2.15	2.17	2.28	2.42	2.54	2.66	2.76	2.83	2.84	2.81	2.67	2.59	2.51	2.46	2.41	2.36	2.32	2.43
Weight of vapor in 1 cubic foot of air	2.01	1.97	1.97	1.95	1.96	1.94	1.90	1.89	1.89	1.92	1.96	1.98	2.02	2.04	2.09	2.13	2.11	2.14	2.15	2.11	2.09	2.05	2.03	2.02	2.01
April.																									
Temperature, degrees Fahrenheit	47.6	46.7	45.9	45.5	45.0	44.8	45.3	46.8	49.0	51.2	53.3	55.1	56.8	58.1	59.0	59.4	59.4	58.7	57.3	54.4	52.3	50.9	49.6	48.4	51.7
Force of vapor, inches, English	.290	.287	.283	.281	.277	.277	.278	.285	.292	.297	.306	.310	.318	.324	.325	.324	.323	.322	.319	.314	.305	.298	.288	.285	0.300
Force of vapor at saturation	.344	.333	.324	.320	.315	.312	.318	.335	.361	.389	.418	.444	.470	.491	.506	.513	.513	.501	.478	.434	.404	.385	.368	.354	0.401
Relative humidity, per cent	84	86	87	88	88	89	87	85	81	76	73	72	68	66	64	63	63	64	67	72	75	77	78	81	76.4
Weight of vapor at saturation	3.96	3.84	3.75	3.70	3.64	3.62	3.68	3.86	4.14	4.45	4.75	5.04	5.31	5.53	5.69	5.76	5.76	5.64	5.39	4.92	4.60	4.41	4.22	4.06	4.57
Weight of vapor, grains	3.33	3.30	3.26	3.26	3.20	3.22	3.20	3.28	3.35	3.38	3.47	3.63	3.61	3.65	3.64	3.63	3.63	3.61	3,61	3.54	3.45	3.40	3.29	3.29	3.43
June.																									
Temperature, degrees Fahrenheit	63.2	62.6	62.0	61.3	60.8	61.1	62.8	65.2	67.6	69.6	71.2	72.8	74.1	75.4	75.9	76.1	76.2	75.3	74.0	71.6	68.3	66.6	65.4	64.2	68.5
Force of vapor, inches, English	.520	.513	.508	.503	.500	.498	.513	.530	.542	.551	.556	.554	.560	.564	.572	.568	.566	.565	.568	.565	.547	.543	.535	.531	0.540
Force of vapor at saturation	.582	.570	.559	.546	.537	.543	.574	.621	.672	.717	.750	.795	.830	.865	.879	.885	.887	.862	.827	.766	.688	.651	.626	.601	0.702
Relative humidity, per cent	89	90	91	92	93	92	89	85	81	77	74	70	67	65	65	64	64	66	69	74	80	83	85	88	78.9
Weight of vapor at saturation	6.51	6.37	6.25	6.12	6.02	6.08	6.41	6.91	7.44	7.90	8.30	8.71	9.07	9.43	9.57	9.63	9.66	9.40	9.04	8.40	7.60	7.21	6.95	6.69	7.74
Weight of vapor, grains	5.79	5.73	5.69	5.63	5.60	5.59	5.70	5.87	6.03	6.08	6.14	6.10	6.08	6.13	6.22	6.16	6.18	6.20	6.24	6.22	6.08	5.98	5.91	5.89	5.97
August.																									
Temperature, degrees Fahrenheit	67.1	66.5	66.0	65.9	65.3	64.9	65.5	67.3	69.7	71.9	73.8	75.6	76.7	77.4	78.3	78.4	78.1	77.5	76.0	73.7	71.4	70.1	69.0	68.2	71.4
Force of vapor, inches, English, of mercury	.600	.592	.587	.582	.579	.575	.584	.607	.626	.638	.645	.650	.646	.654	.659	.652	.650	.650	.658	.648	.640	.631	.623	.614	0.625
Force of vapor at saturation	.661	.648	.638	.636	.623	.615	.628	.666	.720	.773	.822	.871	.902	.922	.949	.952	.943	.925	.882	.819	.761	.729	.704	.686	0.770
Relative humidity per cent	91	91	92	92	93	93	93	91	87	83	78	75	72	71	69	68	69	70	75	79	84	87	88	90	82.5
Weight of vapor in 1 cubic foot of air at saturation, grains troy	7.32	7.19	7.08	7.06	6.93	6.85	6.97	7.37	7.93	8.47	8.98	9.48	9.80	10.01	10.28	10.31	10.22	10.04	9.60	8.96	8.35	8.02	7.76	7.59	8.44
Weight of vapor in 1 foot of air, grains	6.66	6.54	6.51	6.50	6.44	6.37	6.48	6.71	6.90	7.03	7.00	7.11	7.06	7.11	7.09	7.01	7.05	7.03	7.20	7.08	7.01	6.98	6.83	6.83	6.86
September.																									
Temperature, degrees Fahrenheit	60.5	60.4	60.0	59.5	59.2	59.0	59.0	60.7	63.2	65.4	67.4	69.3	70.5	71.5	72.2	72.7	72.1	71.2	69.0	66.7	64.4	63.2	62.0	61.3	65.0
Force of vapor, inches, English	.495	.490	.487	.483	.477	.476	.477	.490	.499	.511	.517	.522	.525	.524	.532	.53	.534	.539	.538	.523	.509	.503	.492	.482	0.507
Force of vapor at saturation	.532	.530	.523	.515	.509	.506	.506	.536	.582	.626	.668	.711	.739	.763	.781	.792	.778	.756	.704	.653	.605	.582	.559	.546	0.625
Relative humidity, per cent	93	92	93	94	94	94	94	91	86	82	77	73	71	69	68	67	69	71	76	80	84	86	88	88	82.5
Weight of vapor at saturation	5.96	5.95	5.87	5.78	5.73	5.69	5.69	6.00	6.49	6.95	7.39	7.83	8.12	8.37	8.55	8.68	8.53	8.30	7.76	7.23	6.74	6.49	6.25	6.12	6.94
Weight of vapor, grains	5.54	5.47	5.46	5.43	5.39	5.35	5.35	5.46	5.58	5.70	5.69	5.72	5.77	5.78	5.81	5.82	5.88	5.89	5.90	5.78	5.66	5.58	5.50	5.50	5.63

The hourly variations of temperature, as they are exhibited in the above tables and diagrams, afford a subject of much interesting speculation. In examining them, we notice at once how much the time of the daily maximum is variable, according to season and locality; but still more striking is the great difference of amplitude, and the more gradual or abrupt ascent and descent of the curves. My object is to present the data obtained by our exploration, and not to enter into an elaborate discussion. I will therefore confine myself merely to point out a few of the causes which co-operate to produce these interesting differences.

The first diagram presents the hourly variations of the temperature at Fort Kearney, Nebr., in June. The mean temperature was 77°.5, Fahrenheit, while at Philadelphia it is only 68° to 69° in June, although the latter place is situated over two-thirds of a degree of latitude farther south, and over 2,000 feet lower. We have no reason to believe that the temperature of June, 1858, at Fort Kearney, has been so much above the average that this result should not indicate a considerable northward bend in the lines of equal temperature for that season in the plains of the Platte River region. It merely confirms prior observations, and verifies the result of theoretical deductions, based upon the situation of that country, in the center of a large continent, far away from any sea-coast, and open toward the north and south. It should be borne in mind that the values for Philadelphia are deduced from a much larger series of observations than those at Kearney, which latter might perhaps be a little above the actual average. Still, these and all the other observations have not been taken on days especially selected for the purpose, but indiscriminately, as the execution of the surveys made it convenient. For that reason they might as well present smaller values than the average. The difference between the warmest and coldest hours of the day at Fort Kearney amounts to 21° Fahrenheit, while at Philadelphia, according to table F, the amplitude is only 15°.4. This, too, is a consequence of the continental situation of the place. The actual amount of vapor in the atmosphere at Kearney was larger than at Philadelphia, on account of its higher temperature, but the relative humidity, the degree of saturation of the air, was less at Kearney. For the same reason, the cloudiness was much less at Kearney, only 3.35, against 6.6 at Philadelphia. (See table G.) Therefore, although a little more heat was absorbed or made latent by the evaporation at Kearney, it was comparatively less than at Philadelphia. The greater clearness of the sky offered less obstruction to the rays of the sun and to their heating influence upon the earth's surface during the day, and to the cooling by radiation during the night. Thus the mean temperature and the amplitude were both increased. The increase of the temperature during the hours of the morning was gradual at Fort Kearney, because the quantity of moisture which was evaporated during that time, and therefore of heat made latent, was considerable. It reached an amount which would justly astonish those not used to such contemplation. From our Table E we see that the minimum amount of vapor in 1 cubic foot of air was 6.38 grains at 5 a. m.; the maximum, 7.41 grains at 10 a. m. In order to supply the difference of 1.03 grains, or, rather, taking the expansion into consideration which has taken place during those hours, of 1.04 grains to a stratum of air of 1 foot thick over 1 square mile, over 5,000 pounds troy of water must be evaporated, and for a stratum of 500 feet, over 2,500,000 pounds are required. If we consider that the evaporation continues with increased intensity after 10 a. m., and that the vapor diffuses itself, although in decreasing quantity, into the higher portions of the atmosphere, we can form an adequate estimation of the heat absorbed in that process, and understand the cause of the slowness of the increase of heat during the morning. The decrease of temperature is quickest toward sunset, because then the source of the heat disappears, but during the night it is not as considerable as we might expect it to be. Although the radiation is great, its effects are balanced, in a measure, it appears, by a partial precipitation of the moisture evaporated during the day, by which a large amount of the heat made latent during the day is again rendered sensible. Besides, the currents of air, which during the day carry the heated air on high, have subsided in the evening. Thus a more rapid cooling of the earth's surface during the night is prevented. The maximum of the temperature was reached at an earlier hour at Kearney than at Philadelphia, namely, at 2½ p. m. instead of 3½ p. m., perhaps, also, on account of the greater lightness and clearness of the atmosphere, but especially on account of the greater intensity of evaporation at Kearney, which caused a more rapid depression of the temperature after the source of the heat had passed the point of greatest intensity; in other words, after the sun had passed the meridian.

The diagram No. VI of the mean daily oscillations of the temperature at Camp Floyd during the first third of November has a very marked shape. The temperature rose rapidly in the morning, because the sky was clear and the humidity exceedingly small, so that only little heat was absorbed by evaporation. As soon as the maximum had been passed, at 2 p. m., it began declining rapidly, and continued thus until about an hour and a half after sunset. By this time the earth's surface had lost the greatest portion of its surplus heat by radiation, and nearly reached the point of mean temperature of the season. The upward currents of air had also probably died out. From this time to sunrise of next morning the temperature appeared to decline uniformly, but at a much lower rate. The amplitude amounted to 28° Fahrenheit, while the greatest mean amplitude of any month at Philadelphia scarcely reaches 16°, and that of November is considerably less.

Still larger amplitudes were obtained from the observations at the end of May, in Woodruff Valley, and in September, at Camp Floyd. The former are represented by the diagram VIII. They both give the most striking illustration of an extremely continental climate. In Woodruff Valley the mean temperature was then 55° Fahrenheit against 56° at Philadelphia, and the mean amplitude 45° Fahrenheit against 15°.4 at Philadelphia. At the time of the observations at Camp Floyd, in September, the mean temperature was 64°.7, while the mean temperature of the month, according to the above tables, is 58°.4 against 57° at Philadelphia, and the amplitude amounted to 48°.3 Fahrenheit against 13°.7 at Philadelphia. The latitude of the former is 45′ south, that of the latter 16′ north of that city, while their elevation above it is about 6,000 and 4,800 feet respectively. Taking into consideration the decrease of temperature due to such considerable elevations, which may be put down as about 18° and 14° Fahrenheit, the great northward deflection of the lines of equal temperature, is again apparent. The following remarks especially apply to the variations in September. The temperature increased at once rapidly after sunrise, because the extremely small amount of humidity on the ground absorbed little heat by evaporation; and it continued increasing nearly at the same ratio until afternoon. The dry and sparsely-covered soil of the plains became intensely heated. The temperature reached its maximum about 2 p. m., an hour earlier than it is reached at Philadelphia, chiefly it appears on account of the greater clearness of the atmosphere, the stronger ascending currents of air, and the greater difference of heat between the heated surface of the desert plains, and the upper regions of the air and the towering summits of the adjoining mountain ranges. The decrease of temperature then began soon after the maximum had been reached; it was strongest between 5 and 7 p. m., about the time of sunset, but continued with considerable force throughout the night. At 7 p. m. the thermometer read already 26° below the maximum, and had attained the mean temperature of the day. Some of the causes which co-operated to produce these results are the following: The radiation was very intense, the more so because the atmosphere was beautifully clear, and the cloudiness of the sky amounted only to 0.7 against 5.5 at Philadelphia as the mean for September. The bare parched soil, on the other hand, gave off its heat comparatively slowly, like a heated brick, and thus prevented the temperature from sinking still more rapidly, as we might expect from a comparison with some of the other diagrams; and it thus cooled gradually until it was heated again by the rising sun. Another cause for the continued strong decrease of temperature during the night was the continued evaporation, which was not interrupted during the night. On account of the scarcity of moisture, its effects were not so intense as they would have been otherwise. If the soil would have been less dry the temperature would have decreased more rapidly toward sunset, but much less during the latter part of the night, when, on the contrary, precipitation would again have taken place, and latent heat thus have become sensible. As it was, only so much could evaporate as rose gradually to the surface from the badly-supplied substrata, and while the refrigerating effects of the evaporation were not intense at any hour, they were continually felt throughout the whole of them.

The temperature curve of Genoa for June shows a remarkable feature. The maximum of temperature took place there at 1.30 p. m., while at Philadelphia it recurs at 4 p. m. I do not suppose that this could have been produced by the same influences which cause the early maximum at San Francisco, although they are scarcely 160 miles apart, but I consider the peculiar situation of our camp the main cause. It was pitched on the rocky slope at the very foot of the main range of the Sierra Nevada, facing a little south of east. During the forenoon the sun burned intensely on this slope and on the sides of the mountains, but early in the afternoon its rays fell obliquely upon the ground, and it soon disappeared altogether behind the mountains. Thus an early maximum was caused, and a rapid decrease of the temperature between 5 and 6 p. m., corresponding to one or the other diagrams at the hour of sunset, which then took place only between 7 and 8 p. m.

The variations of the relative humidity are not less interesting than those of the temperature. Turning at once to the diagrams I will point out some of their most remarkable features, and compare them with the results obtained at Philadelphia, contained in Table F. The most characteristic one is again No. VIII for Woodruff Valley, in the last days of May. It illustrates the extremely arid climate of the interior of Utah. The maximum of saturation at the time of sunrise, at 4.30 a. m., was 74; saturation being 100. If the soil was covered with grass instead of being nearly bare, dew, or rather frost, might then have been formed, under else favorable circumstances, by a very slightly farther decrease of temperature. This, however, was only due to the great depression of the temperature during the night to below the freezing point, not to a large quantity of vapor in the atmosphere, which actually amounted to only 1.5 grains in a cubic foot of air. With the rapid increase of temperature, the degree of saturation decreased so much that at 9 a. m. it was only 22, because the ground was extremely dry, and the little vapor which was formed was carried on high by the ascending currents of air.

While the maximum of the temperature took place at 3 p. m. the humidity, therefore, continued to decrease; at 6 p. m. it was 5.3, and the minimum seemed to take place at about 20 minutes past 6, an hour before sunset, with 4.5. From that time to sunrise of next morning the relative humidity increased nearly uniformly. The amplitude was 69.5 and the mean degree of saturation 29.1. At the same season at Philadelphia, with nearly the same mean temperature, the maximum of saturation at sunrise is about 91, the minimum, between 3 and 4 p. m., about 64, the amplitude, therefore, only 27, and the mean 78.9. A glance at these numbers is sufficient to convince anybody that agriculture can never be carried on there except by irrigation, and they prove, at the same time, that water for that purpose must be exceedingly scarce, so that only a few acres might be cultivated out of stretches of many miles in extent. The plants, however, withstand such extreme changes much better than it might be expected, because the very dryness of the atmosphere protects them from being injured by the night frosts.

At Camp Floyd, in the middle of September, as represented in diagram No. VI, the mean humidity was still less, viz, 21.9; but the amplitude was not as large, only 39; the maximum, at 5.30 a. m., being 42.5, and the minimum, at 3.30 p. m., being 3.5. The corresponding numbers for Philadelphia are 82.5 as mean, 94 as maximum, 67 as minimum at 3 p. m., and 27 as amplitude. We have seen that the amplitude of temperature was even larger at Camp Floyd in September, than at Woodruff Valley in May, and the question arises, why the amplitude of humidity was so much smaller at the former place. The main difference in both diagrams is the smaller increase of humidity between sunset and sunrise. At Woodruff Valley it increased proportionally to the decreasing temperature, perhaps, because the vapor carried off by rising currents of air was replaced by evaporation from a little creek near our camp, or because, perhaps, the prevailing wind brought on as much vapor as was carried off.

At Camp Floyd, on the contrary, the increase of humidity did not keep pace with the decrease of the temperature. Either more vapor was carried off by rising currents than was replaced by the cold air replacing them, or dry wind must have prevailed during the nights.

In August, at Camp Floyd, the saturation was more complete than in September, being 38, and in April it was still higher, equal to 57, with an amplitude of 54.5 and

44.0, respectively; while at Philadelphia it was smaller in April, viz, 76.1; and in August equal to September, viz, 82.5, with amplitudes of 26 and 25, respectively.

In the diagram No. VII for Genoa, Carson Valley, we can again clearly recognize the influences which have affected the variations of the temperature. The minimum of only 11.4 was reached as early as 1 p. m. Then, even before the temperature had decreased, the evaporation from the adjoining widely overflowed meadows of the valley of Carson River appeared to increase the humidity of the air at our camp, perhaps carried there by regular currents of air. To the rapid falling of the thermometer between 5 and 7 p. m. corresponds the irregular increase of the humidity, marked by a dotted line on the diagram. As it appeared irregular, and is evidently due to the peculiar situation of the place, I have eliminated it from Table E, but it can readily be accounted for as being peculiar to the locality. During the hours of the night the humidity increased considerably, in accordance with the decrease of the temperature. The small mean relative humidity of only 30.6 is remarkable, because the loftiest summits of the Sierra in the neighborhood were still covered with snow, the whole lower portion of Carson Valley, many miles in extent, had for weeks been overflowed, and the extensive sheet of water of Lake Bigler commences not more than 2 or 3 miles from Genoa. It indicates that Carson Valley decidedly belongs to the climatical system of the vast deserts of Carson Lake, of the sink of Humboldt River, &c., and that its peculiar climatical features are chiefly derived from them.

The curve No. I of Fort Kearney, also, for June, is much more similar to that of Philadelphia. The maximum is 89.5, the minimum 68.4, while at Philadelphia the maximum is 93, the minimum 64, at 3 and 4 p. m., the amplitude therefore 29, while the mean is 78.9. We thus find, again, that the neighborhood of Fort Kearney, although arid compared with that of the eastern coast, and much less adapted to agricultural pursuits, is still moist compared with that of the desert valleys of Utah.

The diagram No. III, obtained at Fort Bridger in the first days of September, is also very remarkable. The maximum, just before sunrise, about 3 a. m., was 40. The saturation then declined rapidly with the increasing temperature, and was nearly stationary between 9 a. m. and 2 p. m., about 10; then it began to increase uniformly till sunrise of next morning. The mean degree of saturation was only 21.6, the amplitude 30.5. These features can again be explained by the situation of the place and the weather at the time. Fort Bridger is situated in a low meadow, well watered by several branches of a creek. Strong western winds prevailed at the time, which, coming from the arid regions of the Great Basin, were extremely dry. Under their influence the saturation decreased very rapidly with the increase of the temperature. By 9 o'clock, however, the temperature had become sufficiently high to produce a powerful evaporation on the moist surface which balanced the desiccating influence of the wind. With the declining temperature, after 3 p. m., the evaporation becomes also less, and the dry western winds exercised a greater influence upon the saturation of the air than the declining temperature. The relative humidity could, therefore, only increase very gradually and slowly during the night.

I may remark that the difference between the mean values of the relative humidity obtained from the computation of the single observations, in several instances, differs considerably from those computed from the mean of temperature and mean force of vapor of the same observation, the more so the larger the amplitudes of arc. As those obtained in the first-stated manner are, however, more correct, I have given them in the column of means. Apparent errors may thus be explained. The same may be said in regard to the computation of the weight of vapor.

The hourly changes of the quantity of vapor in the atmosphere, represented by the weight of vapor in one cubic foot of air in the lower portion of the atmosphere, has not been illustrated by diagrams, because the values given in the above table were not obtained by direct computation of each observation, but by an indirect computation from the mean values of temperature and relative humidity. If not absolutely correct on that account, still they come very near being so. In the general remarks at the head of this chapter, I have stated that in Western Europe generally the minimum quantity of vapor in the air is to be found about sunrise, that it attains its greatest maximum about 9 a. m., then decreases till toward 4 p. m., and attains a second smaller maximum toward 9 p. m., when it decreases until sunrise; that in winter, however, when the action of the sun is less intense, there is generally only one minimum, about sunrise, and one maximum, about 2 p. m. From our Table F we see that at Philadelphia, probably on account of its situation near the coast, the changes are not so uniform. In January there is a minimum between 7 and 8 a. m., and a maximum between 3 and 7 p. m., with the highest point probably at 6 p. m. The average amount of vapor in 1 cubic foot of air is 2.01 grains, and the amplitude only 0.24 grains. In April there is a minimum about the time of sunrise, from 4 to 6 a. m., a maximum from 11 a. m. to 6 p. m., after which the quantity of vapor decreases until 10 p. m., when it continues nearly unchanged to the time of the lowest minimum. The average amount is 3.43 grains; the difference between the largest and smallest weight, 0.45 grains. In June a minimum takes place at 5 a. m.; the quantity is largest, with little oscillation, from 9 a. m. till 7 p. m., with the highest point at 6 p. m., and then it decreases till morning. The mean quantity is 5.97; the amplitude 0.65 grains. In August 5 a. m. is the time of the minimum; from 11 a. m. to 6 p. m. the quantity of vapor is largest, with the highest maximum at 6 p. m., after which time it decreases till morning. The mean is 6.86 grains; the amplitude 0.83 grains. In September the minimum falls in the hour of sunrise, as in the other months, namely, between 5 and 6 a. m.. The quantity then increases rapidly till 9 a. m.; then very slowly. The maximum takes place from 4 to 6 p. m. The mean quantity amounts to 5.63 grains; the amplitude to 0.55 grains.

The variation at Philadelphia, at least in the above-named months, which alone I have examined, show, therefore, all one decided minimum about and soon after sunrise, and one maximum, of long duration, generally between the hours of 9 a. m. and 7 p. m., which has its highest, but not sharply-marked point, about 6 p. m. Instead of a second maximum at 9 p. m., we find about that hour rather indications of a second minimum.

Our values in Table E, from the central portion of the continent, are altogether different; they prove more than anything else the absolute difference of climate there, and its extremely arid and continental character. In Woodruff Valley, at the end of May, and in Camp Floyd, in August and September, we have the strongly-marked minimum between 4 and 7 p. m., and the equally-marked maximum between 8 and 9 a. m., nearly the reverse of what we have found for Philadelphia. At the same time the average amount of humidity has been very small, and the difference between the maximum and minimum of the day has been from two to three times as large as at Philadelphia. All the features are more distinctly marked than in less extreme climates.

In Woodruff Valley, at the end of May, the sun rises about 4.30 o'clock. The first effect of the rapid increase of the temperature was expansion of the air and vapor, and consequently a slight depression of the weight of vapor in each cubic foot of the expanded air. This depression, although scarcely perceptible, corresponds to the sunrise minimum at Philadelphia, or, rather, it depended upon the same agencies which cause the extension of that minimum beyond the hour of sunrise. It was prolonged somewhat by the upward movement of the warmed air and the vapor contained in it, which began soon after sunrise, and by the circumstance that the little humidity which had accumulated during the night in the soil was rapidly decreasing. Still the evaporation soon became so vigorous that it gained upon the other agencies, and at 8 a. m. the maximum was reached, which, however, was not much above the point which the quantity of vapor had attained at sunrise, just before the depression had taken place. Then, however, most of the available moisture had been consumed, as may be seen from the corresponding diagram of the relative humidity; and, therefore, the increasing expansion of the air and the rising currents gained upon the evaporation, and the quantity of vapor in each cubic foot of air in the lower stratum of the atmosphere was diminished gradually until 7 p. m., when it had reached the exceedingly low amount of 0.35 grains, while the air would have required at that time over 7 grains for its saturation with vapor. This was shortly before sunset, at the time when under ordinary circumstances there ought to have been a maximum. The temperature now sank more and more, while a limited evaporation continued, and both causes combined effected a gradual increase of the quantity of vapor, which continued until sunrise. The average amount in one cubic foot was only 1.08 grains, and the difference between the largest and smallest amount 1.26 grains troy.

At Camp Floyd, in September, the maximum took place at 9 a. m., the minimum, chiefly on account of the earlier setting of the sun, already at 4 p. m., with only 0.45 grains of vapor in a cubic foot of air. The increase lasted then to midnight, when no further change took place until after sunrise at 6 a. m., when the increase commenced again and lasted until the maximum was reached. The stability during the night, notwithstanding the continued decrease of the temperature, must be attributed to the same agencies which have affected the relative humidity, and which I have already mentioned in that connection, namely, rising currents of air on a dry wind from the neighboring deserts. Winds exercise the greatest influence upon the evaporation and conditions of moisture. In general, a wind increases the evaporation considerably, the more so when it happens to be warm and dry. If it is warm and charged with moisture, it either increases the evaporation little or not at all, and if the station is much colder, the moisture of the wind may even be precipitated. A cold wind does not increase the evaporation so much, especially if it is itself charged with moisture, and it can only create precipitation by cooling the air at the station below the point of saturation before it has carried off the surplus moisture of the air from that point; therefore the common saying that a wind is too cold to bring on rain. The average amount of vapor in 1 cubic foot of air at Camp Floyd, in September, was 1.16 grains, and the amplitude 1.44 grains.

At Camp Floyd, in August, the conditions were similar. The maximum took place from 8 to 9 a. m.; then followed a gradual decrease till 6 a. m., when the humidity increased again steadily, as in Woodruff Valley, to the time of the maximum at 9 a. m. Only a slight check was felt at the time of sunrise, but no perceptible depression. The average quantity was 2.59 grains, the amplitude 1.72 grains—more than I have observed at any other point.

At Camp Floyd, in April, the whole conditions were different, as I have stated before, in connection with Table C; and, therefore, the variations were also entirely different. There was a sunrise minimum at 5 a. m., a maximum at 10 a. m., a minimum at 7 p. m., as low as the first one, and a second but lower maximum at 11 p. m. These variations are unlike those at Philadelphia, but similar to those observed in Western Europe. The average amount of vapor was 1.68 grains, the amplitude only 0.49 grains.

The oscillations at Fort Kearney in June were somewhat similar, but the average amount of moisture there was 6.75 grains, much more than I have observed in any month in Utah, and even more than at Philadelphia in June, with, however, a lower mean temperature, and, consequently, more complete saturation at the latter place. The amplitude amounted to 1.10, while at Philadelphia only to 0.65 grains.

The oscillations at Fort Laramie in the first days of August were not so characteristic, but more influenced by contending agencies. Those at Genoa in June are, of course, more similar to the other from Utah, but they exhibit some peculiarities. The maximum took place at 9 a. m., but the minimum as early as 1 p. m., when the same causes mentioned in connection with the relative humidity and the declining temperature caused an increase of the quantity of vapor, which culminated at 4 p. m. The rapid decrease of temperature caused a second minimum at 8 p. m., not quite as low as the first one. The upward currents of air had then subsided, while the evaporation continued in the damp valley. The humidity, therefore, increased again, suffered a slight check shortly after sunrise, the same as at Woodruff Valley, when, as there, it soon continued increasing to the maximum. The mean amount was 2.67 grains, the difference between the largest and smallest quantity 1.62 grains.

The hourly variations of the force of vapor and its absolute quantity are not less abnormal in the region covered by our explorations; but, as they depend upon the weight of vapor and the degree of temperature, and indirectly upon the relative humidity, and are determined by their relative quantity and changes, I may be shorter in my remarks.

Table F shows that at Philadelphia one minimum and one maximum takes place every day, the former about the time of sunrise, when the temperature is lowest and the quantity of vapor smallest, the latter in the afternoon, when the temperature is highest and the quantity of vapor largest, while the relative humidity is not too low. In January the minimum takes place between 6 and 8 a. m., and the maximum lasts, with little changes, from 2 to 7 p. m. The mean force is then 0.170 inches, and the amplitude 0.022 inches. In April, the minimum takes place between 4 and 6 a. m., the maximum lasts from 1 to 3 p. m.; then, however, the decrease is only very slow for several hours. At 11 p. m. there is a slight indication of a second minimum. The mean force is 0.300 inches, the amplitude 0.048 inches.

In June, the minimum takes place from 4 to 5 a. m., the maximum at 2 p. m., but the pressure is high from before noon till 7 p. m. The mean force is 0.540 inches, the amplitude 0.074 inches.

In August, the minimum takes place at 5 a. m., the maximum lasts from 2 to 6 p. m., or we might even say from 11 to 6; the mean force is 0.625 inches, and the amplitude 0.084 inches.

In September the minimum lasts from 4 to 6 a. m., the maximum from 5 to 6 p. m., but the pressure is high from 11 a. m. to 6 p. m. The mean force is 0.507 inches, and the amplitude 0.063.

The means of a single month, however, do not show such uniform results. A glance at the diagrams illustrating the observations at the Girard College, Philadelphia, as published by order of Congress, shows that the pressure varies much in the same month of different years. We frequently find two maxima and two minima as well in winter as in summer.

The most abnormal of our diagrams is again that for Woodruff Valley at the end of May, No. VIII. It exhibits exactly the reverse of the Philadelphia variations. The maximum then took place at sunrise, and the minimum in the afternoon. The cause of this peculiarity will be readily understood. At sunrise the quantity of vapor was not much below its maximum, and the relative humidity so decidedly at its maximum that the great depression of the temperature could not counteract those combined influences. The relative humidity then declined so rapidly that its influence gained upon that of the increasing temperature, and the force of the vapor gradually declined. By noon the temperature had nearly reached its maximum, and therefore the still decreasing quantity of vapor and relative humidity caused a rapid diminution of the pressure, which lasted till near sunset, when it had attained the exceedingly low figures of 0.038 inches. The rapidly increasing relative humidity then raised it, notwithstanding the continued decrease of the temperature, till it reached the maximum at sunrise. The mean force was 0.093, only the fifth part of what it is at that season at Philadelphia, and the amplitude reached the large figure of 0.091 inches.

At Camp Floyd in September, as illustrated by diagram No. VI, the decrease of the relative humidity was slower in the morning; therefore the influence of the temperature gained upon it, and a divided maximum took place at 9 a. m., upon which the decrease of the force became very rapid until it reached its minimum, about 4 p. m.; then, with the increasing relative humidity, it increased first faster then less till near midnight, when the influence of the decreasing temperature became as strong as that of the increasing relative humidity, and the force remained unchanged till sunrise. The mean force was very low, only 0.103 inch, the amplitude 1.29 inches.

The August curve at Camp Floyd is similar, but continues increasing, although less during the night. It shows, however, a bend after sunset in consequence of the very rapid sinking of the temperature at that hour. The mean force, although small, if compared to Philadelphia, was considerably larger, 0.238 inch, and the amplitude was larger than I have observed it anywhere else, 0.157 inch.

In April, at Camp Floyd, I found a sunrise minimum, as at Philadelphia, but a forenoon maximum and an afternoon minimum, as in August at Camp Floyd. The amplitude reached only 0.042 inch. Similar features are presented by the variations at Fort Kearney in June, but the amplitude there was larger, 0.088 inch, and the mean force much higher. In the Laramie curve the evening maximum, which had been small at Kearney, surpasses even the forenoon maximum. The Genoa curve is similar to the August curve of Camp Floyd; but on account of the peculiar local circumstances mentioned above, it has besides the maximum at 9 a. m., a second, although much lower, maximum in the afternoon about 4 p. m., and consequently also two minima, the lowest at 1 p. m., and a smaller one between 9 and 10 p. m.

The diagram for Fort Bridger, for the first days of September, No. III, is peculiar. As far as I can judge from the limited number of observations, there was a maximum at sunrise, for the same reason as in Woodruff Valley, then, on account of the rapidly diminishing relative humidity, a minimum at 9 a. m. By that time the humidity had become so low that it could not decrease much more, and the still increasing temperature created a maximum at 12 m.; at 3 p. m., the temperature and force of vapor were lower; at 6 the temperature had fallen considerably, but the relative humidity had increased comparatively more, and caused a third maximum, even a little higher than the two others, while later the force of vapor became again less, because the temperature became rapidly less.

In order to give a better comparison of the absolute values of the force of vapor, relative humidity, &c., I have arranged the following table, G. It contains the monthly means obtained at the Greenwich observatory, England, as the average of the seventeen years from 1841 to 1857; also the summary of the monthly means obtained at the observatory of the Girard College, Philadelphia, from 1840 to 1845, compiled from the records published by Professor Bache, by order of Congress; and besides the values obtained on our exploration, with the addition of a few means of temperature observed at Camp Floyd by Assistant Surgeons Williams and Moore, United States Army. Those data which have been deduced only from a short series of observations, and are repeated here from Table E, have been marked with letter. For particulars in regard to them I refer to the explanatory remarks to Tables C and D. Those marked *a*, are from the hourly observations in April at Camp Floyd; *b*, from the observations in August at Camp Floyd; *c*, from those in September at the same station; *d*, from Woodruff Valley in the last days of May and the first ones of June; *e*, from Genoa, Carson Valley, in June; *f*, from Fort Kearney, in June; and *g*, from Fort Laramie, in the last days of July and the first ones of August.

G.—*Comparative table of monthly means of temperature, force of vapor, relative humidity, &c.*

	Station.	January.	February.	March.	April.	May.	June.	July.	August.	September.	October.	November.	December.	Mean.
Mean temperature, degrees Fahrenheit.	Greenwich, England ..	38.1	38.5	41.6	46.5	52.9	58.7	61.7	61.4	56.9	49.5	43.8	40.5	49.2
	Philadelphia, Pa	32.3	32.8	42.3	50.6	58.9	68.8	72.8	71.5	64.1	51.3	40.7	32.6	51.6
	Camp Floyd, Utah.....	16.2	29.9	31.9	43.6	54.7	74.7	75.0	72.1	58.4	50.7	34.0	22.0	47.0
					a 42.0	*d* 55.0	*e* 76.3		*b* 69.5	*c* 64.7				
							f 77.5		*g* 67.0					
Force of vapor, inches, English, of mercury.	Greenwich, England ..	0.205	0.203	0.216	0.250	0.300	0.369	0.417	0.426	0.383	0.310	0.260	0.229	0.297
	Philadelphia, Pa	0.173	0.173	0.224	0.293	0.384	0.545	0.611	0.622	0.492	0.312	0.218	0.173	0.352
	Camp Floyd, Utah.....	0.093	0.147	0.130	0.154	*d* 0.093	*e* 0.248		*b* 0.238	*c* 0.103				* 0.150
					a 0.155		*f* 0.628		*g* 0.344					
Relative humidity, saturation = 100.	Greenwich, England ..	89.	86.	82.	79.	76.	74.	76.	78.	81.	86.	89.	88.	81.
	Philadelphia, Pa	85.5	83.7	78.0	76.6	75.6	78.0	76.8	81.6	82.0	79.6	80.4	84.8	80.2
	Camp Floyd, Utah....	83.5	84.5	71.3	51.7	*d* 29.1	*e* 30.6		*b* 38.0	*c* 21.9				†54.
					a 57.0		*f* 68.4		*g* 57.0					
Weight of vapor in 1 cubic foot of air, grains troy.	Greenwich, England ..	2.4	2.4	2.5	2.9	3.4	4.1	4.6	4.8	4.2	2.5	2.9	2.6	3.4
	Philadelphia, Pa	2.06	2.06	2.61	3.35	4.30	6.02	6.69	6.83	5.49	3.56	2.55	2.06	3.96
	Camp Floyd, Utah.....	1.12	1.74	1.53	1.77	*d* 1.08	*e* 2.67		*b* 2.59	*c* 1.16				
					a 1.68		*f* 6.75		*g* 3.78					
Cloudiness of sky, the whole = 10.	Philadelphia, Pa	6.8	6.0	7.0	6.7	6.4	6.6	5.7	6.3	5.5	5.3	6.1	6.5	6.2
	Camp Floyd, Utah.....	4.6	6.2	5.7	5.1	*d* 1.3	*e* 1.3		*b* 0.6	*c* 0.7				
					a 5.2		*f* 3.4		*g* 4.4					

* Estimated. † Estimated at.

This table does not require any further explanation. I will only state that the weight of vapor for January, February, March, and April, at Camp Floyd has been computed from the mean temperature, and the mean forces of vapor of these months, which I found to give, generally, more accurate results than if the mean relative humidity was directly introduced into the calculation. These means, for Camp Floyd, were deduced from three observations each day, at 7 a. m., 2 p. m., and 9 p. m. The means for these single hours were—

In January, force of vapor, 7 a. m., 0.062; 2 p. m., 0.137; 9 p. m., 0.079; relative humidity, 7 a. m., 92.0; 2 p. m., 72.0; 9 p. m., 86.4.

In February, force of vapor, 7 a. m., 0.117; 2 p. m., 0.189; 9 p. m., 0.135; relative humidity, 7 a. m., 89.3; 2 p. m., 76.6; 9 p. m., 87.6.

In March, force of vapor, 7 a. m., 0.114; 2 p. m., 0.160; 9 p. m., 0.118; relative humidity, 7 a. m., 78.3; 2 p. m., 61.4; 9 p. m., 74.3.

During these three months the mountains near Camp Floyd were heavily covered with snow, while in the valley the snow was a few inches deep in January, less in February, and disappeared in March. In April the snow disappeared from the lower mountains, but especially the eastern and northern slopes of the higher mountains, and the principal summits were still covered. In January from 9 to 10 inches of snow (not water) fell at Camp Floyd. In February it began 12 times to snow or rain, but the aggregate amount was very small; in March it snowed 10 times, once with a little rain, but the whole amount was again quite small; in April snow fell at 10 different times and rain at 3, but the whole amount of the precipitation did probably not reach half an inch of water.

EXTREMES OF TEMPERATURE, HUMIDITY, ETC.

After having, in the preceding paragraphs, treated of the values of the daily and monthly changes of temperature, moisture, and barometric pressure, which although extreme if compared with those of the same latitudes in the Eastern States, are the mean values and the rule in the localities where they have been observed, I will close these pages with the enumeration of some of the extreme changes and abnormal conditions recorded on this exploration. The following are actually recorded *differences of temperature between the warmest and coldest time of the day*, and they would, in many instances, be considerably larger, if the maximum and minimum temperatures had been observed. As we generally staid in a camp from afternoon till morning the amplitudes are mostly given between the high temperature of the afternoon and the low one of next morning, which are apt to give a little larger amplitude than the maximum and minimum of the same day would exhibit. We have observed as far east as Little Blue River, in Southeastern Nebraska, October 7th, 3 p. m., 75°; October 8th, 5.45 a. m., 34°; difference, 41° Fahrenheit.

Platte River, below Fort Laramie, September 20th, 3 p. m., 85°; September 21st, 5.15 a. m., 36°; difference, 49° Fahrenheit.

Near the Red Buttes, August 15th, 3.15 p. m., 82°; August 16th, 4.45 a. m., 37°; difference, 45° Fahrenheit.

Upper Sweetwater River, September 9th, 3 p. m., 70°.3; September 10th, 5.45 a. m., 26°.5; difference, 43°.8 Fahrenheit.

Green River, August 30th, 3 p. m., 83°; August 31st, 5.30 a. m., 39°; difference, 44° Fahrenheit.

Black Fork, September 1st, 4 p. m., 79°; September 2d, 5.30 a. m., 35°; difference, 44° Fahrenheit.

Bear River, September 26th, 3 p. m., 56°; September 27th, 6 a. m., 11°.5; difference, 44°.5 Fahrenheit.

Echo Cañon, September 10th, 6 a. m., 25°.5; 1.15 p. m., 75°; difference, 49°.5 Fahrenheit.

West of Weber River, September 11th, 4 p. m., 80°.5; September 12th, 5 a. m., 32°.5; difference, 48° Fahrenheit.

Timpanogos Cañon, September 20th, 3.30 p. m., 83°.5; September 21st, 6 a. m., 35°.5; difference, 48° Fahrenheit.

Camp Floyd, September 17th, 6 a. m., 40°; 12 m., 91°; difference, 51° Fahrenheit.

Camp Floyd, January 3d, 7 a. m., 0°.5; 2 p. m., 31°; difference, 31°.5 Fahrenheit.

Camp Floyd, January 18th, 7 a m., 5°.3; 2 p. m., 41°.7; difference, 36°.4 Fahrenheit.

Camp Floyd, April 8th, 6 a. m., 32°.7; 12 m., 71°; difference, 38°.3 Fahrenheit.

Camp Floyd, April 22d, 5.25 a. m., 20°; 3.15 p. m., 73°.3; difference, 53°.3 Fahrenheit.

Salt Lake Desert, August 1st, 4.30 p. m., 102°; August 2d, 4.30 a. m., 56°; difference, 46° Fahrenheit.

Reese River, May 28th, 3 p. m., 76°; May 29th, 4.50 a. m., 22°; difference, 54° Fahrenheit.

Over 40° difference was frequently observed in Woodruff Valley, the deserts near Carson Lake, and in other valleys of the Great Basin.

As the relative humidity was frequently small, the difference between the reading of the dry and wet bulb thermometers was frequently considerable. We must, however, bear in mind that this difference is no direct measure of the relative humidity. The following are some of the extreme values observed during the survey:

Fort Kearney, October 3d, 3 p. m., dry bulb, 87°.5; wet bulb, 58°.7; difference, 28°.8 Fahrenheit.

Independence Rock, (Sweetwater River,) August 16th, 3 p. m., 91° and 59°.3; difference, 31°.7 Fahrenheit.

Camp Floyd, September 17th, 3 p. m., 90° and 54°; difference, 36° Fahrenheit.

Prince's Creek, Utah, August 2d, 3 p. m., 87°.5 and 56°; difference, 31°.5 Fahrenheit.

In that vicinity, and about that time, the difference reached frequently 30°. At Genoa, Carson Valley, June 16th, 88°.5 and 56°; difference, 32°.5; and for several hours, 30 or 31°. At the same place, June 17th, 2 p. m., 92° and 58°.5; difference, 33°.5; and for several hours, 32°. On June 18th, 1 p. m., 94° and 59°; difference, 35°. June 19th, 12 m., 90° and 56°; difference, 34°; and June 20th, 3 p. m., 101°.5 and 66°; difference, 35°.5 Fahrenheit.

The force of vapor is subject to rapid changes by a change of the wind, and from other apparently small causes, independent of the regular daily variations. We find a change recorded on Big Sandy Creek, near Green River, August 27th, from 6.20 p. m. to 9 p. m., from 0.176 to 0.415; difference, 0.209 inch; and at Genoa, June 16th, from 12 m. to 1 p. m., from 0.204 to 0.088; difference, 0.116 inch in 1 hour, merely by a change of the wind, with a perfectly clear sky; and at the same place, on June 19th, from 11 a. m. to 12 m., from 0.252 to 0.067; difference, 0.185 inch in 1 hour. Some of the lowest values of force of vapor were deduced from observations at the following points: Copperas Springs, near Fort Bridger, September 27th, to 6 p. m., 0.000; Salt Lake Desert, May 8th, 9 p. m., 0.000; Pleasant Valley, Utah, May 9th, 3 p. m., 0.028; Antelope Valley, May 10th, 12 m., 0.027; Camp Floyd, April 21st, 5 p. m., 0.008; Camp Floyd, September 17th, 3 p. m., 0.014; Camp Floyd, January 12th, 7 a. m., 0.025, when the air was saturated with moisture on account of the low temperature; also, January 11th, 7 a. m., 0.026; January 10th, 9 p. m., 0.026; Fort Bridger, September 4th, 3.30 p. m., 0.027; Fort Bridger, September 29th, 10 a. m., 0.022; Woodruff Valley, May 31st, 6 p. m., 0.015.

Extremely small values of saturation, or *relative humidity*, are the following: Copperas Springs, near Fort Bridger, September 27th, 6 p. m., 0; Salt Lake Desert, May 8th, 9 p. m., 0; and at neighboring points, on successive days, 4 and 7; Fort Bridger, September 4th, 3.30 p. m., 3; Fort Bridger, September 29th, 10 a. m., 3; Camp Floyd, April 21st, 5 p. m., 2; April 23d, 6 p. m. and 8 p. m., 11; Camp Floyd, August 8th, 4 p. m., 9; Prince's Creek, August 2d, 3 p. m. and 6 p. m., 8; Woodruff Valley, May 30th and 31st, 6 p. m., 3; June 1st, 3 p. m., 3; Alkali Wells, June 4th, 6 p. m., 7; Walker River, June 8th, 3 p. m., 7; Genoa, June 19th, 12 m., 5; Little Sandy Creek, near South Pass, August 26th, 3 p. m., 8; and as far east as Fort Kearney, October 3d, 3 p. m., 10.5.

It was astonishing to see how little influence, sometimes, rain had on the humidity of the atmosphere, because it was found in the upper regions while the lower atmosphere was dry, and it did not extend far. At Plympton Springs, in the Salt Lake Desert, July 23d, between 3 and 4 p. m., 0.30 inch of rain fell, during a thunder-storm, with hail; our camp was flooded, and after 6 some more rain fell. Still the relative humidity, which at 3 p. m. was 38, at 6 p. m. had only increased to 50. Again, in White Valley, on July 25th, a thunder-storm, with, however, only little rain, was recorded as lasting from 4 to 6 p. m.; the relative humidity at 4 p. m. was 25; at 6 p. m., 28.

APPENDIX F.

TABLE OF DISTANCES,

ALTITUDES, AND GRADES.

APPENDIX F.

TABLE OF DISTANCES, ALTITUDES, AND GRADES.

Names of places.	Intermediate distances, in miles.	Total distances, in miles.	Altitudes, in feet, above the sea.	Difference of altitudes, in feet.	Grade, in feet, per mile.
Fort Bridger	0	0	6, 656	0	0
Summit between Fort Bridger and Muddy Creek	10. 7	1C. 7	7, 653	997	93. 1
Muddy Creek	2. 5	13. 2	6, 992	661	264
Summit between Muddy Creek and Sulphur Creek	7. 2	20. 4	8, 060	1, 068	148
Sulphur Creek	5. 0	25. 4	7, 450	610	122
B ar River	11. 1	36. 5	7, 395	55	5
Summit between Bear River and White Clay Creek	5. 0	41. 5	7, 736	341	68
Camp, 17 miles from the mouth of White Clay Creek	12. 1	53. 6	6, 471	1, 265	104
Mouth of White Clay Creek	17. 0	70. 6	5, 526	945	55
Camp on Weber, 2.6 miles from junction of White Clay Creek	2. 6	73. 2	5, 572	46	17
Ford	1. 5	74. 7	5, 686	114	76
Summit on Parley's Park road, between Weber River and Silver Creek	12. 2	86. 9	6, 891	1, 205	98
Silver Creek	1. 2	88. 1	6, 422	469	390
Summit between Silver Creek and Round Prairie	5. 5	93. 6	6, 715	293	53
Round Prairie	9. 2	102. 8	5, 571	1, 144	124
Near Warm Springs	1. 7	104. 5	5, 556	15	8
Camp on Timpanogos, 12.5 miles above bridge	7. 5	112. 0	5, 246	310	41
Bridge over Timpanogos	12. 0	124. 0	4, 860	386	32
Low ground southeast of and near Lehi	11. 5	135. 5	4, 546	314	27
Bridge over the Jordan River	5. 4	140. 9	4, 540	6	1
Camp Floyd	14. 1	155. 0	4, 860	320	22
Camp Floyd Pass	4. 5	159. 5	5, 234	374	87
Camp No. 1, Meadow Creek	13. 7	173. 2	5, 205	29	2
General Johnston's Pass, Guyot range (summit)	9. 1	182. 3	6, 237	1, 032	113
Camp No. 2, western slope of Guyot range	. 8	183. 1	5, 816	421	526
In Skull Valley	9. 3	192. 4	4, 850	966	103
Camp No. 3, Simpson's Spring, base of Mount Champlin	7. 0	199. 4	4, 850	0	0
In Salt Lake Desert	9. 5	208. 9	4, 370	480	54
Short-Cut Pass (summit)	12. 2	221. 1	5, 347	977	80
Camp No. 4, western slope, Thomas's range	1. 8	222. 9	5, 005	342	190
Foot of slope	12. 6	235 5	4, 298	707	56
Camp No. 5, Fish Spring, Salt Lake Desert	12. 9	248. 4	4, 289	9	0. 6
Camp No. 6, in Salt Lake Desert	29. 7	278. 1	4, 593	304	10. 2
Camp No. 7, Sulphur Spring	2. 6	280. 7	4, 633	40	15
East summit of Tots-arr range	10. 0	290. 7	6, 903	2, 270	227
Camp No. 8, Pleasant Valley	3. 4	294. 1	6, 150	753	221
West summit of Tots-arr range	8. 5	302. 6	7, 150	1, 000	117
Western foot of slope	1. 4	304. 0	6, 675	475	339
Ridge east of Antelope Valley	1. 4	305. 4	6. 995	320	228
Camp No. 9	1. 2	306. 6	6, 658	337	280
In Antelope Valley	5. 3	311. 9	5, 690	968	182
Ridge between Antelope Valley and Spring Valley	10. 7	322. 6	6, 560	870	81
Camp No. 10, Spring Valley	3. 0	325. 6	6, 133	427	142
Un-go-we-ah Mountains (summit)	9. 0	334. 6	7, 530	1, 397	155
Camp No. 11, west slope of Un-go-we-ah Mountains	2. 1	336. 7	6, 600	930	443
In Steptoe Valley	6. 5	343. 2	5, 816	784	120
Camp No. 12, mouth of Egan Cañon	6. 8	350. 0	5, 986	170	25
Mon-tim range (summit)	5. 2	355. 2	7, 135	1, 149	220
Do	3. 1	358. 3	7, 135	0	0
Foot of Mon-tim range in Butte Valley	2. 9	361. 2	6, 148	987	340
Camp No. 13, Butte Valley	6. 8	368. 0	6, 523	375	53
Ridge between Butte Valley and Long Valley	1. 8	369. 8	6, 670	147	81
In Long Valley	4. 7	374. 5	6, 195	475	101
Camp No. 14, near summit of Too-muntz Mountains	5. 5	380. 0	7, 190	995	180
Too-muntz range (summit)	0. 7	380. 7	7, 283	93	132
In Ruby Valley	4. 9	385. 6	6, 034	1, 249	255
Camp No. 15, Ruby Valley	3. 6	389. 2	5, 953	81	22
Hastings's Pass (summit)	5. 7	394. 9	6, 580	627	110
In Valley of South Fork of Humboldt	8. 6	403. 5	5, 640	940	109
Camp No. 16, eastern base of We-ah-bah Mountains	3. 3	406. 8	6, 028	388	118
Summit of We-ah-bah range	4. 0	410. 8	7, 300	1, 272	318
Camp No. 17, Pah-hun-nu-pe Valley, west foot of We-ah-bah Mountains	3. 1	413. 9	6, 018	1, 282	413
In Pah-hun-nu-pe Valley	4. 0	417. 9	5, 660	358	90
Camp No. 18, Pah-hun-nu-pe Valley	9. 3	427. 2	5, 692	32	3
Cooper Range (summit)	8. 7	435. 9	6, 757	1, 065	122
Camp No. 19, Ko-bah Valley, She-u-wi-te Creek	6. 2	442. 1	6, 414	343	55

APPENDIX F.—*Table of distances, altitudes, and grades*—Continued.

Names of places.	Intermediate distances, in miles.	Total distances, in miles.	Altitudes, in feet, above the sea.	Difference of altitudes, in feet.	Grade, in feet, per mile.
Camp No. 20, Ko-bah Valley	17.5	459.6	5,993	421	24
Ridge in Ko-bah Valley	3.5	463.1	6,690	697	199
Camp No. 21, Wons-in-dam-me Creek	3.5	466.6	6,595	95	27
In Ko-bah Valley	3.8	470.4	6,210	385	101
Camp No. 22, east of Pah-rea range	9.9	480.3	6,373	163	16
Pah-rea range (summit)	4.0	484.3	6,440	67	17
In Won-a-ho-no-pe Valley	7.5	491.8	5,443	997	133
Camp No. 23, eastern slope of Pe-er-re-ah Mountains	5.5	497.3	5,870	427	77.5
Camp No. 24, eastern slope of Pe-er-re-ah Mountains	4.9	502.2	6,355	485	99
Pe-er-re-ah Mountains (summit)	4.7	506.9	7,104	749	159
In Reese River Valley	6.5	513.4	5,530	1,574	242
Camp No. 25, on Reese River	2.6	516.0	5,563	33	13
Ridge between Reese River Valley and Woodruff Valley	13.3	529.3	6,483	920	69
In Woodruff Valley	2.1	531.4	6,000	483	230
Camp No. 26, Smith Creek, in Woodruff Valley	5.8	537.2	5,960	40	6
Camp No. 27, Putnam Creek	10.0	547.2	6,325	365	36.5
Se-day-e or Lookout Mountains (summit)	5.0	552.2	7,741	1,416	283
Camp No. 28, Gibralter Creek, west slope of Se-day-e Mountains	3.7	555.9	6,360	1,381	373
Camp No. 29, Middle Gate	14.7	570.6	4,665	1,695	115
Ridge east of Dry Flat Valley	8.8	579.4	4,460	205	23
In Dry Flat Valley	10.2	589.6	4,090	370	36
Ridge between Dry Flat Valley and Alkali Valley	1.2	590.8	4,500	410	341
In Alkali Valley	1.7	592.5	3,960	540	317
Camp No. 30, Alkali Valley	2.6	595.1	3,900	60	23
Camp No. 31, on Carson Lake	16.0	611.1	3,840	60	3.7
Ridge between Carson Lake and Walker's River	24.2	635.3	4,595	755	31
Camp No. 32, on Walker's River	7.0	642.3	4,072	523	74.7
Camp No. 33, on Walker's River	10.0	652.3	4,200	128	12.8
Camp No. 34, on Walker's River	6.0	658.3	4,288	88	14.6
Divide between Carson River and Walker River	6.7	665.0	4,700	412	61.5
Ridge above Camp No. 35	9.3	674.3	4,400	300	32
Camp No. 35, on Carson River	3.0	677.3	4,200	200	67
Camp No. 36, Pleasant Grove, on Carson River	9.0	686.3	4,288	88	10
Chinatown	7.5	693.8	4,360	72	9
Camp No. 37, Carson City, Eagle Valley	11.5	705.3	4,587	227	19
Genoa	13.5	718.8	4,824	237	17
Daggett's Pass, off the route, about 3 miles from Genoa	3.0	....	7,180	2,356	......
Bridge over west branch of Carson River	16.8	735.6	5,698	874	52
Hope Valley	5.2	740.8	6,880	1,182	227
Luther's Pass (summit)	2.2	743.0	7,505	625	284
In Lake Valley	4.6	747.6	6,260	1,245	270
Mail station in Lake Valley	0.5	748.1	6,311	51	102
Johnson's Pass, in Sierra Nevada (summit)	2.0	750.1	7,222	911	455

RETURN ROUTE.

Names of places.	Intermediate distances, in miles.	Total distance, in miles.	Altitudes, in feet, above the sea.	Difference of altitudes, in feet.	Grade, in feet, per mile.
Genoa	0	0	4,824	0	0
Camp No. 2, Eagle Valley	13.5	13.5	4,587	237	17
Chinatown	11.5	25.0	4,360	227	19
Camp No. 3, on Carson River	5.2	30.2	4,300	60	11
Camp No. 4, on Carson River	17.8	48.0	4,154	146	8
Ridge between Carson River and Carson Lake	13.2	61.2	4,460	306	23
Camp No. 5, on Carson Lake	11.8	73.0	3,840	620	52
Camp No. 6, on Carson Lake	12.2	85.2	3,840	0	0
Foot of pass	17.0	102.2	3,960	120	7
Summit between Dry Flat Valley and Alkali Valley	1.7	103.9	4,500	540	317
In Dry Flat Valley	1.2	105.1	4,090	410	341
Ridge east of Dry Flat Valley	10.2	115.3	4,460	370	36
Western base of Se-day-e Mountains	8.8	124.1	4,665	205	23
Camp No. 7	10.4	134.5	5,570	905	87
Ridge between Camp No. 7 and Dodge Valley	3.0	137.5	5,900	330	110
Camp No. 8, Edward Creek, Dodge Valley	8.2	145.7	5,486	414	50
Camp No. 9, western slope of Se-day-e Mountains	7.0	152.7	7,022	1,536	219
Se-day-e or Lookout Mountains (summit)	0.6	153.3	7,260	238	396
Camp No. 10, Smith Creek, Woodruff Valley	7.9	161.2	6,070	1,190	150
In Woodruff Valley	7.9	169.1	6,000	70	9
Divide between Smith Creek and Reese River	2.1	171.2	6,483	483	230
In Reese River Valley	2.5	173.7	5,965	518	207
Camp No. 11, on Reese River	8.3	182.0	5,630	335	40
In Reese River Valley	6.5	188.5	5,530	100	15
Pe-er-re-ah Mountains (summit)	4.7	193.2	7,104	1,574	335
Camp No. 12, eastern slope Pe-er-re-ah Mountains	5.3	198.5	6,285	819	154
Camp No. 13, Won-a-ho-no-pe Creek	5.0	203.5	5,811	474	95
In Won-a-ho-no-pe Valley	4.8	208.3	5,543	268	51
Pah-rea range (summit)	6.6	214.9	6,580	1,037	157
Camp No. 14, Wons-in-dam-me Creek	14.0	228.9	6,595	15	1

APPENDIX F.—*Table of distances, altitudes, and grades*—Continued.

RETURN ROUTE—Continued.

Names of places.	Intermediate distances, in miles.	Total distance, in miles.	Altitudes, in feet, above the sea.	Difference of altitudes, in feet.	Grade, in feet, per mile.
In Ko-bah Valley	9. 9	238. 8	6, 000	595	60
Camp No. 15, Clay Creek, Ko-bah Valley	6. 2	245. 0	5, 998	2	0
In Pah-ho-no-pe Valley	9. 3	254. 3	5, 820	178	19
Camp No. 16, McCarthy's Creek, Pah-ho-no-pe Valley	8. 0	262. 3	6, 184	364	45
We-ah-bah range (summit)	6. 2	268. 5	7, 270	1, 086	175
In Buell Valley	6. 2	274. 7	5, 863	1, 407	227
Camp No. 17, Buell Valley	3. 1	277. 8	5, 998	135	43
In Buell Valley	2. 5	280. 3	5, 813	185	74
Ridge between Buell Valley and Phelps Valley	12. 4	292. 7	6, 523	710	57
In Phelps Valley	4. 4	297. 1	6, 150	370	84
Ridge between Phelps Valley and Butte Valley	12. 7	309. 8	7, 103	953	75
Camp No. 18, near Summit Spring	0. 4	310. 2	7, 057	46	115
In Butte Valley	7. 5	317. 7	6, 268	789	105
Mon-tim range (summit)	8. 5	326. 2	7, 398	1, 130	133
Camp No. 19, eastern slope, Mon-tim range	3. 1	329. 3	6, 828	570	184
Camp No. 20, Steptoe Valley	14. 0	343. 3	6, 193	635	45
Western slope of Un-go-we-ah Mountains	10. 4	353. 7	7, 150	957	92
Do	1. 0	354. 7	6, 918	232	232
Camp No. 21, western slope of Un-go-we-ah Mountains	3. 0	357. 7	7, [illegible]3	525	175
Un-go-we-ah Mountains (summit)	1. 7	359. 4	8, 140	697	410
Eastern slope of Un-go-we-ah Mountains	7. 4	366. 8	6. 480	1, 660	224
Camp No. 22, Antelope Valley	6. 6	373. 4	5, 633	847	128
Tots-arr range (summit)	9. 9	383. 3	7, 060	1, 427	144
Camp No. 23, eastern slope Tots arr Mountains	7. 2	390. 5	5, 927	1, 133	157
Camp No. 24, Crosman Springs, Crosman Valley	14. 8	405. 3	4, 920	1, 007	68
Camp No. 26, Plympton Springs, Crosman Valley	10. 5	415. 8	4, 814	106	10
Ridge between Crosman Valley and White Valley	9. 5	425. 3	5, 657	843	88
Camp No. 25, White Valley	10. 1	435. 4	4, 406	1, 251	124
Camp No. 27, White Valley	1. 5	436. 9	4, 350	56	37
House range (summit)	12. 1	449. 0	6, 674	2, 324	192
Camp No. 28, Chapin's Spring	2. 3	451. 3	6, 530	144	62
In Sevier Valley	7. 5	458. 8	4, 690	1, 840	245
Camp No. 29, Tyler's Spring	8. 0	466. 8	5, 992	1, 302	162
In Sevier Valley	8. 6	475. 4	5, 037	955	111
Summit of Thomas's range	6. 0	481. 4	5, 520	483	80
Base of Thomas's range	2. 0	483. 4	4, 840	680	340
Summit east of Thomas's range	6. 4	489. 8	5, 330	490	77
In the valley	6. 7	496. 5	5, 000	330	49
Camp No. 30, McDowell Mountains	7. 2	503. 7	5, 750	750	104
McDowell Mountains (west summit)	1. 0	504. 7	6, 000	250	250
In the valley between Camps No. 30 and No. 31	2 4	507. 1	5, 330	670	279
McDowell Mountains (east summit)	1. 9	509. 0	5, 830	500	263
Camp No. 31, Good Indian Spring	0. 4	509. 4	5, 771	59	147
Camp No. 32, William Spring, base of Mount Champlin	9. 2	518. 6	4, 558	1, 213	131
Camp No. 33, Prince Creek	8. 7	527. 3	5, 411	853	98
Summit between Prince Creek and Porter's Valley	1. 1	528. 4	5, 852	441	400
In Porter's Valley	2. 3	530. 7	5, 590	262	114
Summit between Porter's Valley and Brewer's Spring	2. 7	533. 4	6, 180	590	218
Camp No. 34, Brewer's Spring	2. 8	536. 2	5, 780	400	143
Oak Pass, Guyot range (summit)	5. 4	541. 6	7, 200	1, 420	263
Eastern slope of Guyot range	2. 0	543. 6	6, 190	1, 010	505
Camp No. 35, Meadow Creek, Rush Valley	6. 8	550. 4	5, 430	760	111
Summit between Meadow Creek and Rush Valley	3. 7	554. 1	5, 700	270	73
In Rush Valley	3. 8	557. 9	5, 140	560	147
Camp Floyd Pass	9. 5	567. 4	5, 234	94	9
Camp Floyd	4. 5	571. 9	4, 860	374	83

SIDE RECONNAISSANCES.

Names of places.	Altitudes, in feet, above the sea.
Salt Lake City, Upper street, near Brigham Young's	4, 300
Salt Lake	4, 170
Depôt camp in Round Prairie, about one mile below Torbert Cañon	5, 786
Mouth of Coal Creek Cañon, 5 miles from Depôt camp	6, 181
Coal Creek, 4 miles below summit, 7 miles up cañon	8, 400
Camp near head of Coal Creek, one-fourth mile from summit, and about 15½ miles from Depôt camp	9, 530
Summit of Uintah range, near head of Coal Creek	9, 680
Camp on Potts's Creek, 7½ miles from summit	8, 050
Five and one-half miles lower down, on Potts's Creek	7, 560
Junction of Potts's Creek with Duchesne	6, 814
On Duchesne Fork, 12¼ miles below mouth of Potts's Creek	6, 280
Junction of Duchesne Fork with the Uintah	5, 345
Summit between Timpanogos River and Kansas Prairie	6, 955
In Kansas Prairie, on east branch of South Fork of Weber	6, 244
Camp on the East Fork of the Weber, one-eighth of a mile from camp of last fall	6, 760
Summit 7½ miles from camp	8, 953
Head of branch of Porter's Creek, 1 mile from summit	8, 754
Fourteen and one-half miles from camp	8, 077
Summit on trail to White Clay Creek	7, 676
Crossing of West Fork of Bear River	7, 395
Summit west of Muddy Creek, 20 miles from Fort Bridger	7, 475

APPENDIX G.

ESTIMATE OF APPROPRIATIONS NEEDED FOR ROADS

IN THE

TERRITORY OF UTAH.

APPENDIX G.

ESTIMATE OF APPROPRIATIONS NEEDED FROM CONGRESS TO PROPERLY IMPROVE THE ROUTES IN THE TERRITORY OF UTAH.

The following letter from Bvt. Brig. Gen. A. S. Johnston, commanding the Department of Utah, to Col. Samuel Cooper, Adjutant-General United States Army, written August 26, 1859, in reference to the roads I have explored and opened in Utah, is here presented *in extenso*, both on account of the value set by the general on the routes I have opened, and of the intimation it gives of his having instructed me to examine certain portions of them with a view to the formation of an estimate for their further improvement:

HEADQUARTERS DEPARTMENT OF UTAH,
CAMP FLOYD, UTAH, *August* 26, 1859.

COLONEL: On Captain Simpson's return from his exploration westward (which has resulted, as has been heretofore reported, in his finding the shortest and best route from this valley to California via Carson Valley, and three hundred miles nearer than any other route from Salt Lake City), believing that the season was so far advanced that he would not be able to examine the country through to the eastern slope of the Rocky Mountains on the most direct course to Fort Leavenworth (which it was expected in the spring he would have had time to do after making the exploration westward), before winter, he was instructed, in furtherance of that object, to ascertain if a route with an easy grade could be found from near the source of the Timpanogos River across to the Uintah River, and down into Green River.

He proceeded to Round Prairie, on Timpanogos River, from which place he commenced his explorations; and I now have the gratification to communicate the result, which will be found in his report from camp No. 3, Round Prairie, Timpanogos Valley, by which the honorable Secretary of War will be informed of his successful exploration on the contemplated eastern route as far as Green River. This discovery, when the route is made passable by the removal of trees and brush, which are the chief obstructions, will enable travelers to avoid making the great detour south, which was unavoidably made by Colonel Loring on his march to New Mexico. I learn from the guide who was employed in the search for the route, that it can be continued without an obstacle, up White River, into either part in which are sources of the Plattes, Arkansas, and various affluents of Green River.

The only question, then, to be determined for the completion of an unexceptionable road from this camp on the most direct route to Fort Leavenworth, through the gold region, which will, from geological indications, no doubt, prove more productive on the western slope than on the eastern, is as to the practicability of getting down from the middle or South Park to the foot of the mountains on the east side.

All the information I have, concurs as to the fact of numerous pack-trails down the eastern slope, which encourages the hope that a good wagon-route may be found, or a good road can be constructed; and I respectfully suggest that for that purpose it would be better to conduct any future explorations from the east side of the mountain.

A part of the tide of emigrants has been turned on Captain Simpson's new road to California via Camp Floyd, and emigrants pass daily, and others with large herds of stock. The road is now well marked, and its natural state is sufficiently good, except a few places, at wide intervals, where the grade should be reduced, for which purpose I respectfully recommend that a small appropriation of money should be asked for from Congress, and also an appropriation for reconstructing a part of the road from this camp to Fort Bridger, which was graded by the Mormon population up the Timpanogos Cañon, and to re-imburse them for their outlay in making that part of the road, and for the expense of building a bridge across that stream, and for grading and bridging such other parts of the road as shall need it.

An estimate sufficiently accurate, upon which to found an appropriation, can be furnished by Captain Simpson, whom I requested to look at the route, on his return, with that view.

Whether the great national route in this region of the Rocky Mountains passes by Fort Bridger or the Uintah Pass, it must pass down the Timpanogos.

The Mormons now charge a heavy toll on the graded road down the cañon and across the bridge. This road should be free from charge to travelers.

The emigrants should not be subjected to the exactions which are made of them at this and several other places on the route. The Mormons and others who charge tolls, should be repaid their outlay, and travelers relieved from a tax which many are ill able to pay.

With great respect, your obedient servant,

A. S. JOHNSTON,
Colonel Second Cavalry, Bvt. Brig. Gen. U. S. A., Comd'g.

Col. SAMUEL COOPER, *Adjutant-General,*
Washington, D. C.

It will be noticed that in the above report General Johnston recommends that the Government re-imburse the Mormon people for the outlay they have made in the construction of a portion of my route from Fort Bridger to Camp Floyd, and that it thus be relieved from the heavy toll which is now exacted upon it. This portion extends for a distance of 12 miles up the cañon of the Timpanogos from its mouth, and the work was executed in the early part of the year 1858, before I explored and opened the route all the way through to Fort Bridger, in the fall of that year.

In order to ascertain the cost of the said turnpike, I addressed the following letter of inquiry to the Hon. W. H. Hooper, Delegate to Congress from Utah:

WASHINGTON, *December* 6, 1859.

SIR: Believing that it would be expedient to have the road from Fort Bridger to Camp Floyd, *via* the valley of the Timpanogos River, entirely free from toll, I respectfully ask for what amount the Timpanogos River Turnpike Company would sell out its interest in the turnpike portion of that road. I am anxious to know, so that if the amount asked is not unreasonably large, I can recommend to the Department an appropriation for the purpose.

I am, sir, very respectfully, your obedient servant,

J. H. SIMPSON,
Captain Topographical Engineers.

Hon. W. H. HOOPER,
Delegate from the Territory of Utah.

*Mr. Hooper's reply.**

HOUSE OF REPRESENTATIVES,
Washington City, March 2, 1860.

DEAR SIR: On the 6th of last December I received a letter from you, making inquiry as to the amount the Timpanogos River Turnpike Company would sell out their road for. Not being able at the time to give the desired information, I stated to you in my reply that I would write to Utah upon the subject and learn whether the company were willing to sell, and upon what terms. From Utah, in answer to my communication on this subject, I learn that, by action of the last legislative assembly, the cañon-road became the property of the Territory; that there was expended in the construction of said road eighteen thousand nine hundred and ninety-seven dollars and sixty-one cents, ($18,997.61,) and for labor in locating the road and supervising the expenditures thereon, one thousand dollars, ($1,000,) making a total cost of nineteen thousand nine hundred and ninety-seven dollars and sixty-one cents, ($19,997.61.)

Should the Government wish to purchase the cañon-road at the before-named amount of total cost, and make the requisite appropriation for so doing, doubtless the Territory will be willing to sell said road for that sum.

I am, sir, very respectfully, your obedient servant,

WM. H. HOOPER.

Capt. J. H. SIMPSON,
Topographical Engineers.

Having now presented some of the grounds for the following estimate, I am prepared to submit it, premising that as the turnpike portion referred to in Mr. Hooper's letter has been, a great deal of it, excavated from the solid rock, and includes an excellent bridge over the Timpanogos, I do not consider the amount expended by the Territory in its construction extravagant.†

* The original transmitted through Bureau of Topographical Engineers, August 2, 1860, to Hon. Secretary of War.

† The details of the routes—at what points they should be improved, and the nature of the improvements—will be found given in my journal of explorations above; and in my report of December 28, 1858, to General Johnston, of my exploration and opening of the new route from Camp Floyd to Fort Bridger *via* Timpanogos Cañon and White Clay Creek. This last report constitutes Sen. Ex. Doc. No. 40, 35th Cong., 2d Sess.

Estimate of cost of the construction and improvement of Captain Simpson's wagon-road from Fort Bridger to California, via White Clay Creek, Timpanogos Cañon, Camp Floyd, and his more southern or return route over the Great Basin.

For portion of road from Fort Bridger to divide between Silver Creek and Timpanogos River, to be expended principally in White Clay Creek Valley	$20,000
To buy out the interest of the Territory of Utah in the turnpike portion of the road, in Timpanogos Cañon, as above	19,997
To improve said turnpike portion by widening it and elevating it sufficiently in places above the contingency of high water in the Timpanogos, and for generally repairing the road all the way from the divide between Silver Creek and the Timpanogos River to Camp Floyd	10,003
Total required for portion of road from Fort Bridger to Camp Floyd	50,000
For route from Camp Floyd to Genoa, *via* General Johnston's pass of the Guyot range, and Captain Simpson's more southern (or more northern) route across the Great Basin (as the War Department may direct), and for making water-tanks	50,000
To carry the road across the first or most eastern range of the Sierra Nevada, from Genoa to Lake Valley, either by the west branch of Carson River, or the Daggett trail, as may be found most expedient by the engineer in charge, and in the latter case the road to join the old one at the summit of Johnston's Pass, or where most advantageous	30,000
Total amount required for the whole road from Fort Bridger to Johnston's Pass	130,000

In the foregoing estimate I have assumed that it would be best for the Government to improve my more southern route over the Great Basin. I have done this for the reason that though this route is 29 miles longer than my more northern route, yet the grades of the former are better, and the grass, timber, and cultivable soil upon it more abundant, and the water equally if not more abundant. Should, however, the Government prefer to improve the more northern route, on which the mail and pony-express are now running, the above estimate will hold equally good, only instead of the phrase "more southern route," that of "more northern route" should be used. Indeed, it might in the low appropriation be left optional with the War Department to apply the money on either route as it might deem best.

So much for the road from Fort Bridger to California. By referring to my journal, under date of August 12, 1859, it will be noticed that I explored a very favorable pass from the valley of the Timpanogos to that of Green River, over the Uintah range of mountains. This pass can be made available for wagons by the removal of the timber in Coal Creek Valley, on the north side of the pass; by the removal of the willows and construction of some causeways in Potts' Creek Valley, on the south side of the pass; and the filling up of some of the gullies in the valley of the Duchesne's Fork. The cost of this would be, say, $20,000. This done, the valley of the Duchesne's Fork of Uintah, and possibly of Green River, would be opened to settlement, and the result eventually follow of a wagon-road communication all the way through from the valley of Great Salt Lake, by the way of the Timpanogos, Coal Creek, Potts' Creek,

Duchesne's Fork, the Uintah River, and White River, to Breckenridge, at the head of Blue River, in the middle park of the Rocky Mountains; from which to Denver City, according to the subjoined letter from Hon. B. D. Williams, there is probably at this date a wagon-road. This route, it will be perceived, will, in connection with mine across the Great Basin, furnish much the shortest route across the continent from the Missouri River, and in addition be of incalculable service in the interchange of commodities between the Mormon population and the people of the gold region about Pike's Peak.

To sum up, Congress should appropriate:

For the road above specified, from Fort Bridger to the summit of Johnston's Pass of the Sierra Nevada *$130,000

For the road from Round Prairie, in Timpanogos Valley, to the mouth of Duchesne's Fork, by the pass of the Uintah range, at the head of Coal Creek 20,000

And for a thorough exploration of the country between the mouth of Duchesne's Fork and Denver City, for the shortest and best route across the Rocky Mountains between those points 20,000

I now give the letter of Mr. B. D. Williams, above referred to:

WASHINGTON CITY, D. C., *January* 18, 1860.

SIR: At your request I write you on the subject of a wagon-road from Denver City, Jefferson Territory, due west to Great Salt Lake City.

I would state that I have just received from Mr. George E. Spencer a plat of a town called Breckenridge, situated at the mouth of French Creek, which empties into Blue River. This point is where the gold was discovered last fall and is about one hundred miles from Denver City nearly west, and about sixty miles beyond the main divide of the Rocky Mountains.

A short history of the prospecting of this country, perhaps, may be interesting. About the month of August last some straggling miners crossed the "snowy range" in search of gold, and, after prospecting for a short time, a portion returned to Denver City for provisions, and made it known that they had made new and good discoveries of gold; at once quite a rush took place for the newly-discovered fields, which were thoroughly prospected before the cold weather set in, so as to satisfy all that there was no humbug in this matter. Several hundred wagons crossed the range in the fall and returned, as late as the 10th of October. John N. Ming, an enterprising merchant at Auraria, fitted out and sent over some wagon-loads of goods which met with ready sale. Since that time there has a company of men obtained from the legislature a charter to build a wagon-road to said point, and are now engaged in prosecuting the same to an early completion. They assure me that they will, by the 1st day of May, have the road fully completed, and that six yoke of oxen can haul 5,000 pounds over the mountains to said point. I am informed that there is but little impediment in getting a good road on to White River.

Then follow that river to where it empties into Grand River, and which is described by Captain Frémont in 1845, I feel satisfied in stating that there can, with but little expense, be a good and permanent wagon-road got, which will be, as you can easily see, about the fortieth parallel of latitude. I cannot speak with the same certainty in reference to the practicability of the road beyond Breckenridge as I can on this side. You will understand that Breckenridge is in the Middle Park beyond the range of the mountains.

I hope that there will be an appropriation made to explore this country, and open a good road across this country. I am assured that it is about one hundred miles nearer than the old road by Laramie, and I am assured by those who know the country well that the snow will not impede the travel in winter.

Hoping this information will be of some benefit to you, I am, respectfully, yours,

B. D. WILLIAMS, *Delegate Jefferson Territory.*

Capt. J. H. SIMPSON, *Topographical Engineers.*

All of which is respectfully submitted.

J. H. SIMPSON,
Captain Topographical Engineers.

DECEMBER 29, 1860.

Col. J. J. ABERT, *Chief Corps Topographical Engineers.*

* I have been informed that the people of California and Western Utah, since my exploration, have been engaged in making the road from Genoa, across the east branch of the Sierra Nevada, by the Daggett trail, to Johnston's Pass. If so, and they have completed it, $30,000 of the above estimated $130,000 may be deducted.

EXPLORATIONS ACROSS THE GREAT BASIN OF UTAH.

APPENDIX H.

MAGNETIC OBSERVATIONS

AND

RESULTS.

APPENDIX H.

MAGNETIC OBSERVATIONS AND RESULTS.

The following table of the magnetic dip (or inclination), declination (or variation), and horizontal intensity of various points along the route from Fort Leavenworth, *via* Fort Kearney, Fort Laramie, and the South Pass, to Fort Bridger, and thence, *via* Camp Floyd, by my new more northern route, to Genoa, in Carson Valley, will not be without interest and value to the physicist as well as surveyor.

The instruments used and experiments resorted to, as well as the method of attaining the ultimate values of the magnetic elements, will be found stated in the following communication of Lieutenant Putnam, Topographical Engineers, my assistant, by whom the observations were chiefly made. The Jones unifilar magnetometer used by us was the one Dr. Kane had with him on his second Grinnell expedition to the Arctic Ocean, in search of Sir John Franklin; and though it was not altogether such in its form or capabilities as I could have wished, yet, for the reason that I could procure no other and there was not time to have one made, I could not do better than to take it. For a paper on the mode of conducting the experiments with this instrument, and with the dip circle (or inclinometer), as well as of obtaining the mathematical value of the elements involved, which has been of great service to us in facilitating our work, I am indebted to Mr. J. E. Hilgard, of the Coast Survey, whose zeal in this branch of scientific research is not greater than his ability, and to whom I have now to express my grateful acknowledgments.

In comparing the declination by the magnetometer (converted into a declinometer) and compass observations on Polaris, as given in the subjoined table, it will be noticed that there is a considerable difference between the results obtained; and that in one instance (at Fort Bridger) it reaches as much as 2° 6′ 50″. At first I was disposed to reject the declinations as shown by the declinometer altogether, supposing that this great difference was owing to a defectiveness on the part of the instrument, but perceiving, on examining the reductions of Dr. Kane's observations in the months of January, February, and March, 1854, at Van Rensselaer Harbor, by Mr. Charles A. Schott, assistant, United States Coast Survey, that he gives the following as a classification of the daily ranges according to their magnitudes, I have come to the conclusion, as the observations were taken with a great deal of care, that the differences have arisen doubtless from the observations by the declinometer having been taken during the day, and those by compass during the night, in connection with the delicate nature of the declinometer, and that the results, therefore, as scientific facts, are worthy of record.

Mr. Schott's classification of Dr. Kane's 17 daily observations is as follows:

Daily range less than 1°	1
Daily range between 1° and 2°	6
Daily range between 2° and 3°	4
Daily range between 3° and 4°	3
Daily range between 4° and 5°	3
Daily range greater than 5°	0

The observations we made were quite numerous, but as they are filed in the Bureau of Topographical Engineers for reference, it is thought best not to incumber the report with them, but only to subjoin a set of each as a specimen of the rest. The results, however, are presented below in a tabulated form, and also graphically on the small charts of the declination and inclination of the needle herewith (see Plate). These charts, I would remark, so far as the data shown across the continent, from Fort Smith, Ark., to the cañon of Chelly, in New Mexico, and from Fort Leavenworth to Genoa, in Carson Valley, are concerned, are an extension by me of the latest charts on this subject from the United States Coast Survey. The Superintendent of the Coast Survey, Prof. A. D. Bache, has kindly furnished me with their latest magnetic charts, and it is a gratification to me, by my explorations in 1849, from Fort Smith, via Santa Fé, to the cañon of Chelly, and by my recent expedition from Fort Leavenworth to Genoa, to be thus able to supply a great deal of magnetic data, which will extend our knowledge of this element over a larger area of our country, and make these charts still more useful.

In addition to the above I would make the following remarks in relation to the electric condition of the atmosphere in the Great Basin. I have noticed that my flannel, when cast off at night before retiring to rest, would evince, by a crackling sound, that it was highly charged. This would frequently be the case in combing one's whiskers, or handling a bear-skin. All this doubtless points to the very dry state, and, therefore, non-conducting power, of the air, and the non-escape of the electric fluid from terrestrial bodies except by the proximity of others.

I would also extract the following from my report of my explorations in the fall of 1858, in Utah, as bearing on this subject:

"It is astonishing to notice the effect of the whirls and gusts of wind upon the magnetic needle, or, more properly speaking, to see the action of the magnetic needle at the time these whirls and gusts are in development. The fact of these disturbances appearing together does not necessarily point to the same cause producing both, but makes it strongly probable that the cause is one and the same in both cases. The needle, whenever these gusts and whirls are in exhibition, would stick either to the north or south end of the bottom of the box, and no change of position could make it stir. Sometimes the effect would be to disturb the needle very much, and to make it point indifferently to any point of the compass. When, however, the gusts would cease, the needle would act normally as usual."*

A somewhat similar phenomenon exhibited itself subsequently at Camp Floyd, in March, 1859, when, however, the weather was fair, though there was some little wind. I was verifying some observations for magnetic declination, by placing a surveyor's compass, on the meridian, immediately over the transit station, with the intention of

* See Senate Ex. Doc., No. 40, 35th Cong., 2d session, p. 28.

reading the declination directly from the needle. The needle, however, I perceived, would not traverse. Supposing the glass cover pressed upon it, I took it off, when the needle moved freely and normally. Finding, however, the wind agitated it too much to allow it to come to a state of rest, I placed the glass back, and found, on a closer examination, that it did not touch the needle. But still the needle would not traverse. I again took off the glass and the needle again traversed freely. I then extended the glass to its place on the needle *gradually*, when I noticed the effect of the proximity was to paralyze the needle, and *that* in proportion to the proximity, so that when the glass was in its place the motion of the needle was entirely paralyzed. The cause, then, of the needle not traversing was the influence of the glass cover in its then abnormal state. Finding the compass to be of no service for the purpose in view, I substituted another in its place, which I found to work well without any signs of disturbing agency. Some days after this I had occasion to again use the first-named compass, when I found the needle acted normally.

The cause, then, of the disturbance above referred to was on account of the accidental abnormal state of the glass cover at the time, and not from any permanent disturbing cause. It is not understood, however, what caused the abnormal condition of the glass of the first large surveyor's compass. Both it and the second surveyor's compass were taken out of their respective boxes just before using them, and the state of the wind was by no means one of irregularity. Besides, if it had arisen from the atmosphere, what affected the one ought to have affected the other, as they had both been subjected to the same handling.

I have thought it proper to note these irregularities in the magnetic needle on account of its bearings upon the accuracy of surveys depending upon its normal state, and the necessity of watching to see that no such disturbing causes are in operation at the time bearings are taken with it. I think there can be no doubt that frequently irregularities, which have been attributed to local attraction, have arisen from this source, and not from the presence of metallic substances to which they have been ascribed; and it is very probable, too, that these irregularities, in all such cases, have been but temporary.* (See, also, Appendix E, pages 78 and 79.)

* Since writing the foregoing I have become acquainted with Mr. W. H. Paine, surveyor and civil engineer, of Sheboygan, Wisconsin, who has furnished me with the following letter, corroborative of the inexplicable character of the abnormal condition of the magnetic needle at certain periods:

"WASHINGTON, D. C., *January* 9, 1861.

"DEAR SIR: Agreeably to your request I will briefly mention some of the observations and experiments which I have made relative to some of the disturbing influences affecting the magnetic needle as used in the surveyor's compass.

"An unfavorable electrical state of the glass covering the needle is a very common cause of disturbance, and its effects are often mistaken for those of local attraction, as it is difficult to determine, by mere observation, whether the one end of the needle is elevated by attraction or the other depressed by a similar cause.

"And when the elevation of one end of the needle from this cause is but slight, the needle is often supposed to be in its normal state when it is not.

"Whenever I have had occasion to use a compass, for several years past, I have proceeded as though I suspected some disturbing influence was having an effect upon the needle, and often, after allowing the needle to become apparently settled, have found that, by breathing upon the glass, or moistening my fingers and bringing them in contact with it, the needle would change its position both in relation to its dip and declination, thus showing that the electric state of the glass affected the needle when it was least suspected.

"For more than two years past I have used a cover or guard, so constructed as to prevent the glass from coming in contact with the clothes of the person carrying the compass, or with other substances, and find that now the needle is but comparatively seldom in an abnormal state.

"Still, there are times when the needle is disturbed, and on two occasions, in particular, I was unable to remove the

I would also draw attention to the fact, which the tables will show, that the usual law which governs the variations in the declination of the needle does not obtain between Fort Bridger and Genoa. At Bridger (longitude 110° 23′ 47″), the declination obtains a maximum of 17° 30′ E.; at Simpson's Spring (longitude 112° 47′ 18″), farther west, it declines to 15° 30′ E.; and still farther west, at Genoa (longitude 119° 40′ 30″), it again has increased to 16° 40′ E.

Mr. Francis A. Bishop, in his report on the Humboldt division of the Fort Kearney, South Pass, and Honey Lake road, speaks of the same thing. His language is: "It will be observed that the magnetic variation increases in going from the Honey Lake (longitude 120° 15′) to the City Rocks (longitude 113° 45′) from 16° 00′ 15″ E. to 17° 00′ 20″ E., contrary to the general law of magnetic variations.*

Captain Whipple's table of magnetic results shows the like irregularity to obtain near the parallel of 35° of north latitude, between Albuquerque (longitude 106° 37′ 52″) and Soda Lake, the sink of the Mojave River (longitude 115° 58′ 46″), though not to the same degree.†

The following is Lieutenant Putnam's communication, referred to above:

SIR: Herewith is presented the results of observations for magnetic elements, *en route* from Fort Leavenworth to Genoa, Carson Valley, in 1858-'59.

The observations for dip and declination were usually made at intervals of about 50 miles along the route; those for intensity could be taken only at a few points, the nature of the observation being such as to require much time and care to determine the necessary data.

The instrument used for obtaining the declination and intensity was the "unifilar magnetometer No. 3;" the dip circle made by Gambey was used for finding the dip or inclination.

To avoid the trouble of locating the meridian, the work of at least one night under favorable circumstances of weather, the magnetic azimuth of the sun was taken, while at the same time another observer measured its altitude with the sextant, and a third noted the time by the chronometer. These data were sufficient, by means of a simple formula, involving the co-latitude of the place, the sun's zenith and north polar distances, to compute the true azimuth, which, with the magnetic azimuth already found, gives the desired declination.

The observations for intensity were of two kinds: experiments of vibration, and experiments of deflection.

1. The experiments of vibration consist in finding the time of one vibration of the magnet, which was suspended horizontally by means of a single fiber of silk. This is best done by noting the time of a large number of vibrations, say 200, and dividing this time by the number.

2. The experiments of deflection, which consist in measuring the angle u, through which the suspended magnet is deflected by another magnet placed at right angles to and a certain distance from the first.

By means of the quantities (t and u) thus found, and the formulas, $m\,x=\frac{\pi^2 k}{t^2}$, and $\frac{m}{x}=\frac{1}{2}\,r^3\tan u$, (in which x is the horizontal component of the magnetic force, m the magnetic moment of the magnet, k its moment of inertia, and r the distance of the deflecting from the suspended magnet in feet and tenths), the value of x may be found.

The dip was obtained as follows: The plane of the circle was first put in the magnetic meridian either by the use of the ordinary compass for the purpose, or by giving it such a position that the needle would stand vertically; this corresponds to a position of the vertical circle at right angles to the magnetic meridian, and by means of the graduated horizontal circle it can be at once brought into the magnetic meridian. In this position both ends of the needle are read. It is then lifted from the Y's, and turned half around its longer axis, replaced, and read again; the horizontal circle is then revolved 180° around its vertical axis, and ends of the needle read again; then the needle is once more turned about its longer axis, and reading taken as before. The same process precisely is gone through with a second needle. If time allows, the poles of each are reversed, and the observation repeated with both. Whenever this is done

---

cause of disturbance by the methods previously resorted to. On both of these occasions other phenomena indicated a highly electrical state of the atmosphere, and to be certain that local attraction was not exerting any influence, I have since passed over the same lines without experiencing any difficulty, or witnessing any of the phenomena then so apparent. I do not attempt to account for the occurrence of this phenomena, but merely submit the facts in the case, although my opinion is that currents of electricity in the air had something to do in the case.

"Yours, very respectfully,

"WM. H. PAINE.

"Capt. J. H. SIMPSON."

* See Ex. Doc. No. 108, H. R., 35th Cong., 2d sess., p. 44.

† See Appendix "G," Pacific Railroad Reports, vol. iv.

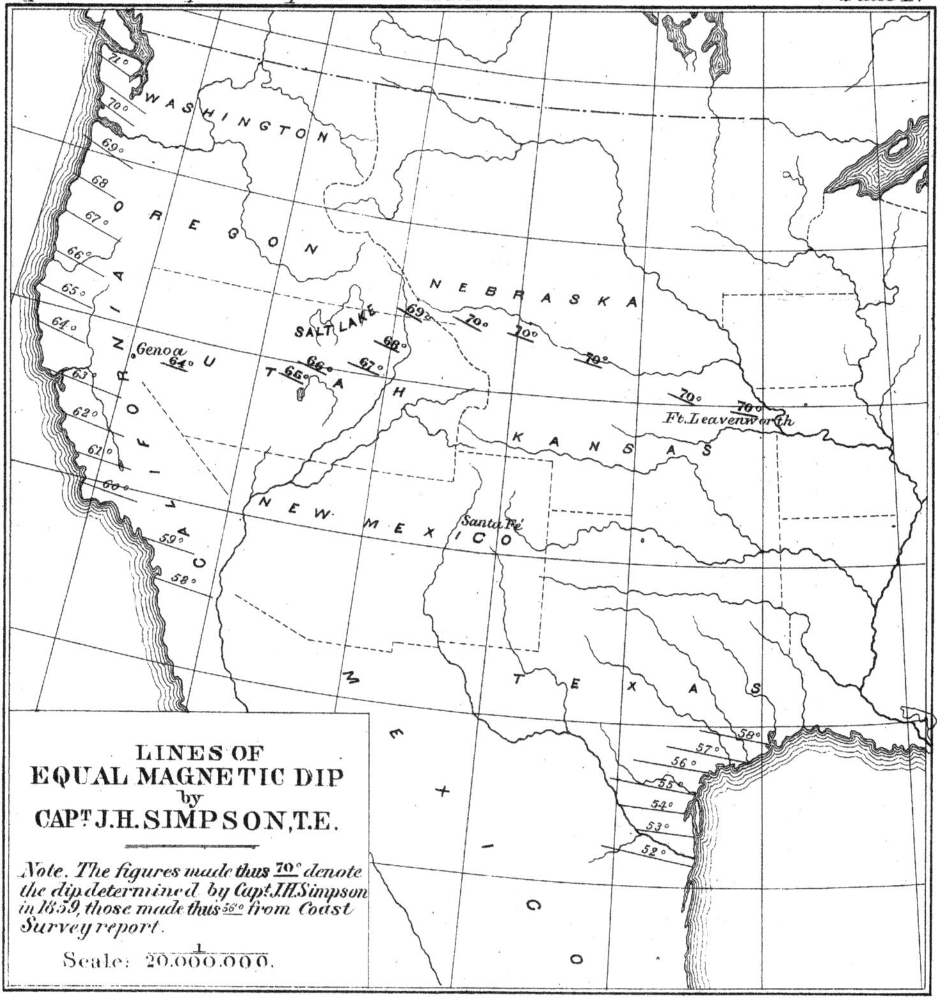

WASHINGTON
OREGON
NEBRASKA
SALT LAKE
Genoa
UTAH
CALIFORNIA
KANSAS
Ft. Leavenworth
NEW MEXICO
Santa Fé
TEXAS
MEXICO

71°
70°
69°
68
67°
66°
65°
64°
63°
62°
61°
60°
59°
58°
64°
66°
65°
67°
68°
69°
70°
70°
70°
70°
70°
58°
57°
56°
55°
54°
53°
52°

LINES OF EQUAL MAGNETIC DIP by CAPT. J.H. SIMPSON, T.E.

Note. The figures made thus 70° denote the dip determined by Capt. J.H. Simpson in 1859, those made thus 56° from Coast Survey report.

Scale: $\frac{1}{20.000.000}$.

a mean of thirty-two observations is obtained, and the errors of eccentricity, imperfect balancing of the needles, and imperfect adjustment of the pivots, are eliminated.

After reaching Washington a constant correction was determined for the declination (rendered necessary by defects of the instrument), facilities for this purpose being obligingly afforded by Mr. Schott, of the Coast-Survey.

I am, very respectfully, your obedient servant,

H. S. PUTNAM,
Lieutenant Topographical Engineers.

Capt. J. H. SIMPSON,
Corps of Topographical Engineers, United States Army.

Table showing the value of the magnetic dip, declination, and horizontal intensity at various points between Fort Leavenworth, Kans., and Genoa, Carson Valley, Nevada, as determined in the explorations of Capt. J. H. Simpson, topographical engineers, in 1858 *and* 1859:

Date.	Place.	Latitude (north).	Longitude (west of Greenwich).	Declination by magnetometer (east).	Declination by compass and observation on Polaris (east).	Dip or inclination, by dip-circle.
		° ′ ″	° ′ ″	° ′ ″	° ′ ″	° ′ ″
May 6, 1858	Fort Leavenworth	39 21 14	94 40 00	11 59 15		69 28 51
June 5, 1858	Little Muddy Creek	39 35 00	95 34 00			69 34 45
June 8, 1858	Vermillion Creek	39 57 00	96 16 03	12 36 42		70 08 59
June 9, 1858	Big Blue River	40 00 00	96 35 00	15 09 46		69 19 30
Oct. 8, 1859	Rock Creek	40 11 00	97 02 00		13 06 00	
June 12, 1858	Big Sandy River	40 12 00	97 12 00	14 39 00		69 32 37
June 15, 1858	Little Blue River	40 15 00	98 10 00	14 43 42		69 50 33
Oct. 5, 1859	Elm Creek	40 30 00	98 30 00		13 18 00	
June 29, 1858	Fort Kearney	40 38 00	98 56 00	14 38 00	14 00 00	70 14 52
July 7, 1858	Camp No. 20	40 40 00	99 54 00	14 16 49		69 37 11
Sept. 30, 1859	Platte River	40 58 30	100 35 00		14 32 00	
July 11, 1858	Camp No. 22	41 05 00	100 50 00	12 04 57		69 46 07
July 18, 1858	Camp No. 25	41 03 00	101 50 00	14 20 44		
July 22, 1858	Ash Hollow	41 21 00	102 03 00			70 02 27
Sept. 24, 1859	North Platte	41 23 00	102 15 00		16 26 00	
July 26, 1858	Chimney Rock	41 43 00	103 30 00			70 15 11
Sept. 20, 1859	North Platte	41 58 00	104 00 00		16 36 00	
July 30, 1858	Fort Laramie	42 12 00	104 31 00	14 24 36		70 02 36
Aug. 7, 1858	La Bonté River	42 35 00	105 22 00	18 22 35		70 15 11
Aug. 11, 1858	Five miles west of Deer Creek	42 53 00	105 57 00	18 28 22		70 28 51
Aug. 15, 1858	Greasewood Creek	42 40 00	107 07 00	20 23 39		70 01 15
Aug. 17, 1858	Sweetwater River	42 38 00	107 25 00	19 41 05		69 53 15
Aug. 23, 1858	......do	42 30 00	108 35 00	19 56 24		69 34 48
Aug. 26, 1858	Little Sandy Creek	42 15 00	109 40 00	20 44 17		68 59 33
Sept. 3, 1858	Fort Bridger	41 20 23	110 23 47	19 36 50	17 30 00	68 05 07
Sept. 11, 1858	Snyder's Creek	40 56 00	111 42 00	19 54 57		67 10 04
April 21, 1859	Camp Floyd	40 13 18	112 08 07	16 34 48	17 10 08	66 29 10
May 4, 1859	Simpson's Spring	40 01 55	112 47 18	16 42 10	15 30 00	66 53 55
May 8, 1859	Sulphur Spring	39 40 36	113 46 19	15 55 25		65 07 07
May 10, 1859	Antelope Valley	39 46 36	114 12 22	16 47 16	16 50 00	65 19 14
May 14, 1859	Eagan Cañon	39 51 46	114 58 15		16 47 00	
May 16, 1859	Huntingdon Spring, east side Ruby Valley	40 00 29	115 19 11	18 05 59		65 25 25
May 19, 1859	Cho-kup Pass	39 53 50	115 44 36	17 02 29		65 19 15
May 22, 1859	Ko-bah Valley	39 44 34	116 10 29	16 43 33	15 55 00	64 55 44
May 28, 1859	Reese River	39 29 29	117 02 41	17 03 10	16 10 00	64 24 52
June 5, 1859	Carson Lake	39 23 37	118 30 01	17 10 42		64 01 59
June 8, 1859	Big Bend, Walker's River	39 08 39	118 56 00	16 55 41		63 36 41
June 15, 1859	Genoa, Carson Valley	38 59 33	119 40 30	16 17 50	16 40 00	64 11 31

The observations for magnetic intensity give for x, the horizontal component of the earth's magnetic force, as follows: At Fort Leavenworth, Kans., May 10, 1858, x=4,368; at Fort Kearney, Kans., June 24, 1858, x=5,0194; at Camp Floyd, Utah, March 25, 1859, x=5,3750.

[Form used.]

Horizontal intensity.—Experiments of vibration.—Camp half-mile south of Fort Leavenworth, May 10, 1858.—Magnet A 67, *Inertia ring,* Z.—*Chronometer* 1821.

Number of vibrations.	Time.	Temperature.	Extreme scale readings.		Time of 200 vibrations.	Calculations.—Observed time of 200 vibrations = 752s. 3. Time of vibrations = 3s. 76. $m\,x = \frac{\pi^2 k}{T^2}$		
	h. m. s.	°			m. s.			
0	4 03 21	67	180	390	....	T	0. 57518	
10	4 03 58	......	......	......	....	T²		
20	4 04 35	......	......	......	....		1. 15036	
30	4 05 12	......	......	......	....	$\pi^2 k$	1. 33940	
40	4 05 50	......	......	......	....			
50	4 06 28	......	......	......	....	$m\,x$	0. 18904	
100	4 09 38	......	......	......	....	* m	9. 54876	
200	4 15 55	......	280	320	12 34			
10	4 16 31	......	......	......	12 33	x	0. 64028	=4. 368
20	4 17 07	......	......	......	12 32			
30	4 17 44	......	......	......	12 32			
40	4 18 22	......	......	......	12 32	$\frac{m}{x}$	8. 90849	
50	4 18 59	......	450	140	12 31	$m\,x$	0. 18904	
	Means ..	......	......	......	12 32	m^2	9. 09753	
						m	9. 54876	

Observer, Capt. J. H. Simpson.

[Form used.]

Horizontal intensity.—Deflections with theodolite magnetometer.—Camp, ½ mile south of Fort Leavenworth, May 19, 1858.—*Magnet* A 67, *deflecting at right angles to magnet* I 10, *suspended.*

[Distance r = 1. 3 feet. Log. = 0. 11394.]

Magnet.	North end.	Circle readings.				Circle readings.			
		No.	A	B	Mean.	No.	A	B	Mean.
			° ′ ″	′ ″	′ ″		° ′ ″	′ ″	′ ″
East.	E.	1	70 53 20	52 00	52 40				
	W.					2	62 51 20	51 00	51 10
	E.	3	70 49 45	48 40	49 10				
	W.					4	62 52 00	45 40	48 50
	E.	5	70 49 40	49 00	49 20				

Mean 8° 50′ 23″

Magnet.	North end.	No.	A	B	Mean.	No.	A	B	Mean.
			° ′ ″	′ ″	′ ″		° ′ ″	′ ″	′ ″
West.	W.					6	62 49 00	48 00	48 30
	E.	7	70 53 00	52 20	52 40				
	W.					8	62 49 20	48 00	48 40
	E.	9	70 54 00	53 20	53 40				
	W.					10	62 49 00	48 00	48 30

Mean 8° 04′ 30″

		Logarithms.
° ′ ″		
Mag. E. 2 u = 8 50 23		
Mag. W. 2 u = 8 04 30		
Mean 8 27 26. 5	$\frac{1}{2}$	9. 69897
u = 4 13 43. 25	r^3	0. 34183
Beginning time 11.25 a. m.; temperature 82°.5.	Sin. u	8. 86769
Ending time 2.40 p. m.; temperature 74°.	$\frac{m}{x}$	8. 90849

Observer, Capt. J. H. Simpson.

[Form used.]

Magnetic dip.—Genoa, Nevada, June 14, 1859.—*Needle No.* 1.—*Observer, Lieutenant Putnam.*

A. S., OR UPPER END.							
Circle east.				Circle west.			
Face east.		Face west.		Face east.		Face west.	
A.	B.	A.	B.	A.	B.	A.	B.
° ′	° ′	° ′	° ′	° ′	° ′	° ′	° ′
63 15	63 14	64 2	64 4	64 9	64 8	64 41	64 37
With poles reversed.							
63 2	63 2	62 31	62 29	65 34	65 33	64 5	64 4
63° 8′ 15″		63° 16′ 30″		64° 51′		64° 21′ 45″	
63° 12′ 22″				64° 36′ 22″			
63° 54′ 22″							

Needle No. 2.—*Observer, Lieutenant Putnam.*

A. S., OR UPPER END.							
Circle west.				Circle east.			
Face west.		Face east.		Face west.		Face east.	
A.	B.	A.	B.	A.	B.	A.	B.
° ′	° ′	° ′	° ′	° ′	° ′	° ′	° ′
63 16	63 14	63 49	63 48	64 36	64 38	64 13	64 14
With poles reversed.							
65 4	65 2	64 46	64 45	64 55	64 56	65 11	65 12
64° 09′		64° 17′		64° 46′ 15″		64° 42′ 30″	
64° 13′				64° 44′ 22″			
64° 28′ 41″							
63 54 22							
2)128 23 03							
Grand mean or magnetic dips............ 64 11 31							

[Form used.]

Magnetic declination or azimuth between the true and magnetic meridian.

Camp one-half mile south of Fort Leavenworth, Kansas, May 25, 1858.—Unifilar magnetometer No. 3.—Magnet I 10.

From magnetic station to magnetic south point (mirror above):

	°	′	″
Limb of magnetometer reads, first vertical........................	67	53	40
Limb of magnetometer reads, second vertical........................	247	52	20
Mean........................	67	53	00

(Mirror below :)

	°	′	″
Limb of magnetometer reads, first vertical	70	07	40
Limb of magnetometer reads, second vertical	250	07	20
Mean	70	07	30
Grand mean of magnetic south point	69	00	15
True south point reads, first vertical	57	01	20
True south point reads, second vertical	237	00′	
Mean	57	01	00

Difference of mean readings or magnetic azimuth 11° 59′ 15″ E.

Lieut. H. S. Putnam, Observer.

NOTE.—In the above case the true meridian had been determined by an observation on Alioth (*e, Ursæ Majoris*) and Polaris, and marked on the ground. In our observations on the march the magnetic azimuth of the sun was observed and the true azimuth (or meridian) determined from the known time, latitude, and declination.

EXPLORATIONS ACROSS THE GREAT BASIN OF UTAH.

APPENDIX H H.

RAILROAD-ROUTES

FROM

THE ATLANTIC TO THE PACIFIC OCEAN.

APPENDIX HH.

RAILROAD ROUTES FROM THE ATLANTIC TO THE PACIFIC OCEAN.

[BY CAPT. J. H. SIMPSON, CORPS TOPOGRAPHICAL ENGINEERS, U. S. ARMY.]

As it may be expected of me, on account of my explorations over different portions of the country lying between the Arkansas and Mississippi Rivers and the Pacific Ocean, that I should express my views in relation to the great question of one or more railroads across the continent, I do not know how I can better do so than to include, as a portion of my report, the following letter which I addressed on this subject to a citizen of Buffalo, January 20, 1859, when I was at Camp Floyd. At that date I had not made the explorations I have since over the Great Basin of Utah, and I will, therefore, premise that what I have said in this letter, in relation to the middle or Beckwith railroad route, I am constrained, from the experience I now have, to modify, so far as to state that, while I do not consider (as I have reported in the introduction to my report) my route across the Great Basin a railroad route, yet I do believe that that suggested by Captain Beckwith, from the south end of Great Salt Lake to the head of the Humboldt, and thence down its valley at least to where it should leave said valley to strike and cross the Sierra Nevada, will be found to be practicable. What should be the line from the Humboldt to and across the Sierra Nevada is a question which, probably, is more open to doubt; though I should gather, from Captain Beckwith's report, that even in this section his grades do not preclude the practicability of the route.*

I will also premise that, as the accumulation of the snows in the high mountain-passes is more due to successive snow-storms, and non-melting of the snow, and thus every storm adding something to the quantity, than to a fall of it at any one period, which might, as often as it occurred, be removed with probably no very great difficulty, I do not consider the snow in the mountains as great a hinderance to a railroad across the continent, on the middle route, as my letter below indicates. With these modifications, I now present the letter as expressing my present views on this subject.

Railroad across the United States, from the Atlantic to the Pacific.

CAMP FLOYD, UTAH, *January* 20, 1859.

DEAR SIR: Your letter of the 9th ultimo I had the gratification to receive by the last mail. You request of me my views in relation to the Pacific Railroad, which you

* See vol. ii, Pacific Railroad Reports.

are pleased to think my familiarity with the country and long consideration of the various projects suggested qualify me to give. My experience in relation to this subject consists in my having made, with Captain Marcy, in 1849, the first survey of the Fort Smith and Zuni route, as far as the Rio Grande, each taking notes for the purpose; thence, to Zuni, I was alone engaged in the reconnaissance, and in my report of this survey I pointed out, for the first time, the great importance to the Government, on the score of grade and distance, of ordering a further reconnaissance of a route in the same direction all the way to the Pacific. My reports of both these explorations have been published by the Government, and they are available to those who may take any interest in the history of explorations in this country. My views in relation to a Pacific railroad differed very much from those of Colonel Frémont and other officers of the Government; but as they did not flatter the public mind into the belief that the project was one of immediate accomplishment, but one, if ever made, only to grow out of circumstances which might be made normal to its accomplishment, they, doubtless, were considered of but little value, and, therefore, excited no attention. It is, however, gratifying to find that the very mode I suggested as being the only one which would bring the railroad at length, if it was to come at all, has, for about two years back, been followed by the Government; that is, by opening the several routes as military, post, and emigration roads, and thus making the circumstances normal to a proper knowledge of the routes, and of the capability of the country in relation to them. The Fort Smith and Zuni route has, since my exploration and reports, been surveyed by Captain Whipple, who extended it all the way to California, and its extension is now being worked by Mr. E. F. Beale, for a wagon-road, under the direction of the Government.

Since my exploration of the route referred to, in 1850, I was over the Santa Fé and Fort Leavenworth route on my return to the States. From May, 1851, to June, 1856, for five years, I was in charge of the General Government roads in the Territory of Minnesota, one of which extended from Saint Paul to Pembina, another from Point Douglass to Lake Superior, another from Mendota to the mouth of the Big Sioux River, and several other roads, all of which, of course, gave me an opportunity of knowing something of the country and climate in that quarter. Since then, during the past year, you are aware of my journeyings to Utah, by Fort Kearney and the North Platte, and of my reconnaissance east and west of Camp Floyd. I mention all this to show my experience in the matters of which I am about to treat, so that my discussion of the subject may be regarded for what it is worth. The mail leaves tomorrow morning, and I am, therefore, obliged to write rapidly and not as fully as I could wish, though my convictions are none the less decided, on account of long consideration of the several routes.

DISCUSSION OF THE SUBJECT.

The public mind has, for a number of years past, ever since the great exodus to California, growing out of the discovery of large deposits of gold in that region, been greatly exercised in relation to the importance and speedy completion of one or more railroads connecting the Atlantic with the Pacific Ocean, across the continent of North

America, and through our national domain. The change created in the minds of men with regard to the real situation of California, in respect to its remote distance from the Atlantic States, by the establishment of a line of steamers on either ocean to the Isthmus of Panama, which would waft the emigrant to the golden port of the Pacific coast, the bay of San Francisco, in one-eighth of the time it was wont to take around Cape Horn; quickly restore him to his friends to tell them what he had seen; and speedily transmit the mails by which the news was kept constantly recurring and fresh, all of which was read by the public with the greatest avidity, have conspired to bring mentally the Pacific coast and its adjoining region very near to us, when, really, in a physical point of view, it is just as far distant as ever.

The consequence has been that what before was believed to be perfectly chimerical, the construction of a railroad across the continent, is now regarded as a thing certain; and not only so, but that it will be accomplished in a few years; people do not say how many, but I suppose they vaguely mean from three to five. Such were the ideas which prevailed ten years ago, and yet not the first certain step has been taken in the consummation of the project. Not a foot of railroad has been laid which may fairly be called a part of the great national railroad, and which has been undertaken with any decided determination to push the road across the continent.

This long lapse of time between the conception of a project of vast importance and the commencement of the undertaking is, however, only the fruit of causes which have been existing all along, and which were first pointed out by the writer, as before stated, in his reports of the Fort Smith route in 1849. Nature remains the same now upon this vast theater between the Mississippi on the east and the Pacific on the west it ever did. The long dreary waste of deserts still are experienced by the toiling, weary emigrant as long and dreary as ever, and the Rocky and other mountains still rear their majestic peaks and ridges, and boldly challenge the strength, energy, and perseverance of the way-worn traveler.

The truth is, facts are stubborn things, and he, be he engineer, statesman, or philosopher, who ignores them, will at length find that he has been following but a vain conceit, which will eventually land him, where an attainable prescience might have forewarned him, into a condition of vain inanity, or, it may be worse, of utter ruin.

We have been led into these reflections by the history of the railroad question, which only within the past two or three years has been approximating toward a solution. In our judgment, facts have been ignored, and desires and vain expectations have been entertained by politicians, and I may say the people generally, which have eventuated in results that might from the first have been anticipated, under reports which it appears to me (in all humility I say it) ought to have dwelt more upon the difficulties of the project, and of the mode in which they are to be determined and met, than upon fanning the public mind with the hot haste which thus far has resulted only in finding, at a late date, from actual observation and experience, that the mode of building the road is, first, to prepare the way by common roads, and opening them to settlement and cultivation, and that then the railroad will normally come, if it comes at all.

Now, all this misapprehension of the failure in regard to the completion of the railroad, as we think, has been owing to two causes, both of which, singly and together, have been operating to produce it. One is the perfect ignorance of the people in respect to the character of the country through which the railroad or railroads are to be built, and, therefore, their inability to realize the true state of the case. The other is the seemingly studious way in which the stubborn facts of the project and unpalatable truths have been kept in the background. I say seemingly studious, for so at first glance it might appear, though I think it has arisen from a habit of mind to dwell, in descriptions of country, upon that which is pleasing, and caring but little to dwell upon that which, though a truth of the greatest importance in the premises, is forbidding; I refer to the almost utter barrenness which characterizes, as a whole, the expanse of country for hundreds, I may almost say thousands, of miles along the several routes. Now, when I speak of the ignorance of the people in respect to the character of the country, I do not speak of it in the way of reproach. Far from it, but only as a fact which they cannot help, and which is common to the most intelligent, and all because, having seen nothing of the same kind in their own experience, they cannot, even by any description which others may give, come up, in their own conceptions, to the utter barrenness and worthlessness, speaking as a whole, which this country throughout nearly its whole extent presents.

For example, the fact may be told a hundred times that the great area of the country, from about two hundred miles west of the States of Arkansas and Missouri, nearly the whole way to the Pacific, is one unmitigated desert (including within this also barren mountains), which a person who has seen it would scarcely take as a gift; and yet, notwithstanding all this, annually you will see bills brought forward in Congress in which the land along the route figures as a very important element in the ways and means to construct the road. Should Congress send out a committee to spy out the utter poverty of the land, as it really exists, it is possible it may be brought to a standpoint from which members will see the fact as it is, and the difficulties on this account, and others may then loom up sufficiently to assure them that the construction of this road will require something more to accomplish it than the legislation which has attended the construction of roads in our densely populated and fertile States, where all is normal to immediate and certain results.

But should not one or more railroads be built across our country? Should not our Pacific possessions and population be brought into closer relation by the quick response of sympathy, social, commercial, and military, which this mode of transit would engender? Should not the trade of the great nations of China and Japan, which by treaty has lately been opened to us, be made available to us as a people and a nation, by the establishment of a hard-iron railway, which, by its slight friction and the steam-car, would rapidly possess us of the rich products of those countries? Does not the quick concentration of troops, necessary in time of danger from threatened invasion, as well as the close bond which should ever subsist between the remotest and all portions of our confederacy, make such a project a *sine qua non* of safety from our enemies from without, and of amity and harmony within?

To all this we most indubitably reply *yes*. But how shall we go to work to build these roads, and what routes shall we take? Shall we have but one road, and that through Northern Texas and Mexico; or shall we take the middle route, through Utah; or would it be best to take the route through Minnesota and the Territories of Nebraska and Washington surveyed by Governor Stevens? Or shall we have two or all the roads?

These have been puzzling questions, as their yet unsettled state shows; but still it seems to us that a solution of them is attainable. The great error, as we think, in the whole of this project has been in the supposition that the road could be built at once, and that all Congress had to do was to will it by legislation. But every project has its normal condition in respect to its accomplishment, out of which naturally and easily is derived the end in view. What, then, is the normal condition which is necessary to the success of so gigantic a railroad scheme? I assert that this condition is in the establishment of the circumstances which will give success to the project. And what are these? Simply those which I have adverted to before, the opening and making practicable by the Government of common wagon-roads along the several proposed lines of railroad-routes, and thus making them military, emigration, and postal routes, by means of which the country will, in eligible locations, be populated; its resources, such as they are, developed; and a knowledge of what really can be done obtained. And I go farther. Not only should these routes be thus established, but Congress, in my judgment, should observe a liberal policy toward the attainment of so important a national good. A comparatively small outlay in this direction will save millions, which may be sunk by the premature commencement of a railroad which might have to be suspended or indefinitely postponed on account of insufficient concurrent means.

Are these circumstances yet normal, on either of the routes, to the successful prosecution and completion of a Pacific railroad?

In respect to the southern route, the policy which is now being observed by the Government, of establishing a military, postal, and emigration road in this direction, must in a few years present a status or condition which will enable the Government and the people to see what really can be done in building a great national road in this quarter.

In regard to the middle or Utah route, the Government, as we think, has wisely made this a military and postal route; and as it has for years been a great highway, it will not be long before the exact status of this road will be known, if it is not already known, in reference to its capabilities and resources as a platform for the proposed railroad.

As it respects the northern or Minnesota route, the Government ought, in the opinion of the writer, also to open and establish a military, postal, and emigrant wagon-road in this direction. This step would not be more productive of advantage to our northwest Pacific Territories of Washington and Oregon than it would be the means of developing the country all along the route, and making the circumstances normal to the expression of its exact condition in respect to the building of a railroad.

As to the question where it is probable the national railroad or railroads will be located, we think it a foregone conclusion that the southern, through New Mexico or Arizona, will be the *locale* of one. We are of this opinion, first, because the grades as determined by the Government explorers are lighter on this route than on either of the others; second, because, if we have a railroad at all, we ought to have one which would be available without intermission the whole year around; and, in order to this, it should be beyond the contingency of obstructions from snow, which could not be the case with the others higher north.

In regard to the route proposed by Senator Benton, and to which Colonel Frémont was most partial, that in the region of the 38th parallel, the surveys by Captains Gunnison and Beckwith show that, from the high grades it would be necessary to overcome, it is entirely impracticable.

That proposed by Captains Stansbury and Beckwith, through Bridger's Pass and by way of Timpanogos, is doubtless far better, in point of grade and practicability, than the one just referred to; but still we think that its cost will never justify its construction, and, if made, that its obstructions by the snows of winter through the high mountain-passes would ever make it an uncertain route.

The route through Minnesota, Nebraska, and Washington Territory, in the region of the 48th parallel of latitude, it might be supposed, from its being still higher north, was out of the question. The facts, however, do not justify such a conclusion. The country, as high as our most northern boundary, and for a number of degrees above it, in British America, has been tried agriculturally, and it is well known that it produces the cereals and all garden vegetables, and some of the succulent fruits in the greatest perfection. The good land, as also the timber regions, approximate on this route nearer than on either of the others. From a map in my possession, copied from one drawn by a Jesuit missionary, the Rev. Peter John De Smet, who kindly loaned it to me for the purpose, I translate the following remark, which applies to the country all along the east foot of the Rocky Mountains, from about the river Maria, a tributary of the Missouri, in latitude 48°.50, to the Saskatchewan River, or latitude 53°—that is, for an extent, following the oblique trend of the mountain range, of for more than 400 miles. His notation is, "All the region which lies adjacent to the Rocky Mountains is agreeably diversified with fertile plains and beautiful forests; lakes and hills give variety to the landscape between the heads and forks of innumerable streams, and wild animals of every kind abound."

Besides, the reverend gentleman, in pointing out to me this region of country, spoke of it in the most glowing terms. He has been for 12 years a missionary among the Indians of Oregon, Nebraska, and farther north in British America, and is probably as well acquainted with all this region as any man living. He acquired the ability of taking notes of reconnaissance in one of the expeditions of Monsieur Nicollet, and has ever since been in the habit of doing so, and plotting his routes. In this connection, I refer you to an extract, herewith, from quite a sensibly-written article entitled "Fraser River," which I find in the last October number of the *Knickerbocker*. The remarks of the writer in reference to the track northwestward which is to mark the direction of empire, and where villages, towns, and cities are destined to spring up, I think, are quite just.*

---

* From an article entitled "Fraser River," in the *Knickerbocker* of October, 1858.

Here is the great fact of the northwestern area of this continent. An area not inferior in size to the whole United States east of the Mississippi, which is perfectly adapted to the fullest occupation by cultivated nations, yet is

This northern route, then, passes over a country which is cultivable for a very considerable portion of its extent. Wood and water are doubtless more abundant upon it than upon any of the other routes; and the grades, according to Governor Stevens, are not impracticable for a railroad. The snows, too, are not so heavy as

almost wholly unoccupied, lies west of the 98th meridian and above the 43d parallel; that is, north of the latitude of Milwaukee, and west of the longitude of Red River, Fort Kearney, and Corpus Christi. Or, to state the fact in another way, east of the Rocky Mountains, and west of the 98th meridian, and between the 40th and 60th parallels, there is a productive, cultivable area of 500,000 square miles. West of the Rocky Mountains, and between the same parallels, there is an area of 300,000 square miles.

It is a great mistake to suppose that the temperature of the Atlantic coast is carried straight across the continent to the Pacific. The isothermals deflect greatly to the north, and the temperatures of the Northern Pacific areas are paralleled in the high latitudes of Western and Central Europe. The latitudes which inclose the plateaus of the Missouri and the Saskatchewan, in Europe inclose the rich central plains of the continent. The great grain-growing districts of Russia lie between the 45th and 60th parallels, that is, north of the latitude of Saint Paul, Minn., or Eastport, Me. Indeed, the temperature in some instances is higher for the same latitudes here than in Central Europe. The isothermal of 70° for the summer, which in our plateau ranges from along latitude 50° to 52°, in Europe skirts through Vienna and Odessa in about parallel 46°. The isothermal of 50° for the year runs along the coast of British Columbia, and does not go far from New York, London, and Sebastopol. Furthermore, dry areas are not found above 47°, and there are no barren tracts of consequence north of the Bad Islands and the coteaux of the Missouri. The land grows grain finely and is well wooded. All the grains of the temperate districts are here produced abundantly, and Indian corn may be grown as high as the Saskatchewan.

The buffalo winter as safely on the Upper Athabasca as in the latitude of Saint Paul, and the spring opens at nearly the same time along the immense line of plains from Saint Paul to Mackenzie's River. To these facts, for which there is the authority of Blodgett's Treatise on the Climatology of the United States, may be added this, that to the region bordering the Northern Pacific, the finest maritime positions belong, throughout its entire extent, and no part of the West of Europe exceeds it in the advantages of equable climate, fertile soil, and commercial accessibility of coast. We have the same excellent authority for the statement that in every condition forming the basis of national wealth, the continental mass lying westward and northwestward from Lake Superior is far more valuable than the interior in lower latitudes, of which Salt Lake and Upper New Mexico are the prominent known districts. In short, its commercial and industrial capacity is gigantic. Its occupation was coeval with the Spanish occupation of New Mexico and California. The Hudson's Bay Company has preserved it an utter wilderness for many long years. The Fraser River discoveries and emigration are facts which the company cannot crush. Itself must go the wall, and now the population of the great northwestern areas begins.

Another effect of the Fraser River discoveries is their determination of the route for the great Pacific Railroad. In view of the facts which we have just stated, it becomes clear that if the population of the United States were evenly distributed from the Gulf of Mexico to the great lakes, the existence of these northwestern areas would draw the lines of travel to the Pacific sensibly to the north. But the Northern States are by far the most densely populated. The center of population is west of Pittsburgh; of productive power, to the east and north of that city. The movement of these centers is slowly to the west and to the north of west. At our present rate of increase, in less than fifty years they will be near Chicago. Their line of direction indicates the track of westward empire, and the general route along which villages, towns, and cities will arise, and therefore the first railroad be built to the Pacific coast.

Beyond and above all possible interferences and obstructions of political or sectional zeal, beyond human control, these great movements of nations and peoples go on without their foresight, and without the knowledge of the earlier generations; yet, working out in beautiful order, and as if with universal consent, and the conspiracy of all the secret forces of nature, their grand and best results.

If we recall, in this connection, the precise position of the *mauvaises terres*, and the rainless, sandy, and uninhabitable areas of the continent, the nature and location of the mountain chains, exclusive of the Rocky Mountain range, extending from latitude 47° to 33°, headed at the south by the Gila River, on whose southern side are the arid, uncultivable tracts of Sonora, and headed at the north by the Missouri River, on whose northern side lie these vast, cultivable and inhabitable areas; if we recall the remarkable deflection to the westward of the Rocky Mountain range in this latitude; if we recall, also, the course of that gigantic stream, which is far greater than the river to which by a mistaken nomenclature, it is made tributary, a stream extending to the very base of the Rocky Mountains, in the region where they are lowest and transits easiest, navigable for steamers for two thousand four hundred and fifty miles from its mouth, and for smaller vessels almost within sound of the Great Falls; if we recall, also, the remarkable deflection to the north of the isothermal lines from the west of Lake Superior, already mentioned, and the position of Columbia River, and remember withal that the first and the great routes of travel are always where nature has scooped out valleys for the passage of great rivers; if we combine all these conceptions with the one first advanced, of the direction of the movement of the centers of population and industrial activity, there remains no room to doubt that even without naming the northwestern areas, that along the valley of the Missouri, over the Rocky Mountains, in the low passes of latitude 47°, and thence by the Columbia and its tributaries to the Pacific, or through the passes of the Cascade range to the splendid harbors of Puget Sound, lies the great route to the Pacific, the belt on which towns and villages will first arise, the strongest link in the union of the Atlantic and Pacific States. The Fraser River discoveries have hastened the result; they have not diverted it.

in more southern latitudes. In addition, the navigability of the Missouri high up in this region will facilitate the construction of the road. These facts certainly are important, and not only show that the country is worthy of the immediate attention of the Government in respect to its development, by the establishment of a military post and emigration route all the way to Washington Territory; but they also point to the day when a railroad will be normal to the then existing state of things, and follow as a natural consequence.

The question of making a railroad across the continent is one, however, of no ordinary magnitude, and it is nothing wonderful that every administration has been backward in taking hold of it. When we reflect that the road will probably be worked at but few points at one time—be probably pushed out from either extreme; that it will not have the dense population of the States immediately about it, whence the necessary labor is to be drawn; that there will be no thousand avenues of commerce by which all the necessary materials and supplies can be conveyed; that there will be but few centers of population whence aid or facilities of any kind can be had; that the road must necessarily pass through a desert where but little or no suitable timber can be found for the superstructure, it may be readily seen why there is such a reluctance in taking hold of so gigantic a scheme. Besides, if it is once taken up, it should be prosecuted to an immediate completion; for, on the supposition that the route is 2,000 miles long (and none of them would be much short of it), if 100 miles of road should be made in a year, it would take 20 years to build it; and during this period a portion of it, if wooden ties are used, will have rotted out twice. If 200 miles are made, which, considering the difficulties in the way, would be a great deal of work, it would take 10 years to build it, and then a portion of it will have rotted out once. These are ugly features, but it is better to look at them in advance than to be startled by them when loss and ruin shall have ensued. The matter would not be so bad if the road could be made profitable as it advances; but this would probably hold true of but the northern one, for the reason that the region through which the others would be laid can never, on account of its sterility, support a dense population, and hence there could arise but little need of commercial facilities until the road should have been made entirely through.

Again, the length of the road would be such, so far as bulky articles are concerned, as to make it ruinous to have them conveyed in this way. The merchant-ships, though slower, would doubtless still monopolize all this heavy, bulky trade. The road would then chiefly have to depend for its support upon passengers, the freight of small packages, and the aid the Government might give it by its transmission of the mails and the transportation of troops and munitions of war. But still its great service in binding the extremes of our confederacy together, and its important use in a military point of view, would doubtless induce the Government to contribute its utmost toward keeping it in operation.

To my mind, scarcely second to the project of a great national railroad across our continent, looms up the important one of a ship-canal through Central America. This, it strikes me, is the great political, commercial, financial, physico-scientific, moral, and religious problem of the age; and, if it could be accomplished, would do more to civilize and Christianize mankind than any and all other projects taken together. It is a gratification to see, by the Secretary of the Navy's report, that the two officers who were sent out by the Government to survey the Atrato River route do not agree in their conclusion as to its practicability. I had been led to believe, from what I had read in the public prints, that the route had been condemned; but this statement of the honorable Secretary leaves a gleam of hope that the great work may yet be accomplished. This Atrato route the late Dr. Foote, when minister to Bogota, brought, as he told me, to the attention of Mr. Webster, then Secretary of State under Mr. Fillmore, and he felt sure, from the information he had obtained upon the subject, that it was well worthy of examination.

This great work deserves the attention of every nation in the world, and, if it cannot be accomplished in any other mode, should be effected by them in conjunction, and thrown open to ships of every clime. A congress of nations for the purpose should, it strikes me, if necessary, be called together, and some feasible plan adopted. But I have carried this letter to an unconscionable length, and will, therefore, not tire your patience any longer by its continuance.

I am, very respectfully, your obedient servant,

J. H. SIMPSON,
Captain Corps Topographical Engineers.

JAMES H. SANFORD, Esq.,
Buffalo, N. Y.

APPENDIX I.

REPORT

ON THE

GEOLOGY OF THE COUNTRY

BETWEEN

FORT LEAVENWORTH, K. T., AND THE SIERRA NEVADA

NEAR CARSON VALLEY.

BY

HENRY ENGELMANN,
GEOLOGIST OF THE EXPEDITION.

LA SALLE, ILL., *December* 29, 1875.

DEAR SIR: I have to-day forwarded to you, by express, the manuscript of my geological report of your exploration of 1858–'59 (two copies), which you had the kindness to send me for revision. I have made no essential changes or corrections, but have only struck out some passages which, at this date, appeared to me irrelevant or out of place. I was inclined to shorten the report materially, but this would have necessitated a rewriting of a large portion of it.

In returning to you the report I have to say that I was much pleased to find that I had really no cause to make any essential corrections. When this exploration was made, the country over which it extended was virtually for the most part a wilderness, partly then trodden for the first time by the foot of the white man. Its mineral wealth had then not been discovered. Now the whole of it is spanned by the iron rail, with many branch roads leading into its distant valleys. It is teeming all over with human industry. The open country has become the domain of the farmer and stock-raiser; numerous coal-mines have been opened at distant points; every mountain and gulch has been explored by the omnipresent miner; steam batteries thunder in its most distant mountain recesses, crushing the ores of the precious metals; and cities have sprung into life and prosperity where then only the squalid Digger Indian hunted the ground-rat. Then the geological exploration was confined to a naturally incomplete reconnaissance within reach of a military escort. Since then, splendidly-equipped geological exploring parties have spent years in closely examining the whole district. Numerous scientists have spent the summer seasons rusticating in the mountains, while mining engineers have professionally traversed it in every direction.

Under these circumstances, the interest with which some parts of this report would have been received at the time when it was written, does, of course, not any longer attach to it. It is, in fact, superseded; but its perusal will show that while it is necessarily fragmentary and incomplete, it represents the general outlines of the geological structure of the country pretty correctly, and contains many diligently-compiled details. In consequence of the non-publication of the report, the credit due to it has, in various instances, been claimed by later observers. In revising the report for publication, I have therefore abstained from making any essential alterations, preferring to let it stand on its merits such as it was originally written, merely eliminating some too lengthy remarks.

I am, dear sir, your obedient servant,

HENRY ENGELMANN,
Mining Engineer.

General J. H. SIMPSON,
Colonel of Engineers, U. S. A., Saint Louis, Mo.

APPENDIX I.

REPORT ON THE GEOLOGY OF THE COUNTRY BETWEEN FORT LEAVENWORTH, KANSAS, AND THE SIERRA NEVADA, NEAR CARSON VALLEY.

[BY HENRY ENGELMANN, GEOLOGIST OF THE EXPEDITION.]

INTRODUCTION.

WASHINGTON, D. C., *July* 19, 1860.

SIR: I herewith submit to you my report on the geology of the country traversed by the expedition under your command in 1858 and 1859, from Fort Leavenworth, Kansas, to the Sierra Nevada, near Carson Valley. Only little has been known, heretofore, of the geology of this whole country, except of its eastern portion, and even there important questions remain unsettled, while the western portion has been altogether a *terra incognita.* By your expedition, therefore, important additions have been made to our knowledge of the geological structure of the central portions of the continent.

Some additional observations have been made in regard to the Upper Carboniferous and more recent formations of Northeastern Kansas. In the remarkable bluff formations of the North Fork of Platte River, below Fort Laramie, mammalian and chelonian remains have been discovered, which indicate their analogy with the interesting deposits of the Bad Lands of White River, famous for the abundance of their terrestrial pre-adamitic fauna; and the general character and succession of the Tertiary strata have been investigated, from the most recent to the oldest, along Platte River, and farther on across the South Pass to the Wahsatch Mountains. The existence of Jurassic strata in the territory of the United States, which had been very problematical till within a short time, when they were first recognized in the Black Hills, by Mr. Meek and Dr. Hayden, on Lieutenant Warren's expedition, has been fully established, and they have been recognized at various points in the Rocky Mountains near North Platte River, and on the eastern slope of the Wahsatch range. The Triassic and Cretaceous Epochs have also been found represented. In the Green River Valley a Tertiary fresh-water formation has been discovered, and in the Wahsatch Mountains an estuary, possibly Eocene Tertiary, deposit. Sandstone and coal formations of apparently Cretaceous age have been observed, considerably developed in that range.

The extensive distribution of coal, partly of very superior quality, from the eastern part of the Rocky Mountains to the Salt Lake country, has been more fully demonstrated, and is of paramount practical importance, bearing upon the question of the best location of a railroad to the Pacific coast.

The physical geography and geological structure of Central and Western Utah, of the so-called Great Basin, has been investigated, and the prevalance of igneous rocks there has been shown, part of which are of great age, while most of them appear to be of comparatively recent origin. In its eastern portion Paleozoic formations have besides been found in most of the mountain ranges; the Upper Carboniferous strata, which had before been recognized at a few points, have been traced as far as 200 miles west of Salt Lake; and decidedly Lower Carboniferous and Devonian strata have been recognized there for the first time in the far-west, the latter, 1,200 miles, in a straight line, from the nearest point where they have before been found *in situ*, as far as is known, in the territory of the United States. The existence of the Silurian formation in the same district has been rendered probable. In the western part of the Basin only a few highly-altered stratified rocks were noticed, together with the eruptive masses.

I have divided the whole distance in five sections, according to their distinct geological and physical characters and configuration. They are:

Section I. The district of Eastern Kansas and Southeastern Nebraska, extending westward from the Missouri River, as far as the older formations reach, including the Cretaceous.

Section II. The plains, comprising the country from the western limits of section I to the foot of the Rocky Mountains.

Section III. The district of the Rocky Mountains, including the area between Fort Laramie and the South Pass, or, in other words, from the eastern foot of the Rocky Mountains to the divide between the waters of the Atlantic and Pacific Oceans.

Section IV. The Green River Basin, extending thence to the axis of the Wahsatch Mountains, to the eastern rim of the Great Basin.

Section. V. The district of Central and Western Utah, the so-called Great Basin, between the Wahsatch Mountains and the Sierra Nevada.

In each of these sections I have given a synopsis of the surface configuration and general character of the district, then a description of the geological formations therein, and finally, some condensed remarks upon the economical geology. Only in section V, I have changed this order somewhat, on account of the greater variety of questions which had to be discussed there.

As the organic remains of the collection have been examined by my friend, Mr Meek, who has, in a separate report, given descriptions of them, and stated the conclusions at which he has arrived by their investigation, I have generally avoided entering into paleontological discussions. By the shortness of the time allowed for the completion of this report, I have been prevented from making some chemical analyses, especially of coal and minerals, which would have given additional practical and scientific interest to the report; but by tests before the blow-pipe I have determined the qualitative composition of some salts and minerals, mostly during our confinement in the winter-quarters at Camp Floyd, which will be found in their respective places. The collections, upon which our main results are based, have been deposited at the Smithsonian Institution, in the museum of which they have been arranged for exhibition, while some duplicates have been sent to the Military Academy at West Point.

A geological map and profile are in the course of construction, which will illustrate

APPENDIX I.

REPORT ON THE GEOLOGY OF THE COUNTRY BETWEEN FORT LEAVENWORTH, KANSAS, AND THE SIERRA NEVADA, NEAR CARSON VALLEY.

[BY HENRY ENGELMANN, GEOLOGIST OF THE EXPEDITION.]

INTRODUCTION.

WASHINGTON, D. C., *July* 19, 1860.

SIR: I herewith submit to you my report on the geology of the country traversed by the expedition under your command in 1858 and 1859, from Fort Leavenworth, Kansas, to the Sierra Nevada, near Carson Valley. Only little has been known, heretofore, of the geology of this whole country, except of its eastern portion, and even there important questions remain unsettled, while the western portion has been altogether a *terra incognita.* By your expedition, therefore, important additions have been made to our knowledge of the geological structure of the central portions of the continent.

Some additional observations have been made in regard to the Upper Carboniferous and more recent formations of Northeastern Kansas. In the remarkable bluff formations of the North Fork of Platte River, below Fort Laramie, mammalian and chelonian remains have been discovered, which indicate their analogy with the interesting deposits of the Bad Lands of White River, famous for the abundance of their terrestrial pre-adamitic fauna; and the general character and succession of the Tertiary strata have been investigated, from the most recent to the oldest, along Platte River, and farther on across the South Pass to the Wahsatch Mountains. The existence of Jurassic strata in the territory of the United States, which had been very problematical till within a short time, when they were first recognized in the Black Hills, by Mr. Meek and Dr. Hayden, on Lieutenant Warren's expedition, has been fully established, and they have been recognized at various points in the Rocky Mountains near North Platte River, and on the eastern slope of the Wahsatch range. The Triassic and Cretaceous Epochs have also been found represented. In the Green River Valley a Tertiary fresh-water formation has been discovered, and in the Wahsatch Mountains an estuary, possibly Eocene Tertiary, deposit. Sandstone and coal formations of apparently Cretaceous age have been observed, considerably developed in that range.

The extensive distribution of coal, partly of very superior quality, from the eastern part of the Rocky Mountains to the Salt Lake country, has been more fully demonstrated, and is of paramount practical importance, bearing upon the question of the best location of a railroad to the Pacific coast.

stratified rocks which have been more or less altered or metamorphosed. In some localities they still exhibit perfectly preserved fossils, in others merely faint traces of organic remains, and in still others their lithological characters show a perfect transition into those of truly metamorphic rocks. Even those which are less altered cannot be sufficiently distinguished from each other, by their lithological characters alone. I therefore have introduced one color for all the rocks which are evidently of Paleozoic age, but which cannot be, with certainty, assigned to any one of the different Paleozoic formations. If, in a range, fossils have been found characteristic of a certain one of these older formations, I have colored the whole range accordingly. In many instances I was doubtful whether I should color rocks as Paleozoic or metamorphic, the transition being so gradual. From the Wahsatch Mountains westward I have marked several deposits with the color adopted for the Post-Pliocene formations, applying the term Post-Pliocene in its widest meaning, that it designates all deposits formed from the close of the Pliocene period to the present day. In that particular district I had thus marked the more solid or regularly stratified deposits, which have been formed posterior to the Tertiary formation, but which I wanted to distinguish from the loose alluvial deposits which have, on the profile, received a distinct color.

I cannot conclude these remarks without thankfully acknowledging the active interest with which Brig. Gen. A. S. Johnston, commanding Department of Utah, did all in his power to further these surveys. For some valuable specimens in the collection, I am also under obligations to Colonel Crosman of the Quartermaster's Department, and to the Assistant Surgeons Dr. K. Ryland and Dr. Charles Brewer, the latter of whom communicated some interesting information about the country south of Utah Lake. Last, but not least, I express my gratitude to my commander for his constant desire to facilitate the acquirement of all possible information, and to promote the interests of the survey in general, as well as for the numerous acts of personal kindness by which I have been favored.

I am, sir, most respectfully, your obedient servant,

HENRY ENGELMANN,
Geologist and Mining Engineer.

Capt. J. H. SIMPSON,
Topographical Engineers, U. S. A., in charge of Explorations.

SECTION I.

NORTHEASTERN KANSAS AND SOUTHEASTERN NEBRASKA.

GENERAL CONFIGURATION AND LIMITS—GEOLOGICAL FORMATIONS—CARBONIFEROUS AND PERMIAN FORMATIONS—CRETACEOUS AND OLDER FORMATIONS—ECONOMICAL GEOLOGY—SURFACE DEPOSITS—WATER—SOIL—TIMBER—BUILDING MATERIAL—COAL—MINERALS.

This district comprises the country along the most eastern portion of our route, extending westward, from the Missouri River near Leavenworth, as far as the older formations, including the Cretaceous, continue near the surface, and exercise a marked influence upon the configuration and general character of the country. As the upper and most western division of these rocks is horizontally stratified, and composed of mostly soft and readily decomposing strata, the evidences of its presence are easily obliterated by the increasing thickness of the more recent Tertiary and Post-Tertiary deposits, and, therefore, the limits of this section are not very distinctly marked. On our route, which is the main route from Leavenworth to Fort Kearney, on the Platte River, and mostly keeps the divide between the Missouri and Kansas Rivers, we cross these limits on the Little Blue, while, farther south, along the principal streams, they stretch much farther westward, in consequence of the deeper erosion of the valleys, and the trend and dip of the strata.

The general character of the country is that of beautifully rolling prairies, such as we find them in Northern Missouri, in Iowa, &c., with seams of timber along the water-courses. It is more broken only in the vicinity of the principal streams, especially the Missouri and Kansas Rivers, and as far as the oldest formations extend, which contain numerous hard strata, forming prominent bluffs and rocky precipices. But at a greater distance from the main arteries of drainage, and where the substrata are softer, the valleys become open and flat, and the country more and more assumes the character of the next section, the plains.

The rocks of this district belong to the Upper Carboniferous and the Cretaceous formations, at some points with a considerable intermediate series of, possibly, Permian, and, perhaps, also of Jurassic and Triassic rocks. The latter seem to be wanting in the northern part of the section, and only to come in gradually toward the south, thus indicating a repetition of the rule of the gradual increase of thickness of the strata, and of the intercalation of new formations toward the south, which has been observed by Prof. I. Hall, in regard to the Lower Carboniferous formations on the Mississippi River. (See Report on the Geology of Iowa, vol. i.) It does not appear to be the consequence of powerful denudations, but rather of a gradual change of level of the surface of the land during the extended period to which these various strata owe their origin. They are, therefore, not exactly conformable, although they have nowhere been observed to be considerably tilted and disturbed.

The geology of this district has lately been investigated by Mr. F. Hawn, in connection with Prof. G. C. Swallow and Dr. B. F. Shumard, and by Mr. F. B. Meek and Dr. F. V. Hayden. To the labors of these gentlemen we are indebted for many highly interesting additions to our knowledge of its geology. I will only mention the discovery of a formation of Permian affinity before unknown on this continent. It was expected that our explorations might throw additional light on some points which cannot yet be considered as fully established, and in regard to which the different investigators have arrived at varying conclusions, but unluckily our line of travel has passed too far north, where only few of the intermediate strata are developed, and where the outcrops are much scattered and covered up by detritus and Post-Tertiary deposits. I can, therefore, not attempt generalizations, and will confine myself to give an account of the observations which were made while, traveling westward, we came successively from the older to the more recent strata.

THE CARBONIFEROUS AND PERMIAN FORMATIONS.

We only find the upper strata of the Carboniferous system, forming the continuation of the Upper Carboniferous series, as it is developed along the Missouri River, and has been fully described by Professor Swallow, in the report upon the geological survey of the State of Missouri. At Leavenworth, nearly the whole third or upper series of the Coal-Measures of the Missouri report is exposed; the stratum No. 1 crowning the hill back of the fort, while at the lower end of Leavenworth City the lowest beds, Nos. 20 to 25 of the series, crop out, and only Nos. 26 and 27 are under the water-level. In the Missouri report the following section is given:

1. 10 feet hard, bluish-gray, ferruginous, subcrystalline, siliceous limestone, interstratified with brown clay. At Fort Leavenworth it is a compact, subcrystalline, grayish and light-buff colored limestone, wholly made up of fossils, numerous *Brachiopoda*, *Fusulina cylindrica*, joints of *Crinoidea*, &c.

2 and 3. 6 feet shales.

4. 3 feet coarse, grayish-white, crystalline limestone.

5. 15 feet bituminous shale.

6. 20 feet blue, buff, and gray siliceous, cherty limestone, interstratified with some shale. (It forms a terrace at the hill back of the fort).

7. 12 feet shale.

8. 7 feet red, yellowish, and gray friable sandstones.

9. 4 feet dark, argillaceous limestone.

10 to 19. 139 feet argillaceous shales, alternating with sandstones and limestones.

20. 8 feet argillaceous, shaly limestone.

21. 3 feet thin-bedded, ripple-marked sandstone.

22. 4 feet bituminous blue shale.

23. 20 feet hard, fine-grained, bluish-gray and buff ferruginous limestone.

24. 5 feet bituminous shale.

25. 2 feet hard, compact, dark-blue limestone.

These rocks continue up the Missouri River until they gradually dip under the water-level, with only a few feet, or none at all, of higher Carboniferous strata intervening between them and the succeeding and overlying ferruginous sandstone of Cretaceous age. Dr. Hayden saw the last of them, on the Missouri, some 50 miles above the mouth of Platte River. At Florence, about 7 miles above Omaha City, they form the bed of the river. On the Platte, they dip under ground near the mouth of Elkhorn River. Farther south, however, a considerable thickness of strata is observed above this series, which, by their organic remains, are characterized as members of the same Upper Carboniferous formation. In their upper portions, gradually Permian types of fossils appear, thus forming a transition between the strata of the Carboniferous and Permian periods, apparently filling the break which exists between the two in the eastern hemisphere. I have myself observed these strata, which we may provisionally call Permo-Carboniferous, on the Republican River, extending as far as 32 miles above its mouth. (See Explorations of Lieut. F. T. Bryan, T. E., 1856. Report of Secretary of War, 1857). The highest strata of this series, in that locality, appear to be identical with No. 11 of Messrs. Meek and Hayden's Kansas section. (Proceedings of the Academy of Natural Sciences of Philadelphia, January, 1859). My collection then only contained Carboniferous types of fossils, which were determined by Dr. B. F. Shumard. Still farther south these upper formations seem to be considerably more developed.

Beyond Fort Leavenworth, on the road to Fort Kearney, the compact limestones of the upper members of the Missouri section form prominent belts of *débris* near the top of the hills, the sides of which, corresponding to a series of argillaceous shales, soft sandstones, and shaly limestones, are mostly covered with detritus. Farther on we frequently do not find the smallest outcrop for many miles.

The compact, siliceous gray and buff limestones were thus noticed near Salt Creek, and again at our first camp, some 8 miles from the fort. There they contain various *Productus*, *Spirifer*, *Chonetes;* numerous *Fusulina cylindrica;* fragments of *Crinoidea*, and various *Bryozoa*. Some miles farther on, near the head of a drain, the same Fusulina limestone is exposed, and below it some argillaceous shales, and a calcareous, micaceous sandstone, with impressions of long, narrow leaves, and a few particles of coal. Near Mount Pleasant, I again found such limestone, while on the branches of Independence Creek, only shales were noticed. Some limestones on the East Fork of Grasshopper Creek still present the same lithological character, but contain numerous *Fusulina cylindrica* of the ventricose variety, and may, perhaps, occupy a higher geological horizon than the Leavenworth rocks. On Clear Creek, 43 miles from the fort, they again appear to be exactly like No. 1.

At the next branch, 2 miles farther on, a similar stratum crops out, some 40 feet above the water, while lower down some layers of yellowish and gray argillaceous limestone are exposed, quite fetid from the large number of organic remains, among which I noticed several *Productus*, *Orthis*, *Allorisma*, *Myalina*, *Bellerophon*, stems of *Crinoidea*, &c., all decidedly Carboniferous forms.

Only on the top of the hill east of Walnut Creek, about 50 miles from the fort, I found the first rock which presents an appearance decidedly different from any I had seen farther east. It is a yellowish limestone, altogether composed of small bivalves of the genera *Pecten*, *Myalina*, *Pleurophorus* (?), &c. About 40 feet lower down, 10 feet of gray and yellowish friable, micaceous sandstone are exposed, above which I found fragments of compact gray limestone, with numerous remains of *Brachiopoda*. Similar limestones continue up Walnut Creek, north of the road.

Although the outcrops along our line of travel were too small and too far apart to base a decided opinion upon, I feel, nevertheless, inclined to consider the stratification of the Coal-Measures not as absolutely regular, with a uniform dip in one direction, but as exhibiting slight undulations, so that we meet with repetitions of the same strata at points where, if the dip was uniform, they would occupy a considerable depth under ground.

I was informed that 6 miles south from Oak Point, on Muddy Creek, a small seam of a good bituminous coal has been found. On the Big Nemaha, at Seneca, 82 miles from Leavenworth, sandstone is exposed in the banks of the creek. On a branch, 2 miles southeast from there, I noticed a seam of good coal, 8 to 10 inches thick. The far-scattered outcrops seem to indicate the following section:

20 feet limestones, compact, siliceous, gray, yellow, or brown, with numerous fossils, joints of *Crinoidea*, *Orthis*, *Chonetes*, *Axinus*, *Posidonia* (?), and *Fusulina cylindrica*, var. *ventricosa*.
20 feet argillaceous shale.
$\frac{1}{3}$ foot calcareous slate, with pyrites and columns of *Crinoidea*.
$\frac{2}{3}$ foot coal.
20 feet or more sandstone.
——— shales.

Limestone similar to the above was also observed at Richmont, $2\frac{1}{2}$ miles lower down on the Nemaha, and still farther down, I am informed, coal crops out. If this is the same seam, the undulation of the dip must be considerable.

From the Nemaha to the Blue, outcrops are very scarce. In the drains off the road and on the slopes, occasionally slabs of limestone are found. On the Vermilion, some miles south of the road, a whitish magnesian limestone is quarried, remarkable on account of the large number of small cavities which it presents, all caused by the weathering out of *Fusulina cylindrica*. A stratum very much like it has been observed near the mouth of the Big Blue River, and No. 22 of Messrs. Meek and Hayden's section presents the same character.

About 14 miles east of the Big Blue, on the top of a hill near the upper road, we find 6 feet of a rock resembling closely the building-stone at Fort Riley, quarried there, near the top of the hills, at the junction of the Republican and Smoky Hill Forks. It is a light buff-colored magnesian limestone, finely granular on the fracture, and nearly made up of fossils, of which, however, only few are well preserved. It is easily dressed, and makes a superior building-stone.

White, green, and gray argillaceous shales were noticed in the drains farther on, and we have now fairly entered the limits of the Permo-Carboniferous formation. Near the Big Blue, in consequence of the deeper erosion of the valley, more rocks are exposed, mostly whitish, grayish, or yellowish, impure argillaceous limestones or marls, partly honey-combed, or containing numerous secretions of flint. The harder layers form terraces and belts of *débris* along the slopes. I noticed in these beds various *Productus*, *Pecten*, *Bellerophon*, columns of *Crinoidea*, numerous *Bryozoa*, and spines of *Archæocidaris;* also the flat tooth of a fish of the *Placodean* tribe. The following is a section compiled from measurements at several points, near the crossing of the Blue, at Marysville:

40 feet slope, apparently underlaid with argillaceous shales and marly limestones, of gray and yellowish colors, and with flint, resembling the following strata.
8 feet limestone, compact, light grayish, and yellowish, in places chalky, and full of fossils.
15 feet slope.
10 feet alternations of such limestones and flint in thin, irregular beds.
30 feet bluish-gray argillaceous shale and calcareous marl, or rotten, chalky calcareo-argillaceous slates.
15 feet alternations of white, gray, or yellowish earthy limestones, and flint in thin layers, with only few fossils.
10 feet slates.
Water-level of the Big Blue River.

Cottonwood Creek, 12.5 miles west of the Big Blue, is the last point on the road where strata of this same series crop out. I observed there 21 feet of a yellow limestone, with finely-grained, earthy fracture, containing numerous *Pecten* of different species, and *Bakevellia,* underlaid by 15 feet of greenish, gray, and purple argillaceous shales. Higher up on the hills more argillaceous shales were noticed.

On the ridge, between the Big Blue and Cottonwood Creek, nearer the latter, a change had been observed in the formation. There, in a drain, several strata were exposed of light-yellowish chalky or arenaceous magnesian limestone, partly vesicular, containing *Bellerophon* and a few other fossils, interstratified with variegated argillaceous shales. They are capped by light-colored arenaceous shales, with ferruginous concretions, changing into yellow or brown soft sandstones, with hard, dark-brown, highly ferruginous portions. While the lower strata form the continuation of the series, which is developed on the Big Blue and Cottonwood Creek, the upper strata belong to

THE CRETACEOUS (OR, PERHAPS, JURASSIC OR TRIASSIC) FORMATIONS.

Neither in these nor in similar strata farther west did I observe any fossils, and their exact position can, therefore, not be determined. To judge from their lithological character alone, I should consider them as beds of transition to the ferruginous sandstones of the Cretaceous formation, the No. 1 of Messrs. Meek and Hayden's Kansas section, which I found farther west; but otherwise they resemble much Nos. 2 and 3 of that section, which have been considered by them as probably Triassic or Jurassic, which may, however, turn out to be likewise Lower Cretaceous, corresponding to the Marly Clay group of Dr. B. F. Shumard, which underlies the sandstone No. I in Texas. (Transactions of the Academy of Science of Saint Louis, vol. I, No. 4, 1860). I did not notice any beds of gypsum or lignite, which have been found in similar formations farther south; but it must be borne in mind that, as I have stated above, these strata thin out altogether toward the north, and near our route are already much less developed than farther south, where the other gentlemen have examined them; besides, that such formations are generally much subject to local changes.

Between Cottonwood and Rock Creeks small outcrops of argillaceous and arenaceous shales were observed, and only nearer to Rock Creek, 20 feet of light-brown and purely quartzose sandstone. On Rock Creek the followiug section was obtained:

On top of the hill, about 150 feet above the creek, there is a layer of dark-brown, very hard ferruginous sandstone, partly even-grained and partly of a coarse, uneven grain. Inside most of the pieces are much lighter colored and less cemented, even friable. Then follow—

80 feet of slope, with occasional outcrops of shale and sandstone, some of which is very compact and finely grained.

40 feet of white, purely quartzose sandstone, with an even and rather fine grain, and easily crumbling. It generally does not show any distinct stratification.

The lowest 30 feet are gray and white argillaceous shales, not all well exposed.

There, also, I did not find any organic remains, except indistinct impressions of wood, in the ferruginous sandstone, on top of the hill. I have, however, little doubt that, if not the whole section, then, at least, this upper bed, is Lower Cretaceous, the No. I of the Nebraska section; and the whole may correspond to the Arenaceous group and Marly Clay group of Dr. Shumard. West of Rock Creek the exposures are scarce, the rocks being too friable, and easily disintegrating. Only on the hills, toward Little Sandy Creek, I noticed strata similar to those on Rock Creek—white quartzose sandstone, overlaid by gray and white argillaceous shales, with arenaceous and ferruginous portions and seams—and higher up large flags of dark-brown ferruginous sandstone. A little farther on, the hills which overlook Little Sandy Creek are capped by white limestone, nearly made up of *Inoceramus* (*Inoceramus pseudomytiloides* and *I. aviculoides*), and in which also a *Baculites* was found. They correspond to No. III of the Nebraska Cretaceous section of Messrs. Meek and Hayden, which is so largely developed on the Upper Missouri. Underneath this rock follows a series of argillaceous shales about 40 feet thick, which seems to be an equivalent of No. II of the Nebraska section; and on the creek the ferruginous sandstone is exposed, apparently the No. I of that section.*

The last small outcrops of the Cretaceous limestones and marls were observed on Big Sandy Creek, and near there, on Little Blue River, but they evidently continue near the surface a considerable distance farther up that river, as we may judge from the growth of timber in the creek bottom. While with Lieutenant Bryan, I found these limestones and marls considerably farther west, near the ninety-eighth degree of longitude, only a few miles south of Little Blue River, and on the Republican, from 74 miles above Fort Riley, near longitude 97° 25′, and latitude 39° 38′—where I observed a section quite similar to that on the Little Sandy—extending about 100 miles, to longitude 98° 45′ and latitude 40° 05′. On Solomon's Fork they are found still farther westward.

---

* Although I have no paleontological evidence that this sandstone is No. I, still I can entertain no doubt in that respect. It underlies the other Cretaceous strata, and is lithologically the same as the rock which I have found largely developed on the Republican River, where, about 75 miles above Fort Riley, it holds the same relation to the *Inoceramus* beds, the same which Mr. Meek, Dr. Hayden, Dr. Newberry, Mr. Hawn, Mr. Pratten, and others have frequently seen in the same position, as well in Kansas as in Nebraska, and in which, at many of these localities, numerous impressions of dycotyledonous leaves have been discovered.

ECONOMICAL GEOLOGY.

I have stated above that the country along our line of travel is a succession of rolling prairies. The surface-deposits above the regularly stratified rocks of the older formations are generally very heavy, and consist of drift-sand, clay, gravel, and soil; at numerous points bowlders are scattered over the surface, partly of granite, but mostly of a very compact, light-reddish quartzose rock.

Water is mostly obtained at a depth of from 40 to 70 feet, at least in the eastern portion of the district. The following sections of wells were obtained:

1. On the upland, 17 miles from Leavenworth:
   - 2 feet of dark clayey soil, highly productive.
   - 12 feet sand and clay, mixed.
   - 5÷6 feet joint-clay, a shaly clay with numerous fissures, which allow the slow percolation of water.
   - 32 feet yellow and brown drift-sand, mostly of fine grain, with little clay.
   - Stiff clay or shale, impermeable to water, on reaching which water was obtained; total depth, 52 feet.
2. On the upland, 33 miles from Leavenworth, near Lancaster:
   - 3 to 4 feet soil, argillaceous, and slightly arenaceous, highly productive.
   - 36 feet drift-sand of yellowish color, free of clay.
   - Below this water was reached, in a fine sand, before having penetrated the substratum of clay; total depth, 40 feet.
3. Half a mile from the latter locality, in the same ridge:
   - 6 feet soil.
   - 12 feet drift-sand.
   - 25 feet joint-clay.
   - 3 feet gravel, in which water was reached; total depth, 46 feet.
4. On the ridge, 38 miles from Leavenworth:
   - 4 feet soil, dark areno-argillaceous, highly productive.
   - 20 feet yellowish tough clay.
   - 30 feet bluish joint-clay.
   - 6 feet white and yellow quartz sand, in which a large supply of water was obtained; total depth, 66 feet.
5. Near Oak Point, on the upland, about 56 miles from Leavenworth:
   - 4 feet soil like the above.
   - 20 feet yellowish joint-clay.
   - 10 feet sand, mixed with some clay.
   - 6 feet gravel, sand, and clay, which seem to overlie the limestone, and in which water was obtained; total depth, 40 feet.

In the western portion, where the sandstones and sandy shales are more developed, it may be more difficult to obtain water; still there are sufficient beds of clay. But the creeks in that portion become dry in summer, because the drainage by these coarse loose sandstones is too rapid, and they retain only some stagnant water in pools.

The Coal-Measures and Permian rocks contain all the ingredients necessary to produce excellent soils, and their stiff clays have been much improved by a mixture with the finely arenaceous deposits which have been swept over the surface from the west. From the above sections it will be seen that the soil is mostly deep, and naturally drained by the substrata. Where, however, the drift-sand reaches too near the surface, the soil becomes too dry, and is, besides, liable to wear out, because the mineral portion of the fertilizing ingredients, once exhausted by a succession of crops, cannot be reproduced from the sand. The marls of the Cretaceous formations, Nos. II and III, can also make highly productive soils; but where the sandstone formations prevail, they are apt to cause aridity, unless the soil happens to be well mixed with the clays of other formations, a fact of which many of the farmers in the western districts had already become aware before the excessive drought of the present season.

The farther we progress westward the more the surface-deposits increase, especially on the uplands, and the country assumes the character peculiar to the following section. The productiveness becomes impaired by the prevalence of arenaceous material and the deficiency of atmospheric precipitation.

The timber is confined to the water-courses, but forests will probably soon spring up at numerous points, as they have done in other parts of the Western States since they have been settled.

Building-material, rock, and good clay for brick, can generally be obtained within convenient distances, and among the clays of the Carboniferous formation, in the eastern part of the district, good fire-clays may be discovered.

Small seams of stone-coal have been found in the Upper Coal-Measures, which can, however, be worked only to a limited extent by "stripping," and it is not likely that extensive thicker beds will be discovered. At some points the lignites which have been observed in connection with the ferruginous sandstones may be of workable thickness. The middle and lower series of the Coal-Measures, as developed on the Missouri River, in the State of Missouri, contain, however, several strata of excellent bituminous coal, which we have little reason to doubt continue far westward at a depth still accessible by well-conducted mining operations on a large scale. As long as a limited demand does not warrant extensive and costly enterprises, the want must be supplied from outside, and farmers would do well to cultivate timber, as they have to do in other prairie countries.

No valuable minerals of any kind are likely to be found in this district, the geological formations not being favorable to their development. Only in Southeastern Kansas, beyond the limits of the district under consideration, outliers of the lead-bearing rocks of Southwestern Missouri might occur.

SECTION II.

THE PLAINS.

GENERAL REMARKS—FROM LITTLE BLUE RIVER TO THE FORKS OF PLATTE RIVER—THENCE TO ABOVE ASH HOLLOW; PROBABLY A PLIOCENE TERTIARY FORMATION—LITHOLOGICAL AND CHEMICAL CHARACTER OF THE ROCKS—FOSSILS—SAME FORMATION AT OTHER POINTS—FROM ASH HOLLOW TO BEYOND SCOTT'S BLUFFS, PROBABLY OF MIOCENE AGE—GENERAL CHARACTER OF THE FORMATION—SUCCESSIVE SECTIONS ABOVE ASH HOLLOW; COURT-HOUSE ROCK, CHIMNEY ROCK, SCOTT'S BLUFFS—FOSSIL TURTLES AND MAMMALS—THENCE TO FORT LARAMIE—TERTIARY STRATA OF VARIOUS AGE—ECONOMICAL GEOLOGY—SOIL—FUEL—BUILDING-MATERIAL.

This section comprises the whole area from the western limits of Section I, on our route near the Little Blue River in Southeastern Nebraska, to the eastern foot of the Rocky Mountains, near Fort Laramie. The surface configuration and general aspect of this district have been described so frequently, that I can confine myself to point out briefly the geological features. It is exclusively occupied by recent formations of Tertiary and Post-Tertiary age, the bulk of which, if not all, are fresh-water sediments. They have not been subject to violent local disturbances, but have been raised, as a whole, by the great continental upheaval, which must have taken place during or at the close of the Tertiary period, and the principal changes which they have undergone are merely effected by erosion. It is difficult to draw distinct limits between the various subdivisions, because the lithological character of fresh-water deposits is variable within short distances; and thus the continuation of the same beds may, at a distant point, appear like an altogether different formation.

Along our line of travel, from east to west, up Platte River, we come successively from the most recent to older strata.

FROM LITTLE BLUE RIVER TO THE FORKS OF PLATTE RIVER.

From the Little Blue to the forks of Platte River we find no rocky strata. The surface is covered with heavy arenaceous deposits, part of which are Post-Tertiary, apparently of the age of the "Bluff" formation, while other portions are, perhaps, older, Pliocene-Tertiary. Along Little Blue River, and in the upland toward Platte River, we find a great thickness of "Bluff" or "Loess" formation, which, also, covers the older rocks, over extensive areas much further to the east. It is there a buff-colored, or light-brownish, finely-grained, earthy argillo-arenaceous sediment, uniform throughout the whole thickness, and contains small *Gasteropoda*, *Helix*, *Lymnea*, &c.

On Platte River, near Fort Kearney, the hills are more sandy and undulating, and no exposures were noticed; but from above the fort to the forks of Platte River deposits are most characteristically developed, which may either form the continuation of the Bluff formation, or may be of Pliocene-Tertiary age. They consist of an arenaceous, light-brownish, or buff-colored material, of mostly a very fine grain, and nearly free of calcareous and argillaceous portions. This sand contains, apparently, the same little shells as the Loess, and exhibits, at some points, indistinct marks of stratification, a slight change in the fineness of the material, or darker lines which indicate a growth of plants during intervals of its formation. Where best developed, this sand rises in high perpendicular walls, and is worn into a maze of intricate ravines, forming a peculiar and frequently highly picturesque scenery. It attains a considerable thickness; single exposures are 200 and more feet high. I had observed the same formation on the Republican River, from the mouth of Frenchman's Fork upward, and along Arickaree Fork to Rock Creek. Dr. Hayden has given a section of the Tertiary strata of White and Niobrara Rivers, in a preliminary report on Lieutenant Warren's expedition in Nebraska and Dakota (Annual Report of Captain Humphreys, Office of Explorations and Surveys, December, 1858, p. 119); but there the strata seem to be developed somewhat differently. Those deposits, which I have designated as Loess, correspond to the Post-Pliocene deposits of that section, the description of which, however, scarcely corresponds to the strata above Fort Kearney on the Platte. The difference may be due to local influences, and the latter strata, perhaps, include the uppermost portion of Dr. Hayden's Pliocene bed, F.

FROM THE FORKS OF PLATTE RIVER TO ABOVE ASH HOLLOW, ON THE NORTH PLATTE.

Near the junction of the North and South Forks of Platte River, the first rocky strata were observed. They continue along the South Fork, cropping out at intervals at one or the other side of the river, and were found most developed in Ash Hollow, where they attain a thickness of over 250 feet. This series is composed of an alternation of loose, finely sandy, and of harder rocky strata, the latter consisting of fine or coarse drift-sand, generally cemented by carbonate of lime, forming more or less calcareous sandstones, and gritty, very impure limestones. Partly they are coarse sandy, partly finely earthy or even on the fracture, and a few are subcrystalline. Their age is, probably, the Pliocene-Tertiary; but I have no paleontological proof of it. They have evidently been deposited before the last great continental upheaval; while they present such an unfinished and recent appearance, that I am inclined to consider them as among the latest formations of the Tertiary period. Moreover, they appear to answer the description given by Dr. Hayden in his above-named section, of the Pliocene strata, F 3. I can, however, not recognize other portions of his No. F in the formations which I have observed on that portion of Platte River.

There is no strongly-marked line between these deposits and the next ones, which are probably Miocene.

The first rock, at the forks of Platte River, is composed of drift-sand mixed with carbonate of lime, and partly porous and not much indurated, partly compact. It is overlaid by the loosely arenaceous deposits described before. The porous kind was found to contain—

Carbonate of lime	45 per cent.
Sand, silica, and some alumina	55 per cent.

In Ash Hollow these strata vary much in appearance; some are white, nearly subcrystalline, and somewhat chalky, irregularly intermixed with loose, sandy portions; in the purer pieces the sand is fine, and can only be recognized by dissolving the rock in acid. Others are buff-colored, of a fine grit, coarse grit, compact, or loosely cemented; a few are even conglomeratic.

In the most calcareous of such rocks, from various localities, I found, by analysis

(Lieutenant Bryan's explorations, 1856, Rep. Sec. of War, 1857), 40 to 65 per cent. of carbonate of lime, while the average contain scarcely a few per cent., and only some select pieces can really be considered as limestones. The softer strata are either purely sandy, or they contain, besides, some lime, generally in chemical connection with silica, and not uniformly mixed through the whole mass, but forming irregular concretions and veins, and root-like bodies. Such concretions I found to be scarcely acted upon by hot concentrated hydrochloric acid, and to consist of—

Silica	79.0 per cent.
Alumina, with traces of peroxide of iron	10.0 per cent.
Water, apparently in chemical combination	4.5 per cent.
Magnesia	1.5 per cent.
Carbonate of lime, mostly in the mineral, as calcia	6.0 per cent.

Many of them, however, contain much more carbonate of lime, and are rather a mixture of carbonate of lime with sand and silicate of calcia.

At a few points only, the lime throughout the stratum has entered into chemical combination with the sand, as in these concretions. Such a specimen, resembling chalk, from the north bank of the South Platte, gave—

Silica	45.5 per cent.
Alumina	15.5 per cent.
Water, partly hygroscopic	14.5 per cent.
Carbonate of lime	13.5 per cent.
Calcia	11.0 per cent.

The stratification, in general, does not differ much from the horizontal; there seems to be a very slight dip to the east. In the details, however, it is irregular; the harder and softer, or coarser and finer, portions of the strata vary considerably in their relative thickness. What appear to be rocky strata are frequently no separate layers, but merely concretionary seams. Wherever large masses of the bluffs have become detached and fallen down, and thus new faces have been formed, they appear quite uniform, without a distinct stratification. After some time, however, the softer portions wear out under the atmospheric influences, while the harder ones, distributed in more or less horizontal lines, are left protruding, and thus indicate the stratification; but as the harder and softer portions are not regularly distributed in the mass, this false stratification is deceptive, and apt to lead to great errors in the estimation of the thickness and extent of the strata.

In these rocks, near the forks of Platte River, I found numerous fossilified seeds of the size of a small cherry-stone, apparently related to the living genus *Celtis*, which have improperly been called *Lithospermum*, which name belongs to a very different living genus of plants. The same were noticed, together with a *Helix*, a few miles above the mouth of Ash Hollow. On the northern bank of the South Platte, 14 miles below the crossing, a silicified fragment of a large bone was obtained; but I am not able to decide whether it originated from these strata or had been washed out from others of a lower geological horizon, higher up the river (see below). At some points these strata contain numerous concretions of sand, of a peculiar shape, part of which are so much like bones of large animals, that many people have been deceived by them.

The same strata were observed by me, in 1856, further south on Rock Creek, a branch of the Republican River, near longitude 102°, where I found similar seeds, and at some points northeast from there, on the upland, toward South Platte River. I then was inclined to consider them as Post-Tertiary. A similar formation, lower down on the Republican River, below the mouth of Frenchman's Fork, and thence to near longitude 97° 20′, may be of the same age, or perhaps a little older. The strata on Lodge Pole Creek, near the Pine Bluffs, present a similar character, and are probably of the same age, or only little older. They are, partly at least, more regularly stratified, and some of them are conglomeratic, or coarse-grit stones; but such differences may be occasioned by the geographical distance of the two points. There I also found the seeds of *Celtis*. The more conglomeratic portion may, however, correspond to No. E of Dr. Hayden's section.

FROM ASH HOLLOW TO BEYOND SCOTT'S BLUFFS.

From Ash Hollow westward, the strata gradually assume a different appearance, and instead of being calcareo-arenaceous they become more purely arenaceous, and finally argillo-arenaceous. The main body of the formation is made up of the very finest, light-brown, or buff-colored sand, with a slight admixture only of clay, just enough to make it hold together, and stand in vertical exposures. Only the lower strata are a little more clayey. But there are interstratifications of coarser sand and sandstones, in which the cement, however, is not carbonate of lime, and which mostly form no regular continuous beds. These strata present numerous precipices and high cliffs, with vertical bare walls and turreted appearance, some of which have attracted the attention of every traveler, and are known as prominent landmarks. On account of the variability of their character it is more difficult to trace their superposition than it would appear on a superficial examination; and the dip does not seem to be quite uniform throughout, but it is generally a few degrees to the east. All my observations combined, leave, however, no doubt that this formation is older than the Ash Hollow series; and the remains of animals in the lowest portion of these strata, near Scott's Bluffs, seem to indicate that it is of the age of the White River formation, viz, Miocene-Tertiary. The total thickness of this series is probably not much less than 1,000 feet, or even more.

At the mouth of Ash Hollow the lowest 30 feet are occupied by a stratum of buff-colored, finely arenaceous material, with no visible cement, but rather compact, capped by the calcareous sandstones. Up the river the arenaceous bed, or beds, rise more and more, and exhibit occasionally harder portions of the same color, like irregular rocky interstratifications, although these are not very prominent. Within 14 miles they attain an altitude of nearly 200 feet, indicating a rise of about 12 feet per mile more than the fall of the river. In a prominent bluff there the stratification is indicated by steps or terraces in the bare escarpment, on which the sand is mostly a little coarser and better cemented, but more in concretions and irregular seams than in distinct layers, and without changing much the uniform appearance of the face. The upper 10 feet are compact sandstone, and the bluff is capped by some strata of the calcareous drift-stone. Near by, a few ledges of a calcareous sandstone, with softer interstratifications, were also noticed near the water-level.

Farther on more rocky interstratifications were observed in the bluffs. If the dip continues unchanged, as appearances seem there to indicate, these strata underlie the last-mentioned exposure; still I hesitate to make a positive assertion. The difference in the appearance might be owing to a slight local change in the development of these strata, because, wherever the arenaceous material has not been the very finest, such seams and concretionary masses of sandstones have been formed. The prevailing color of the rock continues to be the light brown and buff.

The Court-house Rock, about 55 miles from the mouth of Ash Hollow, and 6 miles south of the river, on Lawrence Fork, presents the following section:

1. 10 feet, middle fine-grained, compact sandstone forming its top.
2. 40 feet arenaceous strata, with irregular concretionary ledges of harder sand-rock, coarser than the main body of the strata, and forming steps in the escarpment.
3. 10 feet, a thicker stratum of such sandstone.
4. 50 feet, finely arenaceous, and some argillo-arenaceous material, forming vertical escarpments, but rather soft and not rocky.
5. 10 feet more solid, and a little coarser sandstone.
6. 50 feet fine, loose material, like No. 4, with the two white chalky strata, in which there is a good deal of calcareous substance, and a stratum of coarser loose sand.
7. 105 feet finely arenaceous strata, with interstratifications of more argillo-arenaceous shales.
8. 30 feet buff-colored argillo-arenaceous shales, containing far more sand than clay.

Three hundred and five feet is the total altitude above Lawrence Fork, which would probably correspond to 450 feet above Platte River.

The Chimney Rock is about 11 miles, in a straight line, distant from the Court-house Rock, in west-northwesterly direction. About 2 miles from the river it rises above the sandy hills, presenting a huge column on a conic base. It is remarkable how this slender spire of rather soft rocks could have been preserved in its isolated position, while the same formations all around were demolished. Its upper part is cleft asunder, and threatens to fall down. That it has been higher, and the uppermost portion has been destroyed, within the memory of now living men, may be no idle story. The masses of rock which cover the base correspond to those of the highest strata in the vicinity, and can only have come there by falling from the chimney. A short distance from it we find the bluffs with which it has unquestionably been connected in former times. The following section of the strata was obtained, partly at the Chimney Rock, partly, where I could not climb higher there, from the corresponding strata of these bluffs, which exceed it in height by 130 feet:

a. 130 *feet—the top of the bluff,* not altogether well exposed.

1. 130 feet loose, grayish, and buff-colored sandstone, of a middle fine grain, irregularly interspersed with concretionary masses of a harder sandstone, and with more regular, thicker seams of it, generally forming steps in the slope, 10 to 15 feet apart. The lowest 30 feet form one step, with only a ledge of such rock on top, besides the irregular masses which are dispersed through it.

b. 115 *feet—the chimney itself,* with a diameter of about 50 feet at the base, and only slightly tapering upward.

2. 5 feet, light brownish-gray, loose, middle fine-grained sandstone, with some harder seams, especially on top, where there is also a thin calcareous ledge, like 9.
3. 10 feet, similar loose, middle fine sandstone, free of harder seams and concretions, and of light brownish-gray color.
4. ⅔ foot, seam of hard, finely-grained sandstone, of irregular thickness.
5. 12 feet loose sandstone, like 3.
6. 30 feet, like 2, with irregular, harder seams and concretions, capped by such a harder ledge, varying in thickness from ½ to 1½ feet.
7. ⅓ foot bluish-gray, not very compact, sandstone.
8. 7 feet like 3.
9. ½ foot white seam, areno-calcareous, partly chalky, partly subcrystalline.
10. 12 feet, like 3.
11. ½ foot, white seam, like 9.
12. 15 feet, like 3.
13. 1 foot, like 3, but dark gray.
14. 19 feet, like 3, but light gray and laminated.
15. 2 feet, like 3, in places more or less whitish and slightly calcareous.

c. 223 *feet—the conic base and the pedestal.*

16. 45 feet; dark buff-colored, purely arenaceous shales, so largely developed in the sections given above, and forming also the pedestal.
17. 110 feet; the same, light buff-colored.
18. 8 feet; white, very light rock, chalky and irregularly interspersed with fine sand. It is a mixture of sand with silicate of lime, and quite similar to the rock from the South Platte, an analysis of which has been given on page 261.
19. 60 feet, like 17; the upper portion more argillaceous.

d. Below the base in a ravine.

20. 35 feet, like 7.
21. 5 feet middle fine, gray, loose sandstone.

The total altitude of the Chimney Rock from the base is, therefore, 338 feet; that of the whole section 506 feet; and the elevation of No. 21 above the river may be put down at 60 or 100 feet.

The white stratum, No. 18, may still be seen at the foot of the Perpendicular Bluff, some miles farther west. In Scott's Bluffs it is a few feet above the highest point of the road in the gap, but is there more grayish and arenaceous. Below it we again find the buff argillo-arenaceous strata, No. 19, but here rather more clayey; and the higher layers also correspond to those enumerated above. The height of the white stratum here is estimated at 200 feet above the river, about the same as at Chimney Rock; the stratification, therefore, appears to correspond to the fall of the river. The total altitude of Scott's Bluffs is about 525 feet, including nearly the whole of the preceding section, and some lower strata.

The arenaceous and areno-argillaceous shales continue down to the river, interstratified with a few irregular seams of calcareous or harder and coarser arenaceous material. In these strata highly-interesting organic remains have been discovered lately—fossil turtles and the bones of various mammals. Traveling in forced marches, we were unluckily prevented from collecting much. Some of the bones were submitted to the eminent osteologist, Prof. Joseph Leidy, of Philadelphia, who kindly volunteered in examining them. He recognizes them as belonging to *Deinistis felina*, a large carniverous animal related to the weasel, and to some ruminant pachyderm, perhaps *Oreodon*, which both, like the turtles, occur also in the Miocene formations of the bad lands of White River. The lithological character of these strata seems, likewise, to be similar, and indications are strong that both formations are of the same age, and have perhaps been deposited in the same basin.

In the banks of a ravine, in the lowest strata of the above section, the bones of a huge animal have been found. A Mr. W. W. Wright, of Minnesota, discovered them, and brought to Fort Laramie two leg bones, nearly complete, each over 30 inches long, and a femur. When we passed there on our return, Captain Simpson caused some excavations to be made at the same spot, and we obtained a large shoulder-blade, some vertebræ, ribs, fragments of the ivory of a large tusk, &c. Unfortunately the bones are in a friable condition, or else probably a large portion of the skeleton could have been secured. Although their state of preservation differs from that of the remains of the smaller animals, which are silicified, the former are apparently of the same age, or rather slightly older.

The fossiliferous strata are among the lowest of this series. The next outcrops which I observed on the river present a different character.

If we compare again the above-mentioned section of Dr. Hayden with the formation which we have just described, we find that, although they are not exactly alike, still they show a marked resemblance. The strata in the lower portion of Scott's Bluffs correspond to his turtle and Oreodon beds, B; the next higher one to his C, with the difference, that we find the calcareous matter more concentrated in a few beds; and D is represented by the upper portion of the Chimney Rock section. Dr. Hayden estimated the thickness of B, C, and D at 480 to 580 feet. On Platte River the thickness of this formation is much greater, but then we may have there his bed E, which is between 180 and 200 feet thick, replaced by more finely-grained deposits. If that is not the case, then F must be wanting on the Platte, while farther southwest, on Pole Creek, it is again considerably developed. Dr. Hayden's extensive collections have led to the conclusion that all these beds are probably of Miocene-Tertiary age, and the stratigraphical evidence, which alone I can adduce, does not conflict with this opinion.

FROM ABOVE SCOTT'S BLUFFS TO FORT LARAMIE.

Above Scott's Bluffs still lower strata gradually rise to the surface. They present a decidedly different appearance, but were only seen in scattered outcrops, mostly of no great extent. They are made up of a series of variegated, green, gray, buff, whitish, and reddish argillaceous and arenaceous shales, alternating with sandstones, and some few limestones; and their age must be the Lower Miocene or Upper Eocene. They are probably the same formation which has been observed on Platte River, some distance above Fort Laramie, and may correspond to the *Titanotherium* bed, No. A of Dr. Hayden's section, which he provisionally considers as Miocene. Future investigation can only furnish the elements from which the actual age of this formation can be determined.

The sandstones are partly similar to those in the upper part of the Chimney Rock section, compact or friable, partly more coarse-grained, in consequence of the vicinity of the mountains, which must have existed, although in different profile, at the time of their formation. The few intercalations of limestone do not preserve a uniform character. Some are highly compact and brittle, with an even or conchoidal fracture, and full of seams, and irregular secretions of agatized silex or opal; others are subcrystalline or granular; still others slaty. In an argillo-calcareous ledge in such limestones, 23 miles below Fort Laramie, I found some fossils, *Planorbis, Dentalium* (?), and impressions of long, narrow leaves, probably of some grass.

Nearer to Fort Laramie I noticed prominent outcrops of a coarse, conglomeratic, brown drift sandstone, portions of which contain pieces as big as a hen's egg, and even larger. It overlies light buff, finely-arenaceous shales, such as are so extensively developed farther down the river, and is capped by a light-gray, fine-grained sandstone. These are probably local deposits, and of more recent date than those mentioned last. Captain Stansbury noticed considerable exposures of the same rock up Laramie River.

At the junction of this river with the Platte, near Fort Laramie, the hills are made up of finely arenaceous strata, light-gray, and partly white, from a large percentage of calcareous matter. Some of these are much like the white stratum in Scott's Bluffs and Chimney Rock; others are coarser calcareous or siliceous sandstones, containing concretions or irregular ledges of more compact sand-rock, like the upper members of the Chimney Rock section, and they may perhaps be of the same age, viz., Miocene; but some miles above the fort, and wherever observed farther west, they left the impression upon my mind that they must belong among the most recent Tertiary deposits, and are, perhaps, of the age of the Ash Hollow series, to which they there bear considerable resemblance, and which is probably Pliocene, or that they are partly even more recent. I did not see them capped by any other beds, but they everywhere hold the highest position, either on top of the hills or filling depressions in the older rocks, and are only modified by the latest erosions.

At various points along the eastern foot of the mountains, south of the North Platte, lignites have been discovered, as I have been informed by several officers of the Army. Not having seen them myself, I cannot determine whether they form the continuation of the extensive lignite deposits higher up on Platte River, which underlie the gray, green, &c., argillaceous shales and the sandstones described above; or, if they have been formed in a different basin; nor whether their age is the Cretaceous or the Tertiary.

ECONOMICAL GEOLOGY.

The character of the surface deposits everywhere reflects that of the substrata. As the formations of this district are prevailingly arenaceous, so are also the soils. As far as the "Bluff" formation extends at the eastern end of the section, the soils mostly contain all elements of fertility, but are rather too light and dry; and as the quantity of atmospheric precipitation also decreases westward, the limits of the arable district are reached very soon. Still, large areas are covered with a good and dense

growth of various grasses, among which the short but highly nutritious buffalo-grass, *Buchloe dactyloides*, and a similar one, *Boutelona oligostachia*, are particularly worth mentioning. During the summer months they would afford fine grazing to innumerable herds, especially of sheep. Such is the case in many parts of the district, wherever the soil has a slight admixture of clay; but many hundreds of square miles are too sandy or gravelly to produce much of these nutritious grasses, and must be considered as utterly worthless. The country between Ash Hollow and Scott's Bluffs is of this nature, as are also large areas on the uplands at a distance from the river, along Pole Creek, &c.

The flat river-bottoms in the neighborhood of Fort Kearney are prevailingly sandy. Near the river the upper soil was found only 6 inches deep, light arenaceous and mixed with humus, and of fair quality; the next 4 inches consisted of such soil mixed with much sand, and the subsoil, from a depth of 10 inches down, was composed of nearly pure river-sand, with only little clay. Everywhere about there water can be struck at a depth of a few feet, and therefore the soil is kept moist, and coarse swamp grasses grow abundantly. Tillage will succeed there to some extent, and will be made to pay on account of the lively local demand of the passing traffic.

The most promising point for agriculture on that line is a limited space near the forks of Platte River, at Cottonwood Spring. At Fort Laramie the soil is dry, sandy, and poor, and but little can be grown, the more so because the season is very short, with late frosts and early snows. Small grain could probably be raised at various points in that neighborhood with the aid of irrigation. The same will apply to some valleys at the immediate foot of the mountains, off the main road.

The scarcity, and over-long stretches, utter absence of timber or fuel of any kind, except the dung of animals, have frequently been noticed. Lignite has been found in various localities south of the road, along the foot of the Rocky Mountains, but not near the road, and I have not had an opportunity to examine it; it is probably similar to that of the next section.

Building-material is very scarce in the eastern part of this district, but in the western part, at numerous points, rocks can be quarried, some of which will bear any weight, while others are fit only for light masonry. Part of the houses at Fort Laramie have been built of adobes, and such can be made wherever the strata are slightly argillaceous.

SECTION III.

THE DISTRICT OF THE ROCKY MOUNTAINS.

GENERAL CONFIGURATION AND GEOLOGICAL FORMATIONS—IGNEOUS ROCKS, GRANITES, GREENSTONES—PERIOD OF THEIR ERUPTION—METAMORPHIC SCHISTS—STRATIFIED ROCKS OF THE PALEOZOIC AGE—SILURIAN, DEVONIAN, CARBONIFEROUS, AND PERMIAN FORMATIONS—STRATA OF DOUBTFUL AGE—TRIASSIC AND JURASSIC FORMATIONS—JURASSIC STRATA IN THE BLACK HILLS AND ON PLATTE RIVER NEAR THE RED BUTTES—SECTION OF THE STRATA—THEIR RELATION TO THE CRETACEOUS FORMATION NEAR LA BONTÉ CREEK—SECTION OF THE TRIASSIC ROCKS—THEIR RELATION TO THE JURASSIC AND CARBONIFEROUS STRATA—EVIDENCE OF THEIR TRIASSIC AGE—CRETACEOUS FORMATION—LIGNITE FORMATION—ITS LITHOLOGICAL CHARACTER—ITS AGE—SAME FORMATION FARTHER SOUTH—TERTIARY FORMATIONS OF DIFFERENT AGE—ECONOMICAL GEOLOGY—AGRICULTURE—BUILDING-MATERIALS—COAL, IRON, SALTS.

This section comprises the country from the eastern foot of the Rocky Mountains to the divide between the waters of the Atlantic and Pacific Oceans, from Fort Laramie to the South Pass. The Rocky Mountains in this latitude do not form those compact mountain masses, rising abruptly to a great altitude from a narrow base, and presenting nearly insurmountable barriers, as they do farther south at the Parks; but they have divided into various branches, trending mostly in a western or northwestern direction, and thus they have decreased in altitude and flattened out. There are some considerable elevations, such as the system of the Laramie Peak and the Wind River Mountains, but most of the ranges, although generally presenting bare and rugged declivities, form only quite narrow spurs, which at numerous points fall off entirely, and at others lose their rugged character, and only appear as gentle upheavals of the stratified rocks, with broad, flattened crests. Between these ranges the country is comparatively level, and partly covered with nearly horizontal deposits, and even where it is rough and broken it can scarcely be called mountainous, and presents a surface configuration very different from what it is generally supposed to be in the region of the Rocky Mountains.

The mountains are partly covered with a thin growth of pine, but near the road most of them are entirely bare of timber, or nearly so, and frequently they exhibit rugged walls of granite or other rocks, with scarcely a particle of soil or detritus upon them. The flat portion of the country is an extensive sage-barren, but there is grass along the creeks, and more of it is scattered on the uplands between the sage. The latter grass is of a highly nutritious kind, which the animals like very much, even when it is dry.

Although the main emigrant-route to California and Oregon passes through this section of country, little has hitherto been known of its highly interesting geological features. Besides igneous rocks of different age and metamorphic strata, there are Silurian, and probably Devonian, Carboniferous, Cretaceous, and Tertiary formations; and we have, moreover, found decidedly Jurassic strata, which seem to be developed here over a considerable area. A short time ago the first indications of Jurassic formations have been observed on an expedition under Lieutenant Warren, Topographical Engineers, in the spur of the Black Hills north-northeast of Fort Laramie, by Mr. Meek and Dr. Hayden; and farther west, near the junction of the Wahsatch and Uintah

Mountains, I found more indications of rocks of this period (see section IV), which, therefore, must have a wide range. As they contain highly fossiliferous beds, it is remarkable that they have never been noticed before. Underlying these Jurassic strata there is a gypsum-bearing formation, mostly made up of red, shaly sandstones which in all probability belongs to the Triassic period.

All the strata of this district, even the most recent of the Tertiary formations, have undergone some dislocations, but these latter, like the Tertiary formations of section II, have been raised uniformly as a whole, and overlie, nearly horizontally, the older rocks.

The mountain ranges mainly consist of the upheaved older formations, which have partly been considerably altered, in connection with igneous and metamorphic masses, while in the valleys the more recent strata predominate. We find, however, Cretaceous and Tertiary strata crowning some of the main divides at South Pass, Bryan's Pass, &c.

THE IGNEOUS ROCKS.

Effusions of igneous masses have taken place in this district at different times, partly at an early period, probably toward the close of the Paleozoic era, partly at a much later date. We have evidences of it in the unconformable superposition of the strata of the various periods, combined with the difference in the mineralogical character of the eruptive rocks. These belong to at least two quite distinct groups, the granitic group and the greenstones.

Granites, composed of feldspar, quartz, and dark-colored mica or black hornblende and granitic syenites, closely related to them, form the main body of the eastern chain of the Rocky Mountains south of Fort Laramie, between the North and South Platte, and much farther on. Similar rocks are extensively developed near our route. They were observed in the mountains of the Laramie Peak system, on the divide between Bitter and Horseshoe Creeks, and farther west, near Prele Creek; also in the mountains south of the road, west of Deer Creek. They entirely form the Rattlesnake Mountains from near the mouth of Sweetwater River to the Three Crossings, and part of the Sweetwater Mountains. According to Colonel Frémont, the Wind River Mountains have also a granitic center.

The granitic rock from Horseshoe Creek appears to be composed of reddish-white orthoclase, milk-white oligoclase, quartz, and black mica, which are the normal elements of true granites. That from the Sweetwater Mountains and Rattlesnake Mountains is quite similar, and nearly all the specimens obtained from rocks *in situ* present the same appearance. This, as well as the parallelism and close connection of these ranges, indicates that they are only different spurs of one mountain system. A specimen from Independence Rock contains whitish pellucid orthoclase, a little white oligoclase, much quartz, and greenish-black mica; also some particles of specular or magnetic iron-ore, a frequent occurrence in connection with the eruptive rocks of this district. Only at two points I observed somewhat different granites forming small outcrops.

Among the loose drifted pieces of granitic rocks we find a great diversity of color and composition. They seem to originate from the neighboring mountains, but none of them were observed *in situ*. With them I found pseudomorphous green-colored quartz, shaped after feldspar. Near the South Pass I noticed fragments of a granite containing white mica. As I have not seen any similar rock in these mountains, except in bowlders at Bryan's Pass, southeast from the first locality, and again farther on in the same direction on Cache-la-poudre Creek, a tributary of South Platte River, I suppose that such granites form part of the western branch of the Rocky Mountains, extending from the Park Mountains to the Wind River Mountains. On the west side of South Pass I observed, however, granite, *in situ*, similar to that of the Rattlesnake Mountains.

The greenstones evidently date from a later period than the granites, in which they frequently form dikes. They are composed of white feldspar and green hornblende, and appear to be related to the diorites. Some of them are finely crystalline, and the two minerals can readily be distinguished. In others the hornblende prevails so much that the white feldspar can only be seen on the weathered surface of the rock. Still others are subcrystalline, and form a homogeneous mass of dark greenish-gray color, which is produced by the mixture of the white with the green mineral, the mixed powder of which appears greenish-gray.

These latter rocks can easily be mistaken for basalt, and I should not be surprised if most of the rocks in these mountains which have been described as basalts should, on a closer examination, be found to be such dioritic greenstones. The lithological character of part of these greenstones, especially of the latter description, is such that loose pieces of them cannot well be distinguished from metamorphic slates, hornblende slates, and the like, and their eruptive origin is only proved by their position in dikes. Similar rocks, which are evidently metamorphic, occur on our route and in the adjacent districts. On Horseshoe Creek I noticed pieces of a hornblende rock, with a peculiar concretionary structure like the "schaalstein" of Germany, in which the hornblende seems to envelop numerous small concretions of the size of lentils, and which therefore presents an undulated surface. If not found together with other hornblende rocks which appear to be eruptive, I would at once put it down as metamorphic; but, under the circumstances, not having seen it *in situ*, I hesitate to express a decided opinion.

Greenstones have been observed at various points, between Horseshoe Creek and the Rocky Ridge, a short distance east of the South Pass. They are best exposed on Sweetwater River, in the Rattlesnake Mountains, where they cross the granite in numerous dikes, and can easily be seen on account of the bareness of these mountains. At Devil's Gate I noticed one on each side of the road, and several others near the Gate. One vein has, in former times, filled a large portion of the gap, and may have given origin to it by its disintegration.

From the limited number of observations which could be made in regard to the relative position of strata of different age and the igneous rocks, it has not been possible to determine the exact period of the eruption of the granites and greenstones. The granites are undoubtedly very old. Similar rocks in the eastern hemisphere are not positively known to have disturbed any other than Paleozoic formations, and this seems also to be the case here. The Carboniferous strata have certainly been tilted by the granites, and have been altered in consequence of this eruption. As I could not trace the limits between them and the strata which we refer to the Triassic formation, I cannot decide whether both hold the same relative position to the granites or not, but I am strongly inclined to the opinion that the Triassic rocks are not directly tilted by them.

Other disturbances of the strata succeeded at various times in connection with the changes of the formations. At some points the Triassic, Jurassic, Cretaceous, and more recent strata appear to be conformable; at others, however, we find evidences that upheavals and erosions have taken place in the mean time, and the period of the last general continental upheaval is the close of the Tertiary era or even Post-Tertiary, of which the position of the more modern Tertiary beds affords conclusive proof. It is doubtful whether more than one of these disturbances was accompanied by outbursts of eruptive masses within this district, as we have not observed any plutonic rocks of a more modern appearance than the granites, except the greenstones. The origin of the latter most probably coincides with a second great uplifting of the Rocky Mountain chains, which seems to have occurred toward the close of the Cretaceous or early in the Tertiary period, while the last great changes of the level do not seem to have been accompanied by any violent disruptions of the strata and outbursts of eruptive masses in this section of the country.

THE METAMORPHIC ROCKS.

Many of the older formations of this section have undergone considerable changes in their lithological character, by the immediate influence or secondary consequences of the eruption of the igneous rocks; but completely metamorphosed strata or originally crystalline schists are extensively developed only in the western part of this section, between the Three Crossings of Sweetwater River and the South Pass. On Sweetwater, above the crossings, I observed mica schist, mainly composed of dark-colored mica and quartz, with a laminated texture, also gneiss, made up of white oligoclase, quartz, dark-colored mica, and hornblende (?) with a coarse crystalline granitic texture, and other rocks of a similar character; also some hornblende rocks which may, however, be of eruptive origin. On the Rocky Ridge, east of the last crossing of Sweetwater River, I noticed more outcrops of gneiss (and perhaps granite?), and some of the hornblende rock; but the western portion of this ridge appears to consist chiefly of argillaceous and silico-argillaceous schists, part of which assume a micaceous character, without, however, changing into mica schists. They continue westward, and form numerous outcrops on the eastern slope of the South Pass, until they disappear beneath the capping Tertiary strata. According to Colonel Frémont they thence extend northwestward in the Wind River Mountains.

Similar metamorphic strata, but especially a hornblende slate, are extensively developed some distance south of our route, in the Medicine Bow Mountains. In the eastern portion of this section, at least near the traveled road, there are only few indications of metamorphic strata. I have mentioned that some of the hornblende rocks near Horseshoe Creek may belong to that series, and perhaps also some south of the road, near Prele Creek, where I observed a curious alternation of granite, a crystalline or compact greenstone or hornblende slate and quartz rock.

STRATIFIED ROCKS OF THE PALEOZOIC AGE.

Strata which evidently belong to the older formations have been observed at numerous points, tilted by the igneous rocks; but few of them contain fossil remains, the traces of which have mostly been obliterated by a beginning metamorphosis. Thus we have not been able to determine the age of more than a few of them.

Silurian formation.—I have not observed myself any decisive proofs of the existence of the Silurian formation in this district; but some time ago an unquestionably Silurian coral, *Halysites catenulata* (*Catenipora escharoides*), was found by Mr. Drexler at the Rocky Ridge, a few miles north of the main road. This fossil is generally confined to the upper division of the Silurian formation, and has hitherto been found only in a few specimens lower down, in the upper portion of the Lower Silurian formation. This coral of Mr. Drexler is the first Upper (or Middle) Silurian specimen ever found in the far West. As Dr. Hayden has recognized the Potsdam sandstone, which is at the base of the Lower Silurian, or probably more correctly primordial, farther east in the Black Hills, north of Fort Laramie, (Prel. Report of Lieutenant Warren, Top. Eng. Doc., 1858–1859), we may presume that the Silurian formation occurs at intermediate points along the mountains, but has not been recognized on account of the scarcity of the organic remains.

Devonian formation.—As yet it is not certain whether the Devonian period has any representatives in this section of country. We find it stated in Captain Stansbury's report, that, West of La Bonté Creek, some fossils were obtained which appeared to be Devonian, but we are now able to prove their Jurassic age.

Near the Medicine Bow Butte, at the southeastern extremity of the Laramie Plains, I found, on a previous expedition, a loose, drifted mass of rocks, full of fossils. Dr. B. F. Shumard, who examined them, expressed the opinion that they were Devonian. He says (Expl. of Lieut. F. T. Bryan, Top. Eng., 1856, Rep. Sec. of War, 1857): "They are Paleozoic types, belonging to the genera *Spirifer*, *Chonetes*, *Orthis*, *Orthoceras*, *Conocardium*, &c. They were very badly preserved, and their specific character almost wholly obliterated. From their general appearance, however, I am strongly of the opinion that they represent the Devonian period." As, heretofore, no strata of that age had been observed at any point of the far West, there was still room to doubt the correctness of this conclusion; but since this expedition has proved an extensive development of Devonian strata in Utah Territory (see section V), we may well presume that a more detailed examination will reveal their existence also in this section.

Carboniferous formation.—Rocks of the Carboniferous formation have been observed at several points in the eastern portion of this district. They had first been recognized by Captain Stansbury and Professor Hall, and contain the same organic remains as the Upper Carboniferous formations in the Mississippi Valley. Fossils of this age have been found at the following points along the route:

1. At the Warm Spring Creek, about 13 miles west of Fort Laramie, where limestones are quarried for the use of the fort. The rocks are hard, brittle, mostly subcrystalline, altered limestones and marbles, partly siliceous. They are gray, or variegated gray and red, and contain numerous *Brachiopoda*, especially *Productus*, also *Corals*, and joints of *Crinoidea*, &c.

2. On North Platte River, some 15 miles above Fort Laramie, and some miles farther west, where the road strikes Horseshoe Creek. The rocks there are partly like those of the quarry, partly siliceous altered sandstones, &c.

3. Captain Stansbury obtained Carboniferous fossils at a point some distance south of the road, not far from Prele Creek.

Similar rocks are considerably developed near these localities, but have not furnished any fossils to our collection.

Permian formation.—Hitherto in this part of the Rocky Mountains no strata have been conclusively identified with the Permo-Carboniferous formation of the Eastern Kansas or the truly Permian period.

Strata of generally much altered rocks, the exact age of which could not be determined on account of the scarcity or total absence of fossils, but which apparently belong to the Paleozoic periods, are largely developed in the mountain-ranges of this district. They cap the granites of the Black Hills, far north and south of Fort Laramie. On our routes, we found them on the Platte River, from some miles above Fort Laramie to the upper end of the cañon near the first crossing of the river road. Part of these rocks have already been mentioned among the Carboniferous. I noticed highly altered light-colored sandstones, partly calcareous, or veined with agate, siliceous limestones with secretions of flint and jasper, marbles of various colors, some purple sandstones, &c. They contain traces of fossils, but more perfect ones were only obtained at the localities mentioned above as Carboniferous. Such rocks also crop out at numerous points south of the river, and toward Laramie Peak. On the upper road we find them on Bitter Creek, and on the mountains east of La Bonté Creek.

On La Bonté Creek, some distance south of the road, strongly tilted rocks form several ranges of hills, parallel to each other and to the higher mountains in the south. They present a uniform dip off the latter, and, therefore, steep escarpments in one direction, and more gentle slopes in the other. Sandstones prevail there of white, gray, and brown colors; others are purple or dark brick-red, the latter mostly rather soft. They are interstratified with arenaceous and argillaceous shales and slates; gray, green, bluish, reddish, &c. While the sandstones form the hills, the shaly strata have been more easily eroded, and correspond to the intervening valleys, which are partly occupied by more recent Tertiary formations. They trend generally to north-northwest, and dip strongly to east-northeast over 60°, and at some places they are even vertical. Near the road the trend and dip are much disturbed by local manifestations of the subterranean agencies. A short distance from La Bonté Creek we find formations which underlie Jurassic strata, and are provisionally referred to the Triassic period; and the question arises whether these sandstones and shales are not, perhaps, of the same age, or hold an intermediate position between them and the more calcareous portion of the Carboniferous formation. Further west, near Prele Creek, the mountains south of the road are mainly composed of gray and white and some light red and purple sandstones, with few interstratifications of slates and pure or siliceous limestones. Their dip is variable but strong. They are apparently also Paleozöic. Captain Stansbury obtained there some Carboniferous fossils. The valley of Platte River is generally occupied by more recent formations, and the higher mountains with the older rocks are several miles distant. Near Dear Creek, and for some distance west from there to the Red Buttes, they are partly granitic, but mostly composed of upheaved stratified rocks. At the Red Buttes we find more Triassic outcrops.

The mountains south of Sweetwater River, west of the Devil's Gate, are also mostly granitic, with altered Paleozoic rocks on their slopes. On the east side of the Rocky Ridge I found the last outcrops of this age. They are then succeeded by metamorphic schists.

TRIASSIC AND JURASSIC FORMATIONS.

To within a short period it has been problematical whether the Jurassic and Triassic formations were represented in the territory of the United States, although Middle Jurassic strata are known in the Russian territory, on the northwest coast of this continent. Their discovery was repeatedly claimed, but every time it was found that a mistake had been made. Although some of the strata which Mr. J. Marcou described as Jurassic and Triassic are, perhaps, of that age, still he based his conclusions chiefly upon fossils which have since been recognized as Cretaceous forms, and nearly the whole area which he colored upon his map indiscriminately as covered by those formations, is now well known to be Tertiary and Cretaceous.

On an expedition under command of Lieut. G. K. Warren, Topographical Engineers, in the year 1857, Dr. Hayden collected, in the Black Hills, north of Fort Laramie, a series of fossils, in which he and Mr. Meek recognized the Jurassic formation. The full report of this exploration, and of the highly interesting geological discoveries connected with it, has not been published yet, but a short account of them has been given in a "Preliminary Report of Lieutenant Warren, Washington, 1859, Doc., Secretary of War," and in a paper read before the Academy of Science of Philadelphia, March, 1858.

Our observations fully confirm the conclusion in regard to the Jurassic age of that formation. At various points I observed strata which are evidently coeval with those described by Dr. Hayden, and occupy an analogous position between the Cretaceous and older beds. A few of the fossils of our collection, a full description of which is given in the subjoined report of Mr. Meek, are identical with those of Dr. Hayden, while we have, also, several new ones which, like his, are closely allied to European Jurassic forms. The only disputable point is now, to which horizon of the Jurassic series these strata correspond. Mr. Meek suggests that they are Liassic, basing his opinion chiefly upon the similarity of several of Dr. Hayden's fossils with European species of that age, while our fossils, although from strata which apparently form the continuation of those observed by Dr. Hayden, seem to be more closely related to Middle Jurassic types. We have an *Ostrea*, scarcely distinguishable from *O. Marshii* (*O. Engelmanni*, Meek), a leading type of the Middle Jura of Europe; while a *Pecten* is very similar to *P. lens* (*P. bellastriata*, Meek), which does not occupy a distinct horizon, and furnishes, therefore, no proof *pro* or *contra*. *Belemnites densus*, Meek, has a slight ventral groove, and is thus allied to the *Canaliculati* which are characteristic of the Middle Jurassic formation, and it is perhaps not distinct from *B. eccentricus*, Blainville, of that period. In order to settle this question of age it will, however, be necessary to wait until more complete collections of fossils and accurate sections of the strata can be procured.

All the Jurassic fossils which I obtained in this section of the country were found on North Platte River, close below the Red Buttes, within a few feet of each other, in some strata highly charged with organic remains, and which reach the surface at the lowest central point of an anticlinal exposure. A combination of local upheavals, which cause abrupt changes of the dip, both in direction and degree, and the disconnection of the exposures, prevented me from obtaining a complete section, and from tracing the limits between the Jurassic and older formations; while the overlying strata, at a greater distance from the axis of elevation, have such a slight dip, and are mostly covered over so much with soil and detritus that their succession and relative superposition are not perfectly plain. The difficulty is increased by the scarcity of fossils, of which I did not notice any between the point mentioned and a locality 7 miles lower down the river. The succession of the strata along the river, as far it could be observed, is the following, beginning about 7 miles below the Red Buttes:

1. Dark gray and blue argillaceous slates and marls, with harder seams and concretions of argillo-calcareous marl, the latter mostly inclosing fossils, *Ostrea congesta*, *Baculites*, and a fine new *Inoceramus*, of great size, *I. Simpsoni*, Meek. Fissures of the rock are thickly coated with slender silky crystals of gypsum. These beds, forming an exposure of about 70 feet thickness, evidently correspond to No. III of the Nebraska-Cretaceous section of Messrs. Meek and Hayden, and appeared to be horizontal.

2. A gap probably corresponding to more clays and marls.

3. Sandstones, heavy-bedded, light-colored or brown, and ferruginous, passing down into thinly stratified, partly shaly sandstones, and still lower into brown and gray arenaceous shales, with some seams of sandstone. The observed thickness exceeds 100 feet, and may be much greater. The dip is very slight to the east. These sandstones closely resemble those of the Lignite formations, as well higher up as lower down on Platte River. I did not notice with them any beds of coal, but numerous imperfect marks of fossil plants.

4. A great thickness of sandstones, like the upper ones of No. 3. Underlying them conformably, there are—

5. Dark bluish-gray, apparently altered shales and slates, with irregular seams and concretionary masses of black limestone, which have an even fracture and are hard and very brittle, as if they had passed through a kiln. Seventy feet or more.

6. A remarkable bed, 6 feet thick, of a light greenish-yellow argillaceous substance, which is unctuous to the touch, and readily imbibes water, which renders it highly plastic. It contains gypsum in single crystals and alkaline salts.

7. Over 150 feet more of the dark shales and slates, like 5, with efflorescences of gypsum on the fissures.

8. Sandstones, conformably underlying the shales, of considerable thickness.

9. Shales and slates, dark bluish-black, or light-colored, variegated gray, red, green, &c. About 100 feet.

10. Some beds of brown and gray sandstone, partly slaty, laminated, and calca-

reous, and changing into a gritty, impure limestone. It is fetid, from a large amount of organic remains. This is the rock just referred to, in which I found the Jurassic fossils. It contains one or two species of *Belemnites*, *Pentacrinus*, *Dentalium*, two *Pecten*, two *Ostrea*, a *Gryphæa*, some indistinct fragments of other *Acephala*, and also what appears to be worm-tracks.

11. More shales like 9.

The relative superposition of these strata is not altogether plain, as I have stated above, and from this enumeration of their geographical succession, together with my other field-notes, two different geological sections may be formed. I am not positive which of the two is the correct one. The main point upon which the question hinges is whether Nos. 3 and 4 are Upper Cretaceous, corresponding to the Cretaceous sandstone and Lignite formation higher up on Platte River, or if they are Lower Cretaceous, corresponding to No. 1 of the Cretaceous section of Nebraska, of Messrs. Meek and Hayden.

If the latter view is correct, then the strata appear to be enumerated in our section above in the order in which they actually overlie each other, beginning with the highest. The dip, although slight at that point, appears to be uniformly in the same direction.

Dr. Hayden, in the paper mentioned above (Proc. Acad. of Phil., March, 1858), gives a section of the strata near the Black Hills, in which he assigns this same position to a series of rocks very much like our Nos. 3 and 4. He finds in them, besides indistinct vegetable remains, also seams and layers of dark carbonaceous matter or impure lignite, which I did not observe in Nos. 3 and 4 below the Red Buttes, although lignite may, perhaps, exist in those strata. I found seams of it a few miles west from there, which may possibly occupy this horizon. Farther west, in the Wahsatch Mountains, I have also observed a considerable sandstone formation containing some beds of brown coal, overlying Jurassic strata (see section IV). The few fossils found there point decidedly to the Lower Cretaceous, (or, possibly, even Jurassic) age of that series, and although differently developed, according to local circumstances, it is most likely coeval with No. I of the Nebraska section. These observations, showing that the sandstones at the base of the Cretaceous formations of Kansas and Nebraska extend with increasing thickness to the western limit of the secondary formations in these latitudes, corroborate the opinion that Nos. 3 and 4, although no fossils have been found in them from which to determine their age, may represent that same horizon.

Nos. 5 and 7 of the above section evidently belong together. As no fossil remains were noticed in them, it must be left to further investigations to decide whether they are Jurassic or Cretaceous. In their lithological character they resemble the following Jurassic strata.

The stratum No. 6 is unlike any common rock or shale, and its present condition seems to be due to chemical agencies. I would certainly consider it as quite local, if I had not seen exactly the same substance, in connection with similar shales and slates, on a previous expedition under Lieut. F. T. Bryan, Topographical Engineers, some 80 miles south from there, near the Medicine Bow Buttes. In a piece of it, which had lost all its soluble parts, gypsum, &c., I then found 30 per cent. of alumina, 51 to 55 per cent. of silica, traces of calcia, and much water, which was retained with great force, even when the mineral was heated.

Nos. 8 and 9 then probably correspond to the lowest portion of No. 1 of the Black Hill section, while No. 10 is lithologically similar to Dr. Hayden's A, the highest bed which he considers as Jurassic.

On the other hand there are so many local upheavals in the neighborhood of our section that it is not necessary to consider the strata as altogether conformable. Our No. 1, corresponding to No. III of the Nebraska Cretaceous section, may be an outlier; it has not been observed anywhere lower down on the river. Nos. 3 and 4 may represent the sandstone formation with lignites of the Upper Cretaceous age, of Nos. IV or V of the Nebraska section, which is most characteristically developed farther south on the North Platte, and of which more will be said below. That no beds of coal have been seen cropping out is no proof against their existence, and, besides, the beds of coal are not uniformly distributed throughout the whole thickness of that formation. Nos. 5, 6, and 7 are precisely like some strata which I had, in 1856, observed near the Medicine Bow Butte, resting there upon a gritty limestone which resembles closely our No. 10, but is characterized by its fossils as an equivalent of No. II of the Cretaceous section. They then may form part of No. II or of III. That they are altered, while the other portion of No. III, several miles lower down the river, is not altered, would not be a sufficient evidence against their common age, and the apparent absence of fossils in 5 and 7 is only the result of the metamorphic agencies. No. 5 may, however, occupy a lower horizon than No. 1. No. 8 may be an equivalent of Nos. I or II the Cretaceous section, while with 9, probably, the Jurassic formation begins. A thorough investigation on the spot is required before the question of the relative age of all these strata can be settled.

In Captain Stansbury's report it is stated that a few miles west of La Bonté Creek, north of Laramie Peak, gray sandstone was seen cropping out, overlying the red sandstone which we refer to the Triassic age. Above these were layers of red and light-colored shales, impure limestone, and shaly and thinly laminated sandstone, with some *Brachiopoda*, *Monotis*, &c. These strata were considered as probably Devonian. Besides the fact that the genus *Monotis* is not known to range so low down, it will be seen from the following that the red sandstone spoken of underlies our Jurassic strata, and that the fossiliferous beds are on a parallel with, or at least closely allied to, our No. 10. They also present the same lithological character, not met with in the more recent rocks of this neighborhood, and are therefore probably of Jurassic age. In the mountains south of the Three Crossings of Sweetwater River, I noticed rocks which are petrographically similar to some of the Jurassic beds, and may be of the same age.

Either immediately below No. 11 of the above section, or after a repetition of similar shales and calcareous laminated sandstones of no considerable thickness, the strata near the Red Buttes continue downward in the following order:

12. Gray sandstone, which I did not examine closely, but noticed only from a distance. It corresponds apparently to No. C of the section of Messrs. Meek and Hayden. It occupies the top of the principal of the Red Buttes, probably, together

with some of the higher strata, to a thickness of about 100 feet, and also caps some of the mountains west of La Bonté Creek. Its age is probably the Jurassic.

13. Purple slaty and shaly sandstone, with thin interstratifications of other colors, green, blue, &c., 150 to 200 feet.

14. Some gray sandstone, and much purple slaty sandstone and arenaceous shales, with a thin interstratification of an impure siliceous limestone, and much gypsum; the latter partly in strata, of which there are at least six at the principal butte, each of them over 2 feet thick, partly disseminated throughout the arenaceous material in thin scales and seams, 150 to 200 feet.

15. Hard siliceous sand-rock of considerable thickness, which may belong to an older formation.

The rocks Nos. 13 and 14 do not retain their character unchanged, as is common with such formations. Near La Bonté Creek, the second locality where they are well exposed, I noticed with them heavy beds of white and light-yellowish, fine-grained, friable, quartzose sandstones, and the gypsum is there distributed somewhat differently. The petrographical features of Nos. 13 and 14 are similar to those of No. D of Dr. Hayden's Black Hill section, which is by him there provisionally referred to the Carboniferous period, but in regard to which he states: "It is not easy to determine the age of the bed D. From its stratigraphical position, as well as lithological characters, it might with almost as much propriety be referred to the Permian or Triassic systems as to the Carboniferous." Underlying it he observed beds of bluish and reddish gray, very hard, gritty limestone, 10 to 50 feet thick, No. E of his section, in which he found a smooth, Spirifer-like shell, and *Pleurotomaria*, *Macrocheilus*, and *Bellerophon*, the two latter of which genera are unknown in the Old World in strata above the Carboniferous, but have, in Eastern Kansas, been also found in the Permo-Carboniferous formations. It appears, therefore, that all below No. D of the Black Hill section is Permian or Carboniferous, and, from the remark of Dr. Hayden, "that near the southeastern base of the Black Hills some loose masses of a cherty rock were seen on more than one occasion, under circumstances indicating that the stratum from which they were derived holds a position between the beds C and D, and that several of the fossils which they contain are identical with species occurring in a formation in Northeast Kansas, now known to be of Permian age," it would seem that D is also Carboniferous or Permian. The close similarity which appears to exist between the strata D and Nos. 13 and 14 leads me to suppose that the latter observation may be erroneous, as I hesitate much to refer Nos. 13 and 14 to the Permian age. It is, however, possible that they are altogether distinct.

In the Black Hills, according to that section, the Paleozoic formations appear to be developed on a small scale only, much less than I have observed them near our line of travel, and before further south, and again further west in the Wahsatch Mountains, where they attain a thickness of many hundreds of feet (see section V). It would seem that this is due more to the nature of the upheavals, and perhaps powerful denudations and erosions, than to a difference in their original development. An apparent conformability does by no means involve a positive evidence of undisturbed successive deposition. I have, at numerous points, as well on this expedition as before, noticed heavy masses of brick-red, soft sandstones in connection with the Carboniferous rocks of the Rocky Mountains, which I consider as much older than the beds Nos. 13 and 14, and the lithological similarity alone is a very deceptive evidence of the contemporariness of the formation. I have not observed gypsum with these, but the gypsum is in many instances a secondary formation, which did not originally exist in the rocks where it now occurs, and may, therefore, be found in formations of every age.

Thus far we have no positive evidence of the age of Nos. 13 and 14 of the above section. Such formations contain usually few organic remains, either because the chemical properties of the acid waters in which they may have been deposited did not favor the existence of animal life, or because their traces were obliterated subsequently by chemical agencies connected with the formation of the gypsum. I only found in them the impression of what appears to be the sheath (*ochrea*) of a leaf, such as is, to my knowledge, not known in the Paleozoic era, and is first observed with plants of the Triassic epoch. At the points where I noticed these strata, they are closely connected with Jurassic rocks.

At La Bonté Creek, where the formations underlying them are largely developed, there appears to be a very considerable thickness of strata between them and the limestones of the Carboniferous period, of which I have spoken above, and which is composed chiefly, as far as we could ascertain, of sandstones of white, gray, and brown, brick-red, and purple colors, the latter mostly soft shaly, with interstratifications of variegated shales and slates. Not having had sufficient time for more extended examinations in that interesting locality, where the stratification is much disturbed by local upheavals, I dare not express a decided opinion in regard to the age of this apparently intervening series. I am inclined to think that we have there Permian or Triassic rocks, not observed before developed in a similar degree and with the same features.

An additional evidence of the probably Triassic age of Nos. 13 and 14 is found in the large development of similar gypsum-bearing areno-argillaceous formations further south, in Northern Texas and New Mexico, where they also underlie Cretaceous beds, as stated by Mr. Marcou, Dr. G. Shumard, Mr. Blake, in the reports of Captain Marcy, Captain Pope, Captain Whipple, and others, and in the interesting discoveries made along the Great Colorado and its tributaries by Dr. Newberry, on the expeditions under Lieutenant Ives, Topographical Engineers, in 1858, and Captain Macomb, Topographical Engineers, in 1859. Dr. Newberry there discovered in such formations some plants of the genera *Zamites*, *Petrophillum*, &c., and Saurian bones, which led him also to refer this series to the Triassic epoch. (See American Journal, vol. 28, second series, page 299.) Similar formations are largely developed in the southern part of the Wahsatch Mountains. (See section IV.)

The gypsum evidently existed as such before the eruption of the greenstones. On La Bonté Creek, where the irregularity of the stratification is caused by intrusions of the greenstone, I observed that a thick bed of gypsum, which is considerably bent, has thereby been broken and brecciated, and exhibits numerous fissures radial to the curvature.

In connection with the Triassic formation, I have observed some very instructive instances of complicated stratification, produced by the combined effects of multifarious upheavals.

CRETACEOUS FORMATION.

The middle and lower portions of the Cretaceous formation are not prominently developed along our route. I have, in the foregoing chapter, mentioned that this division of the Cretaceous strata, No. III, and, probably, also Nos. I, II, and IV of the Nebraska section, are exposed above the Jurassic rocks between the Platte Bridge and the Red Buttes, and I have described their character. Farther eastward the overlying Lignite formation covers the surface. Only about two miles above Deer Creek, I noticed gray and brown laminated, impure sandstone, with shaly portions and carbonaceous particles, and found in it some imperfect fossil bivalves, which are referred by Mr. Meek to the genus *Panopaea* and the upper part of the Cretaceous system. The lithological character of the rock corresponds to that of the upmost Cretaceous beds—No. V of the Nebraska section—which are described as yellow arenaceous and argillaceous grit, containing much ferruginous matter; it also closely resembles that of some portions of the Lignite formation. Loose pieces of a hard, brown sandstone, with a species of *Inoceramus* (see Mr. Meek's report), which seems to indicate that the bed from which they come holds a position at the base of No. IV of the Cretaceous section, have been found at several points near the last-mentioned locality, some distance higher up on Platte River, and again a few miles west of the Red Buttes. These specimens apparently have not been drifted far, but I could not ascertain from which strata they come.

I am led to consider the Lignite formation on Platte River, along our route, as Upper Cretaceous, corresponding to the one near Bryan's Pass and the Medicine Bow Butte.

The Cretaceous formation is considerably developed farther south in this section of country. While with Lieutenant Bryan, Topographical Engineers, in 1856, I have observed beds, corresponding apparently to No. IV, on the eastern slope of the Black Hills, near the South Platte. Speaking of them, I remarked (Report Secretary of War, December, 1857, p. 510): "Near the place where Cache-la-poudre Creek breaks through the last chain of rocks to enter the plains, I observed in the sandstones interstratifications of altered sandy shales and shaly limestones. Some of these were highly fossiliferous, full of remains of fishes and shells, and fetid from the large amount of organic matter. The fossils are, however, preserved badly. They are undoubtedly Cretaceous." One of them appears to be *Inoceramus Sagensis*, which, in Nebraska, is confined to the upper part of No. IV.

No. III was then found largely and characteristically developed along Sage Creek, an affluent of North Platte River, near the divide between Platte and Green Rivers, and also on the northeastern side of the Medicine Bow Butte. No. II was observed south of that butte: "There were several layers of a finely-grained, subcrystalline, fetid limestone, which is in some places even bituminous, from the large amount of organic remains which it includes. Other portions contain a great deal of micaceous sand, so much so as to change it into a micaceous sandstone." Fossils were abundant, and evidently of Cretaceous age. Lately the specimens from there have again been carefully examined, and the result shows that this formation is No. II of the Cretaceous series. An *Ammonites* is closely allied to *Ammonites percarinatus*, which occurs in No.

II (more so than to *A. Mandanensis*). Other fossils are young specimens of *Scaphites larviformis*, and still others *Inoceramus fragillis*, both forms of which are in Nebraska confined to No. II. This rock is overlaid by rotten slates and shales, which cannot be distinguished from Nos. 5, 6, and 7 of the foregoing section, and are equally abnormal in their appearance.

LIGNITE FORMATION.

On the Upper North Platte, near Sage Creek, and at Bryan's Pass, and extending east to beyond Medicine Bow Creek, I had then observed a heavy formation of sandstones, including a considerable number of beds of brown coal. In this formation, which reposes upon No. III, in a stratum immediately above one of the coal-seams, I found a number of marine shells, some *Inoceramus*, of which one specimen appears to be *I. tenuilineatus*, which occurs in No. IV, some *Ostrea*, of which one at least is a new species, &c., and from the same series, higher up, I obtained specimens of *Cytherea*, and the characteristic *Avicula Nebraskana*, Evans and Shumard, which occurs in Nos. IV and V of the Nebraska section.

A Lignite, or, rather, brown-coal formation, also occupies a large portion of the country along Platte River from below Deer Creek to near the Red Buttes, and north and south from there. It is mostly composed of white and light-brownish sandstones and argillaceous shales and slates; in the upper portion, also, of arenaceous shales and shaly sandstones. The most eastern point where I noticed it is where the hill-road west of Fort Laramie enters the valley of Platte River, and in the low bluffs some miles below that point. Here I observed light-colored sandstones, mostly not very compact, interstratified with argillaceous and some arenaceous shales of light and dark gray, bluish, and brown colors, and with seams of carbonaceous shales and brown coal. Even the sandstones contain in places particles of coal. The dip is not uniform—from 15 degrees upward.

Up Platte River the formation gains in thickness, and more coal was observed. Heavy strata of mostly white sandstone, alternating with argillaceous shales and slates, and with numerous seams of coal, form prominent escarpments along the river, between Deer Creek and the Platte Bridge. The seams of coal are mostly thin. At one point five of them were observed within a height of less than fifty feet, most of them only from 6 to 10 inches thick; but the shales above and below them were highly carbonaceous and full of vegetable remains, and some of them might be called impure, slaty coal. At other points the carbon appears to have more accumulated, and the seams become thicker, until they form workable beds of coal. A bed of coal on Deer Creek, near the road, is over 6 feet thick, and has long been known, and occasionally been worked for blacksmithing. A description of the coal will be given below.

The trend and dip of these strata are variable; mostly off the nearest mountains, and near Platte Bridge, it is toward the east, so that lower strata rise to the surface above that locality. The thickness of the formation cannot be estimated with any degree of accuracy, but must be considerable, and may reach several hundred feet.

Some sandstones nearer the Red Buttes, No. 3 of the above section, closely resemble those of this Lignite formation, but may perhaps be older. On the ridge, some miles west of the Red Buttes, the road passes by some prominent exposures of white and brownish sandstone, associated with gray and brown shales and slates, and dipping at an angle of 45 degrees to southwest. Interstratified with them I noticed several beds of coal, of which one, immediately underlying the most prominent stratum of sandstone, appears to be several feet thick. The coal was covered with detritus, and I could only obtain some weathered fragments by digging with the knife. It appears to be similar to that of Deer Creek, and is probably of the same age. Its stratigraphical position also leads to this conclusion.

I cannot definitely decide, from the evidence found on our route, whether this Lignite formation is Eocene-Tertiary or Upper Cretaceous, yet it is almost certain that it corresponds to the Cretaceous Lignite formation higher up on Platte River of the age of No. IV or V of the Nebraska section.

I have only obtained a few fossils, and it is not altogether certain whether they actually come from strata of this formation, or from outliers of the Cretaceous beds. It is certainly older than the Miocene formation, and therefore older than the Great Lignite Basin on the Missouri River, which is now generally conceded to date from that period. It is older than Miocene, because we find the Miocene era represented lower down on Platte River by the Scott's Bluff formation (see section II), which is apparently coeval with the Miocene strata of the Bad Lands of White River, and overlies another series of Tertiary strata (see below), which, in their turn, overlie the Lignite formation. No Miocene strata in this part of the country have ever been observed in a disturbed condition, strongly tilted by forces from beneath, while the Platte River lignites have frequently been noticed dipping at an angle of 45°. Another Lignite formation on the Missouri, near the mouth of Judith River, is characterized by its organic remains as Eocene-Tertiary (see various publications of Mr. Meek, Dr. Hayden, and Prof. Leidy). It is considerably disturbed by subterranean agencies, like the Platte River strata, and although the latter are much more and differently developed, this may be the result of local circumstances, and both might perhaps be of the same age (?).

The Platte River formation overlies Cretaceous deposits of the age of No. III of the Nebraska section. A few indications of Nos. IV and V were also noticed, and I am strongly inclined to the opinion that the Lignite formation occupies the horizon of No. IV or V, the same as the not far distant Lignite formation higher up on Platte River, and forms the continuation of it; holding possibly a similar position in relation to the Cretaceous and Tertiary periods, as do the highest Carboniferous strata in Eastern Kansas, between the Coal-Measures and Permian formations (?). Not far from Deer Creek (see above, under Cretaceous formation), I have found in rocks containing particles of coal some casts of fossils which Mr. Meek refers to *Panopœa*, and considers as evidences of the Cretaceous age of the beds in which they occur, the lithological character of which corresponds as well with the decidedly Upper Cretaceous as with the Lignite formations with which they are surrounded.

Close by, and at several other points higher up the river, also near the outcrops of lignites west of the Red Buttes, I have found fragments of *Inoceramus* loose on the surface in a very compact brownish sandstone. This rock is exactly like some of the sandstones of the lignitic series. I have not noticed the *Inoceramus* in the rock *in situ*, and they may possibly have been drifted there; but it is remarkable that they should have been found several times near the lignites, if they are not connected with them.

The Upper Cretaceous brown-coal formation which is developed farther south, in the district of the Rocky Mountains, on the Upper Platte River, Sage Creek, and Bryan's Pass, and which I have mentioned already above, presents a similar general development, only slightly modified by local influences, especially in its upper division, and is composed of an alternation of white, gray, yellowish, and brown sandstones, with some argillaceous slates, brown and gray argillaceous and arenaceous shales, and layers of brown-coal mostly from 6 to 24 inches wide.

Taking all these evidences together, very little doubt remains in my mind that the Lignite formation on Deer Creek should not be of the same age as that on Sage Creek, viz, Upper Cretaceous, and it would require positive evidences to convince me of its connection with the Tertiary Lignite formations farther north.

TERTIARY FORMATION.

Overlying the lignite series we find a succession of strata, which, if we may judge from their color and the material of which they are composed, are probably coeval with those underlying the Miocene (Scott's Bluff) formation below Fort Laramie (compare section II). They extend on Platte River, from the eastern limits of the Lignite formation, to the point where the river begins to cañon and the road crosses back from the north to the south side, and perhaps lower down. They consist of a series of argillaceous shales of drab, green, and gray colors, gray sandstones of a rather fine grain, and some coarse sandstones mainly composed of particles of granite mixed with agate and hornblende rock. The shales contain numerous arenaceous concretions, which, where they are more numerous, form distinct irregular strata. At some points such seams of rounded masses, each only a few inches thick, alternate regularly with seams of clay of about the same thickness, and thus the bare bluffs attain a singularly striated appearance, only interrupted by heavier strata of sandstone. Their stratification is nearly horizontal, and they thus appear to be unconformable to the lignite series. They seem to dip slightly to the east, so that, traveling down the river, we gradually come to higher strata. The whole thickness of the formation does not seem to be more than 200 to 300 feet, but could not be estimated closely. It forms table-hills with precipitous sides, and I did not observe any fossils. The upper or eastern portion is more arenaceous; the buff-color prevails in it, and some of the sandstones are quite conglomeratic, probably on account of the proximity of the higher mountains.

Near Fort Laramie, below the cañon of the Platte, a more recent Tertiary formation is extensively developed in the river-valley and in the adjoining hills, which has been observed also close below the fort, and has been mentioned in section II. It is mainly made up of finely arenaceous strata, which are light-gray or whitish, from an admixture of calcareous substance. Some strata are coarser calcareous or siliceous sandstones, partly concretionary and irregular, like the rocks of the Ash-Hollow formation; but they are generally more friable, and do not form the same fine scenery. The soft arenaceous strata contain, at many points, numerous irregular root-like white bodies, composed of sand and carbonate of lime, or silicate of calcia, which I have also mentioned in connection with the Ash-Hollow rock, and which have occasionally been mistaken for fossils.

Similar formations were noticed far to the west, and, wherever observed, they hold a position which makes it evident that they are among the most recent deposits of the Tertiary period; some of them may even be Post-Tertiary. They are nowhere capped by any others—generally fill depressions in the older rocks, creek-valleys, &c., and are only modified by erosion. Near Fort Laramie they form considerable bluffs, but attain generally less thickness along the road. I observed them in the hills west of Laramie, near Bitter Creek, &c.; also again on the ridge between the Red Buttes and Independence Rock, and at numerous points of the Sweetwater Valley. These deposits naturally change according to the character of the surrounding mountains from which they are formed; they become coarser, conglomeratic, or more argillaceous; therefore, we find strata of a different appearance, but apparently of the same age, in the mountains near Horseshoe Creek, La Bonté Creek, &c. The Tertiary strata in the South Pass will be described in the following section No. IV.

ECONOMICAL GEOLOGY.

Agriculture.—This section of the country is considerably elevated. The lowest points cannot be less than 4,500 feet high, which is given by Captain Stansbury as the elevation of Fort Laramie. This altitude, combined with the climatological character of this region, the remarkably great and sudden changes of the temperature, and the shortness of the summer season, are disadvantageous to agricultural pursuits, but not more so, it would appear, than in the Salt Lake country. The prevalence of sandstone formations is felt unfavorably in the composition of the soils, but I have no doubt that there are numerous points, especially along the creeks, where cultivation would prove successful, although the country at large must remain a desert as long as the present physical conditions last.

Building materials are abundant throughout the district. Rocks, marble, lime, clay for adobes and brick, and even timber, in limited quantity, can be obtained nearly everywhere within a few miles of the road, and at some points there is plenty of it.

Iron.—Iron-ore appears to be largely distributed in the Rocky Mountains. Several of the granites contain the specular ore in so large a quantity that pure pieces of it can be broken off, and we may presume that deposits of the mineral exist with the granites. Pieces of siliceous specular ore, more or less mixed with slate rock, have been frequently noticed among the drift pebbles, and appear to originate from the metamorphic schists or altered rocks. Thus far, however, we cannot conceive how the iron-ore in this region should ever be turned to any use.

We have not observed indications of other mineral veins, nor of gold-bearing rocks. The geological formations at some points appear to be similar to those of the Park Mountains, in the neighborhood of Pike's Peak; but we have so little reliable information in regard to the geological configuration, and the association of the gold in that district, that we cannot now draw a parallel. Long before the gold excitement began in that country, I have heard it stated that some grains of gold had been found in Medicine Bow Creek, but nobody ever succeeded in finding more of it. Still it might be premature to deny its existence altogether.

Salts.—Along some parts of the road, especially near Sweetwater River, we find the soil in places covered with saline efflorescences and salt-ponds, which mostly dry up in summer and leave white incrustations on the surface. These salts are partly carbonates with an alkaline base, partly sulphates, especially of soda and magnesia, not to mention the gypsum, which effloresces from many of the rocks. In Captain Stansbury's report these salt-ponds have been mentioned, and the incrustation of one of them, near Independence Rock, is stated there to be composed of about 58 per cent. of sesquicarbonate of soda, besides sulphate of soda and muriate of soda, which is the composition of the salt called "trona," also found in the natron-lakes of Hungary, Africa, &c.

I took several specimens of such salts in that neighborhood, and have subjected them to a few tests before the blow-pipe. One of them is mainly sulphate of soda, free of carbonic acid and chlorine; another one contains in addition a little carbonate of soda and probably also of magnesia, but no chloride; and a third one sulphate of soda, with a large percentage of carbonate of soda, and some little chloride of sodium, and is similar to the trona mentioned above, although from a different locality.

These salt-ponds, with their concentrated brine, cause the death of large numbers of cattle, which prefer to drink this water because it is salt, and because they always like more to drink from standing pools than from swiftly-running streams. The effect is not sudden, but after the poison has staid some time in the body death follows after a few hours of sickness. The strong and fat are affected as well as the weak and lean. Citric acid and vinegar are said to be antidotes, and we can well account for their beneficial influence; a dose of oil or bacon may likewise be successfully administered.

Coal.—We have seen that coal abounds along Platte River. It is inferior to the stone-coal of the Carboniferous formation, but partly, at least, it is a superior brown coal and a very valuable fuel. In its appearance it is similar to stone-coal, of black color, and mostly great luster, while others present a dull black surface. The streak and powder are dark brown, which is also the color of weathered pieces. When fresh it splits into cuboid fragments, but after being exposed for some time to the atmosphere it becomes laminated. I have not made any tests of the Deer Creek coal, but on a former occasion I have analyzed a coal of the same formation from the Upper Platte River, which closely resembles it (see Lieutenant Bryan's report of 1856), and found in it, by distillation, with slowly increased heat—

45.5 per cent. of fixed carbon;
5.0 per cent. of ashes, partly gypsum;
49.5 per cent. of volatile substance and water.

The coal which I have examined was obtained near the outcrop, and, therefore, not quite fresh. In the interior of the stratum it may be more bituminous. It burned with a long flame, retained its shape in coking, and did not cake at all; on the contrary it split in every direction. The coke was hard and brittle, dark gray, with a metallic luster; it would not withstand much pressure, nor well endure transportation without much loss by slacking. The heating power of such coal is less than that of the stone-coal of the Carboniferous formation, and in weak traveling forges this coal from the outcrops frequently does not afford a good welding heat, but with arrangements specially adapted to it, it can be made to produce the highest heat required in the manufacture of iron. For high furnaces the coke would probably not have sufficient cohesion. It would seem to be less fit for locomotives than for stationary machines, on account of the large grate-surface which it requires; but this obstacle could certainly be overcome.

SECTION IV.

THE GREEN RIVER BASIN.

LIMITS AND GENERAL CONFIGURATION AND FEATURES—NO IGNEOUS AND METAMORPHIC AND PROBABLY NO PALEOZOIC ROCKS—TERTIARY FORMATIONS: THE FORT BRIDGER SERIES—STRATIGRAPHICAL POSITION—SECTION OF THE STRATA—THEIR ORGANIC REMAINS AND EXTENT—THEIR FRESH-WATER CHARACTER AND AGE—THE ROCKS EAST OF GREEN RIVER—THE ESTUARY FORMATION ON BEAR RIVER—OTHER TERTIARY DEPOSITS—CRETACEOUS, JURASSIC, AND TRIASSIC FORMATIONS: IN THE GREEN RIVER VALLEY—ON SULPHUR CREEK—ANALOGOUS STRATA AT THE MOUTH JUDITH RIVER IN NEBRASKA—ON BEAR RIVER AND MUDDY CREEK—AT THE NEEDLES—ON WHITE-CLAY CREEK—ON ECHO CREEK—ON WEBER RIVER AND ITS EAST FORK—JURASSIC FORMATION ON THE SOUTH SIDE OF THE UINTAH MOUNTAINS, ON POTTS'S CREEK AND DUCHESNE FORK—COAL IN SAN PETE VALLEY AND NEAR LITTLE SALT LAKE—THE RED SALT AND GYPSUM FORMATION OF PROBABLY TRIASSIC AGE—ECONOMICAL GEOLOGY—AGRICULTURE—BUILDING MATERIAL—COAL—PETROLEUM—MINERAL SPRINGS—METALLIC ORES—SALTS.

In this section I have comprised the country from the dividing ridge between the Atlantic and Pacific waters, to the eastern limits of the so-called Great Basin. On our line of exploration, it extends from the South Pass to the geological axis of the Wahsatch range of mountains, which passes near Weber River, a short distance beyond the hydrographical axis of that range. It includes the southeastern extremity of Oregon, and the northeastern portion of Utah. I have called it the Green River Basin, on account of the marked basin-shaped configuration of its surface near our route, with the same recent Tertiary strata at its lowest central point on Green River, which gradually rise toward both extremities and crown the dividing ridges at the South Pass and in the Wahsatch Mountains. Its eastern portion, from the South Pass to Green River, and even beyond, presents the character of extensive plains, scarcely interrupted by slight rises of the ground, while the western part embraces the eastern portion of the Wahsatch Mountains, the broadest and most diversified mountain-chain which we have passed on our route across the continent. There the lower formations rise to the surface; the streams have cut out deep valleys and even grand rocky cañons, and subterranean forces have manifested themselves in numerous upheavals and great dislocations of the strata, which are frequently tilted at an angle of 90° and disturbed in every direction.

The eastern portion of the district is a barren waste, rendered so by the prevailing arenaceous character of the formations, the shallowness of the soil in many places, where horizontal strata of limestone and sandstone extend over considerable distances near the surface, and the large quantity of saline efflorescences from the rocks, together with the climatical features of the country; and it would be nearly impassable if it was not for the numerous creeks and rivers which come down from the surrounding high mountains, the Wind River Mountains, the Wahsatch Mountains, the Uintah Mountains, &c., and which along their banks have seams of meadow-land, furnishing subsistence to the animals and relief to the eye tired from the endless dusty sage-barrens and sand-hills. When we approach, however, the foot of the western mountains, we perceive a great change in the vegetation. There are green valleys, diversified with groves of timber, and the mountain-sides and uplands are, besides the wild sage (*Artemisia*), thickly covered with nutritious fodder-grasses, and partly studded with cedar and pine. Still higher up, above the region of the grasses, forests of aspen and pine extend to the loftiest summits, to the region of nearly perpetual snow, greatly enhancing the beauty of the landscape.

In this district we have not found any igneous rocks, although the violent local upheavals indicate their close proximity at various points, and they are prominently developed at the eastern and western borders of the section, nor have we observed any metamorphic and paleozoic strata.

TERTIARY FORMATIONS.

We have observed several formations which we refer to the Tertiary period. Most prominently developed is

THE FORT BRIDGER SERIES,

to which we give that name because Fort Bridger is in the center of the region where it is most characteristically developed and best exposed. This series extends from the South Pass to the divide between Bear and Weber Rivers, thus occupying the greatest portion of this section. Although it consists of several subdivisions, well distinguished by the lithological character of the strata, these are all conformable to each other, and unconformable to the older formations. They are the most recent formations in this section, and we have not found them anywhere disturbed locally by upheavals, but wherever they have been noticed, they exhibit a nearly horizontal position, or rather a slight dip off the surrounding mountains toward the center of the basin. They might, therefore, be supposed to have been deposited after the country had attained its present configuration, but other observations show that this cannot be the case. While they occupy the divides in the eastern ranges of the Wahsatch Mountains and in the South Pass, seams of carbonaceous matter and numerous impressions of plants, *Ferns*, *Equisetum*, &c., which can only have grown on swampy land or in very shallow water, were found many hundred feet lower down in their continuation. Along the valley of Bear River an actual break or fault may be observed. It is evident, therefore, that during and after their formation they have undergone dislocations, not however connected with local outbursts of eruptive masses, and, undoubtedly, coinciding with the great continental upheaval at the close of the Tertiary period. This position of the strata proves that the central and western portion of the continent has not only been raised as a whole solid body, but that the mountain chains, which must have existed as such long before that epoch, have, at the same time, been elevated more than the intervening country. I compare it with the forming of a bubble. The subterranean forces gradually swelled the central part of the continent several thousand feet; the thinner portion of the surface, corresponding to the lowest points far away from the mountains, seems to have yielded most, and to have been raised high as the pressure began. Then those deposits must have been formed. When the pressure again subsided, finding, perhaps, vent in outbursts of igneous masses, and the elevation of mountain ranges at distant points, the bubble collapsed; the mountains, with their granitic centre and base, forming immense solid bodies, retained the position which they had assumed, while the thinner portions of the solid crust yielded more, and resumed the lower position which they still occupy.

This formation, as developed about Fort Bridger, presents the following section in descending order:

1. Arenaceous and argillaceous shales, slates, and shaly sandstones of green color, with interstratifications and concretions of coarser gray and green sandstone, which, at some points, form regular round bodies like cannon-balls. The lower portion contains, also, slaty sandstones and calcareous slates, and thin seams of an oolitic, fetid limestone, forming a transition to the middle portion. The thickness amounts at least to from 200 to 300 feet.

2. Limestones and argillaceous shales, also arenaceous shales, and areno-calcareous slates. The white color prevails. The limestones are partly oolitic, partly subcrystalline, with conchoidal or splintery fracture, partly uncrystalline, earthy, or chalky, also siliceous, arenaceous, and argillaceous; and many of them are fetid on account of the large amount of organic remains which they contain. Over 100 feet.

3. Light colored, mostly white, rather fine-grained sandstones, in thick beds, regularly alternating with mostly light red arenaceous and slightly argillaceous shales, and soft shaly sandstones. Over 200 feet, and perhaps considerably more. These strata may, possibly, be older than Tertiary(?).

The strata No. 1 are peculiarily apt to form prominent bluffs and table-hills, many of which are known as conspicuous landmarks. Generally one of the harder beds of sandstone forms the nearly horizontal top, while in the bare, precipitous sides the shales prevail. These shales are frequently covered with efflorescences of salts. On our road they were most characteristically developed along Black's Fork; they also form the bluffs near Green River, and the upper part of the bluffs around Fort Bridger. They gradually change into No. 2, and while the upper portion appears to contain only few organic remains, the beds of transition and No. 2 are loaded with them. On the banks of Green River I observed, in the fetid oolitic limestone, and the green slates of these beds of transition, remains of fishes, not distinct enough for identification of the species, and obscure impressions of plants; also, crystals of gypsum, and efflorescences of a salt, which proved to be a mixture of sulphate of magnesia and sulphate of soda, while other salts of this vicinity are pure sulphate of magnesia. In the same horizon, near the mouth of Harris's Fork, I observed some gray laminated slates, full of impressions of plants, mostly ferns, and, close by, brown carbonaceous shales, which might, in their continuation, form beds of lignite. The slates, becoming siliceous, form gray, brown, and black compact rocks, with numerous marks of *Equisetum*, &c., and contain seams of fibrose gypsum.

A few feet below them, between layers of green shales, there is a bed of white oolitic fetid limestone, nearly altogether composed of fossils, viz: 2 species of *Melania*, 2 of *Lymnea*, *Unio*, *Planorbis*, &c., a description of which will be found in Mr. Meek's report. The same limestone occurs in the bluff southwest of Fort Bridger (Moore's bluff), and in our collection we have specimens of it from a point 15 or 20 miles southeast of Fort Bridger, at the foot of the Uintah Mountains. Some of the limestones of No. 2, in the quarry near Fort Bridger, contain numerous traces of organic remains, teeth and scales of fishes, &c.

A piece of a fossil leg-bone, about one inch in diameter, which must, therefore, have belonged to an animal of considerable size, was found by a member of the party at the foot of a bluff far south of the road, at the base of the Uintah Mountains. From its green color it is evident that it comes from No. 1, or the beds of transition to No. 2. I was, at the time, unluckily absent on a reconnaissance with Captain Simpson, and was thus prevented from following up this trace, which might have led to the discovery of another of those vast burial-grounds of pre-Adamitic mammalian life, which have made the names of Montmartre and Nebraska famous throughout the scientific world.

On a head branch of Henry's Fork, just beyond the southeast corner of the military reservation of Fort Bridger, some 20 miles from that post, a limestone occurs with a perfectly even conchoidal fracture, and of whitish color, with siliceous secretions, and full of finely preserved *Planorbis*. Although I have not examined that locality, I have no doubt that it is on a parallel with No. 2 of the above section.

Along the road No. 2 forms the lower part of the hills near Fort Bridger. As the strata rise toward southwest, it soon attains the height of the plateau over which the road leads westward. It caps the breaks of Muddy Creek, on Captain Simpson's new road to the Salt Lake Valley, as well as on the old road by Echo Cañon. On the latter it was found a few miles farther on near the crest of high hills, and some strata at the top of the dividing ridge between Yellow Creek and Echo Creek seem to belong to that series.

No. 3 is best exposed in the more elevated western portion of the district. It forms the lower part of the bluffs along Muddy Creek; on the new road, it caps the dividing ridge toward Sulphur Creek, is then interrupted by older upheaved strata, but was found again on the western bank of Bear River, and on the top and on both sides of the dividing ridge toward White Clay Creek. On the old road it also forms the divide toward Bear River, at the Quaking-Aspen ridge, is then interrupted by tilted older formations, extends again from Bear River to the Needles, near Yellow Creek, and beyond forms part of the divide toward Echo Creek, and may extend some distance down that creek. On the western branch of Bear River these strata are found far up and down the stream, extending at least to the mouth of Yellow Creek.

All the fossils in our collection from these rocks are fresh-water forms. In my preliminary report, made at Camp Floyd in December, 1858, I had spoken of the Tertiary formation of Green River as marine. I had done this, before the fossils had been examined, upon the statement of Professor Hall, in Captain Stansbury's report, "that from the South Pass to Fort Bridger the collections are all of marine Tertiary age," which, if taken in connection with the remark of Captain Stansbury himself, that on Ham's Fork very perfect shells were collected, can scarcely be referred to any other formation than that in question. Moreover, some fossils which the same author had figured in Colonel Frémont's report, and described as probably marine shells, closely resemble some of this series, although we now think that they rather represent the estuary deposits described below.

The examination of the fossil remains has not furnished proofs from which to decide upon the subdivision of the Tertiary period to which those strata belong; but from their general character, compared with those further east, we are inclined to consider them as formed in the middle of the Tertiary epoch. No. 1 may correspond to the green, shaly series overlying the Lignite formation on Platte River above Fort Laramie, but they may just as well be altogether different, and deposited in separate basins. At another point of this district we have found beds characterized by their fossils, according to Mr. Meek, as estuary and Eocene Tertiary, which are tilted and appear to be unconformable to these, therefore, more recent strata.

From the sandstone series, No. 3, no fossils have been obtained. As nearly all the older formations on the eastern slope of the Wahsatch Mountains, from the detritus of which they must have been formed, are prevailingly arenaceous, we cannot find it strange that they should lithologically resemble portions of them and still be more modern. Wherever observed they are conformable to Nos. 1 and 2, and unconformable to the older rocks. On the Quaking-Aspen ridge they cap unconformably the strongly tilted coal-bearing strata, and on Bear River, near the mouth of Sulphur Creek, they are nearly horizontal, like everywhere else, while close by the estuary strata are strongly tilted. Although they present the general character of a somewhat older formation, this close connection with the Fort Bridger strata seems to indicate that they belong to the same geological horizon, and are only little older, perhaps Eocene. However, although they differ lithologically from the sandstones in the upper part of the Cretaceous Lignite formation, on the Upper North Platte River, near Bryan's Pass, they may possibly be coeval with them; that is, Upper Cretaceous. The greenish, shaly sandstones, which appear to cap them there (see Lieutenant Bryan's expedition, 1856), may correspond to the green series No. 1 (?). We cannot determine whether they are of marine or fresh-water origin.

From Green River eastward, the lithological character of the formation changes somewhat, although it apparently forms the continuation of the Fort Bridger strata. The prominent table-hills, near the South Pass, must be composed of the equivalents of No. 1. On the summit, and especially on the western slopes of the pass, above Pacific Springs, strata crop out, which I consider as the continuation of No. 2, but which contain a great deal more arenaceous material besides the lime, and perhaps, in consequence thereof, attain a greater thickness. They form a series of white arenaceous limestones and calcareous sandstones, with interstratifications of loosely cemented arenaceous shales and fine sand. Some of the harder ledges are compact siliceous limestones with oolitic portions, like those further west; but they are mostly a mixture of sand and carbonate of lime, and closely resemble some of the strata of the Ash Hollow series. (Section II.)

Red and green and brown coarse shaly sandstones, below the Pacific Springs, and at several points further on, appear to be a local development of the formation, near the foot of the higher mountains. Along Big Sandy I noticed arenaceous and some argillaceous shales, and lower down, some 20 miles from Green River, compact sandstones overlying fine-grained shaly sandstones of white, yellowish, and brown colors. These strata probably form the continuation of No. 3, but present a different appearance, and resemble much more the rocks overlying the Lignite formation on the upper course of North Platte River, east of Bryan's Pass, which there reaches beyond the dividing ridge into the Green River Valley.

Between the South Pass and Green River a great deal of fossil wood was observed strewn over the surface, all silicified, and some of it changed into transparent agate. It evidently comes out of this formation, probably from No. 3, and Captain Stansbury, who followed a road some miles distant from ours, actually observed some fossil trees imbedded in such sandstones, the trunks of which measured nearly 2 feet in diameter. Near there, we find stated in that report, some imperfect specimens of *Nautilus* were collected, which would indicate a marine formation, if we may not presume that these fossils either came from a drifted bowlder, or from a limestone corresponding to our No. 2, in which large *Planorbis* are found, which, when badly preserved, may readily be mistaken for *Nautilus*.

THE ESTUARY FORMATION ON BEAR RIVER.

On Bear River, near the mouth of Sulphur Creek, I observed light-colored shaly slates, gray argillaceous shales, and some strata of sandstone and limestone. The latter is partly light yellowish, coarse-textured, wholly composed of fossils, partly dark-gray slaty, also full of shells, and quite fetid. The outcrop is much covered over by detritus. These strata are considerably tilted; at one point they trend from northeast to southwest, and dip under a high angle to southeast. West of them we find the strata of the lower series of Fort Bridger, with only a slight dip; east of them, a succession of sandstones, to be described hereafter, also strongly disturbed, nearly vertical; but the disturbed condition and imperfect exposure of the rocks prevented me from tracing the exact relations between those different formations.

The fossils collected from these beds belong to the genera *Unio*, *Corbula*, *Melania*, *Paludina*, and *Melampus*. They characterize the formation as a brackish-water or estuary deposit, without any strictly marine forms. Mr. Meek, to whose report I refer for a more detailed enumeration and description of the fossils, among which there are several new ones, considers these strata as decidedly Eocene-Tertiary. The similarity of their organic remains, and their connection with the sandstone series east of them, with *Ostrea glabra* and lignites, indicate that we have here beds formed under similar circumstances with those near the mouth of Judith River, in Nebraska, of which Dr. Hayden has given an account, under the direction of Lieutenant Warren, Topographical Engineers.

These estuary beds are undoubtedly older than the Fort Bridger series, because the beds No. 3 overlie, unconformably, the upheaved mountains of which they form part, on the divide on the old road east of Sulphur Creek; and I hesitate to yield to the paleontological deductions of Mr. Meek in regard to the Tertiary age of this formation. Although, as I have stated, its stratigraphical position is not quite plain at the point where I have observed it, it appears to be closely allied to the sandstone series with *Inoceramus*, *Ostrea glabra*, and coal, which is Cretaceous, most probably Lower Cretaceous, and I am inclined to consider it as an estuary local development in that Cretaceous series. In regard to the analogous deposits of the Judith River, the reader will recollect similar doubts were expressed by Dr. Hayden and Professor Leidy in various communications to the Academy of Philadelphia. Estuary deposits are naturally scarce in all formations, but we have no reason to doubt the possibility of their existence at any horizon; and our knowledge of their fossil fauna is so very limited and so full of startling possibilities, that I am inclined to regard these paleontological deductions as less reliable, especially where few and new species are concerned, because the precedents are few.

I have noticed the formation only at a single locality. In Colonel Frémonts' report, however, Professor Hall describes a fossil from Uintah River, near latitude 41°, longitude 111°, as *Cerithium tenerum*, which is by Mr. Meek considered as identical with a *Melania* from these estuary beds, and a *Turbo* and *Natica* (?) from a point on Muddy Creek, below the crossing of the Salt Lake City road, apparently identical with *Paludinas* from Bear River, while the description of the lithological character of some of the strata of these localities rather corresponds to No. 2 of the Fort Bridger series.

Besides the two formations which have just been described, we have observed some local deposits overlying, unconformably, the older rocks, which, on that account, we provisionally refer to the Tertiary period. On Porter's Creek, the main southern fork of White Clay Creek, and less prominent on the latter stream, we find siliceous conglomerates apparently filling depressions in strata which are probably of Cretaceous age. They are composed of hard sand rock and pebbles of quartz, all rounded, varying in size generally between a hen's egg and a man's head, and imbedded in little sandy matrix, which, although easily yielding to main force, well resists destruction by atmospheric agencies. These conglomerates, therefore, form remarkable turreted bluffs and pinnacles. Their color is mostly gray. Some are brownish or reddish. They must not be confounded with the conglomerates interstratified in that older series of rocks, which have a similar appearance, but generally a more calcareous matrix. Occasionally they include more sandy portions irregularly interspersed, and on White Clay Creek I noticed them underlaid by a few strata of sandstone and shale, both together capping, unconformably, the older sandstones. No fossils have been found in connection with them.

Covering the Tertiary formation, I noticed frequently, especially on the edge of high ridges, bowlders of siliceous rocks, highly-altered sandstones, and the like, some of which contained traces of fossils which appear to be Carboniferous forms. They probably originate from the high mountains in the western part of the Wahsatch range.

CRETACEOUS, JURASSIC, AND TRIASSIC FORMATIONS.

I have already mentioned the possibility of the Upper Cretaceous age of No. 3 of the Fort Bridger series, and the probably Cretaceous age of the formation on Bear River. Along our route no strata are exposed which lithologically correspond to the Nos. II and III of the Cretaceous rocks of Nebraska; but farther south, at Bryan's Pass, I had previously observed them on the dividing ridge, beyond which they probably extend westward into the Green River country, together with the Cretaceous Lignite formation overlying them in that vicinity, and to which the coal strata appear to belong which Captain Stansbury observed at various localities on Bitter Creek. Still lower down on Green River the Cretaceous formation appears to be largely developed.

In the eastern part of the Wahsatch Mountains the Upper Cretaceous beds are not represented, except possibly by No. 3 (?). Sandstone formations prevail there entirely, consisting of more or less compact sandstones, some of which are conglomeratic, and of arenaceous and argillaceous shales, with only a few strata of limestones. Their thickness amounts to many hundreds, perhaps thousands, of feet, and their color is alternately white and red. These strata represent different epochs, the. Tertiary, Cretaceous, Jurassic, and Triassic. Still, their lithological character is so uniform throughout, their stratification so much disturbed, and organic remains were obtained at so few points only, that I have not been able to draw distinct limits between them. Those of the sandstones which appear to belong to the Tertiary formation, and are distinguished from the others by their unconformable stratification, have been described above as No. 3 of the Fort Bridger series.

Underlying these latter, and in close contact with the estuary beds near the junction of Sulphur Creek with Bear River, we find along Sulphur Creek a considerable succession of white sandstones, interstratified with red and gray slaty sandstones and arenaceous and argillaceous shales. Some of these contain conglomeratic seams. They trend from northeast to southwest, and are strongly, some of them even vertically, tilted. A short distance below the crossing of the creek, on the old road, a heavy bed of reddish siliceous conglomerate forms a rugged outcrop over the crest of the hills. Close by, probably overlying it and dipping at a very high angle to southeast, I observed a yellow sandstone with *Inoceramus* similar to *I. problematicus*. A few yards farther east, above the crossing, prominent strata of white, rather fine-grained, soft sandstone, also varying only a few degrees from the vertical to southeast, contain large numbers of *Ostrea glabra*, another species of *Ostrea*, and an *Anomia*, which, by their abundance, make the rock fetid. It is immediately succeeded by coal, the nearest stratum of which is several feet thick, while at least one more follows within a few feet of the first, and is separated from it only by some gray argillaceous shales, but covered over with detritus, and not well exposed. The shales beyond it attain a considerable thickness. Another upheaval, northeast from there, then interrupts the regular succession of the strata, which seem to swing round, and to re-appear higher up the creek with reversed dip, trending from south-southwest to north-northeast, and dipping to north-northwest. At least I observed there a similar sandstone with numerous *Ostrea*, and although I did not see the coal, the supposed place of which, above the sandstone, is occupied by the bed of the creek, I found an indication of it in a hepatic spring, the like of which issues near the first coal. They apparently originate from pyrites in these coal-beds. A spring of petroleum also issues in the continuation of these strata a mile southwest of the crossing of Sulphur Creek, which latter has derived its name from those springs of sulphureous water.

The coal and the sandstone with the *Ostrea* are unquestionably members of the same formation, and the doubt in regard to that implied in a passage of Mr. Meek's report, would never have been expressed if the writer had examined that locality himself, and also the analogous one on White Clay Creek, which leaves no room for questioning the position of the coal in the middle of the sandstone series.

The paleontological evidence seems to point to the Lower Cretaceous (or even Jurassic) age of this formation, and by general considerations I am, likewise, led to consider it as such. It may be an equivalent of those strata which Dr. Hayden, on Lieutenant Warren's expedition, observed at the mouth of Judith River (see Proceedings of the Academy of Philadelphia, May, 1857), which are likewise in close connection with an estuary formation, but appear to be developed on a much smaller scale. They are also strongly tilted, contain coal and *Ostrea glabra* besides other fossils, and were regarded by Dr. Hayden as probably on a parallel with the lowest portion of No. 1 of his section of the Cretaceous rocks of Nebraska, though he suspected from the presence of a *Hettangia* that they might be older.

From the crossing of Sulphur Creek these strata, forming a ridge in the direction of their trend, extend southwest to the East Fork of Bear River, striking it about 1.5 miles below Captain Simpson's road, where the coal must again crop out. They also continue in the opposite direction, forming considerable mountains north of Sulphur Creek, when their trend changes more to north and finally to north-northwest, and they strike Bear River a second time near the mouth of Yellow Creek. In consequence of another disturbance, they crop out again east from there on Muddy Creek below the crossing of the Salt Lake road, where Colonel Frémont found the coal. Captain Simpson discovered it also on White Clay Creek, below the mouth of Porter's Fork, where I observed again, in connection with it, heavy beds of white sandstone with the same *Ostrea*. The latter occur likewise on Weber River, about 1.5 miles above the mouth of White Clay Creek, and again 1 mile below the point where the road, turning westward, leaves Weber River; but I did not find there any coal with them.

Strata of a similar character are exposed at numerous other points. Nine miles west of Bear River they form the Needles, on Yellow Creek, composed of strongly-tilted white and gray, compact, siliceous sandstones, which are partly fine-grained, partly coarse-grit stones, and conglomeratic, and interstratified with mostly reddish shaly strata, arenaceous shales, and shaly sandstones. Most prominent there, is a heavy mass of light-colored conglomerate, composed of rounded siliceous pebbles of the size of hen's and pigeon's eggs with only a few larger ones, thickly disseminated, together with gravel, in a mortar-like matrix. It forms the rugged crest of the hills from which they have received their name. This elevation trends toward the head of White Clay Creek, on which the same rocks were observed near the upper forks, also standing on the edge and partly even tilted beyond the vertical. The dip of the strata along that creek is not uniform, and the slopes are partly covered, so that I was prevented from obtaining a section; but as the dip generally varies between southwest and west we may presume that we come to higher strata the farther we descend the creek, and that those at the upper fork and at the Needles probably correspond to those on the east fork of Weber River near the point where I obtained Jurassic fossils. Some miles below the upper forks, in high mountains on the south side of the creek, yellowish conglomeratic sandstones crop out, also one of a dull reddish color, strongly dipping to west-southwest, and lower down a considerable thickness of alternations of impure whitish sandstones and light-colored argillaceous shales, conformable to the former and likewise containing conglomeratic seams. Near the mouth of Porter's Fork we reach the coal-bearing sandstone mentioned above, and then white sandstones, alternating with red arenaceous slate and red shales. At the lower end of the cañon, the red color predominates; but thence down I noticed again white sandstones, interstratified with gray shales, similar to those above the coal, and perhaps the same strata, because there has been a disturbance and a change of the dip, which is there generally toward west or northwest. Near the mouth of the creek these strata are capped by heavy beds of white sandstone with conglomeratic portions.

Several thick beds of conglomerates occur in this district, though mostly there are only single seams of pebbles within the beds of else rather fine-grained sandstones, not forming separate strata, which indicates that changes in the force of the currents must have taken place while the single beds were deposited. The frequent occurrence of conglomeratic masses proves, besides, that a shore-line cannot have passed far from the present Wahsatch Mountains, which existed probably before the Jurassic and Cretaceous era, although not in their present outlines. This is rendered still more likely by the absence of Jurassic and Cretaceous strata west of these mountains, as will appear from the following section V.

From the mouth of White Clay Creek to Echo Creek, a distance of 5 miles, the same formation continues, with conformable stratification and a slight dip to west and northwest, so that we advance to higher strata. Part of these are brick-red, probably forming the continuation of the red beds at the lower end of the White Clay Creek cañon. Near the mouth of Echo Cañon purple conglomerates are largely developed, and nearly horizontal. They form for some miles high vertical turreted bluffs on the north side of the cañon, while the south side generally presents steep but covered slopes, with only few exposures of rocks, which dip strongly to west-northwest. I was doubtful whether the red conglomerates were conformable; in some places they seem to be so, in others not; but I rather think that they are a local later deposit. The valley is evidently one of erosion, and not one of eruption, with anticlinal strata, as has been stated by others. Some miles farther up, white, yellowish, and dull-reddish, partly conglomeratic, and mostly purer siliceous sandstones form both sides of the cañon, probably corresponding to the lower series, which is exposed also on the upper part of White Clay Creek. Their dip is still to west-northwest, but moderate, although variable. Still higher up we find the divide capped by the sandstones, No. 3.

On Weber River, above the mouth of White Clay Creek, the same formation continues; but the uniformity of the stratification is interrupted in consequence of the proximity of the igneous rocks, which form the limits of this section, and at several points come to the water's edge. Within a short distance I observed the strata dipping to north, west, east, and northwest. From the mouth of Silver Creek to Kamas Prairie the dip is uniformly strong to northwest, and we gradually come again to lower strata, although the ridge of dioritic porphyries west of the river runs nearly north and south. This would rather indicate the pre-existence of the igneous rocks; still, other observations show conclusively that the eruption of part of them, at least, dates after the deposition of the sandstones, and at a comparatively recent period, or else we would not find their tufas, in apparently horizontal position, filling portions of the river valleys which are eroded in these stratified rocks.

Near the point where the road to the Timpanogos leaves the valley of Weber

River, I observed a layer of an impure limestone, with imperfect indications of fossils, but I did not succeed in finding a single specimen from which to identify the formation. Else, the character of the strata is unchanged.

In the northeast corner of Kamas Prairie, at the mouth of the cañon of the East Fork of Weber River, I noticed a gray, very compact, calcareous rock, and up that stream more light-red and gray compact siliceous sandstones, somewhat altered by metamorphic action, and some shaly strata. The cañon follows for a long distance, although not throughout, the trend of the strata, the dip of which varies between north and west-northwest, and is partly very strong, 60° and 70°. Some miles up that stream I found pieces of a gray altered limestone, evidently from an outcrop close by, with numerous traces of organic remains. Although I could only obtain some imperfect *Pecten*, *Ostrea*, and *Pentacrinus*, these, taken together with all the other circumstances, leave scarcely room to doubt the Jurassic age of the formation. (See Mr. Meek's report.)

The high mountains between this point and the head of White Clay Creek, which I crossed with Captain Simpson and a small reconnoitering party, are covered all over with soil, timber, and undergrowth, and therefore afford few data to the geologist. A few red escarpments were observed at a distance near the summits of the Uintah Mountains, of which more will be said below. On the summit of the trail, between Porter's Fork and the East Fork of Weber River, I observed some large masses of white granite, apparently not far out of place.

On another reconnaissance with Captain Simpson, in the summer of 1859, from Round Prairie, on the Timpanogos, to the Uintah River, I obtained a view of the continuation of the Weber River formations south of the Uintah Mountains, where they appear to be a little differently developed, with less conglomeratic portions, although the close connection between the two is evident at the first glance. The axis of the Uintah Mountains bears from east to west at a right angle to the Wahsatch Mountains, and although they may have a center of igneous rocks, and owe their origin to their eruption, these do not appear prominently in the general outlines of the chain, and besides the few blocks of granite mentioned above, I have only noticed near our trail, at their junction with the Wahsatch Mountains, some of the same dioritic porphyries which form the ridge west of Weber River. From north and south stratified rocks cover their slopes, and rise toward the summits, where they form a crest remarkable for its horizontal outlines, with deep intervening chasms and apparently high vertical walls of mostly reddish color.

Near the pass from the heads of Coal Creek, a tributary of Timpanogos River, to Potts' Creek, an affluent of Duchesne Fork of the Uintah River, the ridges are all strewn with pieces of white, highly altered, compact sand-rock, but the first stratum in place, just beyond the summit, is a siliceous conglomerate, followed by red sandstones and conglomerates, and red arenaceous and argillaceous shales, several hundred feet thick, but not well exposed. Near the summit I also obtained some imperfect fossils in a gray limestone, apparently *in situ*, which, however, could not be identified. These red strata are apparently the same which cap the Uintah Mountains farther east, and I have been doubtful whether they occupy a high or low position in the series; in other words, whether they correspond to the Lower Jurassic or Triassic formations which appear to be considerably developed farther south, or to those much more recent strata which we have observed before in the cañon of White Clay Creek, and on Weber River above Echo Creek. The observations in the field were not quite decisive on that point, and the presence of both formations may be accounted for with some degree of plausibility; but the weight of evidence is rather in favor of the more recent age of these rocks. Apparently, the same strata are prominent south from there, and at a much lower level, on the Red Fork of Uintah River, which from these has received its name.

The following is an enumeration of the strata which were observed along Potts' Creek, in descending order, and, although necessarily incomplete as a section, it shows the general character of the formation:

1. Several hundred feet of mostly red sandstones and conglomerates, and red arenaceous and argillaceous shales, with perhaps some strata of limestones. Not well exposed.

2. White, hard sand-rock, only exposed in a short outcrop.

3. Dark red friable sandstone.

4. Some gray slate, mostly argillaceous.

Farther down the creek the lower strata are better exposed, and we find:

5. A considerable thickness of mostly light reddish sandstones, but also white ones.

6. White calcareous shales and slates, and some limestones, some of which are fine-grained with an even fracture, others of an oölitic structure. They contain numerous traces of fossils. I obtained there some joints of *Pentacrinus*, and fragments of *Pecten* and *Ostrea*, which indicate that this rock belongs to the Jurassic age.

7. Light reddish quartzose, not very hard sandstones, probably several hundred feet thick. In an interstratification of finer material I observed numerous *Gasteropoda*, but their generic characters were obliterated.

8. Strata of quartzose sandstone, varying in color from white to red, and of different degrees of hardness, several hundred feet thick. At the junction of Potts' Creek and Duchesne Fork they form high precipitous bluffs, and are there mostly white and exceedingly hard, and some of them contain a large percentage of lime.

These are the lowest strata observed on this river. Continuing down Duchesne Fork we change our course more to the south and southeast, in which direction the strata dip, and we pass them, therefore, in reversed order. I observed successively Nos. 8, 7, and 6. Then followed for several miles, partly corresponding to No. 5, and, perhaps, also to the higher numbers, more loose shaly strata of mostly white color, alternations of generally arenaceous shales, and shaly sandstones, with some more prominent strata of white sandstone, which series reminded me much of some rocks on White Clay Creek and Weber River, and are most probably the same. They are succeeded by a great thickness of white and brick-red sandstones, with much less shaly portions. Where the Spanish trail comes in, we find heavy beds of white soft quartzose sandstone, with only thin intercalations of shales, some of which are red. The river here makes a bend to the east, parallel to the trend of these strata, which therefore continued for many miles along the stream, forming shelved rocky bluffs, some of which may be 300 feet high. For the last 10 miles to the mouth of Duchesne Fork the hills along the river are low, and probably correspond to the lower portion of this white sandstone series.

I have remarked above that Colonel Frémont obtained some fossils on Uintah River, some distance above Duchesne Fork, which apparently correspond to the estuary beds of Bear River, or possibly to the No. 2 of the Fort Bridger series.

The coal has not been observed here; but most likely it exists in the bluffs hidden by detritus, or else at a level not much different from that of these strata. Beds of coal occur at various points farther south, in the Wahsatch Mountains and allied ranges. I have not had an opportunity to examine any of these localities, but from all the information which I have been able to gather I have little doubt that their geological position corresponds to that of the White Clay Creek coal.

On San Pete Creek, a tributary of Sevier River, which in its upper course runs from north to south in a longitudinal valley of the Wahsatch range, several strata of coal have been discovered near the Mormon settlements of Manti and Ephraim, near latitude 39° 25′, and are worked to a limited extent. Governor Brigham Young, in a letter dated 1855, and published in the Deseret News, states in regard to them: "The upper outcropping vein is 3 feet 4 inches thick, and rests upon a stratum of rock below which is another vein from 22 to 24 inches thick, below which is a vein of beautiful coal 5 feet thick;" and the following is an extract from an official report of Brevet Lieutenant Colonel Ruggles, Fifth Infantry, to Brig. Gen. A. S. Johnston, commanding Department of Utah, of a tour of service in San Pete valley, 1859:

"About midway in the mountains bordering the valley on the west there are mines of bituminous coal of apparent considerable extent. The principal stratum is full 4 feet thick, and it crops out at an elevation of nearly 1,000 feet above the valley, and it dips west-southwest at an angle of about 20°. There were five coal strata visible, and the series is surmounted by a well-defined stratum of chalk about two feet thick."

This latter rock resembles the chalky beds of the Upper Cretaceous rocks in Northeastern Kansas. It appears that this valley is situated similarly to that of Weber River, near the geological axis of the Wahsatch range, and the limits of the district belonging to the Great Basin.

We are also credibly informed of the existence of a similar coal in the mountains east of Little Salt Lake and Cedar City; and sandstone formations, probably corresponding to those described above, occur at various localities along the road from Utah Lake to Virgin River.

Red strata, with gypsum and rock-salt, have been observed at numerous points south from our line of survey in the Wahsatch Mountains and their southern continuation. I have not examined any of them, and the red color alone would by no means be a proof of their Triassic age, less so here than in other districts, because we have seen that red sandstones and arenaceous and argillaceous shales pervade all the formations. But if we consider the large development of the Jurassic rocks, in connection with the remarks made in section III in regard to the great extent of the Triassic formation south and east, and their interstratifications of gypsum and salt, there is little room to doubt the Triassic age of these beds, unless we should consider them as Lower Jurassic.

Colonel Frémont, in his report of 1844, mentions that rock-salt is found some miles south of Uintah River. In Captain Gunnison's and Dr. Schiel's reports, red strata, with salt and gypsum, are mentioned from the neighborhood of his trail over the Wahsatch Mountains. In the report of Brevet Lieutenant Colonel Ruggles, it is stated that a stratum of rock-salt has been found in the mountains bordering San Pete Valley on the east, some 20 miles south of Manti, and that it is also represented to have been found in the mountains forming what is known as San Pete Cañon, about 50 miles from the first locality, imbedded in reddish marly clay. Some specimens of it were secured for our collection by the kindness of General A. S. Johnston and Colonel Crosman, Quartermaster-General's Department, United States Army.

From a report of Assistant Surgeon Dr. Charles Brewer, United States Army, of a march from Camp Floyd to the Virgin River in 1859, we learn that beds of gypsum are found near the mouth of Salt Creek Cañon, not far from the town of Nephi, and that red sandstones and shales were noticed at numerous points of the route.

From all these data we may safely conclude that the formation which is now generally, and with much good reason, although without unquestionable proof, referred to the Triassic era, is largely developed in the region of the Wahsatch range, south of our route.

ECONOMICAL GEOLOGY.

Agriculture.—I have spoken above of the desolate character of the Green River region. Still there are numerous points along the river and its tributaries, especially west of it, where cultivation would prove successful. A heavy growth of sage generally indicates a fertile soil, deficient in humidity, and by irrigation this want can be supplied. The lower portion of the Green River Valley, near Brown's Hole, compares in altitude with the Salt Lake region, and the climate of the two does not appear to differ much.

Higher up, toward the Wahsatch Mountains, we find more fertile valleys, like that of Black's Fork, near Fort Bridger, Fort Supply, where Mormons had settled some years ago, the head branches of Henry's Fork, and others, but their altitude above the ocean, being about 6,500 feet, is too great, and their climate, therefore, too cold. The growing season is very short, and the crops are frequently damaged by early snow-storms. Only such plants can be cultivated to advantage as require a short season for their development, and are generally adapted to a much more northern climate; and even they may occasionally be destroyed by the frequently occurring night-frosts in the middle of summer. Settlements in this part of the country will, probably, have to rely upon supplies from outside, and cultivation will scarcely be carried beyond stations put up for some special purpose other than agricultural.

Building material.—Rock, lime, material for brick and adobes, and also timber, are plentiful throughout this district, or can be procured at a moderate cost. Wood, for bridge-building, might be rafted down Green River.

Coal.—I have mentioned above that, according to Captain Stansbury, Topographical Engineers, thick beds of coal crop out south of our road, at various points on Bitter Creek, an eastern affluent of Green River, which are probably a continuation of the coal of North Platte River, which has been discussed in section III.

The Sulphur Creek coal, when fresh, is perfectly black, and has the luster of stone-coal, but it has a brown streak, and is only a superior brown coal of more recent age; weathered pieces are brown, and look much like the coal from Deer Creek (section III); it appears, however, to be of better quality. Captain Stansbury mentions it, in his report of explorations in the valley of the Great Salt Lake, as a bituminous coal, pieces of which, although much weathered, burned in a camp-fire with a bright, clear flame. I had no opportunity to obtain quite fresh pieces, as the outcrop was much covered up; but General A. S. Johnston, commanding Department of Utah, had it tried, and found it so useful for blacksmithing that he secured the locality as a military reservation. To judge from the weathered pieces, it is, however, inferior to the San Pete coal. It contains some sulphur and gypsum. It would be easy to get many thousands of bushels of this valuable material in an open quarry. The Muddy Creek coal is undoubtedly a continuation of the same beds, and the coal of White Clay Creek is, also, the same, or holds a similar position.

The coal from San Pete Valley is the best I have seen west of the Mississippi River coal-basin; but, as the pieces that I saw from there had been obtained by mining from the interior of the stratum, it cannot well be compared with the weathered pieces from Sulphur Creek. It is a bituminous, black coal, with a brown streak, and closely resembles bituminous stone-coal, and as it cokes somewhat it is well adapted to the same purposes. It contains some gypsum; otherwise no analysis has been made of our specimens. At Camp Floyd, it has been extensively used for blacksmithing, and the workmen informed me that it gives an excellent heat, but leaves much ashes, and is inferior to the bituminous coal of Pennsylvania. As this coal may be considered as occurring on the border of the Great Basin, more will be said of it in section V. If a railroad should be built across the continent in this latitude, the coal of the Wahsatch Mountains will obtain paramount importance.

Petroleum.—The spring of petroleum, near the continuation of the Sulphur Creek coal-bed, one mile from that creek, has been mentioned above, and before by Captain Stansbury. He found, in an open country, several small, shallow depressions in the ground, filled with some rain-water, and oil and tar. The fresh oil is green; by exposure it seems to be changed soon into tar of dark-brown color and aromatic taste. This tar, more hardened and somewhat mixed with soil, forms the bottom and sides of the spring. Seldom more than two or three gallons will accumulate, and I could scarcely succeed in filling one bottle with a spoon, because some people had taken it off a day or two previous. Emigrants and Mormons collect it as wagon-grease, and as a liniment for bruises, &c. By boring, I suppose, a considerable supply of the oil might be secured.

Mineral springs.—We only know of the small springs, a few miles west of Muddy Creek, on the old Salt Lake City road. Their water contains some carbonic acid and some salts, and tastes not unpleasantly. It deposits some calcareous tufa, which, at one of the springs, is colored red by a little iron.

Metallic ores were not observed, and the geological formations are such that it would be rather an exception to find any ores associated with them.

Salts.—I have, above, mentioned beds of gypsum and rock-salt, in strata of probably Triassic age; but, as part of them appear to reach beyond the limits of this section, into section V, more will be said of them hereafter.

Efflorescences of salts, on shales and slates, in the neighborhood of Green River, have also been mentioned in the foregoing.

SECTION V.

THE DISTRICT OF CENTRAL AND WESTERN UTAH (NOW WESTERN UTAH AND NEVADA).

LIMITS AND GENERAL CONFIGURATION—THE IGNEOUS ROCKS, THEIR CLASSIFICATION AND AGE—METAMORPHIC AND ALTERED ROCKS—THE STRATIFIED ROCKS—UPPER CARBONIFEROUS AND PERMIAN, LOWER CARBONIFEROUS, DEVONIAN, AND OLD RED, SILURIAN FORMATIONS—THE VALLEYS—THEIR LACUSTRINE ORIGIN—BENCHES AND WATER-MARKS—RIMS OF TUFA—THE DRAINAGE OF THE LAKES A CONSEQUENCE OF EVAPORATION—SPRINGS AND CREEKS—BRACKISH WATER—SUBTERRANEAN RESERVOIRS—HOT AND MINERAL SPRINGS—WARM SPRINGS IN ROUND PRAIRIE, IN KOBAH VALLEY, ON WALKER RIVER, &c.—IMPROVEMENTS IN THE SUPPLY OF WATER—ARTESIAN WELLS—TANKS—WELLS—SOIL AND VEGETATION—AGRICULTURE—MINERAL WEALTH—GOLD, SILVER, LEAD, IRON-ORE, NATIVE SULPHUR, SALT, GYPSUM, SULPHATE OF SODA, SULPHATE OF MAGNESIA, NATIVE ALUM, MINERAL SPRINGS, STONE-COAL, TOPAZ—GEOLOGICAL STRUCTURE OF THE SUCCESSIVE MOUNTAIN RANGES PROGRESSING FROM EAST TO WEST.

On crossing the summit of the Wahsatch Mountains, coming from the east, a section of country is entered altogether different from that on the other side. Its peculiar aspect is pre-eminently derived from a change in the geological formations, and the physical features in general. It forms a part of the region which has been called "The Great Basin," because it has no drainage to the ocean, as all the streams originating there are lost again within its limits, and which comprises all the country between the Wahsatch range to the east, the Sierra Nevada to the west, the divide of the waters of the Columbia to the north, and those of the great Colorado to the south and southeast.

The name "Great Basin," however, gives a wrong impression of its hypsometrical condition, for the profile of the country shows that its outskirts are less elevated than the central portion, which is a lofty upland, with numerous gigantic mountain ranges, equaling in height the Wahsatch Mountains and the Sierra Nevada, while in the southern portion the surrounding heights do not attain a considerable altitude. The surface, moreover, is divided into many systems of drainage, disconnected with each other.

This whole region, as far as it is known, seems to present similar features throughout, which are only modified by the varying elevation of its sections. As other portions of it have been described before, I may confine myself to a few remarks in regard to its general features along our line of travel, between latitudes 39° and 41°, from longitude 111° 25′, near Weber River, to longitude 119° 41′, in Carson Valley.

The whole must be regarded not as composed of separate mountain chains, but as one system, one great continental swell, the relief of which has been shaped by numerous parallel fissures and corresponding mountainous upheavals, running nearly north and south. Of the latter, some consist of stratified rocks, others of stratified rocks with a nucleus of igneous rocks, and still others, altogether, or nearly so, of igneous rocks. Some of them extend continuously, with a considerable elevation, over many miles to unknown distances, others fall off, and are succeeded by others, which cannot be regarded as their immediate continuation, but are rather independent ranges of similar character.

An examination of the eruptive masses leads to the conclusion that, although raised according to one system, the mountains cannot have been called into existence by one great violent effort, but that their formation has occupied a considerable period, probably with intervals of comparative rest; also, that eruptive rocks, and consequently considerable in equalities of the surface, existed long before the parallel ranges were formed.

In the single mountain chains the forces frequently did not exhibit themselves uniformly along their whole axis, but acted with locally more or less increased intensity, thus forming sporadic centers of elevation, from which spurs run out in various directions across the valleys. Such sporadic upheavals are not confined to the principal ranges, but are sometimes independently and irregularly interspersed between them. Thus the general parallelism of the ranges and valleys is not uniformly preserved, but the configuration is much modified by local irregularities.*

Afterward, this compound serrated mountain-system has been partially covered with lakes and large inland seas (some of the more southern and lower portions perhaps by the ocean). The detritus from the mountains filled the valleys partially, forming there lacustrine deposits, and producing that peculiar shape which they now present, after the water has gradually receded, from causes of which we shall speak below. Where the country was less elevated, the lakes naturally covered a large area and the waters subsided slower, burying beneath the accumulating deposits the lower portion of the mountains. In this way only the tops or crests of the mountain ranges have been left standing out like islands in a sea, forming what is now called "Lost Mountains," or "Island Mountains." In this case, then, many of the intercepting barriers became covered, and from a number of separate valleys one main valley was formed.

The disproportion between the mountain masses, alone able to retain atmospheric moisture, and the bottomless accumulations of detritus in such districts, increases the general barrenness of the country to a great extent, and makes it an absolute desert.

*A look at the profile will enable us to account to some degree for the configuration of the surface, as I have described it above. It is well known that the whole continent has been shaped by powerful upheaving forces, which have operated on a line running mainly from north to south. Their duration may have been an extended one, perhaps beginning in the Cretaceous epoch and ending with the beginning of the present era. That corresponding depressions must have taken place in other parts of the globe, may be inferred. Now, we see from the profile that the whole area, from the Missouri River to the Wahsatch Mountains, was elevated as one solid mass, and was disrupted in a few places to the utmost, and, the western or California slope being short, the whole strain occasioned by the upheaval was concentrated on the central portion of the bubble, the basin, and only participated in in some measure by the California slope. The rocks were evidently unable to resist the strain thus created from east to west, and fissures broke open from north to south. They are not quite uniform, because the elevation continued slowly, perhaps during thousands of years, and new fissures opened at various times, wherever the solid surface resisted least, either in the line of or near the older fissures, or independent of them. It cannot surprise us that there should be some running even from east to west, although these are scarce, and not near our line of explorations. As soon as the surface split open, fluid masses from the interior burst out, forming mountains of igneous rocks, and tilted the stratified rocks, which had formed the sides of the fissure.

If we take in account also the rugged and precipitous character of its mountains, naked, or scantily covered with a growth of stunted timber, and the monotony of the expansive valleys, with their dreary sage-barrens, the picture of the country is complete.

IGNEOUS ROCKS.

We find in this district igneous rocks of various description; granite rocks, dioritic porphyries, trachytic porphyries, trachyte (?), phonolitic rocks, greenstone, basalt, pitchstone, lavas, obsidian, pumice, and numerous intermediate forms. They exhibit a close alliance with formations beyond the limits of the Great Basin, in the Sierra Nevada, the Coast ranges, the Colorado Basin, and portions of Eastern Utah.

The systematic grouping of the igneous rocks, according to their analogous composition, the different minerals which they contain as essential and accidental components, and their mode of aggregation, forms an instructive branch of geology, because all plutonic rocks formed within certain, mostly extensive, periods and limits generally bear evidence of it in their composition. They are similar to each other, and belong to the same group, the more so the nearer they approach each other geographically, originating from the same hearth. The history of the igneous rocks of a region, and their relation to the stratified rocks of the different formations, form as essential a part of the geology of a country as the history of the extinct organic life; both together only make the whole.

This department of geology has hitherto been much neglected, because no satisfactory system of classification has ever been fully established. Still, several most distinguished mineralogists and geologists have led the way in Europe, especially Prof. G. Rose, of Berlin. One of the principal obstacles to the study of the igneous rocks is the necessity of numerous and difficult analyses of the feldspathic minerals, which are of primary importance for a systematic classification. An omission in this respect led some of the most noted geologists to make different statements in regard to the composition of the rocks from one and the same locality, and, again, to use the same name for differently composed rocks.

This branch of geology seemed to require special consideration, in a country where a variety of igneous rocks predominate, but it was impossible to gather sufficient material from a hurried examination along the route, the more so because the stratified rocks all belong to a few of the older formations, and are, therefore, affected in the same way by all the more recent protrusions of igneous rocks, however different the respective age of these may be; nor have I had time and means to study the specimens sufficiently and make the necessary analyses, still less to compare them with those from other countries. From a preliminary examination of the large number of specimens, over 160, I have formed some conclusions which I give below, and which we submit for further investigation.

The granitic rocks within the limits of my observations may be readily distinguished from all other igneous rocks of the district. They are the oldest, and do not merge into any of the others. They form the bases of some of the most prominent mountain ranges. I found them in the Wahsatch Mountains, near longitude 111° 50′, and latitude 40° 27′; in the Goshoot Mountains, longitude 114° 05′, and latitude 39° 42′; in the Pe-er-re-ah range, longitude 116° 50', and latitude 39° 30'; in the Se-day-e Mountains, longitude 117° 30', and latitude 39° 13'; and in the Sierra Nevada, in the Carson River Cañon, longitude 120°, and latitude 39°. Rocks of granitic (?) appearance, but of doubtful character, occur also in the Mon-tim range, longitude 115°, latitude 39° 50'.

Mr. Marcou, in his report on Captain Whipple's route, near parallel 35°, although not entering much into the subject, makes distinctions in regard to the age of the granites of different ranges, and I, too, am inclined to consider some of the granitic rocks of this section as much more recent than the normal granites.* My specimens from the Sierra Nevada contain a good deal of green hornblende, besides the mica, which gives them a character not met with, to my knowledge, in the true granites of the eastern hemisphere. Similar granites have been observed by Mr. Blake, near Fort Miller, in Southern California.

The granitic rock from the Wahsatch range, east-northeast of Camp Floyd, is composed of albite, (?), quartz, and green mica, and appears to me much nearer allied to the rocks of the dioritic group, which are of more recent age.

All the other igneous rocks of the section are found merging into each other. I shall confine myself to describe some of the most characteristic ones, and point out their relation to others.

In the Wahsatch range, between the Weber and Timpanogos Rivers, we find a very instructive series of rocks, some of which have the appearance of normal trachyte, or seem to be allied to the andesite, while they probably are porphyritic diorites.†

Prof. Gustavus Rose remarks "that one might be frequently induced to group the dioritic porphyries of this continent together with the andesite which belong to the trachytic group, and is generally more recent than the diorites"; and "that the age and general development of the American dioritic rocks does not seem to differ much from that of the trachytes, while in other countries they approach more the granitic group."

My observations seem to confirm this remark, and I might be inclined to consider this series of rocks as trachytic, if the feldspar, which they contain, although similar in appearance to some varieties of the glassy feldspar, did not differ from it in the degree of fusibility. An analysis would be required to determine its mineralogical position.

I will give a description of the most characteristic specimens of this series:

No. 151 of the collection, from the summit between Silver Creek and Timpanogos River. This rock may be regarded as the most normal of these porphyritic diorites. It has a dark-gray, granular, highly quartzose matrix, which, under the microscope, is

* The name of "granite," has, by some writers, been applied, very loosely, to all rocks of crystalline texture and more or less massive structure, of igneous as well as metamorphic origin. Systematic terminology, however, requires that this name should be confined exclusively to eruptive rocks, forming a crystalline aggregation, essentially of orthoclase, oligoclase, mica, and quartz. They form one group with the syenites, and certain analogous porphyries. They are also not known, with certainty, to have disturbed any strata younger than the Upper Carboniferous.

† Normal trachytes, according to Rose, are mainly composed of glassy feldspar and hornblende, in a feldspathic matrix, without quartz. Quartzose varieties have been separated as trachytic porphyries. Andesite is formed of oligoclase or andesine, hornblende, and brown mica, in a highly quartzose matrix. The diorites are a crystalline aggregation of oligoclase or labradorite, and greenish hornblende, or according to others of albite and hornblende, sometimes with quartz. The matrix of dioritic porphyries frequently contains mica besides these minerals.

dissolved into minute crystals. It contains many small crystals of a white feldspar, also dark-brown mica, and less distinct, but very numerous throughout the matrix, slender columns of dark green hornblende.

No. 149. From the immediate neighborhood of No. 151. It is much less crystalline, more subcrystalline and uneven on the fracture. The matrix is grayish-green (or rather a mixture of bright green, dark brown and white, the colors of the single minerals), with many minute crystals of a greenish-white feldspar, and reddish-brown columnar mica. The small crystals of the latter may, on superficial examination, be readily mistaken for hypersthene. No other minerals are crystallized out.

No. 150. From the same locality; stands between the two preceding ones.

No. 146. From the high conic mountain at the northern end of Round Prairie. The weathered surface is reddish-brown. The gray matrix, granular, and composed nearly altogether of microscopic crystals; it is thickly studded with mostly small crystals of dark-brown mica and some quartz, which is more frequent in the matrix. No hornblende is crystallized, at least not large enough to be recognized.

No. 147. Near the locality of the former. It is the same rock more completely crystallized. It contains little matrix, and besides the feldspar and quartz, and the lamellar hexagonal columns of brown mica, slender columns of greenish-black hornblende can well be distinguished.

No. 148. From the same place. It has again much more dark matrix. The crystals of feldspar are less numerous, but larger; the mica is dark-green, the matrix quartzose, and hornblende could not be distinguished.

No. 152. From the divide between Weber River and Silver Creek. It is a compact, granular, dark-gray rock, more light-colored near the weathered surface. The white feldspar and the hornblende are imperfectly crystallized. Small spots of oxide of iron indicate that more hornblende, or probably mica, has decayed. Other pieces are a little better crystallized.

No. 131. From near the same locality. It contains only little whitish matrix, and is mostly feldspar in tabular crystals, in its appearance much like some glassy feldspar or sanidine, together with many columnar crystals of dark-green hornblende, mostly thin, and a few laminæ of brown mica. This specimen has quite the appearance of a trachytic rock, but still I must consider it a diorite.

No. 153. From Weber River, below Silver Creek. It has only very little gray matrix between the coarse crystals of feldspar, the bright hexagonal laminæ of brown mica, and the grains of quartz. This rock is nearly granitic.

From the above we see that the minerals taking part in the composition of this group of rocks are: a feldspar, dark brown mica, quartz, and dark green hornblende. The latter was found only in well-crystallized specimens, and the want of one or the other of these constituents in some of the rocks must be considered as local. It seems, however, that the more the mica prevails and is well crystallized, the more does the hornblende disappear and quartz come in. This is a rule which has frequently been noticed with rocks of a much older group, the various syenites. We also see how unsafe it is to base upon one specimen, perhaps indiscriminately picked up, any conclusion on the general composition of the igneous rocks of a district, by which we might be enabled to recognize a contemporaneous formation at a distant point.

No. 132. From the hills west of Kamas Prairie. Is a dull gray, finely vesicular rock. It shows a great tendency to crystallization, containing numerous minute, indistinct crystals, of a blackish-green mineral, probably hornblende (not olivine), and some laminæ of brown mica. It may be a vesicular form of the rock No. 152, and belong to the same group, although its lavatic appearance seems to point to a more modern origin.

Rocks similar to one or the other of this series have been found in various localities—near Simpson's Spring (No. 178); in the McDowell Mountains (No. 385); in Butte Valley (No. 240); and especially in the western part of this section, in the Se-day-e Mountains (Nos. 293, 295, and 341), and near Carson River (Nos. 318, 320, 333, 334, and others). They are all composed of a feldspathic matrix, with crystals of feldspar, and either hornblende alone, or hornblende and mica, quartz and mica, or hornblende, quartz, and mica, subject to the same law of mutual substitution. Still I am not certain if all these rocks belong to the same group. The feldspar in some of them may be the glassy feldspar, sanidine, which is characteristic of the trachytic group. They would then have to be called trachytes, trachytic porphyries, and trachytic lavas.

The extreme type of another class of rocks is to be found in No. 181 of the collection, a porphyritic rock from Simpson's Spring, on the eastern rim of the Great Salt Lake Desert. In its compact matrix light pink and white are mixed. It contains numerous crystals of mostly dark-colored quartz, and, somewhat less prominent, but also in large quantity, crystals of light greenish feldspar, orthoclase, with highly perfect cleavage in three or four directions, and, with difficulty, fusible at the edges, before the blowpipe. I also notice many small scales of dark green mica. In some portions of the rock pink prevails, and in others a light greenish-yellow, without any red; but in all the varieties the crystals of quartz are most prominent. This porphyry, if observed alone, might readily be considered as one of the old porphyries, allied and coeval with the granitic group; but I find in the collection a series of specimens which show that it is allied to rocks of a much more modern appearance, and prove, beyond doubt, its close connection with the trachytic porphyries. The feldspar of the other rocks belonging to that group exhibits a more glassy fracture, and a cleavage which is not so perfect in all directions. Most similar to it is the porphyry from Good Indian Spring, in the McDowell Mountains (No. 382), and specimens from Eagle Valley and Carson River, near the Sierra Nevada (Nos. 326, 316, &c.). Allied rocks were frequently met with. The quartz in many of them is highly brittle and perfectly crystallized in hexagonal double pyramids. Others show a certain want of cohesion, which is uncommon with older rocks. This group was found merging, by intermediate forms, as well into the preceding series, as also into others described below, so much so that the position of single specimens becomes doubtful.

Another extreme type is represented by specimen No. 222, from the Ungo-we-ah range. It is a porphyry, with a fine, chocolate-colored matrix and even fracture, inclosing numerous small crystallizations of white feldspar, besides which only minute black particles, probably of hornblende, could be distinguished.

Similar rocks have been found largely developed in many of the mountain-ranges.

The exact nature of the feldspathic mineral could not be determined; it does not seem to be orthoclase or sanidine; perhaps it may be albite. In their general appearance they approach nearest the dioritic porphyries. They do not generally contain quartz or mica, though exceptions are occasionally found, and thus, as well as by close geographical proximity, they merge into the other rocks of the district, especially in those described last.

Most of the rocks of adjoining districts, sometimes described as trap porphyries, must probably be referred to these two groups.

Besides these principal eruptive formations, we find numerous rocks of the pitchstone family, mostly filling veins or forming, at least, other evidently later effusions. Their color is brown or black, with a resinous or semi-vitreous luster. They are generally brittle, and contain water as an essential component; when heated they intumesce and smell fetid. Part of them contain crystallizations of feldspar, probably also zeolitic minerals.

Various other rocks were found, more subordinate and confined to only a few localities, viz, basalt, phonolite, greenstone, pumice, obsidian, and others. They will be described in a subjoined enumeration of the single mountain ranges. Of these rocks, the basaltic, at least if they really should be such, belong to a group entirely distinct from those mentioned before.

Such rocks, which we are used to consider as the products of acting volcanoes—pumice and scoria, have also been formed long before the present era. According to Mr. Blake, pumice, scoria, and charcoal occur imbedded in the Miocene Tertiary strata of California. Therefore their presence cannot be regarded as a conclusive evidence of recent volcanic action, though such may in reality have taken place.

The apparently complete want of distinct limits between these groups of rocks, essentially differing in their extreme types, and their merging by intermediate forms, by steps more gradual than are frequently found with rocks of the same group and locality, has also been observed by Mr. Th. Antisell, in the Sierra Nevada and the Coast Ranges (Pacific Railroad Report, vol. vii). It leads to the conclusion that the subterranean agencies must have been operating during a greatly prolonged period, with intervals not protracted enough to allow a material change in the condition of their hearth. The mineralogical character of the rocks seems to indicate that their formation began prior to the Tertiary period, and continued to the present era. This inference is corroborated by evidences drawn from the relative dislocations of the strata of the western continent. Single portions of the Coast Ranges of California and the Sierra Nevada have undoubtedly been raised at different periods (not considering the first upheaval of the Sierra Nevada by the granitic eruptions). The subdivisions of the Tertiary formation hold there different relative positions at different points, besides being raised, at least partly, from 2,000 to 3,000 feet above their original level. The great dislocations of the strata in and east of the Rocky Mountains also prove that such disturbances have taken place at various times prior, during, and after the Tertiary period; and they seem to have reached their climax in the eruption of these various rocks.

By further investigation we would, probably, be enabled to draw more distinct lines of separation between the different groups, and assign to them their relative age.

METAMORPHIC AND ALTERED ROCKS.

Metamorphic rocks, such as gneiss, mica schist, clay-slate, and others, are but sparingly distributed over this section, and seem to be mostly confined to the immediate proximity to the granites. They occur in the Wahsatch range, the Goshoot Mountains, the Montim range, the Black Mountains near Carson River, &c.; but only in the Sierra Nevada they are more considerably developed. The stratified rocks all over the district have, however, undergone great changes by the influence of the igneous eruptions, either directly, by mechanical force and heat, or by chemical agencies accidentally connected with the outbursts, such as alkaline waters, &c. They have been tilted, and brecciated, and baked; secretions of siliceous matter have been produced, and agate and jasper formed. In numerous places sandstones have been altered into compact flint rock; in others, they have assumed a porphyritic appearance, in consequence of a beginning secretion of crystalline quartz from the siliceous matrix, which has attained a uniform, even texture. I only mention specimens No. 273, from Kobah Valley, and No. 288, from Reese's River.

In slaty rocks such a change cannot be easily traced, because, by being similarly affected, they at once assume the aspect of truly eruptive rocks; and an appearance of stratification cannot be regarded as conclusive evidence of the sedimentary origin. It may be the result of the peculiar circumstances under which a fluid mass has cooled, or of successive volcanic effusions. I have observed several instances where igneous rocks formed what appeared to be regular diversified strata, one above the other, requiring a careful examination to convince me that the rocks were not originally aqueous sediments, and altered or semifused, but truly eruptive. In other instances the distinctions are less obvious. Igneous rocks in such thin strata, like those in veins, generally exhibit a different appearance from those in larger bodies, because they have cooled quicker in contact with cold surfaces, whereby the free play of the molecular attraction and the separation of the constituent minerals is impaired or even forced into a different direction. Instances of that kind will be mentioned in the description of the single ranges of mountains.

In the deserts east of Carson Lake I have observed a mountain of white dolomite, apparently altered from a dark-gray magnesian limestone, which still forms part of the mountain in an unaltered state. For a full description, see below.

STRATIFIED ROCKS.

Little has been known before of the formations in Western Utah, not even along the traveled routes. On the geological map of Professor Hall, in the Report on the Mexican Boundary Survey, a large portion of it is colored as metamorphic, and the remainder is left blank. In Captain Beckwith's report merely "limestones" are mentioned occasionally, but their age had not been determined. That Upper Carboniferous limestones occurred near Salt Lake, was the only fact satisfactorily established. From our investigations in the field and our collections, much important information has been derived. They have largely contributed to our knowledge of the extent and development of the geological formations, and have also proved the existence of some not hitherto known so far West. Referring to Mr. Meek's report, I will confine myself to some general remarks, and describe the rocks more fully in the subjoined enumeration of the single mountain ranges.

Stratified rocks of the Paleozoic age were found extensively developed many hundreds of feet in thickness. A large portion of them belong to the Upper Carboniferous formation, the existence of which near Salt Lake had been proved by Prof. I. Hall, from collections brought in by Captain Stansbury and others. It is principally composed of dark gray and bluish siliceous or silico-argillaceous limestones, with silicious or calcareous slates, and some siliceous or calcareous sandstones.

With this series of rocks, as exposed in the Timpanogos Cañon, west of Lake Utah, I found fragments of *Lepidodendron* in a slate rock, and in the same mountains also a series of bluish-black argillaceous shales, containing a great deal of carbonaceous matter. Captain Simpson obtained there some pieces which are a mixture of such shale with small particles of brittle anthracite. From this we infer that the waters there at one time must have been shallow, and dry land probably near, and that conditions must have prevailed favoring the growth of coal-plants, although, perhaps, not sufficient to produce strata of coal. Examining the shales at several points, I found the carbonaceous matter only disseminated in small particles, but in other places it may be more frequent, and concentrated in pockets, and even strata of coal.

As the indications of coal of true Carboniferous date are more favorable there than at any other point examined in the far West, they ought to be followed up. The question whether stone-coal of the Carboniferous age exists here is of superior importance at the present time, when the communication by rail with the Pacific States has become a political necessity. Even if a railroad should not be located in that immediate vicinity, a thorough investigation of the subject would be desirable. If coal was found in one place, geologists would be enabled to trace it to distant points, even where it is now concealed by overlying formations or recent deposits.

In San Pete Valley, about one degree of latitude farther south, in the same mountain range, a coal has been found superior to any which I have seen west of the Mississippi coal-basin, and which would furnish a most valuable fuel for locomotives. I have not examined the locality myself. It might perhaps be a true stone-coal, and be connected with the above shales; but from all that I have been able to learn about the formation, I am confident that it is an equivalent of the Sulphur Creek coal of more recent origin, and associated with the rocks which are developed on the eastern slope of the Wahsatch range. (See section IV.)*

The Upper Carboniferous strata, wherever observed before in the western portion of the continent, seem to have been formed at the bottom of a deep ocean, which precludes the formation of coal.† Prof. I. Hall, in his Report of the Geological Survey of Iowa, vol. i, part i, p. 138, and also in the Report of the Mexican Boundary Survey, vol. i, makes use of the following language: "The conditions favorable for the production of an extensive deposit of marine limestone are not such as usually accompany the production of coal. * * * The evidences of the existence

* This opinion has since proved correct.

† Mr. Blake, in a paper read before the American Association, has stated the existence of coal-plants in the south-eastern portion of the Rocky Mountains, but the proceedings have not yet been published.

of this ocean in the far West and Southwest during the coal-period amount to almost a proof that the conditions of that area, which now constitutes a part of this continent, were never such as to admit of the production of coal-plants, and the deposition of such materials as make up the Coal-Measures, at least during the latter part of the Coal-Period. In regard to the earlier part of that period, or the time in which the Lower Coal-Measures were formed, we have not at present the means of fully deciding what were the conditions of the central or southwestern part of the continent."

On the other hand, no decidedly Lower Carboniferous strata have ever been found in those regions before, and we have, therefore, been unable to speak with certainty about the non-existence of stone-coal in the western Coal-Measures, the lower portion of which, the equivalent of the coal-bearing rocks of the Mississippi Valley, might have escaped observation in the far West. Not far from the locality of the shales, I have found Lower Carboniferous strata, and the supposition is obvious that these shales might hold an intermediate position as lower members of the Upper Carboniferous or Coal-Measure series. I have not been able to obtain a section, nor to trace the Upper and Lower Carboniferous strata to their line of connection, and, therefore, cannot express a definite opinion in this respect. The shales certainly hold a position not very high in the series, but I doubt whether they correspond to any particular horizon in the Upper Carboniferous rocks of the East.

The upper division of the rocks on Timpanogos River, consisting mostly of light-colored sandstones, some siliceous limestones, and a few red, shaly strata, is characterized by some fossils, which Mr. Meek finds analogous to Permian forms. The difference of their lithological character from that of the Upper Carboniferious rocks lower down in the cañon, favors the supposition that they are distinct from them and actually of Permian age, but the evidence is not conclusive.

Our collection contains fossils which point decidedly to the Lower Carboniferous period as the age of a series of rocks in the immediate vicinity of Camp Floyd, west of Lake Utah. These rocks are also dark-colored, impure limestones, slates, and sandstones. Part of them are much like some of the rocks in the Timpanogos Cañon, while others are much more siliceous, and the fossils are also converted into silex and badly preserved. Among them occurs the spiral axis of an *Archimedes*, a decidedly Lower Carboniferous type, and the first specimen of this fossil yet found in the region of the Rocky Mountains. At many other points strata have been observed, to which we attribute the same age.

Further west, between longitude 115° and 115° 30′, and latitude 40° 10′ and 39° 20′, there is a series of hills and mountains, trending nearly north and south, also made up of rocks of the Carboniferous age, but of a very different lithological appearance. They are several hundred feet in thickness; mostly light-yellowish, more or less arenaceous and argillaceous limestones, with an earthy fracture, also light gray, subcrystalline, siliceous limestones, and a great deal of light-yellowish, arenaceous, and calcareous slates.

The limestones are highly fossiliferous, and the greatest portion of them undoubtedly Upper Carboniferous; but other strata from the outskirts of this formation, not, however, much differing in appearance, are considered by Mr. Meek as perhaps Lower Carboniferous. Distinct limits could not be drawn.

Devonian strata have also been found at several points, and as far west as longitude 115° 58′, and latitude 39° 53′; that is, 1,200 miles farther westward than they have hitherto been found *in situ*, as far as it is known to us. We have good reason to believe that they exist also at an intermediate point in the Medicine Bow Mountains or their neighborhood. (See section III.)

The Devonian rocks are also blue limestones and slates, and do not differ essentially in their lithological character from rocks of the Carboniferous formation. A considerable development of siliceous conglomerates and sandstones, found at a higher level than the Devonian rocks, apparently occupy the position of the Old Red of the English geologists.

As yet we have no conclusive evidence of the existence of Silurian strata in this district; but there is a considerable development of magnesian and siliceous limestones, which circumstantial evidence leads me to consider as belonging to that formation. They contain only a few fossils. Some fragments of *trochiform* univalves, and some coralline forms found in them, do not afford a sufficient criterion, but are not unlike some from Silurian strata of the Mississippi Valley.

West of 116° of longitude these stratified rocks nearly disappear. Indications of them have been found at various points beyond; but they are so thoroughly altered by the influence of the igneous rocks, that no traces of fossils could be found; nor could I decide whether they are altered beds of the Paleozoic formations, or perhaps of a more distant age.

No strata of a period more recent than the Paleozoic have been found in the mountain ranges, along our line of exploration, with the exception of some quite recent formations. If they have ever been formed they must have been swept away entirely. Information communicated by Dr. Charles Brewer, United States Army, seems, however, to indicate that more recent, perhaps Triassic or Cretaceous, strata extend into the basin from the east, across the southern continuation of the Wahsatch range.

No marine Tertiary strata have been observed like those which occur in the southern lower portion of the basin. All the more recent deposits in the valleys are evidently lacustrine and local.

By the numerous pluto-volcanic eruptions the stratified rocks have been much disturbed. In the single mountains they are tilted in every possible direction and degree. Their dip is frequently reversed several times within short distances, and great contortions and faults must have been occasioned. Moreover they exhibit a great sameness in appearance throughout, and are generally badly accessible, and only at long intervals. No section could be obtained under these circumstances. The thickness of these Paleozoic strata, however, is very considerable. Hundreds of feet have been observed of each one of the formations mentioned above, and the whole must be measured by thousands.

THE VALLEYS AND THEIR LACUSTRINE FORMATIONS.

The extensive valleys occupy about half the area of the whole district. Besides some outliers of the igneous and older stratified rocks of the mountains, we find in them indurated strata only at a few points, and these are mostly stratified horizontally, and of evidently lacustrine origin. They impart no peculiar character to the valleys, most of which have derived their configuration from lakes and inland seas, which must have covered a large portion of this country within the present era, after the last great geological changes had taken place, and the continent had attained its present outlines. The valleys are generally formed by corresponding slopes, steeper near the mountains, and so gradually converging toward a center, that it would frequently require instrumental observations to decide whether the ground is horizontal or inclined. In some places we find wide flats many miles in extent. Part of these valleys are not immediately connected with water-courses, but form separate basins, and, when of considerable length, they are subdivided by a rising ground into a number of smaller ones. Others have a regular descent in their longitudinal direction, and a drainage on the surface, sending large volumes of water to lower points, especially during the season of melting snow, while later in the season most of the creeks dry up entirely.

Besides their general shape we have other numerous evidences that large bodies of water occupied the valley at a former period. At some points, as stated above, we find horizontal strata. No fossils have been noticed in them, but their petrographical character clearly indicates a recent origin. Such strata, for instance, were found in Kobah Valley, where it is interesting to observe how the drainage toward Pah-hun-nu-pe Valley was finally effected by the erosion of Swallow Cañon. In many of the valleys regular "benches" of shingle and detritus have been formed along the surrounding heights, and around the Island Mountains, indicating a former beach, sometimes of considerable width. They frequently appear as distinct water-marks of equal height all around. A striking evidence of this kind is found in the Salt Lake Valley, where such a bench-mark can be seen at a glance, extending continuously nearly 20 miles, and more than 200 feet above the present level of the lake, while others are lower down. Captain Stansbury mentions a place at the northern end of Salt Lake where he counted 13 such successive benches, the highest 200 feet above the valley, and he states that the water-marks extend to near the summit of Frémont's Island, which is from 800 to 900 feet high. Less distinct, but still easily recognizable, such benches were observed in most of the valleys, though not in so large number.

Instead of benches, we find at some points a continuous rim of calcareous tufa along the mountains, also proving conclusively a higher state of water at a former period. This was observed especially on a branch of the Great Salt Lake Desert near the Fish Springs, and in the neighborhood of Carson Lake. Such formations may also exist unnoticed in many corresponding localities. They can be readily distinguished from the tufaceous deposits of springs, as noticed at other points of the route. Interesting deposits of this kind and on a more extensive scale have been described by Mr. Blake from the Colorado Desert, in Lieutenant Williamson's Report of the Pacific Railroad Explorations.

The material composing the bottom of the valleys, although differing according to local circumstances, is generally such as cannot well have been formed in any other way than as the slowly increasing deposit of a quiet water. Except in the immediate vicinity of the mountains, where coarser fragments of rocks are mixed with it, it consists of very fine sand or clay, and is mostly an areno-argillaceous impalpable material of light buff-color. Near Camp Floyd, in Cedar Valley, where I had an opportunity to examine more closely, the upper stratum and soil is a finely arenaceous loam; the subsoil very rough, and still more sandy, and exceedingly hard when dry. They make excellent "adobes" or sundried brick, the usual building material of the country. Lower down it changes into nearly pure, very fine sand, with only a few particles of clay. This, when dry, does not appear sandy, but forms compact pieces which readily absorb water and thereby become plastic, though only slightly coherent; a little more water causes it to dissolve into single grains of sand. In such beds, from a depth of 40 feet, we obtained a number of minute fresh-water and land shells belonging to the genera *Spherium* (*Cyclas*), *Lymnea*, *Helix*, *Amnicola*, &c. Near Camp Floyd, so-called saleratus-clay is found (saleratus is an expression frequently used in that region instead of salt, the latter name being reserved for the common salt, the chloride of sodium), a bluish-gray arenaceous clay, in which salts form white crystallizations, films and nodules, mostly consisting of sulphate of magnesia, and a little sulphate of lime and common salt, perhaps also sulphate of alumina combined with the sulphate of magnesia to alum. (See below.) Similar clays are widely distributed. Also coarser sand occurs, in some places like a regular beach; in others, again, as drift-sand or deep, coarse sandy soil.

It would be superfluous to enumerate all the single observations which confirm the theory of the prevailing lacustrine formation of the basin. That the country adjoining Salt Lake and Carson Lake has once been covered with water must strike every observer. Captain Stansbury, in speaking of the Salt Lake Desert, remarks: "These plains are but little elevated above the present level of the lake, and have, beyond question, at one time formed part of it. An elevation of but a few feet above the present level of the lake would flood this entire flat to a great distance, thus forming a vast inland sea." If a rise of the water of a few feet would have such an effect, what would not be the effect of an increase of several hundred feet to the highest water-marks?

We can entertain no doubt that such was the condition of the country at the beginning of the present era, after the last great geological changes had taken place. The position of the latest Tertiary strata, capping the highest summits of the adjoining Wahsatch Mountains, proves that great revolutions have taken place at the close of that period, while the deposits of the basin exhibit not the slightest signs of a disturbance, and occupy exactly such places as they would take, and present such features as they would assume, if those agencies were renewed which led to their formation; in other words, if the country was again covered with water.

The disappearance of the water is connected with the generally increased aridity of the southwestern portion of the territory of the United States, numerous evidences of which have been adduced by all explorers. Some have tried to explain the subsidence of the water by volcanic eruptions and consequent changes of the level; but this explanation, although it may apply to single cases, is by no means satisfactory. Volcanic eruptions would only throw the water to some other point, and not effect a decrease of its quantity; and even if one basin was thus drained, numerous others would be left. Where a region of the size of the Great Basin is concerned we must look for agencies of a more general character. Others explain the disappearance of the water by subterranean outlets. Such outlets may exist in some instances, but it is impossible to assume a subterranean outlet for every sinking creek or river, especially for those nearer to the center of the district. The sinks of all the rivers have bad water in consequence of an accumulation of salts; and the water of Salt Lake is even a concentrated brine, notwithstanding the continual affluence of large volumes of fresh water by the Jordan, Bear River, Weber River, and others. If there was an outlet, the salt water would be carried off, and the lake would become a fresh-water lake.

No such suppositions are required to explain the subsidence of the waters since the beginning of the present era. We only need to examine into the natural course of events. By applying the physical laws, we find that it is all the consequence of the geographical situation, and the topographical features of the country. Evaporation is the great agency which produces so startling effects.

We have a mountainous district with numerous lakes and vast inland seas, elevated from 4,000 to 6,000 feet above the level of the ocean, and surrounded by mountain-ranges as many thousand feet higher, beyond which, to the north, east, and southeast, mountains and elevated plains extend for many hundred miles; while on the west and southwest sides the ocean is nearer, but separated from it by a gigantic range of mountains, the summits of which tower high above the clouds. The country all around will then be well supplied with moisture; soil will be formed and covered with plants best adapted to its properties and location. At such an elevation above the ocean the air is thin, the evaporation fast. Part of the vapors will be condensed again in the same district and on the neighboring mountains, but the remainder will be carried beyond and lost irreparably, feeding rivers which run away to the far-distant oceans. The climate of the country to the north, east, and southeast is too dry, even if we make allowance for a better state of things at that time, and the ocean too distant, to make an adequate return; while, to the west and southwest, the high mountains turn off the clouds, and effectually prevent the passage to the basin of more than a very limited amount of moisture; moreover, as their eastern base is much higher than the western, they will more favor the egress than the ingress of clouds. The loss will be small at first and scarcely felt; but taking place continually through hundreds of years, the effects of it will gradually begin to show themselves. The depth of the waters will diminish inch by inch and foot by foot; the shallowest spots will become dry, but still the country around will be sufficiently supplied with moisture, and capable of sustaining, vigorously, vegetable and animal life. Such seems to have been the condition while human beings lived on this continent. Traditions point to the country around these seas as the home of powerful tribes, which afterward, as the country became more and more inhospitable, emigrated to the south. The remains of ancient towns in New Mexico and Southeastern Utah, of the origin of which, and of the time when they were inhabited, the present generation has no knowledge, seem to indicate a more prosperous condition of the country in former times. It seems also to be an established fact, that then a much more vigorous vegetation existed in some of the central portions of the continent, the remains of which are still found where now only a stunted growth of desert plants scantily cover the barren waste. Volcanic eruptions may have been the immediate cause of the desolation of single spots, but we must look to agencies affecting more equally the whole country, in order to explain the changed state of the present time.

The quantity of evaporated water decreases not in the same measure, as the shallowest places become dry, and therefore the surface of the water becomes smaller, but the quantity of condensed moisture and the humidity of the surrounding country decrease proportionally. The air becomes more dry, and the evaporation, instead of actually decreasing proportional to the surface of the sea, will rapidly increase, and the shore-lines become more and more contracted. The springs, creeks, and rivers will be reduced or discontinue altogether, and the surrounding country become barren and depopulated. Thus the present condition of the basin was produced.

In the southern, less elevated, but warmer, portion of the basin the state of things is even more unfavorable. The quantity of atmospheric precipitation there is merely nominal.

SPRINGS AND CREEKS.

In the spring the snow melts in the mountains, and also the little that is in the valleys and has not disappeared before by evaporation. The water then naturally abounds on the surface. At this time the fissures and clefts of the rocks, the reservoirs from which the springs are fed during the remainder of the year, receive their supply of moisture. Rivulets and creeks run down in every direction. Many of these sink in the absorbent sand of the valleys as soon as they reach the foot of the mountains. Others continue on even to more distant points, until they sink or join larger water-courses.

The water absorbed at one point frequently returns to the surface at a lower place, forced up by an impervious stratum of clay or by a rocky barrier, especially where a valley is contracted by projecting spurs of hills or a branch valley unites with the main valley. Often the water sinks again immediately after the barrier has been crossed, within a few yards of its rise. At other points the water regains the surface because the sand is saturated to its full extent. Thus secondary springs are formed, frequently in the shape of ponds.

At this season the valley deposits absorb a great deal of water, and become miry or overflown at numerous points. During the other seasons the affluence is smaller, many creeks and springs discontinue, and the subterranean reservoirs, formed of the sand at the bottom of the valley which has been saturated in the spring, are emptied by evaporation, and by supplying the springs and creeks with which they connect.

The creeks and rivers form either lakes, the water of which disappears by evaporation, and the surplus of it is absorbed in the wet season by the adjoining sand-flats, or they dry up gradually and sink in the thirsty sand without even forming lakes.

The aridity of the climate and consequent amount of evaporation may be judged from the fact that during our survey the difference between the dry and the wet bulb thermometer frequently indicated a nearly complete absence of moisture in the atmosphere. This was observed even on the shores of Carson Lake and in Carson Valley, at the immediate foot of the Sierra Nevada, under the shadow of its stately pines, with miles of overflowed meadow-land before us.

Most waters contain more or less impurities, from the gradual decomposition of the rocks and soils which they percolate. In consequence of their continued evaporation, impurities and salt substances have considerably accumulated in many valleys, and form efflorescences on the surface. Thus the secondary springs, which issue at low points in the valleys, are frequently impregnated with salts, and all the lakes formed by the sinks of rivers contain bad water.

The mountain springs are in some instances highly calcareous, and some of them deposit considerable tufa. Some others are brackish, containing salts from the decomposition of pyritiferous slates or from other sources. These are partly unfit for use during the dry season, while they may be sweet and palatable during spring, when they run more copiously and mixed with the waters from the melting of the snow.

Although there is a great deficiency of water in general, numerous springs are found at distances convenient for the traveler, especially in the higher portion of the country. Various causes co-operate there to afford a permanent supply. Foremost in this respect is the great elevation of several of the mountain ranges. They retain snow on their summits during a great portion of the year, which not only supplies the springs directly, but also favors the precipitation of atmospheric moisture. Near the highest mountains thunder-storms gather, and rain falls much more abundantly than in wide valleys. By their very bulk they are also enabled to retain more moisture, and thus they afford a more permanent supply than minor ranges. The numerous disruptions of the rocks afford the water access to greater depth, and by a reversion of the dip bring it back to the surface at points which would be devoid of water without. Some of the finest permanent springs on the route are thus formed on the line of contact between the stratified and igneous rocks.

The sinking of the water in the sand favors its preservation. These subterranean reservoirs are impenetrable to the heat, and the water can only evaporate slowly as it rises to the surface by the capillary action, while, if exposed to the open air, it would rapidly disappear. Without this provision not only many springs would be entirely deprived of their supply, but also a general decrease of moisture would take place. A point must be reached where the quantity of water in the basin is so small that the loss by vapors carried beyond its limits is balanced by the gain of atmospheric moisture from outside. We are unable to decide whether this point has been reached or the quantity of water is still diminishing, which is said to be the case in the Salt Lake Valley.

HOT AND MINERAL SPRINGS.

There are also numerous warm and mineral springs in Central and Western Utah, several of which have long ago attracted the attention of travelers, and have been described by Dr. Wislizenus, Colonel Frémont, Captain Stansbury, Captain Beckwith, and others, to which I refer. I only mention the Beer and Steamboat Springs on Bear River, the numerous hot-springs at the western foot of the Wahsatch Mountains, the Hot Sulphur Springs at the eastern base of the Humboldt Mountains, the Boiling Springs near Mud Lake and in the Honey Lake Valley, &c. The water in most of them contains carbonate of lime, sulphate of lime, sulphate of magnesia, some little chloride of sodium, &c. Some are strongly impregnated with sulphureted hydrogen, or free carbonic acid. In the Warm Spring and Hot Spring, near Salt Lake City, common salt is the main mineral constituent.* Several of the springs deposit considerable quantities of calcareous tufa. In some places pure cold springs issue near the boiling hot salt springs, from similar orifices.†

Such hot mineral springs can only be found upon a rocky base, because if running any distance through loose deposits, they would cool, their gases would escape, their carbonate of lime be precipitated, &c., or, in one word, they would more or less lose their thermal character. For this reason we chiefly find such springs in or near the mountains; and where any apparent exceptions occur, as in the case of the spring in Kobah Valley, an underlying rocky stratum must be suspected.

The most interesting of the mineral springs along the line of our survey are the Warm Springs, in Round Prairie, on the Timpanogos, east of Utah Lake. As they exhibit the various stages of the successive formation and discontinuation of such springs, a description of them will be instructive.

Nearly the whole portion of Round Prairie, on the northwest side of the river, is formed of horizontal strata of calcareous tufa, in some places 15 to 20 feet high from the creek, and covering an area of about four square miles. On this common plateau four smaller ones have been formed on the points where the springs have chiefly concentrated their action, and on these the numerous springs are raised, or rather have raised their openings, while a few form basins in the plateaus. Most of the springs have the shape of conical tumuli of various heights, with a circular or oval opening on the top, and an oven-shaped cavity inside, wider at the base than near the rim. Their number is very great if we count all the small ones, and the diameter of the opening varies from a few inches to about 30 feet. Most of them are now dry and filled up to some extent with soil, while others contain more or less water, which is warmer or colder proportional to the quantity of the affluent. The more the deposits of the springs have choked the supplying channels the less water can flow out during a certain time, and the more heat it will lose on the way and on the surface, while the larger and less obstructed affluent will lose less heat in proportion. The temperature of the water varies, therefore, between 80° and 109°.5 Fahrenheit. Most of the springs have no visible affluent or outlet, but the temperature of the water and rising bubbles of gas indicate an affluent, and the exit must take place through crevices in the rock, and makes the ground all around marshy. One of the most beautiful forms a basin 30 feet long, 12 feet wide, and 18 feet deep, in which the water reaches to one foot and a half below the rim. The northern group of springs is distinguished by their high conic shape with a comparatively narrow base. On the western plateau is the highest spring; its cone is about 60 feet high, 100 feet wide on the top, and 200 feet at the base; its total elevation above the Timpanogos must be about 120 to 150 feet. The opening

* This salt may either come from salt-beds at a depth, or more likely it is salt water from the lake, which, by a subterraneous fissure, gains access to the hot spring and is carried up in its main channel.

† In such cases, evidently, the cold orifice was formerly also an opening of the deep-seated hot spring, but the connection becoming obstructed, the open upper part of the channel presented a convenient outlet for cold surface-water.

on the top of this spring is only 12 or 15 feet wide, partly covered with calcareous scum deposited over aquatic plants which float on the water, and on the top of which grass was found growing. This indicates the mode in which the spring openings have been closed up. The top of the spring sounds hollow. The water was found 10 feet deep, and 107° Fahrenheit warm; it flows freely over the rim of the cone, and disappears at the base in the pumice-like tufa which it has deposited, and in the swampy ground around. The warmest spring, of 109°.5 Fahrenheit, is one of the most southern, and forms an elliptical large mound, which evidently has had different openings at different times; now all except one are closed with tufa or filled with scum, and overgrown with a luxuriant vegetation, in consequence of the humidity and warmth. The present outlet is four feet wide and nearly filled up with calcareous scum. It will be closed probably in a short time. The water runs freely over the rim, but disappears before reaching the base of the elevation. Some gas bubbles up in all these springs; it has no smell, and seems to be carbonic acid; but after the water had been kept some time in a bottle, on opening the same a distinct smell of sulphureted hydrogen was perceptible, probably formed subsequently by the decomposition of some sulphate by organic particles. The water contains, in solution, a large amount of solid substances, chiefly carbonate of lime, carbonate of magnesia, sulphate of magnesia, also some carbonate of soda and a little chloride of sodium. I could not detect anything else with the blow-pipe. The tufa, as well the compact, granular kind, which forms horizontal layers, as the pumice-like vesicular, which is deposited by the water running over the rim of the basin and on the plants which grow in the water, is mainly carbonate of lime and carbonate of magnesia. As a curiosity, I mention that the warmth of the springs attract innumerable rattlesnakes. Their principal resort is between the large slabs of tufa at a dry and shattered spring-cone.

A great deal of tufa has been deposited also at Big Spring, northeast of Battle Creek. The water of that spring tastes somewhat like that of the Warm Springs, but is not altogether unfit for drinking.

A spring with similar tufaceous cones, but on a smaller scale, and such formations as indicate an apparently similar origin, were noticed at various points. The one in Kobah Valley particularly attracted my attention. There is an irregularly conic hill, composed of calcareous tufa, some 40 feet high and 150 feet in diameter. Several former orifices can be easily distinguished on it, but the water has forced another outlet a little farther west, where it has formed a lower mound, which is overgrown with vegetation. I could scarcely hold my hand in the water, the temperature of which must be about 120° Fahrenheit. It does not taste considerably sulphurous or salt, but sustains a peculiar vegetation of a yellow color, an *Oscillatoria*, which genus of plants also grows in the hot springs of Iceland, and which smells unmistakably of iodine. It appears that these plants, by their segregating power, have absorbed from the water this substance, upon the presence of which, even in the smallest percentage, the medical properties of some of the most effective mineral-waters are founded. The same may also occur in others of these mineral springs, but generally it can be detected only by chemical analysis.

The hot spring near the bend of Walker River has a temperature of 165° Fahrenheit at the surface. It forms a small pond, from the bottom of which the water is boiling up through several holes, accompanied by bubbles of gas, probably of carbonic acid, and steaming vigorously on the surface. There are no calcareous deposits, but the ground around the spring is covered with salt, which tastes like chloride of sodium. The water must, therefore, contain salt, which, however, does not impair its taste. The salt from this spring has shared the fate of several other salts and specimens of efflorescences of the collection; it has been dissolved in consequence of the upsetting of one of our wagons in Carson River, and we are thus unable to present an analysis of it. The vegetation near this and other similar springs is peculiar, partly on account of the saline nature of the soil, partly on account of the steaming atmosphere which surrounds it, and by which its development is forced very considerably.

Fish Spring, in a branch of the Salt Lake Desert, is similar to the last, but much less warm, so that animals drink the water freely. The springs on the west side of Pah-hun-nupe Valley, on our northern route, are slightly sulphureous.

The Alkali Springs, at the western foot of the Black Mountains, east of Carson Lake, contain a water apparently impregnated with an aggregate of the most offensive ingredients, and tardily oozing from the soil wherever a hole is dug.

IMPROVEMENTS IN THE SUPPLY OF WATER.

In regions like those of Western Utah, where the natural supply of water is limited, and not always to be found at convenient distances, the question attains a paramount importance whether the supply of water cannot be increased by artificial means. Although the greatest portion of the route explored by Captain Simpson is not deficient in this respect, still considerable improvements might be made at some points in order to increase the affluent, prevent the loss of water, and provide for the watering of a large number of animals within the shortest possible time. There are also some long stretches where the traveler would be much benefited if water could be obtained at intermediate points. In the following I will confine myself to general remarks.

From all that has been said of the formation of the valleys, of the material of which their bottom is formed, and of the structure of the mountain ranges, it will appear that in general the success of the boring of artesian wells would be doubtful, except where water is naturally abundant. We do not find in the valleys that alternation of strata, permeable and impermeable to water, which is necessary for the construction of artesian wells. They generally allow the water a free circulation in every direction, and the stratified rocks are too much disrupted to be calculated upon with any degree of certainty. Frequently we would reach igneous rocks with the borer, and then the striking even of a fissure would be merely accidental. In most instances all efforts would prove abortive, and if water was really obtained, it might be warm, or sulphureous, or saline.

In order to increase the supply, we must confine ourselves to the improvement of natural springs, or to following up the water in its subterranean course at the bottom of the valleys between the quaternary deposits and the solid rocks, and gain access to it at favorable points.

Water may be obtained where small and insufficient springs rise to the surface but sink within a short distance. In order to improve them their origin must be examined. If they can be traced to a crevice in the solid rocks, we must try to prevent all loss of water, and excavate and secure large cisterns or tanks. This could be done frequently, at an expense small compared with the great benefit derived from such a work. Where springs are rather formed by exudation from a permeable stratum, or from numerous small fissures, and the water only collects upon reaching a projecting bed of a more solid nature, we would have to consider this as the actual source, which, besides the construction of tanks, would not admit of any considerable improvements. The tanks ought to be placed so that the surplus of one would successively fill the others. The last one would be intended for the watering of the animals, and accordingly be made accessible to them. In their construction special care should be taken to keep the water cool and prevent evaporation; they ought to be provided with a heavy covering. The capacity of the tanks must be enlarged proportional to the more or less permanent flow of the spring. In some instances very large reservoirs could be formed with advantage, by throwing dams across narrow ravines. As a general thing, it is preferable to economize and preserve the supply on hand than to look for a questionable increase of the affluent, because the total quantity of water which the spring is able to furnish during a season may be limited, and a too rapid drainage would only accelerate its exhaustion.

Plentiful springs, which, however, sink within a short distance, or are shallow and easily muddied—of which there are several on the route—would only require a cleaning, and a suitable inclosure to keep off the animals, and a number of small tanks to facilitate their watering. Inclosures and troughs should also be provided where animals would be in danger of falling into the springs or of miring down while thronging round the water.

We have explained before how the water, after sinking in the arenaceous formations of the slopes and valleys, re-appears at points where its progress is intercepted by underlying strata of rocks or beds of clay, and that thus numerous springs are formed in the valleys. These may be improved by similar means.

At other points the water does not actually reach the surface, but comes so near it that it can be traced by a peculiar growth of plants, and be made available. We might, in many instances, obtain water by digging to the solid rock in ravines or washes which descend from high mountains, or in which the drainage of larger districts is concentrated. In them the affluent may be permanent, and originate from deep-seated sources, which would have formed springs unless prevented by the heavy cover of loose absorbent material, or it may be the temporary result merely of the surface drainage. Should it be permanent, and in considerable quantity, it might be made accessible by excavations and secured like the springs; if only temporary, dams could be constructed across the ravine, and thus a large supply of water, at least for a part of the year, could be retained. For experiments of this kind always a narrow point of the ravine should be selected, where the water was likely to be gathered in one stream. A constant subterranean discharge of water may occasionally be reached by shallow excavations or deeper wells at the junction of branch and main valleys, especially where projecting spurs of hills or some beds of rock or clay obstruct and contract the passage.

A plentiful affluent will mostly furnish good water, unless the strata which it percolates are charged with much salt.

We will very seldom obtain favorable results by digging at other points. I have frequently mentioned the reservoirs of water, formed by the absorbent deposits, at the bottom of many valleys, but to strike them, even from the lowest points of the valley, wells would generally attain such a depth as would make them almost useless, and the water would frequently be salt. Besides, we could only distantly guess at the configuration and greatest depressions of the rocky base, and, consequently, the most favorable location for the wells. In order to save time and money, we would in such cases recommend at least a previous examination by means of an earth-borer.

SOIL AND VEGETATION.

From what has been said above, in speaking of the valleys in general, it appears that arenaceous material constitutes a considerable portion of the soil, more or less mixed with clay. Where the former prevails, the soil naturally becomes unfit to sustain any vegetation except a peculiar desert growth; but the more it is mixed with argillaceous material, and the detritus of other rocks, the more nutriment it can afford to the plants. The igneous rocks, by their decomposition, add considerably to the fertilizing ingredients.

From this it would appear that a large portion of the soils must be well constituted for productiveness. There are, however, other causes which generally prevent the spontaneous growth of such a vegetation as we find in more favored countries, and confine the successfully cultivable areas to exceedingly narrow limits. These are chiefly to be found in the meteorological condition of the country. In some narrow mountain-gorges, where there is abundance of moisture, we find a quite luxuriant vegetation; but wherever the country opens out, it assumes the character of barrens and deserts. The growth of the valleys consists mostly of several species of *Artimisia* (sage) and allied plants, becoming more and more dwarfish, and assuming a more sterile character, where the soil is more sandy and poor. In spots which receive moisture only periodically, and have a stiff, clay soil, greasewood is the prevailing vegetation. Places which are subject to overflows, and kept moist during the greater part of the year, favor the growth of wire-grass, and other coarse swamp-grasses; more mountainous localities of this kind are covered with meadows of a tall grass resembling somewhat rye. At still more swampy points, rushes and sedge-grasses occupy the surface. Over dry, deep sandy slopes, an exceedingly nutritious grass is scattered in single bunches, bearing large sweet seeds, which are eagerly sought for by animals and Indians. For the latter, most of the grass-seeds constitute a main portion of their winter supplies. In most of the mountain-ranges, several species of the so-called mountain-grasses abound. They are highly nutritious, and come out very early in spring; and even in midwinter, after a few warm days, young green sprouts may be seen between the matted bunches of last year's growth. Being of a rather dry texture, they retain their nutritious qualities as fodder, in these arid regions, all the year round, and it is principally on them that the cattle subsist.

The growth of timber is confined to the mountain-ranges and some broken sandy slopes. The cedar prevails throughout, but, although the trunk attains a considerable diameter, it generally has the shape of a stunted shrub. A small pine, with eatable seed (*Pinus monophyllus*), accompanies the former, and occasionally the mountain-mahogany and a few other small trees or shrubs are met with. A low growth of willows occasionally borders the margin of springs. Only in the Sierra Nevada, the Wahsatch Mountains, and on the banks of Carson River, larger trees of various kinds were found.

The fall of rain is too irregularly distributed, and altogether insufficient, to sustain a better vegetation. There is no season for the development of more tender plants. The frost is immediately succeeded by drought. Therefore cultivation is confined to points where the soil is good and irrigation possible, of which the light sandy loam is particularly susceptible. Naturally these advantages are only combined in narrow strips, in some mountain valleys, at the foot of the higher ranges, or near very copious springs; districts which form but a small portion of the whole area. A few spots, only, which by the influence of constant moisture have a thoroughly decomposed soil, will bear crops without irrigation, and are in some instances exceeding fertile.

The soil and climate in the neighborhood of Salt Lake are best adapted to wheat, vegetables, and root crops; also, fruit trees, apples and peaches, thrive well. A small New Mexican variety of corn produces well, and is cultivated to a limited extent; still it is frequently killed by frost, and the crop, therefore, uncertain. I have also seen tobacco growing, but the leaves were exceedingly coarse and quite woolly; a wild species of tobacco was found at several points. Cotton has also been raised in the southern part of the Territory, but the success would appear to be very doubtful.

The elevation of the Salt Lake Valley is from 4,200 to 4,300 feet above the ocean. In mountain valleys which are more than 1,000 or 1,500 feet higher, cultivation may prove very uncertain. The late frosts and early cold and snow, common at this elevation, would confine the growing and harvesting seasons in too narrow limits. Still, with a judicious selection of crops, even there permanent settlements might flourish, which have other advantages not enjoyed by those lower down. The same may apply to most of the valleys in the more elevated, central portion of the line of our survey.

MINERAL WEALTH.

Valuable and interesting minerals occur at various points in the western and central part of the Territory of Utah. Some of them are of the highest importance.

Gold.—The route passes through the gold-fields, on the east side of the Sierra Nevada, which lately have created much excitement in California and throughout the country. Close on the road, at Chinatown, on Carson River, near longitude 119° 30′, we found a number of Chinese engaged in washing gold out of the sand, gravel, and bowlders at the mouth of Gold Cañon; among which I noticed pieces of dioritic and trachytic porphyry, and other igneous and metamorphic rocks, forming the walls of the cañon; also brown hematite and quartz. They made use of the "rocker" and "long tom," and were, generally, making from $5 to $8 a day per rocker. The gold there is a fine sand gold, apparently much alloyed, for which the traders were paying $13.50 per ounce. The finer particles must have been swept farther by the force of the current flowing from the cañon. It is evidently a recent deposit, and would at once lead to the conclusion that a larger auriferous bed must be found higher up in the cañon. In fact, a short time before we came there, gold had been discovered some seven miles above, on a branch of this cañon. The diggings there are in a rotten quartz, and paid high. As much as $155 had been made by a man in a day. This is close by the now famous Comstock lode.

Gold has also been found north and south of our route, on the upper course of Walker River, &c.

In the Black Mountains, east of Carson Lake, a quartz-vein was noticed with altered argillaceous slates, gneiss, &c., but the hurried examination did not reveal any indications of gold. We must leave it to more detailed investigations to decide whether gold occurs in the more eastern ranges of Utah. No direct indications have been observed. Still we find at some points metamorphic rocks similar to those with which the gold is frequently associated in the Sierra Nevada; and these ranges seem to have been originated by the same forces which have raised the Sierra Nevada, and to have been subject to the same agencies upon which its metallic wealth seems to depend. Moreover, Mr. Blake, in Captain Whipple's Pacific Railroad Report, mentions gold-diggings in another part of the basin, namely, the Armagosa mine, near the southern road from Salt Lake to California, not many miles beyond the sink of the Mojave River, where the gold was found in connection with calcareous spar.

Silver.—At the time of our survey nothing definite was known in regard to the existence of silver in the basin. Rumors located argentiferous veins in the southern part of Utah. Recently rich silver-ore has been found in the close vicinity of the gold-mines of Carson River, in the so-called Washoe mines, which just now create so much excitement.

Lead.—Minute particles of galena were noticed in an impure brown hematite, or a decomposed, highly ferruginous igneous rock, which crops out in the mountains northeast of Kobah Valley. It appears to be connected with a mineral vein, perhaps of argentiferous lead. Some pieces of galena (sulphuret of lead) were exhibited at Camp Floyd as coming from the vicinity. Ores of lead, and perhaps copper and silver, may exist further south.

Iron-ore has not been noticed near the road, but superior magnetic iron-ore occurs in the mountains near Cedar City, a small Mormon settlement not far from Little Salt Lake, longitude 113°, latitude 38°. An attempt was once made there to manufacture iron, but it failed. I am not aware of the particulars and the reason why, but if the increased demand for iron and its price warranted it, the experiment might be renewed, and the obstacles probably be overcome by an experienced metallurgist, notwithstanding the apparently inferior quality of the coal which is found in that neighborhood, and upon which the manufacturers would have to depend.

Native sulphur is found in the same vicinity. In the collection I have a specimen (obtained from Dr. Brewer, United States Army) which is very pure, but I have been unable to get any information in regard to the quantity and connection in which it occurs. It may be the production of extinguished volcanic action. If it could be obtained in large quantity, as I should judge from the specimen, it would be highly valuable.

Salt is found in great quantity. As the water of Salt Lake is a nearly concentrated pure brine, salt can be got there at a trifling expense. (See Captain Stansbury's Report.) Other saline lakes contain impurities from which the salt cannot be freed so easily. Some of it was observed in many springs, round which it accumulates, but there is usually too little of it to be of much importance.

Near the eastern rim of the basin, in the Wahsatch Mountains, large masses of *rock-salt* are found, partly in pure transparent crystalline pieces, partly strongly mixed with red clay, with which it is associated. The specimens in the collection have been obtained by the kindness of General A. S. Johnston and Colonel Crosman. Salt is thus found in the mountains bordering San Pete Valley on the east, some 20 miles south of the Mormon settlement of Manti (in the latitude of Sevier Lake); also in the so-called San Pete Cañon, and still further south, near Captain Gunnison's trail. I have not examined any of these localities, and can, therefore, not decide to which geological formation the salt belongs. The limited information which I have been able to obtain in regard to it, and considerations of a general geological character, seem to indicate that it belongs to those strata which, in the neighborhood of Salt Lake and Utah Lake, are confined to the eastern portion of the Wahsatch range, but seem to cross it further south toward Little Salt Lake. They have been spoken of in section IV, and may be of Triassic age.

Gypsum is found in similar connection.

Various other salts are found in large quantities.

Sulphate of soda was received by Dr. Schiel as coming from the bottom of Salt Lake. (See Captain Beckwith's Pacific Railroad Report.) A salt, probably the same, forms heavy deposits on the eastern shore of Utah Lake, near Springville. Our specimens have not yet been analyzed. It is a useful article in various manufactures, especially that of soda.

Sulphate of magnesia enters largely into the composition of many salts and saline water in that part of the country. It is formed by the decomposition of various shales.

Native alums were observed in several places. They are formed by the decomposition of metamorphic slates and other rocks, &c., which contain pyrites. Captain Stansbury mentions alum from the northern end of Salt Lake. Dr. Schiel mentions a magnesian alum. All those which I have examined are magnesian alums, in which the sulphate of magnesia replaces, in a great measure, the alkaline component, which, in the common alum, is potassa. No complete analysis has been made by us of any of these alums. I have in the collection a specimen from Tuilla Valley, obtained from Colonel Crosman, and one from the neighborhood of Little Salt Lake, by Dr. Brewer.

The saleratus-clay, which I have mentioned already, seems also to contain it in considerable quantity. A specimen of this clay from Camp Floyd is of gray color, full of white crystallizations and nodules of saline substances, and sometimes whitish throughout. It is also formed by an accumulation of salts from the decomposition of rocks in the clay. The soluble portion contains a little common salt, a great deal of sulphate of magnesia, some sulphate of lime, and a little soda. Probably the sulphate of magnesia is in connection with sulphate of alumina as magnesian alum. It makes good adobes (unburnt brick), as do the other clays of that neighborhood. The salts give this clay valuable properties as building material. Mixed with four parts of sand, it forms a superior plaster, and, stirred up in water, after the heavy part has settled down, it is advantageously used as a whitewash, because it adheres better to the wall than lime-water. This clay was extensively used in the erection of the buildings of Camp Floyd.

Mineral springs.—I have spoken of them in another place. Some of them may have strong medical properties, especially on account of the iodine, of which I have discovered indications in the hot springs of Kobah Valley, of which a description has been given above. It is not unlikely that this powerful remedy might also be found, by analysis, in others of these springs more favorably situated.

Stone-coal.—In speaking of the stratified rocks, I have mentioned that the existence of true stone-coal, of the Carboniferous formation, although possible, is still doubtful, and that those coals which are found in the Wahsatch range, in San Pete Valley, and near Little Salt Lake, are probably equivalents of the coal on Sulphur Creek, &c., on the eastern slope of that range, of which I have spoken in section IV.

As this coal is much used in the Salt Lake Valley, and on account of its geographical proximity to the Basin (the limits of which it seems to cross farther south,) I have to mention it again. The San Pete coal looks like true stone-coal, breaks in cubical fragments, has a dark-brown streak, and is bituminous. It is superior to any coal which I have seen west of the Mississippi River coal-fields, although it may be equaled by the Sulphur and White Clay Creek coal, if they are taken from the depth. It cokes to a certain degree, and can, therefore, be used for all purposes, like coking stone-coal, either fresh or as coke. In case a railroad should be built in that direction, the coal-beds in San Pete Valley or their equivalent at some other point, would probably have to furnish the motive power for several hundred miles of road.

Topaz, perfectly colorless and transparent, and of great beauty and luster, has been found in considerable quantity, loose on the surface, in Colonel Thomas's range. I did not see any in the rock, but it apparently originates from one of the trachytic porphyries in that neighborhood. Its degree of hardness is = 8. Before the blow-pipe it proved infusible, and when strongly heated it was covered with small blisters, but did not show any change of color. It exhibited the re-actions of fluorine, alumina, and silex. (No tests for other elements were made). The largest of the crystals measured scarcely one-third of an inch in the direction of the basal cleavage, which was highly perfect. The crystals were all short columnar, with various modifications, corresponding to the following crystallographic expressions, according to the system—

	Of Rose.	Of Dana.
All the crystals exhibit	$\infty\ c : b : a$	I
	$\infty\ c : b : 2\ a$	$i\breve{2}$
	$c : \infty\ b : \infty\ a$	O
	$4\ c : b : \infty\ a$	$4\breve{i}$
	$2\ c : b : a$	2
Most of them also	$2\ c : b : \infty\ a$	$2\breve{i}$
	$c : b : a$	1
	$\frac{1}{2}\ c : b : a$	$\frac{1}{2}$
Few only	$4\ c : b : a$	4
	$2\ c : \infty\ b : a$	$2\bar{i}$

As none of the crystals have both ends perfect, I could not ascertain whether they are hemihedrally developed, as is most common with the topaz, or have both ends alike. Its pyro-electricity was not examined, nor the polarization of light, but the crystals show very plainly the double refraction.

I will conclude this paragraph with a passage from a letter of Colonel Frémont to the National Intelligencer, dated June 13, 1854, and afterward printed by order of Congress (33d Congress, 2d session, Mis. Doc. No. 8). Colonel Frémont crossed the Wahsatch range near Paravan and Cedar City, and to these points his, perhaps a little too highly colored, observations refer: "They are what are called fertile mountains, abundant in water, wood, and grass, and fertile valleys, offering inducements to settlements. The mountains are a great store-house of materials, timber, iron, coal, which would be of indispensable use in the construction and maintainance of the (Pacific) railroad, and are solid foundations to build up the future prosperity of the rapidly increasing Utah State. Salt is abundant on the eastern border; mountains, as the Sierra de Sal, being named from it. In the ranges lying behind the Mormon settlements, among the mountains through which the line passes, are accumulated a great wealth of iron and coal, and extensive forests of heavy timber. These forests are the largest I am acquainted with in the Rocky Mountains, being in some places 20 miles in depth of continuous forest; the general growth is lofty and large, frequently over 3 feet in diameter, and sometimes reaching 5 feet, the red spruce and yellow pine predominating. At the actual southern extremity of the Mormon settlements, consisting of the two inclosed towns of Paravan and Cedar City, near to which our line passed, a coal-mine has been opened for about 80 yards, and iron-works already established. Iron here occurs in extraordinary masses, in some parts accumulated into mountains, which comb out in crests of solid iron thirty feet thick and a hundred yards long."

GEOLOGICAL STRUCTURE OF THE SUCCESSIVE MOUNTAIN RANGES.

In the Wahsatch Mountains, on crossing Weber River from the east, on the road between Fort Bridger and Camp Floyd, we enter the district which I have comprised in section V. The main body of the divide between Weber River, Silver Creek, and Timpanogos River, is composed of dioritic porphyries, which I have described under the heading of igneous rocks. Near Kansas Prairie, the rocks exhibit a more lavatic appearance, but probably belong to the same group. These igneous protrusions may be regarded as the center of the range. East of them we find more recent stratified rocks, while on the west side the mountains appear altogether composed of strata of the Paleozoic formation. On Weber River, and on the Timpanogos, above Round Prairie, conglomeratic tufas were noticed, made up of these eruptive rocks, imbedded in a finer material of the same origin. These masses have either been deposited in water, or became at least cemented and indurated by its agency.

The interesting warm springs of Round Prairie, and their formation of calcareous tufa, have been described above.

Near the north end of Round Prairie, the first stratified rocks of this section were observed, tilted by the porphyries. These are mostly light-colored, and a few reddish sandstones, a siliceous limestone, and some red, shaly strata. Their age is probably the Permian (see under stratified rocks). The sedimentary rocks continue all the way down Timpanogos Cañon. At its upper end compact siliceous and calcareous sandstones prevail, which may also belong to the Permian formation; while lower down we find more dark-gray, impure, siliceous and slaty limestones, frequently threaded with numerous veins of calcareous spar or dolomite, some of which exhibit many fossil remains, expecially *Brachiopoda;* also dark bluish-gray argillaceous, siliceous, and calcareous slates. In the lower part of the cañon, and at various points south of its entrance, bluish-black argillaceous shales are exposed, containing a great deal of carbonaceous matter, and, on their decomposed surface, crystals of gypsum and efflorescences of sulphate of magnesia. At the mouth of the cañon, again siliceous and calcareous slates predominate.

Of all these rocks I have spoken before, and stated that they all, or partly, represent the upper division of the Carboniferous formation. They present no uniform dip, but are much disturbed and contorted; here horizontal, then bent with a sharp angle, or forming vaults, or folded up so that the continuity of the overlying strata is altogether broken, then rising at once vertically from the bottom of the valley many hundred feet, they again appear horizontal higher up, and thus continue in a gigantic wedge-shaped mountain to a great altitude, as if they had never been subject to any violent actions from underneath—in reality, however, because only the horizontal portion of the strata could withstand destruction, while their bent and crushed continuations did not retain strength enough, and were eventually precipitated down and destroyed.

The cañon forms a chasm in these disrupted strata, not less than 1,500 feet deep, and presenting a picturesque scenery, while the highest summits reach to the region of nearly perpetual snow, over 4,000 feet above the mouth of the cañon. This whole thickness seems to be made up of similar strata; at least the red color which characterizes many of the more modern strata, on the eastern side of the range, was not observed on these peaks.

The Upper Carboniferous formation is developed also at other points in the western portion of the Wahsatch Mountains. Prof. I. Hall recognized it in some fossils of Captain Stansbury's collection, from the vicinity of the Great Salt Lake.

Near the mouth of Dry Creek Cañon, east of the northern end of Utah Lake, a white granitic rock forms a high mount, but I did not notice near our routes any metamorphic schists which Captain Stansbury also observed near Salt Lake. In the hills north of Cedar Valley I noticed a small knob of a similar granite, scarcely reaching the surface, the stratified rocks near which exhibit strong marks of metamorphism.

The general character of the valley of Utah Lake and Jordan River is in all respects like that of the other valleys of the basin, as described above. The mountain range between Utah Lake and Cedar Valley consists of similar strata, apparently of Carboniferous age.

In the hills a few miles west of Camp Floyd, I noticed siliceous limestones, sandstones, and siliceous slates, also shales. By their fossils they are characterized as Lower Carboniferous. (See above under Stratified Rocks.) Similar rocks occur near Old Camp Floyd, at the north end of Cedar Valley. The stratification seems to indicate that the upper portion of Mount Floyd consists of strata which are higher in the series, probably Upper Carboniferous. In this and also the next range west of Rush Valley no igneous rocks were observed, but the dip there, like in all the mountains of the district in general, is variable, and changes frequently within short distances, apparently depending upon local concentration of the subterranean forces at different points of these ranges.

Cedar Valley and Rush Valley form separate basins. The spur of hills in the latter valley also consists of rocks of the Carboniferous formation, but on the road to General Johnston's Pass, east of Meadow Creek, we pass over low outcrops of sandstones, which, although tilted at an angle of 45 degrees, present a quite modern appearance, and seem to be a local formation. Still I am doubtful in regard to their age, not having found any fossils. Near the creek I noticed a low outcrop of fine white friable sandstone, or rather scarcely indurated sand with interstratifications and irregular secretions of gray, hard, brittle, siliceous rock which looks as if it was hardened from gelatinous silex, and is apparently formed from the sand by influence of alkaline (?) water, and of modern (lacustrine) origin.

The mountains west of Rush Valley consist of limestones, &c., like the last ones. The fossils collected in the various passes are mostly corals, and seem to belong to the Lower Carboniferous period. The strata in many instances exhibit strong marks of violent dislocations and altering influences, either heat or chemical agencies. Some appear as if crushed into fragments and then recemented into a regular breccia. In Oak Pass, high exposures of an altered sandstone were noticed, of nearly porphyritic appearance.

We next enter Skull Valley, or by the more southern passes, another branch of the Great Salt Lake Desert, separated from the former only by a low sand ridge. A chemical test showed the efflorescences of salt around Willow Spring to the pure chloride of sodium.

The next range of mountains of considerable extent from north to south, is Colonel Thomas's range, of which the Granite Mountain forms the northern prolongation. In the intervening country we find some more isolated mountain masses and numerous island mountains. Southwest of Willow Spring the hills are composed of altered siliceous limestones and sandstones, with remains of *Gasteropoda*, *Brachiopoda*, Corals, and *Bryozoa*, of Carboniferous age. Further south Igneous Rocks partake in the formations. The central portion of Mount Champlin is composed of the porphyry, No. 181, of the collection, which I have mentioned above (see under Igneous Rocks), and other rocks allied to the trachytic porphyries. Near the base of these mountains I noticed also other rocks, forming dikes and smaller outcrops of perhaps later origin, also vesicular rocks of dark color. All around the mountain, partly covering the igneous rocks, partly as separate, more or less distant, island buttes, stratified rocks were observed, mostly in a highly altered state, limestones, slates, and especially a dark reddish-brown siliceous sand-rock, which at some points attains a quite porphyritic appearance. The McDowell Mountains, further southwest, with their characteristic peaks, are nearly altogether composed of eruptive rocks similar to those of Mount Champlin. They exhibit a most interesting transition among themselves, and between extreme types at other points. Some of them are closely allied to the trachytic porphyries from Carson River and Eagle Valley, on the east side of the Sierra Nevada; others can scarcely be distinguished from some of Weber River, and others again present quite a peculiar appearance. In this neighborhood the Great Salt Lake and Sevier Lake deserts connect with such a scarcely perceptible change of slope, that we are frequently at a loss to tell whether we are in the one or the other.

Colonel Thomas's range, at Pass Short-cut, is composed of stratified rocks, probably of Carboniferous age, which are tilted, as well as covered, by an overflow of a trachytic porphyry of gray color. Some strata are thereby highly altered; sandstones have attained a porphyritic appearance, by a beginning secretion of quartz in single crystals, as in a porphyry. Farther to the south, near the pass on our return trail, the igneous rocks prevail, and only a few highly-altered limestones were noticed, and some layers, in regard to which I was doubtful whether they were originally eruptive or sedimentary. One of the most common rocks there has a peculiar modern appearance, in consequence of its more loose texture. In a gray matrix it contains a great deal of transparent quartz, very brittle and partly crystallized in perfect double hexagonal pyramids, also white glassy feldspar and a little black mica. It has somewhat the appearance of trachytic lava, but is closely allied to the rocks from Mount Champlin. Other varieties have a grayish white or very light pink matrix, containing only few and small crystals of the same minerals, which makes them look vastly different; probably in consequence of a beginning decomposition, or the mode of cooling to which they have been subject, they shell off in rounded masses, forming peculiar knobs, or, if the inner part has been worn out, cavities of various size.

Next follow the House Mountains, which extend from Sevier Lake northward, and are lost in the Salt Lake desert. As far as they have come under my observation, they are entirely composed of stratified rocks, dark-colored siliceous limestones, compact sandstones, and slates. Some of them are highly altered. Only a fragment of a *Trilobite*, apparently of a Carboniferous species, was found near Chapin Spring, and the lithological character of the rocks there points to the same age. Near the north end of this chain the remarkable Fish Springs are found, and not far from them, along the foot of the mountains, horizontal strata of a white calcareous marl, in appearance much like chalk, which must have been deposited in the ancient lakes, and to the formation of which infusoriæ seem to have contributed largely. Near there, I also noticed a water-mark of calcareous tufa lining the mountain-side for a considerable distance. Highly altered stratified rocks also form the main portion, at least, of the hills between this range and the Goshoot Mountains.

The Tots-arrh or Goshoot Mountains are one of the principal ranges of great length and altitude. Their main body consists of stratified rocks, limestones of mostly bluish color, sandstones and slates, which form some of the highest peaks, among them Mount Davis. In the pass from the desert to Pleasant Valley, some fossils of Lower Carboniferous age were found, and also near our camp on the western slope. Many of the strata are strongly altered, sandstones converted into quartzite, &c. Besides, we find some metamorphic rocks, mica schists, argillaceous slate, gneiss, and even granite; but I have not seen any of the porphyritic and other more recent igneous rocks. Pleasant Valley, in this range, seems to follow the line of contact between the Carboniferous and metamorphic rocks. A conglomerate is found in the pass above Red Springs, on the eastern slope. It is mostly composed of more or less rounded pieces of limestone, imbedded in a more areno-calcareous finer matrix of light reddish color. Its age is doubtful, but as it has apparently been deposited in a depression of older rocks, after the mountains had attained their general configuration, it is probably a comparatively recent deposit. In the Goshoot Mountains a considerable quantity of moisture is precipitated and retained, feeding numerous springs, which partly sink and re-appear in the adjoining Crosman Valley, &c.

Next follows the Un-go-we-ah range, between Antelope and Steptoe Valleys, also of great altitude and extent, in which stratified Paleozoic as well as plutonic rocks were observed. On the southern road we find on the east side a great thickness of bluish gray calcareous slates and siliceous limestones, and, toward the summit, with them a calcareous conglomerate, and a trachytic porphyry allied to that from the McDowell Mountains. On the west side limestones are still more extensively developed, mostly siliceous, and of dark bluish and gray color; also slates, and some sandstones. Some of these strata are strongly altered. Near the summit of the pass some fossils were obtained, indicating the Upper Carboniferous age, while others, from the western portion of the range, seem to be Lower Carboniferous. Near the northern road, the brown dioritic porphyries form the bulk of the mountains, while the stratified rocks, bluish gray siliceous limestones, and sandstones altered into flint rock, are confined to the highest summit and part of the western slope. We noticed some interesting instances of the changed appearance of the rocks at the contact between the porphyry and stratified rocks. Near our camp, in Spring Valley, in this range, highly peculiar rocks were exposed, which seem to be the result of a later intrusion, partly pitchstones, partly others of a bluish-gray color, subvitreous and easily breaking into subcuboid fragments. They contain numerous light brown secretions of the size of a pea, with a radiating structure, in the center of which frequently a small grain of feldspar can be observed; they also contain some crystals of black mica. Higher up toward the summit I noticed a local formation of conglomeratic rocks composed of igneous material, and a high knob of porphyry, closely allied to the porphyry from Simpson's Spring at Mount Champlin.

The Mont-tim range, between Steptoe Valley and Butte Valley, is composed of some granite, more recent eruptive masses, and metamorphosed strata, but chiefly of sedimentary rocks of the Paleozoic age. Near the northern road we find, on the east side of the mountains, bluish and gray siliceous limestones threaded with veins of calcareous spar, slates, &c., petrographically much like the formations in the Timpanogos Cañon, but, as some fossils, *Trilobites* of the genera *Homalonotus* and *Proetus*, prove, of Devonian age, or perhaps Upper Silurian. The same again appear near the summit of the pass. Although this is the first point where Devonian strata were noticed, they may occur also farther east, having escaped observation on account of the similarity of their lithological character with that of Carboniferous strata and the scarcity of fossils. A considerable thickness of flint-rock and altered sandstone was exhibited in and near Egan Cañon, probably underlying the Devonian limestones, and also strata of altered slates, much like roofing-slates. On the west side of the range dioritic and trachytic porphyry prevails; also pitchstone was found, and scattered knobs of such rocks extend across Butte Valley, on the west side of which the brown porphyry is again prominent. Near the southern route the range seems to be wholly composed of very compact gray siliceous limestones, in which I found no fossils; but from their similarity to Devonian strata, farther west, I am inclined to consider them coeval. A western spur of the range between the two routes, on the southwest side of Round Valley, is evidently composed of the yellow rocks of Upper Carboniferous age (see below), of which a few doubtful traces were also noticed in the pass to Butte Valley. This valley is closed at the south end by mountains of brown dioritic porphyry, and rocks allied to the pitchstones, forming a spur of a great eruption, which has its center south of Summit Spring, in the next range, and covers a considerable area.

On the northern route the divide between Butte Valley and Long Valley is low, composed of porphyritic rocks and light-colored limestones. Part of these are light gray, siliceous, and subcrystalline, or finely crystalline; others are light-yellowish, areno-argillaceous, and have an uneven fracture. They are characterized, by a large number of fossils, as an Upper Carboniferous formation, but differ much from the other strata of that age, as developed farther east. I may refer to what has been said under the head of Stratified Rocks, and to Mr. Meek's report. West of Long Valley we find similar strata, continuing to the summit of the pass to Ruby Valley, where a blackish eruptive rock, which looks basaltic, but is perhaps allied to the greenstones, forms a considerable protrusion. On the west side, in Murry Cañon, we have again the yellow rocks, but apparently more siliceous and slaty, and less fossiliferous. Their trend and dip are variable, and I did not obtain a section, but the formation must attain a thickness, at least, of several hundred feet. The strata of the spur of hills farther north, in Ruby Valley, show the same color. A few fossils from the gray limestone of an isolated low hill near the road, more resemble Lower Carboniferous types.

On the southern route these light-gray and yellow limestones and slates form the mountains between Butte and Phelps Valleys, north of Summit Spring, south of which they are cut off by the porphyries and allied rocks. In the low divide between Phelps and Buell Valleys, and in some hills farther west, similar light-grayish and yellowish rocks crop out. Some strata there are full of joints of the columns of *Crinoidea*, and a few fossils from that point are considered by Mr. Meek as more like Lower Carboniferous forms. Although the lithological character scarcely would indicate such a division, it may perhaps exist. The presence of Devonian strata, a few miles farther west, is favorable to the supposition that these beds occupy a lower position in the Carboniferous series than those near Summit Spring.

We cross the Humboldt Mountains on the northern route, near their southern extremity, where their great elevation suddenly falls off, and minor ranges appear in their stead. In this latitude the Humboldt Mountains appear to be made up of stratified rocks from their base to the highest summits. I noticed blue and gray siliceous limestones, also flint rock, and a coarse, partly conglomeratic sandstone, perhaps identical with the one in the next range west. These rocks belong probably to the Carboniferous and older formations. Only a small outcrop of feldspathic rock was observed not far from the road. The low ranges farther south, also far beyond our southern route, are formed by the Carboniferous rocks, their yellow color indicating it plainly.

In the next mountains, on the west side of Buell Valley, we again find a considerable development of siliceous limestones and slates, of mostly bluish-gray color, characterized by their fossils as Devonian. They are overlaid in the pass by heavy masses of a coarse siliceous sandstone, and a conglomerate of rounded siliceous pebbles, mostly of a rather dark color, which seem to occupy the position of the Old Red of the English geologists, between the Devonian and Carboniferous formations. A further proof of this I found near Cho-kup's Pass. Its thickness must be considerable. I observed 300 feet of it in a single exposure. On the west side of the pass eruptive masses protrude, which seem to belong to the basaltic or phonolitic group, and are partly vesicular; other rocks close by may either be allied to them or highly altered slates. I also noticed some tufa, a sedimentary local deposit of fine fragments, or ashe , of eruptive origin. McCarthy's Creek marks the line of contact between these different rocks.

In the same range, some miles north of Cho-kup's Pass, on the eastern slope, and again on the west side of the pass, I found a few fossils in gray and bluish limestones. Mr. Meek considers them as Lower Carboniferous. The main body of the range there is composed of siliceous conglomerate, flint rock, and a strongly cemented light-colored or reddish sandstone, which formation attains a thickness of at least several hundred feet. It is most probably an equivalent of the conglomerate farther south, and "Old Red." There we have it overlying Devonian strata, here we find it in connection with Carboniferous rocks. Although the latter are found on the side of the mountain, while the sandstone forms the crest, they seem to occupy a higher geological position. The upheaving forces have exhibited a great local intensity in a direction coinciding with the central line of the ridge. The strata at numerous points stand on the edge, having been tilted up at an angle of 90°, or even more. Thus the originally lower sandstones now occupy the most elevated position in the center. No igneous rocks were noticed near the pass, but they appear to form some hills farther north.

The permanent character of some springs, and the large volume of water, in Pah-hun-nu-pe Valley seems to be, partly at least, the result of the upthrusting of these sandstones and other older strata, which hold a highly elevated position in the neighboring Humboldt and Cooper Mountains, and there, at their outcrops, take up a considerable quantity of water from the melting snows and summer rains; while it is partly due to the circumstance that this valley receives the drainage of the extensive Kobah Valley.

The rocks in Swallow Cañon, between Pah-hun-nu-pe and Kobah Valleys, are dark-gray and blue impure limestones, with numerous small veins of dolomite, also slates and flinty sandstones. They are characterized by their fossils as Devonian (see Mr. Meek's report). This cañon has apparently been eroded by the discharge of the water from Kobah Valley into the less elevated Pah-hun-nu-pe Valley. The former has thus been gradually drained of its lake, the relics of which are still found, not only as marked benches and some tufaceous strata, but as a considerable succession of horizontal layers of shaly sandstones and arenaceous shales, partly calcareous, of gray, yellowish, reddish, and white colors, which form high escarpments at the southwest foot of the island mountain north of Clay Creek, Mount Lowry.

The strata comprising this mountain and the one north from there, near Willow Creek, are mostly limestones of light-gray color, subcrystalline and very compact. Only a few imperfect fossils were noticed in them, some *trochiform* univalves, and some coralline forms, which, according to Mr. Meek, appear to be similar to Lower Silurian species from the Western States. The dip of these strata also seems to indicate that they occupy a lower geological horizon than those of Swallow Cañon, and both evidences, although not conclusive in themselves, lead me to consider these strata as most probably Silurian.

Crossing Pah-hun-nu-pe Valley on the northern road, we find on its west side cliffs of a light-gray, granular, crystalline, magnesian limestone, an agglomeration of small rhomboidal crystals of dolomite, altogether presenting the appearance of many of the Lower Silurian magnesian limestones of Missouri, especially the third magnesian limestone of Professor Swallow. This series is several hundred feet thick, and succeeded by lower strata of a similar character, but more finely crystalline and subcrystalline, like other varieties of the third magnesian limestone. They are underlaid by several hundred feet of coarse sandstones and siliceous conglomerates, which would also correspond to a sandstone in the Missouri series, and perhaps be an equivalent of the Potsdam sandstone of New York. I cannot think that this sandstone and conglomerate should correspond to those in Cho-kup's Pass of the age of the Old Red, although their appearance is similar; then the limestones would be of Carboniferous age, but they are quite unlike any I have observed in that series.

An igneous protrusion, a spur of Mount Cooper, intercepts the further regular succession of the strata. Near by some variegated and altered slates crop out. At some points farther west in Kobah Valley small exposures of similar light-colored silico-magnesian limestones were noticed.

Near the north end of Kobah Valley I found some rock resembling serpentine and other more compact basaltic (?) knobs. The mountains around the western part of Kobah Valley are composed of igneous rocks, mostly porphyries, which seem to hold a position between the dioritic and the trachytic group, and differ much among themselves; some of them present a peculiar appearance, and may be later intrusions. Others appear to be allied to the phonolites.* Only near the southwest end of the valley, again some few stratified rocks of doubtful age were observed, sandstones and altered slates, and some greenish flinty siliceous strata, which have nearly lost the marks of their sedimentary origin, by the immediate contact with the igneous protrusions.

The Pe-er-re-ah range is another of the principal chains. Near our trail it is composed of granite, more recent eruptive, and some highly altered stratified rocks. At the mouth of Simpson's Cañon flint-rock and black and variegated slates were noticed; a little farther on, white, coarse-grained granite, and some more finely-grained

* One specimen from Wons-in-damme (Antelope) Creek, of whitish color and tufalike appearance, resembles very closely specimens from the island of Ischia, near Naples, from the extinct volcano Epomeo, the functions of which are now discharged by Vesuvius. Those specimens are a scoriaceous lava, altered by vapors of hydrochloric acid, which escape from the crater, and have converted the lava partly into kaolin.

porphyritic varieties. At the upper end of the cañon more slates, &c., were observed, but the hills are mostly covered over, and but few rocks exposed. Near the summit I found a trachytic porphyry with a feldspathic matrix and crystals of glassy feldspar and mica, and near by other similar rocks form successive overflows or protrusions, presenting the appearance of stratification. Some of them reminded me distantly of the rocks of Spring Valley in the Un-go-we-ah range, others of the rocks in Kobah Valley, and one is allied to the pitch-stones. The summit and west side of the pass are composed of granite, and only lower down on the west side some more flint-rock occurs.

Where we struck Reese's River, horizontal strata of modern origin were noticed, which must have been formed as lacustrine deposits, partly conglomeratic, partly fine-grained calcareous sandstones, and arenaceous limestones. In the range west of Reese's River, porphyries are largely developed, of mostly light-reddish color, and with crystals of glassy (?) feldspar and mica, and partly of quartz. With them I found some highly altered stratified rocks, especially flint-rock, and a sandstone which had become quite porphyritic by the secretion of crystalline particles of the silex; also some black pitch-stone.

Next follows the Se-day-e range, with subordinate chains. Where it has come under my observation, its main body is nearly altogether composed of plutonic masses, granite, porphyritic rocks, pitch-stones, &c. White granite was found in the center of the range, near the head of Gibraltar Cañon. Trachytic, and, perhaps, some dioritic porphyries are most largely developed. Their color is generally pink or reddish-brown; others are whitish. Those of the latter, at the mouth of Putnam Cañon, exhibit an imperfectly columnar structure. Near the eastern foot of the mountains I noticed various rocks which have evidently erupted at a somewhat later period. There are black and brown pitch-stones, at one place forming a dike, split up by numerous fissures into tabular pieces with glazed surfaces and highly brittle inside; other masses appear as a mixture of the porphyry and pitch-stone, and similar to some lavas; and a large vein is filled with a trachyte which seems to be closely allied to the rock from Weber River, No. 153 of the collection, but contains less quartz and mica. Brown porphyry prevails on the west side, and also in the more western spurs; only in the cañons some local tufaceous sediments were observed, and on Edward Creek a flinty conglomerate and some few other ledges of metamorphosed rocks.

In the park below the Gate of Gibraltar we find extensive deposits of a mostly pure white tufa, apparently formed in a lake which has been drained by the erosion of the Middle Gate. These sediments are formed of finely comminuted trachytic rocks, pumice, &c.; and the siliceous shells of *Infusoria* may have largely contributed to it. They scarcely contain traces of lime. They are apparently identical with those observed by Dr. Newberry on the upper Pitt River, Klamath Lake, &c., and called by him infusorial marls, of which he remarks (Pacific Railroad Report, vol. vii, p. 39), that they have a striking resemblance to pulverized pumice, and have doubtless been formed of similar material. I found the same on Carson River, east of Eagle Valley, where, however, they contain a few per cent. of lime; but a similar formation from the Salt Lake Desert, near Fish Springs, is a calcareous marl.

In the Middle and Lower Gates I noticed porphyry, flint-rock, and signs of other highly altered stratified rocks. Still farther on, a prominent white mountain south of the road was found to consist of purely white subcrystalline and finely crystalline dolomite, evidently altered from a dark-gray magnesian limestone which still forms part of the mountain. The contact between the two modifications exhibits no straight line, but follows irregularly secondary fissures. The stratification is obliterated by the metamorphosis. No fossils were noticed. Close by some slates crop out, and a dike of a greenish decomposed igneous rock.

Gibraltar Creek furnishes a striking example of the repeated sinking and re-appearing of the water, modified in its qualities by the strata which it percolates. At our camping-place in the Middle Gate the water was insufficient, and tasted disagreeably of clay, while lower down it is purified again by the sand. I am confident that it would be easy not only to secure a permanent supply at that Gate, but that a much better water could be obtained, at least during the greatest part of the summer, several miles lower down, and that thus the long waterless distance to Carson Lake could be much shortened.

The Black Mountains form only a comparatively low ridge east of Carson Lake, and are composed of igneous and metamorphosed rocks. The former, as exposed on the eastern slope, are unlike any of the porphyritic rocks, and appear as local protrusions, probably of later date. On the west side, dark-colored vesicular rocks were found in considerable quantity, and above them altered clay slate, gneiss, and compact quartz forming a vein or stratum. Farther north the mountains have a stratified appearance, partly caused merely by horizontal water-marks, and the rocks are black, gray, red, scoriated, vesicular, &c.

Alkali Valley, formerly a branch of Carson Lake, is still mostly a miry salt flat, with a great deal of loose drift-sand on the surrounding beach and benches, especially on the east side.

Drift-sand also covers the greatest part of the hilly country south and west of Carson Lake, as far as the bend of Carson River. In that district rocks prevail similar to those of the Black Mountains. Near the lake we find scoriaceous vesicular outcrops of dark gray and red color and igneous origin, and, lining the hills, a great deal of calcareous tufa, in places enveloping numerous particles of the red rock, and then readily mistaken as such; also, considerable of a sedimentary rock of white color, mostly composed of pumice and other igneous material, and allied to the volcanic tufas. Rocks of the basalt or greenstone group, partly vesicular, were also observed at various points between the lake and the bend of Carson River, and along Walker River, to the exclusion of other igneous rocks, except some in the main divide between the two rivers, which are distantly related to the trachytic porphyries.* One specimen of the latter has a loose porous texture, and contains in the light-gray feldspathic matrix crystals of glassy (?) feldspar and brown mica. Others contain hornblende instead of the mica, especially higher up on Carson River, and appear more allied to those from Weber River.

*I do not think that there are any rocks along our line of survey which can properly be called basalt. Several of the basaltic rocks in the neighborhood of Carson River and Carson Lake resemble more the lavas from Monte Somma and Vesuvius, one especially a lava which erupted as late as 1806, and presents a scoriaceous surface upon which small green crystallizations can be recognized only when the rock has begun to decompose.

Highly altered sandstone was noticed at a few points; and some rocks near the bend of Walker River, and near the hot spring in that vicinity which has been described in a former paragraph, may be either eruptive or metamorphic. Gneiss and quartz-rock were observed between Walker and Carson Rivers, not far from where we struck the latter.

Near the bend of Carson River we also find the unmistakable marks of a former lake, in numerous water-marks and the calcareous tufa on the sides of hills.

Thence up Carson River, the whole formation is plutonic. The rocks are mostly trachytic porphyries, similar to some from the McDowell Mountains, with a flesh-colored or brown feldspathic matrix, and crystals of glassy feldspar, mica, and quartz; others form a transition to the dioritic porphyries and the Weber River group, containing hornblende, mica, &c; they altogether merge into each other, and may be considered as a connecting link between the two groups. Still others are black and vesicular, and conglomeratic tufas occur likewise.

I have already mentioned Gold Cañon, and the infusorial tufas below Eagle Valley. This and Carson Valley are two of the long series of valleys which stretch along the foot of the Sierra Nevada, and in which the eye of the weary traveler is, for the first time, relieved by the aspect of green meadows and cultivated fields. The eastern slope of the Sierra Nevada, along Eagle and Carson Valleys, is mostly covered by metamorphic strata, siliceous and argillaceous slates of various description, and some siliceous conglomerate; but its main body there is composed of white granitic rocks, which were observed on the Daggett trail, in Lake Valley, and Johnston's Pass. (See under Igneous Rocks.) Carson River Cañon is chiefly cut through these white, coarse, crystalline granites. There the contrast of their precipitous, resplendent walls, split up into cuboid blocks, like cyclopean mason-work, and the green foliage, the majestic trees, and foaming mountain-torrent, form an imposing, I might say sublime, scenery not soon effaced from the memory of the beholder.

APPENDIX J.

REPORT

ON THE

PALÆONTOLOGICAL COLLECTIONS OF THE EXPEDITION.

BY

F. B. MEEK,
PALÆONTOLOGIST.

NOTE BY THE AUTHOR.—As may be seen by the date of the accompanying letter to Captain Simpson, this report was prepared as far back as 1860. So many years had, therefore, passed away without any apparent probability of its publication, that I had long since abandoned all expectation of ever seeing it published. I had, however, long back, published brief notices of the new forms collected by the expedition, in the Proceedings of the Academy of Sciences at Philadelphia, thus securing to Captain Simpson's important explorations the credit of their discovery.

After the elapse of so many years without any prospect of the publication of Captain Simpson's report, being aware how very desirable it is that figures and descriptions of all named species should be placed within the reach of palæontologists, I availed myself of the opportunity to prepare figures and descriptions of some of the same species for another report. This, of course, I should not have done, had I known that Captain Simpson's report would be published, even at this late date. The appearance of some of the same species, however, in two different reports is really not a superfluity, as the figures and descriptions appear in connection with reports of distinct explorations, and aid in the elucidation of each, while wider circulation among geologists and palæontologists, of the illustrations and descriptions, will also be secured.

In revising this report at this later date, it has, of course, become necessary to make some changes of nomenclature, &c., to bring it up to our present knowledge of the palæontology and geology of the far West. In doing this, I have tried, as far as possible, by inserting the dates of changes, and by referring to various publications that have issued since the original preparation of this report, fifteen years back, to do full justice to the subsequent labors of others, as well as to my own later publications.

F. B. M.

SMITHSONIAN INSTITUTION, *November* 8, 1875.

APPENDIX J.

REPORT ON THE PALÆONTOLOGICAL COLLECTIONS OF THE SURVEY.

BY F. B. MEEK.

WASHINGTON CITY, *D. C.*, *May* 23, 1860.

Capt. J. H. SIMPSON,
Topographical Engineers, U. S. A.:

DEAR SIR: In the following report, on the fossils collected by Mr. Henry Englemann, the zealous geologist of the party under your command during your late explorations in the far West, you will find figures and descriptions of such new species as are in a condition to be fully characterized. Figures are also given of a few other well-known forms, which are especially interesting in consequence of the fact that they have not hitherto been found at such remote western localities. In addition to these, the collection contains many specimens too imperfect to be satisfactorily identified with known species, or described as new, though quite a number of them are doubtless new to science.

As a large proportion of the collection is from a region of country in regard to the geology of which little is known, I have thought a full list of all the fossils brought in, with references to the localities at which they occur, would be interesting to scientific readers, as well as useful to future explorers. In making out this catalogue, where only generic names could be given, a brief description of some of the more marked characters of the species has, in several instances, been added.

The fossils contained in the collection give evidence of the existence along the line of survey of rocks belonging to the Devonian, Carboniferous, Permian, Cretaceous, Jurassic, and Tertiary epochs.* Those of Devonian age were collected in the region of Humboldt Mountains, near the middle of the Great Salt Lake Basin, at the following points: Latitude, 39° 45′ north, longitude, 114° 45′ west; latitude, 39° 33′ north, longitude, 115° 58′ west; and latitude, 39° 30′ north, longitude, 115° 36′ west.

The specimens obtained at the first of these localities are in slabs of hard dark-bluish limestone, and consist of fragments of *Trilobites* belonging apparently to the genera *Homalonotus* and *Proetus*. These may possibly be Upper Silurian species, but they have so much the appearance, so far as can be determined, of forms occurring in

* Evidence of the existence of Triassic rocks at some places along the line of survey was also observed. It is, however, altogether of a stratigraphical and lithological character, no organic remains having been observed in these beds. (See a communication by Mr. Engelmann and the writer, Proceedings Academy Natural Science, Philadelphia, April, 1860.)

the Hamilton group of the New York series, that, when taken in connection with the lithological characters of the matrix, they leave a strong impression on the mind that they probably belong to about the same horizon.

The fossils found at the other localities mentioned above are, I think, decidedly Devonian types, and also occur in dark-bluish limestone. They consist of *Atrypa aspera*, or a closely allied species, *A. reticularis*, a small *Productus*, and three or four new species of *Spirifer*. As the genus *Productus* is now generally regarded as not dating back farther than the Devonian system, and neither *Atrypa reticularis* nor *A. aspera* ranges up into the Carboniferous, while the species of *Spirifer*, as well as the small *Productus* associated with these, are all closely allied to forms characterizing the Hamilton group, the evidence is nearly or quite conclusive that the rock from which these fossils were obtained belongs to the Devonian system, and I think it will be found to be nearly on a parallel with the Hamilton group.

It is an interesting fact, in case these specimens should really prove to be of the age of the Hamilton series, that at this distant locality they should be found in beds having almost exactly the lithological characters of some of the dark calcareous portions of that formation in New York; while the fossils of the same age found in the intermediate Western States, generally occur in much lighter-colored strata.

It is worthy of note that the localities at which these specimens were obtained are near twelve hundred miles farther westward than such fossils have hitherto been found *in situ*, so far as known to the writer, within the Territory of the United States. It is true that a few fossils, consisting of some *Brachiopoda*, and others similar to *Monotis*, collected by Captain Stansbury from shaly arenaceous beds near the North Platte, three or four days' march beyond Fort Laramie, were formerly supposed to be of Devonian age;* but it is now known that the outcrop there alluded to consists of Jurassic, and probably some Triassic, strata; though the fossils were obtained from the former.

Some specimens belonging to the genera *Spirifer*, *Conocardium*, &c., collected by Mr. H. Engelmann in 1856, near Medicine Bow Butte (latitude 41°, longitude 106° 30′ west), were supposed by Dr. Shumard to be also of Devonian age, but the evidence was not regarded as conclusive, and the fossils were found in an erratic mass, the exact original position of which could not be determined.

The specimens provisionally referred to the Lower Carboniferous epoch were collected west of Lake Utah, near Camp Floyd, latitude 40° 13′ north, longitude 112° 8′ west; and at two or three localities much farther westward, near Humboldt Mountains, already referred to. Those from the first of these localities occur in a hard, compact, dark-colored siliceous limestone, which I am informed by Mr. Engelmann is rather extensively developed in that region. They are all silicified and not in a condition to show very satisfactorily their specific characters, though forms very similar to *Orthis Michilini* and *Hemipronites crenistria* occur among them. There are also, along with these, fragments of *Corals*, *Spirifer*, *Athyris*, and the spiral axis of a species of *Archimedipora*. As the last-mentioned fossil belongs to a genus common in the Lower Carboniferous, and not yet certainly known to range up into the Coal-Measures, and the forms associated with it resemble species occurring in the Lower Carboniferous series of the West, while there is an absence of any exclusively Coal-Measure

* See Captain Stansbury's Report, Great Salt Lake, page 403.

types among them, the weight of evidence is in favor of the conclusion that these dark-colored limestones belong to the lower principal division of the great Carboniferous system.

The other fossils supposed to be of the same age as those mentioned above, are in part from a similar dark-colored limestone on the west side of the south branch of Humboldt River, latitude 40° north, longitude 115° 37′ west; and from a grayish subcrystalline limestone some sixty miles in a southwest direction from the locality just mentioned. The first consist merely of imperfect specimens of *Productus* and *Spirifer*, none of which show enough of their characters to be certainly identified with known species; but, from the position of the beds in which they occur with relation to other rocks hereinafter to be noticed, they would seem to be most probably of Lower Carboniferous age.

A few imperfect specimens collected at various places along the route between Humboldt Mountains and Camp Floyd, indicate that much of the country is occupied by Carboniferous rocks, though it is not improbable Devonian and possibly Silurian deposits may be exposed at several places between these two distant localities, in addition to that already mentioned at which fragments of *Trilobites* were found.*

The specimens I have referred to the Upper Carboniferous epoch are in part from dark shaly beds in Timpanogos Cañon east of Lake Utah, latitude 42° 22′ north, longitude 111° 38′ west; and from extensive exposures of light-yellowish gray, more or less argillaceous, and arenaceous subcrystalline limestones, forming mountain chains between longitude 115° and 115° 30′ west, latitude 40° 10′ and latitude 39° 20′ north. Those from the dark shaly beds at the first of these localities consist of *Spirifer*, *Productus*, *Athyris*, and fragments of a *Lepidodendron*, none of which are known to be identical with described species, but from their general resemblance to Coal-Measure forms, and the nature of the matrix, we may infer with some degree of confidence that they belong to that epoch.

The collections from the yellowish limestone series alluded to above, contain specimens of *Chonetes*, *Productus*, *Spirifer*, *Athyris*, *Pecten*, *Nautilus*, &c., the species being for the most part new, and also distinct from those found in the dark shaly beds at Timpanogos Cañon. One of *Spirifer*, however, seems to be identical with *S. cameratus*, Morton, or closely allied to it, and one of *Athyris* is undistinguishable from *A. subtilita*, Hall (sp.); while the *Chonetes* is quite similar to *C. Verneuiliana*, Norwood & Pratten. From the presence of these Coal-Measure types, and the absence of any well-marked Lower Carboniferous species among the collections from this rock, I am led to refer it, at least provisionally, to the upper division of the Carboniferous system.

Specimens from deposits of the age of the Coal-Measures were collected from limestones on the North Platte, fifteen miles above Fort Laramie, and at several places in Eastern Kansas. The occurrence of rocks of this age at these localities is now so well known, however, as to require no especial notice here.

* There are in the collection from localities a little west of longitude 116°, near Humboldt Mountains, some specimens of hard, compact, bluish and grayish limestones, containing small subcylindrical bodies, some of which present the appearance of small ramose sponges or corals similar to species of *Chætetes*, common in some of our Lower Silurian rocks of the Western States; though I saw none in a condition to show pores, if they exist.

As we now know of the existence of Carboniferous and Devonian formations at these distant western localities, and Silurian fossils have already been identified by Dr. Hayden and the writer from the Black Hills, Dakota, as well as from the South Pass (latitude 108° 30′ north, longitude 42° 12′ west), we may infer that nearly all the principal members of the great Paleozoic series will probably yet be found along the Rocky Mountains, and in the country between them and the Pacific.

In some masses of very hard, light-grayish, compact, silico-calcareous rock from Timpanogos River above the cañon, there are some imperfect specimens of small aviculoid shells resembling the Permian genus *Bakevellia;* also fragments of a coral similar, as far as can be determined, to the genus *Phyllopora* of King. From the analogy of these fossils to Permian forms, and the fact that the bed in which they occur holds a higher stratigraphical position, as I am informed by Mr. Engelmann, than the dark shaly deposits supposed to be of Upper Carboniferous age, farther down the river, there would appear to be some reason for thinking there may be here a representation of the Permian. This supposition would also seem to receive further support from the occurrence at localities not far east of this of Jurassic, and probably Triassic, deposits; still it would be unsafe without more reliable evidence to refer these fossils to the Permian epoch.

There are in the collection from localities in Eastern Kansas, near Cottonwood Creek, on the north side of Kansas River, several specimens of yellowish magnesian limestone, containing apparently the same species of *Pseudomonotis, Aviculopecten, Bakevellia, Myalina,* &c., known to occur at many places in the eastern part of that Territory, in strata that have been referred to the Permian system. As there is, however, in that region a mingling of Upper Carboniferous and Permian types, through a considerable series of beds, it is impossible to determine, from these few specimens, whether the particular outcrops from which they were obtained should be classed with the Permian or the Upper Carboniferous, though they most probably belong to the former.

The farthest western locality at which specimens were collected indicating the occurrence of Jurassic rocks is on the east side of the Wahsatch Mountains (latitude, 40° 48′ north, longitude, 111° 15′ west). They consist of gray, argillaceous, more or less sandy rock, containing fragments of *Pecten, Ostrea,* and stems of *Pentacrinus,* which latter agree exactly with those of *P. asteriscus,* Meek and Hayden, from the Jurassic beds at the Black Hills, Dakota. The strata containing these fossils are associated, as I am informed by Mr. Engelmann, with a series of light-colored and reddish sandstones.

At Red Buttes, on the North Platte, above Fort Laramie, well-marked Jurassic fossils were also collected, in gray argillaceous sandy beds. They consist of fragments of the same *Pentacrinus* mentioned above, and an Oyster, nearly related to *O. Marshii* and *Grypheæa calceola,* Quenstedt, or an allied species, a new species of *Pecten,* near *P. lens** of Sowerby, and *Belemnites densus,* Meek and Hayden.

The strata from which these fossils were collected are clearly of the same age as the Jurassic outcrops at the southwest base of the Black Hills, and, as at that place, hold a position above a series of red arenaceous deposits containing large quantities of gypsum.†

A few fossils of Cretaceous age were found as far west as Bear River, and on

* I have, since writing the above, described this species under the name *Camptonectes bellistriata.*

† No fossils have yet been found in these gypsum-bearing formations, either on the Platte or at the Black Hills, but owing to the fact that those discovered in the overlying Jurassic strata, at both of these localities, are nearly all closely allied to Liassic forms, while similar gypsum-bearing deposits are known to come in above the strata containing Permian types of fossils in Eastern Kansas, it appears possible that they may, in part, represent the New Red Sandstone of the Old World.

several of the tributaries of Weber River, east of the Great Salt Lake. They occur at these localities in whitish and light-yellowish sandstones, and consist of a small *Anomia*, an Oyster like *O. glabra*, Meek and Hayden, and an *Inoceramus* similar to the western species usually referred to *I. problematicus*, Schlot. (sp.).

Deposits of good brown coal and beds of shale were also seen at some localities, associated with the strata containing the above-mentioned Cretaceous fossils, and apparently dipping at the same angle, so as to leave the impression, when the outcrops were examined, that they belong to the same series of strata containing the Cretaceous fossils.*

Cretaceous fossils were also collected from near the bridge on the North Platte, above Fort Laramie. They are *Ostrea congesta*, Conrad, two or three species of *Inoceramus*, with fragments of a small *Baculites*, and occur in gray, soft shaly beds, evidently of the age of No. 2 or 3 of the Upper Missouri Cretaceous series.

There are, likewise, in the collection a few Cretaceous fossils from near Little Sandy Creek, in Southeastern Nebraska, where rocks of that age were previously known to occur. They are in a whitish limestone matrix, evidently belonging to the horizon of the Niobrara beds, or No. 3 of the Upper Missouri section, and consist of *Inoceramus problematicus*, Schloth. and fragments of a small *Baculites.*

Quite a number of specimens in the collection from the Green River country, east of the Wahsatch range of mountains, are of Tertiary age. They evidently came from two formations, as they consist of two distinct groups of fossils, and Mr. Engelmann informs me that the more recent series seems not to be conformable in its dip with the older, which was highly inclined at the localities examined. This older series also differs from the other in being clearly an estuary or brackish-water deposit; while the newer, so far as known, contains the remains of only strictly fresh-water mollusks.

The older formation mentioned above was seen on Bear River, near the mouth of Sulphur Creek, some 30 miles west of Fort Bridger, and but a few hundred yards distant from the outcrops of brown coal and yellow sandstone with *Inoceramus* already mentioned. These beds are chiefly dark-colored and grayish, argillaceous shales, with coarse, dark and lighter-colored calcareous grits. The fossils found in them belong to the genera *Unio*, *Corbula*, *Goniobasis*, *Viviparus*, and *Rhytophorus*;† being just such an assemblage as we might expect to find in an estuary or brackish-water deposit.

The fossils from this region, figured by Professor Hall in Frémont's report, Plate III, are fresh- and brackish-water types, and possibly may be from this horizon. I have always been at a loss, however, to identify, with confidence, the species described in Frémont's report, partly on account of the brevity of the descriptions and the want of more satisfactory illustrations, but also to a great extent owing to the fact that the localities are only given by longitudes and latitudes, which were, at that time, not determined with sufficient precision to know certainly exactly from which one of several distinct formations the specimens were obtained. At one time I was rather

* Since these remarks were written, I have visited this locality, and found the coal-beds there clearly included in the Cretaceous strata mentioned above. (See remarks of the writer on this subject in Hayden's Sixth Annual Report United States Geological Survey of the Territories, 1872.)

† The type of the genus *Rhytophorus* was originally ordered by me to *Melampus*.

inclined to think that the shell described by Professor Hall, in Frémont's report, under the name *Cerithium tenerum*, might be one of the Bear River species of *Goniobasis*, and two other shells described by him in the same report, under the names of *Natica? occidentalis*, and *Turbo paludinæformis*, might be the young of a *Viviparus* found at the Bear River locality, but on these points it is not possible to arrive at any very satisfactory conclusion until some one can be fortunate enough to be able to make comparisons with Professor Hall's type-specimens.

At the time of writing this report, all of the facts known seem to favor the conclusion that the Bear River fresh-water beds belong to the Lower Tertiary.*

The still more modern series mentioned above occupies an extensive area in the Green River country. I am informed by Mr. Engelmann, that it is mainly made up of greenish sandstones and arenaceous shales, with some calcareous beds, several hundred feet in thickness, in which no organic remains were found. Beneath these beds, however, he discovered light-colored shales and limestones, containing great numbers of fossils belonging to a few species, all of which are fresh-water types. Those collected consist of two new species of *Melania*, two of *Limnea*, one of *Unio*, and three of *Planorbis*.†

In some respects a part, at least, of these deposits seem to correspond in a general way with those of the Upper Missouri; that is, they consist of an older series of brackish-water origin (probably in local isolated basins), succeeded by fresh-water formations, extending over much wider areas. It is worthy of note, however, that the fossils found in these Utah [and Wyoming] Tertiary formations are all, so far as known, specifically distinct from those characterizing the Upper Missouri beds, excepting a single species of *Viviparus* already mentioned (*V. Conradi*, Meek and Hayden), which is common to the Sulphur Creek estuary deposits,‡ and those of the Upper Missouri, near the mouth of Judith River. Still, it is probable that we have not yet obtained facts enough to be able to determine whether or not these formations correspond in their details with those of the Upper Missouri.

From what has been said, it will be seen that all the fossils contained in the collection from localities along the line of the survey, in the Great Salt Lake Basin, are from Paleozoic rocks; while all those from Secondary and Tertiary formations were collected from localities east of the Wahsatch range of mountains.§

Very respectfully, yours, &c.,

F. B. MEEK.

* Long after the expression of this rather cautious opinion, I intimated that these beds might possibly be Upper Cretaceous rather than Lower Tertiary; but still felt the want of any positive evidence warranting this conclusion. (See Mr. King's Report Geol. Survey of the Fortieth Parallel, III, 466.) At a still later date (Hayden's Sixth Annual Report Geol. Survey of the Territories, 462, 1873), after having visited the locality, and being forcibly impressed with the fact that these brackish-water Bear River beds are upheaved nearly to a vertical posture, like the marine, decidedly Cretaceous beds at the same place, with the same strike, I was still more strongly impressed with the probability that the former also belong to the Cretaceous. It was my intention at that time to discuss this question more at length, but even before quite closing the page of my remarks in Hayden's Report, just alluded to (which was the last part of the same written), I was suddenly attacked with a severe and dangerous sickness, and merely had a brief note added, saying that "until some decidedly Cretaceous fossils have been somewhere found in or above these beds, they may be left in the Lower Eocene." The weight of evidence, however, favors the conclusion that they belong at the top of the Cretaceous (November, 1875.)

† These seem to belong in part to what has since been called the Green River group (November, 1875).

‡ These are the Bear River beds already mentioned.

§ Some of the facts and conclusions contained in the foregoing remarks were published by the writer, in connection with Mr. H. Engelmann, in the Proceed. Acad. Nat. Sci. Phila., April, 1860.

DESCRIPTIONS OF NEW SPECIES.

DEVONIAN FOSSILS.

MOLLUSCA.

BRACHIOPODA.

Genus PRODUCTUS, Sowerby.

PRODUCTUS SUBACULEATUS, Murchison (?).

Plate 1, fig. 3, *a*, *b*, *c*.

Productus subaculeatus, Murchison (1840), Bull. Soc. Geol. de Fr., XI, 255, pl. ii, fig. 9; and of numerous other later writers.

Shell small, subhemispherical; hinge scarcely equaling the greatest breadth. Ventral valve regularly convex, not produced in front; beak projecting little beyond the hinge; ears small, flattened, and nearly rectangular at their extremities; surface having scattering spines-bases, and marked by fine lines of growth and obscure concentric wrinkles, which latter become obsolete excepting near the beak and on the lateral slopes. Dorsal valve nearly semicircular, distinctly concave in the central and anterior regions, more flattened toward the cardinal border and the lateral extremities of the hinge; surface marked by small concentric wrinkles, and little scattering pits corresponding, apparently, to the spines or tubercles of the other valve.

Length, 0.52 inch; breadth about 0.57.

I am by no means clearly satisfied that this little shell is specifically identical with *P. subaculeatus* of Murchison, the specimens in the collection being few, and not in a very satisfactory condition for comparison. I do not think, however, that it can be distinguished from specimens that have been referred by high authorities in the Old World to *P. subaculeatus.* It nevertheless seems also to be closely allied to New York Hamilton group specimens that have been figured under other names.

Locality and position.—West side of Buell Valley, latitude 39° 30′ north, longitude 115° 36′ west.

Genus SPIRIFER, Sowerby.

SPIRIFER UTAHENSIS, Meek.

Plate 1, fig. 4, *a*, *b*, *c*.

Spirifera Norwoodi, Meek (July, 1860), Proceed. Acad. Nat. Sci. Philad., XII, 308 (not Hall, 1856).
Spirifera Utahensis, Meek (November 20, 1860), last page of extra copies of the above paper.

Shell rather small, trigonoid-semicircular, wider than long, with greatest breadth on or near the hinge-line. Ventral valve very convex at the umbo, sloping abruptly to the front and sides; beak elevated, rather pointed, and more or less arched over the area, sometimes a little twisted to one side; mesial sinus rather shallow, rounded, and extending to the point of the beak, from which it widens and deepens very gradually to the front; area triangular, but wider than high, rather distinctly arched; foramen very narrow, and apparently entirely open. Dorsal valve convex, but much more depressed than the other; mesial fold obscure in the umbonal region, slightly elevated, and rounded at the front. Surface of each valve ornamented by about forty small depressed radiating costæ, some six or seven of which occupy the mesial sinus of the ventral valve, and seven or eight the fold of the dorsal valve.

Length, 0.52 inch; breadth (along hinge-line), about 0.60 inch; convexity, 0.42 inch.

The costæ are all simple, unless a few of them bifurcate in the mesial sinus or on the fold. They generally converge to the beaks, though a portion of those near the lateral extremities seem to run out on the hinge before reaching the beaks. None of the specimens are in a condition to have preserved finer surface-markings, if there were any.

This shell is of the same type as several species found in rocks of the age of the New York Hamilton group in that and some of the Western States, but seems to be distinct from them all.

Locality and position.—Same as last.

SPIRIFER ENGELMANNI, Meek.

Plate 1, fig. 1, *a*, *b*, *c*.

Spirifera Engelmanni (July, 1860), Proceed. Acad. Nat. Sci. Philad., XII, 308.

Shell rather small, semicircular, about twice as wide as long; hinge equaling the greatest breadth, angular at the extremities. Dorsal valve depressed convex; mesial fold rather narrow, but slightly elevated, flattened along the middle, and apparently without plications. Ventral valve very convex in the umbonal region, sloping abruptly to the sides and front; beak pointed, more or less arched; area high, triangular, the hinge side being longer than the lateral slopes, which are usually somewhat angular, generally rather strongly arcuate, or inclined a little backward over the hinge; foramen very narrow, apparently open to the point of the beak; mesial sinus narrow, shallow, extending to the beak, flattened in the middle, and without plications. Surface ornamented by from seven to nine depressed, rounded, simple plications on each side of the fold and sinus.

Length of hinge, about 0.66 inch; diameter from hinge to front, 0.39 inch; height of area, 0.26 inch.

It is probable the surface was also marked with very fine striæ, and possibly granules, as is not uncommon in this section of the genus, but the specimens are not sufficiently well preserved to have retained such delicate ornaments, if they existed.

This species is quite similar in size and form to the last, but may be readily distinguished by its much larger and less numerous plications, none of which are defined on the mesial fold, or in the sinus, as in that species. As near as can be determined from a description without figures or measurements, it seems to be also related to *S. fornacula* of Hall, from the Hamilton group in Illinois (Report Regents University of New York, 1857, p. 115), but has not more than half as many plications.

Named in honor of Mr. Henry Engelmann, Geologist of Captain Simpson's exploring party.

Locality and position.—Devonian of Neil's Valley, latitude 39° 32′, longitude 115° 36′.

SPIRIFER STRIGOSUS, Meek.

Plate 1, fig. 5, *a*, *b*, *c*, *d*.

Spirifera macra, Meek (July, 1860), Proceed. Acad. Nat. Sci. Phila., 309 (not Hall, 1856).
Spirifer strigosus, Meek (1860), last page of extra copies of the above-cited paper.

Shell rather under medium size, subtrigonal, or subsemicircular, considerably wider than long; hinge-line equaling the greatest width, and terminating in rather salient angles. Dorsal valve convex in the middle, compressed toward the lateral extremities; mesial fold narrow, prominent, and angular, especially near the front. Ventral valve more convex than the other, sloping somewhat abruptly from the umbo to the sides and front; mesial sinus narrow, rather deep, with sloping sides continued to the beak, which is pointed and incurved; area of moderate breadth, with well-defined sloping lateral margins, apparently not continued quite to the extremities of the hinge, arched and inclined back over the cardinal margin; foramen triangular, higher than wide. Surface of each valve ornamented by about eighteen to twenty-four moderately distinct more or less bifurcating plications, about six or seven of which usually occupy the mesial fold, and five or six the mesial sinus.

Length of hinge, about 1.19 inches; diameter from hinge to front, 0.63 inch; height of area, 0.16 inch.

The central plication of the ventral valve usually extends along the middle of the sinus nearly or quite to the beak; while the two or three rather smaller ones in the sinus on each side, in most cases, coalesce with those forming the margin of the sinus before reaching the beak. Along the middle of the rather sharp fold of the dorsal valve there is a groove, usually a little larger than those between the other plications, and corresponding to the central plication of the opposite valve. A few of the plications on each side near the mesial sinus and fold sometimes bifurcate once, but the others seem to be all simple. The specimens are not well enough preserved to have retained fine surface-markings, if there were any.

This shell is quite unlike all of the other forms from this region, and I know of no very closely allied species from other localities.

Locality and position.—Same as last.

Genus ATRYPA, Dalman.

ATRYPA RETICULARIS (Lin.), Dalm.

Plate 1, fig. 6, *a*, *b*.

Anomia reticularis, Linnæus (1767), Syst. Nat., ed. xii, vol. 1, 1152; and Encyc. Méthod., pl. 242, fig. 4, *a*, *b*, *c*.
For the long list of subsequent synonyms, with references, &c., see Mr. Davidson's and other extended works on Palæozoic *Brachiopoda*.

Of this widely-distributed species there are quite a number of specimens in the collection from a locality near the south branch of Humboldt River. They are all rather small, and have more the aspect of Upper Silurian than Devonian varieties. As a general thing they are proportionally a little wider than usual; but they vary in this respect, and beyond a doubt belong to this well-known species.

I am not aware of this shell having been hitherto discovered at any locality within the territory of the United States, so far west by between 1,000 and 1,200 miles.

Locality and position.—Same as preceding.

ATRYPA ASPERA, Schloth.

Plate 1, fig. 2, *a*, *b*.

Terebratulites asper, Schlot. (1813), Min. Taschenb., vol. vii, pl. 1, fig. 7.
Atrypa aspera, Dalm. (1827), Vet. Acad. handl., pl. 4, fig. 3, and of many others (not J. Sowerby).
Atrypa squamosa, J. Sowerby (1840), Geol. Trans., 2d ser., vol. 5, pl. 57, fig. 1.
?*Atrypa spinosa*, Hall (1843), Geol. Rept. 4th District New York.

The specimens here referred to the above well-known and widely-distributed species are very small for that shell, and, being in a rather bad state of preservation, cannot be identified with positive certainty. From their general appearance and associates, however, I am led to regard them as probably a variety of that species. It should be explained here, however, that many reliable European authorities regard *A. aspera* as only a more coarsely-marked variety of the common *A. reticularis*.

Locality and position.—Same as last.

CARBONIFEROUS FOSSILS.

MOLLUSCA.

POLYZOA.

Genus ARCHIMEDIPORA, D'Orbigny.

ARCHIMEDIPORA, ——— (?)

Plate 1, fig. 11.

There are in the collection from the dark-colored limestones composing the hills west of Camp Floyd, a few fragments of one or more species of this curious group of *Polyzoa;* but as they merely consist of portions of the spiral axis, it is impossible to make out their specific characters. They are both dextral and sinistral, quite slender, and make about eight turns in the space of an inch.

No species of this genus has hitherto been found in the region of the Rocky Mountains, so far as known to the writer. Several species occur in the Lower Carboniferous series of the Western States; though I believe we have yet no well-authenticated instances of the occurrence of these forms in the Coal-Measure.

NOTE.—Up to this time (November, 1875), I have seen no other specimens of this genus from the Rocky Mountain region.

BRACHIOPODA.

Genus CHONETES, Fischer.

CHONETES VERNEUILIANA, var. UTAHENSIS.

Plate 2, fig. 2, *a*, *b*, *c*.

Chonetes Verneuiliana, Norwood and Pratten (1853), Jour. Acad. Nat. Sci. Phila., III, 1, pl. ii, fig. 6.

This little *Chonetes* is much like *C. Verneuiliana* of Norwood and Pratten; from the typical form of which, however, it differs in having a much broader and more rounded mesial sinus in the ventral valve, which sinus is also bounded by more angular and more diverging ridges than we usually see in *C. Verneuiliana*. Our Utah shell also seems to be more extended on the hinge-line, and has more sinuous lateral margins. Its striæ are exceedingly fine, closely arranged, and appear to increase both by intercalation and division. None of the specimens collected show very clearly the number of spines on the hinge-margin, though there appear to be about five on each side of the beak. No specimens of the dorsal valve were obtained. I am inclined to think it will be found specifically distinct from *C. Verneuiliana*.

Length of hinge, 0.45 inch; diameter from hinge to front, 0.22 inch; convexity of ventral valve, 0.12 inch.

Locality and position.—Near Humboldt Mountains, latitude 39° 57′, longitude 115° 10′.

Genus PRODUCTUS, Sowerby.

PRODUCTUS SEMISTRIATUS, Meek.

Plate 1, fig. 7 *a*, *b*.

P. semistriatus, Meek (July, 1860), Proceed. Acad. Nat. Sci., Philad., xii, 309.

Shell of medium size, greatest breadth on the hinge-line, which is nearly twice the length, measuring from the hinge to the anterior curve. Dorsal valve unknown. Ventral valve *very* gibbous, extremely arched, and greatly produced in front; sometimes provided with an obscure, very shallow mesial sinus, which never extends to the beak; ears triangular, strongly vaulted, extended nearly at right angles to the vertical sides of the elevated visceral arch, from which they are each separated by an oblique, undefined sulcus; beak very convex, distinctly incurved, and extended a little beyond the hinge; surface of the visceral region marked by small, obscure concentric wrinkles, which are crossed by numerous, more or less bifurcating striæ; anterior half smooth, or only marked by fine lines of growth; spines rather long, erect, and scattering.

Length of hinge, 1.19 inches; diameter from hinge to anterior curve, 0.72 inch; length from the beak to the anterior margin of the ventral valve, measuring over its curve, 2.14 inches.

The concentric wrinkles are most distinct on the lateral slopes of the visceral arch, and seem to extend upon the ears. When the radiating striæ are well defined, they form, with these wrinkles, a more or less distinct reticulate style of ornamentation, over the visceral half of the shell. The radiating striæ are generally rather obscure, and number about ten in the space of 0.30 inch.

This species belongs to the group *Semireticulati* of Koninck; its most marked peculiarities are its narrow, strongly arcuate form, produced anterior, and the entire absence of radiating striæ over the whole of the ventral valve, excepting the visceral half. These characters will serve to distinguish it from all the other forms resembling it in other respects, yet known to the writer.

Locality and position.—Timpanogos Cañon, latitude 40° 22′, longitude 111° 38′; in a dark, argillaceous rock, probably of the age of the Coal-Measures.

PRODUCTUS MULTISTRIATUS, Meek.

Plate 1, fig. 8, *a*, *b*.

Productus multistriata, Meek, (July, 1860), Proceed. Acad. Nat. Sci., Philad., xii, 309.

Shell above medium size, breadth nearly double the length, from the hinge direct to the anterior slope; hinge-line longer than the breadth of the shell in front of it; ears moderately large, triangular, distinctly vaulted, and standing nearly at right angles to the swell of the larger valve. Ventral valve extremely ventricose, strongly arched, and provided with a broad, deep mesial sinus, extending from the beak to the front; beak rather small, compressed, and projecting little beyond the hinge. Dorsal valve deeply concave, provided with three broad, obscure radiating prominences, one of which corresponds to the mesial sinus of the other valve, and the other two radiate to the lateral margins in front of the ears. Surface of both valves marked by numerous very fine, obscure, radiating striæ, and destitute of spines, excepting about three near the extremity of each ear, and a few on the anterior slope of the ventral valve.

Length of hinge, near 1.77 inches; length from hinge to anterior slope, 1 inch; greatest breadth in front of the hinge, 1.48 inches.

None of the specimens show concentric lines or wrinkles, but as they are all a little worn, there may have been very fine marks of growth. The radiating striæ are small, very regular, and number about ten to twelve in the space of 0.20 inch; they appear to increase chiefly by intercalation. The swell of the arched portion of ventral valve is very prominent, and has, in consequence of the deep mesial sinus, a more or less distinct bilobate appearance; while the lateral slopes are very abrupt, and its anterior and lateral margins considerably produced. Judging from the few remaining bases of spines on the ventral valve, they seem to have been strong and erect.

Locality and position.—Yellowish limestone series, east side of Long Valley, latitude 39° 57′ north, longitude 115° 10′ west, where it is quite common; probably Upper Carboniferous.

Genus ATHYRIS, McCoy.

ATHYRIS SUBTILITA, Hall (sp.).

Plate 2, fig. 4, *a*, *b*.

Terebratula subtilita, Hall (1852), Stansbury's Rept. Expl. Great Salt Lake, 4, pl. 1, *a*, *b*, and 2, *a*, *b*.
Terebratula? subtilita, Davidson (1857), Monogr. Brit. Carb. Brach., 18, pl. ii, figs. 21 and 22.—Marcou (1858), Geol. N Am., 52, pl. vi.
Spirigera subtilita, Meek and Hayden (1859), Proceed. Acad. Nat. Sci. Philad., IX, 20.
Athyris subtilita, Newberry (1861), Ives's Colorado Report, 126.—Davidson (1863), Brach. of S. India, pl. ix, fig. 7.—Salter, (1861), Quart. Jour. Geol. Soc. Lond., XVII, pl. iv, fig. 4, *a*, *b*.—Meek (1872), Paleont. E. Nebraska 180, pl. i, fig. 12; pl. v, fig. 8; and pl. viii, fig. 4.

There are several characteristic specimens of this well-known shell in the collections from the Coal-Measures of Eastern Kansas, and quite a number of apparently the same species from the Yellow Limestone series so extensively developed in the central region of the Great Salt Lake Basin, near Humboldt Mountains. The specimen figured, which is rather smaller than the average size of its associates, is from the latter locality. Some of the larger specimens are more compressed, and have a more distinct mesial sinus than the one figured. None of those from this distant western locality are in a condition to show the interior; but, so far as can be determined, they present no external differences from Professor Hall's species.

This seems to be one of the most widely distributed species of all those known in the Carboniferous rocks. It ranges from Eastern Ohio, through Indiana, Illinois, Missouri, and Kansas, westward to the middle of the Great Salt Lake Basin, and from Nebraska far into New Mexico. Mr. Marcou also says he has received it from Vancouver's Island;* and Mr. Davidson identifies it from the Carboniferous rocks of England, as well as from India, and it also occurs in South America.

It is a little remarkable that in this country *Athyris subtilita* is, so far as known, peculiarly characteristic of the Coal-Measures, while in England it appears to occur only in the Lower Carboniferous rocks. Mr. Davidson once referred it to the genus *Terebratula*, with a query, not having seen the interior. Several of the specimens, however, found by Dr. Hayden and the writer in Eastern Kansas, in the same beds from which those first described by Professor Hall were obtained, show the internal spiral appendages and other characters of the genus *Athyris*, or *Spirigera*, as it may have to be called.

Genus SPIRIFER, Sowerby.

SPIRIFER (SPIRIFERINA?) SCOBINA, Meek.

Plate 2, fig. 5, *a*, *b*, *c*,

Spirifera scobina, Meek (July, 1860), Proceed. Acad. Nat. Sci., Philad., XII, 310.

Shell rather large, truncato-subcircular, approaching subpentagonal, moderately gibbous, length and breadth nearly equal, hinge-line scarcely equaling the greatest breadth; lateral margins rounding anteriorly and intersecting the hinge almost at right angles; valves nearly equally convex, each provided with from about seventeen to twenty-two rather broad, depressed, occasionally bifurcating, plications. Ventral valve a little more gibbous than the other, and having a shallow mesial sinus, which is very small near the beak, but widens gradually toward the front; beak moderately prominent, incurved; area of medium breadth, with nearly parallel margins, extending to the lateral extremities of the hinge, distinctly arched near the beak; foramen having nearly the form of an equilateral triangle. Dorsal valve moderately convex in the umbonal region; beak rather prominent and incurved; mesial fold depressed, not distinctly defined excepting at the front, where it is generally flattened. Surface of both valves apparently without striæ, but beautifully ornamented by numerous minute regularly disposed granules.

Breadth, 2 inches; length, 1.88 inches; convexity, 1.34 inches.

From about three to five of the plications usually occupy the mesial sinus, and near the same number the mesial fold, in the former of which they are generally a little smaller than on each side. On some specimens most of the plications are simple, while in other instances a portion of them bifurcate, though rarely more than once. The plications are usually about twice as broad as the grooves between. The mesial sinus is never very strongly defined, and sometimes becomes almost obsolete near the beak. Where the surface has been a little worn, the fine granules are entirely oblit-

* I think this an error, however, as I have never heard of any other evidence of Carboniferous rocks there.

erated, but on well-preserved specimens they present a very beautiful appearance under a lens. Scarcely any marks of growth are visible in most cases.

From its regularly granulated surface, and some appearance of punctures seen on exfoliated surfaces, I am led to suspect that this shell may be a *Spiriferina*, but I am not sure that it possesses the internal lamina of that type.

This is a well-marked species, very distinct from all the forms I have seen in any of the Carboniferous rocks of the Western States, and seems not very nearly related to any known foreign species.

Locality and position.—Divide between Long and Ruby Valleys. Latitude 40° north, longitude 115° 20′ west. From the yellowish limestone series, probably Upper Carboniferous.

SPIRIFER (SPIRIFERINA) PULCHER, Meek.

Plate 2, fig. 1, *a, b, c, d, e, f, g, h.*

Spirifera pulchra, Meek (July, 1860), Proceed. Acad. Nat. Sci. Philad., XII, 310.

Shell of medium size, more or less compressed, length from one-half to one-third the breadth; hinge-line equaling the greatest width; lateral extremities often much extended, compressed, and acutely pointed. Ventral valve more convex than the other in the umbonal region; beak rather small, and not very strongly incurved; area somewhat narrow, very slightly arched, or inclined back over the hinge, its margins being subparallel; foramen triangular, a little higher than wide; mesial sinus narrow, well defined, rather deep, and smoothly rounded within, extending to the point of the beak, from which it widens very gradually toward the front; lateral slopes on each side of the mesial sinus of the ventral valve, and its corresponding elevation on the dorsal valve, bearing from seven to nine simple, elevated, rather narrowly-rounded plications. Entire surface ornamented by fine, regularly disposed granules, which, on worn or exfoliated specimens, are seen to be connected with punctures; marks of growth moderately distinct, and more or less arched in crossing the plications and mesial fold.

Length of largest specimen, 1.13 inches; breadth, 3.10 inches; convexity, 0.76 inch.

This is quite easily distinguished from any of its associates, and not very nearly related to any Carboniferous species I have yet seen from other localities. The delicate granulations seen on its surface are also well marked on the surfaces of the exfoliated lamina, and are likewise represented by the usual corresponding punctures on the interior. It varies much in the comparative length of the hinge, though the breadth of the shell is in all cases considerably greater than its length. The individuals having the shortest hinge are also usually more gibbous than the others.

Internal casts of this shell show that it has the mesial septum of its ventral valve well developed, which, with its distinctly punctate structure, requires its removal to *Spiriferina*, whether we view that group as a genus or a subgenus.

Locality and position.—East and west side of Long Valley, and pass east of Ruby Valley. Latitude 40° north, longitude 115° 20′ west. Geological position same as last.

SPIRIFER CAMERATUS, Morton.

Plate 2, fig. 3, *a*, *b*.

Spirifer cameratus, Morton (1836), Am. Jour. Sci. and Arts, XXIX, 150, pl. 2, fig. 3.—Hall (1858), Report Geol. Survey of Iowa, 709, pl. xxviii, fig. 2.—Meek (1872), Palæont. E. Nebraska, 183, pl. vi, fig. 12; and pl. viii, fig. 15.
Spirifer Meusebachanus, Roemer (1852), Kreid. von Texas, 88, pl. xi, fig. 7.
Spirifer triplicatus, Hall (1852), Stansbury's Report Great Salt Lake Exp., 410, pl. ii, fig. 5, (by error pl. 4.)
Compare *Spirifer fasciger*, Von Keyserling (1847), Petsch., 231, pl. 5, fig. 3.

After a very careful comparison of our specimens of this shell with a good series of Morton's species cited above, from the Coal-Measures of Kansas and other western localities, I am left in some doubt in regard to their identity. It is true *S. cameratus* is a variable form, but all the specimens of it I have yet seen are less robust, more finely plicated, and usually have a narrower area. The plications of the Utah specimens are also generally less distinctly fasciculate, though they vary in this respect somewhat.

In some respects our shell resembles a form figured by Prof. Marcou in his work on the Geology of North America, under the name of *Spirifer striatus* var. *triplicatus*, but its plications are coarser and more irregular in their mode of branching, while its mesial elevation is much less prominent and not near so angular.

So far as yet known *Spirifera cameratus* of Morton, is, in this country, peculiarly characteristic of the Coal-Measures, and can always be distinguished at a glance from any of the forms occurring in our Lower Carboniferous rocks. It is an interesting fact, however, that they find in the Lower Carboniferous series of the Old World, forms regarded by the most trustworthy authorities as varieties of *Spirifer striatus*, Martin, which are apparently undistinguishable from Morton's *S. cameratus*. One of Mr. Davidson's figures of *S. striatus* var. *attenuatus* (fig. 13, pl. II), given in his admirable Monograph of the British Carboniferous Brachiopoda, published by the Palæontographical Society, is almost as good a representation of some specimens of Morton's *S. cameratus* as could be drawn; while Mr. Davidson, whose opinion is worthy of the fullest confidence, says he finds so many gradations between this form and the large varieties of *S. striatus*, with coarser, uniform plications, that they cannot be considered distinct species. Yet it is very remarkable that we should have in the Lower Carboniferous rocks of this country very closely allied representatives of the large varieties of *S. striatus* (if not indeed that species itself*), and in the Coal-Measures others scarcely if at all distinguishable from *S. striatus* var. *attenuatus*, while we find no connecting links between these forms at either of these horizons, nor in any of the beds of passage between them.

Locality and position.—Summit Spring Pass, east of Long Valley, and between Long and Ruby Valleys; latitude, 39° 33′ to 40° north, longitude, 115° 12′ to 20′ west. Position, same as last.

* See *Sp. Logani*, Hall, Iowa Report, vol. 1, part 2, pl. 21, fig. 1, 2, 3.

LAMELLIBRANCHIATA.

Genus AVICULOPECTEN, McCoy.

AVICULOPECTEN UTAHENSIS, Meek.

Plate 1, fig. 9, *a*, *b*, *c*.

Pecten Utahensis, Meek (July, 1860), Proceed. Acad. Nat. Sci., Philad., XII, 310.

Shell of medium size, thin, subcircular, much compressed, apparently nearly equivalve, the left valve being slightly more convex than the other; ears small, subequal, triangular, and distinctly flattened; posterior ear truncated nearly at right angles to the hinge, sometimes a little rounded on the truncated edge; anterior ear separated from the margin by a very shallow sinus; surface of the left valve ornamented by rather obscure, unequal, depressed, radiating costæ, and numerous extremely fine, equidistant, thread-like, concentric lines, scarcely visible without the aid of a lens; right valve smooth, or only marked by fine concentric striæ.

Length, about 1.10 inches; breadth, 1.20 inches; length of hinge, 0.57 inch.

Sometimes the radiating costæ are nearly equal, but usually there are two, three, four or more smaller ones between each two of the larger. The smaller costæ generally die out or coalesce with each other or the larger ones before reaching the beak. They are all usually obsolete on the lateral margins, and always wanting on the ears, which are only marked by fine, closely-arranged, concentric striæ.

Locality and position.—Summit Spring Pass, divide between Long and Ruby Valleys; latitude, 39° 33′, longitude, 115° 12′ west. Probably Upper Carboniferous.

CEPHALAPODA.

Genus ORTHOCERAS, Auct.

ORTHOCERAS BACULUM, Meek.

Plate 1, fig. 10, *a*. *b*.

Orthoceras baculum, Meek (July, 1860), Proceed. Acad. Nat. Sci. Philad., XII, 310.

Shell rather small, elongate-conical; section very nearly circular near the smaller end, and slightly oval toward the aperture; sides diverging from the apex at an angle of 8°; septa not oblique, distinctly concave on the anterior side, separated by spaces equal to one-fifth their own greater transverse diameter; siphuncle rounded, nearly but not quite central, a little less than one-sixth the diameter of the shell; surface apparently smooth.

The only specimen of this species in the collection is a fragment, imperfect at both extremities, and about two inches in length, with a diameter at the smaller end of 0.47 inch. Although it retains no surface-markings, there may be fine lines of growth on well-preserved specimens.

In form and proportions this shell is quite similar to two or three species described by de Koninck from the Carboniferous rocks of Belgium. It differs, however, from his *O. Goldfussianum* (pl. xliii, figs. 3 and 4, Animaux fossiles), which it seems to resemble more than any species known to me, in having its siphuncle slightly excentric, though not so much so as in his *O. laterale*, and in having its septa arranged so as to be separated by spaces equaling about one-fifth instead of only one-eighth the diameter of the shell.

Locality and position.—East side Ruby Valley; latitude, 40° north, longitude, 115° 20′ west. Probably Lower Carboniferous.

JURASSIC SPECIES.

RADIATA.

ECHINODERMATA.

Genus PENTACRINITES, Miller.

PENTACRINITES (undt. sp.).

Plate 3, fig. 5, *a*, *b*, *c*.

Numerous fragments of the column and its appendages, of this Crinoid were found in the Jurassic beds near the Red Buttes, on the North Platte. It seems to differ from *P. asteriscus*, Meek and Hayden, characteristic specimens of which also occur at the same locality, in having a more slender and much less distinctly angular column, though it may possibly belong to the same species, the column in Crinoids being very variable in form.

MOLLUSCA.

LAMELLIBRANCHIATA.

Genus OSTREA, Linn.

OSTREA ENGELMANNI, Meek.

Plate 3, fig. 6.

Ostrea Engelmanni, Meek, (July, 1860), Proceed. Acad. Nat. Sci. Philad., XII, 311.—Meek and Hayden (1865), Palæont Upper Mo., 73, wood-cuts A and B.

The collection contains only upper valves of this species, all of which are much compressed, rather thin and subovate, or more less irregular in form. Beak distinctly truncated, and provided with a broad but short area; surface ornamented by from five to about fifteen irregular, moderately distinct, rather rounded, radiating plications, which do not usually extend upon the umbonal region, but become quite distinct at the border, which is usually thin; lines of growth regular and moderately well defined, but not imbricating. Muscular scar rather large, ovate and distinct.

Length (of the largest specimen), 3.50 inches; breadth, 3.0 inches.

This oyster bears some resemblance to *O. Marshii* of Sowerby, but appears to be a much thinner shell, and differs remarkably in the length of the area of the upper value, which is, in none of the specimens brought in, more than one-third as long as in individuals of *O. Marshii* of the same size, nor is it so concave in the middle as in that species; while its plications are not so prominent or angular.

It is also somewhat similar to a form referred by Prof. Jules Marcou in his Geology of North America, pl. iv, fig. 4, to *O. Marshii*. The shell now under consideration, however, is thinner, and differs in being without imbricating marks of growth, while its plications are smaller. In addition to this, the shell figured by Mr. Marcou is now known to be a Cretaceous species, that holds a position far above the horizon from which *O. Engelmanni* was obtained.

This species is named in honor of Mr. Henry Engelmann, of Saint Louis, Geologist of Captain Simpson's expedition.

Locality and position.—Jurassic beds at Red Buttes, on the North Platte, latitude 42° 50′, longitude 106° 40′ west.

GRYPHÆA CALCEOLA, Quenstedt ?.

Plate 3, fig. 2.

Ostrea calceola Roemer (?), Oölite, Geb. tab. 18, fig. 19.
Gryphæa calceola, Quenstedt ? (1856), Der Jura, I, 353, pl. 48, fig. 1–3.

Several specimens undistinguishable from the species cited above were obtained from the Jurassic beds near the Red Buttes, on the North Platte. The specimen figured has the form and other characters of a true *Gryphæa;* but some of the others have the whole beak truncated, and present more the appearance of *Oystrea;* though there seem to be intermediate gradations between these forms. They show clearly the radiating striæ seen on the under valve of *G. calceola*, as known in Europe.

Genus CAMPTONECTES, Agassiz.

CAMPTONECTES BELLISTRIATA, Meek.

Plate 3, fig. 3, *a, b, c, d.*

Pecten bellistriata, Meek (July, 1860), Proceed. Acad. Nat. Sci. Philad., XII, 311.
Camptonectes bellistriata, Meek (1864), Smithsonian Check-List N. Am., Juras. Fossils, 28; and (1865) Palæont. Upper Mo., 77, wood-cuts A, B, C.

Shell of medium size, subcircular, sometimes wider than long, thin, compressed, nearly or quite equivalve; hinge straight and very short; posterior wing small or nearly obsolete, obliquely truncated; anterior wing small, vertically truncated at the extremity, and in the right valve separated from the margin below by a distinct more or less angular sinus, from which a shallow flat groove extends obliquely to the beak; beaks of both valves small, and rather compressed; surface ornamented by numerous fine, arched, bifurcating strae, crossed by extremely small, closely arranged concentric lines, which are often nearly obsolete on the radiating striae over the more convex portions of the valves, but quite distinct in the slender depressions between, to which they impart a punctate appearance.

Length (broad variety), 2.26 inches; breadth, 2.65 inches; convexity, 0.64 inch.

The radiating striæ, of which about six to seven may be counted in the space of one-tenth of an inch near the border on the middle of the valves, are more crowded on the lateral margins, where they curve strongly outward. They are separated by exceedingly delicate impressed lines, and on some parts of the shell occasionally present the peculiarity of bifurcating, and again coalescing at intervals. On the lateral margins the concentric striæ are usually well defined and very regular, so as to form with the radiating striæ a fine cancellated style of ornamentation. Only concentric markings appear to be well defined on the anterior wing of the right valve.

This shell is very closely related to the Jurassic species *C. lens* (= *Pecten lens* of Sowerby), having much the same form, and almost exactly the same style of ornamentation. It differs, however, from all the figures I have seen of *P. lens*, in being usually broader in proportion to its length, and its hinge is also proportionally much shorter, being generally less than one-third the greatest breadth of the shell, while that of Sowerby's species is represented from one-half to three-fourths as long as the breadth of the widest part of the valves below. The posterior wing of our species is also much smaller and obliquely truncated so as to form a much more obtuse angle with the hinge-line.

Professor Agassiz, the founder of the genus *Camptonectes*, informed me that on making careful comparisons of European specimens, he was satisfied that some three or four distinct species have long been confounded under Sowerby's name *Pecten lens*.

Locality and position.—Same as last.

GASTEROPODA.

Genus DENTALIUM, Linn.

DENTALIUM ? SUBQUADRATUM, Meek.

Plate 3, fig. 1, *a*, *b*, *c*.

Dentalium ? subquadratum, Meek (July, 1860), Proceed. Acad. Nat. Sci. Philad., XII, 311.

Shell small, slender, regularly and slightly arcuate, very gradually tapering, flattened or a little concave on four sides so as to present a subquadrangular section, the angles being a little rounded; section of internal cavity circular; surface apparently without longitudinal striæ or marks of growth.

Length, about 1 inch; diameter at larger end, 0.05 inch; diameter at the smaller extremity, 0.02.

This fossil is found in great numbers, associated with fragments of *Belemnites* and *Pentacrinites*, in thin pieces of gray, sandy, calcareous rock. It has the usual proportions and curve of *Dentaliumi;* but the texture, quadrangular form, and surface characters of the shell give it considerably the appearance of *Serpula* and some allied genera. I was at first inclined to suppose it might be an appendage of a *Pentacrinites*, but as it presents no traces of a jointed structure, and has a large internal cavity, this cannot be the case.

Whatever may be the true relations of these bodies, they will probably be of use in the identification of the formation in which they occur, and should not be overlooked by the Paleontologist, in consequence of their doubtful zoölogical relations. I suspect that it will form the type of a distinct genus.

Locality and position.—Jurassic beds on the North Platte, at Red Buttes, latitude, 42° 50′ north, longitude, 106° 40′ west.

CEPHALOPODA.

Genus BELEMNITES, Lamarck.

BELEMNITES DENSUS, Meek and Hayden.

Plate 3, fig. 4, *a. b.*

Belemnites densus, Meek and Hayden (March, 1858), Proceed. Acad. Nat. Sci. Philad., X, 58; also (1865), Palæont. Upper Missouri, 126, pl. iv, fig. 10, *a, b, c*, and pl. v. *a–h.*

Many imperfect specimens of this species were collected from the Jurassic rocks on the North Platte, near the Red Buttes. They agree exactly in all respects with those brought by Lieutenant Warren's expedition from the Jurassic beds at the south-west base of the Black Hills. This species is very closely allied to forms found in the Jurassic deposits of France and Russia; and may, on comparison, prove identical with some one of these foreign species. I have never yet seen an entire specimen of it, though it is quite abundant, and all parts of it can be seen in detached fragments. It probably attained a length of about 4.50 to 5 inches.

CRETACEOUS FOSSILS.

LAMELLIBRANCHIATA.

Genus INOCERAMUS, Sowerby.

INOCERAMUS PROBLEMATICUS, Schloth.

Plate 4, fig. 1, *a* (and 1 *b, c*?).

Mytilites problematicus, Schlotheim (1820), Petrefact., 312.
Mytiloides lobatus, Brong. (1822), Geol. des Envir. de Paris, 215, pl. 3, fig. 4.
Inoceramus mytiloides, Mantel (1822), Geol. Sussex, tab. xxvii, fig. 3; and tab. xxviii, fig. 2.—Sowerby (1823), Min. Conch., v, 61, 442.—Goldf. (1836), Petref. Germ., II, 118, pl. cxiii, fig. 4.—? Roemer (1842), Kreid. von Texas, 60, tab. vii, fig. 5.
Catillus Schlotheimii, Neilson (1827), Petref. Suecana, 19.
Catillus mytiloides, Deshayes (1830), Encycl. Méth., II, 211.
Inoceramus problematicus, d'Orbigny (1843), Paléont., Fr., III, Terr. Crét., 510, 406.—Meek and Hayden (1857), Proceed. Acad. Nat. Sci. Philad., IX, 119.—Meek (1864), Smithsonian Check-List N. Am. Cret. Fossils.—Meek, Palæont. Upper Missouri Basin and contiguous country, 62, pl. 9, fig. 3 *a b*.
Inoceramus pseudo-mytiloides, Schiel (1855), Report Pacific Railroad, II, 108, pl. 3, fig. 8.
? *Inoceramus mytilopsis*, Conrad (1858), U. S. Mexican Bound. Report, I, 152, pl. 5, fig. 6.

Shell rhomboid-ovate, oblique, moderately convex; anterior margin truncated above, from the beaks at first obliquely backward and downward, thence passing by a gentle oblique curve into the base; posterior margin descending obliquely backward, with a slightly convex outline; postero-basal extremity rather narrowly rounded; hinge comparatively short, and standing at an angle of about 60° to 90° from the slope of the anterior margin; beaks oblique, rather convex, but narrow, pointed, nearly or quite terminal, rising little above the hinge. Surface ornamented by distinct concentric undulations, which are subangular, nearly simple, and quite regular on some specimens, but more rounded and irregular on others. Between these undulations traces of finer marks of growth are also sometimes seen.

Length of largest specimen about 3 inches; breadth of same near 1.50 inches.

This is one of the forms that have been very generally referred to *I. problematicus* from western localities, though it may possibly be distinct from that species. The specimens brought in by Captain Simpson's survey are not in a very satisfactory condition, as may be seen by the figure. Since that time I have visited the locality, and collected many others. They show it to vary considerably in form, some having the hinge-line ranging much less obliquely to the axis of the umbones than others. These latter show a slight tendency to have the posterior dorsal margins compressed and subalate, and appear nearly equivalve, while there seem to be various gradations of form between these extremes. The specimen represented by our figure 1 *a*, of plate IV, has the beak and dorsal margin broken away, so that the restoration in dim shade in the figure may not represent exactly the direction of the hinge-line with relation to the umbonal axis. There are also among the specimens that I have seen since first writing this report, considerable variations in the ornamentation, some having very regular, and others irregular undulations. Some, however, such as that represented by our figures 1 *b*, *c*, I think most probably belong to a distinct species from the majority of the others, and seem to be generally smaller and much more regularly undulated. Some of these closely resemble a form that Dr. White has named *I. dimidius*, in Lieutenant Wheeler's report (not yet published at the time of the revision of this report, November, 1875).

If the forms like our figure 1 *a*, Pl. IV, are distinct from *I. problematicus*, I think Dr. Schiel's name, *I. pseudo-mytiloides*, will have to be retained for the species. These shells generally have the beak more pointed and curved downward than in European specimens of *I. problematicus*, and sometimes have the hinge-line ranging at a greater angle with the umbonal axis than in any figures of European specimens of that species that I have yet seen.

The figures 2 *a*, *b*, of Plate IV, represent smaller specimens, with much less oblique beaks and a general outline more rounded. They are probably only the umbonal positions of larger specimens, the specific relations of which remain doubtful.

Locality and position.—Bear River, near the mouth of Sulphur Creek, Wyoming. Cretaceous.

Genus ANOMIA, Linn.

ANOMIA CONCENTRICA, Meek.

Plate 4, fig. 3.

Anomia concentrica, Meek (July, 1860), Proceed. Acad. Nat. Sci., Philad., XII, 311.

Shell small, thin, subcircular or transversely a little oval; lateral extremities nearly equally rounded; cardinal margin rather straight, or but slightly arched; beak very small, marginal, compressed, not projecting beyond the cardinal border; surface of upper valve ornamented by moderately distinct, regular, concentric undulations, and much smaller obscure lines of growth.

Transverse diameter 0.64 inch; length from hinge to the opposite margin, 0.50 inch.

Locality and position.—Same as last.

INOCERAMUS SIMPSONI, Meek.

Plate 4, fig. 4.

Inoceramus Simpsoni, Meek (July, 1860), Proceed. Acad. Nat. Sci., Philad., XII, 312.

Shell attaining a large size, transversely elongated or narrow, oval, gibbous in the umbonal and anterior regions, cuneate posteriorly; anterior side rounded; anal side very long, usually broader than the other, and subtruncate at the extremity; base in young shells semiovate, being more convex behind than in front, in large specimens rounding up very gradually toward the front, and apparently a little contracted or slightly sinuous behind; hinge straight, long, and ranging nearly parallel to the longer axis of the valves; beaks rising little above the cardinal border, rather convex, located very near the anterior extremity; surface ornamented by moderately distinct, rather regular concentric undulations, which sometimes bifurcate on the flanks; lines of growth small, regular, and equidistant.

Length, 8.10 inches; height, 4.35 inches; convexity, about 3.72 inches.

The remarkably elongated transverse form of this shell will serve to distinguish it from any other species yet known in our rocks, resembling it in other respects. Goldfuss figures a somewhat similar form (Taf. cxii, fig. 4 *d*, Petrefact. Germ.) under the name of *I. Cripsii*, Sowerby; though the identity of the specimen from which his figure was drawn with Sowerby's species seems to be doubtful. At any rate, it differs from that now under consideration, in having more pointed beaks, which are much more remote from the anterior end of the shell; it is likewise broader posteriorly than our species, which is much larger and more robust.

In the position and obliquity of its beaks, as well as in some other respects, *I. Simpsoni* resembles a form I have elsewhere referred to *I. Barabini* as a variety *cuneatus;* but it is a much larger shell, proportionally more elongated, and narrower posteriorly, while it comes from a geological horizon far below the known range of any shells yet found associated with *I. Barabini, var. cuneatus.*

The specific name of this fine *Inoceramus* was given in honor of Capt. J. H. Simpson, commander of the explorations across the Great Basin of Utah.

Locality and position.—North Platte, above the bridge; from about the horizon of No. 3 of the Upper Missouri Cretaceous series.

BEAR RIVER FRESH-WATER OR ESTUARY BEDS.

In first preparing this report (in 1860), I referred the fossils from the above-mentioned beds to the Tertiary, believing them to be Lower Eocene. After visiting the locality, however, as elsewhere stated, I was led to believe them much more probably upper beds of the Cretaceous; and now, in revising this report (in 1875), place them together here in a separate division.

MOLLUSCA.

LAMELLIBRANCHIATA.

Genus UNIO, Retzius.

UNIO VETUSTUS, Meek.

Plate 5, fig. 12, *a*, *b*.

Unio vetustus, Meek (July, 1860), Proceed. Acad. Nat. Sci., Philad., XII, 312.

Shell rather thin in young, but becoming proportionally thicker with age, attaining a medium size, transversely-ovate, moderately convex; anterior side rounded; basal and dorsal margins nearly straight and parallel in the young, but the former more convex in the adult; posterior side very long, more compressed, and rather narrower than the other, obliquely truncated above and angular below in young shells, but becoming more rounded with age; beaks small, much depressed, located near the anterior end; surface of young specimens ornamented by fine, regular, concentric wrinkles, crossed on the posterior umbonal slopes of each valve by two sharply-defined linear ridges, which radiate from the beaks nearly or quite to the posterior extremity. On old and medium-sized specimens, these markings become nearly or quite obsolete, excepting near the beaks.

Length of a large specimen, 3.22 inches; height, 1.30 inches; convexity, about 0.60 inch.

The nature of the matrix in which these specimens are imbedded, is such that it was found impossible to remove it from the hinge and interior, so as to see all the details of the teeth and muscular impressions; but by working it away with care from the hinge, I was enabled to determine beyond doubt that it is a *Unio.*

In surface-markings, young individuals of this species bear considerable resemblance to young specimens of *U. priscus*, Meek and Hayden, from the Tertiary deposits of the Upper Missouri, with which I have sometimes thought them identical. Until we can have better specimens, however, of the Upper Missouri shell for comparison, it will be better to keep them separate, especially as the relative geological positions of the beds in which the two forms occur still remain doubtful, while the Bear River beds seem to be very local in Wyoming.

Locality and position.—Brackish- or fresh-water beds on Bear River near the mouth of Sulphur Creek; latitude, 41° 12′ north, longitude, 110° 52′ west: probably belonging to the latest division of the Cretaceous.

Genus CORBULA, Bruguière.

CORBULA (ANISORHYNCHUS) PYRIFORMIS, Meek.

Plate 5, figs. 9 and 10.

Corbula (*Potamomya*) *pyriformis*, Meek (1860), Proceed. Acad. Nat. Sci. Philad., XII, 312.
Corbula (*Potamomya*) *concentrica*, Meek, ib., 312.
Corbula (*Anisorhynchus*) *pyriformis*, Meek (1872), Hayden's 2d Ann. Report U. S. Geol. Survey of the Territories, 298.

Shell transversely-pyriform, nearly or quite equivalve, moderately thick, very gibbous in the anterior and umbonal regions, more compressed and subrostrate behind;

buccal side truncated above from the beaks obliquely forward, rounding rather abruptly into the base below; posterior side much narrower and longer than the other, and very sharply rounded or slightly truncated at the extremity; base semiovate, being much more prominent in the central and anterior regions than behind; dorsal outline declining from the beaks at an angle of about 100°, the posterior slope being distinctly concave. Beaks prominent, equal, incurved, and located half-way between the middle and the anterior end; lunule deeply excavated, but not defined by a distinct marginal angle; escutcheon lanceolate, rather deep, and circumscribed by a marginal ridge; surface marked by fine lines of growth, with usually more or less distinct concentric ridges and furrows.

Length, 1.30 inches; height, 0.85 inch; convexity (of a right valve), 0.39 inch.

This species is quite abundant, but, in all the specimens obtained, the hard calcareous matrix adheres so firmly about the hinge that it is impossible to clear it away so as to see the teeth. Judging from the form of the shell, however, and the fact that it is associated with fresh-water and estuary species, there is little room for doubt in regard to its generic relations.* Most of the specimens are right valves; a few left valves, however, were obtained, which indicate that the species is only slightly inequivalve.

This shell varies much in its surface-markings; some specimens showing only concentric striæ, and others concentric furrows and ridges. At first I thought there might be two distinct species, separable on this character; but, after seeing large collections, I found all intermediate gradations between these extremes, and united the two under the first name.

Locality and position, same as last.

CORBULA ENGELMANNI, Meek.

Plate 5, fig. 13, *a*, *b*.

Corbula (Potamomya) Engelmanni, Meek, (July, 1860), Proceed. Acad. Nat. Sci. Philad., XII, 313.

Shell rather small, transversely subovate, gibbous in the umbonal region; anterior side narrowly rounded; base semiovate, being more prominent toward the front than behind; posterior side narrow, and truncated at the immediate extremity, having a moderately distinct angle extending from the back part of the beaks obliquely backward to the lower part of the slightly truncated posterior end; beaks depressed, located in advance of the middle; surface ornamented by small, very regular, concentric wrinkles; hinge and interior unknown.

Length (of a right valve), 0.39 inch; height, 0.21 inch; convexity, 0.11 inch.

This little shell seems to differ materially in form from the last; but owing to its small size, and the fact that specimens certainly belonging to that species vary in form, I am not quite sure that it may not be a young example of the same. Until specimens showing the intermediate connecting links can be found, however, I prefer to keep them separate.

Locality and position.—Same as last.

*Long after writing the above, I succeeded in working out the hinge, and found it to agree well with that of *Corbula*, and not with *Potamomya*. Mr. Conrad wrote me that he had proposed to found a genus *Anisorhynchus* for its reception, mainly on its apparent fresh-water habits; but I am not satisfied that it is generically distinct from *Corbula*.

GASTEROPODA.

Genus PYRGULIFERA, Meek.

PYRGULIFERA HUMEROSA, Meek.

Plate 5, fig. 6, *a*, *b*, *c*.

Melania humerosa, Meek (July, 1860), Proceed. Acad. Nat. Sci. Philad., XII, 313.
Pyrgulifera humerosa, Meek (1872), in Hayden's Second Ann. Report U. S. Geol. Survey of the Territories, 299.

Shell rather thick, subovate; spire conical, moderately elevated; volutions about five and a half, distinctly shouldered, and more or less angular, last one comparatively large, rounded and contracted below; suture distinct; surface ornamented by about fourteen rather strong, regular, vertical folds or costæ to each turn; folds obsolete on the lower part of the body-whorl, but becoming more strongly defined at the shoulder, where they often terminate in very prominent nodes, so as to give the whorls a distinctly coronate character; crossing these folds or costæ, there are on each volution of the spire about four, and on the last whorl some seven or eight, regular, equidistant revolving lines, or small ridges.

The specimens of this interesting species are too imperfect to afford accurate measurements, but some of them appear to have been, when entire, about 1 inch in length, and 0.60 inch in breadth. One individual (see fig. 6 *b*, plate v), apparently of this species, shows the aperture to be narrow-oval. On this specimen, which consists of scarcely more than the body-whorl, the costæ do not terminate above in as prominent nodes as in others, but merely form small tubercles at the shoulder, which is more sloping than in most of the other specimens.

This species bears considerable resemblance to *Melanopsis armata* of Matheron (which seems to be a *Melania* or *Tiara*), from the Tertiary Lignite formations at the mouth of the Rhone (see Cat. Méthod. Corps Org. Foss. Départ. des Bouches-du-Rhône, plate 37, fig. 12), but differs in having the folds or costæ more distinct, and developed on the whorls of the spire as well as on the last volution. These costæ also in the species under consideration differ in terminating in rounded prominences, while upper ends of the French species seem to be flattened horizontally, and its revolving lines are much more numerous than those of our species.

Long after writing the above, I had an opportunity to examine hundreds of specimens of this shell, and in a very few examples I succeeded in seeing the aperture and columella very clearly. The inner lip is more thickened, and the margin at its base more effuse, and the aperture more angular there than as shown in the figure of the imperfect specimen represented by our fig. 6 *b*, plate v. I have had to establish a new genus for its reception, as it is certainly not a *Melania*, nor a *Tiara*, to which latter I at one time believed it might belong.

Locality and position.—Same as foregoing.

LIMNÆA NITIDULA, Meek.

Plate 5, fig. 14.

Melania ? nitidula, Meek (July, 1860), Proceed. Acad. Nat. Sci. Philad., 314.

Shell subovate; spire conical, moderately elevated; volutions about six and a half, rounded-convex, increasing rather gradually from the apex; suture well defined;

aperture subovate, narrowly rounded below and angular above, scarcely equaling half the entire length of the shell; surface marked by fine obscure lines of growth.

Length, 0.40 inch; breadth, 0.20 inch; apical angle convex, divergence about 40°.

This is a neat little shell, quite unlike any other species known to me from the Bear River beds. In several respects, it resembles some recent species, but it still differs too clearly to be confounded with any of them, even if its geological position did not preclude its identification with any existing species. The specimens do not show the columella very clearly, and I have not been able to see on it the characteristic fold of *Limnæa* quite satisfactorily; but, on re-examination, I am more inclined to believe that it belongs to that genus than to any of the Melanian groups.

Locality and position.—Bear River fresh-water beds, at mouth of Sulphur Creek, Wyoming.

Genus RHYTOPHORUS.

RHYTOPHORUS PRISCUS, Meek.

Plate 5, fig. 4, *a*, *b*.

Melampus priscus, Meek (July, 1860), Proceed. Acad. Nat. Sci. Philad., XII, 315.
Rhytophorus priscus, Meek (1872), in Hayden's Second Ann. Rep. U. S. Geol. Survey of the Territories, 399.

Shell oval, moderately thick; spire depressed-conical; whorls about five, convex or subangular, last one comparatively large, shouldered above, and tapering below the middle; suture well defined; surface marked by rather obscure lines of growth, and small, regular, vertical, or slightly oblique folds, which are distinct on the spire and the upper part of the body, but obsolete below; aperture narrow, angular above, and narrowly rounded below; outer lip apparently sharp, and without teeth or crenulations within; columella provided with one rather strong oblique fold below, and a much smaller less oblique one about half-way up the aperture.

Length, near 0.77 inch; breadth, 0.50 inch; apical angle nearly regular, divergence about 80°.

This shell is very unlike any other fossil yet known in any of the fresh-water or estuary deposits of the West or Northwest, and differs materially from any recent species of which I have any knowledge.

Since writing the above, I have proposed a new genus, *Rhytophorus*, for its reception.

Locality and position.—Fresh-water or estuary beds on Bear River, near mouth of Sulphur Creek, latitude 41° 12′ north, longitude 110° 52′ west; probably latest Cretaceous.

TERTIARY FOSSILS.

MOLLUSCA.

LAMELLIBRANCHIATA.

Genus UNIO, Retzius.

UNIO HAYDENI, Meek.

Plate 5, fig. 11, *a*, *b*.

Unio Haydeni (July, 1860), Proceed. Acad. Nat. Sci. Philad., XII, 312.

Shell under medium size, subelliptical, rather thin, moderately convex; extremities more or less regularly rounded, the posterior margin being sometimes obliquely subtruncated above, and more narrowly rounded below, than the other; basal border semi-elliptical in outline; dorsal side nearly straight along the middle; beaks very small, depressed nearly to a level with the dorsal margin, not eroded, and apparently without wrinkles, located about half-way between the middle and the anterior end; posterior umbonal slopes rather prominently rounded; surface smooth, or only showing obscure marks of growth.

Length, 1.65 inches; height, 1 inch; convexity, 0.60 inch.

The specimens of this species in the collection are not in a condition to show the hinge, though some casts of the interior retain impressions of the lateral teeth, which are comparatively long and straight. These casts also show the muscular impressions to be moderately deep, and the cavity of the beaks rather shallow.

In size and form, this species resembles *Unio nucalis*, Meek and Hayden, from near the Black Hills, Nebraska; but its beaks are less elevated, and not so gibbous; they also appear never to possess the small concentric wrinkles characterizing those of that species; and it seems likewise to be a thinner shell than *U. nucalis*. Some varieties of it resemble *Mya tellinoides*, Hall (Frémont's Rept., 307, plate 3, fig. 1), which is doubtless also a *Unio;* but they always differ from the figure cited in having less elevated beaks, and in being proportionally broader posteriorly. Named in honor of Dr. F. V. Hayden, who has brought many specimens of the species from the Far West. It seems to come from a formation that Dr. Hayden has called the Bridger group.

Locality and position.—Fresh-water Tertiary beds, near Fort Bridger, and south of there, at the base of Uintah Mountains, latitude 41° 40′ north, longitude 110° 10′ west.

Genus GONIOBASIS, Lea.

GONIOBASIS SIMPSONI, Meek.

Plate 5, fig. 1, *a, b, c, d, e.*

Melania Simpsoni, Meek (July, 1860), Proceed. Acad. Nat. Sci. Philad., XII, 313.

Shell elongate-conical; spire attenuated and pointed; volutions about ten, flattened or more or less convex, increasing gradually in size, last one rounded below; suture sometimes linear, in other instances more strongly defined, in consequence of the greater convexity of the whorls; surface marked by fine lines of growth, and small, slightly-arched, vertical folds, which vary in size and regularity on different specimens, and are crossed by small, obscure, thread-like revolving lines; aperture ovate; columella moderately sinuous below; lip somewhat retreating above, and prominent below the middle.

Length, 0.78 inch; breadth, 0.30 inch; apical angle nearly or quite regular, divergence about 26°.

The surface-markings of this species vary considerably on different individuals. The small vertical folds are usually quite obscure or wanting on the lower volutions, but sometimes they are well defined even on the body-whorl; while in other instances they become nearly or quite obsolete on all parts of the shell. The fine thread-like revolving lines are generally equidistant, and number about seven to ten on each whorl of the spire. When well defined, they sometimes impart a slightly nodose character to the folds, particularly near the middle of each whorl. Very often these revolving lines, like the vertical folds, are obscure or quite obsolete, while on other specimens they are distinctly defined on all the volutions.

In most cases, the whorls are very nearly flat, but those of other individuals are more convex. It is possible that these two forms may belong to distinct species, but there are so many intermediate gradations in this respect that I am inclined to regard them as merely varieties of one species.

There are several quite similar forms among our recent Melanians, such for instance as *Goniobasis comma*, Conrad, and *G. athleta* of Anthony, from which, however, this species will be readily distinguished by obvious characters.

The specific name is given in honor of Capt. J. H. Simpson, Topographical Engineers, United States Army, commander of Utah Exploring Expeditions, &c. I am in doubt in regard to the relations of this shell to one of the forms described by Professor Hall in Frémont's Report. Indeed, from first to last, I have had, as it were, to grope in the dark in regard to the fresh-water fossils described in that report, on account of the brevity of the descriptions and unsatisfactory figures, together with the uncertainty of the exact localities from which they were obtained.

Locality and position.—Later Tertiary beds at Ham's Fork, northeast of Fort Bridger, latitude 41° 40′ north, longitude 110° 10′ west. Probably Miocene.

GONIOBASIS ARCTA, Meek.

Plate 5, fig. 5.

Melania arcta, Meek (July, 1860), Proceed. Acad. Nat. Sci. Philad., XII, 314.

Shell rather small, very slender, terete; volutions about twelve, flattened-convex, increasing very gradually from the apex; suture distinctly defined; surface showing an exceedingly slight tendency to develop moderately broad, rather distant, vertical folds, with faint traces of small revolving striæ; aperture ovate.

Length, 0.56 inch; breadth, 0.17 inch; apical angle regular, divergence 15°.

This shell I now rather regard as only a slender variety of the last-described species; but it differs so much from all the specimens I have seen certainly belonging to that variable shell, that, with the collections at hand for comparison, this cannot be clearly demonstrated. It is as much as one-third to one-half narrower, and has two or three whorls more than well-marked specimens of *M. Simpsoni* of its own length; while its whorls differ in being flattened more obliquely above.

The lower part of each whorl rounds abruptly into the suture below, so that the most prominent part is generally just above the suture. This prominence is also continued around the middle of the body-whorl.

Locality and position.—Same as last.

Genus PLANORBIS, Müller.

PLANORBIS SPECTABILIS, Meek.

Plate 5, fig. 7, *a*, *b*, *c*, *d*.

Planorbis spectabilis, Meek (July, 1860), Proceed. Acad. Nat. Sci. Philad., XII, 314.

Shell large, moderately compressed; upper side slightly convex, sometimes a little concave in the middle; periphery rather narrowly rounded below the middle; volutions five and a half, increasing gradually in size, wider than high, depressed-convex, and sloping a little outward above, distinctly convex below; about one-half of each inner whorl on the under side and less than one-fourth above embraced by each succeeding turn; umbilicus rather deep, and one-third wider than the outer whorl; surface and aperture unknown.

Greatest breadth, 1.19 inches; height, 0.25 inch.

This is a fine large species that seems to be quite abundant. It is often found much distorted by pressure, and in this way presents a great diversity of forms and appearances. It resembles several European Eocene and other Tertiary forms; but, so far as I have been able to make comparisons, it seems to be distinct from them all.

Locality and position.—Ham's Fork, in Southwestern Wyoming; from beds now (1875) known as the Green River group.

PLANORBIS SPECTABILIS, *var.* UTAHENSIS, Meek.

Plate 5, fig. 8, *a, b, c.*

Planorbis Utahensis, Meek (1860), Proceed. Acad. Nat. Sci. Philad., XII, 314.

This form differs from the typical *P. spectabilis* in having its volutions, and indeed the whole shell, more depressed, and its periphery more narrowly rounded; while its aperture is proportionally narrower and more oblique. Its volutions also seem to increase more rapidly in breadth. These differences are quite well enough marked to distinguish it specifically, if we could be entirely sure that they are not, partly at least, due to accidental distortion. The type-specimens have evidently been a little depressed by accidental pressure, but still seem to have been naturally more depressed. For the present, I have concluded to view this form as a variety of *P. spectabilis.*

Locality and position.—Same as last.

LIMNÆA VETUSTA, Meek.

Plate 5, fig. 3, *a, b.*

Limnæa vetusta, Meek (July, 1860), Proceed. Acad. Nat. Sci. Philad., XII, 314.

Shell elongate-subovate; spire rather slender and pointed; volutions five and a half to six, compressed or moderately convex; suture well defined; surface nearly smooth, with traces of fine lines of growth, scarcely visible without the aid of a lens; aperture narrow-ovate, apparently rather narrowly rounded below, and acutely angular above, equaling about half the entire length of the shell; columella with a small, comparatively straight, fold.

Length, 0.56 inch; breadth, 0.26 inch.

This and the following form are more like species occurring in the White River Tertiary basin than any yet known in other formations of the Northwest; but they both differ from the White River species in being more slender, in consequence of the less ventricose character of the body-whorl.

Locality and position.—Same as last.

LIMNÆA SIMILIS, Meek.

Plate 5, fig. 2, *a, b* (mag. 2 diam.).

Limnæa similis, Meek (1860), Proceed. Acad. Nat. Sci. Philad., XII, 314.

This form differs from the last in having more convex whorls and a deeper, as well as a more oblique suture. They may possibly be varieties of one species, but, after examining a more complete series than that first studied, I am still inclined to think them more probably distinct.

Locality and position.—Same as last.

CATALOGUE OF THE ORGANIC REMAINS CONTAINED IN THE COLLECTION.

DEVONIAN SPECIES.

BRACHIOPODA.

NAMES.	REMARKS, LOCALITIES, ETC.
Productus ——, undt. sp., No. 350*	West side of Buell Valley; latitude 39° 30′, longitude 115° 36′.
Athyris ——, undt. sp., No. 350	Locality and position same as last.
Atrypa aspera, (Schlot.) Dalm.?, No. 350	Locality and position same as last.
Atrypa reticularis, (Lin.) Dalm., No. 350	Locality and position same as last.
Spirifer ——, undt. sp., No. 350	Locality and position same as last.
Spirifer Utahensis, Meek	Locality and position same as last.
Spirifer strigosus, Meek, No. 351	Buell Valley; latitude 39° 32′, longitude 115° 36′.
Spirifer Engelmanni, Meek, No. 351	Buell Valley; latitude 39° 32′, longitude 115° 36′.
Undetermined fragments of trochiform univalves	Buell Valley; latitude 39° 32′, longitude 115° 36′.

CRUSTACEA.

Homalonotus? —— (fragments)	West side of Steptoe Valley; latitude 39° 47′, longitude 114° 58′.
Prœtus ——, undetermined fragments	Locality and position same as last.

CARBONIFEROUS SPECIES.

PLANTÆ.

Lepidodendron ——, undt. sp., No. 144	In dark shaly beds, Timpanogos Cañon, Utah; latitude 40° 22′, longitude 111° 38′. *Coal-Measures.*
Stems or rootlets of undt. plants	In sandstone, 13 miles west of Leavenworth City, Kansas. *Coal-Measures.*

FORAMINIFERA.

Fusulina cylindrica, Fischer?	Nine miles west of Leavenworth City; east fork of Grasshopper Creek, and on Nemaha and Vermilion Creeks, Kansas. *Coal-Measures.*

POLYPI.

Chætetes ——, undt. sp., No. 402	Massive. Found loose near Rio Virgen; latitude 37°, longitude 114°. Age?
Syringopora ——, undt. sp., No. 184	Similar to *S. ramulosa*, Goldf. Western foot of General Johnston's Pass; latitude 40° 6′, longitude 112° 42′. Probably *Lower Carboniferous.*

* These are the original numbers of the specimens.

Zaphrentis ———, undt. sp., No. 170 .... West of Camp Floyd, in hard, dark, siliceous limestone; latitude 40° 13′, longitude 112° 10′. *Lower Carboniferous.*

Cyathophyllum? ———, No. 185 .... West foot of General Johnston's Pass; latitude 40° 6′; longitude 112° 42′. *Lower Carboniferous.*

POLYZOA.

Fenestella ———, undt. sp. (fragments), No. 201... Hills west of Camp Floyd; latitude 40° 13′ longitude 112° 10′. *Lower Carboniferous.*

Archimedipora ———, undt. fragment, No. 201.... Locality and position same as last.

BRACHIOPODA.

Chonetes Verneuiliana, N. and P., No. 243......... Yellow limestone east side of Long Valley; latitude 39° 57′; longitude 115° 10′. *Upper Carboniferous.*

Productus multistriatus, Meek, No. 243 .... Locality and position same as last.

Productus ———, undt. sp., No. 243............... Specimens imperfect; apparently resembling *P. Rogersi*, Norwood and Pratten, but more produced in front. Locality and position same as last.

Productus ———, undt. sp........................ None of the specimens well preserved. Of medium size; ventral valve gibbous, with a very distinct mesial sinus; smooth near the beak, with obscure radiating costæ, and scattering erect spines on the anterior and lateral slopes; scarcely any traces of concentric wrinkles; abundant. No. 360, Summit Spring; No. 243, west side Long Valley; No 246, pass east of Ruby Valley. All between latitude 39° 33′; longitude 115° 20′, and latitude 40°, longitude 115° 10′. *Upper Carboniferous.*

Productus ———, undt. sp...................... Specimens imperfect, all silicified; somewhat reticulated by the concentric wrinkles crossing the fine striæ on the visceral region; in hard, dark-colored limestone. No. 252, on east side of Buell Valley, latitude 39° 32′, longitude 115° 24′. Probably *Lower Carboniferous.*

Productus ———, undt. sp. (fragments)........... Like *P. semireticulatus.* Siliceous, and in very hard, dark, siliceous limestone. Hills west of Camp Floyd; latitude 40° 13′; longitude 112° 10′. *Lower Carboniferous.*

Productus semistriatus, Meek, No. 144 .... In dark shaly beds, Timpanogos Cañon; latitude 40° 22′; longitude 111° 38′. *Coal-Measures.*

Productus ———, undt. sp .... All fragments; very finely striate, and without concentric wrinkles. Locality and position same as last.

Productus æquicostatus, Shumard? .... North Platte, 15 miles above Fort Laramie; also 2½ miles west of Clear Creek, Kansas. *Coal-Measures.*

Productus semireticulatus, Martin .... Richmond, on Nemaha Creek, and on Big Blue River, Eastern Kansas. *Coal-Measures.*

Productus Rogersi, Norwood and Pratten..........Four miles west of Fort Leavenworth, Kansas. *Coal-Measures.*

Productus Prattenanus, Norwood..................Fragments. Near Clear Creek; on Grasshopper Creek, Kansas. *Coal-Measures.*

Orthis Michelini, (Léveillé) Koninck, No. 218......Pass between Desert and Pleasant Valley; latitude 39° 42′; longitude 113° 50′. *Lower Carboniferous.*

Hemipronites, undt. sp., No. 364 ....Like *H. crenistria*, but apparently more finely striate. Mountains east of Steptoe Valley; latitude 39° 15′; longitude 114° 45′. *Lower Carboniferous.*

Hemipronites crassus, Meek and Hayden.........Two miles west of Clear Creek, Kansas Territory. *Coal-Measures.*

Hemipronites crenistria, Phillips, sp., No. 204......Hills west of Camp Floyd, latitude 40° 13′, longitude 112° 10′. *Lower Carboniferous.*

Rhynchonella ——, undt. sp., No. 185...........Medium size, moderately gibbous, with three plications on the mesial fold and five on each side of it. Latitude 40° 6′; longitude 112° 42′. Probably *Lower Carboniferous.*

Athyris subtilita, Hall, sp., No. 244...............West side of Long Valley, latitude 40°; longitude 115° 15′, in yellow limestone of the age of *Coal-Measures.* Larger specimens of apparently the same species were also found in the *same rock*, between Long and Ruby Valleys; likewise at Fort Leavenworth, Kansas Territory, in the *Coal-Measures.*

Athyris ——, one or two undt. sp..............At Timpanogos Cañon; latitude 40° 20′, longitude 111° 42′. *Coal-Measures.*

Terebratula ?, No. 244...........................Small, subglobose, or subovate; valves nearly equal, having a faint sinus near the front of the ventral valve, and a corresponding elevation in the other; surface marked by regular, moderately distinct lines of growth. West side of Long Valley; latitude 40°; longitude 115° 15′, in yellow limestone. *Coal-Measures.*

Terebratula ? ....Rather small, smooth, much more compressed than the last; ventral valve sinuous near the front. West of Camp Floyd; latitude 40° 13′, longitude 112° 10′. *Lower Carboniferous.*

Spiriferina pulchra, Meek, No. 243...............East and west side of Long Valley; pass east of Ruby Valley; latitude 40°; longitude 115° 20′. *Upper Carboniferous.*

Spirifer scobina, Meek........................Yellow limestone, divide between Long and Ruby Valleys; latitude 40°; longitude 115° 20′. *Upper Carboniferous.*

Spirifer cameratus, Morton.....................Second fork of Grasshopper Creek, Kansas. *Coal-Measures.*

Spirifer cameratus, var. *occidentalis*, No. 356......Summit of Spring Pass; east of Long Valley and between Long and Ruby Valleys; longitude 115° 12′ to 20′; latitude 39° 33′ to 40°. *Upper Carboniferous.*

Spirifer ——, undt. sp., No. 201................In hard, dark-colored limestone, west of Camp Floyd; latitude 40° 13′; longitude 112° 10′. *Lower Carboniferous.*

Spirifer ———, undt. sp., No. 364 .... Above medium size, smooth, width greater than length; hinge equaling greatest breadth; ventral valve with shallow, moderately distinct, rounded sinus. Gray granular limestone, mountains east of Steptoe Valley; latitude 39° 15′; longitude 114° 45′. Probably *Lower Carboniferous ?*.

LAMELLIBRANCHIATA.

Aviculopecten Utahensis, Meek, No. 359 .... Summit Spring; latitude 39° 33′; longitude 115° 12′. Yellow-limestone series, *Upper Carboniferous*.

Aviculopecten, undt. sp. (fragments), No. 243 ..... Large, regularly and distinctly plicated; plications simple, angular, and crossed by regular, distinct, concentric marks. East side of Long Valley; latitude 39° 57′; longitude 115° 10′. Position same as last.

Myalina ———, undt. sp .... Specimens imperfect. Grasshopper Creek, Eastern Kansas. *Coal-Measures*.

Allorisma .... Grasshopper Creek, and 2½ miles west of Clear Creek, Kansas. *Coal-Measures*.

GASTEROPODA.

Bellerophon ———, undt. sp. (casts) .... Two and a half miles west of Clear Creek, Kansas. *Coal-Measures*.

CEPHALOPODA.

Nautilus ———, undt. sp., No. 201 .... Small, subdiscoidal; whorls somewhat embracing, rounded on the dorsum, and subangular around the middle of each side, increasing gradually in size. West of Camp Floyd; latitude 40° 13′; longitude 112° 10′. In dark limestone. *Lower Carboniferous*.

Nautilus ———, (undt. fragments), No. 359 .... Rather large, discoidal; volutions subquadrangular, and but slightly embracing. Yellow impure limestone, at Summit Spring; latitude 39° 33′; longitude 115° 12′. *Upper Carboniferous*.

Orthoceras baculum, Meek .... East side of Ruby Valley.

PERMIAN FORMS ?.*

POLYZOA.

NAMES.	REMARKS, LOCALITIES, ETC.
Phyllopora ?, No. 145	Specimen silicified, and not in a condition to be determined without doubt. Timpanogos River; latitude 40° 35′; longitude 111° 30′.
Aviculopecten, undt. sp., No. 22	Cottonwood Creek, north side of Kansas River, Eastern Kansas, in yellow, impure magnesian limestone.

* There is such a mingling of Permian and Coal-Measure types of fossils through a considerable thickness of rocks in Kansas and some other portions of the West, that it is very difficult to draw a line between these groups; consequently, it is not improbable that a portion, if not all, of the few specimens included in this Permian list, may have been obtained from beds below the horizon at which the line should be drawn between the Permian and Carboniferous systems.

Bakevellia?, No. 145 .... Fragments in hard siliceous rock. Timpanogos Valley; latitude 40° 35; longitude 111° 30′.

Bakevellia parva, Meek and Hayden .... Casts in yellow, impure, magnesian limestone. Cottonwood Creek, north of Kansas River, Eastern Kansas.

Leda subscitula, Meek and Hayden .... Locality and position same as last.

Leda ——, undt. sp .... Similar to *L. bellastriata*, Stevens, but much smaller. Locality and position same as above.

GASTEROPODA.

Bellerophon ——, undt. sp .... Near Big Blue River, Eastern Kansas.

JURASSIC SPECIES.

ECHINODERMATA.

NAMES.	REMARKS, LOCALITIES, ETC.
Pentacrinites asteriscus, M. and H., No. 13 0	East fork of Weber River; latitude 40° 48′; longitude 111° 15′. Also on the North Platte, near Red Buttes.
Pentacrinites ——, undt., No. 417	Portions of column. Near Red Buttes, North Platte; latitude 42° 50′; longitude 106° 40′.

LAMELLIBRANCHIATA.

Ostrea Engelmanni, Meek, No. 92 .... Near Red Buttes, on North Platte; latitude 42° 50′; longitude 106° 40′.

Gryphæa calceola, Quenstedt? .... Locality and position same as above.

Camptonectes bellistriata, Meek .... Locality and position same as above.

GASTEROPODA.

Dentalium? subquadratum, Meek .... Locality and position same as above.

CEPHALOPODA.

Belemnites densus, Meek and Hayden .... Locality and position same as above.

CRETACEOUS SPECIES.

LAMELLIBRANCHIATA.

NAMES.	REMARKS, LOCALITIES, ETC.
Ostrea congesta, Conrad, No. 85	North Platte above the bridge; latitude 42° 50′; longitude 106° 30′. No. 3 of the Upper Missouri section.
Ostrea ——, undt. sp. No. 156	Bear River, near the mouth of Sulphur Creek; latitude 41° 12′; longitude 110° 50′, from a yellowish sandstone.
Anomia concentrica, Meek	Locality and position same as last.
Inoceramus ——, undt. sp.	This shell seems to be closely allied to a form described by Dr. Schiel, in the 2d vol. Pacific Railroad Reports, under the name *I. pseudomytiloides*. Locality and position same as above.
Inoceramus Simpsoni, Meek, No. 84	North Platte, above bridge; latitude 42° 50′; longitude 106° 30′. No. 3 of Upper Missouri section.

Inoceramus ———, undt. sp .... Resembles *I. Mortoni*, Meek and Hayden (which holds a position near the base of formation No. 4 in Upper Missouri), but may be distinct. Found loose at or near the same locality as last.

Inoceramus pseudomytiloides, Schiel .... Five miles east of Big Sandy, Eastern Kansas. No. 3 of Upper Missouri section.

Inoceramus aviculoides, Meek and Hayden .... Locality and position same as last.

Panopæa? .... Apparently a *Panopæa*; but, as the specimens are merely imperfect casts and impressions left in the matrix, it is not possible to identify it with any known species. Above Deer Creek, on North Platte. Probably *Cretaceous*.

Baculites ———, undt. sp .... Small and much compressed. Specimens imperfect. North Platte above the bridge, No. 3 of Upper Missouri *Cretaceous* series; also in same position five miles east of Big Sandy, Eastern Kansas.

FOSSILS OF THE BEAR RIVER FRESH- OR BRACKISH-WATER BEDS.

LAMELLIBRANCHIATA.

NAMES.	REMARKS, LOCALITIES, ETC.
Unio vetustus, Meek, No. 154	Near Bear River, on Sulphur Creek, in estuary beds; longitude 110° 52′; latitude 41° 12′.
Corbula (Anisorhynchus) pyriformis, Meek, No. 154	Bear River, same position.
Corbula Engelmanni, Meek, No. 154	Locality and position same as last.

GASTEROPODA.

Pyrgulifera humerosa, Meek, No. 154	Locality and position same as above.
Limnæa? nitidula, Meek	Bear River, same as above.
Campeloma macrospira, No. 154	Locality and position same as above.
Viviparus Conradi, Meek and Hayden??, No. 154	Locality and position as above.
Rhytophorus priscus, Meek	Same as above.

TERTIARY SPECIES.

LAMELLIBRANCHIATA.

NAMES.	LOCALITIES, ETC.
Unio Haydeni, Meek	Ham's Fork, southwestern Wyoming.

GASTEROPODA.

Goniobasis Simpsoni, Meek	Ham's Fork.
Goniobasis arcta, Meek	Ham's Fork.
Planorbis spectabilis, Meek	Ham's Fork.
Planorbis spectabilis, var. *Utahensis*, Meek	Ham's Fork.
Limnæa vetusta, Meek	Ham's Fork.
Limnæa similis, Meek	Ham's Fork.

TERTIARY FOSSILS.
with some Cretaceous? types.

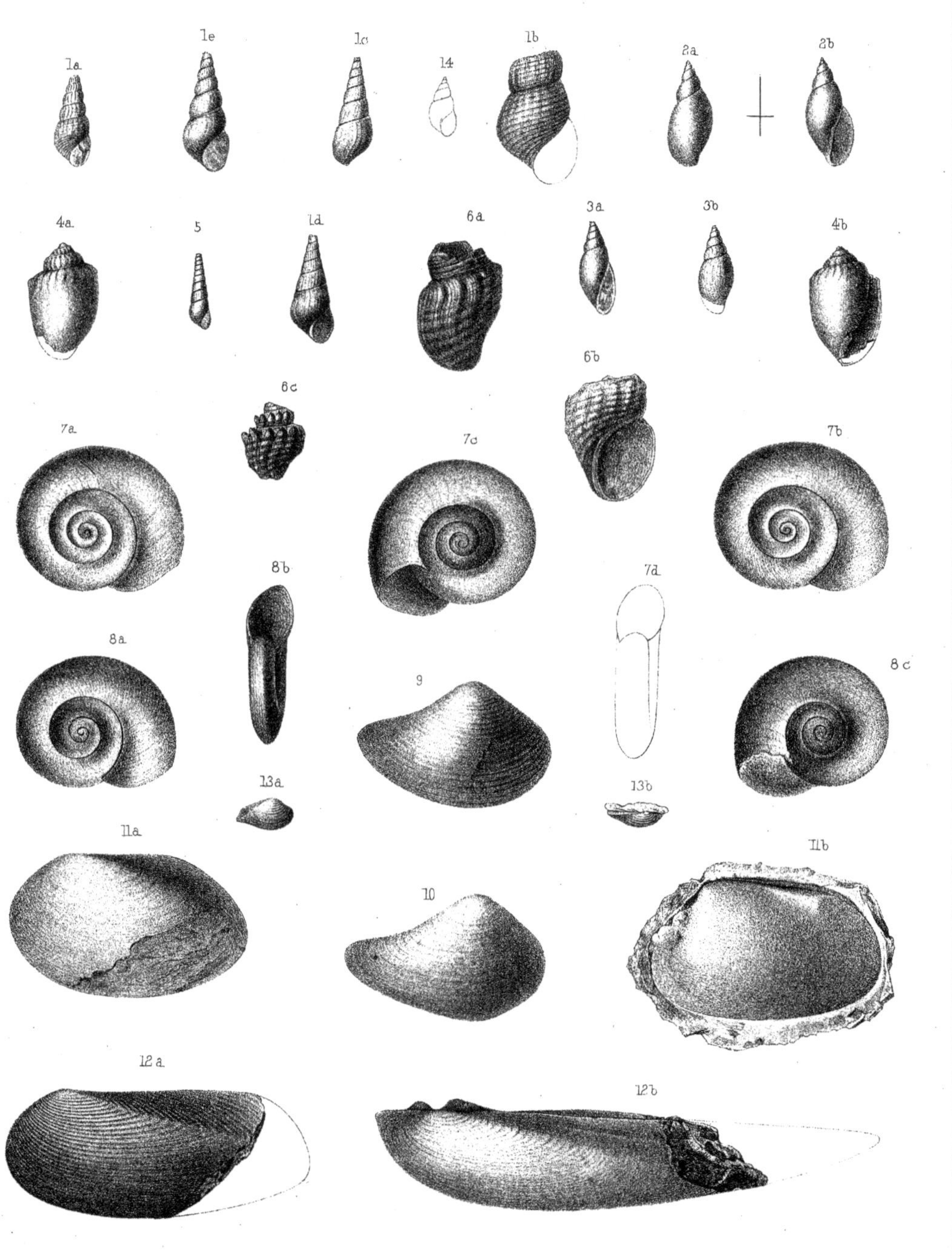

J. J. Young, del.

T. Sinclair & Son, lith. Phila.

PLATE V.

Page.

Fig. 1. GONIOBASIS SIMPSONI 365

1, *a*. Specimen with vertical costæ and revolving lines well defined.
1, *b*. Magnified view of a portion of the same.
1, *c*. View of a specimen with more flattened whorls and less distinct surface-markings.
1, *d*. Another view of the same, showing the aperture.
1, *e*. View of a specimen with more convex whorls and moderately distinct surface-markings.

Fig. 2. LIMNÆA SIMILIS 367

2, *a*. Back view of a specimen magnified two diameters.
2, *b*. Another view of the same.

Fig. 3. LIMNÆA VETUSTA 367

3, *a*. Front view, natural size.
3, *b*. Back view of same.

Fig. 4. *a*, *b*. RHYTOPHORUS PRISCUS, two views 364

Fig. 5. GONIOBASIS ARCTA, Meek 366

Fig. 6. PYRGULIFERA HUMEROSA 363

6, *a*. Dorsal view of an imperfect specimen.
6, *b*. Another view of the same. [Inner lip too thin and base of aperture too round.]
6, *c*. A smaller specimen with more distinct nodes around the shoulder.

Fig. 7. PLANORBIS SPECTABILIS 366

7, *a*, *b*. Upper views of two specimens.
7, *c*. Under view of the former.
7, *d*. Profile view.

Fig. 8. PLANORBIS SPECTABILIS *var*. UTAHENSIS 367

8, *a*. Upper view.
8, *b*. Profile view, showing aperture.
8, *c*. Under side, showing umbilicus.

Figs. 9 and 10. CORBULA PYRIFORMIS 361

Fig. 11. UNIO HAYDENI 364

11, *a*. Specimen retaining most of the shell.
11, *b*. Internal cast.

Fig. 12. UNIO VETUSTA 361

12, *a*. Side view of an imperfect young shell, flattened by pressure.
12, *b*. Dorsal view of a large left valve, the posterior portion of which is broken away.

Fig. 13. CORBULA ENGELMANNI 362

13, *a*. Side view of right valve.
13, *b*. Dorsal view of same.

Fig. 14. LIMNÆA? NITIDULA 363

CRETACEOUS FOSSILS.

1a 2a 2b 3 1b 1c

4

PLATE IV.

	Page.
Fig. 1, *a*. Inoceramus problematicus?	358
a. Side view of a specimen, with irregular undulations.	
1, *b* and *c*. Inoceramus dimidius?	358
Fig. 2, *a* and *b*. Inoceramus ———, undt	358
Fig. 3. Anomia concentrica, upper valve in matrix	359
Fig. 4. Inoceramus Simpsoni	360
A right-side view of type specimen, natural size.	

JURASSIC FOSSILS.

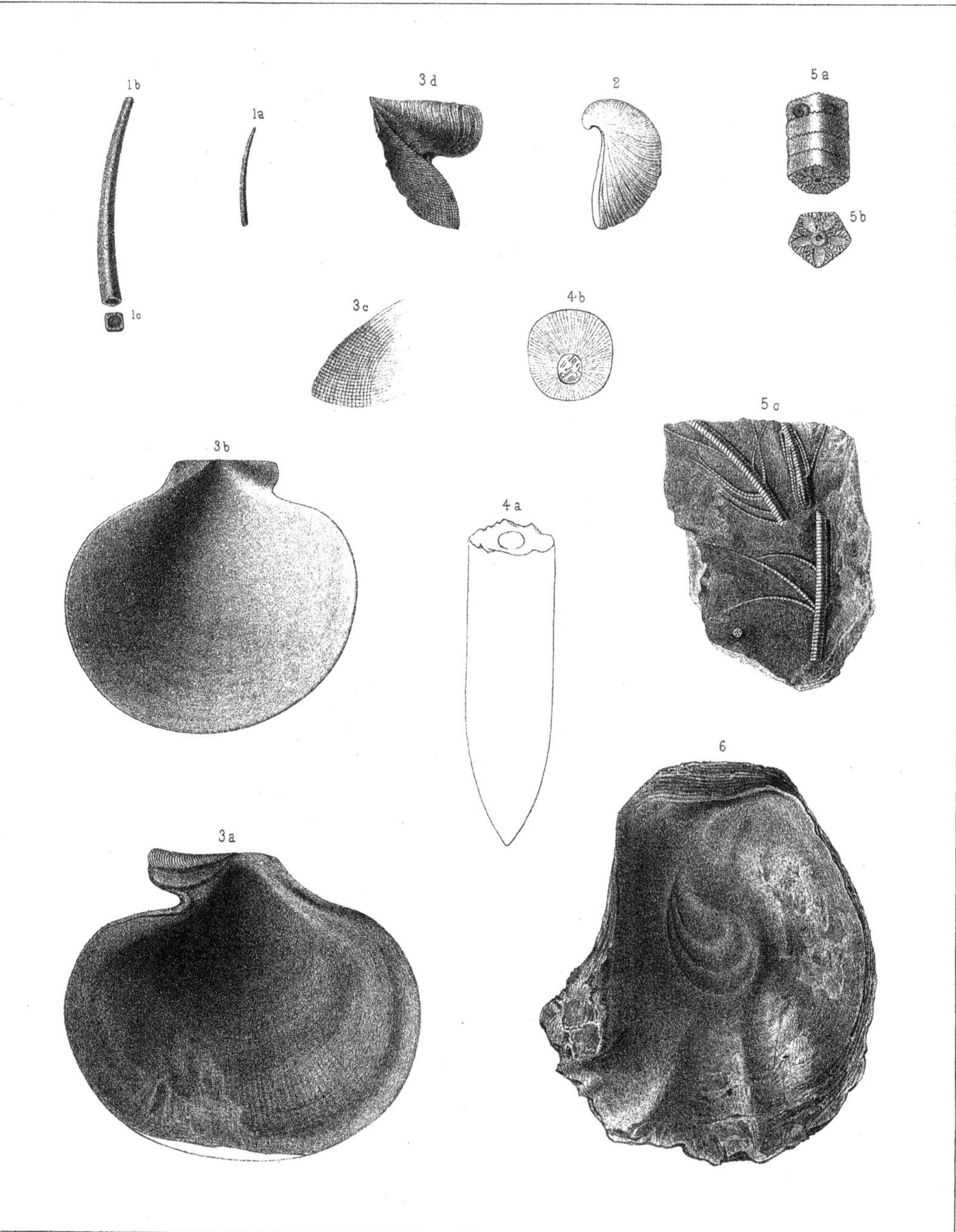

J. J. Young, del.

T. Sinclair & Son. lith. Phila.

PLATE III.

CARBONIFEROUS FOSSILS.

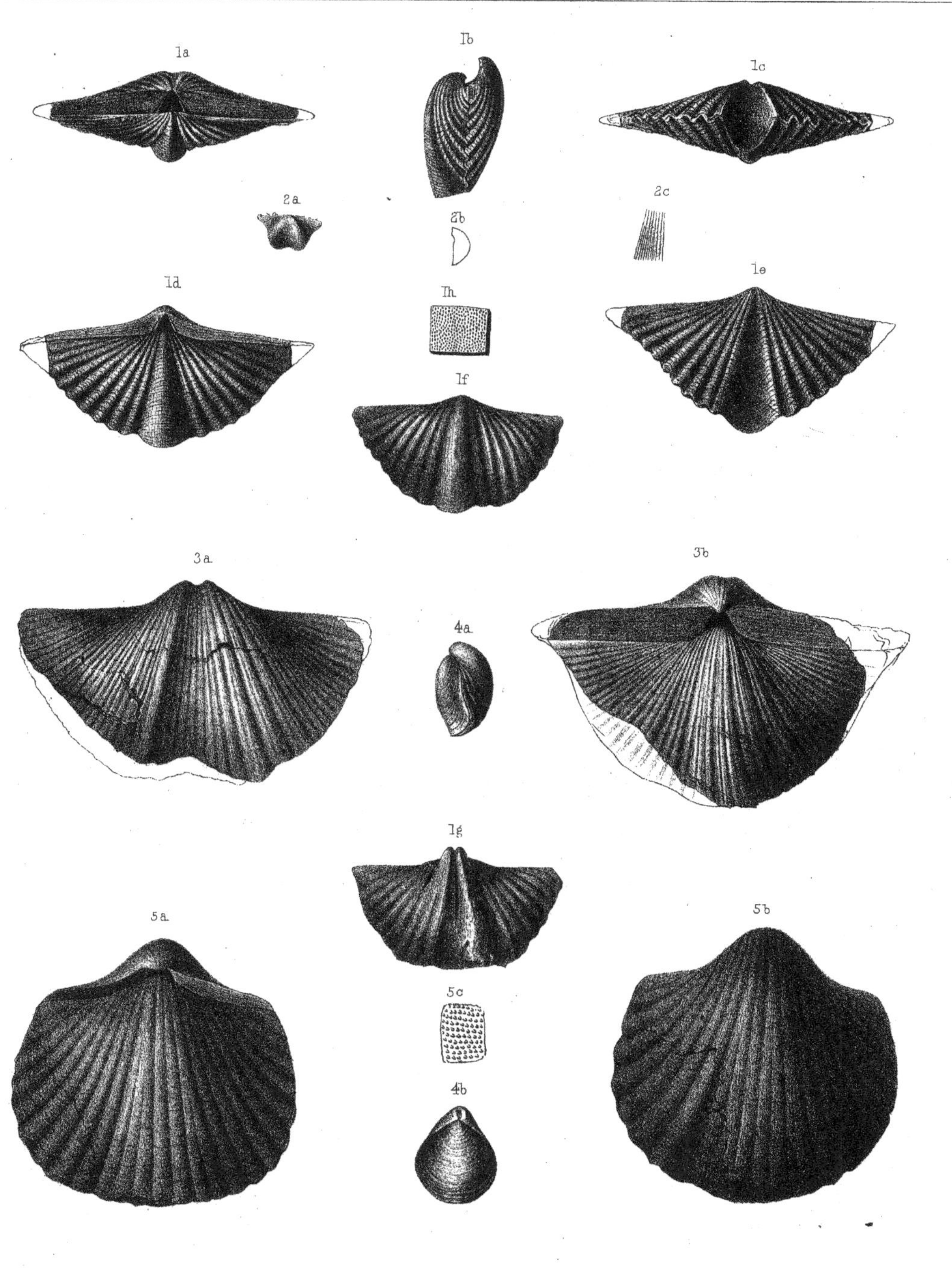

J. J. Young, del.

T. Sinclair & Son, lith. Phila.

PLATE II.

Page.

Fig. 1. SPIRIFERINA PULCHRA 352

1, *a*. Hinge and area view.
1, *b*. Side view.
1, *c*. Front view.
1, *d*. Dorsal view.
1, *e*. Ventral view.
1, *f*. Dorsal view of an internal cast.
1, *g*. Ventral view of the same.
1, *h*. Punctured external surface magnified.

Fig. 2. CHONETES VERNEUILIANA, *var*. UTAHENSIS 348

2, *a*. Ventral valve.
2, *b*. Outline side view.
2, *c*. Enlargement of striæ.

Fig. 3. SPIRIFER CAMERATUS? 353

3, *a*. Ventral view.
3, *b*. Dorsal view.

Fig. 4. ATHYRIS SUBTILITA 350

4, *a*. Side or profile view.
4, *b*. Dorsal view.

Fig. 5. SPIRIFER SCOBINA 351

5, *a*. Dorsal view.
5, *b*. Ventral view.
5, *c*. Portion of granulated surface magnified.

LAEONTOLOGY of
ıpt. J.H. Simpson's
Expls. 1858-59.

DEVONIAN & CARBONIFEROUS FOSSILS.

Appendix J. Plate I.

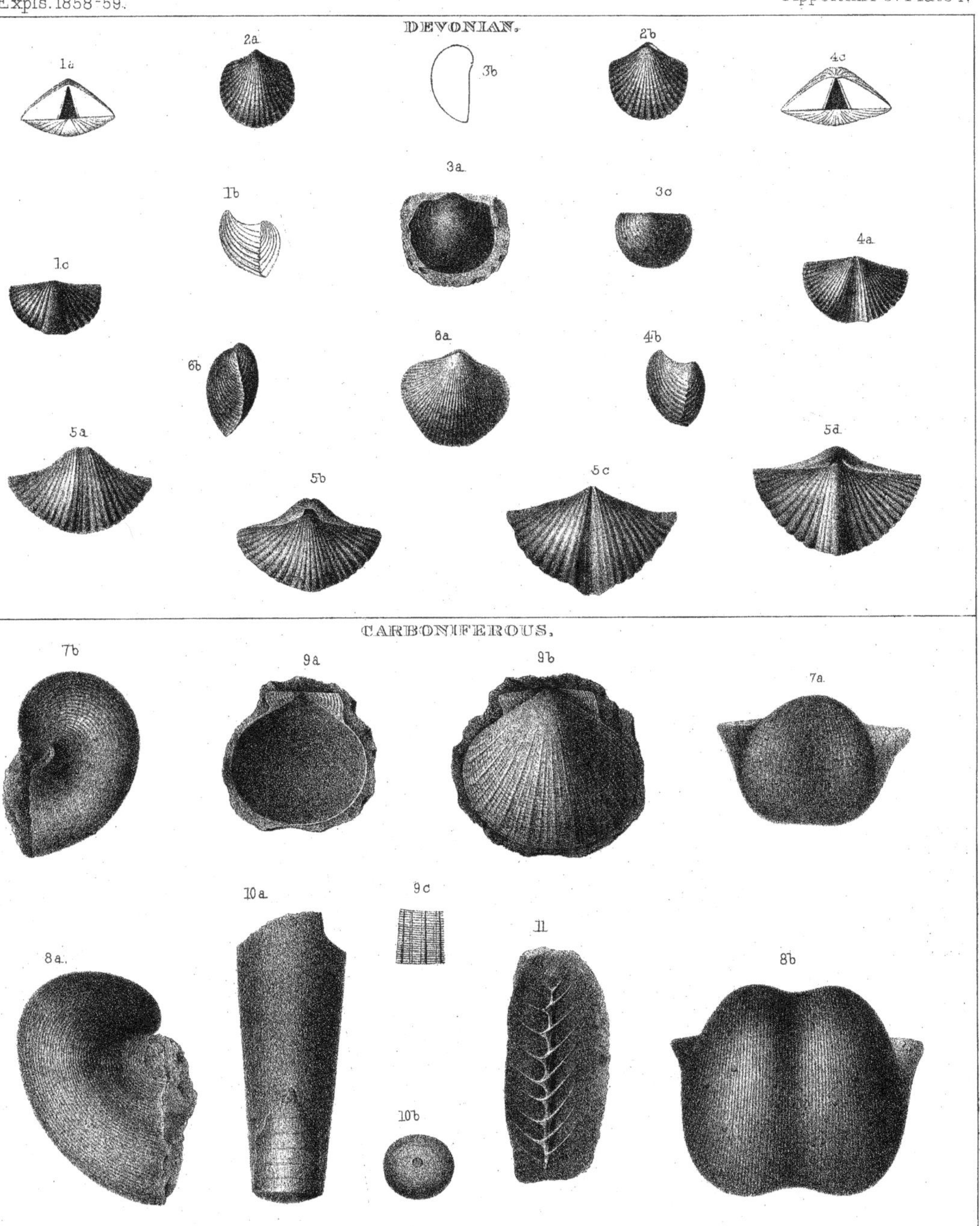

Young. del.

T. Sinclair & Son, lith. Phila.

PLATE I.

APPENDIX K.

ORNITHOLOGY.

A LIST OF BIRDS

BY

PROF. SPENCER F. BAIRD.

APPENDIX K.

LIST OF BIRDS COLLECTED BY CHARLES S. McCARTHY, TAXIDERMIST.

CLASSIFIED BY PROF. SPENCER F. BAIRD.

1. FALCO SAKER var. POLYAGRUS, *Ridgway.*—Prairie Falcon. South Fork Platte; between Butte and Steptoe Valleys; 2 specimens.

2. TINNUNCULUS SPARVERIUS, *Vieillot.*—Sparrow Hawk. Little Sandy River; Scott's Bluff; 27 miles west of Laramie; North Fork Platte; 4 specimens.

3. ACCIPITER FUSCUS, *Bon.*—Sharp shinned Hawk. Big Sandy Creek; 1 specimen.

4. BUTEO SWAINSONI, *Bon.*—Swainson's Buzzard. Bear River, Utah; McCarthy's Creek; Ko-bah Valley; Sweetwater; 4 specimens.

5. ARCHIBUTEO FERRUGINEUS, *Gray.*—Squirrel Hawk. Ko-bah Valley; Needles Creek; Sulphur Creek; 3 specimens. Also eggs Nos. 2329, 2330, in Rush Valley and South Fork Humboldt.

6. CIRCUS HUDSONIUS, *Vieillot.*—Marsh Hawk. Camp Floyd; Turnley's Spring; Bear River, Utah; 4 specimens. Eggs No. 2331, South Fork Humboldt.

7. AQUILA CHRYSAËTOS var. CANADENSIS, *Ridgway.*—Golden Eagle. Steptoe Valley; 1 specimen.

8. OTUS VULGARIS var. WILSONIANUS, *Allen.*—Long-eared Owl. Skull Valley; 1 specimen. Eggs No. 2332 same place.

9. BRACHYOTUS PALUSTRIS, *Bonap.*—Short-eared Owl. Round Prairie; 1 specimen.

10. SPEOTYTO CUNICULARIA var. HYPUGÆA, *Coues.*—Prairie Owl. Fort Kearney; Platte Creek; Horse Creek, Utah; 4 specimens.

11. PICUS VILLOSUS var. HARRISII, *Allen.*—Harris's Woodpecker. Utah; 1 specimen.

12. MELANERPES ERYTHOCEPHALUS, *Swainson.*—Red-headed Woodpecker. Three from La Bonté River; 1 from Fort Leavenworth; 1 Utah; 5 specimens.

13. MELANERPES TORQUATUS, *Bon.*—Lewis's Woodpecker. Sierra Nevada; 1 specimen.

14. COLAPTES AURATUS, *Swainson.*—Flicker. Fort Leavenworth; 2 specimens.

15. COLAPTES MEXICANUS, *Swainson.*—Red-shafted Flicker. North Fork Platte; La Bonté River; 2 specimens.

16. SELASPHORUS PLATYCERCUS, *Gould.*—Broad-tailed Hummingbird. No labels; 3 specimens.

17. Antrostomus nuttalii, *Cassin.*—"Poor Will." Smith's Creek; 1 specimen. Also eggs No. 2834, Ko-bah Valley.

18. Chordeiles popetue var. henryi, *Allen.*—Western Night Hawk. Big Blue; La Bonté River; 2 specimens. Eggs No. 2333, Ko-bah Valley.

19. Tyrannus verticalis, *Say.*—Arkansas Flycatcher. Ruby Valley; La Bonté, Platte, and Humboldt Rivers; 4 miles west of Laramie; 6 specimens.

20. Myiarchus cinerascens, *Lawrence.*—Ash-throated Flycatcher. Valley of Humboldt River; Ko-bah Valley; 2 specimens.

21. Empidonax pusillus ?, *Cabanis.*—Little Flycatcher. Goshoot Pass; 1 specimen.

22. Empidonax obscurus, *Baird.*—Wright's Flycatcher. Ruby Valley; Steptoe Valley; 2 specimens. Eggs (?) No. 2335, Dodge Valley.

23. Turdus migratorius, *Linnæus.*—Robin. Camp Floyd; mountains near Genoa; 3 specimens.

24. Sialia mexicana, *Swainson.*—Western Bluebird. Sierra Nevada; Sweetwater; 2 specimens.

25. Sialia arctica, *Swainson.*—Rocky Mountain Bluebird. Ruby Valley, Utah; 4 specimens.

26. Geothlypis trichas, *Cabanis.*—Maryland Yellowthroat. Fort Leavenworth; 1 specimen.

27. Icteria virens var. longicauda, *Coues.*—Yellow-breasted Chat. Leavenworth; 1 specimen.

28. Helminthophaga celata, *Baird.*—Orange-crowned Warbler. Green River; 1 specimen.

29. Seiurus noveboracensis, *Nutt.*—Water Thrush. Leavenworth; 1 specimen.

30. Dendroica nigrescens, *Baird.*—Black-throated Gray Warbler. Utah; 1 specimen.

31. Dendroica audubonii, *Baird.*—Audubon's Warbler. Utah; 1 specimen.

32. Dendroica pennsylvanica, *Baird.*—Chestnut-sided Warbler. Leavenworth; 1 specimen.

33. Dendroica æstiva, *Baird.*—Summer Yellow Warbler. Fort Leavenworth; Ko-bah Valley, Utah; 3 specimens.

34. Myiodioctes pusillus, *Bon.*—Green Black-capped Flycatcher. Leavenworth; Green River; 2 specimens.

35. Petrochelidon lunifrons, *Say.*—Cliff Swallow. McCarthy's Creek; 2 specimens.

36. Progne subis, *Baird.*—Purple Martin. 27 miles west of Laramie; 1 specimen.

37. Collurio borealis, *Baird.*—Great Northern Shrike. Fort Laramie; Camp Floyd; 3 specimens.

38. Collurio ludovicianus var. excubitoroides, *Coues.*—White-rumped Shrike. Steptoe Valley; Ko-bah Valley; Fort Laramie; between Long and Ruby Valleys; 4 specimens. Also eggs 2336, 2337, 2338, from Humboldt River, Utah.

39. Galeoscoptes carolinensis, *Gray*, Cabanis.—Catbird. Fort Leavenworth; 1 specimen.

40. Oreoscoptes montanus, *Baird.*—Mountain Mockingbird. Ko-bah Valley; South Fork Humboldt; 4 specimens. Also eggs Nos. 2340, 2341, 2342, 2343, 2344, from Ko-bah Valley, Utah; Antelope Valley; South Fork of Humboldt.

41. Harporhynchus rufus, *Cab.*—Brown Thrush. Leavenworth; 1 specimen.

42. Troglodytes aëdon var. parkmanii, *Coues.*—Parkman's Wren. La Bonte River; Sierra Nevada; 2 specimens.

43. Parus atricapillus var. septentrionalis, *Allen.*—Long-tailed Chickadee. Fort Leavenworth; 1 specimen.

44. Eremophila alpestris, *Boie.*—Sky Lark. Camp Floyd; 5 specimens.

45. Chrysomitris tristis, *Bon.*—Yellowbird. Fort Leavenworth; 1 specimen.

46. Pooecetes gramineus var. confinis, *Baird.*—Grass Finch. The eggs No. 2346 were collected at Antelope Peak.

47. Chondestes grammaca, *Bon.*—Lark Finch. Steptoe Valley; Forks of Platte; 2 specimens.

48. Junco oregonus, *Sclater.*—Oregon Snowbird. Camp Floyd; 1 specimen.

49. Spizella socialis, *Bon.*—Chipping Sparrow. Gibralter Creek; 1 specimen.

50. Spizella breweri, *Cassin.*—Brewer's Sparrow. Ko-bah Valley; Goshoot Pass; 3 specimens. Also eggs No. 2348, at Pilot Valley.

51. Spizella ——— ?.—McCarthy's Valley; Green River.

52. Passerella schistacea, *Baird.*—Slate-colored Sparrow. Mount Lookout; 1 specimen.

53. Calamospiza bicolor, *Bon.*—Lark Bunting. South Fork Platte; Chimney Rock; Utah; 3 specimens.

54. Euspiza americana, *Bon.*—Black-throated Bunting. Fort Kearney; Utah; 2 specimens.

55. Hedymeles melanocephalus, *Caban.*—Black-headed Grosbeak. 2 from Simpson's Lake; 2 from between Skull and Rush Valleys; 4 specimens.

56. Cyanospiza amœna, *Baird.*—Lazuli Finch. 2 Sierra Nevada; 1 Gibralter Creek; 3 specimens.

57. Cyanospiza cyanea, *Baird.*—Indigobird. Fort Leavenworth; 2 specimens.

58. Pipilo erythrophthalmus, *Vieillot.*—Towhee Bunting. Fort Leavenworth; 2 specimens.

59. Pipilo maculatus var. arcticus, *Coues.*—Arctic Towhee. La Bonté River; 1 specimen.

60. Pipilo chlorurus, *Baird.*—Green-tailed Finch. Mount Lookout, Utah; 2 specimens. Also eggs No. 2338, from same place.

61. Dolichonyx oryzivorus var. albinucha, *Ridgway.*—"Bob-o-link"—Reed-bird. 115 miles west of Fort Kearney; 4 specimens.

62. Molothrus ater, *Gray.*—Cowbird. 115 miles west of Fort Kearney; 2 specimens.

63. Agelaius phœniceus, *Vieillot.*—Red-winged Blackbird. Utah; 3 from Camp Floyd; Platte River; 5 specimens.

64. Xanthocephalus icterocephalus, *Baird.*—Yellow-headed Blackbird. Bear River; South Fork of Platte; Chimney Rock; 3 specimens.

65. STURNELLA MAGNA var. NEGLECTA, *Coues.*—Western Lark. Big Blue River; Ruby Valley; 2 specimens.

66. ICTERUS BULLOCKI, *Bon.*—Bullock's Oriole. La Bonté River; Sierra Nevada; 2 specimens.

67. QUISCALUS PURPUREUS var. ÆNEUS, *Ridgway.*—Crow Blackbird. Fort Leavenworth; 1 specimen.

68. CORVUS CORAX var. CARNIVORUS, *Baird.*—American Raven. Camp Floyd; 2 specimens. Also eggs No. 2514, Pleasant Springs.

69. PICICORVUS COLUMBIANUS, *Bon.*—Clarke's Crow. Sierra Nevada; Fort Bridger; 2 specimens.

70. PICA RUSTICA var. HUDSONICA, *Baird.*—Magpie. Sweetwater; Carson Valley; 2 specimens.

71. CYANURA STELLERI var. FRONTALIS, *Ridgway.*—Steller's Jay. Sierra Nevada; 1 specimen.

72. CYANOCITTA CALIFORNICA var. WOODHOUSII, *Baird.*—Woodhouse's Jay. 2 Camp Floyd; Mount Lookout; Skull Valley; 4 specimens.

73. PERISOREUS CANADENSIS var. CAPITALIS, *Baird.*—Canada Jay. Utah; 1 specimen.

74. ECTOPISTES MIGRATORIA, *Sw.*—Wild Pigeon. 40 miles west of Fort Laramie; 1 specimen.

75. ZENAIDURA CAROLINENSIS, *Bon.*—Common Dove. Steptoe and Ko-bah Valleys; North Fork of Platte; 3 specimens.

76. CANACE OBSCURA, *Baird.*—Dusky Grouse. Little's Cañon; 1 specimen.

77. CENTROCERCUS UROPHASIANUS, *Sw.*—Sage Cock. 2 Little's Cañon; 2 Pacific Springs; 1 Camp Floyd; 1 Ko-bah Valley; 2 no labels; 8 specimens. Also eggs Nos. 2510, 2511, 2512, from South Fork of Humboldt, and Steptoe Valley.

78. PEDIOCÆTES PHASIANELLUS var. COLUMBIANUS, *Coues.*—Sharp-tailed Grouse. 100 miles from Fort Laramie; 1 specimen.

79. CUPIDONIA CUPIDO, *Baird.*—Prairie Hen. Fort Kearney; 1 specimen.

80. BONASA UMBELLUS var. UMBELLOIDES, *Baird.*—Gray Mountain Grouse. Utah; Fort Bridger; 2 specimens.

81. GRUS CANADENSIS, *Temminck.*—Sand-hill Crane. Humboldt Valley; Simpson's Lake; 2 specimens. Also eggs Nos. 2516, 2517, same localities.

82. BATAURUS MINOR, *Boie.*—Bittern. Marsh near Platte; 1 specimen.

83. NYCTIARDEA GRISEA var. NÆVIA, *Allen.*—Night Heron. Reese's River; 1 specimen. Eggs No. 2515, same place.

84. IBIS GUARAUNA, *Ridgway.*—Glossy Ibis. Simpson's Lake; 1 specimen.

85. ÆGIALITIS VOCIFERUS, *Cassin.*—"Killdeer." Horse Creek; Fort Kearney; 3 specimens.

86. ÆGIALITIS MONTANUS, *Baird.*—Mountain Plover. Horseshoe Creek; South Fork of Platte; Sweetwater; 3 specimens.

87. RECURVIROSTRA AMERICANA, *Gm.*—American Avocet. 4 from Sweetwater; Willet Camp; Avocet Camp; Horse Creek; 7 specimens.

88. STEGANOPUS WILSONII, *Coues.*—Wilson's Phalarope. Steptoe Valley; 10 miles from South Fork of Platte; 3 specimens.

89. Gallinago gallinaria var. wilsoni, *Ridgway.*—English Snipe. Fort Bridger; 1 specimen.

90. Tringa ———?.—30 miles west of O'Fallon's Bluff; 1 specimen.

91. Ereunetes pusillus, *Cassin.*—Semipalmated Sandpiper. Horse Creek; 1 specimen.

92. Symphemia semipalmata, *Hartl.*—Willet. Big Sandy River; 3 specimens.

93. Tringoides macularius, *Gray.*—Spotted Sandpiper. Simpson's Lake; 1 specimen.

94. Actiturus bartramius, *Bon.*—Field Plover. 5 specimens, all from Big Blue River.

95. Numenius longirostris, *Wilson.*—Long-billed Curlew. Utah; Camp Floyd; Carson Lake; O'Fallon's Bluff; Vermillion Creek; 5 specimens. Also eggs 2507, 2508, from Skull Valley; 2509 from South Fork of Humboldt.

96. Rallus virginianus, *Linn.*—Virginia Rail. Ko-bah Valley; 1 specimen.

97. Fulica americana, *Gm.*—Coot. Camp Floyd; 1 specimen.

98. Anas boschas, *Linn.*—Mallard. Big Sandy; 1 specimen. Eggs 2513, Ruby Valley.

99. Dafila acuta, *Jenyns.*—Pintail. Utah; Scott's Bluff; Sweetwater; Camp Floyd; 4 specimens.

100. Nettion carolinensis, *Baird.*—Green-winged Teal. 2 Utah Lake; Fort Kearney; 3 specimens.

101. Querquedula discors, *Steph.*—Blue-winged Teal. Utah; Fort Bridger; Sweetwater; 3 specimens.

102. Querquedula cyanoptera, *Cassin.*—Red-breasted Teal. 2 Spring Valley; Sweetwater; 3 specimens.

103. Spatula clypeata, *Boie.*—Shoveler. Utah; Utah Lake; Pilot Valley; South Fork of Platte; 4 specimens.

104. Chaulelasmus streperus, *Gray.*—Gadwall. Utah Lake; 2 specimens.

105. Mareca americana, *Steph.*—American Widgeon. Camp Floyd; 2 specimens.

106. Aix sponsa, *Boie.*—Summer Duck. Rock Creek, Kansas; 1 specimen.

107. Fulix affinis, *Baird.*—Little Blackhead. Lake Utah; 1 specimen.

108. Aythya americana, *Bon.*—Redhead. Lake Utah; 2 specimens.

109. Erismatura rubida, *Bon.*—Ruddy Duck. Utah; Sweetwater; 2 specimens.

110. Mergus americanus, *Cassin.*—Shelldrake. Utah; 1 specimen.

111. Lophodytes cucullatus, *Reich.*—Hooded Merganser. Fort Kearney; 2 specimens.

112. Sterna hirundo, *Linn.*—Wilson's Tern. Sweetwater; Horse Creek; 2 specimens.

113. Sterna fosteri, *Nuttall.*—Foster's Tern. Ruby Valley; 1 specimen.

114. Podiceps auritus var. californicus, *Coues.*—American Eared Grebe. East side Rocky Mountains; Sweetwater; 2 specimens.

Total of specimens, 258; total of species, 114.

APPENDIX L.

REPORT ON ICHTHYOLOGY.

BY

PROF. THEO. GILL.

APPENDIX L.

REPORT ON ICHTHYOLOGY.

BY PROF. THEO. GILL.

SMITHSONIAN INSTITUTION,
Washington, December 1, 1860.

SIR: I have the honor to forward to you the report on the ichthyology of your expedition, which I have been requested to prepare.

Although few species of fishes were obtained, they are of much interest. Most of them have been fully described in the accompanying report, even when not new, as in the case of the species which is now called *Platygobio communis*. As all the groups to which the respective species belong are in some confusion and not well restricted, I have been compelled to examine the history and nomenclature of not only the genera to which they are referable, but of the allied ones. As in almost all the cases, such genera have been limited in a different manner and considerable modifications introduced, I have always given the full generic characters, founded on a personal examination, or a careful perusal of the descriptions of all the known species of the genera. This I have considered to be the course most advantageous, under the circumstances, to science.

The classification which I have here followed is that which I have proposed and published in the Proceedings of the Academy of Natural Sciences of Philadelphia. It may be considered a modification of that of the illustrious and learned Johannes Müller, whose recent death has been so much mourned by naturalists; it differs from the Müllerian classification in the very different acceptation and restriction of the orders and suborders.

The investigations which have been undertaken in the preparation of the report have been pursued in the Smithsonian Institution; and to the power of availing myself of the excellent Library and Museum of the Institution, such value as the report may have is due.

I am, sir, very truly yours,

THEO. GILL.

Capt. J. H. SIMPSON.

SUBCLASS TELEOSTEI, MÜLLER.

ORDER TELEOCEPHALI, GILL.

SUBORDER PHYSOCLYSTI, (BON.) GILL.

FAMILY PERCOIDÆ, (CUV.) GILL.

SUBFAMILY LABRACINÆ, GILL.

There is found in the Mediterranean Sea a fish which has, from the earliest times, attracted the attention of the inhabitants of the neighboring coasts from the abundance in which it is found and the size to which it attains. By the ancients, as at the present day, it was much esteemed as an article of food, and was called by the Greeks λάβραξ, and by the Romans *lupus*. Of this fish, Cuvier has said (but scarcely with strict correctness) that its appearance and almost all the details of its form recall to mind the *perch*, and that a just idea would be given of it by describing it as a "*large, elongated, and silvery perch*".

From the *Perches*, however, it differs in several characters, which induced Cuvier to separate it generically, and for the name of the genus he adopted the Greek designation of the species. The characters by which Cuvier distinguished it from the Perches were the presence of teeth on the tongue and of two spines to the operculum. It differs also from the true Perches in the armature of some of its bones and by the shorter spinous dorsal fin, the rays in the European and allied American species being always nine, and still more by modifications of the skeleton and among others the small number of vertebræ, of which there are 11 or 12 abdominal and 13 or 14 caudal. The very distinct type represented by *Labrax Japonicus* Cuv. and Val. (= *Lateolabrax Japonicus* Bleeker) has, however, 16 abdominal and 19 caudal vertebræ.

Though Cuvier was the first to properly distinguish the genus, its type had been long previously recorded by Klein as the first of two species, which he placed in a group, for which he used the same name *Labrax*.

That author, in his fifth and last Missal for the Advancement of the Natural History of Fishes,* has devoted his ninth fasciculus to the consideration and description of those fishes provided with two dorsal fins. In this group he includes the Trouts (*Trutta* Klein), in which the first dorsal is sustained by branched rays while the second is adipose, as well as *Mullus*, *Cestræus* Klein, *Labrax* Klein, *Sphyræna*, *Gobio* Klein, *Asperulus* Klein, and *Trichidion* Klein, in which the first dorsal is spinous and the second has branched rays. *Trutta* of Klein is synonymous with the extended genus *Salmo* of Linnæus; *Mullus* embraces, like the Linnæan genus, the *Mulli* and the *Amias* of Gronovius, or *Apogons* of Lacépède; the *Cestræi* are the *Mugiles* of Linnæus; *Sphyræna* is limited to the true species of the genus as now accepted; *Gobio*

* Jacobi Theodori Klein Historiæ Piscium promovendæ Missus quintus et ultimus de piscibus per branchias apertas respirantibus, *Gedani*, Litteris Schreiberianis, 1749.

is equivalent to *Gobius* of Linnæus; *Asperulus* to *Aspro* of Cuvier; and *Trichidion* to *Polynemus* of Linnæus.

The group, it will be thus seen, is composed of very dissimilar elements. From it are also excluded *Perca*, and other genera with the dorsal fins quite as distinct. The Perches are placed in a group of which the character is the presence of only one dorsal entire or sinuate.

Labrax itself is defined* as having as many fins as *Cestræus* (or *Mugil* Linn.); serrated scales; the mouth large, and provided with numerous slender teeth in many rows. Two species are referred to it: the *Labrax diacanthus* Gill (*Sciæna diacantha* Bloch, *Labrax lupus* Linn.); and the *Centropomus undecimalis* of Lacépède, and the moderns. The genus itself is therefore not very unnatural, but its characters are common to many others, especially to *Perca*.

In the second and third volumes of the great "Histoire Naturelle des Poissons", Cuvier and Valenciennes have referred to the genus *Labrax* seven nominal species, six of which are described in the former volume.

Of these, the *Labrax lupus* is the type of the genus, and is distinguished by the spur-like spines of the inferior margin of the preoperculum; the presence of a perfect marginal band of teeth, and of an oval basal patch on the tongue; three spines to the anal fin; and other characters, which have been noticed in the preceding synopsis. To this should the name *Labrax* be restricted.

The second species (*le Bar alongé*, or *Perca elongata* of Geoffroy) is distinguished by finer and more numerous teeth on the inferior border of the preoperculum, and the presence of only two anal spines. The distinctive characters of this species, however, require to be confirmed.

The third species is the *Labrax lineatus* of Cuvier, the common Rock-fish or Striped Bass of the United States. This has been taken as the type of a new genus, for which Mitchill's name *Roccus* is preserved. The characters are given below. To this genus should be also referred the *Labrax multilineatus* described by Cuvier and Valenciennes in the third volume of their "Histoire Naturelle des Poissons".

The fourth species, *Labrax Waigiensis*, has been identified by Bleeker with the *Psammoperca datnioides* of Richardson; if this is correct (and, notwithstanding the discrepancies between the descriptions of the "Histoire Naturelle" and Richardson, such appears to be the case), it belongs to a very distinct genus from the *Labrax lupus*. The teeth of the jaws, vomer, and palatines are described by Richardson as crowded, rounded, and granular, while by Cuvier the teeth on both jaws, the chevron of the vomer, and the palatines are said to be villiform ("dents en velours"): it is also stated by Cuvier that there is a small oval disk at the base of the tongue; by Richardson, the tongue is said to be smooth. In the latter statement, however, he disagrees not only with Cuvier and Valenciennes, but with Bleeker, who also asserts† that there is an oblong patch at the base of the tongue, "lingua basi thurma denticulorum scabra." Both authors agree as to the presence of a single spine to the operculum (although one of the generic characters assigned to *Labrax* by Cuvier was the presence of two spines on that bone),

* Pinnas habet tot quot Cestræus et Mugil: squamas serratas: os magnum plurimis tenuissimisque dentibus multiplici ordine munitum. Voracissimus.

† Natuurkundig Tydschrift voor Nederlandsch Indie, vol. ii, p. 479.

and of a strong horizontal spine at the angle of the preoperculum, above which the margin is pectinated.

The next species in order, *Labrax Japonicus* of Cuvier and Valenciennes, is the type of the genus *Lateolabrax* of Bleeker,* which is widely separated from *Labrax* by the absence of any teeth on the tongue, the increased number of its vertebræ, &c. In the plectroid armature of the operculum, it however resembles that genus.

The last species, *Labrax mucronatus*, is also now considered as the type of a new genus, for which the name *Morone* is accepted. Its generic characters and affinities will be given at length in a subsequent portion of this memoir.

Of the seven species referred by Cuvier and Valenciennes to the genus *Labrax*, five are thus seen to belong to different genera. Nor do any of these genera appear to be unnecessary; but, on the contrary, all of them are well distinguished from each other by characters that ichthyologists must admit are of importance: two of the species, indeed, that were referred to the genus by the French naturalists, do not agree with their diagnosis of that genus, and it is doubtful, indeed, whether they have any near relations with the others. It is not in disparagement of those celebrated and able men that these remarks have been made. The progress of scientific discovery and the examination of better materials have enabled their successors to discover the errors of the founders of modern ichthyology. None could have performed the work at that day better than they.

Having long since, from an examination of the descriptions of various authors, been aware of the confusion and uncertainty in which our American species of the Cuvierian *Labrax* were enveloped, I believed that it might be a useful task to attempt the elucidation of the genus. The results of the investigations undertaken therefor have been published, in the Proceedings of the Academy of Natural Sciences of Philadelphia for April, 1860, as a "Monograph of the Genus *Labrax* of Cuvier."

Most of our general remarks are reproduced, with many additional ones, in the present report. The nominal American species admitted by Drs. De Kay and Storer in the genus *Labrax* amount to seven, and another specific name has been since added by Filippi, an Italian naturalist. It has been attempted to demonstrate, in our monograph of the genus, that all of those nominal species are referable to three true ones. Three of the synonyms apply to one species, and four to another.

Besides the species that have been attributed to the genus by Richardson, De Kay, and Filippi, several others have been described under that name by modern naturalists. Dr. Charles Girard has noticed two of these in the "Proceedings of the Academy of Natural Sciences of Philadelphia" under the names *Labrax nebulosus* and *L. clathratus*. He afterward constructed for them a new genus, which he called *Paralabrax*,

* By a misunderstanding, the name *Percalabrax* has been taken by some authors as the generic denomination of this type. Cuvier (Hist. Nat. des Poissons, i, 55) has remarked, "Nous avons cru, pour plus de clarté, devoir donner un nom particulier à chaque sous-genre; mais ceux qui tiendraient à conserver la nomenclature des grands genres de Linnæus, pourraient placer ce nom sous-générique entre deux parenthèses, comme Linnæus l'a fait en quelques occasions, et dire, par exemple; *Perca* (*labrax*) *lupus*; *Perca* (*labrax*) *lineata*, etc." Temminck and Schlegel, following this suggestion but omitting the parentheses, called the *Perca* (*labrax*) *Japonicus*, *Perca-Labrax Japonicus*, evidently accepting the views of Cuvier as to the limits of the subgenus *Labrax*. Bleeker, quite properly recognizing the generic peculiarities of the species, called it *Lateolabrax*; but Dr. Albert Günther (in the first volume of a Catalogue of the Acanthopterygian Fishes in the Collection of the British Museum, 1859, p. 70), mistaking the meaning of Temminck and Schlegel, has called it *Percalabrax*.

and correctly placed it in the vicinity of *Serranus;* they are indeed very closely related to that genus as now restricted.

Mr. Hill, of Jamaica, in a useful catalogue of the fishes of that island, has also noticed a fish which he referred to *Labrax* under the name of *L. pluvialis*, or the Rainy-weather Chub. It is said by that gentleman to be confounded by the fishermen with the *Labrax mucronatus* (=*Morone americana* of this article), but differs from it by the presence of vertical bars, like those of the common perch of Europe and America. Until more authentic information is obtained, the relations of that species must be entirely conjectural, and it is probable that it has no affinity to the *Labraces.*

GENUS ROCCUS, (MITCH.) GILL.

Synonymy.

ROCCUS *Mitchill*, Report in part on the Fishes of New York, p. 25, 1814.
ROCCUS *Gill*, Proceedings Academy of Natural Sciences of Phila., vol. xi, p. 111, 1860.
LEPIBEMA *Raf.*, Ichthyologia Ohiensis, p. 23, 1820.
SCIÆNA sp. *Bloch.*
PERCA sp. *Bloch and Schneid., Mitchill*, 1818.
CENTROPOME sp. *Lac.*
LABRAX sp. *Cuv., auct. al.*

Labraces with pectinated preoperculum, cycloid or imperfectly ctenoid cheek and opercular scales, lingual teeth developed in a marginal band as well as at the base, and skull with compressed non-diaphanous brain-case and no mastoid projections.

The body is elongate, subfusiform or oblong-ovate, compressed, and with the back anteriorly curved.

The head is compressed, laterally oblong conic. The operculum is armed with two spines, the upper of which is small; the preoperculum pectinated both behind and below; the suborbital bones entire. The muciferous cavities of the lower jaw are not very evident.

Teeth on the intermaxillary, dentary, palatine, and vomerine bones villiform; those on the tongue present in a band along the lateral margins, and in two longitudinal rows, or an elongated oval patch at the base. Interbranchial osselets smooth.

The scales are ctenoid on the body, but on the head, from the nape to the nostrils, and on the cheeks, are mostly cycloid.

The lateral line is straight and continuous to the base of the caudal fin.

The dorsal fins are not united by a perceptible membrane; the anterior fin has nine spinous rays; the second is oblong, with one spinous, and from eleven to fourteen branched ones.

The anal fin is opposite the second dorsal, and has three spinous rays regularly increasing in size.

The caudal is emarginate.

The skull has the brain-case with nearly flat sides below, rectilinear and flat toward the aperture for the last two branches of the fifth nerve, a vacuity on each side between the basioccipital and alispheroid bones, and the postfrontals laterally well developed.

The genus *Roccus* is very closely allied to both *Labrax* as now restricted as well as to *Morone.* From *Labrax*, it differs chiefly in the character of the armature of the preoperculum, and by the absence of the teeth at the anterior extremity of the tongue; the whole margin of the tongue in the latter genus being provided with a band of villiform teeth, and the spur-formed teeth of the inferior margin of the preoperculum calling to mind the genus *Plectropoma* of Cuvier among the *Serrani*. The difference between the last-named genus, or at least some of its species, and *Serranus* is indeed not of as great value as that between *Labrax* and *Roccus*. The only constant character between *Serranus* and *Plectropoma*, as those genera were established by Cuvier, is the spur-like armature of the inferior border of the preoperculum, while *Labrax* and *Roccus* are distinguished, not only by an equally great and constant difference of the preopercular border, but also by the difference of the lingual dentition. As the former character is of as great value in the *Labraces* as in the *Serrani*, consistency will require that if *Plectropoma* and *Serranus* are considered as distinct genera, *Roccus* and *Labrax* should also be so regarded.

The difference between *Roccus* and *Morone* is of even more importance than that of *Roccus* and *Labrax*. The distinguishing characters will be referred to under the diagnosis of *Morone*.

The name which has been adopted for this genus is one given by Dr. Mitchill, in the year 1814, to a medley comprising the *Roccus lineatus* (which he called *Roccus striatus*) and the *Otolithus regalis* (which was designated as *Roccus comes*). The name was solely the result of ignorance, on the part of the author, of the application of the ordinary terms used by naturalists at that day.

As the work in which the name of *Roccus* was first published is very rare and inaccessible, the remarks of Mitchill on his *Roccus striatus* have been extracted to show the character of the work. We are indebted to Mr. Brevoort for the loan of the volume.*

"It has seemed to me proper to make a new genus for this fish and his congeners. He has been supposed by some to be the *Perca nobilis*,† but the position of his ventral fins forbids him to be considered as a *Perca* at all. Besides, if he was a member of the *Perca* family, the specific character of 'eight brown bands' is totally different from the longitudinal stripes that distinguish him, and would rank him among the undescribed species. Besides, he has two dorsal fins, while the *P. nobilis* has but one."

In the first place, the so-called *Roccus striatus* does not differ from the very common European Perch, and from the numerous allied species and genera, in the position of the ventrals.

In the next instance, even if it did so differ, Mitchill had, on a previous page, founded a genus for the same reason as in the case of *Roccus*, and he has given no indications whatever as to how the two are to be generically distinguished.

The two species that are referred to *Roccus* belong to totally distinct families.

Finally, the "*Roccus striatus*" had been indicated previously in four different works.

The name *Roccus* is itself a barbarous latinization of the popular name "Rockfish", or simply "Rock", by which its chief species is known in some parts of the United

* Report, in part, of Samuel L. Mitchill, M. D., Prof. of Natural History, &c., on the Fishes of New York. New York: printed by D. Carlisle, No. 301 Broadway, January 1, 1814. 16mo, 28 pages.

† It is not in any way related to the *Perca nobilis*. According to Cuvier and Valenciennes, that species is the *Chætodon octofasciatus* of Bloch.

States, especially in the District of Columbia, Maryland, and Philadelphia. It has been nevertheless deemed advisable to accept the name rather than to apply a new one. It is scarcely worse than *Lumpus*, *Gunnellus*, *Vogmarus*, *Kangarus*, *Catus*, *Rattus*, and many other names of similar derivation, which have been introduced into systematic nomenclature.

C. S. Rafinesque, in the "Ichthyologia Ohiensis", also proposed for his *Perca chrysops*, in case it should be found to be generically distinct from *Perca*, the name *Lepibema.* He believed it to be distinguished "by the scaly bases of the caudal, anal, and second dorsal fins, the last with some spiny rays, and all the three parts of the gill-cover more or less serrulate, besides the small teeth". Rafinesque suggested that to this genus the *Perca Mitchilli* of Mitchill might "perhaps be found to belong".

The distinctive characters mentioned by Rafinesque alone are very trivial; but *Roccus* is certainly distinguished by the presence of scales between the rays of the second dorsal and anal fins from *Perca*, in which the membrane is perfectly naked. But the opercula are not more completely armed than in *Perca*, nor is there any essential difference in the size of the teeth.

ROCCUS LINEATUS, GILL.

Synonymy.

SCIÆNA LINEATA *Bloch*, Ichthyologie, pars ix, p. 53, pl. 305.
PERCA . . . . . *Schœpff*, Schrift. der Gesells. Nat.-Freunde, vol. viii, p. 160.
PERCA SAXATILIS *Walbaum*, Artedi Genera Piscium, p. 330.
PERCA SAXATILIS *Bloch*, Systema Ichthyologiæ Schneid. ed., p. 89.
PERCA SEPTENTRIONALIS *Bloch*, Systema Ichthyologia Schneid. ed., p. 90, pl. 70.
CENTROPOME RAYÉ *Lac.*, Hist. Nat. des Poissons, vol. iv, p. 225.
ROCCUS STRIATUS *Mitchill*, Report, in part, on the Fishes of New York, p. 25, 1814.
PERCA MITCHILLI *Mitchill*, Trans. Lit. and Phil. Soc. N. Y., vol. i, p. 413, pl. 3, fig. 4.
ROCK FISH *Mease*, Trans. Lit. and Phil. Soc. N. Y., vol. i, p. 502.
PERCA MITCHILLI / LEPIBEMA MITCHILLI } *Raf.*, Ichthyologia Ohiensis, p. 23 (passim).
LABRAX LINEATUS *Cuvier* and *Val.*, Hist. Nat. des Poissons, vol. ii, p. 79.
PERCA LABRAX! *Smith*, Nat. Hist. Fishes of Mass., p. 277.
LABRAX LINEATUS *Rich*, Fauna Boreali-Americana, vol. iii, p. 10.
LABRAX LINEATUS *Storer*, Report on the Fishes of Mass., p. 7.
LABRAX LINEATUS *Ayres*, Boston Journ. Nat. Hist., vol. iv, p. 707.
LABRAX LINEATUS *De Kay*, Zoölogy of N. Y. Fishes, p. 7, pl. 1, fig. 3.
LABRAX LINEATUS *Linsley*, Catalogue of Fishes of Connecticut.
LABRAX LINEATUS *Storer*, Synopsis Fishes of N. America, p. 21; ib. in Memoirs Am. Acad.
LABRAX LINEATUS *Storer*, Hist. Fishes of Mass.; ib. in Memoirs Am. Acad. vol. v, p. 55, pl. 1, fig. 4, 1853.
LABRAX LINEATUS, *Baird*, Report on Fishes of New Jersey Coast, p. —; ib. in Ninth Annual Report of Smith. Inst., p. 321.
LABRAX LINEATUS *Holbrook*, Ichthyology of South Carolina, p. 17, pl. iv, fig. 2.
LABRAX LINEATUS *Gill*, Annual Report Smith. Inst., 1857, p. 255.
LABRAX LINEATUS *Günther*, Catalogue of the Acanthopterygian Fishes in the Collection of the British Museum, vol. i, p. 64.
ROCCUS LINEATUS *Gill*, Proceedings Acad. of Natural Sciences of Phila., 1860, p. 64.

ROCCUS CHRYSOPS, GILL.

Synonymy.

PERCA CHRYSOPS / LEPIBEMA CHRYSOPS } *Raf.*, Ichthyologia Ohiensis, p. 28.
LABRAX MULTILINEATUS *Cuv.* and *Val.*, Hist. Nat. des Poissons, vol. iii, p. 588.
PERCA MULTILINEATA *Les.*, *fide Cuv.*, and *Val.*
LABRAX NOTATUS *Smith*, in Rich. Fauna Boreali-Americana, vol. iii, p. 8, 1836.
LABRAX MULTILINEATUS *Kirtland*, Boston Journal Nat. Hist., vol. v, p. 21, pl. 7 fig. 1; Visitor, p. 53, 1859.

LABRAX MULTILINEATUS *De Kay*, Nat. Hist. of New York Fishes, p. 14.
LABRAX ALBIDUS *De Kay*, Nat. Hist. of New York Fishes, p. 13, pl. 51, fig. 165.
LABRAX NOTATUS *De Kay*, loc. cit., p. 14.
LABRAX MULTILINEATUS *Storer*, Synopsis of the Fishes of North America, p. 22; ib. in Memoirs of American Acad., vol. ii.
LABRAX NOTATUS *Storer*, loc. cit., p. 22.
LABRAX ALBIDUS *Storer*, loc. cit., p. 23.
LABRAX OSCULATII *Filippi*, Revue et Magazin du Zoologie, 2d series, vol. v, p. 164.
LABRAX CHRYSOPS *Gill*, Proc. Acad. Nat. Sci. Phila., 1860, p. 20.
LABRAX OSCULATII *Günther*, Catalogue of the Acanthopterygian Fishes, &c., p. 65.
LABRAX MULTILINEATUS *Günther*, Catalogue of the Acanthopterygian Fishes, &c., p. 67.
ROCCUS CHRYSOPS *Gill*, Proceedings Acad. of Nat. Sciences of Phila., 1860, p. 113.
Not LABRAX CHRYSOPS *Girard*.
Not LABRAX MULTILINEATUS (partim) *Günther*, Catalogue of the Acanthopterygian Fishes, &c., p. 501.

The body is elongated-ovate, with the dorsal outline arched. The height is greatest under the spinous dorsal fin, and there equals twenty-seven hundredths of the entire length from the projecting lower jaw to the concave margin of the caudal fin. The height is nearly uniform under the spinous dorsal; the dorsal outline behind that fin slowly declines to the end of the second dorsal; the abdominal outline ascends much more rapidly from the commencement to the end of the anal fin. Behind the latter fin, the height of the caudal peduncle is about a seventh of the entire length; at the base of the caudal fin, it is equal to a ninth of the same.

The head is conical in profile, slightly depressed at the nape, and thence descends in nearly a straight line to the snout, the latter being scarcely convex. The head, from the lower jaw to the tip of the opercular spine, forms little more than a quarter of the entire length; its height at the nape behind the vertical of the posterior border of the eye is nearly equal to sixteen hundredths of the entire length. The diameter of the eye is more than equal to a quarter of the head's length, and the eye is distant a diameter from the snout.

The pectinated margin of the preoperculum is slightly oblique; its teeth become stronger toward the angle, and are continued on the inferior margin at greater distances for about half the distance between the angle and the articulation with the lower jaw; the anterior limb or margin of the anterior fold is vertical. The operculum has two spines, separated by an oblique emargination.

The first dorsal fin commences over the bases of the ventrals, and is of a triangular form. The fourth spine is longest, and equals an eighth of the fish's length; from thence they gradually decrease in size to the ninth, which is nearly as large as the second. The second dorsal is entirely separated from the first. Its spine is equal to nearly half the length of its longest ray, and somewhat exceeds that of the seventh spine; the last ray is less than half as long as the longest.

The anal fin commences nearly under the fourth ray of the dorsal, and nearly four of its rays are posterior to the end of that fin; the third spine is longest, and exceeds half the length of the first articulated or longest ray. The relative height is the same as that of the dorsal fin.

The caudal fin, when expanded, is emarginated, and its shortest rays form a sixth of the entire length; the longest rays equal a quarter of the same.

The pectoral fins are small, and only equal fifteen hundredths of the length. The first two rays are simple; the third, or longest, is branched.

The ventrals are longer than the pectorals, and equal seventeen hundredths of the length. The spine is more than half as long as the first branched or longest ray.

The number and arrangement of the rays of the respective fins are indicated by the following formula:

D. IX + I. 1. 11; A. III. 1. 9; C. 5. I. 8. 7. I. 4; P. 2. 14; V. 1. 5.

The scales of the trunk are of moderate size, with the nucleus at about the posterior third; thence about ten ridges radiate toward the posterior margin, which is crenated by them. Numerous muricated ridges, terminating in pectinations at the posterior margin, also radiate posteriorly from the same nucleus. The concentric striæ are fine but well marked. The number of scales through which the lateral line passes amounts to from fifty-three to fifty-six, exclusive of the smaller ones at the base of the caudal fin. The number of rows is nine above the lateral line, one through which the lateral line runs, and fourteen below.

The operculum is covered with moderate scales, which have subcentral nuclei and muricated and pectinated posterior margins. Those on the cheeks are much smaller, with the nuclei also subcentral, but with generally entire, or nearly entire, margins. Some of the larger scales near the posterior margin of the preoperculum are pectinated like the opercular ones.

There are on the lower jaw five pairs of indistinct, shallow, muciferous grooves; those of the third and fourth pairs are elongated, the last being under the terminal part of the maxillaries. The fifth pair is obsolete. The maxillaries, on their superior parts, are covered with scales smaller than those of the cheeks; the inferior and posterior portions are naked.

The color is silvery, tinged with golden on the sides below the lateral line, and above with rose. A number of blackish or dusky lines traverse the sides, four of which are above the lateral line; through a fifth the lateral line runs; and there is a variable number of more or less distinct ones below. The head is dark above and silvery on the sides.

The spinous dorsal is punctulated with black, and has a narrow black margin. The soft dorsal is also punctulated. The anal is blackish at its middle and margin between the rays. The caudal is similar to the dorsal. The pectorals and ventrals are immaculate.

The *Roccus chrysops* thus described is undoubtedly identical with the *Perca* or *Lepibema chrysops* of Rafinesque, and the *Labrax multilineatus* of the "Histoire Naturelle des Poissons" and of Kirtland. The descriptions that have been given of the species under those names are meager and unsatisfactory; but the notice of the color given by the above-named authors, and the possession of specimens from the same hydrographical basins as those from which the fishes described by them were taken, leave no doubt as to the identity of the species.

Rafinesque's description of his *Perca chrysops* is, like almost all his descriptions, inapplicable to any known fish, but it agrees with the *Morone chrysops* better than any other species. Rafinesque erroneously attributes to his species six branchiostegal rays, a single opercular spine, eight spines to the first dorsal fin, and places it under the genus *Perca*, all the species of which, he informs us, have naked heads. He suggested for it a new genus, for which he proposed to give the name *Lepibema*, in allusion to the scaly bases of the unpaired fins. Lesueur subsequently sent to the Parisian Museum two specimens of a species which he called *Perca multilineata*, which Cuvier and Valenciennes placed in their genus *Labrax*, adopting for it the specific name of Lesueur. Their description is mostly comparative, it being said to differ from the *Labrax lineatus* by its higher body, shorter head, more feeble teeth, the stronger asperities of the tongue, and especially the larger scales of the maxillaries, which resemble those of *Labrax mucronatus*, while in *Labrax lineatus* they were said to be scarcely perceptible.

The description of the lingual dentition is very unsatisfactory, and no correction is made of the statement made in the second volume that the *Labrax lineatus* has only lateral teeth. It is not so much in the development of the asperities of the tongue that the lingual dentition of the species differs, as in that, while there are two narrow rows separated by a mesial line in *Roccus lineatus*, the rows are broader at the middle in proportion, and coalescent in *Roccus chrysops*.

There were said to be in one specimen sixteen, and in another nineteen, longitudinal dark lines. So large a number is rarely seen; the most constant arrangement is five above, including the one through which the lateral line runs, while sometimes there are several below the lateral line, and at other times they are obsolete. These lines are sometimes straight, but often interrupted.

In the "Fauna Boreali-Americana" of Richardson, a *Labrax* is described in the volume on Ichthyology, under the name *Labrax notatus* (Smith), the Bar-fish, or "Canadian Basse". This species is said to "differ from Mitchill's Basse (*L. lineatus*, Cuvier) in being much more robust, and in being marked with rows of spots, five above and five below the lateral line, so regularly interrupted and transposed as to appear like ancient church-music". It has been suggested by Dr. De Kay that it is the same as the *Perca Mitchilli* var. *interruptus* of Mitchill, but the comparison will apply very well to *Roccus chrysops*, and it is doubtless identical with that species. In the remarks upon the species, it is said, by Dr. Richardson apparently, that "in the more robust form, and in the strong scales of the head, the Canadian Bar-fish resembles the *L. mucronatus* of the United States and the West Indies, and the *L. multilineatus* of the Wabash. The latter has sixteen narrow, black, longitudinal lines on the flanks." It has been attempted to show that the number of lines is not a specific character; and if this is the case, the *Labrax notatus* and *L. multilineatus* are probably identical with each other and with *Roccus chrysops*. The *Labrax notatus*, it is true, is stated by Smith to have but one anal spine and six articulated ventral rays; but this statement is undoubtedly due to a *lapsus calami*, or an error of observation. So great a variation in the number of anal spines, from a nearly allied species, would be in direct opposition to all we know of the peculiarities of the fishes of this tribe, while it is one of the characters of the family to have only five branched rays in the ventral fins. Smith states that he counted fifty-eight scales along the lateral line, a statement which confirms the identity of his species with *Roccus chrysops*.

In the abstracts of Smith's description of *Labrax notatus*, given by De Kay and Storer, the species is said to have the "length, one to two feet". Even if this was so, it would not militate against the idea of its identity with *Roccus chrysops*, although usually large, but an examination of the description of Smith and Richardson reveals no mention whatever of the size of the species.

In the number of Guerin's "Revue et Magazin de Zoologie" for April, 1853 (vol. v, p. 164), Professor Filippi, of Turin, has described a *Roccus*, to which he has given the name of *Labrax Osculatii;* a traveler in America, M. Osculati, having obtained it from Lake Ontario. Filippi has distinguished this species from *Labrax lineatus* very well, alluding to the two longitudinal lines of basal teeth in that species, and attributing to his own a single oval patch. His other characters are the greater height of the body in *L. Osculatii*, which equals a third of the length, while in *L. lineatus* it is a quarter, and the number of scales, which are formulated as $56\frac{9}{15}$ for *L. Osculatii* and $64\frac{9}{11}$ for *L. lineatus.* The true teeth are also said to be more numerous. The distinctive characters of the species are very well stated by Filippi, but his expression of surprise that a fish so common in the United States should not have been noticed by any American naturalist, not even by Dr. De Kay, is uncalled for. Unhappily, the species had been too often noticed, and in De Kay's Ichthyology of New York it appears under no less than three different names. Filippi has mentioned its habitat as the sea and rivers of the United States (*mare et fluviis Confederationis Americanæ*). I know not on what authority it is said to inhabit the sea. It is probably assumed to be found there because the *Roccus lineatus* is. So far as we know, it is confined to the great fresh-water lakes and the western rivers.

As Filippi has already led one naturalist into error regarding the proportions of the species, it seems necessary to state that he must have reckoned the length only from the snout to the base of the caudal fin, and not to its margin. When so measured, the height is a third of the length, but its height in proportion to the total length is only as three to ten.

Specimens of the *Roccus chrysops* are in the museum of the Smithsonian Institution, from Southern Illinois, obtained by Mr. Robert Kennicott, and from the Root River, at Racine, Wis., Toronto, &c., obtained by Professor Baird. It appears to be generally distributed in the rivers of the West.

The specimens from the hydrographical basins of the Ohio River and of the Great Lakes cannot be specifically distinguished from each other; nor can I perceive the difference signalized by Dr. Kirtland in the caudal fins of Ohio and Lake Erie specimens.

In extreme youth, this species appears to be crossed by obscure vertical bands. At a later epoch, these bands are lost, and afterward the longitudinal lines are assumed.

The best descriptions of this species have been published by Professor Filippi under the name *L. Osculatii*, and by the late Dr. De Kay under that of *L. albidus.* The best figure is that given by Dr. Kirtland in the Journal of the Boston Society of Natural History; but the dorsals are erroneously represented as being connected by a low membrane. In the text, they are correctly described as being "distinct".

It is with much hesitation that I have adopted the specific name of Rafinesque. It would have been better for the progress of the science if all the works of that unfortunate naturalist had been ignored.

GENUS MORONE, GILL.

Synonymy.

MORONE *Mitchill*, Report in part on the Fishes of New York, p. 18. (Not defined.)
MORONE *Gill*, Proceedings Academy of Nat. Sciences of Phila., 1860, p. 115.
PERCA sp. *Bloch*, Gmelin, Lac.
CENTROPOMUS sp. *Rafinesque.*
BODIANUS sp. *Mitchill.*

Labraces with a pectinated preoperculum, strongly ctenoid cheek and opercular scales, lingual teeth developed only in a marginal band, and skull with swollen diaphanous brain-case and mastoid protuberances projecting toward the foramina for the last two branches on each side of the fifth nerve.

The body is oblong-ovate and slightly gibbous at the commencement of the dorsal fin.

The head is compressed, laterally oblong-conic. The operculum has two spines, the upper of which is smaller; the preoperculum pectinated behind and beneath; the suborbital bones entire. The muciferous cavities of the lower jaw are very perceptible.

The teeth on the intermaxillary, dentary, vomerine, and palatine bones are villiform. There is only a marginal band on the tongue, which is less perfect at the tip, the asperities being there more scattered. The interbranchial osselets are smooth.

The scales are ctenoid on the body and the entire head.

The lateral line anteriorly convex, but not parallel with the back.

The dorsal fins are united by a low membrane; the anterior has nine spines; the posterior, one. The anal fin has three spines. The caudal is emarginated.

The skull has the brain-case with inflated sides below, swollen and developing into mastoid prominences projecting toward the foramina for the last two branches of the fifth pair of nerves, no vacuity between the basioccipital and alisphenoid bones, and the postfrontals laterally contracted.

The chief distinctive characters of the genus are the presence of strongly-pectinated scales on the cheeks and opercular bones, and the band of villiform teeth on the sides, and of more scattered ones at the tip, as well as the cranial peculiarities.

In the armature of the preoperculum and operculum, it resembles the genus *Roccus*. The slightly gibbous back in front of the dorsal fin and the greater development of the second anal spine are secondary features, which support the natural characters of *Morone* as distinguished from the genus *Roccus*.

For the name of the genus, one used by Mitchill for a group founded in error has been adopted. The name of Mitchill resulted from a misunderstanding of that author regarding the value of the terms made use of by Linnæus. The genus *Perca* was placed by the Swedish naturalist in his section of *Thoracici*. Mitchill, believing that the *Morone americana*, *Perca americana* (*Perca flavescens* Cv.), and *Pomotis aureus* (*Pomatis vulgaris* Cv.), were rather abdominal fishes, considered them to be generically distinct from *Perca*, and consequently gave to them the generic name *Morone*. It is scarcely necessary to state that all the species enumerated have the normal position of the ventrals of *Perca*, and that therefore *Morone* of Mitchill was a mere synonym of

Perca of Linnæus. I have nevertheless chosen to take that name rather than to give a new one.

At least two species are now known of the genus *Morone.* One of them is the well-known "White Perch" of the eastern coast; the other is our *Morone interrupta*, a species that had been erroneously described under the name *Labrax chrysops.*

The synonymy of each species will be given, but a description is only offered of the *Morone interrupta.*

MORONE AMERICANA, GILL.

Synonymy.

PERCA *Schoepff*, Schrift. der Gesells. Nat.-Freunde, vol. viii, p. 159.
PERCA AMERICANA *Gmel.*, Systema Naturæ, vol. i, pars iii, p. 1308.
PERCA *Schoepff*, Naturforscher, vol. xx, p. 17.
PERCA IMMACULATA *Walbaum*, Artedi Genera Piscium, p. 330.
PERCA AMERICANA *Bloch*, Systema Ichthyologiæ, Schneid. ed.
PERCA AMERICANA *Lac.*, Hist. Nat. des Poissons, vol. iv, p. 412.
MORONE RUFA *Mitchill*, Report, in part, on the Fishes of New York, p. 18.
BODIANUS RUFUS *Mitchill*, Trans. Lit. and Phil. Soc. of New York, vol. i, p. 420, Jan., 1814.
BODIANUS RUFUS, Centropomus albus Raf.; Précise des découvertes Somiologiques, p. 19, June, 1814.
PERCA MUCRONATA *Raf.*, American Monthly Magazine and Critical Review, vol. ii, p. 205.
LABRAX MUCRONATUS *Cuv.* and *Val.*, Hist. Nat. des Poissons, vol. ii, p. 81, pl. 121.
BODIANUS RUFUS *Smith*, Nat. Hist. Fishes of Mass., p. 274.
LABRAX MUCRONATUS *Storer*, Report on Ichthyology of Mass., p. 8.
PERCA MUCRONATUS (misprint) *Sw.*, Nat. Hist. of Fishes, Amphibious and Reptile, vol. ii, p. 198, 1839.
LABRAX RUFUS *De Kay*, Nat. Hist. of New York Fishes, p. 9, pl. 3, fig. 7.
LABRAX MUCRONATUS *Ayres*, Boston Journal Nat. Hist., vol. iv, p. 257.
LABRAX MUCRONATUS *Linsley*, Catalogue of Fishes of Connecticut.
LABRAX RUFUS *Storer*, Synopsis of the Fishes of North America, p. 22; ib. in Memoirs of American Academy, new series, vol. ii, p. 274, 1846.
LABRAX RUFUS *Storer*, Hist. of the Fishes of Mass., p. 1; ib. in Memoirs of American Acad., new series, vol. v, p. 57.
LABRAX MUCRONATUS *Baird*, Report on Fishes of New Jersey Coast, p. 8; ib. in Ninth Annual Report of Smith. Inst., p. 322, 1855.
LABRAX AMERICANUS *Holbrook*, Ichthyology of South Carolina, p. 21, pl. 3, fig. 2, 1855.
LABRAX RUFUS *Gill*, Annual Report of Smith. Inst., p. 256, 1857.
LABRAX MUCRONATUS *Hill*, Catalogue of Fish of Jamaica, p. 1.
LABRAX RUFUS *Günther*, Catalogue of the Acanthopterygian Fishes of the British Museum, p. 65.
LABRAX NIGRICANS *De Kay*, Nat. Hist. of New York Fishes, p. 12, pl. 50, fig. 160, 1842.
LABRAX NIGRICANS *Storer*, Synopsis of the Fishes of North America; ib. in Memoirs of American Acad., vol. ii, p. 23, 1846.
GRYSTES NIGRICANS *var.* 1 *Herbert*, Frank Forrester's Fish and Fishing in the United States, vol. i, p. 191.
MORONE PALLIDA *Mitchill*, Report, in part, on the Fishes of New York, p. 18.
BODIANUS PALLIDUS *Mitchill*, Trans. Lit. and Phil. Soc. of New York, vol. i, p. 420.
BODIANUS PALLIDUS *Smith*, Nat. Hist. of Fishes of Mass., p. 294.
LABRAX PALLIDUS *De Kay*, Nat. Hist. of New York Fishes, p. 11, pl. 1, fig. 2, 1842.
LABRAX PALLIDUS *Storer*, Synopsis of the Fishes of North America, p. 22; ib. in Memoirs of American Acad., vol. ii, p. 22.
LABRAX PALLIDUS *Perley*, Report upon the Fishes of the Bay of Fundy, p. 121, 1851.
LABRAX PALLIDUS *Perley*, Descriptive Catalogue (in part) of Fishes of New Brunswick and Nova Scotia, p. 4; ib. in Reports on Sea and River Fisheries of New Brunswick, p. 182, 1852.
LABRAX PALLIDUS *Günther*, Catalogue of the Acanthopterygian Fishes of the British Museum, p. 67.

The history of this species and its nomenclature has been fully discussed in the monograph published in the Proceedings of the Academy of Natural Sciences. It is therefore unnecessary to reproduce it in this report, the species not being an inhabitant of those regions traveled over by the expedition under Captain Simpson.

Günther has recently, in his "Catalogue of the Acanthopterygian Fishes in the Collection of the British Museum", retained the *Labrax pallidus* and *Labrax rufus* as distinct species. We see no reason to change our opinion concerning their identity expressed in our monograph.

MORONE INTERRUPTA, GILL.

Synonymy.

LABRAX CHRYSOPS *Girard*, General Report upon the Zoölogy of the several Pacific Railroad routes, Ichthyology, p. 29 (pl. xi, figs. 1–4).
LABRAX CHRYSOPS *Girard* (figured in Governor Stephen's Report).
MORONE INTERRUPTA *Gill*, Proceedings Acad. of Nat. Sciences of Phila., 1860, p. 118.

The body is oblong ovate, with the back at the commencement of the dorsal fin slightly gibbous. The greatest height under the spinous dorsal equals three-tenths of the length from the snout to the concave margin of the caudal fin. The dorsal outline slightly declines under the spinous dorsal and little more under the rayed. The abdominal outline to the anal fin is convex, and thence ascends quite rapidly in a concave curve to the base of the caudal fin. The peduncle behind the anal fin exceeds a seventh of the extreme length, and at the base is equal to about a ninth.

The head is conical in profile, slightly depressed at the nape, and thence nearly straight to the snout. The head from the snout to the opercular spine forms three-tenths of the length, its length being scarcely less than the height of the body. The eyes are moderate, the diameter being between a fourth and a fifth of the head's length. They are distant much more than a diameter from the snout.

The anterior margin of the preoperculum advances obliquely downward and forward; the pectinate margin is nearly vertical; the distance between the margins near the angle exceeds half the diameter of the eye. The teeth of the posterior margin become stronger toward the angle; the inferior margin is weakly serrated along its posterior half. The operculum has two spines, separated by an oblique sinus; the superior one is blunt and almost rounded.

The dorsal fin commences at a vertical intermediate between the bases of the pectoral and ventral fins and is of a triangular form, the fourth ray being the largest and equaling the length of the pectoral fin; the spines have the same form and arrangement as those of *Morone americana.* The second dorsal is connected by a membrane as in *Morone americana;* its spinous or first ray is little more than half the length of the first articulated one, which itself is nearly as long as the fourth dorsal spine; the fin thence decreases in height toward its last ray, which is shorter than the spinous ray.

The anal fin commences under the fourth or fifth articulated ray of the second dorsal, and about four of its rays are posterior to the termination of that fin; the first spine is short and robust; the second almost two and a half times longer, compressed, and very strong; the third is almost as long as the second, but much more slender. The first articulated ray of the anal is longer than the spines, and about twice as long as the last; the outline of the fin is slightly emarginated.

The first ray of the pectoral fin is, as usual, articulated, but simple; the third is longest and branched, and equals the base of the second dorsal.

The ventrals are about as long as the pectorals; the length of the spine is equal to two-thirds of that of the first or second branched rays.

The radial formula is as follows:

D. IX. I. 12; A. III. 10; C. 4. I. 8. 7. I. 3; P. 2. 14; V. 1. 5.

The scales are of about the same size as in the *Morone americana*, the lateral line running through about fifty besides the smaller ones at the base of the caudal fin; at the region of its greatest height, there are about nineteen rows, of which about one small and six large ones are above the lateral line and eleven beneath. The relative proportions on the different parts of the body are nearly the same as in that species, the chief difference existing on the front of the back, where the exposed portions of the disk are higher and narrower than in *M. americana.* On the cheeks from the orbit to the angles, there are seven oblique rows.

Those on the body are mostly higher than long, with the nucleus at about the posterior two-thirds, with numerous radiating, slightly terminally, muricated, ridges advancing posteriorly, and ending in teeth. About seven radiating ridges advance forward, some of them terminating at the anterior margin within the angles. These are crossed by numerous elevated concentric lines, parallel with the margins. The scales on the sides of the head and between the eyes are also pectinated like those of the body.

The lower jaw has five pairs of mucous pores as in *M. americana,* the fourth pair being largest and deepest, and under the terminal portion of the maxillaries; thence they regularly decrease in size to the anterior pair, which is on each side of the symphysis. The fifth pair is at the articulation of the jaw with the preoperculum, and is continued from the two inferior borders of that bone.

The specimens preserved in spirits have a bright, brazen color, tinged on the back with olivaceous. Along the sides are seven very distinct longitudinal black bands, through the fourth of which the lateral line runs for its entire length. The continuity of the bands below the lateral line is interrupted at the posterior half of their length, and they there alternate with their anterior parts.

The dorsal fins are tinged with purple, and the margin of the spinous one is dark. The anal is of a darker purple toward its anterior angle. The caudal, especially posteriorly and at its middle, is purple. The rays of the pectoral and ventral fins are yellowish, while the membrane of the former is hyaline, and of the latter sometimes minutely dotted.

This species, as will be observed by reference to the synonymy, has been described by Dr. Charles Girard, under the name of *Labrax chrysops* Girard (*Perca* or *Lepibema chrysops* Raf.), to which is also referred, as a synonym, the *Labxax multilineatus* of Cuvier and Valenciennes, Kirtland, De Kay, and Storer. From that species, it is very distinct, and even belongs to a different genus. Cuvier described the ground-color as a greenish-gray on the back and silvery on the belly. This is not the color of *Morone interrupta,* and that species must be therefore distinct from *Labrax multilineatus,* nor can it be the *Perca chrysops* of Rafinesque, which is said to be "silvery with five longitudinal brownish stripes on each side", and have the "head brown above". The description of the *Perca chrysops,* though erroneous in most respects, is as accurate as Rafinesque's generally are, and agree sufficiently well with Kirtland's *Labrax multilineatus,* which is doubtless identical with the Cuvierian species. Even such an observer as Rafinesque would have noticed the deep brazen hue of *Morone interrupta,* and would not have overlooked two of the seven very distinct black bands that run along the sides.

Dr. Girard has stated that there are but six branchiostegal rays in his species; but

I am able to say, from an examination of the specimens used by Dr. Girard himself for description, that it agrees with all allied species in having the normal number of seven, which are developed as in *Morone americana.*

There are preserved in the museum of the Smithsonian Institution three specimens of the *Morone interrupta,* one of which was obtained by Lieutenant Couch at New Orleans, and two larger ones were found at Saint Louis, Mo., by Dr. George Engelmann. The small specimen from New Orleans differs from the two Missouri specimens by the larger second spine of the anal fin, but in every other respect they are similar.

FAMILY COTTOIDÆ, (RICH.).

SUBFAMILY COTTINÆ, (BON.).

GENUS POTAMOCOTTUS, GILL.

Synonymy.

POTAMOCOTTUS *Gill,* Proc. Boston Soc. Nat. Hist.
COTTUS sp. *Agassiz,* Lake Superior, &c.
COTTUS sp. *Girard,* "Monograph of the Cottoids of North America" in Smithsonian Contributions to Knowledge, vol. iii.

Body elongated, anteriorly subcylindrical, and thence declining in height toward the caudal, where it is also much compressed. The skin is perfectly smooth and naked, except sides behind the pectorals.

Head conical or cuneiform in profile, oval above and depressed, and covered by a naked skin. The preoperculum is armed at its posterior margin with a strong spine, curved upward, and below with one or two smaller ones, or tubercles; the antero-inferior angle of the sub-operculum is also armed with a spine directed forward and downward. The other bones are unarmed.

Eyes mostly situated in the anterior half of the head; frontal bones between them of moderate width.

Mouth slightly oblique, and its gape is quite large.

Teeth villiform on the jaws and vomer as well as palatine bones.

Branchial apertures vertical and oblique, entirely separated from each other by a perfect isthmus, as wide or wider than the interval between the bases of the ventrals. There are six branchiostegal rays.

Dorsal fins two, either entirely separate or connected by a low membrane. The first has from six to nine slender spines.

Pectorals rounded, and their rays generally unbranched.

Ventrals nearly under the pectorals, and have a spinous and four (rarely three) unbranched rays.

The genus *Potamocottus* in every respect resembles the *Uranidea,* except in the presence of a band of villiform teeth on each palatine bone. Several species properly referable to this subgenus have been described as true *Cotti.* It is equally closely related to the genus *Cottopsis* of Girard, but is distinguished by its smooth skin. The species named by Girard *Cottopsis gulosus* is a true *Pottamocottus.*

The propriety of retaining the species with palatine teeth in the genus *Cottus* appears to be questionable. Dr. Girard, in his monograph of the genus, published by the Smithsonian Institution, has asserted that when young some species of *Cottus* "exhibit teeth-like asperities on the palatines. This occurs chiefly amongst those having four jointed rays to the ventrals: in *C. Wilsonii*, *C. Bairdii*, and *C. Meridionalis*. *C. gracilis* is the only one of the division with three jointed rays where similar asperities have been noticed." This assertion has not, however, been confirmed by my investigations. An examination of the types of the *Cottoids* described by Dr. Girard, in his "Monograph", has demonstrated that the presence or absence of teeth in the palatine bones is constant in the various species. In the *Cottus Richardsonii*, *C. Wilsonii*, and *C. meridionalis*, teeth are always found on the palatines, in the oldest as well as the youngest individuals. The *Cottus Bairdii* cannot be at present found; but the same is doubtless the case with that species. Many other specimens preserved in the Smithsonian Museum exhibit the same constancy in their dentition.

As to the *Cottus gracilis*, it is said by Dr. Ayres, in his Memoir on the Identity of the North American *Cotti* with the *Cottus gobio* of Europe, that of the very numerous specimens of the Connecticut *Cottus* (*C. gracilis* Heckel), which he had examined, he had seen a single one in which there were a few scattered teeth on the palatines, like those of the vomer; in others, those bones were edentulous. It is probable that that instance is alluded to by Dr. Girard in his mention of palatine teeth having been discovered in the *Cottus gracilis*. An isolated fact like that recorded by an observer who has failed to appreciate the distinctive characters of species of this group cannot, however, be urged as a valid objection to the importance of such characters. Nor could the circumstance that some *Cotti* have teeth when young, which they lose with age, militate against assigning a certain value to a plan of dentition which is constant through life, as well in the young and old. The difference of development alone would be a character of importance. But there does not appear to be even such difference between the dentition of the young and old. In those specimens which Dr. Girard described, the dentition is constant. Palatine teeth are even found in individuals which are much larger than any without. Such is the case with the species now under consideration; such is the case with other species equally large from the Western States.

If the above views are correct, it would then appear to be advisable to separate the *Cotti* with palatine teeth, and place them in another genus, or, at least, a subgenus, to which the name of *Potamocottus* may be given. This group will embrace the *Cottus punctulatus* as its type, and, in addition, *Cottus meridionalis* Girard, *C. Bairdii* Girard, *C. Wilsonii* Girard, and *C. Richardsonii* of Agassiz, as well as *Cottopsis gulosus* of Girard. The genus *Potamocottus* would bear the same relation to *Uranidea* that *Bryttus* does to *Pomotis*, or *Scorpæna* to *Scarpænopsis* of Hoeckel.

The genera *Uranidea*, *Potamocottus*, and *Cottopsis* agree very closely together, both in superficial and anatomical characters, and differ in the most decided manner from *Cottus* and the related genera; to express this divergence, the genera in question should be segregated in a group which may be named *Uranideæ*.

POTAMOCOTTUS PUNCTULATUS, Gill.

The general form of the body is similar to that of the first division of the first section of Girard's *Cotti*. It is elongated, slender, and considerably compressed. Of the extreme length, the head forms three-tenths parts and the caudal fin between a fifth and sixth. The trunk is anteriorly cylindrical, the height being scarcely more than the width behind the pectoral fins. The greatest height is at the commencement of the first dorsal fin, and exceeds a seventh of the extreme length; from thence, the height declines gradually to the caudal peduncle, where it is only equal to a third of the greatest. The breadth also declines uniformly, but more sensibly, to the base of the caudal, where it is very much compressed.

The head is much depressed, and rhomboidal-ovate above. From the snout to the membraneous margin of the operculum, it forms a third of the entirel ength. Its breadth is very great and is only about a sixth less than its length. The height at the occiput is about a half of the length. The snout is anteriorly broadly rounded.

The mouth is quite large; the jaws arched and receding; the distances between the extremities of the maxillaries being equal to the length of the caudal fin. The maxillary terminates under the anterior margin of the pupil. The upper jaw is somewhat protuberant beyond the lower.

The jaws are armed with bands of small, recurved, acute teeth; those on the dentaries are somewhat shorter than those of the premaxillaries, and reach much farther backward, extending to the angles of the mouth; the band is narrow as it recedes backward. At the symphysis of each jaw, there is a narrow interval, separating the bands into two equal parts. The chevron of the vomer and the palatines are also armed with bands of villiform teeth; those on the latter bones are perfectly evident, and almost as large as those of the vomer; they are in bands which are narrowed posteriorly.

The eyes are of the usual size, and situated about midway between the snout and the margin of the preoperculum. The width of the frontal bones between the eyes is about equal to the diameter of the orbit.

The preopercular spine is stout and directed obliquely backward and upward. The one below is small and pointed downward. On the inferior margin is another still smaller. The subopercular spine is moderate, acute, and directed forward.

The breadth of the isthmus separating the branchial apertures is equal to five-ninths of the length of the caudal fin. The branchiostegal bones are of the normal number of six.

The first dorsal has eight rays; the last is connected by a membrane decreasing in height to the second dorsal, where it is extremely low.

The anal fin has about the height of the second dorsal, and commences under its third ray.

The caudal forms between a fifth and sixth of the entire length. Its posterior margin, when fully expanded, is rounded; most of its rays are doubly bifurcated.

The pectorals extend backward to about the vertical of the sixth ray of the second dorsal; all of their rays are simple.

The radial formula is as follows:

D. VIII. 17; A. 13; P. 15; V. I. 4.

The lateral line, from the scapular bones to the end of the second dorsal fin, is well marked; it is then deflected and very obscure.

The color is grayish anteriorly and brownish posteriorly. It is covered with black spots, which, on the head and anterior portion of the body, are very small and numerous, but posteriorly are larger, confluent, and much fewer. The dorsal, caudal, and pectoral fins are quite thickly spotted on the rays; the rays of the anal have also a few spots. The ventrals are nearly immaculate.

This species is perhaps almost the only smooth American Uraneidid which can be at once readily distinguished. A single specimen was obtained by Dr. George Suckley, in the summer of 1859, between Bridger's Pass and Fort Bridger. It is four inches in length.

POTAMOCOTTUS CAROLINÆ, GILL.

By its general form, this species belongs to the group of which the *Potamocottus Richardsonii* is the type, and is nearly allied to that species.

The body is elongated, slender, and compressed. The head forms twenty-eight hundredths of the total length, and the caudal eighteen hundredths. The trunk is anteriorly subcylindrical, and its height equals the length of the caudal fin. The thickness at the base of the pectorals is as great or slightly greater than the height. From the region of greatest height, the body regularly declines to the caudal peduncle, whose height equals a third of the greatest. The breadth declines still more rapidly; at the anus, it is equal to little more than half of that at the base of the pectorals, or to a tenth of the total length.

The head is oval and depressed above. From the snout to the membranous opercular margin, it forms twenty-eight hundredths of the total length; its breadth is about a sixth less than the length. The profile, from the dorsal fin to the snout, is scarcely convex.

The mouth is large; the jaws arched and receding; the distance between the extremities of the maxillaries exceeds a sixth of the entire length, and nearly equals the length of the caudal fin. The maxillaries terminate under the posterior margin of the pupil. The upper jaw extends beyond the lower.

The jaws are armed with acute, curved, approximate teeth; the band on the intermaxillaries is almost entire, and extends with little diminution of width to the extremities of those bones. The band on the lower jaw is separated by a symphysial interval; it diminishes in width to the corners of the mouth. The vomerine and palatine bands are well developed, and about as large as that of the lower jaw.

The eyes are moderate, the longitudinal diameter of the orbit equaling a sixth of the head's greatest length. The distance between the center of the pupil and the snout equals a tenth of the entire length. The interorbital space is scarcely as great as the diameter of the orbit.

The preopercular spine is large, and curved upward; the two inferior are tubercular, the last one smallest. The subopercular spine is acute, and points obliquely forward and downward.

The interbranchial isthmus equals in width about four-ninths of the length of the caudal fin, or a twelfth of the total length.

The first dorsal has eight spines, and is connected with the second by a low membrane.

The anal fin commences under the third ray of the second dorsal.

The caudal fin forms eighteen hundredths of the total length.

The pectoral fins extend backward to the vertical of the third ray of the second dorsal fin; its median or fifth, sixth, and seventh rays are, in one specimen, on the left side, abnormally dichotomous; they are generally simple.

The longest ventral ray equals thirteen hundredths of the total length.

The number of rays and their arrangement are indicated by the formula—

D. VIII. 17; A. 12; P. 16; V. I. 4.

The lateral line is continued in an almost straight direction to the base of the caudal fin. The deflection under the end of the second dorsal is slight. The cutaneous keel in which the pores open is most developed posteriorly.

The color does not differ from that of the nearly allied species. There are four rather darker transverse dorsal bands, one under the first dorsal, two under the anterior and posterior parts of the second dorsal, and a fourth at the base of the caudal fin. The caudal fin and pectoral fins are banded or clouded with darker on the rays. The spinous dorsal is punctulated with darker, especially between the anterior rays. The remaining fins are hyaline. The head above is darker.

The *Potamocottus Carolinæ* is one of the largest species of the genus, and even exceeds the *Potamocottus punctulatus* Gill in size. It is most nearly allied to the *Potamocottus Richardsonii*, but slightly differs from it in the proportions of its parts, and more especially in the character of the lateral line. It is also found in a different hydrographical basin, the specimens described having been obtained by Prof. S. F. Baird, of the Smithsonian Institution, at Maysville, Ky., in the year 1852. They are now in the museum of the Smithsonian Institution, and numbered in the catalogue of fishes of the museum as 2859. The largest specimen is nearly six inches long.

SUBORDER EVENTOGNATHI, GILL.

FAMILY CYPRINOIDÆ, AGASS.

GENUS TIGOMA, GIRARD.

Synonymy.

TIGOMA *Girard*, Researches on Cyprinoid Fishes, &c., (p. 41, sep. copy) in Proceedings Academy of Natural Sciences of Philadelphia, vol. viii, p. 205, 1856.

The body is elongated-ovate or subfusiform in profile, and more or less compressed.

The scales are of moderate and nearly equal size on the different regions of the body. They extend forward to the nape and above the margin of the preoperculum.

The head is rather small, oblong-conical in profile, with a convex or subacuminate snout.

The eyes are of moderate size, and situated entirely in the anterior half of the head. The chain of suborbital bones is narrow.

The mouth is terminal, small or moderate, the maxillary bones ceasing under or near the anterior margins of the orbits; the periphery of the jaws is triangular, semi-elliptical, or oval.

The jaws are covered by thin lips; the lower lips are separated at the symphysis by a wide isthmus. There are no barbels.

The branchial apertures extend forward to or beyond the vertical of the preoperculum, and are separated by a rather narrow isthmus.

The dorsal fin commences near the posterior half of the body, or between the snout and end of median caudal rays. There are about twelve rays.

The anal is nearly intermediate between the bases of the ventral and caudal fins, and is of nearly the same size as the dorsal.

The pectoral fins are of moderate length, and their extremities are more or less rounded, and not acute.

The ventral fins are inserted under, or nearly under, the first rays of the dorsal fin; the first rays are of nearly equal length.

The pharyngeal bones are well developed, curved above, and with the peduncles rather long or moderate. The teeth are compressed and hooked, with or without a grinding-surface, and disposed normally, in two rows; the primary one has four or five teeth, and the secondary (or deciduous?) one or two.

This genus belongs to a group of genera of which the *Leuciscus* of Europe is the type, and it is indeed very closely related to that genus. *Algansea* of Girard is scarcely distinct, differing simply because of the pharyngeal teeth being confined to a single row; and it is by no means certain whether this is a true or permanent character. To this genus *Tigoma* also belongs the so-called *Cheonda cærulea* of Girard, which differs from *Cheonda Cooperi* (the type of the genus) by its narrow suborbitals.

TIGOMA SQUAMATA, Gill.

The body is robust and subovate, compressed, and very gradually diminishing in width toward the caudal fin. The dorsal and abdominal outlines are nearly equally arched. The greatest height of the body before the dorsal and ventral fins equal three-tenths of the length from the snout to the end of the median caudal rays, and is twice as great as the greatest width.

The caudal peduncle is rather slender, and narrowest between the anal and caudal fins; the distance between the anal fin and the base of the caudal equals eighteen hundredths of the total length; the height behind the anal twelve hundredths, and that of its most slender pair ten hundredths.

The head is conical in profile, acutely rounded anteriorly, and with the periphery of the jaws elongated semi-elliptical. The jaws are even; the maxillary bones end at the vertical of the anterior border of the eyes. The length of the head from the snout to the margin of the operculum forms more than a quarter (twenty-eight hundredths) of the entire length; the distance from the same place to the scaly nape exceeds a fifth of the length. The dorsal surface of the head is posteriorly flattened, and anteriorly becomes slightly convex; the outline of the naked portion is elongated subconical, and gradually decreases in width; posteriorly equaling fifteen hundredths of the total length, and anteriorly, from cheek to cheek, one-tenth being scarcely more than the interorbital space.

The eyes are of moderate size, circular, and entirely lateral, but near the profile; they are situated anterior to the plane separating the anterior and posterior halves of the head, the suborbital ring being half-way; the diameter of the eye exceeds a sixth of the head's length (five twenty-eighths), and the center of the pupil is distant two diameters from the muzzle.

The dorsal fin commences midway between the muzzle and end of the median caudal rays. Its base equals a ninth of the total length, its anterior rays fifteen hundredths, and its last more than six hundredths.

The anal fin commences between the sixth and seventh tenths of the length, is smaller than the dorsal fin, and the disproportion between the anterior and posterior rays is less. The base equals an eleventh of the length, the anterior rays thirteen hundredths, and the posterior more than seven hundredths.

The caudal fin is furcate, and its lobes equal; the median rays constitute a ninth of the total length, and the longest equal a fifth.

The pectoral fins are rounded, the third and fourth rays being longest; they equal sixteen hundredths of the total length.

The ventral fins are also rounded, and the third branched ray longest. They are inserted under the first branched ray of the dorsal; their length equals thirteen hundredths of the total.

The number and character of the rays are indicated by the following formula:

D. 4. 7 ÷ A. 4. 6 ÷ C. 9. I. 9. 8. I. 8; P. 1. 14; V. 1. 9.

All the simple rays of the dorsal and anal fins, except the fourth, are rudimentary.

The scales are of moderate size, and mostly suborbicular, with the nucleus subcentral, and with numerous radiating striæ. The lateral line runs through about fifty or fifty-five, and from the dorsal to the base of the ventral fins there are seventeen rows, ten of which are above and six below the lateral line.

The color is a dark purple or purplish-blue, with each scale margined with darker. The fins are of the same color as the body.

Specimens of this interesting new species were obtained by Mr. C. S. McCarthy, the collector of Captain Simpson's party, in the Salt Lake Basin of Utah. The species is readily distinguishable by the margination of the scales with a darker color.

GENUS PLATYGOBIO, GILL.

Synonymy.

POGONICHTHYS sp. *Girard,* Researches on Cyprinoid Fishes, (sep. copy, p. 24,) in Proceedings Academy of Natural Sciences of Philadelphia, vol. viii, p. 187, 1856.

The body is elongated, slender, and sub-fusiform, highest before the dorsal fin. The caudal peduncle is oblong and rather stout.

The scales are of large size, and nearly equal on the sides and front of the back; they advance forward nearly to the region above the vertical of the posterior margin of the preoperculum.

The head is small, forming about a fifth of the entire length; it is oblong-conical in profile, and the cranium is wide, the width of the occipital region being only about a third less than the length of the naked dorsal surface.

The snout is moderately depressed and prominent.

The eyes are of moderate size, lateral but superior, and entirely in the anterior half of the head.

The mouth is rather broad, but of moderate size, the maxillary bones ceasing under the anterior borders of the orbits; the lower closes within the upper. The lower lips are separated at the symphysis by a wide isthmus.

Barbels of moderate size are present at the angles of the mouth.

The branchial apertures extend forward to the vertical of the preoperculum, and are separated by a narrow isthmus.

The dorsal fin commences nearly midway between the snout and base of caudal. It is subquadrate, and has about ten rays; the first three are slender and spinous; the anterior spine rudimentary.

The anal fin is similar in size to the dorsal, and is intermediate between the bases of the ventral and caudal fins.

The pectoral fins are subfalciform, the first rays being longest.

The ventral fins are triangular, and situated under the dorsal fin. The axillary scales are elongated, but not pointed.

The caudal fin is forked and its lobes are equal.

The pharyngeal bones are rather stout and expanded at their angles; the peduncle quite short. The teeth are well developed, much compressed, and furnished with narrow grinding-surfaces; they are in a double row, four in the primary and one in the secondary.

The form which we have above characterized is at least as well entitled to a generic separation from the *Pogonichthys* as typified by the *Pogonichthys inœquilobus* of Girard as many of the genera of Cyprinoids distinguished by naturalists. The only species at present known to belong to the genus is that which has been described by Dr. Girard as *Pogonichthys communis*. From the other species of the genus *Pogonichthys*, it is distinguished by its broad and flattened head and muzzle, the very gradual decrease in width of the cranium, and the large scales. It is also worthy of note that all the typical *Pogonichthyes* are inhabitants of California, while the *Pogonichthys communis* is found in the country east of the Rocky Mountains.

The genus *Platygobio* belongs to a group of nearly allied genera, comprising especially *Gobio* of Cuvier, *Semotilus* of Rafinesque, *Pogonichthys* of Girard, and *Algoma* of Girard. Some of these genera have been widely removed from each other, but all of them appear to be very closely allied. It certainly cannot be in conformity with nature to place genera at almost extremes of the family simply on account of the presence or absence of barbels and the presence of one or two rows of pharyngeal teeth. Such are scarcely generic characters alone, and the latter character especially appears to be inconstant, the second row being perhaps deciduous. At least, there are fishes that have been placed in different genera on account of the presence or absence of the inner row of two or three small teeth, which can scarcely be even specifically, much less generically, distinguished. The barbels, being only tags of skin proceeding from the integument of the maxillary bones, have very little systematic value compared with the barbels, and especially the maxillary barbels of the Siluroids. As the above-mentioned differences are those only which have induced ichthyologists to distribute them, we have no hesitation in bringing the above-named genera together as closely-allied members of the same subfamily. *Algoma* was indeed placed by Dr. Girard among the *Chondrostomi*, but he was probably led to that act by the consideration of the single row of pharyngeal teeth and the absence of barbels, and not on account of the presence of a cartilaginous sheath enveloping the lower jaw. Girard has expressly stated that the sheath is not one of the essential characters of the group as understood by him. Bleeker was therefore incorrect in placing that genus in a group of which the presence of the cartilaginous sheath was the principal distinction.

The following appear to be the distinctive characters of the genera above enumerated:

The genus *Gobio* as admitted by Heckel has a compressed and gradually-narrowed head, with the dorsal surface transversely convex, and declining to the snout. *The ventral fins are under the anterior rays of the dorsal fin.* The scales are large, there being about forty in the typical species along the lateral line. The center of the eye is behind the middle of the head. There are well-developed maxillary barbels.

The genus *Semotilus* of Rafinesque has a head much like that of the *Gobiones*, but it is usually larger, and declines less toward the snout. The bases of the ventral fins are more anterior, being almost entirely *in advance of the dorsal fin.* The scales are comparatively small. The eyes are mostly or altogether in the anterior half of the head. The barbels are also somewhat smaller. The genus *Leucosomus* of Heckel and Girard is strictly identical with this.

In the genus *Pogonichthys* as now restricted, the head is small, compressed, and gradually narrowed to the snout; its dorsal surface is transversely convex, and declines quite rapidly to the prominent snout. The periphery of the jaws is elongated-semi-elliptical. *The ventral fins are under the middle of the dorsal.* The scales are of moderate or rather small size. The eyes are almost entirely situated in the anterior half of the head. The maxillary barbels are small.

The genus *Platygobio* is very nearly allied to *Pogonichthys*, but differs from it by its broader head, the width at the occiput being only about a third less than the naked portion of its dorsal surface; the scales are also larger.

Only one species of *Platygobio* is known. Numerous specimens were collected on Captain Simpson's expedition.

PLATYGOBIO COMMUNIS, GILL.

Synonymy.

POGONICHTHYS COMMUNIS *Girard*, Researches upon Cyprinoid Fishes, (sess. copy, p. 24,) in Proceedings of Academy of Natural Sciences, vol. viii, p. 188, 1856; Girard, Ichthyology of Pacific Railroad Reports, p. 247, pl. lv.

The body is elongated, compressed, and gradually decreases in breadth from the head to the caudal fin. The dorsal outline, anterior to the dorsal fin, is slightly curved to the nostril, and posteriorly nearly straight. The abdominal outline from the ventral fins to the snout is scarcely curved, and behind those fins is almost straight. The greatest height of the body immediately anterior to the dorsal fin equals a fifth of the total length from the snout to the *emarginated border* of the caudal fin, and is twice as great as the width at the same place.

The caudal peduncle is of moderate size, the distance between the posterior angle of the anal fin and the insertion of the caudal equaling fifteen hundredths of the total length, the height behind the anal, thirteen hundredths, and that at the base of the caudal eight hundredths.

The head is conical in profile, flattened and depressed above. The projecting, but flattened, muzzle is vertically rounded. The length of the head from the snout to the margin of the operculum forms a fifth of the total; the upper surface to the scaly nape equals three-fourths of the latter. The width behind equals a ninth of the total length, and at the pupil an eleventh.

The eyes are of moderate size, subcircular, entire, lateral, but near the plane of the superior surface of the head; they are situated entirely in the anterior half of the head, the distance of the pupil from the snout equaling two-fifths of the head's length, and the diameter of the eye itself a fifth of the same. The interorbital space is equal to an eleventh of the total length.

The dorsal fin commences between the fourth and fifth tenths of the total length from the snout, and is higher than long. The base equals a tenth of the total length; the longest ray fourteen hundredths, and the last eight hundredths.

The anal fin commences between the sixth and seventh tenths of the length from the head. Its size is less than that of the dorsal, the base equaling eight hundredths of the total length, the longest ray thirteen hundredths, and the last one seven hundredths.

The caudal fin is forked, and its lobes are equal. The central rays constitute an eighth of the total length, while the longest rays exceed a fifth of the same twenty-one hundredths.

The pectoral fins are emarginated or subfalciform; the longest rays equal a fifth of the length, and are four times longer than the shortest.

The ventral fins are inserted beneath the first rays of the dorsal; the external angles of their bases are distant from each other between six and seven hundredths of the total length. Each fin has a convex margin, and its longest ray equals an eighth of the whole length.

The radial formula is as follows:

D. 3. 6. $\frac{1}{1}$; A. 3. 6. $\frac{1}{1}$; C. 4. I. 7. 8. I. 5; P. 1. 15; V. 2. 7.

The first simple rays of all the fins, except the pectoral, are rudimentary.

The scales are of quite large size, there being about fifty perforated for the lateral line; under the dorsal fin, there are six rows above and seven below the lateral line. Each scale is oblong, or sometimes nearly as high as long, vertical at its base, and rounded behind; there are generally about ten diverging striæ.

The color is reddish-gray or blue on the dorsal region, and on the abdomen is whitish or whitish-yellow. The fins are uniform and colorless.

Numerous specimens of this fish were obtained by Mr. McCarthy, the collector of Captain Simpson's expedition, at Green River, Utah, and in the Platte Valley.

Family SILUROIDÆ, (Cuv.) Bleeker.

Subfamily PIMELODINÆ, (Bon.).

Of this subfamily, there are found representatives of four genera and numerous species in the fresh waters of the United States. These have hitherto, with the exception of the *Noturi*, been referred to one genus, and for that genus the name of *Pimelodus* has been retained.

Now that the *Pimelodi* of Lacépède have been distributed among numerous smaller groups or genera, it remains to ascertain to what group the name *Pimelodus* ought to be restricted, and what names should be applied to the three genera now distinguished among the American *Pimelodinæ*, exclusive of the *Noturi* of Rafinesque.

Lacépède characterized his genus *Pimelodus* simply by the presence of an adipose fin, and included under the name the following species:

PREMIER SOUS-GENRE.

La nageoire de la queue fourchue ou ébranchée en croissant:

1. Le Pimelode bagre, *Pimelodus bagrus* = *Bagrus* sp. Cuv. = *Galeichthys Gronovii* Val. = *Ælurichthys bagrus* B. & G.

2. Le Pimelode chat, *Pimelodus felis* = *Silurus felis* Linn. partim. = *Amiurus* sp.*

3. Le Pimelode scheilan, *Pimelodus clarias* Lac. = *Synodontis clarias* Cuv. = *Synodontis arabi* Val. = *Synodontis schal* Bleeker.

4 Le Pimelode barre, *Pimelodus fasciatus* = *Platystoma fasciatum* Ag. = *Sorubium fasciatum* Gill.

5. Le Pimelode ascite, *Pimelodus ascita* = Embryonic young.

6. Le Pimelode argenté, *Pimelodus argenteus.* = *Bagrus Herzbergie* Val. = *Netuma Herzbergie* Bleeker.

7. Le Pimelode nœud, *Pimelodus nodosus* = *Arius nodosus* Val. = *Auchenipterus furcatus* Val. = *Auchenipterus nodosus* Mull. & Trosch., Bleeker.

8. Le Pimèlode quatre-taches, *Pimelodus quadrimaculatus* = *Hemipimelodus quadrimaculatus* Bleeker.

9. Le Pimèlode barbu, *Pimelodus barbus* = *Bagrus Commersonii* Val. = *Guiritinga Commersonii* Bleeker.

---

* The *Pimelode chat* (*Pimelodus felis*) of Lacépède is chiefly founded on the *Silurus felis* of Linnæus, and the enumeration of the rays of the dorsal and anal fins is taken from the Systema Naturæ, but the mention of the color and partly of the habitat appears to be on the authority of Daubenton and Hauy and of Bonnaterre.

The *Silurus felis* of Linnæus, described on the authority of Dr. Garden as having six barbels and twenty-three anal rays, and as being allied to the *Silurus Catus*, can only be an *Amiurus*, whose nasal barbels have been overlooked. The species of the Encyclopedists described as being from Cayenne, where it is called *Machoiran blanc, Paisani,* and *Petit Gueule*, and whose color is white, is unrecognizable.

10. Le Pimèlode tacheté, *Pimelodus maculatus* Lac., Val. = *Rhamdia maculata* Bleeker = *Pimelodus maculatus* Lac.

11. Le Pimèlode bleuâtre, *Pimelodus cœrulescens.*

This species is described as having two barbels above and two below, besides the supramaxillary ones. It cannot be referred with certainty to any known genus.

12. Le Pimèlode doigt-de-negre, *Pimelodus nigrodigitatus* = *Arius acutivelis* Val. = *Melanodactylus acutivelis* Bleeker = *Melanodactylus nigrodigitatus.*

13. Le Pimèlode Commersonien, *Pimelodus commersonii* = *Pimelodus barbus* Lac. = *Bagrus commersonii* Val. = *Guiritinga Commersonii* Bleeker.

14. Le Pimèlode Thunberg, *Pimelodus Thunberg* = *Silurus maculatus* Thunberg = *Silurus ocellatus* Bl., Schn. = *Arius ocellatus* Val., Bleeker = *Arius maculatus.*

15. Le Pimèlode maton, *Pimelodus catus* = *Pimelodus catus* Val. partim = *Amiurus catus* Gill partim.

16. Le Pimèlode cous, *Pimelodus cous* = *Arius cous* Heckel = New genus near *Glyptosternum cous.*

17. Le Pimèlode docmac, *Pimelodus docmac* = *Bogrus docmac* Cuv., Val., Bleeker.

18. Le Pimèlode bajad, *Pimelodus bajad* = *Bagrus bajad* Cuv., Val., Bleeker.

19. Le Pimèlode erythroptère, *Pimelodus erythropterus* = *Macrones erythropterus.*

20. Le Pimèlode raie-d'argent, *Pimelodus atherinoides* = *Pseudeutropius atherinoides* Bleeker.

21. Le Pimèlode rayé, *Pimelodus vittatus* = *Bagrus vittatus* Val., Bleeker = *Macrones vittatus.*

22. Le Pimèlode moucheté, *Pimelodus guttatus* = *Pimelodus ? guttatus* Bleeker = *Amiurus ? gutata* sp. incert.

SECONDE SOUS-GENRE.

La nageoire de la queue terminée par une ligne droite ou arrondie et sans échrancrure:

23. Le Pimèlode casque, *Pimelodus galeatus* = *Auchenipterus maculosus* Val. = *Trachycorystes* (?) *galeatus* Bleeker.

24. Le Pimèlode chili, *Pimelodus chilensis* = *Silurus chilensis* Linn.

In the year 1817, Cuvier published the first edition of his "Règne animal", and revised the class of Fishes. He formed a family for the *Siluri* and allied fishes, to which he gave the name of *Siluroides.* In this family, he admitted four great genera, *Silurus* Linn., *Malapterurus* Lac., *Aspredo* Linn., and *Loricaria* Linn. The *Siluri* were divided into five sections, the second of which was called that of the *Machoirans* or *Mystus.* The latter name was erroneously quoted as of Artedi and Linnæus in his first editions (Arted. et Lin. dans ses premières éditions); erroneously, for the name of *Mystus* does not occur as the designation of a genus in the special works of either of those naturalists.* It was first applied to a genus of Siluroids by Gronovius in the

* It is applied to species of the genus *Pimelodus* of Lacépède by Artedi in the great work of Seba (Locupletissimi Rerum naturalium Thesauri Accurata Descriptio et Iconibus artificiosis simus expressio per universam Physices historiam); but the third fasciculus, in which the fishes are described, was not published until long after the death of Artedi; and much has apparently been interpolated in that work of which that great ichthyologist was not the author.

first part of his "Museum Ichthyologicum", where two species of the genus *Rhamdia* of Bleeker were referred to it. The name of *Mystus* would have to be then retained for that genus had it not been previously applied by Klein to a genus of Cyprinoids.

The Cuvierian section of *Machoirans* included all those Siluroids which had two dorsal fins, the first of which was rayed and the second adipose. There were consequently referred to it the *Pimelodi*, *Ageneosi*, and *Dorades* of Lacépède. The *Machoirans* were again divided into groups, for which were retained the above names of Lacépède.

Finally, *Pimelodus* of Lacépède was itself taken with the limits assigned to it by its founder, and divided into three subgenera characterized by their dentition.

The first of these was *Synodontis* of Cuvier, which included the third species of the Lacépèdian genus *Pimelodus*—*Le Pimelode scheilan.*

For the second subgenus, the Lacépèdian name of *Pimelodus* was retained. It was intended to include those which had teeth only on the intermaxillaries and dentaries.

The third subgenus was named *Bagrus*, and included those which, in addition to the teeth on the jaws, had a parallel band on the vomer.

To that genus were referred the first,* fourth,† thirteenth,‡ seventeenth,§ and eighteenth|| species of Lacépède's genus *Pimelodus.* The ninth species of Lacépède** was considered as synonymous with his thirteenth. To illustrate the sequence and relative value assigned by Cuvier to his various groups, we subjoin the following extract from his methodical index:

MACHOIRANS (*Mystus* Artedi).
PIMELODES *Lacép.*
SHALS (*Synodontis* Cuv.).
PIMELODES PROPREMENT DITS (*Pimelodus* Cuv.).
BAGRES.
AGENEIOSES *Lacép.*
DORAS *Lacép.*

The next naturalist who circumscribed the genus was Rafinesque. That writer, in the "Ichthyologia Ohiensis", retained *Pimelodus* as the name of a genus, and the characters assigned by him to it were not essentially different from those of Lacépède; he added that the adipose fin is separated from the caudal. By that feature, he distinguished the genus from his *Noturi*, in which there is an "adipose fin very long, decurrent, and united with the tail".

The species of the Ohio referred to the genus so limited were placed in a subgenus called *Ictalurus*, which exactly corresponds to *Pimelodus* as restricted by Dr. Girard in the Report on the Ichthyology of the Pacific Railroad Surveys. The diagnosis of *Icta-*

* *Pimelodus bagrus* Lac. = *Ailurichthys bagrus* Gill.
† *Pimelodus fasciatus* Lac. = *Sorubium fasciatum* Gill.
‡ *Pimelodus commersonii* Lac. = *Guiritinga commersonii* Bleeker.
§ *Pimelodus docmac* Lac. = *Bagrus docmac* Cuv.
|| *Pimelodus bayad* Lac. = *Bagrus bayad* Cuv.
** *Pimelodus barbus* Lac.

lurus given by Rafinesque is, perhaps, the best description of a genus given in his work, and is thought worthy of being copied:

"Head depressed, with eight barbs, one at each corner of the mouth, longer than the others, four under the chin, and two on the snout behind the nostrils. Teeth in two patches, acute and file-shaped. Pectoral fins and first dorsal fin armed with an anterior spine. First dorsal trapezoidal and before the abdominals; second opposite the anal. Body compressed behind, vent posterior and sub-medial. Operculum simple."

By the above limitation, the subgenus *Ictalurus* is seen to partly correspond with that of *Pimelodus* of Cuvier, the teeth being said to be in two patches or only on the jaws. By the description of the condition and position of the fins and the number of barbels, it includes only a small section of the Cuvierian subgenus.

The name *Ictalurus* must be then reserved for some of our Siluroids—for all, if they should be found to be congeneric—for a section, if it is ascertained that several genera are embraced under the subgenus.

Our studies of the Siluroids have convinced us that there are four natural genera found in the United States, three of which were included by Rafinesque in his subgenus *Ictalurus*, but placed at the same time in sections, which received from him various scientific names.

The sections established by Rafinesque were chiefly characterized by the form of the "tail" or caudal fin, and of the eyes, and the number of rays in the abdominal or ventral fins.

The first section was named *Elliops*, and included fishes with the "tail forked. Eyes elliptical. Abdominal fins with less than nine rays."

This group exists in nature, and is of generic value, but the characters given by Rafinesque are not those which essentially characterize it, nor can the name *Elliops* be retained for it.

The name given to a group as a whole must be preserved, and if that group is divided into sections, one of those sections must retain the name of the greater group In Rafinesque's system, *Ictalurus* is the greater group, and in it are included all the North American *Pimelodi*, with the exception of *Noturus*. When Rafinesque divided that group into sections, he should, therefore, have still retained that name for one of them. Such has not been done, but upon each of his sections was conferred another name. As this is in opposition to the rules of nomenclature, *Ictalurus* must be restored to one of his sections, and it is advisable to retain it for his first, and reject the name of *Elliops*. The section with this name is now accepted as a genus; its diagnosis will be hereafter given.

The name *Pimelodus*, it is true, was applied to all the *Ictaluri*, and by that name only are they called. If *Pimelodus* had been of Rafinesque's creation, that name should, therefore, have been adopted; but as Rafinesque has only taken it from Lacépède, with the characters given to it by its founder, it is to be supposed that he intended it to be otherwise restricted. It appears to us that it is no valid argument against the acceptation of Rafinesque's names for genera, if his sections should prove to be such, that he did not apply them specifically.

The section called *Elliops*, on comparison with its type *Pimelodus cœrulescens* of

Rafinesque (not Lacépède), has been found to be identical with *Synechoglanis* of Gill. The most essential characteristics of that genus had been omitted by the former naturalists who had described its species. The present author, not willing to believe that such was the case, although recognizing the similarity of external appearance between the type of *Synechoglanis* and the *Pimelodus cœrulescens*, described it under the new generic name. When an opportunity was at length offered to examine species of the group typified by *Pimelodus cœrulescens*, its generic identity with *Synechoglanis* was evident. We have, therefore, renounced our own name, under which the genus was first truly characterized, and adopt the prior designation of Rafinesque, but, instead of *Elliops*, take the name *Ictalurus*, as previously mentioned.

This second section of Rafinesque's *Ictaluri* was named *Leptops*, and is characterized by the "tail bilobed. Eyes round and very small. Nine abdominal rays Vent posterior. Adipose fins large."

In this section, two nominal species were included, the *Pimelodus viscosus* of Rafinesque and his *Pimelodus nebulosus*. The latter was "said to be totally different from the foregoing, and might perhaps form a peculiar section or even subgenus (*Opladelus*), by the conical head, membranaceous operculum, but particularly, because the first rays of all the fins, except the caudal and adipose, is a kind of soft obtuse spine concealed under the fleshy cover of the fins."

Rafinesque's assertion that his *Pimelodus nebulosus* was "totally different" from the *Pimelodus viscosus* has neither been substantiated by his own description, nor by the observations and explorations of Dr. Kirtland in the same waters as those in which Rafinesque himself pursued his investigations. The *Pimelodus nebulosus* and *viscosus* were doubtless varieties of the same species. The descriptions are mutually applicable to each other, except in those cases where the characters given are evidently fictitious or erroneous, which, indeed, are very frequent.

Rafinesque's fourth section is founded on a species, which, according to Dr. Kirtland, is the adult of the *Pimelodus viscosus* of Rafinesque. The section is characterized as having the "Tail entire, eyes elliptical. Nine abdominal rays. Dorsal fins submedial. Pectoral fins with one flat spine serrated outwards and nine rays. Lower jaw longer."

The only species of this section was named *Pimelodus limosus*. The section in question was designated by the name *Ilictis*. The name, however, should have been spelled *Ilyichthys*, in accordance with its thymology and the rule observable for the composition of names.

Rafinesque has named "a genus" *Pylodictis*, which appears to have been also founded on the same fish that had already been three times indicated in his work. The fictitious genus and species were established only on the evidence of a drawing by Mr. Audubon, of a fish "found in the lower parts of the Ohio and in the Mississippi". That drawing, according to Rafinesque, represented a rayed fin instead of the usual adipose dorsal. Such a feature would be in opposition to that general plan on which naked Siluroids with two dorsals are constructed,* and it is therefore certain that Audubon

* The genus *Phractocephalus* of Agassiz forms no exception to this. A mistake similar to that made by Audubon or Rafinesque occurs in the great work on Brazilian Fishes of Spix and Agassiz. A species is figured in the plates under

had erroneously represented the species, or that the drawing had been wrongfully interpreted by Rafinesque. It is also stated that there is no lateral line. This statement is as certainly false as the other. The remainder of the description applies better to the *Pimelodus* or *Hoplodelus limosus* than to any other Siluroid of the Ohio.

The generic diagnosis of Rafinesque describes the "Body scaleless, conical flattened forwards and compressed behind. Head very broad and flat with barbs, eyes above the head. Two dorsal fins, both with soft rays. Vent posterior."

The numbers of the rays of the fins are not given; but the description of the form of the body and head, the position of the vent, the color, and we may even add the popular name attributed to it, leave no room for doubt as to at least the generic identity of the *Pylodictis limosus* with the *Hopladelus limosus*

Another section, and the last one to be mentioned, into which Rafinesque divided the *Ictaluri*, was placed as the third, and named *Ameiurus*. His generic characters are the following:

"Tail entire. Eyes round. Eight abdominal rays. Vent posterior. Dorsal fin anterior with a spine. Lower jaw not longer. Pectoral fins with one simple spine and seven rays."

This section corresponds to the restricted genus of which the common *Pimelodus catus* and *Pimelodus Dekayi* are the well-known representatives. Rafinesque refers to the section four species which appear to be truly congeneric. Dr. Kirtland, in his "Descriptions of the Fishes of Lake Erie, the Ohio River, and their tributaries," refers to only one of these—the *Pimelodus cupreus*. If we can rely upon the description of Rafinesque, the *Pimelodus lividus* was not known to Dr. Kirtland. It may, however, be the species described by that naturalist as *Pimelodus catus*. There is little doubt that the same is the case with the *Pimelodus melas*. The *Pimelodus xanthrocephalus*, on the other hand, appears to be only a variety of the *Pimelodus cupreus* of the same author.

In identifying the species of Rafinesque, we must, however, bear in mind that his descriptions are generally so inaccurate or vague that of many of them we can never be certain, and we can only have an approximate idea when the zoology of those places which were so unfortunate as to receive his attention has been exhausted. That unhappy man had, nevertheless, a keen appreciation of natural affinities; and had he been less aberrant, he would have ranked far ahead of most of the naturalists of his day.

As to the application of the name *Pimelodus*, it would appear necessary to reserve it for one of those species referred to it by Lacépède which has not been placed in other genera or groups, and which has been retained in the genus by its last monographer.

---

the name of *Heterobranchus sextentaculatus*. It has a long second dorsal, which appears to be furnished with true rays. On this character, Mr. Swainson has founded his genus *Pteronotus*, and, totally deceived as to its affinities, has placed it between the genera *Phractocephalus* of Agassiz and *Sorubium* of Spix in his subfamily of *Sorubinæ;* that group is separated by the subfamilies *Aspredinæ* (composed of true *Aspredinidæ* and of *Eremophili*), and the *Silurinæ* from the subfamily *Pimelodinæ;* both of the latter groups are also composed of genera arranged in a fantastical and unnatural manner. All of the characters of the *Heterobranchus sextentaculatus* indicate its affinity with the *Pimelodinæ*, and it is indeed a true *Pimelodus* of Cuvier and Valenciennes, and, according to the latter, is identical with his *Pimelodus Sebæ*, and consequently belongs to the genus *Rhamdia* of Bleeker, or *Pimelonotus* of Gill. The last two names were published nearly simultaneously, but Bleeker's has probably the priority. Swainson's name could not be accepted, even if correctly applied, as it has been previously given to a valid genus of *Chiroptera*.

The restriction of Cuvier will exclude its application to any except those with teeth only on the jaws.

Rafinesque having conferred a name on those species which had eight barbels, and teeth on the jaws only, the name is excluded from application to any of them.

Subsequent authors have separated other forms referred by Lacépède to the genus. The only species that remained after them, which was not covered by the generic characters of the species separated from *Pimelodus*, was the *Pimelodus maculatus*. For that species the generic name *Pimelodus* must be then retained. That species has been referred by Dr. Bleeker, in his recently-published monograph of the *Silurii*, to a genus to which he has given the name *Rhamdia*, and which had nearly simultaneously, but probably somewhat later, received from myself the name of *Pimelonotus*. As the *Pimelodus maculatus* appears to be generically distinct from the *Pimelodus Sebæ*, the type of the genus *Rhambia*, both names may still be retained.

ICTALURI, Gill.

The body is more or less elongated, compressed posteriorly, and terminated by a well-developed caudal fin. The skin is naked and unprovided with sucking-cups.

The head in profile presents the appearance of a more or less elongated cone, and is covered by a skin which is generally quite thick. It is more or less flattened and broad above, and gradually becomes narrowed to the convex snout. There is never a casque, or helmet. The supra-occipital terminates in a point.

There are eight barbels: the two maxillary constant in the family, a pair in front of the posterior nasal apertures, and two pairs arranged in a curved line behind the lower jaw.

The nostrils form nearly a transverse parallelogram between the intermaxillaries and the eyes; the anterior are suboval or subcircular, and the posterior linear, with a raised margin, from the front of which the upper barbels originate.

The eyes are generally placed in the anterior half of the head.

The branchial apertures are ample, continued from the supero-posterior angles of the opercula to beneath the throat.

ICTALURUS, (Raf.) Gill.

Synonymy.

ICTALURUS *Raf.* Ichthyologia Ohiensis, p. 61.
ELLIOPS *Raf.* Ichthyologia Ohiensis, p. 62.
SYNECHOGLANIS *Gill*, Annals Lyceum of Nat. Hist. of New York, vol. VII, p. 39.
PIMELODUS sp. *Kirtland, auct.*

Body elongated, slender, and much compressed. The caudal peduncle is short but slender, and presents behind the anal an elongated elliptical section.

Head conical in profile, compressed, and with the sides posteriorly sloping downward and outward. The supra-occipital is prolonged backward, and its emarginated apex receives the acuminate anterior point of the second interspinal. The skull is covered by a thin tense skin, through which the sculpture of the bones is apparent.

Eyes large and almost entirely lateral.

Mouth moderate or small, transverse, and terminal. The upper jaw generally protrudes beyond the lower.

Teeth subulate and aggregated in a short laterally-truncated band on each jaw.

Branchiostegal rays eight or nine.

Dorsal fin situated over the interval between the pectoral and ventral fins, higher than long, with one spinous and six articulated rays.

Adipose fin pedunculated and over the posterior portion of the anal.

Anal fin long, and provided with twenty-five to thirty or more rays; it commences near the anus.

Ventral fins provided each with one simple and seven branched rays.

Caudal fin elongated and quite deeply forked, with the lobes equal and pointed.

The genus *Ictalurus* is at once recognized by its forked caudal fin, and its compressed, elongated, and slender body, which gives to it a peculiarly graceful appearance, very unlike that of the stout, obese, and large-headed catfish of our Eastern and Middle States. The head is smaller in proportion than in the *Amiuri*, more compressed, and not covered by so thick a skin; the mouth, as we should naturally expect, is also very considerably smaller. But perhaps the most important distinction resides in the mode of insertion of the supra-occipital or interparietal bone into the head of the second interspinal. A firm and immovable bridge is thus formed, and gives an uninterrupted passage from the dorsal fin to the snout.

ICTALURUS SIMPSONII, GILL.

The body is slender, elongated, and compressed; the height is greatest at the dorsal fin; it is there equal to between a fifth and sixth of the total length from the snout to the concave margin of the caudal; thence it gradually declines for some distance, more rapidly as it approaches the end of the anal fin, the dorsal and especially the abdominal outlines over the anal fin being slightly curved. The caudal peduncle is least high near the middle, where it equals a twelfth of the total length. The greatest thickness is at the bases of the pectoral fins, and is about eight-ninths of the height; thence it quite regularly diminishes to the compressed and thin base of the caudal fin.

The head is compressed, and presents in profile an oblong-conical form; from the projecting snout to the margin of the bony operculum it forms twenty-two hundredths of the total length, exclusive of the lobes of the caudal fin. The height, at the vertical of the margin of the operculum, nearly equals a sixth of the total length, and bears the relation to the length of the head of fifteen to twenty-two. The head above is oblong and nearly regularly decreases in width from the pectorals to the snout; at the vertical of the eyes, it equals three-quarters of the greatest width, and the bony interorbital space only equals three-eighths of the same. The head above is transversely arched posteriorly, and beneath is flat.

The eyes are large and oval, mostly situated in the anterior half of the head on the sides. The largest diameter is between a fifth and sixth of the head's length; the interorbital space is double the diameter.

The maxillary barbels are slender, and extend beyond the opercula. The nasal barbels are very slender, and are scarcely longer than the diameter of the eye. The infra-maxillary barbels are in a curved line nearly parallel with the jaw; the external ones exceed half the length of the maxillary, and are twice as long as the internal infra-maxillary ones.

The branchiostegal rays are enveloped in a thick skin; there are eight, of which the two internal are flattened and largest; the rest are slender, and rapidly decrease in length. The branchiostegal membrane is deeply excavated, and is attached to the throat for about half the interval between the mental fold and the bottom of the emargination of the membrane; the mental fold is itself midway between the emargination and the lower jaw.

The dorsal fin commences at a third of the distance from the snout to the concave margin of the caudal fin; its base equals a fourteenth of the total length, and is scarcly half its height. The spine is slender, and about three-fourths of the length of the longest ray; its posterior margin is nearly edentulous, having but two or three tubercles on the posterior half.

The adipose fin is elongated and falciform, and nearly equals in length (or height) the base of the first dorsal; its base is over the penultimate rays of the anal fin.

The anal fin commences at the fifty-six hundredths of the distance between the snout and the concave margin of the caudal fin; it is situated one twenty-fifth of the same length behind the anus. Its base is more than a fifth of the length of the fish; its greatest height anteriorly (as well as can be judged from the imperfect specimens before us) is somewhat greater than an eighth of the total length, and above two and a half times greater than that of the posterior rays.

The pectoral fins have each a strong compressed spine, smooth on the external margin, and armed with strong teeth directed downward on the internal one. The length is equal to thirteen hundredths of the total length, and that of the first articulated and longest ray to fifteen hundredths. The process of the coracoid bone projects beyond the base of the pectoral spine for a distance equal to the interval between the snout and orbit. The ventrals commence between the fourth and fifth tenths of the length; their length somewhat exceeds a tenth of the total. The second and third rays are longest.

The caudal fin is deeply forked, the longest ray being at least twice as long as the central ones; the latter form a ninth of the total length. The base of the fin is convex. The rudimentary rays advance comparatively little on the superior and inferior faces of the peduncle.

The number of rays is as follows:

D. I. 5. $\frac{1}{1}$; A. 2. 4; P. I. 9; V. 1. 7.

The color of the shrunk alcoholic specimen is purplish-brown above and silvery-bronze on the sides. The free half of the anal fin is darker.

This species is very nearly allied to several of its congeners of the western streams and rivers, but appears to differ from all of them. From the *Ictalurus cœrulescens* (*Pimelodus cœrulescens* Raf.) and *Ictalurus affinis* (*Pimelodus affinis* Girard), it is at once distinguishable by the fewer rays of the anal fin, there being about thirty rays in that of the former and thirty-five in that of the latter. The distinction from the *Ictalurus olivaceus* (*Pimelodus olivaceus* Girard) and *Ictalurus vulpes* (*Pimelodus vulpes*

Girard) appears to be less tangible. As we have not, at present, access to the specimens on which the latter species are based, we have to rely on the descriptions and figures of their describer. As these are not very satisfactory, we are prevented from entering into minute comparison. We can only state that our present species appears to differ from the former by the longer head, the shorter nasal barbels, and the absence of true serration on the posterior face of the dorsal spine. With the *Ictalurus vulpes* it appears to also disagree by the presence of a larger head and a less deeply-forked caudal fin. Other differences will doubtless be found on comparison. It may, nevertheless, be possibly a mere variety of the *Ictalurus olivaceus*. This can only be ascertained by an autoptical examination.

Two specimens of this species, not in any essential respect differing from each other, were obtained by Dr. Suckley in the Big Sandy River of Kansas.

AMIURUS, (Raf.) Gill.

Synonymy.

Ameiurus *Raf.* Ichthyologia Ohiensis, p. 65.
Ictalurus sp. *Raf.* Ichthyologia Ohiensis.
Pimelodus sp. *auct.*

Body moderately elongated, robust, anteriorly vertically ovate and scarcely compressed. The caudal peduncle is also robust, but much compressed, and at its end equally convex.

Head large, wide, and laterally expanded; above ovate, and in profile cuneiform. The supra-occipital is extended little posteriorly, and terminates in a more or less acute point, which is entirely separated from the second interspinal buckler. The skin covering the bones is thick.

Eyes small or moderate.

Mouth terminal, large, transverse; upper jaw generally projecting beyond the lower.

Teeth subulate or acicular, aggregated in broad bands on the intermaxillaries and dentaries. The intermaxillary band is convex in front, of equal breadth, and abruptly truncated near the insertion of the maxillaries. The lower dental band is anteriorly semicircular, attenuated to the angles of the mouth.

Branchiostegal membrane on each side with from eight to nine rays.

Dorsal situated over the interval between the pectorals and ventrals, higher than long, with pungent spinous ray posteriorly dentated, and six branched ones.

Adipose fin short, and inserted over the posterior half of the anal.

Anal fin of moderate length, commencing within a short distance of the anus, and generally provided with from twenty to twenty-five rays.

The caudal fin is short, with a margin sometimes convex, and sometimes truncate or scarcely emarginate.

Ventrals, each with one simple and seven branched rays.

This genus includes our common Eastern American catfishes, and is readily recognized by the broad head covered by a thick skin, the free termination of the posterior process of the supra-occipital bone, the compressed body, and the slightly emarginate or even convex caudal fin, which is not connected with the adipose dorsal.

AMIURUS OBESUS, GILL.

The body is comparatively short and robust. The greatest height exceeds a fifth of the total length from snout to margin of caudal. The least height of the caudal peduncle equals a tenth of the length. The greatest thickness at the bases of the pectoral fins exceeds a fifth of the length.

The head is almost semi-conical in profile, and is above oval and depressed, and declines in nearly a straight line from the dorsal fin to the snout. From the snout to the bony margin of the operculum, it forms a quarter of the extreme length. The greatest width exceeds a fifth of the total length; the width between the cheeks, under the eyes, equals eighteen hundredths of the same. The interval between the borders of the eyes exceeds thirteen hundredths.

The eyes are small and covered with adipose matter; the diameter of one is equal to about an eighth of the length of the head; they are separated from the middle of the snout by more than a tenth of the total length.

The maxillary barbels are slender and extend little beyond the bases of the pectorals. The nasal barbels extend beyond the posterior borders of the eyes. The infra-maxillary are arranged on a curved line parallel with the lower jaw. The external are little longer than the internal, the former about equal the interval between the eyes; the distance between the bases of the two internal exceeds by about a fourth that between the internal and external of one side.

The branchiostegal rays are enveloped in a thick skin; there are nine, the two upper of which are large and compressed. The branchiostegal membrane is deeply excavated, and, as in all the *Ictaluri*, when closed, or not expanded, appears anteriorly as a simple fissure or fold; the mental fold is much nearer the bottom of the emargination than the jaw. The membrane itself is attached for nearly half the distance between the fold and the emargination.

The dorsal fin commences scarcely behind the end of the first third of the length; its length nearly equals a twelfth of the length, as does also that of the spine; its height is about a seventh of the length.

The adipose fin is semi-cordiform.

The anal fin commences at the fifty-four hundredths part of the distance between the snout and end of caudal; its length equals a seventh of the total length, and its height less than a thirteenth; it rapidly increases in height in front, and as rapidly decreases behind.

The pectoral fins are short, their length little exceeding a seventh of the total; the spine equals an eleventh of the length, is moderately stout, externally edentulous, and internally toothed.

The process of the coracoid bone is spiniform, and from the base of the pectoral spine equals seven ninths of its length.

The ventral fins commence slightly behind the fourth tenth of the length; they equal a seventh of the length. The third ray is the longest.

The caudal fin, when expanded, appears to be truncated, and forms fifteen hundredths of the total length.

D. I. $4\frac{1}{1}$; A. 4. 13. $\frac{1}{1}$; C. 7. 1. 15. 1. 9; P. I. 8; V. 1. 7.

The color, in spirits, is olivaceous on the head and body above and laterally, and below and on the abdomen whitish. The membrane between the rays of all the fins is blackish, while the rays themselves are light. The bases of the anal and caudal fins are reddish. The teeth are of a dark-purplish color.

Two specimens of this species were obtained on Captain Simpson's expedition by Mr. McCarthy. The precise locality is not known; but it is supposed that they were obtained in Nebraska.

NOTURUS, RAF.

Synonymy.

NOTURUS *Raf.* American Monthly Magazine and Critical Review, vol. iv, p. 41, Nov., 1818.

NOTURUS *Raf.* Prodrome de soizante-dix nouveaux Genres d'Animaux découverts dans l'intérieur des États-Unis en 1818 *in* Journal de Physique, vol. lxxxviii, p. 421, June, 1819.

NOTURUS *Raf.* Ichthyologia Ohiensis, or Natural History of the Fishes inhabiting the River Ohio and its tributary streams, p. 67; ib. in Western Review and Miscellaneous Magazine, vol. —, p. 361, July, 1820.

NOTURUS *Baird*, Iconographic Encyclopædia of Science, Literature, and Art, vol. i, Zoölogy, p. 216.

SCHILBEOIDES *Bleeker*, Ichthyologiæ Archipelagi Indici Prodromus, vol. i, Siluri (Acta Societatis Scientiarum Indo-Nederlandicæ, vol. iv), p. 258.

SILURUS sp. *Mitchill*, American Monthly Magazine and Critical Review, vol. i, p. 289, and vol. ii, p. 322.

Body moderately elongated, anteriorly subcylindrical, and thence more or less compressed.

Head large, elongated, conic or cuneiform in profile, above ovate and depressed, with a slight longitudinal furrow, branching into a transverse depression on the nape. The skin is very thick, and entirely conceals the bones. The supra-occipital has no connection with the head of the second interspinal.

Eyes of small or moderate size.

Mouth anterior, large, and transverse. The upper jaw projects beyond the lower.

Teeth subulate, and closely aggregated in a broad band in each jaw, which, in the lower one, is interrupted by a linear interval, and in the upper one is continuous; the band of the upper jaw is either abruptly truncated at each end, or prolonged backward by a continuation from the postero-external angle. The lower band is, as usual, attenuated toward the corners of the mouth.

Branchiostegal membrane with nine rays on each side.

Dorsal fin situated over the posterior half of the interval between the pectoral and ventral fins, with a very pungent, short, edentulous spine, and seven branched rays.

Adipose fin long and low, connected with the accessory rays of the caudal fin, and not forming a separate fin.

Caudal fin very obliquely truncate or rounded, and inserted on an equally obliquely rounded base; the rays rapidly decrease in length inferiorly, and there are numerous rudimentary ones, both above the caudal peduncle, where the anterior is united to the adipose fin and forms a continuous keel, and below, where they advance considerably forwards.

The anal fin is comparatively short, and rapidly increases in height for the first half of its length.

The ventrals are rounded, and each has one simple and eight branched rays.

The anus is situated some distance in advance of the anal fin.

The *Noturi* are at once recognized by the peculiarly-formed caudal fin and its oblique insertion on the peduncle, and by the ovate head, with the transversely-depressed nape and median longitudinal groove.

For our earliest information of a species of this genus, we are indebted to Dr. Samuel L. Mitchill; but the description of that naturalist is incorrect, or, at least, his interpretation of the characters observed is erroneous. Subsequent naturalists have, therefore, been much deceived as to its affinities.

The principal error in Mitchill's description is the assertion of the absence of an adipose fin. But this statement is readily reconciled with the features of *Noturus* when it is remembered how low that fin is, and how it unites with the caudal. Mitchill drew attention to the peculiarity of the caudal, and described it as commencing an inch behind the dorsal fin, and thence "continued quite round the tail, and almost to the anal fin. The form is lanceolated and pointed," and "it may be compared to the tail of an eel; the resemblance is nearer to that of a tadpole, when it approaches the period of conversion to a frog." The peculiarities thus noticed and the rest of Mitchill's description leave no doubt as to the true affinities of the *Silurus gyrinus*, and as to the correctness of Rafinesque in afterward referring it to his genus *Noturus*.

Mitchill observed that "the want of serræ to the spines, and of a second dorsal might lead some to remove this fish from the *Siluri* family; but to avoid needless innovation, I retain him here." Mitchill, when inditing that remark, must have forgotten that the type of *Silurus* was without an adipose fin, and that the presence of such a fin was consequently an exceptional rather than a normal character of the Linnæan genus, although the greater portion of its species were provided with it. The want of serræ to the spines is not of as much value as Mitchill supposed.

Dr. De Kay, in his Fauna of New York, introduced Mitchill's description of *Silurus gyrinus* at the end of the *suite* of the *Pimelodi* of the State described in his work, and remarked that "on account of its dorsal spine it cannot be admitted into that genus" (*Silurus* Val.); and the same spine being smooth, and not serrated, excludes it from *Schilbe.* Its natural position in a general arrangement of the *Siluridæ* would seem to be between *Schilbe* and *Cetopsis*, forming a passage, by its simply spinous anterior dorsal and pectoral ray, from one to the other. It may be thus characterized: "No adipose fin; simple spines to the dorsal and pectoral; anal long; caudal pointed, not united to the anal." Important details respecting the teeth are wanting to complete the character.

Having already noticed the true relationship of *Silurus gyrinus*, it necessarily follows that there is no near affinity between it and the genera noticed by De Kay.

The description of Mitchill and the remarks of Dr. De Kay have also led Dr. Bleeker into error. That learned ichthyologist, in his Monograph of the *Siluri*, has formed a distinct genus for the *Silurus gyrinus*, which he has named *Schilbeodes*, and which is interposed between *Hematogenys* of Girard and *Trichomycterus* of Cuvier and Valenciennes, in the subfamily of *Silurichthyoidei* and the group of *Trichomycterini.* Bleeker's generic characters are the following:

"*Schilbeodes* Bleeker.* Pinna dorsalis caudali quam capiti approximata; analis caudali contigua. Cirri 8."

The diagnosis relating to the dorsal fin is erroneous. Mitchill not having mentioned the position of that fin, Bleeker must have assumed that the caudal was not much more than normally extended on the dorsal region of the peduncle, and, noticing the statement concerning the commencement of the fin an inch behind the dorsal, was thus misled. The remarks we have made on De Kay's allocation of the species apply equally to Bleeker's.

The publication of Rafinesque's diagnosis of the genus *Noturus* soon succeeded Mitchill's description of his *Silurus gyrinus*. Rafinesque's first notice of his genus is to be found in volume fourth of the "American Monthly Magazine and Critical Review". It is there said to "differ from *Silurus* by having the second dorsal connected with the tail, or forming a single fin". The description of the single species (*Noturus flavus*) refers only to the color, the caudal fin, lateral line, superior length of upper jaw, the barbels, and the number of rays, most of which are generic characters. Rafinesque's next description occurs in his "Prodrome de soixante dix nouveaux genres d'animaux, &c.", and is substantially the same as that in the Magazine. As the work in which the "Prodrome" is published is inaccessible to most American students, we add the description in a note.* The name of the species is changed by Rafinesque to *Noturus luteus*. The genus is for the third time described by Rafinesque in the "Ichthyologia Ohiensis". It is there said to "differ from the genus *Plotosus* of Lacépède by having the anal fin free", although there is really no connection between the two genera. The remainder of the description differs little from those previously noticed. The specific name of *Noturus flavus* is restored to the species.

NOTURUS OCCIDENTALIS, GILL.

The greatest height is equal to nearly a sixth of the total length, and less than the greatest breadth outside of the bases of the pectorals. The height of the caudal peduncle behind the anal fin slightly exceeds a tenth of the length.

The head is subcuneiform in profile, and above presents an oval form; at the cheeks behind the eyes it appears to be swollen. The length of the head enters less than four times (0.23) in the total length. The breadth at the opercula nearly equals a fifth of the entire length; that between the cheeks behind the eyes is about the same.

The distance between the eyes equals a tenth of the length, and is of nearly the same extent as that between each eye and the middle of the snout. The eyes themselves are small, a diameter not much exceeding a seventh of the head's length.

---

* Bleeker's work not being readily accessible to American students, we extract his remarks in Dutch, which, we must again remind the reader, are founded on error.

"Silurus gyrinus, door Mitchill en 1818 reeds kortelijk doch onvoldoende beschreven, korut mij voor tot de Trichomycterini te behooven. De rugvin schijnt er sell rodert bij de stoortvin te zijn don bij den kop en de aarsvin zon en zeer nabij de stoart vin eindigen. Overigens 8 voeldroden, 7 rugvin en 16 aarsvinstralen. Misscheen een midden vorm tusschen Trichomycterus en Nematogenys."

* 18. NOTURUS. (Abdominal) diffèrent des genres *Silurus* et *Pimelodus* par nageoire caudale décurrente sur le dos jusque vis-à-vis l'anus, et tenant lieu de deux nageoires dorsales adipeuses. *N. luteus,* corps conique comprimée, tête déprimée, 8 barbillons, mâchoire supérieure plus longue, nageoires dorsale et pectorales, queue tronquée, ligne latérale presque droite, couleur entièrement jaunâtre. D. 7; A. 14; P. 7; Abd. 8. C'est une petite espèce: les barbillons sont disposés comme dans les Pimelodes de l'Ohio. Le *Silurus gyrinus* de Mitchill est une autre espèce de ce genre.

The maxillary barbels are slender and scarcely attain to the bases of the pectorals. The nasal barbels extend slightly behind the eyes. The inframaxillary are arranged on a curved line parallel with the jaw; the internal are much more distant from each other than those of one side; the external are about a tenth of the total length; the internal about six or seven tenths as long as the external.

The band of teeth on the intermaxillaries is extended backward from the angles into a point.

There are nine branchiostegal rays concealed in a very thick membrane. The bottom of the sinus of the membrane is very near the mental, the fold being nearly at the end of the third fourth of the distance between the lower jaw and the sinus.

The dorsal fin commences at the beginning of the third tenth of the distance from the snout to the end of the caudal fin. Its length equals a tenth of the length, and is little less long than high. The spine is small and simple, and its length scarcely equal half that of the fin.

The adipose fin is low and thin, begins nearly over the sixth or seventh ray of the anal, and appears, in the single specimen before us at least, to have separated from the accessory rays by a naked interval.

The anal fin commences at the end of the eleventh twentieth of the distance between the snout and end of caudal fin. Its length is not quite equal to a sixth of the total length; it rapidly increases in height toward the middle, where it somewhat exceeds an eleventh of the extreme length. The last rays rapidly decrease in size.

The pectoral fins equal in length an eighth of the total; each has a spine, which enters about eleven times in the length, and which is smooth internally, but on its external border has long serræ. The margin of the fin is rounded.

The coracoid spine is short, stout, and oblique.

The ventral fins commence behind the end of the fourth tenth of the length; each has a length equal to a tenth of the extreme.

The caudal fin is oblong, gradually and obliquely narrowed to the end, which appears to have been nearly truncated.

The supernumerary rays are numerous and well developed, the distance from the anterior to the end of the peduncle being almost as great as the length of the longest rays.

The number and arrangement of the rays is expressed by the following formula:

D. I. 6. $\frac{1}{1}$; A. 4. 11. $\frac{1}{1}$; C. 23. 7. 12. 11; P. I. 10; V. 1. 8.

The color of the single ill-preserved specimen is an olivaceous-brown, light beneath, and with the fins not margined by a darker color.

This species of *Noturus* was collected by Dr. Suckley in the Platte River. It is interesting as being a species of a genus which does not appear to be rich in representatives, and as coming from a more western locality than any other.

HOPLADELUS, (RAF.) GILL.

Synonymy.

GLANIS *Raf.* MSS. American Monthly Magazine and Critical Review, vol. iv.
LEPTOPS *Raf.* Ichthyologia Ohiensis, p. 64.
OPLADELUS *Raf.* Ichthyologia Ohiensis, p. 64.
ILICTIS *Raf.* Ichthyologia Ohiensis, p. 66.
PYLODICTIS *Raf.* Ichthyologia Ohiensis, p. 67.
ICTALURUS sp. *Raf.*
PIMELODUS sp. *Kirtland*, auct.

The body is much elongated, and presents in profile a very slender appearance. It is much depressed, and is anteriorly broader than high.

The head is large, very wide and depressed, laterally expanded, above broadly ovate, and in profile cuneiform. The skin is very thick and entirely conceals the skull. The supra-occipital bone is entirely free from the head of the second interspinal.

The eyes are small.

The mouth is large, anterior, and transverse. The lower jaw projects beyond the upper.

The teeth are in broad villiform bands on the intermaxillaries and dentaries. The intermaxillary band is convex anteriorly, and proceeds to the insertion of the maxillaries, where it is abruptly angularly deflected, and proceeds backward as elongated triangular extension. The band at the symphysis is slightly divided, and anteriorly separated by a small triangular extension of the labial membrane. The lower dental band is anteriorly semi-circular, and attenuated to the corners of the mouth.

There are about twelve branchiostegal rays on each side.

The dorsal fin is situated over the posterior half of the interval between the pectorals and ventrals, and has a spine and about seven branched rays.

The adipose fin is well developed, and has an elongated base resting over the posterior half of the anal; it is very obese, and inclines rapidly backward.

The anal fin commences far behind the anus, is little longer than high, and composed of about fifteen rays.

The caudal fin is oblong, subtruncated, placed on a vertical basis, and with numerous accessory, simple rays, recurrent above and beneath the caudal peduncle.

The pectorals have a broad, compressed spine, serrated or dentated on its external and internal margins, and with the prolonged fleshy integument obliquely striated.

The ventrals are rounded, and have nine rays, one simple and eight branched.

The anus is situated behind the ventrals, some distance behind their bases, and much in advance of the anal fin.

The genus *Hopladelus* is at first sight distinguished by its elongated and anteriorly-depressed body; the depressed and broad oblong head; the bands of very small villiform teeth, and the posterior extension of the upper bands; the small size of the anal, its distance behind the anus, and the recurrence of the caudal fin.

But one species is certainly known.

HOPLADELUS OLIVARIS, Gill.

Synonymy.

SILURUS OLIVARIS *Raf.* American Monthly Magazine and Critical Review, vol. iii, p. 355, Sept., 1818.
GLANIS LIMOSUS *Raf.* loc. cit. vol. iii, p. 447 (Oct. 1818), and vol. iv, p. 107 (without description).
SILURUS NEBULOSUS *Raf.* Journal of the Royal Institution, vol. ix, p. 50, April, 1820.
SILURUS VISCOSUS *Raf.* loc. cit. p. 50.
SILURUS LIMOSUS *Raf.* loc. cit. p. 51.
PIMELODUS VISCOSUS *Raf.* Ichthyologia Ohiensis, p. 64, July, 1820.
PIMELODUS NEBULOSUS *Raf.* Ichthyologia Ohiensis, p. 64.
PIMELODUS LIMOSUS *Raf.* Ichthyologia Ohiensis, p. 66.
PYLODICTIS LIMOSUS *Raf.* Ichthyologia Ohiensis, p. 67.
PIMELODUS PUNCTULATUS *Val.* Hist. Nat. des Poissons, vol. xv, p. 134, 1840.
PIMELODUS ÆNEUS *Val.* Hist. Nat. des Poissons, vol. xv, p. 135 (abstract).
PIMELODUS PUNCTULATUS *De Kay,* Zoölogy of New York Fishes, p. 187 (abstract), 1842.
PIMELODUS ÆNEUS *De Kay,* Zoölogy of New York Fishes, p. 187 (abstract).
PIMELODUS PUNCTULATUS *Storer,* Synopsis of Fishes of North America, p. 151; ib. in Memoirs of American Academy, vol. ii (abstract), 1846.
PIMELODUS ÆNEUS *Storer,* loc. cit. (abstract).
PIMELODUS LIMOSUS *Storer,* Synopsis of Fishes of North America, p. 152; ib. in Memoirs of American Academy, vol. ii (abstract).
PIMELODUS LIMOSUS *Kirtland,* Boston Journal of Nat. Hist. vol. vi, p. 335, 1846.

The body is greatly elongated, and from a lateral view appears to be very slender, slowly diminishing in height toward the caudal; above, it is very much depressed anteriorly, and is rapidly attenuated toward the caudal. The greatest height in front of the dorsal fin is about a seventh of the entire length, while that of the caudal peduncle behind the anal and adipose fins equals a half of the greatest, or a fourteenth of the length. The width at the base of the pectorals is about a third greater than the heigth, and equals a fifth of the length; thence it rapidly diminishes to the caudal peduncle, which, at the base of the fin, is very thin and compressed.

The head, from the projecting lower jaw to the membranous opercular margin, forms little more than a fourth of the entire length. In profile, is elongated conical, or cuneiform, the extreme height at the pectorals being a half of the head's length. Above, the head is oblong, and very flat and depressed. The greatest width equals a fifth of the entire length of the fish, and the eyes a sixth of the same. The sides of the head are slightly convex; otherwise the width nearly equally diminishes to the snout, which is wide and truncated.

The eyes are oval and small, the longest diameter not exceeding a tenth of the length of the head. Their distance from a transverse line parallel with the front of the snout equals three diameters. The interval between each other equals half of the greatest width of the head. Seen from above, they appear to be distant about a diameter from the side of the head.

The maxillary barbels are small and slender, compressed at their base, and with the internal edge rounded. They vary in length, but do not generally much exceed half the length of the head. In one, the barbel on the left side extends to the base of the pectoral. The nasal barbels extend to about the posterior margin of the eye. The inframaxillary ones form the four angles of a transversely-elongated hexagon; the distance between the internal ones is nearly a sixth of the head's length, and that between the external ones exceeds a third of the same ($\frac{8}{26}$). The latter are about half as long as the maxillary, and about twice as long as the internal ones.

The branchiostegal bones appear to amount to twelve on each side; the two internal are wide and compressed and much larger than the others. The branchiostegal membrane is deeply, and when not extended appears to be acutely, emarginated, the emargination extending to the vertical of the posterior border of the eye. The membrane is attached to the throat to within a short distance of the bottom of the emargination. The mental fold is considerably nearer the latter than the jaw.

The dorsal fin commences at three-tenths of the length from the snout over the posterior half of the interval between the bases of the pectorals and ventrals. Its base is equal to about a twelfth of the fish's length, and equals four sevenths of the greatest height. The spinous ray is moderate, and not more than half as long as the second articulated or longest ray; it is entirely enveloped in the skin, and no serratures can be perceived; the skin in which the spine is imbedded is considerably prolonged, compressed, and obliquely rayed or striated.

The adipose fin is elongated, subrhomboidal, advancing slowly outward and backward, very thick at the base, and compressed toward the margin, which is sometimes jagged; it is situated over the last two-thirds of the anal fin, and coterminal with it.

The anal fin commences at nearly six tenths of the distance between the snout and caudal margin; its length is almost equal to a tenth of the same, and its greatest height to a ninth. The rays rapidly increase in length to the middle ones, which are longest. The rays, especially anteriorly and at the base, are enveloped in a thick fat skin.

The pectorals are situated immediately behind the descending opercular margin at less than a quarter of the length. When open, they are horizontal. The four, or longest rays, inclusive of the membranous termination of the spinous one, are nearly equal to a seventh of the entire length. The compressed spine is about half as long as the succeeding rays, and is anteriorly provided with ridges rather than teeth, and posteriorly with tubercular teeth. The membrane continued from it is coterminal with the three succeeding rays, and is striated obliquely forward and interiorly.

The ventral fins commence at the fourth tenth of the length; their bases, if continued backward, would intersect each other at right angles, but the distance by which they are separated behind is nearly equal to their base. Their margins are rounded, and the longest rays are about an eleventh of the length. They cease some distance before the anal fin.

The anus is situated between the ventrals, at a distance in advance of the anal fin equal to a twelfth of the total length; its margin is radiated by ridges. The genital papilla is small and behind.

The caudal fin is scarcely emarginate, and has a straight base; the shortest rays form fifteen hundredths of the total length, and the longest equal sixteen hundredths. Numerous simple rays, enveloped in a very fat skin, are continued on the superior and inferior faces of the peduncle.

The radial formula may be expressed as follows:

D. I. 5. $\frac{1}{1}$; A. 2. 12. $\frac{1}{1}$; C. 20. 1. 7. 8. 1. 10; P. 1. 9; V. 1. 8.

The lateral line is decurrent downward from the angle of the branchial apertures and thence continued along the middle in a straight line to the base of the caudal fin.

The skin is thick, and completely covers the skull, where it has a spongy or wrinkled appearance.

The color is brownish-fawn on the head, blotched with lighter and darker on the trunk, and on the caudal peduncle inclining to reddish. The lower barbels are whitish, like the abdomen and inferior surface of the head.

The *Hopladelus olivaris*, as will be seen by reference to the synonymy, has had the fortune of being described under a large number of names. As several bestowed by the same authors have been brought together as synonymous, the reasons for so doing will be naturally demanded.

For most of the synonyms, we are indebted to Rafinesque, a man that never touched a subject without involving it in confusion. It will therefore excite little surprise to hear that he has described the same species under six different names, and referred it to four different groups, to which he has given five generic names.

The *Silurus olivaris* described by Rafinesque in the third volume of the American Monthly Magazine and Critical Review, p. 355, has been pronounced by Rafinesque himself to be the same as his *Pimelodus nebulosus*, and is consequently the *Pimelodus limosus* of Kirtland.

It is described as follows:

"Body olivaceous, shaded with brown, 8 whole barbs, 4 beneath, 2 lateral thick brown, dorsal fin with 7 soft rays, pectoral fin 10 soft rays, anal fin 12 rays, tail rounded notched, teeth acute."

The above diagnosis, with the exception of those parts relating to the color, number of rays in the anal fin, and form of caudal fin, is applicable to most of the *Ictaluri*. The color is not inapplicable to the *Hopladelus;* the number of anal rays agrees as well with that species as with *Noturus*, and the allusion to the caudal, while it excludes *Noturus*, is referable to *Hopladelus*. The teeth of *Hopladelus* are not, however, well described by the term acute. But as the diagnosis does not suit any other species better, it is doubtless applicable to that one. The difference in the enumeration of the anal rays is probably due to the difficulty of counting them in the thick skin in which they are enveloped.

At page 447 of the same volume of the Magazine, and at page 107 of the fourth volume, the name of *Glanis limosus*, or Mud Catfish, occurs; but there is no description. The species intended is undoubtedly that afterward described as *Pylodictis limosus*, to the subsequent remarks on which we refer.

Rafinesque has best described it under the name of *Pimelodus limosus*. The description is quite creditable to him, as only one serious error occurs. It is stated that there is no lateral line; but there is certainly one present, as in all our North American species. In other respects, the description is sufficiently characteristic, and the number of rays in the anal fin is correctly said to be fifteen. No mention is, however, made of the much depressed head and body, the latter being simply described as "slender". The species is said to differ "from all others by the long lower jaw, &c.", and to attain a length of "about one foot".

The *Pimelodus viscosus* of Rafinesque, the type of his section *Leptops*, appears to be the young of *Hopladelus olivaris*. It is said to have a length of "only four inches", and its color is "brown with bluish and grayish shades covered with a clammy viscosity". The head is described as being "very flat, with a longitudinal furrow above, elongated"; the "anal has fifteen rays and the ventrals nine". Except as to the cephalic furrow, the description so far is not inconsistent with the *Hopladelus olivaris*, but the jaws are said to be "nearly equal" and "the upper hardly longer". This as well as the furrow on the head and the number of rays in the anal fin might tempt us to believe that it was the *Noturus*, but the caudal fin is said to be "unequally bilobed, the upper smaller and white, and the ventrals have nine rays". It is therefore doubtfully treated as identical with the *Hopladelus* until the researches of a naturalist shall show otherwise. It is not mentioned by Dr. Kirtland.

With some doubt, we yield to the opinion of Dr. Kirtland that the *Pimelodus nebulosus* of Rafinesque is the old of *P. limosus*. The species is said to attain a length of from two to four feet. The description is certainly not very characteristic; the species is said to differ from the former by "the conical head, membranaceous operculum, but particularly because the first ray of all the fins, except the caudal and adipose, is a kind of soft obtuse spine, concealed under the fleshy cover of the fins". On account of these differences, it is suggested that the species may belong to a "peculiar section or even sub-genus", for which the name of *Opladelus* is proposed.

No description of the operculum or spines of *Pimelodus viscosus* is given; it is probable that the notes on the two "species" were taken at different times, and that Rafinesque's attention being arrested by the characters mentioned, and not believing that they could have been overlooked by him in the *Pimelodus viscosus*, assumed that a difference existed. It is strange that the jaws should be described as equal, the head simply as "conical depressed", and the body as "conical tapering behind",* and, were not such statements made by an author proverbial for inaccuracy, we might well be excused for believing in the identity of *Pimelodus nebulosus* with a species like the present. The assertion that there are only twelve anal rays may be explained by the subsequent statement that all "the fins are very fat, thick, &c." The eyes of *Pimelodus nebulosus*, as of *P. viscosus*, are said to be round and small; those of our *Hopladelus* are elliptical.

By Dr. Kirtland, the *Pimelodus nebulosus* is considered as "merely the old" of *Pimelodus limosus*. He further remarks that "it is much larger, and proportionally shorter and broader, than the one figured (*P. limosus*). I have never seen the young unless our present species be considered as such."

The *Silurus olivaris* previously mentioned is referred by Rafinesque to his *Pimelodus nebulosus*.

Placing much confidence in Dr. Kirtland's judgment, we have followed him in regarding *Pimelodus limosus* and *P. nebulosus* as identical, but the remark regarding the difference of form excites some suspicion as to his correctness. The degree of differ-

* Rafinesque probably intended to be understood as referring to the "conical" outline of the head as seen from the side, and the depressed dorsal surface. The mention of the body as "conical tapering behind" also doubtless refers to the lateral view.

ence is not mentioned; Dr. Kirtland would, of course, have noticed the characters mentioned by Rafinesque, if they were more than imaginary.

As no other species of *Ictaluroid*, except the *Hopladelus olivaris* and *Noturus*, with fifteen anal rays or thereabouts, has been discovered in the Ohio River by the researches of Dr. Kirtland, we must, for the present at least, regard Rafinesque's descriptions of *Pimelodus viscosus* as well as of *Pimelodus nebulosus* having been based on one of them; they agree best with the *Hopladelus*.

The *Pylodictis limosus*, named by Rafinesque from a drawing of Audubon, appears to be also founded on this species. It agrees tolerably well with the *Hopladelus*, except in the absence of the lateral line, the position of the dorsal over the abdominal fins, and the rayed second dorsal. Audubon probably omitted the lateral line, or did not represent it very distinctly; there is certainly no American Siluroid without it. The last rays of the dorsal being nearly over the bases of the ventrals, the statement, considering the author of it, sufficiently approximates to the fact. The edge of the adipose of *Hopladelus* is frequently jagged or torn, and, being so represented by Audubon, appeared to Rafinesque to be rayed. It is stated that the species "sometimes reaches the weight of twenty pounds" and "bears the names of Mud Cat, Mud Fish, Mud Sucker, and Toad Fish", names which increase the evidence in favor of the identity of Rafinesque's *Pimelodus limosus* and *Pylodictis limosus*.

The descriptions given by Rafinesque in his Monograph of the Siluri of the Ohio are all referred to the above species by their author.

In the twelfth volume of the "Histoire Naturelle des Poissons", Valenciennes describes a species as *Pimelodus punctulatus*, which appears to be also identical with the *Hopladelus*. Specimens had been sent from New Harmony and from New Orleans by Lesueur. It is said to have the form of the *Pimelodus catus*, but with a shorter anal; the lower jaw is the longer; the head very much depressed, and forming a quarter of the entire length, and a fifth longer than wide; the maxillary barbels reach the middle of the operculum; the ossified part of the pectoral spine is half the length of the fin, has its borders serrated in opposite directions, and is prolonged in a soft and articulated point. There are twelve branchiostegal rays and sixteen anal. The color is brown, dotted with black and with irregular black blotches.

The description of Valenciennes answers in every respect to the *Hopladelus*, except as to the number of ventral rays, which is said to be eight. As in every other feature it is applicable to our species, there may have been some mistake in the enumeration, or perhaps even an abnormal variety. It appears to be at least proper to consider the *Pimelodus punctulatus* for the present as identical with the *Hopladelus*.

The description of *Pimelodus æneus* of Lesueur is next abstracted, and Valenciennes remarks that, except as to form and the number of rays, it agrees with his *Pimelodus punctulatus;* he himself remarks that the difference in the number of rays might be explained by the difficulty which the thick membrane in which the rays are enveloped would present to an exact computation. As to form, he objects that the phrase applied to the *Pimelodus æneus*,—"a le corps très-long",—is not applicable to the *Pimelodus punctulatus*, of which the head enters only four times in the length. To this we would answer that the head of *Hopladelus* is certainly only a fourth of the length, but that from the little height of the body the idea derived from a side-view is that the body is very slender, and the character of "corps très-long" is, therefore, quite appropriate. Valenciennes probably did not take this fact into consideration when he observed, in his description of *Pimelodus punctulatus*, that the form was like that of the *Pimelodus catus*.

We have thus united many nominal species. In considering the species of Rafinesque as identical, we have very little hesitation. We have much with regard to those of Lesueur and Valenciennes, and it might, perhaps, have been better to provisionally retain them as distinct. The other course has, however, been preferred, as no other species at all answering to their descriptions can be found.

PLATE I.

ROCCUS CHRYSOPS GILL.

FIG. 1. General form, in which the separation of the dorsal fins, the regular curvature of the anterior dorsal region, and the nearly straight lateral line are to be noticed.
FIG. 2. A scale from the cheek, showing its sub-cycloid character.
FIGS. 3 and 4. Scales from the middle of the trunk above and below the lateral line, illustrating the ctenoid nature of the scales of the body.
FIG. 5. A scale from the lateral line.
FIG. 6. The mouth open, seen in profile.
FIG. 7. The open mouth seen from the front, to illustrate the dentition of the base of the tongue and its sides.

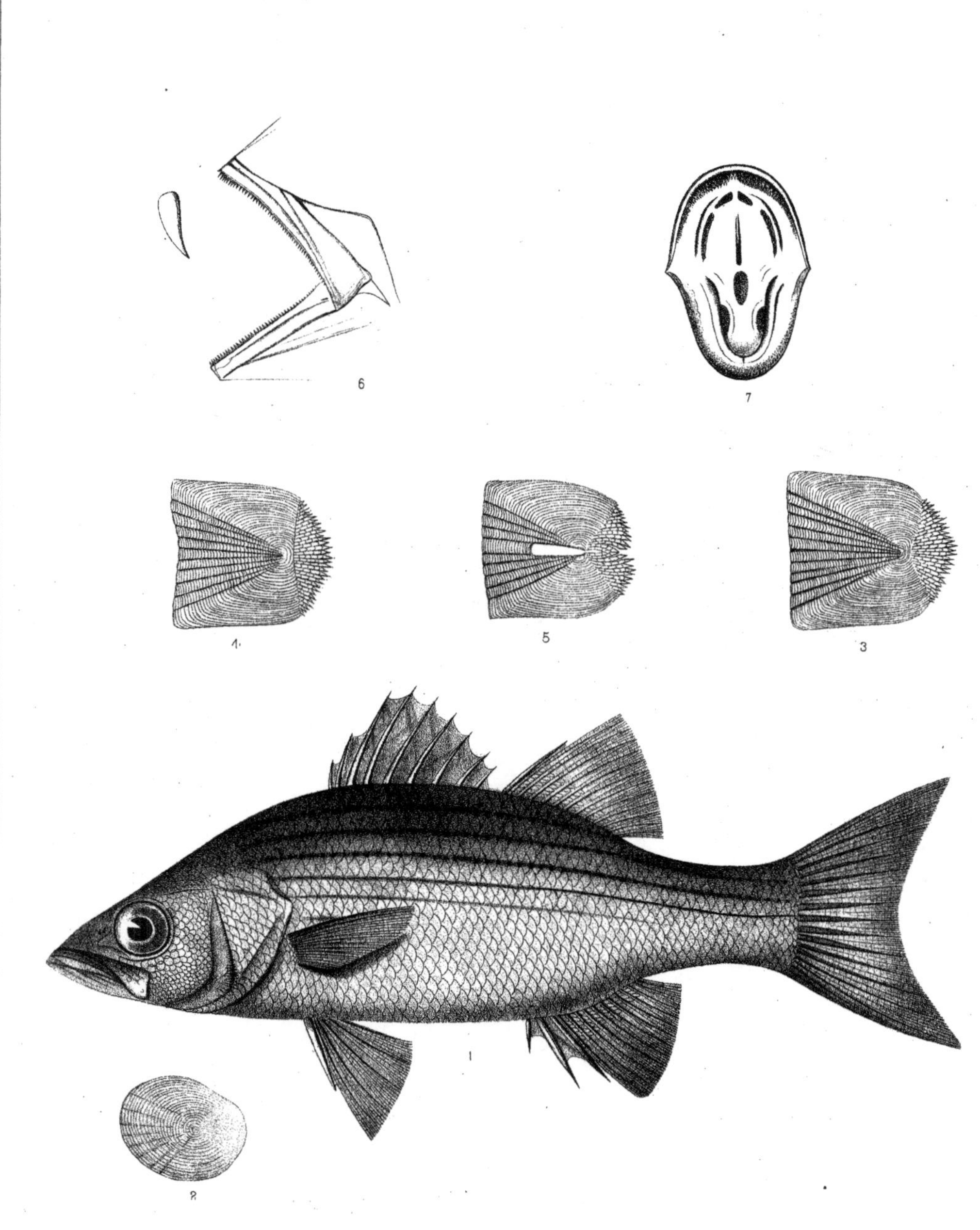

J. H. Richard. T. Sinclair & Son. lith. Phila.

ROCCUS CHRYSOPS GILL.

PLATE II.

MORONE INTERRUPTA Gill.

Fig. 1. Side view of fish. Attention is drawn to the union of the bases of the dorsal fins and the anterior curve of the lateral line.

Fig. 2. A scale from the cheeks, exhibiting its ctenoid structure.

Figs. 3 and 4. Scales from the middle of the trunk above and below the lateral line.

Fig. 5. A scale from the lateral line.

Fig. 6. The open mouth seen from the side.

Fig. 8. The open mouth seen from the front, illustrating the villiform band of teeth on the lateral and anterior margins of the tongue.

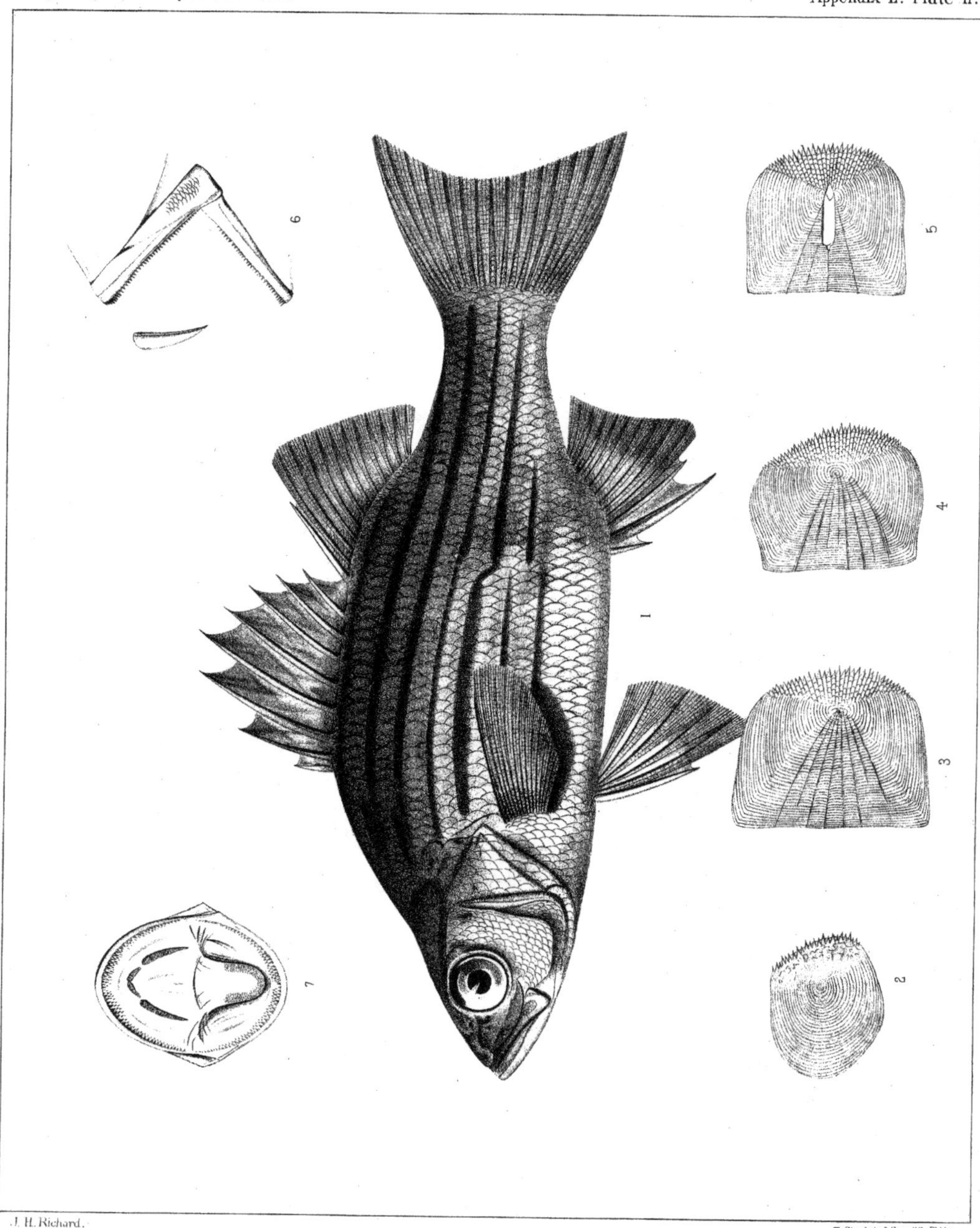

J. H. Richard.

T. Sinclair & Son. lith. Phila.

PLATE III.

POTAMOCOTTUS CAROLINÆ Gill and POTAMOCOTTUS PUNCTULATUS Gill.

The species of the subgenus *Potamocottus* differ from those of *Uranidea* only in the presence of palatine teeth. The generic characters in common with *Uranidea* are the general form of the body and fins, the depressed oval head, the presence of spines only on the preopercular, subopercular, and nasal bones, and the branchial apertures entirely separated by a moderate isthmus.

Fig. 1. *Potamocottus Carolinæ* Gill.

Fig. 2. The same seen from above.

Fig. 3. The head of same from below.

Fig. 4. *Potamocottus punctulatus* Gill.

Fig. 5. Dorsal view of same.

Fig. 6. The inferior surface of the head.

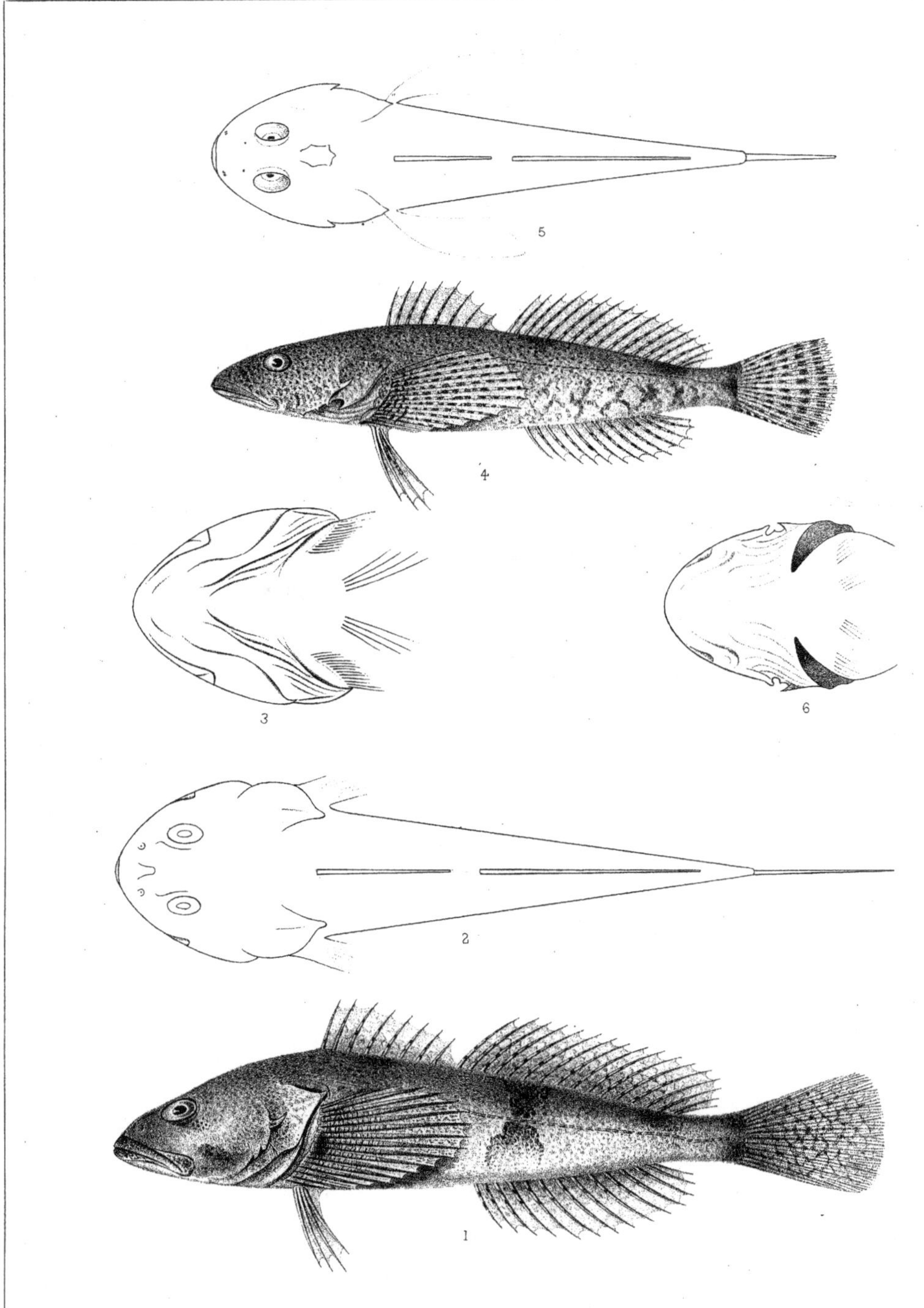

J. H. Richard. T. Sinclair & Son, lith. Phila.

1-3. POTAMOCOTTUS CAROLINÆ GILL. 4-6. POTAMOCOTTUS PUNCTULATUS GILL.

PLATE IV.

TIGOMA SQUAMATA Gill.

Fig. 1. Side view of fish. The form of the head and body, size of the scales, and form and position of the fins are to be observed.
Fig. 2. The superior surface of the head.
Fig. 3. The inferior surface of the head.
Fig. 4. A scale from the side below the lateral line.
Fig. 5. A scale from the side above the lateral line.
Fig. 6. The pharyngeal bones.
Fig. 7. The right pharyngeal bone, representing the surfaces of the teeth.

The grinding-surface of the teeth is not a character of generic importance in the genus *Tigoma*.

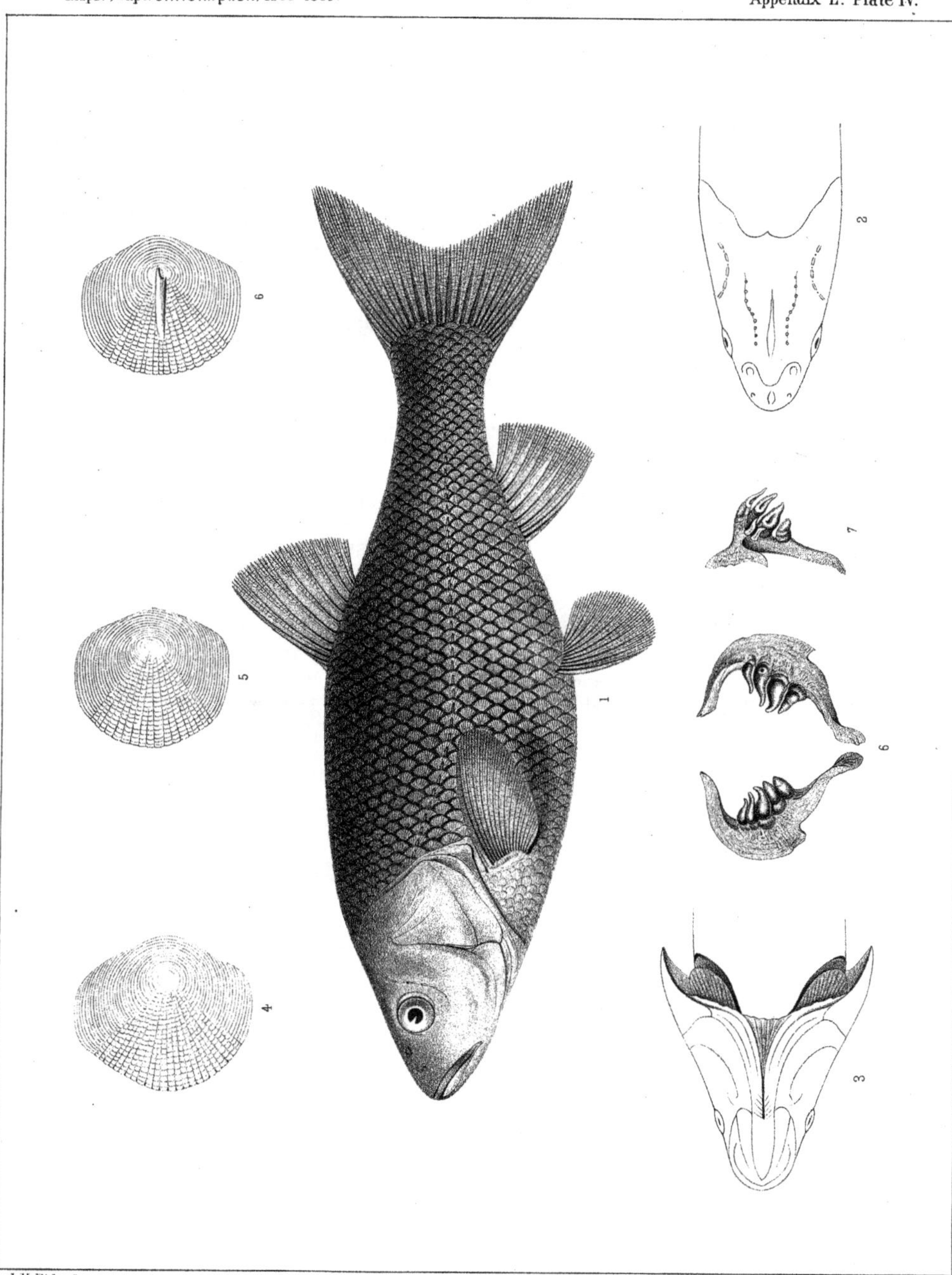

J. H. Richard.

T. Sinclair & Son. lith. Phila.

PLATE V.

PLATYGOBIO COMMUNIS Gill.

Fig. 1. Side view of fish, showing the small size of the head, the large scales, and the form and position of the fins especially the relative position of the dorsal and ventral fins. (The caudal peduncle is represented too slender.)

Fig. 2. The body as seen from above, showing the broad head. (The head does not diminish in breadth so rapidly before the eyes as represented in the figure.)

Fig. 3. The head as seen from beneath, to show the isthmus separating the lips and the width of the isthmus dividing the branchial apertures.

Fig. 4. The pharyngeal bones.

Fig. 5. The pharyngeal bone of the right side, to exhibit the grinding-surfaces of the teeth.

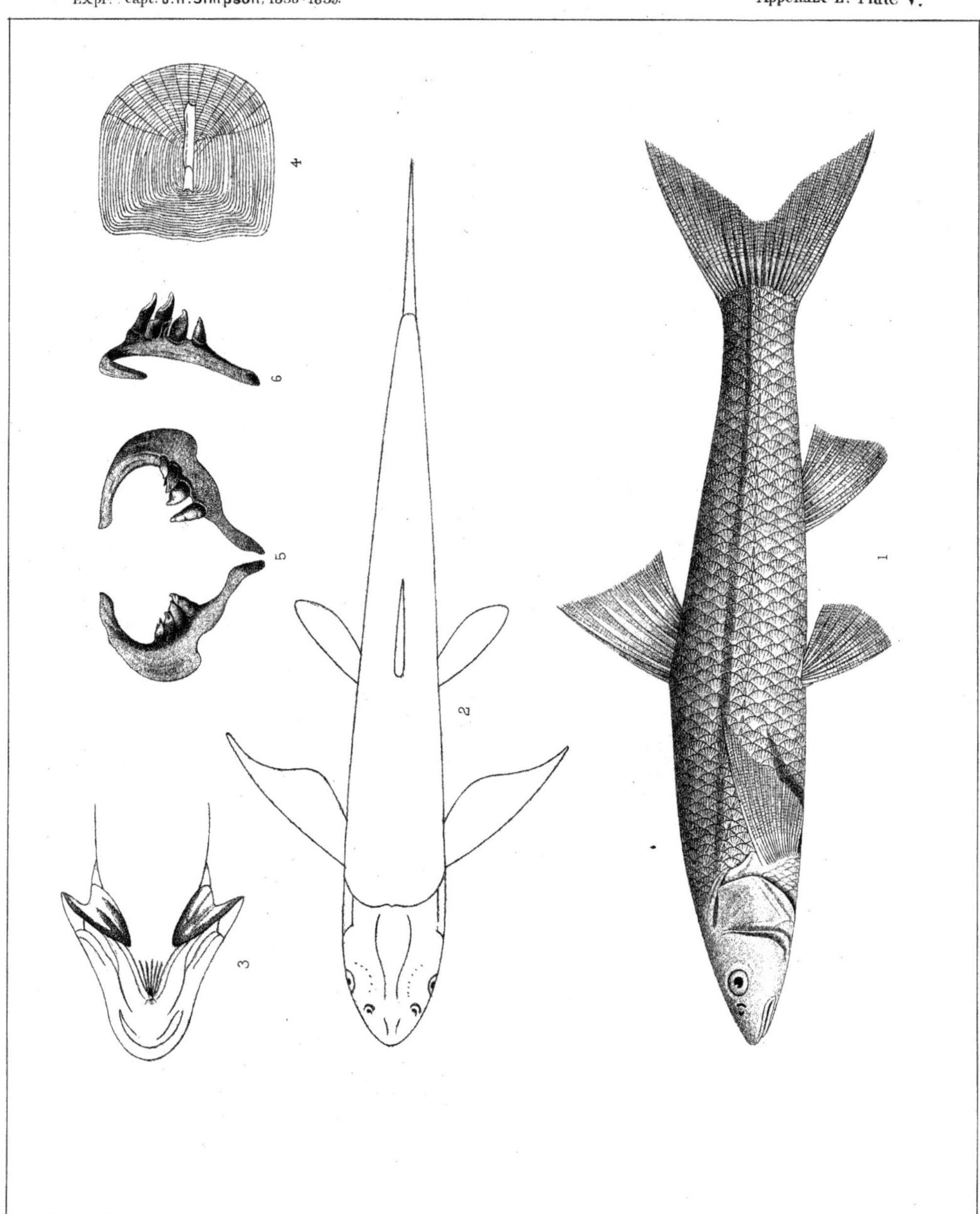

J. H. Richard.

T. Sinclair & Son. lith. Phila.

PLATE VI.

ICTALURUS SIMPSONII GILL.

FIG. 1. Side view of fish, showing the slender body, the form and position of the fins, especially the furcate caudal and the large eyes.
FIG. 2. The head from above, showing the connection of the supraoccipital with the head of the second interspinal.
FIG. 3. The head from beneath, exhibiting the emargination of the branchiostegal membrane.
FIG. 4. The open mouth from a lateral view.
FIG. 5. The open mouth from a front view, to exhibit the dentition.
FIG. 6. The inferior part of the body.

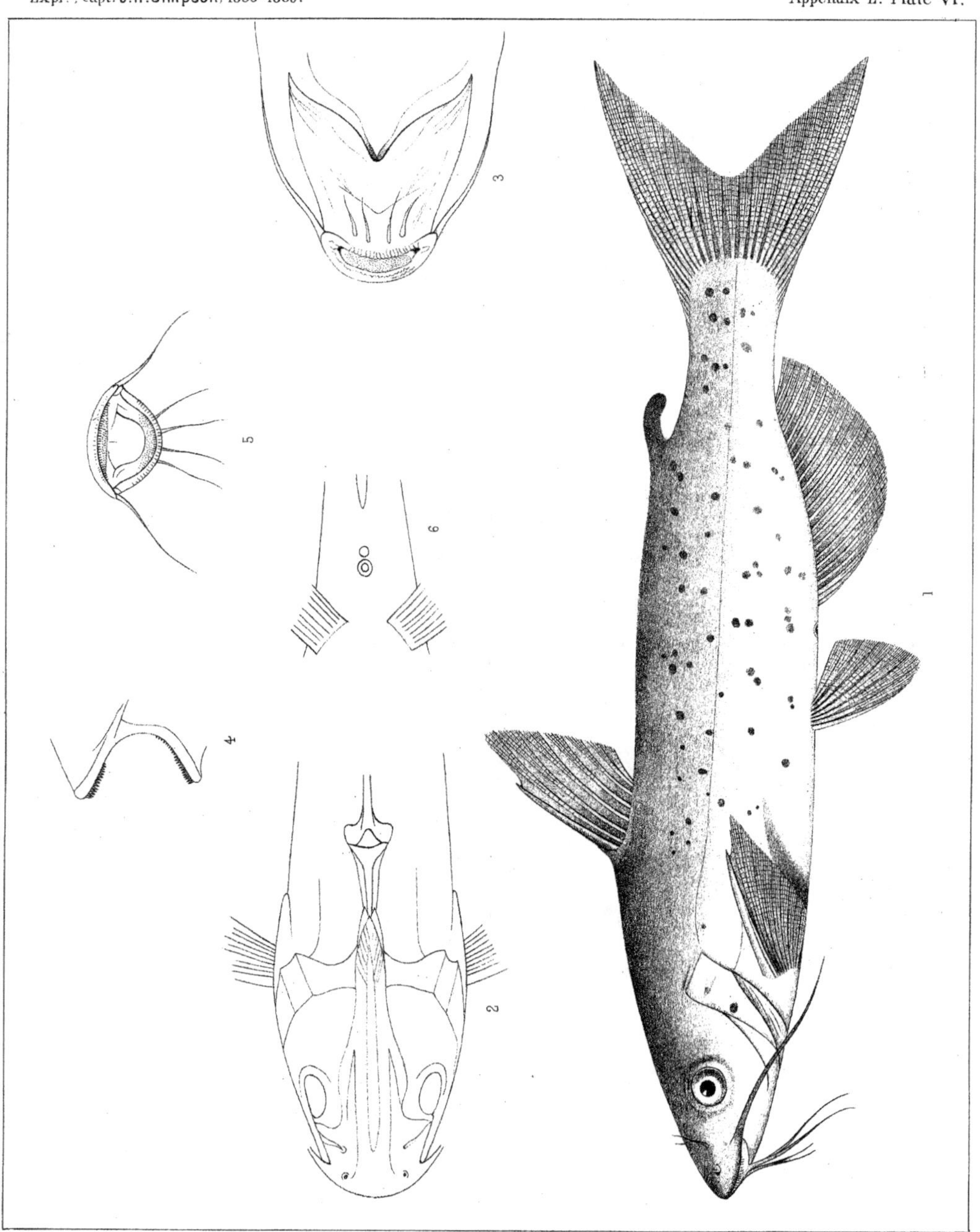

J. H. Richard.

Thos Sinclair & Son, lith. Phila.

PLATE VII.

AMIURUS OBESUS Gill.

Fig. 1. Side view of fish, illustrating the form and position of the fins, especially the caudal.
Fig. 2. The upper surface of the body, showing the shape and breadth of the head.

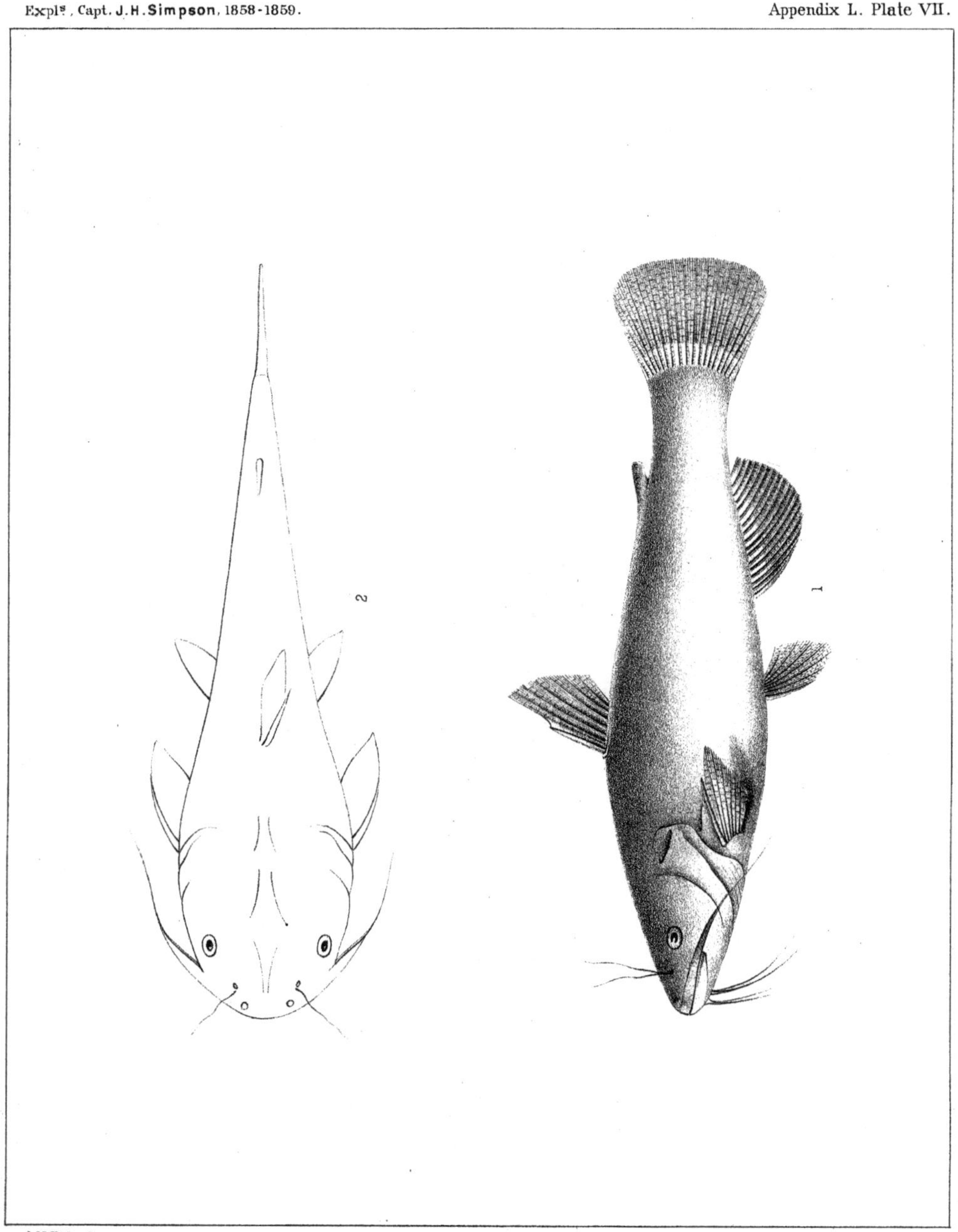

J. H. Richard. T. Sinclair & Son. lith. Phila.

PLATE VIII.

NOTURUS OCCIDENTALIS Gill.

Fig. 1. Side view of fish, showing the peculiar rorm of the adipose, dorsal, and caudal fins.

Fig. 2. View of the dorsal surface, showing the broad head with its T-shaped depression.

Fig. 3. View of the inferior surface of the head.

Fig. 4. The open mouth; the teeth are robust. The lateral extension of the intermaxillary band of teeth is not a generic character.

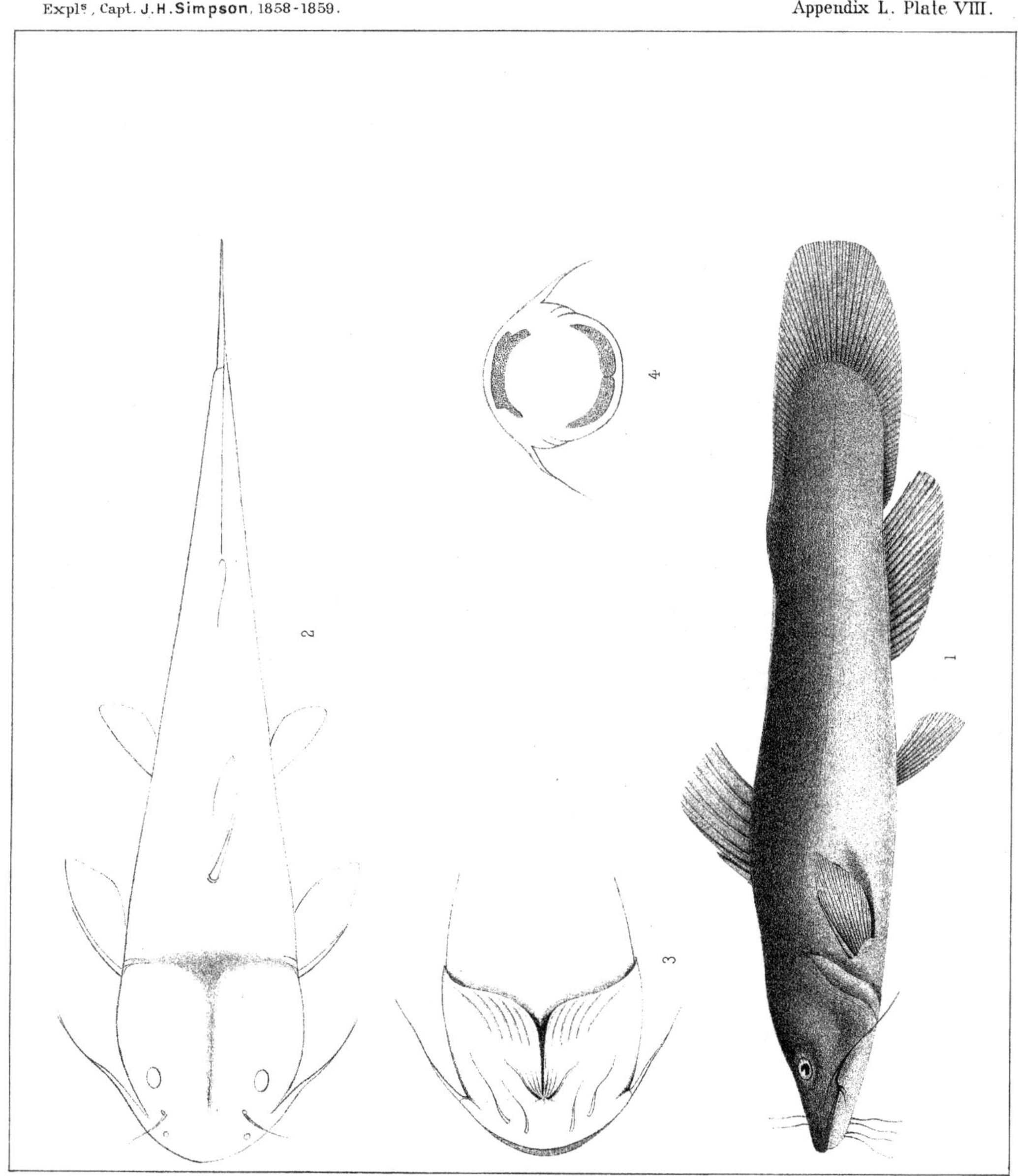

T. Sinclair & Son. lith. Phila.

PLATE IX.

HOPLADELUS OLIVARIS GILL.

FIG. 1. Side view of fish, illustrating the peculiar form of the body and fins.

FIG. 2. Dorsal view of fish to show its width and the form of the head.

FIG. 3. The head from below, with its many (twelve) and broad branchiostegal rays. The lower jaw protrudes beyond the upper.

FIG. 4. The open mouth, with its broad bands of minute villiform teeth, and the posterior extension of the intermaxillary bands.

FIG. 5. Intended to illustrate the appearance of the skin.

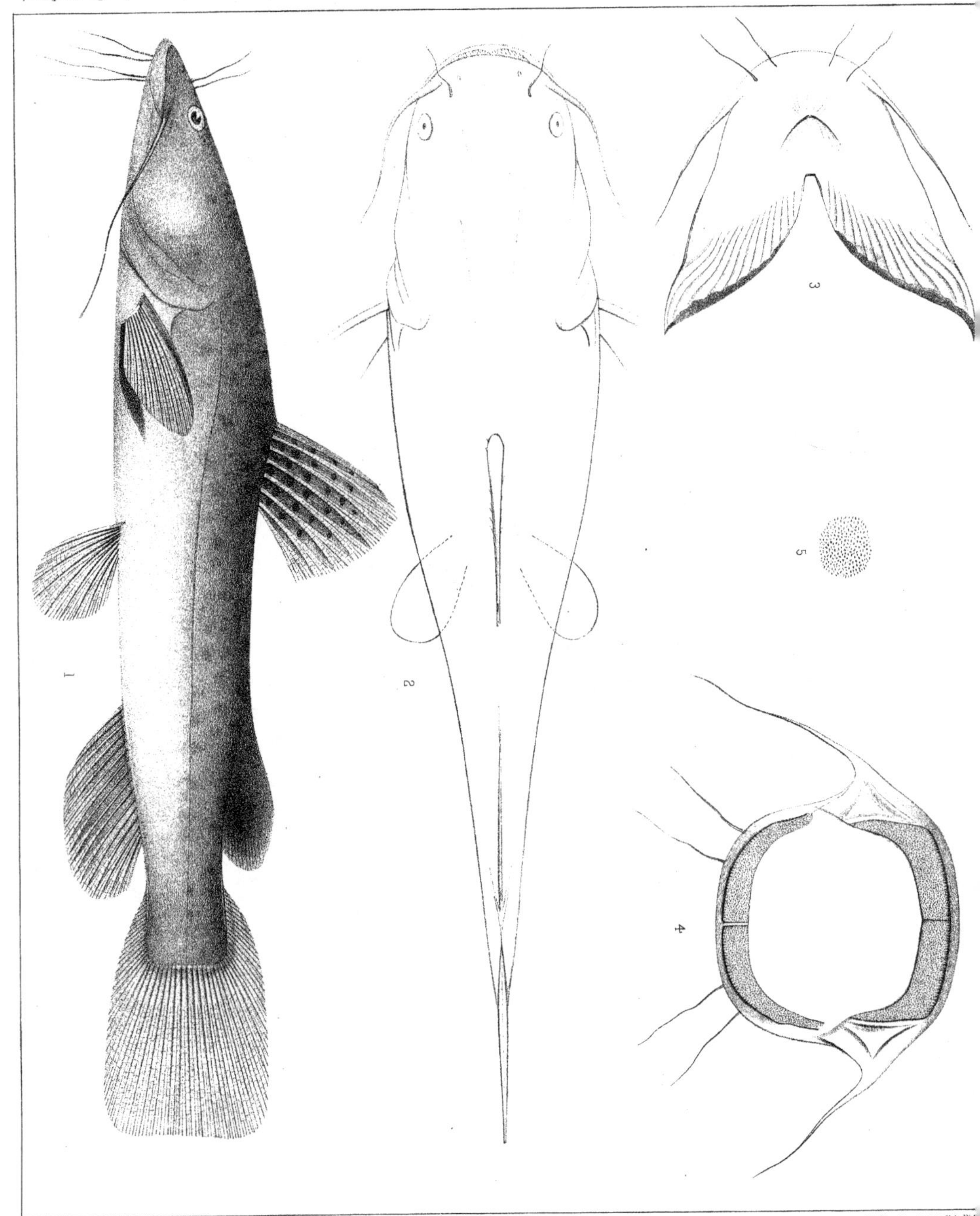

T. Sinclair & Son, lith. Phil.

ILYICHTHYS LIMOSUS GILL.

APPENDIX M.

REPORT

ON THE

BOTANY OF THE EXPEDITION.

BY

Dr. GEORGE ENGELMANN.

APPENDIX M.

SAINT LOUIS, *December* 31, 1860.

DEAR SIR: Want of time has prevented me fully to elaborate the very rich botanical material brought together, under your orders, by my brother, Henry Engelmann, the geologist and meteorologist of your expedition.

I herewith inclose to you an account of a few species, which seem to have a particular, and principally a practical, interest.

I expect to continue my investigations, and hope to submit them, through you, to the scientific public at a future period.

Very respectfuly, &c.,

GEORGE ENGELMANN.

Capt. J. H. SIMPSON,
Topographical Engineers, U. S. A., Commanding Expedition.

ROSACEÆ.

CERCOCARPUS LEDIFOLIUS, *Nuttall in Torrey and Gray's Fl. N. Am.* 1, *p.* 427; *and in his continuation of Michaux's Sylva,* 2, *p.* 28, *t.* 51; *Hooker, i. c. pl. t.* 324; *Mountain-Mahogany* of the inhabitants of Utah.

This small evergreen tree is so well described by Nuttall in both works mentioned that not much remains to be added. His figure, however, is not a very faithful representation. He says that it grows much like a peach-tree, at most 15 feet high, and that the trunk is sometimes as much as a foot in diameter. On the expedition, it was found to grow rarely as a tree, but usually branching from the base, or several stems from one root; its height was from 8–15 feet, and the stems seen had the thickness of 3–6, or, at most, 10 inches. The bark is light gray, tough, smoothish, with superficial longitudinal wrinkles and short transverse scars. The wood is hard, heavy, very close-grained, light reddish-brown, with white sap; medullary rays very numerous, but extremely fine, scarcely visible with the naked eye; the wood is similar to cherry-wood, but harder and heavier. A specimen before me has a diameter of 16 lines, 14 lines of which are wood, showing 24 annual rings, so that each ring has a thickness of not much more than ¼ line. The shoots, or longer branches, have a white, smooth bark, with joints or internodes of about 1 inch in length. The leaves, however, are usually crowded at the end of lateral branchlets, a few lines to 1 or 1½ inches in length closely covered with circular scars. Leaves very thick and leathery, persistent, lanceolate, acute at both ends, entire and revolute at the margin, with a thick midrib, prominent on the lower surface, 9–14 lines long, 2½–3½ lines wide, on a petiole 1½–2 lines long, to the lower part of which adhere lanceolate, brown, scarious stipules. When young, the branchlets as well as the leaves are covered all over with short, curly hair; when older, the leaves become glabrous and glossy on the upper surface, the lower remaining hairy and assuming a rusty color. The sessile flowers are produced in June from the axils of the uppermost leaves of the preceding year's growth, either single or 2 or 3 together; short scarious bracts envelop the base of the cylindrical woolly calyx-tube, which is 3 lines long; its 5-lobed, white limb, 3–4 lines in diameter, is very woolly externally, and less so internally, and bears about 20 or 25 naked, slender filaments, with reniform anthers ½ line in diameter. Immediately after flowering, the silky-feathery style becomes elongated, and carries up with it the detached limb of the calyx; at maturity, the style becomes a twisted, feathery tail of about 2 inches in length; the inconspicuous, linear, hairy fruit itself is about 4 lines long, and remains hid in the persistent, calyx-tube; at its top and base I observe a beard of very curious, stiff, white bristles, less than a line in length, thicker in the middle, and tapering toward both extremities. The fruit seems to be somewhat persistent, as I find it in specimens collected in spring before the flowering-season. About the time of flowering, the young leaves begin to develop at the end of the branchlets, leaving the flowers between them and the leaves of the year before. I generally find 4 or 5 leaves of the same year's growth at the end of each branchlet; they probably fall off when about 15 or 18 months old.

This fine tree, discovered by Nuttall on Bear River, north of the Salt Lake, and near "Thornberg's Ravine" in the Rocky Mountains, was found by the expedition on the Lookout Mountains and other mountain-chains of the basin.

CACTACEÆ.

The geographical limits of the area of this curious American family have been considerably enlarged by this expedition, proving the presence of at least 7 species in the Utah Basin between the thirty-eighth and fortieth parallels, viz: 2 Echinocacti, 1 Cereus, and 4 Opuntiæ. Several species known before have been found in new localities, and 3 new and very distinct species have been discovered, 2 Echinocacti and 1 Opuntia.

MAMILLARIA VIVIPARA, *Haworth, Suppl. p.* 72; *Torrey & Gray, Fl. N. Am.* 2, *p.* 554; *Engelm. Synops. Cact. p.* 13; Cactus viviparus, *Nuttall, Gen.* 1, *p.* 295.

Was collected in the South Pass and on Sweetwater River. It extends from here to the mountains of Colorado and New Mexico, but its most characteristic forms are peculiar to the more elevated plains, where it assumes that cespitose, spreading appearance, from which it has received its name. The mountain form usually makes larger heads, but remains single or branches out very sparingly. Its large purple flowers, with numerous lance-linear, long acuminate, bristle-pointed petals, and its leather-brown pitted seeds, readily distinguish it from allied species.

ECHINOCACTUS SIMPSONI (*spec. nov.**) simplex, subglobosus seu depressus, basi turbinatus, mamilliferus; radicibus fasciculatis; tuberculis laxis ovatis apice oblique truncatis axilla nudis, junioribus leviter compressis basi deorsum productis, vetustioribus obcompressis basi dilatatis; areolis ovatis seu ovato-lanceolatis, nascentibus albo-villosissimis mox nudatis; aculeis exterioribus sub 20 radiantibus tenuibus rigidis rectis albidis, additis supra aculeis 2–5 setaceis brevibus, interioribus 8–10 robustioribus obscuris erecto-patulis, areola florifera sub tuberculi apice arcolae aculeigerae contigua circulari; floribus in vertice dissitis minoribus; ovario abbreviato squamis sepaloideis triangulatis paucissimis (1–3) instructo; sepalis tubi brevis late infundibuliformis orbiculatis seu ovatis obtusis membranaceo-marginatis crenulatis fimbriatis, sepalis superioribus 10–12 ovatis obtusis integriusculis, petalis 12–13 oblongis apice crenulatis cuspidatis ex virescente roseis; stigmatibus 5–7 brevibus erectis, bacca parva viridi sicca umbilico latissimo truncata squamis paucis subinde aculeiferis instructa flore marcescente demum deciduo coronata irregulariter basi seu latere dehiscente; seminibus magnis obovatis obliquis minute tuberculatis, hilo magno ovato subbasilari, embryone circa albumen parcum fere circumvoluto hamato.

Var. *β* MINOR: tota planta, tuberculis, aculeis, floribus seminibusque minoribus.

Butte Valley in the Utah Desert, and Kobe Valley farther west; fl. in April and May, fr. in June and July. Var. *β* comes from the mountains of Colorado. This and the New Mexican *Echinocactus papyracanthus*,† the Mexican *Ech. horripilus*, Lem., and perhaps the South American *Ech. Odierii*, Lem., and *Ech. Cummingii*, Salm, and probably one or two others, form the small group of *Echinocacti*, with the appearance of *Mamillaria* (*Theloidei, tuberculis spiraliter dispositis distinctis*, Salm, Cact. Hort. Dyck 1849, cult. p. 34). They constitute the closest and most imperceptible transition to *Mamillaria* subgen. *Coryphantha*, Synops. Cact., p. 8, which bear the flowers in the axils of the nascent tubercules, the flower-bearing and the spine-bearing areolæ being connected by a woolly groove. In *M. macromeris*, Engelmann, they come from the middle of the tubercule (Cact. Mex. Boundary, t. 15, f. 4), and in the *Theloidei* they advance to the top of the tubercule close to the spines, thus assuming the position which the flowers regularly occupy in the genus *Echinocactus* (see Cact. Mex. Bound. t. 20, f. 2; t. 21; t. 25, f. 1; t. 27, f. 1; t. 28, f. 2).‡

The ovary is also almost naked, like that of *Mamillaria* generally, or has only a few scales, like that of *M. macromeris*. On the other hand, the dry fruit, such as is often found in *Echinocactus*, but never in *Mamillaria*, the tuberculated black seeds, and especially the large and curved embryo, and the presence of an albumen, do not permit a separation from *Echinocactus*.

This species is further interesting because it again strikingly proves that the

---

* An extract of this description was published in the Transactions of the Saint Louis Academy of Sciences, vol. 2, p. 197 (1863).

† The plant I formerly described as *Mamillaria papyracantha*, Plant. Fendl., p. 49; Synops. Cact., p. 8, proves to belong to this section of *Echinocactus*. A closer examination of Mr. Fendler's original specimen shows that the floral areola joins the spiniferous one at the apex of the small nascent tubercules. Thus far Mr. Fendler's specimen, found near Santa Fé, has remained the only one ever obtained of this pretty species.

‡ *Echinocactus brevihamatus*, Engelm., forms an exception. In this species, the flowers are situated exactly as in *Coryphantha*, at the base of the tubercle, and connected with the distinct spiniferous areola by a woolly groove, (see Cact. Mex. Bound. t. 19, fs. 2 and 3).

general appearance, the *habitus*, of a cactus plant, not necessarily indicates its real affinities. Not only is it a true *Echinocactus*, notwithstanding every appearance of a *Mamillaria*, but it is, moreover, closely allied in all its essential characters to the very compact *Ech. intertextus*, Engelm., C. Bound. p. 27, t. 34, in which all traces of tubercules are lost in the straight ribs. It has the same small flowers and the same small dry fruit, containing few large seeds, of similar structure, though not entirely the same arrangement of the spines.

Full-grown specimens of our plant are 3–5 inches high and 3–4 inches in diameter, of dark-green color; tubercules loosely arranged in $\frac{8}{21}$ or $\frac{13}{34}$ order, 8 and 13 spirals being most prominent. They are 6–8 lines long, at base somewhat quadrangular, 6–7 lines wide in the vertical and 4–5 lines in the transverse diameter, becoming subcylindric upward; areolæ 3–4 lines long, a little more than half as wide. The fruit-bearing tubercules are rather stouter and shorter. Exterior spines 4–6 lines long, whitish; interior ones spreading, stouter, and a little longer (5–7 lines long), yellowish and upward deep brown or black; no truly central spine. In the very young plant, the spines, 18–20 in number and only 1–1½ lines in length, are all radiating, closely fitting with their compressed bulbous bases on a linear areola, resembling in shape and arrangement those of *Cereus cæspitosus*. Soon afterward the areola becomes wider, and 6 or 8 short, stout, brown interior spines make their appearance, divergent like the original ones. Next the ordinary arrangement, as described above, takes place.

It seems that quite early in spring the young tubercules on the vertex of the plant begin to form, exhibiting their densely woolly tops, and soon afterward, long before any spines make their appearance, the tips of the smooth brown flower-buds come out. The flowers are 8–10 lines long and of nearly the same diameter, externally greenish-purple, petals yellowish-green or verging to pale purple. The short stamens arise from the whole surface of the tube, leaving only a very small nectariferous space in its base. The fruit is about 3 or 3½ lines long and almost as wide, borne on a very large circular areola, surrounded by a woolly margin (see t. 2, f. 1). It bears toward its top 1–3 scales, sometimes with 1 or 2 small spines in their axils. The fruit usually opens by an irregular lateral slit; falling off, its base remains attached to the areola, as is the case in many (or all? or only all the dry-fruited?) *Echinocacti*, thus producing a basal opening (see t. 2, f. 5). Seeds 1½ lines long in the longest diameter, covered with minute close-set tubercles. The young seedling shows erect, pointed cotyledons, and, when a few weeks old, begins to develop its pubescent spines.

Var. *β* has been received this fall from the Colorado gold-region;* the smallest specimens were 1 inch in diameter, globose, the small tubercules in $\frac{8}{21}$ order, spines 1½–2 lines long, often curved; sometimes 1–3 darker stouter ones in the center. The larger specimens are almost of the size of those of Utah, but often depressed at top; tubercules arranged in $\frac{13}{34}$ or even $\frac{21}{54}$ order, spines only 4–5 lines long, 20–28 external and 6 or 7 internal ones.

This species has been named in honor of the gallant commander of the expedition.

* It here grows and thrives probably at a higher elevation than any other northern Cactus, occupying *e. g.* the gravelly moraines of the Glacial period of Clear Creek Valley, between 8,000 and 9,000 feet altitude, and in the southern part of the Territory, the Sangre de Cristo Pass, 10,000 feet high (January, 1876).

Plate 1. *Echinocactus Simpsoni* as it appears in early spring; on the vertex a young growth of tubercules is visible, their tops covered with wool.

Plate 2. Details of the same.

Fig. 1. Four tubercules from near the vertex, one shows the broad scar where the fruit has fallen off, another one is just developing its spines, exhibiting their points above the thick wool.

Fig. 2. A detached tubercule bearing a ripe fruit.

Figs. 3 and 4. Flowers with the upper part of the tubercule and its young spines.

Figs. 5 and 6. The fruit magnified three times; fig. 5 showing the basal opening, fig. 6 the broad umbilicus.

Fig. 7. A scale of this fruit, more magnified, with two axillary spines.

Figs. 8–12. Seed: fig. 8 natural size, the others eight times magnified; fig. 9 lateral, fig. 10 dorsal, fig. 11 basal view; fig. 12 part of the surface, highly magnified.

Fig. 13. Embryo, enveloped in the inner seed-coat, including also the albumen; magnified.

Fig. 14. Lateral, fig. 15 frontal view of the embryo, magnified.

Fig. 16. Seedling, a few weeks old, magnified.

Fig. 17. Tubercules of the smaller variety from Colorado, in every state of development.

ECHINOCACTUS PUBISPINUS (*spec. nov.*) * parvulus, turbinatus, costis 13 subobliquis compressis interruptis tuberculatis; areolis orbiculatis, aculeis brevibus, rectis seu sæpe curvatis albidis apice adustis velutinis demum nudatis; radialibus superioribus 1–2 robustioribus, longioribus rectis curvatis seu hamatis, ceteris 5–8 brevioribus; aculeo centrali deficiente seu singulo robustiore longiore arrecto sursum hamato; flore ?; fructu ?.

Pleasant Valley, near the Salt Lake Desert, found May 9 without flower or fruit. Plant 2 inches high, 1 or 1¼ in diameter; compressed tubercules 4–6 lines distant from one another, confluent in 13 ribs, radial spines 1–4 lines long, white pubescent or almost tomentose, more so than I have observed it in any other cactus; on the lower areolæ, I find only 5–6 spines, the upper ones a little longer and stouter than the balance; farther upward, the number increases to 10, one or more of the upper ones becoming still stouter and often hooked; at last here and there a single central spine makes its appearance, 5–6 lines long, the strong hook always turned inward or upward. At first, only the dusky point of the spine is naked; with age, the whole coating seems to wear off. In another specimen, I find the spines 8–12 in number, a little longer, more slender, all radiating. The small supraspinal areola proves this plant to be an *Echinocactus;* it probably belongs, together with the next, to the section *Hamati*, Synops. Cact. p. 15.

ECHINOCACTUS WHIPPLEI, *Engelm. & Bigelw, Pacif. R. Rep. IV, Cact. p.* 28, *t.* 1, *Syn. Cact. p.* 15. Var. SPINOSIOR: globosus; costis 13 compressis interruptis; aculeis radialibus 9–11, inferioribus sæpe obscurioribus, reliquis longioribus niveis, 2 superioribus sæpe

* This description has been published in Trans. Acad. St. Louis, vol. 2, p. 199 (1863). It is rather strange that neither this nor the above-mentioned *E. papyracanthus* has ever been found again (January, 1876).

elongatis complanatis curvatis; centralibus 4, summo elongato complanato pergamentaceo flexuoso albo, 3 reliquis paullo brevioribus obscuris omnibus seu solum infimo hamatis; floribus minoribus; ovario squamis sepaloideis 5 oblongis munito; sepalis tubi linearibus margine membranaceis integris mucronulatis, petalis angustis oblongis; stigmatibus 6–7 brevibus in capitulum globosum congestis; bacca ovata parce squamata floris rudimentis persistentibus coronata.

The species was originally discovered on the Little Colorado by Dr, Bigelow, and was found afterward on the same stream by Dr. Newberry; the variety here described was met with more than 5 degrees farther north, in Desert Valley, west of Camp Floyd; remains of fruit, with the withered flowers attached, and some seeds, were found concealed between the spines from which the description has been drawn.* Globose heads 3 inches in diameter, radial spines $\frac{1}{2}$–1$\frac{1}{2}$ inches long, central ones 1$\frac{1}{2}$–2 inches in length; flowers, if I may judge from the withered remains, about 1 inch long; ovary small, bearing about 5 membranaceous scales, the lower triangular, the upper oblong-linear, almost entire, and never cordate or auriculate at base, as they appear in most of the allied species; sepals of tube also narrow, linear, or oblong-linear, 2–5 or 6 lines long, $\frac{1}{2}$–1 line wide, stigmas about $\frac{1}{2}$ line long. Fruit apparently an oval berry, $\frac{1}{2}$ inch long; seed just as it is described and figured in Whipple's Cactaceæ; the tubercules on the seed-coat are extremely minute and distant from one another, each forming a central protuberance on the otherwise flat surface of an angular cell of two or three times the diameter of the tubercule itself; embryo curved about $\frac{3}{4}$ around a rather copious albumen.

CEREUS VIRIDIFLORUS, *Engelm. in Wisliz. Mem. note* 8, *sub Echinocereo; Cact. Mex. Bound. t.* 36; *Synops. Cact. p.* 22.

This is evidently the northernmost *Cereus*, extending to the Upper Platte; it is abundant in Colorado. These northern specimens are 1–3 inches high, 13-ribbed, and show the greatest variability in the color of the radial spines; in some bunches, they are all red, in others white, in others again the colors are distributed without much regularity; sometimes the upper and lower spines are white and the lateral ones red, or a few or even a single one above and below are red and all the rest white; or the lower ones are red and the upper ones white, and all these variations sometimes occur on the same specimen. I mention this to show how little reliance can be placed on the colors or the distribution of the colors of the spines. Central spines wanting or 1 or 2 projecting horizontally, straight or curved upward, white or tipped with purple or all purple, 6–9 lines in length.

CEREUS ENGELMANNI, *Parry in Sillim. Journ. n. ser.* 14, *p.* 338; *Engelm. Cact. Bound, p.* 36, *t.* 57; *Synops. Cact. p.* 27.

Deserts west of the Salt Lake, without flower or fruit. Specimen entirely similar to the one figured in the Cactaceæ of the Boundary. The species seems to extend from the Salt Lake region southwestwardly to Arizona and the Mohave country.

* The botanist of Dr. Hayden's Expedition of 1875, Mr. Brandegee, found it abundantly in Southwestern Colorado (January, 1876).

OPUNTIA SPHÆROCARPA, *Engelm. and Bigelow, Pac. R. Rep. IV, Cact. p.* 47, *t.* 13, *fs.* 6–7; *Syn. Cact. p.* 44. Var.? UTAHENSIS: diffusa, læte-virens, articulis orbiculato-obovatis, crassis, junioribus sæpe globoso-obovatis; areolis subapproximatis; foliis minutis subulatis divaricatis; setis brevissimis paucis stramineis; aculeis nullis seu parvulis nunc singulo longiore recto robusto albido; floribus sulphureis, ovario obovato areolis fusco-tomentosis sub-25 instructo, sepalis exterioribus transversis obcordatis cuspidatis; petalis 8 late-obovatis emarginatis; stylo vix supra stamina exserto; stigmatibus 8 brevibus erectis; bacca obovata areolis plurimis tomentosis stipata; seminibus numerosis irregulariter compressis anguste marginatis.

Pass west of Steptoe Valley, in the western mountains of the Basin, found July 19 in flower and fruit. Joints 2–3 inches long and of almost the same diameter; often over ½ inch in thickness, sometimes almost terete or rather egg-shaped; areolæ 6 or 8 lines apart; leaves very slender and acute, scarcely 1 line long, smaller than in any other of our species except *O. basilaris*, also a western form from the Lower Colorado. Bristles few, and even in old joints scarcely more than ½ line long; spines none, or on the upper areolæ a few short ones, with here and there a stouter one ¾–1 inch in length. Flowers nearly 3 inches in diameter, pale or sulphur-yellow, when fading, reddish; fruit about 1 inch long and half as wide, with a deep umbilicus, and with 20–25 areolæ, which sometimes show a few bristles or a minute spine; seeds very irregular, 2, or, in the largest diameter, sometimes 2½ lines wide.

Unwilling to increase the number of illy-defined species in this most difficult genus, I attach this plant to the only species known to me to which it possibly can be compared, *O. sphærocarpa* from New Mexico, though its fruit is not spherical, has not a shallow umbilicus, and is, at least in the specimen before me, not dry; the latter would be an insuperable distinction, if we might not suspect, what in fact is often the case, that the fruit later in the season would become dry and brittle. The leaves, which heretofore have been entirely too much neglected as a diagnostic character in this genus, and the flowers of the original *O. sphærocarpa*, are unknown thus far.

OPUNTIA TORTISPINA, *Engelm. & Bigelow, l. c. p.* 41, *t.* 8. *fs.* 2–3; *Syn. Cact. p.* 37.

Forks of the Platte; in flower in July. The specimens being very incomplete, I am not quite sure that this is the same species as that of Captain Whipple's Expedition; the joints appear to be somewhat smaller, the areolæ closer together, and the spines shorter (1–1½ inches) and rather weaker; it may possibly prove to be an extreme form of *O. Rafinesquii*, the area of which extends to the Rocky Mountains. Leaves subulate, 2 lines long; flowers 2⅓–3 inches in diameter, sulphur-yellow; ovary long (1–1½ inches), with 20–30 areolæ, with light-brown wool and short bright-brown bristles; exterior sepals obovate, lance-cuspidate; petals 6–8, broadly obovate, obtuse, crenulate; stigmas 6–8, short, erect, as long as the stamens.

OPUNTIA HYSTRICINA, *Engelm. & Bigelow, l. c. p.* 44, *t.* 15, *fs.* 5–7; *Syn. Cact. p.* 43.

A flowering specimen, collected in June between Walker and Carson Rivers, is exactly like one found by Dr. Bigelow on the Colorado Chiquito; it has slenderer and straighter spines than the one figured in Whipple's Report, and approaches somewhat to *O. erinacea*, E. & B., of the Mohave region, in which I now recognize the long-lost

O. rutila, Nutt. in Torr. & Gray Flor. 1, p. 555. Joints 5 inches long, half as wide, obovate; leaves 1½ lines long; areolæ closely set with long straw-colored bristles; lower ones with few and short white spines, upper ones with numerous grayish-red spines, 1½–2 inches in length. Flowers pale straw-colored, 2½–3 in diameter; ovary 1 inch long, with 20–30 white woolly aculeolate areolæ; exterior sepals oblanceolate, squarrose, or recurved at the elongated tip; petals obovate, obtuse, crenulate; style with 8 or 10 short erect stigmas, longer than the stamens. The squarrose tips of the sepals are particularly conspicuous on the bud.

OPUNTIA MISSOURIENSIS, *De Cand. Prod.* 3, *p.* 472; *Torr. & Gray, Fl.* 1, *p.* 555 (*in part*); Cactus ferox, *Nutt. Gen.* 1, *p.* 296.

From the deserts of Salt Lake Valley to Rush Valley; specimens without flower or fruit. Joints small (2–3 inches long), broadly obovate or circular; areolæ closely set; spines numerous, stiff, stout, angular, white, mostly deflexed.

OPUNTIA MISSOURIENSIS, var. ALBISPINA, *Engelm. & Bigelow, l. c. p.* 46; *t.* 14, *fs.* 8–10; *Syn. Cact. p.* 44.

Smith Creek, Lookout Mountains, in Western Utah; flowering in July. By their slender flexuous spines, the specimens approach to var. *trichophora.* Flowers 3–3½ inches in diameter, bright golden-yellow; ovary 1 inch long, with 20 or 25 areolæ, scarcely spiny; exterior sepals obovate, cuspidate; petals about 8, obtuse, crenulate; style shorter than the stamens; stigmas about 5, very short, erect. Some flowers have elongated and very spiny ovaries, evidently abortive.

OPUNTIA FRAGILIS, *Haworth, Suppl. p.* 82; *Torr. & Gray, Fl.* 1, *p.* 555; *Synops. Cact. p.* 45; Cactus fragilis, *Nutt. Gen.* 1, *p.* 296.

Fort Kearny to the North Platte country; in flower in June and July. This is, I believe, the first time that the flowers of this species were collected since Nuttall's discovery of it in 1813. Travelers report that the plant is very frequently seen in the sterile prairies east of the Rocky Mountains, but that it is rare to find them in flower and rarer still in fruit. Since many years I have the plant in cultivation from specimens brought down by Dr. Hayden, but have not been able to get it to flower. Nuttall only informs us that the flowers are solitary and small. In the specimen before me, they are yellow, scarcely 2 inches in diameter; ovary 8–9 lines long; the 13–15 areolæ are densely covered with thick white wool; the upper ones bear a few white spines; lower sepals broadly oval, with a short cusp; petals 5, obovate, rounded, crenulate; style longer than the stamens; stigmas 5, short, erect, cuspidate.*

---

* Through the kindness of Dr. A. W. Chapman, of Apalachicola, Fla., I have received living specimens and fruit of *O. Pes Corvi*, so that I can now complete the description of this very distinct southern species.

OPUNTIA PES CORVI, *Le Conte in herb. Engelm.*; *Append. to Synops. Cact. in Proceed. Am. Acad. Arts & Sc.* 3, *p.* 346; *Chapman, Fl. South. U. S. p.* 145: diffusa, læte viridis; articulis parvis ovatis seu obovatis tumidis sæpius teretiusculis concatenatis fragilibus; pulvillis subdistantibus pulvinatis; foliis teretiusculis ovatis cuspidatis incurvis; areolis junioribus albo-tomentosis setas parcas brevissimas pallidas et plerisque aculeos 1–3 rectos rigidos sæpe basi compressos tortosve obscuros gerentibus, infimis inermibus; floribus flavis minoribus; ovario obovato pulvillos perpaucos fusco-villosos gerente; sepalis exterioribus ovato-lanceolatis, interioribus obovatis cuspidatis; petalis sub-5 obovatis spatulatis obtusis; stylo stamina æquante, stigmatibus 4–5 erectis; seminibus paucissimis anguste obtuseque marginatis in pulpa viscosa baccæ parvæ rubræ sæpe floris rudimentis coronatæ nidulantibus.

Barren sandy places along the coast of Georgia and Florida. Joints 1–3 inches long, obovate tumid, or narrower

OPUNTIA PULCHELLA (*spec. nov.*) :* parvula cæspitosa diffusa; articulis parvis obovato-clavatis; foliis minutis e basi ovata subulatis; areolis confertis, superioribus aculeos albidos rectos, singulum longiorem complanatum porrectum seu deflexum alios brevissimos radiantes gerentibus; floris purpurei ovario areolis 13–15 convexis albo villosissimis et longe setosis dense stipato; sepalis inferioribus lineari-oblongis breviter cuspidatis, superioribus spatulatis; petalis sub-8 obovatis obtusis, stylo cylindrico exserto, stigmatibus 5 linearibus suberectis; bacca sicca setosissima, seminibus crassis rhaphe lata plana notatis.

Sandy deserts on Walker River;† fl. in June.

This is one of the smallest, as it is one of the prettiest, species of this genus. It belongs to the small section of *Clavatæ* (Synops. Cact. p. 46) of the cylindric *Opuntiæ*, but is distinct from all those known to me by its small joints and purple flowers; all the others have, so far as I know, yellow flowers. Joints 1–1¼ inches long, 4–6 lines thick, very slightly tuberculated; leaves scarcely one line long; areolæ crowded, white woolly; larger central spine on the upper areolæ 4–6 lines long, flat, and somewhat rough above, convex below; smaller ones 4–6 or 10, radiating, ½–1½ lines long; flowers crowded, of a beautiful bright purplish-red or deep rose-red color, 1¼–1½ inches in diameter; ovary 4–5 lines long, beset with white capillary spines, 3–5 lines long, 15–20 on each areola; style not ventricose, as is usual in the genus, but cylindric; stigmas slender, pale yellow; berry clavate, at last dry, about 1 inch long, well marked by the conspicuous white-woolly areolæ and their numerous purplish-brown, flexible, hair-like bristles, 4–6 or 7 lines long. These bristles are entirely destitute of the minute barbs which otherwise invariably characterize spines and bristles of *Opuntiæ*. The thick round seeds, 2 lines in diameter, are well distinguished by a broad rhaphe, much wider than I have seen it in any other clavate *Opuntia*.

Plate 3, Fig. 1. Part of a plant of *Opuntia pulchella*, showing a flower-bud and two flowers, natural size.

Figs. 2–4. Bunches of spines, 4 times the natural size.

Fig. 5. Section of a larger spine, more magnified.

Fig. 6. A leaf from an ovary with the axillary woolly and bristly areola, 4 times natural size.

Fig. 7. A fruit.

Figs. 8–9. Seed, 4 times magnified; fig. 9 showing the broad rhaphe.

---

and cylindric, fresh or dark green, usually growing one on top of the other, forming chains of 1 or 2 feet long, at last prostrate; joints fragile, separating as readily as in *O. fragilis*; tumid pulvilli 4-6 or even 8 lines apart; leaves 2½–3½ or 4 lines long, incurved; spines 1–1½ inches long, very straight, when in threes divergent like the "crowsfoot" used against cavalry, whence the name given by the military gentlemen who discovered this species. Flowers 1½–1¾ inches in diameter; sepals and petals less numerous and narrower than in any allied species; ovary about ½ inch long, with only 2 or 3 areolæ on the surface and 3–5 on the upper margin. Fruit obovate, 6–7 lines long, rose-purple, with a shallow umbilicus, oftened crowned with the blackened remains of the flower; areolæ almost obliterated; red pulp very glutinous, including 1–3 or at most 5 seeds, which are regularly shaped, lenticular, with a narrow but thick and very obtuse rim. By its pulpy fruit, this species is widely removed from *O. fragilis*, to which its tumid and fragile joints seem to ally it, nor can it be confounded with any other species, though allied to *O. vulgaris* and *O. Rafinesquii*.

* An account of this species was given in the Transactions of the St. Louis Acad. 2, p. 201 (1863).

† This pretty species was afterward collected, 1867, "among the sage brushes" of Nevada, by Mr. William Gabb, and in the following year by Mr. S. Watson "frequent in the valleys of Western Nevada from the Trinity Mountains to Monitor Valley, 4–5,000 feet alt."

COMPOSITÆ.

The name of "*Wild Sage*", now so familiar to every traveller in our western mountain-deserts, was first used by Lewis and Clarke, in the narrative of their adventurous expedition, to designate several species of *Artemisia* or *Wormwood*, distantly resembling the true garden sage, *Salvia officinalis*, by their gray foliage and aromatic odor. It seems that now this name has, by common use, been restricted to the larger shrubby species, which give a peculiar character to the arid plateaus of Western North America, and which are of the highest importance to the traveller as "furnishing the sole article of fuel or shelter which they meet in wandering over these woodless deserts", as already Nuttall informs us in his genera of North American Plants, 2, p. 142. He states that the "Wild Sage" is his *Artemisia Columbiensis*, which name was by him improperly substituted for the prior name of *A. cana*, described by Pursh from the original specimens of Lewis and Clarke. Torrey and Gray, in their Flora of N. America, 2, p. 418, doubt whether this really is the "Wild Sage" of those travelers, and come to the conclusion that that name was indiscriminately applied to several shrubby species; they further state that the plant given by Governor Lewis to Pursh as "the Sage" is the herbaceous *A. Ludoviciana* found on the homeward voyage on the Missouri River.

I have now the means, through information obtained from Mr. H. Engelmann and from Dr. F. V. Hayden, to throw a little more light on this question, which is not without importance for botanical geography. The two species here in question are—

ARTEMISIA CANA, *Pursh, Fl. Am. sept.* 2, *p.* 521; *Torrey and Gray, Fl. N. Am.* 2, *p.* 418.—Shrubby, with woody stem 2–4 inches in diameter, 2–4 feet (on the Yellowstone, Dr. Hayden) or 2–6 feet high (on the Laramie Plains, H. Engelmann). Stem covered with a light-gray bark, which is separated into many layers of loose shreds connected by smaller transverse fibers, and is readily torn off. Wood light, porous, pale-colored, with very many darker brown medullary rays, easily separating along the division of the annual rings. These rings, or layers, are from ½–1 line in thickness, as stems of 1½–2 inches diameter show about a dozen rings, and are consequently as many years old. The stems are rarely cylindrical, but mostly compressed, knotty, and variously twisted, and often stunted; they are sometimes divided from the base, but oftener bear short and thick branches higher up. The annual branchlets are crowded along the older branches, 8–12 inches long, densely coated with a soft, white pubescence, and crowded with silvery-gray leaves, and bear toward their upper part and on the numerous short and erect lateral branchlets a profusion of small flower-heads, forming a spiked or contracted panicle, interspersed with short leaves. The leaves are flat, linear-lanceolate, entire or (the lower ones) rarely lobed, 1–2 or 2½ lines wide and 1½–2 inches long, the upper ones becoming smaller. The flower-heads are mostly sessile, or nearly so, hemispherical, about 2 lines long and wide; outer scales of involucrum shorter, foliaceous, and canescent (sometimes the lowest ones larger than the flowers, and pointed); inner scales nearly as long as flowers, brownish, scarious, obtuse, cottony-fimbriate on the margins. The flowers are all perfect, usually 5, in some specimens as many as 8 in number, 1½ lines long; ovary glandular, and, when bruised, with the odor of wormwood.

This is the "Wild Sage" of the Upper Missouri (above the mouth of the Yellowstone) and the Yellowstone River, and of the Laramie Plains, but it does not seem to occur west of the Rocky Mountains, as Torrey and Gray (*l. c.*) already state, and Nuttall (*l. c.*) must have confounded it with other species, when he contends that it is "still more abundant on the barren plains of the Columbia River", and that it grows 6 to 8 or 12 feet high.

ARTEMISIA TRIDENTATA, *Nuttall in Trans. Amer. Phil. Soc.* (*n. ser.*) 7, *p.* 398; *Torrey and Gray*, *Fl.* 2, *p.* 418.—Trunk, bark, and wood very similar to that of the last species, but trunk often larger, and usually even more twisted and knotty, with very numerous short and stunted branches, which are repeatedly divided into a great many smaller branchlets; ultimate annual branchlets fascicled, erect, only 3–6 inches long, canescent or silvery, very leafy at base, rather naked upward, bearing strict, rather compact, paniculate spikes, composed of sessile or usually pedunculate spikelets or glomerules of 3 to 6 or 8 sessile heads. Leaves silvery-white on both surfaces, crowded at the base of the branches, and often fascicled on short or stunted sterile branches, narrowly wedge-shaped, 1½–2 lines wide at the obtuse tridentate or trilobed end, narrowed down into a more or less distinct petiole; usually 3–6, rarely 8, lines long. Inflorescence interspersed with short and narrow, undivided, cuneate or spatulate obtuse leaves. Heads of flowers narrow, obovoid, nearly 1½ lines long, not much more than half as wide, with short and obtuse, canescent, exterior scales, and longer, scarious, interior scales, ciliate on the sides. Flowers in some specimens 3, in others often 4–5 in each head, all perfect, scarcely more than 1 line long; ovary quite glandular and with the odor of turpentine.

This is the "Wild Sage" of Utah, and, perhaps, of the whole region west of the Rocky Mountains, where it seems to supplant the more eastern *A. cana.* Nuttall, who first described it, calls it a shrub about a foot high, and as such it appears in the mountains of Colorado; but in Utah it is the largest and most abundant species, usually 2–4 feet high, rarely attaining a height of 6 feet, and then not straight, and with trunks of 3–6 inches diameter; sometimes the smallest bushes have trunks fully as thick as the tallest ones, short and chunky. East of the mountains, in the range of *A. cana*, it ever remains an inconspicuous shrub, lost among the more common species. Near Camp Floyd, specimens were collected bearing white tomentose excrescences of the size of a pea, or larger, undoubtedly galls caused by the sting of insects; the same have been observed on this species in Colorado.

The other species of *Artemisia* collected by the expedition were *A. Canadensis*, Michx., at Bridger's Pass; *A. Ludoviciana*, Nutt., at Sweetwater, Bridger's Pass, Round Prairie, etc.; *A. dracunculoides*, Pursh, on the Sweetwater; and *A. frigida*, Willd., on the Upper Sweetwater River.

CHENOPODIACEÆ.

SARCOBATUS VERMICULATUS, *Torrey in Emory's Report* (1848), *p.* 149. Batis (?) vermiculata, *Hooker*, *Flor. Bor.-Am.* 2, *p.* 128 (1840); Sarcobatus Maximiliani, *Nees in Pr. Maximil. Trav. Engl. ed. p.* 518 (*ex Torrey*), *Seubert in Bot. Zeitung*, 1844, *p.* 753, *cum tab.*, *Lindley in Hooker*, *Lond. Journ. Bot. IV*, *p.* **1** (1845); Fremontia vermicularis,

Torrey in Frémont's First Report, 1843, *Rept.* 1845, *p.* 95, *and Frémont's Second Report*, 1845, *p.* 317, *tab.* 3; Sarcacanthus, *Nuttall in Pl. Gambel*, *p.* 184; Sarcobatus vermicularis, *Torrey in Sitgr. Rep. p.* 169, *in Stansb. Rep. p.* 394, *in Bot. Whipple*, *p.* 130;* *Pulpy Thorn* or *Pulpy-leaved Thorn* of Lewis and Clarke; *Greasewood* of the present travelers and settlers.

This curious and important plant is found on the arid saline plains, principally on clayey soil, which in the wet season is moist, and on the border of salt-lakes, often covering large patches, from below Fort Pierre on the Missouri (*Dr. Hayden*) to the Upper Platte River (*Frémont, H. Engelmann*), and Upper Canadian (*Dr. James*) east of the Rocky Mountains to the plains of the Columbia (*Lewis and Clarke, Douglas, Frémont*), Utah (*Frémont, Stansbury*) through the Basin to Carson Valley (*H. Engelmann*) and down to the Gila River (*Emory*). Though discovered and noticed by Lewis and Clarke (1804) and collected by Dr. James (1819), this shrub was first described, 1840, by Hooker, in his North American Flora, from Oregon specimens, and was doubtfully referred by him to *Batis*. A few years later, it was again described by Nees in his account of the plants collected by the Prince of Neu Wied as a new genus under the name of *Sarcobatus*, and very soon afterward, and without a knowledge of the publication by Nees, again by Torrey under that of *Fremontia*. It is a great pity that this last name had to give way to priority, though at present a much handsomer and showy Californian shrub bears Frémont's name, the wide-spread *Greasewood* of the western mountains and deserts would more fitly have commemorated the bold and hardy pioneer of explorers to the millions, who now do or in time to come will know and value this plant.

The *Greasewood* forms a scraggy, stunted shrub, 2 or 3 to as much as 6 or 8 feet high; in Utah, it is commonly 3–4 feet high. The stems are scarcely ever more than 1 or 2 and rarely 3 inches thick, knotty, flattened, twisted, and often with irregular ridges and holes (the scars of decayed branches); sometimes, however, many straight shoots issue from a single base, $\frac{1}{4}$–$\frac{1}{2}$ inch thick, so straight as to be used for arrows. They are covered with a compact, smoothish or slightly roughened, light-gray bark. The wood is very hard and compact, of light-yellow, in the core light-brownish, color, with very thin annual layers, in younger plants about $\frac{1}{3}$, in older ones $\frac{1}{4}$ of a line or less thick. The oldest stems seen showed 20–25 rather indistinct rings, and were consequently so many years old. The numerous smaller branches have a smooth, shining, white bark, and are beset with white spines at right angles; these spines are indurated branches of two kinds. The sharper and shorter ones are real spines, scarcely ever more than $\frac{1}{2}$–1 inch long; they bear leaves only, or, in the axils of these, female flowers, and are terminated by a sharp point and never by a staminate spike. The other spines are branchlets which did bear such a terminal spike, which, after flowering, has fallen away; they are 1–2 inches long, sometimes even longer, when they are apt to bear also lateral spines. The flower-bearing branches are very often secondary axillary productions closely under the sterile primary branch, which constitutes the spine, so that the spines often appear as axillary to the flower-bearing branches. The leaves are thick and pulpy, linear, or often narrowed toward the base, flattened or even slightly

* Compare S. Watson's Revision of the American Chenopodiaceæ in Proc. Am. Ac. Arts Sc. vol. 9, p. 82 (1875).

channeled on the upper surface, and keeled on the lower one, at least toward the base, leaving a triangular scar after falling off. They are ½–1 inch, rarely as much as 1½ inches long, and ½ line, or sometimes, in the upper half, even 1 line, wide; in young and vigorous shoots, I have seen the leaves flatter, shorter, and broader, almost lanceolate. Their surface usually is perfectly glabrous; in specimens from Carson Lake, however, I find the younger leaves covered with a rough and sometimes branched pubescence. The leaves are sometimes on the lower part of the branches opposite, but commonly alternating in ⅖ order. The staminate and pistillate flowers are both very imperfect, but very different in their arrangement and structure; they usually occur on the same plant, though some plants seem to bear scarcely any but staminate, others only pistillate, flowers. The staminate flowers are crowded into a deciduous spike or ament, terminating the branches. This spike is, before the flowers open, 3–5 lines long and 1½ lines thick, and very compact, exhibiting only the rhombic surfaces of the scales; afterward it elongates to the length of 5–9 lines, showing the deciduous anthers under and between the separated scales. The spike consists of 25–35 peltate angular scales, pointed at the upper end, which cover 3–5 broadly oval anthers, sessile on the rhachis, ½ line long, 2–celled, opening laterally. The fertile flowers are usually solitary in the axils of the leaves and sessile; in some specimens, I find a secondary flower just below the primary one, and sometimes even below a branch, springing from the same axil; sometimes they are aggregated on abbreviated branchlets, forming irregular clusters. The flower consists of a tubular calyx with an inconspicuous rim, investing the lower half of the ovary, which is terminated by two unequal subulate stigmas, lateral in regard to the stem. In the fruit, this rim is enlarged to a broad, circular, spreading wing, 3–5 lines in diameter, green or sometimes red, which surrounds the upper third of the fruit. The flattened vertical seed, inclosed in the membranaceous utriculus, is about 1 line in diameter, and contains a spiral embryo without an albumen, as already demonstrated and figured by Professor Torrey in Frémont's Report.

The Greasewood is found in flower from June to August.

The form from Carson Lake seems to be distinguished not only by the pubescence of the younger parts of the plant, but also by its more squarrose growth, its subdiœcious flowers, and its aggregated fertile flowers and fruits; but the Greasewood of other localities is also often subdiœcious, so that when first described, it was considered a truly diœcious plant.

GEORGE ENGELMANN.

P. Roetter del. T. Sinclair & Son, lith. Phila.

ECHINOCACTUS SIMPSONI ENGELM.

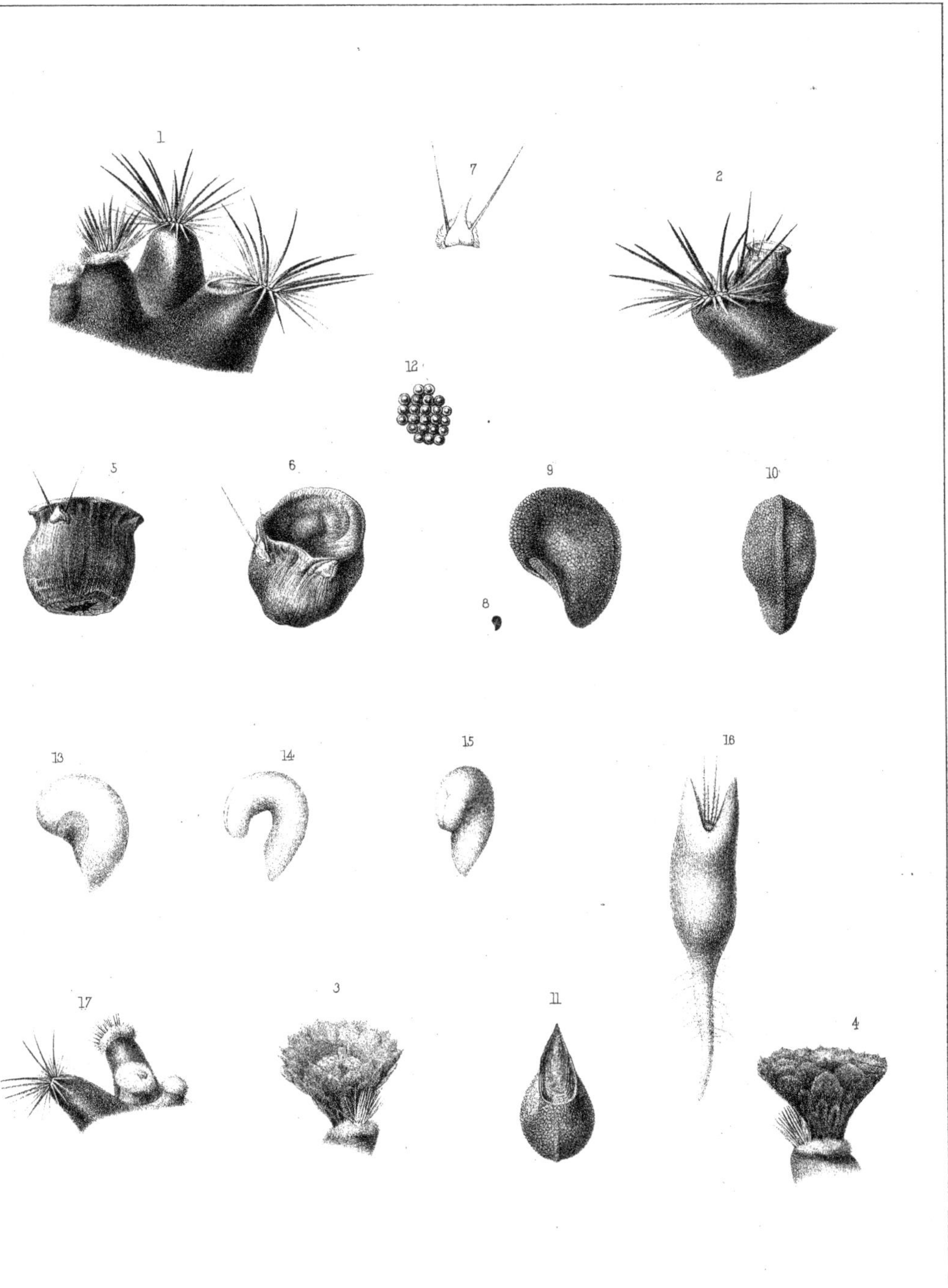

P. Roetter del. T. Sinclair & Son. lith. Phila.

ECHINOCACTUS SIMPSONI ENGELM.

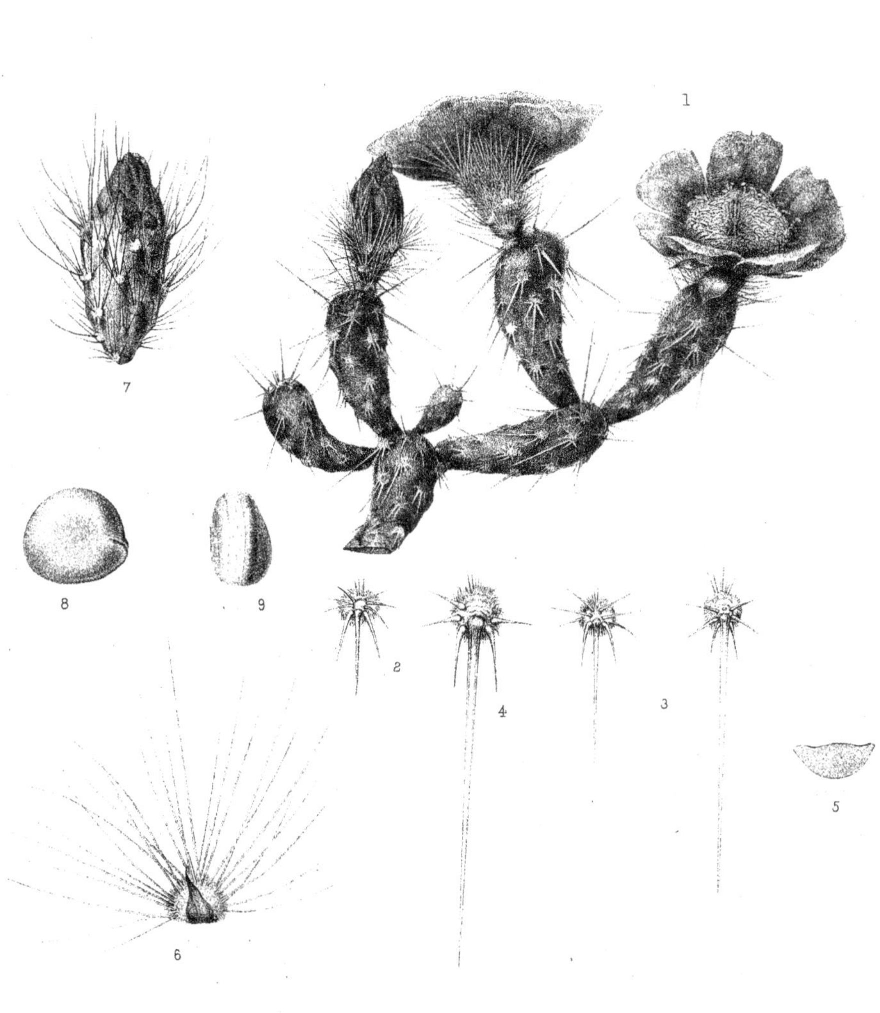

T. Sinclair & Son. lith. Phila.

P. Roetter del.

OPUNTIA PULCHELLA, ENGELM.

APPENDIX N.

POPULATION AND RESOURCES OF THE TERRITORY OF UTAH.

BY

Dr. GARLAND HURT.

APPENDIX N.

POPULATION AND RESOURCES OF THE TERRITORY OF UTAH.

BY DR. GARLAND HURT.

Captain Simpson to Dr. Garland Hurt.

OFFICE TOPOGRAPHICAL ENGINEERS, DEPARTMENT UTAH,
Camp Floyd, U. T., March 1, 1859.

DEAR SIR: I have just asked Mr. Gilbert who would be the best person to refer to for a statement of the population of this Territory, and he mentioned you. Now if you could give me such a statement, I would feel infinitely obliged to you, and would give you full credit for the same in a report which I expect to make to the Government on this subject. I would like to obtain the number and names of the towns and settlements, their respective locations, the population of each, the quality and extent of cultivable soil in their vicinity, the kind and quality of minerals, the saw and grist mills, factories, and other items of information which would be interesting to the public. If you could furnish this information in part or whole, you would be doing the public a great service, and me a very considerable favor.

Very respectfully, your obedient servant,

J. H. SIMPSON,
Captain Corps Topographical Engineers.

DR. GARLAND HURT,
Great Salt Lake City.

Dr. Hurt's reply.

SALT LAKE CITY, U. T., *March* 5, 1859.

DEAR SIR: Your letter of the 1st instant requesting information respecting the towns, population, agricultural and mineral resources, &c., of the Territory of Utah, is just received; and I would say for the present, that while I distrust my qualifications for furnishing such information as will be satisfactory, I shall, at the earliest opportunity, take pleasure in endeavoring to do so.

Yours, truly,

GARLAND HURT.

Capt. J. H. SIMPSON,
Corps Topographical Engineers, Camp Floyd.

AN ABSTRACT STATEMENT OF THE POPULATION, RESOURCES, ETC., OF THE TOWNS AND SETTLEMENTS OF UTAH TERRITORY, MARCH 10, 1859, BY DR. GARLAND HURT.

Brigham City is the county-seat of Box Elder County; has a population of about 800, 1 saw-mill, 1 flouring-mill, and about 2,000 acres of land in cultivation, mostly of a dark, alluvial soil, well adapted to the cultivation of wheat, oats, barley, and potatoes.

Willow Creek has a population of about 600, 1 flouring-mill, and 1,000 acres of land of a quality similar to that at Brigham City.

There is a scattering population in this county of about 400, making the entire population of the county about 1,800.

About 6 miles south of Willow Creek are the Red Springs, so called from the color of the sediment precipitated along the course of the stream formed by them. They afford water enough to propel any ordinary kind of machinery. The water is of a temperature considerably above animal heat.

Ogden City is the county-seat of Weber County; has a population of about 2,000, 1 saw-mill, 1 flouring-mill; and a court-house has been commenced, but not finished. There are about 3,000 acres of land in cultivation in its vicinity, of a quality similar to that above described.

Ogden Hole has about 600 inhabitants, 1 flouring-mill, and about 1,000 acres of good land in cultivation.

Weber Fort has about 400 inhabitants, 1 saw-mill, 1 flouring-mill, and about 600 acres of land in cultivation.

There is also a scattering population in this county of about 600, making the entire population of the county about 3,600.

Farmington is the county-seat of Davis County, and has a population of about 1,000, 1 saw-mill, 1 flouring-mill, a court-house not quite finished, and about 2,000 acres of land in cultivation.

Centreville and its vicinity has a population of about 1,000, 1 saw-mill, 1 flouring-mill, and about 2,000 acres of cultivable land, of a quality similar to that at Ogden City.

There are several other small settlements in this county, embracing a population of about 800; making the entire population of the county about 2,800.

Six miles south of Centreville are the noted Hot Springs, with a temperature but little below boiling-heat, and too well known to require a description at present.

Great Salt Lake City is the county-seat of Salt Lake County, and has a population of about 8,000; several public buildings, the most imposing of which are the new court-house (unfinished), the Tabernacle, the church-store, council-house, and the Social Hall; but, above all these, Brigham Young's superb mansion and Lion House tower with quite an oriental magnificence.

The foundation of the Mormon Temple has been laid upon the Temple Block, and in the spring of 1857 about 300 stone-cutters were engaged in preparing the materials for the building; but (*mysterious are Thy ways O! Lord*) on the announcement of the advance of troops toward Utah, the sound of the war-bugle succeeded the sharp clink of the mason's chisel. The consecrated earth has been carefully restored, and I am informed that no trace of the foundation-work is now to be seen. If this temple should ever be completed, it will be one of the most imposing edifices upon the American continent.

There is a cloth-factory, a sugar-factory, a nail-factory, and several flouring-mills in the suburbs of the city, and about 4,000 acres of fertile land in cultivation.

There are several other small towns in this county, but unimportant, except as forming the habitations of the inhabitants of the farming and grazing districts, and, taken together, afford a population of about 6,000, making the entire population of Salt Lake County 14,000.

Tooele City is the county-seat of Tooele County, and has about 800 inhabitants, 1 saw-mill, 1 flouring-mill, and about 1,000 acres of cultivable land, somewhat inferior to that about Salt Lake City, but produces fine crops of wheat, oats, melons, and potatoes.

Grantsville and E. T. City are villages in the same county, and have each about 400 inhabitants, and about 600 acres of land in cultivation, with a saw-mill and flouring-mill in the vicinity of the latter; making the entire population of this county about 1,600.

Provo City is the county-seat of Utah County, and has a population of about 4,000, 2 flouring-mills, 1 saw-mill, 1 carding-machine, 1 pottery, and about 4,000 acres of land in cultivation in its vicinity, most of which lies upon the banks of the Timpanogos, and near the shore of Lake Utah, and is unsurpassed in fertility by any land in the Territory.

Springville is next to Provo in point of importance, and has about 2,000 inhabitants, 2 flouring-mills, 1 saw-mill, 1 shingle and lathing machine, and about 2,600 acres of land in cultivation of a quality similar to that at Provo.

Springville is a thriving village of enterprising people, but the tragical murder of Potter and the two Parishes, in the spring of 1857, must ever cleave like bird-lime to its history.

Spanish Fork has about 2,000 inhabitants, 1 flouring-mill, and about 2,000 acres of land in cultivation. The land on this stream contains a slight admixture of lime and gypsum, and is celebrated for fine crops of wheat.

A large proportion of the inhabitants are Danes, living in excavations under ground, poorly clad, but industrious and frugal.

Pond-town has about 300 inhabitants, 1 saw-mill, and about 400 acres of land in cultivation.

Payson has about 1,000 inhabitants, 1 flouring-mill, and a saw-mill and lathing-machine in its vicinity. It has about 1,500 acres of cultivable land.

Santaquin has about 300 inhabitants, 1 saw-mill, and about 600 acres of land in cultivation.

Lehi, Lake City, and Pleasant Grove are situated on the northeastern shore of Lake Utah, and have each about 800 inhabitants, 2 flouring-mills in their vicinity, and about 1,500 acres of land in cultivation at each place.

Mountainville, situated in the same neighborhood, has about 400 inhabitants, a saw-mill, and about 600 acres of land in cultivation, making the entire population of Utah County about 12,400.

Nephi is the county-seat, and the only settlement, in Juab County; has about 600 inhabitants, 1 saw-mill, 1 flouring-mill, and about 1,000 acres of land in cultivation, of a quality similar to that at Spanish Fork.

Mount Nebo, the highest peak of the Wah-satch Mountains, is in this county. Salt Creek Cañon, about 2 miles east of the town, is at the foot of Mount Nebo, and is composed on the southeastern side of a solid mass of gypsum, more than 2,000 feet high, which crops out at several points along the side of the mountain for a distance of several miles, showing the quantity inexhaustible. Farther up toward the source of the creek, large beds of rock-salt crop out near the base of the mountain.

Manti is the county-seat of San-pete County, and has about 600 inhabitants, 1 saw-mill, 1 flouring-mill, and about 1,200 acres of land in cultivation. At the base of the mountain, within the limits of the town-corporation, is an extensive quarry of limestone, well adapted for building-material and extensively used by the inhabitants. About 12 miles west of this town is an extensive stratum of stone-coal, much resorted to by the blacksmiths of this and the adjoining counties.

Fort Ephraim has about 600 inhabitants, 1 flouring-mill, and about 1,000 acres of land in cultivation. Extensive tracts of rich meadow-land lie in the vicinity of this settlement. All the tillable land in this county is fertile, and produces abundant crops of wheat, oats, and potatoes.

Fillmore is the county-seat of Millard County, and the destined capital of the new State of Deseret, and has about 800 inhabitants, 1 saw-mill, 1 flouring-mill, and about 1,200 acres of land in cultivation. The state-house at this place, built in 1854 of red sandstone, is one of the most imposing edifices in the Territory. It is designed as the left wing only of the future capitol of the new State. There is a scattering population in this county of about 200.

There is a small settlement in Beaver County, the population and resources of which are unknown to me. The county is said to be better adapted for grazing than agriculture.

Par-o-wan is the county-seat of Iron County, and has about 800 inhabitants, 1 saw-mill, 1 flouring-mill, and about 1,000 acres of cultivable land.

Cedar City, eighteen miles below Par-o-wan, has about 2,000 inhabitants, an iron-manufactory, 1 saw-mill, 1 flouring-mill, and about 3,000 acres of cultivable land.

Stone-coal, iron-ore, and native sulphur are abundant in the vicinity of this settlement. There is a scattering population in this county of about 400.

Harmony is the county-seat of Washington, has about 600 inhabitants, and about 1,000 acres of cultivable land.

A rich mine of lead-ore has been discovered in this county, near the Vagas, from which the Mormons undertook to supply themselves during the war with the United States; but it is said to contain so large a percentage of silver that it could be profitably worked for that mineral.

The most remarkable event in the history of these two counties is the brutal massacre of 139 American citizens at Mountain Meadows, in September, 1857, by

Mormons and Indians, and the confiscation of their property to the so-called Church of Jesus Christ of Latter-Day Saints.

There are several small settlements in the remote counties, but I am not familiar with their population and resources.

Owing to the limited amount of water for irrigation, there is but little room for increasing the area of cultivable land at any of these settlements except at Provo and Ogden.

Perhaps the most valuable meadow-lands in the Territory are to be found upon the shores of Utah Lake. Extensive meadow-lands are also found in San-pete County, Juab County, and in the vicinity of Ogden in Weber County.

G. HURT.

CAPT. J. H. SIMPSON,
Corps Topographical Engineers, Camp Floyd.

Captain Simpson returns his thanks to Dr. Hurt.

OFFICE TOPOGRAPHICAL ENGINEERS, DEPARTMENT OF UTAH,
Camp Floyd, March 26, 1859.

MY DEAR SIR: The statement you have sent me, by the hands of Dr. Forney, of the population, resources, &c., of this Territory, I received last evening, and I cannot express my thanks too warmly for the trouble you have taken in furnishing it. The statistics you give I consider most valuable, and they will form an important part of the report of my reconnaissances.

I am, very respectfully and truly, yours,

J. H. SIMPSON,
Captain Corps Topographical Engineers.

Dr. GARLAND HURT,
Great Salt Lake City.

APPENDIX O.

INDIANS OF UTAH.

BY

Dr. GARLAND HURT.

APPENDIX O.

INDIANS OF UTAH.

BY DR. GARLAND HURT.

The following communication from Dr. Garland Hurt, who for several years was an Indian agent under the General Government in Utah, will be of interest to all who take an interest in ethnological subjects. I cannot agree, however, with the doctor in the idea which he appears to hold forth as to the original disparity of the races, and that any mode of treatment of the Indian tribes which ignores this doctrine, or rather which is based on the doctrine of the original unity of the race, must be attended with failure. I know it is the habit of many excellent and scientific men, as the doctor has done, to leave out in their philosophy a great truth—the greatest that has been divulged to the world—that the great I AM has spoken to man in his ignorance, and has given to him certain primary truths, which if he regard, he will assuredly live in light; but which if he disregard, he will as assuredly walk in darkness himself, and lead others into darkness. Among these great primary truths, I hold, is the unity of the race; and before any one, in my judgment, has a right to disbelieve it, he must first show that the source of knowledge of the Holy One, the Bible, which unbelievers have as yet only served to strengthen by their cavils and objections, is untrue, and therefore unworthy of being received as the grand text-book of individuals as well as of nations. This the history of that work through the ages which are gone, its internal evidences, and its acknowledged bearing on the happiness of the nations of the earth which have sincerely embraced it, show they will never be able to do. So far from it, it is the belief of the writer (however it may be the fashion of the mere moralist to deny it and sometimes to deride it) the greatest specimen of statesmanship is yet to be exhibited in the condition of a kingdom whose controlling officers shall be like Joseph and Daniel of Bible history and Washington of modern times, whose only fear seems to have been lest they should do wrong and run counter to the Divine mind.

Dr. Garland Hurt to Captain Simpson.

WASHINGTON, D. C., *May* 2, 1860.

DEAR SIR: In reply to your inquiries for information concerning the Indians in the Territory of Utah, I would remark that numerous tribes are designated by persons living in the Territory, which, in my opinion, are susceptible of the following divisions and subdivisions, viz:

Utahs: Pah-Utahs, Yamp-Pah-Utahs, Cheveriches, Pah-Vantes, San-pitches, Py-eeds.

Sho-sho-nees: Snakes, Bannacks, To-si-witches, Go-sha-Utes, Cum-um-pahs.
Py-Utes.
Wah-shoes.

The two latter tribes inhabit the country along the eastern base of the Sierra Nevada Mountains, and are not sufficiently understood by me to enable me to speak of them in detail.

The San-pitches speak the Utah dialect, and consequently I have classified them as a subdivision of that tribe, though they are greatly inferior to them in many respects, and the Py-eeds appear to occupy the same relation.

The Go-sha-Utes appear to be a hybrid race between the Sho-sho-nees and Utahs, and the same may be said of the Cum-um-pahs, the difference between them growing out of their relations to the different bands or subdivisions of these two tribes. These mixed bands are known as the Diggers, and commonly called Snake Diggers and Ute Diggers. The Snakes and Utahs proper are well formed and featured, but of a darker complexion than the Indians of the plains east of the mountains.

They are fierce and warlike in their habits, and have been at war with each other for several generations, and are likely to continue hostile. Each of these tribes are also at war with other tribes whose territories border on their own. The Snakes are at war with the Crows and Blackfeet, and the Utahs with the Cheyennes and Arrapahoes. They both, however, profess friendship for the white man. It is the boast of the Snakes, under a chief named Wash-i-chee, that the blood of the white man had never stained their soil.

They occupy the country bordering on Snake River, Bear River, Green River, and as far east as the Wind River. These bands of the Snakes are well supplied with horses and fire-arms, and subsist principally by hunting. Formerly, the buffalo ranged in their country, and formed the principal game; but according to their own accounts, which appear to be corroborated by those of the early trappers, these animals disappeared from their range about thirty-five years ago, in consequence of the severity of the winter, and have not since returned.* At certain seasons, however, these animals visit the Sweetwater and Wind Rivers, whither the Snakes repair every summer and autumn to meet them, and this brings them in contact with the Crows, who regard them as trespassers, and have treated them accordingly, and hence the hostilities between the Snakes and Crows, which will be likely to continue so long as the buffalo continues to range upon these waters.

The inferior bands of this tribe, especially the To-si-witches (White Knives), inhabiting the Humboldt River—who take their name from a beautiful white flint, which they procure from the adjacent mountains, and use as knives in dressing their food—are a

* *Note by Captain Simpson.*—Governor Denver, when Commissioner of Indian Affairs, addressed a letter to Hon. Alexander H. Stephens, Representative in Congress, January 18, 1859, in reference to the proposed new Territory, including the gold-region of the Pike's Peak country, in which he says the following in relation to the range of the buffalo: "Herds of buffalo frequent the plains along the eastern sides of the Rocky Mountains, but none have ever been found farther to the westward. Indeed, there is scarcely any evidence that buffaloes ever crossed that rocky barrier. Their range seems to have been confined almost exclusively to the great valley of the Mississippi." The governor is here evidently wrong, for I have seen a number of skulls of buffalo in Echo Cañon, and in the upper part of the Timpanogos Valley, all showing that at not a very remote period the buffalo roamed west of the Rocky Mountains. Besides, Frémont, in his report of his second expedition across the Rocky Mountains, expressly states (p. 144) that the buffalo ranged west of these mountains up to 1838 or 1840; and the traditions of the Indians, as given above by Dr. Hurt, certainly corroborate it.

very treacherous people; and the Bannacks, Go-sha-Utes, and Cum-um-pahs are not much less so. These latter bands are in the habit of infesting the emigration-road between the Soda Springs and the Bear River and the head of the Humboldt, during the season of emigration to California; and it is believed, and, I think, not without plausible foundation, that persons residing within the setttlements of Utah encourage these spoliations by offering a market for the property thus obtained.

The Utahs proper inhabit the waters of Green River south of the Green River Mountains, the Grand River and its tributaries, and as far south as the Navajo country. They also claim the country bordering on Utah Lake and as far south as the Sevier Lake, as theirs.

They also subsist principally by hunting, and have the same traditions as to the final disappearance of the buffalo from their hunting-grounds that the Snakes have; and it is their efforts to penetrate into the territories of the Arrapahoes and Cheyennes in pursuit of their receding game that have entailed upon them a most destructive war, in which their enemies have the advantage in arms and ammunition, but not in bravery; for it is my opinion, from a familiar acquaintance with them, that there is not a braver tribe to be found among the aborigines of America than the Utahs, none warmer in their attachments, less relenting in their hatred, or less capable of treachery. So complex is their nature that to trust them it is necessary to understand them.

Owing to the disappearance of the buffalo, and the scanty supply of smaller game, which is continually growing less, these Indians are occasionally reduced to the most extreme state of want, and the weaker families are compelled to subsist upon roots, plants, and insects.

Some of the inferior bands of both Snakes and Utahs are almost continually in a state of starvation, and are compelled to resort almost exclusively to small animals, roots, and insects for subsistence.

Among the more vigorous bands, the principal employments are hunting, fishing, shooting, horse-racing, and gambling. All the labor except hunting devolves upon their females, who dress their skins, and make them into clothing or lodges or prepare them for the market. The father holds his female children as his slaves, and demands a stipulated price for them in marriage. Some of their females are well-featured and bring good prices, but generally a few buckskins or a pair of blankets will purchase a bride.

Their females are also excessively addicted to gambling. The mode of gambling with both sexes is quite similar, a number of sticks being used in place of cards. They are so infatuated with this arrangement that I have known parties of them to refrain from eating and sleeping for twenty-four hours at a time, and gamble, with but little intermission.

Between the Utahs proper and the Py-eeds there is a species of traffic which I believe is not known among any other tribes upon the continent. I allude to the bartering of children. So abject and degraded are the Py-eeds that they will sell their children to the Utahs for a few trinkets or bits of clothing. The Utahs carry these children to New Mexico, where they find a profitable market for them among the Navajoes; and so important is it in enabling them to supply themselves with blankets from the Năvajoes, who manufacture a superior article of Indian blankets, that the trade has become quite indispensable; and so vigorously is it prosecuted that scarcely one-half of the Py-eed children are permitted to grow up in the band; and, a large majority of those being males, this and other causes are tending to depopulate their bands very rapidly.

These Py-eeds indulge in a rude species of agriculture, which they probably derived from the Spanish Jesuits, and perpetuate only as a matter of necessity, and that in the most primitive form. Their productions are corn, beans, and squashes. They have no farming-implements, and of course what they thus produce costs them twice the amount of labor that would be necessary with proper facilities.

The Py-eeds are perhaps the most timid and dejected of all the tribes west of the Rocky Mountains, being regarded by the Utahs as their slaves. They not unfrequently take their children from them by force. I have learned from the Utahs, however, that they much prefer obtaining them peaceably if they possibly can; but when pacific measures fail, some of their men prefer to take them by force than to be disappointed.

This is the band of Indians who the Mormons say committed the massacre at the Mountain Meadows in the month of September, 1857; but any one at all acquainted with them must perceive at once how utterly absurd and impossible it is for such a report to be true, for I feel safe in asserting that ten men well armed could defend themselves against the largest force that this band could muster.

Their religious ceremonies are quite simple and primitive, being nearly the same among them all. They recognize but one God, or Great Spirit, whom they call by different names among different tribes; but their conceptions of the attributes of the Deity are generally limited and erroneous. Smoking seems to be one of their religious ceremonies, and is generally indulged in with great solemnity, especially in their national councils.

They are very superstitious, and frequently attribute natural events to supernatural causes, as the changes and eclipses of the moon. Some of them have an idea that anything asked for on the first sight of the new moon will be granted by the Great Spirit.

The sun appears to be with the most of them the embodiment or representation of the Great Spirit, and supplications are frequently made to the rising sun as to a rational being. But in all these ceremonies, their conceptions seem to fall infinitely below a rational comprehension of the object of their adoration, and often developing an inconsistency not easily reconciled with an enlightened idea of true religious devotion.

Their family-relations are patriarchal, and the practice of polygamy is indulged. The marriage-ceremony, being very simple, is often celebrated privately.

In their funeral-ceremonies, the deepest grief is manifested sometimes by inflicting punishment upon themselves. They will, on the death of a principal person, kill their horses, burn their lodges and clothing, and not unfrequently sacrifice their prisoners, cut their hair very short, and refrain from food, in some instances going without eating or drinking for several days.

The females of the bereaved family observe the season of mourning with the most bitter lamentations, and for months after the death of a husband they greet the early morning with loud and piteous cries. But the warrior scorns to weep, and prefers to manifest his bereavement by cutting and carving his flesh, which he sometimes indulges to such an extent as to endanger his own life.

They have no literature, and can scarcely be said to have a history of their own tribes or families. The few traditions that have descended to them are too vague, indistinct, and disconnected to be relied on as a history beyond the first preceding generation.

They are firm believers in charms, legerdemain, and necromancy, and in the management of their sick these superstitious devices constitute their principal treatment, which their patients submit to with the most unbounded faith.

Each band has its medicine-man, whom they treat with great respect and partiality.

Among all the tribes of this region there is the same indisposition to habits of industry, indolence being the rule and industry the exception, and nothing but the keenest impulses of necessity can impel them to action.

But this characteristic they, I believe, only possess in common with all the inferior tribes of our species, and, with a view to their civilization, is an item worthy of much consideration. Intellectually they appear to be as well endowed as most of the native tribes of this continent; yet there seems to be a want of some of those higher intellectual endowments which render our own race progressive and so eminently fit us for the enjoyment of an enlightened government. The discussion of this subject involves a comparison of the races and invites an inquiry into the causes of the disparity that now exists between them, whether that disparity arises out of mental or physical inequality, or both; to what extent that inequality is capable of retarding their progress in the advancement of civilization, arts, and science. It appears to be the opinion of a large number of our modern philanthropists that all beings possessing the human form were originally endowed with an equality that ever forbids the idea of inferiority.

With an eye single to this similarity in physical form, they seem to overlook the mental inequality, or attribute it to a want of culture; and hence the misguided zeal for the improvement of many of the colored races, whose mental inferiority is a fixed and demonstrable fact, which must ever and inevitably define their position in the scale of political importance, and renders the idea of their future elevation to an equality with the Caucasian race utterly preposterous, and can only exist in the misguided wanderings of a perverted imagination. They have shown from their earliest generations their incapacity for any except the most simple forms of government, such as would assimilate them to some species of the gregarious animals, whom they approximate to in this respect and imitate as much as they do the higher orders of their own species.

The conclusions, then, to which we must arrive by this course of reasoning are obvious.

First. That by becoming the constant recipients of our care and sympathy their condition is temporarily ameliorated, but only so during the application of that care and sympathy.

Secondly. By amalgamation we elevate them at the expense of the degradation of the superior race.

Thirdly. By coercion they are made subservient to the intellect of the superior race, and made to bear the burden of their own subsistence, by controlling and directing their physical energies into the channels of usefulness. There is a misguided philanthropy which seems to be constantly directing our energies to the accomplishment of what in the nature of things is utterly impossible, and which it is the province of moral philosophy to correct.

These errors are exemplified in the attempt of our Government, at the expense of millions of treasure, to improve the moral and social condition of the aborigines of the country, who continue to sink lower in degradation and want, and are annually diminishing in numbers. While a small African colony, in the Southern States of the confederacy, under what some are pleased to style tyranny and oppression, have swelled to a powerful nation, infinitely more happy than the Indians or than themselves could be without the controlling influence of the superior race.

These Africans, we repeat, are infinitely more happy and prosperous than it were possible for them to be without the controlling influence of the superior race; while at the same time, instead of diminishing they contribute to swell the sources of the national revenue.

Very respectfully, your obedient servant,

GARLAND HURT.

Capt. J. H. SIMPSON, *U. S. A.*

WASHINGTON, D. C., *May* 5, 1860.

DEAR SIR: Your very valuable letter, in relation to the Indians in Utah Territory, I have just received and read with a great deal of interest. It will constitute an important portion of my forthcoming report. I agree with you in all you say, except as to the original disparity of the races, and the impossibility of their restoration to the same level of physical, mental, moral, and religious condition. The same God who has for wise purposes permitted the degradation of some portions of the human family, can also by His Spirit so breathe upon mankind as to cause them, through the purchased redemption of His only beloved Son, to see each other eye to eye, and to delight themselves in the common blessings of one united family. This view is perfectly consistent to my mind with the coercion, for a time, of the inferior races to labor, of which you speak, and which I believe is one of the divinely appointed means to that end.*

Very respectfully, yours,

J. H. SIMPSON,
Captain Topographical Engineers.

Dr. GARLAND HURT.

*And I might have added that the history of Cherokees, Creeks, Choctaws, Chickasaws, and other tribes in our own country, including the Pueblo Indians of New Mexico, as also that of the inhabitants of the Sandwich Islands, is confirmatory of my position.

APPENDIX P.

REPORT

ON THE

LANGUAGES OF THE DIFFERENT TRIBES OF INDIANS

INHABITING

THE TERRITORY OF UTAH.

BY

LIEUT. C. R. COLLINS,
TOPOGRAPHICAL ENGINEERS.

APPENDIX P.

REPORT ON THE LANGUAGES OF THE DIFFERENT TRIBES OF INDIANS INHABITING THE TERRITORY OF UTAH.

BY LIEUT. C. R. COLLINS, TOPOGRAPHICAL ENGINEERS.

WASHINGTON, D. C., *August* 30, 1860.

SIR: Having received instructions from you to arrange the several lists of Indian words which you have collected in your recent explorations, in a form suitable for the purposes of comparison, I accordingly submit the accompanying comparative vocabulary which I have drawn up, together with a statement relative thereto.

The vocabularies furnish specimens of the languages of the *Utes* or *Utahs*, the *Shoshonees* or *Snakes*, the *Pi-utes*, and the *Washoes*, together with a few numerally, of the *I-at* language.

The result of an examination and comparison of these languages shows quite a similarity between the Ute or Utah, the Shoshonee, and the Pi-ute; while the Washoe is apparently quite distinct in its characteristics.

The few I-at numerals which are given are insufficient for the purposes of classification.

The resemblance of the first three languages to each other seems quite sufficient to warrant the conclusion that they have a common origin, and that the corresponding tribes should be placed in the same primary ethnological group.

This classification is based entirely on the resemblance of language, shown by the vocabulary; it is possible, however, that tribes living in contact with each other may acquire a similarity of language by the adoption of members of one tribe into the other. Captives taken and absorbed into the tribe must necessarily have an influence upon the language. A minute examination of the construction of the language, and particularly of the declination of the verbs, would be a more accurate method of comparison, but would require more material than we at present possess.

In the ethnological classification of Indian tribes given by Schoolcraft, he applies the name of *Shoshonee* to the fifth primary group, located, according to his report, "in the Rocky Mountains, the higher Red River, and the hill country of Texas; and embracing the *Shoshonees* or *Snakes*, the *Bannacks* or *Root-diggers*, and the *Comanches* of Texas." If we assign a place in this group to the *Utes* or *Utahs*, and the *Pi-utes*, it will extend its area westwardly to the base of the Sierra Nevada.*

Further ethnological investigations may result in ascribing to other unclassified tribes a place in the same group.

The language of the *Washoes* appears to bear no resemblance to any of those given in Schoolcraft's collection of vocabularies, nor does it seem to be at all related to the *Shoshonee.*

There is a source of error and difficulty in instituting a comparison between specimens of Indian languages, which arises from the method of obtaining them. The vocabularies are frequently obtained from *different* individuals, who, of course, attempt by the use of the English alphabet to represent the sounds of the words as pronounced by the Indians from whom they are obtained; it is probable if several persons attempt, in this way, to indicate the same Indian word, no two of them would represent it in the same manner, or by the same letters; moreover, as the word is uttered in the Indian's characteristic guttural manner, and there being in an unwritten language no authority for correct pronunciation, the peculiarity of each individual's utterances is likely to be perpetuated in vocabularies made from information obtained from them.

There are several words of different languages in the accompanying vocabularies, which, though spelt differently, are undoubtedly meant for the same words, or at least are derived from the same source; in such cases the sounds of the words, as they are pronounced, generally bear more resemblance than their appearance as they are represented.

Among the cases of similarity of words from the *Ute*, *Pi-ute*, and *Shoshonee*, we find *Pah*, meaning water, to be common to all of them, and it may also be remarked the same word means water in the language of the *Pueblo* Indians of *Jemez* and *Old Pecos*, as given in vocabularies previously obtained.†

The words for face, eye, mother, house, sun, ice, snake, with several others, are common to all of the languages here given, except the *Washoe*, while there are others, which so nearly resemble each other as to point to a common origin, if indeed they are not intended for the same word; these are found in the Indian for nose, beaver, day, summer, winter, &c.

There are frequent instances in these languages of compound words being formed by the union of two or more elementary ones; in some of these cases we know the meaning of all the syllables, or component words; in other cases, some of them may be recognized, and the meaning of others inferred from the meaning of the entire combination. Allowance must be made for the elision due to the junction of several independent words in a compound one. *Pah*, meaning water, occurs as a syllable in the word *Pah*-emp, which means rain; the latter syllable being in all probability derived from *Too-oomp* or sky, thus making *Pah-oomp*, *Pah-emp* or sky-water.

Hail is *Pah-oo-ump;* ice, *Pah-kup;* the element *Pah*, also enters into the words for otter, beaver, duck, and fish, in one or the other of the dialects here given.

* Since writing the above I have observed that Prof. W. W. Turner has also placed the *Utahs* and *Pi-Utes* in the *Shoshonee* group; and has also connected the *Kioway* tribe with the same family. (Pacific Railroad Reports, vol. iii.)

†Journal of a military reconnaissance from Santa Fe, New Mexico, to the Navajo country, in 1849, by Lieut. J. H. Simpson, Corps Topographical Engineers.

The notes which are appended to the vocabulary, give all the necessary information with regard to the arrangement of the different lists of words furnished by their respective authorities.

Very respectfully, your obedient servant,

C. R. COLLINS,
Brevet Second Lieutenant Topographical Engineers.

Capt. J. H. SIMPSON,
Corps Topographical Engineers.

A comparative vocabulary of Indian words.

English words.	Name of tribe.			
	Ute or Utah.[1]	Shoshonee or Snake.[2]	Pi-Ute.[3]	Washo.[4]
God	Shi-ne-babe		Nis-mer-nah	Ti-oni-le.
Devil	Shi-neb	Pi-an-dant	Su-ti	Sem-em-she.
Man	To-wats	Tine-up	Na-na	Sa-li-hou.
Woman	Mam-a-shodo	Wipe	Mo-goh	Se-moh-moh.
Boy	I-pids	Yam-bau	Nat-che	Ma-hou.
Girl	Nange-it	Nah-wich	Tu-ah	Shoul-cum-hough.
Infant, child	Pae-shutz	Tur-ra-fu-ritz	O-ah	Be-gus.
Father	Maw-ah	Ap	Nah	Ta-grih.
Mother	Te-ah	Be-ah	Be-ah	Te-lah.
Husband	Pu-um	Be-wah	Go-mah	Te-bu-mah-le.
Wife	Mah-show-er	Goo-up	No-dug-we	Tun-lian.
Son	To-watz	An-doo-ah	Ud-du-ah	Teng-ane.
Daughter	Pa-ditz	Bi-deh	Ur-bur-dah	Teng-am-ough.
Brother	Tschodge	Dam-mie	Ur-bah-beh	Te-bag-ough.
Sister	Nah-ninge	Nah-wie	Ha-ma	Te-e-sah.
Indian	Noontz	Nu-uh	Ner-mer	En-you-geh.
Head	Tots-ute	Bam-by	Er-sud-pig	La-hep.
Hair	Tots-u-obe	Pong-gush	Wah	Ly-housh.
Face	Ko-bah	Go-bah	Ko-bah	Tic-maish.
Forehead	Hoo-tok-ut	In-gi	Eu-ah	Tic-ca-be.
Ear	Nun-go-bee	Ne-ink	Er-nok-ah	Tip-e-son.
Eye	Poo-ib	Boo-ee	Boo-ee	Te-we-gu.
Nose	Mo-wip	Mo-wy	Mo-be	Te show-e-yep.
Mouth	Tumb-bwap	Tam-bah	Do-bah	Te-hung-ah.
Tongue	Ah-woomp	Igk	E-quah	Tic-mah-doudt.
Tooth	Tah-ump	Muntz	Da-mah	Cey-yect.
Beard	Muns-ump	Go itch	Mas-su-e	Chec-mel.
Neck	Pah-weep	Go-itch	Goo-tah	La-bou.
Arm	Poor-ub	Boor-rah	Ber-tah	La-bough.
Hand	Mu-ur-ve	Maw	Mi-ee	La-dough.
Fingers	Mah-shub	Mas-suck	Ma-gon	De-too-le-sic.
Nails	See-joomb	Mas-sit-dah	See-doo	De-loo-lepe.
Body	Womp-tahb	Kaw-y	Ner-wah	Lah-get.
Belly	Shaugh-ab	Nuh	Coo-he	La-yoh.
Breasts	Ning-oop	Shonk	Ning-oh	Lem-bah.
Man's privates	Wap	Woo-ah	Be-gsh	Te-mon-cush.
Woman's privates	Nig-ump	Die	Sou	Tee-bess.
Leg	Pung-a-boo	Bung-gup	Con-op	Lah-hul.
Foot	Nam-bap	Nump	Ger-ger	Te-my-yept.
Toes	Pee-ret-tombe	Tash-e-toh	Doh-goh	Dee-too-le-sic.
Bone	Obe	Tats-se-oh	Oh-ho	Teah-be.
Heart	Peep	Be	Be-wa	Lew-lah.
Blood	Pap	Fru-up	Per-pe	Tah-soong.
Town, village	Kant	Tah-ah-tits-kau	Nak-got-eh	Teng-a-la-me-lou.
Chief	Ne-ab	Ti-gon-up	Nar-bun-ah	Too-bag-ou.
Warrior	Ni-uk-ne-ab	Noo-ve-ting-up, chana-shun-be-nah.	Nak-ko-et	Co-me-sou-co-leh.
Friend	Tig-a-boo	Hinch, tig-ga-boonch	Ber-ah	Sou-la-deh.
House, hut	Kant	Kant	Na-vie	Lang-ell.
Cup	Kar-tridge	A-woo	Ge-tah	Ching-ou-na-me.
Kettle	Pam-boont	We-wib-too-ah	Op-oh	Ka-wa-lou.
Bottle	Too-pootz	Too-pe-otz	O-tah	Ca-tep.
Arrow	Ou-as-in-too	Hoo-pah	Po-oush	Mas-ke-set.

Vocabulary of Indian words—Continued.

English words.	Name of tribe.			
	Ute or Utah.	Shoshonee or Snake.	Pi-Ute.	Washo.
Bow	Hadz	Ide	Ah-durg	Tak-loh-hot.
Ax, hatchet	Me-pood-pen-en	Oo-hun-ne	Wer-suk-en	E-car-sen.
Knife	Ou-witz	We	We-he	Tow-eng-an-yeng.
Canoe, boat	Ur-ve-shock	Pe-ah-vunk	Sack-ke	Ta-nup.
Moccasins, shoes	Pats	Namp	Moc-co	Te-mo-cougs.
Bread	Pan, (same as Spanish)	To-she-kik-up	To-hut-eca-ba	Tem-lou.
Pipe, calumet	Soonk	Pitch-shemo	To-esh	Bang-dus-duc.
Tobacco	Quap	Too-pah	Pa-moh	Bang-cush.
Sky	Too-wint-up	Too-oomp	Coo-me-bah	To-ma-hum.
Heaven	At-too-wip	War-rah-so-up	Pe-sah	Cum-nac-sa-sa-seh.
Sun	Tap	Tap	Tab-ah	Tou-gil-ah-gu-sots.
Moon	Mur-toads	Moo-ah-tap	Mer-ah	Tee-bah.
Star	Poorts-ip	Tats-in-up	Pah-too-op-a	Mah-la-sung.
Day	Tat-be	Tah-be-dog-e	Tah-bee-no	Ah-bah.
Light	Pau-nin-night-te	Tah-ke	Tah-weep	O-dah-se-weh.
Night	Too-wint	Too-gan-ne	To-kan	
Darkness	Too-or-ip		To-kan-no	Tow-e-day-e-you.
Morning	Itch-cooch	Po-etch-cush	Awa-mooc	Was-leh.
Evening	Tah-wy-e-cup	Tah-y-am-wie	Yong-on	To-pah-teen.
Spring	Tah-mant	Tah-ka-wit-pah-shur	Tad-sah	Se-gah-but.
Summer	Tady	Tods	Tod-yep-a	Am-suc.
Autumn	U-gwunt	E-by-ide	Eu-bau-a	Oh-osh.
Winter	Tom	Tar-kar-wan	Toh-moh	Ca-lesh.
Wind	Nerd	Noo-y	Hey-gwip	Ta-ge-ene.
Lightning	Pan-nuck-shet	Teme-bah-utch	Ter-qua-que-yepa	To-ah-osh.
Thunder	Nun-wint	We-ke	Ner-nah-ah-bah	Tah-hew-e-ach.
Rain	Pah-wars	Pah-emp	Pah-omah	To-ah-osh.
Snow	Nu-bub	Tah-kep-pe	Ter-gra-bah	Ta-dah-ash.
Hail	Pi-ab	Pah-oo-ump	Har gwa-dig-wa	Se-go-gum-oh.
Fire	Coont	Koo-nah	Coo-son	Teh-yo.
Water	Pah	Pah	Pah	Te-mah.
Ice	Pah-kup	Pah-kup	Pah-geh-o-va	Tou-ba-sut.
Earth, land	Too-wimp	Shock-up	Ta-pe	Ha-ow-wa.
Sea	Pah-wad-rid	Sin-ur-bah	Pah-ne-nad	Ta-hou.
River	Too-quint	O-gwint	Hoop	Wa-tah.
Creek	Me-poods-too-quint	Shock-o-bah	Toots-e-hoop	Too-goh-got.
Lake	Me-poods-pah-ardid	Pah-god-dan	Pah-ne-nad	Ta-hou.
Valley	You-ab	Pah-un-up	Yer-per	Ta-moh-wa.
Hill	Pi-ab	Toh-yup	Quid-du-ep	Tou-lou-oug-goh.
Mountain	Ki-be	Quid-u-went	Ki-ebe	Ta-lah-act.
Island	Too-witz-tuck-idge	Che-nump	Pah-soe-a-ted	Tou-me-you-tah.
Stone, rock	Toomp	Timp	To-be	Tah-ech.
Salt	Wi-ab	Ou-gwup	Oug-an-a	Ung-ah-a-per.
Copper	Ung-o-pah-nock-it		Wou-con-you-dip	Wel-kep-kep.
Iron	Pah-nock-it	Port	*Same as knife*	*Same as knife.*
Maize	Co-me	A-nip	Corn	Corn.
Tree	Mah-ab	Op-koo-oer-vant	O-sag-mag-wa	Ki-osh-le.
Wood	Oo-quep	Tsick-up	Koo-nah	Tou-lou-bul.
Leaf	Nung-ah-up	Shamp	Ah-noc-ah	Tou-yah-yet.
Bark	Hash-soop	Ike	Wah-ac-cat	Mah-to-kip-te.
Oak	Que-ub		We-eb	Mal-nah-ge.
Pine	Ah-oomp	Won-go-up	Wo-cue-be	Sou-wah.
Flesh, meat	Too-quab	To-queah	Ah-ber-did-doc	Ta-push.
Beaver	Pah-oontz	Hau-witch	Pah-u-nak	Tah-nesh.
Otter	Pah-vit-zook	Pahn-sook	Pah-n-sang	Cha-wa-wa.
Deer	Too-e	Too-pe	Der-herd	Mem-tah-we.
Grass	Oo-gwoob	Show-nip	Wha-hab-e	Hor-se-pe.
Bison, buffalo	Kootz	Go-witch	Cud-sou	Go-sou.
Bear	Que-aut	Neer-ah	Pad-wah	Ta-ba.
Wolf	Yo-woods	So-wor-rah	Esh-sah	Too-le-seh.
Dog	Cha-ridge	Char-re	We-seg-wog	Cho-coh.
Fox	Tah-bon-ditz	Warn-nes	Wah-he	Mo-gup.
Squirrel	Spiss	Ku-ump	We-dane	Ou-che-le.
Rabbit, hare	Chuck-am	Tap	Cam-me	Pah-lou.
Snake	To-wab	To-quah	To-quah	Ma-a-kee.
Bird	Wid-didge	Te-hunty	Hood-ye-bah	Geh-yonk.
Egg	Nah pab	Po-wood-ge	Ar-no-naugh	Ti-oh-gul.
Goose	Hah-bah-munk	Ne-gunt	Na-giner	Sam-urk.
Duck	Tsug	Pah-e	Per-her	Te-lach.
Chicken	Ham-bung	Shy	Que-nah	Pat-se-en-neh.
Pigeon	Hy-you-en-boong	Hone-dah	Pan-he-ob	Oug-a-hah-di-al-el.
Partridge, (sage hen)	Shee-jeh		Wee-hoop-o-ah	Wah-tel-ah-leh.

Vocabulary of Indian words—Continued.

English words.	Name of tribe.			
	Ute or Utah.	Shoshonee or Snake.	Pi-Ute.	Washo.
Turkey	Pan-dah-mo-witz		Tag-wan	Ou-wha-wee-ap.
Fish	Pah-gah	Pan-que	Pah-gue	Ou-wa-chee.
White	T-shard	Qui-chen	Tah-hoo-qui-dah	Tal-po-po-e.
Black	Too-gut	Hye	Too-hoo-qui-dah	Tal-e-ah-we.
Red	Un-guard	Unga-she-etz	At-soy-qui-dah	Tal-let-leg-eg.
Blue	Tchower	Show-e-tan	Po-eg-gui-dah	Tal-pel-pel-eg.
Yellow	Koi-run-gwat	O-up	O-shy-gui-dah	Tal-sah-se-meg.
Green	Quer-shower	Poo-y	Pe-ega-you	Tal-yah-yeh.
Great, big	Hah-bat	Pe-up	Pa-bac-co	Te-yel-ee.
Small, little	Me-poods	Too-e-gitz	Tot-se	Bah-hah-ging.
Strong	Toot-ten-gee	Too-a-gunt	Oh-hot-a	Tal-sus-sus-eh.
Old	Nan-nan-poods	Soo-a-putz	Moh-ed-dug-wa	Moh-la.
Young	Hah-grut	Hah-witch-che-pah	Pu-et-dub	Tash-lu-tee.
Good	At	Yah	Pe-sau-you	Tung-ou.
Bad	Hods-at	Ked-yant	Ser-ta-yo	Noh-seh.
Handsome	At-um-boon-e-kah	Sa-na-boo-nit	Pe-sa-tah-wep	Oung-oh-we.
Ugly	Hudy-at-boon-e-kah	Ked-sa-nav-oo-wint	Ser-tah-tah-wep	Na-se-eh.
Alive, life	Kody-e-eye	Ka-de-ite	Yert-sung-oh	Yae-e-gep-see.
Dead	Yae-quah	De-ah	Yah-eph	Yo-leh-ee.
Death	Yae-quah	De-ah	Car-de-ma-nicka	Yo-leh-ee.
Cold	Shoop-pwi	E-gint	Ah-dit-se	Tah-was-ka-me.
Warm	Koo-toor-idy	Kah-shit-come-it	Ah-dit-re	Yo-och-rosh-e.
I	Moon-eh	Ne-ah	Ner	La.
Thou	Oom	Ne-ah-mah	Er	Hah-de.
He	Munk	Ich	See-meh	Wak-la-oh-se.
We	Noomp		Tah	Yes-se.
Ye	Moont		Tah-he	*Same as we.*
They	Mah-pat		Er-mir	Teh-eh.
This	Inch		Esh-su	Weh-de.
That	Match		O-ate	*Same as though.*
All	Mah-noon-e		Ser-wa	Meh-lou.
Many, much	Hab-bon	Shout	E-wa	Kah-kahn.
Who	Hung-e		Ha-goh	Go-de-ah.
Near	Tah-ve-noonk		Za-ko	Tah-wad-eh.
Over	Quand-doo		Ac-qui-nog-wa	Kah-wah.
To-day	Tab-by		Tah-ho	Ah-leah.
Yesterday	Ker-erd		Ee-gee	So-at.
To-morrow	Ate-shook	Po-e-chick	Moh-ha	Wat-le-e-yo-geo.
Yes	Hoo-qua	Osh	Ha-ha	Hea-ha.
No	Kods	Kay-ah	Ki	Ac-tag-go.
And	Tam-me		Toh	Tah.
Times, (Fr. *fois*)	Kodz-in-e-tog-e		Me-no	Coo-yah.
Eat	Tuck-e	Took-she-wan	Tuk-ka	Sam-la-yea.
Drink	He-be	Hope	Hep-pe	Sem-ma-yea.
Run	Tog	No-ke-wie	Po-yo-a	Mo-o-see.
Dance	Wippy	No-ah-gin	Net-ga	Lo-see.
Go	Pi-re-que	Me-ag	Me-ah	Key-you-wa.
Come	Kike	Kim	Ke-mak	Pee-ya.
Sit	Kad-de	Cot	Cot-den	Ka-ka-le.
Stand	Woon-e	Woon	Wer-na	Ga-le-ee.
Sing	Ky-e	Tin-ne-koo-up-pun	Ton-ic-wer	Les-me.
Sleep	Pwee	Up-poo-e	Er-we	Les-she-mo.
Speak	Um-by-e	Ti-oog	Yad-wah	Te-ou-i-a-ge.
See	Pone-ne-keh	Poo-ek	A-bo-ne	To-le-ge-he.
Love	Ash-in-de	Ne-ah-cam-wang-yun	Pe-sana-so-bid	Te-com-ca-cam-see.
Kill	Py	Dots-sa-van	Ha-but-sa	Te-at-ke.
Walk	Pag-a-we	O-wid-dah-me-ah-kin	Me-oh-hoo-gok	At-tey-a-li-yu.
Bury	Too-gwe	Nah-goo-in	Ah-goh	Lem-i-yah-we.
Who is that?	Un-gah-rah	Ah-gin-ne-nau-ne-uk	Ha-ja-ou-sou	Go-ding-ah-hah.

[1] Obtained by Captain Simpson from Pete (Un-go-bah), a Ute Indian, who accompanied him as interpreter.
[2] Obtained by Captain Simpson from Tar-a-ke-gan, a Shoshonee.
[3] Furnished to Captain Simpson by Major Frederick Dodge, Indian agent.
[4] Furnished to Captain Simpson by Major Frederick Dodge, Indian agent.

Vocabulary of Indian words—Continued.

English words.	Ute or Utah.	Shoshonee or Snake.
Cañon[5]	We-wuds	
Cottonwood	Shoyp	
To hunt	Pe-shan-gah	Mah-wake.
To hear		Mo-nan-ge.
Willow	Kan-ahb	
To trade	Nar-a-wop	Un-re-mo.
To talk	On-pah-ger	Tig-ren.

[5] The remaining words in the vocabulary were furnished Captain Simpson by Mr. Bean, interpreter and guide, 1858.

Vocabulary of Indian words—Continued.

English words.	Ute or Utah.	English words.	Ute or Utah.
Smoke	Queep.	Mouse	Widges.
Elk	Par-i-ah.	Cat[6]	Moo-sah.
Fly	Mo-pids.	Cricket	Un-sock.
Eagle	Guon-dich.	Grasshopper	Ahr-an-gige.
Feathers	Pe-ah.	Brier	Man-abb.
Crane	Tch-kore.	To meet	Toi-tia.
Trout, salmon	At-in-pah-gah.	To cook	Si-eh.
Mullet	Oo-bug-gah.	To preach, harangue	Om-par-ro-ah.
Chub	We-pah-gah.	To shoot	Ko-que.
Name	Ne-ah.	To gamble	Nah-a-witch.
Love	Pe-mits.	To hit the mark	We-nahr.
Gun	Tum-bu-you.	To miss the mark	Kar-en-qui.
Powder	Queets-owah.	Be still	Ah-gahr.
Lead	Ooo.	Finger-ring	Pan-a-mar-ger-nump.
Caps	Wun-ou-ad-jip.	Foot of mountain	Kan-ne-gub.
Flour	Tu-shu-kunt.	Side of mountain	Pi-ah-bah.
To tell	Pe-sheth-i-na.	Top of mountain	Wig-ki-bah.
To ask	Mi-bwan.	Sore stinking	Pe-keep.
To write	Po-quint-man-ik.	To put down	Rood-zee.
To travel	Pah-nt.	To hide away	Ah-gah-wod-zee.
To move camp	Me-an-bi-que.	To steal	Ee-ying-ah.
To go home	Pi-que-ban.	To fasten or tie	Tap-itch.
To guide	Me-ar-ogi.	To think or remember	Shu-mivi.
Blanket	Pan-shi-mo.	To make	Man-e-kish.
Want	Ash-en-ta.	To give	Mog-ie.
Sugar	Pe-ar-ai-kunt.	To load a gun	To-wods.
Crooked	No-ko-me.	To burn	Koot-sik-ee.
What kind?	Hag-arrh.	To glean	To-in.
This side	E-nunko.	To quarrel	Wah-am-bah.
The right side	In-en-to.	Where	Kuk-ah-bah.
The left side	Man-en-to.	To strike	Que-pi.
Yonder	Moo-ah.	What is the matter?	Mike.
Here	E-bwah.	I said	Mike-nig.
Away off	Mee.	Fight	Ni-o-que.
Close by	In chock-iba.	Angry	Niah.
Hole	Puk-age.	Nothing	Na-vash.
Whip	Wash-e-nump.	Another	Ko-mush.
Lariat	Tshap.	Looking-glass	Nah-voo-nah.
Meeting, gathering	Shu-par-ro.	To win	Quoi.
Rusty	Nah-shants-pe-nok.	To whip	Wit-te-push.
To go on foot	Nam-pah-ut.	To kindle a fire	Koo-ne-ni-te. Koo-neen, yi-te.
To go on horseback	Ko-wi-yo-tspee.	To rub	We-toots-pe-nok.
To lay down	Ah-bee.	To grow	Nau-ni, nau-yi.
To get up	Quer-i-ka.	To cut	Tskebin.
To sit down	Kar-e-wah.	To dig	Ho-ri-eh.
To camp	Me-a-bitch.	Handkerchief	Koo-ret-a-shap.
What for?	Ah-kon-de-ga.	Ramrod	Tskuri-nump.
May be or probably	Um-pug-go.	Flint	Wou-nup.
Cedar	Wahp.	Dry	Tab-ash-e-guipe.
Piñon, pine	Teh-up.	Wet or miry	Pah-we-up.
Pine nut	To-won.	Wagon	Oo-yem-bung-go.
Fir, balsam	Ohmp.	Canteen	O-chalts.
A spring	Tspe-kin.	Brass kettle	Woker-pam-pou-a.
Awl	We-uds.		

[6] The word for Cat given by Mr. Bean is Mo-pids. As he gives the same word for Fly, I have taken the word Moo-sah, which is given for cat, from the vocabulary of Ute words in Captain Simpson's "Journal of a Reconnaissance in New Mexico in 1849." (See Ex. Doc. No. 64, Senate, Thirty-first Congress, first session, page 142.)

Vocabulary of Indian words—Continued.

English words.	Ute or Utah.	English words.	Ute or Utah.
Middle of a thing	Toi-teo-re-roup-punt.	A few	Nan-e-soos.
Cane grass	Pah-gamp.	To shake hands	Moot-sic.
Wire grass	Soe-neep.	To smoke tobacco	Quot-tik-ub-bah.
Coarse grass	O-won-eh.	To go slow	Shan, eep-pah-nt.
To laugh	O-kee-ung-kah.	Midnight	To-i-to-wun.
To cry	Yog-ie.	To-day	Ahp-tab-i.
To kick	Tang-ie.	Time past	Etish.
To take	Kwee.	Now	Ahb.
To catch	Tsie.	After awhile	Pe-nun-ko.
To lasso	We-tsung-ga-wunk.	Very	Tu-ege.
To drive	Tow-washo.	What	Ump-wah.
To herd	Poo-ne-woo-ne.	When	An-oke.
Crow or raven	At-tok-nuts.	Truth	Shumb.
Wolf, (small)	Yodes.	Lie	Tu-ish-er-a.
Backbone	Ho-app.	Horse	Ko-wi-yo.
Ribs	Ow-at-in-bope.	Saddle	Kart-e-nump.
Money, silver	To-shau-pan-a-kañe.	Bridle	Tim-bi-up.
Gold	Waw-pan-a-kañe.	Spur	Tang-i-nump.
Skin or hide	Pove-ah.	Ox	Gets-m-bun-go.
To trot	Pove-yah.	Thick	To-mun-ter.
To gallop	A-po-nah.	Thin	Ko-puk-age.
To stop	Ar-rik-in.	Fat	Yope.
Up above	Pan-unk.	Lean	Kan-n-bitts.
Down below	Pat-sau-unk.	Rich	At-t-nooch.
Say	Ah.	Poor	Tah-gah-pids.
Enough	Oo-na-shump.	Noon	To-i-tab.
Just like	To-an-ow-er.	Cow	Peads-guets-m.
Together	Now-ah.	Horn	Op.
Shirt	Tah.	Cup	Pan-a-koots.
Coat	To-mun-ter-tah.	Spoon	Munt-sook.
Pantaloons	Pemo.	Corn	Koo-me.
Vest	Nah-voo.	Wheat	O-wee-bi.
Leggins	Koose.	Potatoes	We-choon.
Hat	Ki-cho-che.	Squash	Par-ang-ah.
Fall	Pant.	Melon	Shon-ti-kut.
Short	To-bwik-ah.	Sweet	Pe-og-o-munt.
Long	Pa-out.	Sour	Shig-un-tug.
Heavy	Put-te-ant.	Full	Pat-suk-unt.
Light	To-be-puds.	Empty or all gone	To-pit-wa.
To fly	Widge-gue-nung.	Hungry	Tig-i-na-ra.
To understand	Pe-su-ge-wa.	Thirsty	Tong-oou-yay.
All the time	Te-shump.	Sack	Quon-up.

Sentences in English and Utah.

English.	Ute or Utah.
Friend, what do you call this?	Tick-a-boo an-a-ne ah-inch?
I do not know	Tami-i-kotch pe-su-ge-wa.
Where are you going?	Um huk-ah-ba pi-qua?
I am hunting horses	Tam ko-wi-yos' pe-shaw-ger.
May be I saw them yesterday	Um-pug-go tam kuhn poo-in-ka.
Where? do tell me	Huk-ah-bah-oo ish pe-sheth-i-na.
Yonder, the other side of the mountain	Mov-ah inch-kibe quan-ko-up.
I am very hungry	Tam-i-tu-eye tiz-u-na-ra.
I have plenty; you eat with me	Tam hov-on kar-re um-now-ah ti-ki.
Very well, my friend	Tu-ege toy tik-a-bun.
When will you come back?	Um an-oke pe-nun-ko-pe-jee?
May be in one month	Um-pug-go-soos mat-och-yay.
Where will you camp to-night?	Un huk-ah-bah me-a-bitch ahp-to-wun?
Here, close by the spring	E-bwah su-chock-i-ba tspe-kin.
Where is the next water?	Huk-ah-bah ko-mush pah-kar-re?
Yonder, in the middle of the valley	Morah toi-ter-re-wup-punt inch u-ab.
Is there another good road?	Ko-mush at poh-kar-re-ah?
Yes, up this cañon	Oo-wah inch we-wuds pen-unk.
I am now going	Tam ahp pi-qua.
I say give me some bread	Oo-ash-ah tsho-tik-up mo-gie.
I have none; it is all gone	Kats-kar-re-mon-ona tu-pik-wa.
Who ate it all?	Aug-i mon-oke tik-ie?
Your father and mother	Um mo-ants pe-ads non-ah.
It is snowing now	Ahp new-ahp pi-eke.
After, be very cold	Pe-nun-ko tu-ege shu-pe-ki.

Indian numerals.

English.	Ute or Utah.	Shoshonee or Snake.	Pi-Ute.	Washo.	I-at.[7]
1	Shu-ge	Shu-wah	Sur-in	Sac-ka	As-see-to.
2	Wy-in	Wat-too	Wa-ha-you	Has-sla	A-be-ka.
3	Py-in	Pite	Pa-he	Hel-ma	Amo-ko.
4	Whatz-o-win	Wats-so-wit	Wat-se-que	Hah-wha	See-po-po.
5	Man-a-gin	Mah-ne-git	Man-e-ke	To-bal-a-de	Ar-rap-pah.
6	Nah-bah-in	Nah-vite	Na-pa-he	To-bal-do-dal-lau	Ah-seen.
7	Nah-vah-keh-ve	Tah-so-rit	Toc-et-se-gue	To-bal-de-da-bas-ka	Ah-been.
8	Wah-waty-so-vin	Wah-sho-wit	Wo-que-e-gue	To-bal-de-hel-ma	Ah-mo-gue.
9	Show-rump-shin	Shu-wa-ker-ru	Su-me-cot-e-up	Loc-a-lo-le	Pye.
10	Tomb-sho-vin	Sher-wan-it	Su-me-man-a	Loc-a-mo-chum	Hear-a-pye.

[7] The I-at numerals were furnished by Mr. Bean.

Indian numerals—Continued.

English.	Ute or Utah.	Shoshonee or Snake.
11	Shoots-spin-gle	Sher-win-do-in-gin.
12	Wy-in-spin-gle	Wat-te-men-do-in-gin.
13	Py-in-spin-gle	Py-te-to-men-do-in-gin.
20	Wamp-shu-in	Wah-ah-man-it.
21	Ny-in tom-shu-spingle	Wah-ah-man-it-shu-mut-do-in-gin.
22	Ny-in-spingle	Wah-ah-man-it-wat-too-nah-do-in-gin.
30	Pamb-shu-in	Pite-he-man-it.
40	Watz-oo-in-tom-shu-in	Wats-se-won-man-it.
50	Man-e-gin-shu-in	Man-e-gin-man-it.
60	Nah-vam-shu-in	Nah-vah-man-it.
70	Nah-ve-kab-shu-in	Tats-se-won-man-it.
80	Wah-watz-oo-in-tom-shu-in	Wah-she-woon-man-it.
90	Shar-am-shu-in-shu-in-shu-in	She-woon-ne-man-it.
100	Shu-man-tom-shu-in	She-woon-ne-man-it.
1,000	Man-um-tom-shu-in	She-woon-men-do-gin-man-it.

English.	Pi-Ute.	Washo.
11	Su-me-mot-se-po-ke	Tey-yak-loc-a-mo-chum.
12	Wa-ha-mot-se-po-ke	Heska.
13	Pa-he-mot-se-po-ke	Hel-ma.
20	Wa-ha-man-o	Hes-ka-mo-chum.
21	Wa-ha-man-o-su-met-se-wick	Loc-a-te-a.
22	Wa-ha-man-sit se-wick-it	Hes-ka-te-a.
30	Pa-he-man-o	Hel-ma-mo-chum.
40	Wat-se-man-o-e	Hah-wah-mo-chum.
50	Man-e-ke-man-o-e	To-bal-de-mo-chum.
60	Na-pa-e-man-o-e	To-bal-de-dal-coh-mo-mo-chum.
70	Na-toc-se-man-o-e	To bal-de-dal-has-ka-mo-chum.
80	Wo-que-se-que-man-o-e	Ha-wa-wa-mo-chum.
90	Se-ma-cat-a-spa-man-o-e	Loc-i-lo-le-mo-chum.
100	Su-a-man o-nem-ena-a	Loc-a-mo-chum-mo-chum.
1,000	Su-a-man-o-nem-ena-a-len-a	Loc-a-mo-chum-mo-chum-mo-chum.

APPENDIX Q.

JOURNAL

OF

MR. EDWARD M. KERN

OF AN

EXPLORATION OF MARY'S OR HUMBOLDT RIVER, CARSON LAKE, AND OWENS RIVER AND LAKE,

IN

1845.

APPENDIX Q.

JOURNAL OF MR. EDWARD M. KERN OF AN EXPLORATION OF THE MARY'S OR HUMBOLDT RIVER, CARSON LAKE, AND OWENS RIVER AND LAKE, IN 1845.

WASHINGTON, *September* 10, 1860.

SIR: In compliance with your request for information regarding a portion of the route pursued by the expedition to the Rocky Mountains and California under command of Capt. J. C. Frémont, in the year 1845, I inclose you a copy of my journal, which you are at liberty, if it will be in any way serviceable to you, to make such use of as you may think fit.

Truly, your obedient servant,

EDW. M. KERN.

Capt. J. H. SIMPSON,
U. S. Corps Topographical Engineers.

November 5, 1845.—Whitten's Spring. To-day we parted company, the captain passing to the southward with a small party, to examine that portion of the Great Basin supposed to be a desert, lying between the Sierra Nevada and the Rocky Mountains. The main body of the camp, under the guidance of Mr. Joseph Walker, are to move toward the head of Mary's or Ogden's River, and down that stream to its sink or lake. From thence to Walker's Lake, where we are again to meet. I am to accompany the latter party in charge of the topography, &c. Crossing the mountains near our camp, we arrived about 1 o'clock p. m. at several springs of excellent water. These springs spread into a large marsh, furnishing an abundant supply of good grass for the animals. On the 6th, owing to a severe snow-storm, we were obliged to remain in camp. Having no timber but a few green cedars, fires were not very abundant.

On the 7th we commenced our ascent by a steep and rocky road. The snow was falling lightly when we started, but before we reached the summit, we were nearly blinded by the storm. A short descent brought us into a pleasant valley, well watered by several small streams, and timbered with aspen and cottonwood. This is, really, a beautiful spot, surrounded by high mountains, those on the west covered with snow. Crossing a low range of hills, we entered another valley, that takes its waters from the snowy mountains on either side. The stream, after winding among the grass-covered hills, emerges into a plain, through which we could see Ogden's River flowing. Walker has given this creek the name of Walnut Creek, from one of his trappers having brought into his camp a twig of that tree found near its head; a tree scarcely known so far west as this. Camped on Walnut Creek, having made 14½ miles.

November 8.—At about 6 miles from our camp of last night, we struck Ogden's River. It is about 25 feet wide here and about 2 feet deep, with a tolerable current. Crossing without difficulty, we struck the emigrant wagon-trail. Continuing down it for a few miles, we encamped a little below where the river receives a tributary of considerable size, coming from the northwest. Made to-day about 14 miles.

November 9.—Still on the emigrant trail. This has proved of great assistance to our tired animals; they appear to have new life. Met to-day several Sho-sho-nee Indians, who report three separate parties of emigrants having passed this fall. About four miles above our camp of to-night are some hot springs, too hot to bear one's hand in. Walnut Creek empties into the river about 1½ miles below our camp. Made 19 miles.

November 10.—Crossed the river several times. At one point, the high, rocky ridges that bound the bottom came so close to the banks of the river, we were obliged to pass in the water. The timber is principally cottonwood.

November 11.—We left the river to avoid a bend it makes. Ascending some grassy hills, encamped at several springs. Bunch-grass plenty; 11 miles.

November 12.—Continued among the hills for about five miles, when we again struck the river. The country is becoming more open. The hills on the right make a wide sweep from the river, returning to it again at our camp of this evening, November 13. On the left bank the mountains are close and high and rugged in their character. Near our camp on this bank they make a bend forming a valley, through which one would suppose the river to flow. The character of the rocks is changing; more bold, basaltic.

The river presents but little variety, always the same winding, crooked stream. On the 23d November, we arrived at the sink or lake. This lake is about 8 miles long by 2 in width; it is marshy, overgrown with bulrushes, at the upper end. On the eastern side is a range of low hills at the upper, and increasing in height at the lower end of the lake. On the western side is a level plain of clay mixed with sand. The country here becomes more desolate in its appearance. We have been fifteen days on this river, making a distance of nearly 200 miles. The grass has been generally good. The only timber is a few cottonwood trees and willows; the latter are in great abundance on its banks, though very small. The river-bottoms vary from 4 to 20 miles in width. Vegetation failing as we approach the sink, the soil becoming more sandy and sterile. The Indians we first met were better clad than one would suppose; having also a few horses among them. As we approached the sink, however, they appeared much more indigent and shy, hiding from us on our approach; raising smokes and other signs of warning to their friends of the approach of strangers. They belong to the Bannack tribe of Diggers, and are generally badly disposed toward the whites. Walker was attacked some two years since by a party of them numbering, he thought, near 600; these he defeated without loss to his own party. The loss on the part of the Indians numbered 16. Walker was engaged at that time exploring for a route into California, through the Sierra Nevada.

A curious feature of this river is the number of small streams near its banks and immediately in its bed. We tried the temperature of one on the 10th instant with a thermometer graduated to 160°, to which point the mercury rose in a few seconds. From its situation, forming as it does a long line of travel of the emigrant parties, this river will soon become an interesting and noted point in this now great wilderness. Portions of its immediate bottoms may be capable of cultivation; but the bare, sandy bluffs that surround or border it, produce little save bunch-grass, and no timber. Great numbers of ducks and geese are to be found in this region. A small gray duck is of excellent flavor. Provisions becoming scarce. Leaving our camp of the 24th November, on the outlet of the lake, we crossed a low, gravelly ridge, mixed with heavy sand, for 4 or 5 miles; we then struck a level plain resembling the dry bed of a lake, extending to a low range of hills on the western side 10 or 12 miles distant, and from 20 to 25 miles on the eastern side, running in a northeasterly direction, and continuing east of Ogden's or Mary's Lake, probably connecting with some of the high ranges visible from the river on the 18th and 19th. As on the plains on the western side of the Great Salt Lake, the incrustation yielded to the tread of our horses. Nothing can appear worse than the surrounding country; the glare of the white sand, relieved only by the rugged distant mountains, the absence of animal and vegetable life, make up a whole in the way of dreariness and desolation.

The outlet of Ogden's Lake, after running several miles toward the rim of this basin, forms a large marsh in the midst of the sand-hills. Our animals failing, we encamped among the sand-hills, without grass or water.

November 25.—A couple of hours' ride this morning brought us to the outlet of another lake, where we encamped, having ridden twenty-five miles. The water in this stream is running, but is indifferently good. The banks are from 8 to 10 feet high; growth willow. Sand-hills on either side. On the east runs a low rocky range, beyond which are ridges and peaks of higher mountains. About eight miles below us this stream forms a large marsh, hidden from us by sand-hills. Walker tells me that its waters are extremely disagreeable. I found skulls of the natives killed here by Walker's party some ten years since. The emigrants turn toward the California Mountains from the sink of Ogden's River. After a noon halt and rest to our animals, we crossed and continued down the river, camping near the lake.

November 26.—In a southeasterly direction nine miles along the border of the lake. For 30 or 40 yards about its edge in width is a thick growth of bulrushes. It is a very pretty sheet of water; various kinds of fowl in abundance. The greatest length is about 11 miles. On the eastern side runs a low range of burnt rock hills. The lake is bounded on the west by a low range of mountains; about midway on the western side a stream enters it. Slightly timbered; probably cottonwood.

November 27.—In a southern course, over a level for about 3 miles, then crossing a low ridge of sand and burnt rock down an open ravine, leading into a larger plain, we made camp among the sand-hills, at some Indian wells of bad water, thoroughly impregnated with sulphur. These wells, with a little trouble, could be made a good watering-place; but, as they now are, it was with the greatest difficulty that we could procure a sufficiency for our animals. There was plenty of good bunch-grass about camp; no fuel but greasewood. Continuing our route over low, heavy sand-hills, we rejoined Captain Frémont at our place of rendezvous, Walker's Lake. He had reached that point four days ahead of us, having traveled over a mountainous country, finding in his route plenty of grass, water, game, and Indians; the latter very shy, not being accustomed to the sight of white men in their desolate country. The river of Walker's Lake is a fine, bold stream, 30 to 40 feet wide, with considerable current, timbered with fine large cottonwoods, its bottoms covered with a luxuriant growth of grass, wild peas, and rushes. We had anticipated a glorious feast of fish on our arrival at this point, from the glowing descriptions Walker had given us of great quantities of fine salmon-trout which frequent the river and lake. In this, however, we were doomed to disappointment. The fishing season being over, "Carro hoggi" was the only reply we could obtain to our many signs and inquiries after the finny tribe from the few Indians that still lingered about the lake.

To-morrow (November 29) Captain Frémont leaves us again, this time to take his old trail of 1843, while the main body of camp will continue down the eastern slope of the Sierra Nevada, which Walker had discovered when exploring this section of the country some 10 years ago. We will remain here 9 or 10 days to recruit our animals, as many of them are exhausted.

December 8.—Once more took up our line of march. During our stay at our camp on Walker's River the weather has been clear and cold. Thermometer at sunset 23° above zero, and at sunrise 4°. The river frozen hard; it has been a strange mixture of winter and summer. The Indians are of a much lower grade than any I have yet seen. They are, however, very friendly. I visited some of their huts near the mouth of the river. They had some very pretty decoy-ducks, made from the skin of those birds, neatly stretched over a bulrush float. There were four or five old women hovering over a fire of a few willow twigs of six or eight inches in length. I thought if the personification of witches ever existed, these were of them. Their withered bodies, almost entirely naked and emaciated, their faces smeared with dirt and tar, the dull, idiotic stare of their eyes, trembling from cold and dread of our intentions toward them, rendered them to me the most pitiable objects I had ever seen. A couple of children, nestling close to the fire, showed more the signs of wonder in their countenances than fear. Some of these children, notwithstanding the hardships of their lives, only dependent on grass-seeds and the few fish they can catch, any large game being unknown hereabouts, have really lively and interesting countenances; but the expression leaves them with youth; their future, being one of continued privation, soon dulls the light of the eye, and the face becomes heavy and stolid in expression. It was at this camp we have made our first essay on horse-meat. Throwing aside all antipathies I, with the others, enjoyed our meal. On this river, with but a couple of exceptions, is the only *large* timber we have met since leaving the Timpanogos. Traveling three miles on the river and about twelve on the shores of the lake, we made our camp among some low sand-hills. A range of burnt rock hills extends a few miles further back, while on the opposite side of the lake the dark mountains come bluff to the water's edge. No fuel but greasewood and grass. We longed heartily for the fires of our last ten-days' camp, the weather being excessively cold.

December 9.—Camped near the head of the lake. No grass; the water exceedingly bad and salty. Charley, (our cook,) to improve (?) the already horrid taste given to our coffee by the bad water, added some greasewood or other noxious weed, giving it a flavor too unsavory even for appetites as keen-set as ours. This lake is about twenty-two miles in length, and eleven or twelve in the widest part. To the eastward of our camp runs a valley. About twelve miles down it Walker says he found springs of good water and an abundance of good grass, the springs forming a small lake. To-night the horses, driven to desperation by their bad fare, a large number of them eluding the vigilance of the guard escaped to the other side of the lake, where they were found in the morning, having discovered somewhat better grass than we had at our camp.

December 10.—Leaving camp we traveled up a valley leading from the southern end of Walker's Lake, a little east of south; at about eight miles we crossed a low ridge, heavy sand and scattering bunch-grass. Traveling up the general direction of a ravine, in a southeasterly course for about six miles, we made camp late at some springs near the foot of a basaltic rock ridge.

December 11.—Continued our route down the valley in a southerly direction. Walker's trail of two years ago passed to the left of our camp three or four miles. Passed several wells dug by the Indians, but they were dry. Also, a large corral or pen made of sage and cedars for the purpose of ensnaring deer. Continued about six miles into the mountains by a rough and broken road. Were unable to find water. In the evening we encamped among some of the largest sage I have ever seen. This gave us an abundance of fuel, and also served us in constructing pens about our different camp-fires as a protection from the cold. We soon forgot in slumber our lack of water Here we killed our last beef, if what was left of the animal could be dignified by such a name.

December 12.—To-day we obtained a fine view of the great Sierra Nevada from the far north till it faded on the distant horizon far to the south of us. This bold and rocky barrier, with its rugged peaks, separates us from the valley of California. We are to travel along its base till by its lessening height it will offer but a slight obstacle to our passage across it. To the southeast and east of us mountain rises beyond mountain as far as the eye can see. Descending by a break-neck road we reached, toward evening, a small valley, where we made camp. We found a portion of the sand leveled very smooth and some willow hoops lying about, with fresh signs to convince us that the place had not long been vacated by a party of Indians.

December 13.—Still among the burnt rock hills, interspersed with grassy valleys. Descending into a large, open, grassy valley, we fed upon the dry bed of a stream that has both wood and water six or seven miles farther up. Camped at a large spring that spreads into a marsh.

December 14.—Traveled down the same valley. Water rises and sinks, breaking through a rocky ridge to the east; rising again in several cold springs at the entrance of the gap, runs a short distance and forms a stinking lake. Crossing the ridge by an Indian trail, we came into another valley watered by a fine warm stream, in which I took a delightful bath. Good grass and plenty—quite a treat for our tired animals.

The boys brought in some roots they had found near a couple of Indian huts, the inmates having fled at their approach. The root was of some water-plant of good flavor. They were plaited together in ropes, something after the manner of doing up onions at home. Our old cook at fault again to-day, boiling a large piece of rosin soap in our coffee. Rather unlucky just now, when coffee is coffee.

December 15.—The same water of yesterday still finds its way into another valley more to the east. We crossed into this. Its greatest length is from north to south. On the eastern side is a high chain of mountains, about the height of those on eastern side of Utah Lake. The mountains throw out some small streams, which sink before they fairly reach the valley. The road in the forenoon of to-day broken and sandy. We have gained four days on Walker's route of 1843, from camp of December 10 to this place. A better route lies to the right of our road.

December 16.—To-day struck Owen's River. It is a fine, bold stream, larger than Walker's. The same chain of mountains bounds it on the east, while on the western side rises, like a wall, the main chain of the California Mountains. Our rations are becoming extremely scant. The men being all on foot, they feel their appetites much quickened by the additional exercise of walking. A few more days we hope will bring us to the land of plenty.

December 17 and 18.—Still on the river; obliged to keep some distance from it on account of a large marsh. Wild-fowl in abundance. Walker went in search of some salt, which he found, incrusted to the thickness of a quarter of an inch on the surface of the earth. The Indians are numerous here, though they keep out of our sight. They are badly disposed. Colonel Childs had trouble with them here. They shot one of his men. Walker's party killed some twenty-five of them, while on his side some of his men were wounded and eight or nine horses killed.

December 19.—Camped on lake near the mouth of river. Grass poor Ducks and geese plentiful.

December 20. Traveling down the lake. Main California Mountains close on our right within half a mile of us. This lake is somewhat irregular in its shape, lying north and south; is about fifteen miles long, the widest part about seven miles. On the western side there are several capes. It is surrounded by high mountains. Water strong, disagreeable, salty, nauseous taste. There are Indian fires among the rocks within half a mile of us. None ventured nearer. They appear to be well supplied with horses, judging from the quantity of sign. Along the route of to-day we crossed several streams coming from the mountains, some of them dry; all slightly timbered with cottonwood.

December 21.—Leaving lower end of lake, we passed among some sandy hollows, falling into a larger ravine leading south. Passing a good camp for grass and water, the hollow narrowed, bounded by hills of minutely broken black rock, opening afterward into a large plain; camped at some springs on the slope of the main California Mountains; grass, fresh and green, owing to the late rains. To-day we met for the first time the yuca tree, nicknamed by the men "Jeremiah," in lieu of some better title. These trees have a grotesque appearance, a straight trunk, guarded about its base by long bayonet-shaped leaves; its irregular and fantastically shaped limbs give to it the appearance of an ancient candelabra. It bears a beautiful white flower. We passed to-day Child's caché, where, on account of his animals failing, he was obliged to bury the contents of his wagons, among which was a complete set of mill-irons.

December 22.—Passed to-day a salt-lake, half a mile long and about 200 yards wide; leaving this, we turned up a large hollow, for about four miles, to find a camp. At this point there may be a pass over the mountains, judging from the number of Indian trails joining together here. The ascent, however, is very steep, and it was judged advisable not to attempt it, our animals not being in a condition to undergo any such experiments. So we continued our route in a southerly direction, among the foot-hills of the mountains.

December 23 *and* 24.—Still among the hills. On the 23d, a mule was lost, with its pack. Archambeau, Stradspeth, and White were sent back in search of it; returned on the evening of the 24th, with the animal. The mule was loaded with, to us, a very valuable cargo, sugar and coffee, with some of the "possibles," of Stradspeth and White. The mule had wandered up one of the many ravines in the hillsides. When the Indians were discovered, they were sitting very coolly among the rocks, where they had driven the mule, dividing the spoils; there were three of them. Of the sugar they had made a just division, but the coffee was to them perfectly useless. They had already charred and pounded it, without coming to any satisfactory conclusion as to its use. The "possibles" shared the same fate as the eatables. Among the articles a blanket and an overcoat. Being three in their party, and being unable to divide these things equally in any other way, one had taken the blanket, and tearing the coat in two, gave a half of it to each of the others. On our men showing themselves, they fled precipitately, leaving the property behind. Collecting and re-arranging the pack, the men started for camp, bringing with them, as proof of their victory, some bows and arrows, a large sack of sage-seed, about as digestible as sand, and a small sack of some compound, which we could not make out; it was very palatable with coffee, of a dark chocolate color.*

Our Christmas was spent in a most unchristmas-like manner. Our camp was made on the slope of the mountain, at some Indian wells of good water. The yuca tree is here in great abundance, furnishing us a plentiful supply of fuel. The camp-fires blazed and cracked joyously, the only merry things about us, and all that had any resemblance to that merry time at home. The animals, on account of grass, were guarded about a quarter of a mile from camp, higher up the mountain.

December 25.—Christmas day opened clear and warm. We made our camp to-day at some springs among the rocks; but little grass for our animals. Dined to-day, by way of a change, on one of our tired, worn mules, instead of a horse.

Turning from our camp of the 25th into the mountain by an easy ascent, and over a somewhat broken road, arriving on the 27th, on the head-waters of a river.† Continuing down this stream, on the 28th we made camp at its forks. This is the appointed place of rendezvous. There are no signs yet of the Captain. Our pro-

---

*I have seen the same dish among the Indians of California; it is prepared from roasted grasshoppers and large crickets, pounded up, and mixed with, when procurable, some kind of animal grease.

†Now called Kern River.

visions have entirely failed; save the few remaining horses of our cavallada, there was not much prospect of obtaining fresh supplies. To have killed these would have been to deprive us of the means of transportation of our effects and the results of the expedition, in case we are not joined by Captain Frémont in this place. A party of Indians visited our camp, from whom we traded a colt. The hunters brought in a few small deer, the meat extremely poor. A small piece of vension, with as much cold water as one could drink, furnished breakfast, dinner, and supper in one. We became reduced to acorns, and on this swinish food made our New-Year's feast. This forms the principal food of the natives, here and in the valley. Our camp is situated in a beautiful valley, about six miles in length, and well-timbered with pine, cedars, and cottonwood, while the mountains which surround it are of the usual growth of the Sierra, the majestic redwood, &c. The river is a bold stream, coming from the northeast. The Indians inhabiting this region are of the most degraded class, entirely naked, and with scarcely a sufficiency of food to sustain life. I was amused at coming suddenly on a half a dozen of these characters; being armed, they, probably having a dread of pistols, immediately commenced crossing themselves in the most devout manner, at the same time muttering "Christiano, Christiano," the probable extent of their Spanish, hoping to avert any evil intent we might have had toward them.

Since leaving Walker's Lake we have traveled through a country having a few pretty spots, but for the most part a sandy waste, broken by short chains and isolated mountains. Bunch-grass is found among most of the sand-hills. Water, save in the rivers, is not to be had in anything like a sufficiency. Piñon and willow are the principal timbers. From our camp of December 26, toward the south, as far as the eye could reach, lay a continued plain of sand, relieved only by an occasional hill of burnt rock rearing itself above the level, adding, if possible, to the desolation of the scene, with no game, save now and then a hare, and perchance a stray goat. Lizards are here in abundance, and form the principal food of the hungry natives. At our camp the weather has been extremely fine, warm, and sunshine. On the 13th of January there was a severe storm of snow and sleet; a shower followed that soon removed all appearance of winter from the valley, but the mountains retained this, their first winter covering.

January 18, 1846.—Raised camp and traveled about five miles into the mountains, stopping for the night at the hunter's camp, in a pretty valley; snow about two feet deep. An abundance of the most beautiful timber, live-oak, pine, redwood, &c.

January 19.—To-day we reached the summit; snow 2½ feet deep. From here we had the first view of the much-wished-for Valley of California. It lay beneath us, bright in the sunshine, gay and green, while about us everything was clothed in the chilly garb of winter.

On the 21*st January* we reached the valley; our descent was rough and broken; the mountain well watered and densely timbered. Among the foot-hills are beautiful groves of live and other oaks, clear from growth of underwood; the fine grass gives the country the appearance of a well-kept park. We passed two Indian villages; the huts were built of tulé or bulrush. The men entirely naked; the only covering the women possessed was a kind of petticoat made of tulé. The country is much cut up by gullies. The weather is warm like spring, the young grass and some few flowers just putting forth. Notice a small blue flower particularly very abundant.

Crossing several small streams that find their way into the great Tulare Lake, we encamped, on the evening of the 26th of January, on a fine bold stream.* The whole country is well watered, and capable of high cultivation. Oaks and willows in abundance. The river† heads in the Sierra Nevada, running in a west, a little south, and then in a southerly direction. Walker thinking to make a cut-off at the bend, we were obliged to spend a most uncomfortable night at some holes of water, amid a storm of cold rain, with no fuel save a few willows.

January 28.—After searching in vain for the river, we camped, at 9 o'clock at night, among the foot-hills of the Coast range, without grass, water, or fire, having traveled through immense fields of old tulé, the horses sinking at almost every step as deep as their bellies; having to be hauled out only to sink again, owing to the loose rotten soil. This has been the most tedious day we have had since we entered the valley, and particularly trying to our animals in their present weak state. Cloudy and rainy all day.

January 29.—Leaving our miserable camp of last night early this morning, we struck a northerly course, passing a large dry creek timbered with cottonwood, over a plain destitute of vegetation (the grass and shrubbery having been destroyed by the wild horses), we made camp on a large slough.‡ Manuel, to-day, killed a fat wild horse—as acceptable a thing as could have happened, as we were out of meat, and had been so for two days.

January 30.—Continuing down the slough for four or five miles, we struck a bold stream—the San Joaquin. It is heavily timbered with oak and willow. Wild horses and elk begin to show themselves.

February 1.—Jim Connor and Wetowa (two Delawares) tracked a large grizzly bear to his thicket. The whole camp prepared themselves for the attack: after much difficulty, he was killed. This animal was one of the largest size; he must have weighed at least 900 pounds. This acquisition to our larder enlivened the spirits of the men, and mirth abounded at the various camp-fires that night; the song and joke, the accompaniments of plenty in the wilderness, could be heard everywhere.

Continuing up the valley toward Suter's fort, on the 6th we arrived and made camp on the Calaveras, a tributary of the San Joaquin. Messrs. Fabbol and Walker started on ahead to hear if they could obtain any tidings of Captain Frémont. They returned again in the evening in company with Big Fallen, an old mountaineer, known more commonly by the sobriquet of "Le Gros." From him we learned that the captain was at the pueblo of San José with the rest of his camp. The next morning Fallen and Walker started for the pueblo to give him intelligence of our whereabouts, while we would return to the crossing of the San Joaquin to await further orders. Yesterday Jim Secondi (a Delaware) killed another bear, the counterpart of the one killed on the 1st instant.

* The Rio Reyes, or Lake Fork.

† Walker mistook this river for the South Fork of the San Joaquin.

‡ This slough, at high water, connects the waters of the San Joaquin with the great Tulare Lake.

February 11.—To-day we were joined by Carson and Owens, at the crossing. Crossing the river in boats or rafts, made of tulé.

February 15.—To-day we met a party of the boys with fresh horses, sent out to meet us. We passed through the pueblo of San José. The country between the pueblo and the Calaveras is beautiful, and well suited for cultivation; the streams are well timbered with different species of oaks. The flowering season is commencing, adding great beauty to the plains, by their variegated colors. The mission of San José is about twelve miles from the town, situated at the foot of a mountain, on the road from the crossing of the San Joaquin. It was formerly one of the richest missions in the upper country; it presents now but a poor appearance, and shows the evil resulting from the removal of the padres, whose posts were replaced by rapacious "administradors" of government. The building is very large and built of adobes; the roof is of tiles. Long rows of adobe buildings, one story high, used as the dwellings of the native converts, are now in a most dilapidated condition, scarcely affording shelter for the few miserable Indians who still cling to those hearths, where they had been raised, by the kindness of the founders, to something like civilization. The remains of the gardens and vineyards show the care and labor bestowed on the grounds by the fathers. Opposite to the mission, on an eminence, is the Campo Santro; the entrance to it is surmounted by a large cross. From here we can see an arm of the bay of San Francisco. The pueblo of San José is a small town of some 50 or 60 houses, most of them in a very crumbling condition, showing the slothful habits of the people. We arrived about noon at the "Laguna farm," where we rejoined Captain Frémont, who was anxiously awaiting our arrival. Both parties were again united, without any serious accident having happened to either, and both had had their share of hard times.

NOTE.—When separating from Captain F. on Walker's Lake, Walker had given a description of the valley of California, where a river which he *supposed* to be the Rio Reyes (and on which we encamped from the 27th of December till the 18th of January, 1846, the same which is now called Kern's River), enters the valley, the description and the rude map which I made from it, answered to the markings of the country very well. Supposing we had entered the valley at the river Reyes, we crossed the several small streams that find their way into the Tulare Lake, and when reaching the Lake Fork or Rio Reyes, he (Walker) fancied himself on the South Fork of San Joaquin. I remember Walker's telling me that the river made a great bend to the southward, and to make a cut-off, we left its banks, and in expectation of again meeting it, traveled till we found ourselves climbing the Coast range. Walker had fallen into the error on a previous trip years ago, and had, in search of the river, crossed the Coast range toward Monterey. On his return trip he left the country by a more southern pass in the Sierra, which Captain Frémont calls Walker's pass. Walker's old pass was to the northward of this by what is now called Kern River. The mistake Walker made in the name of the river on which we had camped to wait for Captain Frémont was the cause of his failure to make a junction with us, as had been prearranged, at Walker's Lake; Captain Frémont, as will be found by his memoir of 1848, having ascended the Rio Reyes (proper) in search of our party.

E. M. K.

APPENDIX R.

JOURNEYINGS

OF

FATHER ESCALANTE,

FROM

SANTA FÉ TO UTAH LAKE AND THE MOQUI VILLAGES IN 1776.

BY

PHILIP HARRY.

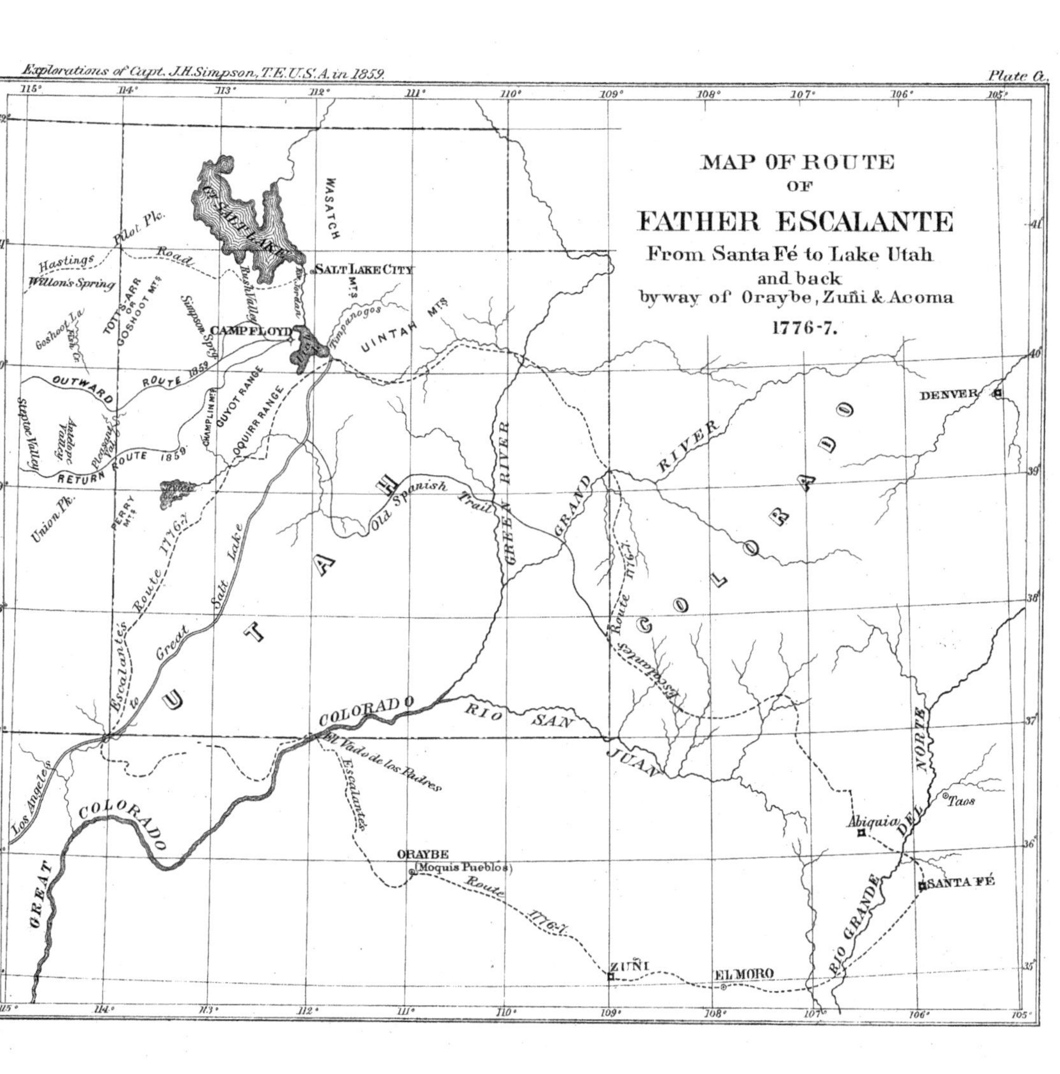
MAP OF ROUTE
OF
FATHER ESCALANTE
From Santa Fé to Lake Utah
and back
by way of Oraybe, Zuñi & Acoma
1776-7.
Gt. Salt Lake
Salt Lake City
Camp Floyd
Wasatch Mts.
Uintah Mts.
Timpanogos
Pilot Pk.
Hastings Road
Willow's Spring
Goshoot La.
Totts-arr or Goshoot Mts.
Simpson Spr.
Bush Valley
Jordan
Outward Route 1859
Return Route 1859
Steptoe Valley
Antelope Valley
Pleasant Valley
Champlin Mts.
Guyot Range
Oquirr Range
Union Pk.
Perry Mts.
Escalante's Route 1776-7
Great Salt Lake to Los Angeles
Old Spanish Trail
U T A H
Green River
Grand River
Colorado
Rio San Juan
El Vado de los Padres
Escalante's
Great Colorado
Oraybe (Moquis Pueblos)
Route 1776-7.
Zuñi
El Moro
Rio Grande del Norte
Abiquia
Taos
Santa Fé
Denver
C O L O R A D O
Escalante's Route 1776-7
115° 114° 113° 112° 111° 110° 109° 108° 107° 106° 105°
41° 40° 39° 38° 37° 36° 35°

APPENDIX R.

THE JOURNEYINGS OF FATHER ESCALANTE, FROM SANTA FÉ TO UTAH LAKE AND THE MOQUI VILLAGES, IN 1776.

By PHILIP HARRY. 1860.

The original manuscript journal of Padre Escalante is said to be in the archives of the city of Mexico. A manuscript copy is in the possession of Peter Force, esq., of Washington, D. C., to whom I am indebted for the inspection and use of it. Below is a summary of the narrative.

On the 29th of July, 1776, F. Francisco Atanacio Dominguez and F. Francisco Silvestre Velez Escalante, accompanied by seven or more other persons, left Santa Fé, N. Mex., crossed the Rio del Norte at the pueblo of Santa Clara, and followed, by way of Abiquiu and the Rio Chama, what is now known as the "Spanish Trail." This is the great route from Santa Fé to Los Angeles, Cal., &c.

I have not had time to translate his journal, and plot in detail his route from Santa Fé to where he struck the Rio Dolores, but have examined it sufficiently to satisfy myself that he followed almost exactly the same route that Capt. J. N. Macomb, Topographical Engineers, lately traveled over, and which the latter has surveyed and mapped. Up to this point on the Rio Dolores, both Escalante and Captain Macomb were on, or at least close to, the "Spanish Trail," crossing the Rios Navajo, San Juan, las Piedras, Florido, Las Animas, La Plata, Los Mancos, &c., at or near the same places.

The point above alluded to on the Rio Dolores is so remarkable that there can be no question of its identity. The river rises in the Sierra la Plata, and flows southwesterly until it reaches this point, whence it makes a sudden bend at a very acute angle, and runs in a direction not many degrees west of north until it falls into Grand River. At the sudden bend above mentioned there are also some extensive and interesting ruins of an ancient Indian pueblo, which are pointedly adverted to both by Escalante and Captain Macomb. Here the routes of Escalante and of Captain Macomb diverge, and Escalante follows the Dolores for many leagues down stream. Then leaving it and going northeasterly, he comes upon a small stream, which he calls the San Pedro, and which falls into the Dolores a few leagues to the westward; he follows it up stream for a short distance, and then taking a still more easterly course gets on to the Rio Francisco (so called by him), a considerable affluent of the San Xavier (Grand River), and which enters the latter some ten leagues to the north. He follows the right bank of the San Francisco, but leaves it before he reaches its mouth, and arrives at the Rio de San Xavier, which is evidently what we call Grand River. Escalante states that the Yutas call it "Tomiche," and he also says that, in the year 1765, Don Juan Maria de Ribera came to the San Xavier at a point a little below the junction with the San Francisco.

He describes the San Xavier as being formed by four smaller rivers or forks (of course he means above his crossing-place), and this corresponds remarkably with the Uncompagre River, Grand River, Smith's Fork, and another large fork, all of which are represented on our maps as coming together a short distance above Escalante's supposed crossing. It seems evident that, after crossing the San Xavier, he follows up stream a different fork from what we call Grand River, but which fork he considers the main river, or San Xavier. The mouth of this fork is indicated on the map of Captain Gunnison's explorations. After having followed this fork for many leagues a little east of north, Escalante comes upon a large "rancheria" of Indians, and procured from them a couple of guides. Hence he travels northwesterly until he arrives at the San Rafael, quite a large river. This is clearly the Blue River of our maps, the main fork of Grand River, and which ought, therefore, to have been so called, instead of the smaller and more southerly branch which goes by that name. He fords the San Rafael at a place where it separates into two branches (probably forming an island), and in other respects describes the locality in such a manner that it might easily be recognized by a person acquainted with the river. From the San Rafael to the San Clemente (now called White River) his course is about northwesterly, and thence nearly west to the Rio de San Buenaventura, which he crosses at a very remarkable ford. This, together with its neighboring landmarks, he describes most minutely. The San Buenaventura of Escalante is evidently Green River, and he strikes it in about latitude 40° 19′, and some 12 or 15 leagues above the mouth of White River, coming from the eastward, and the Uintah River from the westward. He travels down the right bank of the San Buenaventura to within a short distance of the mouth of the Uintah (which he calls Rio de San Cosme), and then strikes westwardly over to the latter, and follows its northern bank until he crosses what is now called Duchesne Fork.

After leaving this, and making his way with great labor westwardly through the Wahsatch Mountains (to which Escalante does not give any particular name), he descends into the more level country at the southern end of Lake Utah, and goes to that lake which he says the Indians call "Timpanogo."

Of this lake and its vicinity he gives a very particular description. He speaks of the rivers that enter it, and of its connection by a narrow outlet with a much larger lake, or body of lakes, to the northward, which are *very salt*, &c.; but this large body of salt water he did not visit.

After spending a few days among the Lake Indians, or "Timpanogotzis," Escalante bends his steps southerly and comes to the Sevier River, which he calls Santa Isabel. He then travels westerly some fifteen or more leagues, in the salt plain through which the river runs, and then leaves it in order to follow a southerly course again, and without coming upon the salt lake or marsh, which he is told that it enters, and subsequently leaves to run westwardly.

By many it has been supposed that Escalante called this river the San Buenaventura, and, moreover, that he asserted it to flow into the Pacific Ocean. I have not seen Escalante's map (if he constructed any), but his journal merely states that, judging from the name which the Indians give this river, and from the manner in which his guide spoke of it, one might be led to suppose that it was the same river as the San Buenaventura, which he crossed further eastward (and, as above stated, in about latitude 40° 19′); but he goes on to say, we could not believe this to be the case, because there was so much less water in the Santa Isabel than in the San Buenaventura where we crossed the latter, besides which the San Buenaventura is joined by many affluents, such as the San Clemente, the San Cosme, the San Damian, and many smaller rivers below the aforesaid crossing place (all of which would increase immensely the volume of water before it could reach the point where Escalante struck the Santa Isabel). So far from his saying that the Santa Isabel debouches into the Pacific, he merely once states, on hearsay, that it enters a salt lake and emerges from it to run westwardly.

His course is now southerly along plains and good traveling-ground until he gets into about latitude 38° 40′. Here, for the first time, he alludes to the fact that the original intention of the party was to reach Monterey, Cal., but that, in consequence of the lateness of the season (it was the 7th of October) and the increasing coldness and inclemency of the weather, he judges it impossible to reach Monterey before the winter sets in with great severity and exposes them to perish by cold and starvation. He therefore persuades his companions to abandon the idea of traveling to the Pacific, and to make the best of their way, by some route hitherto unexplored, to the Moqui villages, and thence back to Santa Fé. In pursuance of this plan he continues southerly, passing the spring of San José (which is probably the same that is so called at this day, and which is near Paravan), and soon after gets upon a small river which he calls the Rio del Pilar (most likely the Santa Clara of Frémont and others). This he follows for some fifteen or twenty leagues and then leaves it, running southwesterly. Continuing on his southerly course he gradually gets as far down as about latitude 36° 20′, meeting occasionally with Indians, who sometimes mislead him and sometimes give him useful, though confused, information respecting the distance of the Colorado River, and the direction in which to find a ford. After traveling a very circuitous route (and living on the meager fare procured from the Indians, for the provisions of the party were entirely exhausted), first southeast, then north, then northeast, then southeast, he gets into the immediate vicinity of the tremendous cañons which inclose and radiate from the Colorado. He now follows up stream, the direction of the river's course, searching for a ford. This course is here north and then northeast. Twice he gets down to the river and tries to cross it, but without success; but, finally, after great labor and fatigue, climbing up and down the almost impracticable cañons and cliffs, and being compelled to kill several horses for food, he finds the ford and crosses the river on the 8th of November, in about latitude 37°, and somewhere between longitude 111° and 112° from Greenwich. With the exception of still having to kill and eat their horses, the hardships of the party are now nearly over. From the ford they ascend along a cañon to the high table-land and find good trails all the way to the Moqui villages, where their wants are relieved. Hence they have no further trouble in reaching Zuni (where there is a mission) and then Santa Fé, by way of Acoma, on the 2d January, 1777.

It may be interesting to know that Escalante found the Moquis opposed to Christianity, which had at one time been introduced among them, but from which they had apostatized. He had some lengthy interviews with their headmen, and tried to persuade them to return to the fold, and to submit to the Spanish government; but although they displayed no hostility, and, on the contrary, were quite friendly and hospitable, they did not show any disposition to come to Escalante's terms, any further than in what might be advantageous to both parties in the way of trade.

On his outward journey to Lake Utah, and again, when he is homeward bound, but still to the westward of the Colorado, Escalante inquires of the Indians whom he meets whether they have heard of any padres (meaning the Padre Garces), or of any Spanish, coming from Monterey to the Moqui villages; but the Indians either know nothing, or are unwilling to say anything about the matter. After crossing the Colorado he does not allude to the subject any more, and the reason for this seems to be, from certain remarks that he makes, that the Moquis were displeased with the Cosninas, their neighbors to the westward, for having brought to them (or allowed to pass through their country) the Padre Garces. It became therefore useless and impolitic for Escalante to say anything about his brother padre, from Monterey, after he had crossed the Colorado, and was in the vicinity of the Moquis.

All this settles the point, it appears to me, that the expedition of Garces to the Moquis had taken place previous to that of Escalante, and that the latter knew of it. Humboldt states that the expedition of Garces was in 1773. So far as we know, and as indicated on a copy of a map that was found in the archives of New Mexico, Garces did not go further eastward than Moqui, but returned to California. The copy of the map above mentioned is in the Bureau of Topographical Engineers, and is dated 1777.

Escalante's journal is written with great precision and clearness, every day's courses and distances are stated, the topographical features minutely described, and a good deal of mineral and botanical information added.

The two padres, Dominguez and Escalante, went on a pacific mission of discovery and propagation of Christianity among the Indians; their companions were evidently actuated solely by worldly motives. It was with great difficulty that Escalante and his brother padre could prevail on the rest of the party to give up the idea of going on to Monterey. They had undoubtedly been considering this—the exploration of a route through to the Pacific coast—as the main object of the expedition, and looked forward to this route as a source of great future advantage and lucrative speculation.

As a matter of special interest I have subjoined a literal translation of Escalante's description of Lake Utah or "Timpanogo."

"At the northern part of the river San Buenaventura there is a range of mountains, which, according to what we ascertained yesterday, extends from the north to the southwest more than sixty leagues, and which in breadth is at most forty; where we crossed it, it is thirty. In this range, and in the westerly portion of it, and in lat. 40° 49′ (*a*), in a direction northwest quarter north (north 33¾° west) from the town of Santa Fé, is the valley of our Lady of Mercy of Timponocnitzis, surrounded by the crests of mountains, whence issue four middle-sized rivers, which water it until they enter the lake, which lies in the middle thereof.

"The area of the valley is in extent from southeast to northwest (*b*) 16 Spanish leagues, which are what we speak of in this journal, and from north to southwest, 10 or 12. It is level, and, with the exception of the marshes, which are found on the margin of the lake, is of a very good quality of soil for every kind of grain. Of the four rivers that irrigate it, the first or most southerly is that of Hot Springs (*Rio de Aquas Calientes*), and, in its wide-spreading meadows, there is sufficient irrigable land for two good settlements (*poblaciones*); the second, at three leagues north of the first one, and having more water, might support a good large 'poblacion,' or two middle-sized ones, with an abundance of land, all open to irrigation. This river, before it enters the lake, divides into two branches; on its banks, besides cottonwood trees, there are large alders. We called it the Rio de San Nicolas. Three leagues and a half to the northwest of this comes the third, and the intervening space is composed of flat meadow-land, the soil of which is good for grain-crops. It is more copious than the two preceding streams, has larger groves of cottonwood, and meadows of good soil, with enough of it irrigable to support two, or even three, good 'poblaciones.' We were in its neighborhood on the 24th and 25th of September, and we named it 'Rio de San Antonio de Padua.' We did not visit the fourth river, though we saw its cottonwood groves. It is to the northwest of the San Antonio, and there is in this direction much level land, and, so far as we saw, good; and, therefore, several 'poblaciones' might be established there. They told us that this stream had as much water in it as the others. We called it the Rio de Santa Aña (*c*). Besides these rivers, there are in the valley many good springs of water, and numerous streamlets that come down from the mountains. What we have just said about the settlements (*poblaciones*) is to be understood as allowing to each one more land than would be absolutely necessary for it, for if merely one square league of arable land were assigned to each 'pueblo,' there might be established in the valley as many 'pueblos' of Indians as there are in New Mexico; for although in the forementioned directions we gave it a certain extent, it is larger; for to the south, and in other directions, it has very extensive bays (*angulos*), and all of them containing good soil. Throughout the whole, there is good and abundant pasturage, and in parts there grow flax and hemp in such abundance that it appears as if it had been sown artificially; and the temperature here is pleasant, for after having suffered considerable from cold ever since we left the river San Buenaventura, we felt warm everywhere in the valley, both by night and by day. Besides these magnificent capabilities, there are found, in the mountains that surround it, plenty of wood for fuel and timber, and many sheltered spots, water, and pasturage adapted to the raising of large droves of cattle and horses. This is as regards the north, northeast, and southeast; to the south, and southwest, there are two other wide valleys, also full of abundant pastures, and with plenty of water; to one of these reaches the lake, and next to the latter there is a large piece of the valley strongly impregnated with saltpeter. The lake is six leagues wide by fifteen long; it runs to the northwest, and by a narrow outlet, as we were told, it communicates with other much larger lakes. This one of the Timpanogotzis abounds in every kind of good fish, geese, otters, and other amphibious animals, which we had no opportunity of seeing. On its shores dwell the aforementioned Indians, who live upon the abundant fish-supplies of the lake, whence the Sabuagana Gutas call them fish-eaters (*Corne-pescados*). Besides this, they gather on the plains seeds of plants, and make a sort of gruel (*atole*) with them; although they add to this the hunting of hares, rabbits, and sage-hens (*gallinas*), of which there is a great abundance. There are also buffaloes not far to the eastward, but the fear of the Comanches prevents them from hunting them; their dwellings are a sort of huts, or 'jacalijos,' of osiers, of which they make also baskets, and other necessary utensils. Their dress manifests great poverty; the most decent which they wear is a coat or shirt (*sago*) of deerskin, and big moccasins (*botas*) of the same in winter; they have dresses made of hare and rabbit skins. They speak the Yuta language, but with a noticeable variation of accent, and even of some words. They are good featured, and mostly without beard. They are found inhabiting most parts of this Sierra to the southwest and northwest—a great many tribes of the same nation, language, and docile disposition as these lake Indians, out of whom might be formed a populous and extensive province.

"The names of the chiefs contained in the sena? above referred to, are, in their language, of the principal chief, Turunianchi; of the second, Cuitzapamichi; of the third, who is the same as our friend Silvestre, Panchucunquibran (which means the orator or speaker); the fourth, who is not a chief and is the brother of the principal chief, is called Pichuchi.

"The other lake with which this one communicates is, as they informed us, many leagues in extent, and its waters are noxious and extremely salt, so that the Timpanogotzis asserted to us that when any one rubbed a part of his body with it he would feel an itching sensation in the moistened part. On its borders, they told us, there dwelt a numerous and peaceable nation, called Paguampe, which, in our language, means throwers or slingers (*echizeros*), which nation speaks the Comanche language, and live upon herbs, drink at the springs and streams of good water that are found around the lake, and have their huts of 'sacate?' and earth (which must be their roofs). They are not considered enemies by the Timpanogotzis—so it was said—but ever since a certain time when they came together, and a man was killed, there has not been the same good fellowship as before. On this occasion the Timpanogotzis entered by the extreme point of the Sierra Blancha (which is the same as that where they are) by a route north quarter west from their country, and by this same route they say that the Cemanlos also make their entrances, which do not appear to be very frequent.*

"The Timpanogotzis call themselves thus after the lake, which they name Timpanogo, and this is a name peculiar to it—for the name or word by which they designate a lake is usually 'Pagariri.'"

* The whole of this last phrase is very obscure, and, besides, I suspect that for *Cemanlos* should be read *Comanches*.—P. H.

Notes to the above description:

(*a*) Escalante's stated latitudes are not to be depended on; his observations must have been made with very rough instruments. His courses and distances, however, are remarkably accurate when compared with our maps.

(*b*) Escalante's courses appear to be magnetic. The variation at the present day is about 17° east.

(*c*) This was probably the Timpanogos River of the present day. The others have various names, such as Spanish Fork, Salt Creek, &c.—P. H.

PHILIP HARRY,
Bureau of Topographical Engineers, Washington, D. C.

INDEX.

64 B U

G.

www.ingramcontent.com/pod-product-compliance
Lightning Source LLC
LaVergne TN
LVHW021239110826
845150LV00002B/356

* 9 7 8 1 4 2 5 5 6 1 7 0 3 *

LIVES

OF THE

QUEENS OF ENGLAND

BEFORE THE

NORMAN CONQUEST.

BY

MRS. MATTHEW HALL.

TAGGARD & THOMPSON,
29 CORNHILL,
BOSTON.
1864.

PHILADELPHIA:
COLLINS, PRINTER, 705 JAYNE STREET.

INTRODUCTION.

These volumes, it is believed, will be found to present the first connected outline of the history of Royal women prior to the Norman Conquest. Most readers are acquainted, through the medium of Miss Strickland's admirable work, with the personal memoirs of Matilda, Queen of the Conqueror, and her successors, who were united by the tie-matrimonial to our English monarchs; yet who can trace even an outline of the life of Editha the Good, her contemporary and predecessor on the throne? Of the stormy and troubled history of Queen Emma, who was wife of two kings, and mother also of two, and who first introduced her Norman countrymen into England, still less is known: nor are there to be found any connected details concerning the wives of those Saxon kings who laid the foundation of our English laws and institutions. No one has been found to go back beyond the era of the Conquest to search amid dusty and worm-eaten records for details illustrative of the vast mine of history, with all its hidden stores of wealth, from the first to the eleventh century. Investigation has commenced from a point more lucid, when Norman conquerors imposed the Doomsday Book as a lasting token of their power.

Woman, possessing, as she ever does, an all-powerful influence over the events of her day, has thrown a bright light over the dark history of the first eleven centuries of our annals, and during that period we discover a succession of important historical events which have occurred through her instrumentality. Were not Roman taste and luxury first made popular in Britain through the influence of Cartismandua, and progressively developed under subsequent female sovereigns, her successors, during the Roman domination, not the least remarkable of whom was the Empress Julia, wife of Severus? Where, in the whole history of this country, is there a page to be found more glorious than that devoted to the British St. Helena, the Empress-mother of Constantine the Great, the self-devoted wife, the patroness of Christianity, the discoverer of the true cross, the builder of churches, the mother of the oppressed,—the glorious career of whose influence has, in a thousand ways, directly and indirectly, descended to our own times with her name and history? Deeply contrasted with these incidents are those forming the groundwork of the life of Boadicea, in whom we behold an instance of the native simplicity of a Briton by birth and education: her fine womanly nature, aroused by unheard-of wrongs to revolt against tyranny and injustice, burst forth, like a torrent which deluged the whole land with blood, into that train of actions which had nearly quenched forever the power of Rome in this island. The family details of Boadicea's history, of whom much has been written, have never before appeared in connection with her life, and without the knowledge of these it is impossible fairly to appreciate the exciting details of her sufferings as woman, wife, and mother—in the delineation of *her* character, no fiction can arrive at the all-powerful force of simple truth.

Passing over Rowena, through whom was introduced the Saxon sway, we may remark that it was to the most excellent and pious Queen Bertha, a Frenchwoman of royal rank, that we were indebted for the primeval establishment of Christianity in Saxon Britain. That faith had, indeed, at an earlier period been introduced and cherished by royalty, but had fallen into disuse. From the time, however, when Bertha set the example, queens and princesses stood forth as the champions of the new creed: it became then *fashionable* to be a Christian; and that same land which had alone, through the merciful intervention of St. Helena, escaped the persecution of Dioclesian, became distinguished for examples of holy votaries to the faith of Christ. Not content with exercising every domestic and social virtue themselves, these Saxon females animated their husbands and lovers to a similar self-devotion in the cause of religion. Many, indeed, of these sceptred women dedicated their whole existence to a religious state of seclusion. Then it was that kings laid aside their crowns and robes of state, and, assuming the monastic garb, at the exhortation of their royal partners, undertook pilgrimages to the Holy See, founded schools or endowed churches, which yet remain to attest their munificence. Such was the spirit which pervaded the Saxon Heptarchy, though the picture had sometimes its dark reverse, as in the characters of Quendrida and Ermenburga—and later still, the singularly beautiful and wicked Elfrida. Each of these royal ladies, whether good or bad actions marked her career, has her own appropriate niche in the annals of the past; and possessed her peculiar influence over the times in which she lived—an influence more or less descending to our remote age, though in few does the benefit conferred on society shine more conspicuously than in that gentle and amiable queen, mother of Alfred the Great, by whose beneficent attention to the education of her sons, some of the brightest rays of light have been shed on our English literature.

Such are a few of the leading features of a period comparatively unknown, and which cannot fail, it is hoped, to prove a useful study to those who desire an introduction to the History of England; for these personal records of the wives and daughters of our early monarchs, form naturally the connecting links between many public events which would otherwise remain detached and unintelligible.

The history of British female Sovereigns before the period of the Conquest had necessarily to be drawn from chronicles which present many legendary records, and which grave writers have sometimes rejected, perhaps too unsparingly; for, as a learned translator* has observed, even legends are of value in recording the history of past times, and in them the germ of important events connected with the establishment and progress of religion may be found. But for the Sagas we should know little of the early habits of northern nations; and to more than one ballad are we indebted for an historical fact, which might otherwise have been forgotten. To the perseverance and study of recluses, who spent their whole lives in producing one work, we owe much gratitude; that they were generally guided by a spirit of truth we cannot doubt, as they were aware that their labours would become known to many a contemporary and rival in whose power it was,

* Benj. Thorpe, F. S. A.; Introduction to Lappenberg's Anglo-Saxons.

even at that day, to confute a writer, if he asserted more than had been handed down by tradition: at all periods there were critics as well as authors, and, as almost every monastery could boast of its learned historian, there was no want of jealous observation of the productions of their literary brethren amongst the monks who filled up their leisure with similar pursuits.

To the bards, who sang their compositions from country to country, was intrusted the sacred task of relating great events: they kept alive in their songs the valiant deeds of heroes; their lays were faithfully repeated by the scribes, who committed them to writing, and, as time wore on, chroniclers sprang up, who, by diligent study, were able to understand and explain much that had become obscure to the uninitiated. The famous Abbey of Glastonbury produced the earliest historian of Britain, who, in the middle of the sixth century, set an example, followed almost uninterruptedly in other monasteries through several ages, till the little less than miraculous invention of printing rendered learning and information easy.

Milton, our greatest and most erudite poet, did not disdain the old legends of the early chroniclers, and has preserved in his history much that it is delightful to read of, and pleasant to believe; and our immortal dramatist sought at the same sources the subjects on which to frame his glorious imaginings.

From the lays of the Welsh bards, from Gildas, and Geoffrey of Monmouth, down to the latest publications which have thrown light on the history of the early British reigns, nothing has been neglected in the work now presented to the public which might conduct to truth, and offer a clear and interesting series of records of those female Sovereigns whose lives are so much less familiar to the English reader than others of a later period, who have found able recent biographers.

CONTENTS.

CARTISMANDUA,

QUEEN OF CYMBELINE.

BOADICEA, "THE WARLIKE,"

QUEEN OF ARVIRAGUS.

GWENISSA THE FAIR,

SECOND QUEEN OF ARVIRAGUS.

JULIA "DOMINA,"

EMPRESS OF SEVERUS.

VICTORIA,* VITURGIA, AND HUNILA,

EMPRESSES OF BONOSUS AND PROCULUS.

* The name of the Empress Victoria's husband has not been handed down to posterity.

ST. HELENA,

QUEEN OF CONSTANTIUS CHLORUS.

CARTANDIS,

QUEEN OF EUGENIUS I.

HELENA AP EUDDA,

EMPRESS OF MAXIMUS.

ROWENA,

SECOND QUEEN OF VORTIGERN.

GUENEVER I.,

QUEEN OF ARTHUR.

GUENEVER II.,

QUEEN OF ARTHUR.

GUENEVER III.,

QUEEN OF ARTHUR.

BERTHA,

QUEEN OF ETHELBERT.

ETHELBURGA "THE SILENT," AND ENFLEDA,

QUEENS OF EDWIN "THE GREAT" AND OSWY.

ST. EBBA, QUENBURGA, SURNAMED "BEBBA," AND SAXBURGA,

QUEENS OF CWICHELME, KYNIGILS, AND CENWALCH.

OSTRIDA AND WERBURGA,

QUEENS OF ETHELRED AND CEOLRED.

QUENBURGA, QUENSWITHA, AND ALFLEDA,

QUEENS OF ALFRED, PENDA, AND PEADA.

HERESWYTHA, SEXBURGA, ETHELDREDA, ERMENBERGA, AND ERMENILDA

QUEENS OF ANNA, ERCOMBERT, EGFRID, AND WULPHERE.

DOMNEVA,

QUEEN OF MEROWALD.

ETHELBURGA AND FRIDOGITHA,

QUEENS OF INA AND ETHELARD.

QUENDRIDA-PETRONILLA,

QUEEN OF OFFA "THE PROUD."

EADBURGA.—ELFLEDA,

QUEENS OF BERTRIC AND WIMOND.

QUENDRIDA II.

OSBURGA AND ETHELSWYTHA,

QUEENS OF ETHELWULF AND BURHRED.

JUDITH OF FRANCE,

SECOND QUEEN OF ETHELWULF.

ELSWITHA, QUEEN OF ALFRED THE GREAT, AND

ETHELFLEDA, "LADY OF MERCIA,"

EGWINA, ELFLEDA, EDGIFA, AND ELFGIFA,

QUEENS OF EDWARD "THE ELDER," AND EDMUND "THE PIOUS."

ETHELGIVA,

QUEEN OF EDWY "THE FAIR."

ELFRIDA,

QUEEN OF EDGAR "THE PEACEABLE."

EMMA OF NORMANDY,

Surnamed "the Pearl."

QUEEN OF ETHELRED "THE UNREADY" AND CANUTE "THE GREAT."

EDITHA THE "GOOD,"

QUEEN OF EDWARD "THE CONFESSOR."

EDITHA "THE FAIR,"

QUEEN OF HAROLD II.

LIVES

OF

BRITISH QUEENS

BEFORE THE CONQUEST.

CARTISMANDUA.

Parentage of Cartismandua — Her father Afarwy leaves Britain — His daughter born — Cymbeline's education — Marriage of Cartismandua — Early habits of splendour—Her arrival in Britain—New coinage of Cymbeline—Children of Cartismandua — Adminius rebels, and flies to Rome — Death of Cymbeline — Cartismandua's possessions—She marries Cadallan—Intermarriages of their children—Caractacus—Habits of the northern tribes—Bericus—British produce — Invasion by Claudius — Cartismandua friendly to the Romans — Re-married to Venusius—They betray Caractacus—Cartismandua separates from Venusius, and marries his shield-bearer — Indignation of the British — Wars with the Scots—The Queen is taken—Her death—Corbred's wars.

THE first British Queen, whose life offers any interest, after the Roman Invasion, is Cartismandua.

She is said to have been great-grand-daughter of King Lud, the eldest of the seven sons of Beli the Great, the heroes of the famous bards, Aneurin, Taliesin, Llywarch Hên, and their followers, whose compositions may be ascribed to the sixth century.[1]

Lud is a favorite with early chroniclers, and his name is preserved somewhat conspicuously in that of the capital of England.[2]

The father of Cartismandua was Mandubratius, or Afarwy, the son of Imanuentius, Prince of the Trinobantes, or people of Middlesex and Essex, whose contentions with the victorious Cassivellaunus, or Caswallon, led to the devastation of the country and the successes of the Romans.

---

[1] Lappenberg's Hist. of England under the Anglo-Saxon kings.

[2] Nennius, Abbot of Bangor, wrote his Historia Britonum about the year 858, and speaks of earlier works to which he was indebted. He is indignant at the name of Troynovant being replaced by that of Lud's Town, as he insists on the tradition, of which the Britons were long proud, of a descent from Brutus, grandson of Æneas; "a fabulous national tradition of Rome;" observes Dr. Lappenberg, "with the faded tinsel of which the vain Britons adorned themselves," in appropriating it to their own nation.

Afarwy had made overtures to Cæsar in Gaul, offering him the means of a second attempt on the country, which offer was gladly accepted; and Afarwy and his son Scæva, together with thirty others of his relations and adherents, placed themselves in the hands of the Romans as hostages, and afterwards accompanied the conqueror on his return to Rome, when Cassivellaunus had been forced to submit to the yoke of the powerful strangers, whose absence from his country he sacrificed much to obtain.

It is not known whether Afarwy had a wife with him when he quitted Britain; but it is supposed that, if so, after her death he espoused a Roman lady, according to the policy adopted by Cæsar, to secure the friendship of the islanders. Cartismandua, there is reason to think,[1] was the offspring of this second marriage, and it was in Rome that she married her cousin Cymbeline, one of the hostages, who, being in due time called back to Britain to assume the royal sway, was accompanied by his bride on his return to the land of his nativity.

Although no particulars of the childhood of the daughter of Afarwy have been handed down to us, the early years of Cymbeline, her husband, have not been suffered to rest in the shade by historians. The hero of Britain, as he afterwards became, and who has been made familiar to us by Shakspeare, was, when a British hostage, educated in Rome, that most polished of cities, and, like the youths his companions in the same circumstances, received eventually an appointment suitable to his rank. Various offices were indeed assigned to the Britons.

Cicero, with true Roman contempt, speaks of Britain in his time as a country from which slaves only could be procured,—alluding to certain captives who had been sent by their conquerors to the circus, where, no doubt, their novel appearance would at that day excite as much interest as any barbarian exhibited on our own stage would do; or the orator might speak in reference to certain Britains appointed to carry the litter of the Emperor,—a post certainly, if ignoble, requiring fidelity to his person. Cymbeline could scarcely be included in Cicero's contemptuous notice, for he not only received a noble education, but was appointed to attend in person on the Emperor Augustus in his wars; in which service he became so distinguished for his valour, that he was rewarded with the honor of knighthood, which carried with it certain peculiar and enviable distinctions.

The Eques, or Roman knight, was permitted to wear rings on his fingers, which no inferior person might display. He was also entitled to wear a dress embroidered with broad guards and studs of purple, which, together with the horse he rode, were provided by the Senate. The British coins of Cymbeline bear the horse-rampant, which shows how proudly the prince regarded the Imperial favour. The Roman knight who had, like Cymbeline, conducted himself valiantly in time of war, *if a stranger and auxiliary*, as in his case, was rewarded with a chain of gold, while a citizen of Rome could only gain a silver one by his valour. By such distinctions the Roman emperors attached foreigners to their service,—a

[1] Carte. Roberts' British History.

politic measure, as was proved by the firmness with which the husband of Cartismandua continued friendly to the Roman interest.

An especial dignity was also enjoyed by the wives of the knights of Rome: to this Cartismandua must necessarily have been admitted. The knowledge of the early associations of the future Queen of the Britons may serve to explain, in some degree, many of the circumstances of her after-life. She was brought up in all the pomp and splendour of a luxurious court, with the throne of Augustus ever before her eyes, and the riches, glory, and honours of the Roman nation continually present to her view. At that time, love of dress and display was carried to a most inordinate height in the Imperial City, and we find Pliny reproving with indignation the monstrous disorders which had crept into the world, following up his remonstrances thus: "But say that women may be allowed to wear as much gold as they will, in bracelets, in rings on every finger-joint, in carcanets about their necks, in earrings pendent at their ears, in stays, wreaths, and chin-bands; let them have their chains of gold as large as they list under their arms, or cross over their sides, scarf-wise; and say that gentlewomen and mistresses may have their collars of gold thickly beset and garnished with massive pearls, pendent at their neck, beneath their waist; that even in their beds, when they should sleep, they may remember what a weight of gold they carry about them; must they therefore wear gold upon their feet, as it were to establish a third estate of women, answerable to the order of knights, between the matrons or dames of honour, and the wives of mean commoners?" From this passage it would appear that golden ornaments on the feet were permitted to Roman knights,—a privilege no doubt prized by all who formed part of the community. Cartismandua, among the rest of the ladies who were married to Roman knights, must have incurred the censure of the historian. It is not surprising, on reflecting to what a height of luxury the ladies of the period had arrived, that in after-times she should have disdained the simple manners of her uncultivated British subjects; and she may be excused if her heart should have reverted and clung in later years to those among whom she had known her earliest enjoyments. The love of splendour in dress must have become habitual to her, and it was but natural that she should sigh for scenes of gaiety so congenial to youth. Cartismandua cannot justly be blamed for this weakness so common to her sex and breeding, nor can it be imputed to her as a crime that she preserved to the last day of her existence her faithful attachment to Rome. This latter feeling was also strongly inculcated and reciprocated by Cymbeline, who is said to have made himself so dear to the Emperor that he was saluted by the honourable title of "Friend to the Commonwealth;" and on his return to Britain, Augustus granted him permission either to pay or receive remittance of the tribute imposed by Cæsar on the Britons, according to his own pleasure. Cymbeline did not avail himself of the generous offer, being desirous to preserve the friendship of the Romans, and to secure for the British youth an opportunity of continuing to make their residence at the capital, where there were so many opportunities of obtaining an enlightened education, the advantage of which he had himself fully experienced.

It would be curious to follow the route of Cartismandua and her husband, in that early age of Britain's annals, when they journeyed towards the land over which the death of Tenantius, Afarwy's brother, had called them to rule. There were then no facilities of travel, and the difficulties were greater than we can now well conceive. The usual passage from Gaul to Britain appears to have been from Boulogne, in Belgic Gaul, to Sandwich, or from Calais to Dover as at the present day. There has been a question as to what description of vessel was used for the service of passing the narrow seas; but those antiquaries who contend for the *coracle*, a frail bark only used for rivers, could have been but little aware of the nature of the Channel. There were, probably, vessels of sufficient weight and power to render the navigation comparatively easy to less experienced sailors than our own; and, of course, all the resources of art, as it then existed, would have been employed, that the royal pair should arrive on their own shores with becoming pomp.

But it was probably at the port of Dowgate,[1] on the Thames at London, that Cartismandua and her husband landed, and from that spot commenced a triumphant entry into the city in one of those chariots, gorgeously painted and adorned with silver, which historians have described with minuteness.[2]

As Cymbeline was a Roman knight, the distinguished friend of Augustus, and a descendant of their own royal family, both himself and Cartismandua must have been welcomed by the Britons with every honour which it was possible for them to offer.

Lud's Town, or London, had even then arisen to considerable importance as "the resort of merchants" and residence of the chief of the Trinobantes, of which state it was the capital. It is said to have contained more dwellings than any other town in Britain; and simple as these were as far as architecture is concerned, they were important in their kind: the Britons did not employ stone for the construction of their dwellings till taught the art of architecture by Agricola,[3] nor was glass used for architectural purposes till some time after the Saxon invasion. The feeling which touched the heart of the noble Caractacus, when he viewed the Roman splendour, might have cast a shade on that of Cartismandua when she first beheld her own future regal abode. Caractacus is said to have exclaimed: "How is it possible that a people possessed

---

[1] Holinshed.

[2] Mauda, Queen of Connaught, the contemporary of Cartismandua, is described as leading her troops to battle, seated in an open chariot, with her crown of gold on her head; [Cæsar brought with him from Britain a corslet richly adorned with British pearls, which he dedicated to Venus. This was one of the spoils which gave the Romans an idea of the riches of Britain. The Scottish and Irish kings wore crowns of gold.] the royal car which conveyed her being accompanied by four chariots, one before, another behind, and two on either side, attended by a great retinue of chariots and horses; while the Queen herself is described as having been apprehensive lest she should contaminate or defile the golden crown and her royal robes with the dust raised by the horses' feet, or the foam proceeding from the mouths of the fiery steeds. See O'Halloran, O'Flaherty, &c., and "Titles of Honour."

[3] Howel.

of such magnificence at home, could envy me a humble cottage in Britain!" The rough warrior had passed his whole life amid these humble, yet, to him, happy abodes of barbarians, whom Diodorus describes at this time as characterised by simplicity, integrity, temperance, and a proneness to dissension. Caractacus looked only on their noble qualities; but Cartismandua had quitted all that art, wealth, and luxury could combine to make life enviable, and like a tender exotic, had been removed from that warm and genial soil, to breathe the air of a land, the customs of which were opposed to all her habits, and which reminded her at each fresh step of what she had left behind; that she shrunk from her allotted destiny, was not therefore surprising.

The royal residence of Dinas Beli, the Palace or Court of Belinus,[1] was a structure in Lud's Town, which extended over the Broken Wharf into the city, till it approached the Gate of Belinus, its royal founder, brother of the Brennus who headed the Gauls and sacked Rome in the time of Camillus. The words Ludgate and Billingsgate[2] are familiar in our own days; and Holinshed assures us, that in his time there were yet remaining the ruins of the Old Palace of Belinus, which had been patched up and converted into warehouses. Belinus's gate was on the banks of the Thames, and is said to have been once surmounted by the king's image, while his ashes were preserved in a golden urn contained in the gateway, beneath which was a haven or quay for ships, it being one of the chief gates or entrances into the capital. Livy, the historian of the Court of Augustus,[3] and contemporary of Cymbeline and Cartismandua, has related the history of Brennus, brother of King Belinus, as Plutarch has also done in his account of Camillus. In the Palace of Dinas Beli, probably, the royal pair were accordingly installed as their future residence.

One of the first acts of Cymbeline in Britain, was to issue an entirely new coinage of tribute-money, bearing the initials of his own name; which was a great advance in art for the Britons, who, up to that time, had been accustomed to use rings of brass and iron, wrought to certain degrees of value, for money,[4] as had been customary among the early Greeks. Many specimens of the coins of Cymbeline, his head crowned with a diadem of pearls, may still be seen in the cabinets of antiquaries. No less than forty gold, silver, and copper coins of this king, of different dies and moulds, have been discovered,—a proof of the extent to which coinage was carried in his reign.[5] Cymbeline is thought to have derived the art itself from his intercourse with the Romans: certain it is, that civilization,[6] during his reign, increased with rapid strides in the land under his rule.

The inscription Cimog on some of the coins of Cymbeline, gave rise to the Cemog, or Denarius, which may be considered the only coin which has a truly British name; and the word TASCIO on the reverse, signifies the Mint or Treasury.

---

[1] Humphrey Llwyd's Breviary of Britain. [2] Holinshed. [3] Milton.
[4] Rapin. [5] Pegge's Essay on the Coins of Cunobelinus.
[6] Rev. P. Roberts on the Early History of the Cymry, or Ancient Britons. Britton and Brayley.

Cymbeline was the first British monarch who stamped his image upon his coins, sometimes with two faces, like Janus, whose temple was closed during his reign. Six of these coins have the obverse only, with the inscription CUNO; and two more, one of which was only found in March, 1849,[1] among a number of gold coins, at the Whaddon Chase, have upon them a horse and wreath; that which was last discovered, was in weight 180 grains; on the reverse was a horse-rampant, an evident allusion to the dignity enjoyed by Cymbeline as a Roman Eques; and on the obverse was a thistle or ear of wheat, doubtless an intimation that corn was supplied to the Romans with the tribute-money.

As the greater number of the coins of Cymbeline have been dug up near Colchester, and bear, besides the monarch's initials of CUNO, the letters CAMY upon them, it is thought that that city was the royal seat of power, as indeed is expressly stated by Dion Cassius. Malden in Essex, and Malton in Yorkshire, have laid claim to being, in former times, the royal residence of British monarchs,[2] each having borne the name of Camalodunum — a mark that Cymbeline at some period resided there,[3] and that the town so named was capital of some district belonging to him: thus, not only were there several Camalodunums, but several cities bearing the name of Venta; Norwich was the Venta or Winchester of the Iceni, and Winchester, now known by the name, was Venta of the Wiccii.

No remains of antiquity can perhaps better convey to the mind the choice of situation selected by our early ancestors for the abode of monarchy, than that spot amidst the Chiltern Hills, in Rockinghamshire, where still appears a high circular mound or keep, in circumference about eighty paces, known to the present day as "Kimble's Castle;"[4] while a little adjacent village bears the same king's name, in defiance of the wreck of time and lapse of centuries. The romantic situation of this strong post would no doubt render it a favourite residence of the Romanized monarch Cymbeline and his consort. From the summit of Belinsbury Hill, which constituted a part of the territory adjacent to this ancient British fortress, we may imagine the eyes of Queen Cartismandua roving at pleasure over an almost boundless prospect of surpassing beauty. In which of the royal British abodes Cartismandua lived is, however, uncertain; or where her children, namely, five sons and one daughter, were brought up.

Adminius, the eldest son, in after times, having offended his father, was exiled the country; on which he placed himself under the protection of Caligula, then Emperor of Rome, who, at his suggestion, undertook that fictitious invasion of Britain, which terminated in the gathering a

[1] Bucks Herald, March 17, 1849.

[2] Allen's History of York.

[3] Dr. Henry assures us that Cymbeline held his court at Malden, which was formerly celebrated for its beauty and magnificence, though only two Roman coins have been found in its vicinity, one of which is held so precious that it is carefully guarded by the bailiffs of the town; both are of the time of the Emperor Claudius.

[4] "The ancient name of the village of Kimble, whenever it occurs in our records, is written Kynebel or Cunobel, and in the Domesday Book is Chenebella."—*Lysons.*

few shells[1] on the coast of Gaul, with which he triumphantly returned to Rome. After this, no more is heard of Adminius, but the Roman writers extol his merits, with those of his brother Togodumnus, who befriended their interest; while they preserve a profound silence as to Arviragus[2] and Guiderius, their brothers, who became afterwards bitter enemies of Rome, and for whose actions our own native historians are the authorities.

This circumstance must have embittered, in no small degree, the domestic happiness of Cartismandua and her family; for the son, who thus disappointed their hopes, was the first-born, and heir to the name and royal honours of the house of Cymbeline. That good king himself, nevertheless, preserved his faith unbroken with Rome during a long reign, which passed usefully to his subjects, and peacefully to both himself and them. Indeed, peace and plenty seem to have marked the era of Cymbeline; yet prosperity did not corrupt him, as is too commonly the case; and it may be presumed that the married life of Cartismandua and her lord, glided smoothly and serenely on with the fair current of time. After a long and glorious reign, Cymbeline died, much regretted by his people; his death being, as they rightly judged, a national loss.

Cartismandua was no longer young at the time of becoming a widow; for her husband had reigned as many as fifty years, according to some authorities.[3]

It was customary in Britain, on the death of a monarch, for his widow or daughter to succeed to the government, if there were no sons; but in this case, there being several princes to inherit the dominions of Cymbeline, they were divided into three portions, of which one was given to Togodumnus, another to Caractacus, while the third portion fell to the widow, their mother. It is, however, uncertain whether either of these states was considered tributary to the other as a minor principality. Laws of Adminius, the eldest of Cartismandua's children, have also been found; but this would rather lead us to suppose he had possessed some share of power during his father's life, and tributary to him, prior to the event of his banishment, which might have led to the act of rebellion that occasioned his father's displeasure.

The territory inhabited by the Iceni[4] was the district which fell to the share of Cartismandua; and this is the first time that a people afterwards so celebrated are named in our histories, Cymbeline being expressly said to have been "King of the Iceni," and the Iceni themselves are mentioned as having studiously laboured to preserve their amity with the Romans.

Norfolk and Suffolk, afterwards distinguished by the name of East Anglia during the Saxon Heptarchy, may be considered as the property by right of inheritance of Cartismandua, and where she probably retired on her widowhood.

---

[1] Dr. Henry. [2] Lewis's History of Great Britain.

[3] Rapin and Henry say Cymbeline reigned thirty-five years: he died, according to Morant, A.D. 42.

[4] Suffolk, Norfolk, Cambridge, and Huntingdon.

The Iceni were not less likely to be faithful allies of Rome, now that Cartismandua reigned over them; and it may be remarked that female government was exceedingly popular at all times in Britain.[1] The fact of the near vicinity of this British district to that part of the country known under the name of Brigantia led to very important results, and opened out a train of events which involved in agitation all the subsequent period of Cartismandua's life. The latent ambition of the character of Cartismandua appeared, unrepressed, after her widowhood; for such must have been the motive which actuated her in her union, shortly after Cymbeline's death, with the Chief of the Brigantes. The mother, by Cymbeline, of a numerous family, Cartismandua could not have wanted scope for the exercise of her affections, and at her mature age, no other reason can be assigned than that she desired still to extend her power. The noble character of Cadallan, Prince of the Brigantes, it must be confessed, might well have won her affection, and may have swayed her choice. Whatever the motive on either side might be, this alliance was entered into, and from that time Cartismandua becomes known to future history as Queen of the Brigantes.

The celebrated district called Brigantia or Galloway, consisted of the large portion of country which extended from the mouth of the Humber to the wall afterwards built by Adrian across the whole breadth of the island, and was inhabited by a chosen body of the Scottish nation, appointed to guard this frontier province from the incursions of the southern Britons, then considered their mortal enemies. This brave, hardy, and adventurous people were distinguished above every other British tribe for their love of liberty, and fought to maintain it as late as the eightieth year of the Christian era, long after all their fellow-countrymen had submitted to the Roman empire.

Brigantia contained many places of great strength and importance, amongst which were Aldborough or Iseur, in Yorkshire, Eboracum or York, afterwards the seat of Roman power in Britain, Carictonium, and Epiake.[2]

Cadallan, chief of the Brigantes, the new husband of the widowed Queen of Cymbeline, was guardian of the young King of the Scots; he had been formerly married to Europeia, a sister of Metallanus, afterwards king, by whom he had several children, the eldest of whom was the famous hero, Caractacus, and the youngest, Boadicea, afterwards so celebrated for her heroism and misfortunes.[3] It is rather remarkable that two princes should have been conspicuous at the same time in our annals, each bearing the name of Caractacus, one the son, the other the step-son, of Cartismandua; a circumstance which has created no small confusion among historians: that they are quite different persons, may be plainly established on examining the particulars of their times with attention.

The precise date of the marriage of Cartismandua to Cadallan is not given, but it was shortly followed by other alliances among their families not less important; the Brigantine princess Boadicea being given in mar-

---

[1] Tacitus. [2] D'Anville. Hutchinson's Durham.

[3] Scott, Anderson, and Nesbitt.

riage to Arviragus, son of Cartismandua, while his sister became the wife of Caractacus, son of Europeia, who, perhaps to distinguish him from his contemporary and namesake, the King of the Britons, was designated Urickfras, or the Strong-armed. These ties no doubt were intended still further to strengthen the states of Britain, and on the part of the Brigantines, to fortify themselves against Rome in case of necessity; but unfortunately events did not occur in the course which had been anticipated.

One of the first important changes was the death of Metallanus, King of Scots, who leaving no children, the throne devolved upon Caractacus, his nephew; for the laws relative to succession among the Picts were different from those of the Celtic and Teutonic nations, the sons inheriting by right of their mother:[1] thus Caractacus obtained the crown as the son of Europeia; by his elevation the daughter of Cartismandua became the Queen of the Scots,—a brilliant event in the life of her aspiring mother. But it must be named that Cadallan did not himself live to witness his son's accession to power; he died at an early period after his union with Cartismandua, leaving his consort with entire control over the kingdom of Brigantia, now hers in her own right,[2] which, joined to that of the Iceni, gave her as much influence throughout the island as could possibly be enjoyed by either her children or step-children.[3] Well might the heart of the Roman Queen of the Britons be lifted up, in beholding her noble and fortunate offspring blessed with peace, prosperity and power, and herself the friend and ally of a nation so mighty as that of Rome; as an instance of the esteem in which she was held, it is recorded that a large sum of money had been lent to her husband Cadallan by that people,—a circumstance which, though gratifying in the beginning, in the end proved disadvantageous to her interests.

Some account should here be given of a people so singular as the new subjects of Cartismandua,—the Brigantes, who are said to have been the same tribe as the Meatæ, who eventually settled north of the Wall of Adrian.[4]

The Caledonians and Meatæ, in war and peace, closely resembled each other. Their arms of warfare consisted of a short spear, a broadsword, a dirk, and javelin, with a small target for self-defence. They had neither towns nor villages, houses nor towers; living only in huts, they, like the Britons of the south, had for their subsistence, chiefly milk, the flesh of cattle, and the game killed by their own hands. They were swift and sure-footed, could patiently endure toil, and every hardship. They had horses which were small in size and fleet, and were accustomed to use chariots in warfare, in which they rushed to the thickest of the battle. It is related that in long marches they used a preparation, a quantity of which, no bigger than a bean, sufficed to prevent all sense of hunger and thirst. They were in the habit, like the Britons, of painting and tattooing their bodies, whence they are thought to have obtained the name of *Picts*. In war they cast aside the wolf-skins, which they were accus-

[1] Palgrave. [2] Dr Henry. [3] Carte, &c.
[4] Ridpath's Border History.

tomed to wear over their left shoulder, girt with leathern thongs,[1] and appeared on the field of battle almost naked, like the Roman gladiators, wearing round their neck, collars or torques, formed of twisted iron wire, which they regarded as great ornaments, and prized as highly as the other British tribes did theirs of silver and gold;[2] their greatest pride was to exhibit their skins punctured as they were, and painted with the figures of divers animals, flowers, and the heavenly bodies.

There is every reason to believe that the pictures represented on the body of each individual were an index to his history, and like the hieroglyphics of the ancient Egyptians, handed down records from generation to generation.[3] Such an art, rude as it was, displays no small ingenuity; this opinion is corroborated by the fact, that these figures were afterwards transferred to the shield or banner of the person to whom they belonged. The "marks of the Britons," as they were called,[4] may be regarded as a personal species of heraldry, often recognisable in their names, as in that of "Pen-dragon," the appellation of the family of King Arthur of renowned memory,—the head of a dragon being his device.

It is remarkable that nearly all the ancient British names were expressive of colour;[5] and Camden, who makes this observation, adds that "the most common names of the Britons at present, Gwyn, Dû, Goch, Llwyd, were derived from white, black, red and russet; so that it seems not at all extraordinary that the whole nation should have taken their name from the several tints used in the general practice of painting themselves: and the inhabitants also, both ancient and modern, take their name from colours." The plants called madder were not only in constant requisition for home use, but, next to tin and wool, constituted a great article of commerce with the continent; it was thought by Pliny to have been the same as the plantain of Gaul. Not only married women, but young maidens, are said to have anointed and dyed their bodies with the juice of this plant; some indeed stained themselves all over with its deepest dye, till they became, in colour, like Ethiopians,—a fashion much esteemed. In this guise they attended solemn fasts and festivals, without any other attire,[6] though this seems to have been only the practice for certain offices of religion.

Such was the people amongst whom Cartismandua, refined by birth,

---

[1] Hutchinson's Durham.

[2] Smith and Meyrick. Howel's Med. Hist. Angl.; and Herodian.

[3] O'Flaherty says the figures were printed with ink, by iron marks.

[4] By Tertullian, "Britannorum stigmata."

[5] The following list is given on the authority of Camden:—
Cogidumnus and Argentocoxus contain *coch* or *goch*, red.
Mandubratius, Cartismandua, Togodumnus, and Bonduca contain *dû*, black.
Venusius and Immannentius contain *gwyn* or *uen*, white.
Cuniglas contains *glas*, blue.
Cingetorix and Arviragus contain *aure*, or gold colour.
Some of the above names were derived from the Romans, as the word *werith*, green, from *viridis*, by which the identity of the names Arviragus and Prasutagus is proved, *werith* and *prasinus* both signifying green.

[6] Pliny, Speed.

education, and association, found herself in command A change at this time seems to have taken place in her character, and brings it out in a stronger and less pleasing light than it has hitherto appeared.

From the period of the banishment of Adminius, Rome had become a rendezvous for all disaffected Britons. Bericus, a rebel, who had fled thither, having been received and protected by the Emperor Claudius, who refused to deliver him up on application from Togodumnus, King of the Britains, that prince was so offended,[1] that when the next application was made by the Romans for the tribute-money, they met with an indignant refusal, and were, moreover, so fiercely attacked by the passionate Guiderius that they scarcely escaped with their lives: in their haste, they fled to the shelter of those fortresses they had prudently established to guard against a sudden surprise.[2]

The Britons followed up this attack by prohibiting all commerce with Rome.[3] The news of this decree annoyed the Romans greatly, as much of the British produce had become necessary to them; particularly the metals,[4] which they prized highly. Pliny says that the best mirrors were anciently made with a mixture of copper and tin; and that in his time those of silver were so common, that they "were used even by the servant-maids." These metallic mirrors were very much in request amongst ancient nations. The Egyptian women, whenever they went to their temples, carried one in their left hand.

Pliny observes that such was the luxury of the Romans, that it was simply reckoned a piece of elegance to consume, in the ornaments of coaches and the trappings of horses, metals which their ancestors could not use even in drinking vessels, without being astonished at their own prodigality. Nero and his wife shod their favorite horses with gold and silver.

We learn also from Pliny, that the lead mines of Britain were very productive during the first century, especially that at Comeristwith, in Wales; so much so, that the Britons had limited the amount of the yearly quantity to be wrought and transported over the sea. Pliny relates a marvellous story of one of the miners and a favourite crow, which was so tame, that it daily flew and followed him wherever he went. "This man, being one day at work in a valley where the first mine was known to be, laid his purse and girdle beside him, and set to work earnestly, according to his usual custom. The crow kept flitting about him, till it molested him so much that he got angry and menaced the bird. The crow, on this, seized the girdle and purse in its beak and flew away. The man, in despair, at the thought of losing his money, threw aside his tools, and set off in pursuit. By this he saved his life, for he was scarcely out of the mine when it fell in and killed all his fellow-workmen."

British wicker-work,[5] also, was a commodity highly prized at Rome,

---

[1] Milton, Rapin, Speed. [2] Holinshed. [3] Ibid.

[4] Lead, in the form of *ceruse*, was in great request among the Roman ladies as a cosmetic. Plautus introduces a waiting-woman refusing to give her mistress either ceruse or rouge, because, in the true spirit of a flattering Abigail, "she thought her quite handsome enough without them."—*Bp. Watson*

[5] Holinshed.

and much inconvenience was experienced by the Romans from the loss of all this produce, when Togodumnus thus checked the commerce between the two countries. Not the least was the deficiency in payment of the tribute-money, so regularly transmitted by Cymbeline during the whole of his long reign; for though the Romans held Britain in contempt, her money was acceptable.[1]

Claudius despatched an army to reduce Britain to obedience. Aulus Plautius, a man of consular dignity and great wisdom and valour, was, with Cneius Sentius, appointed to the command; he was accompanied by Vespasian, afterwards Emperor, and various other noted persons, among whom was the young Titus, who in this war greatly distinguished himself, and on one occasion was so fortunate as to save his father's life.[2] Four legions, with auxiliaries and cavalry, in all constituting a force of 50,000, embarked for Britain, when an amusing incident occurred,—the soldiers beseeching Plautius, with great earnestness, "not to lead them against a people inhabiting a region beyond the limits of the world:" so barbarous were the Britons considered by these civilized Roman soldiers, that Plautius had the utmost difficulty in getting them on board the vessels.

On their arrival, the Romans were guided by Bericus to the parts of Britain inhabited by his friends; but so bravely were they opposed by the natives, that although in the contest Caractacus[3] and Togodumnus were slain, Plautius was compelled to write off to Claudius to come to his assistance.[4] The aged Emperor, immediately on his arrival, advanced into the country of the Trinobantes, and took possession of Camalodunum.[5] After this he laid siege to the city of Winchester, where Arviragus, who, by his brother Guiderius's death in this contest, had become King, had stationed himself. The Romans first besieged Venta; but afterwards, it was proposed to Arviragus that he should divorce his Queen, Boadicea, and espouse Gwenissa, the daughter of Claudius, at the same time acknowledging the Roman supremacy. These terms being acceded to, peace was agreed on between the Roman Emperor and his barbarian son-in-law.

During the stay of Claudius in Britain, he is said to have endeavoured to reduce the Brigantes also under the Roman yoke. It is worthy of

[1] Hegesippus says, of Britain, "When we would deprive men not only of the privileges of Rome, but, in a manner, of the conversation of mankind, we send them thither, and banish them out of the world."

[2] Suetonius, Milton, Dr. Henry.

[3] This Caractacus, or Caradoc, was son of Cymbeline and Cartismandua. The victory of Plautius, the Roman general, was honoured with an ovation, and when he went to Rome, the Emperor in person came forth to meet him, giving him the right hand all the way.

[4] Speed.

[5] Claudius, aware of the terror created among the Britons by the appearance of an elephant, well fenced with iron, having on its back a tower full of men, such as Cæsar had brought over with his army, caused some to be brought to Britain on the present expedition. On the former occasion the sight of that monstrous walking battery, moving into the Thames, had effectually frightened the Britons from the opposite shores.—*Lewis, Rapin.*

notice that Seneca, who is said to have lent money to the husband of Cartismandua, writes thus of Claudius; and Camden,[1] who gives the passage, considers it a clear proof that their submission was not enforced, but voluntary; —

> "'Twas he whose all-commanding yoke
> The furthest Britons gladly took;
> Him the Brigantes in blue arms adored,
> When the vast ocean feared his power,
> Restrained with laws unknown before.
> And trembling Neptune served a Roman lord."

It was natural that Cartismandua should receive the Romans amicably, though the acquiescence of her subjects in an alliance with their hitherto hated foes, must have been rather the result of necessity than free will, as subsequent events proved. Whether Cartismandua was personally introduced to the Emperor, is not positively stated; but assuredly a princess known in infancy to the mighty Cæsar, and educated at his court, would readily confirm with Claudius the friendship Cymbeline had during his life preserved unbroken. It is true that two of her sons had thrown off that alliance, and called forth the angry indignation of the "masters of the world," but they had paid with their lives the penalty of opposition. Policy clearly directed Cartismandua to avail herself of the Roman protection, and she appears to have seen cause to remain their ally and friend to the last.

After the return of Claudius to Rome, the war broke out afresh, through the resentment of Caractacus at the injuries done his sister, Boadicea, whose cause he warmly espoused; and we afterwards find Arviragus, after he had become sufficiently powerful, abandoning his allegiance to Rome, forsaking the daughter of Claudius, and reconciling himself to Boadicea. Vespasian, at the head of the Romans, defeated the allied forces of the Britons, and fearing Cartismandua would espouse the cause of her children, he, after taking the city of Camelon, hastily marched into Galloway or Brigantia, and took possession of the city of Carrick. It was at that place, the capital of the territories of Cartismandua, that Vespasian received the oaths of allegiance of the Brigantes, who despaired of recovering their freedom.[2] Cartismandua being herself desirous to maintain peace, and, moreover, indebted to them a large sum of money, was placed in a difficult position. Her son, whose character proves him to have inherited her own ambition, had been forced into submission, Vespasian requiring him to come in his own person, casting aside his royal attire, and appearing in the humblest apparel, a suppliant for pardon and protection: this the proud Queen was obliged to acquiesce in, however galling she might find it.

Not long afterwards Vespasian was recalled by Claudius to Rome, and we do not hear any more of Arviragus from this date, except as the ally and friend of the Romans, whose protection was thus secured to both Cartismandua and himself.

Aulus Plautius being left at the head of the Roman affairs in Britain, at a time when a dangerous illness prevented his attending to the neces-

[1] Mag. Brit. [2] Holinshed.

sary duties of the war, the Romans were in danger of losing as much as they had gained, when Ostorius Scapula, a man of noble descent, and great experience both in peace and war, was appointed Pro-Prætor in the place of Aulus Plautius. He had no sooner arrived than that general expired at Camelon, where he was residing at the time:[1] he had survived the departure of Vespasian only two years, during which time the warfare had been carried on in Kyle and Galloway against the brave Caractacus.

After the arrival of Ostorius, the Britons made a fierce irruption into the territories in alliance with Rome, but were repulsed with great slaughter. Among the friends of the Roman Empire, the Iceni till then might be numbered, who had "by their own request" kept up an amicable footing: these were the subjects of Cymbeline and Cartismandua, and had consequently been uninjured by the war. When Ostorius, to protect himself from his disaffected neighbours, attempted to build a chain of forts between the Nen and the Severn, the Iceni themselves flew to arms. They were, however, defeated, and Marcus Ostorius, son of the Roman general, for saving the life of a fellow-citizen in the engagement, was presented with the civic crown. Those of the Brigantines who had rebelled were also obliged to make terms of peace, and the Silures alone maintained the contest under the brave Caractacus, son-in-law of Queen Cartismandua.[2]

About this time the Queen of the Brigantes had married Venusius, a British chieftain, one of the most skilful generals of his time. This prince, called by some writers Prince of the Jugantes, possessed many noble qualities; but whatever motives led to this marriage of Queen Cartismandua, it is generally allowed to have proved most unfortunate to the parties themselves, to their country, and to their allies, the Romans. Both British and Roman authors concur in the praise of Venusius, whose coins have been preserved, and may be seen represented in some of their histories. New accessions to the dignity and possessions of the already powerful Cartismandua must have accrued from this match, and at first no symptoms appeared of the evils about to ensue. Yet a period of calamity for Britain, and bloodshed for Rome, was preparing. While all seemed to submit to the Roman supremacy, one high and haughty soul had scorned to tamper with the freedom of his country. Caractacus had already struggled boldly for his sister's sake; he now reappeared in arms against Rome, and battle followed battle during the space of nine

---

[1] Plautius was interred in the church of Claudius and Victoria, which Vespasian had built on the banks of the river, near the city; the body of the Roman pro-prætor had been previously burnt, and the ashes inclosed in an urn after the Roman fashion. The Picts and Scots afterwards adopted this mode of burial. [Holinshed.] "The British *cairn* was a heap of stones thrown over the urns in which they deposited the ashes of the dead. These were placed in a stone chest within, termed by the Welsh and Irish by a word denoting a *bed*, and by the British word signifying *sleeping-place.* There were no inscriptions, but a few triplets committed to memory handed down, by oral tradition, the names and deeds of the departed." [Smith and Meyrick.] Bania, an Irish queen, was interred in the hill called, from the circumstance, Knockbane. [O'Flaherty.]

[2] Tacitus.

years, Britain becoming the scene of a succession of contests, which ended only in the defeat of that heroic and vainly persevering chieftain.

In the last fatal encounter which took place at Caer Caradoc,[1] in Shropshire, A. D. 51, the Britons were completely defeated, the wife and daughter of Caractacus were taken prisoners, one of his brothers was forced to surrender at discretion,[2] and the unfortunate prince himself, who was so severely wounded that he with the greatest difficulty escaped from the field of battle, was compelled to seek an asylum with his mother-in-law, Queen Cartismandua, who was at the time residing at Dunstaffnage, one of the royal cities of the Brigantes: the heroic chief, judging by his own heart, trusted that his mother-in-law, though an ally of Rome, would respect his misfortunes, and protect his person in this hour of extreme exigency.

A dark cloud now overshadows the character of Cartismandua, who, instead of extending the protection which Caractacus had hoped to find, at once abandoned every feeling of affection and compassion, and mindful only of her own interest, delivered up her unfortunate son-in-law to the Roman general.

If anything could be advanced in extenuation of such an act, it might be the fact that the daughter of Cartismandua was in the power of the Romans, with several other members of the family of Caractacus; perhaps fear for her daughter's fate, should she neglect to deliver up the enemy of Rome, might have had some influence on her conduct, together with alarm for her own safety and that of her kingdom. Before she decided to betray the unfortunate Caractacus, Cartismandua, it appears, consulted her husband, and her doing so seems to show that she still hesitated. Self-interest, however, prevailed; and she reflected that to protect and shelter Caractacus would be to violate her own faith with the Romans; and she reasoned, that to give him up, would, perhaps, be the ultimate means of saving his life, as well as that of her daughter, while both, as relatives of hers, might be respected by the conqueror. Amid these conflicting arguments, Venusius, anxious to conciliate his wife and preserve the kingdom, is said to have assented to yield up the unfortunate prince.[3] Without loss of time, therefore, a secret messenger conveyed to Ostorius Scapula the tidings of the important prisoner awaiting his disposal.[4]

Some authors have endeavoured to increase the odium which this act has fixed on the memory of the Queen, by attributing it to the envy she felt towards the Picts, whom she desired to behold in the same state of thraldom as her own countrymen, the Britons. Others have ascribed the act to the vanity of her ambition to shine as a powerful ally of Rome, and a hope of aggrandisement, to which she sacrificed all the better feelings

---

[1] Tacitus, Warrington, Holinshed, Speed, Lewis, &c.

[2] Until very recently it was customary for a society of gentlemen to meet annually on the hill Caer Caradoc, so famed for being the scene of the defeat of the hero whose name it bears, whose praise they celebrate on the occasion in prose or verse. On one of those occasions an admirable extempore poem was delivered by the Rev. Mr. Sneyd Davies. [Pennant, Lluyd.]

[3] Speed, Holinshed, Warrington, Dr. Henry.

[4] Scott, &c.

of her nature; be this as it may, certain it is that the Romans overwhelmed her with favours in consequence. Cartismandua is accused of having thrown Caractacus, chained, into prison; but it is to be hoped that those writers are correct who state, that the first fetters which bound the person and wrung the soul of the heroic victim were those with which he was bound by the Romans, a strong party of whom were instantly dispatched, who, coming secretly and suddenly on Caractacus, seized the wounded hero, and conveyed him to the presence of Ostorius. Unconquered even then, the chief addressed these words to the Roman general: "I have been beaten, and lost my liberty, rather through my perfidious step-mother's deceit than the strength of thy arms; it is my duty to submit to the conqueror; but remember thine is, to follow the laws of clemency." Ostorius asking him in what manner he should use him, "In the same," answered Caractacus, "as thou wouldst wish to be used, if thou wert my prisoner." [1]

The joy of the Romans at this unexpected piece of good fortune was unbounded; the unfortunate King was sent, with his whole family, to Rome, to grace their triumph; and ornaments of honour were decreed to Ostorius, who still remained in Britain.[2]

Let us consider next the consequences of giving up Caractacus, to Cartismandua herself.

In the first place, the infamous deed drew upon the Queen and her husband the hatred of the whole British people;[3] but they were obliged to suppress their feelings, for Venusius and Cartismandua were under the all-powerful protection of the Roman Empire; their indignation did not, however, less fiercely burn to avenge the injuries of Caractacus. Loaded with benefits, the treacherous sovereigns for a time had cause for apparent rejoicing in the success of their perfidy, if wealth and power were the aim of the step they had taken. Cartismandua beheld herself raised to a pinnacle of greatness unknown in Britain before her times; her pride is thought to have risen with her fortunes, and she became dazzled by the sunshine of such great prosperity. Luxury seemed now her sole aim, and its necessary corruption followed.[4]

The just jealousy of Venusius had been awakened by the levity Cartismandua displayed in her conduct towards one of her own or her husband's train, a shield-bearer, called Vellocatus.[5] Cartismandua is said to have taken advantage of her husband's displeasure to execute an intention which she had long fostered, to abandon him altogether; an open separation was at once effected, and the Queen, careless of opinion, set no bounds to her will, and in defiance of all decency, espoused the armour-bearer in public, either according to Roman or British custom, after which she caused her new spouse to be proclaimed king.[6] The reasons that

---

[1] Pineda's History of the Brigantes. [2] Dr. Henry.

[3] Camden says, that the yielding Caractacus up to the Romans, obtained wealth from them for the Queen, as though she had *sold him over to his enemies;* that this wealth procured luxury, which led to all the evils which followed.

[4] Milton. [5] Lappenberg.

[6] Henry, Malcolm, Lewis, Holinshed, Tacitus, Milton, Stowe.

induced Cartismandua thus to degrade her dignity are unknown, nor is it conjectured how Venusius, whose noble qualities, except in one instance, were generally admitted, could so suddenly have become hateful to her; the Queen's heart seems to have been changed, and the elevation of fortune to which she had of late attained by unworthy means, altogether destroyed her former principle.

The last act of Cartismandua, the elevating Vellocatus to the supreme dignity, proved the ruin of herself and family; it exasperated the people to such a degree, that the whole kingdom was in commotion. Venusius was by all parties esteemed the lawful husband of Cartismandua, and so general was the abhorrence felt at the conduct of the Queen, that they scorned to be ruled by her, and resolved to support her injured husband's right to the throne.[1] The neighbouring states supported this determination, being, as well as the Brigantes, jealous of the ambition and authority of Cartismandua.[2]

The flower of the British youth, having assembled under the conduct of Venusius, attacked the Queen in the heart of her own territories, of which the chief city had declared for Venusius.[3] This unexpected defection in her own subjects was fatal to the Queen's cause. After many sharp encounters she was reduced to such extremities, as to be on the point of falling into the hands of the brave warriors whom she had so much injured. To escape was impossible; no alternative remained, but to apply for help to the Romans, and to them Cartismandua knew her appeal would not be in vain; in fact, the experience of her Roman allies had already caused them to foresee the danger into which the Queen had now fallen. At Cartismandua's request, some bands of horse and foot soldiers were sent to her aid. Several encounters took place between the Roman forces and those of the Queen's enemies; but the former at last prevailed, and were enabled to deliver the Queen from her perilous situation: her person was saved, but she was forced to yield up the possession of her kingdom to Venusius.

The war which domestic dissensions had begun, now involved the foreign foe: up to this time Venusius, who had lived in amity with his Queen, had respected and been respected by the Romans, her friends and allies;[4] now that they openly protected her against his interest, his resentment was unbounded, and he, from this period, vowed vengeance on Rome; and though he had only taken up arms to avenge his own wrongs, he henceforth resolved to engage in a war of hatred against the powerful Roman Empire.[5] The struggle, henceforward, was not for liberty, but for vengeance; and Venusius gave his skilful enemies unexpected trouble.[6] During the three years which ensued, we have no more mention of Cartismandua, who probably had sought shelter and protection at Camalodunum, with her great allies. Her security was, however, shortly endangered; for the camp which Ostorius had established amidst the Silures (the general still persevering in his design of erecting the chain of forts between the Nen and the Severn) was attacked by the Bri-

[1] Malcolm, Lewis, Speed. [2] Tacitus, Holinshed. [3] Camden.
[4] Tacitus. [5] Ibid. [6] Milton

tons in a body, who surrounded the officer commanding the legionary cohorts, and, but for sudden succour from the neighbouring garrisons, would have cut to pieces the whole corps. As it was, the præfect of the camp, with eight centurions and the bravest of the soldiers, were killed on the spot.[1] These and other reverses exasperated and harassed Ostorius, while the Briton's fiercest wrath was aroused by hearing that he had declared he would extirpate the very name of the Silures. A foraging-party of Romans, and the detachment sent to their support, were soon after put to the rout, and two whole auxiliary cohorts, sent in quest of plunder, became prisoners of war to the fierce Britons. Overcome by the continued anxiety of this varying war, Ostorius sunk with fatigue, A. D. 55, when Aulus Didius was appointed to the command of the Roman forces in the island.[2]

During the interval which preceded the arrival of Didius, Manlius Valens, and the legion he commanded, had hazarded a battle, in which they were defeated by the Silures.[3] The first step taken by the new general was to invade the territories of Corbred, King of Scots, who had succeeded to the crown on the imprisonment of his brother Caractacus, and till this time had preserved amity with Rome. This step was taken at the express request of Queen Cartismandua.

The territory of the Picts, on the borders of Scotland, had been assigned to Caractacus for his life, and when that chieftain died, the Romans laid claim to it as reverting to them. This was represented to the Scottish King, who, at the head of an army, had advanced to the scene of warfare, by a herald from Aulus Didius, who ordered the inabitants of Galloway to depart from that district, and make way for the Romans. The herald of haughty Rome would have been put to death, but was spared out of regard to the laws of arms. Scarcely was the message received, when Corbred learnt that Cæsius Nasica had entered Galloway with a Roman legion, to the great terror of the inhabitants,[4] who, in the engagement which ensued, were defeated by their skilful enemies.

Corbred, who had distributed his men in several castles and fortresses for better security, advanced to Epiake, to obtain advice and assistance from Venusius. He took possession of that city, and left the Brigantes to defend it against their mutual foes.

At this juncture, Queen Cartismandua contrived, by some stratagem, to seize the persons of Venusius, his brother, and several of his family, whom she threw into prison at Epiake; by which one would infer that a party in her favour had still existed among her own people. It is said that the Queen was induced to hazard this daring step, to prevent her husband and his family assisting the Scotch King, as had been stipulated by the late alliance made with Corbred. It would seem that Venusius

[1] Tacitus.

[2] "Didius was a tame, inactive officer, whose great age prevented his performing anything remarkable in the war; indeed, he never risked his own person in any single engagement, but acted by the medium of his officers, content to keep the enemy in subjection, without seeking to add further honours to those he had before accumulated."—*Tacitus.*

[3] Tacitus.

[4] Scott, Holinshed, &c.

himself must have afterwards escaped, as he appears, soon after, opposing Cartismandua in a sharp engagement, in which the Queen, aided by her Roman allies, came off victorious. On this last event, the brave warrior certainly fell into the hands of his relentless wife. Historians relate, that when Corbred heard the tidings of what had befallen Venusius and his family, he hastily retreated towards Epiake.[1] Finding, however, upon his return there, that the cause of Cartismandua was nearly desperate, and that she had resolved to put her prisoners to death,[2] his arrival became the signal of triumph over the fated Queen, who was now in his power; and her enemies were released. The punishment inflicted by the Scottish King on Cartismandua, which immediately followed, marks how deeply he had felt injured by the wrongs of his brother Caractacus, who, like himself, was her step-son, both being children of Cadallan, her former husband.

It appears that Cartismandua was immured alive; her advanced age unconsidered and unpitied. This horrible though deserved death is an indication of the spirit of the times, in which such savage vengeance was considered virtue. From her birth to her grave, Cartismandua's life had been one of vicissitude and irritation. The exile of her father, and loss of his dominions, her marriage and return to Britain, which she looked upon as in itself an exile; the fatal disobedience of her son Adminius, the disaffection of Guiderius and Arviragus from the Roman interest, in which her own was bound up, and the union of her daughter with the declared enemy of Rome; all these events must have filled the heart of the Queen with constant agitations, while the necessary struggles to maintain her power kept her in ceaseless action and alarm; till at length, the unprecedented step she was led into by her ungoverned will, cancelled all her former triumphs, and covered her with disgrace and ruin.

After his signal act of vengeance, Corbred advanced against Cæsius Nasica, whose forces he routed; and from that time forward, an unremitting and successful war was carried on against the Romans, the Brigantes remaining unsubdued during the whole reign of Vespasian.

---

1 Scott, Guthrie, Holinshed.

2 Camden.

BOADICEA "THE WARLIKE."

"War! war! no peace! peace is to me a war!"

The Pictish Princes—Cadallan—Metallanus—Boadicea's claims on British sympathy—British mothers—The Castle of Maidens—Education—Marriage and wrongs of Boadicea—Caractacus rouses himself—Arviragus throws off the Roman yoke — Defeat of the Britons — Roman triumph — Will of Prasutagus—Manner in which it was respected — Seneca as usurer — Outrages of the Romans—Rage and grief of the Britons—Boadicea's resolve—Corbred moved to help her—Insolent answer of the Romans—Taking of Mona—Boadicea's magnificent speech and prayer to Adraste—The hare—Preparations for the fight—Camalodunum—Omens—Fate of the city—Successes—Cruelties — St. Albans taken—The Wheel of Fortune turns—Reaction—Defeat of the Britons—Death of the Queen.

THE disastrous fortunes of Boadicea have furnished a theme for many an historian and poet: and a more dramatic subject could scarcely be discovered throughout the whole of our British annals: as a wife, a queen, a patriot, and a mother, Boadicea was for her heroism in misfortunes unequalled. Spenser, commenting upon the surname of "Victorious," bestowed upon this ill-fated Queen by the Britons, says she was one—

"Who, whiles good-fortune favoured her might,
Triumphed oft against her enemies;
And yet, though overcome in haplesse fight,
She triumphed o'er death in ennemis despight."
Faerie Queene.

Little indeed in accordance with the actual history of Boadicea was that triumphant title: her misfortunes might rather, like Priam's, have given her a right to the sad distinction he claimed—

"The first of men in sovereign misery."

Who has not felt sympathy for

"——The British warrior-queen,
Bleeding from the Roman rods;"

and with tears of commiseration followed her, when she

"Sought, with an indignant mien,
Counsel of her country's gods!"

The word "Boadicea" is variously written—Bonduca, or Voadicea, or Woda, the letters b and v being used indiscriminately, as in Spanish, by British writers; according to one commentator, "the woman of the sword" is the real meaning of the term: others say that the really British name was Aregwedd Buddig, or "the Victorious," "Buddig"[1] being "Boo Tika" upon the coins of the Queen.

[1] "Beadaighe." The word "Buddig" is preserved in an ancient poem, in conjunction with those of Beli the Great and Mynogan, his predecessor.—*Rev. P Roberts.*

The mother of Boadicea, Europeia, was a daughter of King Evenus II., and a descendant of Agasia, princess of Britain.[1] Through her, Boadicea might, as King Henry VII. long afterwards did, have laid claim to the honours of a royal Trojan ancestry; on the side of her father also, who boasted himself the descendant of Scota, she derived her origin from the Egyptian monarchs.[2] If this exalted birth could confer happiness, how brilliant and glad might have been the destiny of Boadicea!

The family of Boadicea had early became distinguished by its fidelity to the throne. Cadallus, her grandfather, had signalized himself by his protection of the infant children of Durstus and Agasia, during the period they were excluded from the succession on account of their minority; when one of these young princes became king, as Evenus II., Cadallus filled the office of Regent.

The gratitude of Evenus caused him to reward this tried and faithful friend by the gift of the territory of Brigantia, together with other estates; and when, after the death of Cadallus, dissensions arose among his sons as to the division of their patrimonial inheritance, the King himself undertook to adjust their difference. To the eldest son, Cadallan, afterwards the father of Boadicea, he awarded the greater part of the family estates in Brigantia, with supreme authority over the rest; constituting, in fact, a sort of petty sovereignty. Angus was apportioned to the second son, and the remainder of Brigantia to the third: after which, the Scottish King, in person, proceeded to Epiake, where, in the most conspicuous part of the city he caused a statue, in honor of his departed friend, to be erected.[3]

Cadallan, who was married to Europeia, niece of King Ederus, the next prince who sat on the throne, fixed his residence at Carictonium, in the county of Carrick, and there several of his children were born. As the sons of Pictish princesses inherited the crown by right of their mother, it was thought that Cadallan aspired to the supplanting of the young monarch to whom he had been appointed guardian, but he gave a very convincing proof of the uprightness of his intentions in that respect.

The King, for his vices, had been thrown into prison by the people; and one of the persons about the court, under the impression that he might gain favour with Cadallan, secretly entered the dungeon and assassinated him. The Regent, filled with horror and indignation, put the murderer to death for the crime, and instead of availing himself of this event for an act of treason, instantly proclaimed Metallanus, his wife's brother, king. This prince possessed a character totally different from his predecessor, and swayed the sceptre for the space of thirty years in undisturbed peace and harmony.

During the reign of Metallanus, Cadallan, who had lost his wife Europeia, entered into a second alliance; the lady whom he selected was

---

[1] Tacitus, Speed, Guthrie, Anderson, and Nesbitt.

[2] See Rev. P. Roberts on the Early History of the Cymri, or Ancient Britons

[3] Pineda, Boetius, Polydore Virgil, Holinshed.

Cartismandua,[1] widow of Cymbeline, the deceased King of the Britons, whose eventful life has just been related in this work.

At the period of her second marriage, Cartismandua, as has been shown, had a numerous family by her first husband. The family of Cadallan consisted of three sons and a daughter; of these Caractacus was the eldest, the daughter was Boadicea.

This princess has the highest claims on British sympathy, from the fact of her having been born, nursed, and bred among her countrymen. She had no leaning to the Roman invaders of the soil; Britain alone had her heart; and the freedom of her country, for which women, as well as men, in her time lived and died, was her ambition.

Her mother's country was the *southern* portion of Scotland, now known as the Lowlands; consequently the habits and manners of those people governed her education and character, and the sentiments displayed throughout her after-life, were caught from those associations.

Among the ancient women of Britain it was a thing to cause suspicion of a wife's fidelity, if her child were reared by any other than the mother. The British matron did not consider it fostered with due care, unless nursed at her own bosom; for she would have dreaded a degeneration from the parents, as well as danger to the infant's life.[2] On the birth of a son, it was usual for the mother to place the first food on the point of her husband's sword, and to insert it in the child's mouth; at the same time she offered a devout prayer to the gods of her country, that the babe might at some future period end his life amidst the swords and javelins of his enemies on the field of battle.[3] We are not actually told that a female child was desired to share the same fate; but as in those days women ever attended upon the warlike expeditions of their husbands, there is little doubt but that the spirit with which Boadicea the Warlike was reared, tended to the same purpose.

In the Isle of Skye, a famous fortress existed in those times, in which the use of arms was taught by a woman; it was called Dun Sgathach; but the scene of the education of the princesses of the Pictish nation, was the celebrated Castle of Maydens, situated in the vicinity of Holyrood House, Edinburgh. Camden, after describing that monastery, proceeds to state that over the edifice, "within a park well stocked with deer, hares, and conies, hangs a mountain with two tops, called Arthur's Chair, from Arthur the Briton. On the west side, there mounts up a rock to a mighty height, steep and inaccessible on all sides but that which looks towards the city, upon which stands a castle, so strongly fortified with a great number of towers, that it is looked upon as impregnable. This the Britons called 'Castle Myned Agned,' and the Scots, 'The Maiden's Castle,' and 'The Virgin's Castle,' because the maiden princesses of the blood-royal of the Picts were kept here."[4]

---

[1] The date of this marriage cannot be very easily determined: it occurred between the years 2 and 29. Cymbeline died A. D. 2, and Metallanus in 29, who is expressly stated to have survived Cadallan; but the date of Cadallan's second marriage and that of his death are undiscovered.

[2] Holinshed.

[3] Solinus.

[4] The Castle of Maidens, afterwards called Edenburgh, from Aidan, one of the

"Here were the daughters and grand-daughters of Pictish monarchs kept in strait custody, and appointed to learn to sewe and worke, till they came to years of marriage."[1] The study of warlike achievements was, therefore, not the only occupation of the female sex.

There is much interest in inquiring into the kind of implements made use of in this primitive condition of society. The ancient British needle was made of bone, and resembled that used for the heads of arrows. The Welsh word "Nedwydd" literally implies, sharp-pointed wood; the British word "Gwaell" signifies a needle, bodkin, skewer, or brooch, and singularly enough is a denomination made use of for several bones; thus "Gwaell y goes" is the spindle-bone of the leg, and "Gwaell yr Yswydd," the shoulder-blade bone, which perhaps was split for needles or bodkins.[2]

With the rude implements described, the skins of animals which had been killed in the chase[3] were sewn together, either with leathern thongs or vegetable fibres.

Another favorite employment of the early British maiden, was that of weaving baskets, and the structure of these baskets was so much admired by the Romans, that they not only introduced them into Italy, but even adopted the British name for the *bascawd*, terming them *bascawdæ*.[4] The daughters of modern England and Scotland, who are so familiarly acquainted with the many domestic uses of the basket, must not forget that they owe its invention to the native island maidens who preceded them, nineteen centuries ago. Amongst these, no doubt was the royal Boadicea, who was instructed in all such feminine accomplishments as existed in her time. Nor are we left wholly in ignorance of the associates of her infancy, for several Pictish princesses of that date are noticed by our historians. These were Crifanga and Nairia, who were both daughters of Pictish monarchs. The first lady married in A. D. 15, Lugad Ribdearg, King of Ireland, who had by his second queen, Devor-

---

Scottish kings, was built by the same British king who founded the city of York, whence we discover him to have been of the Pictish race. He was named Ebranke; and the town of York, where his remains reposed, was formerly denominated Caer Ebranke, or Eboracum. From Maiden Castle in Stanmore, in the North Riding of Yorkshire, ran the old military way, called the Maiden Way, because it began at Maiden Castle, and which passed through the ancient town of which the vast ruins yet remaining below Kirkby Thore, in Westmoreland, [north-west of Appleby, upon the river Eden,] are called by the people there *Whely Castle*. This old town is about 300 yards in length, and 150 in breadth, and has three entrances on each side, with bulwarks before them; Roman urns and coins are frequently dug up there.—*Ency. Brit.*

About a mile from Dunstable, in Bedfordshire, is the encampment called Maiden Bower, 2,500 feet in circumference, environed by a ditch and a rampart. Near Leighton Buzzard is a similar one; and on the road from Bedford to Eaton Socon a third may be discerned. See Camden.

[1] Holinshed.

[2] Smith and Meyrick: Costumes of Ancient Britons. This work refers to the Archæologia for some pictures of these bone needles.

[3] Smith. [4] Hope's Essays, &c.

gilla, a son, named Crimthan.[1] This Crimthan subsequently married Nairia, daughter of Laoch, another Pictish king, and assumed from his wife the surname of Niadhnar.[2] It was usual for Pictish princes to assume the name of their wife or mother, from the custom which existed among them of conveying the hereditary rights of their monarchs through the female line. On the death of the king, a new member of the royal family was selected as his successor, who always laid claim to the throne "by the spindle side," and was presented to the people as his *mother's* heir.[3] It seems probable that some connexion existed between one or both these princesses with Boadicea, as at a subsequent period, Crimthan, step-son of the former, and husband to the latter, made himself conspicuous for an expedition into Britain to aid his friends and relatives the Picts and Scots, against their formidable enemies, the Romans. He is said to have returned to Ireland laden with the spoils of the Roman legions, amongst which were "a suit of armour, embossed with gold and gems, a military cloak with golden fringe, a sword with figures of serpents upon it in chased gold, and a brace of greyhounds joined together by a silver chain, of which the price was estimated, according to the primitive custom of barter, at the value of three hundred cows."[4]

Boadicea had very early lost her mother, and was destined to be deprived of her other surviving parent; a particularly trying circumstance for her, as it placed her more completely under the influence of her haughty step-mother Cartismandua. This position must have had a powerful influence on her after-life. Another important event which happened A.D. 29, was the death of her uncle, King Metallanus, who leaving no children, the race of Fergus became extinct, and the crown was adjudged to Caractacus, son of Europeia, the King's sister.[5]

On the elevation of Caractacus to the throne, the ambitious Cartismandua sent to negotiate with that king and his sister, the alliances which united in one firm and double tie the royal family of North and South Britain; it was probably about the same time that the princess Boadicea became united in marriage to Arviragus, the third son of Cartismandua. Through her children, the Queen of the Brigantes might thus control both extremes of the country, and her own individual power was by no means limited as leader of the mighty people which formed a barrier between the two.

The Iceni were the people over whom Arviragus ruled; they are named by Tacitus as being very rich and prosperous, and had been unshaken by the war with the Romans.

The country of the Iceni was divided between the Magni and Coritani, who possessed all the country from the Stour in Essex to the banks of the Humber and the Don. Caistor, near Norwich, was the capital town

---

[1] The death of Devorgilla, mother of Crimthan, who was a princess of Denmark, and Lugad's second wife, so affected that prince that he put a period to his own existence. O'Flaherty, O'Halloran, Warner, Keating.

[2] O'Flaherty.

[3] Palgrave's Saxon Commonwealth.

[4] Moore's History of Ireland.

[5] Duncan's History of Scotland. Caractacus became king A. D. 28. Holinshed.

of the Iceni Magni, who dwelt between the Stour and the Nen. On the other hand Leicester, called Ragæ, was the capital of the Iceni Coritani, who dwelt between the Nen and the Humber and Don.[1]

Amongst these people were two Roman stations, Camborita or Cambridge, amongst the Magni; and another at Lincta or Lincoln, amongst the Coritani; and so late as A. D. 48, the people preserved their friendship with Rome. Probably this was owing to the rule of Cymbeline, and doubtless his widow and children had endeavoured to maintain the good understanding which existed. The Trinobantes and Cassii being their southern neighbours, and the Brigantes those to the north, assisted in preserving this state of peace, those nations being allies of Rome. The Carbanii adjoined them on the west.[2]

Arviragus and Boadicea, it appears, resided at Norwich, which city was termed by the Romans "Venta Icenorum," the "Winchester" or royal city of the Iceni. A Roman castle, about three miles distant, was supposed to have been built by Cæsar.[3]

For some years after the marriage of Boadicea, we gain no further information respecting her than that she became the mother of two daughters and a son, who were educated in Britain; and with them was brought up a son of one of the brothers of Boadicea, who was surnamed Galgacus or Galdus, from the circumstance of his living among strangers, and who afterwards became a distinguished personage.

The circumstances attending the arrival of the Emperor Claudius in Britain have been already related, and the separation of Arviragus and Boadicea. The object of the Romans was to disunite the British princes, the better to establish their power. They wished to divide Arviragus from the Scottish interest, and with this view the daughter of Claudius had been proposed for his wife. Aulus Plautius is said to have first suggested the measure.[4] Arviragus consulted with his Britons, and their consent gained, peace was made between the British king and Roman emperor. Deputies were sent to Rome for the princess, and the unfortunate Boadicea, on pretence of some "private ground for displeasure," was formally divorced from her husband, and with her children, placed in confinement, where, to add to her grief, one of them died. This unjust proceeding was deeply resented by the Britons, to whom Boadicea was dear; the story of her wrongs roused every heart in the kingdom. It was not the least felt by the heroic king of Scotland, who hastened to rescue his beloved sister from her ignominious and unmerited thraldom.

Boadicea was, probably, confined in the capital of her own dominions, viz., Norwich; otherwise, the scheme which was adopted by Caractacus might not have been so successful. The Britons, placing themselves under arms, are said to have forcibly carried off the Queen and her children from their prison, and conveyed them into Wales to the protection of Caractacus, to whom a great portion of that country belonged, for he is particularly denominated King of the Silures by some historians. This

[1] Hoare's Notes on Giraldus Cambrensis. [2] Hoare.
[3] Parkins's Norwich. [4] Holinshed. Grafton's Chronicle.

people inhabited Wales and the Marches, and at this time Shrewsbury was one of their chief towns. That this was the heart of the territories of Caractacus in South Britain, appears from its neighborhood afterwards being the place of his final defeat.[1] Here, then, Boadicea was received by one who was her faithful friend in adversity, and the meeting of such a brother and sister under circumstances like theirs may easily be conceived. The indignation of Caractacus, once aroused against the Romans, was destined to be felt by them without cessation for a long series of years:[2] at present their measures were entered into and determined upon in relation to the future only, for they waited the result of impending events.

The next summer brought to Britain the Roman princess, who was formally united to Arviragus; and as if no measure should be neglected to gratify the Romans, and insult the discarded Queen, it was determined in counsel that the children of Arviragus, by his first marriage, should be excluded from the succession, and that the regal power should devolve on the offspring of the present marriage.

After the unsuccessful battle fought by the friends of Boadicea, when the Roman chiefs and Arviragus retired to London, Caractacus retreated first to York, and afterwards to Carrick. Thither an embassy from Plautius followed him, demanding the reason of his opposition to the Roman authority. Caractacus's answer was, that he had just cause for his conduct in the injuries that his sister Boadicea, and her son Guiderius, had sustained, and were likely to sustain, through their counsel and means; and so little was he disposed to make any amends for what was done that he thought it more reasonable that the Romans should quit the island of Britain, unless they had made up their minds to have not only the Britons, but the Picts and Scots, for their perpetual enemies, if only for the defence of their ancient liberty and freedom. The Roman ambassadors having returned with this answer, Plautius was highly indignant, and threatened revenge on the author of such high and contumelious language against the majesty of the Roman empire.[3]

Things being arranged to the satisfaction of the Roman Emperor, Claudius returned to Rome, leaving Arviragus in possession of the sovereignty—if such it could be called under the present circumstances, his Queen being a Roman, and her allies, Aulus Plautius and his forces, having a sort of military rule under him, in which he was compelled to acquiesce. Arviragus, however, for a time preserved his faith. He even united with the Roman general to chastise the Britons for the abduction of Boadicea, against whom a battle was fought; but the Queen's adherents being overthrown, the affection for her was such that the very next day the people of Lancashire, Yorkshire, and Derbyshire flew to arms, and the Roman force, with the two leaders, Arviragus and Plautius, was compelled to retreat to London, lest an escape to the continent should be necessary; and in the emergency, Plautius sent to Rome for two more legions to support his authority.[4]

[1] Holinshed. [2] Tacitus. [3] Holinshed.

[4] Caractacus, King of Scots, was elected chieftain in this war, undertaken in

These events were followed by a general meeting of the friends of Boadicea, at Shrewsbury, in which Caractacus was invested with the sole command of the forces to be raised among the Britons, Scots, and Picts. In the following spring the hosts of these three nations were collected in Yorkshire, to make another struggle in favor of the Scottish princess. After a sanguinary contest, Arviragus and Plautius again retreated on London, and Caractacus and his friends to York, and thence to Epiake. The Roman general sent soon afterwards an embassy to Caractacus, which received the haughty answer suggested by the freedom of spirit in which Caractacus had been brought up.

After this, Arviragus suddenly assumed in his own person the sole command, disdaining the intervention of the Romans. Vespasian, afterwards Emperor, was sent over by Claudius to compel him to submit; that general laid siege to Exeter, where Arviragus, having come up with his forces, gave him battle, though no decided victory was gained on either side: the next day the King was reconciled to Vespasian by the interference of Queen Gwenissa; but afterwards deserting his wife, Arviragus fled to Shrewsbury, where a reconciliation took place between him and his much-injured Queen, Boadicea. The fate of Gwenissa belongs to her biography.

Arviragus once more on the British side, the affairs of Boadicea wore a more favourable aspect. The chiefs of Britain united their forces again in Yorkshire, but before an engagement could take place, Vespasian fell upon the army of confederates, and it was almost cut to pieces in spite of its brave defence. Arviragus himself was prevented only by his attendants from falling on his own sword; they carried him by main force from the field of battle. The Pictish King, who had joined in this struggle, beholding the destruction of his people, desired not to survive them; he threw away his arms and regal ornaments, and sitting down on a stone, as one distracted, was slain by some of the Romans who followed up the pursuit. Caractacus escaped into his own country.[1]

Vespasian next besieged Camelon, and forced it to surrender from famine: to that town had been carried the regal ornaments of the Pictish King, of which the Roman General secured possession.[2] They consisted of a crown, with other jewels; and we are told, that with these was a sword, which had a haft of gold and purple scabbard, very finely wrought and carved, which Vespasian ever after wore with much pride in his wars.[3]

Camelon was now peopled with Romans by Vespasian, and endowed with the liberties and privileges of a Roman city. A temple to Claudius was built on the banks of the Carron, in which two statues were set up

his sister's defence, [Holinshed,] by the general desire of the people, and promised to join the allied forces at Shrewsbury in the spring. Congist, King of the Picts, also added his friendly assistance at this juncture. [Ibid.]

[1] See Life of Gwenissa. [2] Holinshed.

[3] Holinshed. When Arviragus threw off the Roman yoke, it is likely he fortified those places which were most convenient for their invasion, viz., Richborough, Walmer, Dover, and Hastings.—*Chronicles of Dover Monastery, printed in Leland's Collectanea.*

by order of the general, one of which represented Claudius, and the other the goddess Victoria. Vespasian subsequently marched into Galloway, and took possession of Carrick, where he received the oaths of allegiance of the people, who, till then, had held out in the cause of the Queen and liberty. It was probably to this town that King Arviragus came to meet the victorious Roman, to whom he had, with consent of his adherents, offered to submit upon honourable terms. Vespasian, on this occasion, desirous of humbling the pride of Arviragus, refused to make any terms, unless he would come in his own person, and in private attire, a condition probably more galling to him than any other which could have been imposed. Resistance was, however, useless. He divested himself of his royal costume and equipage, and, coming to Vespasian in the humble manner he had dictated, was not only pardoned, but restored to his former station. Hostages were, however, required for his fidelity, and a fine imposed, not only on every chief who had rebelled, but on every city which had joined in taking up arms against Rome. The British laws were abrogated, Roman ones were substituted, and a Roman judge was appointed over every province, for the preservation of peace and Roman discipline.

Arviragus is no more mentioned in history, except as an ally of the Romans, with whom, during the rest of his long life, he maintained terms, and even assumed the greatest respect for the Roman Senate. The fame of his valour effaced all beside in the Roman mind, now that he was subservient to the will of the strongest; and the poet Juvenal, who, in some complimentary verses addressed to the Emperor, mentions him thus:

"Some captive king, thee, his new lord, shall own;
Or, from his British chariot headlong thrown,
The proud Arviragus comes tumbling down."

It was considered a subject of glory and triumph, even for the Roman Emperor to aspire to conquer or make captive this heroic chieftain.[1] Arviragus is said to have been more fierce in war than any of the princes, his contemporaries; yet, in peace, no one could be more mild or more jocose. He is said to have enacted new laws, and confirmed those of his ancestors, and to have distinguished himself for the princely munificence with which he rewarded persons of merit. His selfishness and cruelty to both his wives is lost in the turbulence then called bravery.

The next point which historians give us of Boadicea's history unites her name with that of Prasutagus, King of the Iceni, her husband, who appears to be the same as Arviragus, King of the Iceni, and which name he seems to have borne after the death of his mother, Queen Cartismandua.[2] One circumstance might account for the new name of the King of the Britons: his second wife, Gwenissa, laid aside her Roman name, and adopted one purely British; and as it was usual among the ancient Britons, when they embraced the faith of Christ, and were baptized, to

[1] In compliment to Vespasian, for his valour displayed in Britain, on his return to Rome he was met by the Emperor without the gates of the city, who gave him the right hand as they walked,—a mark of very great esteem

[2] Rapin.

adopt new names from the Greek, Latin, or Hebrew, it is not unlikely that the king adopted it when, with Gwenissa, he received the Christian faith. As the British word Gwerydd (for Arviragus) contains the basis of *viridis*, *green*, conveyed in the word Prasutagus, and the custom of Britain was to specify some particular colour in the name of the individual, this alone seems to set the question of identity, which has been raised, beyond further doubt.[1]

Arviragus, or Prasutagus, as we may now call him, anticipating the rapacity of the Romans, left, by his will, the Emperor Nero co-heir with his two daughters, making no mention whatever of Queen Boadicea; for the husband of Gwenissa, who, at her death, had left a son as her heir, could only hope by such a division as that made in the will to secure his family from injury.

No sooner, however, was he deceased, than the officers of Nero seized on his entire effects in their master's name, his kingdom was spoiled by the Roman centurions, his house ransacked by slaves, his kinsmen treated as captives of war, and the wealthiest of his subjects amongst the Iceni despoiled of their estates, under the pretext furnished by the will; this last injustice was done at the instigation of the colony settled at Camalodunum or Colchester, with whom the soldiers co-operated, hoping hereafter to be able to take the same license themselves; thus, many who had settled even in that city, were expelled from it on the same pretence. The temple erected to Claudius, appeared to those Britons who remained in Camalodunum, a badge of their eternal slavery, for the priests employed in it under pretence of religious services due there, wasted or embezzled every man's property for their own private use.[2] This was not enough for the cupidity of the oppressors. Catus Decianus, the Roman procurator, endeavoured to bring all the people's goods under a new confiscation, by disavowing the remitment of Claudius; fresh taxes were imposed on lands and cattle;[3] and to crown all, those Britons who had been drawn in by the rich philosopher Seneca, Nero's counsellor, to borrow vast sums of money under his promises of easy loan, and licence to repay at convenience, were suddenly compelled to repay all at once, with great extortion. Among the number of those who had entered into such a snare as to entangle themselves in debt to Seneca, was the father of Boadicea, who had obtained the money through Roman usurers.[4] "The King of the Iceni," as he is here called, would rather seem to have been Cymbeline or Venusius, than the brave Cadallan, father of Boadicea and Caractacus; and if either of these, the word "father" might be intended to signify "step-father;" it was certainly one of the three; and in any case, on the death of Arviragus, such a debt must necessarily devolve on Boadicea, as the representative of those princes. The unfortunate Queen, a widow, in the hands of merciless creditors and unrelenting enemies,

[1] There is some diversity of opinion as to the place of interment of this celebrated British monarch,—whether, as some relate, he was buried in the temple of Claudius at Gloucester, or at London; nor is the exact date of his death specified.

[2] Stowe, Echard, Milton.

[3] Warrington.

[4] The amount due was forty sesterces.

vainly remonstrated against the injustice of their proceedings; at length, infuriated by her reproaches, and unrestrained by any feeling of humanity, the brutal soldiery to whom she was given up, encouraged by their more brutal leaders, subjected the ill-fated Boadicea to the common punishment of the scourge, while the fate of her unhappy daughters was even more hideous than her own. Their immortal wrongs blacken the page of history, which has no record so atrocious.[1] The tide of accumulated injuries was now at its height, and the fury of a whole nation burst forth in one overwhelming current, to overflow the land with the blood of enemies whom no laws had restrained.

Ages have passed by, yet the heart still bleeds at the record of this noble woman's wrongs. From the moment of this outrage, the heart of the Queen was deadened to all feelings but those of vengeance, stung with shame, crushed with unmerited disgrace, and bowed by agonies that found no name; while Boadicea resolved still to endure life, hateful as it had become to her, in the sole hope of wreaking a fearful vengeance which should atone for her unheard-of injuries.

No lack of sympathy was shown for the wrongs of Boadicea by her generous and loyal-hearted Britons. One and all, the inhabitants of the Roman colony of London excepted, determined to unite in freeing their country from the yoke of a people who could perpetrate such crimes, more hateful since the victims were the weak and defenceless. The injuries long oppressing themselves, had been, up to this time, endured; but this outrage armed them all in one common cause, and they felt that the hour for a final struggle had arrived. At this time the Roman writers themselves acknowledge that the violence and injustice of the Emperor's servants gave the Britons just cause to lay aside their private animosities, and aid their Queen in the recovery of their lost liberty. The daughter of Cadallan placed herself at the head of her devoted partisans, and the disunion which Cæsar had hailed as one of the happy causes of his success, was at once extinguished in the bosoms of the British chiefs; one spirit alone animating the mass—the desire to avenge the injuries of their Queen,—a cause which embraced the personal wrongs of each individual. But before the actual outbreak of the tremendous insurrection which filled all the Roman empire with amazement and consternation, secret councils were held by the chieftains to concert measures for their rebellion. Among these was Venusius, who with his party had warmly espoused the cause of Boadicea; and at these meetings the Queen is said to have personally addressed her faithful ministers on the subject of their mutual wrongs. One of the evils of the Roman yoke on which she insisted, was the introduction of vices unknown in Britain, except through the medium of those jesters and buffoons, whom their tyrants encouraged to corrupt the nation. These persons were employed, it would appear, in the theatres at Camalodunum and Caerleon,[2] which had become colonized by Romans, and where the novelty of such spectacles

[1] Tacitus, Stowe, Milton, Echard.

[2] The remains of the Roman theatres are yet to be seen in some parts of Britain, as Caerleon, in Monmouthshire, &c.

as theatrical shows or entertainments would create vast astonishment and admiration, and doubtless obtain many followers among the uninformed Britons. Boadicea, in her celebrated address to her noble chiefs, stigmatized these persons as "Rome's instruments and Britain's vipers;" remarking that "Tiberius, though extremely covetous, would have been glad to have made peace, and Nero would still have followed his fiddling trade at home, had not the discords of Britain been fomented and kept alive by his fiddlers here!" From this address we discover that there had been a party among the Britons in favour of Rome; and that this still existed appears from the Londoners withholding their support to the approaching insurrection, for which they were destined afterwards to suffer severely.

The Trinobantes, and neighboring states, are said in the outset to have warmly espoused the cause of the Queen, and joined her with their forces. To these different states Boadicea had from time to time addressed herself, in epistles composed for the inhabitants of such towns and provinces as had united in resolving to throw off the Roman yoke, and which treated not only on that, but on other subjects of national importance; for the Queen, we are informed, was "well versed in letters,"[1] which is not surprising, as the Roman intercourse with this island had been long enough carried on to enable her to become acquainted with Latin forms of literature; and we find that in this early period the Britons were not only possessed of traditions, but had written records of their own affairs,[2]—the characters, indeed, being peculiar to their age, and the knowledge of them limited to the persons of highest rank only, and the Druids. Gildas, the British poet and historian, attributes the scarcity of British records to the artifice of their enemies, the Romans, who were anxious to destroy every memorial of past times with the Druidical religion, by whose ministers they were preserved.[3]

The Queen had, in the first instance, dispatched a messenger to her brother Corbred, King of the Scots, father of Corbred Gald, a young prince whom she had herself nursed and educated at her own court, and who passed many years with Boadicea amid the chequered scenes of her eventful life.[4] She complained in bitter terms of the injuries inflicted on herself and her daughters, by which she, his only sister, had been brought to extreme misery, and assured him that the Britons were ready to arm in her cause. Corbred was deeply moved by these sad tidings. He sent

---

[1] Bale reckons both Arviragus and Boadicea among the authors of Britain.

[2] Gildas.

[3] Conquovar Mac Nessa, King of Ulster, A. D. 48, ordered the precepts of the Druids of Ireland to be committed to writing.—*Toland.*

"In private the ancient Scots were accustomed to use for writing, ciphers which did not resemble the letters of other nations, but rather the characters used by the Egyptians, being figures of animals made into the form of letters, as appears from the characters on the ancient tombs to this time; and though these ancient hieroglyphics are now lost, they have a kind of writing peculiar to themselves, which was once in common use, and those who have the ancient speech pronounce the aspirations and dipthongs better than any of the rest."—*Holinshed.*

[4] Scott.

a herald to Catus, the Roman general, requiring him to obtain reparation from those Romans who had so basely treated the British Princesses. If this was not done, the King declared he would himself be her avenger. The Roman general's reply was full of contempt and ridicule. He scornfully upbraided Corbred for interfering with the Roman officers' affairs, "who were above taking notice either of his sister or her daughters, and at liberty to treat them as other women, according to their pleasure."

Corbred, indignant at this new insolence, hesitated no longer, but making an alliance with the Picts and people of the Isle of Man, soon raised a strong body for the enterprise, intended to act with the forces raised by the Queen in her own behalf. But before these could form a junction, a sudden and unlooked-for event precipitated the rebellion into an outbreak. This event was the reduction of the Island of Mona[1] by Suetonius Paulinus, then head of the Roman forces in Britain. This celebrated general was sent to Britain in the year 61, by Nero, to take the command of the Roman forces. He was already distinguished for merit and military talent, and to this was joined the strongest impulses of ambition, for he had formed a determination that his successes in Britain should equal those of Corbulo in Armenia. To reduce the whole island was his ultimate aim. His first undertaking was, however, the reduction of the Ordovices, or people of North Wales. These were the inhabitants of the present counties of Denbigh, Carnarvon, Merioneth, and Montgomery.[2]

The Ordovices received that name at the time of their conquering Worcestershire, Warwickshire, and North Gloucestershire; it signified the "Great Huiccii," or "the Honourable Wices;" and after their expulsion thence, other British settlers in that part were called Wigantes or Huiccii.[2] This seems to be the people who were ranged under the standard of Venusius, who had warmly espoused the cause of Boadicea.

Agricola, at that time only twenty years of age, had accompanied Paulinus in his expedition against the Ordovices, and resided with him at his head-quarters. Under this great commander, the young warrior acquired that experience which, at a subsequent period, enabled him to accomplish the reduction of the island; the cherished hope of Suetonius himself, though he did not live to accomplish his high aim.

The people whom Suetonius had resolved to not only subdue, but extirpate and destroy, were brave, warlike, and devoted to their religion; the enterprise presented, therefore, very great difficulties: it was the more desirable to accomplish, because this spot, the court of ecclesiastical and civil justice, had become a rendezvous for every British malcontent. To enable himself more effectually to reduce this island, Suetonius withdrew the veteran soldiers from Camalodunum, little foreseeing the disastrous consequences which might arise from leaving so important a hold unprotected against their enemies. About this time, Petilius Cerealis[3] received from Nero an appointment in Britain, to occupy the place of Vettius Volanus, who, for his mildness of disposition, was recalled. Petilius was

---

[1] Anglesey. [2] Life of Agricola. [3] Green's History of Worcester.

[4] Tacitus and Hume say that Petilius was first sent over A. D. 70.

very unlike his predecessor; already distinguished as a skilful veteran, in the war against Civilis, the Batavian chief, he was well suited to propagate the terror of the Roman arms in Britain. Suetonius himself was also remarkable for his severity; so that the Britons were oppressed in every way. Such was the state of things when the Roman general penetrated for the first time as far as Mona, the seat of their mysterious worship, and now crowded with inhabitants, many of whom had sought its shelter as a last retreat.[2]

For the purpose of the intended invasion of the island, Suetonius caused ships to be made with flat bottoms, for a steep, uncertain shore. "In these the foot were conveyed over; the cavalry followed, by fording in shallow water, or swimming, and leading the horses. On the shore stood a motley troop of armed men, mixed with women running up and down among them, dressed like Furies, in *black garments*, their hair dishevelled, and torches in their hands. The Druids also attended, lifting up their hands to heaven, and uttering dreadful execrations. The novelty of the sight so struck the soldiers, that they stood as it were motionless, exposing themselves to the enemies' weapons, till, animated by the exhortations of their general, and encouraging one another not to fear an army of women and madmen, they advanced, bore down all they met, and involved them in their own fire. Garrisons were afterwards placed in the towns, and the groves, sacred to their bloody superstitions, cut down; for it was their practice to offer the blood of their prisoners on their altars, and consult the gods by the entrails of men." Such is the relation Tacitus gives of the taking of Mona; and the spot in Anglesey where Suetonius and his barbarous legions butchered the unoffending Druids is still shown at a ferry, called Porthamel, across the Menai Straits. The horrors of such a slaughter baffle description; men and women alike fell victims, and deluged their own altars with their blood. Suetonius expected, now that he had effected his object in reducing Mona, that the whole of Britain would be reduced to the Roman yoke; but he was altogether deceived in his calculation: while yet employed in arranging matters for the security of his new conquest, he received the alarming news that the whole country was in a state of revolt.

The tidings of what had been done by Suetonius Paulinus had become very quickly known through the island, and reached the ears of Boadicea. She saw that the moment was arrived for the decisive stroke. The veteran troops had been called from Camalodunum, to assist Suetonius in the reduction of Mona; and Boadicea perceived that the city might easily be taken by her forces. The Scottish succours from Corbred had not arrived; but the warlike Queen determined not to delay her intended plans for their arrival. Prior to the approaching contest, Boadicea, in conformity with the customs of her times, determined to encourage her followers, by addressing them on the subject of the strife in which they were about to engage. For this purpose she mounted an eminence raised of turf, from which she could be seen by the whole assembled multitude, amounting to as many as 80,000 men. The appearance of the Queen is said to have

---

[1] Tacitus.

struck awe into the heart of each beholder, by the dignity and majesty of her demeanour. In person, Boadicea was of the largest size, her face was beautiful, but fierce and stern; some annalists say, "terrible of aspect, savage of countenance." Her complexion was brilliantly fair,[1] and her yellow locks, which were spread all over her shoulders, reached down to her hips. She wore a plaited tunic of several colours, drawn close about her bosom, and over that a vestment made of some stuff of British manufacture, fastened by a clasp, and adopted in compliment to the southern natives; the chequered robe beneath being the produce of the north of Britain. About her neck she wore a thick collar, or chain of gold, esteemed a mark of the highest command, and expressive of the dignified quality of the wearer. She addressed the whole assembly, in a voice loud enough to reach the ears of the most distant of her eager auditors who crowded around her, many of whom were women.

Her speech was as follows:—

"My friends and faithful subjects,—I do believe that there is no man here who is ignorant how much freedom and poverty are preferable to bondage and wealth.

"Since the Romans have been acquainted with this island, there is no indignity, however vile, no cruelty, however grievous, which we have not suffered.

"Are we not contemned and trodden under foot by those who have studied only to become our lords and tyrants? Are we not bereaved of our riches and possessions? Do we not till their land, and pay them all manner of tribute, even for our persons? Amongst other nations, death is a deliverance from slavery; but with the Romans, the dead do still live, even to augment their riches.[2]

"And can we hope for mercy at their hands, who have already treated us so barbarously? Even he who taketh a wild beast, will at first cherish it, and seek by gentleness to win it to familiarity. Are we not, then, the authors of our own misery, in suffering them to set foot in our

---

[1] The ancient British maidens were remarkable for a dazzling whiteness of skin, which, accompanied by a ruddy and florid complexion, was thought to be produced by the humidity of the climate. [Xiphiline.] Fedelmia was so noted for her fair complexion as to be surnamed "White as silver." Carbrey Ninfear, King of Leinster, in order to obtain the hand of this princess from her father, Conquovar Mac Nessa, King of Ulster, was compelled to cede a large portion of his territories. Three fruitful tracts of land, extending from Loch-au-Choideagh and Tara to the sea were, by Carbrey's consent, annexed to the dominions of Conquovar, as his daughter's marriage settlement. [O'Flaherty, Keating.] Boadicea, Claudia, and St. Helena, are especially noted for beauty of complexion. [Xiphiline.]

[2] It is supposed that the expression in the speech of Boadicea (given by Dion Cassius) which refers to *taxation* thus—"We are forced to pay for the bodies of our very dead," relates to the impost of the Romans on those Britons buried according to national custom, instead of being burnt like the Romans; and that a high price was demanded for the privilege of burying the higher orders in their best garments, and laying by their side their axe and dagger, as we have often had instances in the openings of cromlechs,—a custom to which the Britons continued obstinately to adhere.

island? We should have slain them afar off, and driven them back even as we did Cæsar.

"Better were it to lose our lives in defence of our country than to drag on a miserable existence in servitude.

"Wherefore, my well-beloved citizens, friends, and relations, let us, while the remembrance of our ancient liberty remains, seek to recover, not only the name of freedom, but the enjoyment of liberty itself. Let us set an example to posterity. Let us not forget what we have once been; for, if so, what can we expect of our children, brought up in misery and bondage?

"I do not recall these things to rouse you to rebellion, for I well know you sufficiently abhor the Roman name, neither do I seek to put you in fear of what might happen hereafter; but I would return my hearty thanks and commendations, that you do thus willingly obey my summons, unawed by your powerful oppressors, and proving yourselves prompt, zealous, and courageous, and willing to live or die for your Queen and country. Do your enemies outnumber us? Regard their strength. We do so much exceed them, that our army is strong as stone walls, and one of our targets is of more value than all the armour they bear. The victory will soon be ours. They must soon be our captives. Yet, should we loose the field, we may easily escape the calamities of a defeat; for their heavy arms will impede their pursuit, and the hills and marshes will intercept them.

"*We* can endure hunger, thirst, cold and sunshine; they live in tents or houses: baked meats, wine and oil, are necessary to them; if these fail or the summer sun oppress them, they languish and consume: but to us, every herb or root is meat, every juice an oil, water is pleasant wine, and every tree affords a habitation.[1]

"Besides this, the country is well known to us, and we have many friends; but the Romans are strangers, and without succor in case of need. We can swim over every river, naked or clad, while they require mighty ships to convey them.

"Let us then courageously attack them, and let us teach them that hares and foxes can never match with wolves and greyhounds."

At these words Boadicea released from beneath her mantle a hare, which had been purposely concealed;[2] and the sight of this prognostic of success was received with loud shouts by the people, who hailed it with a loud shout, and vented freely their indignant feelings against the ill-treatment of their Queen.

---

[1] Hares, fowls, geese, and fish, the Britons were by their religion forbidden to eat.

[2] The hare released by Boadicea is generally supposed to betoken the fearfulness of the Romans. The hare was used by the Britons for the purposes of divination: and though they never killed it for the table, from the delight which they took in breeding it, they kept numbers about the courts of their chiefs. The idea of a hare-warren, and the model of a park, were originally derived by us from the primeval Britons. [Whittaker's Manchester.] An instance of one of the warrens yet exists at Kimble, in Bucks, once the abode of King Cymbeline. The speech of the Queen seems to infer that the fox was also held in veneration by the people.

Boadicea now recalled their attention, while she proceeded with her prayers or supplication; wherein she especially addressed herself to the deity of woman worshipped by the British people, under the name of Andate or Andraste, their Goddess of Victory;[1] and this appeal, as well as her former speech, is worthy of a more enlightened age.

"I thank thee, O Adraste," were the words she used, "and call upon thee, not as a ruler such as Messalina, as Agrippina, or as Nero, which last is called a man, but is indeed a woman; but I call upon thee as the goddess of our British warriors, whose wives are no less brave and valiant than themselves. I beseech thee, since I am Queen of this mighty people, to grant them health, liberty, and victory over the wicked, insatiable, and luxurious Romans, whose lives are devoted to covetousness and cruelty. Let not, I beseech thee, the tyranny of Nero and Domitian any longer prevail. That thou wilt be our helper, our defender and our saviour, I heartily beseech thee!"

At the conclusion of this dignified and affecting prayer, Boadicea departed to prepare for battle.

This appeal to Adraste, the female goddess, is rendered so much the more affecting, when we learn that no less than five thousand females had enlisted in the cause of their royal countrywoman, wholly bent to avenge her wrongs, or perish in the contest.[2] This was peculiarly meritorious, as every individual who went to the war with the sovereign, took his or her own expenses, the service being esteemed one of honour to those who engaged in it.[3] In those times the women had no less courage than the men, and on all occasions like the present, every stout British maiden or married woman, unless about to become a mother, marched with her husband and brothers to the defence of her country. Even the women advanced in years accompanied the army, encouraging the men to valour, and assailing the enemy on their approach with stones, while the younger of their sex fought among the ranks, side by side with the men. On departing for the strife, they had a religious custom of slaying the first living creature that they found, in whose blood they not only bathed their swords, but also tasted the same, in the assurance that they were about to obtain some great and noted victory. Many hoary priestesses followed the British armies, clad in white garments bound with a brazen girdle, and having their feet naked, whose office it was to sacrifice the prisoners of war, and by these victims predict the success of the strife. To render themselves competent to share the dangers of the field of battle, the British women laboured incessantly to equal the opposite sex in strength; despising alike heat and cold, they travelled barefoot or in rude carriages, and had their food trussed behind them on their horses or their own shoulders, never refusing to undergo any labour or fatigue assigned to them by their leader.[4]

[1] Andate, or Andraste, was the British Goddess of Victory, who had a temple at Camalodunum, and to whom the Britons sacrificed their prisoners of war.—*Ancient Universal History, from Dion Cassius.*

[2] Holinshed.

[3] Ibid.

[4] A woman of the Cimbri, rather than survive a defeat, would kill even her own flying relatives, and having strangled her infant, and cast it beneath the

The Britons, animated by the speech of their heroic Queen, set out against the Romans; Boadicea first attacking the colony of Camalodunum.[1]

The following account is given of the state of Camalodunum, which yet was incomplete, or in progress, and laid out, as will be seen, rather for pleasure than security, while it was rendered defenceless by the abstraction of its garrison of veterans:—"Camalodunum, the standing court or palace royal of their kings, while Cymbeline lived, was now become the centre of pleasant retirement to the Romans, not the rendezvous of their power. The outside state of the town seemed very flourishing; for, besides the old palace, and other buildings of the Britons (for the Romans, saith Segonius, did not use to destroy the buildings they found), it had a senate-house for consultations, *a theatre for plays*, that goodly Temple of Claudius, and undoubtedly, as well they as the rest, answerable to the Roman magnificence. The colony lay open on all sides, the better to enjoy free walks and air about; yet safety was not altogether neglected, though pleasure was rather sought than strength.[2] It had no trench, no palisades, nor other defence about itselfe; but it had the majestie of the Roman name (a reputed wall of brass), the aire of a fresh conquest, and sundrie strength in the marches or pale of the province, where the Roman garrison watched and warded in castles, sconces, and other presidiary places."[3]

The city was, as may even yet be observed by the ancient remains, in a progressive and imperfect state, and on this account was chosen by the Britons as their first point of attack;[4] they had another and a still stronger reason, the great hatred they entertained for the veteran soldiers.

The inhabitants of the colony are said to have had warnings of their approaching ruin. A noise as if of contention was heard in the court,

---

chariot-wheels, ended the horrid scene by her own self-destruction. Lucius Antoninus, one of the Roman generals in Britain, in making application to Rome for fresh succours, stated that their enemies were never more cruel and fierce, not only the men, but also the women, who cared not for the loss of their own lives, so that they might die revenged.—*Holinshed.*

[1] This celebrated place, first taken by Claudius, A. D. 44, and garrisoned with veterans of the second, ninth and fourteenth legions, had since that period been the seat of the Roman government, being sometimes also called Colonia, as appears from some money of Claudius, inscribed COL. CAMALODVN; and by medals the Emperor had struck in honour of his conquest, bearing on one side his own effigies, with the legend, "TI. CLAUD. CÆS. AUG. GER. P. M. T. R. P. XII., IMP. XIIX.;" and on the reverse a plough, drawn by an ox and a cow yoked, driven by a man; above them, COL. CAMALODUNUM AUG." Plautius, the proprætor of Camalodunum, had been recalled A. D. 48, after which Ostorius Scapula, his successor, had withdrawn the chief part of the veteran legions from the place; to which measure is attributable the destruction of the colony by Boadicea; because the Trinobantes, who had been awed by the presence of that military force, were thus encouraged to unite with the Queen's forces in their stroke for freedom.

[2] According to Tacitus, "the Roman generals attended to improvements of taste or elegance, but neglected the useful. They embellished the province, but took no care to defend it."

[3] History of Colchester. [4] Hoare. Notes on Giraldus Cambrensis.

and a great tumult in the theatre, that scene of vicious entertainment which had been censured by Boadicea, in her address to the Britons; for she knew that they participated in these entertainments, and had become accustomed to intermingle familiarly with their former enemies. Perhaps the Druidesses were concerned in these supposed supernatural sounds—for such they were considered, "seeing that no man there either spake or mourned."[1] These weird priestesses seem to have been acquainted with the art of ventriloquism, and were in some of their mysteries accustomed to conceal themselves in certain recesses, and by giving forth sentences or sounds when invisible to their listeners, to create the utmost astonishment.[2] The signs of the approaching calamity, as viewed by the Romans of Camalodunum, prove them to have been quite as superstitious as their less-informed neighbours, the Britons. Certain houses or buildings, appearing like a colony in ruins, are said to have been seen in the river Thames, and the sea between the island and Gaul appeared to flow with blood.[3] To crown all these evil omens, the image of the goddess Victoria set up by Claudius, *without any apparent cause*, fell from its base, and lay extended on the ground, with its face averted, as if that deity yielded to the enemies of Rome. This last certainly looks much like a contrivance of the Druids, which is the more probable, as women are said to have rushed here and there, in restless ecstasy among the people, with frantic screams, denouncing impending ruin: "Destruction is at hand! destruction is at hand!" Such were the hideous clamours heard "*in a foreign accent*,"[4] which are said to have penetrated even into the very council-chamber of the Romans, filling their hearts with terror and dismay, so that they clearly perceived that secret enemies mixed in all their deliberations. Suddenly, while an undefined fear was on the people of Camalodunum, Boadicea, with her countless multitude, appeared before the place. The Romans had but a few soldiers, and in the utmost alarm, sent off to Catus Decianus, procurator of the province, for a reinforcement. That officer could spare only two hundred men, and those but half armed, to assist them in their great extremity. It appears, however, that the temple of Claudius was strongly fortified, and there they resolved to make their stand, without, however, concerting any measures for their defence, being

[1] Tacitus, Speed.

[2] An oracular stone is mentioned by the author of the "Celtic Druids," known by the name of "the Great Cannon:" it rests upon a bed of rock, where a road plainly appears to have been made, leading to the hole, which, at the entrance, is three feet wide, six feet deep, and about three feet six inches high. Within this aperture, on the right hand, is a round hole, two feet diameter, perforated quite through the rock, sixteen feet, and running from south to north. In the above-mentioned aperture a man might be concealed, and predict future events to those that came to consult the oracle, and be heard distinctly on the north side of the rock, where the hole is not visible. This might make the credulous Britons think the predictions proceeded solely from the rock deity. The voice on the outside was distinctly conveyed to the person in the aperture, as was several times tried. The circumference of this rock is ninety-six feet.

[3] "The sea was purpled with blood, and at the ebb tide the figures of human bodies were traced on the sand."—*Tacitus.*

[4] Tacitus

taken so entirely by surprise, from the profound peace which had seemed to exist around them prior to this unexpected assault, that neither palisade nor ditch was thrown up, nor were any of the women, the aged, or infirm, sent out of the garrison. The colony was therefore taken with ease, and laid waste with fire and sword; the temple, where the military had sought to secure themselves, was laid seige to by the Queen and her exulting chiefs, and after holding out for two days, was taken by storm. Such was the carnage, that it is computed not less than from 70,000 to 80,000 fell on the occasion, aged persons, women, and children, alike falling victims to the Britons' too just fury. It is necessary to the veracity of history to add, awful as the picture is to contemplate, that the mandates of carnage were given by the stern Queen herself. Her vengeance extended yet further, being, as is generally believed, excited by the conduct of Seutonius in Anglesey, on whom she was desirous of retorting, by her cruel justice; nor can the horrors of Paganism appear in darker colours, than the picture of this revenge. Punishments, even for the women,[1] were invented, too hideous to be contemplated, that in nothing should the Romans be outdone in evil.

After this terrible sacrifice to vengeance, both the priests and warriors indulged in carousing and feasting in the wood called Andates, and in the several temples, especially that of the goddess Andate, invoked by Boadicea in her address. Boadicea then headed her warriors again, and set forth in quest of further victory. It was, no doubt, by the great Roman road which led from Colchester through the middle of the county of Essex, towards Bishop Stortford, &c., in Hertfordshire, that Boadicea pursued her course. This way is, in modern days, known as Stane Street.

Petilius Cerealis, at the time when these dreadful occurrences took place, was at Verulam, and marching in haste thence towards Colchester, "to rescue that which was already lost," was encountered by the furious Britons.[2] The ninth legion, under the command of the renowned conqueror of Batavia, was routed, the foot-soldiers *all slain*, and Petilius himself, with his cavalry, was forced to escape to his camp for safety, where he entrenched himself for a time, "not daring to attempt anything farther." The pursuit was followed up with great slaughter, 6000 Romans being slain, and about 3000 of the confederate Britons. Catus, the procurator, was in the engagement, and, being wounded, made his escape into Gaul.[3]

---

[1] Of whom some of the noblest were treated by Boadicea, as they had been by Suetonius. Nero was, in the end, obliged to recal Suetonius, because he was considered an unfit person to compose the alarmed minds of the Britons, from having both permitted and inflicted so many cruelties.—*Hume.*

[2] The ninth legion had received an accession of force from Germany, of eight auxiliary *cohorts* and one thousand horse.—*Tacitus.*

[3] "At the bare tidings of the disasters encountered by the Romans, Catus, like a tall man, took to his heels, and sailed into Gallia."—*Speed.* "Posthumus, the camp-master, durst not resist Boadicea, and refused to fight against her; indeed such terror had she infused into her enemies, that this fear had become quite general."—*Tacitus.*

After the conquest of Camalodunum, the Queen had been joined by the forces of her brother, the King of Scots, who had aided her in the defeat of Petilius[1] and his troops.

The successful Boadicea pursued her career towards Verulam, at that time a place of greater importance than London itself, the royal seat of Cassibelaunus; it had become a 'municipium' of the Romans A municipium was very different from a colony, such as Camalodunum, which was a city from which the inhabitants were expelled, to make way for the new-comers;[2] it was an enfranchised city, which possessed every privilege of Roman citizens, "having senators, knights, and commons; magistrates and priests, censors, ediles, quæstors, and flamens."[3]

The devotion shown by the Britons of Verulam to their conquerors, had obtained for them this signal favour; and it was to punish them for this, and for their secession from the customs and religion of their ancestors, that Boadicea was induced to attack the town. Verulam had been compassed with walls by the Romans, and the great Watling Street, by which the warlike Queen had approached the place, passed quite through the city. The modern St. Albans has been erected within the limits of the ancient city; but though some portion of its walls were standing in the days of Holinshed, and by him described as substantially built, the modern ruins do not afford much information of the extent of the original foundations. Of the richness and beauty of the place, a better idea may be obtained from the researches made in the reign of the Saxon King Edgar, by Eldred, then Abbot of St. Albans, who was desirous of enlarging the religious establishment there, which had been founded by Offa, King of the Mercians. It occurred to the zealous prelate that some relics of the ancient Roman Verulam might be obtained, and on digging amid the ruins, he discovered a number of pillars, portions of antique work, thresholds, door-frames, and sundry other pieces of fine masonry for windows, &c., well adapted for the purpose of beautifying the religious structure he desired to adorn. Of these also, "some were of porphyrite stone, some of divers kinds of marble, touch, and alabaster, besides many curious devices of hard metal; in finding whereof, he thought himself an happy man, and his success to be greatly guided by St. Alban."[4] The good abbot also found "many pillars of brass, and sockets of latten, alabaster, and touch, all which he laid aside by great heaps, intending to employ them in laying the foundation of a new abbey, but died before he could commence the building."[5] The examination of the things already discovered by Eldred, was prosecuted by his successor, Abbot Eadmer, and led to a further search in the ancient walls of the city, which was rewarded by the discovery of numerous other pieces "of excellent workmanship." The emissaries of the abbot, in the progress of their researches, came to some vaults underground, "in which stood certain idols, and a number of altars, very superstitiously and religiously adorned, as

[1] Agricola served under Petilius "in an ordinary capacity, [A. D. 70.] and shared the common dangers of the war." [Tacitus.] Petilius Cerealis had encountered the Brigantes in many battles, Venusius holding him at bay, and remaining to the last unconquered. [Milton.]

[2] Holinshed. [3] Pennant. [4] Holinshed. [5] Ibid.

the pagans had most probably left them in time of necessity. The images were formed of sundry metals, and some of them of pure gold, and the altars were richly covered. Eadmer removed all the ornaments from the altars, and appropriated them to his own building, and destroyed an immense number of these idols, which were only admirable for beauty of construction, but unavailable in point of material. Many curious pots, jugs, and cruses of stone and wood were taken up by him, most artificially wrought and carved, with an immense quantity of household stuff, as if the whole furniture of the city had been brought thither for the purpose of being hid in the vaults." The spot of this singular discovery seems to have been used as a place of burial; for Eadmer is said to have found there pots of gold, silver, brass, glass, and earth, some of which were filled with ashes and bones, and the mouths turned downwards, which vessels being broken in pieces by the abbot, the metal was melted, and reserved for the purpose of garnishing the church.[1]

The fact of the discovery of such a quantity of rich furniture, in such a spot, is accounted for by the alarm which the people naturally felt on the approach of the Queen, after her recent successes. The wealth of the place is expressly mentioned as one of the causes for the attack of Boadicea, it being the site of one of the British Mints: the word VER may be distinguished on the coins, though the name of the reigning prince is not legible.[2]

This noble seat of Roman grandeur combined with British industry, shared the fate of Camalodunum, being laid waste with fire and sword;[3] and so general a scene of carnage ensued, that the loss of the Romans and their allies, on the occasion, is said to have amounted to 70,000 men.[4] The fate of the municipium has been chronicled by the pen of Spenser, who, in character of the Genius of the place, says:—

"I was that city which the garland wore
Of Britain's pride, delivered unto me
By Roman victors, which it won of yore;
Though nought at all but ruins now I be,
And lie in mine own ashes, as ye see.
Verlame I was: what boots it what I was,
Sith now I am but weeds and wasteful grass?"

Ruins of Time.

It is necessary to turn from the footsteps of the ruthless Boadicea, and to trace the progress of the Roman general from Mona, where he was staying at the time of these signal losses.

Suetonius, on receiving news of these disasters, quitted Anglesey, and with the greatest intrepidity marched through a hostile country towards London,[5] by the great British road, called Watling street,[6] which ran

[1] Holinshed; who observes that "numbers of vessels of a similar kind, though of finer earth, of six or eight gallons a piece, were found, A.D. 1578, in a well at Little Massingham, in Norfolk: and also in Henry VIII.'s reign, containing old British coins and those of the Roman Emperors."

[2] Pennant.

[3] Girald. Cambrensis.

[4] Tacitus, Speed, C. Daniel, Howel.

[5] Giraldus Cambrensis.

[6] The noted Watling Street, which was the direct road from Chester (the city of the Legions) to Dover, did not enter London, [Dr. Stukeley,] but in its course

immediately from Wales by Wroxeter Wall, High Cross, Towcester and Verulam, to London; and necessarily he was compelled to pass through the dominions of the Iceni in Leicestershire and Northamptonshire.[1]

Notwithstanding the many difficulties and dangers which necessarily attended this progress through a hostile country, Suetonius Paulinus succeeded in reaching London in safety.

The Roman general was at first doubtful, whether he should not fix on that place as the seat of the war; many considerations, however, deterred him; and the smallness of his own army, as well as the fatal temerity of Petilius, made him determine by the sacrifice of one province to secure the rest.[2] Vain were the prayers and tears of the wretched inhabitants, nothing could shake the resolution of Paulinus, or divert him from his plan, when once laid out in his own mind. The signal for a march was given, and those only were left behind who by advanced age or weakness could not follow.[3]

The Queen had not forgotten that in the season of her deepest sorrows, when all other Britons had flocked from every quarter of the island to her standard, the Londoners alone had hung back; this act had marked them out as objects of especial indignation and vengeance, and too soon was her wrath to fall on all that were found; she advanced upon the city, took it, and put to the sword all that were found. Thus had she well gained the surnames of "the Warlike" and "the Victorious!"

A change was, however, at hand; the wheel of fortune was turning, and the period that was to terminate her frantic vengeance was approaching. Suetonius, though he had forsaken the city of London, had not removed far distant, having encamped his forces in the neighbourhood, in a quadrangle of about 130 feet in extent.[4]

It was a moment of terrible excitement for the contending parties, when the respective leaders, prior to the contest which was to decide their fortunes, impressed upon the multitudes who were assembled, their hopes of success and sentiments of patriotic courage and enthusiasm. With very different hopes were they inspired. The Queen's countless throng, elated with conquest, and certain of success, was without order of battle. Their wives and children were brought with them, as witnesses of their valour,[5] or assistants in the fight, while those intended as spectators only, were placed in waggons around the spot fixed on for their engagement. The waggons or carts used as land carriages by the Britons prior to the introduction of the conveniences and luxuries of life by the Romans, were thus employed in warlike expeditions, and the chariots

---

from Verulam, and Elstree or Snellamasis, crossed the Oxford road at Tyburn, and thence ran to the west of Westminster [Higden] over the Thames, and onward into Kent. From Tyburn this road proceeded over part of Hyde Park by May Fair, "through St. James's Park to the street by Old Palace Yard, called the Wool Staple, to the Thames; there formerly stood an old gate, one part of the arch of which is still left, but not Roman. On the opposite side of the river is Stane Gate Ferry, which is the continuation of this street to Canterbury, and so to the three famous sea-ports, Rutupiæ, Dubius, and Lemannis."

[1] Hoare's Notes on Girald. Cambrensis. [2] Girald. Cambrensis.

[3] Tacitus, Speed, [4] Hone's Every-Day Book. [5] Sharon Turner.

they used as conveyances for travelling accommodation being rendered equally available both for peace and war. On the chariots of war, however, immense drums were constructed, by stretching skins over them, which emitted very powerful sounds.

The British chariots, called by them *Esseda*, and by Tacitus *Covini*, were guided by the principal warrior; the Britons esteeming it most honourable to drive the car into the thickest of the enemy's ranks, and to distinguish themselves by braving every danger: it was the custom for a number of combatants to mount together on the same vehicle. The practice of fighting in chariots, in use among the Britons, has been compared to that among the Trojans of old, as described by Homer; but this difference existed with the Greeks and Trojans, that the driver of the chariot was secondary in rank to the chief of high renown who fought.

In one of these warlike cars, such as we have described in the history of Cartismandua, appeared Boadicea and her two daughters, who sat before her. The Queen drove through the ranks of her faithful followers, and, in turn, addressed herself to the several nations who had assembled in her behalf: "This was not," she said, "the first time that the Britons had been led to battle by a woman; but now she did not come to boast the pride of a long line of ancestry, nor even to recover her kingdom and the plundered wealth of her family." She took the field, like the meanest among them, to assert the cause of public liberty, and to seek revenge for her body, seamed with ignominious stripes, and her two daughters, injured beyond forgiveness.

"But the avenging gods," urged the Queen, "are now at hand. A Roman legion dared to face the warlike Britons; with their lives they paid for their rashness; those who survive the carnage of that day, lie poorly hid behind their entrenchments, meditating nothing but how to save themselves by an ignominious flight. From the din of preparation, and the shouts of the British army, the Romans even now shrink back with terror;—what will be the case when the assault begins? Look round and view your numbers. Behold the proud display of warlike spirits, and consider the motives for which we draw the avenging sword. On this spot we must either conquer, or die with glory: there is no alternative. Though a woman, my resolution is fixed; the men, if they please, may survive with infamy, and live in bondage."[1]

The army of Suetonius amounted to 10,000 men, while that of Boadicea was said to be 230,000. The Romans consisted of the 14th Legion,[2] the standard-bearers of the 12th, and the vexillarii of the 20th Legion, which was under the command of Agricola: there were various reinforcements from the neighbouring places besides. Pœnius Posthumus, master of the 2nd Legion, called Augusta, had been appointed to lead the forward-guard, but refused the orders of his general with contempt, and withdrew from the approaching engagement; after the battle, he was so grieved at having lost his share of the glory, that he slew himself.[3] The great disparity of men between the Roman and British forces, would

[1] Tacitus. [2] Ibid. [3] Girald. Cambrensis, Speed.

have deterred Suetonius from hazarding an engagement, had he not been greatly distressed from want of provisions. He, however, relied on the Roman valour, and prior to the onset, addressed his soldiers in terms calculated to animate them to do their utmost. "Despise," he said, "the savage uproar, the yells and shouts of undisciplined barbarians. In that mixed multitude the women outnumber the men. Void of spirit, unprovided with arms, they are not soldiers who come to offer battle; they are dastard runaways, the refuse of your swords, who have often fled before you, and will again betake themselves to flight, when they see the conqueror flaming in the ranks of war. In all engagements it is the valour of a few that turns the fortune of the day. It will be your immortal glory, that with a scanty number you can equal the exploits of a great and powerful army. Keep your ranks, discharge your javelins, rush forward to a close attack; bear down all with your bucklers, and hew a passage with your swords! Pursue the vanquished, and never think of spoil and plunder. Conquer, and victory gives you everything."[1]

The engagement began. The Roman legion presented a close embodied line: the narrow defile gave them the shelter of a rampart. The Britons advanced with ferocity, and discharged their darts at random. In that instant the Romans rushed forward in the form of a wedge; the auxiliaries followed with equal ardour; the cavalry, at the same time, bore down the enemy, and, with their pikes, overpowered all who dared to make a stand. The Britons betook themselves to flight, but their waggons in the rear obstructed their passage. A dreadful slaughter followed: the cattle falling in one promiscuous carnage, added to the heaps of the slain. Tacitus, who gives the foregoing account, concludes by remarking, that "the glory of the day was equal to the most splendid victory of ancient times!"—a confession somewhat humbling to the Roman's pride, one would think, who has just before admitted the greater number of the foe consisted of *women*. Dion Cassius assures us, that the field was not won without difficulty. The cruelty and sanguinary conduct of the Britons on former occasions, were now, if possible, exceeded by the Romans. It is said that not less than 80,000 Britons were left dead on the field, while of the Romans, 400 only were slain, and as many wounded. The surviving Romans interred their vanquished foes, according to their quality, near the place where the battle was fought, known to this day, from the circumstance, as *Battle Bridge*.[2]

---

[1] Tacitus.

[2] The ancient camp, called Ambresbury Banks, near Epping, has by some been considered the scene of the final defeat of Boadicea by Suetonius. "To me," says Gough, "it appears rather to have been a resting-place for the Queen's army after her march from Camalodunum." This spot, which is opposite the park of Copt Hall, and on the south-east side of the London road, was described by Smart Lethieullier, Esq., in a letter to the celebrated antiquary, Mr. Gough. "This entrenchment is now entirely overgrown with old oaks and hornbeams. It was formerly in the very heart of the forest, and no road near it, till the present turnpike-road from London to Epping was made (almost within the memory of man) which now runs within a hundred yards of it; but the entrenchment cannot be thence perceived, by reason of the wood that covers it. It is of an irre-

The conduct of Pœnius Posthumus, after the successful termination of the engagement has been mentioned already. The 11th, 13th, and 14th Legions were liberally rewarded for their bravery by Nero.

Boadicea, on beholding the entire overthrow of her army, determined to put an end at once to her life and misfortunes. Her own lofty spirit was unsubdued, but she scorned to become the spectacle of common gaze in a Roman triumph, as she full well remembered was the fate of her brother, the noble Caractacus, nor could she stoop to be the vassal of her conquerors' will. Like Cleopatra, she determined by poison to terminate her existence, consistently preserving to the last the faith she held with her people, whom in her speech she had assured that she would not survive a defeat, to live either in infamy or bonds.

The heroic and unfortunate Queen was interred with honour by her faithful British followers. Some, who think the last decisive battle was fought near Winchester, then a royal city, say that her remains were carried thither in state for interment;[1] but so divided are historians on the subject, that Salisbury Plain has been asserted to be the site of the fierce contest, and Stonehenge itself the spot where the bones of the Queen were laid.

This mysterious monument, the *Cor Gaur* of the Britons, would, indeed, have been fitting for the resting-place of a woman so renowned, whose "great despair" required some emblem which should, for ages after her, excite awe, terror, and amazement in the mind.

Boadicea, during thirty-two years, had enjoyed the rank and dignity of a queen, without either prosperity or happiness accompanying the regal honours. Deserted by her husband for another, her children branded as illegitimate, she had evinced, under every trial, a spirit worthy of her race. On being restored to the position she formerly enjoyed as queen-consort, she employed her influence for the benefit of the people, and kept faith with the Romans till, on her husband's death, they themselves roused, by their conduct, the spirit of "the Lioness," as Gildas calls her, and brought upon them her resentment and revenge. Even long before, her heart must have bled for the bitter trials of her gallant bro-

gular figure, rather longest from east to west, and on a gentle declivity to the south-east. It contains nearly twelve acres, and is surrounded by a ditch and a high bank, much worn down by time; though where there are angles, they are still very bold and high. There are no regular openings like gateways or entrances, only two places where the bank has been cut through, and the ditch filled up very lately, in order to make a straight road from Debden Green to Epping Market. The boundary between the parishes of Waltham and Epping runs exactly through the middle of this entrenchment; whether carried so casually by the first settlers of those boundaries, or on purpose, as it was then a remarkable spot of ground, I leave to better judgments to conjecture. As I can find no reason to attribute this entrenchment either to the Romans, Saxons, or Danes, I cannot help concluding it to have been a British oppidum, and perhaps had some relation to other remains of that people, which are discoverable in our forest. It is distant from Fifield, where the cells and forge were lately discovered, about ten miles; and about eight from Navestoke Common, where we visited the Templum Alatum."—*Gough's Camden, in Essex*, vol. ii. p. 49.

[1] Hoare (see Notes on Girald. Camb.) says the spot is extremely doubtful; it was certainly south of London, and he thinks somewhere in Surrey.

ther Caractacus, whom she had beheld given up, after his honourable defence of her own wrongs, to the insults of his enemies, and led in triumph to Rome. Boadicea the Warlike, displayed on all occasions, an heroic spirit and incredible valour, worthy of the celebrity she obtained in her own and succeeding times.

Many Britons were taken prisoners in the last fatal battle, but, nevertheless, great numbers had escaped. These would have renewed the contest, but the death of the Queen defeated their purpose, and they were forced to submit to their fate and to disperse.[1] At the close of the battle, the two unfortunate sisters, daughters of Boadicea, completely armed, were still fighting on the field. The Romans made them their prisoners, and conducted them to the presence of Suetonius, who, to his honour, expressed to them the greatest indignation at the treatment they had formerly experienced, and promised to make whatever reparation was possible.[2] Nor did he falsify his word. The eldest princess was married, a few months after, by his arrangement, to Marius, the Roman who had wronged her,[3] and whom historians call the brother-in-law of Boadicea, the youngest daughter of the late Queen,[4] who, with her mother's name, inherited her undaunted character and her misfortunes.

Marius was crowned with a golden crown, and appointed to govern part of the conquered country; the district was in the neighbourhood of Kendal, and the prince being called also "Westmer," it derived from him the denomination "Westmereland."[5] It was peaceably ruled by this prince during five years, the whole of which time he maintained amity with his protectors, the Romans, and distinguished himself by prudence, valour, and wisdom. Coel, his son, received a Roman education, and succeeded to the throne in after-years, paying the usual tribute-money to the Emperors: his son Lucius was the first Christian King of the Britons, of whom mention will be made in the history of Gwenissa. Marius died A. D. 78, and was interred at Carlisle.

A fear of the rival claims of Boadicea, the sister of his wife, had induced Marius to banish her from his territories, she being entitled to share the queenly honours of her sister. Her fate was as disastrous as that of her mother, and she had shared every vicissitude of her fortune; and though the wife of Marius withdrew from the struggle, her spirit was yet unconquered. The subjects of Marius were hers by right of inheritance, and loyally attached to her service and person, as well as to that of her sister. Her cousin, Corbred Gald, King of Scots, had been her associate in infancy; and gratitude for his nurture, entitled her to expect his support and assistance in opposition to the Roman power. Boadicea accordingly assembled a numerous army composed of Britons, men of Brigantia and of the Isle of Man, resolving to struggle for the vengeance which she still considered incomplete. She put to sea with her forces, and landed in Galloway, the whole of which was at that time in possession of the Romans, and at Epiake they had fixed their headquarters.

---

[1] Stowe, Milton. [2] Holinshed. [3] Scott, Holinshed.
[4] Hearne's Curious Discourses. [5] Holinshed.

The precise spot where the younger Boadicea landed is not stated; but she is said immediately after to have marched in the dead of night, unknown to the Romans, to the place where her enemies had encamped. Coming thus suddenly on the tents of the unprepared Romans, Boadicea and the Britons slew many of their most valiant leaders with their soldiers, and would have entirely destroyed the whole of their forces, had not Petilius, the Roman general, been alarmed, and prepared great lights or torches of pitch and resin, which being thrown into the faces of Boadicea's troops, enabled him to discover and repulse them. By this means the Romans gained time to put themselves in order and defend their camp until the morning; for being apprehensive of further danger, they did not quit their tents to pursue the flight. When daylight arrived, they made an onset on the Britons and put them to the rout.[1] Next day Boadicea went to Epiake, which she fired, and in it the whole Roman garrison was destroyed.

It was some little time afterwards that Petilius pursued and routed the followers of the Princess Boadicea, and made her his prisoner; it occurred in the following manner:—A Roman legion[2] had been deputed to seize her person, and by means of using great expedition, laid an ambush, by which stratagem they contrived to enclose her with a great part of her followers. On being captured a second time, expecting to be put to a barbarous death, she is said to have followed the example of the Queen, her mother, and put a period to her existence. Other writers affirm that she was brought alive into the presence of Petilius, and interrogated by him respecting her enterprise; upon her making a courageous answer, she was slain on the spot by his soldiers: it is not, however, certain that Petilius himself either designed or commanded the death of Boadicea the Younger.[3]

Agricola, on returning to Rome after the defeat and death of Boadicea, was, for his brilliant successes, raised to the patrician rank by Vespasian, and soon after to the government of Aquitaine. Tacitus writes thus of him, during his consulship: "Though I was then very young, he agreed to a marriage between me and his daughter, who certainly might have looked for a prouder connexion." The nuptial ceremony was not performed till the term of his consulship expired. Soon after Agricola was appointed Governor of Britain, with the additional honor of a seat in the pontifical college. He arrived in Britain A. D. 78, and governed during the reigns of Vespasian, Titus, and Domitian. Having resolved to subjugate the island, and render it of actual service to Rome, he carried his arms northward, defeating the Britons in nearly every encounter.[4]

---

[1] Holinshed.

[2] A legion consisted of six thousand men; a cohort was six hundred—a tenth of a legion, though "chief cohorts" sometimes contained a thousand men.—*Rapin.*

[3] The following year, A. D. 73, Petilius was succeeded by Julius Frontinus, a man of eminence and information, distinguished as a lawyer and soldier, and as much renowned for virtue as talent.

[4] In a decisive action which took place in Caledonia, in the neighbourhood of the Grampian Hills, the Scots, with their heroic chieftain, Galgacus, were de-

Agricola, who had previously subdued all the southern states, after the defeat of Galgacus, fixed a chain of garrisons between the Firths of Clyde and Forth, to secure the Roman province—for such Britain had at last become—from the invasion of the northern barbarians.[1] Another important and glorious act was performed by his orders. The Roman fleet sailed round the northern point, and made the first certain discovery that Britain was an island. The cluster of islands called Orcades, till then wholly unknown, were in this expedition added to the Roman empire; "Thule, which had been concealed in the gloom of winter, and a depth of eternal snows, was also seen by our navigators."

Pennant believed that the Roman fleet anchored under the rock of Dumbarton Castle on one occasion. A fragment of an old building crowning one of the summits, has been conjectured to be the remains of a Roman pharos, or light-house. Agricola's rampart, and that raised by Lollius Urbicus, terminated in this neighbourhood, and traces of the latter (raised under Antoninus Pius, and popularly known as Graham's Dyke) may be seen not far from Dumbarton.

The Castle of Dumbarton, or Dun Briton, signifies "Town of the Britons." This ancient fortress was originally called Arcluid or Alcluid, "the Place on the Clyde," and was capital first of the Caledonians, and afterwards of a British or Welsh kingdom established in that district. It is fifteen miles from Glasgow. Bede, who wrote in the eighth century, says in his time it was one of the chief British fortresses. It was afterwards taken and held by the Saxons, and recovered again from them by the Picts. At last, in 756, Edbert, the Northumbrian king, forced the garrison to surrender for want of provisions.

---

feated, the loss on the side of the Britons being estimated at 100,000 men. [Sir R. Philipps, Tacitus.] The speech of the heroic pupil and nephew of Queen Boadicea on this occasion, which is given in the pages of Tacitus, strongly sets forth the oppression of the Romans, their ambitious artifices, and their vices, and affords a noble sample of the genuine outpourings of a heart inspired by the spirit of true liberty. To use the language of the commentator of the historian who records the speech of Galgacus, "the ferocity of a savage, whose bosom glowed with the love of liberty, gives warmth and spirit to the whole speech. Neither the Greek nor the Roman page has anything to compare with it. The critics have admired the speech of Porus to Alexander; but excellent as it is, it shrinks and fades away before the Caledonian orator. Even the speech of Agricola, which follows immediately after it, is tame and feeble when opposed to the ardour, the impetuosity and the vehemence of the British chief." [Murphy's Notes on Tacitus.] After the defeat and death of his sister Boadicea, Corbred, the Scottish King, had retired to his own dominions, where he died in peace, leaving three sons, all minors, Corbred, Talcan, and Brek; of whom the first had been educated by Queen Boadicea, and was surnamed "Gald," or "Galgacus, "the Fighter of Battles." [Holinshed.] Galgacus was buried at Dunstaffnage, where a sumptuous monument was erected to his memory, on which were engraved all his actions, and pillars were placed around his tomb. [Scott.]

[1] Murphy's Tacitus.

GWENISSA THE FAIR.

Political influence of Women—A Deputation sent to Rome to fetch Gwenissa as the bride of Arviragus—Customs of Roman betrothals—Gwenissa's family—She is supposed to be illegitimate — Lines of Harding on the Marriage of Arviragus and Gwenissa—The flowery mead—Gloucester built in honour of the event—Crowns of gold—The Emperor Claudius returns to Rome—Festivities in his honour—Beauty of Gwenissa—The love of her Husband for her—Its transient duration—He breaks with Rome — Gwenissa as Winner of Peace—Vespasian remains in Britain — Asserted visit to Britain of Joseph of Arimathea — The Twelve Hides of Glaston — Change in the fortunes of Gwenissa — Arviragus forsakes her for Boadicea—She dies of grief in giving birth to her son Marius.

Here is a father now
Will truck his daughter for a foreign venture,
Make her the stop-gap to some canker'd feud,
Or fling her o'er, like Jonah, to the fishes,
To appease the sea at highest.—*Sir Walter Scott* (*Old Play*).

Was never king more highly magnifide,
Nor dredd of Romans, than was Arvirage.—*Spenser*.

THERE are few histories which do not present instances of the political influence of woman. The wife, the daughter, the mother, or the friend, has, in innumerable cases, become the arbitress of the destiny of an empire; and frequently has it happened, that her happiness, sometimes even her life has been offered up as a sacrifice to her country's welfare. Such was the case with Gwenissa, one of the most interesting queens of Roman Britain.

The circumstances of the divorce of Arviragus from Boadicea have been already recounted, and how he assented to the proposals of Claudius, to receive his daughter Gwenissa in marriage, after having made a formal declaration of his submission to the Roman empire. A deputation was therefore dispatched to Rome, to bring over to this country the royal lady who was to replace the repudiated Queen.

The laurel, the badge of joy and victory, was usually affixed by the Romans to their letters of dispatch after success against the enemy,[1] and was the emblem of the successful termination of the expedition undertaken by Claudius. It was also a custom, in the Roman form of betrothal, for the bridegroom to send to his bride a simple *iron* ring, which did not contain any stone, but was symbolical of the lasting bond of which it was the type. In Britain, as well as Gaul, at this time, these rings were worn on the middle finger.[2] At Rome, the number of rings on a person's hand denoted the high rank of the wearer, and many of these bore engravings of Harpocrates, and of the Egyptian deities. In

[1] And also placed on the spears and javelins of the soldiers.—*Pliny*. [2] Pliny.

the reign of Claudius no gold seal or ring was permitted to bear the portrait of the Emperor, without an act of especial license; but Vespasian, some time after issued an edict permitting rings and brooches to bear the imperial image. The simple iron ring was accordingly conveyed to the Roman Princess by the ambassadors of the Emperor.

The beautiful Gwenissa, on her father's side, was directly descended from Anthony, the Triumvir, and the gentle and virtuous Octavia, sister of the Emperor Augustus. Antonia the younger, daughter of Octavia, by her marriage with Drusus, brother of Tiberius, had two sons, Germanicus, and Claudius—the father of Gwenissa, whose paternal ancestors were therefore the noblest in Rome. Her maternal relationships are not, however, so easily determined.

Shortly before Claudius had departed for Britain, he married Messalina, the mother of Octavia and Britannicus. By his first union with Plautia Urgulanilla, he had an only son. This lady, to whom he had been married in the reign of Tiberius, was repudiated by her husband with great ignominy, being convicted of infidelity, and other crimes. Claudia, the innocent offspring of her guilt, was condemned, at the age of five months, to be exposed at her mother's door. Subsequently to this, Claudius took Ælia Petina, a lady of high birth for his wife, her father being of consular dignity. After bearing a daughter to the Emperor, named Antonia, Ælia Petina was divorced, but on very slight grounds. Now, if Gwenissa was the legitimate daughter of Claudius, she must have been the offspring of his first or second marriage; yet is her name unnoticed by Suetonius, who enumerates, in exact succession, the several wives of Claudius, and mentions not only Antonia and Octavia, but even the illegitimate Claudia.[1] It appears more likely that Gwenissa was the daughter of Ælia Petina, than that Claudius should have offered to Arviragus a lady—only his daughter by adoption—in order to procure such a peace as might enable him to appear in Rome without disgrace; which is the opinion some commentators on this subject have adopted.[2]

On the site of the modern Hospice de l'Antiquaille, at Lyons, formerly stood the Roman palace of Claudius, who was a native of that city. There, at some period, the Emperor and his family had resided; but at the time of which we are writing, Messalina held her court in Rome. To Gwenissa, who was residing there under the care, it may be presumed, of a dangerous and too celebrated step-mother, the imperial embassy was addressed. The emissaries of Claudius departed from Britain in the autumn, and returned in the following spring, bringing over the young princess in safety.[3] The quaint lines of Harding thus record the arrival of the Roman bride:—

"Thene Claudius sente for dame Gennyce,
His doughter fair, full womanly to see;
She came in haste, as then it might suffyce,

[1] Grafton calls Gwenissa illegitimate.

[2] Rev. P. Roberts' Notes on British History.

[3] Geoff. of Monmouth, Brut y Tysilio.

To come oute from so farre lande and countrie,
And in a mede with floures of greate beauté,
Wedded they were; where Claudius then made
A cytee fayre, Cayre Glowe[1] to name it had."

Gwenissa was welcomed with great honours on her arrival, and her reception from her aged father was affectionate in the extreme. The nuptial rite was afterwards performed with much solemnity,[2] as the poet relates—

"In a mede with floures of great beauté,"

in presence of the whole court of both the British King and Roman Emperor, their generals and the soldiery. So great a concourse must have required a much larger space than the customary dwellings of the Britons, and not inappropriately the royal espousals were celebrated under the broad expanse of the blue sky, with the enamelled carpet of green turf, bespangled with the first flowers and fairest promises of spring, spread out beneath the feet of the young and lovely bride.

The pageant at this inauspicious marriage was imposing, and the mind may easily picture the divers characters there assembled: the aged Emperor, his young daughter, the haughty Arviragus, who had made even his new father-in-law tremble by his power and bravery, and whose feelings must have been divided between exultation and remorse; the statesmen, the generals, and legions, contrasting with the rough and uncivilized forms and garb of the native Britons.

Like many other royal nuptials, the semblance of joy supplied the place of its reality. But to the young bride all seemed fair, and she appears to have been quite content with her lot. At her suggestion, Arviragus proposed to his father-in-law the erection of a new city on the scene of their espousals, commemorative of the occasion. Claudius willingly assented, and in person laid the foundation of a city to which he gave his own name, calling it Claudio-cester, now Gloucester. It contained a temple to the Emperor in which, if Tacitus is to be depended on, he received the honors of a deity. The Romans ever worshipped their rulers, in the empire, with extravagance, and the affability and generosity Claudius testified towards the Britons, in which perhaps he was desirous of securing their future goodwill for his daughter, having made a very favorable impression, the Britons perhaps followed their example in this respect without disinclination.

The building of the Roman city proceeded with alacrity, and as soon as it was completed, a Roman military establishment was placed there, by consent of the Britons; in this arrangement Claudius testified not only his desire to secure his conquests, but to afford a security for the future safety of his daughter. An army of regular legions, and a large body of auxiliaries, had accompanied Claudius into Britain, from which due ar-

[1] William of Malmesbury ascribes the building of the city of Gloucester to Claudius, the father of Gloui, who, he says, was his son "by a British girl named Gewissa."

[2] Lewis, Harding, Tanner.

rangements were made by selecting the persons most fit to colonize the new Roman station.[1]

As if to leave nothing incomplete, the marriage of Arviragus and Gwenissa was a second time celebrated at Lud's Town, the capital of the Trinobantes, where it was followed by many regal festivities, and the crown was formally placed on the head of the British King and his Roman bride. The crowns of our ancient British sovereigns were mostly made of pure gold, though it appears from some ancient coins, that Cymbeline also wore a fillet of pearls.[2] They were worn on nearly all state occasions, whether in battle, in processions for religious festivities, or on the occasion of meeting in council, not only by the Kings, but the Queens also. We are expressly informed of an untoward accident which occurred to the Queen of Cathir the Great, whose golden crown was *stolen* from her at a grand convention, held at Tara, A. D. 141.[3] Some of these golden crowns were afterwards displayed by Claudius on his triumphal entry into Rome, among other spoils taken from the Britons; they were of beaten gold, and one—a present from Spain to the Emperor—weighed seven pounds, while another, he had received from that part of Gaul called Comata, weighed as much as nine pounds.[4] A British naval crown of gold was, moreover, placed by Claudius close by the civic crown, over the gate of the Imperial Palace of Rome, in token of his victory over the British sea, when he crossed it.[5]

The period of Claudius's visit to Britain is by some said to have been extended to two years, while others say a few months only. As soon as peace was established, and Arviragus settled in the government, as a tributary of Rome, the Emperor bade a final adieu to his son and daughter, and returned to Rome, being everywhere received with the honors of a conquering hero; a triumphal arch was erected at Boulogne, commemorative of his victories over the Britons. He entered Rome in triumph, attended by his captives of war; the Empress Messalina following him at a distance as he proceeded through the city, in a chariot magnificently adorned. On arriving at the capital, Claudius mounted the steps on his knees, supported on each side by his two sons-in-law, Silanus and Pompey.[6] The surname of Britannicus was awarded to the Emperor

---

[1] "About the middle of February, 1818, some men in the employment of Sir W. Hicks, Baronet, while digging up the roots of an old ash-tree, which they were employed to fell, at Cooper's Hill, about four miles from Gloucester, came to a large stone that excited their curiosity. On removing it, they discovered a flight of steps leading to an apartment, in the centre of which was a cistern about a yard square; in clearing the room, the skulls of a buffalo and a bullock, with horns complete, and the remains of a fireplace with a quantity of wood-ashes, were likewise found. A fortnight afterwards, four more apartments were discovered; in one of which is a very curious tessellated pavement (the tessera are cubes of about half-an-inch), also the remains of several urns and figured tiles of Roman pottery. The walls of one of the apartments, and also the passages, are painted in *fresco*, with alternate stripes of purple, yellow, and scarlet, all of which are beautifully shaded and curiously ornamented with scrolls and a border. These interesting remains of antiquity have probably existed for upwards of seventeen centuries."—*Journal of Science and the Arts*, 1818, No. IX, p. 144.

[2] Selden. [3] O'Flaherty. [4] Pliny. [5] Echard. [6] Ibid.

for his exploits; and he, on his part, directed it should be borne by his son by Messalina.[1] Presents of triumphal ornaments and chains of gold were adjudged to the several officers who had accompanied the expedition, as we find on record by inscriptions yet extant,[2] the senate moreover decreed that annual games should be established in honor of this event; and for some time after the return of Claudius, Rome was filled with every kind of festivity, dramatic representation, horse-races, bear-combats, pyrrhic dances, and gladiators.[3] Such were the rejoicings in commemoration of the peaceful conquest of Britain by Claudius, through the agency of his daughter's charms.[4]

That the personal attractions of the daughter of Claudius were of no mean stamp, is evident from her having been surnamed "the Fair." This Queen is only known to us by the name of Gwenissa, and not by the one she had borne in former years in the land of her birth. This is remarkable, but it was a custom with the Romans, and often with the Britons, to change the names of foreigners into their own peculiar dialect; and probably the fair stranger received hers from the Britons on account of her personal beauty, the word Gwen literally signifying, in the dialect of the island,[5] a "lovely" or "fair" woman: the Roman Venusia, or Venus, might have been associated, and the British *Gwenissa*, thus formed, which, if written in Saxon, is sometimes Winifred (the g, v, and w being often interchanged)—a name used by the Britons to designate "Fair Countenance," and by the Saxons a "Winner or Procurer of Peace."[6]

After the first splendours of her marriage were passed, and her father had departed, Gwenissa the Fair might, perhaps, have heaved more than one sigh for the luxurious scenes of her youth. Imperious destiny, however, had fixed in Britain her future home, and so great an ascendency had the young Queen obtained over the mind of the fascinated Arviragus, that he seemed to value her as his chief good, while, by the gentle sway of beauty and goodness, she obtained from all those who surrounded his person, unqualified admiration.[7] The passion, however, which her beauty had illumined, was of transient duration. After a time, the "late remorse" of Arviragus awoke, to remind him that for her and her father's interest he had been compelled to divorce his earlier-chosen, and once not less-beloved Boadicea, and that the mother of his children was suffering for her sake. Perhaps Arviragus, who had steeled himself against the pangs of conscience for a time, became their prey when he was able to perceive the true state of his circumstances, and that his apparently splendid position was simply a condition of slavery. Impatient at his bondage, he at length resolved to assume, in his own person, the grandeur and consequence of a sovereign, and to assert his power over both the Romans and British people, whom he had been appointed by Claudius to rule merely as his deputy. Haughty, arrogant, and overbearing, his conduct displeased the civilized Romans so much, that not choosing to submit to

[1] Echard. [2] Pliny. [3] S. Turner.
[4] Univ. Hist., S. Turner. [5] Josephus. [6] Butler's Lives.
[7] Geoff. of Monmouth.

the ostentatious display of wealth and power in a barbarian, they resented his attempt. Arviragus took this as a pretext for breaking off his faith with his allies, the countrymen and friends of his Queen. Information was forwarded to Claudius that Arviragus had declared his independence, on which the Emperor despatched Vespasian to reduce him to obedience. The struggle was again renewed, and the Roman general laid siege to Exeter. Arviragus marched to its relief, and a battle took place, in which much loss was sustained on both sides. At this critical juncture, the character of Gwenissa shines forth in a very pleasing light. She had been much afflicted by the hostilities which had arisen between her father and her husband, and undertook, in person, the difficult task of arranging an accommodation between the hostile parties. The day after the battle, Gwenissa, in her character of the "Winner of Peace," had an interview first with one party, and then with the other, and through the influence of her beauty and solicitations, succeeded in reconciling them to each other. The result of her successful mediation was, that the Romans and Britons united their rival forces, and proceeded in harmony to London in each other's company, and afterwards Arviragus paid the tribute-money to Vespasian, as formerly agreed upon with the Emperor.[1]

The especial request of Queen Gwenissa detained Vespasian in Britain, during the following winter.[2] The unsettled state of the country made her consider the presence of this distinguished leader in some measure necessary to her own safety, and the late defection of her husband might have raised some suspicion of his fidelity to herself in her mind. This, the prolonged stay of Vespasian was calculated to dispel, and welcome, no doubt, must the society of this brave and excellent man have been at the court of Roman Britain. The future Emperor of Rome had fought no less than thirty battles under Claudius and Plautius, had subdued two mighty nations, and twenty towns, with the Isle of Wight, then called Vectis; for his military exploits he was rewarded with triumphal ornaments, the sacerdotal dignity, and consulship; nor was the renown of the young Titus, his son, who served under him in Britain, much inferior to his own, as numberless inscriptions in Germany, and in this country, are yet remaining to attest.[3] While these distinguished guests were staying in Britain, the court resided at Lud's Town. It was about this date that Arviragus probably commenced the Castle of Windsor for his royal abode, though it is by some ascribed to a later period.[4]

While Vespasian yet tarried at the court of Arviragus and Gwenissa, an event happened which William of Malmesbury records as a remarkable piece of ecclesiastical antiquity. He states, that when St. Philip the Apostle, after the death of our blessed Lord, was in Gaul, promulgating the doctrines of Christianity, he received information that all those horrid superstitions which he had observed in the inhabitants of that country, and had vainly endeavoured, with the utmost labour and difficulty, to overcome, originated from a little island at no great distance from the continent, named Britain. Thither he immediately resolved to extend

---

[1] Biog. Brit. Holinshed.
[2] Harding's Chronicle.
[3] Echard.
[4] Holinshed.

the influence of his precepts, and despatched twelve of his companions and followers, appointing Joseph of Arimathea, who, not long before, had taken his Saviour from the cross, to superintend the sacred embassy.[1] On their arrival, Vespasian interested himself very warmly in their behalf with both the King and Queen, to whom he related a miracle concerning St. Joseph :—

Vespasyan praied the kyng,
The quene also, to be to hym good lorde
And good ladye, which they graunted in all thing.
* * * *
All this he told the king and eke the quene,
And prayde them his supporters to bene.[2]

The royal protection was granted to the strangers, at the request of the Roman general, and they were hospitably entertained by Arviragus,[3] who, to compensate them for their hard and toilsome journey, bestowed on them, for a place of habitation, a small island, which then lay waste and untilled, surrounded by bogs and morasses. To each of the twelve followers of St. Joseph, he appointed there a certain portion of land called a hide, sufficient for one family to live upon, and composing altogether a territory to this day, denominated "The Twelve Hides of Glaston."[4]

This account of the first introduction of Christianity into Britain, singular and romantic as it may seem, is not undeserving of attention, as it is well known that St. Paul preached to the utmost bounds of the west; and we have excellent authority for believing that some of the

---

[1] Norman authorities have assigned to Joseph the credit of being an apostle to Britain, and they are supported by the approving opinion of Cardinal Bona and Geoffrey of Monmouth. His pretensions have been defended by Theophilus Evans in his Drych y prif Oesoed, and the learned Charles Edwards in his Hanes y Ffydd. Leland tells us, that he met with the fragment of Melkinus in the library of Glastonbury; by which he concluded, that Melkinus had written something of the history of Britain, and particularly something concerning the antiquity of Glastonbury, and Joseph of Arimathea. But this story, says Leland, "he sets on foot without any certain author," which makes this learned antiquary dissent from him. And elsewhere, when speaking of the Glastonbury tradition, he observes, "that twelve men are said to have come hither under the conduct of one Joseph; but not Joseph of Arimathea." Bishop Stillingfleet, in his Origines Britannicæ (ch. i,), has ably examined all the circumstances connected with this tradition, and has satisfactorily proved the improbability of the mission of Joseph of Arimathea to this country. No mention, too, is made of it by Gildas, Bede, Asserius, Marianus Scotus, or any of the earliest writers.—*Chronicles of the Ancient British Church, anterior to the Saxon Era*, p. 16.

[2] Harding.

[3] It is said that Arviragus was converted by St. Joseph, and received the baptismal rite. [Nennius.] St. Joseph also gave him a shield, white as silver, on which was figured a cross —

Which shelde, by Joseph exhortacion,
He bore on him in feldes of werre alwaye,
And in his baners and cote armour gaye.
Harding's Chronicle.

These arms were used throughout Britain, that each man might know his nation by them.

[4] Collinson's Somersetshire; Biog. Brit.

Apostles actually preached to the Britons. Theodoret,[1] who asserts this, declares the Britons were converts to St. Paul; and states, that Aristobulus, a bishop ordained by St. Paul, and sent to Britain as a missionary, was martyred A. D. 56. There is, indeed, every reason to believe, that the Christian faith was early promulgated in Britain,[2] and many converts made prior to the defeat of Queen Boadicea. If Vespasian was at all instrumental in establishing it here, it is singular enough, as his son Titus was the destroyer of Jerusalem, and disperser of the Jews throughout the world.

Pomponia Græcina, wife of Plautius, a lady of the court of Gwenissa the Fair, is thought to have been a believer in the Christian faith. This Roman matron was accused of having embraced a strange and foreign superstition, for which crime she was condemned to be tried by her husband. According to the custom of the times, Plautius convened her whole family and relations for this purpose, and in their presence tried her for her life and fame; after which he pronounced her innocent of anything immoral.[3]

---

[1] A bishop of the fifth century.

[2] Gildas fixes the event in the eighth year of Nero's reign.

[3] Pomponia Græcina, returning to Rome after the death of her husband, perhaps in company with the imprisoned Caractacus and his family, became acquainted with Claudia Rufina, [Gladys Ruffyth, in the British dialect,] daughter of that British prince, and with her is named in the Epistles of St. Paul, as being "saints of the household of Cæsar." She ever after her trial led a retired life; but though this has caused many writers to esteem her of the Christian faith, it did not deter Ovid from addressing to her the fourth Book of his Metamorphoses. Her friend Claudia, with her husband and family, mingled in the most brilliant circles of Rome, and are numbered among the most eminent early Christians. [Saxon Martyrology; Archbishop Usher.] They were friends of the poet Martial, who addressed an Epigram to Aulus Rufus Pudens, on the happy occasion of his marriage to Claudia; and another to the young lady herself, on the same subject, as well as some complimentary verses on her beauty, from which the following is an extract: —

"From painted Britons how was Claudia born!
The fair barbarian how do arts adorn!
When Roman charms a Grecian soul commend,
Athens and Rome may for the dame contend."

[Liber IV., Epigram 13.] A book of Epigrams and an elegy on the death of her husband are said to have emanated from the genius of this royal lady, [Baleus; Female Worthies,] who, when her father Caractacus obtained leave to return to Britain, remained behind at the court of Rome, where she was afterwards united to A. R. Pudens, who was a Roman knight and of senatorial rank, as well as a philosopher of the Bononian sect. Linus, who had been honoured by an Epigram of Martial being addressed to him, is named with Pudens and Claudia, by St. Paul in the second Epistle to Timothy. The apostle visited Rome A. D. 62, eleven years after Claudia went thither with her father. It is even asserted that Timothy, the disciple of Paul, was a son of Claudia by Pudens, [Rowland's Mona Antiqua,] and that it was owing to the impression made by his preaching that, A. D. 156, [Geof. of M. gives the date of Lucius' *death* as 156. Nennius gives 167 as the date of his *conversion*; Bede 156,] King Lucius addressed a letter to Eleutherius, then Pope of Rome, requesting further instructions on the Christian faith. [Rowlands.] In consequence of this application, SS. Fagan and Dervan were sent over to Britain, who, on their arrival, baptized the King and Queen,

Gwenissa the Fair was perhaps not only a patroness of the disciples and missionaries of the new faith, but the mild doctrines they promulgated might have influenced her many acts of generosity and kindness. But the crisis of her destiny, delayed for a time, was at hand. Arviragus, who had increased his power by timely submission until he had become a terror to the neighbouring kings, at last, elevated with pride, again resolved on asserting his power, and, joining a confederacy of chieftains who had assembled at Shrewsbury, amongst whom was Caractacus,[1] was, as has been related, then reconciled to Boadicea.

The news of the final desertion by Arviragus of his fealty and his love, so deeply affected the unfortunate Gwenissa, whose unmerited affection was thus spurned, that, overcome by the extremity of her grief, the hour of maternal anguish was prematurely brought on, and, in the midst of her sufferings, she expired.[2]

The son to whom Gwenissa gave birth, survived, and received the name of Marius, to which was afterwards added that of "Westmer." With the death of Gwenissa ceases all information regarding the earlier British Queens, no record having been preserved of any until we come to those who were adventitiously so. In resuming the line we have to introduce a Roman-born subject.

---

with their family; whose example was imitated afterwards by their subjects, the inhabitants of Essex, Sussex, and Surrey; [Weever; Stillingfleet;] and thus the doctrines of Jesus became established in the island. Many churches were built by Lucius, particularly those of Winchester and Westminster, which last occupied the spot on which now stands the venerable Abbey of St. Peter. In the subsequent persecution under Dioclesian, it was pulled down, and a temple to Apollo erected from its ruins.

Lucius, the first Christian monarch of Europe, was called "Lever Maur," or "the Great Light;" because he assumed for his badge "the Star of Jacob," which may be seen upon his coins; two of which bear the impression of the Cross, with the royal initials, L. U. C.

The glorious example of Lucius and his queen was followed in Scotland, A. D. 185, when Donald, brother of Ethodius, became king. This prince sent ambassadors to the reigning pontiff, St. Victorinus, requesting him to send over to him some religious men to instruct himself and his subjects in the Christian faith. On their arrival the king, queen, and many of the nobility and people, embraced the faith with great zeal, though idolatry was not extirpated from the country for many years after. [Scott's Hist. of Scotland.]

[1] Geoffrey of Monmouth, Holinshed. [2] Caxton's Chronicle.

JULIA "DOMINA."

Julia born in Phœnicia — Julia Mæsa, her sister — Beauty and talents of Julia Domina — Her abstruse learning — Her ambitious views — Her arrival at the Imperial City — She is noticed by the Empress—Her success—Her admirers—Severus — The Augury — The Marriage of Julia — Children of Severus—Caracalla and Geta — Eastern Expedition of Severus — Julia becomes Empress — They go to Britain — Advance to Caledonia — Difficulties and Trials on the Campaign — Fulgent lays siege to York — Cruelty of Severus — Superstition of the Emperor — The Court at York — Luxury and pomp — The Emperor's death — Enmity of the Antonines — Return to Rome — Fratricide — Grief of Julia — Severity of Caracalla — Supposed marriage to her Step-son — His Murder — Julia dies — Her Sister's children — Her character as regards Britain.

THIS celebrated woman was not descended from an illustrious family, her father Bassus being merely a priest of the sun at Emessa, a town of Phœnicia; and Julia Soæmias, her mother, had another daughter also, who is known in history as Julia Mæsa, and who became equally distinguished with her sister.

The eldest daughter, whose fate it was to become elevated to the throne of Severus, the Roman Emperor, was by nature gifted with the most rare beauty, so that she charmed all those who approached her; which impression was rendered permanent by the superior talents which accompanied her personal endowments. The mind of Julia, however, was little in accordance with her personal qualities, for malice and dissimulation were its characteristics. The study of philosophy, geometry, and the various sciences, from an early age, was her pursuit, though not commonly the taste of her sex; and this afterwards rendered her capable of enjoying the society of learned men, for she could converse freely with them on any subject; and not only did she think correctly, but her address was easy and graceful, and her manner of writing elegant; so that on her elevation she proved herself competent to manage the most delicate affairs of the cabinet.

Julia, to all the shining qualities calculated to give her influence, added ambition. She was inspired with the presentiment, that hers would be a high and brilliant destiny; and her acquaintance with judicial astrology had led to a knowledge of the prediction that her husband "should one day become Emperor!" The path of glory seemed to open before her: full of hope and expectation, she quitted the obscure town to which she owed her birth, for Rome, the theatre of the world, which she judged a worthy sphere for the display of her charms and her genius. Julia Domina was accompanied by her sister, no less eminently endowed in mind and person than herself.

Scarcely was she arrived at the Imperial City, when she attracted the notice and was taken into the protection of the Empress Anna Faustina.

In a city so devoted to magnificence and display, the lovely sisters could scarcely have failed to be admired. Julia, who was truly Syrian in her character, delighted in sports, shows, and every sort of diversion that could gratify the senses. The high spirits in which she appeared at these festivals, set forth her beauty to the most dazzling advantage, and always ensured some fresh conquests. A crowd of lovers was soon at her feet, and among the number, Septimius Severus, then only a Roman tribune. At the time this bright star of foreign lustre appeared in the horizon, with her combination of attractions, Severus, who had lost his first wife, Martia, was revolving in his mind a second marriage. He, like Julia, had certain presages of his future greatness; some augurs, whom he had consulted respecting a wife who would be likely to forward his ambitious views, being acquainted with the prediction concerning Julia, informed him of it, and gravely recommended the lovely Syrian as a suitable match. The superstitious Severus readily conceived they were destined for each other,[1] while her ambition, and the assurance that her husband should arrive at empire, had more influence on his heart than even her beauty. Already the favorite of the Emperor, he had great interest at court, and made so good an appearance, that Julia did not doubt of his being a man whose preferment was certain. She readily accepted his offer, and thus the first grand step towards the accomplishment of the prophecy was fulfilled. The nuptial ceremony was solemnized in the Temple of Venus, near the Imperial Palace; the Empress Faustina not only honouring the espousals with her presence, but resigning her own apartment on the occasion for the use of the newly married pair.

Severus was by birth an African,[2] and had obtained from the Emperor Marcus Aurelius the offices of quæstor, tribune of the people, and prætor; after which he was proconsul of Africa.[3]

At the time of Julia's marriage, he was the father of three children by his first wife, one of whom was the afterwards unworthily celebrated Caracalla. This prince was born at Lyons, where his father had formerly been stationed as Governor of Gaul, during the war of the usurpers. His mother, Martia,[4] was a native of Britain,[5] and at the time of her marriage, Severus was a tribune under Marcus Aurelius Antoninus. As Caracalla bore the name of Bassianus, many have esteemed him the son of Julia,[6] but that name, perhaps, was given him as a compliment to her, as, soon after Severus quitted Gaul, and while Bassianus was yet a child, Martia died, and Severus entered into his second marriage: the daughters of the first union were both called Septimia, from Severus himself, who

[1] Spartian.

[2] Born A. D. 146, at Leptis or Lepris.—*Crevier.*

[3] Spartian.

[4] Martia or Mary; Owen's Pedigrees.

[5] Crevier; Lewis's Hist. of Brit.; Spartian; Owen's Pedigrees; Lives of the Empresses.

[6] Wootton, in the History of Rome, says both Bassianus and Geta were children of Julia, the second wife of Severus, whom he married after the death of Martia, his first consort; but this does not seem to be the case, from a careful examination of the many points in the history of these princes.

derived it from his father, Septimius Geta.[1] Two years after her marriage, Julia gave birth to a son, at Rome,[2] named Geta, from his grandfather. The fact of the two brothers being the offspring cf different mothers,[3] accounts for many minute points in their after-history. The eldest-born was by the woman who derived her origin from a British family, whose history has not, however, reached us, on account of the Roman contempt for a subdued nation; the younger enjoyed from the cradle, every honor and privilege of a Roman citizen by birth and education. Yet was Severus particularly partial to the children of Martia, and after his marriage with Julia, is said to have even erected statues to the memory of his former wife, at the request of his son Bassianus, who could not be pacified in any other way, under the contempt shown for his mother, whose alliance was considered ignoble.[4] This occasioned a preference among the Romans for the son of Julia, which, added to the misfortune of his losing his mother, Martia, at so tender an age, and being committed to the care of a jealous stepmother, were unfavourable circumstances, in themselves sufficient to account for the many bad features displayed in the character of Bassianus "Caracalla"[5] during the latter years of his life. In childhood especially tender-hearted, the earnest entreaty of this young Gaul had obtained from his father, on the reduction of Byzantium, a mitigation of the punishment to which that city and Antioch had been condemned,[6] which tender emotions of affection and sympathy were entirely extinguished before the young prince had arrived at the imperial power.

The causes which led to the expedition of Severus into the East, and taking of the cities of Byzantium and Antioch, being immediately connected with his elevation to the throne of the Cæsars, require to be noticed here. At the time when Julian received the imperial power, the vast armies of Rome were commanded by three several leaders, each possessed of wisdom and experience, yet differing in character, and each alike in the one point of anxiety to succeed to the throne of Pertinax: they had an equality of force, three legions being at the disposal of each; but the army generally decided, in such cases as theirs, the fortune of the day; and of the three competitors for power—Pescennius Niger in Syria, Clodius Albinus in Britain, and Septimius Severus in Illyricum,

[1] Crevier. [2] Lives of Empresses. [3] Echard.

[4] Lewis; Lives of the Empresses.

[5] Both before and after his father's death, Bassianus appeared often in the dress peculiar to the Gauls, from which he derived the name by which he is chiefly known in history—Caracalla. The cassock of this name, which Caracalla rendered fashionable in Rome, was originally Gaulish; it was a long garment reaching down to the ancles, [Echard,] and resembled the habit of a modern monk, being sometimes worn with, and sometimes without, a hood or cowl. [Aurelius Victor Tenacius de Re Vestiaria Rom., Hoffman. Lexic. Univ.] By some the name of Caracalla, given on this account, is regarded as a reproach thrown on the prince's origin. The love of dress of Caracalla is seen also by his appearing in a dress peculiar to the Alemanni whom he had conquered, and wearing false hair of the same colour as theirs. [Dio Aurelius Victor.]

[6] Crevier.

the latter was destined to succeed on this occasion. The empire had long been the goal of his ambition, and from the time of his marriage till his elevation to power, Severus is said to have been always guided by the counsels of Julia, to which he was principally indebted for that high reputation with the soldiery which, in the end, induced them to proclaim him Emperor. He lost no time in undertaking an expedition into the east against Niger, whom he succeeded in making his prisoner. Cruelty was a prominent feature in the actions of Severus throughout his career of triumphs; he put his enemy to death, and the same fate was afterwards shared by his wife and children: most of the senators, his adherents, lost their lives, and the remainder were banished. Those cities which befriended Niger, were also severely punished; of which number were Byzantium and Antioch, in whose behalf Caracalla interfered; while the Empress, who on this, as on every other occasion, had accompanied her husband, interposed in favour of her native city, Emessa, and obtained its pardon from the Emperor.

It would cause too long a digression to relate all the circumstances of the arrival of Severus at imperial power. Suffice it to record, that his entrance into Rome was one of the most triumphant of those times of pomp and exhibition.

The vanity and pride of Julia were fully satisfied with the honours heaped on both her husband and herself. Crowns of flowers and of laurel were showered upon them as they passed by the shouting citizens: the senators, in state attire, met them at the gates with greeting; fires, made of perfumed wood, were lighted in every street: on Julia was conferred the title of August, given always to the wives of their Emperors,[1] besides those of Mother of the Republic and of the Armies, and several other complimentary titles, expressly invented for this occasion. She thus saw fulfilled to the letter the prediction of her future grandeur, on which she had relied. Her pride naturally rose with her prosperity; she insisted on the full privileges of her newly acquired dignity, and intoxicated with her position, treated the greatest persons in the empire with haughtiness and contempt.

Severus meantime was anxious to secure the fortunes of his children by Martia. He accordingly gave one daughter to Aëtius, whom he raised to the consular rank, and bestowed the other on Probus, who already was a consul, and who was offered, on this occasion, the government of the city of Rome, which, however, he was politic enough to refuse,[2] and hoping to ingratiate himself with the new Emperor, gave as his reason, that the honour of being his son-in-law was, in his opinion, infinitely greater than that employment.

Severus, desirous to determine who should be his heir, was so anxious, that the subject invaded his rest, and in a dream he learnt that his successor was to be named Antoninus. Regarding this as an infallible prediction, he brought his favorite son, Bassianus, into the camp, and gave him the name of Marcus Aurelius Antoninus, in presence of all the legions.[3] This son actually did reign after him, as history attests;[4] and

[1] Selden's Titles of Honour.
[2] Lives of the Empresses. [3] Ibid. [4] Ibid.

it is a circumstance which Spartian remarks as very singular, that Severus should have omitted, when he wrote the history of his own life, any mention of his first wife, this prince's mother, to whose memory the statues were raised at Caracalla's request.

In order to withdraw his sons, and still more, perhaps, his wife, from the pleasures of Rome, to which she was attached beyond all bounds, Severus availed himself of the excuse afforded by an irruption from North Britain into the territories in the south of the island which were under the Roman empire, to undertake an expedition to Britain.[1] He was accompanied by Julia, his two sons, and two Roman legions.[2] On his arrival, he encountered the rebel Britons in an engagement, when some were reduced to submission, and the rest fled into Caledonia, whither they were pursued by the warlike Emperor.[3]

At the time Severus undertook this expedition, he was advanced in years, and so broken with infirmities, that he had to be carried in a litter; yet, impelled by his indomitable spirit, he proceeded through woods and morasses to the farthest parts of Caledonia. He surmounted all the fatigues of the march, and many fierce encounters which took place between the Roman and Pictish forces. Julia was with her husband throughout the whole of this trying campaign.

One of the foes of Severus in Britain was Fulgent, a relative of Martia, mother of Caracalla. In this campaign with the Scots he fought against the Romans with great bravery, having procured some Picts to assist him in the war, and many inhabitants of the islands adjacent to Britain, as well as the Britons themselves. It is said that he laid siege to York, which was relieved by Severus marching to its aid, and in the contest which followed, Fulgent received a mortal wound. That Severus fell has also been asserted, but this is untrue, as he was prevented by age and infirmities from personally engaging in the contest.

During this warfare the armour of the northern Britons and Caledonians consisted of a small shield and a spear; they wore also a sword depending from their naked bodies, which were painted over with the figures of animals.[4] The cruelty of Severus was in this campaign as conspicuous as ever: a speech of his is on record, of which the following quaint lines are a translation:[5] he commands an indiscriminate slaughter of his enemies:

"Let none escape your bloody rage —
With terror let all die;
Spare not the mother, nor the babe
Which in her womb doth lie."

From this we discover that women mingled with the strife, even women about to become mothers, and who were fiercely sentenced to be slaughtered by the unfeeling Emperor.[6]

---

[1] Warrington. [2] Geoff. of Monmouth. [3] Ibid. [4] Guthrie.

[5] It is translated from the Greek by Mr. Leigh, in his "Select and Choice Observations of the Roman Emperors."

[6] Fifty thousand Romans perished in the expedition of Severus into Scotland, though no battle was fought, through ambuscades of the enemy and fatigue in

On entering York after his success against Fulgent and the Caledonians, a circumstance occurred confirmatory of the superstitious character of Severus. A Temple of Bellona stood at that time in Eboracum, and in front of it a small column, called the "martial pillar," whence a spear was thrown when war was declared against an enemy.[1] Severus, on entering the city, proceeded towards that spot with the intention of offering a sacrifice, but on his way thither was met by a Moor wearing a cypress garland about his head, — a circumstance considered so unlucky, that the Emperor ordered him to begone out of his sight: when the man, who was of the class of soothsayers, and, being an African, respected by Severus, who was himself of that quarter of the world, saluted him with these words: "Totum fuisti, totum vicisti, jam Deus esto victor,"[2] and offered to conduct him on to the temple. This was thought by the Emperor to foretell his death; and another prognostic was added when he quitted the temple after the sacrifice had been offered, for some of the black beasts appointed to have been slain are said to have followed the Emperor to the palace. All the Romans, and more especially Severus, regarded this last as one of the worst of omens, and a warning of the approach of death.[3]

---

cutting down woods, building bridges, and drying marshy grounds. Julia must have witnessed much during this season. Severus is said to have observed with great accuracy the lengths of the days and nights of the summer and winter while in Caledonia, which could not have been done without a stay of at least six months. He pursued his course, laying waste by fire and sword, in spite of his gout and all difficulties, till peace was brought about by a concession of the disputed territory, and the Caledonians delivering up their arms. On this occasion it was that Caracalla had sought to murder his father in the sight of the whole Roman and British army. The Emperor, in presence of his soldiers, was in the act of concluding a treaty, and the Britons were presenting their arms in token of submission, when Caracalla, who stood behind, suddenly drew his sword, and would have killed his father. Severus, turning at that moment, beheld the sword raised to destroy him: without betraying any surprise, or uttering a single word, he pursued the business in hand, received the arms of the Britons, and signed the treaty. When he had returned to his tent he sent for his son; and Papinian, captain of the guard, and Castor, his chief chamberlain, being present, reproached Caracalla for his wickedness. Then offering a drawn sword to him, he said, "If your ambition to reign alone prompts you to imbue your hands in the blood of your father, execute your impious purpose rather in this place than in the sight of the whole world and in the presence both of our friends and enemies. If you are not yet abandoned to such a degree as to murder your father with your own hand, order Papinian to commit the parricide: you are emperor, he must obey you!" This speech neither affected Caracalla at the time, nor rendered his conduct more dutiful for the future.

[1] It is supposed that the site of this building was in or near the street called St. Saviour-gate, as in digging the foundation of some houses on the north side of it, many years ago, large quantities of the horns of several kinds of beasts were discovered, and the probability is increased when we consider its vicinity to the Imperial Palace. [Allen's Hist. of York.]

[2] Spartian. Leigh's Choice Observations.

[3] The structure which was called the Prætorian Palace is supposed to have occupied the whole space of ground extending from Christ Church, through all the houses and gardens on the east side of Goodramgate and St. Andrew's Gate, through the Bedern, to Aldwark. The royal baths in all probability occupied a

During the residence of Severus in Britain, with the exception of the period occupied in the Caledonian war, he constantly held his court at York. It was a military colony, governed by both military and municipal laws. The Emperors sat at times in person in the Prætorium, in the chief tribunal, to give laws to the whole empire; and the rescript of Severus and Antonine, *de rei vindicatione*, is dated from this ancient city;[1] York or Eboracum, may therefore be regarded as a miniature picture of Rome, and as possessing a just claim to the titles with which it has been dignified by Alcuin, of Britannia Orbis, Roma altera, Pallatium Curiæ, and Prætorium Cæsaris. In its form it resembled ancient Rome, for in a plan of the city left by Fabius, Rome is represented in the form of a bow, of which the Tiber was the string: and "the Ouse has not inaptly been called the bowstring of York." Both these rivers run directly through the cities which they water, and have contributed to their ancient splendour and ultimate consequence.[2]

The city, in the reign of Severus, was arrived at the height of its grandeur and consequence. "The prodigious concourse of tributary kings, foreign ambassadors, and other persons of distinction, who crowded the court of the sovereigns of the world at this period, when the Roman empire was in the zenith of its power, in addition to the emperor's own magnificence, his numerous retinue, the noblemen of Rome, or the officers of the army, all which would necessarily attend him, must have exalted Eboracum nearly to the summit of sublunary grandeur."

Julia "Domina," the chosen partner of Severus, the inseparable companion of his progresses east or west, even to the extreme bounds of the north, held within the walls of the Prætorian Palace her own imperial state. With her was her sister Julia Mæsa, who shared her brilliant fortunes, and never quitted her up to the latest period of her existence.[3]

For a space of time not less than two years, while the court was held in Britain, the island natives beheld before their eyes a spectacle novel and imposing,—grandeur and luxury, in all their varied forms of dress and equipage. No wonder that the consequence was a final loss of their own simple tastes and unaspiring habits. As early as the time of Agricola, the Roman fashions were imitated by the Britons, and especially their dress, proud buildings, baths, and elegant banquets.[4] A Roman British female is exhibited in Smith's costumes, taken from the reverse

---

considerable part of this extent, [Drake; Allen,] for the Romans were peculiarly partial to their hot and cold baths.

[1] Universal History.

[2] Allen.

[3] At a later epoch of our history, this Roman palace became the residence of the Saxon and Danish kings of Northumberland, and then of the earls of the district, until the reign of Edward the Confessor. The palace, when in possession of Tosti, Earl of Northumberland, brother of Editha, Edward's queen, was plundered and burnt by the enraged populace. It fell afterwards into the hands of the crown; but as the English kings did not reside there, the building became neglected. More recently still "the Guildhall," as the palace of Severus had been named in more modern times, was appropriated to the Dukes of York.—*Allen's York.*

[4] Milton.

of a coin of Carausius. She is habited in the *gwn* and *pais*, just like the Welch peasantry of the present time; except that the former, instead of opening before and wrapping over, appears a copy of the Roman tunic. All the Brito-Roman coins and bassi-relievi agree in exhibiting the tunic as worn over the pais, with sleeves, as at the present day in Wales, descending only down to the elbows.

While the Romans in Britain progressed in the vast undertakings assigned to them by Severus, the Emperor himself remained at York, suffering from severe illness, from which he never recovered. Caracalla, who had returned from his expedition against the Caledonians, not content with so near a view of the imperial diadem as was presented by the fast-ebbing current of his parent's existence, endeavoured to hasten his last moments by exciting a mutiny among the Roman troops, whom he caused to proclaim himself Emperor. Severus, hearing of what had passed, caused the principal offenders to be brought into his presence, who prostrated themselves before him, and supplicated forgiveness.

The nobles of Severus wondering how he could govern so vast an empire in his feeble and diseased state, he remarked that "he ruled with his brain, not with his *feet*," alluding to the gout from which he was then suffering. This had long been a trial to the Emperor, for on returning the second time from the East to Rome, he declined the proffered honour of a triumph, because the gout prevented his riding in the state chariot used on such occasions. When in Caledonia, he was carried in a litter.

When he felt himself dying, he caused his urn to be brought, and having taken it into his hand, said: "Thou shalt contain him whom the world could not." Some say that Julia and her son Geta were staying in London[1] when Severus died; but that they were present at the last fatal scene, appears from the address that Severus is said to have made to his sons prior to his death: "Agree among yourselves; enrich the soldiers; contemn all others."

This Emperor, who was indebted for his elevation to the legions, entertained a particular regard for the soldiery, and, out of gratitude, had conferred many benefits on them,—among which was an indulgence which injured the discipline of the army. The soldiers had hitherto been required to live in a state of celibacy, but Claudius permitted to them the rights and privileges which attached to the married state.[2] Severus went further, and gave them leave to marry. Before his time the Roman camp had no place of accommodation for women. Might not Severus have acted in this, as in many other instances, from the influence of his Empress, the attendant of his numerous campaigns, and partaker of his cares and dangers?

[1] The Emperor's infirmities preventing his own progression through the British states, Julia's visit to the south was probably for the purpose of transacting business, and to join the court of Geta, held at London during his father's visit to Caledonia; for the south of Britain was left under his control, — a politic arrangement of Severus, to prevent differences between the brothers. Of Geta, who was an extravagant admirer of horses, we are told an equestrian statue was found near Bath. — *Collinson.*

[2] Murphy's Tacitus. See notes.

The Emperor plainly foresaw the contention that would arise between his sons after his death respecting the empire. After addressing them, as before related, he bade them read in Sallust the dying speech of Mycipsa to his children, in which they would find this expression: "By concord, small possessions increase; by discord, great ones are wasted." After this parental exhortation, he uttered the following words: "I received the Republic everywhere troubled; I leave it at peace *even among the Britons;* bequeathing to my Antonines,[1] old and lame as I am, an empire which will prove firm, if they be good,—but weak, should they turn out evil."[2]

Such were the last moments of Severus, who died in the Imperial Palace at Eboracum, whose walls not long after were destined to witness the dissolution of another Roman Emperor, Constantius Chlorus, a very different character from its present inmate. The remains of the deceased Emperor were buried in a spot about two miles and a half distant from the city,[3] called, from the circumstance, Severs-hill, to the present day. Of the three singular hills, called Severus'-hills, the centre one is the smallest, and is about twenty-seven yards above the level of the surrounding country; the others are about thirty-five yards in height.[4]

A small arch yet exists in Rome to the memory of Septimius Severus, Caracalla and Julia.

Severus had been raised to the empire A. D. 195, and died A. D. 212, after a seventeen years' reign, aged 66. During the last two years his sons had shared in his sovereignty, as Antonines. He is said to have been inexorable to his enemies, but kind to his friends, and rough and untractable in his manners, though exact in his distribution of justice. In his time food was provided to the Roman people, even without asking, whenever it was needed, and the soldiers loved him for his excessive liberality, and for permitting them to have their wives in their quarters. The greatest pleasure of the Emperor was to do good to all around him, and Galen, the prince of physicians, who lived in his time, and attained the age of seventy, declares that Severus kept constantly by him a great store of treacle, and other expensive remedies, to relieve such as wanted them, by which means he saved the lives of many persons. Of this number was his Greek secretary, Antipater, son of Piso, to whom Galen dedicated his treatise on treacle, and who wrote the history of the reign of his imperial master, Severus. Arria, also a lady of distinction, was saved by this remedy; she was much esteemed by Severus, because she applied herself to the study of philosophy and the reading of Plato. Severus[5] may be ranked among the *literati* of his own era, for he wrote

[1] The title accorded the two young Cæsars, his sons. [2] Spartian.

[3] In the township of Holdgate and parish of Acomb. — *Allen.*

[4] Leigh, Rudulphus, Camden, and Drake.

[5] Coins of Severus and of Julia have been dug up at Aldborough in Yorkshire, and other parts of Britain. A valuable deposit of Roman coins was dug up near Morton in Yorkshire, consisting of a very large quantity of denarii in excellent preservation, chiefly coins of Severus, Julia, Caracalla, and Geta. They were contained in the remains of a brass chest, supposed to have belonged to a Roman legion, and to have been deposited, on some sudden alarm, in the spot which it

the history of his own life; while Julia, who successfully applied herself to letters and philosophy, patronized every art, and was the friend of every man of genius; amongst other proofs of this, it was at her request that Philostratus undertook his life of Apollonius Tyanæus.

According to Gibbon, the nurse and preceptor of Caracalla were both Christians. Origen, also, who died in 253, says in his 6th Homily, "The power of our Saviour's kingdom reached as far as Britain, which seemed to lie in another division of the world." Yet Severus is himself said to have been a persecutor of the Christians. It was agreed by the two brothers, Caracalla and Geta, that they should return to Rome[1] with the Empress-Mother. They set out, bearing with them the ashes of Severus in a golden urn, the same which had been brought to the dying Emperor. On their way so many contentions arose from mutual jealousy, that it was feared they would destroy one another; and on one occasion Geta would have fallen a sacrifice to the poison prepared for him by Caracalla, but for the fidelity of his servants.[2] Julia, as though she had been mother to both, endeavoured by every possible means to reconcile them, but without success; their animosity increased to such a degree that they even ate and lodged separately, and each stood upon his guard against the other. On their arrival in Rome, they immediately divided the imperial palace between them, as they could not agree to live together. "No communication was allowed between their apartments, the doors and passages were diligently fortified, and guards posted and relieved with the same strictness as in a besieged place." The two Emperors, one of whom was but twenty-three, and the other a year younger, met only in public, and then in the presence of their afflicted mother.

Every posthumous honour was awarded to the memory of Severus, and on the arrival of the brothers at Rome the first act of Caracalla and Geta

---

had quietly occupied afterwards during a period of almost sixteen centuries.—*Allen's York.*

A thick coin in middle brass, of Julia, is said to have borne on the obverse a fine head of the Empress, with the legend, "Julia Domna Pia Felix Augusta." The reverse exhibited a full length figure of Venus; the legend merely, "Felicitas Publica," with the usual S. C. (meaning by order of the Senate) inscribed on the field.—*Journal of Science.*

A considerable quantity of clay moulds, or matrices, for the coining of Roman money, were turned up some time since at Lingwell Yatt, near Wakefield. Several crucibles for melting the metal were also found at the same time, and in some of the moulds there were coins yet remaining. A number of clay moulds for casting coins were also discovered in the parish of Eddington, Somersetshire, having the impressions of Severus and Caracalla, with their Empresses, Julia and Plautilla. Some of these moulds are lodged in the Ashmolean Museum, Oxford.—*Collinson.*

[1] According to some authorities, Caracalla, on his father's death, proceeded direct to London, where the Empress and Geta were staying, with the hope of prosecuting his claims on the empire in that quarter: for it too soon became apparent that only one of the brothers could reign, and that the other must fall. The Romans would have preferred Geta for their Emperor, for he was, both by his father and mother, a Roman; but the Britons rejected him, desiring Bassianus "Caracalla," their own countryman by the mother's side, to be advanced to the supreme dignity.

[2] Wootton.

was to perform the Emperor's Apotheosis or Deification, with the usual ceremonies. The whole city assumed the garb of mourning. Next, an image was made of wax, to represent exactly the deceased Emperor. This was laid on a stately ivory bed, magnificently adorned with cloth of gold, and placed at the entrance of the palace. On the left hand were seated the whole body of the senators in black, on the right the ladies of the highest quality in plain white habits, without jewels or other ornaments. This lasted for seven days, during which time the physicians resorted to the image as though it had been a real patient, still signifying that they had less and less hopes of the Emperor's life; at which words the mourners always gave a groan. At last, when they had declared his death, the noblest and youngest of the senators carried the bed upon their shoulders through the Via Sacra to the Old Forum, on each side of which were erected two large scaffolds, one filled with young boys, and the other with young maidens, all children of the highest quality, who sang solemn and mournful hymns and songs in honour of the dead. After these were ended, the senators and knights again took up the bed and carried it out of the city into the Campus Martius, where a beautiful pyramid of wood, with several stones, had been erected. The first story was square, being a sort of chamber filled with various sorts of combustible matter, and richly adorned on the outside with cloth of gold, ivory statues, and fine pictures; the second of a similar character, but smaller size, had the four sides open; the third was still less; after which was a fourth, and, indeed, many other successive stories, each decreasing in proportion, till the last ended in a point. The bed and statue were placed in the second story, in presence of noblemen and gentry of every nation, who desired to do honour to the deceased. Then the Roman knights rode on horseback round the pile in a certain order, to the sound of warlike instruments; afterwards persons in chariots, in purple robes, who represented the most celebrated Roman commanders and emperors; after this Caracalla and Geta, the successors of Severus, fired the pile with torches, and consuls, senators, and knights followed their example. It was wrapped instantly in flames, and from the top an eagle was let fly, which was out of sight in an instant, amid the shouts of the spectators, who, believing the bird carried the Emperor's soul to heaven, from that time forward paid him the same homage they rendered to the immortal gods.

The disunion which existed between the brothers did not diminish, and they continually had recourse to the Empress, who officiated as mediatrix. A negotiation was set on foot respecting a division of the empire, but this plan, first proposed by Geta, was broken by Julia, who desired to keep her sons together, and foresaw the step would lead to the ruin of the state. On this occasion she threw herself at their feet, begging that they would divide her too between them. She had omitted no opportunity before of reconciling her sons, and now by her prayers and tears established an appearance at least of concord between them. Accordingly, medals were stamped with the images of the two brothers joining hands, and surrounded by the motto "Happy Concord."

Caracalla, who ever listened with respect and apparent deference to the arguments of the Empress, agreed to abide by her decision, and had arranged to meet his long-divided brother in her apartments, for the purpose of a lasting reconciliation. The heart of Julia beat with joy at the prospect of witnessing so tender a reunion, and the meeting so earnestly desired actually took place in her presence; it was then that, in the midst of a conversation which had commenced among the reunited members of the divided family, some centurions who had been concealed in the apartment, rushed suddenly with drawn swords upon the young and helpless Geta. Vainly did Julia cast her maternal arms around her child to shield him from death. In the dreadful struggle she received a wound in the hand from his assassins, and beheld on one side the horrid spectacle of Caracalla animating and assisting the murderers, upon the other, Geta falling dead at her feet, her own person being covered with his blood.

The fratricide flew to the Prætorian camp, where he fell prostrate before the statues of the tutelary deities of the camps. Supported by the army he next hurried to the Senate, and prevailed on that obsequious assembly to declare in his favour. His brother's funeral over, Caracalla returned to the palace, where he found the Empress-Mother surrounded by her women, bewailing in the most moving manner the death of her son. His first impulse was to put them all to death, but passion yielded to pity, and he showed great kindness to Julia, to whom he even ordered that the same honours should be paid as were rendered to himself. The heart-breaking scene might have moved one even more stern than that stony-breasted Emperor; and indeed, what were all the world's honour's to Julia at that moment—a widowed wife, deploring the loss of an only and dearly-beloved son! But the silent reproach of those who surrounded the Empress, revived the fury of the murderer, and he commanded them to disperse, on pain of death; while, to prove that he was in earnest, he ordered that one of the terrified mourners should be led away to instant execution. Fadilla, the unfortunate victim of his anger, was daughter of Marcus Aurelius, and sister of Commodus, both Emperors; she herself had rendered state-services, by pleading the cause of the people, and preserving the life of a Roman emperor, besides having quelled an insurrection. All this was overlooked by Caracalla, who only beheld the tears shed in the first moment of grief for the death of the young and blooming Geta—a tribute due to the bereaved Empress. This severity had the effect expected, and silenced all remonstrances from the women. Fadilla, the personal friend and confidante of Julia, was the first of a series of victims, termed "the friends of Geta." It is said that no less than 2000 persons of both sexes suffered on this occasion, amongst whom was Papinian, the most eminent lawyer in Rome, the particular friend both of Severus and Julia; his crime was having declined composing a defence for the Emperor, for he observed "It is easier to commit fratricide than to justify it!" Rome was filled with mourning, and the loss of Severus was regarded as a public calamity. Even before he quitted Britain, the sanguinary Caracalla had ordered the death of his wife Plautina. For the sake of the city, for the sake even of Caracalla himself, Julia suppressed her own sufferings; she saw the necessity of resuming her influence over the government, which Caracalla allowed; and during the whole of his reign, she administered the chief affairs of the State, "with a jus tice that supported his authority, and with a moderation that sometimes corrected his wild extravagances." On one occasion she remarked to the Emperor how much he exhausted the people by his rapacity; that they were no longer able to pay their accustomed taxes: Caracalla's reply was characteristic of himself, "I shall have whatever money I want as long as I can command a sword."

Advanced in life, Julia still possessed the attractions of beauty, a lively imagination, a firmness of mind, and strength of judgment seldom bestowed on her sex. Spartian, and some other authors, have related that Julia consented to become the wife of Caracalla, and that their nuptials were publicly celebrated, which, if true, would have allied her to the murderer of her only son; but others consider Caracalla to have been only her step-son, which is under every point of her history apparent.[1] The tale seems to have originated in a scandal of the Alexandrians, who called her Jocasta because she lived at court after the death of Geta. Dion plainly intimates that she durst not do otherwise, since any concern for the son she had lost might have cost her her life; and he relates that she secretly mourned over the extravagances of Caracalla, passing the greater portion of her time, during the latter years of her life, in the society of learned men. She would hardly have acted thus, if guilty of such a crime. Julia did indeed accompany the Emperor to the East, but they were not residing at the same spot when he was murdered.

Maternianus[2] wrote to Caracalla, then at Edessa, informing him that he had heard Macrinus repeat a prediction that himself was to arrive at the imperial power. Julia was at time staying at Antioch, and the Emperor, who was at Edessa, had given her instructions in his absence to read all his dispatches. Fully empowered to do so, when the letter of Maternianus fell into Julia's hands, she read it, and transmitted it to Caracalla; but before it reached him, Macrinus, who attended him there, had received private information of the circumstance direct from Rome.[3] Caracalla was driving a chariot at the public shows, when a packet was handed to him containing the letter of Maternianus, and passing them to Macrinus to read, the future Emperor found it among the rest.

The particulars of Caracalla's murder need not be dwelt on here; the assassin had been hired by some military conspirators, and at the end of three days Macrinus received from the army the predicted dignity of Emperor. By his orders, Caracalla's body was burnt, and the ashes conveyed to Antioch to Julia, who was overwhelmed with her new affliction. Some say she mourned but the loss of that power which she so much loved, and to which she had sacrificed her feelings. She had, to this advanced age, retained the title of Augusta, and a great part of the business of the government passed through her hands: Macrinus gave her to understand that she was to retain the dignity of Augusta, with its

[1] Had this scandal of Julia, however, been true, both Herodian and Dion Cassius were ready enough to admit anything against Caracalla, and they do not even mention it.

[2] Captain of the Guards at Rome.

[3] By a courier from Ulpius Julianus, his particular friend.

rank, and to have the honour of continuing guards for her person. On this she resolved no longer to devote her thoughts to death, but to continue to live according to her former dignity. Macrinus soon, however, discovered a cabal with the soldiers, in which she was engaged; so that he hastily ordered her to withdraw from Antioch. This sudden change decided her as to what course she would adopt, and abstaining from food, she died, it is said, either of inanition or poison, unable to live as a subject,[1] after a life passed in the enjoyment of supreme power. This event took place A. D. 217, fifteen years after the death of Severus.

The vicissitudes of the life of Julia did not, till the last, affect her spirit or disarm her fortitude. A gifted woman, elevated from a humble station to the highest pinnacle of earthly splendour, her hapniness is problematical. The dreadful death of her only son, and the extravagant follies of Caracalla, must have corroded at her heart, amidst all the stately honours and dignity she so much coveted. During the latter period of her existence, her chief enjoyment was that fertile one afforded by the society of the learned, whom to the very last she fostered and protected. If her youth was charged with folly, the qualities she displayed during her after-life may atone for her errors, looking upon her as a public character. She was always disposed to intercede with Severus, and avert his severity, and from her Caracalla received wise counsels. Literature and science followed her footsteps, or sprung up afresh from the decline into which they had fallen. To her, perhaps, were the children of her sister Julia Mæsa, who was with her when she died, indebted for the advice which led them on to their future greatness.[2] The failings of Julia have been severely visited by historians. Such failings in exalted persons may remind us of the imperfection of all here below. Had Julia's career been less brilliant, less exposed to temptation, she had perhaps exhibited fewer of those imperfections, which the higher the object is placed, become the more manifest.

In her character as a British sovereign, her acts appear to advantage, as she certainly helped to refine the manners of the rude people amongst whom she sojourned.

---

[1] Echard.

[2] Julia Mæsa, after the death of the Empress, her sister, was ordered to quit the country. During the twenty years she had spent at the imperial court, she had acquired an immense fortune, and contracted splendid alliances. She retired to her native city, Emessa, taking her wealth with her, and accompanied by her two daughters and their sons,—for each was a widow, and had an only child. Bassianus, a son of one of these daughters, became priest of the sun at Emessa; and the troops perceiving his strong resemblance to their favorite Caracalla, and, moreover, bribed by his mother, at the instigation of Julia Mæsa, declared him Emperor. Perhaps the anticipation of Julia Domina's connivance at some such enterprising scheme had caused the severity shown to her by Macrinus. Bassianus, afterwards well known as Heliogabalus, proved so unworthy, that the army soon repented of their choice, and, attracted by the virtues of his cousin Alexander, son of the other daughter of Julia Mæsa, they raised him to the imperial power; in which capacity, after the murder of Heliogabalus, being guided by his mother's excellent counsels, he displayed, during thirteen years, remarkable wisdom and prudence. His death took place A. D. 235.

VICTORIA, VITURGIA, AND HUNILA,

EMPRESSES OF THE WEST.

Zenobia and Victoria—Influence of both—Character of Victorinus—His Murder, and that of his Son—Marius chosen by the Empress—His history and fate—Posthumus succeeds—Ælianus—Tetricus appointed by Victoria—Constantius Chlorus in Britain—Victoria's sudden death by the treachery of Tetricus—Aurelian's Roman triumph—Viturgia and Proculus—Bonosus the Pedagogue—His rise—Aurelian bestows Hunila upon him—He proclaims himself Emperor of Britain, Gaul and Spain—His death—Probus settles a pension on Hunila.

THE vast Empire of Rome, at the period of the accession of the Emperor Aurelian, A. D. 270, was divided between two rivals in talent, in fame, and at the last, in misfortune,—Zenobia, Empress of the Eastern division of the Roman territory, and Victoria, the not less deservedly celebrated Empress of the West.[1] It is not without pleasure, that in so distant a period we hail the name which our present beloved Sovereign has engraven on each true British heart,—a name destined to be illustrious; for the Empress Queen of Gaul, Spain and Britain, occupied a position among the most distinguished of her times, and by her character and actions illuminated the darkness of the Western hemisphere. "Aurelia Victoria Augusta" possessed such vast power, that she raised as many as six candidates to the imperial dignity, in defiance of the Roman arms, while to the last fatal scene of her existence she maintained the supreme authority over those she had exalted, and over the people whom she had appointed them to rule.

The "Heroine of the West," as Victoria has been designated, was not of British birth, though Britain was included under the dominions over which she held control; she was a native of Gaul, and by her adroitness succeeded in persuading[2] Posthumus, on his elevation to the empire, to receive her son, Marcus Victorinus, for his colleague in power. The assumption of the purple by Posthumus is placed in the year 265, when he was proclaimed throughout Gaul, Spain, and Britain; so highly was he esteemed by Valerian, that when appointed to the government of Gaul, that Emperor wrote to the people in these terms of commendation: "He is one whom I esteem above the rest, and think the most worthy of all to represent the Prince." Among the list of thirty tyrants who aspired to the imperial power during the reigns of Gallien and Probus, we accordingly find those of Victoria, Victorinus, and Posthumus.

The enterprising Victoria was little inferior in merit to her celebrated contemporary, Zenobia; she possessed great courage and ambition, and no sooner had she accomplished her project of securing the empire for

[1] Gibbon.

[2] Gibbon.

her son, than her superior qualities began to unfold themselves. It was Victoria who really governed the state, though business was transacted in the name of her son and his colleague; so extraordinary a power had she over the minds of the soldiery, that she could rely on their executing her every wish. Trebellius Pollio, in his account of the "Usurpers," has introduced Victoria to cast contempt on Gallien, by a contrast between himself and the boldness of the women of his time. Victorinus was generally governed by his mother's politic counsels, who, for her valour and masculine courage, was styled "Mother of Armies." By her assistance he opposed Lollianus, whom he defeated and slew in a sharp battle, remaining sole master of Gaul, together with his mother, who was associated with him under the title of Augusta.[1] The influence exercised by the Empress in this situation is compared, by a modern writer,[2] to that possessed by Mammæa in an earlier period of the Roman history, and considered to have been "at least as constitutional."

Cologne was the seat of the Imperial Government of the West, and Victoria, who resided in that city, exercised, in her son's name, all the functions of royalty, while he devoted himself to a life of pleasure, although he is said to have been by nature endowed with every quality requisite to form a hero; and to have equalled Trajan in bravery, Antoninus in clemency, Nerva in gravity, Vespasian in managing the public money, and Pertinax and Severus in his care of the military discipline. The author,[3] who considered "no one ought to be preferred to Victorinus," somewhat contradicts his commendation, when he adds, that his besetting vices "drowned all his good qualities, and cast such a blemish upon his reputation, that no one dares to record the virtues of a man whom all own to have deserved the doom which, in the end, overtook him."[4] This doom could not be averted by all the virtues of his mother.

On his first elevation to power, Victorinus had controlled his evil passions; but afterwards, imagining his high rank raised him above control, disregarding fear or censure, he threw off the restraint, and lost the affections of his soldiers by his immoral conduct towards their wives.[5] The plot formed in consequence against the life of Victorinus succeeded so suddenly, as scarcely to leave him time to name his son Victorinus Augustus as his successor. This step, in the event of any emergency, had been advised by Victoria, who appears to have foreseen the fate of her son. The heavy wound her mother's heart received in his loss, did not deprive her of her presence of mind. She instantly caused her grandson to be proclaimed Emperor, and assumed an unlimited power in his name. The honours thus secured proved, however, fatal to the child; for the murderers of his father, in fear of their personal safety under the dominion of Victoria, succeeded in effecting the death of the young Emperor almost immediately after.

Victoria's mind did not, however, sink under this double misfortune; from henceforward she resolved to preserve that throne, which, during five years, she had maintained in her son's name. She determined to

---

[1] Echard.
[2] Sir F. Palgrave.
[3] Julius Alexianus.
[4] Univ. Hist.
[5] Lives of the Empresses.

govern over the whole empire, by electing some general who should entirely depend on herself. Marius appeared to her well fitted for this purpose, and accordingly she proposed him to the legions, and so well employed her powers of persuasion in his behalf, that she obtained his election as Emperor.[1]

Marius was by trade an armourer, which cast some ridicule on his election; but he was possessed of "intrepid courage, matchless strength, and blunt honesty."[2] In conformity with the terms on which Victoria had assisted in his elevation, she was suffered to enjoy the solid power, while the honours of the government rested on him. At the time he received the purple, notwithstanding his mean origin, he had, after passing through every inferior degree, arrived at the dignity of a general; yet so hurt was he one day at an allusion to his former condition made by one who had worked under him in his shop, to learn the trade, and who came to congratulate him when Emperor, that he received him with the greatest contempt. This unexpected conduct so provoked the man, that he killed Marius on the spot, exclaiming as he stabbed him: "This very sword you made yourself."[3]

Posthumus, the colleague of Victorinus, succeeded, and reigned for seven years.

In the year 266 a new opponent for the empire arose at Mentz, in the person of Ælianus,[4] but he was defeated by Posthumus,[5] who, however, so displeased the soldiers, by not yielding up the city to be plundered, that they put him and his son, the younger Posthumus, to death; when Ælianus assumed the imperial diadem, and was proclaimed in that part of Gaul bordering the Rhine, while the rest was, that which had been governed by Victorinus.[6] That Desidianus Ælianus had governed the Roman troops in the north of England, during the reigns of Valerian and Gallian, appears by an inscription found in Northumberland.

Trebellius Pollio writes concerning Victoria, that after she had beheld her son and grandson slain by the soldiers, and the others in succession cut off, she stirred up Tetricus, a man of a noble family, and chief ruler of Aquitaine, to seize the rule; and by largely bribing the legions, Victoria at length caused him to be proclaimed Emperor, together with his son Cæsar, throughout Gaul, and he was soon after acknowledged in Spain and Britain.

Tetricus, who was related to the Empress-Queen Victoria, was, at the time of his elevation, commanding a part of Gaul; and as soon as Victoria had procured his nomination, she sent an express to inform him of his new dignity, exhorting him not to refuse an honour conferred upon him by the army. He received the imperial robe at Bordeaux, and

---

[1] Lives of the Empresses. [2] Gibbon. [3] Lives of the Empresses.

[4] "Lollianus and Ælianus are supposed to be the same."—*Gibbon.*

[5] Some coins of Posthumus were found in a Roman vase, which contained others of the Emperor Valerian, and was dug up by some workmen in a field, at Charlton, in Cheshire, where they had been buried three feet below the surface.—*Journal of Science and the Arts.*

[6] Univ. Hist.

shortly after showed himself worthy of his election and the Queen's patronage, by the courage and judgment he displayed during the war in Spain. In his absence in that country, Victoria held the entire government of Gaul, and conducted every affair of the state, according to the arrangement she had made with Tetricus. Placing herself at the head of her army, she maintained her authority independent of the Roman arms; for after successfully making head against Gallien, after placing in succession her son, grandson, and Marius on the throne, she had raised Tetricus to the empire, in spite of the power of Claudius. Coins of brass, gold, and silver, were coined in her name, and bore her impression, specimens of which were still to be seen at Treves, in the time of Pollio. Even during the reign of Aurelian, she opposed the imperial arms with an undaunted spirit. At that time Tetricus was in Britain, and Aurelian despatched Constantius Chlorus to that country to oppose him.[1] It is not certain whether Victoria herself was ever in this island, but a city in Scotland bears the name of the heroine. So great was the renown of this Queen, that it had not only filled all Gaul, but had spread to the limits of the Eastern Roman Empire. Zenobia, the competitor of Aurelian, heard with pleasure of the grandeur of the "Heroine of the West," and is said to have desired nothing so much as to join her forces to those of the Amazonian Queen, that they might together conquer the whole world![2]

Tetricus had at first yielded to the desire of Victoria, to enjoy the supreme authority; but as soon as he was securely fixed in power, he resolved to shake off the sway of a woman. Victoria, deeply wounded at his ingratitude, would have revenged herself; but Tetricus, aware of her intention, put a period to her existence, within a few months after he had received from her the gift of an empire. Thus, in the very height of her power and success, this remarkable woman, distinguished for her powers of mind and masculine judgment, was cut off by means of the very agent which she had herself created, in hopes of securing the continuance of her sway.

It is thought that the traitor Emperor had expected by this means to ingratiate himself with Aurelian, at whose feet he shortly after threw himself, to be dealt with according to his pleasure.[3] At this critical juncture, when Victoria was no more, and Tetricus in his power, the Gallic army was attacked by the forces of Aurelian, when, fighting without a leader and without order, it was easily cut to pieces. By this decisive victory, near Châlons upon the Marne, the Emperor Aurelian obtained the dominion of Gaul, Spain, and Britain. The year 274 witnessed his triumphal entry into Rome, which was conducted in the most superb manner, and graced by the presence of Zenobia and Tetricus. The captives of the several conquered nations, on this memorable occasion, followed the triumphal chariot with their hands tied behind them. The Eastern Queen was so loaded with jewels, that she could scarce support their weight, but was compelled to stop from time to time to take

[1] Morant's Colchester.
[2] Lives of the Empresses.
[3] The reign of Tetricus lasted altogether for six years.

breath: some Egyptians of rank, taken at the defeat of Firmus, and the principal lords of Palmyra, did honour to this ceremony. Amongst the rest were seen Tetricus; his son accompanied him: both were attired in the Gallic costume,—trowsers, a saffron tunic, and a purple mantle, "one of the earliest instances of French fashions," remarks Lady Morgan, "recorded in the pages of history."

The Romans were surprised that Aurelian should cause a woman, and a Roman senator, who had been Consul, to mix in the procession with the Goths, Vandals, and other barbarians; but the Emperor justified his conduct on this point to the Senate, and ever after treated Tetricus with the greatest kindness, to repair the affront put upon him, calling him at times his "colleague," and at others honouring him with the empty title of "Emperor."

Victoria was more happy than either Zenobia or Tetricus, in having escaped by death[1] the indignity of appearing in this humiliating scene. She left her fame untarnished by disgrace, to descend with the memory of her virtues to succeeding ages.

The renown of Victoria inspired the women of her times with high projects and haughty daring. Through the suggestions of Viturgia, wife of Proculus, that robber chieftain afterwards assumed the imperial power at Cologne.[2] Viturgia was seconded in her ambitious project by Sampso, a woman of as much spirit and daring as she herself possessed, endowed with a manly courage. Proculus had first armed two thousand slaves on his own behalf; after which he entered the army, became Tribune, and had the command of several legions, which instigated him to attempt the purple. Further stimulated by his wife, and supported by the people of Cologne, he caused himself to be proclaimed Emperor in that city, and was afterwards acknowledged throughout the western division of the Roman Empire, including Britain. Proculus was, however, defeated by Probus, and taking refuge with the Franks, from whom he pretended to derive his origin, was delivered up to the Emperor, and punished as he merited.

The famous Bonosus, the colleague in power of Proculus, was of Spanish descent, but his parents were of British birth,[3] and his father taught the rudiments of the Latin language, then the vehicle of all learning in a public school. Bonosus had entered the army very young, and from a soldier worked his way up through the successive intervening degrees, till he became a general under Aurelian. The Emperor who had made him Governor under Rhætia, gave him for his wife a princess of the blood-royal of the Goths, whom he had made his prisoner during his twenty years' war against that people. Hunila, and nine other Gothic women, in the habit of the other sex, had fought in an engagement between Aurelian and Cannabaud, a Gothic prince. After the battle, in which Cannabaud was slain,[4] some of these females were found dead on

---

[1] Some say that the Queen died a natural death.

[2] Univ. Hist. Gibbon.

[3] Some say his mother was of Gallic origin.

[4] The chariot drawn by four stags, which Aurelian took from this Gothic prince, was used by him afterwards in his triumphal entry into Rome.

the battle-field, and others taken prisoners by the Romans. The latter, among whom was Hunila, were entertained by Aurelian in a manner suitable to their sex and dignity. When peace was made with the Goths, Aurelian exacted some of the sons and daughters of their chiefs as hostages, that the youths might be trained up near his own person, and the damsels be educated in the Roman fashion. Hunila and the other noble Gothic women, were given afterwards in marriage to his principal officers, in the hope that the two nations might be cemented by these close and endearing connections.[1]

Hunila was distinguished beyond her companions for beauty, wit, and virtue; and in giving her to Bonosus, the Emperor calculated, through her means, on becoming acquainted with the great men among the Goths, who he hoped would, in feasting and drinking with Bonosus, discover to him their secret views and designs.[2]

Bonosus, however, having through neglect caused the Roman fleet on the Rhine to be burnt by the Germans, was so afraid of being punished, that he assumed the sovereignty, and caused himself to be proclaimed Emperor by the troops under his command,—a position in which he maintained himself longer than was expected, his sway extending over Gaul, Spain, and Britain. The last a country which has been named "an isle fertile in usurpers."[3]

Bonosus had, however, like Victorinus, a vice which counterbalanced his good qualities, that of inebriety. He was a slave to Bacchus, and is said to have been able to drink as much as ten men, without being in the least disordered;[4] this was the cause of his downfall. After fighting several battles with Probus, the Emperor who succeded Aurelian, he was finally defeated in a sharp engagement, when he died by his own hand, to avoid falling into the hands of the conqueror.[5] When Bonosus hanged himself, his well-known failing caused the jest to be passed upon him, that "there hung a bottle not a man."

Probus destroying the rebellious Gauls, however, not only spared the life of Hunila, on account of her virtue and beauty, but settled an annual pension upon her, and suffered the sons she had borne to Bonosus to enjoy their patrimonial estate.[6]

---

[1] Gibbon. [2] Univ. Hist.

[3] Nearly all the Thirty Tyrants were, like Bonosus, persons of mean birth, who had become exalted through their merit, being considered as models of virtue and ability, and raised at first by the Imperial notice, had afterwards assumed the purple; the term Tyrant then signifying not an abuser of power, but simply an usurper.—*Gibbon.*

[4] Echard, Univ. Hist. [5] Ibid.

[6] Probus was the first Emperor who permitted Gaul, Spain, and Britain to plant vineyards and to make wine. At the first coming of the Romans, the Britons were unacquainted with the vine, but a licence being granted by Probus for its cultivation, it soon became a very common produce. An early account of London informs us that, in the metropolis itself, we had one vineyard in East Smithfield, another in Hatton Garden (which is at this time called Vine-street), and a third in St. Giles's in the Fields. The various other Vine-streets in Bloomsbury, Westminster, Lambeth, and the Borough, have had a similar origin.

The Irish corna, or horn, was not devoted by our ancestors to martial purposes alone, but used to quaff their mead, a custom with the Danish hunters even in the present day.—*Walker.* The ancient Scots, as well as the present Highlanders, drank in shells; hence, in the old poetry, we often meet with the expression, the "chief of shells," and the "halls of shells," while to "rejoice in the shell," meant to feast sumptuously and drink freely.

The poems of Ossian describe Bosmina, when sent by her father Fingal on an embassy of peace, as bearing in her right hand a sparkling shell, and in the left an arrow of gold,—the first the joyful mark of peace, the latter the sign of war. Allusion is also made by the poet to the wine of the strangers, *i. e.* the Romans, and the wax [wax-lights are often mentioned as among the spoils] taken in their warfare; this was during the expedition of Severus into the northern parts of Britain.

ST. HELENA.

Daughter of Coel, the Hawk-faced—Particulars of her birth—Her accomplishments and virtues—Constantius in Britain—Carausius—Romantic stories of Helena—Disputes as to her birth—Colchester claims the honour—She marries Constantius—Her children—Reverses—Galerius and Valeria—Constantius and Theodora—Maximian—Helena's self-devotion—Empty honours—Constantine at Rome—The four Empires—York—Character of Constantius—Persecution of Christians—Theodora's children—Constantia—Death of Constantius—Excellent conduct of Helena to Theodora—Power she enjoyed—Fausta and her father: The Plot discovered, and its punishment—Policy of Helena—Expedition of Constantine against Maxentius—The Cross—Conversion of the Emperor—Cities founded in honour of Helena—Helena's writings—Tragedy of Fausta and her son—Helena undertakes the care of the children of the Emperor—At eighty, Helena undertakes her journey to the East—The finding of the Cross—Relics—Her death—Honours to her memory—Traces of Helena in Britain—Her Causeway.

"Coell ruled the realme in lawe and peace full well,
A doghter had he, and none other heyre,—
Eleyn that hight, farre passing good and fayre."
Harding's Chronicle.

"Of all the Christian world, that Empress most renowned,
Constantius' worthy wife."—*Drayton's Poly Olbion.*

In such terms as these are we introduced by the poets to the Empress Queen, St. Helena, whose fine character and whose romantic history afford a most brilliant and pleasing subject for biography.

Coel,[1] King of the Britons, the father of Helena, by some surnamed "the Hawk-Faced," began to reign over that portion of territory known in the present day as Essex and Hertfordshire, in the year 238,[2] and added the principality of North Wales to his dominions shortly after, by his marriage with Seradwen, its heiress, a princess descended of the royal house of Eudda,[3] whence in still later times came the—

"Pendragon kings of Uther's royal race,"

amongst whom was the celebrated Arthur.

The wife of Coel was the only daughter of Cadfan, son of Conan ap Eudda, King of Wales.

It is supposed by some writers that one daughter alone was born to the royal pair, the princess afterwards known as St. Helena; there were, how-

[1] Harding, Kennet, Baronius, Lewis, Polydore, Virgil, Baleus, and many others, assert that Helen was daughter of Coel, King of the Britons.

[2] Colchester Chronicle.

[3] Sir John Price, Warrington, Rowlands.

ever, three children; of whom the eldest was Tiboen, or Helena; the second, Guala, the British name of Julia; and the third, a prince who bore the maternal family designation of Conan.[1] Of this prince, who, on his father's death, retired, to govern over the northern territories acquired by his mother Seradwen, which are placed by one of our writers[2] at the wall of Antoninus, history almost entirely loses sight in following the more splendid fortunes of his two royal sisters, Helena and Julia; the one destined to create a new line of Emperors in the Roman world; the other, to transmit to her descendants that imperial dignity, which, through the royal current of the Pendragon family, descended to Cadwallader, the last British Prince of Wales of Roman descent, and passed on to the family of Tudor, of which Henry the Seventh was the first, and our present Sovereign Lady, Victoria, the latest royal representative.[3]

Helena was a name derived from the Greek, signifying "pitiful," and given in later times to Coel's daughter, by the Romans, on account of her compassionate disposition. Her true British name was Tiboen,[4] thus written in some Welch lines quoted by Mr. Rowlands:—

"Tiboen ferch Coel Godebog
I Grêd a gafoàd y Grôg."

Many other titles were borne by this excellent princess, such as the surname of "Lueddog," and the noble name of Flavia obtained on her marriage with Constantius, the descendant of Vespasian, who derived it from that Emperor, through his own great-uncle, Claudius Gothicus. The title of Augusta was added when Helena was made Empress; consequently, by some historians she is called Flavia Julia Helena Augusta; her brilliant fortunes towards the close of her long career acquired her, moreover, the epithets of "the Prosperous" and "the Powerful;" and to crown the virtue and piety of this memorable princess with the highest distinction, the religious of after-ages have awarded to her the veneration of a saint; so that the name of St. Helena has descended to us with more than mere mortal celebrity.

---

[1] Or, Cenan ap Coel; Rowland's Mona Antiqua.

[2] Carte, Gibbon.

[3] The following table exhibits the House of Eudda:—

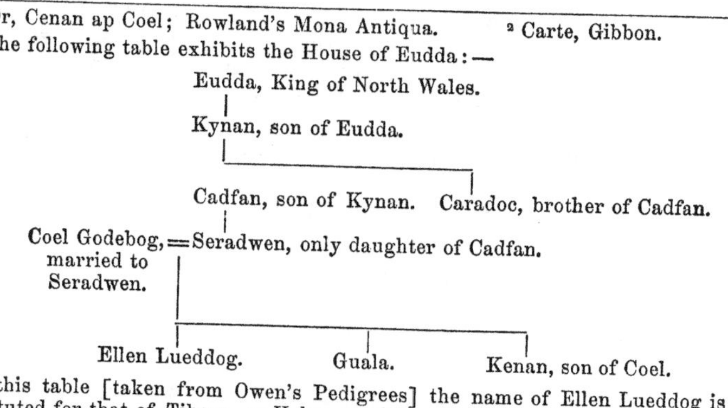

In this table [taken from Owen's Pedigrees] the name of Ellen Lueddog is substituted for that of Tiboen, or Helen, used by Mr. Rowlands, and for Dyfyn, the name attributed by Sir John Price to her.

[4] In the north of England, Tibby is still used as an abbreviation of Helen.

Roman and British writers differ in many particulars respecting the life of the daughter of Coel. Those Greek and Latin authors who were her contemporaries, writing with the party-spirit of their times, have testified a partiality to the side of their own country, whenever its honour became placed in collision with that of Britain. As regards the history of a princess of British birth, the testimonials of her native historians are probably most to be depended upon, and may be considered as surer guides to truth.

The principal evidence extant, respecting the birth of St. Helena, is that of the "Colchester Chronicle," preserved in that city. According to this document, her birth took place at Colchester, about A. D. 242, four years after her father mounted the throne.[1] This testimony is not only universally admitted by British historians, and confirmed by foreign writers, but borne out by the local traditions of that neighbourhood; for from ages past, even to the present day, it has been the boast of the inhabitants of Colchester, that St. Helena was born there; and in commemoration of the holy cross which she afterwards discovered, the arms of the town are a knotty cross between four crowns.[2]

The erroneous idea taken up by some authors, of Helena being an only child, seems to have arisen from the superior pains bestowed on her education by her father, who destined her to become his successor on the throne. To be Queen of the Britons, even then, was a high and glorious destiny; but Coel could scarcely have imagined to what an eminence she would rise, when he predicted, from the precocity of Helena's talents, the distinction she would attain; and, in consequence, determined that her brother and sister should receive as their inheritance his northern states,[3] and the southern be appropriated to her, his eldest-born. Coel, however proud of her acquirements, could not then have contemplated, in this favourite child, the future Roman Empress,—one with whose name all the Roman as well the British Empire, should resound; nor could he dream that the daughter of a Pagan prince should lead the bright procession of Christian converts onward to an immortal and imperishable kingdom, unlike his, never to pass away! Yet such was the career marked out by Heaven for the Empress Queen of Constantius, the daughter of the British Coel.[4]

---

[1] Morant's Colchester, Baleus, Lewis.

[2] The following is the entry in the beginning of the ancient Record Book of that city, commonly called the Oath Book, which by the hand appears to have been written about the beginning of Edward III.'s reign; A. D. 242, Helena filia Coelis nascitur in Colocestria." Morant's Colchester, Baleus, Geoffrey of Monmouth.

[3] At a later period, probably after Cenan ap Coel's death, the Princess Julia, marrying Edern ap Padarn, a northern prince, inherited her mother's Welsh estates.—*Owen's Pedigrees.*

[4] Leland, Camden, Glastonbury Historian, &c. Among those who call Helena a native of Britain, without naming Colchester, were Butler, Polydore Vergil, and Flavius Julius Dexter. St. Ambrose, Cedrenus, Nicephorus, cited by Gibbon, and other modern writers, deny that she was a native of Britain. Camden tells us, only one author states she was born at Naissus; and Drake calls her a native of York, from a speech made by some English orators at the councils of Constance and Basil,—an opinion, he thought, which received confirmation from the anonymous panegyrist of her son Constantine.

Gifted by nature in a preëminent degree, Helena's beauty surpassed that of any of the British maidens, her companions;[1] she possessed, moreover, "an innate brightness of wit, eloquence of speech, and elegant manners," which added still greater charms.[2] In a knowledge of the liberal arts, she is said not only to have surpassed her own countrywomen, but those of every other nation; and she was particularly distinguished by her taste for music, in which she had attained great proficiency. Spenser, in his "Faerie Queene," thus celebrates the praises of our Island Princess, whom he calls—

"Fayre Helena, the fairest living wight,
Who in all godly themes and goodly praise
Did far excell, but was most famous hight
For skill in musicke of all in her daies,
As well in curious instruments as cunninge laies."

There seems to be no doubt that Helena was both a musician and a poetess, for certain literary works attributed to her are even now said to be extant; among which are noted a volume of Greek poems,—for Helena was deeply read in Hebrew, Greek, and Latin lore.[3] Even a royal lady of modern times might have been proud of the compliments lavished on the daughter of Coel by historians; one calling her "both fair, and wise, and good, and well lettered,"[4] while another designates her "a noble lady and a learned."[5]

She had arrived at her eighteenth year[6] when the event occurred which drew her forth from her studious life, and shed the first bright ray on the path of her future greatness. This was her marriage to Constantius, at that time only in the dawn of his own rising fortunes.

Flavius Valerius Constantius, surnamed "Chlorus," according to some historians, from the green garments he wore in childhood, or from his pale complexion, was of imperial descent, his mother Claudia being niece of the Emperor Claudius Gothicus.[7] His father, a noble lord of Illyria, was a native of Naissus, the capital of the Dardanian nation, which consisted of a great part of Mœsia, and there the earliest years of Constantius were passed. There also the orders of Aurelian, under whom the youth first bore arms, reached him. For these reasons the city was, in after-times, embellished by the filial affection of his son, Constantine the Great, with many noble buildings.

Though Aurelian never visited Britain in person, he was a great deal in Gaul during the wars with the usurpers; and Constantius also was there, no doubt, at that time, having entered the army at the age of fourteen, and being at the time of Aurelian's accession in his twentieth year, A. D. 270. Three years after, when Zenobia and Tetricus were being paraded in Rome, in the triumphal procession of Aurelian, Constantius was distinguishing himself, and obtained a great victory for the Romans, at Vindomessa, in Switzerland. He afterwards was known as the "con-

---

[1] Owain's Chronicle. [2] Baleus. [3] Caxton.
[4] Holinshed. [5] Ibid. [6] Geoffrey of Monmouth.
[7] Vie de Constantin; Leigh's Choice Observations.

queror of Spain,"[1] and was received into the body-guard of Probus. On the defeat of Bonosus and Proculus, by a singular coincidence we find Constantius, Carus, Dioclesian, and Maximian, walking together in triumphal procession into the Roman capital, each of whom were subsequently raised to the empire. Constantius afterwards commanded a legion as Tribune; and the Emperor Carus, who made him Governor of Dalmatia, had some thoughts of naming him his successor, instead of the worthless Carinus, his son. After Carinus and Numerican, sons of Carus, the empire devolved on Dioclesian, A. D. 284. It was to oppose Carinus that Dioclesian first created Maximian Cæsar; and afterwards, on the death of that Emperor, he saluted him as his own colleague and partner in the imperial dignity, A. D. 286.[2]

According to Platina, Constantius obtained a great victory in Gaul, under Probus, when several thousand German mercenaries were slain, through his bravery in renewing the fight after an unsuccessful engagement; and, in consequence, peace was restored to the province. It is certain that his uncle Claudius fought against the Gauls under Posthumus. The same author dates this event in A. D. 281, in which year Maximian Herculeus is said to have made himself master of Britain, it being ten years after Carausius was slain. We find that Dioclesian sent Maximian into Gaul to quell an insurrection, about two years before the creation of the Cæsars (Constantius and Galerius), and that he was afterwards created Augustus by Dioclesian.[3]

There seems every likelihood that in this campaign Constantius acted in co-operation with Maximian, but there is an error as to the date, as the victory of Probus occurred many years earlier, and most likely that was the date of Helena's marriage.

There seems no doubt that it was during the wars of the Empire against the usurpers in Gaul that Constantius paid his first visit to Britain.

One of the most formidable enemies of Rome at this period was Carausius, a man of great bravery, but mean birth, employed by the Empire to guard the frontiers of Britain from invasion. Maximian, then associated with Dioclesian, who had ordered him to be stationed at Boulogne for that purpose, finding he had turned the power invested in him to his own advantage, ordered him to be put to death; but Carausius escaped into Britain, where having many followers, he assumed the purple, and caused himself to be proclaimed Emperor. Maximian, unable to contend at the time until a fleet was prepared, permitted him to continue in his assumed power; and at this time Carausius boldly issued a medal, associating himself with Dioclesian and Maximian, of which the legend was—"THE PEACE OF THE THREE AUGUSTI."[4] After several years, Allectus was sent to reduce him to dependence on the Empire; but that traitor, uniting in his schemes, at first governed in his name, and afterwards betrayed and killed him, and ruled in his own behalf for the space of three years as Augustus. The Britons, oppressed by the tyranny of Allectus, placed

[1] John Rous, Colchester Chronicle, Geoffrey of Monmouth.

[2] Butler, Gibbon. [3] Platina. [4] Hoffman's Univ Lexicon.

themselves under the command of Asclepiodatus,[1] who, after slaying Allectus, assumed the supreme power for a time, and in his turn was doomed to fall in a contest with Coel, father of St. Helena.

The deceased Asclepiodatus was a Briton by birth, and by descent Duke of Cornwall:[2] he was also a prætorian præfect, and led the Roman fleet; so that both he and his predecessor, Allectus, had assumed the supreme power in the Roman name. When, therefore, Coel conquered Asclepiodatus, it became necessary to vindicate the Empire, for he was not only a Briton, but king by ancient right of descent; and the Romans, fearing all authority in the island would cease to exist, despatched Constantius Chlorus to redeem their tarnished honour, and revive the laurels of his country.

Coel, having openly become, by the train of circumstances just detailed, the enemy of Rome,[3] Constantius, on his arrival, proceeded to lay siege to the city of Colchester, the capital of his dominions, which, as some say, was bravely defended for three years, but at length relieved, upon the Roman general entering into a treaty with the King for the hand of his daughter, "the fayre Helena." Some relate that Coel, knowing that Constantius was "a wise and bold man,"[4] and noted for bravery, sent, on his own part, ambassadors, to offer peace and submission to the Roman power, provided he was allowed to retain his kingdom, on payment of the usual tribute. With this Constantius complied, and Coel confirmed the treaty, by bestowing on the general the hand of his daughter[5] when "Constantius espoused her with much honour."[6]

A romantic, but somewhat improbable, incident has been related of the first introduction of Constantius and Helena. It is said that the nurse, or "attendant maiden," of the princess, dreading the dangers to which her youth and beauty might be exposed, if she were beheld by any of the lawless soldiers of the Roman army then besieging the city, disguised her young mistress in humble attire as a poor maiden, and concealed her in the house of a countryman; but the precaution was in vain. The chance of war conducted Constantius to her retreat, who was so charmed

---

[1] Bran ap Lyr, or Asclepiodatus, [Rowland's Mona. Antiq.] began to reign A. D. 232, and his power lasted thirty years; he much injured the Roman authority, and the news of his death gave great joy at Rome. [Holinshed.] The sister of Asclepiodatus was called Bronwen, the White-Necked; and Harlech Castle was anciently called Tôr Bronwen, because it was the place of her abode. [Pennant's Snowden.]

Carausius, keeping for his own use the booty he took from the Saxon pirates, made Maximian think that he connived at their piracies. The wealth earned by his exploits and reputation caused him to be hailed Augustus by the Britons. He is said to have built vessels of war, and the many medals struck by him, impressed with various devices and inscriptions, testify the pomp and splendour of his reign. One of the coins of Carausius bears the ensigns of the Eternal City; and, as Sir F. Palgrave remarks, "it is very remarkable that the wolf and the twins are copied upon the rude mintage of Ethelbert, the Bretwalda or Emperor of Anglo-Saxon Britain."

[2] Carew's Survey of Cornwall. [3] John Rous, Morant. [4] John Rous.

[5] Geoffrey of Monmouth, John Rous, Warrington, Morant. [6] Caxton.

with Helena, that he carried her off. On discovering, however, much to his surprise, that she was the King's daughter, he made her his wife.

To this important incident, if it really did occur, may be attributed some of the stories which have been circulated to the disadvantage of Helena, disputing the legality of her union with Constantius. The *Colchester Chronicle* itself mentions her, in some instances, as "*Concubina;*" and it becomes rather an important question, to inquire into the exact particulars of her union with Constantius.

The word "concubina" is sometimes used "*in bonem partem*" for a wife as well as a concubine, and, in relation to Helena's tie, simply meant a lady of inferior dignity to the daughter of Maximian, whom Constantius espoused at an after-date. Marianus Scotus, who boldly defends Helena, says that she who was "a King's daughter, a Cæsar's wife, and an Emperor's mother, was no concubine." Two authors, however, have stigmatised her memory with this accusation — Julian, the apostate, and Zosimus; of whom the former was an Emperor of Rome, who tried, by every means in his power, to subvert the attempts made by Helena and her son Constantine to establish the Christian faith; the latter a Greek historian and a pagan, who is noted by ecclesiastical writers, as remarkable for the prejudice with which he has treated the Christian Emperors, and especially for his severity towards Constantine the Great.[1] St. Ambrose, the only respectable witness against Helena,[2] asserts a startling fact, that Helena was first seen by Constantius in his march from Persia (when passing through Nicomedia), at an inn in the little town of Drepanum, where he had fixed his quarters.[3] Had this circumstance been known to Zosimus, the declared enemy of Constantine, he would not have failed to make use of it. Several other historians say, that the union of Constantius with Coel's daughter was not legal.[4] The author of the History of Colchester, adopting the record of that city, says: "The constant tradition amongst us has always been, that Helena had by Constantius her son Constantine born *before marriage;* but, soon after the birth, he married her, and adopted him." This tradition, preserved in the old British memoirs, is published by Geoffrey of Monmouth, and other authors of various times and nations, of whom Michael Alford, who wrote expressly on the subject, cites no less than seventy.[5]

There are, on the other hand, many who declare Helena to have been the lawful wife of Constantius. That elaborate writer, Mr. Butler, in his memoir, says, "*it is certain she was married to him;*"[6] and Crevier, in his "Lives of Roman Emperors," speaks thus on this important point: "Some, even Christian authors, have disputed the marriage of Constantius, and thus rendered illegitimate the birth of Constantine. But, in

---

[1] Aikin's Biography. [2] Crevier.

[3] St. Ambrose and Nicephorus both relate the same story, and the former has been copied by several French writers.

[4] Eusebius, Orosius, St. Jerome, Cassiodorus, and Bede. [5] Morant.

[6] At Naples is still extant an inscription, in which Helena is styled the wife of Constantius. In two others, to be seen in Gruter, she is distinguished with the title of Augusta, which was never given, as is well known, to a concubine.

reality, this opinion seems to have had no other foundation[1] than Helena's being of greatly inferior rank to her husband.[2] That excepted, everything conspires to make us look upon her as united to Constantius by a lawful alliance; the distinction which Constantine always enjoyed at Dioclesian's court, where he held the first rank next to the Emperor; the very circumstance of his being an hostage, which supposes him to have been dear to his father as a son destined to succeed him; and the great encomiums given by panegyrists to the chastity of Constantius, whom his son is praised for having imitated, which make it probable that Constantine was the legitimate son of Constantius Chlorus." Indeed, had any further proof of this been wanting, it was furnished afterwards by an address made to Constantine himself, on the occasion of his marriage to Fausta, daughter of Maximian, by his learned and elegant, but unknown panegyrist, who speaking of Constantius, says: "He had freed the provinces of Britain from slavery; you ennobled them by your origin!"

The enemies of her faith sought thus to disparage her memory; but the fact of a Roman Emperor, as Constantius afterwards became, having espoused a British woman, was, in those days, sufficiently extraordinary to create comments on the legality of the tie. Gwenissa, daughter of Claudius, is not even named by Roman writers, in their disdainful contempt of her alliance with the British Arviragus; and Helena's son is stigmatized as illegitimate, no doubt from similar reasons. The daughter of Coel was held to be a match beneath the dignity of the Roman name; yet it is not impossible that hers was what is yet known *as a handfast marriage* in Scotland, the country from the neighbourhood of which her mother came, and that this had given colour to the account of her son's illegitimacy. That Helena possessed great attractions, even in the eyes of one of the most wise and accomplished senators of Rome, is unquestioned; and the gentleness and amiability of Constantius in times of peace, as renowned as his bravery in war, must have confirmed the attachment of the island princess. Ample testimonials exist of the tender affection which subsisted between them, an affection still more strongly cemented by the birth of a son, to be afterwards known as Constantine the Great,[3]—a title bestowed on him for his many shining talents and great actions. Whether Britain or Dacia[4] was the birthplace of this

[1] Some writers call Helena "obscuri generis." Julius Flavius Dexta calls her "a chief woman of Britain," and Mr. Lewis, "a king's daughter," denying the assertion of her mean origin. As her father was "master of the horse to the Emperor," some have called her a housekeeper's daughter; from that arose the title of "Comes Stabuli, or constable" (Lewis); but others again designate her as Stabularia, from her having built a church afterwards over the manger in which our Lord was laid at his birth. As well as the encomiums of historians on her virtue, she was, according to Polydore Vergil, "a very virtuous woman." See other authors, who speak of her in terms which could not have been bestowed on one who was exceptionable in one of the first of woman's attributes.

[2] Gibbon dismisses the question by saying, "We are obliged to confess that Helena was the daughter of an innkeeper."

[3] Platina's Lives of the Popes.

[4] That Britain was Helena's own birthplace and that of her son Constantine is, according to Camden, "what all historians who have written on that subject, ex-

prince has been a subject of dispute, literary and national, as well it might, for honours are coveted by all; but the general opinion is that Constantine was born at Colchester, the native city of Helena, and can consequently be claimed as British. This would never have been questioned, but that Helena, subsequently to her marriage, at times accompanied her husband in his foreign campaigns. Nor is it the least convincing proof of the legality of Helena's tie with Constantius, that the latter entrusted this son, the child of his dearest affections, to the maternal care of Helena for his education, knowing that her enlightened and cultivated mind fitted her for so arduous a task.

It is an acknowledged fact, that in the history of nearly all those individuals who have attained an eminent distinction for great or good qualities, the hand of a mother may be traced as implanting the first seeds which riper years have matured. How honourable was the appellation of Cornelia, mother of the Gracchi! How high a lustre is still shed on the name of Helena—when added to it is that title which speaks volumes in her praise—the mother of Constantine the Great!

Mr. Morant, in his History of Colchester, says, the city walls were most probably built in the times of the Romans. He remarks, "the west wall reached as far as St. Helen's Lane. On the north and east side the castle was secured by a ditch and rampart of earth. This rampart is thrown up upon a wall that formerly encompassed either the castle or the palace of Coel, on the site whereof the castle is built, the buttresses, and other parts of which, have been lately discovered." That Colchester had strong walls and a castle subsequent to this period, is a fact attested by the remains of both, even in the present day. The castle was built by Edward the Elder, who also repaired the city walls; and, says the same writer, "if there were any remains of Coel's palace, he might perhaps bestow some pains in repairing that too, and making it a kind of fortification. The present castle was built after the Norman Conquest."

As the walls of London are said to have been built by Helena about this date,[1] Colchester was very probably fortified at the same time; for Constantius would naturally be anxious to defend his capital against the hostile incursions of neighbouring princes. Many writers attribute the walls of Colchester to Helena rather than to her father,[2] and it is

---

cept Cedrenus and Nicephorus, affirm with one voice." Julius Fermicus, a Christian writer, who lived soon after the death of Constantius, says, in his work "On the Error of Profane Religion," that Constantine was born at Tarsus, near Nicomedia, in Bithynia, a town of Dacia. Others fix his birth at Naissus, near the Dardanelles (Bayle's Dictionary); but there the son is confounded with the father. (See Camden and Butler.)

[1] Miscellaneous History. The creeks about Colchester and the Mersey Island are celebrated for their fine oyster-beds: this fact alone rendered it a favourite residence with the Romans. It was from this people we first learnt the art of fattening our oysters in artificial beds, the feeding-pits being first invented about ninety years before Christ, and the place where they were first constructed was upon the shore of Baiæ. Even as early as the reign of Vespasian, the British oyster was deemed famous among their luxurious Roman conquerors, and thought worthy to be carried into Italy. [Whittaker; Britton and Brayley.]

[2] Stowe, John Rous.

beyond question that Constantius, who displayed great talent in architectural designs, assisted his consort in the undertaking. Britain is said to have owed many of her public works and ornaments to Constantius, who invited over architects from abroad to assist in carrying out his plans for the advantage of the people and security of the Roman government. The city of Worcester is said to be of his foundation.[1] It is not, therefore, surprising that the oldest parochial church in the city should bear the name of St. Helen. Chlorendon Park, near Sarum, in Wiltshire, received from him its name of "Chloren," which, some say, had been given him by the Britons on account of his wearing a long train which was carried after him, this being the toga or robe which betokened his rank as a senator of Rome. Chlorendon, now Clarendon Park, says Mr. Kennet, "is a park the size of which exceeds any park in the kingdom; in the north part of which, next Chloren, is a church covered over with ivy, called Ivy Church; and to give credit to a late poet, the park had in it twenty groves, each of which was a mile in compass, and it contained a house of the king's within it, but long since dilapidated." In the time of Constantius, a fortification was built by that prince on the side of the down near Sarum, of which the ramparts are yet remaining; it bore the name of Chloren, like the park in which the Roman King of Britain designed to make his own residence.[2]

For some years after Coel's death Constantius remained in Britain, adding improvements for the public benefit, and maintaining the security of the Roman interest. During this interval he paid the customary tribute on his own account to the Roman Emperor.[3]

Several children were born to the Roman King of Britain; the name of the eldest does not appear. A quarrel had arisen between him and his younger brother Lucius, and he was unhappily killed by the latter; for which Constantius exiled the fratricide from Britain, appointing him to dwell in Aquitaine. The penitent prince subsequently embraced the Christian faith, and entered the Church, first becoming an elder, and afterwards bishop. "He built a house of prayer, in which he and his followers worshipped God."[4]

---

[1] Green's History of Worcester.

[2] One of the groves in Chlorendon Park yet remains to attest its Roman origin, being composed of chesnut. The chesnut was first introduced into Britain from Lydia by our Roman conquerors, and, in all likelihood, first by Constantius himself.

[3] Lewis.

[4] As this prince's history does not appear again in conjunction with that of Constantius and Helena, it may be named here, that Constantine, his brother, after his own conversion and accession to the empire, promoted Lucius to several ecclesiastical situations; who finally went into Rhetia, accompanied by his sister Emerita, and near the city of Augusta, converted the Curienses to the faith of Christ. He was put to death in the Castor Martis, and buried in the city of Augusta, where his festival was kept on the 3d of December. The truth of these particulars is attested by the abbey founded by Prince Lucius, and an ancient hymn composed to his honour, entitled "Gaude Lucionem." Emerita, daughter of Helen, also was martyred in Trinicastell, where her brother Lucius dwelt. [Hermanus Schedelius, Holinshed.]

During the interval between the death of Coel and Constantius mounting his throne in Britain, and that in which he succeeded to the Roman empire, this great man made more than one campaign abroad; and under all the changing vicissitudes of the roving life of Constantius, Helena and her first-born, Constantine, were his constant companions.

The daughter of Coel afterwards accompanied her husband in his campaigns abroad. We are expressly informed[1] that Constantius, who "surpassed all others in his endeavours to increase the Roman commonwealth,[2] accompanied by his *wife*, Flavia Helena Augusta, passed out of Britain into Germany, attended by an infinite number of Britons, of whom it is thought the city Bretta derived its name."[3] Constantius was founder of the city of Constantine, in Normandy. The sea adjoining Bithynia, from this Empress also, was called Helenapontus, or Hellespont."[4]

A period of reverse, however, was at hand, which was destined to throw a deep shade over the mother and son. The details which led to this misfortune must necessarily be given.

About six years after those revolutions in the mighty empire of Rome, which had associated Dioclesian and Maximian in the cares of supreme power, the joint Emperors agreed to elect two Cæsars as their colleagues, each of whom, by being appointed ruler over a certain portion of dominions belonging to them, should render assistance in preserving order over their extended empire. The persons on whom their choice fell were Galerius and Constantius, and to the proposed honour about to be conferred one only condition was affixed, one calculated to insure the dignity of those elected, that of each becoming the adopted son, or rather son-in-law, of the two Emperors. It was previously determined by Dioclesian and Maximian, that in case of the newly created Cæsars being already married, they should repudiate their wives, and be left free to espouse the imperial brides destined to them. Galerius was originally a shepherd of Illyria, but had afterwards become a soldier of Rome; his character was a mixture of cruelty and bravery. His pride at such an advancement to fortune made him willingly agree to put away from him his wife, for he also was married, and he received the hand of the fair Valeria; by which the general who had led his army before the victory, became second only in rank to his imperial father-in-law Dioclesian, and his colleague. Had his worth been far greater, he might well have been proud of receiving the hand of a bride so amiable as the highly gifted Valeria, who, as well as her mother, stood high in the estimation of the Romans: he dismissed, therefore, without a sigh the partner of his humbler fortunes, and took his new honours cheerfully. With Constantius Chlorus the circumstances were different in all respects.

The beautiful Flavia Theodora was not indeed the daughter of Maximian, but of his wife, the Empress Galeria Valeria Eutropia, by a noble Syrian who had died shortly after the birth of this, their only child. The widow's beauty had attracted many admirers, and amongst others

---

[1] By Lewis, in Hist. of Britain.
[2] John Rous.
[3] Lewis.
[4] John Rous.

Herculeus Maximian, who, though in person more calculated to inspire terror than love, was successful in his suit. Eutropia being dazzled by the prospect of an imperial diadem, as soon as her appointed time for mourning was at an end, gave her hand to Maximian, and the first link was wrought by that step for the future fortunes of Theodora. From that time Rome had two reigning Emperors, and two Empresses had presided over the female world of Rome, Prisca and Eutropia, entirely different in character, though so nearly allied in rank and dignity. Prisca, wife of Dioclesian, adorned the throne by her virtue and good sense, while a Christian by practice as well as precept, she viewed without distrust or jealousy her beautiful rival Eutropia, who, naturally disposed to gaiety and diversion, though she had, at her first elevation, cautiously concealed her levity of character, soon yielded herself up to its dictates. Entirely indifferent to her husband, she encouraged admirers, and allowed the attentions of a handsome Syrian; yet so far was Maximian from resenting Eutropia's conduct, that he appeared blind to this intimacy. His great desire for an heir who might perpetuate the honours of his family was vainly indulged during some years. When, therefore, the infant Maxentius was born, in spite of the evil reports of his wife's fidelity, he hailed the event with transports of joy, and brought the child up with the utmost care and expense as his own son and heir to an empire. The near relationship of Constantius to his Empress was one reason why Maximian had determined to ally him with his daughter-in-law; and he had, moreover, stipulated with Dioclesian that he should become his successor in the Empire. It was known to both, that the person whom their policy selected was already the husband of a British woman of royal lineage, whose inheritance he now enjoyed, and by whom he had, moreover, become father of several children; but it did not enter into their minds to compare the obscure Helena with the brilliant, beautiful, and witty Theodora, or weigh in the same balance the petty throne of a British State with the imperial diadem of Rome!

The struggle was great in the mind of Constantius. Nevertheless the imperial will could not be thwarted, though Constantius betrayed an evident reluctance to the marriage with Theodora; he could not forget that by divorcing himself from Helena, still tenderly beloved, an ignominious stain would be cast on the birth of her young son Constantine, now in the bloom of youth and hope.

It is said that the earnest solicitations of Helena alone decided him; regardless of herself at this trying moment, she was earnest in her exhortations to her husband to accept a step so calculated to promote his present personal advantage. He consented, accordingly, to a separation from Helena; and Dioclesian, by taking every step necessary to give publicity to their divorce, furnished the world with the most conclusive proof that their marriage had been valid.[1] After every necessary step had been taken, Constantius espoused Theodora at Milan, and was forth-

[1] Platina, in his "Lives of the Popes," says, "Constantine was the son of Constantius by Helena, whom yet he afterwards divorced to gratify Herculeus."

with invested with the government of Gaul, Spain, and Britain, with the enviable title of Cæsar,[1] for which he had sacrificed so much.

Theodora, shortly after her marriage, returned with him into Britain, accompanied by her mother; but while to her he became, and remained to the last, a faithful, kind and affectionate husband, his feelings towards Helena may be best conceived by the fact of the first act of his newly acquired sovereignty being to present his divorced Queen, the mother of his son, with the robe of imperial purple, by this means testifying to the world, his own sense, that she was in every respect deserving of the high rank to which he had been elevated, and which fortune alone had denied to her.

Notwithstanding this empty honour, the fate of Helena was rendered still more severe, by Constantine being taken from Britain, and from her care, by his father, and placed at the court of Dioclesian, as a hostage for his mother's fidelity to Rome. The jealous caution with which, from that moment, he was watched in all his movements, proves not only his legitimacy, and the regard by which he was esteemed by his parents, but the Emperor's fear, lest sooner or later, like Bonosus and Proculus, he should assume the sovereign power in Britain, to which his birth by Helena, and right as grandson of Coel, justly entitled him. While still an inhabitant of the imperial palace of Dioclesian, the situation of Constantine was evidently that of a dependent guest and suspected captive,—a state of bondage exchanged only for a worse, when upon Constantius requesting his son might be permitted to accompany him on his return to Britain, the Emperor, to avoid complying with the desire of the father, sent the prince to join the army in Persia and Egypt under Galerius;[2] there the young Briton distinguished himself in the Egyptian war by his valour during several severe actions; and there, until his father's approaching death recalled him to Britain, he remained, spending the best years of his life in the society of those who were enemies of the Christian faith, which in after-times he was called upon to protect, and separated from the nearest and dearest of his own relatives.

At this time four imperial courts were established in the Roman world, in different directions: that of Dioclesian, who maintained the govern-

---

[1] Every preliminary being settled, the ceremony of inaugurating the new Cæsars was performed. On the first day of March, A. D. 292, Dioclesian having assembled the troops in a place about three thousand paces distant from Nicomedia, ascended an eminence, presented Galerius to the soldiery, and, with their consent, invested him with the purple. The same honour was probably conferred on Constantius by Maximian in some one of the cities of Gaul or Italy.

The two Cæsars had every attribute of imperial power but the title of *August*, which remained with Dioclesian and Maximian. They had the tribunitian authority, the name of Emperors, that of Fathers of their Country, and of the high priesthood. Constantius, however, as noblest by birth, though adopted by the second of the Augusti, was considered the first of the two Cæsars, and on all public monuments his name, to which he had added that of *Herculeus*, was placed before that of Galerius. The anonymous author of Constantine's life, published by Valesius, writes in express terms that Constantius divorced Helena to marry Theodora, and Eutropius that Constantine was the fruit of an obscure but lawful matrimony.

[2] Crevier's Roman Emperors.

ment of Asia and Africa, and as prior Augustus, had supreme power over the rest of the empire; that of Maximian Herculeus who governed Italy and Spain; of Galerius, who ruled Illyria, Thrace, Macedonia, and Syria; and of Constantius, who had received Gaul and Britain. The latter showed his affection for the country which had given birth to Helena and Constantine, by fixing the seat of his government at York, whither his bride and the Empress, her mother, had accompanied him.

There, while the meek and excellent Helena, with pious fortitude, was mourning in her lonely widowhood, the loss of a beloved husband, and separation from a dearly cherished son, Theodora, at the distance of a few hundred miles, enjoyed the sweet intercourse of daily association in conjugal affection, which Helena had lost, with one who could not have been known without commanding love and reverence. Constantius, indeed, never acquired that surname of "Great," which admiring ages had reserved for his son by Helena, but he certainly merited, by his public virtues, the appellation of "the Good." Apart from his selfish repudiation of Helena, he exhibited many excellent qualities, and was looked upon as the father and friend of the people.[1]

So mild and moderate was the Roman Cæsar in his dominion, that during the greater part of his reign tranquillity prevailed in Britain. His habits were regular, and he respected virtue Securely resting on the affections of the people, who loved him for his own goodness, and anxiety to promote their happiness, Constantius did not consider it necessary to exhibit the pomp and ostentation of the Roman Emperors; so great an admirer was he of simplicity, that when he did give an entertainment, he borrowed of his friends plate to furnish his table: one of the sayings ascribed to him was this, "that he had rather the riches of the state should be dispersed in several hands than locked up in one coffer." Dioclesian differed in opinion from Constantius, and blamed him for levying so few taxes that his treasury was empty, observing that "a prince ought not to be poor." On which we are told that this great man sent for the richest of the inhabitants of York and informed them that he was in want of money, and should be glad if they would show their attachment by a voluntary gift. His treasury was soon filled; when Constantius remarked to the Roman envoy of Dioclesian that, "he had just collected together those things that had long been his;" adding, "I left them in the keeping of their possessors, who, as you see, have been faithful to their trust." The deputies returned to Rome filled with admiration, of not only the ruler but the people: and Constantius on his part, restored to his subjects the money they had so readily contributed for his service.[2]

In no particular did Constantius become more conspicuous than in his forbearance towards the Christians during the frightful persecution which signalized the reign of Dioclesian. This ancient "reign of terror" began in the family of the persecutor himself, and, sad to recount, was first instigated by a woman. The mother of Galerius had inflamed that prince against Christianity, who, in his turn, instigated Dioclesian to extirpate

[1] Green, Crevier, Warrington. [2] Crevier.

the faith of Christ, and spread the worship of their own gods. The Emperor first ordered his wife Pisca, and Valeria, the young wife of Galerius, to assist in sacrifices made to idols. Both ladies had received the baptismal rite, and had been encouraged by their own learning and genius to seek the society of those orators and writers who explained their new faith. But they knew that if they disobeyed the command of the Emperor, whatever his assumed regard for them, they must expect to die. Love of life, weakness of faith, or easiness of temper, led them, therefore, in the end, to worship those idols their hearts refused to acknowledge; a weakness in such high examples which many readily followed, while others stood forth in defence of their faith, and, to the number of 17,000, fell victims for conscience, sake. The church in Nicodemia was levelled with the ground, and the very next day an edict appeared, depriving all Christians of their rank, and of the benefit of the laws, and exposing them to torture.[1]

The persecution, which raged at that time, spread throughout the Roman world, two provinces alone excepted; these were Gaul and Britain, which escaped by the timely interposition of the merciful and humane Constantius.[2] That prince, though compelled with reluctance to demolish the Christian churches throughout his dominions,[3] preserved the persons of the followers of Christ from harm; yet he could not prevent some of the atrocities which marked this period of bloodshed. Among the British martyrs were Aaron and Julius, A. D. 303, and St. Alban, who are said to have suffered cruel torments: a church was afterwards raised[4] to the memory of each. This persecution endured for two years and two months throughout the Roman Empire, when many persons of both sexes suffered death;[5] it was happily terminated in A. D. 305 by Constantius becoming Emperor. To try the hearts of his courtiers, Constantius proclaimed that all those who forsook the worship of the true God, should be banished the court, and that heavy penalties and fines should be imposed upon them; thereupon, all those who were base enough to serve him only for their own views went away, forsook the true God, and worshipped idols, by which means he found out who were the true servants of God, and whom he intended to make his own, thinking rightly that such as were faithful to their God, would prove so to him.

Did the inhabitants of Britain, as some have asserted, owe this interposition of Constantius in favor of Christianity to his own belief in its doctrines, or to his recollection that it was the religion of his divorced Queen, St. Helena? We have high authority for the fact, that Constantius was distinguished for Christian piety, and had been the founder of a metropolitan see at York. Some say that Constantius had received the faith and rite of baptism in the seventh year of his empire, Pope Syl-

---

[1] Milner. [2] Ibid.

[3] Eusebius. Amongst others, the splendid minster of Lucius, at Westminster, was levelled to the ground at this epoch.

[4] In the city of Caerleon, where they were interred. A choir of nuns graced the church of Julius, and a famous order of canons that of Aaron.

[5] Kippis, Milner.

vester officiating in the solemn ceremony; and we are assured that it was the constant desire of Helena to advance the Christian faith, which first stimulated this Emperor to favour the Christians. If it be true that Helena was herself a professor of its doctrines prior to her divorce, it must have deeply affected the heart of Constantius to behold her, on that painful separation, so entirely resign herself by its influence to her hopeless fate. The widowed wife and childless mother had submitted to her lot in so meek and uncomplaining a manner, as to prove her just claim to the title of Christian, and her example must have had its effect. Released from the matrimonial tie, she sought not again to enter into the married state, and most probably the reflections in this season of bitter trial in the life of Helena, laid the foundation for her own future greatness as well as that of her son.

In memory of this period of suffering, the African marigold has been placed in our floral calendars on St. Helena's day, August 18th, as it is a flower betokening grief, or distress of mind, and is thus appropriately emblematical of the feelings of the deserted Empress.[1] There is also a sentiment attached to the blossoms of the flower called helenium, which resemble small suns, of a beautiful yellow colour, and is said to have been produced by "the tears of Helena."

It is not positively certain that Helena[2] or Constantius were Christians at this period, though there seems some foundation for the supposition. That Christianity had obtained a footing in Britain long ere this, has been shown, and that it was professed even in the family of Constantius himself is equally certain.

During the residence of the Emperor at York, the Empress Theodora had borne him six children, all of whom were educated in Britain; the sons were Dalmatius, Julius Constantius, and Annibalianus: the daughters were Constantia, Anastasia, and Eutropia. To all Constantius proved a kind and tender parent, but the first of these royal princesses, Constantia, requires some especial notice, as her after-history becomes much connected with that of Helena and her own half-brother, Constantine.

At a very early age, Constantia studied the works of Arian, and became from the first his sincere disciple, though he had not then acquired any name, and at a subsequent time she was his powerful patron. Constantia was influenced in adopting the sect of Arianism, being already a Christian, by her friend and preceptor, Eusebius, Bishop of Nicomedia. She was singularly steady in her opinions, once formed, nor could she be won over to those of others; but her peculiar views caused afterwards much disadvantage and inconvenience to a church which required unity

[1] The African marigold blossoms all the year round, and was, therefore, termed by the Romans the flower of the calends — in other words, of all the months. The flowers are said always to turn towards the sun, and to follow his course from east to west. Thus Marguerite of Navarre, the maternal grandmother of Henry IV. chose it for her device, with the motto, "Je ne veux suivre que lui seul," intimating that all her thoughts and affections were turned towards Heaven, as the marigold towards the sun. See "Language of Flowers."

[2] Baleus calls Helena the most Christian mother of Constantine, and Lluyd tells us that the young prince was brought up by her in the Christian faith, which she herself professed.

in its several members for its support.[1] The princess was endowed with rare beauty, and possessed also "masculine courage, discretion, prudence and virtue; she had a judgment which penetrated the most solid affairs, much eloquence, and unshaken firmness and resolution, and a happy art of reconciling any differences which arose among those who surrounded her." Constantia's character and profession of faith might have caused Constantius to show leniency to the Christians, even were he not himself a believer in the sacred truths of religion.

It was not long after this cruel persecution that Constantius was called from his earthly dominions. He was seized with his last illness while occupied in an expedition against the Picts and Scots, and finding his life drawing towards its close, the Emperor's heart naturally yearned to behold the son who had been snatched from him just on his arrival at manhood. A messenger conveyed to Galerius the request of his dying colleague, that he would send home his son as soon as possible.[2] Galerius delayed, as long as he could, the fulfilment of this duty. For a long time past he had regarded the "son of Helena" with the eyes of a jealous rival, and, seeking his destruction, had on various occasions placed him in positions of certain peril. Constantine's life had been risked against the Sarmatians in war, but he returned victorious to Galerius, carrying with him the enemy's king as his prisoner; and the Emperor regretted the conquest which spared the British prince. On another occasion, Constantine, ardently desirous to win renown and honour, undertook, by persuasion of Galerius, to fight with a wild beast in the theatre. The spectators, in wonder, beheld the animal slain by the youthful prince; but Galerius smiled, for he meant yet further to ensnare him into danger.[3] At last, however, the prince perceived his aim, and resolved to escape from court to Britain, and join his father. At this juncture, the news of the dangerous illness of Constantius reached him. Surrounded by the spies of Galerius, who watched his slightest movement, he made his escape by stealth. His perils were numerous, and in order to evade pursuit and retard the speed of those who sought to overtake him in his flight, Constantine was forced to resort to the expedient of maiming at every post the horses which were not necessary for his flight—a crue resource, yet, under his circumstances, excusable, for he was no doubt flying for his life, besides his desire to behold his dying parent.[4] In this way he succeeded in reaching Britain, where he arrived only a few days before his father breathed his last, and on proceeding to York, had the melancholy satisfaction of beholding once more his mother, from whom he had been so long and painfully divided.[5]

Constantius, during the brief interval which intervened between the arrival of Constantine and his own death, was requested to name his successor in the Empire, to which entreaty he gave the following memorable reply: "That he would have none other than the most pious Constantine," thus setting aside the claims of the children of Theodora in favour of his son by Helena, and giving a final proof of his attachment to his

---

[1] Lives of the Empresses. [2] Milner. [3] Lewis.

[4] Gibbon calls this "a foolish story." [5] Milner, Lingard.

first wife, and the legality of her union with him. His decision was received with approbation by the army, and the purple robe was thrown over the prince's shoulders, who on this occasion is said to have shed tears, and clapped spurs to his horse, to escape the importunities of all those who pressed around him to proffer the imperial dignity.[1] How different had been the conduct of Caracalla, another Emperor's son, on a similar occasion!

A. D. 306, Constantius died, fourteen years after he had become Cæsar, having enjoyed the dignity of Emperor the two last years of his life;[2] his memory was held in such esteem, that he was afterwards deified. His last mortal remains were deposited at York, in the Church of St. Helen, in Aldwark. This building stood near the walls of the city, but there are no remains in the present day. Some suppose that it was erected by Constantine on his conversion, over the remains of his father, especially as the name of St. Helen is affixed to the building. The main street, which now bears the name of Aldwark, to mark its antiquity,[3] was so designated by the Saxons; it adjoins St. Anthony's Hall, and the Roman Imperial Palace, described in the life of the Empress Julia, is supposed to have extended from Christ Church to this street.[4] Camden relates that the remains of Constantius were discovered in a vaulted tomb within a little chapel at York, and adds "on the authority of several intelligent inhabitants of that city, that when this vault, which had by tradition been marked as the place where the ashes of Constantius reposed, was opened, a lamp was found burning within it, but which was soon extinguished by the communication of the air; for it was a Roman custom to preserve lights in their sepulchres for a long time, which art they accomplished by the *oylines* of gold resolved into a liquid substance."

Helena, who had passed the prime of life, for she was now in her fifty-fourth year, in a quiet obscurity, at a distance from those whose presence would have made life so dear, was now destined to emerge from her solitude, and assume an eminent position in the vast theatre of the world. It was she who had implanted the first principles of virtue in the bosom of the great Constantine, who had set in motion all those secret springs which were to bear him onwards to glory and greatness, and she was called upon in her own person to direct the career of that victorious child.

Without ambition for herself—for that failing had never formed part of Helena's character—she had none of those vain-glorious emotions which usually animated her contemporaries; all her feelings were absorbed in one, that of ennobling the name of the beloved son who had blessed her too brief union with Constantius, and who in spite of difficulties had inherited his imperial destiny. To guard that son from the

[1] Leigh's Choice Observations.

[2] In 1283, when preparations were making for the erection of Caernarvon Castle, a body, supposed to be that of Constantius, was discovered there. King Edward gave orders that it should be honourably re-interred in the Church of St. Publicius, a descendant of the family of Helena.—Matthew, West, Pennant.

[3] *Ald* implies old, and *wark* a building.

[4] Allen's York; Milner's Church History; Green's History of Worcester.

perils of his high station, to assist him by her maternal advice, derived from the many years' experience of her own royal sway, and in her late humbler position, was the coveted duty of this exalted and estimable woman, and worthily did she acquit herself of the important office. If Helena did not witness either the arrival of her long-lost son, or the last moments of her departing Constantius, it is certain that no sooner was Constantine recognised successor to the Empire, than she repaired to the Imperial Court of York; and many places in that city and the north of England yet remain to attest by her name that there she was once present.

Theodora, her mother, and her children, were now become the guests of Constantine; they continued in the Imperial Palace, and under this painfully distressing change in their destiny, beheld nothing in the conduct of the new Emperor, or of his amiable mother, which could in any way remind them, by the smallest neglect or humiliation, of the bitter loss they had sustained. On the removal of the court from Britain, they accompanied it into Italy.

Not less difficult and trying was this sudden change of situation for Helena, than was that in which she had been divided for ever from her husband. She was now called upon daily to meet and associate, in the bonds of affection and kindliness of spirit, with the widowed Empress who had supplied her place on the throne of Constantius; and to guard over and protect her and her children, as the nearest ties of one so dear to herself. This hard duty, accompanied with all the recollections of the departed Constantius, Helena achieved. She had exchanged the dignity of Queen of the Britons for the more elevated rank of Empress-Mother of Rome. The dutiful Constantine, now that he had attained the sum mit of grandeur, desired only to make use of his new power to serve that mother whom he had always loved and reverenced. He publicly testified the immense debt of gratitude he felt was due to her long-tried affection by raising her at once to all the dignities of a Roman empress. He caused her to be proclaimed Augusta in his armies, introducing her to the soldiery with more distinction than Agrippina had ever enjoyed;[1] Helena not having had the dignity of Augusta during the lifetime of Constantius,[2] it was bestowed on her by her son, as though he desired to compensate her for the deprivation of an honour by her divorce, which she had been entitled to. He likewise caused medals to be struck, bearing her effigy, with her names, Flavia Julia Helena. One of these coins has, on one side, a female standing with a branch in her right hand, and the inscription "securitas Republicæ," and on the other side, the words Flavia Julia Helena, round the head of the Empress.

Ancient inscriptions style Helena "Venerabilis et pietissima Augusta,"[3] and some of these give to her the imperial attributes.[4]

Many stones yet extant bear the attributes of Empresses given to Helena, such as "Venerabilis Domina," "Clarentissima," "Charissima," and "Domina nostra."[5] Besides these dignities, Constantine admitted

[1] Butler. [2] Selden's Titles of Honour.
[3] Green's Worcester. [4] Selden. [5] Butler.

Helena to council, as Alexander Severus had formerly done his mother Mammæa; and thus was the Empress-Mother enabled to confer on her country a train of benefits almost unexampled, while the hitherto enslaved island of Britain, under its new rulers, emerged from barbarism, and began to taste the many advantages of civil and religious freedom. It was to the influence of Helena, at this period, that Britain was indebted for some of its greatest and most durable benefits; for not only had Constantine admitted her into his councils, but he gave her power to carry out all she might desire to achieve for her country, by placing her at the same time at the head of his exchequer. In doing so he paid the highest compliment to her discretion, as monetary resources were at that moment in the greatest requisition, and Helena did not act in a manner to make the Emperor regret his confidence had been so reposed.[1]

From the period of the death of Constantius, to that in which Maxentius was defeated near Rome by Constantine, there was an interval of six years. This period was doubtless occupied in adjusting the affairs of Gaul and Britain, over which Constantius had especially ruled.

Leland speaks of the City of London as enlarged and fortified by Constantine at the request of Helena.[2] The manner in which the walls were built was discovered at a later date, in laying the foundation for a new wall.[3] They are thus described by William Fitz Stephen, who died in 1171 : "The wall of this city is high and great, continued with seven gates, which are made double, and on the north distinguished with turrets by spaces; likewise on the south, London hath been enclosed with walls and towers, but the large river of Thames, well stored with fish, and in which the tide ebbs and flows, by continuance of time hath washed, worn away, and cast down those walls."

The Saxon Chronicle confirms the fact of the existence of these walls, by saying that "in 1052, Earl Godwin, with his navy, passed along the southern side of the river, and so assailed the walls."

While these great works progressed, Constantine made every arrangement for the public security and welfare of Britain. He divided the country into five provinces, named Britannia Prima, Valentia, Britannia Secunda, Flavia Cæsariensis, and Maxima Cæsariensis.[4]

Constantine appointed that each of these five provinces should be ruled by a vicegerent, five rectors, two consulars, and three presidents; but from that time till the reign of Valentinian, no account is given of the

[1] Some money of Constantine is said to have been discovered in the walls of the ancient city of Allcester.—Kennet.

[2] Lewis, Hist. of Britain.

[3] Stowe.

[4] Holinshed. The countries they comprehended were as follows: —

The 1st province, or Britannia Prima, the east part of England, from the Trent to the Tweed.

2nd. Valentia, [or Valentina,] the left side, from Liverpool to Cockermouth.

3rd, Britannia Secunda, that part of the isle which lay south, between the Trent and the Thames.

4th, Flavia Cæsariensis, all that country between Dover and the Severn, including Cornwall and Wales.

5th, Maxima Cæsariensis, or Scotland.

manner in which the government was conducted after the son of Helena quitted his native country.

In early youth Constantine had allied himself to Minervina, supposed to be a British lady, by whom he had a son named Crispus. He afterwards had espoused Fausta,[1] daughter of Maximian, the enemy of Christianity, a lady who was the half-sister of Theodora, the Empress of Constantius. Maximian had contracted this alliance for Fausta from motives of state policy. Twice driven from his throne by the unworthy Maxentius, his adopted son, Maximian took refuge with Constantine, who at that time was residing in the palace of Trèves.[2] Though the Emperor could scarcely forget a revolt which Maximian had formerly kindled against him at Marseilles, he received him with the utmost generosity and clemency. Maximian repaid this by raising a new plot against his life. He endeavoured to gain over his daughter Fausta to send away the Emperor's guards during the night, and to leave his apartment open to him. Presents, prayers, promises, and threats were employed to seduce the unhappy Empress. If she betrayed her father by a word, she knew it would be to die; if silent, her husband's life was the price at stake. At last she promised obedience to Maximian, but conjugal affection led her to discover his secret to Constantine. The Emperor could not believe his aged father-in-law capable of such treachery, and sacrificed the life of an eunuch to prove the fact. The unfortunate victim, of a class held in no esteem except as serviceable to their master, was placed on the couch of Constantine, who dismissing his guards, concealed himself in the chamber. In the dead of night, Maximian entered, and finding the passage cleared for his approach advanced to the bed, when he buried his poniard repeatedly in the slave's bosom, exclaiming, "My enemy is dead. I am master of the Empire!" The sight of Constantine changed his joy to despair; he beheld with horror the threatening countenance of his supposed victim: the day of grace was past; Constantine pardoned him not again, and he fell a sacrifice to his insatiable ambition![3]

This was the first[4] who fell by the death-doom of one merciful by nature, but who gained sternness and severity by the circumstances of his own fortunes. In Maximian, the colleague of his late imperial father, Constantine destroyed the father-in-law of Theodora, the husband of Eutropia, the father of Fausta, and grandfather of his own sons. It seemed a horrible alternative, yet certainly no safety on a throne could have been enjoyed, had Maximian continued to exist.

[1] Three sons of Constantine by the Empress Fausta were afterwards placed over the provinces. Constantine, the eldest, over the Gauls, Spain, and Britain; Constans over Illyricum, Italy, and Africa; and Constantius over the East.

Constans was founder of Caer Segont, which was also called Hengaer, the old town which stood by the site of the modern Caernarvon.—*Kennett.*

[2] The city of Treves was honoured with the title of Augusta; it was a Roman colony, and the residence of several emperors, who had the care of superintending their possessions in Gaul.

[3] Hist. Universelle.

[4] At a later period Licinius, the husband of Constantia, his sister, and her son, were put to death by him; but the fate of Licinius was deserved, when his crimes towards the wife and daughter of Dioclesian are considered.—See Gibbon.

Perhaps this conspiracy against the life of Constantine alarmed the maternal feelings of Helena, and actuated her conduct in future towards the sons of Theodora. These three young princes, Dalmatius, Constantius, and Annibalianus, had been promoted by Constantine to the order of nobility, out of respect to their being of his family; in consequence of which they all wore a purple robe with golden guards.[1]

Helena, who always preserved her authority over her son, and is said to have rarely exerted it in a bad cause, showed much wisdom and prudence by the care she took to prevent the rise of these princes, brothers of Constantine, who were of noble birth by their descent from Maximian. There were no instances of the sons of Emperors remaining in a private station, and Helena feared that though in reality they had no right to the empire, which was *elective*, they might perhaps, urged by ambition or by evil counsellors, forget their allegiance to Constantine, and disturb the tranquillity of the State. The Emperor Constantius had desired that his dominions, undivided, should devolve on her own son, and the army had sanctioned his choice. Helena had no share in this arrangement, which, however, being made when the three brothers of Constantine were still minors, she resolved to maintain, and by her prudent precautions effected her purpose. She kept them always at a distance from the court and from employments, sometimes at Toulouse, at other times at Trèves, or in some other distant city, and last of all at Corinth, where she fixed their abode.[2] Julian the Apostate, afterwards Emperor of Rome, already alluded to as having stigmatized Helena's marriage as illegal, who was himself the descendant of Theodora, designates the conduct of Helena in this instance as "the cunning artifice of a stepmother;" but Tillemont esteems it good policy, founded on the opinion that they had no right whatever to the throne; and indeed the sequel of Constantine's family history, which will be given hereafter, proves how prudent were the precautions of Helena.

As we do not hear more of Eutropia and Theodora, it would seem not unlikely that after the death of Maximian, and the separation of these princes from the court, they quitted the palace of Constantine for the more calm retreat which their children were permitted to enjoy at a distance from the crimes and ambition which pervaded the atmosphere of the Roman State.[3]

At the time Constantine was proclaimed in Britain, Maxentius, son of Maximian, invaded Italy,[5] where he was now exercising great tyranny over the Romans in the city of the Emperors; and many of those who were exiled sought protection in Britain at the court of Constantine,

[1] Zosimus. [2] Crevier's Hist. of the Roman Emperors.

[3] Helena, in quitting Britain, had, according to Geoffrey of Monmouth, been accompanied by the three brothers of King Coel, her uncles, Llewelyn, Trehearne, and Marius. Llewelyn, at a subsequent period, espoused a Roman lady, by whom he became father of Maxen Wledig, or the Illustrious, of whom it will be necessary to speak in another part of this work, as the husband of Helena ap Eudda.

[4] Though Constantine had been made Emperor of the West, the prætorian guards had, in a tumultuary manner, declared Maxentius Augustus at Rome. [Platina.]

whom they stirred up by their representations to march to Rome and oppose the tyrant. Among other acts of oppression of which Maxentius recently had been guilty, was that of putting to death St. Katherine, a near relative of Constantine, at Alexandria, whose sacred body, adds our authority, "was miraculously carried by angels from Alexandria to Mount Sinai."

Constantine, having assembled a powerful army, marched against Maxentius. On arriving in the neighbourhood of Rome, the Emperor encamped over against the bridge Milvius, now called Ponte Mole, two miles distant from the city. The enemy's forces were superior in point of numbers, but Constantine earnestly implored the protection of the one supreme God. After his prayer, a little before noon, as he was traversing the country with a part of his army, he beheld in the sky a cross of light, with this inscription, "By this shalt thou conquer." The following night he is said to have seen our Saviour, who commanded him to make a representation of the cross which he had seen, and use it in battle. The Emperor obeyed the Divine command, and thus as early as the fourth century originated the famous banner called Labarum[1] or Standard of the Cross, which wholly displaced the ancient standard of Rome.[2]

Maxentius was defeated, and by the breaking of a bridge of boats, which by his own command had been thrown over the Tiber, was drowned in his flight.[3]

To commemorate these events, in which the heart of the Empress-Mother must have deeply shared, the senate afterwards câused a triumphal arch to be built to the honour of their pious and valiant Emperor. This arch is yet to be seen in Rome. A statue was also erected to Constantine in one of the public places of the city, where he appeared holding a large cross in his hand, instead of a lance, and by his own order the pedestal bore the following inscription:—"By this salutary sign, the true mark of courage, I have delivered you from the yoke of tyranny, and restored the senate and people of Rome to their ancient glory."[4]

Constantine the Great was the first who displayed a cross in a shield on the imperial arms, on his helmet, and on the shields of his soldiers.[5]

Whether Helena was converted to Christianity before her son,[6] as some

---

[1] Butler's Lives. The Roman custom of carrying a banner called *Labarum*, in Tertullian's time, in their armies, gave rise to the practice of banners being carried in public processions. The Labarum was worshipped both by commanders and private men. On it was painted an eagle, the ensign and the tutelary bird of the empire. From hence it is, that ensigns are called sacred in processions, and that they are saluted, and the effigies of saints of both sexes are painted thereon, because they are the patrons of parishes.—*Roma Antiqua*, p. 76.

[2] Lesly, Bishop of Ross, reports a similar story respecting Hungus, King of the Picts. He states, that the night before the battle between Athelstan, King of Northumberland, and Hungus, King of the Picts, a bright cross, in form of that whereon St. Andrew, the tutelar saint of Scotland, suffered martyrdom, appeared to Hungus; who, having gained the victory, ever after bore the figure of that cross on his banners.

[3] Butler, John Rous. [4] Butler. [5] Clavis Calendaria.

[6] St. Ambrose says that Constantine was happy in being born of such a mother

authors assert, or not till after the appearance of the miraculous cross which Constantine beheld, she received the right of baptism from the hands of Sylvester, Bishop of Rome, who on this occasion was endowed with imperial dignities which were confirmed to his descendants.

A story is on record concerning the conversion of Constantine, which states, that when the Emperor was, while in the prime of age, afflicted with the leprosy, and his recovery despaired of, Helena offered up prayers for her son's restoration to health.[1] Gower, who introduces this circumstance in his "Confessio Amantis," says that every remedy resorted to having failed the physicians of the Emperor ordered him to be bathed in the blood of children whose ages were under seven years. The necessary number of infant victims was collected, but Constantine's mercy prevailed; he grieved to think of the lives about to be sacrificed —

"By cause of him alone.
He sawe also the greate mone,
Of that the mothers were ungladde,
And of the wo the children made;
Whereof that his harte tendreth
And such pitie within engendreth,
That him was lever for to chese
His own bodie for to lese,
Than see so great a mourdre wrought
Upon the bloude, which gilteth nought.—Book ii.

The children and their mothers were remanded home, the latter praising and blessing Constantine, and praying for his restoration to health. The Emperor, on the other hand, having no hope on earth, commended himself to God alone. The same night Peter and Paul are said to have appeared to him in his sleep, and ordered him to send to Mount Celion for Sylvester and his clergy, who would cure him of his disease; "at the same time they commended his charity towards the children."

Constantine, as on a former occasion, was obedient to the order received in his vision. Sylvester obeyed the summons with joy, and seized the opportunity to preach the faith to the master of the world. Constantine requested to be baptised, and for this purpose the same vessel was employed which had been prepared for the blood of the victims. On being immersed in the holy water, "the scales of his body fell off, till nothing remained of his great malady, his body as well as his soul being cleansed and purified."

Such is the legend: we are further informed by the poet, that the Emperor sent for his mother, "Queen Eleyne;" and that, by their joint persuasions and influence, the Roman people were admitted to the rite of

---

as St. Helena, who found for him a divine help which filled him with courage, and placed him above the greatest perils. A truly great woman, who had it in her power to bestow on the master of the Empire something beyond all that he had already. Crevier, on the contrary, says that Helena had long been engaged in the superstitions of idolatry, and that it was by the conversion of her son that God thought proper to bring her to Christianity, which she embraced with a sincere heart and enlightened mind.

[1] Lewis's Hist. of Great Britain.

baptism,[1] "of which their most holy Empress had previously set them the example."

"This emperour, which hele hath found,
Within Rome anone let founde
Two churches, which he did make
For Peter and for Paules sake;
Of whom he had a vision,
And yafe thereto possession
Of lordeshippe, and of worldes good."[2]

Platina[3] tells us that Constantine left Constantinople for the hot baths, for the recovery of his health;[4] but discredits the story of the Emperor's being afflicted with leprosy, and says, it is not mentioned by any Christian or profane author.

Whether the story was founded on fact, or not, Pope Adrian I., in after times, asserted, in support of his supremacy, that Constantine the Great, the first Christian Emperor, having been converted to the truth, baptised by Pope St. Sylvester, and cured of his leprosy, had, out of gratitude, when he founded his new capital, Constantinople, freely resigned Rome, and made to the Popes the absolute and eternal donation of the Sovereignty of Italy and of the Western Empire.

In the same year that Constantine vanquished Maxentius, he is said to have also bestowed on the Bishop of Rome the Imperial Lateran Palace, A. D. 312, in which, in the following year, 313, Pope Melchiades held a synod in the apartment of the Empress Fausta, wife of Constantine. It is interesting and curious to discover the Popes in possession of this edifice as early as the fourth century; and in later times to hear the famous Pope Gregory comparing Bertha, Queen of Ethelbert, the Kentish monarch, to the pious St. Helena, because, like her, she yielded up her royal abode for the service of the papal missionaries.

The baptismal font of Constantine, which was preserved in the Palace of the Lateran, having become nearly ruinous, was restored and beautified by Leo X.

"The hall of Constantine, in the Vatican, one of the last works of the immortal Raphael, was commenced under the same Pontiff (Leo X), and terminated after his death, and that of the artist, by Giulio Romano and Gian Francesio Penni. This apartment is adorned by four grand compositions, each of the series occupying one side of the chamber. The first represents the Vision of Constantine, with the miraculous appearance of the Holy Cross; the second and largest is the Victory of Constantine over Maxentius; the third, the Baptism of the Emperor; and the fourth, the Donation made by him to the Church. On the basement of this apartment are represented the figures of several of the Roman Pontiffs, who had been distinguished by superior piety; each of whom appears to be seated in a niche, and to be attended by two angels, who support his mantle, or assist in holding the book which he is employed in reading. Among them are the sainted Pontiffs, Pietro Damaso, Leo, Gregory, and

[1] The painting of the Baptism of Constantine, by Christoforo Roncalli, adorns the Lateran Palace.

[2] Gower's Confessio Amantis, book 2. [3] And Socrates. [4] Butler's Lives.

Sylvester. On the base of a column, at the foot of the picture which represents the baptism of Constantine, is inscribed, "CLEMENS VII, PONT. MAX. A. LEONE X. COEPTUM CONSUMAVIT."[1]

Constantine first beheld Rome on the occasion of his triumph over Maxentius: at that time he made some stay in the capital; but he never fixed his residence there; and from that time to the twentieth year of his reign, we always find him, by the dates of his laws, and by other historical monuments, both in war and in peace, either at Milan, at Arles, or in Illyricum, while his visits to Rome[2] appear to have been rare. Notwithstanding which, in that city remains are yet found which testify his affection for his excellent mother.

The ruins, also, of the private baths, built with great magnificence in Rome, for Helena's use, by her son, still bear the name of Thermæ S. Helenæ.[3] These baths, in the Villa Ursinia, are still among the objects of interest shown to strangers, being almost entire: they bear at the entrance the following inscription:—

"D. N. Helena Ven. Aug. Mat.
Avia. Beatiss. . . . . . .
Thermæ . . . . Istria;"

"which (says Montfaucon) we have therefore set down, because otherwise delivered by others. On the left hand going out, is the Neustriæ way, and on the right the Labicane, leading to the tomb of the Empress Helen."

Several new cities were afterwards founded by Constantine, in honour of his mother, to which he gave the name of Helenopolis. One of these was situated in Palestine. Another was Drepanum, in Nicomedia, which he beautified and fortified, exempting it from all taxes: this town was favoured more particularly from the regard which the Empress herself entertained for it, from the circumstance of St. Lucian the Martyr having been interred there; she herself assisted in commemorating the spot. "This was named Helenopolis, as well as other cities, in her honour, and not because she was born there, as some have erroneously supposed."[4] The city where Constans was slain was called the City of Helena.

The grand object of Constantine and of Helena, from the time of the victory over Maxentius, seems to have been the propagation of the Christian faith. The Empress instigated her son to piety and alms-deeds;[5] and after three hundred years had rolled away, under the domination of Emperors hostile to the creed of Jesus, its followers beheld one of British birth arise as a protector to the rights of their Church. They now first experienced peace and quietness, and to become a Christian was legal. Indemnity was made to those professors who had been injured, and the ministers of God were treated with honour.[6]

The heads of the several provinces belonging to Rome were directed to promote the Gospel; and though, like Constantius, the Emperor would not oblige them to profess Christianity, he forbade them, by their præfects, to sacrifice to idols. Even beyond the bounds of his own Empire, Con-

---

[1] Roscoe. [2] Crevier. [3] Butler's Lives.
[4] Procopius. [5] Butler. [6] Milner, Baleus.

stantine still sought to promote the good cause; for, in a letter to Sapor, King of Persia, he zealously pleads for the Christians of his dominions. He destroys idol temples, prohibits impious pagan rites, puts an end to the savage fights of gladiators, stands up with respectful silence to hear the sermon of Eusebius, Bishop of Cæsarea, who furnishes him with the volumes of the Scriptures, for the use of the churches; he orders the observation of the festivals of martyrs, has prayers and reading of the Scriptures at his court, dedicates churches with great solemnity, makes Christian orations himself, one of which, of a considerable length, is preserved by the historian, his favourite bishop: directs the sacred observation of the Lord's Day, to which he adds that of Friday also, the day of Christ's Crucifixion, and teaches the soldiers of his army to pray, by a short form made for their use.[1]

Among other improvements, Constantine abolished the barbarous punishment of crucifixion; and from the time that the sign of the cross appeared to him in the battle against Maxentius, the cross, as a figure, began to be reverenced and esteemed. Theodosius afterwards made a law that no image of the cross should be graven in stone, marble, or in earth, lest men should tread on it.[2]

Constantine also forbade the private use of divination, though he still allowed the public use of it in baths and temples; he afterwards abolished the worst branches of sorcery and magic. Finding the idolaters still addicted to their rites, he took another step, that of publicly exposing the mysteries which had hitherto been kept secret, melted down golden statues, and caused brazen ones to be drawn by ropes through the streets of Constantinople; and some of the temples, which had been scenes of horrible wickedness, he destroyed. In Egypt the famous cubit, with which the priests were wont to measure the height of the Nile, was kept in the temple of Serapis. This, by Constantine's order, was removed to the Church of Alexandria. The pagans beheld the removal with indignation, and ventured to predict that the Nile would no longer overflow its banks. Divine Providence, however, smiled on the schemes of Constantine, and the Nile the next year overflowed the country in an uncommon degree. In this gradual manner was Paganism overturned.[3]

As for Helena, Rufinus calls her faith and holy zeal *incomparable*, and says she kindled the same fire in the hearts of the Romans. One of our early writers, speaking of the piety of Helena,[4] says, "She persevered to the end of her days, with the evangelic Anne, in holy widowhood, entirely devoted to the Christian religion." There are authors who record that it was through her that persecution ceased, and peace was restored to the Church.

[1] Milner's Church History. "Galerius, tormented with sufferings from an incurable disease, published an edict taking off the persecution from the Christians, and allowed them to rebuild their places of worship, desiring them to pray for his health. He expired a few days afterwards."

[2] Polydore Vergil.

[3] For many benefits conferred on the Church, Constantine was, after death, canonized by the Greeks, who keep his festival on May 21st.

[4] Baleus. Gregory the Great recommends her as an example to Bertha, Queen of Ethelbert.

Such an understanding of heavenly philosophy is she said to have arrived at, after a knowledge of the Gospel, that she early produced treatises—

On the Providence of God, 1 book.
On the Immortality of the Soul, 1 book.
The Rule for Right Living, 1 book. (To the ever-august lord, her son.)
Epistles to Constantine, 1 book.
Of her Revelations, 1 book.
Pious Exhortations to her son, 1 book.
To Pope Sylvester, many epistles.
To the Abbot Antonius, many epistles.[1]
Certain Greek Poems, 1 book.

All which are stated by Ponticus to be still extant.

Hitherto, from the period of his coming into power, nothing is recorded of Constantine that takes from the excellence of his character. But whatever virtues might exist in those times, the savage nature, yet unsubdued by a continuance of the usages of the blessed faith of Christ, would occasionally break forth, and some unexpected act of cruelty or revenge appears in history, as if to contradict the good attributed to its heroes.

This was the case in regard to Constantine, who, generally represented as just and merciful, yet committed acts which can scarcely be reconciled with such a reputation, and in these the influence of his mother appears to have been of no avail.

It would seem that, at the time when the son of Fausta was about ten years of age, Crispus, the son of Constantine by his first wife, Minervina, became the object, some writers say, of the love, some of the jealousy, of his mother-in-law. Be the cause what it might, Fausta, it appears, was bent on the destruction of the young prince, and made accusations against him to his father, which entirely embittered his mind.

It was at a grand festival in honour of the twentieth year of Constantine's reign, when the court was at Nicomedia, that in the midst of enjoyment, and unsuspecting of evil, Crispus and several of his friends were arrested, carried away to judgment, and after a brief examination by persons already instructed to find them guilty, they were condemned, some to death, others to banishment, which was to end in the same punishment. Crispus was sent to Pola, in Istria, where he was soon after put to death.[2]

The vengeance of Fausta was now satisfied, and the stern justice of Constantine executed; but Helena's affliction knew no bounds at so severe and unlooked-for an act, and she felt convinced, not only that the prince was innocent of the intention to conspire against his father, of which he was publicly accused, but that he had secret enemies, who ought to be brought to light, and receive the reward of their crime.

In her endeavours to discover these, revelations of a character for which

---

[1] Anthony, the holy hermit, who is described as a man "wrapped wholly in contemplation," was by birth an Egyptian. [John Rous.] His manner of living was severe, his food being bread alone, and water his beverage; his single meal in the day was taken at sunset. This man did much to reform mankind in Constantine's reign, and Helena oftentimes, both by letter and messengers, recommended herself and her *sons* to his prayers. [Platina.]

[2] Gibbon.

she was not prepared, were made, by which Constantine became aware of the infidelity of the Empress Fausta herself, to whose representations he had yielded, and had sacrificed his son. Rage and jealousy now took possession of his mind, and without waiting for more proofs of the frailty of his wife, he determined that her life should pay the forfeit of her treachery.

It is recorded that Fausta met her death in the bath, in which she was suffocated by the steam, "it having been heated to an extraordinary degree."[1]

Helena heard of this second act of retribution with feelings of deep regret and sorrow, and is said to have, in her character of his mother, reproved the Emperor with great severity for his cruelty in both instances: and this is recorded to have been the sole occasion on which a difference ever existed between her and her son. The accusations and the vengeance were both common to the times, and frightful as the facts are, the loss of human life did not affect the world as it does in more civilized days; otherwise it is difficult to find excuses for Constantine, who is accused by some authors of more than one act of cruelty irreconcileable with his boasted clemency. Considering his profession of the new faith, and his opposition to the old, he had doubtless sufficient enemies ready to blacken his character, whenever there was a possibility of misrepresenting the truth. This may also account for the accusations which have been made against Helena herself, of having been the accuser of Fausta, and the instigator of her son's vengeance against his wife.

The death of Licinius is another stain cast on the fame of Constantine, who, having condemned him as an accomplice in the designs of Crispus, affected to listen to the prayers of his agonised sister, and appeared to consent to his banishment to Thessalonica; but he was, soon after his arrival there, murdered by the imperial order.

Helena, after the catastrophe of their mother's death, took upon herself the education of the children of Fausta.

About A. D. 325 happened one of the most interesting events in Church history—the Council of Nice. It is not certain that Helena was present on this remarkable occasion; but, as her son presided at the assembly, it is very likely that she did so likewise, for she generally not only accompanied him wherever he went, but sat in council, and aided him with her wisdom and experience.

Helena is thus described, when, at the advanced age of eighty, she undertook an expedition surprising at her years: "Her life was constantly happy, at least after the elevation of her son to the throne of the Cæsars. She saw that only son reunite under his power the whole extent of the Roman dominion, and three grandsons seemed to promise her that the Empire would be perpetuated in her posterity. Add to this, perfect health, and an unimpaired vigour of mind, preserved even in her old age. So many prosperities were not to her, as they too often prove, a means of seduction, but, on the contrary, an inexhaustible fund *of grateful acknowledgment and piety towards God.*"[2]

---

[1] Gibbon. [2] Crevier.

The great enterprise for which, more than any other action in her life, Helena has been celebrated, was a journey into the East, for the express purpose of discovering the true cross on which our Saviour had suffered. This grand undertaking was made at the distance of more than three hundred years from the Christian era, and attests the exalted piety of the Empress. Some say she desired to adorn the churches and oratories in those sacred spots, noticed in the history of our blessed Lord, and to relieve the poor[1] of those parts; others, that visions, admonitions in sleep, or divine warnings, had led to the design which drew Helena to the Holy Land; and St. Paulinus declares no worldly motive could have directed her steps; it was the pious one alone of discovering the true cross. A letter from Constantine was dispatched to Macarius, Bishop of Jerusalem, ordering him to make search for the sacred relic on Mount Golgotha of Calvary. Tradition had pointed out the spot where it was to be found, and it is said that Helena had been favoured with an especial revelation to aid her search.

Accordingly, the aged Empress set forth, attended by an imperial retinue, and at the head of a large army, taken for that purpose out of Britain;[2] whence some have derived her surname of "Lueddog," Elen Lueddog, signifying "Elen with the *great army.*"

The desire of Helena to admit her own countrymen to a share in this great and glorious enterprise is highly interesting; for it shows that in her honoured position of Roman Empress she still remembered that she was Queen of the Britons. The Emperor himself accompanied her as far as Byzantium.

On her arrival at Jerusalem, Helena is said to have convened a large assembly of Jews, of whom she requested information concerning the spot of which she was in search. They refused to point it out; upon which Helena threatened to put them to death.[3] On hearing this, they reluctantly confessed that Judas—an ominous name—one of their number, could give the necessary information. This man, however, who was really acquainted with the place, was as resolute as his brethren; and it was not till after he had passed several days without food in a dry cistern or pit, where he had been placed by order of Helena, that hunger conquered his resolution, and he made known the secret, by leading the impatient Empress to the spot.[4] When arrived there, the search was by no means easy. The Emperor Adrian, who had delighted in the profanation of those sacred places, had, about 200 years before, buried under great heaps of earth the place where the holy sepulchre existed, not far distant from the spot of the crucifixion, and had built upon a platform over the place, which was paved with stone, a temple to Venus, while above the sepulchre he had raised a statue of Jupiter.

It was necessary to remove the whole of this edifice, and afterwards to clear away the mass of stones on which it rested, as a preliminary step to the necessary discovery; this done, they had to dig very deep to discover the former surface. No difficulties could, however, deter Helena

---

[1] Rufinus, John Baleus.

[2] Lewis's Hist. of Great Britain.

[3] Caxton says by *fire*.

[4] Eusebius, Caxton.

from accomplishing her pious object. After a vast quantity of earth had been removed, and all the rubbish of the buildings they had demolished, the sacred grot was discovered wherein the Lord's body had rested,[1] and whence it had arisen in a glorified state.

After they had dug a little deeper still, they discovered three crosses; and here a new and unexpected difficulty arose—for they could not determine which of these crosses was the one that had borne the Saviour of Man. The superscription was indeed found, but it was not attached to any one of them. Judas could not tell the Queen which was the true cross, and Macarius suggested that a miraculous proof should be demanded of God concerning its identity. The Empress, the bishop, and others, therefore, went to the house of a lady of quality, who was very ill, in the city. On arriving there, the Empress having herself made a prayer aloud,[1] the bishop applied the crosses, and the sick person was restored instantly at the touch of the true cross. Many historians relate this as a fact; and add that, by touching it, a dead person also was restored to life. According to Caxton, Judas had laid the three crosses in the middle of the city, and while there awaiting some demonstration from God, at about noon a young man's body was carried forth to burial. Judas detained the bier, and laid on it first one of the three crosses, then a second, and after that a third, when the dead was restored to life. Sozomen relates this incident, as he tells us, from report only; and Mr. Butler says it deserves little credit. Some, indeed, consider the whole story of the Inventio Crucis, or Finding of the Cross by Helena, as a mere fiction; and Salmasius, in his "Treatise de Cruce," p. 296, endeavours to prove it such, on account of the supposed inscription; "for where was the necessity of a miracle for distinguishing the cross on which our Saviour suffered, from those of the malefactors, if the above-mentioned inscription was found near it; as it would plainly appear, from the hole and nails, which of the crosses it had been affixed to, though even the two other malefactors, as is probable, had their inscriptions."[3] Eusebius, however, mentions indirectly the discovery of the cross, in the letter of Constantine addressed to Macarius about building the church, and describes the two magnificent churches which Helena built, the one on Calvary, the other on Mount Olivet;[4] it is therefore, no refutation of these historians, though perhaps some embellishment may have been added to the main facts.[5]

---

[1] Caxton. [2] This prayer is recorded by Rufinus, Hist. lib. x., cap. 8.

[3] Keysler's Travels. [4] Butler.

[5] Polydore Vergil, who relates the fact of Helena's finding the three crosses, says, "it was easy to perceive Christ's cross by the title which then did remain, albeit sore wasted and corrupted with antiquity."

Judas is said to have possessed a family memorial of 326 years' standing, naming the place which Helena desired to discover, which document he presented to the Empress, and thus the cross was found. Subsequently Judas, who was a Hebrew, received the baptismal rite, and the name of Queriacus was bestowed on him by Helena; he lived to become a bishop, and suffered martyrdom. The Romans appointed a festival in his honour on the 3rd of May, which was subsequently called Holy Cross Day.

Platina tells us the cross was discovered by Helena on the 3rd of May, during the Pontificate of Eusebius, but the calendar appended to Cooper's account of

The Empress, who had presided in person over the whole work, was overwhelmed with joy at finding herself in possession of such a treasure; she cut the sacred cross into two pieces, the largest of which was enclosed in a rich silver shrine, and placed under the care of Macarius, Bishop of Jerusalem; it was afterwards annually exposed to the adoration of the people, sometimes oftener, in proportion to the number of pilgrims who resorted thither to worship it. The second portion of the cross was sent as a present of inestimable value to Constantine, who was at Constantinople, and there, at certain periods, it was uncovered and exposed to the adoration of the public with much solemnity. Fragments, as is well known, of this cross have been dispersed all over Christendom.

About three hundred and fifty years after the discovery of the cross, an Anglo-Saxon nun wrote the description of a journey of pilgrimage made by two of her countrymen[1] in the eighth century, who travelled to the Holy Land through Asia Minor. After tracing their progress, the writer, who was of the monastery of Heidenham, says: "And then they came to Jerusalem, by that place where the Holy Cross of our Lord was found. There is now a church in this place, called the Place of Cavalry; but St. Helen, when she discovered it, enclosed it within the boundaries of Jerusalem; and there stand three wooden crosses, in front of the east court of the church, near the wall. These are not within the church, but withoutside, under a covering; and there is that garden, near where the sepulchre of our Lord was. This sepulchre was cut in the rock, and that rock stands upon the ground; it is four-square within, and narrow towards the top; and the cross of that sepulchre stands now upon the top; and there beside is built an admirable house; and on the east side, in that rock, is the door of the sepulchre, by which men enter into it to pray; and there is the bed where the body of the Lord lay; and there stand about the bed fifteen golden basins of oil, burning day and night; that bed is on the northern side, within the sepulchre, and is on the right hand of the man as he goes in to pray there. And there, before the door of the sepulchre lieth a great stone, like to that which the angel rolled away."

Such is one of the earliest accounts of the sacred edifice which was erected over the spot of our Lord's Sepulchre,[2] where part of the cross found by St. Helena was deposited. The splendour is said to have rivalled that of Heliogabalus's Temple of the Sun, "its walls being lined with precious marbles, its roof covered with beaten gold, while in the shower of light which fell upon its dome, Helena affected to image and perpetuate the angelic glory to which the fane was dedicated." [3]

A modern writer[4] describes the building in these terms: "The form

---

the most important Public Records of Great Britain (vol. ii. p. 489), fixes the date on the 3rd of May, A. D. 326, in the twenty-first year of Constantine's reign, the thirteenth of the Pontificate of Sylvester, and the first after the Council of Nice.—*Butler*, vol. v., p. 564.

[1] St. Willebald and St. Wunebald. See Miss Lawrence's interesting work, History of Woman in England.

[2] Milner's Hist. of the Church of Christ. [3] Lady Morgan.

[4] Light's Travels in Egypt, Nubia, the Holy Land, and Cyprus.

of the body of the Church of the Holy Sepulchre is circular, over which is a heavy cupola. In the body of the church are entrances to the three chapels of the Greeks, Armenians, and Latins, and to the cells of the monks, who are kept there for the service of the church. The chapels are fitted up in the style of the sect to which they belong; the Greeks and Armenians with pictures, the Latins with images. In the centre rises an oblong building of wood, of twenty feet in length by ten in breadth, in which is a cupola, open at top. One half of this contains the Sepulchre of our Saviour, the other is fitted up for the chapel of the Copts. A small space enclosed by low railings surrounds the entrance to the Sepulchre. I confess I had been prepared to see something like a tomb, and was rather disappointed, on entering, to find myself in a mean chapel, where the altar, of plain white marble, occupied a space of six feet in length, two in breadth, and in depth about two feet and a half, leaving only room in front fit to kneel. It covers, according to the tradition of the place, the tomb of our Saviour, of whom a miserable picture is hung on the tapestry over the altar; this is lighted by forty-five silver lamps, suspended in six rows from the cupola. I followed the example of my guide in kissing the altar, kneeling and bowing my head over it.

"From the Sepulchre, I was led to a flat stone of six feet in length, and three in breadth, forming part of the pavement of the body of the church where our Saviour's body was anointed after it was taken from the cross; near which were the tombs of Godfrey and Baldwin, two of the sovereigns of Jerusalem during the Crusades. They are now enclosed, and concealed from view within the wall, their existence and appearance not being interesting to the Armenians, who new modelled the church.

"The attempt to bring everything connected with the crucifixion of our Saviour under the same roof, surprised me. In one part of the church is an elevated piece of rock, enclosed in a sort of chapel, in which the crucifixion took place; three small square pieces of marble, in the centre of which is a pole, mark the spot where the crosses of our Saviour and the malefactors were fixed; and in another, close to this, is a chapel, dedicated to the place where the ceremony of nailing to the cross was performed; underneath is an excavation, where St. Helena found the cross; and a little further off is the tomb of Nicodemus the Jew, who is mentioned in St. John, chapter iii.; but by what authority he is buried here I do not know. To complete the show, a fragment of a granite column, about two feet high, said to be taken from the palace of Pontius Pilate, and described as the pillar to which our Saviour was attached when he was scourged, is placed in another chapel. But I will not tire the reader by dwelling longer on the relics of this church, which are made the objects of contention between the different sects, and are by turns possessed, as each has money to purchase the right to them from the Turkish chiefs, who of course are anxious that such contests should occur."

Mr. Light, seeing the anxiety to crowd all the relics of the Saviour under one roof, the Sepulchre in particular being so near the place of crucifixion, doubts whether it was the actual burying-place of our Lord, and thinks that the early Christians, from their zeal, neglected to examine among the tombs further from the city for the real Sepulchre. He says:—In the Valley of Jehosophat there are caverns which have evidently been tombs, many of them with a stone portal, and bear marks of great antiquity. The text in Scripture says, the stone was rolled away, which certainly applies more to a vertical than a horizontal position, the supposed situation of the present tomb, and is contrary to the custom prevalent of burying the dead in tombs excavated in the sides of rocks, of which memorials are to be found in all parts of the East. As I made these observations before I read Dr. Clarke's account of Jerusalem, I was much gratified in finding his opinion coincide with mine."

The same author goes on to observe:—"Within the limits of the Aga's seraglio or palace are said to be the place of confinement and judgment-hall of our Saviour, the spot where he was scourged, and that in which the cross was kept before it was used for the crucifixion, and where it was left by the Empress Helena after she found it on Mount Calvary."

Helena, likewise, was desirous to evince her piety by monuments, raised in the several other places rendered sacred by our Lord's sufferings. She destroyed at Bethlehem the Temple of Adonis, by which Adrian had, about a hundred years before, profaned the place where Christ was born, and raised instead, a church to the incarnate Son of God. She built another upon the Mount of Olives, on the spot where our Saviour ended his abode on earth by his glorious ascension. In both these works she was assisted by the liberality of her son, but she had the first share in the design and execution of them.[1]

The lamented author of the "Crescent and the Cross"[2] thus describes his visit to the Church of St. Helena, at Bethlehem:—"Entering by a very low door and long passage, almost upon hands and knees, I stood up under the noble dome of the Church of St. Helena. The roof, constructed of cedar-wood from Lebanon, is supported by forty huge marble pillars, showing dimly the faded images of painted saints. The whole

---

[1] Both these edifices are described by the early Saxon writer of the Life of St. Willebald, in the eighth century, as having been seen by that bishop, who, when he visited the Mount of Olives, "came to the church on that mount from which our Lord ascended into heaven. And in the midst of the church stands a plate of brass beautifully wrought, and it is square. This is in the midst of the church, on the place where our Lord ascended into heaven; and in the middle court is a quadrangle, and there are little glass lamps, and round about these lamps is glass to enclose them. And this is why they are enclosed, that they may keep alight both in rain and sunshine. This church is, moreover, very broad, and without a roof, and there stand two pillars just withinside the church, against the northern and the southern walls. These are in remembrance of the two men who said, 'Ye men of Galilee, why stand ye gazing up into heaven?' And that man who can pass between the wall and the columns, they say he is free from his sins.

"Then he went to the place where the angels appeared to the shepherds, and then to Bethlehem, where our Lord was born. This place was formerly a cave, and now it is a house, cut four-square in the rock, and the earth is dug away round about, and a church is now built over it. And on the place where the Lord was born now stands an altar, and another smaller altar is there, and when they celebrate mass in the cave, they take that smaller altar and carry it within. This church, which stands above, is built in the form of a cross, and it is a glorious building."

[2] Eliot Warburton.

building is silent, dirty, and neglected-looking, but of noble proportions. From its court are parted off the different chapels belonging to the rival sects. The Armenian is the handsomest and wealthiest of these, as its friars are by far the most respectable.

"The Chapel of the Nativity is a subterranean grotto, into which you descend in darkness, that gives way to the softened light of many silver lamps suspended from the roof. Notwithstanding the improbability of this being the actual place of the Nativity, one cannot descend with indifference into the enclosure, which has led so many millions of pilgrims, in rags or armour, during 1800 years, from their distant homes. It is, however, impossible to recognise anything like a reality in the mass of marble, brass, and silken tawdry ornaments; and one leaves this most celebrated spot in the world with feelings of disappointment."

Mr. Turner is still more minute; these are his words: "I descended a staircase and entered a grotto, said to be the site of the stable in which our Saviour was born; it lies east south-east, and west north-west, and is thirty-seven feet six inches long, and fourteen broad. At the easterly end, on the supposed site of the birth, is built an altar, six feet three inches long, and fifty-eight feet six inches deep, formerly belonging (as indeed did the whole church) to the Catholics, but now usurped by the Greeks, with whom the Armenians have lately bought a share. This altar, lying north north-east, and south south-west, is above, adorned with mosaic, laid by Helena, but now ruined, and with Greek pictures of saints, &c., and lighted with fourteen silver lamps, belonging to its present possessors. The grotto, *i. e.*, the whole, is lighted by twenty-six silver and silver-gilt lamps, the property of the Catholics. To the west-south-west of the site of the birth, fourteen feet distant (in which are included three steps, cut from the naked rock), is another altar (lying north by east and south by west, and contained in an interior grotto), the site, it is said, of the manger in which our Saviour was laid: this altar is fifty inches long, and thirty-five and a half deep. To the east south-east of the manger, five feet six inches distant, is another altar, supposed to be on the spot where stood the Magi, when they offered their gifts to Jesus. Both these are hung with appropriate pictures; and the one on the site of the manger is lighted by five silver lamps. This interior grotto measured seven feet ten inches, by eight feet nine inches, and is embellished by four small columns standing near the supposed site of the manger, one of verd antique, one of pink, and two of white marble; these were also placed by St. Helena. At the westerly end of the church is a door leading to a large natural cave, in which is shown, first, from the door to the right, an altar, covering, it is said, the spot where Joseph retired to pray, after the delivery of the Virgin; second, to the right, an altar, where are thought to have been buried the Innocents murdered by command of Herod; under it is a large hollow; third, turning into a passage on the left, an altar upon the sepulchre of St Eusebius; fourth, in the same passage, an altar upon the sepulchre of Santa Paola and her daughter; opposite to which, fifth, an altar on the sepulchre of St. Jerome; and sixth, turning to the right, a chamber, said to have been the tomb where St. Jerome taught. The only thing belonging to the

Greeks and Armenians here below, is the altar, on the site of the birth; under this is a small hole, which they have embellished with a silver plate, for the pilgrims to kiss."[1]

It appears from St. Ambrose, that Helena was, out of contempt, called Stabularia by the Jews and Pagans, not as Baronius thinks, because Constantius lodged at the house of her father *in Britain*, but because she herself founded this Church at Bethlehem where the stable stood in which Christ was born, and which the enemies of the Christian name turned into ridicule. St. Ambrose writes thus of her: "They say she was first a stabularia, or one who entertained strangers, and so became known to Constantius, who afterwards arrived at the Empire. A good stabularia, who sought so diligently the crib of the Lord; who chose to be reputed as dung, that she might gain Christ!" This commentary might also have referred to another grand work of Helena, which was a kitchen for the support of the indigent and hungry poor at Jerusalem.

In this manner Helena directed the State revenues which her son had placed in her hands to the purposes of religion and benevolence. Paulinus, Epist. XI. ad Severum, reproaches the Empress-Mother with abusing the exchequer; but Fuller,[2] who refers to this charge against Helena, thinks that the word "abuti" should be rendered, "a full and free use of those treasures" her son had employed her to distribute.

Saint Paulinus[3] writes of the discovery of the cross through the zeal of the Empress Helena, and lavishes praises on the faith of Constantine. The epistle which he addressed on this subject to Sulpicius Severus is edifying, for it gives a just idea of the mother's piety, and the religion of the young prince, her son: —

"I am persuaded that it is not out of season that I inform you how the cross has been found, and recognized, to edify your faith by the history of an event which is too important for one to be ignorant of. It is easy to see, that he who knows not the detail, would with difficulty understand how this cross, which has been discovered by revelation, was the true one, on which the Lord willingly expired for us; but it cannot be doubted that if it had fallen into the hands of the Jews, who are always watching to weaken the faith of Jesus Christ, they would have torn it to pieces, and reduced it to ashes. For those who had sealed the Sepulchre would not have failed to destroy the remembrance of it, and they would not have suffered the preservation of the cross to afford an excuse for worshipping Him whose resurrection they would not acknowledge, though attested by the opening of the tomb, and the uselessness of the seals they had placed upon it to hinder the rising from the dead which they apprehended. It is, therefore, in vain that we demand why the cross remained buried in the earth, since, if it had not been so, above all during the time of the persecutions, which have succeeded to the hatred of the Jews, and almost surpassed their cruelty, it is evident that all the remains would have been entirely destroyed; for one may easily imagine with what fury those per-

[1] Turner's Tour in the Levant.

[2] Worthies of England, vol. i. p. 500, edit. 1840.

[3] Bishop of Nola.

sons would have destroyed the cross, who have expended their violence on the place where it had been deposited. The Emperor Adrian thought that by despoiling this sacred spot, he would succeed in undermining and extirpating the faith of the Christians: with this view he decorated a statue of Jupiter in the place where Christ died, and Bethlehem was in like manner profaned by the impure Temple of Adonis. He hoped, so to speak, to pluck up the Church by the root, and to shake it from the foundation, if idols became adored on the spot where Jesus Christ was born to suffer, suffered to rise again, rose again to reign, and was judged by the world, that in his turn he might judge the world. Alas! it has pleased the all-powerful God to expose himself to these outrages, and even to permit profanation of sacrilegious men in the spot where he was crucified for the salvation of the human race. Over the cross, which had shaken all nature with earthquakes, by the eclipse of the sun, and by the dead rising from their graves, the idol of the Devil was raised; his altar smoked with the funeral pile of the beasts which were sacrificed to him; the name of God was conveyed to dead images, while He who is the living God, and the resurrection of the dead, was loaded with opprobrium, and blasphemed as a man who was dead, and dead by the shameful punishment of the cross. In Bethlehem, where two animals had recognised their master, and the manger of their Lord, men, disowning their Saviour and their God, have paid a superstitious worship to the infamous love of mortals, and to dead bodies. That place in which wise men from the distant climate of Chaldea had adored the Eternal King, whose cradle had been revealed to them by a new star, and had offered their presents, had the Romans rendered sacred to impure and barbarous passions. In that spot where, during the night, lighted by the star, the shepherds, accompanied by a multitude of angels, and transported by a celestial joy, repaired to render homage to the new-born Saviour, impure females, amidst effeminate men, have wept for the death of Adonis, and the grief of Venus. Alas! what piety may be able to expiate such prodigious impiety! In the place where the sacred tears of the Saviour's infancy had been heard, shameful ceremonies retain the cries of those who utter the lamentable complaints of Venus.

"This shame to the age lasted till the time of Constantine, which touches our own. This prince merited to be the model and Chief of Christian princes, by his own faith and that of his mother Helena, who, by Divine inspiration, when this circumstance was made known to her, sighed for the happiness of beholding Jerusalem; and being proclaimed August with her son, besought him to give her permission to visit the places made holy by the traces of our Lord, and by the mysteries which He had wrought for us. She desired by the destruction of temples and sacrilegious idols, to purge these holy places from the contagion of impiety, and to restore them to their original holiness; for it was necessary that the Church should resume its rights, and recover its first lustre in that place where it had received its birth. The Emperor did not hesitate to consent to all that she wished, and his august mother devoted the treasures with which she had been entrusted by him, in lavishing on the pious works which she projected every richness that could be withdrawn thence. It was with all the grandeur and magnificence which depended on herself, and which religion required, that she adorned noble churches in every place where her Divine Redeemer had accomplished the healing mysteries of mercy.

"Helena desired, in these magnificent works, to pay to Christ the homage of an Empress; but she did not, at the same time, omit to perform those works of mercy and goodness, which are more pleasing in the eyes of God than any temples wrought with hands. It was her delight to relieve the poor, the orphans, and widows, by her charity; and as she travelled from place to place through the Holy Land, and more intimately surveyed the spots on which she desired to erect monuments to mark the glory of the Lord, and her own pious zeal in His service, she left in the hearts of all, abundant testimonies to her own vital religion. Helena especially honoured those virgins who were consecrated to God; and having one day assembled all who resided at Jerusalem, she gave them an entertainment, at which she waited on them herself."

Suidas, who notices this humility of mind and Christian modesty in the Empress of the Roman world, towards women of the monastic order, says: "She often assembled, and seated, and ministered to them with her own hands, setting before them the victuals, and handing the cups, and pouring water over their hands, so performing the part and office of a maid-servant."

"She loved simplicity; and in the common prayers of the faithful, she mixed with the other women, without taking any particular or distinguished place. She visited the principal churches of the East, and left, wherever she went, proofs of her Christian and religious liberality; nor did she pass by the chapels of the meanest towns, where her delicate sense of humility led her to appear amongst the women at prayer in a most humble garment. She was able to indulge her pious charity in these respects, because the Emperor, her son, confiding in her prudence, gave her leave to draw upon the imperial treasury for whatever sums she pleased."[1] Whilst, therefore, "Helena travelled all over the East with royal pomp and magnificence, she heaped all kinds of favours both on cities and private persons, particularly on soldiers, the poor, the naked, and those who were condemned to the mines, distributing money, garments, &c., and freeing many from oppression, chains, and banishment."[2] By these and a thousand other actions, Helena proved herself the "common mother of the indigent and distressed."[3] "She herself built more churches than any woman before her time or since,[4] to say nothing of those numerous edifices of another kind, suggested by her benevolence."

Of this latter class was the kitchen founded at Jerusalem by the Empress, thus described by Mr. Turner: "We visited the kitchen of St. Helena, which is a large edifice, well built of yellowish marble, and having its two doors adorned after the Gothic fashion. It is still used by the Turks for the purpose for which it was originally instituted, being

[1] Crevier.
[2] Butler's Lives.
[3] St. Gregory the Great.
[4] Green's Worcester.

a kitchen endowed by the Sultan for the benefit of the poor, and of Turkish travellers. The Turks have divided it into several apartments, of which some are ovens, some stables; and above they have built a mosque and a bath."

The Church of the Ascension, which stands on the loftiest of the three summits of the Mount of Olives, in the centre of the village of Mount Olivet, on the very spot whence our Saviour is thought to have ascended to heaven, was built, it is said, by St. Helena, and, says Warburton, "from the roof may be obtained the most interesting, if not the most striking, view in the world." The holy spot whereon our Lord is supposed to have stood, was enclosed by the Empress with an octagonal building, roofed by a round dome. "On each side of this building, except where is the door, are two small columns (fourteen in all) of coarse marble, with highly ornamented capitals. The circle of the inside was sixteen feet two inches round, and the dome about thirty-five feet high from the ground. Within is a stone, thirty-one inches by twenty-one, said to have been the last earthly substance that Jesus trod on. This stone contained an impression, which, says tradition, is the print of Jesus' foot. A higher authority,[1] however, says, our Saviour ascended from Bethany. Near the stone is a recess (to make which the symmetry of the building is spoiled, and a parcel of stones are heaped up to cover it on the outside) for the Turks and Arabs to pray in. All the pilgrims kiss the stone very devoutly. Of the court in which the building stands, each side is about one hundred feet, but the shape is irregular. Here the Greeks, Armenians, Syrians, and Copts, have each an altar (the Armenians have two) of stones, rudely piled,[2] of the Mosque of Omar. In the kitchen, which has a small dome, supported by four square clumsy columns, are some of the original caldrons of Helena, of which, one of the largest that I measured, was fifty inches round, and thirty inches deep. A mituctee, or superintendent, is sometimes sent from Constantinople, to honour a distinguished visitor here: she has a residence in the kitchen, and takes care that the guest be well provided: in this case the poor are neglected, as the fund is eaten up by the numerous attendants that always accompany a distinguished Turk."[3]

It must be interesting to the generous friends of the poor and needy, who in our own days have fed the hungry and clothed the naked, in similar institutions, to revert to the primary institution founded on this principle in a remote age in that Holy City which, in religious interest, exceeds every other in the earth. Nor was this the only other embellishment added by Helena to the churches she had already founded; for, about one hundred paces south-east of the Holy Sepulchre stands the convent of St. Peter, also the work of the Empress. It is now in the possession of the Turks, who have converted it into a tanner's yard and stables; several broken pieces of columns are attached to the walls.

[1] Luke, chap. xxiv.

[2] The village itself stands on the summit of a mountain, and commands a complete view of Jerusalem, from which it is about twenty minutes' distance.—*Turner.*

[3] Turner's Tour.

Scarcely a spot celebrated in Scripture passed unregarded by the observant and pious Helena: churches arose in all directions, convents adorned the desolate places dedicated to the service of Christ: Nazareth, Bethlehem, Arimathea, testify the zeal of the Empress in her holy undertaking. The finest convent in the Holy Land, that at Nazareth, was erected by her orders, and is thus described: "The church of this convent is very large and handsome: there is a grotto under it, to which visitors descend by a handsome marble staircase: it was there, they say, that the angel Gabriel appeared to the Virgin. The natural ceiling of the grotto is left; but a very handsome altar of sculptured marble is built in it; and there are still seen two columns of granite, placed, it is said, by Helena, to mark the spot; of one of which the lower part is broken off, so that it is upheld by, and hangs from, the stone roof, which is here looked on as miraculous. Out of the grotto, a short passage leads into a small cave, said to have been the kitchen of the Virgin."[1]

Of the convent of St. Catharine, at Bethlehem, Dr. Wittman writes:—"As we approached the convent, in which we were received with great hospitality, we passed beneath the ruins of an ancient gateway, and afterwards entered a lofty building, erected by St. Helena, anciently styled the Temple, but now the Convent of St. Catharine. It is ornamented with at least fifty lofty and beautiful columns of marble, of the Corinthian order, and has on its walls the remains of several fine paintings in fresco of Scriptural subjects, representing the apostles, patriarchs, &c. The beauty and symmetry of the Temple have been in some measure destroyed, by a portion of it, which they have converted into a chapel, having been divided off by the Greeks, who received permission from the Turks to do so, on their consenting to pay an annual contribution."

"Ramla," says the same traveller, "the ancient Arimathea, was the seat of government in the theocratic days of Israel; here Samuel judged the people, and here the elders of the Hebrews assembled to demand a king to rule over them." Here St. Helena, having gathered the bones of the martyrs out of the marshes, and placed them in coffins, built over them a church called the Church of the Forty Martyrs. Light, who visited the subterraneous Church of the Holy Martyrs, says, "the ruin may be dated from the time of the Crusades. Close to this there is a large reservoir, which is ascribed to St. Helena, the roof being supported by arches and pillars of the Gothic or Saracenic architecture, the length being not less than one hundred feet, and the breadth forty."

Among other foundations ascribed to Helena, are the Convent of St. Tecla, in the island of Cyprus, and the Convent of Santa Croce, built on the summit of the ancient Mount Olympus: the latter is said to have been small, but built with great solidity.[2]

---

[1] Turner's Tour.

[2] Mr. Turner says: Under it are subterraneous chambers, of which three have been opened, and found to contain rich priestly habits; of these the Turks took possession; there remains a fourth unopened, of which the priests conceal their knowledge till they shall find an opportunity of opening it unknown to their tyrants. The door of the convent is guarded by a portcullis; the church is small and mean. I found it full of about one hundred and fifty Greek peasants, who were bowing and praying to a cloth, on which was embroidered a cross."

When the idea of searching for the cross first inspired the Empress, she is said to have exclaimed, "I behold Calvary, I behold the field of battle—but where are the spoils and the trophies? I seek the standard of salvation without its being displayed to my view! I am elevated on a throne, and the cross of my Saviour lies buried under a dunghill! I see myself amidst a superb court, and the triumph of the Son of God is buried in ruins! How can I believe that I have been redeemed, if I do not behold the victory of my Redeemer?"[1] Her glorious enterprise was indeed achieved, and when the precious relic of the Divine nature upon earth was presented to her enraptured view, she worshipped, not indeed the senseless wood, but Him who had suffered upon it. Yet this very circumstance led to a result on which the pious Empress had not counted—no other than the worship of relics—a superstitious observance which has continued ever since to prevail wherever the Romish faith has prevailed. The first originator, then, of the material worship which so essentially characterises the Roman Catholic, in contradistinction to the real Christian or Protestant faith, was the unconscious mother of Constantine. Before her time, no cross was ever venerated by the followers of our Lord, nor were material objects combined with the principles of the Christian faith. The apostles, the primitive fathers of the Church, the martyrs of Dioclesian, had alone the true God before their eyes; but now a new object of interest arose, and a new tradition attached importance, solemnity, and honour, to places and things; to the former, as the abodes of our Lord on earth, to the latter as relics rendered sacred by His touch.

The portion of the cross, forwarded to Rome, was divided into portions, each of which was destined to form the foundation for some new edifice, dedicated to Christianity. Over these sacred relics was built, amongst others, the magnificent edifice of St. Peter at Rome. The possession of a portion of the Holy Cross was esteemed in itself sufficient to render any spot sacred and hallowed. Spires and domes arose in countless numbers to testify the fact. Other relics besides were found to be peculiarly sacred; the garments of the apostles, the bones of departed saints, began to acquire value in the Christian mind. The belief which could not attain by faith to a spiritual knowledge of the facts of the redemption, was forward in recognising and receiving objects known and attested by their connexion with the Divinity and His followers.[2]

To the great influence of Helena was also to be attributed the removal by Constantine of the court from Rome to Byzantium, where the Emperor founded for himself a new capital, which, from his own name, derived that of Constantinopolis, or "the city of Constantine." The more

[1] Ambrose, Theodoret.

[2] An order of the Cross (or Croisade), consisting of ladies only, was instituted in 1668 by the Empress Eleanora de Gonzagua, a namesake of the mother of Constantine, and wife of the Emperor Leopold, on the occasion of the miraculous recovery of a little golden cross, wherein were enclosed two pieces of the true cross, out of the ashes of part of the palace: though the fire had burnt the case wherein it was enclosed, and melted the crystal, the wood had remained untouched by the devouring element! —*Ency. Brit.*

immediate vicinity of this city to the localities which the Empress-Mother desired to adorn with edifices for Christian worship, was the main object in her view, and the Emperor seconded the design, under the impression that they might by fixing their residence there, more easily direct the persons employed to carry out their mutual enterprise. In the end, however, the removal of the court to so distant a spot produced the ruin of the Roman Empire, by diverting the strength of the heart of the government to so remote a portion. It is singular enough that the renowned city of Constantinople, first chiefly re-edified and ennobled by Constantine, son of Helena, should at last have been lost, and bereft of all Christian religion, by an Emperor called Constantine, whose mother also bore the name of Helena, A. D. 1460.[1]

The mother of Constantine the Great visited Constantinople the same year that the cross was discovered, A. D. 326. In that new capital of the world the Empress "founded temples exceeding in splendour, if not in beauty, the antique monuments of pagan worship, and strangely contrasting with the chill catacombs and subterraneous crypts of the early congregations of Christians. The first church raised by Constantine, under the influence of Helena, was dedicated to the Divine Wisdom, clothed in a female form, under the invocation of St. Sophia. Even the foundation of the imperial city itself was ascribed to the inspiration of the Virgin Mary, who was chosen its tutelary guardian."[2]

Among other decorations of the Forum itself, there were, according to Suidas, "two columns of Helena and Constantine, with a cross between them, having the inscription 'Unus Sanctus,' 'there is One Holy.'"

The fame of Christianity spread far and wide, amidst all the external honors paid to the faith; and as Helena, with her splendid train of Roman and British followers, progressed through the East from place to place, great multitudes of converts, amongst whom were illustrious Indians, Iberians and Armenians, and many others of a meaner sort, received the baptismal rite, and swelled the imperial train.[3]

During the period that Constantinople was re-edified, Constantine resided at Nicomedia, surnamed "The Beautiful," the capital city of Bithynia, which, for greatness and magnificence, has been compared to Rome, Antioch, and Alexandria.[4] Thither Helena repaired, to join her son, as soon as she had accomplished her designs in the East, carrying with her the precious testimonials of her pious search. On arriving, she related to the Emperor how she had discovered the holy cross, and by what prodigy it had been distinguished from those found with it, and also the superscription which had been separated from the cross. The Emperor was deeply affected, and still more so when his mother presented to him some of the sacred nails used by the Jews in the crucifixion of

[1] Stowe. "In 1472, on the 27th of May, when Mahomet II., Prince of the Turks, took Constantinople, he beheaded the Christian Emperor, Constantine, and, putting his head on the top of a lance, caused it to be borne with derision through the Turkish camp. At the taking of the city there was also a horrible tempest of thunder and lightning, which buried about eight hundred houses."

[2] Lady Morgan [3] Suidas. [4] Lemprière.

our Lord.[1] For scarcely had that precious cross, which Helena prized more than all the riches of the Roman Empire, at length been placed in her possession, than she remembered that she had not the nails, and had accordingly sent to desire Judas to search for them likewise. He obeyed the order, and after having dug in the earth for some time, is said to have found them shining as gold, and to have borne them to the Empress, who, on beholding them, worshipped them with great reverence. One of these nails she put into a bridle for the horse her son rode upon,[2] and another she reserved for the helmet he was accustomed to wear in battle;[3] for both her affection and piety united in the hope that these sacred relics would preserve her beloved Constantine uninjured from his foes.[4]

The iron rim, which formerly adorned the helmet of the Roman Emperor, and was made from one of the nails used in the crucifixion, is still in existence. It is about three-eighths of an inch broad, and a tenth of an inch thick, and constitutes the most important part of the famous iron crown of Lombardy, with which the Emperor Napoleon Buonaparte in modern times caused himself to be invested at his coronation; being attached to the inside of it all round. Upwards of 1500 years have passed away since this crown was presented to Constantine by his mother, and, says an intelligent writer, "there is not a speck of rust upon it; which I was desired to notice as a permanent miracle, by the chanoine who called my attention to that fact. The crown itself consists of a broad circle of gold, set with large rubies, emeralds, and sapphires, and is kept in the Cathedral of Monza, over an altar, closely shut up within folding doors of gilt brass. This exhibition is attended with some ceremony, and the cross is not usually taken down from its elevated position to gratify curiosity by a nearer view; but we were more fortunate. The crown is kept in an octagonal aperture in the centre of the cross; it is composed of six equal pieces of beaten gold, joined together by close hinges; and the jewels of embossed gold ornaments are set in a ground of blue and gold enamel; which, to me, was interesting, as it exhibited an exact resemblance to the workmanship of the enamelled part of a gold ornament now in the Ashmolean Museum, which once belonged to King Alfred, and is the most curious piece of antiquity in that museum."

Constantine the Great, at the beginning of his reign, wore the simple laurel and radiant crowns used by his predecessors in the Empire, but was the first Roman Emperor who made use of the diadem of pearls and rich stones; and the fashion, not only of the crown, but of the coronation of Constantine, was afterwards followed by the rest of the monarchs of Europe.[5]

St. Gregory of Tours assures us that the third of these sacred nails

---

[1] Platina's Lives of the Popes.

[2] One of the nails Constantine made into a horse's bit, which he used in battle.—*Platina.*

[3] St. Ambrose. Caxton's Golden Legend.

[4] Burton's Rome

[5] Selden's Titles of Honour.

was thrown into the Adriatic by the Empress herself,[1] during a storm (perhaps on her homeward passage, as we are told she conveyed the holy treasure herself to her son), in consequence of which the sailors entered on that sea, as sanctified, with fastings, prayers and singing hymns, even to his own day.[2]

Two more of the precious nails are noticed by a modern writer, of which one was to be found in the Treasury of St. Mark at Venice, and the other in the church of the Benedictine Monastery at Catania: the latter, by its miraculous powers, prevented the destruction of that edifice in the overwhelming eruption of Ætna in the year 1669, when the lava flowed all round the monastery, and left it standing amidst liquid fire unhurt!

Amongst the bridal offerings presented by Hugh the Great, son of the King of France, to Athelstan, the English monarch, on the occasion of his soliciting the hand of the Princess Edilda, daughter of Edward the Elder, for his wife, was the sword of Constantine the Great, whose name, as that of its former possessor, was inscribed upon it in letters of gold; and upon its pommel, rising up above the rich plates of gold, was to be seen one of the four nails of the crucifixion. That one of the nails did fall into the hands of the French King, is a fact recorded by Burton;[3] and we are told that when Hugh presented this famous sword to King Athelstan, it was accompanied by other sacred relics—a portion of the true cross enclosed in crystal, and a fragment of the crown of thorns; which last precious memorials were presented by the English monarch to the Abbey of Malmesbury.

Helena, having first built a church upon the ground where the cross was found, *returned* and brought the nails with which our Saviour's body was fastened, as a present to her son.[4]

The cross which Helena conveyed to Rome on her return, was placed in a silver case set with gold and precious stones,[5] and was deposited in the Sessorian Church,[6] or rather in the edifice sometimes so called, because it stood upon the site, or to speak more properly, near a great building named Il Sessorio, the Temple of Venus and Cupid. This pagan edifice was destroyed by the pious Constantine on the occasion of his founding the Church of Santa Croce, and the remains of the structure are yet visible as you enter the vineyard near the church. Santa Croce is one of the seven principal churches of Rome, and situated within the walls of the city, upon the top of Mount Esquiline.[7] At the time it was built by Constantine, that part of Rome was much more inhabited than in the present day, as is evident from the adjacent ruins. "It now stands quite alone, with no buildings near it, amidst groves, gardens and vineyards; and the number of mouldering ornaments and tottering arches that surround it, give it a solemn and affecting appearance. It is remarkable for the antiquity of its shape."[8]

This church, built by Constantine at the express request of Helena,

---

[1] Or her son,—Platina, from Ambrose.

[2] Butler, Platina.

[3] Antiquities of Rome.

Platina's Lives of the Popes.

[5] Ibid.

[6] Ibid.

Burton, Roman Itinerary.

[8] Burton.

derived its name of "Santa Croce" from the circumstance of the Empress herself depositing in it some pieces of the holy cross and a part of the earth taken from Mount Calvary; some of the latter was placed under the church, and the rest over the roof.[1] Here also were deposited two of the thorns, one of the thirty pieces of silver, a part of the cross of the *Good Thief*, one of the nails used at the crucifixion, and the superscription on the cross in Hebrew, Greek and Latin; the latter, which was in red letters and much damaged, was as follows:—

"HIESVS NAZARENVS REX IVDAEOR."

This last relic was discovered in A. D. 1492, during the Pontificate of Innocent VIII, in a little leaden chest, where it had been concealed above one thousand years.

Without more minutely describing the interior of this beautiful church, suffice it to say, that by a door or gate you descend to the Chapel of St. Helena, into which no female is permitted to enter except on the 20th of March, which is the anniversary festival of the consecration of the church, and then no men are admitted. The ceremony of the consecration of Santa Croce was performed by Pope Sylvester.[2]

Constantine erected many other churches:[3] one of these was dedicated to the two martyrs, "St. Marcellinus the Presbyter and St. Peter the Exorcist, and stood in the Via Labicana."[4] He built a church to St. Paul, and also another to St. Peter, which last stood not far from the heathen temple of Apollo, and was erected at the instigation of St. Sylvester. This famous person had been banished by the tyrants, but when Constantine favoured Christianity, he left Mount Soracte, whither he had retired, and came to Rome, where he obtained great influence with Con-

[1] Keysler, Eustace, Burton.

[2] It was in the year 1601, when Rubens was staying at Rome, that he executed a commission he had received from the Archduke Albert to paint three pictures for the Church of Santa Croce di Gierusalemme, connected with which he had formerly borne the cardinal's hat. One of these pictures represented the *Finding of the Cross*, and the others, the Crucifixion, and the Crowning with Thorns. These pictures, which were very remarkable as specimens of the style of painting of this great master in the art at that period of his career, were brought to England in 1811, and sold the following year by auction. [Noel's Translation of the Life of Rubens.] The Crucifixion afterwards, on its way by sea to Count Woronzow, at St. Petersburgh, was unhappily lost. Rubens painted twelve pictures, representing events from the history of Constantine, formerly in the Orleans Gallery, but now scattered through different private collections in England, several of which display great beauties. "These sketches—for they are not finished pictures—were brought to England with the Flemish portion of the Orleans Gallery, in 1792. The history of this grand acquisition, the dangers encountered by the purchaser, a Mr. Slade, and the artifices to which he had recourse in their removal; the indignation and threats of the French painters, crowding round the packages, and in despair to see this rich collection carried out of their country, would form a striking chapter in the biography of pictures. The twelve sketches of the history of Constantine were valued, as a series, at £1000; but no one having come forward to purchase them, they were unfortunately, we must allow, dispersed among various purchasers, and brought double the sum."—*Mrs Jamison's Notes on the Life of Rubens.*

[3] Milner.

[4] Platina.

stantine. He was made Bishop, A. D. 314, as successor to St. Melchiades.

"The Constantinian Church," called the Lateran, was also built and richly endowed by Constantine.

These churches, like those in the East, were distinguished for their holy relics. One, that of St. Giacomo Scossa Cavalli, is said to have derived its name from the following circumstance. A cart-load of relics, among which was the stone designed for the sacrifice of Isaac, another on which Christ stood when among the doctors in the Temple, some holy earth which had been brought from Jerusalem, and even, it is said, some drops of the blood of our Saviour, were despatched from the church of Santa Croce di Gierusalemme to that of St. Peter; when stopping at this spot, neither whipping nor any other means could induce the horses to go a step further. Accordingly the occurrence was considered a divine intimation, and the whole of the relics were deposited on the spot.[1]

In the Church of St. Peter in Vinculo, at Rome, are said to be the identical chains which bound St. Peter, both at Rome and at Jerusalem: at the latter city, St. Helena found a relic of the chain by which she judged St. Peter had been fastened, and therefore determined to offer it to the Pope, who possessed another fragment. It was received by him with much pomp and solemnity, and it is said that the identity was proved by the two chains uniting of their own accord when brought in sight of each other!

Pope Julius II. (A. D. 1503–1513) pulled down half of the Old Church of St. Peter's at Rome, and laid the foundation-stone of the new edifice himself. It was built cn the plan of Michael Angelo.[2] Of the dome of this celebrated building, built under Pope Sixtus V., the following particulars are interesting, inasmuch as they commemorate our heroine, the Empress. It is said of the great artist, Michael Angelo, that having heard some one praise the Rotunda as an unparalleled work, he observed "that he would not only build a dome equally large, but build it in the air." He made good his assertion: the honour of the undertaking and design of the dome at St. Peter's is due to him. This amazing structure rests on four pillars, of ninety palmi in diameter, each of which is adorned with a white marble statue, twenty-two palmi high, without the pedestal. The first is St. Veronica, by Francesca Mochi; the second is St. Helena, by Andrea Bolgi; the third, St. Andrew, by Du Quesne; and the fourth, St. Longinus,[3] by Bernini, who also designed these orna-

[1] Keysler's Travels.

[2] Roscoe's Leo the Tenth.

[3] The sacred lance, which pierced our Saviour's side, was formerly preserved with the statue of Longinus, but it is now kept in the general repository for relics over the figure of St. Veronica. It is said that St. Helena discovered the iron of the lance. It was subsequently divided into two parts: the point was kept in the imperial palace at Constantinople, the other division in the Church of St. John of the Rock. It seems to be uncertain whether the division was made by Constantine II., who wished to give the point to Charlemagne; or whether Baldwin, while he was King of Constantinople, pawned it to the Venetians, from whom it was recovered by St. Louis, King of France. However, in 1492, Bajazet II., Sultan of Constantinople, sent the part which did not contain the point, as a present to Innocent VIII.; a bribe to induce him not to protect his brother Zezim, who dis-

ments.[1] Over each of these four statues is a fine tribune, or gallery, from whence, several times in the year, the relics, which are kept in a particular chapel, are exposed to public view.

In the vaults under the pedestals of each of the four statues an altar is erected, on which the history of the saint whose statue stands over it is represented in mosaic-work, by Fabio Christofore, from the designs of the famous Andrea Sacchi. Under these four altars are steps leading down to the other subterraneous vaults, which are full of excellent mosaic, that being the only work which could be proof against the dampness of the place. This mosaic-work was formerly the pavement of the whole Church of St. Peter.[2]

It has been objected that two out of the four principal niches in this church, those which are formed in the vast piles that support the dome, and which of course face the altar, should be appropriated by saints whose very names exist only in a legendary tale, viz., Saints Veronica and Longinus, while a third is devoted to St. Helena, whose statue, though she was a princess of great virtue and eminent piety, might stand with more propriety in the porch near the statue of her son; for in the early ages of Christianity the honour of being deposited within the church was reserved to martyrs, and Constantine had merely requested to be allowed to lie in the porch of the Basilica of the Apostles, which he had himself erected in Constantinople. On this account it is thought that the statues of apostles, the principal martyrs, doctors and bishops, should alone have been admitted into St. Peter's Church. Eustace remarks that

puted the throne. The Pope sent a solemn embassy to receive it, and for a long time it was preserved in the Vatican. In 1500 it was placed in a magnificent chapel, where was the statue of Longinus; but when this chapel was destroyed by Julius II. it was removed to the case of St. Veronica, where it has remained ever since. Benedict XIV., in one of his works, assures us, that while he was canon of this Basilica, he had the exact measure of the point sent him from the Chapel Royal at Paris; and that, after comparing the two together, they corresponded so exactly that no manner of doubt could remain as to the identity of the two relics. These relics were exhibited on Good Friday and other days. No one is allowed to visit the place where they are kept, unless he has the rank of a canon. And those sovereigns or illustrious persons who have sought this privilege have first the honorary dignity of canon conferred upon them. — Burton's Antiquities of Rome.

[1] Bernini, by the niches he made in the pillars for the above-mentioned four statues, and especially by the stairs along the foundations of the pillars, for going down into the vaults, or *Sacra Grotte*, was censured for having weakened the foundations to a great degree, and soon after a cleft discovered itself in the cupola, occasioned by a violent clap of thunder. Bernini was near losing his head for this unlucky accident, but saved it by his success in removing and erecting the obelisk in the Piazza Navona. Michael Angelo, the designer of this dome, was apprehensive of such an accident; and earnestly desired that these four pillars, with their foundations, should not be in the least altered or meddled with. In the year 1700 this cleft in the cupola was widened by an earthquake. [Keysler's Travels.] The four supports of the dome of St. Peter's Church are about 240 feet in circumference, and 178 in height. Each of the four has two niches in front, one above the other. In the lower ones are statues of saints, and some of the most precious relics are preserved in them. St. Veronica has her veil or sudarium, St. Helena has part of the true cross.—*Burton.*

[2] Keysler.

"the pictures, or rather the mosaics which have been substituted in the place of the original pictures, may be objected to on the same ground as the statues, as many of them represent persons and events totally unconnected with the sacred records, and sometimes not to be met with even in the annals of authentic history." The candid and judicious Erasmus would have the subjects of all the pictures exhibited in churches taken exclusively from the Holy Scriptures, while the histories of saints, when authentic, he thinks might furnish decorations for porticos, halls, and cloisters; had this advice been followed, many useless, some absurd, and a few profane representations might have been banished from the sacred place.

Shortly after her return from Palestine, Helena was taken ill. "The Empress, perceiving her last hour approach, gave her son excellent instructions concerning the government of his empire, and the manner in which he should regulate his own affairs and those of his family, both temporal and eternal. She commended to his care the legacies which she had made to virgins, and to the Church, as well as certain institutions for poor persons and widows, and the rewards which she was desirous of making her servants and the army, in proportion to their merits and the time they had been in her service. As for the territories she possessed in the Eastern and Western Empire, she bestowed them all on the young Cæsar, the child of Constantine, who himself remained seated near her, kissing her hands, and bathing them with his tears. She was more afflicted with the sorrowful necessity of quitting him, than with the approach of death; and, collecting all her remaining strength, she gave him final advice, worthy of a mother and of a Christian princess. When she had communicated all her wishes for his august family and for the empire, she spoke no more, except to supplicate mercy from God: at length, in the midst of the consolations of her faith, full of hope and merit, she departed, to receive in heaven a crown more glorious than that of which death had deprived her." [1]

The spot where Helena expired was, according to some writers, Nicomedia, by other accounts Constantinople, and some fix it at Rome. There is no division as to the day of her death, which is admitted to have been August 18th; but there is a difference of opinion as to the date, some thinking she died in the same year the cross was discovered, others making it one year or two years later. Thus, A. D. 326 is given by some as the date, A. D. 327 by others, and A. D. 328 by the rest.

If in 326 this event is fixed, it was the eightieth year of the Empress' age, and the twentieth of her son Constantine's reign.

"Constantine, anxious to pay to the last mortal remains of his mother, that respect which he had never refused her during her life,[2] caused the mournful ceremony of her funeral to be performed with extraordinary pomp and magnificence. By his orders, a porphyry vase, said to be the

---

[1] Butler.

[2] Constantine paid to his dying mother, "as he had always done, every duty of filial piety. His tenderness and respect for so worthy a mother, is one of the finest traits of this prince's life."—*Crevier.*

largest and richest in the world, was made, to contain, not only the ashes, but the whole body of this princess. This vase or urn consisted of one entire piece of porphyry, and the carvings upon it represented a lion and horsemen, with various other figures in bas-relief, without any heathenish emblems, these ornaments being in a middle taste of architecture, resembling those on the triumphal arch of her son Constantine. According to Crevier, the body of St. Helena, having been enclosed in this splendid urn, was conveyed by Constantine's directions to Rome, to be deposited in the tomb of the Emperors, within the walls of the city, and magnificent fêtes were held in Rome for the space of three months upon this mournful occasion. Constantine, afterwards thinking that a monument to her own memory alone would be more worthy of this excellent parent, erected a round building outside the city, to receive her honoured remains. This splendid mausoleum was situated near the road to Palestrina, on the Via Lavicana, about three miles from Rome.

According to Nicephorus and others, Helena's body was removed, two years after, from this mausoleum to Constantinople, and buried there; and Constantine, afterwards dying in Nicomedia, was interred with her. In the pretty Church of the Panthenorator, at Constantinople, may be seen the tombs of Constantine and St. Helena, each raised about eight feet high on a column, the summit terminating in a point cut into four sides, in the fashion of a diamond. "While Constantinople was in the power of the Venetians, they took the body of St. Helena from its tomb, and carried it to Venice, where it is now preserved entire. They attempted the same thing with the body of Constantine, but did not succeed: the two tombs are of red jasper, and to this day two broken parts are to be seen on that of Constantine, where they made the attempt."[1]

As, however, Nicephorus did not live till the fourteenth century, later historians have preferred believing the Torre Pignattara, at Rome, to be the tomb of this famous Empress;[2] and Bower, in his History of the Popes, tells us that this costly sepulchre, made by Constantine, had been plundered by thieves in the time of Innocent II. (A. D. 1143), and the body carried off by them from its tomb. An earlier account places the removal of Helena's body from Rome in 849: yet are the remains of the Empress even to this day worshipped in the Church of the Franciscans at Rome, called Ara Cœli, where they are said to repose in a rich shrine of porphyry, under the high altar, as related by several authors,[3] though no record exists of the truth of this assertion. Pope Anastasius IV. found the porphyry sarcophagus,[4] said to have contained Helena's remains, and "which, being dug up under Torre Pignattara, was damaged in several places. The Pope removed it to the Lateran Church, intending it for his own tomb, for he was a regular canon of that church. At his death, Anastasius was buried in the Lateran, in this tomb of porphyry: another account says, the Pope was disappointed of his intention, and that it has remained empty ever since. The ruins of the vast mausoleum of St.

[1] Travels of La Broquière, translated by Johnnes.

[2] Burton's Rome: Keysler.

[3] Keysler, Butler.

[4] Bower's Hist. of the Popes.

Helena were cleared by Pope Urban VIII. (1644), the structure having been much damaged by the barbarians. This Pope, desirous to preserve the memory of Helena, caused a chapel to be erected there, which he consigned to the protection of St. John de Lateran. From the Church of San Giovanni Laterano, the splendid urn is said to have been removed to its present resting-place, the Vatican Museum, by Pope Pius VI.: it rests there in the Sala a Croce Greca, with the Sarcophagus of St. Constantia, the daughter of her rival Theodora, the second wife of Constantius.[1]

In the year 1095, Notkar, Abbot of Hautvilliers, in the diocese of Rheims, wrote a history of the translation of the relics of St. Helena from Rome to that abbey, which was performed in 849, previous to the spoliation of her sepulchre by thieves. That author gives an authentic account of several miracles, wrought through the intercession of the saint, of some of which he testifies himself to have been an eye-witness, and the rest he learnt from the persons on whom they had been performed.[2] Part of this work, which Mr. Butler assures us is well written, was published by the Messieurs de Ste. Marthe and by Mabillon, and almost the whole is inserted by the Bollandists in their great work. The entire MS. copy is preserved at Hautvilliers, with an appendix, written by the same author, containing an account of two other miracles performed by the relics of this saint.

"In 1095,[3] Stephen of Blois and Adela, daughter of King William the Conqueror, with several members of the noble House of Blois, attended the religious festival of the removal of St. Helena's honoured remains to a place which had been prepared for them in the neighbourhood of Hautvilliers. The ceremony took place, October 28th, 1095, on the festival of St. Simon and St. Jude. Notkar, Abbot of Hautvilliers, who presided on this occasion, and was the original suggester of that posthumous honour to the sainted Empress, thus describes the pageant: "At last the long-desired day arrived, and fell on a Sunday; all the great lights of the monastic order attended, with many archbishops and bishops; and of the secular powers were present Earl Stephen and Adela, his wife, Constance, daughter of Philip, King of France, wife of Hugh, Earl of Treves, Stephen's brother, with many others, respectable in their way, whom I shall not here enumerate. Not only France, but even Lorraine, delighted to send her pious sons to the obsequies of such a queen; for how should not all Christianity applaud her to whom all are so greatly indebted! There is a certain place, in prospect of all Hautvilliers, called by the inhabitants Montescola, where, on the high brow of a hill, a promontory stretches out into a convenient flat, fit for the reception of such venerated limbs. Here a tent was erected, large enough to accommodate the Earl and Countess, with their family, and all those of the sacred

[1] The present state of Torre Pignattara, as described by a traveller of our own times, is a small church, and a still smaller dwelling for the priest who has the care of the church, both being enclosed in a round circular brick wall of very bad architecture.

[2] Butler.

[3] Ibid.

order. A consultation was then held as to what hour of the day the ceremony should take place, and we agreed that it should be after the mystery of the Holy Resurrection had been celebrated by Hugh, Bishop of Soissons; this being over, brethren of proper gravity were selected, who carried the relics of so glorious dust to the appointed place of interment, where the golden urn was opened, and enclosed with the bones was found this writing: 'Corpus Sanctæ Helenæ Reginæ, matris Constantini, sine capite. The body of St. Helena the Queen, the mother of Constantine, saving the head.' The sacred pledges were then deposited in another vase and re-interred, &c." The noblest person there present, Earl Stephen, who as highest in rank, was appointed to present the offering at the tomb; and he still further gratified the monks of Hautvilliers, by granting them some valuable privileges and immunities. Many miracles were said to be afterwards wrought at this tomb, which became no small source of gain to the Monastery of Hautvilliers.[1]

After the death of Helena,[2] Constantine showed a particular kindness to Constantia, the daughter of Theodora. This princess, after the deaths of her husband and son, accepted an invitation to her brother's court, where she had first shared in the influence of Helena over the Emperor, and subsequently, during the absence of the Empress-Mother in the East, had filled her place near his person. After death had deprived Constantine of his much-cherished parent, Constantia acquired an entire ascendency over her brother. Constantine also raised the brothers of Constantia, and their children, in dignity at this period; and the event proved how much more advantageous had been the previous severity of Helena, even to the princes themselves, than the indulgence of the Emperor; for by raising them, he gave umbrage to his own sons, who were no sooner in possession of the kingdom by his death, than they ruthlessly massacred their uncles and cousins.[3]

The Arians of this period owed their protection to Constantia's influence with the Emperor, which she exerted as much as possible to ameliorate their sufferings. Arius, the founder of the sect had been excommunicated, and forbidden to enter Alexandria. The Princess afterwards was instrumental in procuring his recall, through the instrumentality of one of his followers, a priest, supposed to have been Acacius, who succeeded Eusebius of Cæsarea. This personage insinuated himself into the Princess' confidence, and at length succeeded in making her believe that the disgrace of Arius had been brought about by his bishop's malice, through envy at the esteem in which he was held by the people, and that he was not tainted with the belief for which he had been condemned by the Council of Nice. Constantia adopted his views very forcibly, but dared not address Constantine on the subject. At last being seized with a severe illness, in which she feared her death approaching, she desired

[1] Lives of the Princesses of England, by Mary Anne Everett Green.

[2] "After Helena's death, Constantine erected to her honoured memory, in the middle of a great square in Constantinople, her own statue and his, with a large *cross in the middle.* He likewise erected her statue at Daphne, near Antioch, and several other places in Italy."—*Butler.*

[3] Crevier.

the Emperor, as her last request, to admit the priest to his favour, whom she had honoured with her own friendship, and listen to his conversation in matters of religion; adding, that she feared his government would receive a fatal shock from the persecution and banishment of innocent people. Constantine, who was tenderly attached to his sister, promised to attend to her request, and admitted the priest from that time into his confidence; who so effectually worked upon the Emperor's mind, that he secured the recall of Arius from exile; who, after making a written declaration of his faith, conformable to the doctrines laid down in the Council of Nice, and swearing it to be his true belief, was again received by Constantine into the Christian Church.[1]

The Church of St. Constantia at Rome is situated near that of St. Agnes (without the Porta Pia, or Nomentana): it was formerly the Mausoleum of the Princess Constantia, and at a period still earlier than that, a temple of Bacchus. "The tomb of this British princess, or rather the temple in which she was interred, is of circular form, supported by a row of coupled columns, and crowned with a dome. Behind the pillars runs a gallery, the vaulted roof of which is encrusted with ancient mosaics, representing little genii playing with clusters of grapes, amidst the winding tendrils of the vine. The tomb of the saint, a vast porphyry vase, ornamented with various figures, once stood in a large niche, directly opposite the door; but as the body had been deposited many years ago under the altar, the sarcophagus was transported to the Museum of the Vatican. The *Sala a Croce Greca*, in the Vatican, containing the above relic of antiquity, is supported by columns, and paved with ancient mosaic: it is furnished with statues, and lined with bassi-relievi.

"Both the removal of the sarcophagus and the placing the body of the Princess as a saint under the altar of the mausoleum, then converted into a church, were performed by orders of Pope Alexander the Fourth.

"The sarcophagus of St. Constantia, formed with its lid of one block of red porphyry, is beautifully ornamented in basso-relievo, with little infant Cupids employed in the vintage, and bordered with tendrils and arabasques,—an appropriate device for the locality to which the last remains of Constantia were consigned by her brother,—the Temple of Bacchus, and where for ages they remained undisturbed."[2]

St. Helena[3] was canonized for the great act of bringing the true cross from Jerusalem to Italy.

> "Herself in person went to seek that sacred cross,
> Whereon our Saviour died; which found, as it was sought,
> From Salem unto Rome triumphantly she brought."
>
> *Drayton's Poly Olbion.*

The feast of the Exaltation of the Holy Cross was celebrated by the

[1] History of the Arians. [2] Eustace's Tour.

[3] The Greeks venerate Constantine and Helena together on the 21st of May. In the old style Holy Rood Day was celebrated on the 26th of September. The day of the death of the Empress has received the name of St. Helen's Day. The Church of Rome has ranked this pious princess among her saints, and celebrates her festival by an express service.

Roman Church[1] on the 14th of September, and also at Jerusalem by the Greeks and Latins as early as the year 335. The first occasion of this festival was the miraculous appearance of the cross to Constantine, and the subsequent discovery of that sacred wood by the Empress-Mother, St. Helena.[2] The 14th of September is called Holyrood Day. In former times every church had its rood-loft, which was a gallery across the nave, at the entrance of the chancel of the church, on which the holy rood or cross, when perfectly made, had the image of our Saviour extended with that of the Virgin Mary and St. John on each side. This representation alluded to a passage in St. John (chapter xix. v. 26), Christ on the Cross saw his mother and the disciple whom he loved standing by. This was called the rood, and it was placed over the screen which divided the nave from the chancel of our churches, and conveyed to our ancestors a full type of the Christian Church. The Church militant was represented by the nave, the Church triumphant by the chancel, intimating that all who would go from the one to the other, must pass under the rood, or in other words, carry the cross and suffer affliction. Instances of the rood may be seen in Norwich and Winchester Cathedrals.

That in Norwich Cathedral was erected by Bishop Hart. It is at present the organ loft, on which was erected the principal rood or cross: beneath it was situated Holyrood Chapel, in which Jesus' mass was sung once every week.

To the Chapel of the Sepulchre, in Winchester Cathedral, which is a dark chapel below the organ stairs, there used formerly to be great resort in Holy Week, to witness the Mass of the Passion of our Saviour, as yet celebrated in the Roman churches on the Continent. On the walls of this chapel are discovered rude paintings of the taking down from the cross, the lying in the sepulchre, the descent into limbus, and the appearance of our Lord to Mary Magdalen, from whose lips the word "Rabboni" is seen to proceed, with kindred subjects.

Since the 8th century the festival of the Exaltation of the Holy Cross has been removed by the Latin church to the 3d of May, which is called Holy Cross Day, or the Day of the Invention of the Cross; it being

[1] In the year 642, Heraclitus restored to Mount Calvary the true cross, which had been carried off, fourteen years before, by Cosroes, King of Persia, upon his taking Jerusalem from the Emperor Phocas; in memory of this event the festival of the Exaltation of the Cross was afterwards held on the 14th of September.—*Ency. Brit.*

[2] The ecclesiastical emblems with which St. Helena is represented are these; she is crowned, with a large cross in her arms, of a tall stature, and she is also occasionally depicted with a *beard*, and *tied to the cross*. S. Borgia de Cruce Veliternâ, c. 27, &c. At the foot of the Velitern Cross, beneath the figure of our Lord, is a circular compartment, with a half-figure of a woman, having a nimbus round the head, the hair curled, and adorned with a band, as if of pearls, and in a rich jewelled dress. This may be conjectured to be the Empress Helena, to whom was granted the favour of finding the true cross, and who is represented in several ancient crosses. On the reverse side, in the centre compartment, is an Agnus Dei, enamelled upon a field of gold, without nimbus or banner, which are usually found in this emblem of the Lamb which is so frequent in early Christian art. In the oldest examples, as in this, the colour of the cross is red.—*Pugin's Glossary of Ecclesiastical Architecture.*

supposed that the event took place about the month of May, or early in the spring of the year 326.[1]

One of the earliest Christian writers has composed two hymns for the occasions of Holy Cross Day and Holy Rood Day, and they may be found in the Roman breviary. One of these alludes to the passion flower, which has obtained the name of the Holyrood flower, not only because it flowers at this period of the year, but because the leaves, tendrils, and different parts of the flower, have been supposed, by the religious, to represent the instruments of our blessed Saviour's passion; whence the name Passi Flora, and the great veneration in which it is held in some foreign countries: the five stamens have been compared to the five wounds of Christ, the three styles to the nails by which he was fixed to the cross, the column which elevates the germs to the cross itself or to the pillar to which he was bound, and the rays of the nectary to the crown of thorns.[2] The common passion flower, which lasts a long while in blossom, generally goes out of flower after Holyrood.

In the primitive ages of Christianity, before churches for divine worship were common, service was often performed under a cross raised in some convenient place. Such was St. Paul's Cross in London, where the practice continued until the Reformation. Such was also the antique cross in the Market-place of Halifax, Yorkshire. The cross being a sign used in civil contracts, it became usual to touch or swear by it before reading and writing in transactions relative to public and private business, and crosses were erected in the open places of towns and cities, where even to this day fairs, marts, statutes, and markets are held.[3] Sermons were preached at these spots, and public pageants or processions usually commenced from them or terminated there: hence Edward I. erected crosses at every place where the corpse of Queen Eleanor rested on its way to interment, desiring those spots to be considered holy. Every churchyard in early times had its cross, on which the bodies of the dead were placed while the service was read; every turning in the road had also its cross, and the boundaries of parishes had the same marks.[4]

At Leighton Buzzard, in Bedfordshire, is a relic of considerable antiquity, in the form of a Gothic cross of stone, beautiful even in decay; it stands in the open area of the Market-place, and is supposed to have withstood the operations of time for more than 500 years, but by whom or on what occasion it was erected, even tradition does not attempt to reveal; its form is pentagonal, in height thirty-eight feet: the upper story is divided into five niches, each containing a statue; the first is in an episcopal habit, the second represents the Virgin and Jesus, the third appears to be designed for St. John the Evangelist, the others are too mutilated to be defined.

In the centre of the square at Halifax, a little higher in the street than the cross, stood a Maypole used by the Romans in their celebrated festival called Floralia, which usually commenced on the 4th of the Calends of May. The feasts held at that time were called Maxima, and were kept by costly banquets and oblations. Constantine the Great forbade these entertain-

[1] Butler, Burton. [2] Hortus Anglicus.
[3] Green's Hist. of Worcester. [4] Clavis Calendaria.

ments, but they were renewed by Honorius and Arcadius in the first year of their empire, and in Britain, under other forms, have descended to our own times.

Nothing can exceed the affection the Britons testified for the memory of their excellent Empress, St. Helena. To this patroness of churches innumerable sacred edifices have been dedicated throughout our island; to enumerate the whole of them would be impossible. Far and wide, edifices, crosses, roads, and other monuments, have been raised to perpetuate her goodness.

In Colchester, the native place of St. Helena, most things have reference to her and to her finding the cross; the streets in particular exemplify this, the main street representing the shaft or body of the cross, and Head Street and North Hill the transverse part of the same.[1] In the parish of St. Nicholas, in that city, there is a cave bearing this princess' name; and the chapel, a place of great antiquity, is said to have been founded by the Empress herself. Just within the entrance of Colchester Castle are also exhibited some clumsy images of Helena and Constantine, carved in stone, but manifestly of modern date. A curious testimonial to the Empress exists in King Henry the Fifth's Charter to the City of Colchester, the initial letter of which represents St. Helena before the cross finely illuminated.[2]

In London, where Helena held her court alternately with Colchester, a religious edifice, to the east of Crosby Square, was founded by William Fitzwilliam, in commemoration of the discovery of the cross by St. Helena. It is said to have been built A. D. 1210, and was called "the Priory of St. Helen's the Less." The Church of St. Helen's the Great stands north-east of Threadneedle Street.

In Yorkshire[3] abundant traces exist of St. Helena; in York four churches bear her much-loved name: attached to one, an ancient edifice in the parish of Leeds, was a medicinal well, yet in existence. There was also Burgh Wallis, near Doncaster, St. Helen's Foord, at Wetherby, and St. Ellen's Chapel, at Wilton, which last was founded by Sir William Bulmer in the reign of Henry the Eighth; one in Werkdyke, another at Kilusea, in the Holderness wapentake, with the churches of Skipwith, Stillingfleet, Thoranby, in the Ouse and Derwent wapentake. In Cornwall there is a church dedicated to St. Helen, and the Church of Elstow or Helenstowe in Bedford, since turned into a monastery, is also named as having this Queen for its patron saint.

There are churches dedicated to St. Helena at Derby, Warrington, East Medina in the Isle of Wight, Norwich, Worcester, and Abingdon. St. Helen's, Worcester, is one of the most ancient edifices in that city.[4] The ancient hospital of St. Helen, at Abingdon, when refounded in 1533, received the denomination of Christchurch.[5] In Monmouthshire churches exist of St. Helen's name: there is also one at Wilton, a town situated in a vale on the Humber, dedicated to her.

St. Helen's Porch is yet in existence in the mean church of St. Helen's,

[1] Morant's Hist. of Colchester. [2] Britton and Brayley.
[3] Allen's Hist. of York. [4] Green's Worcester. [5] Magna Brit.

Auckland, a village so called from the name of the Empress. In 1844, in the month of April, the tongue of the bell of St. Helen's, Auckland, dropped out, which, after having been divested of the rust which had been accumulating from time immemorial, was found to bear this inscription: "Sancta Helena, ora pro nobis," also a bishop's mitre and crest, with the initials A. and W. at right angles. Very superstitious ideas were formerly attached to bells.[1]

At the east end of the side-aisles in Durham Cathedral are gates leading into the east transept, commonly called the Nine Altars. One of these altars was dedicated to St. Aidan and St. Helena.[2]

This interesting part of Durham Cathedral is thus described:—

"In the eastern or highest part within the church were the nine altars, dedicated and erected in honour of several saints, and of them taking their names, as the inscriptions thereof will declare; the altars being placed north and south, one from another, along the front of the church, in an alley the whole breadth thereof. In the middle of which front was the Altar of the Holy Fathers, St. Cuthbert and St. Bede, having all the aforesaid altars equally divided on either hand, on the south four, and on the north four.

"On the south were the following:—

"1. The Altar of St. Oswald and St. Lawrence.

"2. The Altar of St. Thomas of Canterbury and St. Catherine.

"3. The Altar of St. John the Baptist and St. Margaret.

"4. The Altar of St. Andrew and St. Mary Magdalene, being the outermost altar towards the south.

"On the north side of St. Cuthbert and St. Bede's Altar, were these four following:—

"1. The Altar of St. Martin and St. Edmund.

"2. The Altar of St. Peter and St. Paul.

"3. The Altar of St. Aidanus and St. Helena.

"4. The Altar of the Holy Archangel, St. Michael, being the outermost towards the north.

"Over each of these altars is a window representing the history which is attached to it. On the north side, the third was the picture of St. Aidane and St. Helena, with the like windows and lights as the rest, presenting the picture of St. Aidane in his episcopal attire, with a crosier in his hand, whose soul after his death was represented to be carried to heaven in a sheet by two angels. In this were some part of the history of Christ, and the picture of a king and two other saints; as also the picture of St. Helena in a blue habit, she being a princess; which contained the story of the religious of all orders of her sex, and her resorting often to their churches, and the picture of Our Lady and the Angel Gabriel appearing to her, and the Holy Ghost overshadowing her, with the lily springing out of the lilypot; and underneath the middle stone-work were four angels. Above were four turret windows, with four apostles; and the picture of God Almighty above all, in another little window, with Christ in his arms."[3]

---

[1] Fosbrooke's British Monachism.

[2] Hutchinson's Durham.

[3] This extract is taken from the "History and Antiquities of Durham Cathe-

It would almost appear that the subject of the Conception had been expressly selected for St. Helen's window, from the fact that a slur had been thrown on her bright fame by the second marriage of her husband, and that the lily springing forth from the lilypot was an emblem of her innocence.

"A Popish chapel, dedicated to St. Helen, was in use in Queen Elizabeth's time, in Halifax in Yorkshire, near the remains of which, in the present day, is a remarkably fine well, bearing also the name of the Empress. Very near St. Helen's Well, a spot yet bears the name of Halliwell, or Holy Well Green.[1] It was common among the early Christians to dedicate remarkable springs to particular saints, to whose merits any cures they might perform were attributed. Upon the saint's day whose name the well bore, the people were wont to assemble to make their offerings or vow to her, a custom which was afterwards changed to that of adorning the well with boughs and flowers, and entertaining themselves with music, dancing, eating cakes, and drinking ale. The Chapel of St. Helen, at Halifax, is now converted into a cottage, but, it can be seen, has been a place of greater account: in one of the walls they show you a large stone, which is called the Cross," continues the historian of this place, "which is sometimes visited by strangers, who at the same time inquire for the well; and from the behaviour of some of them, the inhabitants concluded they were Papists, whose zeal brought them hither to behold this once famous place, of which their forefathers were despoiled. Clarke Bridge, Halifax, seems to have been first built by the clergy, to enable them to pass more conveniently from the church to the Holy Well on the opposite bank."

The worship of springs and fountains is of very ancient date, as appears from heathen authors and Christian monuments, and among many other British customs, was kept up by the Saxons long after their conversion to Christianity. This appears from injunctions and canons made to forbid them. In 967, it appears from some constitutions of Edgar, taken from a Saxon penitential: "We teach that priests shall abolish all heathenish superstitions, and forbid the worship of wells, and of trees, and of stones." Here an allusion is also made to the stone altars erected in the fields, of which many remains may be found. The same penitential contains a prohibition against "vowing or bringing alms or offerings to any wells, or stones, or tree, or to any creature, but only in God's name to God's church." A Saxon homily of Bishop Lupus, mentions some, who, being seduced by the devil, in their afflictions vow their alms either to well or stone; and in another, he cautions men against worshipping wells or trees. This foolish custom of worshipping and bringing

dral," to which the reader is referred for an account at length of the other eight altars.

[1] "I have the copy of a deed without date, but which, by the witnesses, must have been executed between the years 1279 and 1324, wherein William de Osete grants an assart in Linley to Henry de Sacro Fonte de Staynland, which shows that the name of the above Holy Well is no new conceit, but a real piece of antiquity, perhaps much older than the time of this deed." —*Watson's Hist. of Halifax.*

offerings to trees and fountains continued after the Conquest, as appears by a synod at London in 1102, by the constitutions of Walter, Bishop of Worcester, in 1240, and the injunctions of Oliver, Bishop of Lincoln, in 1280; which two last forbid the worshipping of Cerne and Roll's Well, St. Edward's Well, near St. Clement's at Oxford, and St. Laurence's Well, near Peterborough.[1] The superstitious veneration paid to St. Winifred's Well needs scarcely to be mentioned.[2]

After the accession of Constantine to the imperial dignity, Helena is said to have revisited her native country. It is on record, that she did so after her return from Palestine, which is unlikely at her extreme age: at an earlier date she most probably returned to Britain, either to visit her grandson Constans, or to inspect the government which Constantine had entrusted to his delegates. Kennet, in his "Parochial Antiquities," declares, that "after Helena discovered the cross, and on her return homewards, she built a castle of her own name in Silesia, and another in Spain, near Callacium, which we now call Cales; and first arriving in Ireland, which was but a short cut from Spain, and thence steering for North Wales, landed at Aber Segont, near that fair walled town which we now call Caernarvon, where Constans, her grandchild, had built a city." Within the old town there still stands a little chapel, and a delicate spring of running water close by, both bearing St. Helen's name, in memory of her landing there; and from the gates of this city is both a crossway and also a cross of stone, standing in Bivio. Between the two ways, ariseth a great causey of hard durable stone, for such is the nature of those stones that they will not wear away, the way on each side being worn out knee-deep, which the inhabitants call Sarn Elen Weddaw, *i. e.*, St. Helen the Powerful's Causeway, and runneth southward through the rocky ragged straits of the mountains, even to the south parts of the kingdom."[3]

The noted Sarn or Llwybr Helen, the Causeway or Path of Helen, which is a road through North Wales, supposed to have been made by this Queen,[4] is thus described by Pennant:—"This road is now entirely covered with turf, but by the rising of it, is in most parts very visible; beneath are the stones which form it, and it extends in all its course to the breadth of eight yards. There are tumuli near it in various places, it being very usual for the Romans to inter near their highways. Close to the part in question (where this road appears for the first time on a common) is one, in which were found five urns; the whole materials of it are composed of burnt earth and stones, with several fragments of bricks, which had been placed round the urns to keep them from being crushed."

The causeway of Helen also ran under the summit of the vast Berwyn mountains, being there an artificial road called Fordd Helen, or Helen's way,[5] and those also in Llanbadyr Odyn in Cardiganshire, and from

[1] Mag. Brit.
[2] Morant's History and Antiquities of Essex.
[3] Kennett's Parochial Antiquities.
[4] Pennant.
[5] Pennant, from the annotation on Camden.

Brecknock to Neath in Glamorganshire, passed under the name of this great Empress. Pen Caer Helen is a lofty hill, about twenty-four miles from Segontium: Pennant ascended to the summit, in hopes of discovering more of Helen's noted road, but without success. Mars ar Helen, or the Field of Helen, is also the name given to another part which Giraldus considered the course of the road. Of the Via Devana, the same author remarks: "There is no Roman road so perfect as this; like the Via Occidentalis, it bears the name of Sarn Helen. The foundation of almost all the roads through Wales have, in fact, been attributed to St. Helena, the mother of Constantine.[1]

[1] Kennett's Parochial Antiquities.

CARTANDIS.[1]

Eugenius slain in battle—Decree of Maximus—Prayers of the widow and noble ladies—The Picts interrupt their devotions—Appeal of Cartandis to Maximus—His generous sympathy—He sends her escorted to Carrick—Attack of Pictish robbers—She returns to the Emperor—Enmity of the Picts—Their remonstrances—Scene of the Picts and Cartandis before Maximus—Her agony and entreaties—Success of Cartandis through the good feeling of the Emperor.

THE history of this Queen forms a touching episode in the life of Maximus the Roman, who ruled in Britain in the fourth century. She was the wife of Eugenius I., King of Scots,—a princess of the blood royal of Wales, and is cited as an instance of connubial affection.

Eugenius was slain in a fatal battle fought against Maximus, who had invaded Scotland; and his body which was discovered among heaps of the dead, was interred, by order of that leader, with the honour and ceremony usually bestowed on the funeral of Roman princes. Afterwards an edict was passed, that by an appointed day all the Scots should quit that part of the kingdom, under penalty of death or imprisonment: they were likewise required to surrender their houses and possessions to such persons as were nominated by the Romans. In consequence of this decree, many took refuge in Ireland, the Western Isles, Norway, and Denmark; while the few who remained were either taken prisoners by the Picts, then in alliance with the Romans, or enlisted from pure despair in the service of their enemies.[2]

Cartandis, widow of the deceased King, learning that his remains had been consigned to the earth under another form of religion than her own,[3] was distressed with apprehensions for the repose of his departed spirit, and from the moment of his funeral obsequies had remained constantly on the spot, which contained the relics of all that was dear to her, occupying herself in particular prayers and devotions for the soul of the dead. Many noble ladies were with her, who, joining in her mourning, united their own devotions with hers, for their husbands and other relatives who had been slain with Eugenius in defending their country, and were interred at the same place.

While occupied in this manner, the Picts, who had first instigated Maximus to issue the edict of banishment, arrived at the spot and interrupted them in their sorrowful duty, by acquainting Cartandis with the penalty attached to the neglect of the Roman mandate. The supplica-

[1] This is a variation of the name of Cartismandua. [2] Holinshed, Scott.

[3] She was probably of the sect of Pelagius, who was a Welshman.

tions of Cartandis and her attendants to be left unmolested were vain; the fierce Picts insisted on their complying with the decree, and enforcing their commands with violence, they ill-treated and insulted many of these noble and unfortunate women.

The Queen, accompanied by some of her British relatives, two gentlewomen, and a male attendant, repaired in person to the presence of Maximus, to complain of the indignity which had been offered her. She addressed a pathetic remonstrance to that general, soliciting his permission for herself and her maidens to continue in that country during the remainder of their lives, even though it were in the most servile state, provided that at their death they might be interred in the same grave as their husbands. Maximus, compassionating the misfortunes and affliction of Cartandis, whose conjugal affection he could not but admire, assigned to her the city of Carrick for an abode, with certain other revenues for the maintenance of her royal dignity.

The generous Maximus also appointed some persons to attend Cartandis for her protection while on her progress to a village not far distant from Carrick: scarcely, however, had the Roman escort safely conveyed her thither, and departed, after receiving her farewell and thanks, having, as they thought, left her in security, than a band of Pictish robbers on horseback was encountered by the ill-fated party. The fierce troop put the groom of Cartandis to the sword, and not only roughly treated her female attendants, but despoiled them and their royal mistress of all they possessed. Cartandis, however, succeeded in effecting her escape back to Maximus; the Roman general being converted from a foe into a friend. He received her with all the honour and respect due to her rank and sufferings, and, as nearly as he was able, restored to her the value of the property of which she had been deprived: the remainder was soon after regained, upon the capture of the robber Picts, who were punished with death for the outrage which they had committed.

Cartandis, on this, became a mark for the enmity of the Picts, when they learnt how kindly Maximus had received her, and how severely he had punished those who had despoiled and insulted her. They sent a deputation of nobles of their nation to complain to him of his having thus taken part against them in favour of a woman who was their enemy, and, moreover, a prisoner and in their power. For her sake, they said Maximus ought not to have put to death men who were friends of theirs, and allies of Rome: they proceeded to require that, in conformity with the proscription which had been issued, Cartandis should be despoiled of her possessions, and detained a captive in Britain.

Cartandis was herself present at the interview of Maximus with the Pictish chieftains, and had to support a scene of great trial, before the Roman general surrounded by the powerful soldiers of the empire, as she listened as these barbarians proceeded in discussing the future destiny they desired to be awarded her. When they came to that part of their embassy which concerned her imprisonment, and she perceived their design was to send her to Wales, her former country, in opposition to that wish nearest her heart, she broke forth into a passionate lamentation, bewailing in piteous accents her miserable fate, and entreating rather that her life might be offered upon her husband's tomb.

Raising her clasped hands to Maximus, she besought that generous prince, in the most earnest and pathetic manner, that he would be pleased to permit her either to pass the sad remainder of her present widowed state in the manner she found most conformable to her feelings, or else to take it from her at once. At this moving spectacle, all present, the Picts alone excepted, were deeply affected, and the sorrow-stricken Queen obtained her supplicated boon: the request of the Pictish nobles was refused, and Cartandis, having a portion assigned to her, suitable to her royal birth and dignity, received permission to depart into whatever quarter of the country she pleased, and was suffered to live from that time forward, under the protection of the mighty Roman name, unmolested and undisturbed.[1]

---

[1] Holinshed.

HELENA AP EUDDA.

Parentage of Helena—The aspirants for her hand—Her Father wishes her marriage—Maximus proposed—Conan objects, but consents at length—Deputation—Character of Maximus—He arrives at Southampton—Promise, and ceremony of Marriage—Dream of Maxen-Wledig, a Welsh romance—Caernarvon—The Fort—The Will—Kynan-Meriadec of Armorica—Maximus and his bride at Trèves — St. Martin of Tours — The devotion of Helena to him — Gratian's fate — Ursula and the "Eleven Thousand" victims — Successes of Maximus—Reverses—His death, and that of his son Victor—The Tears of Helena, and her Fountain.

THOUGH Helena ap Eudda is less distinguished in British History than her illustrious relative and sainted namesake, the mother of Constantine, her character, and the particulars of her life, are not devoid of interest, as affording an instance of female influence, and as one of the earliest patrons of Christianity.

The father of Helena was son of Caradocus, Duke of Cornwall, the ancient tin country, and grandson of the Asclepiodatus,[1] or "Bran ap Llyr,"[2] so noted in the times of Constantius. Eudda,[3] or Octavius, as he was denominated by the Romans, Duke of the Wisseans,[4] had married Guala, sister of St. Helena, and received with her, as a bridal dowry, the kingdom of North Wales, it being the second time that territory had been conveyed to a new line of monarchs, by marriage with a daughter of that royal house. Eudda and Guala, by their union, connected in one the families of Wales and Cornwall; and the vast possessions thus united under their control, were destined to become, in process of time, the marriage-portion of their only child Helena,[5] whose noble inheritance caused her to be sought by many an aspiring adventurer. The young princess herself, who was born at Caer Segont, or Caernarvon, possessed qualifications which rendered her worthy of her lofty destiny. The increasing years of her aged parent made him anxious to see this child, who was his sole heir, settled in marriage with some prince, whose merits entitled him to succeed to the regal dignity; and fearing, least in the

[1] Rowland's Mona Antiqua.

[2] Bran ap Llyr is celebrated for his valour, and as being the ancestor of Arthur and all those heroes who contended against the Romans, Saxons, and Danes for the freedom of their mountain-district.—*Geoffrey of Monmouth, Lappenberg.*

[3] Or Ederus, sometimes written Paternus or Padarn, Edern ap Padarn, or "with the crimson cloak."—*Owen's Cam. Biog.*

[4] The Wiccii, or people of Worcester, over whom Venutius had formerly reigned.

[5] Warrington, Gibbon, Pennant.

event of his own death, without some previous arrangement to that effect, other aspirants to the crown might spring up, Eudda called a council of state, to take the subject into consideration. The king inquired of his assembled nobles, which of his family they would prefer to reign over them at his death, and the majority were desirous of securing peace to the nation, by bestowing the Princess Helena on some noble Roman. Several members of the British senate dissented in favour of Conan Meriadec,[1] the king's nephew, who was present, whom they wished to become their ruler. Caradocus, Duke of Cornwall, son of Trahewrne, and cousin of St. Helena, gave his opinion in favour of Maximus, the Roman senator—a person not only allied to the imperial family, and educated in Rome, but his own cousin, being a son of Llewelyn, his father's brother, and equally related with himself to the royal family of Britain. This proposition met with general approbation, except from Conan, who himself aimed at the crown, and was much displeased at it: the matter, however, being arranged in favour of Maximus, Conan consented that Mauritius, his son, should become the ambassador of Eudda to the imperial court.

Accordingly, Maximus was duly informed by Mauritius of the intentions of King Eudda to honour him with the hand of the lovely Helena, with the reversion of the crown in perspective. The embassy met with an honourable reception at the court of Rome, where Mauritius was nobly entertained; and Maximus greatly pleased with the brilliant prospect that awaited him, undertook the journey into Britain.[2]

Flavius Clemens Maximus was born in a second marriage of Llewelyn, the brother of Coel, with a Roman lady. The place of his birth is differently stated: Spain, Rome, and Britain contend for the honour. His near relationship to the imperial family had caused him to be educated at the capital with great care,[3] and by his bravery he rendered himself worthy of the distinction at which he eventually arrived.[4] The poets write of him as a robber-chief; but lofty talents he no doubt possessed. Long before Maximus was invited to Britain by Eudda, he had made that country his residence, having been called thither to repel the Picts and Scots: his noble conduct towards Cartandis, which has been named in her Life, gives a favourable view of his character.

At the time when the British embassy reached him, Maximus was contending with Gratian and Valentinian for a third share in the Roman Empire, which they had refused to accord him: his progress towards the island-home of his future wife was marked by the subjugation of several cities of the Franks, while his train was speedily augmented by a large number of followers. This popular chief arrived in safety at Southampton. But his expecting father-in-law regarded his martial array as having a hostile aspect, and, struck with sudden fear, ordered his nephew Conan immediately to raise an army to oppose his further progress.[5]

The tidings of the misunderstanding which had arisen in the mind of

[1] Palgrave. [2] Polwhele's Cornwall. [3] Daniel.

[4] In Lluyd's Brev. of Brit. he is called "the Robber of Richborough."

[5] Geoffrey of Monmouth.

Eudda having reached the Roman prince, he consulted with Mauritius as to the course which it would be best for him to take. They determined to send twelve aged men, bearing olive-branches in their hands, to Conan. This embassy was admitted to a hearing, and it was stated that Maximus had come from the two Emperors of Rome on a visit, the object of which was peace and not war; when Conan and others persuaded Eudda to desist from his contemplated hostilities. After this, Maximus was conducted by Conan to London, where he had an interview with Eudda. Prior to their meeting, Caradocus and Mauritius had privately consulted with the King, when the former strongly urged the suit of Maximus, and ended with the following words: "Should you refuse him, what right could you plead to the crown of Britain against him; for he is the cousin of Constantine, and the nephew of King Coel, whose daughter Helena possessed the crown by an undeniable right?"[1] The King acquiesced, and the people, being uniformly in favour of the match, Maximus was promised the hand of Helena ap Eudda, and the rich inheritance she derived from her parents.[2]

The nuptial ceremony took place at Caernarvon, where Eudda resided and held a royal court. There yet exists, in the Welsh language, a fabulous story relating to this circumstance, which is called "the Dream of Maximus."

Lady Charlotte Guest has devoted herself to the translation of this national composition, "The Dream of Maxen Wledig, or The Glorious," of which the following is an extract. That very interesting tradition, so poetically connected with the subject of this biography, is composed in these terms:—

"Maxen Wledig was Emperor of Rome, and he was a comelier man, and a better and a wiser, than any emperor that had been before him. While hunting one day, he fell asleep and had a dream, in the course of which he came to an island, the fairest island in the whole world; and he traversed the island from sea to sea, even to the farthest shore of the island: valleys he saw, and steeps and rocks of wondrous height, and rugged precipices; never yet saw he the like. And thence he beheld an island in the sea, facing this rugged land; and between him and this island was a country of which the plane was as large as the sea, the mountain as vast as the wood; and from the mountain he saw a river that flowed through the land, and fell into the sea. And at the mouth of the river he beheld a castle, the fairest that man ever saw; and the gate of the castle was open, and he went into the castle; and in the castle he saw a fair hall, of which the roof seemed to be all gold; the walls of the hall seemed to be entirely of glittering precious gems; the doors all seemed to be of gold; golden seats he saw in the hall, and silver tables; and on a seat opposite to him he beheld two auburn-haired youths playing at chess; he saw a silver board for the chess, and golden pieces thereon. The garments of the youths were of jet-black satin, and chaplets of ruddy gold bound their hair, whereon were sparkling jewels of great price, rubies and gems, alternately with imperial stones; buskins of new cordovan leather on their feet, fastened by slides of red gold.

[1] Geoffrey of Monmouth.

[2] Roberts's Notes to British History.

"And beside a pillar in the hall he saw a hoary-headed man, in a chair of ivory, with the figures of two eagles of ruddy gold thereon; bracelets of gold were upon his arms, and many rings upon his hands, and a golden torque about his neck, and his hair was bound with a golden diadem. He was of powerful aspect; a chess-board of gold was before him, and a rod of gold and a steel file in his hand, and he was carving out chess-men.

"And he saw a maiden sitting before him in a chair of ruddy gold: not more easy than to gaze upon the sun when brightest, was it to look upon her by reason of her beauty. A vest of white silk was upon the maiden, with clasps of red gold at the breast; and a surcoat of gold tissue was upon her, and a frontlet of red gold upon her head, and rubies and gems were in the frontlet, alternating with pearls and imperial stones; and a girdle of ruddy gold was around her. She was the fairest sight that man ever beheld.

"The maiden arose from her chair before him, and he threw his arms about the neck of the maiden, and they two sat down together in the chair of gold; and the chair was not less roomy for them both, than for the maiden alone. And as he had his arms about the maiden's neck, and his cheek by her cheek, behold, through the chafing of the dogs at their leashing, and the clashing of the shields as they struck against each other, and the beating together of the shafts of the spears,[1] and the neighing of the horses and their prancing, the Emperor awoke.

"And when he awoke, nor spirit nor existence was left him, because of the maiden whom he had seen in his sleep, for the love of the maiden pervaded his whole frame. Then his household spake unto him, 'Lord,' said they, 'is it not past the time for thee to take thy food?' Thereupon the Emperor mounted his palfrey, the saddest man that mortal ever saw, and went forth towards Rome.

"And thus he was during the space of a week. When they of the household went to drink wine and mead out of golden vessels, he went not with any of them; when they went to listen to songs and tales, he went not with them there; neither would he be persuaded to do anything but sleep. And as often as he slept, he beheld in his dreams the maiden he loved best; but, except when he slept, he saw nothing of her, for he knew not where in the world she was.

"At length Maxen sent for his wise men, and told them of his dream; and by their advice he sent messengers into different parts of the world, to discover the place and lady of whom he had dreamt. At the end of the year they returned without success, and he was very sorrowful. Then Maxen went to the spot where he had slept, and pointed it out himself. 'Behold, this is where I was when I saw the dream, and I went towards the source of the river westward.' On which thirteen messengers set forth on the track prescribed, and at last, in the great ship, they crossed the sea, and came to the island of Britain. And they traversed the island

[1] When sleep had first come upon Maxen, "his attendants stood and set up their shields around him upon the shafts of their spears, to protect him from the sun, and they placed a gold enamelled shield under his head. And so Maxen slept." To this the passage above refers.

until they came to Snowdon. 'Behold,' said they, 'the rugged land that our master saw.' And they went forward until they saw Anglesey before them, and until they saw Arvon[1] likewise. 'Behold,' said they, 'the land our master saw in his sleep.' And they saw Aber Sain,[2] and a castle at the mouth of the river. The portal of the castle saw they open, and into the castle they went; and they saw a hall in the castle. Then said they, 'Behold the hall which he saw in his sleep.' They went into the hall, and they beheld two youths playing at chess, on the golden bench. And they beheld the hoary-headed man beside the pillar, in the ivory chair, carving chess-men. And they beheld the maiden sitting on a chair of ruddy gold. The messengers bent down upon their knees—'Empress of Rome, all hail!' 'Ha, gentles,' said the maiden, 'ye bear the seeming of honourable men, and the badge of envoys.[3] What mockery is this ye do me?' 'We mock thee not, lady; but the Emperor of Rome hath seen thee in his sleep, and he has neither life nor spirit left because of thee. Thou shalt have of us, therefore, the choice, lady—whether thou wilt go with us and be made Empress of Rome, or that the Emperor come hither and take thee for his wife?' 'Ho! lords,' said the maiden, 'I will not deny what ye say, neither will I believe it too well. If the Emperor loves me, let him come here to seek me.'

"And by day and night the messengers hied them back, and when their horses failed they bought other fresh ones. And when they came to Rome, they saluted the Emperor, and asked their boon, which was given them, according as they named it. 'We will be thy guides, lord,' said they, 'over sea and over land, to the place where is the woman whom best thou lovest; for we know her name, and her kindred, and her race.' And immediately the Emperor set forth with his army, and these men were his guides. Towards the island of Britain they went, over the sea and over the deep. And he conquered the island from Beli, the son of Monogan, and his sons, and drove them to the sea, and went forward even unto Arvon. And the Emperor knew the land when he saw it. And when he beheld the Castle of Aber Sain, 'Look yonder,' said he; 'there is the castle wherein I saw the damsel whom I best love;' and he went forward into the castle and into the hall, and there he saw Kynan, the son of Eudov, and Adeon, the son of Eudov, playing at chess. And he saw Eudov, the son of Caradawc, sitting on a chair of ivory, carving chess-men. And the maiden whom he had beheld in his sleep, he saw sitting on a chair of gold. 'Empress of Rome,' said he, 'all hail!' and the Emperor threw his arms about her neck; and that night she became his bride.

"And the next day in the morning, the damsel asked her maiden-portion. And he told her to name what she would, and she asked to have the island of Britain for her father, from the Channel to the Irish Sea, together with the three adjacent islands, to hold under the Empress of Rome; and to have three chief castles made for her, in whatever

[1] Caern-arvon. [2] Segont.

[3] Each of them wore one sleeve on the front of his cap, as a sign he was a messenger, that no harm should be done him in passing through hostile lands.

places she might choose on the island of Britain. And she chose to have the highest castle made at Arvon. And they brought thither earth from Rome, that it might be more healthful for the Emperor to sleep, and sit, and walk upon.[1] After that the two other castles were made for her, which were Caerlleon and Caermarthen.

"Then Helen bethought her to make high roads from one castle to another throughout the island of Britain. And the roads were made. And for this cause are they called the roads of Helen Luyddawc, that she was sprung from a native of this island, and the men of the island of Britain would not have made these great roads for any save her."[2]

Caernarvon, the scene of this romance, afterwards became celebrated as the birthplace of Edward II., the first Prince of Wales. The river Seiont, from which the place derived its ancient name, rises in the heart of Snowdonia, and forms the lakes of Llandberis in its passage, which rather inclines to the southwest, till it turns abruptly to the north to reach the sea beneath the mighty towers of Caernarvon. The ruins of Segontium are yet distinguishable on a planted hill near its exit, where the view of Caernarvon, with its castle and the coast of Anglesey, across a great arm of the sea, is hardly to be paralleled for beauty.[3] Near the steep bank of the river Seiont, at a small distance from the castle, is an ancient Roman fort. Near the corner of one of the walls, is a heap of stones,[4] the ruins of a tower the foundation of which was accidentally discovered some years ago. This place seems intended to secure a landing-place from the Seiont at time of high water; and Pennant says: "I was informed that in Trer Beblic, on the opposite shore, had been other ruins, the work of the same people." At a small distance above this, and about a quarter of a mile from the Menai, is the ancient Segontium, to the use of which the fort had been subservient. It forms an oblong, of very considerable extent, seemingly about six acres, placed on the summit of rising ground, and sloping down on every side. It is now divided by the public road; but in several parts are vestiges of walls; and in one place appears the remnant of a building made with tiles, and plastered with very hard and smooth mortar; this seems to have been part of a hypocaust. At present a public road passes through this station, beyond which the Romans had only a small outpost or two in this country.[5]

At Segontium the Empress Helena ap Eudda had a chapel of her own, of which the author of the "Mona Antiqua" assures us the remains were in existence in his days.[6] A well, near the fort, even now bears the name of the princess, and some very slight remains of ruins are to be seen adjacent, which tradition informs us is the spot upon which the chapel of the Empress stood.

A Triad has been preserved, which goes at some length into the expe-

---

[1] Geoffrey of Monmouth; Carew's Cornwall.

[2] This great work was apparently the same as that commenced by St. Helen, the Empress.

[3] Skene's Rivers. [4] Pennant. [5] Pennant's Wales.

[6] Rowland's Mona Antiqua.

dition undertaken by "Kynan Meriadec and his sister Helen, surnamed Luyddawc,[1] or Helen of Mighty Hosts, the children of Euddav," for the purpose of supporting the claim of Maximus to the imperial throne. They raised an army of 60,000 men in Britain, and proceeded with it across the sea to Armorica, A. D., 383: the desolation caused by this abstraction of its inhabitants from the island, is said to have been the remote cause of the Saxon invasion.[2] This is another version of the colonization of Bretagne, noticed previously.

The great reputation Maximus had acquired in Britain by his military successes against the Picts and Scots, had gained the affections of the people, whose predilection was still further confirmed by his marriage with Helena. From this time they identified their own views with his, and he was constrained to accept the purple in accordance with their wishes.[3] The accession of Maximus is placed in the year 383; he afterwards declared to St. Martin, that "he had accepted the Empire with regret, but that he was prepared to defend by the sword that diadem which had been bestowed by Heaven."

After his marriage, Maximus, with the flower of the British youth, who had rallied round his standard, had returned with his bride into Gaul,[4] where he established his court at Trèves, and in defiance of his imperial opponents, assumed to himself the dignity of an Emperor of Spain, Gaul, and Britain. Gildas remarks, that he "stretched out his wings" from the seat of his empire, "to Spain and to Italy," levying taxes on the barbarous nations by the mere terror of his name; and the moderation of the government of the Usurper, during whose reign not a single enemy or rebel perished, otherwise than in fair and open warfare, forcibly demonstrates the willing allegiance of the nations over whom he ruled.

St. Martin, who had, A. D. 374, been elected Bishop of Tours, and as an apostle, had diffused the light of Christianity throughout Gaul, destroying all the temples of heathenism, was received with every mark of respect and honour by the Emperor Valentinian, then in that country.[5] When the holy bishop waited upon the Emperor at Trèves, Maximus made him sit at his table with the most illustrious persons of his court. He was placed at the right hand of the Emperor, who, in drinking, commanded his servants to give him a cup, that St. Martin might receive it again from him; but the bishop bestowed it in his turn on the priest who had accompanied him on his journey,—a holy boldness, which, far from displeasing, gained him the favour of the Emperor, and of his whole court.

The wife of Maximus, the beautiful Helena, who now held the rank of Empress of the West, insisted on waiting upon the venerable priest whilst partaking of his scanty repast, as if she were of mean estate. Of this pious British woman, Sulpicius Severus writes thus, in his Dialogue on the Virtues of St. Martin: "By day, and by night, the Queen hung

[1] Conan and Helen are here represented as brother and sister.

[2] Lady C. Guest's Notes to the Mabinogion.

[3] Palgrave.

[4] Warrington.

[5] Ency. Brit.

upon the words of Martin, and like her example in the Gospel, washed the holy man's feet with her tears, and wiped them with the hairs of her head. Martin, whom no woman had ever approached to touch, could not escape from her assiduities, or rather submission. She thought not of the wealth of a kingdom, the dignity of empire, the crown and the purple; nothing could remove her from the posture she had taken at his feet, till having asked her husband's consent, they together compelled Martin to accede to her request, that she herself, without the aid of servants, might be permitted to prepare him a banquet. The blessed man was reluctantly obliged to yield. The chaste preparations are made by the hands of the Queen, the seat is placed by her, the table drawn to it, the water supplied by her own hands; she serves the food which she had cooked, and while he partakes sitting, she persists in placing herself on the floor at a distance, with the customary respect shown by servants, imitating their modesty and humility in all she does. Herself mixes the wine for him to drink, herself hands it to him; and supper being finished, she collects the fragments and crumbs of the bread which he had partaken of, rightly judging them, by the faith in her, to be more precious relics than an imperial banquet. Blessed woman! deserving to be compared in piety with her who came from the ends of the earth to hear the wisdom of Solomon—if we consider merely outward history; but if we compare the faith of the Queen, which we may do, apart from the majesty of the mystery contained in the Scripture narrative, the one came to *hear* the wise man, the other obtained grace, not only to *hear*, but to *serve*. * * * The Queen, on this occasion, ministered like Martha, and heard like Mary."[1]

St. Martin employed his influence with Maximus to preserve the Priscellianists, who were persecuted by the clergy in Spain. The Bishop of Tours would hold no communion with men whose religious principles induced them to shed the blood of mankind; and he obtained the lives of those whose death they had solicited.[2]

---

[1] St. Martin introduced the monastic system into Gaul, and his example was followed by his relative, St. Patrick, the Hibernian apostle. Martin resided in a cell made of twigs interwoven, and many of his disciples occupied caverns. No one had any property, or bought and sold, but all things were common. No art was exercised but writing, in which the juniors alone were occupied; the seniors devoting their time to prayer. They rarely left their cells, except to assemble at the place of prayer. They took their refection together, after the hour of fasting. None but the sick drank wine. St. Martin is frequently represented giving his cloak to a beggar, probably from having introduced the garb. Many of his followers were clothed with a stuff made of the *bristles of camels*, a softer habit being esteemed criminal. These habits were anciently worn by British monks also, as well as those of Gaul, and hats formed of the same. The *camblet* cloth of a later period was made of goats' wool.

The camels' or goats' hair shirt reached from the elbows to the knees: the hair material was worked into fine threads, and woven by weavers on purpose. One similar to them, belonging to Becket, was washed by his chaplain; they were commonly infested with vermin.

The feet and legs were usually bare; the Anglo-Saxons received their visitors by hospitably giving them water to wash their feet and hands, and wiping them with a towel. — Fosbrooke's Brit. Monachism.

[2] Ency. Brit.

Gratian,[1] then twenty-eight years of age, had made himself conspicuous by the protection of the Christians, for which he was hated by the whole heathen world, whose worship he intended to abolish utterly.[2] He was still contending for the Empire with Maximus, and sent Ambrose, Bishop of Milan, to him, to sue for a peace, to which Maximus seemed to incline, while, in reality, he appears to have conspired against the life of his enemy. As this is the greatest blot on the character of the Christian Maximus, it appears worthy of particular detail.

Gratian had offended the veteran soldiers, by sending some Alans against Maximus, in preference to themselves, and numbers in consequence revolted to Maximus, who made them large promises of reward. This alarmed Gratian, who fled to Paris, whither Maximus, after defeating the Alans, pursued his imperial foe, and fixed his camp without the city. After five days, occupied in slight skirmishes, with no particular advantage on either side, first the Moors, and then the rest of the army, deserted to the side of Maximus, and Gratian, with three hundred horse only, made his escape to Lyons, other cities refusing him admittance. Maximus, who aimed at his oppenent's personal destruction, followed with his army, but not succeeding by force of arms, had recourse to the following stratagem.[3] He caused letters to be sent to Gratian, informing him that his wife was on her way to visit him. The unfortunate Prince crediting the information, repaired to the banks of the Rhone, which runs by the city, to meet her, believing her to be approaching, and overjoyed in the prospect of their meeting. When he opened the litter, and expected to clasp her in his embrace, he was treacherously murdered by Andragathius, an adherent of Maximus, who, with other ruffians, had been hired to assassinate him. By his death Maximus became undisputed master of the Western Empire.[4]

This event has left a stain on the otherwise bright fame of the Emperor Maximus; so imperfect is the virtue of the greatest hero of those times.

Having rendered himself master of Gaul, Maximus colonized it with British soldiers, and next attempted to appease his envious rival Conan, who, jealous of his successful suit with Helena, and subsequent elevation to the Empire, had laid waste some of his territories in Britain. To silence this competitor, Maximus bestowed on him a portion of Gaul, called Armorica at that time, but after that date known under the name of Bretagne, or Little Britain.[5] This cession was made A. D. 384.

[1] A burgher of a British municipal town.—Orosius. [2] Echard.

[3] Echard's History of Rome. [4] Echard, Howel, Med. Hist. Angl. Palgrave.

[5] Dr. Lappenberg, in his "England under the Anglo-Saxon Kings," remarks on this subject: "This settlement has given a name, as well as a distinct character and history to the province of Bretagne. Though that country had, from the earliest times, by descent, language, and Druidism, been related to Britain, yet the new colonists, who were followed by many others, both male and female, served unquestionably to bind more closely and preserve the connexion between Bretagne and the Britons of Cornwall and Wales; and but for this event, the heroic poetry of France and Germany had probably been without the charm cast over it by the traditions of the Sangraal, of Tristan and Iseult, and of Arthur and Merlin. But Britain was thereby deprived of her bravest warriors, and thence the more easily became an early prey to foreign invaders."

15 *

Maximus, after this, sent an embassy to Cornwall, to demand from the King the hand of his daughter Ursula, for Conan; and the young princess, and a numerous train of British females, many of whom were married women, quitted for ever the shores of their native country. Abundance of fables have been written of their number, the adventures that befell them, and the glorious death they encountered from the savage Huns.[1] They were martyred near the Lower Rhine, and buried at Cologne, where a tomb was erected over their remains, and a great church built on the spot.[2] This well-known edifice became celebrated to all time for the tomb of St. Ursula, and her "eleven thousand" holy companions. St. Ursula, "who was the mistress and guide to heaven of so many holy maidens, whom she animated to the heroic practice of virtue, conducted to the glorious crown of martyrdom, and presented spotless to Christ, is regarded as a model and patroness by those who undertake to train up youth in the sentiments and practice of piety and religion."[3]

The sisters of the order of St. Ursula are, in the Roman Communion, the instructresses of young females, and their establishments, those of Ursuline Sisters, are well known all over the continent.

In the poem we have before quoted, called "the Dream of Maxen," he is said to have spent seven years in Britain, and after that returned to Rome, making many conquests by the way in the countries through which he passed. He laid siege to Rome, but had made no progress at the end of a year, when succours from Britain reached him. These were "the brothers of Helen Luyddawc," with a small host of Britons, "and better warriors were in that small host than twice as many Romans."

"And Helen went to see the hosts, and she knew the standards of her brothers. Then came Kynan, the son of Eudav, and Adeon, the son of Eudav, to meet the Emperor. And the Emperor was glad because of them, and embraced them.

"Then they looked at the Romans as they attacked the city. Said Kynan to his brother, 'We will try to attack the city more expertly than this.' So they measured by night the height of the wall, and they sent their carpenters to the wood, and a ladder was made for every four men of their number. Now when these were ready, every day at mid-day the Emperors went to meat, and they ceased to fight on both sides till all had finished eating. And in the morning the men of Britain took their food, and they drank until they were invigorated. And while the two Emperors were at meat, the Britons came to the city, and placed their ladders against it, and forthwith they came in through the city.

"The new Emperor had not time to arm himself when they fell upon him, and slew him, and many others with him. And three nights and three days were they subduing the men that were in the city and taking the castle. And others of them kept the city, lest any of the host of Maxen should come therein, until they had subjected all to their will.

"Then spake Maxen to Helen Luyddawc: 'I marval, lady,' said he, 'that thy brothers have not conquered this city for me.' 'Lord Emperor,' she answered, 'the wisest youths in the world are my brothers. Go

[1] Butler. [2] A. D 453.—Sigebert's Chronicle. [3] Butler's Lives of Saints.

thou thither and ask the city of them, and if it be in their possession thou shalt have it gladly.' So the Emperor and Helen went and demanded the city. And they told the Emperor that none had taken the city, and that none could give it him, but the men of the island of Britain. Then the gates of the city of Rome were opened, and the Emperor sat on the throne, and all the men of Rome submitted themselves unto him."

How far the dream of Maximus is in accordance with the general facts of history it is difficult to say. There is no doubt that Maximus was one of the most heroic and successful of Roman emperors, and it is equally certain that Helena accompanied him in his wars abroad. Both Roman and British authorities concur in the narrative of his conquests and great enterprise.[1]

Helena had three sons by Maximus, of whom Victor was the chosen companion of his martial expeditions. Publicius, his brother, retiring from the world, assumed the religious habit, and to him the Mother Church of Segontium was dedicated. "It stands about half a mile south-east of the town, and from its royal patron, who was canonized at his death, bears the name of Llan Peblic, or Publicius."[2] This church and the chapel of Caernarvon were bestowed by King Richard II. upon the nuns of St. Mary's at Chester, on account of their poverty.

"The dress of Pabo post prydain, called the 'Pillar of Britain,' as seen on his tomb, is a specimen of that worn by a royal priest in the time of Publicius. Pabo, who was contemporary with the sons of Helena, and the founder of Llan Pabo in Anglesey, is clad in a long dalmatic, partly opened at the sides, and bordered with fur. Round the neck and down the front, is a border of lace, richly studded with pearls. St. Jestin ap Geraint, a prince of the Devonshire Britons, who lived a century later than Pabo, is habited in a cope, fastened on the breast with a rich fibula; beneath this he has a short mantle or scapular over his tunic. This mode of dress was of the highest antiquity, and remained in vogue for royal personages till the time of Henry V. In his right hand the saint holds a staff, not unlike the augural staff of the ancients."[3]

The brilliant career of Maximus was destined to a sudden close. Valentinian, on being driven from Italy by Maximus, obtained assistance from Theodosius, Emperor of the East, who subdued his hitherto successful rival at Aquileia, A. D. 388. The inhabitants of the city seeing, or fancying they saw, despondency in his hitherto buoyant spirit, abandoned him in his first reverse, stripped the Emperor of his regal ornaments, and carried him bound to Theodosius. The generous Emperor would have pardoned him, but those who surrounded him, perceiving the clemency he designed to execute, hurried Maximus from his presence, and ordered his head to be cut off, even without the Emperor's mandate.[4]

Thus fell Maximus, the first to bear the name of Wledig, or "Illustrious,"—a surname equivalent to that of Emperor, afterwards borne by

---

[1] Palgrave.
[2] Pennant.
[3] Smith and Meyrick's Costumes of Britain.
[4] Echard.

the Roman princes of his family in Britain: his dominions were annexed by Theodosius to his own, and afterwards transmitted to his son Honorious, who became Emperor of the West.[1]

Victor, son of Maximus, had been slain with his father at Aquileia, and some of his most dreaded relatives and friends were put to death as an example: the rest were pardoned; "so that," says the Chronicle, "under so merciful a conqueror, they felt not that they were conquered."[2]

The wife and daughters of Maximus seem to have been taken prisoners, probably at the surrender of Aquileia. Theodosius sent for them out of their confinement, settled an honourable pension upon them for their lives, and charged "a near kinsman of their own" to take care of their interests, and see that nobody oppressed them.[3] This statement differs from the one given in our national histories and traditions, from which it would appear that Helena was in Britain when Maximus died. The spot on which the Empress received the fatal tidings of the death of her husband and son, is still pointed out in Wales,[4] in the beautiful vale of Festiniog, where the springs called Fynnon Helen are supposed to have been derived from her tears.

One of the sons of Helen had entered the cloister, a second died a violent death abroad; for the third, Cunetha, it was reserved to transmit the honoured title of Wledig, with the maternal inheritance, to his children, among whom it was divided at his death. The original patrimony of Cunetha was in Cumberland and some neighbouring districts; and the Triads celebrate his praise, as being the first in this island who granted lands and privileges to the Church.[5] Wales was divided by Cu-

[1] Warrington, Howel, and Daniel.

[2] Such of these princes as were driven by the Saxons from their possessions embraced a religious life, and were ranked with the children of Bran and Brechan, under the appellation of "the three holy families of Britain." Theodoric, [Owen's Cambrian Biography,] son of Tethwald, King of Caermarthen in Wales, resigning his crown, settled as a hermit at a spot since known as Tintern. In that place, surrounded by rocks, he designed to pass the remnant of his days in solitude and peace; but the success of the Saxons compelled him to arm in defence of his country, and he was slain at Mathern, near Chepstow, by a mortal wound in the head. His body was buried on the spot where he fell, and Bishop Godwin saw his remains, which had been deposited in a stone coffin. [Stillingfleet and Powel.] At a later period Tintern was a place of refuge for two other monarchs, who also left the spot to encounter a violent end: Kilwulf, King of Wessex, being dragged thence by his subjects, against his will, A. D. 610, to act once more as their leader; and Edward the Second, who fled there from the pursuit of his guilty queen, Isabella. Marcella, daughter of the slain hero, Theodoric, hermit of Tintern, named Olaf King of Ireland, became mother of Brechan, who inherited her estates in Wales; so that Caermardhin took from him its ancient name of Brechonia, or Breconia, in British Brechniock, in English Breknock: [Powel; Girald. Camb.:] thus an Irish historian remarks that, "Brecknock town and Brecknockshire have caused the glory of Ireland, that gave them the name of honour, which they hold to this day; and Ireland to glory in them, that gave their king's son, Marcella, their lady, and all that country in her right." [Hanmer's Chronicle.]

[3] Echard.

[4] Girald. Camb.

[5] Sir John Price.

netha among his sons; and its several provinces yet bear the names of those early British princes: Cardigan, especially named as a part of their grandmother Helena's territory, was so called from Caredic, son of Cunetha.[1] Of the whole family, Eneon Urdd, or "the Honourable," was most distinguished. His son, Caswallon Caw Hir, or the "Long-Handed," fixed his royal abode in Mona in 443; and, as the eldest branch of the Cynethian family, received homage from the princes, his contemporaries.

[1] Owen's Cambrian Biography.

ROWENA.

Vortigern, hoping to establish order in Britain, invites Hengist and Horsa—Arrival of the Saxons—The feast at Thong Castle—The fatal Was-heil—Rowena's beauty—Dress of Saxon ladies—Marriage of Vortigern—His first wife—Gods of the Saxons—The Irminsula—Discontent of the Britons—Excommunication and separation—Vortimer proclaimed King—Fury of Hengist—Rowena's artifices—She poisons Vortimer in a nosegay—Vortigern consults Merlin—History of Ambrosius—The fortress in Snowdon—The massacre at Ambresbury—The Valley of Vortigern.

THE pressure of the Barbarians, those "many-nationed spoilers," had obliged the hitherto triumphant Romans to concentrate their attention and all their power in their own country, and, by degrees, they withdrew their forces from the remote provinces which owned their sway, until Britain was altogether abandoned by them, and left to the British princes, who were forced to carry on continual warfare with the savage Picts, and that people called the Scots of Ireland, settled on the west coast. The Saxons also came occasionally, to "fright the isle from its propriety," by their incursions; and the endless quarrels of the chiefs for supremacy, plunged the whole land into such a state of anarchy, that Vortigern, who then filled the uneasy throne of South Britain, may be excused, in his despair of establishing order, for forming the resolution of seeking protection and assistance from the powerful and restless German freebooters, whom he had hitherto looked upon as enemies.

In an evil hour for the freedom of his country, Vortigern summoned to his aid the unscrupulous adventurers, Hengist and Horsa, and Britain became their prey.

The loves of Vortigern and Rowena have become the property of the romancer, and some historians reject the traditions respecting them; but yet the story is as often repeated as omitted by chroniclers, and is by some attested as worthy of credit. There is a probability about it, which, while it interests, enlists the reader in its favour.

Nennius, Geoffrey of Monmouth, and their followers, tell the story of Rowena's fatal charms, and she is named in the Welsh Triads as Ronwen. She was the daughter of the Jutish captain, Hengist, who, after he had successfully assisted Vortigern against his foes, had established himself and his party in the country: rejoicing to find themselves powerful chiefs, who were lately banished adventurers, expelled from their own shores.

When, at first, the Saxons stood before the King, says Roger of Wendover, he asked them respecting the faith and religion of their ancestors, on which Hengist replied : "We worship the gods of our fathers, Saturn, Jupiter, and the other deities, who govern the world, and especially Mercury, whom, in our tongue, we call Woden, and to whom our fathers dedicated the fourth day of the week, which, to this day, is called Woden's Day. Next to him, we worship the most powerful goddess, Frea, to whom they dedicated the sixth day, which, after her, we call Friday." "I grieve much," said Vortigern, "for your belief, or rather, for your unbelief; but I am exceedingly rejoiced at your coming, which, whether brought about by God, or otherwise, is most opportune for my urgent necessities. For I am pressed by my enemies on every side; and if ye will share with me the toil of fighting, ye shall remain in my kingdom, where ye shall be had in honour, and enriched with lands and possessions." The Barbarians straightway assented, and having made league with him, remained at his court.

Hengist had received as the reward of his helping arm, from the grateful Vortigern, a fertile and commanding tract of land, on the Thames, called by the Britons, Ruoihin, and by the Saxons, Thanet. As soon as Hengist was fairly established, he sent for new allies to his native country, and his welcome summons was speedily answered by the arrival of a host of relations and friends, all greedy for gain. But the most attractive personage amongst these, and one on whose power the wily Jute most depended, was his beautiful daughter Rowena, celebrated, wherever she had been seen, for her surpassing loveliness and grace, "a prodigy of beauty, and the admiration of all men."

There is a tradition generally repeated, that Hengist's modest demand, on being requested by Vortigern to name the price of his services, was merely as much land as he could cover with a hide; this being of course granted, the cunning freebooter had it cut into thongs, and thus managed to procure a considerably larger share than was intended. However this may be, he became possessed of a great portion of the country, and built or appropriated numerous castles, which he fortified, and where his followers established themselves.

It was at one of these, to which, it seems, he had given the name of Thong Castle, the situation of which is variously asserted (some chroniclers insisting on its being at Doncaster, others, that it was in Kent), that Hengist entertained the somewhat weak and luxurious Vortigern, and there, at a grand banquet, he introduced his fascinating daughter Rowena to the Prince.

In order to do the more honour to his guest, Hengist commanded the beautiful maiden to wait upon him during the repast, according to the fashion of the time, and Vortigern was not slow in taking the bait held out. At the first glance his eye had been dazzled by Rowena's beauty, and the smiling grace with which she presented him with a golden goblet, uttering, at the same time, in silver accents, the words of greeting—"Wæs heal, hlaford Cynyng," "*Health to thee, Lord King,*" entirely subdued him. From her lips he immediately learnt the customary answer, "Drinc heal," and his fate was sealed.

Drayton, after detailing this scene, goes on to say that the enamoured monarch—

"Kuste hire[1] and fitte hire adoune, and glad dronk hire heil,
And that was tho in this land the verst was-hail.
As in langage of Saxoyne that me might ever iwrite,
And so wel he paith the hole about, that he is not yet voryrte."

From that time "was-heil" and "drinc-heil" were the usual phrases of quaffing among the English, though Drayton thinks the custom had long before existed, both in Saxony and other nations.

The dress of the Saxon ladies is thus described, and we may suppose Rowena appeared, on this memorable occasion, similarly attired:—"They wore linen, dyed of divers colours, under the gown, and to this part of the dress belonged those close sleeves seen under or within those of the upper garment. The gown frequently was embellished with bands of different colours, or embroidery about the knees and at the bottom. On their heads they wore a veil, coverchief, or hood, which, falling down upon the forehead, was carefully wrapped round the neck and shoulders; sometimes they wore over their shoulders a cloak, with a hole cut in the middle, for the purpose of passing the head through. Their shoes, commonly of black, were plain, and sometimes slit down the middle of the instep. The predominant colours for female dress were green, blue, and light red; sometimes pink and violet, but rarely perfect *white*."[2] Purple was worn only by kings and queens.

Hengist himself is represented as of "pleasing address, engaging and condescending behaviour, and of sound judgment."[3]

In "Smith and Meyrick's Costumes" he thus appears: "With a four-pointed helmet, like those worn in France in the ninth century, and a breast-plate precisely similar to those worn in that country in the reigns of Lothair and Charles the Bold; some say he wore 'scaly mail,' and surcoat of fur. The chieftain's spear was broad and heavy, his convex shield armed with a boss. His long red hair was worn flowing down; he was stout in person, and freckled. When unarmed, his head was adorned with a wreath of amber beads, and round his neck was suspended a golden torque. His banner was red, and exhibited 'the picture of the white prancing steed,' at once the hieroglyphic of his name, and a symbol of the deity he worshipped."

As Hengist is said to be only about thirty at the time he arrived in Britain, his daughter Rowena must have been extremely young. At first, on Vortigern's declaring his passion for her, the artful father pretended to think her too lowly for so great an alliance; this assumed opposition, of course, increased the ardour of the royal lover, and his entreaties soon convinced both father and daughter that the objection was merely fanciful.

The object of the Jute was attained, and almost immediately the marriage of Vortigern and Rowena took place.

---

[1] Winsemius, the historian of Friesland, relates with much gravity as a fact, that *kissing* was unknown in England till the fair Rowena, Hengist's daughter, in the character of cupbearer, pressed the beaker with her lipkens, and saluted Vortigern with a kus-ên (a little kiss).—*Sir R. Phillips.*

[2] Smith and Meyrick.

[3] Rapin.

Vortigern had united himself previously to his marriage with Rowena, to a British lady of royal birth, by whom he had three sons, Vortimer, Categrin, and Pascentius, and one daughter.[1] This lady had been divorced to make way for the new marriage, and here the history of the Saxon invasion strongly resembles that of the Roman, four hundred years earlier. The divorced Queen of Vortigern may be compared to Boadicea, who was repudiated to make way for her husband to marry another: in these instances, as in that of the Spanish Florinda, the ill-treatment of a woman introduced the enemies of her country.

Vortigern's first wife was much loved by the people, more particularly because she was a Christian, while Rowena, her rival in the King's affections, was a lady of "uncowght beleue,"[2] in other words, a Pagan; moreover Vortigern had promised Rowena full liberty to exercise her own religion.[3]

As the rites of that religion are remarkable, a brief account of the idolatrous worship in which Rowena had been educated, may be excused.

The Saxon temples, in which their idols were worshipped,[4] were surrounded with inclosures, and it was considered profanation to throw a lance within the assigned boundary. The chief of the deities were the Sun and Moon, from whom, the former a female, and the latter a male deity, were named the two first days of their week. Tuesco, or Tiw, gave a name to the third day, but of him nothing is known. Wednesday was named from Woden, or Odin, the God of War, and renowned ancestor of Rowena herself, who is computed to have lived in the third century. Thor was another deity, and Friga, the wife of Woden, was venerated on Friday, as was Seterne on Saturday. There was besides Friga, several female deities, as Rheda and Eostre, to whom they sacrificed in March and April, Eostre giving name to the festival of Easter; and Herthus, or the Earth. There was a female power called an Elf, who appeared to have answered to Venus; Hera, the Goddess of Plenty, and Hilda, Goddess of War.[5] The offerings to these deities varied according to circumstances and seasons, consisting of cakes, of cattle, and sometimes even of human beings. The most celebrated and singular idol of the Saxons yet remains to be described. It stood at Marsburg, and bore the name of Irminsula. The edifice in which it was placed was spacious, elaborate, and magnificent, but had no roof. The idol itself, the largest in all Saxony, was constructed, it is thought, of wood, and represented an armed warrior; "its right hand held a banner, in which a red rose was conspicuous; its left presented a balance. The crest of its helmet was a cock; on its breast was engraven a bear, and the shield depending from its shoulders, exhibited a lion in a field full of flowers." Such was the extraordinary figure which was the principal object of adoration in the

[1] The author of "Britannia after the Romans" thinks that Rowena was the Christian wife of a monarch who leaned strongly towards Druidism, and a queen most anxious to reconcile the British and Saxon tribes to each other.—*Miss Lawrence's History of Woman.*

[2] Fabian. [3] Robinson. [4] Turner.

[5] Turner; History of the Anglo-Saxons.

temple Pictures of the Irminsula were to be found in other Saxon temples, which proves the high veneration with which it was regarded.

Both men and women served in the pagan temples of the Saxons; the former sacrificed, the latter divined and told fortunes. The priests, in the hour of battle, took their favourite image from its column, and carried it to the field, and after the conflict was over, the captives were immolated to the idol. There were certain days, also, on which the soldiery, clothed in armour, and brandishing an iron cestus, would ride round about their idol, and afterwards dismounting, kneel before it, and offer up prayers for success in their warfare.

The Irminsula was thrown down and broken, and the fame it had acquired destroyed by Charlemagne, in the year 772; its destruction occupied half the Gallic army three days, the rest being under arms; the vessels of the temple being appropriated, together with vast wealth, by the conquerors. The column on which the image had stood, being thrown into a wagon, was buried in the Weser, where it was found in the succeeding reign; and the Saxons attempting to rescue it, fought a battle on the spot called the Armensula. They were repulsed, and the image hastily thrown into the river; whence it was subsequently conveyed to the choir of a new church, built in the neighbourhood, at Hillesheim, and employed to hold lights at the festivals. After many ages of neglect, its rust and discoloration were removed by Meibomius and a canon of the church.[1]

Such were some of the extravagances of the Pagan idol-worship, which was introduced into Britain at the marriage of Rowena, and being protected and patronised by Vortigern whose chief idol was Rowena herself, threatened to choke the scattered seeds of Christianity which had sprung up in different parts of the island.

The first coming of Hengist had been, no doubt, welcomed by the helpless Britons as a deliverance from threatened bondage; the increase of his possessions might not, perhaps, have awakened jealousy, had not the advancement of a foreigner and a pagan to the position of Queen-Consort, and the consequent divorce of their Christian country-woman alarmed them, and pointed out the necessity of expostulation. Whatever the British nobles might have felt at first, they dissembled their indignation, and the earliest intimation of their feelings which Vortigern received was a visit from Wodine or Vodinus, Bishop of London, a man of singularly devout and exemplary character. That priest, having learnt that the Queen had been dismissed by her husband, went to him and remonstrated freely with him on the subject, telling him how great a crime he had committed in dismissing his lawful wife, who was a good and virtuous woman and excellent Christian; he added, moreover, that he had deeply offended against the laws of God and man, by marrying a Saxon, who was an enemy to the Christian faith, and whose father was aiming at the crown of Britain, and resolved to subdue it to the thraldom of the Saxons. Vortigern, abashed by the Bishop's honest reproof, acknowledged his crime, prayed God might pardon him, and made a confession of his guilt to the

[1] Turner.

holy man, full of penitence, auguring well for the future. Upon this Hengist, who in an adjoining chamber had listened to all that had passed, came in with fury, and upbraided Vortigern for being so dejected after his marriage. To completely emancipate his son-in-law from such an adviser, he slew the Bishop and several other religious men who resided with the King, and would have killed his son Vortimer also, had he not saved his life by a precipitate flight.[1]

Vortigern was next excommunicated by St. Germanus and the whole synod of bishops, on account of his marriage with the heathen Princess Rowena.[2] His crimes and follies had rendered him so much an object of detestation among the people, that in the year 464 a General Assembly of the British States was convened by the nobles of London.[3] On this occasion Vortigern was upbraided as the author of all the country's calamities, and the crown being taken from his head was placed on that of his son Vortimer.[4] The deposed King was then sent as a prisoner into Wales, and Rowena, who had been also made captive, was confined in the Tower of London. The object of this severe treatment was to prevent any children of her's in future aspiring to the throne, to the exclusion of the issue of Vortigern's first wife; for Rowena, at the time of her imprisonment, was expecting to become a mother, and shortly after gave birth to a son.[5] This was a cruel reverse of fortune, but Rowena does not appear to have possessed acute feelings; beautiful as an angel as she is represented to have been, her character does not present us with any of the gentle virtues which adorn the sex, except, indeed, the persisting in a determination to adhere to the fortunes of her own family, which owed its aggrandisement to herself, may be considered as one of them.

Hengist, after learning the imprisonment of his daughter and her husband, had to arm himself against the united forces of the Picts, Scots, and Britons, who, headed by Vortimer, fought four battles; in one of which Horsa, on the side of the Saxons, and Categrin, brother of Vortimer, were slain fighting hand to hand,—a proof of the animosity which fired the rival chiefs.[6] Hengist, during the interval, spared neither age nor sex, burnt public and private edifices, slew the priests at the foot of their altars, and even nobles and bishops were sacrificed to his indignation.[7] In the end, however, fortune favoured Vortimer, and the Saxons, with Hengist, were forced to fly from the kingdom. During the six or seven years which followed, the British King employed himself in the restoration of Christianity, and rebuilt the churches which the Pagans had destroyed.[8] At the end of that time his life fell a sacrifice to the artifices of Rowena, who had bribed one of his attendants to poison him.[9]

Some of the best years of this dangerous beauty's life had been passed

[1] Weever, Scott. This scene is supposed to have taken place at Ambresbury in Wiltshire, and the great massacre of the Britons at Stonehenge, but antiquarians dispute on this point.

[2] Roger of Wendover.
[3] Warrington, Scott.
[4] Fordun
[5] Roger of Wendover.
[6] Speed.
Hume.
[8] Howel.
[9] Fordun, Brut. Tysilio, Howel.

in prison,[1] but it would seem that this confinement was not very rigorous, owing to the generosity of the disposition of her step-son.

Rowena was anxious to recover her lost power, and reflecting what disasters Vortimer had caused the Saxons in England,—that she was herself a captive, her husband deposed and in prison, and her father a fugitive from his possessions, she determined to procure the death of the royal Vortimer. To this step she was led by her father's instigations, and, it is thought, with the connivance of her infatuated husband.

Rowena employed as her agent on this occasion a young man, attendant on Vortigern, whom she engaged in her service by the promise of a great reward. The event is thus recorded :[2]—"Disguised as a gardener, the Queen's emissary appeared one morning before the King, when he was taking the air in his garden, and presented him with a nosegay of flowers sprinkled with poison." As soon as Vortimer was sensible of its effects, and perceived that his death was inevitable, he called the nobility into his presence, and exhorted them to a manly defence of their country. He made it his last request that they should erect his sepulchre on the seashore, on the spot where the Saxons were accustomed to land. Some say that his tomb was prepared during his lifetime, at the entrance into Thanet, the scene of their last fatal struggle, in which Vortimer was the conqueror; and that the monument was called Lapis Titulo, in modern times "the Stoner."[3] However the King directed that his remains should be deposited therein, under the impression that the image and relics of a dead warrior would inspire the same terror he had infused when alive. For some reason not assigned, the Britons disregarded this request, and interred the heroic prince at Caer Ludd, or London.[4]

Perhaps some of the British nobles were prevented from complying with the last wishes of Vortimer, by the influence of Rowena, who no sooner found that her scheme had answered all her hopes, than she contrived, by flattery, to persuade the nobility to re-establish her husband upon the throne. This step was decided upon in a general council of state; and as soon as Vortigern was again made King, he sent into Germany, desiring Hengist to come over secretly, with a few attendants, lest if he came in any other manner, it might cause the Britons to rebel.—A. D. 461. The machinations of Rowena were thus far successful; her husband had recovered his crown, she was again a Queen; and her infant son, who had been born during her solitary sojourn in the Tower, was acknowledged the heir to the kingdom of Britain.[5] Under this promising aspect of affairs for the Saxons, Hengist was encouraged to set sail for Britain, with three thousand armed followers.[6] If the departure of her father had made Rowena "sad," as the historian informs us,[7] his return must have filled her heart with joy.

---

[1] Scott.

[2] Evans's Mirror of Past Ages, from an ancient MS. [3] Warrington.

[4] The following authors are unanimous in believing Vortimer to have been poisoned:—Evans ("Mirror," p. 106); Verstegan, c. 5, p. 129; Fabian, p. 76; Matthew Westminster, p. 120.

[5] Warrington. Langhorne says that no children were born to Vortigern by Rowena.

[6] Fordun. [7] Tanner.

Hengist now asserted his friendship for Vortigern, and his desire to support the claims of his own grandchild, the son of Rowena, whom he feared might be slain by the Britons, and who, Vortigern being aged and infirm, and unlikely to have more heirs, had the only claim to the throne.

The weak and superstitious Vortigern is said to have consulted Merlin as to the fate of himself and his son by Rowena, and received for answer that they should be burnt to death by Uther and Ambrose. These princes had a prior claim to Vortigern on the British throne. Their brother Constans, who had entered a monastery when a child, was, by Vortigern's contrivance, brought thence, on the death of Constantine, his royal father, to assume the crown,—A. D. 448.[1] Vortigern had afterwards caused him to be murdered, and seized on the vacant throne, to the prejudice of the junior princes, Uther and Ambrose, who, it was supposed, fled for safety into Bretagne.[2] This, however, was not the case, for Ambrose was detained in Britain by his mother; and is known afterwards as "Emris Wledig," or "Emperor," the title borne by his illustrious ancestor, Maximus: this was his Welsh title; the Roman one was Ambrose Aurelian.

After the departure of the Romans from Britain, many private Roman families had remained established here, forming a sort of clan of their own. The mother of Ambrose was one of these; her birth was very noble, for her parents were said to have worn the imperial purple,[3] but the name of her father has been purposely suppressed, though he is called a Roman chieftain, and of consular dignity. She is accused of having violated her vows as a vestal virgin.[4] This, however, seems to have been a fiction, invented by the enemies of the mother of Ambrose. Both herself and children had been educated by Guiteline, Archbishop of London; and Cirencester, the Roman city, is said to have been the scene of her espousals to their father Constantine.

On the death of Constans, her eldest son, his widowed[5] Queen, dreading that the cruel Vortigern should aim at the destruction of her other children, had lived in a state of complete seclusion. The young Ambrose gave such extraordinary evidence of his mathematical powers, that it was spread abroad as a rumour by the superstitious common people, that he was the offspring of a demon in human form, who had associated with his mother. The Queen desiring to conceal the rank of his father, favoured the conceit, and thus the youth early obtained the name of Merlin, "the Magician."[6]

Vortigern had, by the advice of his nobles determined to build an impregnable fortress in Snowdon, and collected the necesary materials to accomplish his design. To his surprise, these all disappeared in one

[1] Constantine, son of Solomon, King of Armorica, was elected and crowned at Silcestre, A. D. 433.—*Geoffrey of Monmouth, Holinshed.*

[2] Turner. [3] Bede. [4] Nennius.

[5] The emissaries of Vortigern, entering the bedchamber of young Constans, cut off his head, and carried it bleeding to Vortigern, who, feigning the utmost horror and astonishment, immediately ordered the deaths of the murderers! His next act was to assume the regal power.—*Warrington.*

[6] Langhornii Chronicon.

night. On consulting with his wise men as to the cause, they told him the building would never stand unless it was sprinkled with the blood of a child who was born without a father. The country was searched far and wide, when a cluster of boys at play were overheard to charge one of their companions with being an "unbegotten knave." This child was the Merlin of whom we have been speaking, and who, with his mother, was instantly brought into the presence of the royal Vortigern, his greatest enemy. The Queen was forced to keep up her deceptive story, by owning the youth the offspring of the being of supernatural powers; and Merlin was sentenced to be sacrificed. In this cruel emergency, the wisdom of the boy was the means of saving his life. He confounded all the wise men of Vortigern by his questions; and having explained why Vortigern had failed in his erection of the castle, by founding it on a morass, had the good fortune to be set at liberty. Merlin obtained great reputation by the circumstance alluded to, and many prophecies were afterwards imputed to him, the repetition of which was forbidden, in after-days, by the Council of Trent.[1]

When Vortigern, desirous of learning his future destiny, and that of the son of Rowena, appealed to the royal prophet, he received the answer which sincerity alone could have dictated,—a quality for which Ambrose Aurelian was ever remarkable, and distinguished by it from his contemporary chieftains.[2] This excellent prince was afterwards leader of the Britons against the Saxons;[3] his valour is said to have been equal to his modesty, and the latter was conspicuous in so learned a prince. It is particularly stated that he was skilled in mathematics and astronomy;[4] and to him the town of Ambresbury, in Wiltshire, owed its origin.

The British nobles had, on the arrival of so many armed warriors, under Hengist, felt very indignant, and prepared for war. Rowena informed her father, as usual, of what was to be expected; who sent to Vortigern, offering to retain such only of his followers as the King pleased; but requested an interview on the subject. Thus, under the appearance of peace, he concealed the most artful scheme.

Vortigern is said to have accepted an invitation from Hengist to a banquet at Ambresbury, with about three hundred of his nobles; and on this occasion it was, that the whole of the followers of the British King were slain by the Saxons, and Vortigern himself detained a prisoner. Among those slain was Vodinus, who, at Vortimer's instigation, had formerly reproved Vortigern for divorcing his Queen and marrying Rowena.[5] The haughty and insolent King, who is truly described as

---

[1] Pennant (from Nennius). "There were two Myrddins, or Merlins; one the minister and archbishop of Ambrosius, who succeeded Vortigern, and built Stonehenge called Myrddin Ambrosius, and whose skill in bringing the stones from Ireland, obtained him the name of Enchanter; and the Myrddin, or Morvyn, a British poet and prophet, contemporary with Taliessin, who lived in the following century, and died in Bardsey."—*Sir R. Phillips.*

[2] Turner.

[3] Hume.

[4] Gibbon.

[5] Langhornii Chronicon.

"neither wise in counsel, nor experienced in war," oppressed by the Saxons, and pursued by Aurelius, who took up arms after the death of Vortimer, fled for refuge into Wales, to a castle among the mountains of Caernarvonshire.

The valley of Vortigern (Nant y Gyrthyrn) is described as an immense hollow, to approach which says Pennant, "we ascend from Nefyn for a considerable way up the side of the high hill, and after a short ride on level ground, quit our horses. Fancy cannot frame a place more fit for a retreat from the knowledge of mankind, or more apt to inspire one with full hopes of security from any pursuit· embosomed in a lofty mountain, on both sides bounded by stony steeps, on which no vegetables appear, but the blasted heath and stunted gorse; the hind side exhibits a most tremendous front of black precipice, with the loftiest peak of the mountain Eist soaring above; and the only opening to this secluded spot is towards the sea, a northern aspect, where that chilling wind exerts all its fury, and half freezes during winter, the few inhabitants." [1]

Nennius places the scene of Vortigern's retreat near the Teibi, in Cardiganshire; but (says Pennant) "I believe that the historian not only mistakes the spot, but even the manner of his death. His life had been profligate, the monks, therefore, were determined that he should not die the common death of all men, and accordingly made him perish with signal marks of the vengeance of Heaven." The guilty monarch was, it is said, destroyed in the castle wherein he had taken refuge, by lightning, together with the rest of the inmates; or else they were burnt to ashes, together with the structure itself, by the contrivance of the Britons.[2] Pennant proceeds thus with his description of the spot: "Just above the sea is a high and verdant natural mount, but the top and sides worked by art. The first flatted, the sides marked with eight prominent ribs from top to bottom. On this might have been the residence of the unfortunate Prince, of which time has destroyed every other vestige. Till the beginning of the last century, a tumulus, of stone within, and externally covered with turf, was to be seen here; it was known by the name of Bedd Gwrtheyrn. Tradition having regularly delivered down the report of this having been the place of Vortigern's interment, the inhabitants of the parish, perhaps instigated by their minister, Mr. Hugh Roberts, a person of curiosity, dug into the cairn, and found in it a stone coffin, containing the bones of a tall man.[3] This gives a degree of credibility to the tradition, especially as no other bones were found with it,—no other tumuli on the spot; a proof, at least, of respect to the rank of the person, and that the place was deserted after the death of the royal fugitive about the year 465."

Rowena's history is littled noticed after the seclusion of Vortigern.

[1] The glen is tenanted by three families, who raise oats, and keep a few cattle, sheep, and goats, but seem to have great difficulty in getting their little produce to market.—*Pennant.*

[2] Howel.

[3] Kennett's Parochial Antiquities.

That she survived her husband, and still persevered in her feelings of resentment against the Britons, was believed, since she is accused of the death of Ambrose Aurelian, who is said to have been poisoned, in revenge for his share in her husband's death; "for she was very skilful in the art of poisoning."[1] Some writers, however, ascribe the deed to Pascentius, brother of Vortimer, who would be his rival for the crown; and a third account represents the philosopher King to have been slain in battle, fighting against his Saxon foes, and states that Stonehenge was erected over the spot where his remains were deposited, or else to commemorate the slaughter of those noble Britons who were massacred by the Saxon Hengist.[2]

---

[1] Oliver Matthew's Abbreviation of divers most true and ancient Britannic Chronicles, &c.

[2] Howel, Med. Hist. Ang.

GUENEVER I.

The beauty of the three Guenevers — Parentage of Arthur's first Queen — The Earl of Cornwall—Tintagel Castle described—Uther the Terrible, and his love for Igwerna—The Merlins—Gorolois and his wife—Uther marries the widow of Gorolois — Birth of Arthur — The Comet — Pendragon—Love of Arthur for his wife—She is carried off by the Duke of Somerset—Confined at Glastonbury —The Abbot obtains her release—She accompanies Arthur in an expedition against the Scots—First of the Twelve Battles—Guenever taken prisoner—She dies at Castle Dunbar—Tomb of Guenever and her maidens.

THE three Queens of Arthur the Great, the poetically-immortal adversary of the Saxons, were alike remarkable for their personal beauty, and for being honored with the name of Guenever, most probably in addition to some other appellative, and in reference to their pre-eminent loveliness. That they were, as some writers have imagined, but one individual, is clearly an error; as not only does their history, on careful examination, connect itself with the three successive portions or epochs of the life of their warrior-lord, but their parentage was different, and the place of their interment dissimilar. In giving them a place among the Queens of England, the opinion is followed of those authors who state that they were three separate princesses, bearing the name of Guenever, who, in turn, shared the regal honours as Queen-Consort.[1]

Every one of the many different readings of the word Guenever[2] has reference to beauty: it expresses "white as silver." A dazzling whiteness of skin, produced by the humidity of the climate, is said to have been a striking characteristic of woman in Britain at all times. "With her complexion ruddy, eyes blue, her hair long, and of a yellow colour, suffered to flow carelessly over the shoulders." The sex is described as "tall in stature, stately and dignified in manners, and in personal strength and vigour of mind so nearly approached to that of man, that softer sentiments often subsided, and made way for respect and awe."

High birth was intimated by the addition of Gwen, Vren, or Bren, to the name of any person. Eight Scottish monarchs bore the denomination of Eugenius, or Huganus,—the Owen, or Oeneus, of the Welsh, Evenus, or Eneas. The woman's name which corresponds is Gwenus;[3] the same as Venus, the goddess-mother of that hero Æneas, from whom the British kings, as late as Henry VII., pretended to derive their descent. We are expressly told that Arthur's first wife was so remarkably beau-

[1] Langhornii Chron., Lewis's Hist. of Great Britain.

[2] Camden. See Life of Gwenissa, p. 92. [3] Ibid.

tiful as to excel all the other ladies of Britain; on which account she was called Gwinne, "a word, in the Welsh tongue, signifying *fair*."

This beautiful Queen of the Britons was daughter of Corytus, or Gwryd Gwent;[1] though some go further a-field, and say that her father was king of Biscay.[2] She was of Roman descent, and had been educated, up to the time of her marriage, by Cador, Duke of Cornwall, who was her near relative.[3] Arthur, having established peace, married "a fayre ladye, and a gentel, that Cador, the Earl of Cornwall, had long since nourished in his chamber." We are not exactly told that Guenever was crowned, but that she was "made Queen;" therefore she no doubt enjoyed the honours of being consort of Arthur.

Guenever, it seems, was brought up from infancy by Cador, Duke of Cornwall,[4] called "her near relative." Cador was son of Gorolois, Duke or Earl of Cornwall, by Igwerna, the mother of King Arthur, and his "*own chamber*," or residence, was the famous Tintagel Castle, in Cornwall.

This castle, celebrated in romantic annals as the birth-place of Arthur himself, thus appears to have been the abode of his Queen during childhood. Carew describes the Castle of Tintagel thus: — "Half the buildings were raised on the continent, and the other half on an island, continued together, within man's remembrance, by a drawbridge, but now divorced, by the downefaln steepe cliffes on the farther side, which, though it shut out the sea from its wonted recourse, hath yet more strengthened the island; for in passing thither, you must first descend with a dangerous declyning, and then make a worse ascent, by a path,

---

[1] Langhorne. [2] Stowe.

[3] Biog. Brit. Caxton says she was his own cousin,—a fact corroborated by Stowe.

[4] Before Athelstan's time, the Earls of Cornwall retained the title of Duke or King; that monarch annexed it to his crown, but allowed the Duke or Earl the privilege of royal jurisdiction and crown right, the giving of liberty to send burgesses to Parliament, and appointing a sheriff, admiral, and other officers, which continued in the duchy till 1337, when the Parliament settled the duchy on the eldest son of the King of England, at the time when Edward the Black Prince was created Duke of Cornwall.

The eldest son of the King of England is born Duke of Cornwall, in respect to which he is of age at the very day of his birth, so as to claim living and seizing of the said dukedom. This, however, was first settled on the King's eldest son by Edward III.; and it is to be observed that it does not descend by virtue of that monarch's grant to the heir of the crown of England in general, but to the son, and him the first-begotten son of the King. So Richard de Bourdeaux, son of the Black Prince, who died without coming to the crown, was not Duke of Cornwall by birth, but was created so by charter; nor was Henry VIII., after the death of his brother, Prince Arthur, Duke of Cornwall, because he was not the eldest-born son. Sir Walter Raleigh estimated the settled revenue of the Prince of Wales, arising from the mines in Cornwall, at £20,000 sterling.

The Earls of Cornwall made Launceston Castle, Liskeard, Rostormel, and Moresk, at different times their place of abode; but since Edward III.'s time, when Trematon came into their possession, these residences ceased to be made use of, and fell into decay and ruin. The ancient British dialect was spoken in Cornwall till the time of Henry VIII., when the introduction of the English liturgy paved the way for its disuse.—*Magna. Brit.*

through his stickleness occasioning, and through his steepness threatening, the ruine of your life, with the falling of your foote. At the top, two or three terrifying steps give you entrance to the hill, which supplieth pasture for sheepe and couyes; upon the same I saw a decayed chappell. Under the island runs a cave, thorow which you may row at full sea, but not without a kind of horrour at the uncouthnesse of the place." Norden more particularly describes the island as being "by a very narrow, rockye, and wyndinge waye up the steepe sea-clyffe, under which the sea-waves wallow, and so assayle the foundation of the ile, as may astonish an unstable brayne to consider the perill, for the least slippe of the foote sendes the whole body into the devouring sea; and the worste of all is highest of all, nere the gate of entrance into the hill, where the offensive stones so exposed hang over the head, as while a man respecteth his footinge, he indaungers his head, and looking to save the head, indaungers the footinge. According to the old proverbe, 'He must have eyes, that will scale Tintagel.'"[1]

Secluded and wild as was this spot, the rumour of the charms of the fair Igwerna, mistress of the castle, had spread far and wide, and had reached, among others, Uther Pen-Dragon, "the Terrible," the reigning Prince descendant of Asclepiodatus, the famed Duke of Cornwall, who was contemporary with St. Helena.

Uther, who had just become a widower, is said to have first beheld Igwerna, the greatest beauty of her time, at a banquet held in London. He sought, without success, to win her regard by every means his passion could suggest; but the lady fled from his importunities, and, with her husband, Gorolois, returned to Tintagel Castle, whither she was pursued by Uther in disguise. The magical skill of Merlin[2] was called to his

---

[1] Magna Brit. Norden says that most of the buildings were in ruins, but by the view annexed to this account, it appears that those on the mainland were standing in his time. Leland says: "Shepe now fede within the dungeon; the residews of the buildings of the castle be sore wetherbeten and yn ruine, but it hath bene a large thing."

[2] The names of two Merlins are given in the Ancient Triad, in conjunction with that of Taliesin, as the three principal bards of the isle of Britain: —

Merlin Ambrose.

Merlin, the son of Morfyn (Merlin Silvester, or Caledonius).

And Taliessin, the chief of bards. [Taliesin, in the sixth century, wrote a poem on the Battle of the Trees, which is yet in existence; and in which he likens the words in the Ogham, or secret letters of the Welsh, to twigs or branches of trees. Mr. Darces seems to think that this is an allusion to the original system.]

Merlin Ambrose, or the Magician, already mentioned in the Life of Rowena, was a Druid of British or Welsh birth. Merlin Silvestris, born in Caledonia, also a celebrated Druid, lived about a century later, about 570, and dwelt in the city of Alcluid. The fact that Magi, or Druids, dwelt at the court of Brudi, who was converted and baptised by St. Columba, in 536, proves that the Order had not been so completely extirpated in Britain by the Romans as is generally supposed. [Toland's History of the Druids.] Rodarchus the Munificent, who reigned in Britain in the sixth century (A. D. 561), had two wives — one named Llangwrith, and the other Ganieda. Merlin the Prophet was brother of Ganieda: he had accompanied Feredarus, General of the Venedati, when he made war on Guenolous, the King, and so also had Rodarchus, his brother-in-law, and is thus noticed in

aid, who pourtrayed to the lady, by means of a shadow which he raised on the wall, the form of one who was destined to be her future husband. Uther, at length, disguised as Gorolois, deceived the beautiful Igwerna,[1] and it is said that Arthur was the offspring of this deceit. Some attribute the story to the policy of Gorolois himself, who desired to conceal his wife's frailty or misfortune; but the fact that Uther was compelled to the artifice of representing her husband, attests the truth and loyal integrity of the deluded fair one.[2] Not long after Gorolois fell by the hand of Uther, and that prince immediately married his widow.[3]

The birth of Arthur took place at Tintagel Castle,[4] a few hours only before the death of Gorolois, the event being attended by the appearance of a comet, which Uther beheld at Winchester, and which prodigy was explained by Merlin, whom the king had sent for, to denote the birth of a son, who should arrive at great power; and also of a daughter, whose sons and grandsons should successively enjoy the kingdom of Britain.

At Tintagel Castle is yet shown the hall and the bed of King Arthur, his way to church, &c.; and in the neighbourhood everything grand, uncommon or inexplicable, is attributed to him.[5] The author of the Legend of King Arthur says:—

"Of Brutus' blood, in Brittaine borne,
King Arthur I am to name;
Through Christendome and Heathynesse,
Well knowne is my worthy fame.

"And in the Castle of Tintagill
King Uther mee begate,
Of Agyana[6] a beauteous ladye,
And come of hie estate."

Both Guenever and Arthur could lay claim to a Roman ancestry, in token of which Arthur bore the celebrated surname assumed first by his father Uther the Terrible—that of Pendragon, which, in the British tongue, signifies Dragon's Head. The princes to which this epithet was appropriated are spoken of by the poet as

"Pendragon Kings of Uther's royal race!"

Geoffr y of Monmouth: — "Lo! then comes another from the hall of Rodarchus, King of the Cambri, to meet the conqueror, who had married Ganieda, and was happy in a beautiful wife. She was the sister of Merlin. And Rodarchus orders garments, hawks, hounds, swift steeds, gold, shining gems, and goblets, which Guierlaudus had carved in the city Sigeni, to be brought, and presents and offers them one by one to the prophet." "We thus see," says Toland, translator of this passage, "that Merlin the Wild was no mean person. His sister Ganieda was nobly married, and he himself, for his vaticination, which was a prominent part of the Druidical office, received a present which might have suited an emperor."

[1] Thrale's Retrospections. The name of Igwerna, Arthur's mother, signifies an eel or serpent, and perhaps the famed banner of her husband had some allusion to the circumstance.

[2] Antiquities of Glastonbury; Fabian. Buchanan likens the tale to that of Jupiter and Alcmena.

[3] Biog. Brit.; Merlin's Prophecies.

[4] Geoff. of Monmouth.

[5] Borlase, Hearne.

[6] Ibid.

Uther's famous ensign was the picture of a dragon with a golden head. The dragon, being considered an emblem of destruction, was depicted on the Roman standards of that epoch, and Uther, desirous of attaching the remnant of the Romans in Britain to his interests, adopted the fierce ensign to signify his descent from their emperors. The dragon had been displayed on the banners of Rome in an exhibition given to the people by the Emperor Gallien, and at the time of Uther, similar shows or spectacles were common throughout the remotest provinces of the Roman Empire; in Britain they were patronized by Uther, and afterwards by his son, King Arthur.[1] Cadwallader, their descendant, afterwards bore the red dragon on his banner, and Henry the Seventh, proud of his descent from the Roman line of princes, followed this example at the battle of Bosworth,[2] which brought in the line of Tudor, the ancestors of Queen Victoria.

In spite of all this, the very existence of Arthur has been questioned, though the son of Henry the Seventh was named after him, and many ancient writers attest the truth of his history. At the time of Uther's death,[3] Arthur was only fifteen or eighteen years of age, and from that date, A. D. 516, he reigned for a period of twenty-six years; the people he ruled were the Silures, and he is termed King of Gwent,[4] then the British metropolis of the nation.

Guenever the Fair had no children by Arthur, who, however, is said to have "loved her wonder well and dearly."[5]

---

[1] In the battle between Edmond Ironside and Canute, the Red Dragon of Wessex was unfurled. Henry III. placed it as his standard in Westminster Abbey, prior to his visit there, and had it carried before him at the battle of Lewes; and Edward III. also exhibited it at the famous field of Cressy. — Willemonte's Regal Heraldry.

[2] This banner of Henry VII., which afterwards gave rise to the office of Rouge Dragon among the heralds, was of white and green silk, in imitation of the one Cadwallader had used in his wars, who had singularly enough believed that, at some future period, one of his posterity should wear the English crown The dragon and the greyhound were the supports of the royal arms of Henry VII. and Henry VIII.: the former, as soon as he became king, having procured a true statement of his descent from Cadwallader. — Pennant.

Juliana Berners says that Arthur bore "three dragons, and over that another shield with three crowns."

Another national emblem, *the leek*, is said to have been first used at this epoch. In the days of King Arthur, St. David [uncle of Arthur — he was Archbishop of Menevia] won a great victory over the Saxons, having ordered every one of his soldiers to place a leek in his cap, for the sake of distinction; in memory whereof, the Welsh to this day wear a leek on the first of March."—Walpole.

"I like the leeke above all herbes and flowers;
When first we wore the same, the field was ours.
The leeke is white and greene, whereby is ment.
That Brittaines are both stout and eminent.
Next to the lion and the unicorn,
The leeke the fairest embleym that is worne."

Harleian MS., 1977

[3] Uther is said to have died from drinking the water of a poisoned well.

[4] Dr. Borlase, Howel, Kippis, Buchanan, Hearne. [5] Caxton.

A strange event is on record as having called forth the affection and courage of Arthur in his wife's behalf. Melvasius, Duke of Somerset, had by stratagem succeeded in carrying off the Queen from her husband, and kept her confined during the space of a year, in a castle near Glastonbury. As soon as the brave and injured King discovered the place of Guenever's concealment, he hastily collected his friends in Cornwall and Devonshire, and besieged the disloyal prince. While, however, one party was assaulting the town, and the other defending it, the monks, headed by the Abbot of Glastonbury and Gildas Albanius, fearing the consequence of this intestine discord, entered into the midst of the contest, and persuaded Melvasius to restore Guenever to her husband. For their successful mediation on this occasion, the monks were rewarded by both parties with a gift of considerable territory.[1]

Guenever afterwards accompanied her husband in an expedition against the Scots. On this occasion Arthur fought the first of the twelve famous battles ascribed to him, which took place on the banks of the river Duglas, in Lennox:[2] he four times encountered his foes in the same locality. In one of these fierce struggles "20,000 Picts and Scots were slain on one side, and 30,000 Britons on the other;[3] so great was the slaughter, that the river was dyed with the blood of the slain, whose bodies were borne down its banks with the stream to the sea. Next day the British camp was rifled, and many rich spoils taken. Among the prisoners was Queen Guenever, wife of Arthur, with a great number of ladies, her attendants, and other gentlewomen. All the booty was divided by lot among the conquerors; the captive queen and her maidens, with several noble prisoners, and much spoil, fell to the share of the Picts, by whom they were conveyed to Angus, and secured in the Castle of Dunbar, a

---

[1] Langhorne's Chron.; Turner from Caradoc ap Llancarvon. [2] Stowe.

[3] Holinshed, by mistake, places this engagement in 542. He says it was fought on the banks of the Humber; and that in it both Arthur and Modred, his nephew, were killed.

Aspatria is a long straggling village, standing on the ridge of a hill. In removing the earth of a barrow which stood on a rising ground, called Beacon Hill, about two hundred yards north of the village, in the year 1790, a human skeleton was found in a sort of rude chest, or kistvaen, formed by two large cobble-stones at each side and one at each end. The skeleton measured seven feet from the head to the ancle-bone; the feet were decayed and rotted off, and the other bones soon mouldered on exposure to the air. On the left side, near the shoulder, was a broad sword, five feet in length, the guard of which was elegantly inlaid with flowers; on the right side lay a dirk, or dagger, one foot and a half in length; the handle appeared to have been studded with silver. Part of a gold fibula, or buckle; an ornament for the end of a belt, a piece of which adhered to it; a broken battle-axe; a bit, shaped like a modern snaffle; and part of a spur, were also discovered here. On the stones that enclosed the west side of the kistvaen, were various figures, rudely sculptured, but principally representing circles, having a cross within each relief. The learned antiquary, Hayman Rooke, Esq., from whose account these particulars are extracted, was induced to suppose, from the above emblematical delineations, that the person here deposited was interred soon after the dawning of Christianity; and also to infer, from the rich ornaments contained in his sepulchre, that he was a chieftain of considerable rank. This has been sometimes considered the tomb of Arthur. — Britton and Brayley.

place of great strength, where they remained in confinement the rest of their lives," [1] The ill-fated Queen did not long survive this sad stroke of fortune; she died at Castle Dunbar, and was buried in the fields of a town called Megle, in the county of Angus,[2] about ten miles from Dundee.[3] Arthur is said to have in person attended the funeral obsequies of Guenever, over whose remains a sumptuous tomb was afterwards erected.[4] The ladies who had shared her captivity were, at their death, interred in tombs placed around that of their Queen and mistress. The tombs of Guenever and her maidens were yet pointed out in the days of Holinshed; as that historian relates, and from him we learn that a story was current even then respecting the sepulchre of the Queen, viz., that if any woman should chance to tread upon it, she would remain barren, as Guenever the Queen herself had been. "In consequence," says Langhorne,[5] "the women regard that monument of antiquity as a pestilent place, not even venturing so much as to look upon it, not only fearing the tradition for themselves, but teaching the same to their daughters, and bidding them also to beware of its influence." [6]

---

[1] Scott. [2] Rapin. [3] Scott. [4] Ibid.

[5] Langhorne places the death of Guenever I. in 511—the year in which Æscus, the Saxon King of Kent, died; but Arthur did not become king till 516, according to general history.

[6] Langhorne, Hector Boetius, Holinshed.

GUENEVER II.

Bridal festivities of Guenever, daughter of Uther ap Credawgal, at Carlisle—Arthur's Chamber—The Round Table—The Knights—The salt—The minstrels—Their accomplishments—The lady in her bower—The sweet key of Gwynedd—Customs at feasts—Grandeur of Arthur—Arthur a Christian—Arthur and Guenever in Brittany—The Fairy Morgana—The Coronation at Caerleon—Concourse of Kings—Guenever and the White Pigeon—Great ceremonies—Dubricius struck with the vanity of worldly grandeur—Retires to a cell—Arthur desires to be buried beside Guenever.

THE bridal festivities of the second Queen of Arthur, who bore the same name as her predecessor, that of Guenever,[1] were destined to form the theme of many a quaint and courtly ballad, familiarly known in modern times. This Guenever, who was daughter of Uther ap Credawgal, was united to Arthur at Carlisle, where might be seen as late as the times immediately preceding the Conquest, an ancient building, situated near the Church of St. Cuthbert, denominated Arthur's Chamber, supposed to have been part of the mansion of the British monarch.[2] The following lines from the ballad of the Marriage of Sir Gawain, allude to Guenever :—

"King Arthur he lives in merry Carleile,
And seemély is to see;
And there with him Queen Genever,
Yt bride so blithe of blee.

"And there with him, Queen Genever,
Yt bride so bright in bower;
And all his barons about him stoode,
Yt were both stiff and stoure.

. . . . .

"King Arthur welcomed them there right all,
And Genever, his queene,
With all the Knights of the Round Table,
Most seemély to be seene."

The date of these second nuptials of Arthur is given as 511; the battle of Bannesdown Hill, which overlooks the vale of Bath, having been fought immediately before.[3] As this, the twelfth battle fought by Arthur against the Saxons, was crowned with victory, the King, desirous of commemorating the occasion, had established that famous order of knight-

[1] Laughorne's Chron. [2] Britton and Brayley's Cumberland.

[3] Langhorne, Howel, Camden, Stowe.

hood whose members were designated Knights of the Round Table. The motto assigned to the order was characteristic of an ancient Briton: "Spread be my board, round as the horizon, and ample as my heart, that there may be no first or last; for odious is distinction, where merit is equal."[1] The number of these knights was limited to twenty-four, the King himself making the twenty-fifth.[2] Lothaire, husband of Queen Anna, Arthur's sister, was the first knight created by Arthur;[3] a great compliment to his brother-in-law, who is described as "a worthy prince, hardy, bounteous, manly, and right chivalrous." The creation of similar orders, on occasions of public rejoicing, had been customary from the earliest periods of our history; and several cities, among which may be mentioned Windsor, have laid claim to being the scene of the earliest investiture of this order. At Winchester, which disputes the point with Windsor, there may yet, says Evans, be seen "King Arthur's Round Table,"[4] hanging in the great hall, where the Saxon kings were subsequently accustomed to hold their feasts; this hall is supported by marble pillars, and is in the King's House, on the west side of the city of Winchester. The table, which bears the name of the monarch, is formed of one solid piece of wood, round which are cut several names in the Saxon characters, though only one, that of Lancelot, is legible,—a knight who takes a prominent part in the history of Guenever, the third of Arthur's Queens.

At Penrith a large circle may still be seen, which, after the lapse of centuries, retains the name of King Arthur's Round Table. It is supposed that this monarch introduced the fashion of round tables afterwards into Gaul, as they became very prevalent in that country, where every knight had at *his back* a squire with his armour in waiting.[5] This royal military order seems to have cultivated music; for a tune, called the "Prelude of the Salt,"[6] was always played whenever the salt-cellar was

[1] Sir R. Phillips. [2] Leland, Pennant. [3] Harding.

[4] Evans's Notes to Old Ballads. When Edward the First conquered Wales, in 1284, he held a Round Table, and celebrated his victories with dance and tournament. The concourse of English nobles on the occasion was prodigious, and numerous foreigners likewise graced the assembly with their presence.—*Pennant.*

[5] Marie de France, an Anglo-Norman poetess of the thirteenth century, the contemporary of Henry the Third of England, whose famous "lays" are in the British Museum among the Harleian Collection, No. 978, has one, the fifth, called "The Lay of Lanval," a knight of King Arthur's Round Table, who, being falsely accused by the Queen of having insulted her beauty, is, by the orders of Arthur, tried for the offence at Cardiff, and delivered by a beneficent fairy, who conveys him to the isle of Avalon. There are in all 646 verses on the subject. M. le Grand has translated this lay into prose in his "Fabliaux." There is also an ancient English metrical version of it, by Thomas Chestre.—*Hay's Biography.*

[6] Salt was, from the earliest times, highly esteemed, and admitted into religious ceremonies. As a mark of league and friendship, Jews, Greeks, and Romans held it sacred. Formerly, on Ascension Day, the old inhabitants of Nantwich piously sang a hymn of thanksgiving "for the blessing of the brine;" and Mr. Pennant, who thinks the custom of Saxon origin, says "that a very ancient pit there, called the 'Old Brine,' was also held in great veneration, and till within these few years, was annually, on that festival, bedecked with boughs, flowers, and garlands, and was encircled by a jovial band of young people, celebrating the day with song and dance."

placed before King Arthur's Knights at his Round Table. The nuptials of Guenever II. were graced by many gaieties; not only were the knights of the Round Table established on the occasion, but not any of the ceremonies usually observed at the marriage of the ancient British princes were neglected.

No public festivity, great feast, or wedding, was duly solemnized in Wales, without the attendance of the bards and minstrels. There was one class of musicians, a member of which was especially appointed to attend on the nuptial festivity. This musician was required to be a ready waiter at table, and also an expert carver of every species of fowl. At the weddings of any of the royal family, his office was to wait on the bride.

A picture in an ancient MS. of the British Museum, represents Arthur and his Queen at table in their royal robes, with their crowns, and surrounded by their attendants: in the front of the picture is a musician playing on what appears to be a *violin*, while a page on bended knees, offers a cup of refreshing beverage, as the reward of his minstrelsy.

The court bard lodged with the governor of the palace: the Prince was accustomed to bestow on him an ivory chessboard; the Princess, a golden ring. If the Princess called for a song after retiring from table to her own apartment, this bard had to sing to her highness in a low voice, lest he should disturb the performers in the hall. The subject was said to be on *Death* (not a very lively theme), but the word is probably misinterpreted, unless it was intended, like the skeleton at Egyptian feasts, to remind the lady of her mortality.

The marriage-fine of the bard's daughter was one hundred-and-twenty pence, her nuptial present thirty shillings, and her portion three pounds. The chief of the musicians was entitled to the marriage-fine for the daughters of all the inferior musicians or bards of the district, who paid twenty-four pence on their marriage; a proof of the antiquity and authority of this office.

The poets and minstrels contended for prizes of skill: at these Eisteddfods, or British Olympics, judges were appointed to decide on their respective merits. "Although it is probable these assemblies of bards were subjected to certain restrictions, there is no instance of such being the case before the days of Cadwallader, who died at Rome, A. D. 688. "Cadwallader, it is said, being at one of these assemblies, with his nobles, a minstrel came thither, who played in a key so displeasing, that he and all his brethren were prohibited, under a severe penalty, from ever playing on it any more; but were ordered to adopt that of Mwynen Gwynedd, or the sweet key of Gwynedd." [1]

There was another custom worth notice, which concerned the bards. The nuptial feast being concluded, a Pencerdd, or chief musician, was constituted Cyff Cler, and seated in a chair surrounded by the other bards standing, who made him the subject of their merry and ludicrous compositions, to raise mirth in the company. He was that day to make no reply, but on the next he was to divert the hall at the expense of the

[1] Pennant.

inferior bards, and was also to compose a poem upon a subject given him suitable to his dignity.[1]

There were not many dishes used by the ancient Britons at their feast, nor various kinds of cookery. "They served up fish, the flesh of tame animals, wild-fowl and venison, either boiled, broiled or roasted. Tame fowl they never brought to table; ducks, hens, and geese were indeed reared for amusement, but their feelings were spared the sacrifice of beholding the favourite bird of yesterday a victim on the board of to-day. In their kitchens they used spits and earthen pots; platters formed of wood, earth and even pewter, covered their tables. The knives and forks of the inmates or guests hung at their girdles, in the same case with the dagger, called by the ancient Scotsman, *Bidoc.* Side tables were also provided, on which might be seen drinking-cups of wood, horn and earth, one of silver usually being there also, and sometimes of shell. There was a distinction in the mode of placing themselves at the feast. The superiors or chiefs of the party occupied a table in the centre of the great hall, while their retainers sat upon benches raised but a little from the ground, and arranged in a circle around them; they were attended on by youth of both sexes. After eating, the chieftain called for a cup of wine or ale, and drank to the person who sat on his right hand, and the same cup being afterwards filled to the brim, was passed round the circle to each person in succession. Women not only had a place at the festive board, but were treated with much honour, and were accustomed to retire, as in more modern times, before the other sex indicated any symptoms of the effect of their potations."[2]

From many passages in Le Grand's Fabliaux, it appears that the custom of reclining on beds or couches during meals still subsisted, and to eat on the same trencher or plate with any one was considered a great mark of friendship. At great entertainments, the guests were placed two and two, and only one plate was allotted to each pair. In the romance of Perceforest, it is said, "there were eight hundred knights all seated at table, and yet there was not one who had not a dame or damsel at his plate." In the romance of Lancelot du Lac, a lady whom her jealous husband had compelled to dine *in the kitchen,* complains, "it is very long since any knight has eaten on the same plate with me."[3]

A peace of twelve years' duration followed the second nuptials of King Arthur. In this interval he acquired much renown by his splendour and magnificence, and foreign princes sought his friendship.[4] Norway and Denmark owned his supremacy, and Arthur sought to reduce Gaul, then a province of Rome. He laid siege to Paris, and reduced the city to such extremities that Flollo, the governor, offered to meet the King in single contest to decide the struggle, according to the chivalry of the day. In this encounter Flollo was slain, and Paris became the property of the British hero. Such is the account given by our ancient historians. Arthur, on this, established his court in France, and assumed for the royal coat of arms, quarterly, France and England. These arms,—afterwards

[1] Pennant's Wales.
[2] Macpherson.
[3] Notes to Le Grand's Fabliaux.
[4] Kippis, Biog. Brit.

to be seen in Glastonbury Abbey, on the head of which it was bestowed by the King, in divers panels of the wainscot of the abbot's apartment, and over the chimneys,—were "vert, a cross bottone, argent, in the first quarter our Blessed Lady, with our Saviour in her right arm, and a sceptre in her left, all or."[1]

That Arthur was a believer in the Christian faith, is evident from the fact of his making a cession of certain of his territories to the Saxon Prince Cerdic, on condition of his becoming a Christian.[2] Leland, who describes the seal of Arthur, which he had himself seen in the Church of Westminster,[3] declares that upon it the monarch appeared holding in his right hand a sceptre with a fleur-de-lis on the top, and in his left hand "orbem cruce insignitum,"[4] plainly inferring a sovereignty over both France and England.

The successes of Arthur have been described as so wondrous as to belong rather to fiction than history, and it has been doubted whether Arthur ever held any dominions in Gaul. However this may be, tradition that he had such a sway still lingers in Brittany, as a modern writer tells us, in describing a visit she paid to Caerduel, situate in the parish of Pleumeur Bodorr, "the lovers of romance will hardly think that labour lost which places them on a spot so celebrated in the chronicles of the period as the favourite residence of King Arthur. Here places and names surround us, with which the Romances of the Round Table have made us familiar, but to which fancy has assigned a locality in fairy-land, rather than in any veritable portion of the earth's surface. Here the half-fictitious personages whose adventures have in so many forms amused us, and the mystic performers of those deeds which have bequeathed to Europe an heroical literature of her own, have 'a local habitation and a name.'"[5] "Here it was," says M. de Fremenville, "that Arthur, surrounded by his noble peers, Lancelot, and Tristan, and Caradoc, and Yvain, and the rest, held a brilliant court, of which his wife, Guenarchan and the beautiful Brangwain were the ornament and pride."

"It is certain, at least as certain as anything can be relating to a period so remote, and at best but semi-historic, that Arthur possessed dominions in Brittany as well as in Wales, during the early part of the sixth century. In the romances which celebrate his adventures, we find him as often in one country as the other."[6]

The reminiscences attached to Caerduel, are not the only ones in this neighbourhood which relate to King Arthur, if the antiquaries of this country may be believed. "There is, at no great distance from this spot, and just off the coast, a little isle called Agalon, or Avalon, and here, as the Bretons most jealously maintain, and not at Glastonbury, according to the more generally received tradition, was the tomb of the monarch. The well known fable of his existence in fairy-land, and his

[1] Hearne's Antiquities of Glastonbury.

[2] Dr. Borlase.

[3] Selden believed it a fact that Leland did see the seal here alluded to.

[4] Selden's Titles of Honour.

[5] Mrs. Trollope, in "A Summer in Brittany."

[6] M. de Fremenville.

return at some future period to rule again over his faithful Celts on either side the Channel, a tradition firmly believed by the peasants in some parts of Brittany to the present day, has been explained under the hypothesis of his having died in the Breton Avalon in this manner. The fairy Morgain, whose name ought to be written Morgwen, and means 'whiteness of the sea,' was a Druid priestess living in that island. It is known that these mysterious priestesses usually dwelt on the most wild and savage promontories of this rugged coast, or in the still more inaccessible islands which surround it. On that shore of the isle of Avalon which is opposite to the main land, there are extensive quicksands; and the supporters of this explanation think, that Arthur's loss among these, upon some occasion when his love of the chase, or some other adventure, had taken him to this mysterious and sacred isle, was poetised into the story of the fairy Morgwen having detained him prisoner in her enchanted isle." [1]

Arthur had early distributed his possessions on the continent among his followers, and Normandy is said to have been allotted to Bedoer, his butler. During the nine years that France is said to have been the monarch's residence, he arranged everything for the preservation of tranquillity in his territories there. At length he returned to Britain, and considering some solemn demonstration of power necessary after so long an absence, he resolved to be again crowned, with every possible grandeur which such a great occasion could demonstrate. The feast of Pentecost was approaching, when King Arthur called together an assembly of his British subjects at Caerleon, in Monmouthshire, for this august ceremony to be performed.

The ancient city of Caerleon or Caergwent, is described by Giraldus Cambrensis, in his Itinerary through Wales in the year 1188, when he attended Baldwin, Archbishop of Canterbury, in his journey there; the object of the prelate not being, as is generally supposed, the conversion of the Welsh to Christianity, which had been early established in their country, but that of preaching a crusade for the recovery of the Holy Land, which, by the dissensions of the Christian princes, had lately been lost. There can be no doubt that the description of Giraldus affords an accurate representation of the state of that place in the twelfth century.

"It is called Caerleon, the City of the Legions; for 'Caer,' in the British language, signifies 'city,' or 'castle,' and because the Roman legions which were sent into this island, were accustomed to winter in this place, it acquired the name of Caerleon. This city is of great antiquity and fame, and was strongly defended by the Romans with brick walls. Many remains of its ancient magnificence are still extant, such as splendid palaces, which once emulated, with their gilded roofs, the grandeur of Rome; for it was originally built by the Emperors, and adorned with stately edifices, immense baths, temples, and a theatre, the walls of

[1] Mrs. Trollope. "From Kaerduel," continues the same author, "we walked to Penos Guirec, and there breakfasted, and then proceeded to Trecastel. It is a very remarkable line of coast, presenting, without any of the grandeur and sublimity of high cliffs, a scene of savage wildness and rugged barrenness which I have rarely seen equalled."

which are still standing. Here we still see, both within and without the walls, subterraneous buildings, aqueducts, and vaulted caverns, and what appeared to me most remarkable, stoves so excellently contrived as to diffuse their heat through secret and unperceivable pores. The city is pleasantly situated on the banks of the navigable Usk, and surrounded with woods and pasture."

Among the ruins of Caerleon, various antiquities have been from time to time discovered, of many of which a catalogue was preserved by Camden and his continuator.

The views in the neighbourhood of Caergwent are extensive and fine, but the mighty Roman city has sunk down to a miserable village, the ruined walls of which, on the south and west side, alone remain to attest its former greatness. A modern traveller writes thus respecting this spot of ancient celebrity: "The Roman walls are still visible, but the facing stones have long since been removed for private uses. Near the centre of the field, adjoining to the west wall, is the theatre (or more properly the amphitheatre), mentioned by Giraldus. The form of it only remains, no traces of its walls being discoverable; the diameter of the area is very large, and is bounded with a high circular entrenchment of earth. There is very little extant of the castle, which is of a later age; and the keep is remarkably lofty. Modern Caerleon contrasts in a melancholy manner with the grandeur of its ancient state, for it contains scarcely a single decent house!"

Not to modern Caerleon, but to that ancient Roman city which shone resplendent in art and grandeur, must the reader transport himself, to witness the second coronation of Arthur the Great, the supposed conqueror of Gaul, the hero of the ancient Britons, to whom nothing seemed impossible. The city was conveniently situated for the concourse whom the King had invited thither on this solemn occasion. Among the royal guests are named the Kings of Scotland, North and South Wales and of Cornwall, the Archbishops of London, York, and Caerleon, with many British princes, besides the Kings of Ireland, Iceland, Gothland, the Orkneys, and Norway.

So great was the splendour of this solemn festival that all the fronts of the houses are said to have been laid over with gold in honour of the occasion, after the custom of the Romans of that time. The British historian, who has handed down to us the particulars of the eventful ceremony, remarks, moreover, that "there never were assembled at any festival so many men and women of rank; so many steeds, hawks, and hounds; nor was there such a display of precious stones, golden vessels, and dresses of purple and fine linen, as there; for there was no one, even beyond Spain, desirous of distinction, who did not come to partake of the general satisfaction. There were also many who, uninvited, came to be spectators."[1] Arthur and Queen Guenever were invested with their crowns in the following manner:—

"When the company was assembled, the three Archbishops were called upon to robe the King, and place the crown upon his head; and

[1] Holinshed, Geoffrey of Monmouth.

Dubricius (Archbishop of Caerleon) was appointed *to sing the sacred service.* Arthur, when he entered the church, was arrayed in his royal robes, and supported by the other two Archbishops; and before him went four persons, bearing each a drawn sword, this being his privilege as general. The four persons were—Arawn ap Cynfarch, King of Albany; Caswallon law hir, King of Gwynedd; Meyric, King of Dyfed; and Cador, Earl of Cornwall. As he went on, the conventual train, on all sides, sang the best poetical compositions to the sound of musical instruments."[1]

"The Queen also, on her part, entered the church after him," though, according to Geoffrey of Monmouth's account, she went to the other church, which agrees better with what is said of the populace running from one church to the other. "This, and some other minute circumstances, give to the author of this description the air of one who had been a spectator."[2]

Whether the ceremony was performed in one church, or at the two different edifices, it is needful here to pursue the narrative of Tysilio. Guenever, according to his description, "entered the church after her husband, dressed in her royal robes, her crown on her head, attended by bishops and nuns, and the four wives of the four above-mentioned chiefs, each bearing a white pigeon in her hand.[3] When she had entered the church, the service began, which had been composed and set to music in the best manner ever known; and the people ran from church to church to listen to the different services.

"When the service was over, the King and Queen returned to the palace, changed their dresses, and entered the great hall to the banquet; Arthur and his attendants taking their places at one end of the hall, and at the other Gwenwhyfar, and the ladies in her train, as it was the custom for the Queen to do, when the King held a court, and had guests by invitation.

"When all the company were properly seated, Cei arose, and taking with him a thousand men, superintended the distribution and arrangement of the viands, as Bedwyr, comptroller of the cellar, with a thousand of his men, did those of the mead, which was served in vessels of gold and silver. All these had dresses of yellow ermine. Neither was the number or dress of those who waited on the Queen inferior to theirs who waited on Arthur.

"Hence it was that no court in Christendom could vie with that of Britain in customs or regulations. For all the men who attended on Arthur were in uniform, as were also their wives; and the ceremonial rules of behaviour were alike to all. And as no female, of any description, would admit the addresses of a man undistinguished by military excellence, the men were the more valorous, and the women more chaste.

"After the banquet, the company went out of the town to see a variety of games, and more especially the exercises with the lance; and what-

[1] Chron. Tysilio. [2] Rev. J. P. Roberts.

[3] This seems either to have been a part of the ancient ceremonial, or to have been an allusion to the feast of Pentecost.

ever were the game devised, the walls were crowded with female spectators, each of whom recommended her favourite to notice, which caused the men to exert their abilities to the utmost. Prizes for the victors were also given by the Sovereign, at his own expense.[1]

"Thus the festival continued for three whole days, and on the fourth, those who attended it were gratified by ample presents,—some by a grant of cities or castles, and others by vacant bishopricks. And on this occasion Dubricius, Archbishop of Caerleon, retiring to live as a hermit, surrendered his see; for, considering how long a preparation had been made for a festival of three days only, and struck with the perishable nature of worldly enjoyments, he resolved to prepare for the eternal joys of heaven."[2]

The translator of the foregoing Chronicle of Tysilio remarks, that this sentiment attributed to Dubricius, whatever he might think of the mode he pursued, is finely impressive; for surely, if transient pleasures require so much preparation, those which are eternal demand one more serious.

Although in the midst of coronation festivities, here must we break off the records concerning Guenever, the second of Arthur's Queens, of whom nothing more has been handed down, than an account of the exhumation of her remains, which, at her death, were interred at Glastonbury. This lady was so much beloved by Arthur, that at his own death he requested to be interred by her side, a desire fulfilled with fidelity by his British subjects.

---

[1] 'Some guests the while, as various likings sway,
With tables* or with chess beguile the day.'
The Knight and the Sword.—*Breton Lays.*

[2] Chronicle of Tysilio, translated by Rev. P. R. Roberts.

* Tables was a game resembling trictrac or backgammon. Both chess and tables were mentioned by Robert of Gloucester, in describing King Arthur's coronation—"Wyth pleyinge at tables, other atte chekere."—*Warton's History of English Poetry.*

Chess, a favourite Asiatic game, was either introduced into Europe by the Saracens of Spain, or learned from the Greeks or Turks by the pilgrims in the Crusades.—*Notes to the Fabliaux by M. le Grand.*

GUENEVER III.

Guenever, daughter of Gogauranus—The sisters of Arthur—Curious story of Fedelmia and her friend—The children exchanged—The invasion—The "hag's" visit—Explanation and secresy—Change in the manners of Arthur and his Court owing to the Pictish Princess—The enchanted mantle—Queen Guenever's disgrace—Sir Cradocke's triumph—The Three Battle-Knights of Britain—The Three Gift-Horses—The three Chaste Women—The fatal horn—King Mark's Queen—Tristan and Iseult—Queen Guenever and Lancelot—King Arthur's Castle at Camelot—His Courts—The King's nephews—Schools for British youth—Arthur quits his Court—Mordred's conduct—Battle of Camelford—Morgwenna and her maidens—Arthur's death—Constantine's cruelty—Guenever retires to Caerleon—Interred there—Discovery of Arthur's tomb.

THE third and last Queen of Arthur, like the two former, was known by the name of Guenever; her father was a King of the Picts, of gigantic stature, called Gogauranus,[1] who had also two sons, Durstus and Garnardus, Kings of Pictland.[2] From this it would seem that the new bride of Arthur was daughter of the King to whom his sister Ada had been married. Anne[3] and Ada, both very beautiful princesses, the children of Uther Pendragon by Igwerna, were both married on the same day; Anne, the eldest,[4] to Lothaire, King of the Picts, and Ada, the youngest, to Gabranus, or Goranus, who ruled over the Scots.[5] This double nuptial ceremony was performed at London,[6] and the princesses were given away by their uncle Aurelius Ambrosius. Goranus had been previously married to a lady named Ingeanach, of whom the following curious story is recorded, and which, as it seems much more likely that she was mother of Guenever III., than the Princess Ada, who was Arthur's own sister, is here given.

Eochaidh, or Eugenius, son of Eana Cinsalach, King of Leinster, had been banished from Ireland, by Niell, the monarch, and, with his consort, Fedelmia, sought an asylum in Scotland, with her friend Ingeanach, wife of Goranus, son of Domangard. Both ladies were on the point of becoming mothers, and being brought to bed on the same night, partly for convenience, and partly from regard to each other, had been lodged in the same apartment, no other person being admitted to their chamber but the female attendant whose presence was necessary on the occasion. Fedelmia brought forth two sons; Ingeanach only a daughter, and all her children being girls, she had passionately desired a son. This having

[1] Langhorne. [2] Ibid.

[3] Called by Langhorne, Arthur's "twin-sister," "gemella soror."

[4] Scott. [5] Carew, Kippis, Rowlands. [6] Holinshed.

also been the wish of her husband, whom she desired to please, Ingeanach besought her friend to substitute one of her sons for the daughter to whom she had given birth. The exchange was readily made, and the infant prince received with embraces of affection by Ingeanach. As soon as the Queen's attendants were admitted, and learnt that a prince had just been born, they carried the happy tidings to Goranus, who, unsuspicious of any fraud, received the infant with the greatest endearments, named it Eugenius in honour of his friend, and treated it as his own.

On the death of Niell, Eugenius or Eochaidh, returned into Ireland, and took possession of Leinster, his own patrimony, over which he ruled for many years. His wife and son, whom he sent for from Scotland, joined him there: the latter, who succeeded him on the throne, had received the name of Brandubh.

Meanwhile, Goranus had settled the succession upon his supposed son. At his death, Eugenius was, therefore, crowned King of the Scots, without opposition. No sooner had he settled his affairs than he prepared for an invasion of Ireland, grounding his pretensions to that kingdom on his royal descent. He landed with his forces in Leinster, and commenced plundering the inhabitants. Brandubh, then king, perceiving how incompetent his forces were to contend with those of his enemy, gave himself up as lost; and his despair was augmented by the Scottish King's sending to demand of him a heavy tribute, under the penalty of spreading fire and sword through his dominions. At this critical juncture, his mother, Queen Fedelmia, who lived with him, volunteered to go in person to Eugenius, having a scheme of her own, by which she hoped to persuade him to retire out of the province. On her arrival at the Scottish camp, the Queen demanded an audience of the royal leader. So extraordinary a request led the King to imagine that the lady was distracted; but he nevertheless acceded to her petition. She then boldly expostulated with him upon the subject of his invasion, represented the cruel havoc he was making in Leinster, and bravely inquired what had provoked him to so barbarous and unwarrantable an undertaking. Eugenius, indignant at being thus called to account, replied roughly, that "it was not necessary for him to answer every *old hag* who should ask him questions;" and then ordered her to quit the camp. Whereupon Fedelmia told him "that his own mother was as much a hag as herself, as she would soon convince him, if he would grant her a private audience, for she had a secret to disclose that was of the utmost importance to his interest." The King, who was all curiosity to hear what she had to say, having granted her request, Fedelmia thus addressed him: "Sir, I told you that your own mother was such a hag as myself, which is literally true; for I am your mother, and Brandubh, the King of Leinster, whom you seem resolved to drive out of Leinster, is your own brother; and to evince my honour and veracity upon this occasion, I beseech you to send instantly to your supposed mother, the Queen Dowager of Scotland, who, I am confident, will assert the truth, and confess that you are my son; only let me entreat you to cease hostilities and outrages upon the province until the messenger returns." The astonishment of the King was great at what had been revealed by Fedelmia, and so important did he consider the relation she had given him, that he instantly dispatched a messenger into Scotland to his mother, desiring she would come to him into Ireland with all possible haste, as her presence was absolutely necessary relative to the most tender circumstance which had occurred to him during his whole life. Queen Ingeanach complied with the request of her son, and on her landing in Ireland was conducted to the camp. The King of Scotland then acquainted her with the occasion of his message, and the surprising account he had heard from the Queen of Leinster, and desired she would satisfy him as to the truth of the discovery, and declare on her honour whether he was her son or not. The lady openly confessed the whole intrigue between herself and the Queen of Leinster, and convinced the King as to the fact of his birth, who desired that they would keep the matter secret, lest his right to the crown should be disputed, and an attempt be made to prevent the succession of his family to the throne of Scotland; for if the tribe of the Dalriada were informed he was not the son of the deceased monarch, they would dispute his title, and disturb his government. The ladies bound themselves to secrecy; a peace was immediately made, and a strict friendship established with Brandubh, the King of Leinster; and Eugenius, withdrawing his forces from the island, returned into Scotland.

Very unlike was this Queen to her predecessors in character—for we read of Guenever II., that no court in Christendom was more remarkable for female purity than hers, where the men were brave, and the women free from reproach—and no sooner had Arthur become allied to this Pictish princess, than a change took place in the manners of the court; nor does the fame of Guenever III. herself escape. Not only was Guenever unfaithful to her royal lord, but the brave Arthur, the hero of his times, who had been so tenderly attached to his two former Queens, followed the bad example of his present wife.

A story is related of an enchanted mantle, the property of which was, that none but a modest and pure woman could wear it. It was justly reckoned one of the greatest curiosities of Britain, and as such is frequently alluded to by the old Welsh bards.[1]

This extraordinary garment was brought to Carlisle, where the court was then staying: it was the third morning of May. "God speed thee, King Arthur," said the dwarf who exhibited this robe, the pattern and nature of which were rare to behold; "and God be with thy fair Queen Guenever. I have brought a curious article of female costume, well-shaped, and fair to look on, which I wish her majesty to try on; but it has one small fault,—it will neither keep shape nor colour a moment on any lady that hath done amiss." On this, all the knights in the court began to be in fear for their ladies; but not so Queen Guenever, who forthwith advancing, boldly seized the mantle, and threw it at once over her person, to make the first trial, when, lo! says the ballad—

"From top to toe it shiver'd down,
As though with sheers bestradde.

"One while it was too long,
Another while too short,
And wrinkled on her shoulders
In most unseemly sort.

[1] Sir Henry Ellis.

"Now green, now red, it seemed,
Then all of sable hue;
'Beshrew me,' quoth King Arthur,
'I think thou be'st not true!'"

On which remark, the Queen indignantly casts down the mantle, with severe reproaches to her lord, saying, as she departs to her chamber—

"'I had rather live in desarts,
Beneath the greenwood tree,
Than here, base king, among thy groomes,
The sport of them and thee!'"

Sir Kaye next called on his lady to essay the wonderful garment: "Here, put on this mantle, if thou art innocent; but if thou art guilty, bide where thou art, come not near it." How did the knights laugh, and the ladies titter with mirth, when they beheld the mantle shrivel and shrink together! the lady cast it from her, and followed Guenever to her chamber. Another trial was made; but at the first touch, this sensitive garment shrunk up "to a tassel and a thread." At last, Sir Cradocke's lady made the attempt, and with complete success; for the magic robe fell into as elegant and decorous folds as any matron could desire. Queen Guenever, who, from her chamber beheld this, burst forth into passionate exclamations of envy, and, coming down into the company, declared the mantle had been falsely won; she was thereupon reproved by the owner, who told the King freely, that she stood in need of chastisement, for her bold speech and too free carriage.

Warton was of opinion, that the ballad of "The Boy and the Mantle" was taken from an old French piece, entitled, "Le Court Mantel," quoted by M. de St. Palaye, in his "Mémoires sur l'ancienne Chevalerie:" the tale also resembles that of Ariosto's Enchanted Cup. The old stories possessed by other countries of King Arthur, were imported originally from Britain, according to Sir Henry Ellis. The currency of the story is a proof, at least, that there was no want of satire at Arthur's court, and probably no lack of matter for its exercise.

While the owner of the mantle was reproving Guenever, a wild boar ran by, which he seized, and having killed, laid the head down before the court, saying, "No man, whose wife has done him wrong, can carve that!" Several hid their knives, unwilling to risk the attempt; some others affected they had none; but all who did try failed, Sir Cradocke alone excepted. A golden horn was then produced by this ill-omened stranger, who filled it with wine. "Let any knight, whose wife hath erred, try to drink out of that." "It was spilt on the shoulder of one, on the knee of another, and in the eyes of a third; nor could any drink a drop but Sir Cradocke, who won the horn and boar's head, while his dame carried off the magical garment, accompanied by the envy and acclamations of the whole court.

Cradocke, or Caradoc, was surnamed strong-armed. His warlike achievements obtained for him the dignities of a Knight of the Round Table, and he was made lord of the "dolorous tower," destined for the confinement of state-prisoners. The Triads style him one of the *three* battle-knights of Britain; and Arthur himself called him the Pillar of

Wales. His praises were celebrated by Aneurin Gwawdrydd, "the Monarch of the Bards," who flourished about 570, in his poem entitled, *Godod'in:* and the Triads style his fleet war-horse Lluagor, "one of the *three* gift-horses of Britain." Caradoc, however, possessed a still greater treasure, as we have seen, in his wife, a princess whom the triads notice as "one of the three chaste women of Britain;" who possessed three rarities, of which herself only was reputed worthy—her mantle, her golden goblet and her knife."[1]

A horn, adorned with gold, is mentioned in the poem called "La Mort d'Arthur," possessing such virtue, that no lady untrue to her husband could drink out of it without spilling the wine: this enchanted horn had been sent to acquaint Arthur with Guenever's frailty, but was intercepted by King Mark, whose queen, with one hundred of her ladies, tried to drink out of it, and "only four could drink without spilling!" There is another characteristic story told of the Queen of Mark: these popular tales are almost all we have to guide us as to the habits of the day, and have therefore their value.

Many, indeed, is the fiction interwoven with the history of Arthur's time; and difficult is it to separate the true from the false. Caradoc and Tristram, and indeed, most of the knights whose achievements have been handed down in ballads to posterity, have left their names attached to numerous spots of legendary interest.

The famous legend of the Queen of Mark runs as follows:—

Morrough, one of Arthur's newly created knights, brother of the Queen of Leinster, was sent by Anguish or Angus, King of Ireland, into Cornwall, to demand of Mark, its king, a tribute won from him in single combat. Payment was refused, but Mark offered to meet the ambassador in single combat, to decide their strength of arms. Sir Tristram, or Tristan in the French romances, undertook the share of Mark in the engagement, in which he dealt so fierce a blow on his opponent's skull that, returning to Ireland, he died of the wound. Tristram himself was wounded by a spear, which had been poisoned, and he departed also for Ireland, to seek a cure in the country where the poison had been prepared. While at court there, his skilful performance on the harp made a great impression on all the household of King Anguish, and won for him the heart of the beautiful Isod, or Isolde, the monarch's daughter. Her love was returned; but as true love always finds a cross, the Queen, by private intelligence and other means, learnt that Sir Tristram was the person to whom her brother owed his death-wound; upon which discovery he was banished, not only from the court, but also from the kingdom. On his return, Mark was so interested by the recital of the charms of the Irish princess, that he despatched Sir Tristram to Ireland again, as his own ambassador, to seek the hand of Isolde for himself. "La Belle Iseult," as French romances call her, returned with her former lover to Cornwall, where her marriage with Mark was celebrated with much joy and solemnity. But the renewed acquaintance of the lovers had revived the flame which should now have been extinguished. Again Sir Tristram sought to en-

[1] Le Grand's Fabliaux, *notes*.

tertain his fair mistress with the sweet strains of his harp; and on one of these occasions he became a victim to the aroused jealousy of Mark, by whose hand he was slain; so that the historian remarks "his love, which began with the harp, ended with the harp."[1] The father of Isod, who doated on her, had built for her, before she left Ireland, a castle upon the walls of Dublin, called Isod's or Isolde's Tower. It stood near "a void room called Preston's Inns, which, in those times, served as a place of recreation for the monarchs of the country;[2] and, not far from Dublin and from Isod's Tower, is a chapel with a village, named Chapel Isoud, which was afterwards built by King Anguish, 'in remembrance of his child, and for the good of her soul.'"[3]

The chronicles of the times abound with instances of Guenever's gaieties; and in the merry court of Arthur, filled with knights and chivalry, many strove to obtain the notice of the fair Pictish Queen, who presided over their assemblies. In the curious metrical romance, entitled "La Mort d'Arthur," the greatest part of the poem consists of the exploits of Sir Launcelot du Lake, King of Benwike, his amours with Guenever, and his refusal, for her sake, of the beautiful daughter of the Earl of Ascalot. At the conclusion of the tale, both Launcelot and Guenever assume the religious habit, in token of their repentance.[4]

It was usual for knights to wear the sleeve of their lady love or mistress upon their arms. Elayne, the fayre maiden of Aslotot, gave Sir Launcelot "a reed sleeve of scarlet, wel embroudred with grete perlys."[5] This love-token the gallant knight of the Round Table ventured to display at a tournay, which circumstance very seriously displeased his royal mistress, Queen Guenever, who, like other enamoured dames, could brook no rival. Nevertheless, Sir Launcelot's fidelity to the Queen, though often tried in that fickle court, was so firm that legends tell of his having been visited by a fair love-sick damsel, who assuring him the Queen could not possibly be informed of his trespass, he chivalrously answered, "Though she should never know it, my heart, which is constantly near her, could not be ignorant." One of the four knaves or varlets of the French playing-cards bears the name of Lancelot, in memory of that valiant hero.

The circle which surrounded the King and Queen of this chivalrous time appears to have been more merry than moral, and extremely splendid.

"King Arthur at Camelot kept his court royall,
With his fayre quene, Dame Guenever the gay;
And many bold barons sitting in hall,
With ladies attired in purple and pall."

"Cadbury Castle, called by ancient topographers *Camalet*, was situated on the eastern side of the parochial church of Cadbury," at the northern extremity of a ridge of high hills, commanding an extensive prospect over Meadess and the Blackdown summits in Devonshire. "Its

---

[1] Dr. Hanmer, Caxton, Book of Houth.
[2] Holinshed.
[3] Dr. Hanmer.
[4] Wharton's History of English Poetry.
[5] Art of Needlework.

form," says Mr. Collinson,[1] "is neither entirely circular nor square, but somewhat between both, conforming to the shape of the hill. Part of it seems to have been hewn out of the solid rock, and is defended by four ditches, and within is a still higher entrenchment of a circular form, which was the citadel or *Prætorium*, but vulgarly called King Arthur's palace."

The rampart is composed of stones, now overspread with earth, and has only one entrance from the east, which is guarded by six or seven ditches. The area contains upwards of thirty acres. Within it and in the ditches, have been found at different periods, many noble relics of the Roman Empire.[2]

This ancient fortification, which, by its name, signified "Tower of War," is called by Drayton, "King Arthur's Ancient Seat;" and many places there and in the neighbourhood bear the name of that British King. His Round Table, his Kitchen, his Well, have been transmitted to our times, and even a road across the fields, under the Castle, is known as King Arthur's Hunting Causeway.

The following lines of Drayton commemorate this ancient British seat:

"Like Camelot what place was ever yet renowned?
Where, as at Caerleon, oft he kept the Table Round;
Most famous for the sports at Pentecost so long,
From whence all knightly deeds and brave achievements sprung."

According to the British Triads, the principal courts or palaces of Arthur were the following:—Caerleon, on the river Usk, in Wales; Celliwig, in Devon or Cornwall; and Penrhyn Rhionedd, in the north.

The feast which Arthur held at his coronation at the first of these places, is there also spoken of as one of "The three honourable feasts of the Isle of Britain."

Among the many distinguished characters who graced the court of the chivalrous Arthur, were Mordred and Gawainus, two of the King's nephews, the sons of Lothaire, by Anna, daughter of King Uther, "the Terrible." For the eldest of these princes the Queen is said to have entertained a very strong attachment. Both of them were natives of her own country, the land of the Picts; and though the admirers of Arthur have loaded the memory of Mordred, his destroyer, with every opprobrious reproach, the British Triads state that he was remarkable for his "gentleness, good nature, and agreeable conversation," and that it was "difficult to deny him any request."[3]

The manner in which these princes became associated with Arthur's nobles, was thus:—Their father, Lothaire, on the death of Uther, laid claim to the British crown on the score of Arthur's illegitimacy, he having married Anna, daughter of the deceased King,—a proof she was not Arthur's twin-sister, as Langhorne has asserted, but born after Igwerna's marriage. Finding this argument ineffectual, Lothaire united with the Saxons and Colgrim, who ruled in Northumberland, against Arthur.

---

[1] History of Somerset.

[2] Leland, Camden, Stowe, Selden.

[3] Turner's Anglo-Saxons.

He was defeated, and afterwards entered into an alliance, by which it was stipulated that Lothaire should preserve peace with the Scots, and aid Arthur against his Saxon foes; the condition being that Arthur should enjoy the crown during his own life, but that when he died, it should descend to Mordred or his sons, if he had any.[1] This treaty had answered very well for Arthur at the time when it was made, after the death of his first Queen, who was childless, and when he had himself no prospect of issue. Nor had he any children by Guenever the Second, as far as history records; yet the third Guenever, the faulty Queen, became the mother of several. There were two sons, called Noe and Llechan.

According to the agreement of Arthur and Lothaire, Mordred, the eldest son of the latter, took up his abode at the court of Arthur, as his destined successor; and his brother, the young Gawaine, also accompanied him into Britain for the purposes of education: the name of Sir Gawaine figures prominently in many of the romances of this epoch.

In Arthur's time, there were many schools in England for the education of youth; every monastery, indeed, receiving pupils. Paulinus, the disciple of Germanus, resided in the Isle of Wight, where he received pupils for education; and Dubricius, the Archbishop of Caerleon, had a school "in a place abounding with woods:"[2] to this last, perhaps, the young Pict was transferred. St. David, his great uncle, paid a visit to the establishment of Paulinus, who, we are told, used "to sup in the refectory, but had a scriptorium, or study, in his cell, being a famous scribe."

Lothaire, who had been the first-created knight of Arthur's Round Table, was afterwards appointed to rule over Norway and Denmark; and Gawaine became ruler of Lothian, in Scotland, the patrimonial estate or inheritance, but tributary to his uncle, the King of the Britons;[3] while Thametes, his royal sister, becoming the mistress of Eugenius, King of Scots, had by him a son, St. Kentigern, afterwards Bishop of Glasgow, a prelate of royal blood, who became a great favourite of Brudeus, King of the Picts.

Morgwenna, or Anna,[4] sister of Arthur, after her husband's death, entered on the Druidical office of priestess, in one of the islands anciently so celebrated for those rites, upon the coast of France; later still, we

---

[1] Holinshed. [2] Fosbrooke's British Monachism.

[3] Lothaire's dominions included all the lands about Pentland to the Forth, which were from him called Lothian. He was also rightful heir to the throne of Norway, being of the lineage of King Sichelm. The Norwegians had elected Riculf for their king; but Arthur, who had invaded Norway and Denmark, killed the usurper, and placed his brother-in-law upon the throne, who immediately resigned Lothian, in Scotland, to his son. — Harding, Brit. Bray.

Langhorne calls Lothus the ruler of Laudonia, and brother of Augusellus and Urianus. [Turner also says Lot was brother of Urien, and son of Cynfarch, and that Anna's marriage with him united the Kings of the Northern Britons in consanguinity with Arthur.] It was Augusellus bore the sword at Arthur's coronation: we do not hear that Lothus was present on that occasion.

[4] Whether Morgwenna and Anna are the same admits of a doubt.

trace her to Avalon, and find her attendant on the bed of her dying brother, King Arthur.

Arthur, finding it necessary to take up arms against the Romans, and to quit the country for that expedition, made the necessary arrangements for government during his absence. He accordingly declared publicly, that should anything happen to himself, Constantine, the son of Cador, Earl of Cornwall, a nobleman much loved by the people, was the person he desired to succeed to his crown: by which it would seem that he did not consider Guenever's sons his heirs. During his temporary absence, Mordred was placed at the head of the government, as regent, and Arthur commended the Queen, his wife, to his protection.[1] This done, the King departed to battle with his enemies, little expecting what would transpire in his absence.

Mordred, who had always expected to succeed to Arthur's crown in the event of his death, was so much exasperated on learning that Constantine had been preferred to him and to his children, that he remonstrated with the King, and ventured to remind him, before his departure, of the agreement made formerly with his father.[2] King Lothaire was dead, and Arthur now made that an excuse for considering the agreement at an end; Mordred and his friends were accordingly silenced for a time, but no sooner was Arthur gone than Mordred began to endeavour to establish for himself the claim to what he conceived his rightful inheritance.

His designs, however, did not at first discover themselves openly. Perhaps Mordred would never have carried them to such lengths, had he not been secretly favoured by Queen Guenever, who was attached to him, and from the first had desired to promote his views, and those of her countrymen, the Picts.

When first Mordred had settled at the court of Arthur as heir apparent to his crown, he had received the hand of the daughter of Gawolan, a British lord much esteemed by Arthur, and sister, as is supposed, of the historian Gildas.[3]

Although Mordred had formed this alliance, and had offspring by his wife, he is said to have encouraged the Queen's passion privately, while both conspired against his uncle's crown. He was not long in assembling a party in his favour, composed of Picts, Scots, and Bretons, and of their cabals Guenever was not ignorant, having, as we are told, been "too

---

[1] Biog. Brit., Robinson.

[2] Buchanan.

[3] Opposite Uphill, in Somersetshire, is the lofty island of Steep Holmes — a vast rock, inaccessible except by two passages, the summit sandy and unfruitful, producing few shrubs or vegetables. In this solitary spot, Gildas Badonicus, the ancient British historian and philosopher, surnamed "the Wise," pursued his literary studies, disturbed alone by the noisy sea-gulls, which build their nests amid the crevices of the rocks. Here, while the country was wasted with civil strife, was composed his celebrated work, "De excidie Britanniæ." But not even in this forlorn place of refuge did he long remain unmolested. A band of pirates, who had fled there to escape justice, settled in the island, and, by degrees, stripped the sage of the little he possessed, till, obliged to forsake the island, he betook himself to the Monastery of Glastonbury. He died about 570. — Collinson's History of Somerset.

familiar with Mordred." To fortify himself still more strongly against his uncle, Mordred entered into an alliance with the Saxons under Ethelbert, the first King of Kent, who held his court in the town of Richborough, in the Isle of Thanet.

Arthur, meanwhile, had been apprised of the deep injuries which he had sustained, and leaving his nephew Hoel, King of Armorica, to pursue his affairs abroad, returned with all haste to Britain. He succeeded in landing in Kent, where, at Richborough, a bloody battle was fought, in which, though many of Arthur's friends were slain, Mordred was defeated and forced to fly to Winchester, whither the King pursued him. He was again defeated by Arthur at that city, and forced to fly into Cornwall.

The final contest between the King and his nephew took place about a mile and a half from Camelford,[1] on the banks of the river Camblan, in Cornwall. Numbers fell on both sides during the engagement: the army of Mordred was totally routed, the Prince himself slain in the battle, while his brother Gawaine, who fought on the side of his patron the King, also lost his life. Arthur, mortally wounded, was conveyed from the field by his friends. His sister Morgwenna,[2] as recorded by all credible historians, with her attendant maidens, conveyed the dying King in a barge along the shore to the Usella, which they ascended, and committed him to the care of his friends at Glastonbury, in Avalon, Somersetshire. There, in the monastery, Arthur remained during the brief period which preceded his death, for his wounds proved mortal. Finding himself becoming hourly weaker, he resigned his crown to Constantine, the son of Cador, whom he had previously nominated his successor. Notwithstanding the tender care bestowed on the King by Morgwenna and her maidens, who were well versed in the female Druidical accomplishment of healing, Arthur died of his wounds, May 21st, A. D. 542.[3] Fearful that the news of his death would cast a damp over the Britons, and infuse courage into their Saxon foes, it was industriously circulated that Arthur was recovering; and Taliessin sang that Morgwenna had promised that if her brother remained a long time with her, she would cure his wounds; hence it happened that the return of Arthur was, for many ages after, one of the fondest hopes of the British people.[4]

As for Constantine, he was crowned by Arthur's subjects on the King resigning his crown, and this event was followed by the murder of the two young sons of his rival, Mordred, attributed by some authors to Constantine himself, though he had given them a promise of safety. This King is said to have cruelly slain the royal youths in the church with their two governors, even in the arms of their mother, to whose lap they flew for shelter, vainly beseeching her to protect them, nor could the intervention of the Abbot avail, who threw his cope over them, hoping that respect for his sacred robe would have withheld the murderers. Some attribute the deed to revenge for the death-wound of Arthur having

[1] During this battle, in which Mordred was killed and Arthur mortally wounded, the sun is said to have been twice eclipsed!

[2] Called by romancers "The Fairy Morgana."

[3] Warner's Glastonbury.

[4] Turner.

been dealt by Mordred, others to a resolution to extinguish the race of Mordred, lest they should aspire to the regal power which they might justly claim from their grandmother, the sister of King Arthur.

On the dispersion of the clergy, Cuillog, the widow of Mordred, and her brothers, retired into Anglesey, where they built cloisters for religious purposes.[1] As Arthur had disinherited the young princes, sons of Cuillog, it is not surprising that their uncle Gildas, the British historian, omitted the name of King Arthur in his work, or that he spoke ill in it of Constantine, who was his nephews' murderer, besides using many angry expressions in his epistle.[2]

It was only for a short time that Constantine preserved his power: the Saxons effected a landing in Britain, and after sustaining a defeat from them, he fled to Wales with his wife and children, where for some years he maintained his royal state. On the death of his Queen, he became weary of the world, and retired secretly into Ireland, where he spent some time in ministering to the poor. At last, becoming known, Constantine was persuaded to resign his crown to his son, and profess himself a monk in the Monastery of St. David,[3] being a sincere convert to the Christian faith.[4] He was afterwards sent into Scotland by the bishop of his diocese, to instruct the people there in the faith, and while in that country suffered martyrdom, for which, many years after, he was canonized as a saint; and many Scottish churches, according to Holinshed, were, in his time standing, built by the bishops of that country, and dedicated in the name of St. Constantine.[5]

To return to Queen Guenever. At the time that Mordred was first put to flight by Arthur, she was residing at the city of York,[6] but tidings being brought to her, that Mordred was unable to defend himself against the King, "she was sore dread, and had great doubt, and wist not what was best all for to be done; for she wist well that her lord, King Arthur, would never of her have mercy for the great shame that she had him done; and took her away privily with four men, *without more*, and came to Caerleon, and there she dwelled all her life's time, and never was seen among folke her life living." She professed herself a nun in the Church of St Julius the Martyr, at Caerleon;[7] and by the date discovered on her tombstone at Ambresbury, in Wiltshire, must have lived to a very advanced age. The monastery in which the Queen was buried, had been erected by Aurelius Ambrosius, Arthur's uncle, for the maintenance of three hundred monks, to pray for the souls of the British noblemen slain by Hengist. The Queen's tomb, says Rapin, was found there "within the last century." This author, thought the circumstance of Guenever surviving her husband for fifty years, threw discredit on the fact, but as she was the third of his wives, and not long united to him, she might not have been thirty years of age at the time of the King's death.

The tomb of Guenever III. was more costly than that of her husband. "On its coverture it had, in rude letters of massy gold, R. G., A. D. 600.

[1] Holinshed, Milton.
[2] Rowland's Mona. Antiqua.
[3] Butler, Holinshed.
[4] Old Welsh MS.
[5] Howel, however, declares that, at the end of a three years' reign, Constantine was slain by Conanus, and buried at Stonehenge.
[6] Caxton.
[7] Ibid.

The bones within this sepulchre were all firm, fair, yellow-coloured hair about the skull, and a piece of the *liver* about the size of a walnut, very dry and hard. Therein were found several royal habiliments, as jewels, veils, scarves, and the like, retaining, even till then, their proper colour; all which were afterwards very choicely kept in the collection of the Right Honourable the Earl of Hertford, and of the aforesaid gold, divers rings were made, and worn by his lordship's principal officers."[1]

Arthur's first consort reposed in Scotland; his second was interred at Glastonbury: to that monastery the King was conveyed after the fatal battle of Camelford, and the desire he had more than once fondly expressed, to be laid by the side of his second wife, was faithfully complied with by his friends; the funeral obsequies being managed by his sorrowing sister Morgwenna with the greatest privacy, for the reason already mentioned, although many British nobles attended the mournful ceremony.[2] The body of the King was placed sixteen feet deep under the ground to prevent the Saxons offering any indignity to the royal remains, in the event of their discovering the grave, the knowledge of which was kept a profound secret.[3] Many other British monarchs were interred in this famous place of sepulture, amongst whom were Coel, Kentwin, Edward the Elder, and Edmond Ironside.[4] The illustrious dead, whose remains lay in mouldering state in this abbey, were buried under the body of the church in three large vaults, supported by two rows of strong massive pillars.

The body of Arthur was not discovered till 640 years after his death;[5] it took place in the reign of Henry II., A. D. 1172.[6] That King, at the time of the reduction of Ireland, "was passing through Wales, and at Pembroke was received with regal dignity by the Welsh, on which occasion one of their bards, playing upon the harp, sang to the King, whilst he was at dinner, of the exploits of the great Arthur, wishing him the prosperity and victory which had attended that monarch. In the ballad an allusion was made to the place of Arthur's burial, said to be between two pyramids in the holy churchyard at Glastonbury, many feet deep. On his return from Ireland, the King informed Henry de Blois, then Abbot of Glastonbury, of what he had learnt from the ballad of the bard, and desired him to dig and search for the bones of the great King."[7] The abbot did so, and, as some say, found these bones in the manner described by our historians,[8] among whom was Giraldus Cambrensis, who was an eye-witness of the fact. Some, however, say that this discovery was not made till 1189, after the accession of Richard I., when Henry de Saliaco was abbot, who was created in the first year of Richard's reign. Mr. Hearne considers this more probable than that it took place under Henry de Blois, the brother of King Stephen.[9]

King Henry II. informed the Abbot that he had heard from the Welsh bards that Arthur lay buried between two pyramids, very deep. The monastery contained two stone pillars, with many inscriptions illegible from the injuries of time and the antiquity of the writing. The tallest

[1] Gough's Sepulchral Monuments. See Jones's Stonehenge restored, and Mr. Ray's Itinerary, 1662, who was shown her gravestone.

[2] Warner's Glastonbury. [3] Ibid. [4] Willis's Abbeys. [5] Collinson. [6] Warner. [7] Ibid. [8] Leland, Stowe. [9] Hearne's Glastonbury.

of these was twenty-six feet high; the sculpture upon it could not be understood. Between these two pyramids "Arthur's body was found" buried, and marked in a hollow oak deep in the earth. There was found a cross of lead and a stone thereupon, and letters written within the cross turned towards the stone, which letters, says Higden, "I read and handled in this manner: 'Hic jacet sepultus inclytus rex Arturus cum Genevera uxore sua secunda in insula Avalonia,' *i. e.*, 'Here lieth buried the noble King Arthur, with his second wife Guenever, in Avalon.' The bones were laid in the grave, so that the two parts of the grave toward the head contained the man's bones, and the third part, towards the feet, contained the woman's bones. There the yellow tresses of the woman's hair were found whole and sound, with fresh colour;[1] but a monk touched the hair covetously with his hands, and anon it fell all into powder." The bones of Arthur himself are described as being of extraordinary size, and were identified by the ten wounds in his skull. The bodies of the King and Queen had been laid fifteen feet deep in the ground, as the "singer of gestis" had reported to the King, in the hope that they would not be discovered by the Saxons, and were marked, as before related, for their identity; and the discovery of them in this singular manner quite staggered the opinion held till then by the Welsh, that Arthur was still alive, and would return again to reign over his faithful people, and make them an independent nation.[2]

"After the spectators had gratified their curiosities, the abbot and his monks, with great satisfaction and reverence, took all the remains of the two bodies out of their separate coffins, and putting them into decent chests, made for the purpose, they deposited them first in a chapel, in the south alley of the church, till such time as a monument, suitable to the dignity of a king and queen, could be made for them, in the middle of the presbytery of the choir; where, in finishing the church, they erected a stately mausoleum of touchstone, nobly engraven on the outside, in which they placed the King's body by itself, at the head of the tomb, and the Queen's at his feet, being the east side of it." This inscription was then placed:—

"Hic jacet Arturus, flos Regum gloria regni,
Quem mores probitas commendant laude perenni."[3]

---

[1] Sharon Turner.

[2] The poet thus records the popular belief: —

"But for he skaped y[t] battel y[e] wys,
Bretons and Cornych seyeth thus
That he levyth zut perde,
And schall come and be a king aye.
At Glastyngbury on the queer,
They made Arter's tombe ther,
And wrote with Latin vers thus:
Hic jacet Arturus, rex quondam, rexque futurus."
[Chron. of Kings of England; Fabian.]

[3] Five different epitaphs are attributed to Arthur's tomb, and some Saxon poetry was written to his memory. — Collinson.

And over Queen Guenever's bones was the following inscription:—

"Arturi jacet hic conjux tumulata secunda,
Quæ meruit cœlos virtutum prole fecunda."

The remains of the royal Arthur and his Queen were after this allowed to rest in peace until the year 1248, when, we are informed that King Edward I. and his wife Queen Eleanor, partly out of devotion, and partly out of curiosity, came to Glastonbury, "attended by many of the topping men of the nation, clergy as well as nobility;[1] where, upon the 19th of April, they caused King Arthur's tomb to be opened, and both the shrines to be taken out of the monument, which when the Court and its attendants had thoroughly viewed, King Edward opened the shrine wherein King Arthur's bones lay, and Queen Eleanor the chest wherein were those of Queen Guenever; and then each of them taking the respective bones out of their respective chests, they exposed them on two credences, on side-tables, near the high altar, till the next morning, for every one that had a mind to gratify their curiosity; and early the next morning, being the Wednesday before Easter, the King and Queen, with great honour and respect, wrapt up all the bones (excepting the two skulls, which were set up, and to remain in the treasury) in rich shrouds or mantles, and placing them again in their separate shrines, the King put into that of Arthur, an inscription setting forth what they were. And then the King and Queen fixing their royal signets to each chest, they caused the chests to be placed in the old mausoleum,[2] where they remained undisturbed about two hundred and fifty years, that is to say, till the dissolution of the abbey, in the days of King Henry VIII.; and "then this noble monument," saith Speed, "among the fatal overthrows of infinite more, was altogether rased at the dispose of some then in commission, whose over-hasty actions and too-forward zeal in their behalf hath left unto us the want of many truths, and caused to wist that some of their employments had been better spent."[3]

"At the same period of the dissolution of monasteries, was destroyed a little table, containing the story of the discovery of Arthur's tomb, and the leaden cross, with the inscription which had been set up in the monastery, and were seen by the great antiquary, Leland;[4] the cross, in particular, which had been placed there for exhibition, by command of the Abbot of Glastonbury, was regarded as one of the greatest curiosities of the abbey."[5]

---

[1] The king paid this visit in the sixth year of his reign, accompanied by Queen Eleanor, for the purpose of celebrating the feast of Easter, at his own expense, and was received with very great ceremony. The particulars of the royal visit, with the account of the second exhumation of the bodies of Arthur and Guenever (which took place on the Wednesday morning), are extracted from Mr. Eyston's "Little Monument," contained in the Appendix to Warner's History of Glastonbury.

[2] The abbot, Henry de Saliaco, is reported to be the author of the lines placed on his tomb.—*Hearne.*

Fabian places the translation of Arthur's remains into the new tomb in the year 1180; Biog. Brit. in 1189.

[3] Appendix to Warner's Glastonbury, from Eyston's Little Monument, &c.

[4] Biog. Brit.

[5] Warner.

BERTHA.

The daughter of Caribert—The two maids of honour—Dangerous confidences—The entertainment given by Ingoberga to her husband—The wool-spinner—The King's anger—The Queen's divorce—Her rival's advancement—The Queen retires to a convent—Bertha's education—Proposals of marriage from King Ethelbert of England declined on account of religion—Mirofleda supplanted by her sister—Excommunication and death of Caribert—Consent of Bertha, and arrival of the newly-married pair in England—Reside at Canterbury—Bertha's zeal in the Christian faith—Pope Gregory and Augustine—Fear of the Roman missionaries—Ethelbert receives them well, and becomes a convert—Churches—The Pope's letters—Conversion of Redwald—Story of Edwin—Bertha's death—Epitaph—Eadbald's remorse—He marries Emma.

BERTHA is a Princess whose name cannot but excite peculiar interest, for her claims on the respect of posterity are no other than having first introduced Christianity amongst the princes of the Saxon Heptarchy.

She was the daughter of Caribert, King of Paris, by Ingoberga, his first Queen; and though some have supposed her their only child, she had two sisters, both of whom assumed the religious habit, one at Tours, the other at Poictiers. Notwithstanding Caribert was four times married, these three daughters were his only offspring; so that the kingdom, at his death, devolved on his brother; the French laws not permitting the reign of a woman.

The father of Bertha is said to have been passionately fond of the chase, for which amusement the fair Ingoberga was too often neglected. The Queen, in her sorrow for this desertion, confided her trouble to two young girls, her attendants of honour: in an evil hour was this imprudent communication made.

One of these maidens had escaped from the distasteful retirement of a conventual life to the more attractive scenes of a court; the other, an accomplished dancer and singer, was gifted with rare personal beauty. At their artful suggestion, the Queen invented a novel amusement for her husband, in hopes of securing more of his society, on which occasion the talents of her companions were exhibited. The King's admiration, on witnessing the performance prepared for his enjoyment, passed all bounds; and the unhappy Ingoberga soon saw that her plan had but too well succeeded; the actresses in this scene were soon her declared rivals in her husband's affections. She was so indignant at the infidelity of Caribert, that she determined to mortify and humble him in return for the insult offered to herself. The father of these girls was a common wool-spinner, and Ingoberga, who was aware of the circumstance, ordered him to come to her palace, and follow his usual avocation of spinning. While he was thus employed, she took Caribert into her apartments to witness his labours. The stratagem so enraged the King, that he immediately expelled Ingoberga from the palace, and having divorced her, Miroflede, the eldest daughter of the wool-spinner, was elevated to the post she had enjoyed, both in his throne and heart.

The Queen sheltered herself in the seclusion of a convent under her misfortune, whither she was probably accompanied by her children. She devoted herself to prayers and charitable deeds; and Gregory of Tours speaks of her as a woman of great wisdom, and constant practical piety, "unceasing in prayer, in mortification, and almsgiving;" besides which she set at liberty many persons suffering under the horrors of slavery.[1]

Under the superintendence of such a mother, the young Bertha had no doubt many advantages: she was possessed of great beauty and virtue, and so much esteemed for both, that even during the life of his father, the Saxon prince, Ethelbert, had made proposals for her hand. His overtures met, at first, with a decided refusal, on account of his religion; for not only Caribert and Ingoberga were Christians, but their daughter professed the same faith; while Ethelbert, and the Saxons, over whom he ruled, were pagans. Subsequently, Bertha consented to the match, on condition of being freely permitted to pursue the religious exercises in which she had been brought up,[2] and to enjoy the counsels of Luidhard, Bishop of Soissons (or Senlis): this request being accorded, she gave her hand to Ethelbert.

Ingoberga must have deeply felt the parting from her daughter, her two other children being separated from her; and her heart was still more wounded by the conduct of their father, whose affections, estranged from herself, had not long been retained captive by the insolent Miroflede, who had been supplanted by her younger sister.[3] The latter had not only procured her disgrace, but was promoted to her queenly dignity. The clergy, however, so strongly felt the disgrace the King brought on himself and the country, by marrying a nun who had broken her vows, and who was the sister of his former consort, that they excommunicated both Caribert and his wife: the former consoled himself in the society of a new favourite, but died soon after, in 670. Ingoberga survived the last of her rivals, and died A.D. 578, at the age of seventy, twenty-seven years after she had been deprived of the regal dignity.[4]

On the arrival of Bertha in Britain, she and her husband Ethelbert took up their residence at Canterbury. The young foreign Princess soon became very popular among the Saxons: her accomplishments won their hearts, and her irreproachable conduct their esteem: her beauty also pleaded powerfully in her favour with them. Bertha was exceedingly zealous for the propagation of her faith, and the earnestness she threw into her exertions for the good cause ensured success. She made use of every legitimate art which her address could employ, to reconcile Ethelbert to the principles of Christianity, and her exertions were at length

[1] Of this, Ingoberga is one of the earliest instances on record.

[2] Turner, Bede, Huntingdon.

[3] Anecdotes des Reines et Régentes de France.

[4] Mezeray, Hume, Anecdotes des Reines et Régentes, &c.

successful. Pope Gregory the Great, for that end, had employed the zealous Augustine; but the honour of so great an enterprise as the bringing of a whole nation from the darkness of paganism to the light of the Gospel, is mainly due to the influence of Bertha.

Besides Luidhard, several French chaplains attended on her, and an old temple, situated a little without the walls of Canterbury, had been assigned to her use for the performance of Christian worship.[1] Many persons about the court of Ethelbert, who soon after succeeded to the crown, were disposed in favour of the new faith by the exemplary conduct of Bertha and Luidhard.[2] Some were made at once converts, others were willing to become so: such being the state of affairs in Kent, Bertha, perceiving the harvest was plenteous, but the labourers few in number, made an application for help in her pious labours; first to the French, her own countrymen, and failing there, probably from the influence of her mother's rivals at court, appealed next to the Pope. Gregory the Great, the reigning Pontiff, was ambitious on his own part, of shining in an undertaking so glorious as the conversion of Britain.

The Pontiff's feelings had first directed him to the enterprise, at the sight of some beautiful children exposed in the Roman slave mart;[3] and, when, in answer to his inquiry whence they had come, he was told they were Angles: "Not Angles, but angels, [4] if converted," was his celebrated punning reply. The circumstance had fixed the desire on his mind; when, therefore, Bertha, "Queen of the Angles," and the daughter of Ingoberga, whose piety was known, and whose humane interest had so often set captives free, made an appeal to him on a subject which he had so warmly espoused, he lent a willing ear to her request.

Regarding her favour, protection, and influence, as happy omens for the success of a Christian mission, he deputed Augustine, a monk of Rheims, and forty other persons, among whom were Mellitus, Justus, Paulinus, and Rufinian, to undertake a voyage to Britain, to accomplish the arduous enterprise.

It was a perilous undertaking, in the opinion of the Roman missionaries, who, before they had proceeded many miles, sent back Augustine to the Pope, with an entreaty that they might be excused from the office, and not be sent to a fierce and infidel nation, whose language they did not understand. Gregory would not admit their expostulations, and having written to that effect, exhorting them to persevere, they proceeded on their unwelcome expedition, taking with them French interpreters. They performed the voyage safely, and landed in the Isle of Thanet. On their arrival, they informed Ethelbert that they had come to offer him heaven

[1] Bower's History of the Popes; Butler's Lives of Saints.

[2] Butler, Bower, &c.

[3] Gregory is said to have written to Candidus, steward of the patrimony of St. Peter in France, to buy such English slaves as were to be sold in that country, under the age of seventeen or eighteen, and send them to Rome to be brought up in the monasteries. As they were pagans, the Pope desired they might be attended in their journey by a Presbyter to baptise them, should he find any of them in danger of dying on the road. [Bower's History of the Popes.]

[4] Bede.

and eternal happiness, in the knowledge of a God, with whom the Saxons were unacquainted.

Ethelbert, through Bertha's influence, received the messengers of Christ with hospitality, and at the end of a few days appointed a meeting with them in the Isle of Thanet. It was a Saxon superstition that spells were ineffectual in the open air, and on this account, it was arranged that the interview between Ethelbert and Augustine should not take place in any dwelling.

The procession of the Papal missionaries bore in its front a standard, on which was depicted a silver cross, with an image of our Saviour painted; as it advanced, litanies were chanted. Ethelbert's apprehensions were increased at the unusual spectacle; but the priestly train having taken seats by his command, the Gospel was preached and listened to with the utmost attention by the Kentish King.

Ethelbert was not immediately convinced of the truth of the new doctrine propounded; he, however, graciously replied to Augustine and his followers, of whose sincerity he was fully persuaded, promising that no opposition should be offered in his endeavours to obtain converts; but, on the other hand, that they should be entertained during their stay in Britain. He accordingly ordered suitable provision to be made for their maintenance, and assigned for their abode a mansion in the city of Canterbury.[1] By their holiness of living and excellent precepts, the priests obtained, from that time, universal respect and subsistence through the beneficence of Ethelbert, and the patronage of such Saxons as were won over to their belief. They daily performed the services in the church, which was dedicated to St. Martin,[2] in presence of the Queen, who went thither to pray. This ancient edifice, still used for divine service, stands on the side of a hill rising on the left hand of the road leading to Deal, within half a mile of the city walls; the body of the church is built of Roman bricks, of an architecture prior to the Saxon invasion.

The learning, piety, and good example of the excellent Queen Bertha amply supported the Roman missionaries, in this their original condition, and her zeal and piety were eventually rewarded by the conversion, not only of the King, her husband, who was first to embrace the new faith, but of the whole nation, who followed the example of the throne. So much may be accomplished by individual exertions; in spite of a weak frame, a mighty and a powerful heart can achieve wonders; and thus had Bertha the glory of succeeding in her vast design of turning thousands from darkness and ignorance to the light and knowledge of the purest faith. The King was baptized on Whitsunday, A. D. 597, about a year after the arrival of Augustine.[3] Many others received the holy rite, un-

---

[1] Their lodging is said to have been in the parish of St. Alphege, in a place called Stablegate, which was then used as an oratorium by the King's household. [Thorne, Coxe, Roger of Wendover.]

[2] Augustine and his followers first met to sing, to pray, to say mass, and to baptise in St. Martin's Church, till, on Ethelbert becoming converted, they gained permission to build new and repair the old churches throughout his dominions.

[3] MS. Chronicles of Canterbury; Dugdale.

biassed in their persuasion; for Ethelbert, though he now seconded the Papal emissaries, desired that nothing should be done by compulsion. The very ancient font which still exists in the Church of St. Martin, at Canterbury, is said to be the same that was used at the baptism of Ethelbert.

A small edifice of great antiquity, called St. Pancras Chapel, had been used by the Saxon King, prior to his conversion, as a private temple. It still stands to the east of the hospital in Canterbury, and to the south-east of St. Augustine's monastery. The materials and architecture are Roman, and it is only thirty feet long by twenty-one in breadth. St. Martin's Church is some distance to the east of St. Pancras.

The chapel of St. Pancras was afterwards purified by Augustine, and the idol placed in it was broken. The edifice was dedicated by the Roman bishop in the name of St. Pancras, a youth of fourteen, who suffered martyrdom under the reign of Dioclesian, in the persecution, A. D. 304. This was the first church dedicated by Augustine, and the altar in the southern porch, at which, after Ethelbert's conversion, he was accustomed to celebrate mass, still stands there; it occupies the spot on which had been placed a statue of the King.

Ethelbert was not content with patronising Augustine and his followers; upon his conversion he resigned his palace in Canterbury for their use, and retired to Reculver, in the Isle of Thanet, where he erected a royal residence for himself and his successors.

According to Bede, there was already in existence, in the east part of Canterbury, when Augustine arrived, a building of about two or three hundred years old, which occupied the site of the present cathedral, and was the same as that given to the Roman missionaries. Augustine repaired and enlarged the edifice, dedicating it in the name of Christ.

In 938 this church had become little better than a ruin by the attacks of the Danes, the walls being uneven, and in some places broken down, and the roof in so threatening a condition it could not be entered with safety. The fabric was repaired by Archbishop Odo; but the roof he built was burnt by the Danes, 1011, and only the walls remained. Canute restored the edifice; but, after his time, it again fell to decay, so much so, that in 1070 Lanfranc was compelled to rebuild it almost from the foundation, though even then the ancient walls were not entirely thrown down.

Behind the choir of Canterbury Cathedral, in the chapel of the Holy Trinity, erected about A. D. 1184, in honour of St. Thomas à Becket, stands the ancient patriarchal chair, in which the archbishops are enthroned; and which, tradition records, was the regal seat of the Saxon Kings of Kent. It is formed of three pieces of grey marble, cut in panels; the under part being solid, like that of a seat cut out of a rock.

The under-croft, or crypt, over which the choir of Canterbury Cathedral is raised—undoubtedly the most ancient part of the building—is considered Saxon, and supposed to be that part of the old edifice left standing by Lanfranc. The walls are perfectly destitute of ornament, and everything presents the aspect of the most venerable antiquity. Of the pillars, some are round, others twisted, and neither in shafts nor capitals are there two of them alike. The circumference of most of the shafts is about four feet, and the height of shaft, plinth, and capital, only six feet and a half. From these spring semicircular arches, making a vaulted roof of the height of fourteen feet.

The church architecture of the Saxons seems to have been of the Roman style, and an adaptation of the buildings found by them on their arrival here. The Britons had, shortly before the coming of the Saxons, besides their wattled and wooden churches, some stone edifices, like those of St. Martin and St. Pancras, at Canterbury, but not constructed in a style resembling the edifices which followed the doctrines of the supreme Pontiff. "They had no crypts under them for reliques; they were not supported by arches and columns; these arches and columns were not adorned with the images of saints and legendary stories; their shape was not cruciform; they had no oratories in the aisles, nor were they glazed. This was the *Roman style*, as precisely delineated by Bede, Eddius, Richard Prior of Hexham, and contradistinguished from the British."[1]

Before Augustine's time many Saxons had been converted by the Welsh and Irish clergy, but their native buildings were as mean as the British. After the arrival of the Roman missionaries, and the conversion of Ethelbert, it became fashionable to adopt whatever was connected with the Papal power, and to decry the native arts. At a later period the Saxon prelates were either educated at Rome, or attached to its doctrines, hence they patronized the Roman style of architecture in the edifices erected under their superintendence in Britain. Of this number were Ninian, who built the stone church at Whitherne[2] (Candida Casa) in Galloway; Benedict Biscop, founder of one at Weremouth; Naiton, who solicited Abbot Ceolred to send him architects to construct a church after the Roman fashion; and Wilfred, who built the church at Hexham, with others mentioned by Bede. As the Saxons, at their coming to Britain, did not understand masonry, they had to send for foreigners to build their churches and monasteries. Thus the sculptures which adorn our capitals and arches, and are designated the Saxon ornaments and Saxon style, were not *invented*, but patronized by that people, and were as different as possible from the British forms of architecture, being derived from the more cultivated and polished Romans.

There had been established in Britain, long before the arrival of Hengist, a Roman architecture: while the same style as our Anglo-Saxon churches is found to prevail in the East, to the surprise of those who know that those buildings were erected prior to the arrival of the Saxons in Britain. All the principal churches in the East were, however, built by a British Queen, as related in the Life of St. Helena, to whom the Pope compared the pious Bertha, Queen of Ethelbert; and they, like the Anglo-Saxon churches, had a Roman origin. Helena was the greater part of her life in Britain, and her husband Constantius was a great architect, which facts simplify the whole matter.

The crypt or undercroft of Canterbury Cathedral, ascribed by Arch-

---

[1] Ledwich. [2] Lappenberg.

deacon Batteley to the believing Romans,[1] "remained unalterably the same amid all the conflagrations and repairs the cathedral underwent,"[2] and singularly enough, the *capitals* of the columns, and the Egyptian hieroglyphical figures upon them, carry us back to the age of Constantine, "son of Helena," who had served in the Egyptian wars under Galerius. These figures are delineated by Ledwich in his interesting work.[3]

Bertha, anxious to promote the good cause, and spread the Gospel to the farthest bounds of the kingdom, engaged some persons to come over to her from France to assist in the pious undertaking. Gregory, on his part, enjoined Augustine to remove the idols from the heathen altars, but not to destroy the altars themselves; because the people held the spot sacred, and would therefore be more likely to carry on the Christian worship in its precincts. The people were in the habit of feasting at their pagan festivals, on the offerings of the altar, after they had been presented, together with their priests: the Pope desired Augustine not to encourage such entertainments among the converted Anglo-Saxons. By his order Augustine visited France, and was ordained Archbishop of the

---

[1] Osborne says it was founded before A. D. 742.

[2] Ledwich.

[3] Antiquities of Ireland (Observations on Saxon and Gothic Architecture).

No. 1 has on it the cat, adored in Egypt, and supposed to supply a cure against the bite of asps and other venomous animals: a symbol of Isis.

No. 2. An Egyptian grotesque—a hawk killing a serpent. The hawk worshipped in Egypt for freeing the country from snakes, scorpions, and other reptiles.

No. 3. An ideal quadruped, resembling the Egyptian gryphon, having the beak, talons, and wings of an eagle, and body of a lion. The gryphon was sacred to Osiris. It is here represented killing some noxious bird or serpent.

No. 4. A gladiator or criminal engaged with a lion.

No. 5. A horseman with a cap and trowse.

No. 6. A sheep, to which the Egyptians paid divine honour.

No. 7. An equestrian figure.

No. 8 is a purely Egyptian figure—a double-headed Anubis bestriding a double-headed crocodile; Anubis being inseparably the companion of Isis.

No. 9. A man sitting on the head of another, holding in one hand a fish, and in the other a cup: an allusion to Isis.

No. 10. A double-headed monster.

No. 11. A bird destroying a crocodile, or some serpent of the lizard kind.

No. 12. A satyr resting on two deer.

No. 13. Two birds on a Roman masque.

No. 14. A grotesque, with the head and comb of a cock, the body and arms human, the shoulders winged, with the feet and tail of a satyr, playing on a violin with a bow; behind is a scalene triangle. Opposite is another grotesque, blowing a trumpet, with the head and horns of a goat, the lower extremities human. That these are Egyptian hieroglyphical figures is confirmed by various authors. The triangle denoted Orus, son of Isis and Osiris. From the figures on the capitals contained in the crypt, it was likely to have been an Iseum or Roman chapel, sacred to Isis, and an early imitation of Roman models. There seems little doubt that this building was erected long prior to the coming of the Saxons, by the Romans, most probably under Constantine. The grotesques exhibited on the capitals were mostly confined to crypts, and derived from the eccentricities of Egyptian superstition. Similar instances are to be seen in the vaults at Hexham, which, like Canterbury, was a Roman station; and in which may be found fragments of Roman inscriptions, grotesque figures, and much carved stone work." [Porphyry, Tertullian, Montfaucon, Hutchinson.]

English by the Archbishop of Arles. After he returned, he sent a deputation to Rome, to inform the Pope of the success of his mission, and to request the solution of some theological questions. An embassy from Gregory brought back the answers required, with instructions to the priests to exert themselves in the diffusion of the light of the Gospel; they brought over vessels and vestments for the altar, copes, relics, &c., with a letter and presents to King Ethelbert. The Pope's letter to the Anglo-Saxon monarch, bears date the 10th day of the Calends of June, A. D. 601,[1] and may be seen in Bede, or in the History of Radulf de Diceto: the one here transcribed is from the latter:

"*Pope Gregory to Ethelbert, King of the Angles.*

"Glorious son, guard with solicitude the faith which thou hast divinely received. Hasten to spread the Christian faith among the peoples subject to thee; multiply the zeal of thy rectitude in their conversion; proscribe the worship of idols, and destroy their temples. For God himself will render the name of your glory even more glorious to posterity, seeking as you do his honour among nations saved. So it was that Constantine, the most pious Emperor, reclaimed the Roman state from the profane worship of idols, and subjected it to Almighty God. And thus it came to pass, that this man vanquished by his praises the fame of the ancient princes, and surpassed his predecessors by continued well-doing."

"*Pope Gregory to Bertha, Queen of the Angles.*

"We bless Almighty God, who hath graciously vouchsafed to reserve for your reward the conversion of the people of the Angles. For, as through the memorable Helena, the mother of the most pious Constantine, Emperor of the Romans, the hearts of the Romans were kindled to the Christian faith; so, by the zeal of your glory, we are confident the mercy of God is operating among the people of the Angles."

"*Pope Gregory to Augustine, Bishop of the Angles.*

"Who may suffice to recount what gladness has arisen in the hearts of all the faithful, that the people of the Angles, by the operation of the Almighty's grace, and by thy brotherly labour, have, upon the expulsion of the darkness of error, been penetrated by the light of the holy faith; that with integrity of mind they now trample on the idols to which an insane fear had before subjected them; that they are prostrated before Almighty God in a pure heart; that from the lapses of wickedness they are tied to the restraints of holy preaching; that in soul they are brought under, and in understanding are lifted up to, the divine precepts; that they humble themselves even to the earth, in order that their mind may not rest in earth. Of whom is this work but of Him who saith 'My father worketh hitherto, and I work.'"

Many rich vestments, vessels, relics, and a pall, given by St. Gregory to St. Austin, were afterwards kept in the monastery of St. Austin, at Canterbury. Their original inventory, drawn up by Thomas of Elmham, in the reign of Henry the Fifth, is preserved in the Harleian Library,

[1] Bede.

and published by Mrs. E. Elstob, at the end of a Saxon panegyric on St. Gregory.

"The pall sent by Gregory, was for Augustin to say mass in. This *pallium* sent by the Popes to archbishops, is an ornament worn upon their shoulders, with a lappel hanging down upon the breast and back. It is made with white lamb's-wool and spotted with purple crosses."[1] The first Christian Emperors gave this imperial ornament to eminent bishops; it is recorded as one of the gifts bestowed by the British Emperor Constantine on Pope Sylvester.

The letter of Gregory to Augustine directs that the pallium shall only be worn during the solemnity of mass. It likewise directs that bishops for twelve places, subordinate to his own see, shall be appointed, amongst which was to be one for London, who was to be consecrated by his own synod, and to receive a pallium from Rome. A bishop of York is to be ordained, with power to ordain twelve subordinate bishops, and the Pope expresses his design of bestowing on him also the pall. The Bishop of London was to take precedence of his brother Bishop of York, as being first ordained, but to have no power over him.

Mellitus, the Roman Abbot, who came to England in 601, was consecrated by Augustine, Bishop of London, 604, and having succeeded Laurentius in the Archbishopric of Canterbury, died April 24, 624.

There had been a progression of events, meanwhile, in other parts of Britain. Three more kingdoms, Northumberland, East Anglia, and Essex, had become established; the last of these was founded by Uffa, the survivor of twelve Saxon princes, who had landed on the eastern coast of Britain about five years after Bertha's marriage. Redwald, King of the East Angles, had been brought up in the pagan doctrines; but, through the incessant exertions of King Ethelbert, was led to renounce the worship of idols, and in 609 was baptized at Canterbury.[2] The dominions of Redwald comprised Norfolk, Suffolk, Cambridge, the Isle of Ely, and part of Bedfordshire.[3] The Kings of East Anglia had several royal residences, one at Rendlesham in Suffolk, and another at Ely: at the first of these Redwald built a church, on his conversion to Christianity. The principal abode of Redwald was at Kaninghall, of which the ruins are yet to be seen, near which coins and various antiquities have from time to time been dug up; and Thetford, another royal abode of East Anglia, is even now filled with ruins of religious houses above all other towns in England.

The conversion of Redwald led to very important results. The court of this Prince had become the asylum of the fugitive Prince Edwin, who, when an infant, had been deprived of his patrimonial inheritance, the crown of Northumberland, by Ethelfrid the Wild, who had married his sister Acha, both being children of Alla, first King of Deira. Finding, after a time, that his life was no longer secure at the Northumbrian court, Edwin sought the protection first of Cadwan, King of Wales, who dwelt at Caer Segont, whose wife was a relation of Quenburga, his own consort,

[1] Butler. [2] Rapin, Turner, Butler. [3] Usher, Whittaker, Butler

daughter of Ceoil, King of Mercia. The protection afforded by Cadwan, gave umbrage to Ethelfrid, who shortly after repudiated Acha.

Edwin, however, finding that Cadwan was in danger from his stay, left his retreat, and wandered from court to court, no Prince daring to protect him, through dread of his formidable enemy. Such was his life during twenty-seven years, until, at the age of thirty, he obtained an asylum with the East Anglian King, and by his amiable qualities and noble demeanour, engaged the respect and esteem of Redwald and his subjects. Ethelfrid offered rich presents to the East Anglian, to induce him to deliver up his guest, or put him secretly to death; but the King after withstanding many such offers, at last was tempted to *deliberate*, feeling his inequality in strength to Ethelfrid.[1] At this moment, which threatened such peril to Edwin, an unexpected friend arose. The unfortunate Prince was made acquainted by the Queen of Redwald of what had transpired. His confidence in her husband's honour and generosity had at first won her regard, and his many amiable qualities riveted her esteem.

Edwin would not avail himself of the opportunity thus afforded for escape, but waited calmly the result. Meanwhile, the Queen sought her husband. Availing herself of her well-known influence, this noble-spirited woman resolved, if possible, to save her husband from the dishonourable act he was about to commit. She told him: "It stood not with the high and sacred state of a King, to buy and sell the bodies of men, as it were a petty chapman; or that which is more dishonourable and slave-like, to sell away his faith, a thing which he ought to hold more precious than all the gold and gems of the whole world, yea, than his own life."[2]

While Edwin was, therefore, yet occupied in pondering over this unexpected turn of affairs, the messenger of the Queen, whose name, which should have been written in letters of gold, as a glory to her sex, is unfortunately lost, informed him that Redwald had been inspired with better thoughts, and refused to yield up his guest.[3]

The Queen carried her generous influence yet further; for, at her request, Redwald levied an army, and marched against Ethelfrid. The Northumbrian King was slain in the engagement which followed, when Redwald completed his triumph, by entering Northumberland as its conqueror; and far from taking for his own any portion of that district, placed Edwin in security on the throne of his ancestors.[4] This magnanimous conduct procured for Redwald the dignity of Emperor of the Saxons in Britain, and entitled him to be called the "*British Aristides.*"

The "Villa Regia," or seat of the Northumbrian monarchs, was Osmundthorpe, in Yorkshire; at which place may still be seen a piece of stained glass, representing a King with a crown, sword, and shield, bearing the arms of the Kingdom of East Anglia, while a local tradition relates, that at that spot, Edwin, King of Northumberland, was hospitably entertained by Redwald, and reinstated in his dominions.[5]

In spite of this fine action, worthy of a Christian, after returning into

---

[1] Hume, Rapin. [2] Camden, from Bede. [3] Rapin.
[4] Allen's History of York. [5] Hutchinson, Rapin, Hume.

East Anglia, Redwald is said to have relapsed into idolatry, the very same year,[1] though without wholly forsaking the Christian faith; for, in the temple in which sacrifices to Odin were performed by his order, was contained two altars, *one dedicated to Christ, and another to idols.* The latter, Bede assures us, lasted to the time of Adulf, King of East Anglia, his own contemporary, who mentioned that he had seen it when a boy. So singular a combination rather promoted than retarded the progress of Christianity, by awakening the attention of the people. The return to idolatrous worship of Redwald, is ascribed to the influence of his Queen, who is described by Langhorne as "a woman of great mind and remarkable prudence, but too much given to idolatry." Guthrie says: "Though she possessed the virtues, she had not the graces of Christianity, being averse to its religion; yet, the generous protection she afforded to Edwin, and the noble sentiments with which she inspired her husband, together with the great veneration the nation had for her family, give us the highest idea of her spirit and good sense."[2]

At a subsequent period, Ethelburga Tate, the daughter of Queen Bertha, became the wife of Edwin, with whom, perhaps, an acquaintance had commenced at the court of Redwald, during his exile.

The husband of Queen Bertha, besides assisting Sebert, his nephew, (converted through his means), in the erection of the Monastery of St. Peter's, Westminster, built the Cathedral of Rochester, which he dedicated to St. Andrew. To him belonged the glory of abolishing idol-worship throughout his dominions, and of either closing the temples of paganism, or converting them to the service of Christ. In all his great undertakings, Ethelbert was assisted by Queen Bertha, though her name does not prominently appear, except on the occasion of the grand religious revolution, brought about through her pious zeal, and which may be said to have occasioned an intercourse with foreign countries, which greatly tended to improve the Saxons.

The remains of Queen Bertha, whose death preceded that of Ethelbert, were deposited, at her death, in the porch of the Church of St. Martin, at Canterbury, where also rested those of the future saint, Augustine, who died before his regal friend and patron, and of Luidhard, the French bishop,—the new cathedral of Canterbury being yet unconsecrated.[3]

After the loss of Bertha, Ethelbert, probably feeling the blank in his domestic happiness occasioned by that circumstance, married a second Queen; yet at his own death, in 616, he was buried by the French Princess's side, in St. Martin's Porch, within the Church of St. Peter

---

[1] Echard, Guthrie.

[2] Sigebert, her son by a former husband, being sent to France on her marriage to Redwald, the usurper of his rights, became the dependant guest and *protégé* of Clothair, the French monarch, and eventually, on the death of his half-brother, Earpwold, mounted the East Anglian throne. Edwin, restored to his inheritance of Northumberland, declined, on Redwald's death, the proffered crown of his benefactor, awarding it to his son Earpwold, whose mother had so befriended him in adversity.

[3] Chron. of W. Thorn.

and St. Paul.[1] His remains were afterwards deposited under the high altar in the same church,[2] and a light was kept constantly burning before his tomb.[3] The memory of his piety and virtues caused him to be afterwards canonized as a saint, and to be honoured, on February 24th, the day of his death, in Roman and Saxon martyrologies under the name, endeared in our own times, of *Albert.*

The epitaph on Queen Bertha, preserved by Leland, may be translated thus:—

"Adorned with virtues, here lies the blessed Queen Bertha, who was in favour with God, and greatly beloved by mankind."

About the middle of the eighth century, another Queen of Kent distinguished herself by her exertions in favour of Christianity. This was Aldeburga, wife of Ethelbert, who reigned jointly with his brother, Eadbert, A. D. 725. While the King, her husband, was still a heathen, Aldeburga re-established the deserted church of St. Martin, and the hymn and the prayer were again heard within its consecrated walls.[4]

In 616, Archbishop Lawrence consecrated the new edifice at Canterbury, and removing the body of St. Augustine thither, buried it in the north porch.

If Ethelbert's object in choosing a second consort had been to secure a protector for his young family, he certainly erred in judgment; for his second consort was unworthy to succeed the pious Bertha. Eadbald was his father's successor, and had no sooner mounted the throne, 616, than he married the Queen, his mother-in-law, with whom he was passionately in love, she being very young and very beautiful.

Laurentius, successor of Augustine, finding not only that Eadbald, after this marriage, had returned to idolatry, but that his example had influenced his subjects to do the same, prepared to depart into France, his preaching here producing so little fruit: Mellitus and Justus, his companions, had already quitted the country, but he resolved, before he did so, to make one more effort to reclaim the abandoned son of the great Ethelbert and pious Bertha, the protectors of the Christian faith. He was perhaps the more induced to take this step, by the fact that Eadbald, since his crime, had "been troubled with frequent fits of madness, and oppressed of an evil spirit,[5] his guilty conscience being its own accuser. Suddenly appearing before the King, the good prelate threw off his vestments, exhibiting to Eadbald a body torn with stripes and bruises. The King inquired who had dared to treat in such a manner one of so high a rank as the Archbishop; when he was told that St. Peter, Prince of the Apostles, had appeared to him in a vision, and bestowed on him that

---

[1] The ridiculous Latin lines upon Ethelbert, given by Stowe and Weever, are thus rendered:—

"King Ethelbert lieth here,
Closed in his polyander:
For building churches sure he goes
To Christ without meander."

"Rex Ethelburtus hic clauditur in polyandro,
Fana pians certe Christo meat abque meandro."

[2] Bede. [3] Polydore Vergil. [4] Palgrave. [5] Bede.

chastisement, with a severe reprimand, for his intending to desert his charge. Eadbald was so struck by the miracle, that he returned to his former faith, and divorcing himself from his mother-in-law, received the rite of baptism from Laurentius. The people, imitating their ruler, were also restored to the faith of Christ.[1] Mellitus and Justus were recalled from France by Eadbald, the former to the see of Rochester, and the latter to that of London, but the Londoners could not be persuaded to receive him, Eadbald having less influence than his father. The King passed the rest of his life in piety and penitence; and to expiate his sins, founded a college within the walls of Dover Castle, which Wightred, one of his successors, removed into the town, and stored with twenty-two canons, dedicating it to St. Martin, A. D. 725.[2]

The converted King married Emma, daughter of Theodobert, King of Austrasia, now Lorraine. This lady became the mother of three children, Ermenred, Ercombert, and Enswitha. The eldest son died in his father's lifetime, but Ercombert was destined to revive the faded glory of his family; Enswitha, emulating the piety of her grandmother Bertha, of blessed memory, founded the Abbey of Folkestone, in Kent, and, having assumed the religious habit, presided over it as abbess till her death, when her name and virtues were enrolled in the saintly calendar, August 31st, the day of her departure from this life.

Eadbald reigned twenty-five years, and dying, was interred near his father, in a little chapel built by himself, in honour of the Virgin Mary. Queen Emma, whom one of our poets[3] has designated as—

"Lady Emme, of France the chosen flower,"

died the following year, and was laid by the side of her husband, both their remains being deposited at the altar of St. John.

---

[1] Rapin, Hume.

[2] This edifice was afterwards rebuilt, in Henry the First's reign, by Archbishop William Corbeil, A. D. 1132, whose successor, Frebold, placed Benedictine monks in it, and called it "The New Work at Dover." It was surrendered November 16th, 27 Henry VIII., the yearly value being £232 10*s.* 5½*d.*

[3] Bradshawe.

ETHELBURGA "THE SILENT," AND ENFLEDA,

QUEENS OF EDWIN "THE GREAT" AND OSWY.

Marriage of Ethelburga to Edwin—Paulinus—His zeal—The Life of Edwin attempted—A daughter, Enfleda, born—She is dedicated by her father to God—Pope Boniface—His letters—Coiffi, the priest—His famous speech and act—Edwin becomes a Christian—Hilda first appears—Numerous converts in Northumberland—Edwin's progresses—The Tûfa—Edwin killed in battle against Penda—Eadfrid murdered—Ethelburga seeks protection with her brother, the King of Kent, accompanied by Paulinus—She sends her sons to France: they die there — She founds a nunnery, and takes the veil — Her acts of charity — The Danes — Enfleda demanded in marriage by Oswy — The voyage and the jars of oil—The marriage—Enfleda builds the Monastery of Tinemouth—Wilfred—Enfleda's daughter dedicated to God—Cædmon, the poet—The Synod at Whitby—The mother and daughter—The spirit of the Abbess.

THIS lady who, unlike the generality of her sex, became renowned for taciturnity, and Enfleda, her daughter, were Queens of Northumberland. Their history being intimately connected, it has been thought better to unite the record of their lives.

Ethelburga "Tate," or "the Silent," was the daughtor of Ethelbert and his pious Queen Bertha, and was educated in the Christian faith. Ethelburga's beauty and virtues were destined to atone to Edwin the Great, King of Northumberland, for his many troubles.

Edwin was twenty-three years of age when he mounted the throne, and at the time when he married Ethelburga, was in his thirty-first year. Quenburga, whom he had espoused when very young, had not lived to behold her husband reinstated in his rights: she died while he was an exile, leaving two sons, Osfred and Edfred.

It was about the year 624 that Edwin sent ambassadors to the court of Kent, to demand the hand of the Princess Ethelburga. Her parents were dead; but their son Eadbald sat upon the throne, and Edwin was most desirous to strengthen himself by an alliance with him. Eadbald gave his consent to his sister's marriage; but not without making certain stipulations, which were rendered necessary by Edwin's being a follower of Paganism. As Ethelburga was a Christian, her brother required that she should be allowed to follow that religion without restriction, and be permitted to have her own ministers to officiate. Edwin, on receiving this answer by his ambassadors, undertook that he would not in any way whatever oppose the Princess in her religious exercises, but would, on the contrary, permit her, and all whom she might bring with her, to follow their faith according to the principles of Christianity. More than this, he declared that he would himself embrace that doctrine, if, on examination by means of wise men appointed for the purpose, it should prove more holy and worthy of God than his own. On this, Ethelburga was promised to Edwin, and Paulinus, "a man beloved of God," ordained bishop, that he might accompany the royal bride into Northumberland.[1] It was hoped that this excellent prelate, by his daily exhortations, and exercising the mysterious offices of the faith, would not only confirm the hearts of the Princess and her attendants, but prevent their becoming corrupted by the society of the Pagans.[2]

The marriage of Ethelburga, the Christian, to the Pagan King, Edwin, was solemnised at the royal city of York, A.D. 625.[3]

It was on Easter Sunday, in 626, the year following, that an attempt was made on the life of Edwin, by a person in the employ of the King of Wessex. Eumer—for so the man was called—under pretence of conveying a message, obtained admittance to the royal presence, when, drawing his dagger, he rushed on the King. The faithful Lilla, one of Edwin's officers, perceiving his master's danger, interposed his own body, and received the wound, which had been dealt so violently that the dagger, after piercing Lilla, even wounded Edwin; before, however, the assassin could repeat the blow, he was despatched by the royal attendants.[4]

Scarcely had the grateful King returned thanks to the gods for his own preservation, when Paulinus appeared with the welcome tidings that his Queen Ethelburga had just been safely delivered of a daughter, its birth supposed to have been hastened by the alarm of the recent event. Paulinus immediately gave thanks to Christ for both these joyful occurrences, and upon that, strove to persuade the King that through his prayers to the Saviour, Ethelburga had been enabled to bring forth her child in safety. Edwin, delighted with the words of the priest, and the happy tidings of which he had been the bearer, promised, that in case God would grant him life and victory over the King who had armed the hand of an assassin against him, he would renounce the worship of idols. As an earnest of this promise, he delivered over his newly-born daughter to Paulinus, to be forthwith consecrated to the service of Christ. Enfleda — for that was the name bestowed on the royal infant — was the first baptized of the Northumbrian nation. The solemn rite was performed on Whitsunday, and twelve other members of the royal family were baptized with the little princess.[5]

Malton, in Yorkshire, was the birthplace of Enfleda, and the scene of Edwin's escape from the dagger of Eumer. The King had a royal villa at this place, where he was at that time residing. Brompton, a village between Malton and Scarborough, was another royal residence of the Kings of Northumberland.[6]

---

[1] The first Abbot of Bardney, named Deda, according to Bede, described Paulinus as tall of stature, a little stooping, his hair black, his visage meagre, his nose slender and aquiline, his aspect both venerable and majestic.

[2] Bede. [3] Hutchinson, Harding. [4] Hume

[5] Bede. [6] Allen's History of York.

As soon as Edwin recovered from his wound, which was at first alarming, he marched against the West Saxons, and having defeated his enemies, put to the sword all those who had sought his life.[1]

His consort, emulating the glory of her mother Bertha, had, in the meantime, left no argument untried which could influence her husband to adopt the Christian faith, and extended the same care towards his Northumbrian subjects.[2] Pope Boniface, learning the exertions made by Ethelburga for the propagation of the doctrines of Christ, encouraged the undertaking, by himself addressing a letter to Ethelburga, exhorting her to persevere in her holy purpose; he sent, at the same time, a letter to her royal husband. Of these letters, both of which are preserved by Bede, we select that addressed to Ethelburga, who was the undoubted means of introducing the faith into Northumberland.

"The copy of the letter of the most blessed and apostolic Boniface, Pope of the city of Rome, to Ethelburga, King Edwin's Queen.

"To the illustrious lady, his daughter, Queen Ethelburga, Boniface, Bishop, servant of the servants of God. The goodness of our Redeemer has, with much providence, offered the means of salvation to the human race, which he rescued by the shedding of his precious blood, from the bonds of captivity to the devil: so that making his name known in divers ways to the Gentiles, they might acknowledge their Creator by embracing the mystery of the Christian faith, which thing, the mystical regeneration of your purification, plainly shows to have been bestowed upon the mind of your highness by God's bounty. Our mind, therefore, has much rejoiced in the benefit of our Lord's goodness, for that he has vouchsafed, in your conversion, to kindle a spark of the orthodox religion, by which He might the more easily inflame in His love the understanding, not only of your glorious consort, but also of all the nation that is subject to you. For we have been informed by those who came to acquaint us with the laudable conversion of our illustrious son, King Eadbald, that your Highness also, having received the wonderful sacrament of the Christian faith, continually excels in the performance of works pious and acceptable to God; that you likewise carefully refrain from the worship of idols, and the deceits of temples and auguries, and having changed your devotion, are so taken up with the love of your Redeemer, as never to cease lending your assistance for the propagation of the Christian faith. And our fatherly charity having earnestly inquired concerning your illustrious husband, we were given to understand, that he still served abominable idols, and would not yield obedience or give ear to the voice of the preachers. This occasioned us no small grief, for that part of your body still remained a stranger to the knowledge of the supreme and undivided Trinity. Whereupon we, in our fatherly care, did not delay to admonish your Christian Highness, exhorting you, that with the help of the Divine inspiration, you will not defer to do that, which, both in season and out of season, is required of us; that with the co-operating power of our Lord and Saviour Jesus Christ, your husband also may be added to the number of Christians, to the end that you may thereby enjoy the rites of marriage

[1] Hutchinson and Burke. [2] Hume.

in the bond of a holy and unblemished union. For it is written, 'they shall be in one flesh.' How can it be said, that there is unity between you, if he continues a stranger to the brightness of your faith, by the interposition of dark and detestable error? Therefore, applying yourself continually to prayer, do not cease to beg of the Divine mercy the benefit of his illumination; to the end, that those whom the union of carnal affection has made in a manner but one body, may, after death, continue in perpetual union, by the bond of faith. Persist, therefore, illustrious daughter, and to the utmost of your power, endeavour to soften the hardness of his heart, by insinuating the Divine precepts; making him sensible how noble the mystery is which you have received by believing, and how wonderful is the reward, which, by the new birth, you have merited to obtain. Inflame the coldness of his heart by the knowledge of the Holy Ghost, that by the abolition of the cold and pernicious worship of Paganism, the heat of Divine faith may enlighten his understanding, through your frequent exhortations; that the testimony of the Holy Scripture may appear the more conspicuous, fulfilled by you, 'The unbelieving husband shall be saved by the believing wife!' For to this effect you have obtained the mercy of our Lord's goodness, that you may return with increase the fruit of faith, and the benefit intrusted in your hands; for through the assistance of His mercy, we do not cease, with frequent prayers, to beg that you may be able to perform the same. Having premised thus much, in pursuance of the duty of our fatherly affection, we exhort you, that when the opportunity of a bearer shall offer, you will, as soon as possible, acquaint us with the success which the Divine power shall grant by your means, in the conversion of your consort, and of the nation subject to you; to the end, that our solicitude, which earnestly expects what appertains to the salvation of you and yours, may, by hearing from you, be set at rest; and that we, discerning more fully the brightness of the Divine propitiation diffused in you, may, with a joyful confession, abundantly return due thanks to God, the giver of all good things, and to St. Peter, the prince of the apostles."

This letter finishes with a trait of friendliness somewhat singular, and no doubt agreeable to the female receiver: "We have, moreover, sent you the blessing of your protector, St. Peter, the prince of the apostles, that is, a silver looking-glass, and a gilt ivory comb, which we entreat your glory will receive with the same kind affection, as it is known to be sent by us."

The letter of Pope Boniface to Edwin was, in like manner, accompanied by presents: these were, "a shirt with one gold ornament, and one garment of Ancyra,[1] named in the epistle. Edwin had, in the first instance hesitated to embrace the new doctrine, but the efforts of Ethelburga were destined to be crowned with success. The King had promised her that he would examine the foundations on which the new faith rested, and that if he found them satisfactory he was willing to become a convert.

[1] Ancyra or Angora, a city of Galatia, spoken of by Pliny and Strabo, formerly the seat of the Gauls. It was there that the particular kind of cloth made of goats' wool was dyed, and underwent the process called *camlet*, which "gave it its water colour."

Accordingly, he held several conferences with Paulinus, canvassed the arguments he proposed with the wisest of his counsellors, retired frequently from company, to resolve in solitude that all-important question, and at length came to the desired conclusion.

A year had passed in anxious deliberation on the truth, when, "attended by Paulinus, Edwin entered the great council, requested the advice of his faithful Witan, and exposed to them the reasons which induced him to prefer Christianity to the worship of paganism. Coiffi, the high priest of Northumbria, was the first to reply, whose faith was shaken by repeated disappointments. He attempted to prove the futility of the pagan religion by his own misfortunes, and avowed his own resolution 'to listen to the reasons, and examine the doctrine of Paulinus.' He was followed by an aged thane, whose discourse offers an interesting picture of the simplicity of the age. 'When,' said he, 'O King, you and your ministers are seated at table, in the depth of winter, and the cheerful fire blazes on the hearth in the middle of the hall, a sparrow, perhaps chased by the wind and snow, enters at one door of the apartment and escapes by the other. During the moment of its passage it enjoys the warmth; when it is once departed, it is seen no more. Such is the nature of man. During a few years his existence is visible; but what has preceded or what will follow it, is concealed from the view of mortals. If the new religion offer any information on subjects so mysterious and important, it must be worthy of our attention.' To these reasons the other members assented. Paulinus was desired to explain the principal articles of the Christian faith; and the King expressed his determination to embrace the doctrine of the missionary. When it was asked, who would dare to profane the altars of Woden, Coiffi accepted the dangerous office. Laying aside the emblems of the priestly dignity, he assumed the dress of a warrior, and, despising the prohibitions of the Saxon superstition, mounted the favorite charger of Edwin. By those who were ignorant of his motives his conduct was attributed to temporary insanity. But disregarding their clamours, he proceeded to the nearest temple, and bidding defiance to the gods of his fathers, hurled his spear into the sacred edifice. It stuck in the opposite wall; and, to the surprise of the trembling spectators, the heavens were silent, and the sacrilege was unpunished. Insensibly they recovered from their fears, and, encouraged by the exhortations of Coiffi, burnt to the ground the temple and the surrounding groves."[1]

Alcuin has celebrated the fame of Coiffi in his poem on the Church of York.

The King, now changed in heart as well as doctrine desired to receive the rite of baptism, which was performed with much solemnity during the festival of Easter, at the Church of St. Peter, in York, Paulinus himself officiating. On this great occasion, which took place A. D. 627, many Northumbrians, both of the nobility and meaner classes, received the same rite. Of the number was Hilda, a young Saxon girl of royal birth, being great-niece of Edwin: then she was fourteen years of age

[1] Bede.

only, but she lived to become one of the most distinguished characters of her time.

The simple church whose interior was the scene of this imposing spectacle, so new and interesting in a nation of unbelievers, at the time was constructed of wood, but was afterwards re-edified with stone by the King, who made it a cathedral, constituting Paulinus archbishop of the see.

Crowds now began daily to flock to Paulinus to receive the baptismal rite, and it is on record of that venerable prelate that, being at one time staying with the King and Queen at Yeverin, in Northumberland, he was employed for six-and-thirty days, from morning till night, in instructing the throng that pressed forward to receive the new doctrine, whom he baptized in the river Glen. Churches and oratories were as yet unbuilt, and thus, as among the primitive Christians, rivers were brought into use by Paulinus, especially the Swale, as at the royal mansion in the neighborhood of that river Paulinus most commonly resided with the King.[1] Edwin is also said to have dwelt at Auldby, about six miles from the city of York. Christianity had now fairly dawned on Northumberland.

The Roman altars and temples had been laid in the dust, and a general indifference to religion prevailed at the time when Saxon mythology was introduced; and this was now supplanted by the pure doctrine of a revealed religion, which quickly spread, and with such good effect throughout the north, that it is said, a woman and her infant might have passed, without danger or damage, from sea to sea,[2] so rare had acts of injustice become.

Having procured peace with the other Kings, his contemporaries, Edwin employed himself in progresses through his own territories, for the redress of the injured—enacting just laws for the public protection. He carefully repaired the roads throughout Northumberland, making them safe and commodious; and so minutely did the King regard the comfort of his people, that every spring by the way-side was provided with a bowl, for the refreshment of travellers.[3]

Thus, by his nobleness and intrepidity of character, Edwin became renowned as the greatest Prince of the Saxon Heptarchy. "His dignity," says Bede, "was so great throughout his dominions, that his banners were not only borne before him in battle, but even in time of peace: when he rode about his cities, towns, or provinces, with his officers, the standard-bearer was wont to go before him. Also, when he walked along the streets, that sort of banner which the Romans call Tufa, and the English Tûf, was, in like manner, borne before him." This was a globe, or a tuft of feathers, fixed on a spear.

It was unfortunate for Northumberland to lose so good a monarch in the zenith of greatness. After a reign of seventeen years' duration, Edwin, in the forty-eighth year of his age, perished in battle against Penda, King of Mercia, together with Osfred, his youngest son by Quenburga: Eadfrid, the eldest-born, afterwards imploring the protection of

[1] Lives of the Saints [2] Howel. [3] Hutchinson.

Penda, who was his relative, was murdered by him in violation of his oath.[1]

Edwin had four children by Ethelburga; two of whom only survived him, Ulkfren and Enfleda. The claims of these children of Edwin were set aside in favour of Eanfrid and Osric, of whom the former took possession of Northumberland, and the latter of Deira; while the people, strange to say, after such an example, on losing their Christian King, reverted to a state of paganism.

Ethelburga adopted the alternative which alone remained for safety to herself and family. Taking with her, her children, and Uffi, the son of Osfred, who was now an orphan, she determined to seek the protection of Eadbald, King of Kent, her brother, who had married Emma, a French princess. Accordingly the Queen placed herself and family under the protection of Bassus, a faithful chieftain, and fled by sea into Kent, A. D. 627, where the royal fugitives were honourably received, first by Honorius, and afterwards by Eadbald himself; who bestowed on Paulinus, the faithful friend and adviser of his sister, who accompanied her on this occasion as in all others, the see of Rochester, in which he passed the remainder of his days; bequeathing to the church there, at his death, the pall which he had received from the Roman Pontiff.[2] A great number of precious ornaments, which had belonged to King Edwin, were conveyed by Paulinus into Kent at the same time; among them were a large golden cross and a golden chalice, consecrated for the service of the altar, which were preserved in the Church of Canterbury.[3]

Ethelburga retained her daughter with her, but fearing her sons' safety insecure in this country, sent them together to the court of her relative, King Dagobert, in France, where they afterwards died. When she first arrived from Northumberland, Eadbald had presented her with some land in Kent, where the royal widow founded a nunnery, afterwards dedicated to the honour of the Virgin Mary and St. Mildred, one of the later abbesses. This was the first founded of the three celebrated Kentish monasteries; the second, at Folkstone, being built by Enswitha, daughter of Eadbald; and the third, at Minster, in Thanet, by Queen Dompena, in A. D. 664.[4] Ethelburga's was founded in 633,[5] when the amiable Queen exhibited to the English people the novelty of a Christian widow taking the veil,—a step which, from her high example, afterwards became customary amongst the Queens of the Anglo-Saxons.[6]

From this time till her death Ethelburga devoted herself wholly to acts of charity; and when snatched from the world, she was interred in the nunnery of which she had been the foundress. That edifice, afterwards converted to a monastery at a later period, suffered much from the rapacity of the Danes, by whom it was rifled no less than three times in the space of thirty years, during the ninth century: it came at last to

[1] Lingard. Hume, Hutchinson. The remains of Edwin were interred at Streaneshalch, or Whitby, which became the repository of those of the different members of the Royal Family.—*Howel.*

[2] Mac Cabe. [3] Bede. [4] Phillipotts.

[5] Smith's Notes on Bede. [6] Hutchinson, Leland.

the see of Canterbury.[1] The memory of St. Edwin the Great was honoured till the time of Henry VIII.; and a small church in London, near Newgate, some have conjectured was named after St. Ewen, or Andoeni.[2]

Oswy, and his brother Oswin, meantime had divided between them the Northumbrian monarchy, the former governing in Bernicia, the latter in Deira.[3] It is not certain whether Ethelburga was yet alive when an embassy arrived at the court of Eadbald from the former of these princes, demanding the hand of her daughter, the Princess Enfleda, in marriage. The account of this embassy is very interesting, and characteristic of the times. Oswy commissioned Utta, "a man of great gravity and sincerity," who was much esteemed for his good qualities and truthfulness of character, to become his ambassador into Kent. Utta was commanded to travel by land to his destination, but to return home by sea; on which account he addressed himself to Aidan, Bishop of the Church of Deira, during the reigns of Oswy and Oswin, beseeching his prayers for the prosperity of his voyage. Aidan blessed Utta and his companions, and commended them to the protection of Heaven, delivering to Utta, at the same time, some jars of hallowed oil, with these words: "I foresee that whilst you are at sea, a sudden tempest will come upon you; remember to cast into the troubled waters the oil that I give you, and speedily the tempest shall be assuaged, and the sea be calmed, and you shall have a prosperous voyage." All these things were fulfilled according to the prophecy. Enfleda and her train had to encounter a tempest on their way to Northumberland, the account of which is given by Bede, who had been told the story by one who had it from Utta's own mouth.[4]

Eadbald had, as we have seen, not only the honour of giving his sister Ethelburga in marriage to Edwin, but afterwards of bestowing her daughter Enfleda on Oswy. It is necessary to mention here the relationship which existed between King Oswy and the Princess of Kent. Edwin, father of Enfleda, was brother of Acha, wife of Ethelfred the Wild, and therefore uncle of her son Oswy. Thus, Enfleda and Oswy were first cousins; at the time of her marriage, which took place A. D. 642, the Princess was only in her sixteenth year, while Oswy was about thirty. She was fortunate in her match, for he was one of the most interesting princes of whom we read in the history of the Saxon Heptarchy.

Treading in the footsteps of her illustrious mother and grandmother, Enfleda distinguished herself not only by the patronage she afforded to religious men, but by the religious edifices she founded. Not long after her arrival in Northumberland, Oswin, her husband's brother and partner in the government, was slain at Gilling, near Richmond, in Yorkshire; and the Queen built a monastery on the spot, which we learn was completed before the year 659, the Abbot of which, Trumhere, was afterwards made Bishop of the Mercians. No trace of the edifice now re-

[1] Camden, Dugdale, Butler.

[2] It stood at the north-east corner of Warwick-lane.

[3] Holinshed.

[4] Hutchinson's Durham, Biog. Brit.

mains, it having been entirely destroyed, A.D. 897, by the Danish chiefs, Hinguar and Hubba.[1]

Trumhere, who was the third bishop in Mercia, was an Englishman, and related to Queen Enfleda. He had been instructed and ordained in Scotland, and Oswy, at the solicitation of his Queen, had granted him the place where Oswin had been slain, on which he built the Abbey of Ingethlingum Gilling, of which he himself became Abbot; whether this was the same edifice raised under Enfleda's patronage, or one adjacent, does not appear.[2]

The Monastery at Tinemouth was likewise built by Enfleda, in commemoration of St. Oswin,[3] whose shrine was there preserved.

> "Queen Enfled, that was King Oswy's wife.
> King Edwin, his daughter, full of goodnesse,
> For Oswyn's soule a minster, in her life,
> Made at Tynemouth, and for Oswy causeles
> That hym so bee slaine and killed helpeles;
> For she was kin to Oswy and Oswyn,
> As Bede in chronicle dooeth determyn." — Harding.

Enfleda bestowed her royal patronage on one who was destined to attain the greatest celebrity; this was Wilfrid, a Northumbrian, who, when very young, came to York, where Oswy held his court. On his arrival he was introduced to Queen Enfleda, who, seeing the youth, then only fourteen, was handsome, polite, and in every respect of a promising appearance, offered him a situation at court. This was worth the acceptance of Wilfrid, but he modestly declined the favour, telling the Queen that his disposition induced him to seek for retirement. On which Enfleda, pleased with that declaration, promised to use every means in her power to facilitate the execution of his design. She accordingly placed him under the care of a chief officer of the King's household, who was engaged to go to the Monastery of Lindisfarne, with the intention of entering that religious community. The isle of Lindisfarne, on the coast of Northumberland, was the episcopal seat of Aidan, an Irishman, and a Culdee of Iona, who had been sent for by Oswald, who bestowed it on him as an episcopal see, and in person attended his ministry. When Aidan preached, as he did not perfectly understand the Anglo-Saxon tongue, the King was interpreter; for during his exile in Ireland he had learnt the language of that island. Aidan's preaching was recommended by his practice. Bede says: "He was a man of the greatest modesty, piety, and moderation; having a zeal for God, but not fully according to knowledge, for he kept the Lord's Day of Easter according to the custom of his country." Under this famous prelate Wilfrid passed some years in study, and the exercise of Christian piety, at the end of which time his observation leading him to discern errors in the Church of the Scots, he resolved to visit Rome, for the purpose of learning the rites of

---

[1] Dugdale, Tanner.

[2] Holinshed.

[3] The death of Oswin, with which Oswy appears to be chargeable, from the lines cited, is said to have taken place in 651. He is described as having been "tall and handsome in person, affable in manners, and courteous to rich and poor," which caused him to be "beloved by all." — Holinshed.

the Church in that city. Having obtained the consent of the brethren, and taken leave of the Abbot of Lindisfarne, Wilfrid repaired to his friend and patron, Queen Enfleda, and acquainted her with his design. The resolution of the youth pleased that royal lady, who accordingly sent him into Kent, where her cousin Ercombert had succeeded to the throne of Eadbald, and requested that King to send him to Rome in an honourable manner.

The request of Elfleda was attended to, and Wilfrid was accompanied on the occasion of his journey by another youth, Benedict, or Biscop, who also desired to visit the city of the apostles; this pair afterwards make a great show in Anglo-Saxon history.[1]

Enfleda had borne her husband a daughter, called Elfleda, who, when only a twelvemonth old, was dedicated, by a vow of King Oswy, to serve God in a state of perpetual virginity. On the occasion of the sanguinary battle of Winwidfield, near Leeds, Oswy vowed, prior to the engagement, that if God would grant him the victory, he would not only so consecrate his infant child to His service, but would also build a monastery to His honour. The day was gained by Oswy; King Penda, his enemy, with many nobles, fell on the field, and the vow was duly performed.[2] To signalize his gratitude, Oswy commenced, in the year 657, building the famous double monastery of Whitby, then called Streaneshalch from a watch-tower or light-house which stood on the cliff on the eastern side of the harbour; it was situate on a bold and precipitous shore. The monastery was designed for monks and nuns of the Benedictine order, though Malmesbury says it was for women only, and the King invited the celebrated St. Hilda to undertake the government of the double community.[3] This royal lady the sister of Hereswide, Queen of the East Angles, who was noted for her exceeding piety and great goodness, had been invited by St. Aidan to come over from France, on the death of her sister, and had settled in a small nunnery on the river Were; she remained there one year, at the end of which she was made Abbess of the numerous society congregated in the Monastery of Hartlepool. From this place, at the end of several years, she was called, by the message of King Oswy, to superintend the Monastery of Whitby. This religious foundation, which was built by Oswy, and dedicated to St. Peter, always bore the name of its first Abbess, so great was the veneration in which St. Hilda was held by the people there.

The princess Elfleda, agreeably to her father's vow, had been professed a nun in the monastery where Hilda at that time resided; but on the holy Abbess removing to Streaneshalch, went thither also, and first becoming a novice, ruled afterwards over the establishment.[4]

Cædmon, the great poet of the Anglo-Saxons, owed his first patronage to the Abbess Hilda, and the earliest specimens of literature of that era were produced in the Abbey of Whitby. Bede says: "There was in this house a brother, who, when he heard verses out of Scripture, would, with much sweetness and humility, turn them into English poetry." The

[1] Lives of the Saints, Bede.
[2] Holinshed, Allen's History of York.
[3] Allen, Butler.
[4] Holinshed, William of Malmesbury.

books of the convent were in the Latin tongue, used also in the greater part of the service; but Cædmon rendered the Scriptural subject into the vernacular tongue. This man was only a neat-herd, and he dreamt that a stranger came to him and bade him compose a song. He replied, "I cannot;" but the command was repeated, and a subject, "the creation of all things," given. The wondering cow-herd awoke at dawn of day, and proceeded to the steward of the household of the Abbess Hilda, to relate this wonderful dream, and the verses he had in his sleep composed. This person conducted him to the presence of the venerable Abbess, who was surrounded by scholars and learned men; he was ordered to repeat his verses. He did so, to the delight of his attentive audience. His powers of poesy were found to be no dream, but a waking reality; and Hilda earnestly encouraged him to continue to compose his poems in his native Saxon tongue, to assist him in which efforts she transferred the peasant to the school of her convent, and diligently and unremittingly superintended his education. This was no mean alteration in the fortunes of Cædmon, for the school of Hilda was the nursery of the great men of her times. Six of her scholars subsequently were elevated to the episcopal chair: Bosa, John of Beverley, and the second Wilfrid, filled successively the See of York; Hedda became Bishop of Wessex, and Tatfrith and Ostforus Bishops of Worcester.[1]

At the time that Hilda was Abbess of Whitby,[2] a famous synod was held there, to fix the time for the celebration of Easter; great differences having previously existed in the British Church on the subject of Easter, which was kept by the British after the manner of the Eastern Church, on the fourteenth day after the full moon, on whatever day of the week it happened, and not on Sunday, as we at this day observe it.[3]

The following interesting account of this memorable council is extracted from the late Dr. Lingard's invaluable work on the Anglo-Saxon Church:—

"Oswy and his people followed the Scotch missionaries, but Queen Enfleda, who had been educated in Kent, and Oswy's son Alchfred, who attended the lessons of St. Wilfrid, adhered to the practice of the Romish Church. Thus, Oswy saw his own family divided into opposite factions, and the same solemnities celebrated at different times within his own residence. Desirous to procure uniformity, he summoned the champions of each party to meet him at Whitby, and to argue the merits of their respective customs in his presence, A. D. 664. On the one side stood Agilbercht, a Gallic prelate, at that time Bishop of Winchester, who chanced to be on a visit to the King; with Romanus, the chaplain of Queen Eanfled; Wilfrid, the chaplain of Prince Alchfred; and Jacob, a deacon, who had remained in Northumbria ever since the flight of Paulinus. On the other, were ranged Colman, the Bishop of Lindisfarne; Cedd, who had been ordained by the Scots Bishop of the East Saxons; the Abbess Hilda, and the Scottish clergy. Both Agilbercht and Colman, as foreigners, were but imperfectly acquainted with the vernacular language. Agil-

[1] Bede. [2] Allen's York.

[3] The best account of the Easter controversy will be found in Dr. Smith's Appendix to Bede's Ecclesiastical History, No. 9.

bercht, therefore, placed the defence of his cause in the hands of Wilfrid; but Colman would not accept the services of a substitute, and Cedd was appointed his interpreter,—an office which he discharged to the satisfaction of all parties.

"The King, after a short preface on the benefit of uniformity, called upon Colman to begin. He alleged, in defence of the Scottish custom, first, the example of St. John the Evangelist, who was said, in books, to have kept Easter on the fourteenth day of the lunar month; second, on the Paschal canons of Anatolius, which ordered it to be kept on the same day; and on the practice of Columba, and his successors in the isle of Iona, by whom he (Colman) had been educated, and appointed Bishop of Northumbria. Wilfrid, in answer, said, that Colman was in error with respect to St. John, who, at a time when condescension was requisite, kept the Pasch at the same time with the Jews, on the fourteenth day, whether it were a Sunday or not; whereas, the Scots kept it only on that day, when it happened to fall on a Sunday; neither could he appeal to the Paschal canons of Anatolius, for Anatolius followed a cycle of nineteen years, which the Scots did not; a manner of reckoning, by which he never kept the Pasch till the fourteenth day was begun; whereas the Scots often kept it before the thirteenth day was ended. With respect to the practice of the Abbots of Iona, an obscure isle in the Scottish sea, their authority ought not to prevail against that of the universal Church, and the decree of the great Council of Nice.

"Colman rejoined that these abbots were holy men, who could not be supposed to have done wrong; to which Wilfrid replied, that, cut off as they were, by their situation, from the rest of the world, they might be excused under the plea of ignorance; but that, if Colman and his clergy, now that they knew the decrees of the Apostolic See, or rather of the universal Church, refused to conform, they would undoubtedly sin. Columba might have been a great man, but Peter was a greater, on whom our Lord had built his Church, and to whom he had given the keys of the kingdom of heaven. At these words Oswin, who had hitherto been silent, exclaimed, 'Colman, is it so?' Receiving an answer in the affirmative, he resumed with a smile, 'Who then is the greater in heaven, Columba or Peter?' All replied, 'Peter.' 'Then,' said the King, 'will I obey the decrees of Peter; for if he, who has the keys, shut me out, who is there to let me in?' The bystanders applauded the witticism; and the conference broke up. The result was, that Hilda and Cedd, and several of the Scottish clergy, passed over to the party of Wilfrid; and Colman, after a short interval, taking with him his own adherents, and about thirty natives, returned to his parent monastery in the Isle of Iona.[1]

"The conference at Whitby established harmony in the Anglo-Saxon Church, but the Picts, Scots, and Britons, maintained their opinion for many years after. In 701, Adamnan, Abbot of Iona, who had adopted

---

[1] Colman, a monk of Iona, and successor of Finan as Bishop of Lindisfarne, disliking Oswin's decision against the British mode of keeping Easter, threw up his bishopric, and returned to Ireland, where he built two monasteries. He wrote a book in defence of his own opinion relative to the keeping Easter, another on the ecclesiastical tonsure, and an exhortation to the inhabitants of the Hebrides.

the Roman method during his visit to the court of Alfred of Northumberland, reclaimed the northern tribes. In 710, Naitan, King of the Picts, after consulting Ceolfred, Bishop of Wearmouth, ordered the Roman computation to be followed throughout his dominions; but it was not till 715 that the monks of Iona, whom Adamnan could not convert, yielded the point to the arguments of Egbert, an Anglo-Saxon missionary. Elfod, Bishop of Bangor, established the Catholic computation of Easter, in North Wales, in the middle of the eighth century, and still later, in 777, in South Wales, from which time no more controversies have arisen on that subject." [1]

This celebrated council derives no small interest from the fact of its having united, in a view to obtain an insight into the truth, so many of the most celebrated individuals of that age.

Oswy died A. D. 670, his reign having lasted twenty-eight years, and was interred in Streaneshalch monastery, with truly regal solemnity. The widowed Queen, retiring to that place, which contained the last remains of her beloved husband, assumed the religious habit, having determined, like her mother, Queen Ethelburga, to pass the remainder of her life in the exercises of religion. The next ten years from that time, the royal mother and daughter resided together among the holy sisterhood, over which St. Hilda presided. In 680, that pious Abbess departed this life in her sixty-sixth year, after having passed through a long and trying illness, when the Princess Elfleda was elevated to the situation left vacant by her loss, the Queen continuing still to reside with her daughter.

As late as 1776, it was an opinion entertained there, that Hilda rendered herself at times visible, on particular occasions, in the Abbey of Streaneshalch, or Whitby, where she so long presided. At a particular time of the year, in the summer months, at ten or eleven in the forenoon, the sunbeams fall in the inside of the northern part of the choir; and it is then that the spectators, who stand on the west side of Whitby churchyard, so as to see the most northerly part of the abbey, past the north of Whitby Church, imagine they perceive in one of the highest windows there, the resemblance of a woman arrayed in a shroud. Though we are certain this is only a reflection, caused by the splendour of the sun's beam, yet report says, and it is constantly believed among the vulgar, to be an appearance of Lady Hilda, in her shroud, or rather in her glorified state.[2]

The Abbess Elfleda, was highly esteemed by St. Theodore of Canterbury, and by St. Cuthbert, from whom she received frequent visits; and on such occasions, it was her custom to entertain her visitors at her own table: this appears from an account given by the venerable Bede. Other authorities inform us, that the Abbess would often go abroad to make her own visits, and mingle with her own relatives. The brothers of El-

[1] Lingard; Antiquity of Anglo-Saxon Church.

[2] There is a tradition concerning the snake-stones which abound at Whitby, that the place was formerly infested by snakes, which, being driven over the cliff by Lady Hilda, lost their heads in the fall, and by her prayers were afterwards transformed into stones. — Allen's York.

fleda received her visits and sought her counsels. King Alfred, the youngest of these princes, was watched over by her on his death-bed; and afterwards we find the excellent Abbess striving to reconcile Archbishop Wilfrid and the party which was opposed to him. Elfleda was, indeed highly esteemed by the great men of her times, and Theodore, Archbishop of Canterbury, in a letter addressed to her, designates her "the wisest lady." Eddius, in his Life of Wilfrid, says, "that by her wise counsels, Elfleda was ever the best adviser and comforter of the whole province; and she did much service during the minority of Osred, her nephew, by her exertions for the promotion of peace."

Under the care of Elfleda, many missionaries and scholars were sent forth from the establishment.

The 51st Letter in the Collection of St. Boniface, is addressed to an abbess abroad, named Adolana, by "Elfled, handmaiden of the ecclesiastical household," who commends to her care another abbess, her own pupil, who from infancy had desired to visit Rome, and requests her to give such information as might be useful respecting the journey thither. The letter had apparently been consigned to the care of Boniface, on one of his journeys to the imperial city.

Queen Enfleda, on her death, was interred at Streaneshalch, in the Church of St. Peter, where rested the remains of Kings Edwin and Oswy, and many other distinguished persons of those times. Elfleda died at the age of forty, and was likewise interred in that edifice. The revenues of Streaneshalch had been greatly augmented by the royal daughter of Oswy and Enfleda, and the monastery continued to flourish till the year 867, when that part of England was laid waste by the Danes, and it was altogether annihilated, "so that the very name was lost in its ruins, and the place remained desolate till near the time of the Norman Conquest, when a few huts being erected in the place where the town had formerly stood, it took the name of Presteby,[1] because it was in the neighbourhood of the ancient residence for monks, and after that was called Whiteby or Whitby,[2] a word signifying "the white dwelling" or "town."

---

[1] Allen's Hist. of York.

[2] This famous monastery is familiar to the lovers of romantic lore, as the scene of part of Sir Walter Scott's beautiful poem of Marmion, the allusions in which, relating to this celebrated pile and its rulers, and the learned notes attached, may satisfy even the most severe antiquary; few could be more instructed in the mystery of the craft than the poet, who has rendered interesting and classical every spot named in his writings.

ST. EBBA, QUENBURGA, SURNAMED "BEBBA," AND SAXBURGA.

The child Ebba's adventures—She enters a convent—Marries Cwichelme—Seeks the court of her brother Oswald — Her influence — Quenburga — Birinus — Kynigils — Saxburga repudiated — Penda's vengeance — Bebba and Bebbanburgh—Bamborough Castle—Oswald and Aidan—The silver dishes—Oswald's charity — The blessing — The Hermit's adventure — Oswald slain — The limbs of Oswald — Ostrida his niece — Ebba the Saint — The double Monastery — Saxburga and her husband reconciled — Conversions — The Plague — The Queen Regnant.

THE lives of these Queens are intimately connected; their names being repeated together in the history of their times; but though the events in which they bore a share were of importance, their individual history does not occupy a very large space.

Ebba, whose piety earned for her the honours of canonization, was the only one of the children of Queen Acha who was not the companion of her flight, after the battle in which her husband Ethelfrid the Wild lost his crown and life, Ebba, then quite a child, fell into the hands of the conquerors as prisoner; but by her quickness and intelligence contrived to elude the vigilance of her guards, and, flying from pursuit, came to the banks of the Humber, where, finding a boat, she is said to have put to sea alone, and, unaided by any human being, safely arrived at that point of land or promontory which stretches into the sea in the mouth of the Forth, and from the circumstance bore, and still bears, her name, being called St. Ebba's Head. The bishop of the diocese received the little wanderer, who assumed the religious habit, following the profession of a nun for many years, and setting an example of superior sanctity to the whole of her sisterhood.

In process of time she quitted her convent to become the wife of Cwichelme, King of Wessex, whose power was shared by Kynigils. Cwichelme was that King of Wessex, who sent an assassin to rid him of his enemy, Edwin of Northumberland, whose loyal subject, Lilla, devoted his life to save him.

Of the married life of Ebba, little is known, but on becoming a widow, she sought the court of her brother Oswald, who had succeeded to the throne of Northumberland; and there she had an opportunity of exercising her pious powers, for her brother greatly venerated her character, and was much guided by her counsels. He had married Quenburga, daughter of Kynigils, a wife worthy of so excellent a monarch; and it was while he was in Wessex, soliciting her hand, that he had the glory of assisting Birinus, the missionary, in his task of converting the King, to whom he became sponsor on his baptism, and many of his subjects, to Christianity.

The two Kings, in commemoration of the occasion, afterwards erected Dorchester[1] into an episcopal see, of which Birinus was made Bishop. Oswald was united to Quenburga, and thus became both father and son to the converted monarch. Cwichelme, and his son by Ebba, were also baptized at the same time, Birinus being sponsor to the King, whose death occurred soon after his conversion.

Kynigils afterwards founded Winchester Cathedral, under the direction of the pious and successful missionary.

Although Kynigils and his brother Cwichelme had become Christians, Cenwalch, son of the former, yet remained an adherent of the Saxon idolatry, nor could any persuasions influence him to become a convert. This prince, during his father's life, became the husband of Saxburga, daughter of Wibba, King of Mercia, and grand-daughter of Crida, founder of that monarchy,—a princess, who, by her great spirit, talents, and courage, afterwards occupied an important and distinguished position in the Anglo-Saxon Heptarchy. Nor was this the first matrimonial tie which had united the thrones of Wessex and Mercia. The reigning King of Mercia, the fierce and warlike Penda, who had bestowed Saxburga on Cenwalch, was only half-brother of that lady, although a son of Wibba.[2] His mother was a Princess of Wessex, a descendant of the noble race of the Gewissaæ;[3] and had, besides, a daughter who married Cadwallo, King of the Britons.[4] On the other hand, that Saxburga, and her brothers Kenwald, Eoppa, and Eawa, were the children of a different wife, is not generally known.

Saxburga was destined to experience the strangest vicissitudes of fortune; on the death of the Christian King, Kynigils, her father-in-law, A. D. 643, her husband being elevated to the throne, dismissed her from his court *with ignominy*, and gave her rank to a princess whom he "more favoured."[5] Historians universally admit that no just cause existed why such a step should have been taken by Cenwalch.[6] This took place in the year 642, but the perpetrator of such an act of injustice was condemned to undergo a severe punishment. It was not likely that Penda, the most warlike of the Mercian Kings, would permit so deep an insult to be offered to a member of his family without retribubution. To avenge his half-sister Saxburga, he therefore made war on Cenwalch, and succeeded in expelling that King from his dominions about the third or fifth year of his reign.[7] The fugitive prince was received at the court of Anna, King of East Anglia, where, for some time, he remained in security; but what became of Saxburga at this epoch of her history we are not informed.

Quenburga, sister of Cenwalch, now Queen of Northumberland, the

[1] In Oxfordshire, formerly a city, but now a village. It first belonged to the West Saxons, and afterwards to the Mercians.

[2] Palgrave, Holinshed. [3] Geoffrey of Monmouth. [4] Speed.

[5] Lingard. [6] Speed. [7] Holinshed, Palgrave, Roger of Wendover.

year following her marriage, presented her husband with a son, whom he named Ethelwold. The Queen herself had, after leaving her father's court, assumed the surname of "Bebba," which was commonly adopted by the consorts of the Northumbrian monarchs in commemoration of the wife of Ida the Firebrand, founder of that monarchy, in whose honour that prince had founded the city which, in modern times, is known as Bamborough.[1] Ida had originally sailed from the shores of the Baltic, with his consort Bebba and twelve sons, at the head of a body of Angles, in a fleet of forty vessels, and was received at Flamborough Head with joy by some of his own countrymen, with whose aid he subjugated Northumberland, Durham, and some of the south-eastern counties of Scotland, founding, in the year 559, a distinct and independent monarchy.[2]

Though some have said that the chief town of the Kingdom of Northumberland, which gave its name of Bebbanburg to a large district or tract of land, extending southward, was named after Oswald's queen, there is no doubt that it was first called "Bebban" from the queen of Ida. It is certain that Quenburga was called "Bebba" after her union with Oswald; she is thus named by the poet Harding in his Chronicle:—

> "King Oswold wedded Beblam his wife to bee,
> Kynge Kyngilles doughter full faire to see."

Oswald and his Queen resided at the royal city of Bebbanburgh, of which the following account has been given by the chaplain of Henry II., in 1192:—"Bebba is a very strong city, but not exceeding large; containing not more than two or three acres of ground. It has but one hollow entrance into it, which is admirably raised by steps. On the top of the hill stands a fair church, and in the western point is a well, curiously adorned, and of sweet, clean water."[3]

More modern historians thus describe this interesting spot:—

"Bamburgh Castle, in the origin, was one of the castella built by Agricola on his third campaign; the Roman wall is close to the verge of the hill on which this celebrated fortress is situated. For providing the garrison with a supply of water, which the besiegers could not cut off, there was in most castles a well, which was sometimes curiously concealed within the thickness of the walls. There are draw-wells in the Castles of Dover, Canterbury, Rochester, Colchester, Carisbrook, &c. In the old Norman town of Newcastle, the well is very curiously concealed within the wall. The great well of Bamburgh had long been forgotten, when, in December, 1770, it was accidentally discovered in lowering the floor."

The great draw-well of Bamburgh Castle is described as "a dark and rugged shaft excavated within the keep, through the rock of stone, to the amazing depth of a hundred and fifty feet," and as being "equalled only by the draw-well of Beeston Castle: this stupendous work is ascribed to the Norman Lords of Bamborough."

"The Saxon Castle of Bamburg having been destroyed, A.D. 993, it is probable that the church shared the same fate, and remained in ruin through the chief part, if not the whole, of the dark and troubled cen-

---

[1] Bede. [2] Turner. [3] Simeon of Durham.

tury which succeeded. Neither the church nor the castle is mentioned again till the reign of William Rufus; but before that period the castle, at all events, had been rebuilt; and under the early Anglo-Norman kings, the vill of Bamborough rose into existence. The castle was accessible only by an acclivity winding under the south-east front, through an ancient tower; and formerly it was defended also by a ditch cut through a narrow isthmus communicating with the mainland. Within the first bailey, there is another ancient gateway; and beyond, proceeding between walls, partly of artificial masonry, and partly formed by the precipitous cliff, we pass below a massive Norman round-tower which commanded the critical pass. The inner bailey, in which the keep is situated, is a level space of great area, surrounded by various buildings, now no longer devoted to military occupations, but appropriated to ministries of charity and peace. The space covered by the walls of the castle measures eight acres; and not less than fifty-six acres of rock, warren, and sand-hills are included within its domain."[1]

The youth of Oswald had been passed in exile in Ireland, and when Aidan, the Culdee, arrived to instruct his subjects in the Christian faith, the King appointed him to a see in the island of Lindisfarne, which may be seen seven miles to the north of Bamborough; the Fern isles being opposite the royal residence of Oswald, and the cliffs of Dunstanburg rising to the south.

The preaching of Aidan was so successful, that in seven days, no less than fifteen thousand persons received the baptismal rite.

King Oswald was the first prince of our Saxon rulers, who is recorded to have been served in silver dishes.

"When he was once sitting at dinner on the holy day of Easter, with the aforesaid bishop (Aidan), and a silver dish full of dainties before him, and they were just ready to bless the bread, the servant, whom he had appointed to relieve the poor, came in on a sudden, and told the King, that a great multitude of needy persons from all parts were sitting in the streets begging some alms of the King; he immediately ordered the meat set before him to be carried to the poor, and the dish to be cut in pieces and divided among them. At which sight the bishop, who sat by him, much taken with such an act of piety, laid hold of his right hand, and said, 'May this hand never perish!' Which fell out according to his prayer, for his arm and hand being cut off from his body, when he was slain in battle, remain entire and uncorrupted to this day, and are kept in a silver case, as revered relics, in St. Peter's Church in the royal city."

The Northumbrians might well obey such a ruler with love. The following distich is on record of Oswald:—

"Quis fuit Alcides? Quis Cæsar Julius? Aut quis
Magnus Alexander? Alcvdes se superasse
Fertur; Alexander mundum, sed Julius hostem,
Se simul Oswaldus, et mundum vicit, et hostem."[2]

Queen Bebba was herself as much celebrated by her admirable con-

[1] Gibson.

[2] Camden.

duct, as the saintly King, her husband, for his holiness of life. Of this, the following instance has been transmitted by one of our chroniclers:—

"A hermit, of extraordinary sanctity, desirous of ascertaining whether any other person surpassed himself in purity of life, was, in answer to his meditations, told by revelation, "that King Oswald was more holy, though he had wedded a wife." To the King accordingly the pious hermit repaired, desiring, with holy zeal, to be informed concerning his "course of life." On which Oswald, in the true spirit of that love and confidence which reposed on the purity and virtue of his beloved partner, referred the hermit to her, bidding him carry to her his ring with his commands, "that she should entertain him as though he were her own royal spouse." Queen Bebba failed not in strictly obeying her lord's mandate; but, while she shared with the holy man the regal repast, she showed him that it consisted only of bread and water, no other food being permitted to him, thus exhibiting an example of that self-denial by which purity of life is alone attainable. When night came, the hermit, expecting to pass it as Oswald himself was in the habit of doing, was more surprised than pleased when the Queen caused him to be cast into a cold water bath, according to the habit of the prince he wished to imitate!

"Gladly, and right early on the morrow, did the venerable man take leave of the Queen, and, having restored to King Oswald his ring, frankly acknowledged that his own entire life was not so holy as one of his days and nights." [1]

No further mention of Queen Bebba is made till after Oswald's death. The title of Bretwalda,[2] or Emperor, was accorded to this King in the year of his son Edilwold's birth; peace and plenty were the characteristics of his reign. At last Penda, King of Mercia, envying his neighbouring potentate's prosperity, took up arms against him. The two kings fought at Maserfield, in Shropshire, August 5th, 642, and Oswald fell in the engagement. The spot where the monarch was slain was called from the circumstance, Oswald's tree, abbreviated into Oswestry.[3] The cruel victor caused the body of the prince to be cut into pieces, which, being stuck on stakes, were dispersed over the battle-field as so many victorious trophies. Some old verses say that it was the head and hands only of the unfortunate prince that were thus exposed; the translation is as follows:

"Three crosses raised at Penda's dire commands,
Bore Oswald's royal head and mangled hands,
To stand a sad example to the rest,
And prove him wretched who is ever blest.
Vain policy! for what the victor got
Proved to the vanquish'd king the happier lot;
For now the martyr'd saint in glory views
How Oswy with success the war renews:
And Penda scarcely can support his throne,
Whilst Oswald wears a never-failing crown." [4]

The Church, to which Oswald was justly dear, rendered every posthu-

[1] Harding's Chronicle.

[2] An imitation of the dignity of Emperors of the West.—Lappenberg.

[3] Pennant's Wales.

[4] Ibid.

mous honour to his memory, and not only was he raised to the dignity of a saint, but his claim to the honour was supported by various miracles.[1]

The widowed Queen Bebba had used the interest of her brother-in-law Oswy, the now reigning monarch, to obtain from Cadwealla permission to bury the head and arm of Oswald.

Hardinge in his quaint chronicle has these lines:

> "King Oswy to Cadwall did enclyne,
> And Oswald his hed and arme had leue to burye,
> Which he betoke to Queen Bebla in hye,
> Who closed them in silver fayre and clene,
> And them betooke to Saynte Aydan, I ween."

The venerable Bede records the same. "Oswald's head and arm were conveyed by King Oswy to the sorrow-stricken Queen, who religiously enshrined the precious relics in a silver case and conveyed them to St. Aidan, by whom they were carefully deposited in St. Peter's Church, in the royal city of Bebbanburgh."

Of Bebba we learn no more. Her infant son was deprived of his inheritance for a time by the usurpation of Oswy: at the death of that king he mounted the throne, being but sixteen years of age at the time, and preserved his power during the remainder of his life, transmitting it when he died, to Alfred, the natural son of Oswy.

---

[1] An engraving in Strutt's Regal Antiquities, represents the King setting out with his army against the Mercian monarch, and, in another plate, gives a delineation of the battle, with Oswald falling from his horse, wounded by the Mercian king. These drawings are taken from a MS. (Harleian, 1981) preserved in the Royal Library at the British Museum; which, by the writing and dress of the figures, appears to have been written and illuminated at the commencement of the fourteenth century. They are contained in a psalter at the bottom of the leaves. The MS. was presented to Queen Mary, in 1553, by Baldwin Smith, a citizen of London.

The town (which is near Severus's Wall) taking the name of Oswald's Tree, from the cross or tree the King had erected there. The MS. account of the town, written in 1635, has the following: — "There was an old oake lately standing in Mesburie, within the parish of Oswestry, whereon one of King Oswald's arms hung, say the neighbours by tradition."

Oswald's Well is situated a little to the west of the free-school of Oswestry, and is supplied by a spring flowing from the elevated ground above it. The well is a small square basin, in a recess formed by a stone wall, and arched over. On the back is a rudely sculptured head of King Oswald, and the front was secured by an iron grate. A second recess of the same kind is divided from the former by a slight stone wall, and in this recess there is water also, which was perhaps granted for common uses, whilst the other may have been held sacred. There was formerly a chapel or cell near it, but no vestige of either remains; and the well itself is in a very ruinous state, but the water is good. There is a tradition that when Oswald was slain, an eagle tore one of the arms from the body, and flying off with it, fell down and perished upon this spot, from whence the water gushed up, and has continued to flow ever since, as a memorial of the event. The title of "Baron of Oswaldistre" is now held by the Duke of Norfolk. — History of Oswestry.

A monastery was founded on the place of Oswald's martyrdom, dedicated to the memory of that sainted king, but no evidences either of its foundation or dissolution exist. Leland, in his time, names the cloister as having been standing within the recollection of persons then alive.

The remains of St. Oswald being afterwards found by his niece Ostrida, Queen of the Mercians, were solemnly enshrined in the Abbey of Bardney, in Lincolnshire, and the King's banner hung over his tomb at her cost, and worked by herself.[1] At a subsequent period, the relics of departed royalty were removed by Ethelfleda, Queen of the Mercians, to the Abbey of St. Peter at Gloucester, where they were deposited on the north side of the upper end of the choir. In that cathedral a fair monument of the murdered prince is still remaining, with a chapel set between two pillars of that church.[2]

Bishop Aidan,[3] the friend and counsellor of the ill-fated Oswald, survived his royal master nine years. In 651, when Penda, at the head of the Mercian army, ravaged Northumberland, he came to Bamborough, and sought, but in vain, to take that royal city by force. He afterwards encompassed it on the land side with wood and thatch, which he caused to be set on fire, and the flames soon rose above the walls of the citadel. Aidan was at this time on the Farn Island, two miles from the mainland; and seeing the danger of the garrison, invoked the Divine aid against the machinations of the enemy; on which, according to Bede, "the wind suddenly changed and bore the flames upon the camp of the besiegers," who were thus compelled to desist from further assault. Aidan was in the King's Vill, not far from Bamborough, when he was visited with his last illness: for he was in the habit of resorting to a church in the village of Bamborough, where a little chamber had been erected for him on the western wall of the edifice, that he might conveniently reside there when he made excursions into the adjacent country. The Bishop had other similar accommodations provided for him in several of the King's country-seats, having no place of his own but his church, and a few fields about it. In his sickness they set up a tent for him, adjoining the west side of the church of Bamborough, and there he died.

Ebba, sister of Oswald, who was aunt as well as sister-in-law of Quenburga "Bebba," after she had returned into Northumberland, founded successively several nunneries, and became noted for her sanctity.

The nunnery upon the Derwent, in Durham, was founded by this widowed Queen of Wessex, and, from her name, called Ebchester. It was built, A. D. 660, and Oswy, brother of Oswald, assisted in this pious work, perhaps as some atonement for usurping his nephew's place. The small, irregular village of Ebchester is described by Camden as "occupying the brow of a steep declivity overhanging the Tyne."

St. Ebba, in her widowhood, resumed the religious habit which she had worn when a child, and retired to the same establishment in which she passed her early years. She was foundress of the celebrated monastery of Coldingham in the Marshes, below Berwick, in Scotland, which

---

[1] Willis's Abbeys.

[2] "Oswy afterwards took the head of Oswald from Bardney, and interred it in the church of Lindisfarne: it attended the faithful monks of that place in prosperity and adversity, till at length it found 'a safe resting-place in the bosom of St. Cuthbert,' where it remained until the outrages of Lee, and other malefactors of evil memory." — Gibbon, Harding, Speed.

[3] Brit. Sancta.

establishment she governed herself as Abbess until her death, which did not take place till she had arrived at a very advanced age. This celebrated double separate monastery was visited by the famed St. Cuthbert, by invitation of the Abbess Queen, who was desirous that her people there should be edified by the instructions of that holy man,—a request most readily complied with.

The history of St. Ebba is much connected with the public events in her time, proving the influence she maintained by her own excellent conduct.

At one period this Queen presided over Camwode Abbey, during the reign of her nephew Egfrid. St. Etheldreda, then Queen, having obtained her husband's permission to take the religious vows, professed herself a nun in Camwode Abbey, "the convent of Ebba, the King's aunt," receiving the veil from the hands of Bishop Wilfrid.[1] Etheldreda remained in the establishment, under the protection of St. Ebba, till her flight to Ely.

Again St. Ebba's name comes prominently forward; for Egfrid had imprisoned Wilfrid on his return from Rome; and during the space of nine months every art had been practised to induce the bishop to confess that the Pontiff's decision had either been a fabrication, or purchased by presents. Threats and promises, however, failed in moving Wilfrid, who was at length happily liberated, at the earnest prayers of the Abbess Ebba, on his subscribing to a condition that he would never more set foot within the territories of Egfrid.[2]

After the completion of Coldingham, St. Ebba assumed the government of the establishment, and presided over it till her death, which took place A. D. 683, having survived her husband as many as forty-five years. At some period, it is said that "St. Cuthbert informed Elfrid, a priest, by revelation, where the bones of St. Ebba and St. Ethelgifa, and many other saints, might be found, which, on his discovering the place, were first exposed by him as holy relics, to be worshipped by the people, and afterwards placed with the body of St. Cuthbert."

Cenwalch, after the just vengeance of Penda had caused his abdication, retired to the protection of Anna, King of east Anglia, a pious and excellent monarch, who took upon himself to reprove his guest freely for his ill-treatment of Queen Saxburga. Sigebert, king of Essex, also remonstrated so strongly in favour of the Queen, and so powerfully urged the principles of the Christian faith, that at last Cenwalch became a convert, and in 648 received the baptismal rite[3] from Felix, a Burgundian priest, who, after being seventeen years Bishop of East Anglia, was elevated to the Archbishopric of Canterbury.[4] An entire change seemed to have taken place in the heart of Cenwalch, who now received his Queen Saxburga back. Some, indeed, say that she had been reconciled to him prior to his conversion. The question naturally suggests itself, was this Queen herself of the Christian persuasion? Her brother Penda was

[1] Bradshawe's Life of St. Werburga; Richard, Prior of Hexham.

[2] Lingard's Antiquities of the Anglo-Saxon Church.

[3] Bede. [4] Rapin.

certainly one of the bitterest persecutors of the Church throughout the whole period of the Saxon Heptarchy. Still Saxburga might have embraced the doctrine at the time of the conversion of Kynigils, and perhaps this was the cause of her repudiation, more especially if they became reconciled to each other either on the eve of the conversion of Cenwalch or immediately after that event.

These two important events to Saxburga, her husband's conversion and her own reconciliation to him, were succeeded by another not less gratifying. Their nephew, Cuthred, son of Cwichelme, entered into a negotiation with Cenwalch relative to his restoration to his dominions. The conversion of Cenwalch first induced him to assist him in his difficulties, and to receive him at Ashendon,[1] in Bucks, where the preliminary arrangements were made between the two kings, and the remuneration settled upon for the services rendered by Cuthred on the occasion. It was there stipulated that all that part of the kingdom which lay northward from the river Thames, and the extent of which was computed at 3000 hides,[2] containing within its limits as many villages, should be held hereafter by Cuthred for his principality:[3] these lands granted to Cuthred lay near Ashendon, where the agreement was made, and amounted to about a third part of the kingdom of Cenwalch.[4] After this arrangement, Cuthred successfully aided Cenwalch in the enterprise of recovering the crown, which he had forfeited through his own errors. Cenwalch and Saxburga from that time forward seem to have lived in the most entire harmony: this lasting for a long succession of years, must have repaid Saxburga for all her past affliction. The husband, no longer a Pagan in heart, showed in every action that he was worthy to profess the mild doctrines of Christianity, and became a blessing to himself and others.

The first employment of Cenwalch on his recovery of the throne, after fulfilling his contract with Cuthred, was to complete the edifice at Winchester which had been founded by his father, and built under the directions of St. Birinus, Bishop of Dorchester. It was completed in 648, and in a style of magnificence unusual in those times. St. Birinus came to Winchester when it was completed, and solemnly dedicated the building in the name of the Holy Trinity and of Saints Peter and Paul. The same year the holy prelate died, and though in the first instance buried at Dorchester, where he usually dwelt, his remains were eventually transferred to Winchester Catheral.[5]

It is not stated that either Cenwalch or Saxburga quitted Britain during the fatal visitation of the plague in Britain. The following is, however, a Welsh record concerning a princess called Saxburga, and who probably was the same:—"When the plague and famine had ceased its long ravages, those Saxons who had had the good fortune to escape, sent intelligence to Germany of the thinness of the population in Britain, represent-

[1] Or Æscendune, in the forest of Brentwode, included in the territory of Wessex. — Kennet, Lipscombe.

[2] Lipscombe's History of Bucks. [3] Palgrave. [4] Bede.

[5] Holinshed, Milner, Anglo-Saxon Chronicle.

ing how easily a new settlement might be made. Accordingly a vast number of men and women landed in the north, under Queen Sexburgis, and settled in Britain, from Norway to Cornwall, without opposition from the Britons. By 'Norway' the Welsh Chronicle here means Northumberland, sometimes called Albany. In the Highlands of Scotland two districts were formerly entitled Norway and Denmark, because colonized from those countries, which frequently occasions a confusion in the mind of readers unacquainted with the fact, when referred to in our histories under those names."[1] The date of that event, 664, makes it possible that this was no other than Saxburga, the Abbess-Queen of Kent.

Cenwalch survived the desolating scourge of the yellow plague about eight years, having reigned altogether thirty-one years, three of which he had passed in exile. He died in 672, giving, at the last, a most convincing proof of his respect for Saxburga, by bequeathing to her the administration of the affairs of the state, a step the more remarkable, as it was quite unprecedented. Saxburga is, in fact, the solitary instance of a Queen-Regnant during the entire dominion of the Anglo-Saxons.[2] The measure was imprudent; and the people, disdaining to fight under a woman, not long after the death of Cenwalch, rebelled against the widowed Queen, and displaced her from the high office which had been confided to her by her husband's will. Some, indeed, say that the Queen continued in power during the space of two years;[3] and others, that for half that period, her power was shared by Egwin, and that he, after her death, reigned one year by himself,[4] and was then succeeded by Kentwin.[5] However this might be, the kingdom seems to have been divided for ten years among the Ealdormen, after the decease of Cenwalch, and the short period during which Saxburga held her authority over the people. During that space of time, however brief, Saxburga proved herself in every respect worthy to discharge the duties of her office. One of our old chroniclers describes this Saxon Queen-Regnant as having "levied new forces, and preserved the old in their duty," ruling her subjects with moderation, and overawing her enemies; in short, that "she conducted all things in such a manner, that no difference was discoverable, except that of sex." It was a misfortune to her people to lose such a ruler, whose character seems to have combined some of the characteristics of her dauntless brother Penda, possessing his splendid talents without his defects.

[1] Roberts's British History.
[2] William of Malmesbury.
[3] Matthew of Westminster.
[4] Bromton, William of Malmesbury.
[5] Bromton

OSTRIDA AND WERBURGA,

QUEENS OF MERCIA.

Ostrida marries Ethelred, the youngest son of Penda—Elfwin slain—Archbishop Theodore endeavours to reconcile the Kings — Ostrida removes the bones of Saint Oswald — Abbey of Bardney — The miracle of the pillar of light — The standard — Embroidery — The spinsters—Visit of Ethelhild—Holy dust—Its effect—Ostrida slain—Ferocity of the times—Ethelred abdicates—He becomes Abbot at Bardney—Kenred makes a pilgrimage to Rome—Werberga enters a convent.

OSTRIDA was the youngest of Oswy's daughters by his Queen, Enfleda, and was born in the year 657, the fifteenth of her father's reign, about the period when her sister Alfleda was united to Peada, the eldest son of the Mercian King. This princess was lineally descended from Ida, founder of the Kingdom of Northumberland, on her father's side; while on that of her mother, grand-daughter of Bertha and Ethelbert, she claimed her origin from the French monarchs, and the famous hero Woden, the common ancestor of the Anglo-Saxon princes. Bradshawe, writing of Ostrida, calls her "a beautiful lady, of noble lineage, born in the north part."

The death of Oswy took place when Ostrida was only thirteen years of age, and her half-brother, Egfrid, formerly a hostage at the Mercian court, became King.[1] It was in the seventh year of Egfrid's reign that Ostrida married Ethelred, the youngest of Penda's sons, who had been on the throne about three years.[2] Notwithstanding this alliance, two years afterwards, Ethelred, though a peace-loving prince, made war on Egfrid, who had invaded his dominions. The cause of the dispute between these near relatives was this: some towns in Mercia had been taken in the reign of Wulphere, and Ethelred demanded restitution from Egfrid of the province of the Lindiswaras.[3] In a great battle, fought near the river Trent, Elfwin, a youth of eighteen, brother of Egfrid and Alfleda the former Queen of the Mercians, was unhappily slain—a prince who was dear to both nations for his mother's sake.

This painful occurrence would have caused the war to break out more fiercely than ever, but for the timely interposition of Theodore, Archbishop of Canterbury, who succeeded in reconciling the two Kings and their people, without any one being put to death on the occasion. The usual mulct for a murder was, however, paid by Ethelred to King Egfrid.

[1] Holinshed.

[2] Speed, Palgrave, Leland.

[3] Natives of Lincolnshire.—Lingard, Rapin, Bede.

It is thought that the lasting peace which followed, and even Ethelred's secure possession of the crown he wore, were secured to him by the fact of his being united to Ostrida, the Northumbrian princess; for, though the *were* for Elfwin's death was paid, he recovered the possession of the disputed territories A. D. 679.

Ostrida was present at a grand general witenagemote, held at Heathfield (now Bishop's Hatfield, in Hertfordshire), by her husband, which was attended by all the chief prelates of the Saxon Heptarchy, the object of the meeting being to preserve the English Church from the heresy of the Eutyches. On this occasion, King Ethelred made large donations to the Abbey of Peterborough, besides confirming previous grants. Ostrida appended her name to the new donation made by the King at this assembly—"I, Ostrida, Ethelred's Queen, confirm it." This signature is preceded by those of Theodore, Archbishop of Canterbury; Wilfred, Archbishop of York; and Sexwulf, first Abbot of Peterborough, but at that time Bishop of Lichfield; and after the Queen's name appear those of Adrian, the Pope's legate; Putta, Bishop of Rochester; and Waldhere, Bishop of London. Before the grant of King Ethelred was signed, the Pope's letter was read, ratified, and confirmed by the council.[1]

One of the most interesting acts of Queen Ostrida was her removal of the bones of her uncle, King Oswald, to Bardney Abbey,[2] in Lincolnshire.

The Abbey of Bardney, founded by King Ethelred,[3] is thus spoken of by Bede, in his account of some miracles which attended the translation of the relics of that sainted king. "There is a noble monastery, in the province of Lindsey, called Beardeneu, which Queen Ostrida and her husband Ethelred much loved, and conferred upon it many honours and ornaments." It was here that she was desirous to lay the venerable bones of her uncle. The fulfilment of her purpose brought to light a strong point of feeling in the minds of the Mercians. "When the wagon in which these bones were carried, arrived towards evening in the aforesaid monastery, *they that were in it refused to admit them,* because, though they knew him to be a holy man, yet, as he was originally of another province, and had *reigned over them as a foreign king, they retained their ancient aversion to him even after death.* Thus it came to pass that the relics were left in the open air all that night, with only a large tent spread over them." Small respect seems here to have been shown to the wishes of the royal lady, their Queen and mistress. A miracle was requisite to discover to them their error: through the whole night, from the wagon up to the heavens, was seen a pillar of light, visible throughout the province of Lindsey; and the next day, the very brethren who had refused to receive the royal relics, prayed to God to permit them to be deposited among them. Accordingly the bones, being washed, were put into a shrine which they had made for that purpose, and placed in the church with due honour; and that there might be a "perpetual memorial" of the royal Oswald, "they hung up over the

[1] Saxon Chronicle, Dugdale, vol i. 67, Turner.

[2] Fabian says "the Abbey of Bourdeaux."

[3] Willis's Abbeys.

monument his banner, made of gold and purple."[1] This standard had been wrought "by no hands, as ye may guess," but those of Queen Ostrida herself, who, by her own industry, and at her own cost, decorated the tomb in which the hallowed relics of her departed relative were deposited.[2]

During the seventh century, much talent was exhibited by our Anglo-Saxon countrywomen in the art of embroidery: women of the highest rank excelled in the accomplishment, and the example was followed by others. The products of this feminine industry and skill were usually devoted to the Church and its ministers,[3] and were esteemed so valuable as to become heirlooms, bequeathed by their owners to those most dear to them. The needles of illustrious women were busy, from the fair Ostrida, who wrought the tragedy of a murdered uncle, to the Norman Matilda, who depicted upon canvas the heroic actions of a warlike husband. The Anglo-Saxon ladies excelled in needlework and gold embroidery, and also were acquainted with the arts of weaving and dyeing. The last is alluded to by St. Aldhelm, in these words: "The shuttles, not filled with purple only, but with various colours, are moved here and there among the thick spreading of the threads, and by the embroidering art they adorn all the woven work with various groups of images." Spinning was, indeed, so common an employment of the female sex, even among women of royal blood, that the will of King Alfred terms the members of his family who were of the female side, "the spindle side;" so that the modern term of "spinster" has descended to us in allusion to those unmarried, and able to devote themselves to feminine accomplishments more exclusively.

The banner of Ostrida is said to have been wrought of purple and gold: a robe worn by Aldhelm was constructed of a purple ground, composed of delicate thread, upon which appeared black circles; and in those circles were wrought the figures of peacocks, of an ample size. Such was the taste of the seventh century, in which age abundance of goldsmiths and jewellers were to be found ready to assist the fair patronesses of their art; of whom Bede says, that they were skilled in collecting "remarkable and precious stones, to be placed among the gold and silver, which were mostly of a ruddy or aërial colour." It was customary with the sovereigns of the Heptarchy to present rich garments, vases, bracelets, and rings, to their witenagemote and courtiers, which example was followed by their queens-consort.[4]

The superstitions of the days in which Ostrida lived are well attested by the miracles related by the venerable Bede. One of those is connected

[1] Bede.

[2] Speed, Butler, Harding.

[3] An example of the clerical costume of the seventh century may be seen in the church of Malmsbury, in Wilts, in the figure of St. Peter, who, with other apostles, is wrought, in the south porch of that edifice, in basso-relievo; the date given by Fosbrooke is 675; the work is Saxon, and sketched in 1801. The double keys in the right hand of St. Peter (head of the Church); book, with jewels, of the New Testament in the left; the robes are becoming and well-disposed, jewels on the border of the neck, feet bare. The doorway at the entrance of the same church, exhibits the figure of a religious, in basso-relievo, dressed in the simple monk's habit, hood, &c.—*Fosbrooke's Brit. Monachism.*

[4] Sharon Turner.

with the Queen, who, at the time, was on a visit at Bardney Abbey. Ethelhild, sister of the abbot, came there to pay her respects to her royal mistress, from her own convent, which was not far distant. The conversation happening to turn on the uncle-saint of Ostrida, Lady Ethelhild remarked, she had been an eye-witness of the pillar of light which reached from earth to heaven, before alluded to. The Queen thereupon added, that the very dust of the pavement, on which the water that washed the bones had been spilt, had already healed many sick persons.[1] The abbess, upon hearing this, desired that some of the said dust might be given her, which she tied up in a cloth, and putting it into a casket, returned home. Not long after, a visitor at the monastery was suddenly seized with an evil spirit, so that none could bind him, and the abbess, with one of the nuns, was sent for to his assistance. All efforts to assuage his madness were fruitless; but suddenly the abbess had recourse to the holy dust in the casket, which she had received from Queen Ostrida. When a small portion was given to the sufferer, and after the priest had prayed over him, he had a quiet night, nor was he ever after disturbed by his old enemy. Bede, who related this adventure of Ethelhild, speaks of her as "a certain venerable abbess of that name, who is still living."

Ostrida's union with Ethelred lasted for twenty years, during which she had but one son, who received the name of Ceolred.[2] A sad fate overtook her soon after this period: she was upon a journey through North Mercia, and was attacked and slain by the people of the district over which her husband ruled; these were the South Humbrians, or people of the territories which lay south of the Trent. This treasonable act is supposed to have been committed by the heads of the State, who raised an insurrection to revenge on Ostrida the death of Peada, their former King, murdered by Alchfleda, the Queen's half-sister. Unlikely as such a cause might be, that circumstance having occurred when Ostrida was yet in her cradle, it has been assigned by our historians, in the absence of any evidence as to the real one which occasioned the Queen's untimely end. This tragical event affords an example of the ferocity of the times: it happened A. D. 697, Ostrida being forty years of age, half of which she had resided among the people to whom she owed her undeserved death. Ethelred had reigned twenty-three years with much honour, when he was bereaved of his consort. The little care taken either by himself or his son to discover the murderers, has led to a suspicion that the King personally connived at the circumstance; or, that the murderer was too nearly connected with him to be denounced. Whether this was the case or not, it is a fact, that the cruel death of Ostrida so affected the mind of Ethelred, that from that time he could not discharge the duties of royalty, but resigned his regal dignity and dominions to Kenred, his nephew, son of Wulphere. whether sorrow for her loss, or penitence for his own share in the crime, induced this, is unknown.

Kenred was arrived at maturity, and the son of Ostrida was still too

[1] It had the virtue of expelling devils from the bodies of persons possessed.—*Bede.*

[2] Speed, Rapin, Langhornii Chron., Palgrave, Holinshed.

young to govern; so that in his abdication Ethelred consulted the wishes of the discontented nation. He assumed the monastic habit of the Benedictines, and having first taken the vows at Bardney, became abbot of that monastery, which had been patronized by his consort when living, afterwards her place of abode, and where her last mortal remains now reposed.[1]

Ethelred abdicated in 704,[2] the time of his entering the cloister; and eight years after became abbot. He discharged the duties of his station for four years only, at the end of which he died at an advanced age, having survived Queen Ostrida nineteen years. The royal founder and Abbot of Bardney was interred in that monastery, where his tomb was still to be seen in the days of William of Malmesbury. The piety and munificence of Ethelred and Ostrida caused their names to be numbered among the Saxon saints.

The royal donation of a crown temporal in these times was "found wanting," when weighed in the balance with the crown eternal, which prince and peasant alike strove to obtain. In the hope of a reward in heaven, Kenred returned the present of a kingdom to his cousin Ceolred, the son of Ostrida, and making a pilgrimage to Rome, passed the residue of his life there in penance and devotion; he had been accompanied in his devotional expedition by Offa, King of Essex, who had married a sister of Ethelred and Wulphere. Kenred died at Rome, A. D. 711.[3]

Ceolred, after an eight years' reign, died King of Mercia, and was buried in the chapel of Mary, at Litchfield Cathedral, where stood the shrine of St. Chad. He left no children by his Queen Werburga, who, like her namesake, the daughter of Wulphere and Ermenilda, received the honours of canonization. Of the family whence the royal Werburga, wife of Ceolred, sprang, historians leave us in ignorance. When her husband died, Werburga entered a monastery, probably that in Holy Island, where she was residing at the time of her death, which event is placed by the Saxon Chronicle in 782–783, and is given by Hoveden in these words:—"Werburga, formerly Queen of the Mercians, then abbess, ceased to live here, that she might live for ever with Christ, anno 783."

Werburga had arrived at a good old age, in the habitual practice of piety and virtue; her character is given in these words: "Like the holy widow, Anna the prophetess, she never departed from our Lord's temple, serving God night and day, in abstinence and prayer, for the space of sixty-five years. For the latter part of that time she was abbess of the monastery, and showed no less humility in governing others than she had before in obeying."[4] Beautiful, at all times, is Christian humility; but how much more so when viewed amidst the attributes of pomp and power, as in a queen towards her subjects, or an abbess to the flock committed to her charge! Werburga was not a solitary instance; for another Queen, named Richthryda, adorned this period of the Saxon Heptarchy by embracing the desired employments of another life, it being her office "to carry oil with lamps before the great ones of the Lord."

---

[1] Willis's Abbeys.

[2] Willis says 712, and that Ethelred was abbot only four years.

[3] Holinshed, Pennant.

[4] Brit. Sancta.

QUENBURGA, QUENSWITHA, AND ALFLEDA.

The daughters of Penda—Penda's warlike propensities—Queen Keniswitha accepts the care of Oswy's son — Quenburga's marriage — Peada and Alfleda — Stipulations — Peada baptized at Carlisle — Penda's opinions — Influence of females in conversion — Quenburga's devotion — Court of Alfred a monastic school—Alfred's death—Quenburga returns to her father's dominions—Retires to Dormund Caistor—The three sisters all become nuns—Penda's death—Death of Peada—His wife, his mother, and his mistress suspected of his murder—Oswy seizes his dominions—Two young princesses take the veil.

"Keneburg in this our sainted front shall stand,
To Alfred the loved wife, King of Northumberland."
Drayton's Poly Olbion.

QUENBURGA and Quenswitha were sisters: their father Penda, King of Mercia, had a very numerous family by his Queen, who also bore the name of Quenswitha. Four princes, Peada, Wupher, Ethelred, and Merowald, became noted Kings of the Saxon Heptarchy. Mercelin, a fifth, was celebrated for piety, and has been entered on the saintly calendar;[1] while, besides the two daughters already named, whose honourable career has transmitted their names to posterity, may be mentioned their sisters Quendrida, Idaberge, and Walburga, the last of whom wore the crown-matrimonial of Sussex.

The father of this remarkable family maintained his power for thirty years, which he spent in continual wars with his neighbours. His adventurous spirit "hated peace worse than death." Five Kings of the Anglo-Saxons perished in contending against his arms, besides the renowned Edwin and Oswald. Penda, in his sister Saxburga's cause, turned his arms against Northumberland, and penetrated as far as the capital city of Bamborough, setting fire to every habitation in the line of his march. Oswy, the Northumbrian monarch, warned by the fate of his kingly predecessors, made every effort to conciliate his formidable enemy. He not only sent him the most valuable presents, but delivered over his second son, Egfrid, as a hostage into the care of Queen Keneswitha, wife of Penda. It was on this occasion that a match was proposed, which it was hoped would establish a lasting peace between the two hostile nations. This was the marriage of Alfred, eldest son of Oswy, by Enfleda, the Kentish princess, to Quenburga, daughter of the Mercian King. This tie, which took place shortly after, was very important in its consequences. On the occasion of Quenburga's coming to Northumberland, she was accompanied by her eldest brother Peada, who

[1] Speed, Rapin, Malmesbury, Fabian, Butler.

then beheld and fell in love with Alfleda, half-sister of Alfred, the King's illegitimate daughter, by a lady bearing the same name, and who was sister of Egfrid, and of another Alfred often mistaken for the son of Enfleda, who had married Quenburga.[1]

Peada[2] demanded Alfleda of Oswy for his bride, but Oswy refused to accede to the proposal of the Mercian prince, unless he would become a convert to the faith his daughter professed. The royal husband of his sister Quenburga was a firm believer in Christianity; she was mainly instrumental in persuading Peada to embrace its holy doctrines; and that he did this from a sincere conviction, appears from the answer he made when interrogated on the subject: he remarked, with much warmth, "that no consideration, not even the refusal of Alfleda, should provoke him to return to the worship of Wodin."

Peada was accordingly baptized prior to his union with Alfleda; the ceremony was performed by Bishop Finnan, and all his train received the sacred rite with him. This interesting event was witnessed at Carlisle. This city had arrived at great consequence under the Romans, and though afterwards ravaged by the Picts and Scots, was still, for its ancient splendour, accounted a city. When, in a later period, Egfrid, the brother of Alfleda, reigned in Northumberland, he gave the city to St. Cuthbert; and Bede paid a visit there in 686, at the time St. Cuthbert was bishop of Lindisfarne, and describes the walls, which the townspeople took him to see, and a fountain or well of admirable workmanship, which had been early constructed by the Romans.[3]

Before Peada quitted Mercia, in 653, he had been crowned by his father King of Leicester, so that Alfleda might be considered by her marriage Queen of that portion of the Heptarchy. At this period Mercia was divided into two parts, called North and South Mercia, the river Trent forming the boundary between them; the southern division, which belonged to Peada, was called also the Mediterranean, or Middle Angles, and contained 7000 households. The young Queen was conducted by her husband into his dominions, attended by his train, and by four Christian priests, Cidd, Betti, Adda, and Diuma, whom he engaged to instruct his subjects in the new faith.[4] It had been expected that Penda would oppose his son's conversion, as he was a great enemy to Christianity; but either all religions were alike to him, or he treated the subject with complacency for the sake of a son much beloved; for not only did he suffer, and indeed promote, first the marriage of Quenburga to the pious Alfred, but afterwards the conversion of Peada, and the alliance stipulated as its result to take place with Alfleda. More than this, he admitted Chris-

[1] The second Alfred, King of Northumberland, was brother of Egfrid, who succeeded Oswy, of whom they were illegitimate children. The first Alfred, who married Quenburga of Mercia, reigned over Deira, but at his death the people of that district revolted in favour of Egfrid. The youth of the second Alfred was passed in exile in Ireland, whence he was afterwards recalled to assume the crowns of Bernicia and Deira.

[2] Lingard, Biographia Britannica, Holinshed.

[3] Britton and Brayley, Holinshed, Rapin, Lingard.

[4] The first three were Angles, the last an Irishman.—*Bede*, lib. iii. c. 21.

tianity among the Mercians, but in doing so forbade that the Pagan rites should be intermixed with those of the Christians, as had occurred in Essex. This fierce King is said to have "especially hated and despised those who, after they had embraced Christianity, lived in a manner unbecoming their profession," as did Eadbald and other converted princes of the Heptarchy, whom he regarded as "despicable wretches who would not obey their God, in whom they believed."[1]

The Northumbrian missionaries were successful in propagating their belief. The Queen herself employed her influence over the heart of her husband in behalf of the Christian faith, and in seconding its apostles in their work among his subjects. Thus it is a most remarkable fact, that Mercia, as well as Kent and Northumberland, the three most considerable kingdoms of the Heptarchy, were indebted for conversion to the influence of the female sex.[2] Alfleda had only to recall to her mind the bright examples of Bertha and Ethelburga to receive encouragement in the glorious task. Peada, her amiable consort, the first Christian King of Mercia, was a prince of superior understanding, worthy of his exalted dignity, and possessed of talents which commanded the esteem and admiration of all who knew him.

The heart of Quenburga, Queen of Deira, like that of Alfleda, was more set upon the kingdom of heaven than on any earthly diadem. She was singularly devout and pious, and her exhortations prevailed with her husband, King Alfred, that they should live together as brother and sister, rather than as husband and wife: in those times such instances of devotion were esteemed the most exalted proof of religion.

Through the influence of the Queen of Deira, the court of Alfred became converted into a kind of monastic school, of regular discipline and Christian perfection, according to the prevalent notion.

Alfred, however, having died during his father's life-time,[3] Quenburga returned to the dominions of Penda, her father. She had resolved to pass the residue of her days in religious seclusion, and selected for her retreat from the world, a town in the confines of Huntingdon and Northampton, called Dormund Caistor. That spot suited her inclination for retirement, but was not the most healthy, being in a moist and fenny situation. Some say that a monastery had already been built there by Prince Wulpher, her brother; but the general opinion is, that Quenburga herself founded the establishment for Christian virgins, over whom she presided as Abbess;[4] and this seems most likely, as the town, since called Caistor only, was changed, at that date, from the name of Dormund Caistor to Kunneburg-ceaster, or the town of Quenburga. Into this holy retreat, the three sisters of the widowed Queen retired, the Princesses Keneswitha, Quendrida, and Idaburga, who were all consecrated at Godmanchester.[5]

Great changes, meanwhile, befell the Christian abbess, Quenburga. Her husband was dead, and she had devoted herself to God. She had now to mourn in solitude for the warfare and loss of her father Penda, his

---

[1] Rapin, Roger of Wendover. [2] Hume, Rapin. [3] Brit. Sancta.
[4] Dugdale, vol. vi., p. 1621. [5] Butler.

foe being her father-in-law, King Oswy. The particulars of this battle have already been related. Penda died as he had lived, a Pagan, and his death was that of a hero, on the battle-field. Thirty captains were slain fighting on the Mercian side on that eventful day, and those who did escape, of their party, were drowned in their flight, in the river Winwid.[1] Among the prisoners taken on the field of strife were the widowed Queen of Penda, Keneswitha, and Egfrid, her hostage, brother to Queen Alfleda.

These were painful tidings for the ears of the royal sisters of Mercia, to Peada and his consort, and the three sons of the deceased king. They were followed by a yet more tragical event, the sudden and mysterious death of Peada.[2] The catastrophe of his murder occurred during the festival of Easter, but the true author of the deed is unknown. Three persons stand charged with the crime. The amiable Alfleda, his consort, whose irreproachable life renders such a deed most improbable. Oswy's mistress, who was a Pagan, of whom Robert de Swapham, quoted by Speed, remarks, "this blot is taken from the Christian lady, Alfleda, and brands the face of her that most deserveth it."

The third party accused of Peada's death, is his own mother, the captive Queen Keneswitha. This charge is so unlikely to be true, as to need no refutation. Of the three accused parties, Oswy's mistress seems most likely to have been guilty, and perhaps her daughter was made the tool of her intrigues on this occasion: this opinion derives strength from the fact, that on Peada's death, Oswy seized his dominions, and held them, with the rest of Mercia, till driven thence by Wulphere, brother of the deceased monarch. After the death of Peada, the name of Alfleda, his consort, disappears from the Chronicles.

It is worthy of remark, that the children of Penda, so notorious an opponent of Christianity, were all distinguished for their extraordinary piety. All his four sons, who in succession ruled over Mercia, actively supported the new doctrine, and their sisters became famous in the calendar of saints.[3]

St. Keneswitha was very young when she lost her father, and having resolved to consecrate herself to God, she took the veil in the Monastery of Dormund Caistor, over which her sister, the foundress, presided as first Abbess. Her elder sister, Quendrida, assumed the religious habit with her. These two young votaries are described by historians, as being "eminent for holiness."[4] As for their royal protectress and sister, Quenburga, she was "a mirror of sanctity, so that many virgins of all ranks and degrees resorted to her monastery, to be instructed in the rules and exercises of a religious life; and while the daughters of princes reverenced her as a mistress, the poor were admitted to regard her as a companion, and both the one and the other honoured her as a parent."

---

[1] Winwidfield, near Leeds.

[2] Holinshed, Rapin, Robert de Swapham, Speed.

[3] Ingulphus.

[4] Palgrave.

HERESWYTHA, SEXBURGA, ETHELDREDA, ERMENBURGE, AND ERMENILDA.

Religious enthusiasm—Church building—Queen Hereswytha, "the mother of many Saints"—Her husband, King Anna—Etheldreda and Thonbert—She retires to a monastery—Her second marriage to Egfrid—Their establishment—Egfrid's remonstrance—Etheldreda goes to a convent, accompanied by Bishop Wilfred — Architecture and Church Music patronised by Wilfred — Anger of Egfrid—Their separation: he re-marries—Ermenburge persecutes Wilfred—Anglo-Saxon carriage—Wilfred's trials — Sexburga's piety—Her daughter—The Abbess Hildelitha—The Convent of Minstre—Ermenilda's, and her young daughter Werburga's, piety—Murder of the young princes, Wulfade and Rufin —Werburga's profession — The Abbess Etheldreda's edifying death — St. Audrey's lace, and St. Etheldred's chain—Ely Monastery—Sexburga's happy death—The butterfly shadow—Miracles—St. Werburga, the Patroness of Chester—Ely Cathedral—Antiquities—The stone cross of Etheldreda.

THE distinguishing feature of the seventh century was religious enthusiasm. It was a period when self-negation was looked upon as the prime virtue, and females in high position thought it incumbent upon them to devote their lives to self-sacrifices, of a nature which, in these days, do not carry with them the eminent character of virtue which they were then thought to bestow.

Monkish writers naturally enlarge on the holiness and purity of a life of celibacy, and infinite credit has been given to many persons in those remote ages, whose acts, considered by them worthy, were calculated to cause unhappiness and discontent to others. Of this kind was the conduct of several of the consorts of the Saxon monarchs, who, consenting to become wives, did not comprehend the duties of the state into which they had entered, and adopted the habits of recluses in the midst of a court; disappointing the hopes of the country, which looked to them to become the mothers of princes who should perpetuate the line of succession, and whose example of attachment and tenderness to the husbands they had accepted should afford an example to their female subjects.

Mistaken piety led many royal wives into a perfectly opposite course to what is an evident duty, and much inconvenience, as well as vexation, ensued in the State in consequence. But whatever are our present notions, the ascetic behaviour adopted at this early period of history was looked upon as a proof of every Christian virtue, and was probably a natural reaction from the licentiousness of Paganism.

Unbounded praise is bestowed by most Roman Catholic writers on those Queens who converted their palaces into nunneries, and looked upon their husbands as merely brethren of a community, whose earthly love it was their duty to repudiate, and with whom it was praiseworthy to live on terms of the strictest severity. Occasionally the partners of these holy and religious ladies shared their enthusiasm, and devoted themselves to the same life; but in some cases it was different, and the whole country was thrown into a ferment in consequence of the domestic troubles ensuing.

To have erected and endowed a church or a monastery is always spoken of by early historians as the most praiseworthy of acts, and almost countless are the edifices raised in the seventh century to prove the zeal of the new converts to the true faith. The Queens of Ercombert, Egfrid, and Wulphere were not the least amongst those pious personages, who strove to gain the approbation of man and the favour of Heaven by expending enormous sums on religious buildings.

Not one of the princes of the Anglo-Saxon Heptarchy was more eminent for piety than Anna, King of East Anglia, who had sheltered Cenwalch from the indignant wrath of his fierce brother-in-law Penda, King of Mercia; nor was there a more excellent and amiable princess than Hereswytha, his consort, who for her own piety and the holiness of her offspring, has been entitled the "mother of many saints." Of her first husband, to whom she bore a son and a daughter,[1] no account is accurately given: three sons and three daughters were the offspring of her union with King Anna. The sons of Hereswytha were Jurminus, Adulphus, and Erkenwald; her daughters were Ethelburga, Sexburga, Etheldreda, Oslave, and Withburga.

Sexburga, whose education had been carefully attended to (for women at this time were highly instructed), became the wife of Ercombert, King of Kent, who was remarkable both for his zeal in religion and his patriotism. He was first to establish the fast of Lent in his division of the Heptarchy, where he razed the temples of heathenism, and extirpated the idolatrous worship so long prevailing. Queen Sexburga encouraged her husband in all his religious undertakings, sharing in his exertions, and confirming his resolution by her counsel and example. "Thus," says the Chronicle, "while her virtue, humility, and devotion excited the admiration and reverence of the people, her goodness and unbounded charity gained for her more especially the love of the poor. Although she had married in obedience to the will of her parents, she would have preferred the cloister to a palace, a church to matrimony, and the service of Christ to worldly empire."[2]

Etheldreda[3] was the destined wife of Thonbert, an Englishman of

---

[1] St. Sethrid, Hereswytha's daughter by the first husband, was honoured by the early English as a saint, though her name is not contained in any calendar. She succeeded St. Fara, abbess and foundress of Faremoutiers, in France, in her high office, and was honoured, on the 6th or 7th of May, as St. Sethrid, or Sessetrudis. — Butler's Lives, Jan. 10 and Dec. 7.

[2] Bromton.

[3] The uncertainty of orthography in former times is well exemplified in the name of Etheldreda. Its abbreviation is Eldrude, a compound of Saxon and British, from "Ell," the reduplicative pronoun, and "drud," "illustrious" or "well-beloved." — Butler.

noble birth. From her infancy she had been distinguished by her humility and devotion, which led her, in conformity with a custom at that time enjoined by the Church, to take upon herself a vow of perpetual celibacy, devoting herself entirely to the service of Christ. This vow she never violated, though she twice entered the connubial state. She was induced to accept Thonbert for her nominal husband, in conformity with the wishes of her parents, and with him she is said to have lived for three years, as a holy sister, in accordance with her early vow. He was Prince of the Southern Girvii, having authority over Rutland, Northampton, and part of Lincolnshire, those districts being ruled by their own princes, who were subject to the Kings of Mercia. To this domain was added the Isle of Ely, upon his marriage with Etheldreda, to whom it was given as a bridal dowry.[1] At the end of two years, Etheldreda's father, King Anna, with his son Jurminus, was slain in battle by Penda, and the death of her husband followed shortly after. Returning into solitude, the young widow could now uninterruptedly devote herself to religious duties, and humble herself before Him who "loveth those whom he chasteneth."

Her mother Hereswyda, to whom she was tenderly attached, and who, on the death of King Anna, had retired to France with her own sister Hilda, and entered the Monastery of Chelles, died at this time.

The famous Monastery of Chelles, five leagues distant from Paris, on the Marne, though founded by Clotilda, Queen of France, was chiefly endowed by St. Bathilde, a Saxon Queen. Hilda had resolved to end her days in that establishment, but the loss of her sister broke the tie which bound her to the spot, and she suffered herself to be prevailed on by St. Aidan to return into Northumberland, where she is afterwards distinguished as the Abbess of Whitby.

The deaths of Thonbert and of Hereswyda occurred in 655, and the year after Adulphus succeeded to the throne of his father Anna, Etheldreda remaining in Ely, occupying herself in "fasting, prayer, vigils, and penance." Vainly, however, did the widowed princess seclude herself from the world. The fame of her beauty and her virtue had spread, and attracted the attention of Egfrid, one of the most powerful Kings of the Saxon Heptarchy, who then governed Northumberland, and he desired to obtain her in marriage. Etheldreda, however, refused to become his wife,

> "Though her sister Sexburge moened her tenderly;"

until the Prince urged his suit with such importunity, promising that her vow should be held sacred, that she yielded her consent;

> "And at the maryage was great solemnyte,
> Trumphes, honoures, on every side,
> Great cost and royalte."[2]

This word, however, is written indifferently—which is sufficiently confusing—Etheldrida, Etheldrith, Adelfrida, Adelthrid, Ediltrudis, or Audrey. The name of Etheldreda signifies "noble advice." [Camden.] Hereswy*tha* is indifferently written with a *d* or *th* — the sound being the same.

[1] Butler, Bradshawe. [2] Bradshawe.

Ely was probably the scene of the nuptial festivity, as King Egfrid came there to seek his bride.[1] Five years had been passed by Etheldreda in widowhood when, by her second espousals to Egfrid, she became Queen of Northumberland.

During twelve years from the date of this union, Etheldreda resided with her consort as his sister, not as his wife; for neither the affection of the husband, the authority of the king, or any other inducement, was of any avail in inducing her to break the vows she had made to Heaven. Egfrid, on the other hand, felt such respect for his wife, and was so much affected by the example of her virtue, that he allowed her full liberty to fast, watch, and pray, and to devote her time to acts of piety and charity, during that space of time; but his own youth, and the great desire of his subjects that he should have heirs, at length led him to make representations, not indeed to Etheldreda herself, whose reproof he feared, but to Bishop Wilfred, who possessed the entire confidence of the Queen, and she was in the habit of consulting him on all occasions. Etheldreda had bestowed on him, with the consent of her husband, Hexham, which she is believed to have obtained as her own bridal dowry from Egfrid, for an episcopal see; and Wilfred built in it a church and monastery, the structure of which surpassed any in England. Italian architects, masons, and glaziers[2] were hired to assist in its erection, and it was furnished with plate and holy vestments, besides containing a large collection of the Lives of the Saints, and a noble ecclesiastical library.[3] Sacred music was first patronized in Northumberland in Etheldreda's time. St. Acca, a subsequent Bishop of Hexham, himself a learned musician and author of many literary productions, especially of a religious nature, retained in his service for twelve years a famous singer named Maban, by whose instructions the use of church music and singing of anthems was revived, and who introduced many Latin hymns before unknown in the northern churches.[4]

Several charitable institutions, founded in different parts of Wilfred's diocese, were encouraged by Queen Etheldreda.

---

[1] Butler.

[2] The art of making glass was known in Britain before the coming of the Romans, and improved by them. It was lost in the invasion of the Saxons, but afterwards imported among them, A.D. 664, for the ornament of churches and religious edifices, as Bede tells us, though not used till after the Conquest, in private dwellings. Specimens of Saxon glass may be seen in Westminster Abbey, cemented into the tomb of Edward the Confessor: they are small square or diamond-shaped pieces, not more than an inch in length, and lined with gold leaf. Similar ornaments were seen in a tomb discovered in repairing Rochester Cathedral, though of rather a later date.

[3] Lives of the Saints.

[4] Biog. Brit. This Acca was interred in Hexham Church, where one stone cross was placed at his head and another at his feet. When, three hundred years afterwards, his tomb was opened, his burial-clothes were found in a state of entire preservation, and a wooden tablet, of the form of an altar, was discovered, which had been placed on the breast of the deceased prelate. It was joined with silver nails, and bore an inscription. Such was the mode of interment in those days used for a bishop among the Angles.

Bishop Wilfred, appealed to by Egfrid on the subject of Etheldreda's vow, did not feel at liberty to decline the commission intrusted to him of interfering in this matter, and accordingly addressed himself to the Queen on the subject of her husband's wish. Etheldreda now plainly perceived that the only method of enabling her to keep her resolution, was to endeavour to induce Egfrid to live in a state of separation from her; Wilfred represented, accordingly, to the king that it was the desire of his wife to enter into the seclusion of a monastery. The prelate's entreaties and the importunity of Etheldreda herself at last extorted from the King a consent that she should depart from the court of Northumberland, [1] and follow her wish in this respect also. Having succeeded in gaining the consent of the King, Etheldreda took an important step, in which she was advised by Wilfred; she repaired to the Monastery of Coldingham, beyond Berwick, of which Ebba, "the King's aunt," was Abbess, and there professed herself a nun.[2] She received the veil from the hands of Wilfred himself, and on the occasion expressed her joy by remarking "that she never thought herself a Queen till she was professed, and thus solemnly contracted to the King of Heaven." [3]

Etheldreda remained for some time under the protection of the Abbess Ebba; but at the end of a year from the time of her profession, Wilfred informed the royal nun that Egfrid had formed a design, either by persuasion or compulsion, to make her return to his court. To avoid this alternative, Etheldreda quitted the convent and fled to the kingdom of East Anglia, for greater safety. She was accompanied in her journey by two maidens, and the monkish Chronicles inform us that at every place where they rested on their way thither, "our Lord showed them miracles." [4] It is supposed that Ovin, an old and faithful steward of the Queen, attended their flight.

Adulph, who is sometimes called the "natural brother of Etheldreda," received the fugitives; and in due course of time, Etheldreda, assisted by him, erected on her own estate, the Isle of Ely, a double monastery.[5] This edifice was founded in A. D. 672.[6] As soon as it was completed, Etheldreda assumed the government. Wilfred himself attended in person at Ely, to assist at the ceremony of the Queen's election as abbess.

This prelate had, as it is natural to imagine, incurred the severe anger of Egfrid, nor was that anger appeased even after he had taken another wife. The new Queen was Ermenburge, sister-in-law to the King of

[1] Bede, Milton, Lives of the Saints. [2] Holinshed.

[3] Butler. [4] Lives of the Saints. [5] Canwod Abbey. — Bradshawe.

[6] To this period may perhaps be ascribed the foundation of a structure by Etheldreda in the locality now known as Ely Place, Holborn. The work of that Queen has long since fallen to decay; but Shakspeare, on the authority of Holinshed, informs us that the Bishop of Ely dwelt at a palace in what is now called Ely Place — which residence was noted by some of our writers for its strawberry gardens, vineyards, and meadows. On the spot where Queen Etheldreda's foundation existed, was erected, in 1320, the antique chapel bearing her name, of which Newcourt, in his "Repertorium Londinense," written in 1700, says, "is, to this day, a very fair, large, old chapel."

Wessex,[1] who, unwilling to encourage so great a power as that possessed by Wilfred in the kingdom, irritated the King still more against him; and her mortification at the freedom of the bishop's strictures on the violence of character, soon led to open hostilities between them.

Ermenburge[2] now employed every means to ruin Wilfred in the King's opinion, and her task was the less difficult as Egfrid was already so much incensed. She gained also an ally in Theodore, Archbishop of Canterbury, who was induced to assist her views, owing to misrepresentations, of which he afterwards became aware; for the present, however, he only listened to the grievances brought forward by the Queen, and was prevailed on to depose Wilfred from his dignity, after he had spent ten years in endeavouring to establish the monastery of which he was the support. Richard, Prior of Hexham, speaking of Ermenburge, says: "In her heart Satan stirring up the seeds of hatred against the said bishop, by her tongue incited the King's mind to expel the priest;" and it appears that the Queen was the more displeased, because Hexham, part of Etheldreda's dowry received from Egfrid, had been bestowed on that prelate. It is plain that all parties, Queen as well as bishops, had an interested motive for the disgrace of Wilfred.

Accordingly Theodore parcelled out his great diocese, consecrating Bosa to the see of York, for the Deiri; Eata to that of Lindisfarne, for Bernicia; and Eadhead to the church of Lindissi, or great part of Lincolnshire, which Egfrid had won from Mercia. This great division of Wilfred's bishopric took place A. D. 678. Wilfred on this appealed to the Pope. He raised no clamour, for he dreaded either disturbances or schism, but was sufficiently well acquainted with the canons to perceive the irregularity and nullity of many steps taken against him. He accordingly embarked for Rome, where having pleaded his own cause, he returned to England, and repairing to the presence of Egfrid, handed to him the sealed decrees of the Pope. That prince, having first caused them to be read by the prelates of his own faction, who were at that time present in the apartment, declared that they had been obtained by bribery, and commanded that Wilfred should be committed to prison. The order was obeyed, and during the space of nine months Wilfred was subjected to the most rigorous treatment. It is said, everything but the clothes which he wore was taken from him, and all his adherents were dispersed in different directions. Queen Ermenburge herself took possession of his case of relics, which she hung up in her chamber, and carried about with her in her chariot wherever she went, making an outward display of piety but little in accordance with her conduct.

The following curious account of a lady's carriage exists in an Anglo-Saxon MS. in the Harleian library. It represents the carriage of a lady of rank, of a rather later period than that of Ermenburge: "it has uprights fixed before and behind, with a body, shaped like a hammock, suspended between; the whole, and in particular the spokes of the wheels, are painted with various colours. The lady to whom the gay vehicle belongs, wears on her head a double veil, and has a perforated mantle

---

[1] Eddius.

[2] Lingard.

over the shoulders; her upper gown, which scarcely descends below the knees, is embellished with a border of needlework edged with beads. The sleeves descend only as far as the elbows, and are of considerable width, in shape resembling those now most fashionable. Beneath is worn an under garment, with long tight sleeves, reaching to the ground, so as almost to cover the feet."[1]

Wilfred's composure of mind is said to have been so great under his reverses, that his guards overheard him singing psalms in his dungeon: a bright light also is said "to have issued from that dark chamber, which alarmed his guards, and Wilfred having performed an extraordinary cure on the sick wife of their governor, that person refused any longer to guard him; so that the King, for safety, removed him to another prison."[2]

At length Ermenburge was seized with a dangerous illness while staying at the Monastery of Ebba. The King's aunt was struck with the belief that her malady was caused by the indignation of Heaven for her conduct towards Wilfred; a notion fostered by the abbess, on whose remonstrances at her injustice to that excellent prelate, Wilfred was set at liberty, his relics restored, and his companions sent back to him, on condition, however, that the bishop should never more set foot within the territories of Egfrid. He accordingly retired from Northumberland, and solicited the protection of Brithwald, nephew to the King of Mercia, who granted to him land, on which he built a monastery. Egfrid's emissaries, however, discovered his retreat, and the Mercian was alarmed by his threats; so that Wilfred, unwilling to endanger his friend's safety, quitted his place of refuge, and fled into Wessex.[3] But Wilfred's trials were not yet over; for Irmenigild, sister of his persecutress, was Queen of Wessex, and, influenced by Ermenburge, so harassed the prelate that he was glad to avail himself of the invitation of Ethelwald, King of Sussex, to reside in his dominions. One prince had remained his firm friend throughout, namely, Alfred, illegitimate brother of Egfrid. When, therefore, in 685, Egfrid was slain, Ermenburge's influence expired with him; as Egfrid had no issue, Alfred became his brother's successor on the throne, and Wilfred was immediately reinstated in all his honours at Hexham, and appointed to the see of York and monastery of Ripon.

For this the prelate was in a great degree indebted to Theodore, Archbishop of Canterbury, his former persecutor, then arrived at an advanced age, and subject to frequent fits of sickness. The Archbishop sent to Wilfred, and desired him to meet him at London with St. Erkenwald, bishop of that city, brother of Etheldreda. In their interview he confessed all the actions of his past life, and observed, "the greatest remorse I feel is, that I consented with the King to deprive you of your possessions, without any fault committed on your part." He then earnestly entreated that he might be permitted to make all the restitution that was left in his power. Accordingly he wrote letters to King Alfred, to Ethelred, King of Mercia, and to Elfleda, Abbess of Whitby and others, and thus made ample amends to Wilfred for his ancient hostility.

Queen Ermenburge, not long after her husband's death, A. D. 685

[1] Smith and Merrick. [2] Butler's Lives. [3] Lingard.

assumed the religious habit in the monastery of her sister, at Carlisle, founded A. D. 686.

The Farn island,[1] the largest of the group, and the nearest to the mainland, is celebrated for having been the residence of St. Cuthbert during nine years. "In that spot he devoted himself to prayer and fasting, after having borne the charge of the priorate of Lindisfarne, and thither numbers came to be edified."

The island on which he dwelt is about eleven acres in extent, and the basaltic rocks with which it is bordered rise abruptly, on the south-west side, to a height of about eighty feet above the sea: the north is entirely exposed to the winds and waves. The site of the buildings erected by the holy recluse has been ascertained, consisting of his oratory, cell, hospitium, and fountain; and the chapel, which had fallen into decay, was restored and roofed by Archdeacon Thorpe.

It is recorded that "when the coffin of St. Cuthbert was brought by the monks of Lindisfarne to the spot where the city of Durham is now built, no power could move it thence." The monastery was, therefore, of course, erected there.

Sexburga, after the death of Ercombert, had departed from England and repaired to France, accompanied by her unmarried sister Ethelburga, and her youngest daughter Ercongeca. Her eldest daughter, Ermenilda, had been previously married to Wulphere, King of Mercia. Her sons were Egbert and Lothair, of whom, hereafter, mention will be made.[2]

Sexburga, her daughter and sister, all received the religious veil in France. At this time there were very few conventual establishments in Britain, and it was customary with the Anglo-Saxon princes and nobles to send their children into France to be educated in the monasteries there. The most celebrated of these establishments, which were really schools for education, and noted for resort by the English, were Faremoutiers, Briège, Andelie, and Chelles. Etheldreda, at some period of her life, is said to have resided at Faremoutiers:[3] perhaps it might have been while waiting for the completion of her edifice at Ely.

At the time the royal princesses of England arrived, Hildelitha was Abbess of Faremoutiers. Ethelburga joined her pious flock, but was at a subsequent period recalled to her native country to assume the government of the celebrated Abbey of Barking, which had been built for her reception by her brother Erkenwald, Bishop of London, a princely prelate, whose virtues afterwards caused his relics to be worshipped in a famous shrine dedicated to him in St. Paul's church.

---

[1] Farne, is a corruption of the Celtic word *fahren*, a recess. Holy Island was called Lindisfarne, from the Lindis, a rivulet which empties itself into the sea from the opposite shore.

[2] Dugdale.

[3] St. Fara was the name of the foundress of the Monastery of Faremoutiers, and is supposed to have been the first abbess. Hildelitha, who afterwards presided there, returned to England to assist Ethelburga in the management of Barking Abbey. St. Sethrid, the daughter of Hereswyda, afterwards held the government of Faremoutiers, prior to her union with King Anna. Etheldreda is esteemed third Abbess of Faremoutiers. According to Holinshed, both Sethrid and Ethelburga became Abbesses of Briège. — See *ante*, p. 266, note.

Ercongeca made her profession either in Briège or Chelles; it is not known to which place Sexburga retired, though she seems to have spent the six following years in France. Sexburga, even during her husband's lifetime, had earnestly desired to devote herself exclusively to the service of God, in a state of religious seclusion; and in order that others, at least, might be enabled to attend on the divine service night and day without impediment, she had commenced erecting a nunnery in the isle of Sheppey, on the coast of Kent, having obtained a grant of land for that purpose. Some say that this was given by her son Egbert, who succeeded his father on the throne, but the building appears to have been commenced during the lifetime of Ercombert,[1] though not formed into a community till A. D. 664.[2]

The establishment consisted of seventy-four nuns in all, who were assembled there by the widowed Queen, who had either taken on herself previously the monastic vows and veil, or did so at this time, when in her own person she assumed the government of the monastery.

The ruins of this little edifice, called Minstre, in the isle of Sheppey, have survived the lapse of ages to commemorate their royal foundress. The buildings attached to the monastery were some twenty miles in compass. The original edifice was destroyed by the Danes, but rebuilt in 1130, and consecrated by William, Archbishop of Canterbury, to the honour of the Blessed Virgin Mary and St. Sexburga: it subsisted in the hands of Benedictine nuns till the dissolution of abbeys, at which time the "building of Minstre[3] was valued at the annual sum of 129*l.* 7*s.* 10½*d.*; some part of it is now converted into a parish church, in which are divers funeral monuments, supposed to have been removed out of the adjoining chapel, some of which make a show of wondrous great antiquity."

It is said, that a desire still further to seclude herself from the world afterwards induced Sexburga to seek the solitude of Ely, and to this may be added a wish to dwell under the same roof as Etheldreda, her much-loved sister, who had obtained even then an extraordinary reputation for sanctity. It would appear that this arrangement was made by Sexburga at the period of Wulphere's death, who had succeeded Penda on the throne of Mercia, and who, during the life-time of Ercombert, had espoused her daughter Ermenilda,[4] Princess-Royal of the house of Kent.

Wulphere had heard of the virtues and piety of Sexburga's daughter with admiration,[5] and professing himself a Christian, undertook, at the time of his union with her, to extirpate the remnants of paganism from

---

[1] Dugdale says the edifice was completed in 675. Weever gives as the date 710 (an obvious error). Dugdale numbers the nuns at seventy-seven.

[2] Weever. [3] Ibid.

[4] She (Ermenilda) was heiress-apparent to the dignity of her father's kingdom. — Bromton.

During her government of the Monastery of Minster, Sexburga's mind had to sustain a severe shock in the criminal conduct of her son, King Egbert, who was under the necessity of paying the weregild, or fine, imposed on a murderer by the Saxon laws.

[5] William of Malmesbury, Butler.

Mercia,[1] where the Christian faith had been already introduced by his deceased brother Peada. Worldly motives delayed the performance of this promise, and "the humble and patient" Ermenilda strove in the interval to soften the fierce temper of her warlike husband. She educated her family in the pure principles of the Christian faith, and daily performed with her only daughter Werburga, the whole of the church service. "This young princess, early distinguished for surpassing piety, was wont to spend many hours daily on her knees in private prayer; she also observed with diligence the fasts enjoined by the religion she professed."

The sons of Ermenilda were Wulphade, Rufin, and Kenred, who emulated their mother's example of virtue and goodness. These Princes were taught in the faith of Christ by St. Chad, who also baptized them. This prelate was Bishop of Litchfield, and had a cell or hermitage in a forest, to which the young Princes were at times accustomed to resort for instruction. The ill-fated youths were, however, destined to come to an untimely end. The circumstances which led to their sad fate were these: Werbode was a knight of Wulphere's court, very powerful, and his influence was great over the mind of Wulphere, to whom he had rendered great services in arms; so that he readily obtained his promise to give him the beautiful Princess Werburga, his daughter, provided her own consent could be obtained. The news of Wulphere's promise much grieved the Queen and her sons, who all confirmed Werburga in her refusal of his suit, more particularly Ermenilda; for Werbode was a pagan, and had induced Wulphere to waver in his intentions regarding the true faith, and at length to renounce it and follow the worship of idols. When the knight found that these young Princes stood in his way to Werburga's favour, he resolved on their death. An opportunity soon offered. He discovered that the royal youths visited St. Chad[2] at times, under pretence of hunting; and contrived that Wulphere should be stationed in a place where he could see his sons pass on one of these occasions, having previously informed him of their secret religious object. The King's passion at beholding them on such a mission was so furious, that he gave an order for their execution; but no sooner was the cruel deed perpetrated, than he was filled with remorse and penitence, and though too late to redeem the loss of his children, threw himself on the pity and devotion of the Queen and St. Chad, and having entered into commune with himself, became a convert to the Christian doctrine, abo-

[1] "There still remained, in the kingdom of Mercia, an excessive and inveterate Pagan barbarism. But Queen Ermenilda, the handmaid of God, having been instructed by her parents in the apostolic alphabet of the first teacher, St. Augustine, by her sweetness, by her soothing exhortations, by her manners and benefits, softened their untamed dispositions, and exhorted them to the sweet yoke of Christ and the rewards of everlasting blessedness; while the perverse and most rebellious she repressed by her power: nor did she rest until she extirpated the idols and demoniacal rites, and filled the kingdom of the Mercians with churches and priests." — Bromton's Chronicle.

[2] "Chad travelled about, not on horseback, but, after the manner of the Apostles, on foot, to preach the Gospel in towns, the open country, cottages, villages, and castles."—*Bede.*

lished heathenism in Mercia, and by his endeavors and example, propagated the Christian faith. The bodies of Wulfade and Rufin were placed by the Queen in a sepulchre of stone, and over the spot where they were interred this afflicted mother and her penitent husband founded the Priory of Stone.[1] Wulphere afterwards founded Peterborough Cathedral.

The beautiful Werburga had resolved to devote her life to the service of God, and had refused on that account many suitors for her hand, amongst whom was the Prince of Wessex, who waited upon her with rich presents, to receive the same answer as other aspirants.

Upon the change which took place in the religious views of the King, Werburga no longer dreaded his resentment, and ventured to disclose to her father her intention of embracing the religious profession. To this Wulphere was averse, and testified much grief; but so earnest were the supplications of the Princess, that he at length yielded to her wish.

"Wulphere, in person, conducted his beloved child to Ely in great state, accompanied by his whole court. On their arrival there, they were met at the gate of the monastery by the royal abbess, St. Etheldreda, with the whole of her religious family in procession, singing holy hymns. Werburga, falling on her knees, then begged to be admitted as a penitent. She obtained her request, and Te Deum was sung, after which she went through the usual trials with great humility and patience, exchanging with joy her rich coronet, purple silks, and gold, for a poor veil and a coarse habit, and resigned herself into the hands of her superior, to live only to Christ. King Wulphere, his three brothers, and Egbert or Egbright, the Kentish King, Adulph, King of East Anglia, and the great lords of those respective states, were all present at the solemn ceremony, being entertained by the Mercian King with a truly regal magnificence."[2]

Meanwhile Etheldreda, as Abbess of Ely, afforded the holy sisterhood over whom she presided, a constant example of Christian perfection. She was very strict in the duties of her religion, eating only once a day, except on great festivals or in times of sickness. "She would rarely wash in a hot bath, unless just before any of the great festivals, as Easter, Whitsuntide, and the Epiphany; and then she did it last of all, after having, with the assistance of those about her, first washed the other servants of God then present."[3] She was in the habit of wearing woollen clothes, never making use of linen; and it was her custom never to return to bed after matins, which were sung at midnight, but to continue in the church at her devotions until morning. She seems to have rejoiced in pains and humiliations. The physician, Cynefrid, who attended her in her last illness, and was present at her death, relates that she had a very great swelling under her jaw, which he was ordered to lay open. This operation performed, she was more easy for two days, so that many thought she might recover. At the time she had suffered most pain, she had been much pleased with that sort of distemper, and said: "I know that I deservedly bear the weight of my sickness on my neck; for I remember,

[1] In Staffordshire.—Stowe, Leycester, Butler.

[2] Butler.

[3] Bede.

when I was very young, I bore there the needless weight of jewels; and therefore I believe the Divine Goodness would have me endure the pain in my neck, that I may be absolved from the guilt of my needless levity, having now, instead of gold and precious stones, a red swelling and burning on my neck." The third day after the incision made by her physician, "the former pains returning, she was soon snatched out of the world, and exchanged all pain and death for everlasting life and health."[1]

Etheldreda had fulfilled her duties as abbess for seven years, and she was deeply mourned by her little flock, who were sincerely attached to her for her many virtues and goodness.[2] The 23d of June, the anniversary of her death, which took place A. D. 679, has ever since been esteemed her festival day, in which the honours of a saint are accorded to her, and her name may still be seen in English prayer-books as St. Audry. "At a fair held on the causey, in the isle of Ely, which is called St. Audry, much ordinary but showy lace was usually sold, whence St. Audry's lace became quite proverbial, and passed into the corruption of *Tawdry*, a word used to denote not lace only, but any other part of the female costume which was gaudy in appearance.[3] A certain chain also, made of fine small silk, bears the name of St. Etheldred's Chain, perhaps in allusion to the necklaces worn by the Queen, when a child, at the East Anglian court. The Saxon women had several ornaments for the arms and neck, similar to that ascribed to Etheldreda, studded with brilliants, collars, earrings, and bracelets; these a mother was permitted by law, at her death, to leave to her daughter; and by the same legal authority had the right of conveying to her son, her land, slaves and money.

Sexburga, after her sister's death,[4] presided as Abbess of Ely for twenty years, with great advantage to the convent and neighbourhood. In her time the structure of that venerable building, of which the ruins alone at present afford a noble specimen of Saxon architecture, was completed. As soon as the building was in a fit condition, Sexburga removed the holy remains of the Abbess into it. By the particular desire of the Abbess-Queen, her body had been placed in a coffin of wood; from this her humility is plainly to be discovered, for persons of consequence in her days alone were interred in stone coffins. Queen Sexburga, her sister, performed the interesting task of translating her relics, in 694, in the sixteenth year of her own government at Ely. Bromton, in his Chronicle, tells us that St. Sexburga, "inflamed by a divine zeal, prepared to have her venerable bones transferred to the church; and not having a stone suitable for concealing so heavenly a treasure, of her kindness appointed certain persons to seek a stone of the kind, and having found one, to bring it by ship to the Monastery of Ely; for the isle of

---

[1] Bede. [2] Fuller's Church History of Britain. [3] Clavis Calendaria.

[4] Drayton writes thus of her: —

"Sexburg, some time queen to Ercombert of Kent,
Tho' Ina's loved child, and Audrey's sister known,
Which Ely in those days did for her Abbess own."
Poly Olbion.

Ely is, by the nature of the place, entirely surrounded by waters and marshes, whence it is destitute of stones of the sort.[1] They applied to a small town at no great distance, named Grantchester,[2] which was at that time much reduced, and but scantily inhabited; by the well of which they found, as it were prepared by Providence, a stone exactly suited for the sepulchre, wherein, afterwards, a certain grace of the Divine operation was very remarkable, since it appeared that the quantity of the stone thus providentially found was, as if purposely, exactly that required by the dimension of the virgin's body. They found, also, a lid very like a sarcophagus, likewise of the appearance of marble, and of the proper size and evenness, and without any incongruity or dissimilarity of the parts."

Having fulfilled this purpose, they returned without meeting any obstacle. "Whereon Sexburga, rejoicing in the benefit of the divine gift, blessed God, who doeth wonderful things. Now when the day determined upon for transferring the body of the holy virgin from a wooden coffin to the stone mausoleum arrived, on opening the previous coffin, the venerable body was found entire, without any sign of corruption, as though it had been recently buried on the same day. The blessed Wilfred, Archbishop of York, was present at this spectacle. There was also, for the greater evidence and certainty of the truth, the aforesaid physician, Kinefrid, who had been present at her death, and had opened the tumour of which she died. He, recollecting the wound which he had formerly made on her body, approaching and carefully examining it, recognised it to be the same, wondering at the marvellously curative power of God on the dead; for there remained of the scar only the slightest mark, the size of a thread, and that becomingly surrounded and concealed with what might be *the shadow of a butterfly*. The brethren stood on one side, and the sisters on the other, blessing God with hymns and praises; while St. Sexburga entered with a few, religiously and devoutly to wash the remains of her sister, and after a short space called out from within: 'Glory be to the name of the most high God' And that what was done might be with the approbation and in the presence of witnesses, she summoned certain who were more worthy of participating in so great secrets, who, on the removal of the pall and the exposure of the countenance, beheld the body of the virgin undecomposed, and more like one sleeping than dead. At length, having carefully wrapped the body in precious vestments suitable to preserve so great a treasure, with a great and manifold chorus of exultation, they carry it to the church, and place it in a new sarcophagus with honour."[3]

Many miracles are said to have been wrought afterwards, by the de-

---

[1] There were no quarries in Ely, but the brethren were sent by Sexburga into Cambridgeshire, to procure a stone coffin, which they were ordered to fashion with their own hands. The stone they discovered was found to fit exactly the size of the virgin abbess' body, having in it a hollow place, equally adapted to the size of the head. The coffin found for Etheldreda was a relic of ancient Roman art: it was a white marble coffin, most beautifully wrought.—*Polwhele Bede*

[2] Near Cambridge.

[3] Chron. Bromton, Reg. Northumb., Bede.

vout application of the relics of St. Etheldreda, and of the linen cloths taken off her coffin.[1]

The venerable Bede has written a Latin poem[2] on the discovery of the relics of St. Etheldreda, which is a curious specimen of the literary composition of the times in which he lived.

It is not quite certain whether Ermenilda retired to Sheppey during the life of Wulphere, and took her mother's government of the monastery there; or whether she deferred entering on a religious life till the death of her consort, which took place in 675. Wulphere was interred at Litchfield,[3] and as his only surviving son, Kenred, was still too young to govern, he left the crown to his own brother Ethelred.

One of our early chroniclers writes thus of the royal widow: "Upon the famous King Wulphure, therefore, after a reign of seventeen years, passing to the eternal kingdom, although his pious wife Ermenilda bewailed her social calamity, nevertheless, with her whole soul wounded in love, she exulted in the liberty of Christ. She forthwith betook herself to the most excellent Monastery of Ely, where her parent Sexburga, daughter of Anna, King of the East Angles, and sister of St. Etheldred, among bands of virgins, was shining as the moon among stars, and where her daughter Werberga humbly served God in virgin integrity. Here, therefore, this Ermenilda laid aside all earthly hope and regal ornaments, and put on the yoke and armour of Christ, with the religious habit of the monastics." As Abbess of the Monastery, after Sexburga's death, Drayton writes of her thus:—

> "King Wulphere's widowed pheere, Queen Ermineld, whose life
> At Ely is renowned;"

while Bradshawe, in even more courtly language, styles her "a noble Margaryte of high magnificence," and a "rose of paradise full of preeminence."[4]

Sexburga departed this life on the 6th of July, 699, at an advanced age. Her remains were deposited near those of her sister, in the Cathedral Church of Ely,[5] though some have thought her interment took place at Canterbury, where her husband, King Ercombert, lies entombed.

Ermenilda was third Abbess of Ely, but could not have become so till twenty-four years after her husband Wulphere's death, when she must have been very aged. This venerable Princess is compared, by Drayton, to her cousin Ermenburga, wife of Merowald, Wulphere's brother, in the following stanzas:—

> "Two holy Mercian queens so widowed, saints became;
> For sanctity much like, not much unlike in name."

Ermenilda passed to the heavenly kingdom in the month of February, A. D. ——,[6] when her remains were interred with those of her mother

[1] Butler. Bede relates this account in the words of Kinefrid, the physician.

[2] Eccles. Hist., lib. iv., c. 20.

[3] The word "Litchfield" means, in the Saxon, "Field of the Dead."—*Dr. Johnson.*

[4] Life of St. Wereburga.

[5] Millar.

[6] February 13th, on which day, after death, she was honoured among the English female saints.

and aunt, and, as Bromton expressed it, "having been tossed, she rested in the Lord."

Werburga, her successor, the fourth Abbess of Ely, was induced by the persuasions of her uncle, King Ethelred of Mercia, to quit that establishment for the purpose of undertaking the general charge of the religious foundations throughout Mercia, in which he desired to establish a strictly monastic discipline. Through the liberality of Ethelred, the Abbess Werburga founded several monasteries: those of Trentham and Hanbury, in Staffordshire, and another at Weedon, a royal palace of Northamptonshire.[1] She herself resided at Hearburg, near Stamford, or at Croyland. At the time she died, Werburga was at Trentham; but by her own express wish, her remains were conveyed to Hanbury for interment. The author of her Life assures us that her relics were venerated at Croyland till the ninth century, when they were removed to Leicester.

In 708, nine years after the death of Werburga, her body was taken up, in presence of King Ceolred, his council, and many bishops, when it was found incorrupt and entire, and placed in a costly shrine. In the reign of King Alfred, the shrine of St. Werburga, for fear of the Danes, was carried to West Chester; and the valiant Ethelred, Earl of Mercia, who had married the daughter of that monarch, built and endowed with secular canonries a stately church, as repository for these holy relics, which afterwards became the cathedral. The body of the saint fell to dust, soon after its translation to West Chester.

St. Werburga is considered the especial patroness of the city of Chester: and Malmesbury tells us that "the praises and miracles of these two women (Ermenilda and Werburga), and particularly of the younger, are there extolled and had in veneration; and though they are favourable to all petitions without delay, yet they are more especially kind and assistant to the supplications of women and youth." He speaks of a circumstance which occurred in his own time. "This St. Werburga lies at Chester, in the monastery of that city, which Hugo, Earl of Chester, ejecting a few canons, who resided there in a mean and irregular manner, *has recently erected.*"

The relics of Werburga being scattered in the reign of Henry VIII., her shrine was converted into the episcopal throne in the same church, and remains in that condition to this day, being "one of the most remarkable monuments in the county of Cheshire, and a rich specimen of Gothic architecture in the early part of the fourteenth century. This monument itself is composed of stone, ten feet high, embellished with thirty curious pieces of antique images of Kings of Mercia, and other princes related to this saint, the names of whom were inscribed upon scrolls held in their hands. These figures, having been much mutilated, either at the Reformation or during the civil war, were restored, but in a bungling manner, about the year 1708.[2]"

---

[1] Weedon, once the royal site of Wulphere's palace, was afterwards converted into a nunnery, at the entreaty of Werburga, who presided over it. The Danes destroyed the edifice; but Werburga's memory was preserved by a fair chapel there, dedicated to her sainted memory.—*Green's Worcester*, *Pennant.*

[2] Lysons's Mag. Britannia; Willis's Abbeys; Butler.

Some further account is here necessary of the Cathedral Church of Ely. Many abbesses in succession followed Werburga in the establishment there, whose names, however, are not on record till A. D. 870, when the monastery was ravaged by the Danes, and shortly after occupied by a college of secular priests. In the reign of King Edgar, the Abbey was refounded by Ethelwold, Bishop of Winchester, and the structure appropriated to the use of monks only of the Benedictine order, though the dedication was made in the name of "the Blessed Virgin and St. Audry."[1]

The following is one of the narratives of the monks respecting the relics of their holy foundress: On a former occasion, the corpse of Etheldreda was seen through a hole which the Danes broke in her coffin: a priest, more forward than the rest, prying too busily, and endeavouring to pull the envelope out by a cleft stick, the saint drew back the drapery so hastily, that she tript up his heels, and gave him such a fall as he never recovered, nor his senses, afterwards. Bishop Athelwold stopt up the hole, and substituted monks for the priests. Abbot Brithnoth transferred hither the body of Withburga, the foundress' sister; and when, afterwards, in the time of Abbot Richard, some doubts were entertained about the incorruptibility of the foundress, nobody presumed to examine her body, but they contented themselves with uncovering that of her sister, who was found to be in such good preservation, that she seemed more like a person asleep than dead: a silk cushion lay under her head; her veil and vestments all seemed as good as new, her complexion clear and rosy, her teeth white, and her lips somewhat shrunk.[2]

In 974, when the Monastery of East Dereham, in Norfolk, which King Anna had founded for his daughter Withburga, was destroyed by the Danes, the remains of that princess were translated to Ely, and interred with those of her sisters, Sexburga and Etheldreda. The regal remains of the three ladies, and of Ermenilda, were afterwards removed into the new church of Ely by Abbot Richard,—a solemn and imposing ceremony. Edgar Atheling, and some of the English nobles, having previously defended the isle of Ely against William the Conqueror, that warlike prince paid a visit to the convent, and made an offering at the altar of St. Etheldreda,[3] which is dedicated to St. Peter and St. Etheldreda.

The foundation of the present Cathedral Church of Ely was laid in the reign of Henry the First, son of William; and history, which gives us the accurate date of each portion of this interesting structure, assigns the latest part of the building to the year 1534. The removal of the choir, which took place in 1770, was a very great improvement. The original choir contained the relics and shrines of St. Etheldreda, Sexburga, Ermenilda, and Withburga; it was bounded by a stone screen, and niches still remain in the columns to mark the place whence it was removed. It is said that Bishop Mawson had agreed with an artist to fill the window of the choir with modern stained glass. The middle light of the five was

[1] Millar's Cathedral of Ely.

[2] Gough's Sepulchral Monuments, from Malmesbury de Gestis.

[3] Dugdale.

to have contained a whole-length figure of St. Etheldreda, and below it the royal arms: the others were likewise to have had their embellishments. This agreement was made not long before Bishop Mawson's death. He had advanced a considerable sum of money, and sufficiently provided by his will for the rest. The artist, however, was unable to fulfil his contract; a part had, however, been accomplished, and was put up. The heads of St. Paul and St. Etheldreda were completed, which are in two windows in a room at the Deanery.

Later improvements, even in our own times, have been made in this noble edifice. A magnificent painted window was presented to it by the Rev. Bowyer Sparke, one of the canons of the church. It occupies the south-east angle of the lantern, and is of noble dimensions, being forty feet in height. It is designed to commemorate the foundress, by representations of her marriage, and of her consecration as abbess; whilst the four great lights of the window contain, under gorgeous canopies, the figures of Etheldreda as Queen, her father Anna, King of the East Angles, her first husband Thonbert, King of the Girvii, and her second husband Egfrid, King of Northumberland: in the second row, she appears as Lady Abbess of Ely, with Wilfred, Archbishop of York, by whom she was consecrated, and her successors in the government of the monastery, Sexburga and Ermenilda. This great and beautiful work was completed by Mr. William Wailes, of Newcastle, in little more than three months, at a cost of 600*l*.[1]

The lover of English antiquities will linger with delight, to trace, in "that beautiful part of the building called the 'Octagon,' several of the most important historical passages in the life of the pious Etheldreda. These events are depicted upon small clusters of very slender columns, which connect the arches of this part of the building. Beginning at the right side of the north-west arch, the first of these represents her reluctant marriage with Egfrid; the second, her taking the veil in the Monastery of Coldingham; the third, her pilgrim's staff taking root while she slept by the way, and bearing leaves and shoots; the fourth, her preservation, with her attendant virgins, on a rock surrounded by a miraculous inundation, when the King pursued her with his knights, to carry her off from her monastery; the fifth, her instalment as Abbess

[1] Millar's Cathedral of Ely.

"The same liberal benefactor [Mr. William Wailes] proposes to present another painted window, by the same artist, to the south transept, and the church is likewise indebted to him for originating, by a noble gift, the restoration of the south-west transept, which has added so greatly to the beauty of the cathedral. The design for the eight great windows at the east end of the choir, for filling which with painted glass, the late Bishop Sparke left £1500, is nearly completed. Mr. A. B. Hope has undertaken to restore one of the pinnacles of the east end of the church; Lady Mildred Hope to restore the beautiful cross in the eastern gable, and the crocketting which leads up to it; and Mr. H. R. Evans, who has been so long and so honourably connected with the chapter, as steward of the manors, &c., has undertaken to defray the expense of opening and restoring the great lantern of the western tower, which is now concealed by a plaster vault to the floor of the bell-chamber, and of thus bringing into view the most beautiful system of Norman arcading which is to be found in any cathedral in this kingdom." —*Bury Paper.*

of Ely; the sixth, her death and burial; the seventh, a legendary tale of one Brithstan, delivered from bonds by her merits, after she was canonized; the eighth, the translation of her body.

"There yet exists in Ely Cathedral, a relic of very great antiquity; it is the lower part of a stone cross with its square pedestal, found many years ago at Haddenham, in the isle of Ely, and placed by Mr. Bentham, historian of the building, in the west end of the southern aisle, under an arch in the wall. The inscription on the pedestal is very legible.

"This cross was erected to the memory of Ovin, the steward and minister of Queen Etheldreda, a monk of great merit, who had accompanied her from the province of the East Angles; and the cross itself is supposed to be a work of the latter end of the seventh, or the very beginning of the eighth century."[1]

---

[1] Description of Ely Cathedral; Brit. Sancta.

DOMNEVA.

Lady Eva—Marriage with the son of Penda—The Queen takes the veil in her husband Merowald's life—She founds the Abbey of Minstre, to atone for the murder of her brothers by Egbert—"The Deer's course"—Pious *ruse*—Fate of Thunor the murderer—The humility of Mildred—Leobgitha's verses—Gold and silver ink—The Abbess Eadburga—The letters of St. Boniface to the pious Abbess—The Danes—Mildgitha retires to Estrey—Estrey Court—The sepulchres of the murdered princes there—Mildburga and her father—Their tombs in the Abbey of Wenlock.

DOMPNEVA, or Domneva, appears to be a Roman abbreviation of Lady Eva, or Domina Eva,[1] of which an instance occurs in the name of Julia Domna, wife of Severus. Ermenburga, Eva, or Dompneva, are used indiscriminately for the Queen of Merowald, son of Penda, in our histories: as there is another Ermenburga, Queen of Egfrid, this abbreviation is adopted to distinguish her from others. Ermenred Clito, King of Kent, had by his wife Oslave, daughter of King Anna, another daughter besides Dompneva, who was called likewise Ermenburga,[2] and one called Eormengitha, both of whom became nuns: his sons were called Ethelred and Ethelbright.[3]

Merowald, who was destined to marry Domneva, was King of Herefordshire, or the West Hecanas,[4] over which he had reigned three years. Both this princess and her cousin Ermenilda seem to have been given by their parents in marriage to the Mercian princes, sons of Penda, in the hope of securing a friendship between that royal house and the East Anglian.

At this period the kingdom of Kent had arrived at the highest pinnacle of greatness: the glorious Ethelbert and his amiable consort had transmitted their virtues to their descendants. The alliance of the royal family of Kent was sought with avidity by the other princes of the Heptarchy. It has been seen that the Princess Enfleda had married Oswy of Northumberland, and Etheldreda, the sister of Sexburga and Oslave, became the wife of Egfrid. Domneva and Ermenilda united the kingdoms of East Anglia, Kent, and Mercia. These matrimonial alliances are, in fact, a key by which alone the history of the Saxon Heptarchy can be properly understood.

In spite, however, of her marriage, and, it is said, by the consent of

[1] Written indiscriminately, Dumnona, Dompnena, Dormenilda, and Dormengylda.

[2] Ebba or Eaba, Eva or Gaffe, as the name is spelt indifferently in the same Saxon manuscript; it is sometimes written Eadburge, Idaburga, and Elburg; St. Ebba is also at times converted into St. Tabbs.—*Butler*.

[3] Speed, Rapin.

[4] Lappenberg's Anglo-Saxons.

her husband, Queen Domneva assumed the religious veil:[1] it appears that she became Abbess of Minstre, in Thanet, about the year 670, King Merowald being yet upon the throne. The circumstances which occasioned the erection of this famous monastery are remarkable; and as Domneva was herself the foundress and first abbess, they belong especially to her history.

The two brothers of Queen Domneva had been committed by their dying father, Ermenred, to the care of their uncle Ercombert, King of Kent, who, as long as he lived, fulfilled the sacred trust reposed in him with the honour which might have been expected from so excellent a prince; but when he died, his power, and with it the guardianship of the young Ethelred and Ethelbert, who were still in their minority, devolved on his son Egbert, who regarded these princes, his cousins, as dangerous rivals to his power. He is accused of having employed a Thane, named Thunor, to put the orphans to death;[2] and to prevent discovery of the crime, directed that their bodies should be interred beneath the royal throne in the palace of Estry, in Thanet, the place where they were usually residing under his protection. Heaven, however, would not permit such a crime to escape detection, nor suffer Egbert to pursue in security his guilty career. It is related that a miraculous light, falling on the spot where the bodies of the ill-fated brothers had been deposited by their murderer, revealed their holy relics; and the alarmed monarch was induced, by the united representations of St. Theodore, Archbishop of Canterbury, and St. Adrian, Abbot of St. Augustine's, whose councils were seconded by the clamours of the people, to send into Mercia to seek pardon of Domneva, Queen of Merowald, the sister of his victims, for the heinous crime he either perpetrated or permitted, and to offer to indemnify her for their loss by the usual Weregild, or compensation for murder.[3]

The custom of paying a blood-fine, called Weregild or Manbôt, did not belong solely to the Saxons Compositions for murder existed among the Jews, and also the Greeks, as is apparent from Nestor's speech to Achilles, in the Iliad; and even till a recent period among the natives of Ireland the same custom prevailed, the price of a man's head being termed by them his *eric*.[4] Spencer, in his "View of the State of Ireland," writes thus of these cases of composition for murder: "The Brehon, that is, their judge, will compound between the murderer and the friends of the party murdered which prosecute the action, that the malefactor shall give to them, or to the child or wife of him that is slain, a recompense, which they call an Eriach; by which vile law of theirs many murders amongst them are made up and smothered. And this judge being, as he is called, the Lord's Brehon, adjudgeth, for the most part, a better share unto his lord, or the head of that sept (or family), and also unto himself for his judgment, a greater portion, than unto the plaintiffs or parties grieved."

On the arrival of Queen Domneva in Kent, Egbert appeared before her in a very sorrowful manner, imploring her pardon, and laying before

[1] Brit Sancta.

[2] Sax. Chron., Sim. Dunelm.

[3] Butler.

[4] Sir John Davies.

her a great many rich presents. The Queen generously pardoned her royal cousin, but declined accepting any of his offerings: her request to him was, that he would grant her a place "in Tenet," where she might build a monastery in memory of her two brothers, with a competent maintenance, in which she might, with the virgins devoted to God and obliged to her, pray to the Lord to pardon and forgive the King for their murder. Egbert assenting, asked the Queen "how much land she desired to have?" who replied, "only as much as my deer can run over at one course." This being accorded, the animal was let loose at a place called Westgate, in presence of the King, and many of his nobles and people, who all crowded towards the spot where the deer was led in expectation of the event. Among the spectators was Thunor, the King's agent, and the real murderer of the Princes, who cried out that Domneva was a witch, and the King a fool for suffering so noble and fruitful a soil to be taken from him by the decision of a brute. Whilst the King and others around him were diverted with seeing the deer run, "this man endeavoured to put her by, with riding across and meeting her." While thus endeavouring to defeat the pious object of Domneva, the wrath of God fell on him; for, as some say, "the earth opened and swallowed him," or, as we may with greater credibility receive it, "a fall from his horse" occasioned his death; the spot being ever after called "Thunor's Leap," while the place where he was buried yet bears the name of this wretched man. At the sight of the signal judgment which had fallen on Thunor, the King is said to have "very much feared and trembled."[1]

Thunor's Leap was, according to Lewis, the old chalk-pit, which he supposes to have been first sunk when the Abbey and Church of Minstre were built, the bottom of which, in process of time, became overgrown with grass, when the crafty monks invented this fable to frighten the poor people of the neighbourhood. Immediately adjoining this spot formerly stood a beacon, it being some of the highest land in that locality, and it was here that King Egbert had taken up his position, in order that he might be able to see the deer run almost all the way.[2] "The Deer's Course," as it is called by the monks, was nothing more than a lynch or balk, cast up as a boundary, to divide the two capital manors of Minstre and Monkton, in the island, and very probably existed even before the former was granted to Domneva.

"The tame deer of the Queen was to obtain for her royal mistress as much land as it could run over at a breath; the favourite animal having finished her course, from one side of the island to the other, and run over in length and breadth forty-eight plough lands (or ten thousand acres), followed the Lady Domneva, while the King, on his part, returned thanks to Christ Jesus, and surrendered to his illustrious cousin the whole tract of land which the deer had run over; St. Theodore, the devout Adrian, and others who were present, hallowing the gift with their blessing."[3] This donation Egbert afterwards confirmed to the ecclesiastical posterity of Domneva by charters, recorded in the book of St. Augustine's,[4] to the infringers of which he added a frightful curse.

[1] Chron. of Thorne. [2] Lewis. [3] Thorne, Weever.

[4] Weever had himself seen these charters, as he assures us in his work

Domneva accordingly founded her new minster, dedicating it to the Blessed Virgin Mary, and to the name and honour of her murdered brethren.[1] A difference of opinion exists as to the exact date of the foundation, some saying it was commenced in 664 and completed in 670, others that it was commenced only at the latter year.[2] It has again been doubted whether Queen Domneva herself ever ruled the establishment. Drayton says she passed the residue of her days—

> "Immonaster'd in Kent, where first she breathed the air;"

yet we afterwards trace her as president of another religious community in Mercia. It is, however, highly probable that on the completion of the structure, Domneva superintended it until the arrival of her daughter, St. Mildred, who had been sent to France, to the Monastery of Chelles, for her education, that she might be fitly prepared to govern the edifice of her mother's foundation.[3] All things being made ready for her, Mildred was sent for, as the person most fit for the situation of abbess; and on her arrival the Mercian Princess was consecrated to that holy office by Theodore, Archbishop of Canterbury, having previously taken the veil at the Monastery of Chelles. Seventy young women at the same time received the nun's veil, to form a community for their royal mistress, having been selected either from birth or merit. Among the number was Ermengitha, the aunt of Mildred, who was afterwards so much renowned for piety that her tomb, about a mile distant from the monastery, became a favourite resort for devout pilgrims.[4]

Mildred behaved with so much humility amongst her followers and pupils, as rather to make herself their servant than their mother and mistress; for she desired more to be loved than to be feared; and much more effectually brought her sisters on the way of religious perfection by her example than by her authority.[5] This abbess was celebrated as a saint after her death, and in her honour two parish churches in London were dedicated, St. Mildred's in the Poultry and St. Mildred's in Bread-street. According to Wilson's English Martyrology, St. Mildred died in 674; but this is an error, for she was not till after that Abbess of Minster, and her name is to be found subscribed in the Council of Beckenham, A. D. 694.[6] This great council was held by Withred, King of

---

[1] Butler, Weever.

[2] Dugdale, Thorne. Leland is wide of the mark in naming 596, and also Speed, who says Queen Ermenburga (or Dompneva) lived A. D. 590; these dates would, as Dugdale remarks, have been long before her time.

[3] The Church of Minster is the most ancient structure in the island of Thanet, and has three aisles; in the choir are eighteen collegiate stalls; on the floor of the church, and under the porch, are several large flat gravestones, of very great antiquity; on the top of the spire of the steeple was formerly a globe, above which rose a cross, covered with lead, and upon this a vane, surmounted by a cross of iron, emblem of the power and superiority of Christianity over the earth; but these fancied monuments of idolatry were removed in the year 1647, by one Calmer, a rigid Calvinist, who had obtained the sequestration of the living by the refusal of Dr. Casaubon to take the covenant.—*Dugdale.* Minster was sometimes called St. Mildred's Monastery.—*Weever.*

[4] Lives of Saints.

[5] Spelman.

[6] Hist. of the Church of Great Britain, 1674.

Kent, and Berthwald, Archbishop of Canterbury, and in it many things were concluded in favour of the Church. Five Kentish abbesses were present on the occasion, and not only subscribed their names and crosses to the constitutions concluded therein, but their subscriptions were placed not only before and above all presbyters, but also above that of Botred, a bishop present in the council. These abbesses' names are worthy of record; they were Mildred, Etheldreda, Æte, Wilnolde, and Hereswide.

That writing was a female accomplishment in the Saxon times, appears from a letter to St. Boniface from Leobgitha, a nun of St. Mildred's Monastery under Eadburga, sister of Domneva, the Abbess who succeeded Mildred. From Leobgitha's letter, it seems that it was customary for the nuns not only to read but to write Latin: she concludes her letter by saying, "Beneath are some verses which I have striven to compose according to the rules of poetic tradition, not with confident boldness offering them, but desiring to excite your superior mind, and ask your aid. *This art I learned from the institution of Eadburga*, who ceaselessly versifies the sacred law." The following is a translation of the lines in question by a modern author of talent:[1]—

"Oh! may the Almighty, all-creating King,
Who in his Father's kingdom shines in light
Ineffable, to thee aye safety bring,
And grant thee endless joys in glory bright."

Golden ink was used by the Anglo-Saxons, and sometimes silver ink. Their red ink was made of vermillion or cinnabar; sometimes manuscripts were written with purple ink, and capital letters with an ink composed of vermillion and gum. The black ink used by the Saxons in England during the eighth, ninth, and tenth centuries, preserved its original blackness much better than that used in succeeding ages.

Eadburga was abbess of St. Mildred's Minster from the death of that princess till the year 751; and to her many of the letters of Boniface are addressed. This venerable prelate, who was a native of Wessex, had been sent over as a missionary into Germany, to preach to the idolaters there; Eadburga watched over him with a solicitude truly maternal, and the excellent Boniface exhibits in his correspondence with the royal abbess every token of esteem and respect. In one of his letters he styles her "the most honorable maiden, and most beloved Lady Eadburga, distinguished for the wisdom of her monastic government."[2] In one of the earliest epistles, Boniface styles himself "an humble deacon," and solicits the lady-abbess to accept some cinnamon and frankincense, and a *silver pen*.[3] In the 28th of this collection of Boniface's letters, also addressed to Eadburga, the Bishop entreats her to write the Epistles of St. Peter *in letters of gold*, "to inspire carnal men with the greater respect to that apostle," whom he calls the patron of his mission.

St. Eadburga built a new church in honor of St. Peter and St. Paul, and as soon as it was completed, caused the body of St. Mildred to be translated into it.[4] It was, together with that of Eadburga, in 1055,

[1] Miss Lawrence. See "Records of Women of England."
[2] Bonifacii Epist. [3] Lawrence's Hist. of Women. [4] Butler, Brit. Sancta.

translated to Canterbury, where they were deposited in St. Gregory's Church, by Archbishop Lanfranc.[1]

According to some writers, St. Mildred's Monastery was entirely destroyed by the Danes in 978, but another account, given by Thorne, fixes its destruction in the year 1011, at the time of Sweyn's invasion.

Mildgitha, the sister of Mildred, retired to the Monastery of Eastry, not far from Canterbury, which Egbert had himself built to atone for his crimes.[2] At a subsequent period Eastry, the manor of which Egbert had vested in the Church, was given to Christ Church, Canterbury, by Ethelred the Unready, for the support of the monks' kitchen.[3] An ancient tradition affirms, that the altar-tomb, placed at the east end of the little chapel which belonged to Eastry Court, was the sepulchre in which the bones of the two murdered brothers of Queen Domneva were enshrined, and over which a light constantly hovered.

The three sisters, Mildred, Mildgitha, and Milburga, foundress of the Abbey of Wenlock, in Shropshire, were all canonized.

The body of King Merowald, which had been enclosed in a wall of the church of the Abbey of Wenlock, was found at the same time as that of his daughter, Milburga.[4] Domneva, who is called "the virtuous mother of three virgin saints," had only one son by Merowald, who did not survive his infancy; so that his crown devolved on his younger brother Mercelyn, son of Penda, who likewise dying without issue male, the little kingdom of Herefordshire became re-united to the powerful territory of Mercia.

Queen Domneva survived her husband many years, and is frequently mentioned by our historians. Besides the Monastery of Minster, this Queen was foundress of a nunnery at Ebbsfleet, in the isle of Thanet;[5] but it was at Gloucester that she spent her remaining years after her widowhood.

---

[1] A deed of King Edward the Confessor, confirming certain privileges to the Church of St. Augustine, at Canterbury, runs thus:—

"Wherefore, I, Edward, king, by the grace of the King of Kings, and prince of the Angles, after long banishment being returned to my kingdom, by the will of the only compassionating God, and sitting again on the throne of my fathers, do grant and decree that the church which King Ethelbert, at the advice of the blessed Augustine, founded in honour of the Apostles Peter and Paul, and enriched with gifts, in which the bodies of the King himself, and of all the Bishops of Canterbury, and of the Kings, might be placed, be free, with all its appendages and adjacencies; seeing that, indeed, in the same church the above-named King lies buried, and the virgin Mildreth, beloved of God, rests, begotten of his stock. I also, being sprung of the same king's stock, and, by God's help, possessed of his kingdom, do deliver up the isle of Thanet, which King Egbert granted, by hereditary right, to the venerable Queen Domneva (to the mother, to wit, of St. Mildreth, as much as a hind had gone over in its course, for the slaying of her two brothers, Ethelbred and Ethelbert, whom, by order of the same king, Thunur, hateful to God, struck down by an unjust death, whom forthwith celestial vengeance terribly followed by cutting him off."—*Thorne's Chronicle.*

[2] Butler's Lives.

[3] A. D. 979, Philipott.

[4] Philipps, Bromton, Drayton.

[5] Speed, Tanner, Dugdale.

ETHELBURGA AND FRIDOGITHA,

QUEENS OF INA AND ETHELARD.

Invasion of Ivor and Ina—Conditions of the Conquerors—Marriage of Ethelburga to Ivor—His death, and her marriage to his successor, Ina—The arch of Taunton Castle—Ealdbryht Clito besieged by Ethelburga—The "Western Key of the Kingdom"—The Laws of Ina—Guala—The learned men of Ina's time—The Abbey of Glastonbury, and its rich endowments—Ethelburga's pious project—The splendid banquet and the contrast—Its effect on the King—Discourse of Ethelburga—The Crown resigned—Ethelard—Preparations for a pilgrimage to Rome—Departure of the King and Queen as pilgrims—Arrival in Rome—Religious acts—The Saxon school of Ina at Rome—Romescot—Return to England of the royal pair—Death of Ina—Ethelburga at Barking—Cuthberga, Abbess of Wimbourne—Canonization of the Abbess-Queen—The three daughters of Ina—Fridogitha's liberality—Her piety and pilgrimage—Her death and canonization—St. Frideswide.

ETHELBURGA, and her brother Ethelard, the husband of Fridogitha, were descended from Cerdic, founder of the West Saxon monarchy. Their father was Ethelwald, son of Cenwalch, King of Wessex, by Saxburga, sister of Penda.

Two adventurous chieftains from Armorica, Ivor and Ina, having entered into an alliance,[1] invaded the British coast with a fleet, and committed great devastations, especially in Wessex, then governed by Kentwin, son of Kinegils. Ivor, who was son of Alan, King of Bretagne, having won from Kentwin Cornwall, Devon, and Somerset, was offered the peaceable enjoyment of the conquered territories, provided he would allow Kentwin to retain possession of the remainder of Wessex, and would marry Ethelburga, that prince's cousin. At the time this proposal was made, both armies were drawn up in each other's sight in hostile array: arms were, however, laid aside on Ivor's accepting the terms. Ethelburga accordingly became the wife of the chief, and Ivor succeeded the famous Cadwallader, called "the Blessed," who, after a life of warfare, ended his career as a pilgrim to the holy shrine, having named his relative Ivor as his heir, who accordingly took possession of Wessex. On his death, in the year 690, both his kingdom and his widow were appropriated by Ina, his companion in arms.

The circumstance of Ethelburga being the wife of both these princes, and the similarity of their names, has caused some confusion in the not a little entangled web of this portion of history, so conflicting are the narratives of the British chroniclers.

As Ivor, however, disappears early, and Ina is a character of impor-

[1] Palgrave, Geoff. of Monmouth.

tance, it is sufficient to know that Ethelburga was his queen, of whom he appears to have been passionately fond. Nevertheless, a lady is mentioned as his mistress, for whose abode he constructed a building over an arch within his castle of Taunton, in Somersetshire,—a fortress founded by him for his own residence, in the year 700, and for the purpose of securing his conquests against the disaffected nobles of the surrounding district.[1] This arch the Queen, jealous of her rival, is said to have destroyed after her husband's death, together with part of the castle, to be revenged upon her. The statement, however, is apparently erroneous.[2]

The remains of the ancient castle of Taunton, founded by King Ina, are on the west side of the town, and are thus described:[3]—"The old building, being one hundred and ninety-five feet in front, had a circular tower at each end, of which one only is now remaining. The other, with the west end, has been long since destroyed, and a large house built in its room, that has been for many years a boarding-school for young ladies. The west end or wing is the shortest, being sixty-five feet in length, and was lately standing, as it was originally built, allowing for the injuries it had suffered from the cannon of its enemies, or rather from its greater enemy, time. The whole building had a flat roof, with parapet walls, and embrasures for guns; but part of the roof, within the memory of man, has been taken down, and the present erected in its stead. On viewing the back part of it, there could be lately discerned some breaches, made by cannon, in the old wall, which was judged, from its appearance, to be part of the castle built about the eleventh century."[4]

Of this edifice Ealdbryht Clito had obtained possession and had secured himself there.[5] This Saxon chief was one of those pretenders who so frequently disturbed the tranquillity of the latter part of King Ina's reign. The Queen very materially assisted her husband in opposing them; she herself laid siege to Taunton, and after compelling Ealdbryht to withdraw into Sussex, levelled the fortress with the ground. This act probably gave rise to the report of her having pulled down a part of the building from other motives. The castle was soon after rebuilt and fortified, and denominated the "Western Key of the Kingdom."[6]

The date of the destruction of Taunton by Ethelburga, was A. D. 721 or 722, according to the Saxon Chronicle. Ina afterwards directed his forces against the South Saxons, amongst whom Ealdbryht, after his defeat, was wandering in exile; he was finally slain by his antagonist;[7] when Ina had the satisfaction of witnessing the complete re-establishment of peace in his dominions.

To the period of these intestine divisions in Mercia may perhaps be referred the building of the ancient castle of Desborough, in Bucking-

---

[1] Collinson.

[2] Sir Benjamin Hammett wrote to Dr. Toulmin, stating that it had recently been altered by himself into a room, after a lapse of twelve hundred years.

[3] Dr. Toulmin's History of Taunton.

[4] A Bishop of Winchester erected a new castle there about the date of the Conquest.

[5] Saxon Chronicle. [6] Dr. Toulmin. [7] Collinson's Somerset.

hamshire, which, some think, was named after Ethelburga, who is occasionally called Desburga.[1]

The laws which Bede has transmitted to us of Ina, testify to his character, which appears worthy of admiration: his zeal for religion, and desire to promote its interests, are a great feature in these laws. They were made at the instance of his father Kenred,[2] his bishops Edda and Erkenwold, his Ealdormen, and other witas in council assembled. One of these enjoins the baptism of infants within a month after their birth, under severe penalties, which penalties are greatly increased if it died unbaptized; another releases a slave from his master's jurisdiction forever, if he does servile work on a Sunday by his order; a third lays a fine on such as should strike in the church; a fourth orders the regular payment of tithes, with several others of a similar tendency. These laws of Ina are thought to have especially favoured the Britons, placing them in as advantageous a position as their conquerors.

It has been asserted that Ina himself set the example he desired to see followed, of intermarriages with the Saxons and British, by espousing Guala,[3] daughter of Cadwallader; but there is so much confusion of dates respecting this event, that it is difficult to come to a conclusion as to the facts. Milton, who names the marriage in his history, seems very doubtful about it; and historians are obliged to slur it over, evidently not being able to give the necessary details. It was not probable that during Ethelburga's lifetime, Ina should have made this alliance, as nothing is recounted of her divorce or resumption of lost dignity, circumstances very often occurring in these times; and the name of Ethelburga continually occurs throughout the long reign of Ina, both as a sharer of his warlike successes and his domestic peace. It seems more reasonable to suppose, that the similarity of names, and their repetition in the same family, may have led the chroniclers into error, than that injustice should have been done to the wife to whom Ina was so much attached.

The great respect shown by Ina to the distinguished scholar who illustrated his reign, St. Aldhelm, and also to the celebrated Winfreth, better known as Boniface, proves the worth of his own character, and the superiority of his mind.[4] Both these great men exercised a powerful and salutary influence on the acts of Ina, and both have left names capable of giving lustre to any reign.

One of the most memorable services to the Church, performed by Ina, was the rebuilding and endowing the magnificent old British Abbey of Glastonbury, which he did for the repose of the soul of a murdered kinsman, and which was a more Christian method of proving his piety than the signal revenge he thought himself bound to take on the murderers. Nothing could equal the splendour he lavished on this favourite building, and the riches he continued to shower upon it. It is recorded that he

[1] Camden.

[2] See the Preamble to his Laws: "I, Ina, with the counsel of my father Cenred."

[3] Lambert's Archives; Winchester Chronicle; Rudborne.

[4] William of Malmesbury.

adorned the chapels in the most sumptuous style; "garnishing and plating them over with two thousand six hundred and forty pounds' weight of silver, and erecting an altar which he ornamented with two hundred and sixty-four pounds' weight of gold;" besides this the chalices, censers, candlesticks, and robes, embroidered and enriched with gems and carving of the most elaborate description, were innumerable.

Baldred, a sub-king of Wessex, almost equal to himself in power and riches, vied with Ina in gifts to this world-famous monastery; and the names of Ethelburga and Ethelhard appear in the charters of 725,—the latter styling himself "the Queen's brother."[1]

Ina and his Queen also granted donations to Old Sarum, which, from some records contained in the Bodleian and Cottonian Libraries, appears to have been immediately under the protection of the Saxon princes. The following record is very curious, as it probably informs us of the only churches there in those early times; it begins thus:[2] "I, Ina, king, for the salvation of my soul, grant unto the church of St. James, in Saresbyrig, the lands of Fokenham, for the use of the monks serving God in that church. Whoever shall presume to infringe this my munificence, let him, in the day of judgment, be placed on the left hand of Christ, and receive the sentence of damnation with the devil and his angels." Then follows the grant of Ethelburga, his consort, to the nunnery of St. Mary, in Sarum: "I, Ethelburga, wife of Ina, king, &c., for the salvation of my soul, grant to God, and the nuns serving God in the church of St. Mary, in Saresbyrig, the lands of Beddington, with their appendages, &c."

Ethelburga had, for a length of time, endeavoured to persuade her husband, then in the decline of life, to relinquish the concerns of the world, and receive the habit of a monk. The King at last, after a long and fortunate reign of thirty-seven years, laid aside his regal dignity, through her exhortations, aided by the effect produced on his mind by the ingenious device with which they were accompanied.

The following incident, important in its results, is singularly characteristic of the time:—The royal pair one day paid a visit to one of their country residences, where a splendid banquet awaited their arrival, which was served with all the pomp and splendour attendant on regal luxury. Ethelburga resolved to convert this occasion to a useful moral lesson on the subject nearest to her heart. As soon as the King and Queen, with their cortège, had departed, the festive hall was, by her orders, scattered with filth and rubbish; while on the very bed, lately appropriated to their own repose, was placed a swinish litter. Scarcely had the travellers proceeded two miles on their road than Ethelburga made an excuse to return, and Ina, with much courtesy, assented to her request. His surprise was excessive on re-entering the hall, lately the scene of mirth and festivity, to perceive the disgusting change. In silent astonishment and displeasure he gazed upon the scene before him. When informed that it had been so directed by the Queen, he demanded

[1] Hearne's Glastonbury; Dugdale.

[2] Phillips's History of Old Sarum.

from Ethelburga an explanation of this strange mystery. She smiled, and answered: "My lord and husband! this is not, indeed, the noisy hilarity of yesterday: here are no brilliant hangings, no flattery, and no parasites: here are no tables weighed down with silver vessels; no exquisite delicacies to delight the palate: all these are gone like the smoke and wind. Have they not already passed away into nothingness? And should not we feel alarmed who covet them so much, because we shall be as transient? Are not all such things, are not we ourselves, like a river, hurrying, heedless and headlong, to the dark ocean of illimitable time? —unhappy must we be if we let them absorb our minds! Think, I entreat you, how disgusting those things become of which we have been so enamoured. See to what filthy objects we are attached. In these loathsome relics we may see what our pampered bodies will become. Ah! let us reflect, that the greater we have been, and the more powerful we are now, the more alarmed should be our solicitude; for the greater will be the punishment of our misconduct." [1]

The reflections of Ethelburga, thus strangely prefaced, were by no means uncommon in early times, when strong contrasts were often brought to bear on worldly pleasure. The singular and impressive lesson was not thrown away on the intelligent mind of Ina, who immediately determined on what was then held as the highest act of piety, namely, to make a pilgrimage to Rome. His first step was to renounce the temporal dignity of his earthly kingdom, to prepare himself for the one immortal. He forthwith resigned his crown, by will, to his brother-in-law Ethelard, and then made every necessary preparation for the religious life on which he proposed to enter; assuming a plebeian dress, renouncing his rank, and living in a private and retired manner with his beloved Ethelburga, who joyfully aided him in carrying out his good resolutions. It is even said that, during this period, Ina lived by the labour of his own hands, as was the custom of many of the religious of his times.[2]

Ethelburga accompanied her husband to Rome, assuming a masculine habit, probably for her protection on the journey, and, as is also asserted, retaining it on her arrival in that city.[3] They resided there, not far distant from each other, in a poor and private manner, "unlike, indeed, the dignity to which they had been accustomed, but filled with mutual love, charity, and devotion." [4] They passed their time in constant exercises of religion and benevolence; among which may be mentioned the founding of the Saxon school by Ina at Rome, for the benefit of such of his countrymen who might seek an education in that city, with a church for their service, and to provide convenience for their interment. To support these foundations, and the English residents there, Ina is said to have imposed the tribute of a penny on every family in England, which was sent to the Papal See under the name of Rome scot, or Peter's

[1] William of Malmesbury, S. Turner. It is to be regretted that the place which was the scene of this remonstrance is not positively mentioned: one of Ina's palaces and a castle was at Somerton, in Somersetshire, thirteen miles distant from Wells.—*Collinson.*

[2] Hume, Tanner. [3] Bicknell. [4] Butler.

pence.[1] The establishment of this tax is, however, more frequently attributed to Offa than to Ina.

Some authors state that Ina and his Queen died at Rome; others, that Ina, returning to England, shut himself up in a cloister, where he ended his days. According to Willis, the remains of this glorious monarch of the Angles repose in the middle of the body of the church of Wells (founded by himself), opposite to the north porch.

Queen Ethelburga is said to have entered into the Abbey of Barking after her return, her sister-in-law, Queen Cuthburga, Ina's sister, being abbess of the establishment; and when Cuthburga became Abbess of Wimbourne, in Dorsetshire, Ethelburga presided over the congregation of Barking till her death, after which she received the honours of canonization.

Ethelard was named by Ina his successor, as he had no male heirs. Camden, however, mentions three daughters of Ina, of whom he relates a story similar to that of the three daughters of King Lear, and which is supposed by some of the editors of Shakspeare,[2] to have suggested to the immortal bard the subject of his play. Ina is said to have inquired of these princesses, on some occasion, not only whether they loved him then, but whether they would continue to do so during their lives, above all others, to which the two eldest swore earnestly that they would. But the youngest and wisest of them, unwilling to flatter her father, told him honestly, "That albeit she did love and reverence him, and so would whilst she lived, as much as nature and daughterly duty at the utmost could expect; yet she did think that one day it would come to pass, that she should affect another more fervently, meaning her husband, when she was married, who being made one flesh with her, as God by commandment had told, and nature had taught her, she was to cleave fast to, forsaking father and mother, kith and kin." This is all we hear of the daughters of Ina, whether by Ethelburga or Guala, and Camden gives it from an anonymous authority.

Ethelard became king in 729, trod in the footsteps of his illustrious predecessor, and in all his undertakings was assisted by his Queen Fridogitha, who especially distinguished herself by the generosity she displayed in her donations to the Church, on which she bestowed the greater part of her own patrimony. The first year of their accession to power, both the King and Queen liberally endowed the Abbey of Glastonbury. Fridogitha herself bestowed on it the manor of Brunantun (or Brompton-Ralph), containing within its limits five hides of land, which remained in the possession of the monks till after the Norman Conquest, when King William gave it to Sir William de Mohun.[3]

Among other acts of religious charity, Fridogitha prevailed on her hus-

---

[1] Every family, possessed of goods to the value of twenty pence in Wessex, paid a yearly tax of a penny as "King's alms." This tax, collected at Lammas, was paid to St. Peter and the Church of Rome; hence it was at first called "Rome scot," and afterwards "Peter's pence." [Weever, Matthew of Westminster, Dugdale, &c.]

[2] Johnson and Stevens.

[3] Collinson's Somerset, iii. 505; Dugdale.

band to bestow the manor of Taunton on the church of Winchester; a truly regal gift, as Taunton, at that very time, was the chief seat of the Mercian sovereigns. Some writers assert Taunton to have been the gift of Emma, Queen of Ethelred the Unready; but as it is not named among the manors bestowed by that Queen, it is much more probable that it was given by Fridogitha. Ethelard gave, on his own part, seven manses or dwellings for peasants.[1] This donation was made rather more than three hundred years before the Conquest of the Normans in England, and in the interval, such a remarkable share of immunities, prerogatives, and privileges were appended to it, as are hardly to be found in the description of any other manor in the Norman survey.

In 737, Fridogitha undertook a journey to Rome, accompanied by Forthere, Bishop of Sherborne, in Dorsetshire. This prelate is described as "a man of praiseworthy erudition, especially in the Holy Scriptures,"[2] and is numbered among our early writers. On the Queen's return to England, she abandoned all her earthly possessions, and devoted herself exclusively to the service of God. At her death, she was interred in the Cathedral of Winchester.

The daughter of Ethelard and Fridogitha, who emulated the pious example of her mother, became one of the saints of the Anglo-Saxon Church, under the name of St. Frideswide.

---

[1] Dugdale; Toulmin's History of Taunton.

[2] Matthew of Westminster.

QUENDRIDA-PETRONILLA.

Melo-dramatic legend of Quendrida—King Offa screened by monkish writers—Unknown crime of Petronilla—Exposure in an open boat—Stranding of the beautiful stranger on the Welsh coast—Meeting of Offa and Quendrida—Fascination of the young King—Opposition of his parents—The royal marriage—Death of both Offa's parents—Offa's early deficiencies—Sudden change—Beornred's wars—His defeat—Offa's dyke—The Emperor Charlemagne—His letters and presents to Offa—Demand in marriage of Prince and Princess—Interruption of the friendship of the two Kings—Close of the French ports—Alcuin the Learned—Harmony re-established—The Princess Eadburga's marriage—Young Ethelbert, King of East Anglia—His proposal for the hand of the beautiful Etheldritha, youngest daughter of Offa—Excellent character of Ethelbert—His arrival in Mercia—Omens—Rich gifts and grand retinue of the bridegroom—Etheldritha, at her window, admires the beauty and grandeur of her lover—Quendrida's envy and hatred—Offa's welcome—The Queen's treacherous proposal—The chair of state—The canopy and the well—The murder accomplished—Despair of the bride—Her anathema—She leaves her father's court—Offa's remorse—Banishment of the guilty Queen—The spoils she took—Robbers—Her deserved fate—Offa builds cathedrals—The shrine of St. Ethelbert—Divine judgment on Offa's race.

THE history of Quendrida[1] has in it so much of melodrame, that, but for the repetition of her story by several chroniclers, great part of it would be considered fabulous. It is probable that the Monk of St. Alban's, in his account, has said more than the truth, in order to screen King Offa, the founder of his abbey, from the reproach of a foul murder which stained his reign, and has thrown all the odium of a fearful crime on the Queen; but other historians tell of her guilt,[2] and recount her strange adventures, therefore they cannot be rejected in a record of her life.

Tradition does not acknowledge Quendrida as an Anglo-Saxon,[3] but insists that she was of Frankish birth, and her name Petronilla; that for some crime not specified, she had been condemned by Charlemagne's officers of justice to be exposed in an open boat, and sent adrift at the mercy of winds and waves. The frail bark was borne onwards until it stranded on the Welsh coast, and there, in an evil hour, the beautiful stranger's half-lifeless body was found, and the fair-distressed conducted to the presence of the young Prince, whose destiny she was to become. She told

[1] The name is variously spelt Drida, Cynedrida, and Cynethryth; but the *th*, in British, is pronounced like *d*, and the above spelling has been adopted as less difficult to the eye, in this, as in other cases.

[2] Roger of Wendover; Sax. Chron.; Vita Offæ II.

[3] Lappenberg, Bromton.

her story artlessly, and with tears and entreaties for succour, related how she was the victim of conspiracy, being of the royal house of Charles the Great, whose mind had been poisoned against her; that she was innocent of all guilt, and had been most cruelly persecuted, the only reason for which treatment she traced to her rejection of the addresses of one who was hateful to her.

Her youth, her beauty, her eloquence, and her sorrows, immediately won the confidence of those who had saved her; and young Offa's heart became at once the prey of her bright eyes, more seducing in their tears. Deeply grateful for his commiseration, she is said to have exclaimed: "God, who frees the innocent from the snares of the wicked, has now happily placed me under the wings of your protection, has changed my misery to joy, and has made me feel more glad of my exile than I ever felt in the land that gave me birth."[1]

The fascinated Offa gave the rescued beauty in charge to his mother Marcellina, who, however, it seems, had even in the beginning, some doubts as to the truth of her story; but Quendrida, secure of her conquest, had no fears, and did not conceal her haughty disposition or her proud aspirings. All the remonstrances of both Offa's parents were vain, and the infatuated Prince made the dangerous waif thrown on his shores the partner of his fortunes, without hesitation. "The match was fatal" to both father and mother, who did not live a year after their son's marriage.

Of Offa himself strange marvels are related, as that he was lame, blind, and dumb from his birth, but recovered all his faculties suddenly, when the usurper Beornred persecuted his parents, and oppressed his country. Till this time he was called Winfrith, but the name of Offa was then bestowed on him, because of the similarity of the occurrence to that recorded of the Danish Offo, or Uffo, son of Wærmund, "King of Angeln."[2]

Offa (called the Second) was of the royal house of Wibba, and son of an Ealdorman, called Thingfrith; he appears to have been the nearest relative of King Eanwulf, if not his grandson, as in one of his charters he calls himself. In early life he had continually to contend with the turbulent chief Beornred, who had usurped the government of Mercia, but over whom he at length triumphed; his dominion was not, however, firmly established till Beornred's death, in 757.[3]

For a series of years he was occupied in repelling the incursions of the Welsh; and the famous dyke, known by his name, was formed by him, from the mouth of the Dee to the Wye, to keep out his troublesome neighbours. It is interesting, in many parts of that country, to trace remains of the deep boundary, which is still descernible.[4]

---

[1] Speed, Vita Offæ, Turner. [2] Nennius, Alfred of Beverley, Saxon Chronicle.

[3] William of Malmesbury.

[4] In the year 777, Oswestry was taken by Offa from the Britons, and the kingdom of Powis was reduced to the western side of the celebrated ditch still known by his name.

This ditch, called Clawdd Offa, extended from the river Wye, along the counties of Hereford and Radnor, in Montgomeryshire, from Pwll y Piod, an ale-house on the road between Bishop's Castle and Newtown; thence it passes northward,

The ceaseless contentions of these times carry the historian in a perpetual circle of bloody wars and usurpations, until he no longer wonders that the poet-chronicler Milton lost all patience, and exclaimed "Such

near Mellington Hall, near which is an encampment, called Caer-din, by Brompton Mill, where there is a mount; Lunor Park, near Montgomery, Forden-heath, Nantcribba, at the foot of an ancient fortress, Leighton-hall, and Buttington Church. Here it is lost for five miles; the channel of the Severn probably serving for that space as a continuation of the boundary. Just below the conflux of the Bele and the Severn, it appears again, and passes by the churches of Llandysilio and Llanymynech, to the edge of the vast precipitous limestone rock. From this place, it runs by Tref y Clawdd, over the horse-course on Cefn-y-bwch, above Oswestry, then above Sellatyn; whence it descends to the Ceiriog, and then to Glynn, where there is a large breach, supposed to be the place of interment of the English who fell in the battle of Crogen. It then goes by Chirk Castle, and below Cefn-y-wern, crosses the Dee and the Ruabon-road near Plas Madoc, forms part of the turnpike road to Wrexham, to Pentre-bychan where there is a mount; then by Plas Power to Adwy'r Clawdd, near Minera, by Brymbo; crosses the Cegidog river, and through a little valley, upon the south side of Bryniorkyn mountain, to Coedtalwrn, and Cae-dwn, a farm near Treyddin Chapel, in the parish of Mold (pointing towards the Clwydian hills), beyond which there can no farther traces be discovered. It seems probable that Offa imagined that the Clwydian hills, and the deep valley that lies at their base, would serve as a continuance of this prohibitory line: he had carried his arms over most parts of Flintshire, and vainly imagined that his labours would restrain the Cambrian inroads in one part, and his orders prevent any incursions beyond these natural limits, which he had decreed to be the boundaries of his new conquests. "It is observable," says Pennant, "that, in all parts, the ditch is on the Welsh side; and that there are numbers of small artificial mounts, the sites of small forts, along its course." These were garrisoned, and seem intended for the same purpose as the towers in the famous Chinese wall — to watch the motions of their neighbours, and to repel hostile incursions. The folly of this great work appeared on the death of Offa: the Welsh, with irresistible fury, despised his toils, and carried their ravages far and wide on the English marches. Superior force often repelled them. Sanguinary laws were made by the victorious Harold against any that should transgress the limits prescribed by Offa. The Welshman that was found in arms, on the Saxon side of the ditch, was to lose his right hand.

"There is a famous thing,
Called Offa's Dyke, that reacheth farre in length,
All kind of ware the Danes might thither bring;
It was free ground, and called the Britons' strength.
Watt's Dyke, likewise, about the same was set,
Between which two the Danes and Britons met,
And traffic still, but passing bounds by sleight,
The one did take the other pris'ner streight."

The great dyke and fosse, called Watt's Dyke, is little known, notwithstanding it is equal in depth, though not in extent, to that of Offa, with which it has been frequently confounded. Of the formation of this dyke, as to time or occasion, no authentic information can be found. It runs nearly in a direction with that of Offa, but at unequal distances, from five hundred yards to four miles. The space intervening between the two was considered as free ground, where the Britons, Danes, &c., might meet with safety for commercial purposes.

Watt's Dyke appears at Maesbury, and terminates at the Dee, below the Abbey of Basingwerk. The southern end of the line is lost in morassy grounds, but was probably continued to the river Severn. It extends its course from Maesbury to the Mile Oak; from thence, through a field called Maes-y-garreg Lwyd, between two remarkable pillars of unhewn stone; passes by the town, and from

bickerings to recount, met often in these our writers, what more worth is it than to chronicle the wars of kites and crows, flocking and fighting in the air?"

"Nothing," however, observes the learned Lappenburg, "would more raise the wars of Offa above this contemptuous mention of the great epic poet of England, than if it were ascertained how far all these chiefs were influenced by the mighty ruler of the Franks, Charles the Great. If any reliance can be placed on the monkish biographer, the Kings of Kent, previously to the invasion of that state by Offa, had applied to Charles for aid and protection. The menacing letters of the Emperor were unheeded by the Mercian, and in the course of years their mutual success united the lord of the Germanic insular realm with the chief of the Roman continent. Charles sent to Offa, or as he himself expresses it, "the most powerful ruler of the East to the most powerful ruler of the West," many costly presents, the catalogue of which has been preserved, though not that of the presents sent in return, which to us would have been of far greater interest."[1]

In a letter extant of Charlemagne[2] to Offa, mention is made of a Hunnic sword and belt and two silken mantles. The Emperor calls the King his "brother," but this is probably merely in courtesy, and cannot be admitted as an argument of his being related through his Queen Quendrida, as some have thought.

The friendship of the two courts was interrupted by a discord of some moment.

Geroaldus, Abbot of St. Wandrille or Fontenelle, had frequently been employed by Charlemagne in his missions to the court of Mercia, This prelate was sent thither to demand the hand of Offa's daughter for his son Charles. His negotiation was, however, unsuccessful; for though the very friendly intercourse between the two kings had warranted the request, Offa refused to grant Eadburga to the French prince, unless Bertha, daughter of Charlemagne, were bestowed on his own son and successor, Egfrid, who is described as being "the only joy and pride of his parents." The desire of Offa to form a high alliance for his only son

---

thence to Old Oswestry, and by Pentreclawdd to Gobowen. the site of a small fort called Bryn y Castell, in the parish of Whittington: runs by Prys Henlle and Belmont; crosses the Ceiriog, between Brynkinallt and Pont y Blew forge, and the Dee below Nant y Bela; from whence it passes through Wynn-stay Park, by another Pentreclawdd, to Erddig, where there was another strong fort on its course; from Erddig, it runs above Wrexham, near Melin Puleston, by Dolydd, Maesgwyn, Rhos-ddu, Croes-oneiras, &c.; goes over the Alun, and through the township of Llai, to Rhydin, in the county of Flint; above which is Caer Estyn, a British post; from hence it runs by Hope Church, along the side of Molesdale, which it quits towards the lower part, and turns to Mynydd Sychdyn, Monachlog, near Northop, by Northop Mills, Bryn-moel, Coed y Llys, Nant y Flint, Cefn y Coed, through the strand-fields, near Holywell, to its termination below the Abbey of Basingwerk. A dyke and rampart, similar in appearance, and not unlike in name, runs through the counties of Wilts and Somerset, called Wans Dyke, perhaps from Gwan, a perforation. [History of Oswestry.]

[1] Dr. Lappenberg's History of England under the Anglo-Saxon Kings, translated by Benjamin Thorpe, F. S. A.

[2] Wilkins, Malmesbury, Leland.

and heir was extremely natural, but Charlemagne was indignant at the presumption of the demand.

It is remarkable that this Princess Bertha, her father's especial favourite, was afterwards, or perhaps at that very time, secretly united to Angilbert, one of the most learned men of his time, who became Abbot of the powerful Monastery of St. Riquier, in Picardy. Bertha is described as being "the softened image" of her great father, in mind, voice, aspect, and bearing.[1]

The fathers, therefore, contended for the honour of their respective priceless treasures; but Charlemagne's anger seems to have been excited beyond bounds, and he immediately ordered the French ports to be closed against the Anglo-Saxon merchants. Thus all intercourse between the two nations was reciprocally interdicted. There had always been a great repugnance among the Saxon kings to intermarriage with foreigners, of which few instances occur prior to the time of Edward the Elder, whose sisters contracted splendid foreign alliances. Bertha, Emma, and Judith, were among the few solitary instances of a prior date; and after Edward the Elder was Emma of Normandy, whose tie with Ethelred was the first step to the Norman conquest.

The learned Saxon Alcuin, the friend and confidant of Charlemagne, was despatched to England as ambassador, to restore the broken amity of the two realms, which had not been destined to be of long duration. In a letter of Alcuin, quoted by Malmesbury, is the following passage: "I know not what is to become of us. Some dissension, which seems to have been fomented by diabolical skill, has arisen lately between King Charles and King Offa, so that all communication by sea is forbidden to the merchants on both sides. It is said, that I am about to be sent to England for the purpose of establishing peace."[2]

The object of Alcuin's mission was accomplished, and harmony was re-established between the rulers.

The hand of Eadburga, which had been refused to the French Prince, was given to Bertric, King of Kent, heir-apparent to the throne of East Anglia, in the event of the death of Ethelbert, a young and amiable prince who yet remained unmarried. The union of Bertric and Eadburga took place in 787, Aldric, the father of that king, being also associated in the government.[3]

Ethelbert had resolved to devote his whole life to the service of God, and not to enter the married state; but his courtiers overruled this resolution, and persuaded him to seek the alliance of some princess worthy of perpetuating his royal race. Ethelbert had heard of the beauty and virtues of Etheldritha, the youngest of the daughters of King Offa, and his friend and confidant, Earl Oswald, strongly urged him to demand her hand. A council was held, at which the nobles of East Anglia were all present, together with Laonorine, the Queen Mother. Every person there assembled, except that royal lady, approved of the proposed marriage, and it was settled that it should take place.

---

[1] Angilbert's Carolus Magnus.

[2] Turner.

[3] Sax. Chron. and Asser's Life of Alfred.

On the part of the Mercians, Humbert, Archbishop of Litchfield, had suggested Ethelbert to Offa as a suitable husband for his daughter, and was seconded by Unwona, Bishop of Leicester.[1] The excellent character of the Prince rendered the match in every way desirable, and the Mercian King invited him to his court to celebrate his nuptials with the fair Etheldritha. When Ethelbert's proposal was thus accepted it was settled that the marriage should take place at the same time as that of her sister Elfleda with Ethelred, the Northumbrian King. The nuptial ceremony for both the royal couples was arranged to be performed at the ancient Mercian palace of Sutton Wallis, near Hereford, whither Ethelbert was to repair for the purpose.

On the day previous to that eventful one when

> "Our kindred all within the halle,
> The wedding feast arraye;
> When the song shall sound, and the dance goe rounde,
> And the musicke merrilie playe,"[2]

the young King of the East Angles departed on his journey towards Mercia, full of hope and expectation, attended by a retinue of his own nobility. In conformity with his usual custom prior to commencing his journey, he heard mass with habitual attention and devotion. Late in the evening Ethelbert arrived in the neighborhood of Sutton,[3] where, instead of entering the town, he ordered his tents to be pitched, that he might pass the night in the open country. Some East Anglian nobles, however, were deputed to proceed to the palace of Offa, and announce his arrival, with the cause of his coming, and at the same time were instructed to present to the Mercian King some rich gifts prepared by Ethelbert, his future son-in-law. They were most graciously received, and Offa signified his approbation of the East Anglian's suit.

Ethelbert, after a night harassed with frightful dreams, which seemed to forbode some impending calamity, sent forward his chariots and packhorses laden with rich baggage, well-stored chests, and provisions; and accompanied by an immense number of men on foot and horseback, followed himself, with a magnificent band of his knights, arranged in due order. The approach of this cavalcade was soon rumoured through the town, and at length reached the palace of King Offa. Amongst others who were attracted to behold the sight was Etheldritha, the maiden daughter of King Offa. From a window of the lofty palace of her father, she beheld the young King Ethelbert and his knights entering the courtyard. She marked with a woman's interest the splendid spectacle, and then hastened to her mother to speak to her of the manly beauty of Ethelbert, of the stately nobles, the valiant knights, and the wondrous splendour of his retinue, Queen Quendrida listened to her daughter's enthusiasm, and her malice and envy were alike excited by the narrative.

---

[1] This see was removed from Dorchester to Leicester in 737. It eventually merged into the present Lincoln bishopric.

[2] "The Greye Baron," from Dovaston's Legendary Ballads.

[3] Offa had another royal residence at Tamworth, where his successors, Kinwulf, Beornwulf, and Buthred, afterwards resided.

She had opposed the marriage from the first, disliking Ethelbert for his religious devotion; for, being an unbeliever herself, Christian observances were hateful in her eyes. She had been deeply mortified that her daughters should have been unable to form foreign alliances, and had even persecuted the Archbishop of Litchfield and the other bishops, because, in the marriages she sought for her other daughters, they had opposed her policy, as ruinous to Mercia; and now nothing could exceed her vexation when she found that she was likely to be foiled in her last expectation; meanwhile Offa, delighted to receive Ethelbert, his daughter's bridegroom, bestowed on him a paternal embrace, accompanied with the words, "Welcome, my son; welcome, my son-in-law, welcome! You shall henceforth be regarded as my favourite child!" Quendrida stood aloof, beholding the joy of the meeting with a scowling brow, and revolving in her mind how to make Ethelbert feel the effects of her resentment.

Unsuspicious of her designs, Offa afterwards repaired to his wife, to ascertain when it would be convenient to her that her daughter's marriage should be celebrated. It was then that Quendrida spoke as follows:—

"The subject is one which requires very grave consideration. You are well aware that the petty princes of the East Angles have long desired to obtain dominion over the Mercians. You have full knowledge of the hereditary enmities, and the mutual injuries inflicted upon each other by both these kingdoms; and now I am greatly deceived, if ambition rather than affection has not attracted Ethelbert to this court. Marriage is the pretext, friendship the cloak, which have served the purpose of the keen spy, who would judge for himself the weakness that accompanies your advanced years, and the best means of insuring your destruction. You should regard your guest, not as a lover, but as a hostile commander; for it is in the latter capacity he has appeared before you, accompanied by numbers of soldiers, large enough for an army—too large for the purposes of peace.

"Suppose he marries your daughter, and that such is the sole cause of his coming; then by right of that marriage he will regard himself as your heir, and entitled to succeed you on the throne. As an impatient heir, he will daily wish for your death; and all that you now peacefully enjoy, he will constantly seek for, and as sedulously struggle to acquire. You prepare a rod of chastisement for yourself; you knot together the whip with which you will hereafter be beaten, if you give to one like this, pretensions to be your successor. Make him your son-in-law, your life is in peril, and your crown in danger; or if life be long spared to you, it must be passed amid the terrors of fear; you exchange the independence of a free king in your own dominions for the trembling timidity of an Eastern slave.

"Suppose, on the other hand, that you now reject his alliance, and that you allow him, justly offended with the treatment he has experienced, to withdraw from your kingdom, there can be no doubt that you expose yourself to as great a danger as that which you desire to escape. He now knows the roads of your kingdom — he requires no spy to tell him what parts of it are the most accessible for his troops — how it can be best assailed, or what are the points on which you will rely for your defence. He has seen and has noted your age and your infirmity; and all he has to do is to make as a pretext for hostilities, the affront to which you have subjected him, and on the instant he proclaims war, he begins the destruction of your kingdom, and deprives you of life.

"There is but one of two modes of escaping from the danger and perplexity entailed upon you by the coming of this guest; either he will in a short time cause your death, or you now must cause his — in my mind a just and fitting punishment for his presumption."

When Quendrida finished speaking, Offa sighed deeply, and after considering for a few moments, answered her thus:—

"Your discourse has, in sooth, convinced me that I am reduced to a dangerous and pitiable plight; for I plainly see that on this side there is imminent peril, and on the other irretrievable infamy.[1] Far, far, however, be from me the detestable crime that you suggest; a crime which, if once committed, would bring eternal opprobrium upon me and my successors."

He quitted her presence, and soon after rejoined his royal guest with an appearance of tranquillity which covered the real anguish which preyed upon his mind. A magnificent banquet was served, with costly wine,[2] accompanied by music, singing, and dancing. The two Princes sat down together to the entertainment, and the day passed away in joy and merriment. But Quendrida, with "murder in her smile," meantime had prepared a tragic ending to the scene. Close by the couch which Ethelbert was to occupy at night, she caused a magnificent throne to be placed, over which was erected a royal canopy, the sides of it decorated with rich hangings. Beneath this chair of state there was a deep well. Such was the contrivance on which she had decided, and having seen that all was sure, she joined Offa and Ethelbert in the banqueting hall. There, entering into a lively conversation, she after a time inquired of the unsuspicious Ethelbert — "Will you not come, my son, and visit the maiden who is to be united to you in marriage? She anxiously awaits a visit from you in my chamber, and will, no doubt, hear with pleasure the words of love, when pronounced by her intended husband."

Ethelbert rose at once and attended Quendrida to the fatal spot, whence his attendants were at the same instant excluded. The Princess was not there, as her expectant lover had supposed, but Quendrida, turning suddenly round, said: "Seat yourself there, my son, until she arrives." The young King obeyed, and the moment he took his seat on the throne, the platform on which it was erected gave way beneath him, and in a mass fell with him and upon him into the gulph beneath,[3] where, by the aid of assassins concealed in the neighbouring apartments by the Queen, he was speedily suffocated; for Quendrida aided her confederates by flinging on the unfortunate Prince the pillows, bedding, hanging, and tapestry, lest the sound of his dying groans and shrieks should betray her

[1] Bromton.

[2] Wine was said to be "the drink of the elders and the wise," and only seen at the tables of the great.

[3] The Monk of St. Albans, &c.

crime To complete the deed, the scarcely lifeless body was decapitated by the order of the relentless Quendrida.

That this horrible act was entirely perpetrated by the Queen without the knowledge of Offa, appears the more unlikely, since it is certain that he immediately after invaded East Anglia, and annexed it to his own dominions, which would seem to betray the motive of the deed.[1] So suddenly, indeed, did he march thither, that no measures could be taken for its defence, and it was added easily to his other conquests.

The innocent bride Etheldritha, becoming suddenly conscious of the horrible truth, in the midst of the general consternation which filled the palace had yet found time to convey warning of her parent's treachery to the East Anglian nobles who had accompanied Ethelbert, so that they were able to make their escape, while the unfortunate Princess herself, in her consternation and despair, filled the air with lamentations, and even in the extremity of her anguish was led to curse the authors of her being, and prophetically to denounce the vengeance of Heaven which was about to punish them for their awful crime. To Quendrida she declared in words, as if inspired, that her only son Egfrid would not live three years longer, and that she should herself die in a few months, overcome with equal misery and despair to that she had caused.

Etheldritha instantly abandoned her father's court, and in the Monastery of Croyland, in Lincolnshire, received the habit of a nun, preferring rather "to be as a serf in the house of the Lord, than to dwell as a queen in the palace of sinners;" in that solitary retirement, at a distance from the vain pleasures of the world, she passed in sadness and contemplation the remainder of her days.

Offa, after the deed of murder had been perpretated, took to his chamber for three days, which he passed without nourishment, sighing and weeping, his mind apparently occupied by the deepest grief. Whether from remorse or disgust, he avoided the sight of his guilty Queen, and commanded that Quendrida should be removed at once from court to one of the most remote and solitary places in Mercia, to be placed there in the closest confinement. He did not put her to death, but professed to desire that the prolongation of her life would afford her time for repentance. He suffered her, however, to carry to her prison an immense treasure, "the spoils of the oppressed." She had with her the instruments of her doom; for these heaps of accumulated gold and silver induced robbers to attack the mansion in which she dwelt, for the sake of so splendid a booty; and the Queen, being seized by the marauders, who little heeded her dignity, was flung into a deep well, where, bruised and maimed like her ill-fated victim, she expired in torment. This Lady Macbeth of her time is said to have been called by the Saxon name of Leog, signifying "a queen to be feared." Offa witnessed the retribution of Heaven, on the author of what was perhaps a crime in which he had participated; he lived, moreover, to repent. Desirous of re-establishing his character in the estimation of the world, and to appease his remorse, or quiet the soul of the murdered prince, he paid great court to the clergy, and as-

[1] Turner's Anglo-Saxons.

sumed the monkish devotion of his times. He even undertook a pilgrimage to Rome, to obtain absolution from the hands of the supreme Pontiff. He was ordered to erect a cathedral over the remains of Ethelbert; and on his return the Cathedral of Hereford[1] was built, whither, as soon as it was completed, he removed the mangled relics of the ill-starred prince, which had been dishonourably buried, at the time of the murder, on the bank of a small river near the palace. The edifice was then solemnly dedicated in the name of the royal martyr, who had been previously canonized by the Pope.

The shrine in which the ashes of St. Ethelbert repose is yet in existence, and an exact representation of the original may be seen in Strutt's Anglo-Saxon Antiquities. "It consists of a curious piece of enamelled copper, lined with oak, which last is supposed to be part of the floor on which the murder of the saint was committed. The machine held by the two attendants, on which the dead body lies, appears to be the bier on which the corpse was carried on the shoulders of attendants to the place of sepulture. The writing on the tablet held by the attendant priest, is so obliterated as to render it impossible to be decyphered."

Offa, who is said to have bestowed a tenth of his goods on the Church, having richly endowed the Cathedral of Hereford, founded also the Abbey of St. Alban's; and surely if the practice of saintly virtues claimed canonization, the honour was merited by Ethelbert, who, when living, was beloved and admired of all for his goodness and piety. One of the sayings attributed to him was the following: "That the greater men were, the more humbly they ought to bear themselves; for the Lord putteth proud and mighty men from their seats, and exalteth the humble and meek."[2] In the centre of the Abbey of St. Alban's may be seen a rude painting of the monarch, with an inscription underneath, setting forth that it was founded by Offa in 793.

The Abbey at Bath was likewise of Offa's foundation;[3] he enriched the church at Westminster, and made also rich gifts to Canterbury, and other places far beyond his own dominions.

Retributive justice pursued all his family; his daughter Alfleda, married to Ethelred of Northumberland, was beheaded, by her husband's orders, before a year of her marriage was past. It is said that this pair were united at the very time of the murder of Ethelbert; and Strutt has published a curious picture from an ancient Saxon book in the Cottonian Library, representing the double marriage of the sisters, as if the nuptial

---

[1] Weever. [2] Holinshed.

[3] After Ethelbert's murder, Offa had removed to Bath, which city he had conquered after it had been more than two hundred years under the dominion of the West Saxons, who had rebuilt the Roman walls, employing in that task the ruins of temples, mausoleums, and triumphal arches, devastated in their conquest under Ceaulin and Cuthwin, A. D. 577. Roman sculptures had been inserted in these new walls for ornament. Thus the city was remodelled according to the Saxon taste, and the Temple of Minerva converted into a Christian house of nuns, dedicated to St. Peter: in this foundation Offa placed a society of secular nuns. — Collinson.

ceremony with Ethelbert had actually taken place,—which is not unlikely, the better to secure the victim.

Ethelred of Northumberland was put to death by his subjects in the year of Offa's demise, and his son Egfrid, on whom his hopes were placed, died within a few months of his father: thus the line of Offa became extinct, and in the person of Egbert, the glorious Mercian kingdom became merged in that of Wessex.

Offa's grave was accidentally discovered in the churchyard of Hemel Hempstead. "In digging a vault, the sexton, when he had excavated the earth about four feet below the surface of the ground, found his spade strike against something solid, which, upon inspection, proved to be a large wrought stone, the lid of a coffin; and under it was found the coffin entire, which was afterwards taken up in perfect condition; but the bones contained therein, on being exposed to the air, crumbled to dust. On the lid of the coffin is an inscription, partly effaced by time, but still sufficiently legible decidedly to prove that it contained the ashes of the celebrated Offa. The coffin is about six and a half feet long, and contains a niche or resting-place for the head, and also a groove on each side, for the arms, likewise for the legs; it is curiously carved, and altogether unique of the kind." [1]

[1] Monthly Magazine, vol. xxvi. Oct. 1st, 1808.

EADBURGA.—ELFLEDA.

Pride of Eadburga—Prince Egbert's banishment—He seeks shelter with Offa, is refused hospitality—Flies to the court of Charlemagne—The Queen's influence; her jealousy, and vindictive character—Infatuation of her husband—Her hatred of Worr—Her attempts to ruin him—Resistance of Bertric—The banquet—The poisoned cup—Death of the King and his friend—Flight of the Queen—She seeks the court of Charlemagne; is well received there at first—Her beauty and her gifts—Change of public estimation—Charlemagne's sarcastic offer—The incautious reply of the widow—The Emperor's contempt—His bestowal of a convent on her—Her conduct as Abbess—Her expulsion and degraded position—Her arrival at Pavia and destitution—Her death in misery—Her quaint epitaph—Detestation of her memory—Title of Queen not allowed by Anglo-Saxons—Egbert's succession—The contrast of the sisters—The Abbess of Croyland—Witlaf's sojourn and gifts; his attachment to Etheldritha—The Danes—Elfleda, daughter of Kenulf—Her son Wistan—Rejected offer of Berferth—Murder of Wistan.

Eadburga, the daughter of Offa, who had married Bertric, King of Kent, is said to have "borne herself very highly, on account of her parentage."[1] Her pride was ill-founded, for she inherited the worst qualities of her mother, without any of her father's merits, being disdainful, capricious, and of violent passions. She is accused of having incited her husband Bertric to banish Prince Egbert, the true heir to the crown, on pretence of his being engaged in a conspiracy against him: there are, however, writers who say that Egbert fled from the court of the West Saxons, because his father-in-law Bertric had attempted his life; his reason for the young prince's destruction being to remove a competitor for the throne, the title of Egbert, as son of Alchmond, though set aside in his favour, being superior to his own. The fugitive prince, whose story somewhat resembles that of Edwin of Northumberland, sought protection with Offa. But that monarch was not more kindly disposed towards him than his daughter and her husband, and Egbert was finally compelled to seek his safety with Charlemagne in the court of France: in that country it was that the royal exile acquired the accomplishments which enabled him, at a future period, to become so shining a character on the English throne.[2]

It is very probable that Eadburga used her influence with her infatuated husband, to prevent his doing justice to Prince Egbert, even if she had not been the original cause of his misfortunes; for every act of her life proves that her power was exerted to an evil end, and to offend her, or to stand in the way of her will or her interest was at once to create in her an implacable enemy. She exercised unlimited control over her hus-

[1] Speed. [2] Hume

band, who opposed her in nothing, and allowed her absolute dominion in all the concerns of the kingdom. When other plans failed to revenge herself on those she considered her enemies, she had a means to which she did not hesitate to have recourse, namely, poison; and it is said, that on more than one occasion she availed herself of her dangerous knowledge of the property of drugs, to get rid of persons obnoxious to her. Her success in these modes of vengeance, was, however, destined, in the end, to cause her downfall, and "she fell into the pit which she had digged for another," as her mother Queen Quendrida had done before her.

Amongst the courtiers of Bertric was a young Ealdorman, named Worr, distinguished for worth of character and for accomplishments, to whom the King was extremely attached, and who had, in consequence, excited the jealous hatred of Eadburga. Having used every art to destroy her husband's confidence in his friend, she resolved to effect their separation by her customary method, in order to have no rival in the regard of Bertric. But she did not contemplate the event which occurred, and which at once deprived her of power and influence for ever.

At a repast, at which both Worr and the King were present, she presented the former with a cup, previously drugged by her own hand, of which he unsuspectingly drank, but at the same time, by an accident which she did not foresee, Bertric, taking the goblet from his friend, before she could prevent him, finished the remainder of the poison, and both, seized instantly with agony, expired before her eyes together.[1]

The King being dead, Eadburga, justly fearing the punishment she so well deserved, and knowing that she had incurred the hatred of the people, not only by this, but by many other crimes, without delay hastened to fly from the palace, and eventually contrived to make her escape into France, taking with her all the riches and treasures she had been able to secure. Eadburga, thus laden with precious gifts, presented herself before the French throne, and there, at first, her beauty and liberality procured for her a courteous reception; but the taunts and mockery by which she was afterwards repulsed, abundantly prove how soon the false Queen lost the esteem of her royal entertainer. Charlemagne was reminded by her presence, that her hand had been refused by the proud Mercian sovereign, her father, to his favourite son Charles. As if in retaliation, the monarch is said to have offered Eadburga, who was now a widow by her own act, the choice of either himself or his son, in these words:—

"Eadburga, say, which do you choose for your husband; myself, or my son, who now stands beside me?" To which the Queen, with characteristic levity, returned: "If I am to have my choice, I select your son, because he is the younger of the two." On which the great King, smiling, answered: "If you had chosen me, you should have had my son; but since you have preferred him, *you shall have neither*."

Charlemagne, after thus venting the spleen he yet felt on the score of his early disappointment, seemed to relax in his enmity, and gave to Eadburga a splendid monastery, where she, exchanging her lay habit for that of a nun, presided, unworthy as she was, as abbess, during a few

[1] Hume, Speed, Echard.

years.[1] Her evil disposition, however, unable to reconcile itself to this privacy, led her to conduct herself so ill in that capacity, that she was driven from her own establishment with infamy, and reduced to the attendance of one solitary female servant. Finally, Eadburga, daughter of the powerful Offa, who had once been "clothed in purple and fine linen," excluded from the society of all her former associates, was reduced to such a condition of miserable poverty and contempt, that, abandoned, shunned, and abhorred by all, she was forced to beg her daily bread in the streets of the city of Pavia, where she ended her days. Her case was publicly known, and many eye-witnesses attest these facts,[2] which are given on the authority of Alfred the Great to Asser.

The following epitaph was written for this Princess, and is here introduced more for its peculiar quaintness of expression,[3] than its appropriateness to one so burthened with crimes unalluded to therein :—

"I was, I am not; smiled, that since did weep;
Labour'd, that rest; I wak'd, that now must sleep;
I played, I play not; sung, that now am still;
Saw, that am blind; I would, that have no will.
I fed that, which feeds worms; I stood, I fell:
I bade God save you, that now bid farewell.
I felt, I feel not; followed, was pursued:
I war'd, have peace; I conquer'd, am subdued.
I moved, want motion; I was stiff, that bow
Below the earth; then something, nothing now.
I catch'd, am caught; I travel'd, here I lie;
Lived in the world, that to the world now die."

So universal was the detestation in which the crimes of Eadburga were held by the West Saxons, that upon the death of Bertric, previous to their electing a new king, they made a law that no female should reign in their country, and forbidding the wives of their future monarchs to assume the title of Queen, on pain of their husbands being deposed.[4] In consequence of this law, Redburga, wife of Egbert, was deprived of the regal honours,[5] and also Osburga, Ethelwulf's first wife. Through its infringement in favour of Judith, his second consort, who was solemnly crowned, Ethelwulf had nearly been deprived of his kingdom and authority. The law remained in force till the reign of Edgar, after which it fell into neglect and ceased to be observed, the wives of the Saxon Kings being always styled Queens or Reginæ, and sharing with them in the coronation solemnity, being anointed, crowned, and sitting in the chair of state by their side; the particulars of which honours, derived thenceforth through their royal partners, are yet extant.[6]

Egbert, the eldest son of Alchmond, was, on Bertric's death, recalled from France, and being the sole surviving descendant of the race of the mighty Odin, became King of Wessex, and finally chief of the Saxon Heptarchy.

---

1 Speed. 2 Ibid. 3 Heywood's History of Women.

4 Saxon Chronicle.

5 The King's wife bore the title of *hlafdig*, or lady. — Sim. Dunelm.

6 Selden's Titles of Honour.

On comparing the conduct of the two sisters, Etheldritha and Eadburga, we are almost tempted to believe that the difference in their parentage, which some authors have asserted, really did exist, and that the former was not the daughter of Quendrida.

During the space of forty years, the gentle and unfortunate recluse Etheldritha lived at Croyland, in the exercise of every virtue, for which she became so revered, that her name was, after death, included in the saintly calendar. Hospitality, not the least feminine or least Christian virtue, was extended by her to the fugitive prince Witlaf,[1] when persecuted by King Egbert. Witlaf was sheltered by Etheldritha during a period of four months, in consequence of which circumstance he added to the privileges granted to the monastery by preceding kings, that of sanctuary within the five waters of Croyland. He also gave his purple coronation robe, "to be made into a cope for the use of the priest who ministered at the holy altar,"[2] and his golden veil, embroidered with the Fall of Troy, to be suspended against the walls at his anniversary or birthday; and besides these gifts, those of his gilt cup, embossed with figures of vine-dressers fighting with dragons, which he called his crucibolum, and the horn which he used at his table, for the elders of the monastery to drink out of at festivals, and to remember him in their prayers." This charter was dated A. D. 833. The worthy Abbess, on her death, was interred at Croyland, on which occasion the grief of Witlaf was so poignant that he could hardly be withdrawn from her tomb. As a still further testimony of his affection and regard for her memory, he caused his Queen Celfred, and their son Wimond, at their death, to be interred by her side.[3] But, as if the spirit of Ethelbert was still raging for vengeance on Offa's race, in the year 870, Croyland Monastery was ravaged by the Danes, who broke open all the tombs in hopes of plunder. "There were on the right hand of St. Gutlac's tomb, the monuments of Cissa, Beccelin and Abbot Siward; on the left, the tombs of Egbert, the secretary of Gutlac, St. Tatwine, St. Etheldritha, Queen Celfreda, and Wimond." Being disappointed of their object, these barbarians laid the bodies on a heap, and setting fire to them, burnt the church and convent together, three days after their arrival.[4] Previously to this desecration, Beornwulf, who became King on his brother Witlaf's death, A. D. 838, when marching through Croyland, had despoiled the monastery of all that Witlaf and the Mercian Kings had bestowed upon it, having seized on all the money he could find there, with a vast number of jewels and other ornaments bestowed for decorations on the church.[5] At a later period, the King, however, made restitution to Croyland for this robbery.[6]

Wimond, who had formerly married Elfleda, daughter of Kenulf, was deprived of his rights as heir to Witlaf, by his uncle Beornwulf: nor was this all. Beornwulf and his son Berferth together, concerted to put to

[1] Sometimes spelt Withlaf and Wightlaf. [2] Dugdale. [3] Willis's Abbeys.

[4] Dugdale, Willis, Ingulphus. [5] Roger of Wendover.

[6] He died 852, and during his reign, which lasted thirteen years, the name of his consort, Queen Sethred, accompanied by the title Regina, was frequently appended to his in the royal charters granted to the church of Worcester; an additional proof that the law made in Wessex did not affect the other Queens of the Heptarchy.

death Wistan, son of Wimond and Elfleda, an amiable and pious prince, who, led by his disposition to religion, left his affairs, on Witlaf's death, in the hands of his mother, who is esteemed a queen by our writers, and of his nobles. Berferth, knowing Elfleda's hand would convey a strong title to the sovereign power, sought her for his wife, though in reality his aunt by relationship.[1]

In conformity with this plan, Berferth sent his messengers to ask the Queen's hand in marriage. Elfleda, however, was utterly unconscious of the perfidious plot of her pretended lover, and deferred sending any answer till she had consulted with her son and the nobles of the land.

Wistan was accordingly requested to give an opinion respecting the proposed match, when he gave the following answer:—

"My dearest mother, bear in mind that Berferth, who now seeks you as a wife, is both my cousin and your gossip; that he who received me at the sacred font of baptism, was as my father to a new generation unto life. Attend but to my counsels, and you shall be given to a husband that will never die; for those who marry themselves unto Christ, and accept Him as their bridegroom, shall receive as their dowry a glorious principality in the kingdom of heaven."

"Let it be as you have said, my son," replied the Queen; "I will never wed Berferth, nor any mortal man."

Wistan, assured by his mother of her determination to pass the remnant of her days in virtuous widowhood, revealed to the messengers of Berferth the canonical impediments to any marriage between that prince and the Queen.

Berferth, on receiving the answer to his matrimonial proposition, resolved on vengeance, to effect which occupied his entire thoughts. Under the pretence of peace and affection, he sent to invite the young Prince, his godson, to an interview, who, suspecting no injury, came, with his attendants, unarmed to the spot appointed, called, to this day, "Winstanstow." Thither Berferth also repaired with his followers, but they were all privately armed. At meeting, Berferth, taking the Prince a short distance from his friends, requested permission to embrace him as his godson. "Approach, my son," said he, "and bestow upon me the kiss of peace." Wistan on this walked towards him, saying, "In the name of Holy Peace, that which is God himself, I kiss thee, so that in His name I may be kissed by thee." Berferth, who had at that moment no respect for his King, or regard for the laws of God, stealthily drew his sword, and striking the Prince on his head, while in the act of embracing him, he shattered the skull to pieces, while one of his followers ran the royal victim through the body with a sword. The rest of the young King's attendants were also put to death. This crime was perpetrated June 1st, 849; but the judgment of Heaven fell on Berferth for the deed, who, even on the spot, was seized, it is said, with a raging madness, so that he was never permitted by God either to marry the Queen, or mount to the throne which he desired.[2]

[1] Capgrave.

[2] Concerning St. Wistan, consult William of Malmesbury, book ii., ch. 13; and Harleian MS., 2253, *De Martyrio S. Wistani.* He is commemorated on June 1st.

QUENDRIDA II.

The grand-daughter of Offa's Queen—Her great abilities and the high position she holds in the state — She is left guardian to her young brother Kenelm — Her sister Burganilda attached to the young King—His tutor Ascobert—The traitorous designs of Quendrida on the life of Kenelm—Ascobert agrees to aid her plans — Kenelm's dream — His uneasiness — He informs his nurse, who interprets it — Aware of his danger, he removes to a secure place — The Castle of Kenilworth chosen as his abode—The family of the Kenelms—The hunting excursion to Clint Wood—The murder of the young Prince, and concealment of his body in a pit—Quendrida mounts the throne—Is suspected by the people —Driven from the government, which is given to her uncle Kenulf—She assumes a religious habit, but retains her patrimony, the Abbey of Winchcomb—Touching legend of the revelation at Rome of the death of Kenelm—Discovery of the body—Canonization of the murdered Prince—Chapel built—Quendrida's scorn—The judgment of Heaven on her—Her death.

THE name of Quendrida is unfortunate in its repute; for Quendrida, the grand-daughter of the guilty Queen of Offa, inherited the bad qualities of the degraded Queen who disgraced the high lineage of Charlemagne, which she claimed.

Elfleda, daughter of Offa and Quendrida, after the death of Ethelred, King of Northumberland, had united herself to Kenulf of Mercia, fourth in descent from Wibba, the father of the warlike Penda. Kenulf had succeeded to young Egbert's short reign, and soon became distinguished by the virtue and piety of his conduct, By her marriage with Kenulf, Elfleda had three children, Quendrida, Burganilda, and Kenelm. Another daughter of Kenulf, named Brenna, became Queen of the Picts, but it does not appear whether she was also his daughter by Elfleda, or some former consort.

Even during the lifetime of Kenulf, the Princess Quendrida took her seat in the witenagemote of Mercia; so that it is probable that either some principality had devolved on her by inheritance through her mother, or by gift of her father, or else she was indebted for the honour of a place in the council to her father's partiality and her own talents. In the witenagemote held in London, in 811, Elfleda, her mother, and Quendrida, were both present, as appears from the signatures, among which is that of Quendrida, who styles herself "the King's daughter."

From this fact of Quendrida having been honoured with a seat in the State councils of her father's reign, she must have early entered into, and become acquainted with power, and learned to love that dominion which she afterwards abused.

A monument of Kenulf's piety arose in a stately abbey, at Winch-

[1] Palgrave.

comb, in Gloucestershire, the Mercian capital. Kenulf, at his death, was interred within its sacred walls. He had reigned twenty-four years, and died a natural death, a circumstance worthy of record in those days, leaving his crown to his young son Kenelm. This is recorded in the following quaint lines:—

"In the foure and twentithe yere of his kyngedom
Kenulfe went out of this worlde and to the joye of hevene com;
It was after that oure lord in his moder alyghte,
Eigte hondred yer and neygentene, by a countes rigte,
Seinte Kenelm, his yonge sone, in his sevende yere
Kyng was ymad after him, they he yong were."[1]

On his deathbed Kenulf had besought his eldest daughter Quendrida to take charge of the young Kenelm, his heir, then, as these lines assure us, only seven years of age.[2] In thus entrusting the infant King to Quendrida, Kenulf overlooked the more amiable Burganilda, his younger daughter, and made a false estimate of the character of his children. They were, indeed, very different in disposition; for though the aged King might esteem Quendrida, by her abilities, more competent to fulfil the duties of guardian to her brother, Burganilda is said to have loved the little Kenelm with a sister's affection, even to his life's end;[3] while the ambitious Princess Quendrida planned only how to get rid of the innocent child, who was an obstacle in her path to the sovereignty.[4] The heinous crime which the Mercian Princess apparently meditated from the first, is the more appalling from the exceedingly amiable character of the little King, her brother, which very early disposed him to acts of piety and virtue.[5]

Quendrida began her scheme by attempting to destroy Kenelm by poison, and for that purpose caused a strong draught to be prepared, which she offered to him with her own hand, but it failed to take the effect she had anticipated, so that for this time she was foiled of her intention.

Ascobert, tutor or personal guardian of the young Kenelm, had long beheld Quendrida with a lover's admiration. This man the Princess corrupted from his duty, by the gift of a large sum of money, and a promise that she would favour his suit. As this would render Ascobert the sharer with Quendrida in the regal power, he undertook to put his young charge to death.[6]

About this period the monkish chroniclers inform us that the young King, having fallen asleep, dreamt a miraculous dream. He saw a tree stand by his bedside, and "the height thereof touched heaven, and it shined as bright as gold, and had fair branches full of blossoms and fruit. And on every branch of this tree were tapers of wax burning and lamps alight, which was a glorious sight to behold; and he thought that he climbed upon the tree, and Ascobert, his governor stood beneath and

[1] Vita S. Kenelmi, MS. Coll. Trin. Oxon. No. 57, Arch.

[2] Caxton, Holinshed, Palgrave, Butler, Speed; Brit. Sancta.

[3] Langhornii Chron. [4] Brit. Sancta. [5] Caxton.

[6] Brit. Sancta, Palgrave, Lingard.

hewed down this tree he stood on; and when this tree was fallen down, the holy young King was heavy and sorrowful, and he thought there came a fair bird which flew up to heaven with great joy."

Kenelm, on awaking, in much wonder, related this dream to his nurse Wolwelyn, who, on hearing it, was much grieved, and interpreted it to signify that his sister and the traitor Ascobert had falsely conspired his death; "for," said she, "he hath promised Quendrida to slay thee, and it signifieth that he smiteth down the tree that stood by thy bedside, and the bird that thou sawest fly up to heaven, signifieth thy soul, that angels shall bear up to heaven after thy martyrdom." [1]

Whether any previous observations of the nurse had led her thus to interpret the dream of the young Prince, or whether a supernatural power of divine inspiration, as is asserted, guided her in this interpretation, her admonition was not thrown away on her young charge, who betook himself forthwith to a more secure place of abode. To this circumstance is to be ascribed the first foundation of the noble structure of Kenilworth, a word which literally means King Helme, or Kenelm, his "wearth" or "place of safety." [2] That the young monarch resided there, is plain from the remainder of the particulars of his sad history, which all connect themselves with the immediate neighbourhood. The residence of Kenelm [3] continued to be a royal palace till the reign of Henry III., who granted it to a member of the Kenelm family, "in whose family," says Weever, "it is thought to be continued at this day, in the person of Lord Clinton." He subjoins a curious article on the name of Kenelm, and asserts that all the persons in whose name the word Helme is compounded, of whom he gives a list, were originally of one family.

The youth and innocent life of Kenelm did not, however, influence the feelings of his treasonable guardian. The fatal catastrophe soon arrived. One day Ascobert, pretending to take him out on a hunting excursion, led him astray into a wood, named Clent,[4] where he fell an easy victim. After cutting off his head, the murderer drew the body into a great valley, between two high hills, where he dug a deep pit, into which he threw the royal corpse, and laid the head upon it.[5] This deed accomplished, Asco-

[1] Caxton's Golden Legend. [2] Weever's Ancient Funeral Monuments.

[3] "King Helme, his home" (Sax.), was at one time united to the see of Hereford. Kenilworth, according to Dugdale, was an ancient demesne of the crown, and had in the Saxon times within its precincts a castle, which stood upon a place called Holme Hill.

[4] Caxton's Golden Legend; Langhornii Chron.

[5] A MS. Psalter presented to Queen Mary, in 1553, by Baldwin Smith, a citizen of London, contains the representation of Kenelm, King of Mercia, hunting with his attendants. There is a difference of opinion among authors as to whether accident or design caused the death of the young King; and Malmesbury, who inclines to the former opinion, concisely informs us that his sister Quendrida, without any malicious intention, was the innocent occasion of his death, without, however, relating the particulars of the accident. More modern authors accuse Quendrida of the crime. According to the MS. Psalter, which contains the picture referred to, he was murdered August 16, A. D. 819, and the illuminator agreed with the opinion that Quendrida was author of the crime. A second engraving from the MS. Psalter represents the regicides in the act of throwing the dead body of the King into a pit.—*Strutt.*

bert returned to claim his promised reward from the partner of his guilt. It does not, however, appear that he received any share of the administration, though he became the accepted lover of the guilty Quendrida, who, overjoyed at her success, lost no time in assuming the regal dignity, and at the same time commanded that, upon pain of death, no man should speak of the unfortunate Kenelm. The Queen, thus arrived at the summit of her guilty ambition, was, nevertheless, watched by a Power higher than any on earth. Suspicion had naturally attached itself to her of being author of the late King's death, as the only person benefited by it, but as yet no one dared to accuse her. Still the Mercians disdained the government of a female as much as the West Saxons, and having had an instance of the deposal of a queen by that nation, in the excellent but inefficient Sexburga, wife of Cenwalch, were not slow in availing themselves of the precedent. They accordingly deprived Quendrida of the authority she had usurped, and for which she had not hesitated to shed the innocent blood of her own brother, and placed upon the throne, in her stead, her uncle Ceolwulf.[1]

On this event Quendrida testified some signs of contrition, whether sincere or otherwise, by assuming a nun's habit. Although she had lost her crown, she still retained her patrimonial inheritance, the Abbey of Winchelcomb, bequeathed to her by her father, over which she now assumed the government. She could only have kept the supreme power a very short time, for the death of her father Kenulf, and accession of Kenelm, are fixed in the year 819; and Ceolwulf, who, succeeded herself, and reigned *two years*, must also have begun to reign at the same date, for he was deposed in 821, by Beornwulf, a Mercian, whose only title to the crown was opulence and power. If, however, as Holinshed tells us, Ceolwulf did not mount the throne till 823, the length of Quendrida's reign would be extended by several years.

After her deposition, Quendrida is frequently mentioned in the English councils with the titles of "Abbess" and "Heiress of Kenulf." That she was a nun at the time of the Council of Cloveshoe, appears also from one of them. She was, however, compelled by King Beornwulf to compound with Wulfred, Archbishop of Canterbury, for the land which her father had wrested from him.[2]

The death of the ill-fated Kenelm has formed the favourite theme of many a monkish chronicler, and given birth to the following touching legend. His fate had been revealed at Rome by the appearance of a white dove, which alighted on the altar of St. Peter's, when the Pope was at mass, and let fall from its beak a scroll, on which were inscribed, the following words in letters of gold:—"In Clent, in Cowbage, Kenelme, kynge born, lyeth under a thorne, his head off-shorne." Mass being over, the Pope showed the scroll to the people, but no one present except an Englishman, could inform him of its meaning. On which he sent an embassy to England, to Archbishop Wulfred and the clergy, desiring that the spot called Cowbage, in the wood of Clent, named in the scroll, should be searched throughout. The papal mandate was obeyed, and

[1] Lingard. [2] Ibid.

the result was the discovery of the body of the young King. It follows that many miracles are said to have attended the discovery of his holy relics. The legend goes on to tell how a white cow was instrumental in directing attention to the spot so much sought for. "This cow belonged to a poor widow, and being daily driven into Clent Wood, was used to find its way to the valley where Kenelm was buried, and though it remained without nourishment throughout the whole day, at night returned with the other animals in better condition than they, and would yield more milk."[1] The name of Cowbage had been given to the valley in consequence, and the fact had become so well known, that the Archbishop and his friends found the place without difficulty.

The people of Mercia dared not remove the body, for fear of Quendrida's anger; but the Archbishop and his friends, less scrupulous, transferred the mangled remains of the murdered monarch with great solemnity to the Abbey of Winchcomb, where they were enshrined, and from that time treated as those of a saint; Kenelm being shortly after canonized by the supreme Pontiff.[2] The record proceeds in the true spirit of

---

[1] Caxton.

[2] The Chapel of St. Kenelm is mentioned by Nash in his History of Worcester, as an ancient structure on the south-east side of Clent Hill, in the parish of Hales Owen, an insulated district belonging to Shropshire, although part of the chapel-yard is said to be in Staffordshire: the author remarks, "It is no easy matter to reconcile the tradition of the place (which fixes the spot where the murder was committed, and the body first interred at Cowback or Cowdale, within the parish of Clent), with the legendary account of it; for the legend affirms that a spring of water gushed out on the discovery of the royal infant's body. Now, in the field still called Cowbeck there is no spring of water, and yet not only long tradition has determined that for the spot where Kenelm was murdered, but the words above cited [one version of the legend runs: "In Clent Cow-batche, Kenelme, king bearne, lyeth under a thorne, heaved and bereaved."] point it out expressly to have been in Clent Cowback. [Both Higden and Butler say that Cowdale Pasture, where the well was situated, was in the south part of Staffordshire, on the borders of Worcestershire.] At the east end of St. Kenelm's Chapel is a fine and plentiful spring, and, till of late years, there was a well (now, indeed, filled up) handsomely coped with stone, and much resorted to, both before and since the Reformation, by the superstitious vulgar for the cure of sore eyes and other maladies. This well is mentioned in a court-roll of Romsley Manor, second of Edward IV., when the jury present "quod Johanna Haye occupat cenutærium et fontem St. Kenelmi, &c." Now, unless we suppose that the site of the present chapel was the ancient Cowback, and the limits of Clent since contracted into a narrower compass (for both the chapel and spring, together with part of the cemetery, are now within the manor of Romsley and parish of Hales Owen), we must either entirely reject the legend, supported as it is by the remains of the holy well and the chapel, which still bears the name of St. Kenelm's, and affords besides a very ancient specimen of rude Saxon sculpture over the south door, corresponding with that early age; or else we must adhere to the traditionary spot of his murder and interment, the present Cowback; and in that case it will be difficult to account for the holy well, and the erecting of the chapel at the distance of near a mile from the true place of interment."

"My opinion on this obscure point is, that Kenelm was murdered in the field now called Cowback, but the corpse was buried in or adjoining to the site of the present chapel, on the erecting of which, to the honour of this royal youth (who was soon after canonized for a saint), and the great resort of persons who came thither to make their offerings at his altar, the artful priest who officiated there,

monkish credulity, "That when the saint's body was brought to the abbey, the bells sounded without the help of man, and rung of their own accord. Quendrida, the abbess, hearing the noise then inquired, 'What all this ringing meant?' whereupon she was informed that the body of her brother Kenelm was being brought into the abbey; to which she answered scornfully, 'That is as true as both mine eyen ben falle upon this boke.' And on this, beholding with indignation a solemn procession of clergy and people pass by her window to honour his funeral, she took up her Psalter, and read, as it were, against him the imprecation of the 108th Psalm, in which, when she had proceeded as far as that verse, 'This is the work of them who defame me to the Lord, and who speak evil against my soul,' her eyes suddenly fell out of her head upon the very verse she was reading, and stained the book with her blood. Quendrida's primer was kept for a testimony of this miracle, in the Abbey of Winchcomb, till the dissolution of that house, it still retaining the marks of her blood." Not long after the Abbess-Queen expired most wretchedly, and her body unhonoured by funeral pomp, was cast forth, to use the words of the legend, "into a foul mire:" and who is there that reads the record of Quendridas's crimes and their deserved punishment, but must regard the death of the young Kenelm as enviable in comparison, and perceive that, even on this earth, there is a retributive justice awarded to the guilty!

finding a spring of water in the chapel-yard, which might possibly have some medicinal virtue in it, most likely trumped up this tale, which, in those days of ignorance and superstition, easily met with credit, and thereby drew a still greater number of persons hither, in hopes to find a cure for their bodies as well as their souls.

"With regard to the fabric, no part of it except the south door appears older than Henry the Third's time, and I am rather inclined to think it of later date; but the arch and columns of the south door are undoubtedly part of the old Saxon chapel which was erected here soon after the discovery of King Kenelm's body.

"As this chapel was never privileged with the right of sepulture, no monuments or inscriptions occur, nor are there any arms or other ornaments in the windows. The tower is a very elegant piece of Gothic architecture, and rudely adorned with niches and pinnacles.

"On the outside of the chapel wall, fronting the south, is carved a rude figure of a child, with two fingers of the right hand lifted up in the ancient form of giving the benediction. Above the head of the figure is carved a crown, which projects several inches from the wall. No doubt the whole was meant for a representation of St. Kenelm." [Nash's Worcestershire, copied from Antiquities of Shropshire: see also in Nash's work, p. 107, and in Gentleman's Magazine, vol. lxxii. p. 1177, a picture of the Chapel of St. Kenelm.]

OSBURGA AND ETHELSWYTHA,

QUEENS OF ETHELWULF AND BURHRED.

The mother of Alfred the Great — Earl Oslac, her father, cup-bearer to King Ethelwulf—Wars with the Danes—The King first intended for the Church—His choice of the cup-bearer's daughter—Her virtues and industry—Needlework of the Anglo-Saxon ladies — The five sons of Osburga — Her daughter Ethelswytha married to the King of Mercia—The title of Queen revived—The Danes overrun Mercia—Subdue Burhred, and force him to abandon his country—He dies at Rome—His Queen follows him, and dies on the road—Alfred's infancy — Prayer of Osburga — The story of the illuminated book of Saxon verse—The children's anxiety—Alfred's resolution and success—The pilgrimage to Rome of Ethelwulf, accompanied by his young son — Uncertainty respecting Osburga—Ethelwulf's return with Judith, the French princess—Death of Osburga.

No biography could be more interesting than that of the mother of the great Alfred, the most endeared monarch of the Anglo-Saxon race; a true hero, whose deeds are authenticated, and who is not a visionary object of the admiration of posterity, like the renowned champion, King Arthur, of romantic celebrity. Unfortunately, too little of her to whom Alfred owed his existence is known. Osburga was the daughter of Earl Oslac, a descendant of Whitgar, the nephew of Cerdic; consequently her station, though inferior to that of the monarch whose wife she became, was dignified, and her birth equal. Her father Oslac filled the post of cup-bearer to King Ethelwulf, which was one only entrusted to a personage of great fidelity, and in whom the utmost confidence could be placed. This was important in an age when poison was so frequently resorted to by enemies, to rid themselves of those they dreaded or hated.

Ethelwulf had succeeded to the kingdom of Wessex after the death of his celebrated father Egbert, who had had to wage continual war with those redoubted invaders the Northmen, and, though often victorious, left his kingdom still threatened by them on every side. Ethelwulf's character was by no means warlike: he had been educated by a priest, Swithun or Swithin, of Winchester,[1] and had even, it is said, taken the post of sub-deacon of the same church when he was called to the throne. His life of seclusion probably rendered him, at the beginning of his reign, little ambitious, and he was content to choose as his wife, instead of some foreign princess of higher pretensions, the good and pious Osburga, the daughter of his cup-bearer, whom he had probably opportunities of knowing and esteeming.

---

[1] William of Malmesbury.

As Osburga is never named by historians as remarkable for personal attractions, her merit, no doubt, recommended her to the notice of the sovereign; her "industry," as well as her piety, is, however, the theme of all the chroniclers;[1] and from the few anecdotes which have been handed down respecting her, there is reason to suppose that she, like many princesses who preceded her, was acquainted with literature, which, at that time had attained a very remarkable height of excellence, owing to the exertions of learned churchmen.[2] It would have been interesting to posterity, if the writers, who mention Queen Osburga's diligence, had described some of the elaborate work which occupied her leisure; such performances being considered so important, that a minute account of them was not looked upon as beneath the dignity of history. There have come down to us many charming and curious specimens of Saxon art in the form of needlework,[3] of which details are given; and from the talent in the family of Osburga, her own may be surmised. We know that some of her great-grandchildren, daughters of Edward the Elder, were particularly noted for their skill in this feminine accomplishment, and that her piety also was inherited in an eminent degree by her children.

Queen Osburga had five sons,[4] all of whom, except the first, who died in infancy, successively wore the English crown after their father's death. The youngest of these princes was born A. D. 849, at Wanating, or Wantage,[5] a royal manor-house of the Anglo-Saxon monarchs, where Osburga was at that time residing. This child, no other than he who was afterwards known as Alfred the Great, seems from his earliest infancy, to have awakened the tenderest interest in those around him, especially of his fond parents, whose favorite he is reported to have been. As soon as the Prince was old enough to receive the instructions of any preceptor, he was consigned by his mother to the care of St. Swithin,[6] then Bishop of Winchester.

Besides the five sons of Osburga, she had a daughter named Ethelswytha,[7] who was probably one of the eldest-born of her children: she was married to Burhred, King of Mercia, who had solicited the aid of her father against the refractory Britons, then under Roderick the Great, ravaging his kingdom. The powerful King Ethelwulf, joining his forces with those of Burhred, however, compelled the Britons to obedience; and the marriage of Ethelswytha took place at Chippenham, in Wilt-

---

[1] Palgrave, Turner, Kemble.

[2] Asser calls Osburga "fœmina nobilis, ingenis, nobilio et genera."

[3] Standards were woven by Danish ladies, of which strange marvels are related by Asser.

[4] Bayle, Raleigh. [5] In Berkshire. [6] Spelman.

[7] The names of Saxon women were generally significant of some circumstance in their own destiny, or the history of their family. Thus, Æthelswytha signified *very noble;* Selethrytha, *a good threatener;* Elfhilda, the *elf of battle;* Beage, the *bracelet;* Ethelfritha, *noble and powerful;* Adeleve, the *noble wife;* Eadburh, the *happy pledge;* Heaburge, *tall as a castle;* Eadfled, the *happy pregnancy;* Adelfleda, the *noble pregnancy;* Ælfgiva, the *elf-favour;* Eadgifa, the *happy gift;* Æthelgifa, the *noble gift;* Wynfreda, the *peace of man;* Æthelheld, the *noble war-goddess;* Ælfthyth, *threatening as an elf.* [Turner.]

shire, with great pomp and rejoicing, during the festival of Easter,—the union being a highly popular one.

It was on this occasion that both Ethelswytha and her mother Osburga received the title of Queen, and were allowed all the honours and dignities annexed to the rank, forfeited through the crimes of Eadburga, daughter of Offa, King of Mercia, and since then not accorded, by the Saxon law, to the wives of their sovereigns.[1] Ethelswytha afterwards subscribed her name, in conjunction with her husband, in the manner exemplified in the Old Register, at Worcester, as "Ethelswyth Regina." This Queen also affords rather a singular instance of a Queen of England being permitted by law, in that day, as at present, to give a contract as a *femme sole.* In the Chartulerie of the Abbey of Abingdon, she alone bestows lands, by charter, to Cuthwulf, her servant.

Ethelswytha shared her husband's subordinate throne for twenty-two years; at the end of which time the still-encroaching Danes, removing from Lindsay to Repton-upon-Trent, took up their quarters there for the winter, and compelled Burhred to fly from his dominions, which they farmed out to Kilwulf, one of Burhred's household servants, contingent on his surrendering it to them at command. All Mercia was now overrun by the Danes, under their King Healfdene; their insolence, increased with their successes, and their ravages and cruelties were extreme. Burhred, unable further to contend with such foes, left his kingdom, and sought an asylum at Rome, where he died very shortly after his arrival, and was buried in the church of Santa Maria, belonging to the Saxon

---

[1] Osburga herself was the second queen who had been denied the privileges of royalty in Wessex; neither enjoying the royal title, nor the seat by her husband's side in the chair of state, which probably encouraged an idea of her birth being ignoble. [Speed.] The first who suffered from the crimes of her predecessor by this diminution of the dignity usually accorded to the queenly state, was Redburga, wife of Egbert, and mother of Ethelwulf, who during the long period of thirty years, in which her husband governed Wessex, never was permitted to assume the title and state of the queen-consort. It would have been strange indeed if Ethelwulf had insisted on these grants in favour of his wife which the people had refused to his mother, who, for aught we know, might have been yet alive when Osburga became his queen. The character of Redburga, however, differed very much indeed from that of her pious and gentle daughter-in-law; she is, in fact, compared, by one of our old writers, to Jezebel, for inciting her husband Egbert, to whom the title Ahab is applied, to one of the most remarkable steps of his reign, by which she proved she possessed the influence over her husband, denied in the honours she ought to have received, though exerted in a bad cause.

At Redburga's suggestion, Egbert forbade the Welsh, on pain of death, to come beyond Offa's dyke, the boundary between England and Wales. This edict commanded that all the Britons, or Welsh, should, with their wives and children, depart out of their lands, cities, towns, and castles, in England, "to Wild Walshe above Offa ditch," and also to Cornwall, Scotland, and Ireland. After which edict (issued about A. D. 766) had been complied with, Egbert gave the land the name of England.

The above deed is attributed to a desire to gain over the territories of the Britons into their own possession, and the writer styles the Saxon King Egbert "cruel," and his Queen Redburga "his cruel and covetous wife." [Oliver Mathew's Abbreviation of divers true and auncient Brutaine Chronicles.]

school.[1] Ethelswytha, who had not at first accompanied her husband, whom she hoped some fortunate revolution would eventually restore to his throne, finding that no chance of the ascendency of his better fortune remained, determined to join him in his exile; and we learn from the Saxon Chronicle, that in the year 888 she set out on her pilgrimage for that purpose, accompanied by the Ealdorman Beeke, who carried with him the alms of King Alfred, and of the people of Wessex, to the city of Rome. It was not destined that Ethelswytha should reach the goal she sought, for she was taken ill and died on the way. She was interred either at Pavia or Ticino.[2] Such was the history of the only daughter of Ethelwulf and Osburga.

Osburga, after her daughter's marriage, which probably took place when she was extremely young, devoted herself to the care of her sons; and of her is told the charming anecdote, so often repeated, and so full of touching interest, of her exciting her youngest boy to learn.

It is recorded that Osburga was one day seated in the chamber with her children, holding in her hand an illuminated book of Saxon poetry[3] (how precious would be the volume, could it be recovered!), which the brothers were eagerly looking over. Observing their admiration, and taking advantage of it, their mother observed, playfully, "Whichever of you shall first learn this book, shall have it as a gift." All were delighted at the idea, Alfred, the youngest, in particular, who, looking up into her eyes, gravely asked her if she were really in earnest. She assured him that she meant what she said, as she desired to see her sons learned men. Upon this the child begged that the book might be entrusted to him to carry to his master, and he shortly after returned with it, able to recite all the poems it contained. Of course the beautiful prize was awarded by the gratified Osburga, who hailed this first indication of her favourite son's perseverance[4] with maternal delight!

Alfred required all a mother's care in his early life, as he was afflicted with a painful malady from an infant; and many were the vows offered up for his recovery at various shrines. Osburga's prayers, at a certain church in Cornwall, were supposed to have, at length, relieved him of his complaint to a great extent. As his health, however, was always delicate,

---

[1] Saxon Chronicle. [2] Ingulph.

[3] Writing books, as a monastic employment, was usual in the earliest times. Among British monks, David had a study, or writing-room, and began the Gospel of St. John, in golden letters, with his own hands. The Anglo-Saxon artists possessed eminent skill in the execution of their books, and the character which they used had the honour of giving rise to the modern small beautiful Roman letter.

In the statutes of the regular canons are two verses, specifying that they had simple girdles, tablets, combs, needles, thread, a style, paper or parchment, ink, and a pen-case. Du Cange mentions a singular kind of scribes, called Biodiatores, who wrote books and letters in the manner of embroiderers, so lightly representing the object that it almost escaped the sight.

The custom of carrying a pen behind the ear is ancient. In the Life of St. Odo is the following passage: "He saw a pen sticking above his ear, in the manner of a writer." — Fosbrooke's British Monachism.

[4] This anecdote is sometimes told of Judith, the step-mother of Alfred.

it might have been the cause of his father resolving to make him the partner of his pilgrimage to Rome, though the child was then only five years of age, and the charge of him must have been a most anxious one. Osburga saw him depart, no doubt, with painful hope; and the result of her husband's journey, however happy for her son, showed that her presentiment of evil was but too well founded as regarded herself.

It is unexplained for what reason, at this time Osburga appears no longer to share the throne of Ethelwulf; whether they parted in fulfilment of some vow, common at this period, which might have had reference to the health of Alfred, or whether, as was equally common, she was repudiated, that her husband might be at liberty to marry the Princess Judith, of France, remains in uncertainty. Some writers have asserted that, though no longer acknowledged Queen, Osburga, after this marriage, resumed her duties, and superintended the education of her children,[1] which is not impossible, as the new Queen was only twelve years old, but is little probable.

Asser, the contemporary and friend of Alfred, wrote his biography, yet, strangely enough, he tells nothing of the remaining history of Osburga. That she died before her favorite son became king is certain, and it is most likely before the death of her husband; but this is left to conjecture, though some assert that it was to divert his grief for her loss that the pilgrimage to Rome of Ethelwulf was undertaken.[2]

Her tomb was shown at Coventry, where her memory was cherished, and she was canonized as a saint, according to the custom of the day. From this circumstance it may be thought that she retired into a convent, and died in the odour of sanctity.

---

[1] Lappenberg.

[2] Leland calls her St. Osburga, and her death has been stated as happening in 855.

JUDITH OF FRANCE,

SECOND QUEEN OF ETHELWULF

Motives of Ethelwulf for his visits to the Court of Charles the Bald — Beauty of the Princess Judith — Attachment of Count Baldwin of Flanders — Ethelwulf's offer accepted — Splendid Marriage of Judith to Ethelwulf — Royal presents — Ethelwulf takes his bride to England — They are ill received — Ealstan, Bishop of Sherburne, excites Ethelbald to rebellion — Offence given to the Church — Ethelwulf proclaims Judith Queen, in despite of opposition — Ethelwulf yields to his son to avoid bloodshed — Judith crowned — Prayers on the occasion — Alfred and his young mother-in-law study together in retirement — Ethelwulf's death — Ethelbald forcibly marries his widow — Displeasure of the people and the clergy — He becomes penitent — Separates from Judith — She sells her dower, and travels, on her return to her father's court, through Flanders — Meeting of Judith and Baldwin — Consequences of her stay — Anger of Charles the Bald—She is placed in a convent—Rescued by her brothers—Elopes with Baldwin—Enmity and final forgiveness of the French King — The children of Judith — Matilda, wife of William of Normandy—Ballad of the imaginary adventures of the "King's Daughter."

It has been already related that Ethelwulf made a pilgrimage to Rome, taking the capital of France on his way, both as he went and as he returned, with his young son Alfred.

The beautiful Princess Judith might have attracted his visit on the second occasion, as policy had directed his first. His piety led him to all the celebrated shrines throughout the country, and there were few churches at which he did not offer up his vows. He passed a year in Rome, not only in pious exercises, but in viewing all the remains of the former glory of the Imperial City, even then filled with the ruins of its greatness.

Probably the acquaintance he then made with the habits of foreign nations, and the desire to see his own country improved in learning and civilization, might be his inducement to the step he afterwards took in uniting himself with foreign interests. If Osburga were still living it is difficult to reconcile his conduct with his former attachment to the mother of his children.

When, in 855, the English king arrived at the court of Charles the Bald, accompanied by his youngest son, Alfred, then in his sixth year, the Princess Judith, his destined mother-in-law, was only between eleven and twelve years of age. No overtures were, however, at that period made respecting the French Princess, but on Ethelwulf's departure from the court of her father, the train of the royal pilgrims was attended, by his orders, with a truly regal retinue of Frenchmen to the borders of his realm.

Ethelwulf, having arrived at the Imperial City, had the satisfaction of presenting to the Pope the valuable gifts he brought thither for his acceptance. Alfred had, young as he was, already paid one visit to Rome, having been sent there by his father to be consecrated King by the Sovereign Pontiff. On that occasion Leo had received the little English Prince as his own adopted son, and the gifts now offered by Ethelwulf to the Pope were intended as an acknowledgment of his personal gratitude for the Pope's generous behaviour towards his favourite child. These articles consisted of a crown of pure gold, weighing four pounds, two golden tassels called Bancas, a sword adorned with pure gold, two golden images, and four Saxon dishes of silver gilt; besides this there were several gorgeous dresses. These various presents are enumerated by Anastasius, a contemporary of Ethelwulf. Besides these offerings to the Pope, Ethelwulf made a perpetual grant of three hundred mancuses[1] or marks per annum to the Roman See, one-third of which sum was to be appropriated by the Pope, another to the support of the lamps of St. Peter, and the residue for the lamps of St. Paul's. A donation in gold was likewise presented to all the Roman clergy and nobles, and one in silver to the people.[2] The English King remained twelve months at Rome, during which he rebuilt the Saxon school which had been founded by his predecessor Ina, King of the West Saxons, and which, through the carelessness of some English residents, had the year before been destroyed by fire; and as a proof of the humane disposition of this King towards the English, it is deserving of mention here, that when he learnt it was customary for public penitents and exiles to be bound with iron, he obtained an order from the Pope that no Englishman should be put into bonds for penance.

Ethelwulf revisited the court of France in the month of July, 856, and it was then that he became a suitor for the hand of the beautiful Judith. Young, however, as this Princess was, she had already become an object of interest in the eyes of one who was by nature gifted with rare personal endowments, possessed of ambition, and capable of the highest undertakings. Baldwin of Flanders, or "the Forester," was as much distinguished by his courage as by his strength of arm, from which he was surnamed the Iron-Arm or Iron-Hand; he was of tall and noble stature, and his countenance beautiful. He had entered the field for the first time under the command of Charles the Bald, in the war that King had undertaken against the Saracens, who had invaded the borders of

[1] The value of a Saxon *mancus* or *mearc* was thirty pence, and it was equal to six shillings of their money, though, about A. D. 1194, it rose to the value of thirteen shillings. That the Saxons coined gold money is certain, and the mancus was their only piece of gold. They were accustomed to reckon by the pound, the shilling, and the mancus. The mancus was about the weight of our present half-crown. -- Spelman, Account of Gold and Silver Coins. Asser does not say whether they were mancuses of gold or silver. Hoveden calls them mancuses of silver pennies.

[2] In the Camere of Raphael, in the Sistine chapel at the Vatican, among the pictures of princes who have been benefactors to the Holy See, is one bearing the inscription, "King Astulphus, under Pope Leo IV., made Britain tributary to the Blessed Peter." Leo reigned from 847 to 855, during which time Ethelwulf was King of England.

Guienne, and also against the Normans, who had made several inroads into the French kingdom. In these wars Baldwin obtained much distinction, and was accounted the most valiant warrior of the time. Having a situation near the King's person, he was often in the habit of seeing the Princess Judith,[1] whose notice he attracted by his assiduity and attention. So entirely did Baldwin win her respect and affection, that before the period of Ethelwulf's visit to France, we learn that he was betrothed to her in marriage. Nevertheless, Charles the Bald, for state reasons, hesitated not to break off this earlier contract in favor of the more splendid alliance with the King of England, setting at naught every obstacle which intervened on either side in a match more particularly unsuitable from the great disparity in age of the parties. Accordingly Ethelwulf and Judith were betrothed and married[2] in the following October. The ceremony of the espousals took place in the palace of Verberie, when the nuptial benediction was bestowed by Hincmar, Bishop of Rheims, who at the same time placed upon the head of the little bride a diadem, and hailed her as a queen. An account of this interesting ceremony of Judith's marriage and coronation, when a double benediction was pronounced on her, first as a spouse and then as a queen, is yet extant. The magnificence of Judith's crown is even mentioned in a prayer on the occasion.

Presents worthy of the royal personages concerned in this marriage were mutually given, after which Ethelwulf determined on his return to England,[3] and took shipping with his youthful bride. During his stay at the French court, the news he had received from England was of a nature to disturb even bridal festivities. An insurrection had been raised against him, by Ealstan, Bishop of Sherborne, and Eanwulf, Earl of Somerset, at the head of which his eldest son Ethelbald had placed himself.[4] Ealstan, to whom Ethelwulf had been indebted for his own prosperity, had become his enemy on finding his influence on the decline, and incited Ethelbald to rebellion, on the plea that his father, who lived the life of a monk, ought to pass the residue of his days in religious seclusion, as he had begun them, and give up the government in his favour, as Ina and Cadwalla had done, who, like Ethelwulf, had gone on pilgrimages to Rome, but had first abdicated their crowns. Ethelbald had expected, when his brother Athelstan died, that his father would have made him King of Kent; but finding not only that this was not done, but that Alfred, his father's favorite, was consecrated King by the Pope, he feared Ethelwulf intended to prefer him as his successor on the throne. A natural thirst after power, and the dictates of an ill-disposed mind, combined to draw him over to the schemes of Ealstan; and the people were so much disaffected by the absence of their monarch, and the prospect of an infant heir to the throne, that these considerations, added to the unpopular nature of the new match entered into by Ethelwulf, prepared the way for a revolt. When, therefore, the newly-married pair returned to their dominions, the rebels went so far as to prohibit the

[1] Marcus d'Assigny's Hist. of the Earls of Flanders. [1] Sharon Turner.
[3] Asser. [4] Milton, Holinshed, Turner.

King's entrance into his realm; taking for their ostensible pretext, that Ethelwulf had not only dignified his new wife with the title of Queen, without the consent of the country, but had eaten at the same table with her, and placed her by his side in a chair of state, by which he had violated the law made by the West Saxons on the death of their King Bertric; by which they considered themselves absolved from their allegiance; and Ealstan and Ethelbald forbade him to enter England with his outlandish wife.[1] Everything appeared to threaten civil war,[2]—the father and son were opposed at the head of either party—when the friends of both interfered to prevent bloodshed, and it was agreed that Ethelbald should receive from his father the whole of the ancient kingdom of Wessex, which was the western division of his territories, while the King himself should govern the eastern portion, comprehending Kent, Essex, and Sussex:[3] the latter was the district the late King Athelstan had enjoyed, and by far the least considerable portion. Some of Ethelwulf's courtiers representing this to him, and wishing to persuade him not to sign the treaty with Ethelbald, the excellent monarch replied, that "he would not purchase the territories he had ceded to his son at the price of civil warfare;" and added prophetically, that "even could he so obtain them, Ethelbald would soon recover them through his death."[4] On one point, however, Ethelwulf was less placable—he insisted on the honours due to his Queen Judith, whom he continued to treat with the same respect and affection, notwithstanding the displeasure it occasioned in the kingdom.[5]

Amid the general dissatisfaction at the infringement of the West Saxon law, which pronounced it illegal for a Queen of England to wear the diadem of state, Ethelwulf convened the three estates of his kingdom, to sanction the ceremony of Judith's coronation, as well as to ratify the instrument by which he had bound himself and his people to pay over a tribute to the Holy See.

The ceremony of Judith's coronation[6] was performed with all possible

---

[1] Milton.

[2] To use the words of Dr. Lingard:—"It is some confirmation of the story told by Asser, that while, from the reign of Offa to the extinction of the Mercian monarchy, we have many undisputed charters, subscribed by the consorts of the Kings of Mercia, with the title of Regina, there is not one in which any consort of a King of Wessex does the like during the same period. The most early instance in which that title is given to a wife of a King of Wessex, in any contemporary document, occurs, if I mistake not, in the reign of Edmund (anno 945), when Ethelgive, making her will, declares her intentions to her lord the King, and her lady the Queen, and bequeaths to her lady the Queen thirty mancuses of gold, and her land at Westwick. It has been supposed that queens were crowned, because in some MSS. the order for the coronation of a queen follows that for the coronation of a king; but this proves only that both orders were contained in the original from which the copy was made."—Hist. and Antiquities of the Anglo-Saxon Church, by Lingard, vol. ii., p. 34.

[3] Hume. [4] Rapin. [5] Raleigh.

[6] The particular sort of crown worn by the early Queens of England has not been described. Alfred and his successors, to Edward the Confessor, wore the commonest and most ancient form of crown. Edred and Edmond Ironside had coronets like those of our earls, having fewer points, but those points raised higher

solemnity: the form of the service used on this interesting occasion has been preserved by Du Chesne, and is worthy of notice, as supplying the only record extant of the phraseology used at the inauguration of a queen-consort.

The conclusion of the marriage ceremony constitutes the earlier portion of this form. After the ring has been given, with the exhortation, "Take this ring, the sign of fidelity and love, and the bond of marriage union, that no man may separate those whom God hath joined, who liveth and reigneth for ever," the Queen is blessed in the following words:—

"We invoke thee, Holy Lord, Omnipotent Father, Eternal God, for this thine handmaiden, whom, in the divine dispensation of thy Providence, thou hast caused to grow up from her youthful blossoming to this joyful time. Give her richly of thy fear, that she may go on full of truth before thee and all men, from day to day, unto better things. May she receive, rejoicing with us, largely of thy heavenly grace, from the kingdom above; and thence, being guarded by the strength of thy mercy from all adversity, be deemed worthy to live for ever."

The rather long and elegant prayer offered at the anointing the head of the young and beautiful Queen, here followed, in which it was supplicated that she might possess "the simplicity and meekness of the dove;" after which the coronation took place in the following words:—

"May the Lord crown thee with glory and honour, and place upon thy head a crown of spiritual precious stones, that whatever may be typified by the brightness of gold, or the changeful splendour of gems, may ever shine forth in thy life and conduct; which may He grant, to whom be honour and glory, world without end."

Then follow the blessings, thus:—

"Bless, O Lord, this thine handmaiden, thou who rulest the kingdoms of kings through all generations.

"Accept the offerings of her hands, and may she be replenished with the blessings of the fruits of the earth, of the heavens, of the dews, of the

---

and pearled at the top. In some coins of Harold, that King wears a diadem of pearls round a helmet; which was common with other West Saxon Kings, who sometimes wore it on their bare heads. The coins of Offa represent that monarch with a crown of pearls and other materials, similar to that used by Constantine the Great; and his successors, Berthulf, Burghred, and Kenwulf, wore the same kind of diadem. Aldulph, in the seventh century, wore the ordinary plain fillet or diadem, when King of East Anglia. — Selden's Titles of Honour.

The coins of Alfred represent his head encircled with a simple diadem, after the most common and ancient fashion; and there is not an instance among the Anglo-Saxons of any imperial crown till Edward the Confessor, who had a crown much like that of the Eastern Emperors. [Notes of Spelman.]

Spelman tells us, that in the arched room in the cloisters of Westminster Abbey, where the ancient regalia of the kingdom are kept, upon a box, which is the cabinet to the most ancient crown, is an inscription, as follows: "Hæc est princi palior corona quâ coronabantur Reges Ælfredus, Edwardus, &c.," and the crown is of a very ancient work, with flowers, adorned with stones of somewhat a plain setting. This, by the inscription, appearing to have been the crown of Alfred and his successors, is to be supposed to have been made by his orders, and that when he was become universal King of the Heptarchy

depths, from the heights of the ancient mountains, and from the eternal hills.

"May the blessing of him who dwelt in the bush come upon her head. Grant to her showers from heaven, the fatness of the earth, abundance of corn and wine, that their people and their posterity may obey them, and this nation bring honour to her and to her children."

The service concludes with a short prayer, probably the same still said after the Communion, and truly beautiful and simple as it is, claims no small interest from the fact of having been in use among our ancestors no less than a thousand years ago.

Ethelwulf and Judith, after these ceremonies were over, retired into Kent, where they resided in a state of privacy better suited to the tastes of both, than the glare and splendour of public festivities. Ethelwulf had rightly appreciated the character of Judith, when he bestowed on her the queenly honours which, next to his own affections, he deemed essential to her happiness, and to the maintenance of her dignity in the eyes of his people. However just that law which had emanated from the crimes of Eadburga, and was expressive of the national abhorrence of caprice and cruelty, he considered it unjust that the young, innocent, and royally-descended Judith, should be, for that reason, deprived of her deserved rights. The grave insult offered to both himself and his young bride on their arrival in England, must have been deeply felt both by the young Queen and her more mature consort. If, however, Ethelwulf had in the first instance offended his people, by conferring on a foreigner the forfeited distinctions of queen-consort, they were afterwards induced to acquiesce in his wishes by their love for himself, which his sweetness of disposition had obtained, so that in a short time, all objections ceasing, Judith appears to have enjoyed undisputed her royal prerogative of sitting in the chair of state by her husband's side.[1]

The anecdote before related in the Life of Queen Osburga, respecting the first learning of Alfred the Great, can scarcely be referable to Judith, as she was almost a child herself when the young Prince first came under her notice; and as he is spoken of as singularly precocious, his learning at five years old is not extraordinary; whereas, if he was twelve, as some assert, before he learnt to read, there is a difficulty in crediting the astonishing capacity he so early is said to have displayed. Ethelwulf, his father, had been instructed by the same personage to whom his son's education was entrusted; and as his health was delicate, like most sickly children, he most probably began learning very early. Judith had come from a court infinitely more refined than that of England, and being so nearly his own age, could enter into the precocious boy's studies, and no doubt assisted them; the ladies of her time and nation being well accomplished, although Alfred complains of the ignorance of his countrymen in general, when he came to the crown. There exists, doubtless, some confusion of dates, which has caused the characteristic story told by Asser, to be attributed indifferently to the mother and step-mother of Alfred. It is certain, that Judith's stay in England was but short, even

[1] Selden's Titles of Honour.

though she was twice Queen; but a few years at so early an age, and with children of great genius, can do wonders when the seed is once well sown.

Ethelwulf survived the partition of his dominions only two years, which period he passed in acts of justice and charity. The reign of Ethelwulf terminated A. D. 857, after he had sat twenty years on the throne, and his remains were interred in the Cathedral of St. Swithin, at Winchester.

No children remained by his marriage with Judith, and the dominions over which the King had ruled, were left by his will to his second son Ethelbert, and after his death, to Ethelred, his younger brother, in case of whose decease they were to devolve on Alfred. This was, in the end, the order in which they were inherited by the Princes, and finally, as will be seen in the Life of Alfred's Queen, were divided by him amongst his own family. The three younger sons of Ethelwulf had already shown themselves worthy of their parentage; but Ethelbald, the eldest, had not only rendered himself hated by the people for his arbitrary government and profligacy, but for the unfilial conduct he had displayed to his father. No sooner was Ethelwulf dead, than Ethelbald took advantage of the unprotected state of the widowed Queen, who, then little more than fourteen, was left exposed to the trials and dangers of foreign enmity. Her extreme youth, her great beauty, and the disparity of age between her and the late King, may well excuse her, even if she herself consented to the proposal of Ethelbald to make her, immediately on his father's death, his queen.

Turner, in his History of the Anglo-Saxons, refers to the Saxon Chronicle and Bede, as authorities for supposing that by law a son might wed his father's widow, and a brother his sister-in-law; but in these cases there is ample proof that the act was not according to law, but in contradiction to it, from the open indignation expressed by the people, and especially the priests, when the violent and arbitrary Prince, in spite of all opposition, announced his will.

This step is rendered the more remarkable, from the fact that Ethelbald had been the most forward in opposition to the entrance of Judith into the country, after her nuptials with Ethelwulf. Liberty of choice was of course denied to Judith, and she probably saw the propriety of yielding with a good grace to necessity.[1]

The second nuptials of Judith were accordingly celebrated at Chester, greatly to the disgust of the nation.

If the marriage of Ethelwulf with the French Princess had given offence, that of his son with the widow was infinitely more disliked; and the clergy, taking part with the general community, protested altogether against what they represented as sinful in the extreme. The clamours rose loud and high, and at length Ethelbald was alarmed. His health was failing,—his temporary passion for his young step-mother had, perhaps, faded,—his religious scruples awoke, as often happens with princes too late, and he gave way to the remonstrances of Bishop Swithin, little

[1] Turner, Holinshed, Burke, Caradoc, Milton.

regardless of the fair and youthful cause of his people's anger. It caused him, apparently, no struggle to part from Judith,[1] who could have desired nothing better than to relinquish a dignity which had been forced upon her, perhaps in both instances.

It would appear that she was now obliged to retire from court, while Ethelbald passed the remainder of his days in penitence so deep, as to leave regret behind him when he died, only three years after.

French historians assert, that though her marriage with Ethelbald was dissolved at the instance of the Bishop of Winchester, no church censure was passed upon Judith; and the Pope's interference in her favour, when she had, by her brother's assistance, escaped from the convent in which she was afterwards placed, appears strong presumptive evidence that both her marriages had been of a compulsory character, and that this was well known to his Holiness, who regulated his conduct accordingly.[2]

Judith, free to return to her native country, was now permitted to sell the possession she had received as her dower, and, with considerable wealth, set forth on her journey.

She is said to have passed through Flanders, then under her father's rule, as her safest route to escape danger. A secret motive, however, may have been the hope of a renewal of her intercourse with Baldwin, who, still remembering her extraordinary beauty and his former attachment, and advertised of the great riches she brought with her, received her with great courtesy. In short, Baldwin testified so much regard and devotion, that when Judith expected to depart for France, she was so gently detained, that she was in no haste to quit that country. Some accounts, however, state, that even in this, Judith acted not from her own free will, being forcibly detained by her handsome wooer, whose excuse was, that even in her childhood he had been promised her hand,—a circumstance which inspired pity for a disappointment so great, and enlisted many on his side.

The French King, Charles, apprehensive, perhaps, of his daughter's partiality for Baldwin leading to some indiscretion, commanded her not to delay her journey; and to manifest his displeasure, either at her having lingered so long, or at her second marriage with Ethelbald, ordered her to be confined within the walls of the Convent of Senlis, but at the same time to be treated with all the respect due to a queen.[3] Under the guardianship of Bishop Erpuin, the young widow resided there in a style of regal splendour; the spot itself is described as "that pleasant and healthy abode, the royal nursery, where the Kings of France were accustomed to send their children: some Roman arches of their palace, enclosing a wild fragrant garden, were standing a few years ago."[4]

A learned writer has been severe on Judith,[5] calling her an "undutiful girl of ungovernable passions." Widows were peculiarly protected against violence, and it was a crown prerogative among the Franks that no female of the royal family could marry without her parent's consent; therefore Judith was to remain under *mundbyrd*, or wardship of Church and State, till she should either resign herself to widowhood or remarry.

[1] Rudborn. [2] Palgrave. [3] Ibid. [4] Lingard. [5] Palgrave.

Charles appears to have designed the hand of Judith for the King of Navarre, for whom she entertained the strongest aversion, a sentiment which had increased in proportion to the progress of her regard for Baldwin. According to some, the alternative of entering the cloister was offered; but the peremptory mode of dealing with the young Queen points out the influence under which her two former marriages had taken place, and shows that it was expected she would yield implicit obedience to the will of her imperious father. After having been twice given away in marriages against her will, Judith, in the present instance, determined to evade one so displeasing to herself as that now proposed. Her brother, Louis the Stutterer, who was in his father's secrets concerning Judith, fully appreciated the injustice with which she was treated, and encouraged her in her resolution of accepting no husband but Baldwin. Accordingly, at a time when Charles had left Louis to officiate as Regent of the kingdom during his own absence, a few months only after Judith had been sent to Senlis, Baldwin carried off the fair prize, with the connivance of her brother, and was supported on this occasion by the Germans also. Judith had, it appears, contrived to elude the vigilance of her guards, and in a disguise prepared for that purpose, escaped from the convent-wall, and was soon, with her lover, beyond the reach of pursuit.

One account states that the lovers repaired together to the possessions of Lothaire, the brother of Judith. This prince, who is described as being "lame and unhealthy, but humble, affectionate, diligent, and pious," was of an excellent disposition, and resided, in his office of Abbot, at St. Germain l'Auxerrois. From this place Baldwin sent Judith, to whom he had been married without delay, to Flanders; and the troops which Charles sent to recover his truant daughter, and who followed her route, were signally defeated.[1]

The perpetration of so daring an act as the abduction of the descendant of the mighty Charlemagne, a daughter of the royal house of France, spread great terror among the Flemings, amongst whom Baldwin held the office of grand-forester. Charles, himself, breathed nothing but revenge, threatening not only to make war on the Flemings, but utterly to destroy their whole nation. He first, however, ordered Baldwin to send his daughter home; but not being obeyed, he caused Anselm, Archbishop of Rheims, to excommunicate him for having forcibly carried off a widow.

This sentence of excommunication obliged the newly-married pair to undertake a journey to Rome, where, on their arrival, they cast themselves at the feet of Nicholas the First, the Sovereign Pontiff. Count Baldwin then declared, that "he had used no blandishments, no deceits, or violence, against Judith, who had followed him of her own accord, without even her brother Louis reclaiming her." He prayed, therefore, that of his singular clemency, and for his love to the Christian people, he would grant him remission, and endeavour by any means to soothe the mind of the King, to mitigate his anger, and to find some way of peace with him. The suppliant prayer of the "Iron-handed" chief, added to the tears of his lovely young wife, had such an effect on the pious Pontiff,[2] who from

[1] Mezerai. [2] Lingard, Mezerai.

the first had disapproved of the sentence of excommunication, that he not only interdicted that decree, but sent two bishops, Rhodoald Portuensis and John Ficodensis, to the French King, as ambassadors, to intercede from himself in Baldwin's favour.[1] The papal embassy proceeded to Soissons, where Charles was staying, and where the angry King assembled a council of Gallic bishops to receive them, it being the second time they had been convened respecting the subject of Baldwin's marriage. Finding he could not prevail against Iron-Hand in warfare, Charles had procured the condemnation of his new son-in-law in that pious assembly by the *Gregorian Law*.[2] Now, on their being a second time convened, various opinions arose, and much discussion followed the announcement of what had been done by the supreme Pontiff. As regarded the request of the Pope to Charles, the King thought something ought to be yielded to his prayer; and fearing lest the hitherto unsubdued nation of Flanders should join the Danes,[3] who were threatening invasion of France both by sea and land, "the King swallowed the indignity, and suffered himself to be at length prevailed upon. He requited a signal injury with an uncommon benefit; not only making peace with Flanders, but receiving Baldwin into his friendship, he ratified and approved the marriage of his daughter."[4]

Judith and her husband were, on this occasion, admitted to a private interview with the King, who gave orders that their nuptials should be celebrated by costly feasts and public expressions of joy, A. D. 863,[5] though he would not assist in person at the ceremony, which was performed at Auxerre, whither the French nobles were convened for that purpose. Hincmar, Archbishop of Rheims, who had married Judith to Ethelwulf while yet a child, refusing to unite her to Baldwin on the present occasion, the ceremony was performed by the Bishop of Noviomagus.[6] After this the pair retired into Flanders, where they resided with much magnificence; Charles having conferred the government of that country on Baldwin, as the dowry of his daughter, together with the title of Earl, by which dignity Baldwin obtained a position among the Peers of France.

The lands appropriated to Baldwin consisted of all that tract which lies between the rivers Scheld and Somme, and the ocean, and were bestowed on the understanding that the Earl should employ all his forces to defend that territory from the Normans. The success of the Earl did not in this equal his courage, for the barbarous Normans overran all Flanders, and laid it waste with fire and sword, taking possession of many towns, one of which was Ghent, which they plundered. Baldwin had, hoping to arrest their depredations, built the city of Bruges, A. D. 856, and fortified it with a strong castle, called the Burgh; and the lands that had been laid waste, were, by his orders, recultivated. In the centre of Ghent, also, we may yet see the dark, battered towers of the castellated

---

[1] Annales Flandriæ.

[2] Although they are said to have favoured Baldwin in their hearts.

[3] Turner. [4] Annales Flandriæ, [5] Hist. of the Earls of Flanders.

[6] Lingard.

palace of Baudouin, "Bras de Fer." The second Baudouin added the fortifications which defended the birthplace of Charles Quint.[1]

It is not recorded whether Judith appeared at the French court after her reconciliation with King Charles. Three years after her marriage, her father and mother were publicly crowned at Soissons, A. D. 866 : but the heart of Charles was estranged from his consort by another, and had he not feared the consequences, he would have repudiated her. Queen Ermentrude was not long an obstacle in his way; she died October 6th, 869, to the joy of her husband, who, far from regretting her loss, regarded the event as a benefit, and married her rival Richelda in the following year. Ermentrude died at the Abbey of St. Denis, in the church of which her remains were deposited. Many vicissitudes had been experienced by her children during her own life. One of her sons, Louis, was surnamed "the Stammerer," from a natural defect; another, Lothaire, called Le Boiteux, or "the Cripple," had preceded her to the tomb, in 866; a third, Carloman, died, also, in 866, after having had his eyes put out by the orders of his unfeeling father.[2] Seldom, indeed, was any father so despotic as Charles the Bald. Carloman had been devoted to a religious life against his own will, and to escape taking the vows, fled the country, for which offence he was condemned by a synod of national bishops to *lose his eyes*. He appealed to Adrian II., the reigning Pontiff, who took his part in so warm a manner that Charles resented it as an insult. The French clergy supported Charles, and a conference terminated the dispute ; the Pope abandoning Carloman to his fate, the unfortunate Prince underwent the savage punishment to which he had been condemned.

The unfortunate Carloman was afterwards harboured by his uncle, Louis le Germanique, and maintained in a monastery out of charity. Charles, King of Aquitaine, was a fourth brother of Judith, who had likewise several sisters, all of whom became abbesses. Of the four sons of Charles the Bald by Richelda, Pepin, Drogo, Louis, and Charles, all died young, and the last when his parents were in great distress.[3]

The domestic tyranny Judith had personally experienced could have left her little to seek of happiness in the French court, and from the nature of her union with Baldwin, it may be presumed that their marriage was a happy one. They were blessed with several children, and though Charles, their first-born, died in infancy, the second boy, named after his father (thought by some to have had the peculiarity of baldness which distinguished his grandfather the French King, from his surname), lived

---

[1] Lingard. "Besides these, many good works are recorded of the Iron-Handed Forester, such as monasteries endowed and charities judiciously and generously bestowed. If not of regal or even noble birth, the nobility of good actions has conferred celebrity on his name, so that it matters little how historians differ as to his genealogical descent. Those, however, who are satisfied to leave the traditions of the Flemings unnoticed, place this heroic chief, in their genealogies, as the son of Count Odoaire, son of Count Ingelrain, both hereditary Counts Foresters, whose epitaphs were to be seen, in the last century, cut on stone, at Bruges [Palgrave.]

[2] Anecdotes des Reines et Régentes de France.

[3] Palgrave.

to inherit the earldom as Baldwin "the Bald." When her first child died, "Judith sorrowed much, attributing it to the want of mother's milk, and she determined herself to nourish the next babe, named after its father. The Lieutenant Bailli, of Tournay, expatiates upon the maternal conduct of 'Madame Judith,' a reproach to the matronly luxury and self-indulgence of his times. Baldwin II.'s manly vigour did credit to his mother's tenderness: he afterwards had abundant locks of hair, though he called himself 'le Chauve,' in honour of his grandfather."[1] Rudolf, his brother, become afterwards Count and Abbot of Cambray, which city, and the country surrounding, had been purchased by his father.[2] Gunadilde, daughter of Baldwin and Judith, married Wifred, Earl of Barcelona.

Earl Baldwin I. is said to have given good laws to the people of Flanders, over whom he ruled sixteen years, and at his death was interred in the convent church of St. Bertin, at St. Omer's.[3]

Baldwin "the Bald," who succeeded his father, espoused Elstrude, a Saxon princess, daughter of Alfred the Great, and grand-daughter of Ethelwulf, the first husband of Judith.[4] Thus was, no doubt, revived the tie of affection and interest between the Princess of France and her pupil and companion in literature, King Alfred. Nor is it the least interesting point in the history of Judith and her family, that from the son of this marriage was derived, in the female line, our Norman race of kings; Matilda, Queen of William the Conqueror, being the immediate descendant of Arnold the Great, son of Baldwin the Bald and Elstrude of England. It is singular that though there were no children from the marriage of Judith and Ethelwulf, their descendants, in two distinct lines, should have so long ruled the realm of England.

The adventures of Judith, arranged according to the poet's fancy, are the subject of a curious poem, contained in a Collection of Ancient Ballads:[5] it is entitled "An excellent Ballad of a Prince of England's courtship to the King of France's Daughter, &c." (to the tune of 'Crimson Velvet'), and may interest the lover of antique traditions.

The song begins by stating that, in the days of old, the Queen of France had a daughter who was "lovely faire," and that a Prince of England, exiled and outcast, yet noted for his merit, coming to her father's court, an attachment between him and the Princess ensued. The King disapproving the match, they agreed to escape together from thraldom.

"The ladye soone prepared
  Her jewells and her treasure:
Having no regard
  For state and royal bloode
In homely poore array,
She went from court away,
  To meet her joye and heart's delight,

---

[1] Palgrave, Hist. of Normandy and England.

[2] Hist. of the Earls of Flanders; Ducarel's Norman Antiquities.

[3] Hist. of the Earls of Flanders.

[4] Ducarel.

[5] The editor gives it from an ancient folio MS., collated with another in black letter, in the Pepys Collection.

"Who in a forest great
Had taken up his seat,
To wayt her coming in the night.
But lo! what sudden danger
To this princely stranger:
Chanced, as he sate alone!
By outlawes he was robbed,
And with ponyards stabbed,
Uttering many a dying grone."

The Princess, "in her strange attire," escapes without recognition to the forest, only to find her royal lover weltering in his blood on the ground. She gives vent to the most passionate exclamation of grief, and endeavours, "with her golden haires," to staunch the wounds; but her efforts and prayers are alike useless.

"All in vaine she sued,
All in vaine she wooed;
The prince's life was fled and gone."

Bewailing her own destiny, and her lover's hard fate, she passes the night in mourning over his remains, and resolves not to return to the court of her father.

"To my father's court
I return will never,
But in lowly sort
I will a servant bee."

Whilst she is thus lamenting, a forester, all in green, coming by, inquires the cause of her affliction. She tells him her *brother* lies slain by her side, and requests him to direct her to some situation where she may obtain servile employment, in these words:—

"'Where may I remaine,
Gentle for'ster shew me,
Till I can obtaine
A service in my neede?
Pains I will not spare.
This kinde favour doe mee;
It will ease my care;
Heaven shall be thy meede.'

"The for'ster, all amazed,
On her beautye gazed
Till his heart was set on fire.
'If, faire maid,' quoth hee,
'You will goe with mee,
You shall have your heart's desire.'
He brought her to his mother,
And above all other
He sett forth this maiden's praise.
Long was his heart inflamed,
At length her love he gained,
And fortune crowned his future dayes.

"Thus unknowne he wedde
With a king's faire daughter:
Children seven they had,
Ere she told her birth;

Which when once he knew,
  Humbly he besought her,
He to the world might shew
  Her rank and princely worth.
He cloathed his children then
(Not like other men)
  In partye colours strange to see.
The right side cloth of gold,
The left side to behold
  Of woollen cloth still framed hee.
Men thereatt did wonder;
Golden fame did thunder
  This strange deed in every place.
The King of France came hither,
It being pleasant weather,
  In those woods the hart to chase.

"The children then they bring —
  So their mother willed it —
Where the royall king
  Must of force come bye.
Their mother's riche array
  Was of crimson velvet;
Their father's all of gray,
  Seemelye to the eye.

"Then this famous king,
Noting everything,
  Asked how he durst be so bold
To let his wife so weare,
And decke his children there
  In costly robes of pearle and gold?
The forrester replying,
And the cause descrying,
  To the king these words did say:
'Well may they by their mother
Weare rich clothes with other,
  Being by birth a princesse gay.'

The king, aroused thus,
  More heedfullye beheld them,
Till a crimson blush,
  His remembrance crost.
'The more I fix my mind
  On thy wife and children,
The more methinks I find
  The daughter which I lost.
Falling on her knee,
'I am that child,' quoth she;
  'Pardon me, my sovereign liege.'
The King perceiving this,
His daughter deare did kiss,
  While joyfull teares did stopp his speeche.
With his traine he tourned,
And with them sojourned.
  Strait he dubbed her husband knight;
Then made him Erle of Flanders,
And chiefe of his commanders:
  Thus were their sorrowes put to flight."

ELSWITHA, WIFE OF ALFRED THE GREAT, AND ETHELFLEDA, "LADY OF MERCIA."

Romantic legend of the meeting of Alfred the Great and Elswitha — Albanac's family—The nocturnal visit—The daughters—The father's resolve—The choice offered—Marriage of Alfred and Elswitha—Sudden illness of the bridegroom—Connubial affection—Passage in Boethius—Famine in England—St. Swithun—Children of Elswitha—Her happiness, and fondness for her husband—Athelney—The Danes—Dangers—Generosity of Alfred—Monastery founded—Alfred's Will—Eadburga and Elswitha—St. Mary's, Newminster—Learning of Ethelfleda—Lady of Mercia—Her numerous fortresses—The captive Welsh Queen—Fleance, son of Banquo—Ancient Welsh customs—Candle-bearer's perquisites — Death of Ethelfleda — Mourned by King Edward—Elfwina dispossessed by her uncle—Ethelfleda buried in St. Peter's, Gloucester.

A SINGULARLY romantic legendary account exists of the first introduction of Alfred the Great to his future consort Elswitha. Alfred, like Haroun al Raschid, was fond of visiting and informing himself of the condition of every class of his subjects. On one occasion he set out, accompanied by a courtier named Ethelbert, and in his rambles stopped at the house of Albanac, a chieftain of rank and power, whose name would indicate his descent to have been rather British than Saxon. This nobleman received his sovereign with welcome, and his wife and three daughters, all of whom were extremely beautiful, attended on him, as was the custom. The dignified deportment of Elswitha, one of the young Saxon ladies, and the grace and elegance of her person, eclipsed that of her sisters at supper, when waiting upon the King. Alfred was much attracted with her charms, and praised her beauty in glowing terms. The impression made upon him was observed by Albanac, who, when the company separated for the night, communicated his suspicions to his wife. The King, on his part, at retiring, had confided to Ethelbert his admiration of Elswitha, who, with a courtier's tact, approved of his choice. Next morning, when day broke, Albanac presented himself at the door of his royal guest, requesting immediate admittance. The King bade him enter; on which, to his surprise, he beheld Albanac, with a drawn sword in his hand, conducting his three daughters, who, clad in the deepest mourning, seemed overwhelmed with the most poignant distress. "What is it I see?" exclaimed Alfred. "A father," returned Albanac, "whose honour is more dear to him than life itself. You are my King, and I am your subject, but not your slave. You are well acquainted with my illustrious ancestors, and it is now proper you should know my sentiments. Last night you discovered a particular attention to my daughter. If you have conceived the idea of dishonouring my house, you see the sword that shall in an instant sacrifice these unhappy victims, willing to sacrifice themselves; but if a pure flame is kindled in your breast, my alliance will not disgrace the crown: choose, therefore, and name her that is born to such distinguished honour!"

This somewhat abrupt proceeding, the legend goes on to say, did not displease Alfred, who, appreciating the noble and daring courage of the father of Elswitha, immediately professed his readiness to make her his wife, and she was soon afterwards Queen. That the King had chosen his partner wisely, was proved by subsequent events. Elswitha was virtuous and amiable, and inspired her noble husband with a lasting affection for her.

It is a subject of pleasing contemplation to trace the feelings of Alfred on the subject of connubial affection, which appears from his writings, wherein he expresses himself in terms of enthusiasm. A passage in Boethius, translated by Alfred, runs thus: some additions to the original being made by the King, these are given in italics:—[1]

"Liveth not thy wife also! She is exceedingly prudent and very modest. She has excelled all other women in purity. I may, in a few words, express all her merit; this is, that in all her manners she is like her father. She lives now for thee, *thee alone. Hence, she loves naught else but thee. She has enough of every good in this present life, but she has despised it all for thee alone. She has shunned it all, because only she has not thee also. This one thing is now wanting to her.* Thine absence makes her think that all which she possesses is nothing. Hence for thy love she is wasting, and full nigh dead with tears and sorrow." "Alfred dwells on the 'vivat tibi' of Boethius with manifest delight, and dilates upon the thought as if with fond recollections of the conduct of his own wife, who shared his adversity with him."

Such legends as these are valuable as showing the habits and manners of the times, and prove how lawless and turbulent they were, when no confidence was placed in the honour of those the highest in power, when their gratification was at stake. Alfred himself was superior to the period at which he lived, and a few years afterwards suspicion would not have fallen on him; but at this time, he was only just come to the crown, and, being still very young, had not as yet had an opportunity of proving to his subjects his rare and remarkable worth.[2]

The real history of his marriage is merely that his wife Elswitha was the daughter of Ethelfrid,[3] surnamed Mucil, Ealdorman of Mercia; and that her mother was nobly born, being Edburga of the royal house of Mercia. Alfred was just twenty when he married, and during the nuptial festivities, which lasted several days, he was seized with an alarming malady, from which, it is said, "he enjoyed scarcely a day's respite during more than twenty years of his useful and active life."[4]

He never, however, allowed the acute pain of his malady to interfere

[1] Sharon Turner.

[2] Lingard, however, alludes to opinions of his character in early life, which probably accounts for the suspicions of Mucil: he quotes St. Neot and Asser.

[3] Lingard. [4] Lappenberg.

with his manly resolution; and by the force of his extraordinary will, contrived to master his bodily sufferings, which are, indeed, said rather to have strengthened his mental energy.

The year of Elswitha's marriage, A. D. 868, was noted for a terrible famine, felt in all parts of Europe, so that in some places the living are said to have fed upon the bodies of the dead! And it is further said, that this famine was followed, in 869, "by a great mortality of man and beast." The tutor both of Alfred and his father, Swithun, Bishop of Winchester, died at this time, and desired to be buried in the open churchyard, instead of the chancel of the minster, where the ashes of the great reposed, "that the drops of rain might wet his grave; thinking that no vault was so good to cover his grave as that of heaven." The popular Scottish proverb and superstition contained in the following lines, probably arose from the expression he used:—

"Saint Swithin's Day, if thou dost rain,
For forty days it will remain;
Saint Swithin's Day, if thou be fair,
For forty days 'twill rain nae mair."

Asser, who frequently saw the mother of Elswitha, calls her a venerable woman, "illustrious and pious," and from the time of her husband's decease, she had ever lived the life of a true widow.[1]

Elswitha had five children, Edward the Elder, Ethelwold, Ethelfleda, Ethelgitha, and Elswitha, of each of whom some account will be given. Besides these she had several who died in infancy, one of whom, Edmund, had been intended by Alfred for his successor on the throne. Elswitha was deeply attached to her husband, and to judge from his character, her own conduct, and the merits of her family, she was not only a good wife, but a happy mother

The companion of Alfred in prosperity, Elswitha shared with him his adverse fortunes. At a moment when almost every friend and adherent had forsaken the King, we find him contriving the erection of a fortress, in a place of security, his first object being to remove Elswitha and her children to a spot free from danger, which he happily succeeded in effecting. After nine successive years spent in bravely encountering those fierce enemies of England, the Danes, Alfred retreated for temporary security into the little isle of Athelney,[2] a spot of rising ground on the north side of Stanmoor, bounded on the north-west by the river Thone, over which there is a wooden bridge, still called Athelney Bridge. "Alfred built a castle in Athelney, and made it a very strong hold, and forcing a way unto it by a bridge or causey; for guard of the way, he built on either side a tower." This ever-memorable place was anciently environed with almost impassible marshes and morasses, and could only be approached by a boat:[3] it had, moreover, a very large wood of alders, which harboured stags, wild goats, and other beasts." Such was the place of refuge of the King and Queen and their children, who lodged in a small

[1] Sharon Turner.

[2] A contraction of the Saxon word, meaning "Isle of Nobles."

[3] Malmesbury.

house belonging to St. Athelwine, formerly a hermit there, son of King Kinigilfus.[1]

During this period of adversity, it is on record that Alfred experienced many privations, one of the greatest being the want of provisions: so that of a severe winter, which set in under such unfavourable circumstances for the royal family, a characteristic tale is told. The King's attendants were one day out on the perilous expedition of fishing, for the Danes were near,—a requisite duty to provide for the daily necessity, from which Alfred and Elswitha were alone exempted. The King employed himself with reading, the Queen with her domestic occupations. At this moment a poor pilgrim, passing the gate, implored the monarch for a morsel of food. Alfred, calling to Elswitha, requested her to give the man a portion of her provision. It is said that their whole store consisted of but one loaf, and the equally humane Queen hesitated a moment in the act of charity. Alfred, however, was not to be deterred by any selfish consideration from his generous purpose. He readily bestowed the half of his slender store on the mendicant, consoling himself and his Queen with the reflection, that the benevolent hand which could supply the necessities of five thousand with but five loaves and two fishes, would doubtless provide for their future wants. Satisfaction and resignation accompanied this beneficent action, which was rewarded by the speedy return of their companions, laden with an ample store of provisions.[2]

After Alfred quitted this retreat, and had subdued his enemies, he founded on the spot a monastery for Benedictine monks, to commemorate his gratitude to Heaven for the shelter it had afforded to himself and his family: this religious foundation was liberally endowed both by Alfred and his successors on the throne.[3]

Elswitha enjoyed the society of her beloved and excellent husband for

---

[1] Biog. Brit.

[2] Spelman relates the story of the pilgrim as of his mother, not his wife, though he thinks it was the latter who was with the King; Judith having returned into France, and Osburga being dead. After the deed of charity, the King, falling asleep, dreamt of St. Cuthbert, who came to announce to him, in reward of his charity, that he should be restored to his kingdom, and that his servants would speedily return with abundance of fish. His mother, who also had fallen asleep, was called by the King, who declared his dream to her, and learnt she had dreamt the same thing, which, while they were yet busy recounting to each other, was in part realised by the return of their attendants.—Spelman.

[3] A jewel of gold, enamelled like a bulla or amulet, to hang round the neck, circumscribed, in Saxon characters, "Alfred ordered me to be made," was found there. It is now in the Ashmolean Museum. An engraving of it may be seen in Gough's Camden (70).—Turner.

The monastery Alfred built in Athelney was of wood. It was borne upon four main wooden pillars, and enclosed round about with cancellings or chancel-work; they having not then the use of glass, nor other means to shut out the violence of weather, and yet let in sufficient light, than by fine open-work carvings, and lattices of window-work, of which (to express the curiosity) Malmesbury says that they were carved *opere sphærico*. According to Spelman (see notes), there were four cancells, choirs, or chapells, surrounding the *area* or *auditory* of the church.—Spelman, Life of Alfred, p. 166.

nearly twenty-eight years:[1] the two last which preceded his death, which occurred A. D. 900, were marked by a great increase of suffering from the malady by which he was afflicted.[2] During the latter part of their union, the royal pair, hand in hand, restored and patronized many female religious communities. The nunnery at Shaftesbury was founded by the King, and when completed, Alfred placed in it his daughter Ethelgive, who assumed the government of the infant establishment, while several females of the first distinction hastened to profess themselves her disciples.[3]

Elswitha herself founded the Abbey of St. Mary, at Winchester, aided, as some say, by the King. This edifice, known also as Nunnaminstre, or the New Minstre, was situated in the east part of the city, on the north side of the cathedral, with which it was parallel; but from the unhealthiness of its situation, and too great proximity to the cathedral, was afterwards removed to Hyde Meadows.

King Egbert had entailed his estates, by his will, on his male descendants, to the exclusion of females: "to the spear-side and not to the spindle-side." Ethelwulf, his son, after making his second son Ethelbert King of Kent, bequeathed at his death to the remaining three, certain lands, which were to come eventually to the survivor. Alfred, surviving his two elder brothers, made a new agreement, that the survivor should enjoy the personal estate of the other, and with it the lands bequeathed by Ethelwulf. Before, however, Alfred's will was made, he assembled the Thanes of Wessex, at Langdon, "lest any one should say that I had defrauded my kinsfolk;" for by the same agreement it had been stipulated with Ethelred, that all real property, acquired by grant or purchase, should be left to the nephews of the survivor. Wherefore Alfred's will states, that if any of the lands which he left to females had descended to him from Egbert, he desired his heirs male to take the lands, and give to the females an equivalent in money. The Saxon Thanes having approved the King's title to the property, the following day he divided his lands among his two sons, his three daughters, his two nephews, his cousin Osferth, and his wife Elswitha. To each of his sons he left five hundred pounds; and to the Queen and the three Princesses, her daughters, four hundred pounds each, at that time no inconsiderable sum of money.[4] Besides these, he left certain sums to his ealdormen, servants, and bishops; fifty mancuses of gold to fifty priests, fifty to the poor ministers of God, fifty to poor people in distress, and fifty to the church in which he should be buried.[5] To Queen Elswitha he also bequeathed three towns; Wantage, the birth-place of Alfred, was one of these, where stood a palace of the Saxon Kings.[6] The manor of Ethandune,[7] with other Berkshire lands, were also mentioned in the will of Alfred as left to Queen Elswitha. She had also other property, some of which was bestowed by herself on Glastonbury, and afterwards confirmed to that church by King Edgar.[8]

[1] Speed. [2] Walter Raleigh. [3] Lingard.
[4] Biog. Brit. [5] Lingard. [6] Lysons's Mag. Brit.
[7] Eddington, near Hungerford.—Lysons.
[8] Winchcomb—the name of which signifies "the Valley of Battle," given, in

On the death of Alfred, Queen Elswitha retired to the Abbey of St. Mary, Winchester. Eadburga, daughter of Edward the Elder, was abbess of this establishment, which followed the Benedictine rule, and was so popular that her name as patroness of the abbey was joined to that of the Virgin Mary, to whom it was dedicated. Elswitha, admiring the virtues of her grand-daughter Eadburga, and also witnessing the tranquillity enjoyed by her daughter the Abbess of Shaftesbury, resolved to pass her declining years in religious seclusion. In the establishment and society of the Abbess Eadburga she died, A. D. 904, having survived her excellent husband only four years.

The remains of King Alfred were at first interred in the Cathedral of Winchester; and we learn from Asser that a magnificent monument of precious porphyry was erected to his honour, who was renowned as "the truth-teller"—one of the most noble of all characteristics in either sovereign or subject.[1] In compliance with his father's will Edward the Elder caused the edifice of Newminster to be completed, and it was consecrated on the advent of St. Judoc, A. D. 903, being at the first only a house and chapel for the learned monk Grimbald. The foundation and chief parts of the building had been laid and built by Alfred during his life, and Grimbald, the first to set the King to the undertaking, was designed by him to be the first Abbot. The monastery was situated on the north side of Winchester Cathedral, with which it was parallel, and there wanted room for some of its parts: it was placed so near the cathedral that the singing-men in the choir of the one were easily heard into the choir of the other, and this gave occasion of many differences about it. The place being so "straight and hard to be enlarged, the King was fain to pay the Bishop a mark of gold for every foot of land which he was forced to buy, that he might have commodity sufficient for the shops or work-houses for his monks' offices[2] belonging to the monastery.[3]

Edward the Elder, on the completion of the structure, placed in it secular canons, under St. Grimbald as abbot;[4] after which he caused the remains of his father, King Alfred, to be conveyed thither, with solemn pomp and magnificence, from the adjacent cathedral. The body, also, of Queen Elswitha, which had been at first entombed in St. Mary's Abbey, Newminster, was also, by his orders, conveyed thither, to be deposited with that of her husband. It was not, however, ordained that they should repose on this spot of their own selection; its contiguity to Winchester Cathedral, and unhealthiness of the situation, caused the subsequent removal of the religious establishment to Hyde Meadows, without the city, in the reign of Henry I., at which period it was known as St.

A. D. 965, to Glastonbury, by Queen Elswitha — was still in the hands of the monks of that establishment at the time of the Norman survey.

The Saxon Queen, says Turner, "had her separate property; for, in a gift of land, she gives fifteen mancuses, calling them a part of the land of her own power. She had also officers peculiar to her household; for the persons with whose consent and testimony she made the grant, are called *her* nobles."

[1] Asser says this tomb was erected in St. Peter's, Winchester.

[2] Annals of Winchomb, 905.

[3] Spelman. [4] Butler.

Grimbald's Monastery. The learned Beauclerc and his Saxon Queen Maude, the descendant of Alfred and Elswitha, in whom were united the interests of the Norman and Saxon cause, attended in person the removal of the bones of that king and queen to the new edifice of Hyde Abbey. The monks of St. Grimbald's, in solemn procession on the occasion, carried with them the relics of three saints, as well as the remains of Alfred and Elswitha. During the civil war of 1142, Hyde Abbey was burnt to the ground, and a great part of its treasures perished in the flames: the edifice was, however, rebuilt in the reign of Henry II., and restored to its former rank and splendour, which it retained till the destruction of religious houses at the Reformation, at which period it was reduced to a heap of ruins.[1]

Ethelfleda, the first-born of Alfred's children by Queen Elswitha, was esteemed the most learned, as she was the most remarkable, woman of her time, and singularly distinguished for masculine spirit and abilities. This princess conferred on her country many benefits; and her promptitude and valour saved it more than once from those rapacious ravagers, the Danes. In talent she more nearly resembled her glorious father than any of his children; and equally to her mother was she indebted for those noble qualities which made her illustrious. At a very early age, Ethelfleda was married to Ethelred, Earl of Mercia, who, being in an infirm state of health, was frequently prevented attending to the care of government. His place was, on these occasions, well supplied by his wise and learned consort, whose great foresight and prudence in the conduct of public affairs were acknowledged from the first. There are records extant which prove that she took part even in her father's councils.

After Alfred's death, Edward the Elder bestowed anew on his sister and her husband conjointly, or perhaps only confirmed, the government of Mercia, with the title of "Subregulus Merciorum" to the Earl. Accordingly in an instrument of Werfred, Bishop of Worcester, to that church, made A. D. 904, the royal couple are both together styled in the Saxon tongue Æthred, the Alderman or Duke, and Ethelfled, the *Lords* of Mercia. A period of twenty-four years must have elapsed between the date of this charter and the one first mentioned. Other charters granted by this princess bear her signature alone, thus, "Ego Ethelfled consensi."

Ethelfleda's piety, according to the opinion of that time was great. After the birth of a daughter, she resolved to devote herself solely to a life of heroism and the care of her country's good, instead of indulging in the happiness of maternity; and her husband, sickly and weak both in mind and body, did not oppose her will. She, therefore, threw off all the weakness of her sex from that time, and appears in history rather as a general than as a mother or wife. She founded monasteries, as one at Gloucester testifies, and it was there that Ethelred, dying, was entombed, in 912.

---

[1] In our own times, the site of the building where Alfred and Elswitha rested, gives place to the county Bridewell, a few remnants marking the antiquity of the hallowed spot.

After his death, conjointly with her brother, Edward the Elder, she exerted all her energies to repel the Danes, and by her counsels and acts greatly aided the King.

As soon as Ethelfleda became a widow, Edward made a partition of Mercia, apparently with her full consent, annexing London and Oxford to his own dominions of Wessex, and committing the other portion of the government to her care.[1] From this time till her death, a period of eight years, Ethelfleda held sovereign rule with the title of Lady of Mercia, and the extraordinary martial talents she exhibited during this season of power procured her the honourable titles not only of "Queen," but of "King" also, as if those of Countess-lady, which she possessed, were inadequate to express her heroism.

Her attention was chiefly directed to the necessity of erecting fortresses in different parts of the kingdom, to prevent the Danes from extending their territory, and of checking their inroads; for many fastnesses had fallen into the hands of those dangerous intruders, who could thus hold the whole country in fear and subjection. At Hereford, and at Witham in Essex, Edward built strong places; and in the same year of her becoming a widow, the Saxon Chronicle records that Ethelfleda, "on the Holy Eve called the Invention of the Holy Cross," came to Shergate, and built the fortress there, and another at Bridgenorth in the same year. A monastery, dedicated to St. Barnabas, was likewise founded by the "Lady of Mercia," at Brunnesburgh,[2] that year, which shortly after fell to decay.

One of the royal palaces of King Offa was at Tamworth, whence many charters of succeeding sovereigns were dated. This town became, in 913, the residence of Ethelfleda, who restored it from the ruinous condition in which it had been placed by the incursions of the Danes. She erected a tower there, "in the fore part of the summer," says the Chronicle, on the artificial mount upon which the present castle stands. In the same year, before Lammas, "the Lady of Mercia," built a fortress at Stafford; this being the first authentic record given of that town.

Early in the summer of 914, Ethelfleda built a fortress at Eddesbury, and late in the autumn of that year, another at Warwick. Dugdale, who refers the foundation of Warwick Castle to Ethelfleda, tells us that there was a mound of the same form there, and with terraces similar to that of Durham Castle. In 915, Ethelfleda caused the dungeon of Warwick Castle to be made, which is a strong tower or platform, upon a large and high mount of earth, artificially raised (such being usually placed towards the side of a castle or fort which is least defensible), the substance whereof is yet to be seen.

In 915, "after mid-winter," was built the fortress of Cherburg, and that at Warburton; and the same year, before mid-winter, one at Runcorn,[3] also the town of Warham, and Fadesbury, both named by Roger of Wendover.

---

[1] Bromton, Leland, Dugdale.

[2] In Cheshire.

[3] Runcorn, in Cheshire, on the banks of the Mersey, was originally built by the renowned Ethelfleda. The river here suddenly contracts from a considerable breadth to a narrow channel, by a projecting point of land from the Lancashire

In those days there were very few defensible places, such as we now call castles, which rendered it very difficult for the English to defend themselves from the incursions of foreign invaders; a defect which gave great advantages to William of Normandy, who was so sensible of the fact, that after the victory of Hastings, he neglected not to raise "a sufficient store of forts throughout the realm."[1] Ethelfleda had, before the Norman Prince, perceived the danger which this deficiency caused in England, and her exertions in this respect, to defend the country from the Danes, cannot be too highly appreciated. Ingulphus justly observes of this Princess, who, by some one is styled a "restorer of the brick," that in respect of the fortresses she built, and the armies she managed, she might have been thought a man."

Ethelfleda exerted herself successfully against the Welsh, preventing them coming to the aid of the Danes. This glorious achievement was accomplished in 916, when "the Lady of Mercia," at the head of a large army, entered Wales, and stormed Brecknock, where she took the "King's wife," and thirty-four of her attendants, prisoners.[2] This event, by which the Welsh became tributary to Mercia, occurred within three nights of the feast of St. Cirisius, and in Wales was called "*Gwaith y Dinas Newydd*," or "the Battle of the New City." The object of Ethelfleda, in this expedition, was to punish the Welsh for having put to death the innocent Abbot Egbert.

The Queen whom Ethelfleda made her captive, was Angharad, the wife of Owen. The name she bore was correspondent to the English word Anne, and was exceedingly popular in Wales, three other Queens being distinguished by it, all worthy of notice. The first Angharad was Queen of Roderic the Great, and mother of three princes, among whom that monarch divided his dominions prior to his decease, building for each, in his peculiar district, a royal residence; from which time the brothers were known as "the three crowned Princes," each wearing, on his helmet, a coronet of gold, or broad head-band, indented upwards, and set and wrought with precious stones.[3] The only daughter of Meredith,

side; and opposite Runcorn-gap, as the above strait is denominated, Ethelfleda erected a castle to defend this extremity of her vast domain.

"Not a vestige of this building can be seen; but its site is marked by the name of *the castle*, given to a triangular piece of land, surrounded with a mound of earth, jutting out into the river, guarded on the water-side by ledges of rocks and broken precipices, and cut off from the land by a ditch six yards in width. The parochial church stands above the Castle-rock: its foundation was probably coeval with the castle, but was certainly prior to the Conquest, since Nigel, Baron of Halton, bestowed it on his brother Wolfrith, a priest, in the time of the Conqueror."—Britton and Brayley.

When Alfred repaired and restored the different castles which had been demolished by the Danes, he, for the first time, built of stone many of those which had formerly been constructed of earth: of this number was Norwich Castle. "Alfred's Castle" there was afterwards entirely destroyed by the Danish King, Sweyn, father of Canute the Great."

[1] Dugdale, Saxon Chronicle.

[2] Powel, Caradoc of Llancarvan.

[3] Sax. Chron., Caradoc of Llan: "Y Tri Tywysoc Talaethiæ" (the three bandlet-wearing princes).

son of the Queen Angharad, whom Ethelfleda captured, bore her grandmother's name, and married the ambitious Llewelyn ap Seisyllt, who, in her right, mounted the throne A. D. 1003, and, as he afterwards added North Wales to his dominions, united the three principalities which Roderic had divided among his sons, from one of whom, in fact, he claimed his descent.

Both the houses of Tudor and Stuart have been derived from Roderic the Great; the wife of Rhys ap Twdwr, ancestor of Owen Tudor, the father of Henry VII., being descended from Angharad, Queen of Llewelyn ap Seisyllt, by a second marriage with Cynfyn Hirdref. The house of Stuart is derived from Nesta,[1] grand-daughter of Angharad; her parents being Griffith ap Llewelyn and Ranulf. Fleance, son of the Banquo murdered by Macbeth, sought safety and shelter in the court of Griffith, in North Wales, but returned the kind reception there given him by the seduction of the Princess Nesta, or Agnes, who gave birth to a son, named Walter.[2] Fleance paid the forfeit of his life for his breach of faith, and the unfortunate Princess was reduced, by her father's orders, to a condition of servitude. The misfortunes of his parents were much felt by their son Walter, whose temper was violent, as is shown by the manner in which he resented insult. Being one day reproached with his ignoble origin by a young man with whom he had quarrelled, he killed him on the spot. To protect himself from punishment, he fled to Scotland, where he succeeded in obtaining a post among the English attendants of Margaret, Queen of Malcolm, and conducted himself so well, that he was soon advanced in the royal favour, and became steward of Scotland, and receiver of the revenues of the realm.[3] From the office held by Walter, he derived the surname of Stewart, and his descendants bore the same; not only the royal house of Stuart, but many noble Scottish families are derived from this source.

It may be thought curious to mention here some of the ancient Welsh customs as concerned their Queens.

The Queen had, by the laws of Wales, a fine for *saraad*, or offence, which might be committed three ways:—

Firstly: "When her protection shall be violated," that is, "the right to conduct beyond the bounds of the country, without pursuit and without obstruction."

Secondly: "When she shall be struck in anger;" or,

Thirdly: "When a thing shall be forcibly taken out of her hand."

The fine for this very unmanly treatment of a crowned head was to be only "*one-third* of the King's saraad, the gold and silver excepted. Now, the fine for the King's saraad was as follows:—"One hundred kine; a silver rod, with three knobs at the top, and three at the bottom, which shall reach from the ground to the King's face, when he shall sit in his chair, and as thick as his ring-finger; and a golden cup, which shall

---

[1] Nesta is used in Wales for the Greek Agnes: in the Greek, it means *chaste.* The French write it Ignatia.—Camden's Remains.

The same name applied to a man is exemplified in that of Ignatius Loyola.

[2] Caradoc, Lluyd. [3] Warrington.

hold the King's full draught, and as thick as the nail of a ploughman, when he has ploughed seven years; and a gold cover, *as broad as the King's face*, and as thick as the edge of the cup." Now, as the gold and silver was to be *excepted* in the fine for the Queen's "saraad," the value of little more than thirty-three cows was all the compensation that she was entitled to for the insults above named.

The Queen occupies a low station, also, in the arrangements made for the interior of the palace. Every one of the King's officers has an appropriate place in the hall, but the King's wife occupies her solitary chamber,[1] where she is waited upon by a single attendant hand-maiden; a steward, "who is to serve her in her chamber with meat and drink;" and a page, "who is to convey messages between the chamber and the hall, keep the keys of her coffers, and supply the chamber," and two or three inferior attendants: "and it is further enacted, that when the Queen shall will a song in her chamber, let the bard sing a song respecting Camlan,[2] and *that not loud*, lest the hall be disturbed." So that it would seem her enjoyments were to be considered only as second to those of her guests and subjects, who assembled to carouse over their meal.

Among the inferior attendants of the Queen, one was a candle-bearer, whose pleasant perquisite is to be "all the tops he shall bite off the candles, also the broken bread and fragments that fall over the Queen's dish."

No female domestic seems to have been employed in the King's household, except the Queen's handmaiden, the baking-woman, and the laundress. These last two were allowed the right of protection,—the baking-woman as far as she could throw her kneading-bat, the laundress as far as she could throw her washing-beetle.

These laws, generally speaking, place the value of every ordinary woman at one-third of that of her husband, and arrange that, in cases of separation by mutual consent, the joint property should be fairly shared between them.

"If husband and wife separate, the husband has the swine and the sheep; if only one kind, to be shared. Goats are to the husband. Of the children, the eldest and youngest to the husband, the middlemost to the wife. The household furniture to be shared, but the milking-vessels, except the pail, to the wife; the husband, the drinking-vessels and riddle; the wife, the sieve. The husband has the upper stone of the hand-mill; the wife, the lower one. The upper garments are the wife's; the under garments, the husband's; and the kettle, coverlet, bolster, fuel, axe, settle, and all the hooks except one, the pan, trivet, axe, bill, ploughshare, flax, linseed, wool, and the house-bag, to the wife; if any gold, it is to be shared between them. The husband to have the corn above the ground and under, and the barn, the poultry, and one of the cats; the rest to the wife. To the wife, the meat in the brine, and the cheese in the brine; those hung up belong to the husband. The butter, meat, and cheese, in cut,

[1] In Brittany, even at the present day, the wife is the least cared for of the family, and is expected to attend on the others.

[2] The battle in which Arthur fell.

belong to the wife; also, as much meal as she can carry between her arms and knees, from the store-room to the house. Their apparel to be divided."[1]

"The wife had an exclusive right to her jewellery and wearing apparel," and the wife of a "privileged or *free* man might lend her under garment, mantle, headcloth, and shoes, without consent of her husband, and can give meat and drink unrestrictedly, and can lend the furniture. The wife of the 'taeog,' or bondsman, could only lend her head-covering, and of her houshold utensils, only her sieve and riddle; and these, but at the distance she can be heard calling, with her feet on the threshold. The reasons for these restrictions, in regard to the wife of the bondsman, was probably owing to the fact that the household goods, and even the clothing, were the property of the bondsman's master."[2]

On the capture of Queen Angharad, the Welsh King, Owen, fled to Derby, where he was kindly received by the Danes. Ethelfleda, apprised of this, followed Owen thither with her army; and in 918, the Saxon Chronicle informs us, that "with the help of God, before Lammas," she conquered that city, with all that thereto belonged. The Queen, on this memorable occasion, had nearly lost her life through her heroism. Speed compares her to Zenobia, saying, that her person was in the greatest danger when endeavouring to enter the gate, multitudes of the Danes resisting her progress; she, however, persevered and succeeded in entering the town, though many of her officers fell in the encounter, and four of her warriors, who guarded her royal person, and were most dear to her, were slain when fighting by her side, by Owen, the Welsh King;[3] a circumstance which was to her "a cause of sorrow." Caradoc, describing this struggle, says, that when Gwyane, Lord of the Isle of Ely, Ethelfleda's steward, perceived the Queen's danger, he set fire to the gates, and rushing furiously on the Britons, entered the town; on which, Owen, finding he was overmatched, chose rather to fall by the sword, than cowardly to yield himself to a woman. Boadicea appears revived in this account.

The year 920 witnessed the recovery of Leicester and York from her enemies, the Danes. Leicester was taken early in the year, without loss, and the greater part of the army that belonged to it, submitted to her At this period the character of Ethelfleda again reminds us forcibly of her illustrious father. The historian of the city of Leicester[4] says, "she relieved in many places the distresses of mankind, which the horrors of war had made miserable. The city of Leicester she beheld with the tenderest compassion, which had been honoured by a royal residence, but whose beauty and strength had fallen to decay by the annihilating power of war. Its miserable inhabitants she succoured; its wasted dwellings she bade to rise from their ruinous heaps in pleasing order. She repaired its fortifications, and built a wall that encompassed the city, of such amazing strength that it is called by Matthew Paris *indissoluble*. "The foundation of the wall is discoverable in many places at this day; and

---

[1] Ancient Laws and Institutes of Wales, p. 38.

[2] Miss Lawrence's History of Woman in England.

[3] Saxon Chronicle.

[4] Thoresby.

such is the tenacity of the mortar, that whenever the inhabitants of Leicester have occasion to remove any part of the foundation, the stones of which it was built are found almost inseparable."

After the reduction of Derby by Ethelfleda, the Yorkists promised, and confirmed, some by agreement, and some with oaths, that they would be in her interest.[1] On the submission of York, the independent organisation of the "Seven Burghs" was broken up.[2]

After an eight years' reign, and many glorious acts, Ethelfleda died at Tamworth. This event, which occurred twelve nights before midsummer, 920, was felt by the public, who loved and venerated her, as their own private loss, and deeply mourned by King Edward, who, at the time deprived him of this beloved sister and faithful ally, was staying at Stamford. Directly the intelligence of the death of Ethelfleda reached him, the King rode to Tamworth, where he received the allegiance of all the people of Mercia. Not only the subjects of Ethelfleda rendered homage to Edward, but the three Kings of North Wales sought him for their lord; and on his proceeding to Nottingham, which he secured and fortified, all the Mercians there, whether Danish or English, espoused his cause. Thus the influence of the royal Lady of Mercia, even after her death, procured for her brother the universal homage of those tribes whom she had compelled to acknowledge her power.

A share of power for a time was permitted by Edward to rest in the hands of Elfwina, only child of Ethelfleda, who had been formerly placed by her mother under the King's guardianship,[3] but of this she was afterwards deprived by Edward, on the plea that she had promised marriage to Reynold, the Danish King, "*without his knowledge.*" Whether or not this was a true charge, the Princess was "deprived of all authority,"[4] and conveyed as an honourable captive into Wessex. Her imprisonment took place "about three weeks before mid-winter," so that the duration of her power was short. From this time the name of Ethelfleda's daughter disappears from English history, Mercia being annexed by Edward to his own dominions. Caradoc of Llancarvan considers that Edward's unjust conduct to his niece brought upon him the troubles which followed in his kingdom. Turner, however, remarks that, in the latter part of Edward's reign, a peculiar spirit seemed to have excited the Anglo-Danes; an argument in favour of Edward having been obliged to act as he did from motives of personal security, and to defend himself from the danger of Elfwina's directing her power against the security of the State.

The remains of Ethelfleda were deposited in St. Peter's, Gloucester, in the southern porch, where they were discovered in the time of Archbishop Thurstan, on the occasion of the foundations of the church being

[1] Saxon Chronicle.

[2] The Five Burghs were "Lincoln, Nottingham, Derby, Leicester, and Stamford. Chester and York could only be joined in a more direct alliance; but when there was a common action among them, they were called the 'Seven Burghs.'"

[3] Caradoc of Llancarvan.

[4] Saxon Chronicle, Palgrave.

30

enlarged.[1] The following lines are translated from Henry of Huntingdon on the fact of the contemporaries of this princess honouring her with the title of King:—

"Mighty Elfleda! maiden, thou should'st bear
The name of Man: — though Nature cast thy frame
In Woman's softer mould—yet he could fear
Thy matchless might! Let him resign his claim,
And, maiden, do thou change thy sex's name.
In grace, a queen—be hence a king in might,
And ages shall renounce proud Cæsar's fame,
To gaze on thine, as on a fairer light!
So, maiden, fare thee well! surpassing queen, good night!"[2]

---

[1] Malmesbury.

[2] O Elfleda potens, &c.

EGWINA, ELFLEDA, EDGIFA, AND ELFGIVA,

QUEENS OF EDWARD THE ELDER AND EDMUND THE PIOUS.

Romantic tale of Athelstan's mother—The loves of Egwina and Edward—Dream of the Shepherd's daughter—The nurse of the King's children—Adoption of Egwina—The bright light—Edward's second wife Elfleda; her seven children—His third wife Edgifa—Edgifa's lawsuit and will—Athelstan and Beatrice—Goda's dishonesty—Education of the family of Edward the Elder—Eadburga the nun: her choice—Edward's death, and his son Ethelwerd's—Athelstan named as successor—He provides for his family—Beatrice marries Sihtric, King of Northumberland—Edgifa marries Charles the Simple—Her trials and story—Edgifa and Elfgifa sent to Germany—Their marriage-list of the sisters—Hugh the Great and Edilda—The marriage presents—Revived fortunes of Edgifa and her son, Louis d'Outremer—Restoration and imprudence—Harshness of Louis to his mother—The widow of Edward the Elder still goes on with her lawsuit—Edmund the Pious—St. Dunstan—The precipice—Elfgiva—Legend—Explanation of the dream—Edmund assassinated—Reay Cross on Stanmore—Monasteries—Edred and St. Dunstan—Edwy the Tyrant; his ill-usage of his grandmother—Edgar re-establishes her in her rights—She bestows her property on the church—Her death.

THE marriage of Edward the Elder with the beautiful maiden Egwina is not an ascertained fact; but she was the mother of one of the greatest and the most worthy of the Kings of England, and the preference of Alfred for him above his other grandchildren, as well as of Edward above all his sons, might lead to the conclusion that he was considered legitimate, although his birth was brought forward as a reproach to the good and learned Athelstan by the disaffected among his subjects. The legend of the loves of Egwina and Edward is told by several chroniclers: by William of Malmesbury, who at the same time calls her "illustris fœmina;" and Florence, who does the same, naming her "mulier nobilissima." It is, therefore, by no means improbable that she really was the wife of Prince Edward. The story is thus told:—

In the time of King Alfred there was a shepherd's daughter, a young maiden of extraordinary beauty, who had so singular a vision in her sleep that it became the theme of the whole neighbourhood, and reached the King's ears. She dreamt that as she lay on her bed, a bright light, as of a full moon, shone forth from her body and illumined all England. The nurse of King Alfred's children was told of this dream, which by her was repeated to the Queen, who told it to her husband. Alfred was so much struck with the fact, that he had the maiden sent for, and received her into his house, adopting her from that time and treating her as his own child. She remained, therefore, under the nurse's care

Prince Edward who was not at the time at home, returned in due course, and visiting his nurse, was astonished and delighted with the addition to the family. The extreme beauty of Egwina, which seemed to make an impression on all, did not fail to fascinate the young prince. Whether Egwina's birth was known to King Alfred to be noble, and that, aware of her having been concealed as the shepherd's daughter, he did not oppose the passion of his son, or whether they were united before he knew of it, is not ascertained. Athelstan, and a sister called Beatrice, were born to Edward; and from the first, his subjects then, and the world since, might agree that he was the bright light of his mother's dream, for he filled all England with a glory never known before.[1]

Egwina appears to have died immediately after the birth of her daughter, and Edward was free to make what alliance he pleased. Very soon after her death, he married Elfleda, daughter of the Saxon Earl, Etheline. He had not then succeeded to the crown, but in 901 he was crowned, with his queen, in great pomp, at Kingston-upon-Thames.

Elfleda bore seven children to her husband, and Edward found himself a widower for the second time, for her life seems to have ended prematurely. He, however, in a short time appears again as a husband, having married a lady of high birth, named Edgifa, the daughter of Earl Sighelm.

This Queen, almost immediately after marriage, became involved in the intricacies of a lawsuit. Her father Sighelm had engaged part of his land in a mortgage, and after his death it was redeemed by the oath of Edgifa, which by the Saxon laws was considered as equivalent in value to the worth of the money which Sighelm had paid to the mortgagee, but for which he had neglected to obtain a charter of release.[2] The Queen's will, which may be seen in the Appendix to Lye's Saxon Dictionary, where it is translated from the Anglo-Saxon into Latin, throws much light on this singular transaction, and on the habits of Queen Edgifa's days.

In her will, Edgifa declares to the Archbishop of the Convent of Christ's Church, at Canterbury, how the land of Cowling came to her, viz.—"That her father had granted to her the land and deed, as he rightfully acquired it, and his ancestors granted it to him. It happened that her father borrowed thirty pounds of Goda, and delivered to him this land as surety for the money, and he held it seven years. Then it happened that all the Kentish men were in the war at Holme. But Sighelm, her father, was unwilling to set out for the wars in any one's debt, and therefore repaid to Goda the thirty pounds, and bequeathed the land to Edgifa, his daughter. When he had fallen in battle, then Goda denied the payment of the money, and kept possession of the land for six years. Then Berksige Deyring,[3] persisted in affirming it, till at length the nobles who were there, counselled Edgifa to purge the land of her father of so great a sum of money; and she accordingly made oath, in the presence of the whole people at Arlesford, and there cleared her father concerning the

[1] Lappenberg, Fl. Wigorn, William of Malmesbury. [2] Palgrave.

[3] A Saxon lawyer?

repayment, by oath, of the thirty pounds. She was not, however, allowed to enter on possession of the land, until her friends had prevailed upon King Edward to prohibit Goda from holding it any longer, on pain of losing all he possessed; whereupon he gave it up. It happened afterwards, in course of time, that the King expressed so much displeasure to Goda, that he gave him in an account of the deeds and lands which he possessed. And the King, therefore, delivered him and all his privileges, with the deeds and lands, to Edgifa, to dispose of as she pleased. Then she said, that she dared not, for fear of God, so retaliate on him as he had deserved of her; and she restored to him all his lands, except two caracutes at Osterland. But she would not return the deeds until she knew how far he would abide by them in respect to the lands which were to be his." These were, doubtless, the lands held by mortgage from Sighelm; and that Edgifa understood the character of the man whom she had to oppose in this legal contest, is evident by the subsequent events, as the will itself declares, to which we shall have occasion to advert hereafter.

Edgifa had two sons by Edward, Edmund and Edred, and two daughters. Of the second marriage one son remained, and six daughters. Of the first, Athelstan and Beatrice, who were educated at a distance from Edward's court, under the care of his sister, the Lady of Mercia; there, though separated from their step-mother Edgifa, they preserved a tender affection for her, and for the numerous offspring of Edward, their father; of which many proofs occurred after the death of the King.[1]

Edward, in the careful education of his children, followed the example of his father's wisdom. His daughters have been compared to those of Charlemagne, with whom a similar course was adopted. Their early years were devoted to the acquirement of solid knowledge, and the accomplishments prized at the period were theirs; nor was the use of the distaff and spindle neglected by the Princesses; so that their minds and bodies were always occupied—the surest method by which good conduct can be preserved. Very precious and elaborate specimens in "raiments of wrought needlework" and early English embroidery, are said to have been produced by the diligence of these "King's daughters."[2]

The sons of Edward had equal means afforded them of gaining the information necessary to constitute good princes.

A story is related of Eadburga, the youngest of Edgifa's daughters,

---

[1] Turner's Anglo-Saxon.

[2] The skill of the daughters of Edward in spinning and weaving is praised in the highest terms by our historians, and they were likewise instructed with the greatest possible care in the art of needlework: so renowned was their talent with the distaff that the term "spinster" is said to have been derived from these royal ladies. With such noble examples before them for contemplation, it is not to be wondered that we learn that the leisure hours of the Saxon women (even of the first rank) were spent in spinning and such like servile employments; neither was it any dishonor for the lady of the house to be among her maids, helping them and performing the duties of the house in common with them, while the lord was with his men, assisting and overlooking them; many instances of which may be brought to prove the ancient simplicity and plainness of their manners.—*Strutt's Saxon Antiquities.*

when only three years of age. The princess was led by her father into a room; in which the King had previously placed in one part a quantity of rings and bracelets; and a chalice, with a book of the Gospels, in another. The child was desired by her father to make her choice between them, when disregarding the vain ornaments of a transitory existence, she ran to those objects dedicated to religion. Edward, tracing in the infantine act a predilection for the service of Heaven, exclaimed with fervour, as he clasped her in his arms, "Go whither the Divine Spirit calls thee: follow with happy footsteps the spouse whom thou hast chosen!"[1] Accordingly the royal child was consigned to the care of her grandmother, Queen Elswitha, who resided at the convent at Winchester. She dwelt, for many years after, among that holy sisterhood, distinguishing herself by acts of piety and humility.[2] Monkish chroniclers relate of her rare humility, that "she would at night, secretly remove the socks[3] worn by the several nuns, and after having washed and *carefully anointed* them, replace them on the beds of her sleeping companions."[4] Long after her death, the acts of Eadburga were fondly recounted by the religious of the nunneries of Winchester, and Pershore in Worcestershire, at which last place her "sacred relics had been deposited, but were afterwards exhumed by Bishop Ethelwold and placed in a rich shrine, the Abbess Elfleda having covered them with gold and silver."

A. D. 925.—At the time of Edward's death he was residing at "Farndon, in Mercia,"[5] which is by some supposed to be Faringdon, in Berkshire.[6] A few days later the King was followed to the tomb by Prince Ethelwerd, the son of Elfleda, his former Queen. Both father and son were interred with regal solemnity in the New Monastery of Winchester,

[1] William of Malmesbury. [2] Lingard.

[3] *Socca*, or socks, were sometimes made of leather, as it appears these of the nuns were, by the "anointing" mentioned.

[4] "In the eighth and ninth centuries, the Anglo-Saxons wore stockings reaching halfway up the thigh, called by writers of the period "*hose;*" the most general material being linen, although "*skin hose*" and "*leather hose*" are likewise often mentioned. Over these stockings bands of cloth, linen, and leather, were worn, commencing at the ankle and terminating a little below the knee, generally bound round the leg like the haybands of a modern ostler, but sometimes crossing each other, as they are worn to this day by the people of the Abruzzi and the Appenines. In some illuminations of the period a sort of half-stocking is represented over the hose, instead of the bandages, having the tops generally embroidered, and these appear to have been called *socca*, or socks. They wore boots or buskins, but generally shoes (*sceo* or *scho*); slippers also appear to have been worn, called *slype-sceo* and *unhege-sceo*. The shoe is mostly painted down the instep, secured by a thong, the material being commonly leather, but the Anglo-Saxon princes and high ecclesiastical dignitaries are often represented with shoes of gold covered with precious stones. The shoemaker's seems to have been a comprehensive trade, and to have united some that are now very distinct businesses. He says in an ancient Anglo-Saxon dialogue: "My craft is very useful and necessary to you. I buy hides and skins, and prepare them by my art, and make of them shoes of various kinds, and none of you can winter without my craft." He subjoins a list of the articles he fabricates: — "Ankle-leathers, shoes, leather hose, bottles, bridle thongs, trappings, flasks, boiling vessels, leather neck-pieces, halters, wallets, and pouches."

[5] Saxon Chronicle. [6] Lysons's Mag. Brit.; Holinshed, Raleigh.

near the remains of Alfred the Great, whom Ethelwerd is said to have greatly resembled in person, manners, and literary attainments. The double loss must have fallen heavily on the bereaved Queen and her family. Ethelwerd, the deceased Prince, had been a youth of great hopes, and perhaps Edward had anticipated his early death; for a few days before he expired, he summoned Athelstan to his presence, and having declared his desire that he should succeed him on the throne, piously admonished him as to his future conduct and mode of government. Thus Edgifa beheld Athelstan, the son of the shepherdess Egwina, raised by his father's will to the throne, in preference to her sons Edmund and Edred, still infants, as well as to the exclusion of Edwin, the surviving brother of Ethelwerd. The choice of Edward seems to have been grounded in this instance on the predilection of his father, the wise Alfred, for this his favourite grandchild, and Athelstan was accordingly crowned, with but one dissenting voice, at Kingston.[1]

It was the first care of Athelstan to provide for the future welfare of the numerous family of the deceased King. Within the course of a few months, his sister Beatrice was given away in marriage, some think, sacrificed, to Sihtric, King of the Northumbrian Danes, who was only baptized on the occasion, and died within a year, when much confusion ensued for the succession.

The first and third daughters of Elfleda, Edward's second Queen, devoted themselves to a life of celibacy: these were Edfleda, "who assumed the sacred robes of a nun; and Ethelhilda, who continued to wear a humble lay habit: both renounced the pleasures of this world, and were at their death interred near the remains of their mother at Winchester." Their sister Edgifa was married, during King Edward's life, to Charles the Simple, King of France, and the same year of Athelstan's accession, returned an exile with her son, and placed herself under the protection of the English King.

Edgifa is said to have been distinguished above her sisters for merit and genius. Through the treason of Robert, Count de Vermandois, Charles the Simple had been imprisoned in the Castle of Peronne; while Raoul, son of Richard, Duke of Burgundy, caused himself to be proclaimed King, and crowned at Soissons, A. D. 923, though he acted only as Regent during Charles's imprisonment. Edgifa had made every possible effort to procure the release of her husband, but in vain. She fled to secure her son's life, and after a six years' captivity, the unfortunate Charles died in his prison, worn out with sorrow and misery.

Edgifa returned in sorrow to the home of her childhood, and continued to reside there with her son Louis.

Henry I., son of Conrad, King of the Germans, and Emperor of the Romans, had demanded for his son Otho, a sister of Athelstan in marriage. The English King had four sisters, available alike in beauty, though of dissimilar ages, two of whom he sent to the Emperor; these were Edgifa and Elgiva, children of Elfleda. The Emperor Henry bestowed the former on his own son Otho, who succeeded him in the

---

[1] Athelstan is said to have first worn a crown of pure gold.

empire, so that the Princess became eventually Empress of Germany. Her sister Elgifa was given in marriage by her father-in-law, the Emperor Henry,[1] to a personage who is always named as "a Duke who resided near the Alps." Where this undefined locality might be, historians, copying each other, are content to remain ignorant.

Another of the daughters of Edward was given by Athelstan to Louis, Prince of Aquitaine.

The numerous daughters of Edward the Elder may be thus enumerated:

Beatrice, Queen of Northumberland, wife of Sihtric.
Edfleda, and Ethelhilda, nuns.
Edgifa, Queen of Charles the Simple.
Edgifa, wife of Otho, Empress of Germany.
Elgiva, married to "a Duke near the Alps."
Edgiva, wife of Louis, King of Aquitaine.
Elfleda, wife of Louis, King of Provençe.
Eadburga, nun at Winchester; and
Edilda, married to Hugh the Great, Count of Paris.

The affairs of France remaining unchanged, it became the policy of Athelstan to reconcile himself with the successful ruler.[2] Charles the Simple was still in captivity, and Hugh the Great, called Count of Paris, was all powerful. Negotiations were, therefore, entered into for the marriage of his youngest sister Edilda.

Adulf of Flanders, grandson of King Alfred, through his daughter Elswitha, and nephew of Athelstan, conducted the embassy, and in the name of Hugh, brought over an immense number of precious gifts, which he displayed before the nobles at Abingdon.

These presents consisted of Oriental spices, hitherto unknown in England, brilliant gems, especially emeralds, many fleet horses, and other gifts worthy of being more especially described.[3] Amongst them, "a vase composed of onyx, and sculptured with such a subtle artistic hand, that as it was looked upon, the harvest-field pourtrayed upon it seemed to incline in waving bends upon its surface, the vines to bud forth, as if with a rich germinating juice, and its engraven men to move, as if endowed with life; whilst its shining and polished surface reflected, as if it were a mirror, the mimic face and form of the beholder." Another present was "the sword of Constantine the Great, bearing the name of that Emperor, inscribed in letters of gold; while upon its pommel, rising up above the rich plates of gold, was to be seen one of the four nails used in the crucifixion." This valuable gift was accompanied with the lance of Charlemagne, used in his wars against the Saracens, and the famous pennon which had belonged to that Emperor, by whom it was displayed in his war in Spain. "A diadem, rich with thick gold and precious jewels, the lustre of which dazzled the eyes of the beholders." A particle of the true cross, enclosed in crystal, and of the crown of thorns,

[1] Holinshed. [2] Lappenberg. [3] William of Malmesbury.

encased in a similar manner, were also among the offerings of the princely suitor.

Athelstan received the bearers of these treasures with great courtesy, and having accepted the proposal of Hugh for the Princess his sister, directed that the holy cross and sacred crown should be deposited in the Abbey of Malmesbury.[1]

Edilda, said to have been the most beautiful of all the sisters, was united to Hugh the Great, A. D. 926: this was a tie which doubly united the nations of France and England, and entailed singular consequences; for when Charles the Simple died, A. D. 929, at the castle of Peronne, two competitors alone remained for the French crown, the Count de Vermandois and Hugh the Great.

At this time, the abilities of Edilda's sister, the exiled Queen Edgifa, were once more called into action. She resolved to make one more effort in behalf of her child, in whom she hoped to see the royal line restored. She applied to William, Duke of Normandy, a generous prince, allied by blood to the royal family of France, and who saw in the enterprise much advantage to be gained to himself. The Duke by his credit with the French nobles, engaged them to recall Louis. The French, either from love to their ancient masters, or fearing the troubles which the competition of Herbert and Hugh would cause, sent deputies to England, to bring back the son of Edgifa. This princess, rendered cautious by experience, hesitated before delivering the young Louis into the hands of the deputies, at the head of whom was William, Archbishop of Sens. She exacted from him, in his own name, and that of the nobles and the nation, not only hostages, but a promise to be more faithful to him than they had been to Charles the Simple: the conditions were accepted, and the Princess gave up her son; nor had she cause to repent it. Edgifa herself accompanied him in triumph to Boulogne, where, on their arrival, they were met by Hugh the Great and other French nobles, who united in taking the oath of fealty to him, and received him with every demonstration of joy, while the people sincerely rejoiced in the return of their sovereign. The sincerity of the nobles at this juncture is, however, questionable; for Edgifa is said to have returned to England, to obtain succours from her brother, King Athelstan, and herself heading the forces, a complete revolution was effected; Louis was triumphantly placed upon the throne, and peace restored to the kingdom. The spectacle was thus afforded of the grand-daughter of the Great Alfred heroically emulating her ancestor, by leading an army composed of English and French indifferently. Louis, only seventeen years of age, was proclaimed King at Boulogne, and afterwards conducted to Laon to be crowned, which ceremony was performed on the 20th of June, A. D. 936, by Artold, Archbishop of Rheims, in presence of more than twenty bishops, Hugh the Great, and the rest of the nobility of France. There is no reason to doubt that both the widowed Queen of Charles, and her sister Edilda, the wife of Hugh, were present at this triumphant ending of long disappointments. The coronation was rendered still more interesting by the

[1] William of Malmesbury.

marriage, at the same time, of Louis to his young cousin Gerberga, daughter of the Emperor Otho.[1]

Edgifa finding the nobles sought to govern in her son's name, and that, fearing she might obtain the regency, they were opposed to her residing in France, retired into England, where she remained at Athelstan's court till 938, when Louis, who resided at Laon, sent for her to assist him with her advice. She therefore returned to the court of Louis d'Outremer,—for so he was called from his sojourn in England. In France, however, Edgifa became involved in a new series of troubles, from her too open friendship with the House of Vermandois, always odious and displeasing to the reigning family. With singular imprudence, she allowed herself to become attached to Herbert,[2] the second son of that Count of Vermandois who had made her husband his prisoner at Peronne, where he died.

So offended and jealous was Louis at his mother's conduct, that he caused her residence at Laon to resemble a sort of honourable imprisonment. At last she contrived to escape from her guardians there, and some time after, although she had attained a mature age, married her youthful lover Herbert, then only twenty, at St. Quentin, for which act her son dispossessed her of the royal revenues she had so long enjoyed.[3] The following year, Edgifa gave birth to a son, Stephen of Troyes, but died in 953, in her confinement with a daughter, the Princess Agnes of Lorraine. Such was the fate of the sister of Athelstan, her son's policy inducing so much harshness to a mother to whom he owed his crown, his early safety, and careful education.

Lothaire, the grandson of Edgifa by Louis d'Outremer and Gerberga, succeeded his father at the end of a long reign of thirty-eight years, and was followed by another son of his own, Louis the Fifth, the last of the Carlovingian race; but during the reigns of these three nominal kings, the real power was held by Hugh the Great, who had married Edilda, and afterwards by their son, Hugh Capet, who, on the death of Louis the Fifth, seized the crown, A. D. 987, being the first sovereign of that royal house whose late misfortunes resemble those of the Stuarts. From Hugh Capet, was lineally descended Eleanor de Montfort, the wife of Llewelyn, the last of the Welsh Princes, from whom Henry VII. claimed his maternal descent.

The widowed Edgifa, Queen of Edward the Elder, during all these changes of fortune, was still unable to establish her claim to her patrimonial inheritance. After her husband died, the dispute was renewed, as we learn from the statement in the Queen's will, to which we return, as it runs through the web of this complicated history: "Then King Edward died, and Athelstan came to the throne. Then Goda, availing himself of the opportunity, went to King Athelstan, and besought him to require of Edgifa the restoration of his deeds, which he did; and she restored him all, except the deeds of Osterland; and he with his own hand released to her that paper (or deed), and humbly gave her thanks

[1] De Menin's Treatise on the Anointing and Coronation of the Kings and Queens of France.

[2] Historic Anecdotes.

[3] Rivalité de la France et de l'Angleterre.

for the rest, and moreover he gave her his oath that the compact should stand good to her children, born and unborn, for ever. And this was done in the sight of Athelstan and of his nobles, at ——, near Lewes. And Edgifa held the land and deeds during the lives of his two sons, who succeeded him."[1]

On the death of Athelstan, after a sixteen years' reign, A. D. 941, the Queen of Edward the Elder had the satisfaction of beholding her eldest son Edmund raised to the throne, who had obtained the surname of "the Pious." The new monarch was then in the twentieth year of his age,[2] having been only four years old at the time his father died. The coronation took place at Kingston; and the same year, 941, Edmund was united to Elfgiva, by whom he became father of Edwy and Edgar, who afterwards sat on the throne. The birth of this last prince, in 943, took place at a vill close by Glastonbury, which from that circumstance derived the name Edgarlei, which it still retains. At the time Prince Edgar was born, St. Dunstan is said to have heard voices which seemed high up in the air, and which sounded as if intoning a psalm and giving utterance to these words: "Peace shall prevail amid the Church of the English during the time of the boy who has been born, and of our Dunstan."[3]

Glastonbury was especially favoured by Edmund. It is said that one day, when the King was out hunting, he set forward with his dogs in advance of his suite in the pursuit of a herd of deer which had been roused by their horns, and that stag and hounds, reaching a steep precipice, plunged into the abyss and were dashed to pieces; the King, eager in the chase, dashed after them so furiously that he was unable to check his horse, and on the moment when death stared him in the face, he uttered a mental prayer that if he could be saved, St. Dunstan, whom alone of all people living he had injured, should receive ample compensation. The horse arrived on the very edge of the precipice, stopped suddenly,[4] and the King's life was saved, as he believed, by the intercession of the holy man. Returned home, Edmund sent for Dunstan, and commanded him to ride with him to Glastonbury. There, having first offered up his prayers, Edmund took Dunstan by the right hand and led him to the sacerdotal throne, on which he placed him with these words:—"Be thou the Prince in this place, its potent possessor, and the most faithful abbot of this church; and whatsoever may be here wanting to thee, either for the advancement and increase of divine worship, or for the sustentation and administration of the sacred monastic rule, I will, with a devout heart and royal munificence, supply thee." Dunstan accordingly laid the foundation of a glorious church, and as soon as the building was completed, assembled in it a company of monks. Edmund bestowed a charter of privilege on the abbey, A. D. 944. This charter was inscribed in golden letters in a copy of the Evangelists, presented by Edmund to the church, a beautiful illustration of Saxon art. In the charter, after the King had

[1] Lives of the Saints.
[2] Turner says eighteen: Antiquities of Glastonbury.
[3] Flor. Wigorn.
[4] Ibid.

signed his own name, the following persons attested the deed, Eadred, the King's brother, and Edgifa, his mother, in these words: "I, Edgifa, mother of the King, have confirmed the aforesaid gift."[1]

As the signature of the King's wife is not there, this grant probably took place after the decease of that most excellent woman, whose remains were interred at Shipton, or Shaftesbury,[2] and she became venerated as a saint for her many virtues. Her solicitude for the relief of the indigent, and charity in procuring the liberty of slaves, are particularly noticed by our monkish chroniclers, whose pages are filled with testimonials to her goodness. Of her, William of Malmesbury declares: "She was a woman always intent on good works, endowed with such piety and sweetness, as privately to redeem prisoners, and readily to bestow on the poor even her most precious garments. This Queen is said to have been remarkable for the beauty of her person, and so skilful, and admirable in the works wrought by her hands, according to the fashion of her times, that even envy itself, finding no fault, was compelled to praise. Malmesbury assures us that St. Elfgifa was not only eminent for her virtues during life, but for her miracles after death. He declares that she was favoured with the gift of prophecy, and in his work entitled "De Gestis Pontificium" may be seen an account of the miracles of this Queen, originally in metre, but written there in prose, and according to the author's own statement, when "he was young," before A.D. 1125.[3]

One of these miracles is thus given, but as it concerns Edgar, her youngest son, who could have been only an infant, either the good Queen must have survived the date usually assigned as that of her death, for many years, or else it must have been performed by her step-mother Queen Edgifa. The widow of Edward the Elder was so popular with the English, that many of the subsequent Queens of England, till Emma of Normandy, who died shortly before the Conquest, assumed hers as a sort of surname in addition to their own; thus Emma was called Emma Elfgiva,[4] or the "Help-Giver." The legend stands thus:—

---

[1] Hearne Monasticon, vol. i.; Warner.

[2] The Monastery of Shaftesbury is said to have been built by Elfgiva, Queen of Edmund, in conjunction with her son Edgar, for nuns, and at her death she was not only interred there, but miracles are said to have been afterwards wrought at her tomb. Shaftesbury, once a village, but now a city, was built on the declivity of a hill, and a stone, transferred from an old wall to the chapter-house of the monastery, had this inscription:—"In the year of our Lord's incarnation, 880, King Alfred, in the eighth year of his reign, founded this city." Some say that Elfgiva did not die till 971 or 972, and that in the last of these dates she attested a charter to Glastonbury. In the days of Malmesbury and Ethelwerd miracles were still worked at the tomb of St. Elfgiva. "She was much afflicted by her wicked son Edwy, but comforted by his brother Edgar. God was pleased, for some years before her death, to try her with long and tedious illnesses, with which she was purified like gold in the furnace, and fitted for the heavenly palaces, to which she was called A.D. 971. Her festival is celebrated on the 18th of May, according to Britannia Sancta, which calls her the mother of Edwy and Edgar."

[3] William of Malmesbury, Miraculæ S. Elfgifæ.

[4] It will have been observed that the letters *f* and *v* are used indifferently in Saxon.

Edgar one day, out hunting, pursued the chase to the extremity of the forest, and alighting there to await his friends, threw himself on the ground beneath the shade of a wild apple-tree beside a stream, where he fell asleep. A female hound, apparently large with whelp, came to rest at the monarch's feet, and aroused the sleeper. The hound was mute, but the whelps within barked as if for joy. The surprised King, raising his eyes, beheld two apples successively fall into the stream, which in doing so caused a sound to be emitted from the splashing bubbles of the disturbed waters, resembling the words, "Well is thee! well is thee!"[1] Shortly after the King perceived a small empty pitcher, followed by a large one filled with water, floating down the stream, and as if the waters were like to a whirlpool, the larger strove to empty its contents into the smaller one, but without success, for it escaped empty from every such attempt, though it dashed saucily against the side of the larger vessel.

On Edgar's return, he sought his mother, to whom he knew God had revealed many things, and desired the meaning of what he had seen. The Queen directed her son to tranquillize his mind, and having delayed her reply till the following morning, addressed her son in these words:—

"The barking of the whelps, while the mother was quiescent, signifies that those who are now in power and doing well (though evil-disposed), will remain silent; but that, after thy death, worthless, wicked, debauched spendthrifts, as yet unborn, will be found to arise and bark against God's Church.

"As to the one apple falling in quick succession after the other, so that from their collision as they fell a sound was emitted, which seemed to convey the words, 'Well is thee,' this signifies, that from thee, who are now as a tree shading all England, shall issue two sons; and those who favour the pretensions of the second shall destroy the first, and then the promoters of their opposing parties shall say of each of the young Princes, 'Well is thee,' because he who is dead shall be reigning in heaven, and he who is living shall be reigning in this world.

"Then as to the larger pitcher not being able to fill up the smaller with its contents, that is intended to designate the nations of the Northmen, which are more numerous than the English, and who will, after thy death, attack England; and although they will make many attempts to supply the losses suffered in their ranks, by fresh accessions of their compatriots, shall never be able to fill up with their soldiers this corner of the world. On the contrary, our Angles, even when they seem to be most completely subdued, will have vigour and strength enough to expel them, and the land shall be theirs, as it is in accordance with the will of God, and so shall remain until the time pre-appointed by Christ."[2]

Edmund married a second wife, as we learn from the Saxon Chronicle, who survived him; this second consort was Elfleda of Damerham, daughter of Ealdorman Elgar,[3] who adopted the name of Edgifa, in consequence of which circumstance great confusion occurs, in the Chronicles

[1] "Wel his the."
[2] William of Malmesbury; Gest. Pont. Ang
[3] Saxon Chronicle.

attributing to one Queen the acts of the other, so that it is difficult to distinguish them.

When only in his twenty-fifth year, A. D. 946, the young monarch Edmund was slain by a robber, named Leolf, at Puckle-kirk, in Gloucestershire,[1] on the occasion of his celebrating the mass-day of St. Augustine, which was customary with the Saxons.

Edmund had formerly enacted some severe laws against thieves, and pecuniary punishments proving inefficient, had commanded that the oldest in every gang should suffer the extreme penalty of death.[2] This was the first time that the life of man had been taken for theft, and it cost Edmund his own.

Leolf was a notorious robber, banished for his crimes. He suddenly presented himself to the King, forcing his way into the palace, whence Edmund indignantly ordered him to be expelled; he fiercely resisted the cup-bearer, to whom the order was given, and who endeavoured to obey the royal mandate. On this, the exasperated monarch rushed on Leolf and seized him by the hair, when the robber drew his dagger and stabbed the youthful prince to the heart. Edmund did not die instantly, but the wound in his breast proved mortal. The assassin was despatched forthwith by the royal attendants.[3]

Edmund the Pious, after a short reign of six years,[4] thus died in 946, leaving his two children so young, that in a council held to settle the succession, they were adjudged unfit to reign, and the crown awarded to their uncle Edred.

It was in the reign of Edmund, the son of the sainted Edgifa, that the celebrated Reay Cross, or Ray Cross, was placed on Stanmore, on the confines of Westmoreland and Yorkshire, bearing upon it the *arms of England and Scotland sculptured on the opposite sides.* It was erected in testimony of Edmund's grant of Cumberland (which district he had obtained by the conquest of Dunmaile, its King) to Malcolm, King of Scots, on the condition that Malcolm should hold it of him, and protect the northern parts of England by sea and land against hostile incursions. From this circumstance the eldest sons of the Scottish monarchs from that time were styled "Governors of Cumberland,"[5] and the Cross was placed as a memorial of the divisions of the two kingdoms.

Queen Edgifa is frequently noticed during the reign of her younger son Edred. Having heard that St. Ethelwold, Abbot of Glastonbury, had resolved to go to France to study the Holy Scriptures, the Queen, considering the Prelate's absence would be no small loss to the kingdom, prevailed upon her son to stay his journey, and make him Abbot of Abingdon in Berkshire. She assured Edred that Ethelwold had not only wisdom enough to suffice for himself, but to guide others, and that he needed not to seek in foreign lands for what he possessed already, and she begged him not to let so great a man depart the country; the King was delighted to hear this assurance from his mother, and acted on her suggestion.[6] It

[1] Saxon Chronicle.
[2] Rapin.
[3] Hume, Raleigh, Lingard.
[4] Britton and Brayley.
[5] Camden's Britannia, 1594.
[6] Wolstan Vit. S. Ethelwold.

was Edred who, in the latter part of his reign, repaired the Abbey of Abingdon, which had been built by King Ina, but had fallen to decay and ruin.[1] In this great undertaking the Abbot and monks were assisted by grants of money from the royal treasures, and the most material benefit was conferred upon them by the donations of the Queen-Mother.

Ethelwold, who by Edgifa's influence had been made Abbot of Abingdon, was afterwards made Bishop of Winchester.

At the time when Edred was endeavouring to persuade his friend and adviser Dunstan, Abbot of Glastonbury, to accept the see of Winchester, which he had declined, as being unfit for it, Edred entreated his mother, Queen Edgifa, to invite the prelate to dinner and add her persuasions. "I know," said the King, "dearest mother and Queen of the broad empire of the English, that our mutual friend Dunstan loves you the most of living beings, and that he takes an especial delight in the good works that you do; because, whatever he counsels you for the sake of eternal life to perform, that you are sure willingly to accomplish, whether it be in giving alms for the subsistence of the poor, or in the bestowal of donations for the advancement of churches.[2] Therefore is it, that I have confident hope that if you beseech him to do that which it is becoming in me to ask, and in him to perform, he cannot justly refuse a compliance with your request. It is a thing perfectly manifest to all persons, that he ought to hold the highest rank in the priesthood. This is as plain to us as that we are his inferiors in wisdom, and in all that duly merits honour and respect in this life, as we are sure that he who is King of the English is a more powerful monarch than any of the other kings of the earth. Address him, then, with that winning eloquence which belongs to women: struggle, in order that the grace which you have obtained in his eyes, may gain from the servant of God a compliance which cannot but tend to aid in releasing us from the bonds of sin."

The Queen-Mother, in obedience to the words of her son, invited Dunstan to come to her, and sought, by her arguments, to induce him to relax in his resolution, but he remained unmoved. "I am unwilling," said he, "lady, that thou shouldst ask of me aught that it would hurt my conscientious feelings to concede, or the refusal to concede which may give offence to thee. I am not ignorant how difficult it is for each of us to plead his cause before the tribunal of Christ, much less how difficult it will be for a man to obtain an acquittal in those cases in which he has acted as the adviser or the judge of others. If, however, these considerations cannot produce any impression upon thy mind, I would desire to add another, and such as may be esteemed that which mainly must prevent me from receiving a bishopric. I see that my lord, the King, suffers under a constant languor, that his life is endangered by it, that he cannot endure to be parted from me for a moment, because he has made me as if the father of a sovereign, and the master of an entire kingdom."

As the Queen-Mother still persisted in urging him to accept the mitre, notwithstanding his repeated refusals, he, somewhat agitated, said to her

[1] Magna Brit. [2] Lives of the Saints.

"Most assuredly, the episcopal mitre shall never cover my brows in the days of this thy son."[1]

From this conversation Dunstan departed, with his mind much agitated. The next day, however, he informed the King that, after his interview with Edgifa, he had, on his return home, beheld a vision of St. Peter, who struck him, saying, "This is the punishment for your refusal, and a token to you not to decline hereafter the primacy of England." The King, not perceiving his friend's artifice, who desired to be all or none, interpreted the vision to his own mind, asserting that it foretold he was to be Archbishop of Canterbury.[2]

In 955, the death of Edred deprived Edgifa of her son, and Dunstan of a firm friend. His nephew Edwy, eldest son of Edmund, succeeded him, a prince then in his sixteenth year. He not only manifested an open antipathy to the clergy, but deprived many prelates of their benefices, and even went so far as to banish Dunstan from the kingdom. These measures gave great umbrage to the people; but they were still more displeased, and loudly and vehemently did they express their indignation, when they beheld the manner in which Edwy treated his aged grandmother, the venerable Queen Edgifa. Upon some unknown pretext, she was despoiled of all she possessed, and reduced to a state of indigence and privacy.[3] Eadmer, writing of the injuries Edwy inflicted on his grandmother, says, "He afflicted immensely *his mother, the glory of all England, the consoler of churches, and the supporter of the oppressed*, and after having taken away from her the property belonging to her, cruelly and barbarously degraded her from her previous dignity." For this ill-treatment no other cause is apparent than the favour with which the Queen had always regarded the clergy.

As regards her patrimonial estate, we find that the Queen's own Charter runs thus:—"At length Edred died, and Edgifa was despoiled of her whole inheritance. When Leofric and Leofstan, the two sons of Goda, seized from Edgifa the two aforesaid lands at Cowling and at Osterland, and said to the young Edwy, who had then been elected, that they were more rightfully theirs than hers. And so it was settled until Edgar." The reign of the oppressor was, however, prematurely brought to a close. The people rebelled against Edwy, and placed his brother Edgar, a boy of twelve years of age, on the throne, which caused Edwy to die of grief soon after.

Edgar was no sooner made king than he annulled all the oppressive acts of the preceding government. Attention was forthwith paid to the injuries of Edgifa, who now recovered her often-disputed patrimony.[4] The Queen's Charter says of King Edgar, that "he and his nobles decreed that they (viz. Leofric and Leofstan, the sons of Goda) had committed a wicked robbery, and they decreed the inheritance to be hers, and had it restored. Then Edgifa received by the King's permission, and in presence of him and all his bishops, the said deeds, and laying her hand on the altar, gave the land to the Church of Christ, viz., to the convent

[1] Osbern, Vit. St. Dunstan; Acta Sancta; Aug. Sacra.

[2] Turner's Anglo-Saxons. [3] Lingard. [4] Ibid.

(of Christ's Church at Canterbury), and for the quiet of her soul; and denounced that Christ, with the whole assembly of heaven, would bring evil on him for ever, who should at any time pervert or make void this bequest. Thus this inheritance came to the convent of the Church of Christ." No doubt the harassed Queen saw that this was the only plan of securing the property, as the Church would guard its own.

Appended to an antique picture of Queen Edgifa are the following lines commemorative of her donations to the Church; in it her name is written, as is sometimes the case in our old authors, Eddeva or Edyve:—

"Edyve, the good queene and noble mother
To Ethelstane, Edmund, and Eldred,
Kinges of England, every each after other,
To Christ's Church of Canterbury did give indeed,
Monketon and Thorndenn, the monkes there to feede;
Meyham, Cleene, Cowlinge, Osterland,
East Farleugh, and Lenham, as we beeleve;
The yeare Dom. MLXI. of Christ's incarnation."

In the subscriptions of King Edgar's Charter of Privilege to Hyde Abbey, by Winchester, which is yet remaining in the valuable library of Sir Robert Cotton, are contained also the signatures of Elfrida, that monarch's queen, and Edgifa, his aged grandmother. They are written in letters of gold, in a hand of that age: "Ego Edgifu, prædicti regis avia hoc opus egregiam crucis taumate consolidavi." Selden observes that Edgifa durst not style herself any other than "the king's grandmother," on account of the law passed in Wessex through the crimes of Eadburga; for so "avia," as well as "avea," denoted, of which many instances in those times are on record.

Edgifa died August 25th, A. D. 963.[1]

[1] Notes to Lye's Saxon Dictionary, whence the Queen's will has been extracted.

ETHELGIVA,

QUEEN OF EDWY THE FAIR.

Ethelgiva's relationship to the young Prince Edwy the Fair—Her extreme beauty — St. Dunstan's character and history — His contentions with the Devil; his temptations and triumphs—The fame of the Saint—St. Dunstan's mortification to find the young King married—The forced coronation—Flight of the King—Anger of the nobles—Rage of the Bishops—Discovery of the weeping Bride—Insults to Edwy and Ethelgiva—Passionate words of the Mother of the young Queen—Fury of Dunstan—Sympathy of the People for the Royal Pair—Ethelgiva refused the title of Queen—Edwy's dislike to the ambitious Prelate—The evil spirit at Glastonbury—Flight of Dunstan—His dangers from his enemies, the married priests—Security of the Royal Lovers—Seizure of Ethelgiva: horrible vengeance—She is sent to Ireland—Odo's representations to the King—His despair — His troubles — His brother Edgar — Recall of Dunstan—Divorce pronounced against Ethelgiva—Excommunication of Edwy—Recovery of Ethelgiva, and attempt to return—Waylaid on her journey—Hamstrung and starved to death—Broken heart of Edwy—He dies—Buried at Winchester.

THE history of Ethelgiva's life is a sad episode, and presents a picture of crime, cruelty, and bigotry rarely equalled in the annals of any country. She must have been of royal blood, as she is said to be so nearly allied to her husband that the fact furnished a pretext for the injuries inflicted upon her by her ruthless enemies. No narrative can more strongly illustrate the extraordinary power of the Church, and the persistance of its servants, than the tale of Edwy's persecuted wife. She is represented as so remarkably beautiful, that Edwy, prior to his accession, had been unable to resist the fascination of her charms, and is supposed to have married her in secret. On this step all the after misfortunes of the enamoured pair seem to have depended. The monkish writers who have told her story are generally desirous to avert blame from St. Dunstan, through whom the misfortunes of Ethelgiva arose, and it is their object to prove that no marriage whatever took place between the lovers; that Ethelgiva, her mother, was of infamous character, and that the conduct of Prince Edwy was worthy of all reprehension. That there was imprudence in the connection there can be no doubt, and it is possible that they might have been within the forbidden degrees of relationship; but nothing could excuse the extreme and persevering cruelty with which their fault, admitting it to have existed, was punished by the severe and haughty churchman whose will was resisted by the young King.

Perhaps the bitterness of St. Dunstan to the unfortunate pair may be better understood when the circumstances of his own life are considered.

The tender feelings he had once himself experienced might have been expected to cause him to look with indulgence on the natural weakness of youth; instead of which the memory of his sacrifices seems to have rendered him fiercely severe and implacable in his resolution to root out every tendency to yield to the impulses of passion or affection. Whatever the failings of Edwy might be—and his subsequent conduct showed that he had many—the severity of St. Dunstan may be looked upon as having fostered instead of correcting them.

Dunstan was born of a noble Saxon family, at the beginning of the reign of Athelstan.[1] His precocious talents induced his parents to send him for instruction to a famous school at Glastonbury, where his remarkable genius soon developed itself. His bodily health was infirm, but his mental powers were extraordinary. Not only in abstruse learning was he soon distinguished, but in all the lighter literature, such as "heroic poetry, songs and ballads," which was then highly prized. His influential friend Wulfhelm, Archbishop of Canterbury, introduced him at the court of Athelstan; but his haughty and contemptuous bearing, as well as his superiority, gained him more enemies than friends, and the absurd charge of magic was brought forward against him by the jealous ignorance which could not comprehend his amazing information. He was waylaid and attacked by enemies, by whom he was maltreated and left for dead, having been cast into a bog. From this, however, he escaped, was received by a relative, the Bishop of Winchester, and counselled by him to devote himself to a monastic life.

But the world still had charms for the accomplished Dunstan, and he next appears living altogether in the society of, and protected by, a rich matron of royal descent, named Ethelflaed, cultivating the arts of music, painting, and sculpture, in all of which he excelled;[2] his works in metal, such as bells, crucifixes, and censers, were of admirable execution. His fame continued to increase, and reports of miracles performed by him became current. King Athelstan and his court came to visit Ethelflaed and her celebrated guest, and showed him great honour. A miracle he then performed was bruited abroad; it was asserted, that through his power, no sooner had the royal cupbearers poured out the mead from their vessels than they found them instantly filled anew.

At this time, it seems, the heart of the learned Dunstan became the prey of beauty, and he passionately loved a fair maiden from whom Wulfhelm, the Bishop of Canterbury, was anxious to separate him. His reason appears to have been disturbed by the struggles of his mind on this occasion, for his resistance to advice and entreaty was long and resolute. At length the Bishop had recourse to prayer, and implored Heaven that some worldly misfortune might cause him to see the path of duty with more clearness. The evil prayed for arrived, perhaps either in the death or infidelity of her he loved. Dunstan was seized with a dangerous fever, on recovering from which he had no longer any opposition to make to the

[1] Turner, Vita S. Dunstani.

[2] Bridferth, Osbern, &c. In Hickes there is an engraving from one of St Dunstan's drawings, representing the Saviour.

proposal of his zealous relative; and, considering himself called to the holy state, he embraced a monastic life at Glastonbury. Here he began a career of austerity before unparalleled;[1] he built himself a cell too short to allow him to lie at length, and here he wrought at his forge, when not engaged in prayer: he slept little, and his food was almost too scanty to sustain nature. He believed that the Foul Fiend was always on the watch to surprise him, and he thought it necessary to be constantly on his guard against his attempts. Too much learning had no doubt made him mad, and fostered by his solitude, the malady became confirmed. All was, however, by his admiring and bigoted brethren imputed to him for holiness, and their wonder was daily fed by the miraculous tales they heard of devilish forms visiting the cell of Dunstan, and contending with that pious and holy recluse. The Fiend would sometimes thrust his head in at door or window, and insult his ears with profane and foul language. Once the Father of Ill ventured too far, and Dunstan, appearing not to observe him, waited until his tongs were red hot, when suddenly darting forward, he seized the tempter by the nose, who yelled so loud that the hideous noise was heard throughout the whole country.

The solution of this mystery probably is, that the ignorant monks were alarmed at the noise made by the fire in his furnaces, as he prepared the metals on which he wrought.

Every year the fame of Dunstan increased, till at length he was drawn from his retreat, and took up his permanent place at court as chief minister to King Edmund, having been previously made Abbot of Glastonbury, with an enormous revenue. His influence from this time knew no bounds, and his will was paramount in all things. When young Edwy, therefore, came to the crown, it was not likely that he would allow his power to be disputed, or surprising that he should desire to sweep from his path those who dared to oppose him. Of course, when so young a man as Edwy held supreme power, Dunstan expected to have still more authority, and nothing could exceed his anger when he found himself thwarted on the very threshold by the discovery of the King's marriage without his sanction. His representations, that Edwy should separate from Ethelgiva, were unattended to, and nothing but murmurs attended his command that she should not be admitted to a share in the solemnity of the coronation.

The ceremony was performed at Kingston, on a raised platform, in sight of all the people, Archbishop Odo officiating on the occasion. Edwy was remarkable for his handsome person, from which he was called The Fair, and was at the time only in his seventeenth year, a circumstance which might have called for leniency. A magnificent banquet, befitting such an occasion, had been prepared for Edwy and the Saxon nobles; but while the latter were indulging in the rude and noisy merriment accompanying such entertainments, Edwy, watching his opportunity, escaped to society more congenial to his taste, perhaps rejoicing to be able thus to avoid the excessive drinking which was certain to form a feature at these festivals. The Saxon nobles, however, perceiving his

[1] Lappenberg.

absence, were indignant at their entertainer showing them so little courtesy, and loudly expressed the displeasure they felt at the young King's forgetfulness of their dignity.[1] St. Dunstan and the prelate Kynsey were appointed by them "*to bring the King back to the festive board.*" These two ecclesiastics, equally offended with the Saxon nobles, accepted the mission, and angrily leaving the scene of festivity, with a suspicion of the cause of Edwy's absence, not a little irritated and incensed by the disrespect shown to themselves as representatives of the Church, in common with the other guests, but more especially from his acting thus against their known and expressed disapproval of the alliance into which Edwy had entered,—sought the retreat of the imprudent host.

Entirely throwing aside all respect or consideration, the two prelates burst into the apartment of the King, whom they found, as they had expected, in the company of his young wife and her mother. The King, forgetting in the happiness of the moment all but his escape from an irksome ceremony, had taken off and laid on one side the crown of state, that crown which he had not yet been able to share with the woman whom he loved, and was caressing Ethelgiva with fondness, and soothing her mortification at not partaking in the splendour he did not prize alone,—when these rude intruders invaded his privacy.

A most strange and unbecoming scene ensued. With violent language they insisted on the King's returning to the banquet, loading Ethelgiva and her mother with the bitterest threats and reproaches, and heaping on them the most insulting and opprobrious epithets; and then, resolving to accomplish their purpose, forcibly replaced the diadem on the head of Edwy, whom they dragged from his seat, and literally compelled to return with them to the revellers in the banqueting-hall.[2] This was no easy task; for the terrified women clung to him as to their protector, and force only constrained them to separate from him.

At this moment Ethelgiva, the mother of the young wife, turning her eyes on Dunstan, exclaimed in a burst of anger, "How unmeasurable must be the audacity of this man, who has thus ventured to intrude himself upon the privacy of a King! You have threatened me with death by strangulation, but I shall have you doomed to the mutilation of your limbs, and to perpetual banishment."[3]

These passionate words were fatal. Dunstan, enraged at the resistance and the confidence displayed, saw plainly that both the mother and daughter had obtained an influence over the heart of the young Edwy, which the monk had intended to appropriate; and as the elder was the most likely to bias the King in favour of her own views, Dunstan's rage seems to have been peculiarly directed, at this time, against her. It is thought that Dunstan was really ignorant of Edwy's actual marriage to the daughter of Ethelgiva, which may palliate in some degree the violence of his conduct, anxious as he was to prevent the union. On the other hand, the existence of such a tie, and the circumstance of Ethelgiva being denied the usual honours of Queen-Consort, may excuse the ambitious and indignant mother the fury of her resentment. We are told by

[1] Saxon Chronicle. [2] Malmesbury, Wallingford, &c. [3] Osbern.

some chroniclers that he was not married, and that on the coronation-day Ethelgiva and her mother visited Edwy, it being the object of the latter to persuade the King to marry "*one or the other* of them;"[1] but she probably desired him to proclaim his union to his subjects, and thus, without further delay, enable her daughter to wear the crown.[2] Edwy might have been too much in dread of the ecclesiastical authorities to disclose the important fact, and hence his anxiety to pacify both his wife and her mother. The powerful individuals who headed the combination against Edwy's marriage, on finding the tie really did exist, and that it was impossible to be prevented, directed their fury against both the young Queen and her mother, vilifying them in the most atrocious manner.

The conduct of Dunstan meanwhile, instead of producing the results he expected enlisted sympathy for Edwy and his Queen, and the ancient enemies of the proud Abbot were not slow to take advantage of the occasion. Ethelgiva was accepted as the wife of the sovereign, and the star of the prelate declined. Availing herself of Edwy's unconcealed dislike of Dunstan, the young and injured Queen hastened to take revenge, and by his consent, constituted herself mistress not only of all the property and title-deeds belonging to the community of Glastonbury, but of the personal property of Dunstan also; and, at the same time, a decree of instant banishment was issued against him by the King, upon charges from which he was unable to clear himself. The monkish chronicler proceeds to state, that at the time the persons sent to drive the brethren from their monastery were superintending the inventory of the ecclesiastical goods and property subjected to confiscation, there was heard, on the western side of the church, the harsh, ringing laugh of a demon, "which sounded like the wheezy voice of a gleesome hag." It was heard by St. Dunstan himself, and he responded to it in these words: "Foe to mankind, do not rejoice so much; for however great may be thy joy now in seeing my departure, thy grief will be twice as great when God, to thy confusion, shall permit my return." Dunstan saw no safety, for the present, but in flight; but scarcely had the vessel proceeded three miles from

[1] Bridferth, Osbern, and Eadmer.

[2] Those writers who assert that Ethelgiva was not lawfully united to Edwy are supported by several modern authors of the Roman Catholic persuasion, as Dr. Lingard, Dr. Milner, &c. Hallam blames Dr. Henry for calling her Queen and a lawful wife, without intimating that the nature of her tie with Edwy was at the least considered equivocal. Dr. Lingard divides the writers on Ethelgiva's history into two classes — those who wrote before, and those who wrote after the Conquest. Of the first were Bridferth of Romsey, who is followed by Osbern and Eadmer. Neither of these last had, it appears, seen an ancient Life of Odo, written in Anglo-Saxon, Cott. MSS., in British Museum (Nero E. 1 *b.*), which has formed the groundwork of the later Lives of that prelate, and is another authority quoted by Dr. Lingard. A second Life of Odo is another source, of which the author, supposed to be either Eadmer or Osbern, is doubtful: it describes the coronation scene from Bridferth, and then turns to the ancient Life of Odo, the words of which it seems almost to adopt. The additions in this seem like an attempt to reconcile the narrative in the Life of Odo with the account of Osbern, as if the pages of both the latter were open before the writer at the time the MS. was written Malmesbury wrote the story of Ethelgiva twenty or thirty years later

land, being bound for Flanders, where the exiled monk meant to take refuge, when the emissaries of Queen Ethelgiva's mother appeared on the beach, resolved on the destruction of Dunstan, had he remained but a few moments more on shore.

Another abbot was chosen amongst the enemies of Dunstan, Elsy being appointed to Glastonbury, and the abbey was filled with *married* priests, a state which he had resolutely extirpated amongst the clergy, its former community being all displaced. The downfall of Dunstan took place in 956, and was followed by that of other members of the Church, who, despoiled of their property, were driven into banishment.

The reaction of so great a triumph appears to have been too great for the mind of the youthful monarch, who now, surrounding himself with evil counsellors, and feeling his power unlimited, gave way to excesses, which, perhaps, but for the imprudent and injudicious fury of Dunstan, might never have been either in his wish or his reach. Rapacious favourites, young like himself, inexperienced and unprincipled, urged him to the most dangerous and impolitic acts. He despoiled monasteries, and seized possessions, making powerful enemies on all sides; but his chief crime was his conduct to his venerable grandmother, Edgifa, whom he deprived of all her possessions, as has been before related in her life.

The King's marriage had been *legal*[1] as far as the actual ceremony, but it was contrary to Church laws, Edwy and his wife being too nearly related, or "too sib," as the Chronicle has it; and consequently, as the Church would not recognise their union, an open war ensued between Church and State, the successive contests of which occupy the whole of this short and troubled reign.

Carried away by the stream of success, neither Edwy nor Ethelgiva allowed themselves to fear, and held their former enemies in contempt; but the unrestrained license of the court, and the indulgence shown to profligate and exacting ministers, soon disgusted the country, and new troubles began. Odo, Archbishop of Canterbury, conducted the party of Dunstan, who, though in exile at Ghent, was far from having abandoned the hope of ultimate triumph. The discontented clergy fomented the disaffection everywhere ripe; a rebellion broke out in Mercia and in the north, and Prince Edgar was proclaimed King, although only thirteen years of age.

The ill-fated Ethelgiva was alone in her palace in Wessex, her husband, being forced to absent himself in consequence of these accumulating troubles, considered her in perfect safety; but Bishop Odo's emissaries were on the watch, and a strong party of his troops surprised the place, when the Queen was seized upon, dragged forth, and a hideous

[1] The Charter, Cod. Dipl. No. 1201, which is in every respect an authentic document, mentions her as Ælfgyfa, the King's wife; and this in addition to herself was witnessed by her mother Ædelgyfa, by four bishops, and by three principal noblemen of the court. "If (says Mr. Kemble [Kemble's Saxons in England]) that charter be not genuine, there is not one genuine in the whole Codex Diplomaticus, and I cannot see the shadow of a reason to question it, as Lingard has done."

vengeance accomplished. Her beautiful face was seared by a red-hot iron, and she was forced on board a vessel, which carried her off a prisoner to Ireland.

Odo, on this, immediately repaired to Edwy, and endeavoured to represent to him the necessity of yielding, doubtless concealing from him the extent of the punishment he had inflicted on the unfortunate Ethelgiva, which, however, he was not slow to learn, when his agony and rage may be conceived.

Mercia and Northumberland now rose to place Edgar on the throne, and Edwy, whom these events had forced to fly about from place to place, entered, at length, into an arrangement with his young brother, that the river Thames should form a boundary to divide their respective principalities. No sooner was this effected than Edgar, upheld by the priesthood, annulled all the acts which had been passed against them by Edwy, recalled Dunstan from his exile, and reinstated the Queen-Dowager in her former rank and dignity. It must have been a great triumph to the enemies of the ill-fated Ethelgiva, to behold Dunstan, on the death of Coenwalch, Bishop of Worcester, chosen his successor in that see, and consecrated by Archbishop Odo. A still greater was afforded by the solemn sentence of divorce pronounced between the King and herself, by Odo, on the plea of their too near relationship.[1] The sentence was given by the Church A. D. 958.

The revengeful prelate had determined, at all costs, to uphold the canonical law of marriage, and his act proves how fully assured he was that violence or death alone could divide those who loved so tenderly as this ill-fated pair. Nor was this the last stroke of vindictive power exercised: Edwy himself underwent the sentence of excommunication,—a fact mentioned by Malmesbury alone, of all who have recorded the events of this most harshly-treated monarch's reign.

Some have supposed that it was the Queen's mother who was seared with the iron brand; but the object of the Archbishop was to destroy utterly that fatal beauty which had enslaved the King. The attempt was, however, fruitless: the effect of the searing-iron was in a few months entirely obliterated; and, restored to her former beauty, Ethelgiva, notwithstanding the sentence of perpetual exile issued against her, quitted Ireland, with the design of rejoining her beloved Edwy at Kingston. She was on her way thither when, at a short distance from Gloucester, she was intercepted by the spies of Odo, who once more obtained possession of their prisoner, retaining her until they could receive the orders of that prelate. Odo commanded that Ethelgiva should be tortured in the most horrible manner that could possibly be devised, and accordingly the frightful operation of hamstringing was put in force on her delicate limbs. This brutal sentence perpetrated, the young and beautiful Queen was left, without food or attendance, to linger on a bed of straw, till, at the end of a few days, death, more merciful than her heartless persecutors, released her from her sufferings.[2]

---

[1] Saxon Chronicle. [2] Malmesbury.

Edwy, as unfortunate as his hapless consort, whose greatest crime seems to have been fidelity to the last, was not long destined to survive the loss of one so dearly loved. A series of afflictions pursued and overwhelmed him; rebellion—a younger brother preferred before him—his divorce and excommunication, together with the reversion of every decree made against his own enemies and those of Ethelgiva,—all combined, were too much for his mind to support. He sunk into a state of extreme melancholy, which, at the end of his stormy reign of four years, terminated his existence. The remains of the broken-hearted sovereign were interred at Winchester, the favourite city of the West-Saxon monarchs.

ELFRIDA,

QUEEN OF EDGAR "THE PEACEABLE.

Edgar's volatile Character — Wulfreda, the nun — Ethelflede the Fair, mother of Edward — Her death, and Elfrida's beauty — Ethelwold's mission — His deception, and marriage to Elfrida—Misrepresentation to the king—Ethelwold's son —Hunting—The tribute of wolves' heads—The concealed beauty—Ethelwold's confession to his wife—Her resolve—Her conquest—The murder in the forest —Marriage of Edgar and Elfrida—St. Dunstan—Elfrida's power—Contentions —Ventriloquism—Ely—Ordwulf, the giant—Dissolute clergy—Coronation at Bath — King Edgar's death — Edward the Martyr — His cruel murder—Ethelred's tears: the whipping with wax candles — Pledging — Miracles — Penitence of the Queen postponed — Saxon verses — Dunstan's anathema — Murder of Brithnoth, Abbot of Ely — Ethelred asserts his will — Elfrida returns to Warewell—Her religious edifices—Wulfreda ejected from Barking—Death of Elfrida —Royal grant to the convent.

THE severity of St. Dunstan, which had been so inveterate towards the unfortunate Edwy, relaxed singularly in regard to his successor, Edgar, whose habits and propensities do not appear to have differed much from those of the King, his brother, whom he superseded. But he was so young that time was before the ambitious churchman to mould him to his wishes, and to secure all that he desired for the good of the Church, and for the well-governing of the country; for Dunstan was a man of too intelligent a mind to sacrifice one to the other.

Many romantic tales are related in ballads and Saxon poems, of the volatile affections of the young King. He is accused of having carried off a nun, or at least a novice, from the Abbey of Wilton, where she was residing, and forcibly detaining her. This fair one is called Wulfreda,[1] and she became the mother of a daughter, who afterwards dedicated herself to a religious life; she having herself retired to the Monastery of Barking, founded by Edgar, in expiation of his act.

The first wife of Edgar is called Ethelflede the Fair, or the White; and sometimes also, for some unexplained reason, *the Duck*;[2] she was the mother of Prince Edward, who succeeded Edgar on the throne; but she died early, and it was soon afterwards that Elfrida became his wife.

The extraordinary beauty of the only daughter and heiress of the aged Ordgar, Ealdorman of Devonshire, made her hand the prize coveted by many a youthful Saxon noble; and such lively pictures of the young lady's beauty had reached the court of Edgar, that the heart of that monarch, apparently extremely susceptible, was set on fire by the reports.

[1] Malmesbury, Brompton, Osbern.

[2] Lappenberg.

He instantly formed the design of securing to himself so great a treasure, and directed Ethelwold, his minister and friend, who was at most times his confidant and adviser, a noble whom "he much loved and trusted," to repair to the residence of Elfrida's father, and ascertain whether her beauty was indeed such as had been reported. The secret object of this mission was revealed to the courtier in these words: "Go to the noble Baron Ordgar of Devonshire, see if his daughter be as fair as men speken of; and if it be so, I will have her unto my wife."

Ethelwold obeyed;—he discovered that report had not exaggerated, but rather fallen short of the truth in its picture of the charming Elfrida, and so much was he enraptured with the young lady on their first interview, that, wholly forgetting his object in seeing her had been to advance the suit of another, and that other his sovereign, he earnestly desired to obtain the lovely heiress for himself. He accordingly, without betraying the real object of his visit, proposed to her father that a union should take place between himself and the lady; and Ordgar, who was not ignorant that the noble Ethelwold, besides being a fair young knight, worthy, and, moreover, "well with the King," was a man certain of his fortunes, being the favorite of his royal master, considered the proposal so advantageous, that he accorded his consent to the match, provided also that the King himself was agreable to it,[1] a point which involved some difficulty to the lover of Elfrida.

Edgar had, in earliest infancy, been placed by his father, King Edmund, under the care of Alfwenna, a noble lady,[2] the mother of Ethelwold, who, in consequence, had, with three younger brothers, been the playmates in childhood, and trusty friends and companions in riper years, of their future sovereign: indeed, it was to the powerful influence of Athelstan, the husband of Alfwenna, an East Anglian nobleman, whose royal descent and extensive authority had procured for him the denomination of "Half-King," that Edgar was mainly indebted for his elevation to the throne of Northumberland and Mercia during his brother Edwy's lifetime, and subsequently, for the kingdom of all England. To testify his gratitude, Edgar erected East Anglia into an Earldom, Athelstan being the first who enjoyed the title and authority of Earl over that district, an honour afterwards enjoyed by Ethelwold at his death.[3]

Knowing how high the suitor for his daughter's hand stood with the King, the Ealdorman felt no doubts, when the Earl engaged to obtain the desired consent to his proposed nuptials with Elfrida: it was a task which required, under his circumstances, very nice management, yet he succeeded to his utmost desire; for, on his return to court, he so much undervalued the charms of Elfrida, as completely to put an end to the King's anxiety about her: he represented her as "handsome enough in the face, but a deformed cripple in body." Edgar at once, on this, ex-

[1] Caxton's Chronicle.

[2] Lingard; Parkins's Norwich. The name Alf-wenna, signifying "Half-Queen,' implies very high rank and power in its possessor.

[3] Athelstan assumed the religious habit of a monk at Glastonbury prior to his decease; his wife, Edgar's foster-mother, was buried in Charteris Nunnery, in Cambridgeshire, an establishment of her own foundation.

pressed his indifference to the match without reserve; whereupon Ethelwold rejoined:—"Sir, she is her father's heir, and I am not rich of lands; and if you would consent, and grant that I might have her, then should I be rich enough." "In God's name," quoth the King, "I consent thereto." Then Ethelwold thanked the King, and returned into Devonshire, and after having "spoused the damsell," he dwelt in that country.[1]

Not long after Elfrida's marriage, her husband, in an evil hour, informed her of all that he had done to deceive King Edgar, who had desired to marry her, and to obtain her for his own wife, confiding in her professed affection, that she would hear the tale with pleasure; but as soon as she was made acquainted with these particulars, "she loved him no more, from that time forwards, as she had done before."[2] In due time she presented Ethelwold with a son, who repaired to court, and solicited Edgar to become sponsor for the infant, which was granted, and the child was named Edgar. Ethelwold, after this condescension on the part of the King, felt more secure than ever from suspicion. The English courtiers had, however, viewed with envy and dissatisfaction the Earl's rich advancement by his marriage; and it was whispered at court, that whatever pecuniary advantages Ethelwold had obtained, his gain was at least an hundred-fold greater in having espoused "the fairest woman that ever was seen."[3] Thus, Edgar too soon became acquainted with the truth, and felt a redoubled curiosity to behold the woman whose beauty, celebrated before, had become so much more renowned as Earl Ethelwold's wife.

Dissembling the resentment which agitated his bosom, Edgar, who was accustomed to devote much of his time to the chase, devised a hunting-party,[4] for which the real object was an excuse to visit Devonshire, of which Elfrida's father was Earl, and in which county Ethelwold had hitherto secluded his wife in a state of the strictest privacy, with the hope of guarding her beauty from the monarch's eye. The Earl himself formed one of the party on this momentous occasion. As they approached the house in which Elfrida dwelt, the King informed Ethelwold of his intention to behold the lady whose charms he had heard so highly extolled. The alarmed noble vainly endeavoured to dissuade the King from his purpose; but, unable to succeed, as a last resource hastened forward to apprise Elfrida of the dreaded honour. Some say that the terror felt by Ethelwold at this hour of expected discovery, first wrung from his

[1] Caxton, William of Malmesbury. [2] Caxton. [3] Ibid.

[4] Edgar was remarkably fond of the chase; so much so that he would frequently hunt on a Sunday. Dunstan reproved him for this, and he owned and amended his error. In his reign it was a too common habit with the clergy to neglect their duties, and mix with the laity in the pleasures of gaming, hunting, dancing, and singing, besides which they lived openly with their concubines or wives. As might be expected, the habits in such a court were not very select. Edgar himself was most devoted to the hunting of the wolf, and he rendered an essential benefit to the country by imposing on Judwal, King of Wales, an annual payment of 300 wolves' heads; in the fourth year this payment ceased, for the want of wolves. It was usual to pay this Welsh tribute at Winchester, whence Wolvesey Castle has derived its name.—Hume, Malmesbury.

lips the confession to his wife of the artifice his affection had led him to employ, for the sake of obtaining her hand, while he earnestly besought that she would array herself as unbecomingly as possible, to conceal her beauty from Edgar's eye.

The Earl had misjudged his wife's character, in making this appeal to her good feelings. Hers was not a nature to forgive the man who had robbed her of a crown, and bestowed on her merely the coronet of an earl's wife. The knowledge of the King's approaching visit awakened all her ambition, and she resolved not to let the opportunity escape of securing his attention. She had secretly pined in the retirement to which Ethelwold's prudence had consigned her. She had sighed, but hitherto in vain, to exhibit her beauty and wealth, in all their pomp, at the splendid court of the monarch, who was a known admirer of female loveliness. The moment so auspicious was at hand, and if lost might never be renewed. Her heart full of contempt, amounting almost to hatred, for the man who knelt to sue her to adopt the course he desired, she promised to comply with his wish, but her promise was merely a deception to put her husband off his guard. When Edgar arrived, attended by his agitated friend, Elfrida, to his distraction, appeared before her sovereign in a dress resembling that of a bride. The vesture was as rich and costly as she could render it; her golden hair was finely combed, and part of it hanging down in luxuriant curls; her head was crowned with jewels, and a chain of diamonds about her neck gave splendour to her unparalleled beauty.[1] The enraptured monarch had no sooner beheld the lovely apparition, than he resolved, cost what it might, to obtain so rich a treasure. For the time, however, he dissembled his anger against Ethelwold, and seeming to think lightly of her beauty, bade her farewell with apparent indifference. His first step was to order a place of entertainment to be prepared for Elfrida and her husband, in return for their hospitality, near the wood in which they were to hunt, and to which he might repair when his sports were over.

On his return to the spot prepared for his accommodation, King Edgar beheld Elfrida holding in her arms her infant son, his namesake and godson, whom Ethelwold presented to him. On this the sovereign embraced and kissed Elfrida the mother, and became from that moment so much distracted with love, that he could obtain little rest, ever meditating how to obtain her. His schemes were at last determined, and the King acted accordingly. Eight days after, a parliament was called at Salisbury, at which all the magistrates of the land were present. Then Edgar subjected to their consideration his project for the safe custody of Northumberland from the incursions of the Danes; and it was settled that Ethelwold should be appointed governor of York and the adjacent country. This was a deeply planned scheme, apparently intended to honour the Earl to whom he had so recently made a visit, but who was not intended to reap the fruits of the promotion.[2] The Earl was found shortly after murdered, in the Forest of Wherwell, in Hampshire, where it was supposed he had been attacked by robbers when passing through its gloomy

[1] Heywood's History of Women. [2] Dugdale.

shades; but there is no doubt that they were armed men instructed by King Edgar to lie in wait for his former favourite, who, by his orders, barbarously murdered him. Another account given is, that the King's own hand dealt the fatal stroke; that Ethelwold, in passing through the forest, encountered, either by chance or design, his formerly attached but now revengeful master; that the King and Earl conversed for some time with apparent cordiality, till, on arriving at the thickest part of the wood, Edgar suddenly drew his dagger and stabbed the Earl to the heart.[1]

While some accounts fix the Forest of Wherwell as the scene of the gloomy tragedy, others point out Harewood Forest, in the north of England, as memorable for the murder of the unfortunate Earl, which indeed is noted by the traditions of the neighborhood. Mason the poet thus describes the spot:—

> "A darkling dell, which opens in a lawn,
> Thick set with elms around,"—

and in his well-known play, has represented the Countess Elfrida as an angel of light and goodness, full of truth and constancy. Warner, who visited the scene of the Earl's murder, describes it in his work as being half a mile beyond the ancient Castle and Forest of Harewood.

There is an ancient ballad or "Song of King Edgar, showing how he was deceived of his love," which contains these lines:—

> "Thus he that did the king deceive,
> Did by desert his death receive."

No sooner was the news of the murder brought to court, than Edgar "sent for the widow of the glorious Ethelwold, Lord of the East Angles,[2] to come to London, and straightway made her his Queen;[3] and on the same day that the nuptials were solemnized, the King and Queen Elfrida appeared together in public, both of them wearing crowns on their heads; by which act the people plainly perceived who was the author of the Earl's death, and consequently made no exertions for the discovery of the murderer."[4]

"But," say the chroniclers, "on the morrow morning after their marriage and public appearance with their crowns, Dunstan, Archbishop of Canterbury, came into the King's lodging-chamber, and boldly asked him 'who that was that he had with him?' and it being answered 'the Queen,' the good Archbishop plainly replied, 'that it was against the laws of God and holy Church, to be united to one whose son he had been godfather to, in respect of their spiritual kindred; after which time," continues the historian, "Elfrida never loved St. Dunstan; yet he ceased not to admonish the King of that fault, though to little purpose."[5]

---

[1] It is added, that a natural son of Ethelwold passed closely at the time, when the King asked "How it pleased him?" To which the youth servilely replied, "Very well! if it so please your grace, for whatsoever pleaseth you, ought not to displease me!" The answer saved his life; and Edgar afterwards tried to extenuate his murder of the father by lavishing favours on his son.

[2] Flor. Wigorn.

[3] Parkins's Hist. of Norwich.

[4] Gaillard's Rivalité.

[5] Malmesbury. Dugdale.

At this very time, when the marriage festivities were going on, began a series of misfortunes to the country in the shape of pestilence and conflagrations. London was devastated by the latter scourge, and the Cathedral of St. Paul was reduced to ashes. Of course the monks did not fail to attribute these events to the indignation of Heaven. Nevertheless, population increased; Edgar remained popular with his subjects, for his public acts were all deserving of praise, and showed both energy and wisdom. He has been blamed for the favour he showed to the Danish settlers, but his expeditions against the Welsh and other disaffected nations, were satisfactory, and brought him both fame and profit.

The date of Elfrida's marriage is fixed by the Saxon Chronicle in 965, an obvious mistake, as her name appears appended to a charter in the year 964; it is therefore very likely that Roger of Wendover is correct in assigning the nuptials to the year 963.

The solemn coronation of Elfrida soon followed her marriage, notwithstanding the reproaches of Dunstan, Archbishop of Canterbury. It is not, however, certain that Edgar was crowned with her then, but at a later period she shared with him that solemn pageant of royalty. Thus having reached the height of her ambition, Elfrida endeavoured to extinguish her remorse, and atone for her crimes, by erecting a monastery on the spot where Ethelwold had been slain. Aylwin, his brother, had succeeded to the Earldom of East Anglia; he was founder of the Abbeys of Ramsey and Huntingdon, where his statue may yet be seen.[1] The last Earl of East Anglia was Harold, the son of Godwin, and it is somewhat remarkable that his wife was not only, by her marriage to him, Countess of East Anglia, but exchanged that title, like Elfrida for the more exalted one of Queen of England.

Notwithstanding her ambition, Elfrida could hardly expect to receive higher honours than those accorded to the former consort of Edgar, Ethelflede the Fair, who, in some records of Edgar's reign, is styled only "the King's wife," but never the *Queen*.[2]

Yet while the other consorts of those sovereigns of the heptarchy who had maintained their independence after Edgar, were permitted to enjoy that title which Elfrida had bought at so high a price, it was not in her nature to be content with the honours due to the husband only, and reflected from him. Elfrida had worn the crown on her wedding-day, and thus attired, sat like Judith in her chair of state by the side of Edgar; and though we find her afterwards styled frequently "the King's wife," she had also the enviable title of *Regina* accorded to her. A charter granted by Edgar to the Church of Worcester, A. D. 964, the year after his marriage, was signed by Elfrida thus: "Ego Elfyred *Regina* consensi et signo crucis confirmavi;" while another to the Church at Ely, was also attested by her as "Regina."[3]

In King Edgar's Charter of Privilege to Hyde Abbey, by Winchester, which is yet extant, in a hand of that age, in letters of gold, may also be found the signature of Queen Elfrida. First appear the manors and

---

[1] Parkins. [2] Carter and Dugdale. Selden's Titles of Honour.
[3] Cott. Lib.

donations of Edgar, Dunstan, Edmund, and Edward; then the subscription of the Queen, who takes precedence of Edgifa, the King's grandmother, that venerable friend and patron of the pious and good during several reigns, the aged relict of King Edward the Elder.

"I, Alfdrid, the lawful wife of the aforesaid King, by my bequest establishing monks in the same place, with the King's permission, have made the mark of the cross." Then follows: —

"I, Eadgifa, grandmother of the aforesaid King, have confirmed this excellent work by the sign of the cross."

The fact of the words "with the King's permission" being inserted, shows that it was not a common custom for the King's wife to attest these charters. In this last document the name of Regina is omitted.

After the second innovation of the law for Elfrida, it ceased to be regarded in Wessex, and from that time forward we find the Saxon Queens of England were, as a matter of right, crowned, anointed, and seats of state provided for them by the side of their husbands on the most public occasions, besides which they bore the title of "Regina" or "Queen."

The Book of Grants, presented by Edgar himself to the Cathedral of Winchester, bearing the date A. D. 966, and written entirely in letters of gold, in the old Saxon character, contains a curious and ancient illumination. The book is in the Cottonian Library, marked "Vespasianus A. VIII.," and an engraving from it may be seen in Strutt's Regal and Ecclesiastical Antiquities, where the following description is given: —

"Edgar is here delineated as piously adoring our Blessed Saviour, who appears above seated on a globe, to show his empire, and supported by four angels, emblems of the four gospels; under his feet are two folding-doors, intended, perhaps, to represent the entrance into the bottomless pit, which is so placed to convey the idea of his triumph over Death and Hell; in his left hand he holds the book of judgment, which is to be opened in the last day."

Strutt supposes the figures on the right and left of the King to be Cuthbert, the Saint of Durham, and Etheldreda, Abbess of Ely. On the opposite page is a Saxon inscription in capital letters of gold, thus translated into modern English:—

"Thus sits that God alone who made the heavens
Whilst humbly Edgar the king pays his adoration."

To quote further from Strutt, "as there has been extraordinary pains taken in the writing and ornaments of this book, and as it was written (which appears by the date) at the very time of Edgar, it is more than barely probable that this is not only an exact delineation of the habit of that monarch, but also (to the best of the illuminator's power) a true portrait of him." The following is the description of the colours of the original:—"The garment of our Saviour is a dark blue, and the lighter robe is gold; so also is the oval he sits in, the book he holds, and the doors under his feet. The angels are dressed in white, and the shadowed part is gold, as well on the habit as on the wings. The king's cloak is a dark blue, edged with gold, his coat a deepish crimson, and his hose a dark brown; his book and crown are gold. The saints, on each side of him, are in blue, and the lighter-coloured part of their garments is gold, as well as the ornaments they hold, and the glory over their heads."

Edgar was one of the greatest friends the Church ever had in this country. He is said to have built forty monasteries, to have completed Glastonbury, which his father had founded, and to have adorned the religious edifices of Abingdon, Thorney, Burgh, and Ramsey, besides founding a building for nuns in Winchester.

Elfrida was present, A. D. 969, at a witenagemote of considerable importance, held at Winchester in the royal palace. In that year Edgar gave instructions to St. Dunstan, Archbishop of Canterbury, and Sts. Oswald and Ethelwold, the Bishops of Worcester and Winchester, to expel all the clerks from the larger monasteries of Mercia, and replace them with monks. This expulsion was in consequence of the dissolute life they led. The clerks who were expelled, desired to prefer a complaint against the severity of Dunstan, in the King's own presence; and they were met by the Archbishop in the witan at Winchester, the King, Queen, nobles, and clergy being assembled on the occasion. After Dunstan had uttered his defence, the clerks prayed to be restored, and those who held possession of their offices removed. Dunstan spoke not, but hung down his head as if in reverie;[1] but it is said that at this moment a figure of our Lord, affixed to the standard of the cross, appeared in an elevated position in the palace, and a voice was heard saying, "Let it not be done — let it not be done; well have ye judged, ill would ye change." The King and all present, at first astonished and terrified to death almost by this extraordinary appearance, filled the air with their shouts, and assented to the sacred decision.

Ethelwold, one of the three prelates appointed to survey the monasteries, was a pupil of Dunstan, and some of the expelled monks had tried to deprive him of life by poison. It was Ethelwold, who, by Edgar's order, commenced the restoration of the monasteries which had either fallen into decay or been ruined by the Danes.[2] Ely was the first monastery repaired; it had been destroyed by the Danes, A. D. 970, and instead of filling it with nuns as before, Ethelwold placed in it a company of monks, under Brithnoth, one of his own society or establishment, whom he constituted abbot. Brithnoth governed Ely in that capacity eleven years, at the end of which his history becomes identified with that of Queen Elfrida, as will be seen in the course of this memoir. The restoration of Medehamstede, after it had laid waste for nearly a hundred years, was commenced in the same year as that of Ely by Ethelwold, and

[1] It appears evident that this scene was got up by Dunstan, whose knowledge of mechanics, ventriloquism, optics, &c., enabled him easily to impose on the uninformed personages with whom he had to do. The charge of magic has always been made against the learned in the sciences in all unenlightened times, and it was a great temptation to one who had a great end to gain, the feeling that he could so well deceive, without a chance of detection.

[2] Ethelwold, Bishop of Winchester, in a great famine, sold all the sacred vessels of his church to relieve the poor, saying, "That there was no reason why the senseless temples of God should abound in riches, and lively temples of the Holy Ghost should want them."—Howel, Med. Hist. Ang.

when completed it received the name of Peterborough, which has descended to modern times.[1] Leland relates that Edgar assisted Ethelwold in rebuilding Medehamstede, by the persuasion, some say, of his first wife, Ethelflede the White; but the date of the restoration of this abbey proves that it was Elfrida, and not Ethelflede, by whose counsel he acted. When St. Paul's, in London, was endowed by Edgar with twenty-five mansions and a considerable sum in money, Ethelflede is said to have added her own donation of two lordships, which royal gifts were afterwards confirmed by Ethelred and Canute. These, and the donation of the island of Portsea, to the New Minster, at Winchester, have been attributed to Ethelflede, but appear much more like the acts of Elfrida, who was desirous of purchasing peace with the Church which she had offended. That Elfrida, as well as Edgar, took an active part in the restoration of clerical institutions is evident. In the Cottonian Library is extant a reformation of the monastic life of both sexes, written in King Edgar's time, wherein he takes care of the monks, and his wife Elfrida of the nuns.

Elflede[2] "Candida" (the White), Edgar's first wife, had left him two children, Edward, afterwards surnamed the Martyr, and a daughter called Editha, who entered into the seclusion of a conventual life.[3]

The children of Edgar by Elfrida were two sons, of whom the eldest, Edmund Atheling, died in his father's lifetime, A. D. 971, and was interred with princely honours in the Monastery of Rumsey, Hampshire."[4] The youngest of the royal children bore the name of Ethelred, to which was afterwards added the surname of "the Unready," and with his mother's beauty, he inherited some, at least, of her bad qualities.

Not long after the death of her son Edmund, Elfrida lost her father, Earl Ordgar, who was interred at Exeter. In the year of his decease, A. D. 971, this nobleman[5] had commenced an abbey at Tavistock, in Devonshire, which he filled with monks. The edifice itself was on a very grand scale, and not completed till 981; it was finished by Ordulf, the Queen's brother, a person described as of gigantic size and stature, whose figure, and also some of his bones, were exhibited there; but the Danes destroyed the building, about ten years after its completion. Malmesbury records, amongst other instances of the personal strength of Ordulf, that when the drowsy warder of Exeter delayed on one occasion to open the gates, he burst them open, demolishing also the stone jambs on which they hung.

Elfrida seems to have accompanied her husband on most occasions of importance, and probably the King's leisure intervals were passed in her society, though his infidelities are said to have been great. We are told that the Saxon princes had a palace situate to the north of St. Albans,

[1] Chron. Peterburgens; Ingulphus: Vit. S. Ethelwold.

[2] The name is written at times, Egelfleda and Eneda; also Ethelfleda and Elfleda.

[3] Gaillard's Rivalité, &c.

[4] Ramsey and Rumsey were quite different places, though each was distinguished by a convent; that of Ramsey was in Huntingdonshire, and built by Elfrida's brother.

[5] Turner, Roger of Wendover.

the site of which is now occupied by King's Bury, to which they were wont to resort at times for their favourite amusement of fishing. "At this royal abode there was a great fishpool, of about twenty acres, which, by the festivities displayed on it, was a great inconvenience to the neighbouring Abbey, till Abbot Ailric procured it, in exchange for *a cup of rich workmanship*, of King Edgar. He had afterwards the embankment cut away, and the waters dispersed; but the situation is still pointed out by Fish Pool Street, in the lower part of St. Albans." The palace itself was not finally demolished till the reign of King Stephen.[1]

The dissolute lives of the clergy during this reign have been already noticed, and, indeed, a great laxity of morals appears to have prevailed among all classes. At this time there were so many Danes in the country, who gave themselves up to drinking and idolatry to such an excess, that they were hardly governable. To repress the vice of drunkenness, the Winchester measure was instituted. Edgar ordained a size, by certain pins in the pot, with a penalty to any that presumed to drink deeper than the mark. Gold and silver nails were also ordered by Dunstan for this same purpose, and were put into the drinking-vessels to prevent inebriety and quarrels. These pins, nails, or pegs, were fastened in the pots, whence the phrase "to drink to the pin," a feat only acquired by long practice.[2]

Edgar also commanded a new coinage, the old having been so reduced, by the fraud of cheating clippers, that scarcely any piece was found to be of worth, when its value was tested in the scales.[3]

There is no doubt that London and Winchester were frequently chosen residences of Edgar and Elfrida, and most probably Worcester, where their son Ethelred II. afterwards erected a tower, called "King Edgar's Tower," because the statues of that King and his two Queens, Elfleda and Elfrida, are placed on its eastern front.[4]

In 972 Edgar and Elfrida were solemnly crowned at St. Peter's, Bath, the ceremony being performed by Dunstan, on the 11th of May, the feast of Pentecost. St. Oswald assisted in the ceremonies of consecrating and anointing Edgar and his Queen. For seven years previously Edgar had laid aside his crown, a penance imposed by Dunstan, for his crime in carrying off the nun Wulfreda of Wilton; he now resumed the insignia of royalty in public, and surrounded by his peers, to whom, on this occasion, he presented the customary gifts. The royal robes, worn by Edgar

[1] Britton and Brayley.

[2] The custom of drinking to the pin is thought to have been introduced by the Danes themselves, who fixed a pin inside of their wassail-bowl.—Hardy's Notes on William of Malmesbury.

[3] That the byzant or besant, an ancient Greek coin of gold, which was named from ancient Byzantium, and issued by the Greek emperors, was used in England, is proved by the fact that St. Dunstan purchased of King Edgar the estate of Hindon, in Middlesex, for 200 byzants. The coin was generally current in England before the Norman Conquest, and has been introduced in armorial bearings. The value of one byzant, according to Dr. Henry, was nine shillings and fourpence.—Notes to Le Grand's Fabliaux.

[4] Green's History of Worcester.

at his coronation, are described as of immense value, on which account the King afterwards bestowed them on Glastonbury, as a decoration for the altar.

> "Much bliss there was, by all enjoyed,
> On the happy day named Pentecost;
> Crowds of priests, and throngs of monks,
> In council sage were gathered there." [1]

Not long after this grand event, Edgar, who seems to have been to the full as fond of pomp and parade as his consort Elfrida, summoned his subreguli at Chester.[2] Kenneth, King of Scots, was among the first to do him homage, and was followed by his nephew, Malcolm of Cumbria, and Maccus, King of Mona and the Isles, by the Princes of Galloway, and the Cymric tribes.[3] During this meeting at Chester, Edgar one day purposed to go by water to the Abbey of St. John the Baptist, and obliged eight of these tributary princes to row him in a barge upon the Dee, Kenneth MacAlpine being one of the number. This king had received Lothian from Edgar, on condition that he should annually attend Edgar's principal feasts, and do him homage for that district. The English king gave him several houses for his entertainment during his journey, and made him many handsome presents, such as one hundred ounces of pure gold, many silken ornaments, and rings with precious stones.

Amid all the honours accorded to royalty, the highest in such a gay and glorious court, Elfrida must have had her heart's utmost desires fulfilled; but her triumph was not destined to last; and could she have foreseen how little real happiness was to be gained by her crime, even her first steps in that career had perhaps been stayed. Her successes and glories were terminated, in the twelfth year of their marriage, by the King's death, who was then only in the thirty-second year of his age, though the sixteenth of his reign. He died July 8th, 975, and was interred at Glastonbury, with every regal honour. The tomb was, at a later period, 1052, opened[4] by Abbot Ailward, when the King's remains were re-interred within a large shrine covered with gold and silver, and inlaid with beautifully moulded images in ivory, which had been Edgar's own present to the Church.

---

[1] Saxon Chronicle.

[2] Edgar was, in person, small and thin, [a picture of him may be seen in Wynkyn de Worde,] which caused Kenneth to remark with surprise that so many provinces should yield obedience to a man so insignificant. The speech reached the ears of Edgar, who led his guest apart into a wood, and producing two swords, bade him choose one of them. "Our arms," said the king, "shall decide which ought to obey the other; for it will be base to have asserted that at a feast, which you cannot support with your sword." Kenneth, in much confusion, remembered his hasty observation, and "apologised for it as a joke."—Turner.

[3] Palgrave.

[4] The opening of the tomb is said to have been attended with several miracles. Not only was the royal corpse fresh and incorrupt, but the abbot, seeing it was too large for the receptacle prepared for it, having profanely hacked it with a steel instrument in his hand, to his own horror, and that of the spectators, torrents of blood burst forth from the wound. The abbot afterwards became insane, and died a violent death!—Saxon Chronicle.

Immediately the King's death became known, two mighty factions arose, which threatened to lead to a civil war. The King's will had declared that the crown should devolve on Edward, the son of his first wife, an amiable Prince, then in the thirteenth year of his age; but the ambitious Elfrida desired to secure the throne to her son Ethelred, then but a child of about seven, and objected to Edward's claim, that his mother either had not been lawfully married to Edgar, or that the young prince was born before their coronation, and that he was illegitimate, besides which the Queen alleged he was of a harsh and cruel disposition.[1] As Elfrida had always possessed great influence with the late King, she had acquired many friends, who now became partizans in favour of Ethelred's succession;[2] but many of the nobles who were acquainted with her imperious temper, dreaded the consequences of her being placed as Regent at the head of the State, which must have been the case if Ethelred was elected king, and of this number was the Queen's old enemy, Dunstan, still the most powerful person in the kingdom, to whom even monarchs had been forced to submit. It was this prelate who stepped forward in the emergency, to carry into effect the claims of Edward, knowing that he was supported by the wishes of the people generally, and by Oswald and other bishops and nobles, who desired the late King's will to be respected. Dunstan, indeed, was the last person in the world who was willing to suffer such a diminution of his own power as would have been the result of Ethelred's advancement, when his mother Elfrida was directly his opponent; he accordingly convened an assembly of nobles at Kingston, for the purpose of crowning and anointing Edward. The faction of Elfrida, among whom was Alfer, Duke of Mercia, formally declared against the ceremony taking place; the Queen herself, who was present, objected on account of the Prince's illegitimacy, which rendered her son the legal heir.[3] At this crisis Dunstan appeared, bearing in his hands the banner of the crucifix, accompanied by young Edward, whom he presented to the lords as their rightful monarch, declaring that he would himself be responsible for their Prince's conduct, whom he would regulate as his father's tutor and prime-minister. This promise of Dunstan united the wavering minds of the assembled lords, and Edward was received with universal joy.[4] Taking the youth by the hand, Dunstan marched directly to the church, accompanied by the other bishops, and followed by a great crowd of people, where he anointed him King, in spite of the opposition of Elfrida and her party, who were overwhelmed with grief at the priest's triumph.[5]

This public acknowledgment of Edward by Dunstan proves the validity of his mother's marriage, and the base artifice Elfrida had employed against him. Had he really been illegitimate, as an author observes who was of that opinion himself,[6] Elfrida might justly be excused for desiring the true heir to become king.

---

[1] Brit. Sancta, Lingard. [2] Hume.

[3] Brit. Sancta, Osbern, and Capgrave. [4] Holinshed. [5] Henry.

[6] Holinshed says, Edward was born of a nun named Elfleda, and not of Edgar's Queen.

Even after the coronation was over, the Queen still continued to strive by all possible means to get Ethelred's claim acknowledged, and so far inveigled Edward by her flattery, that he suffered her to order all the affairs of the kingdom, retaining for himself merely the title of King. At the same time he was, if possible, still more devoted to St. Dunstan and his followers than his father had been, so that the nation had every hope the reign would be prosperous and happy. All these expectations were, however, frustrated by the Queen's ambition, who could not rest tranquil. She opposed Dunstan in all ways, and her friends, the opponents of the Church in general, destroyed the monasteries which Edgar had built. It will be remembered that the enemies of Dunstan and Ethelwold, among the clergy, had been ejected, on account of dissolute conduct, from their offices. Elfrida, to strengthen the party of Ethelred, declared herself openly their patroness, the highest affront which could have been offered to Dunstan; besides which she tried to bias the minds of the great in favour of her son. Mercia and Earl Alfer sided with her and with those who protected the disgraced clergy. Essex and East Anglia, with their Earls, sided with the King and Dunstan, to whose will he was subject, and who therefore was possessed of great power, yet had to cope with one who was as ambitious as himself, and perhaps even more unprincipled as to the means of gratifying the passion. There was every prospect of a civil war, when Elfrida perceived another method of attaining her object; she joined in a conspiracy to assassinate Edward, and accident shortly after furnished her with an opportunity of effecting her purpose.[1]

The young King had shown, from the first, every mark of respectful attention to Elfrida, to whom he had presented the county of Dorset as a dowry, affixing to it a royal dignity.[2]

The monarch was returning from a hunting excursion in Dorsetshire, near Wareham, not far from which stood Corfe Castle, the residence of his mother-in-law and of her son Ethelred. While his companions were earnestly pursuing the game, Edward was left alone, and perceiving the walls of the castle in the distance, he hastened thither to pay his respects with his accustomed courtesy to his mother-in-law, who, on perceiving him, with feigned affability welcomed, and invited him to alight and refresh himself. This, however, Edward declined, but requested a cup of wine to be brought him, and at the same time inquired for his brother. Whether Elfrida had premeditated this treachery towards her son-in-law, or whether the favourable opportunity suggested this act of cruelty, remains uncertain; she, however, commissioned one of her creatures[3] to stab the King in the back, while in the act of drinking. Edward, finding himself wounded, spurred his horse to rejoin his friends, but from loss of blood fell from his seat, and one of his feet being caught in the stirrup, he was dragged for some time by the affrighted animal, who being at length arrested near a house on the road side, the mangled corpse was found there by some domestics of the Queen, who had tracked him thither by the blood, and by commands previously received from Elfrida, they

[1] Gaillard's Rivalité, and others. [2] Turner.

Knyghton and Burke say the Queen herself did the deed.

threw the body into a well.[1] As Roger of Wendover relates, "The wicked woman Alfdritha, and her son Ethelred, ordered the corpse of the king and martyr, St. Edward, to be ignominiously buried at Wareham, in the midst of public rejoicing and festivity, as if they had buried his memory and his body together; for now that he was dead, they grudged him ecclesiastical sepulture, as when he was alive they robbed him of royal honour." The young Ethelred, however, deserved not the blame even of a participation in this cruel transaction; for he had tenderly loved the King his brother, and wept bitterly on hearing the news of his death. Elfrida, unable to pacify him, was so much offended, that it is added, "having no rod at hand, in the violent paroxysm of her anger, she seized some tapers that stood before her, and beat the boy so severely that she had almost killed him, too, upon the spot. So terrified was the child that he never after could endure to have any of those sort of candles lighted before him."[2] The tapers of the middle ages were from *five to seven pounds weight*, and being placed in candlesticks of silver, formed an ornament for the bedchamber of ladies. King Alfred, it is well known, caused his candles to be adapted to the measurement of time. Elfrida's correction was, therefore, by no means of a gentle kind.

A MS. Psalter, preserved in the Royal Library at the British Museum, having been formerly presented to Queen Mary in 1553, by Baldwin Smith, a citizen of London, contains an engraving which represents Edward hunting, and his visit to Corfe Castle. The same attendant who offers the King a cup of drink, is seen there stabbing him with a dagger. One of our modern customs, that of pledging each other at table, arose from the circumstances attending the death of Edward. The old Saxon mode of pledging, when two persons drank together, was as follows:—"The person who was going to drink, asked any one of the company that sat next him, whether he would pledge him. On which, he answering that he would, held up his sword or knife to guard him whilst he drank; for while a man is drinking he necessarily is in an unguarded posture, exposed to the traitorous stroke of some hidden or secret enemy; this practice originated from the treacherous conduct of Elfrida to her son-in-law."[3]

The friends of the deceased King soon discovered the remains of their murdered sovereign, and having burnt the body, interred the ashes at Wareham.[4] But the deed was not destined to be thus passed over, for "the innocent victim" of Elfrida "was ennobled with the grace of miracles."[5] The King's body, on the night of the murder,[6] had been carried into a cottage where a poor woman dwelt, who was maintained by the charity of Elfrida: she was blind, but is said to have been restored suddenly to sight. This miraculous circumstance, being reported next morn-

[1] Gaillard's Rivalité, &c. [2] Holinshed. [3] Strutt.

[4] Gaillard, &c. [5] Roger of Wendover.

[6] In 1245, Pope Innocent IV. ordained that the day of Edward's murder should be kept as a festival: the exact date of the event was March 18th, 979 (Brit. Sancta). He had reigned three years.

ing to the Queen, much affrighted her.[1] The report of the miracle spread, and multitudes are said to have resorted to the tomb, whereon such a celestial light was shed, that the lame were enabled to walk, the blind to see, and the dumb to speak; all who laboured under any infirmity being healed.[2] "Among the rest, the murderess took her journey thither. Having mounted her horse, she urged him to go forward, when, lo! he who before outstripped the winds, and was full of ardour to bear his mistress, now, by the will of God, stood immovable; nor could her attendants move him at all with their shouts and blows: their labour was still in vain, when another horse was put in his place."[3] Neither the horse which the Queen rode, nor any other, would approach the spot, in spite of whips and spurs, and every other means tried to make them go forward. On which the murderess perceived "how great had been her offence against God, in shedding the blood of the innocent; and she repented deeply of her sin,[4] and gave up her intention of visiting the tomb, resolving to pass the rest of her days in penance and prayer:" of this resolve she evidently put off the accomplishment. So many miracles indeed were wrought by the sainted King, who, for his death, was surnamed "the Martyr," that it was thought desirable to transfer his relics to a more fitting receptacle. Some say, this holy ceremony was performed by his sister St. Editha; others relate that Earl Elfery, who was one of the most forward partizans of Elfrida, and had been one of those who destroyed the monasteries of the monks, bitterly repenting of his fault, removed the King's sacred body from that mean place, three years after, with great solemnity, to the monastery at Shaftesbury.[5]

The Saxon Chronicle[6] notices Edward's murder in these terms:—

"There has not been 'mid Angles
A worse deed done
Than this was,
Since they first
Britain-land sought.
Men him murdered,
But God him glorified.
He was in life
An earthly king;
He is now after death
A heavenly saint.
Him would not his earthly
Kinsmen avenge,
But him hath his Heavenly Father
Greatly avenged.
The earthly murderers
Would his memory
On earth blot out,

[1] Brit. Sancta. A church was afterwards built upon the spot, to commemorate the restoration of the blind woman to sight.

[2] Roger of Wendover.

[3] Ibid.

[4] Holinshed, Roger of Wendover.

[5] "Though, even this way, he did not escape condign punishment, being eaten with worms in the following year."—Roger of Wendover.

[6] Saxon Chronicle; Brit. Sancta.

But the Lofty Avenger
Hath his memory
In the heavens
And on earth wide spread.
They who would not erewhile
To his living
Body bow down,
They now humbly
On knees bend
To his dead bones.
Now we may understand
That men's wisdom,
And their devices,
And their councils,
Are like nought
'Gainst God's resolves."

Ethelred "Atheling," or the "Noble," for whom Elfrida had been guilty of so great a crime, was too young at the time to be considered an accomplice in her guilt, yet it was with no small repugnance that the prelates and thanes bestowed on him a crown bought with the price of blood.[1] Dunstan more especially felt this, yet was compelled to anoint Ethelred, a measure not to be avoided. The ceremony of inauguration took place at Kingston-on-Thames, Sunday, April the 24th.[2] The new monarch, who is described as "a rare youth of a graceful person, fair countenance, and lofty stature, received the royal diadem from Dunstan of Canterbury, and Oswald of York, in the presence of ten bishops and the rest of the assembled clergy and nobles."[3] Dunstan is said on this occasion to have been moved, by a prophetic spirit, to declare to the young Prince, all the calamities to which the kingdom would be exposed during his reign in the following words:—"Because thou hast aspired to the crown by the death of thy brother, whom thy mother hath murdered, therefore hear the word of the Lord: the sword shall not depart from thy house, but shall furiously rage all the days of thy life, killing thy seed, till such time as thy kingdom shall be given to a people whose customs and language the nation thou now governest know not: neither shall thy sin, the sin of thy mother, and the sin of those men who were partakers of her counsels, and executors of her wicked design, be expiated but by a long and most severe vengeance."[4] Dunstan survived this event nine years, at the end of which he died, A. D. 988, after having witnessed the reigns of five monarchs, and part of that of a sixth, viz., Ethelred.

This last event took place many years before the decease of Elfrida, who survived her worst enemy and greatest rival. Indeed, it was probably the ascendency of the Queen's faction which embittered and shortened Dunstan's life; for Edward the Martyr, ruled by his counsels, would have carried on everything as Edgar his father had left it; but, as Dunstan had perceived from the first, the ascendency of the mother of

[1] The usual atonement for murder, called the Weregild, was paid by Elfrida at the time of Edward's death.—Lingard.

[2] A. D. 979.

[3] Roger of Wendover.

[4] Holinshed.

Ethelred, and such as took part with her under her son's authority, was likely enough "to turn all upside down."[1] One of the motives attributed to Elfrida for the commission of Edward's murder, was her desire to subvert the authority of Dunstan. In this, however, she was unsuccessful, and gained only the popular aversion; for neither remorse nor hypocrisy could ever reinstate her in the public opinion.

But even yet Elfrida's crimes were not ended: in the year 981 another murder stained her guilty hand. Turner remarks as singular, the fact that this circumstance of the murder of Brithnoth, first Abbot of Ely, by Elfrida, should have escaped historians in general, being merely noticed in the following manner in the history of Ely:[2]—"It happened that, on a certain day, the Abbot Bridnod set out for King Ethelred's court, on affairs of the Church. When near Geldesdune, on his way through the wood called New Forest, he is said to have turned aside in search of some secluded spot for prayer, where, by accident, he discovered the Queen Ælstritha engaged under a tree, in her practices of witchcraft. The Queen uttered an expression of consternation at being detected, but the holy man, inwardly troubled, retreated as quickly as possible from the spot, and proceeded on his way to the court. Here he was magnificently received by the King, and having speedily accomplished the purpose of his journey, was on the point of returning home, rejoicing in the royal munificence. Not willing, however, to shame the Queen, though abhorrent, he first went to seek an interview with her, which she, when aware of his coming, desired might be strictly private, under a pretext of her requiring spiritual counsel. Summoning some women of her household, devoted to her will, she gave orders that he should be put to death. That no wound might appear on the body, the perpetrators were instructed to pierce him beneath the armpits with *bodkins* till he expired. Whereupon she cried out as if terrified by a sudden calamity. The servants and companions of the Abbot run to the spot, and hear with groans, of the previous arrival and sudden death of their master: with much grief and lamentation they place his body on a vehicle, and convey it back to Ely, where, not detecting any visible marks of violence, they commit it to the tomb. Thus was the first abbot of the holy church of Ely martyred,[3] by the contrivance of a good-for-nothing woman, preferring to fall into human hands, rather than to transgress the divine law, earning for his soul eternal joy in heaven, where he shall reign with all saints.

"As to the Queen, no one presumed even to whisper a suspicion, or bring an evil report upon her. And this matter might have continued to be hidden from all, had not she herself, by the divine mercy, been seized with compunction for her witchcrafts and abominable practices, and especially for the death of the glorious King Edward, her eldest son, to whose murder, (to make a way to the throne for Ethelred, her subsequent issue) she confessed, and for which deed she raised, at her own expense, the Convent of Werewelle. Here she spent the remainder of her days

[1] Holinshed. [2] Gale's Scriptores Hist. Elieni.

[3] Some records place the event in A. D. 981.

in grief and penitence, and detailed with groans and anguish, the manner in which she had slain Bridnod, Abbot of Ely, as above related."[1]

Elfrida's motive in this act, was as usual, her desire for power. The whole of the isle of Ely, had been purchased of King Edgar for a small sum, by Ethelwold, Bishop of Winchester, one of the Dunstan party, who in the year 970, placed in the monastery he had renewed, an abbot and monks, for whom he obtained many privileges from the monarch, with whom he was a great favorite. This abbot was Bridnoth, one of his own monks. Elfrida, after Ethelred's advancement to the throne, still maintained her spleen against Dunstan. Brithnoth had come to court on this occasion concerning matters connected with his church, and having *succeeded* in his mission, was about to depart with a joyful heart, when the Queen interfered and caused the Abbot's assassination. The "magic practices" he was said to have witnessed, were probably some of the Danish rites, or she had been consulting the wise-women on her own future destiny and that of Dunstan. Brithnoth had ruled Ely eleven years from his first appointment, and on his death, Elsy, or Elfsy, was appointed abbot in his place, by King Ethelred.[2] The brotherhood of Ely had their suspicions on the suddenness of their former abbot's decease, but the power of Elfrida silenced all. Not long after Brithnoth's murder, we find that, at the invitation of Bishop Ethelwold, the young King and his mother went, with several of the nobility, to visit the church of Ely, and took the opportunity to go in procession to the tomb of St. Etheldreda; when the young monarch, having a great love and affection for the Saint, promised, in the presence of all who were there assembled, to become from henceforth her devoted servant. In consequence, Ethelred afterwards, on several occasions testified great kindness and regard for that church, and as a particular mark of favour, was "pleased to grant that the head of the church of Ely should hold and enjoy the office and dignity of Chancellor in the King's court: the like he also granted to two other churches, viz., St. Augustine's in Canterbury, and Glastonbury, thus dividing the chancellorship between the abbots of those three monasteries, who were to enjoy the office by turns."[3]

Elfrida was obviously desirous of making her peace with the offended clergy through the grants of Ethelred, then but twelve years of age. Of course it was she who held the administration of Church and State affairs, for a weakness of character was apparent in Ethelred from an early age, which was in a great measure attributable to the tyrannical and arbitrary influence maintained over him by his mother. As the King grew older this influence gradually declined, until Elfrida, finding herself the object of popular aversion, became aware that her power was at an end: on which, pretending to be moved by her conscience, she determined to bid farewell to the court,[4] and to close her days in a monastery, the usual resource of baffled ambition in these days. She accordingly founded in

---

[1] Rog. of Wend.

[2] Dugdale.

[3] Dugdale; who places the visit of Ethelred in his brother's reign; but as Bridnoth was dead, and Elfsy abbot, it was plainly during his own.

[4] Lingard.

986, the Monastery of Werewell,[1] in expiation of the deaths of her first husband, Earl Ethelwold, and her son-in-law, Edward the Martyr; and within the walls of this edifice, of the Benedictine order, the yet beautiful Elfrida, renouncing her worldly grandeur, the incentive to her many crimes, exchanged the robes of royalty for sackcloth, and having professed herself a nun, dwelt in mourning and great penitence, a great part of her remaining life;[2] here she practised every kind of austerity. "Her flesh, which she had nourished in delicacy, she mortified with haircloth at Wherwell,"[3] sleeping on the ground, and afflicting her body with all kinds of sufferings,[4] such as fasting and various kinds of penance. Although the weregild, the price of murder, had been paid, the guilty Queen was a prey to remorse and apprehension, and among other self-inflicted punishments, is said to have "worn armour, made of little crosses, which she thought could alone secure her from an imaginary phantom, or evil spirit, which incessantly haunted her imagination."[5] Nor was private mortification enough; Elfrida tried to atone for her misdeeds by the publicity of her repentance, yet could she never reinstate herself in public opinion.[6] She expended large sums on the poor, and in building churches and monasteries, to the amount of her whole patrimony.[7] Elfrida founded a monastery at Andover, and another at Ambresbury in Wiltshire, a town on the Upper Avon. This last was founded A. D. 980, in expiation of the murder of Edward the Martyr; it was of the Benedictine order, and commended to the patronage of St. Mary, and St. Meliorus, a Cornish saint, whose relics were preserved there.[8]

Another abbey, or rather a small nunnery, was erected by her at Reading, on the spot now occupied by St. Mary's Church, being the third edifice founded in 980, the year after King Edward's death:[9] Henry I. suppressed this A. D. 1120, but the following year built a magnificent abbey there for two hundred Benedictine monks, which he dedicated to the honour of God, our Lady, and St. John the Evangelist, and appropriated to its use the revenues of the earlier foundation.

Elfrida's rapacity is seen in all her actions. Wulfreda, the injured nun of Wilton, had presided many years over the Monastery of Barking, when some dissensions arose between her and the priests of Barking, who referred their cause to Elfrida, requesting her to eject Wulfreda, and assume the goverment in her own person. To this proposal Elfrida readily assented, and on the Queen's assuming the presidency of the Monastery of Barking, Wulfreda was forced to retire to a religious house, which she had founded at Horton, in Devonshire.[10] Elfrida presided at Barking for twenty years, at the end of which, while still residing there, she was seized with a violent sickness, and in the probable dread of approaching dissolution, repenting the injury she had done Wulfreda, she caused her

---

[1] "Wherwell."—Dugdale.
[2] Dugdale, Brit. Sancta.
[3] Roger of Wendover, Holinshed.
[4] Clavis Calendaria.
[5] Lingard.
[6] Holinshed, Gaillard, Bicknell, Lysons's Magna Brit. Dugdale.
[7] Leland, Camden, Speed.
[8] Britton and Brayley.
[9] Britton and Brayley.
[10] Britton and Brayley.

to be reinstated in her former situation. Seven years afterwards Wulfreda died in London, whither she had retired to avoid the Danish army then invading England. This retaliation of Elfrida on her former rival in the King's affections, at so distant a period, marks how deeply the feelings of jealousy and revenge were implanted in her bosom.

Elfrida retired from Barking to Wherwell, where she died in 1002, in a state of extreme penitence, and at a very advanced age.[1] King Ethelred granted Wherwell, in the year of his mother's death, a charter of confirmation, on account of its being the place in which she ended her days, and which contained her last remains.[2]

---

[1] Dugdale. [2] Ibid.

EMMA OF NORMANDY,

SURNAMED "THE PEARL," QUEEN OF ETHELRED "THE UNREADY," AND CANUTE "THE GREAT."

The Pearl of Normandy—Parentage of Emma—Quarrels settled—Emma's Marriage with Ethelred, 1002, at Winchester — She receives the popular name of Elfgiva—Unsuitableness of Ethelred—His personal appearance—The songs of Gunnlaugr the Scald—The Sagas: their value—Danegelt, its odiousness to the English—Massacre of the Danes on the Eve of St. Brice—Gunilda's fate—Her anathema — Emma's sorrow concealed — The neglect of Ethelred towards his wife—She appeals to her brother—Anger of the Duke of Normandy—Reconciliation — Hugh and Alwyn — Siege of Exeter—Oath of fealty to Emma's unborn babe—Birth of her son, Edward the Confessor—Alfred, the eldest son, set aside on account of a prophecy — Emma flies from the troubles in England, with her children, to Normandy—Remains there two years—They are followed by Ethelred—"Unready" a title fitting for the weak King—London Bridge is broken down—Edmund Ironside—Algitha at Malmesbury Abbey — Death of Ethelred—Canute marries Emma—Her weight in gold—Influence of Emma—Mutual attachment—Danish Dandies—Drinking-cups—Back-gammon—Poets — Story of Canute and his courtiers — Splendid gifts to abbeys — The King's verses—Vauland, the smith—Hardicanute and Gunilda—King Olaf—Death of Canute—Earl Godwin's power — Treacherous letter to Emma's sons—Murder of Alfred — Suspicions — Harold — Emma's exile and return — Hardicanute — The gilded ship — The dwarf Mimicon — Death of Hardicanute — Edward succeeds—His conduct to his mother—The trial of the ploughshares—Triumph—Death of Emma.

The first alliance between the English and the Normans, who afterwards ruled England with such despotic sway, took place in 1002, when Emma, who for her beauty was surnamed "the Pearl of Normandy," became the wife of Ethelred, the reigning monarch.

The family of Emma was of Scandinavian origin. Rollo, or Robert, her great-grandfather, after an unsuccessful invasion of England, in the reign of Alfred, had turned his arms against the natives of the neighbouring coast of France, who, finding themselves unable to oppose their warlike invaders, offered Robert a settlement in their territories. Charles the Simple, then on the French throne, yielded to Rollo part of the Province of Neustria, and bestowed on him at the same time the hand of his daughter Gisla, on condition that the Dane should do him homage as a vassal. The territory ceded to Rollo from that time went by the name of Normandy; and the Duke, when he died, bequeathed it to his son, Duke William I., who held it for twenty-five years. This prince was succeeded by Richard his son, then a minor, whose wife was Agnes, daughter of Hugh the Great, Earl of Paris, by whom he had no children. Bv Gunnora, his second wife, he had three sons, Richard, Robert, and

Mauger; and three daughters, Emma-Agnes, Helloie or Alix, and Maud. The eldest of these princesses, named after Richard's first consort, was afterwards Queen of England, Alix espoused Geoffrey, Earl of Bretagne, and Maud became the wife of Eudes, Earl of Chartres and Blois.

Ethelred, King of England, had quarrelled with Duke Richard I., on some subject which has not been handed down to us. A fleet was prepared by Ethelred for the invasion of Normandy, and Richard, on his part, arrested all the English pilgrims and merchants in his dominions, some of whom he threw into prison, while others he condemned to death. Pope John XV. employed his legate Leo, Bishop of Treves, to reconcile the contending princes. Leo visited first Ethelred, and afterwards Richard, and, at his request, commissioners were appointed to meet at Rouen, when it was agreed that all ancient causes of dissension should be forgotten, that a perpetual peace should subsist between the King of England and the Marquess[1] of Normandy, their children born and to be born, and all their true liege-men; that every infraction of this peace should be repaired by satisfactory compensation; and that neither prince should harbour the subjects nor the enemies of the other, without a written permission.[2] This, the oldest treaty now extant between any of our kings and a foreign power, is drawn up in the name of the Pope, and confirmed by the oaths and marks of one bishop and two thanes on the part of Ethelred, and of one bishop and two barons on the part of Richard:[3] it was signed at Rouen, March 1st, 991.

In the eighth year after Ethelred's accession, he had married Ethelgina, daughter of Earl Thorold, by whom he had five children, Edmond, surnamed Ironside, for his strength of mind and body, Edwy, and three daughters. The Queen dying in 1002, Ethelred sent ambassadors to Normandy to demand the hand of Emma, sister of the reigning duke, Richard II. It is not unlikely that some overtures had been made at an earlier period, prior to Ethelred's first marriage, for this beautiful princess, who was then but a child; for Roger of Wendover says that Emma was the cause of the quarrel between her father and Ethelred, but no particulars have reached us.

Duke Richard II. gave a most honourable reception to the English embassy. The negotiation for the marriage was speedily concluded, and the same year that witnessed the death of Ethelgina, saw the young and blooming "Flower of Normandy" solemnly bestowed on the recently widowed King. In Lent, 1002, the new Queen came over to England, attended by a numerous retinue of French men and women.[4] The nuptial ceremony was performed at Winchester, which, from that time, became a favourite residence of Emma, and was the spot in which she passed the earlier years of her married life. Both Saxon and Norman chroniclers unite in representing the youthful Queen Emma[5] as in a pecu-

---

[1] The title of Marquess or Duke is indiscriminately used, in the treaty, for the father of Emma.

[2] Malmesbury says that the subjects of either Prince were to be provided with passports under seal, in travelling through the other's dominions.

[3] Lingard.

[4] Ingulphus, Gale, Saxon Chronicle.

[5] Gemma and Ymma, Imma and Eme are various readings of the name Emma.

liar degree gifted with elegance and beauty; so that many flattering epithets had been bestowed on her—as "the Pearl," "the Flower," or "the Fair Maid" of Normandy. As she readily adopted the manners of the English on her arrival, she became so much beloved by them as to receive the popular surname of Elfgifa, the Elf or "Fairy Gift," and is called in the Saxon Chronicle Emma Elfgiva: several of her female predecessors among the queens-consort of England having, as has been before named, assumed this title, in honour of the wife of Edmund the Pious.

Ethelred was much older than Emma, being about thirty-four years of age at the time of his second marriage, and in some respects exceedingly unsuited to win the affections of the young and lovely bride whom he had selected. The son of Elfrida, who had perhaps herself witnessed the second nuptials of Ethelred, or at least lived to counsel them, inherited his mother's beauty of person, with many of its accompanying vices. He is represented to have been "a tall, handsome man, elegant in manners, beautiful in countenance, and interesting in his deportment;"[1] yet Malmesbury characterises his personal appearance, sarcastically calling him "*a fine sleeping figure.*" Amongst other weaknesses, he was open to flattery, as is evident from the patronage he afforded to Gunnlaugr the Scald, who, having sailed to London from Norway, presented himself to the king with an heroic poem which he had composed on the *royal virtues.*

The adulatory style of this composition, which the author sang before the English Monarch, may be seen by the following lines:—

"The soldiers of the King, and his subjects,
The powerful army of England,
Obey Ethelred,
As if he was *an angel of the beneficent Deity.*"

Ethelred, having listened to the poet, bestowed on him in return for his verse "a purple tunic, lined with the richest furs, and adorned with fringe," and gave him an appointment within the palace. On his departure from the court, in the following spring, Gunnlaugr received from his royal patron a gold ring, of the weight of seven ounces, accompanied by a request that he would return in the autumn. The Scald visited Ireland and sang: "the king there wished to give him two ships, but was told by his treasurer that poets had always clothes, or swords, or gold rings given them. Gunnlaugr accordingly had a present of fine garments and a gold ring." In the Orkneys he was rewarded with a silver axe.

The Scalds were persons of some importance, and having much in their power, were generally well treated by those monarchs who were anxious for their good report. They were, says Laing, a kind of "wandering scholars, natives generally of Iceland, and a class of more consequence than mere amusement at a court could have made them."[2] They were, in fact, the recorders of events, and many of their songs, or sagas, are family annals. "They were frequently employed as messengers and

which some say is identical with Amy, in Latin written Amata and Eutrophine, in Greek it signifies a *good nurse,* or help-giver, as the Saxons say.

[1] Turner, from Gunnlaugr Saga. [2] Laing's Norway.

ambassadors, who carried the tokens which monarchs or nobles exchanged with each other. These tokens were not merely gifts, but had a meaning known to the personages, and accredited the messenger." Such personages were necessary at a time when reading and writing were rare accomplishments amongst princes.

"The language of the Scalds seems to have been understood at the courts of all the branches of the Scandinavian people; the same Scald appears to have visited on business or pleasure the courts of Rouen, of England, of Denmark, Sweden and Norway, and there is no mention of any difficulty arising from difference of language in any of the transactions of individuals. These were frequently adventurers passing from the service of one monarch to another."[1]

The sagas are extremely valuable, as the Scalds recorded the passing events of the time, and any falsehood or exaggeration would have been detected by contemporaries.

Ethelred had made the alliance with Normandy from policy, to gain aid against his formidable enemies, the Danes, who at that time were incorporated among the English, and led a careless and easy life, treating them as though they were their servants and drudges, while their wives and daughters became slaves to their pleasure, whence they had even obtained the epithet of "Lord Danes." Great part, indeed, of England had a government according to Danelagh. All this had been brought about by the pusillanimity of Ethelred, who, instead of meeting his foes in fair and open strife, had bought off their hostilities by a yearly sum of money, known under the name of Dane-gelt, long the most odious tax felt in England. Every year these intruders became more dangerous and increasingly powerful, and by degrees settled in the very heart of his dominions. Ethelred, therefore, in marrying Emma, whose mother Gunnora, was descended of an eminent Danish family, expected the alliance would be instrumental in obliging the Danes to ameliorate their conduct,[2] if, indeed, he could not obtain of Duke Richard's assistance to wholly extirpate them from the country, which groaned beneath their tyranny. In these calculations, however, Ethelred was grievously mistaken. The Normans and Danes were, as has been shown, descended from the same stock,[3] and the Norman Duke did not perceive any motive sufficiently strong, as regarded his own interest, to induce him to embroil himself in war with the relatives of his mother for the sake of entering into the schemes of the husband of his sister Emma. Whether Ethelred was so blind as to believe that his new ally would sanction the unparalleled act of cruelty of which he was guilty, in the very year of his marriage, and almost before the rejoicings for that event were over, it seems hard to believe; yet so puffed up was the weak King with his notion of newly-acquired power that, instigated by his favourites, he gave orders for a general massacre of the Danes throughout the country. The day before

[1] Laing's Norway. [2] Echard.

[3] "The Earls of Rouen are descended from Gange Rolf; they have long reckoned themselves of kin to the chiefs in Norway, and hold them in such respect, that they always were the greatest friends of the Northmen, and every Northman found a friendly country in Normandy, if he required it."—Snorro.

St. Brice's Day, secret letters were sent by Ethelred to every city, commanding the English at an appointed hour to destroy the Danes by fire and sword.[1] Neither age nor sex was spared—men, women, and children being mercilessly slaughtered; the Saxon females even falling on their helpless foes, unarmed, and on a day of festival, maiming with scythes and reaping-hooks those whom they could not kill. Amongst those who perished was Gunilda, sister of Sweyn, the Danish monarch, who had been given as a hostage for the treaty of peace concluded between her brother and the perfidious Ethelred. Having embraced Christianity, and married Palling, a Saxon courtier, she had settled in this country. This noble lady beheld her husband and children massacred before her eyes: she herself was killed by strokes from a lance. In the agony of her grief for the loved ones who were falling around her, her words to the Saxon murderers were, "God will punish you, and my brother will avenge my death." Her prophetic denunciation was fulfilled, for England not long after sunk beneath the Danish yoke.[2]

Those who seek an excuse for such an act on the part of Ethelred, assert that he had cause to suspect the Danes of a plot to murder him and his Witan, and to seize upon the kingdom. This was the pretext for the atrocious action of which he was guilty, and which, instead of consolidating his power, annihilated the peace and security of the kingdom. At a moment when he had just formed an alliance with Emma, descended of the same blood as the victims, the policy of this massacre was singularly shortsighted. The young Queen's horror must have been extreme when she found that the solemnities and festivities of her marriage were thus converted into a scene of general bloodshed and mourning. The spirit of the ruthless Elfrida seems to have governed Ethelred on this occasion; and perhaps Emma's indignant sorrows were checked by him as violently as when his mother had beaten him "with waxen candles," when mourning over the murder of his own brother, Edward the Martyr, the victim of her ambition.

There were other causes for trouble in the mind of Emma, who, though possessed of unrivalled beauty, had failed in securing the affections of her husband. From the time of their marriage, the King had neglected her company, and associated with unworthy favourites, both male and female.[3] Emma felt this deeply: she had been idolised by her own countrymen, and was beloved by her new Saxon subjects. Young, lovely, learned, and highly accomplished, she felt that the treatment of Ethelred was so degrading to her merit, that she resolved at length to return to Normandy. Roger of Wendover seems to infer faults on her side, as well as on that of her husband; but he acknowledges that "the King was so petulant to his wife," that he would scarcely admit her to his intimacy; and she, on her part, "proud of her high descent, and irritated against him, blackened him in no small degree to her *father*."[4] The Duke of Nor-

[1] Rapin compares the Danish massacre to that of the Romans under Boadicea. The day selected for it was Sunday, too, the festival of St. Brice, when they were unarmed and taking their bath.

[2] Rivalité de France et de l'Angleterre.

[3] Holinshed.

[4] It should be her *brother*.

mandy, on receiving the account sent by Emma of her ill-treatment, despatched messengers to fetch her back to her own country; but, alarmed at the probable consequences, Ethelred thought it better to reconcile his Queen, which having effected, the Norman ambassadors returned without her. From that time, however, the Duke exhibited much coldness towards Ethelred, doubtless being aware of the hollowness of the apparent reconciliation; and when Ethelred sought his assistance against the Danes, he could not obtain attention to his request.

The expectations that Emma's marriage would turn out very advantageous to England, therefore, failed altogether. The Normans, on the contrary, instead of procuring defenders for England, brought across the sea "place-hunters" and ambitious men, craving money and dignities;[1] and this introduction of the Norman was the first link of a chain of events which led to the entire subversion of England, and afforded an opportunity for William of Normandy to lay claim to the throne, which he obtained by art and force of arms.[2]

Two persons had come over to England in the train of Emma, who were destined to act a prominent part in her eventful career, and had been received with great honour by Ethelred. These were Hugh and Alwyn, both Normans by birth. The latter was of high rank, being a relative of the ducal family, and accordingly had escorted the young Queen in the capacity of "counsellor or guardian."[3] On his arrival he was made superintendent of the royal household, and created Earl of Southampton. The courage and fidelity of Alwyn were afterwards of great service to Ethelred during his wars against the Danes; and at a later period still his history becomes involved more particularly with that of Queen Emma, to whose fortunes he ever remained a firm and tried friend. Hugh, the other Norman attendant on the Queen, was, at her request, created Governor of Exeter,[4] with the title of Earl of Devonshire. Emma herself was "Lady" of Exeter. He does not appear to have been equally faithful, to judge by the events which followed.

In the year succeeding that of Emma's marriage and the Danish massacre, Exeter was besieged by King Sweyn (A. D. 1003); for that Ethelred had privately put to death all the Danes in the several cities of England, had reached the ears of the brother of the injured Gunilda, who, at the head of a great navy, landed in Cornwall, burning with rage and indignation. Exeter bravely sustained a siege from the Danes for the space of two months, but at the end of that time was finally taken "by the treachery of Hugh, its governor, the Queen's countryman." On the surrender of the city, Sweyn put all to fire and sword, and razed it to the ground, besides taking great plunder.[5]

Turketil, at that period, describing the condition of the English to Sweyn, says, "a country illustrious and powerful; a king asleep, solici-

[1] Thierry's Norman Conquest.

[2] Holinshed. [3] Milner. [4] Caradoc, Fabian, Saxon Chronicle.

[5] Exeter was afterwards restored by Canute, but appears to have been still attached to the Queens of England; for after the Conquest, we find it holding out against William, under Githa, the mother of Harold.

tous only about women and wine, and trembling at war; *hated by his people*, and derided by strangers; generals envious of each other; and weak governors, ready to fly at the first shout of battle." [1] It is said of Elfric, a Saxon bishop of that time, that "he considered the state of things so bad that he believed doom's-day to be approaching, and the world very near its end." [2]

About this time, Emma was called to be present at a very affecting and remarkable scene, peculiarly characteristic of the superstition of the times. The Queen had already become mother of one son by Ethelred, to whom the name of Alfred had been given, and she was a second time about to give birth to a child, who afterwards wore the crown under the title of Edward the Confessor. The great rapidity and progress of the conquests of the Danes, owing to the pusillanimous and tardy conduct of Ethelred, justly surnamed "the Unready," from being never prepared to face his foes, caused a great council to be held, to deliberate on the affairs of the kingdom, then nearly overrun by the enemy. On this occasion, Queen Emma was present; and Ethelred, being desirous of appointing a successor, requested the opinion of the council. Some recommended Edmond "Ironside," son of his first Queen, so surnamed on account of his bodily strength, while others gave the preference to Alfred, the son of Emma, still in his infancy: yet, it having been predicted by one of the assembly that the former should enjoy but a very short life, and that the latter should perish immaturely, the wishes of all concentred on the child of which the Queen was then pregnant; and the King, assenting to this election, the nobility took an oath of fealty to the unborn babe.[3] In the first compartment of the screen which adorns the chapel of King Edward the Confessor, at Westminster, this subject is represented. In this piece of sculpture Queen Emma appears standing in the midst of a large assembly, with her left hand upon her waist. All the figures appear to have the right arm extended upwards, as if in the act of swearing allegiance.[4]

Emma gave birth to her son Edward at Islip, in Oxfordshire, and the second compartment of the before-mentioned screen in the chapel of St. Edward represents the event. It is curious on account of its containing in sculpture the ancient form of a state-bed:[5] in the back-ground are two of the Queen's attendants with the infant prince in their arms. At a subsequent period, Edward the Confessor received the town which had been the scene of his nativity, from his mother, Queen Emma, for his own maintenance; and long after, when he came to the throne, he bestowed that place, among other royal gifts, on the Abbey of Westminster, so that it became the country-residence first of the abbots, and then of

---

[1] Malmesbury; Kemble's Saxons in Britain. [2] Turner.

[3] Life of Edward the Confessor; Neale's Westminster Abbey. [4] Neale.

[5] A bed, of a very simple construction, is exhibited in Strutt's Saxon Antiquities, plate 13, fig. 2. It seems to be nothing more than a thick boarded bottom; the covering is very thin, and the pillow stiff and hard; in short, from the view of the whole together, ease was but little considered. This (though so rude in appearance), being a royal bed, is ornamented with curtains, which are fastened to the top, but they had also others that slid with rings on an iron rod.

the deans of Westminster. In Edward's original charter, he speaks of it in terms thus translated:[1] "Edward, king, greeteth Wlsy, bishop, and Gyrth, earl, and all my nobles in Oxfordshire. And I tell you that I have given to Christ and St. Peter at Westminster, *that small village wherein I was born*, by name GITHSLEPE,[2] and one hide at Mersie, scot-free and rent-free, with all the things which belong thereunto, in wood and field, in meadows and waters, with church and with the immunities of the church, as fully and as largely, and as free, as it stood in mine own hand; and also as my mother Emma, upon my right of primogeniture, for my maintenance, gave it me entire, and bequeathed it to the family."[3]

Emma and her children had been sent to the Isle of Wight for safety, from Winchester, which was threatened with destruction by the advancing army of Sweyn; Ethelred himself remaining in London, in a state of inactivity and apprehension, neither daring to assemble or to lead an army against his enemies, "lest the nobles of his realm, who had been unjustly treated by him, should desert him in the battle, and give him up to the vengeance of his foes." Tormented by these distressing apprehensions, the wretched King secretly withdrew from the city of London, and arriving at Southampton, crossed over to the Isle of Wight, whence he dispatched Queen Emma, with his two sons Alfred and Edward, and their guardians Elfhun, Bishop of Durham, and Elfsey, Abbot of Peterborough, into Normandy to Duke Richard her brother, who received them with honour and respect. Eadric, too, King Ethelred's kinsman, crossed over with the Queen, and a hundred and forty soldiers, and resided with her two years, attending her with great state. They crossed the sea in the month of August.[4] The Bishop of London also accompanied the Queen and her family as their protector.[5] The royal party carried with

---

[1] Kennett's Parochial Antiquities. [2] Islip.

[3] The King appears to have claimed the power, not only of disposing of the benefice or fee after the death of the tenant, but also of controlling the distribution of his other possessions. Hence the vassal in his will was always anxious to obtain the confirmation of his superior, and to make provision for the payment of what was termed by the Saxons the *heriot*, by the Normans the *relief*. Elphelm, after leaving his heriot to the King, concludes his will in these words:—"And now I beseech thee, my beloved lord, that my last testament may stand, and that thou do not permit it to be annulled."

The heriot was to be paid "within twelve months from the death of the last possessor: and was apportioned to the rank which he bore in the State." [Lingard, Sir H. Ellis, &c.] The payment preserved the estate in his family, if he died intestate, or was remitted in case of his falling in battle in his lord's service. In the stormy season of Ethelred's warfare against the Danes, and probably with a view to the future welfare of her children, in the event of her quitting England for her brother's protection, Emma adopted this precaution. The heriot, or bequest of Queen Elfgifa, in 1012, we are told, was as follows: — "She left the King six horses, six shields, six spears, one cup, two rings, worth one hundred and twenty mancuses each, and various lands."

The word *heriot* signifies "habiliments of war," and Canute was the first who established the compulsory heriot in England.

[4] Roger of Wendover, Fabian, Ran. Higden.

[5] "And the King sent Bishop Elfhun, with the Ethelings Edward and Alfred, over sea, that he might have charge of them."—Roger of Wendover.

them the treasures of Ethelred, either for security, or to obtain, through their medium, assistance from the Duke, in the recovery of their kingdom;[1] among other valuables, Queen Emma took with her, "an incomparable copy of the Gospels, such as had never before been seen in Normandy," which she presented to the Church of St. Peter.[2]

Having obtained a favourable reception for herself,[3] and ascertained the friendly disposition of her relatives towards Ethelred, Queen Emma persuaded her husband to throw himself on the hospitality of his Norman neighbours. Accordingly, "when King Ethelred heard of the honourable reception they had met with, he followed himself in the month of January, and laid all his troubles before the noble Duke, who much compassioned his calamities, and soothed his grief with words of consolation."[4]

Some authors relate that Ethelred, and Edmund "Ironside," secretly embarked at the same time as the Queen, and personally escorted her to the home of her youth.[5] The Saxon Chronicle, however, which calls Emma "the Lady," states that, after her departure to Normandy, the King left the fleet[6] at mid-winter, and went to the Isle of Wight, "and was there during that tide; and after that tide, he went over the sea to Richard, and was there with him until such times as Sweyn was dead." The same record places Emma's visit to Normandy, in 1013. Ethelred was very splendidly entertained by his generous brother-in-law.

On the death of Sweyn, the people recalled Ethelred, although the fleet, and also the Danes, had elected Canute as his father's successor. Ethelred, with his usual *unreadiness* to avail himself of fortune's favours, would not venture to England till his son Edmund Ironside, whom he sent over to ascertain the disposition of the people, had returned, when having been informed that, "if he would make haste" all things were favourable, he departed for England, with certain succours afforded by the brother of Queen Emma. The people testified great joy at his return, and Ethelred, on his part, swore new allegiance to them, and promised to reform his administration. The return of Emma to England could not have been productive of much comfort to her at this time, when the greater part of the country was, as in the reign of Alfred the Great, overrun by the Danes. In spite of promises, hopes, and aspirations for better things, nothing seems to have prospered.

Famine, pestilence, and war, distinguished the unfortunate reign of Ethelred, and taxation burthened the people. The year of the King's

[1] Echard. [2] Jumièges.

[3] Rouen, the residence of the ducal family, "was anciently called Ruda or Rudaburg; whence the Earls of Normandy were called Ruda-jarlar, the Rouen Earls, not Earls of Normandy." During the period that Emma resided abroad, with her brother, Elfsy, Abbot of Peterborough, "who was there with her, went to the minster which is called Boneval, where St. Florentine's body lay. There found he a poor place, a poor abbot, and poor monks; for they had been plundered. Then bought he there, of the abbot and of the monks, St. Florentine's body, all except the head, for five hundred pounds; and then, when he came home again, then made he an offering of it to Christ and St. Peter."—Saxon Chronicle, Milton, Laing's Notes on Snorro.

[4] Roger of Wendover. [5] Harding. [6] Which lay in the Thames.

return was marked not only by a renewal of the war, but by another unlooked-for event. "On the eve of St. Michael's mass, came the great sea-flood wide throughout this land, and ran so far up as it never before had done, and washed away many towns, and a countless number of people."[1] But adversity, thus poured forth in full measure on the sovereign head, failed in its effect, and Ethelred was still oppressive, weak, and irresolute; thus, though at the head of a powerful army, he was unable to maintain his royal rights; his son Edmund could not even prevail on him to head his troops in person. The weak King, even feigned illness, as an excuse for remaining in London, where he alone fancied himself to be secure.

On his return, Ethelred had ordered the army, which lay at Greenwich, to be paid 21,000*l.*,[2] and sent a general invitation to all who would enter his service. Many flocked around him, and among the rest "came King Olaf, with a great troop of Northmen, to his aid." Of this great leader, it is said that "he had in his ship 100 men armed in coats of ringmail, and in foreign helmets. The most of his men had white shields, on which the holy cross was gilt; but some had painted it in blue or red. He had also had the cross painted in front on all the helmets, in a pale colour. He had a white banner on which was a serpent figured." The dress of Olaf must have been costly, for mention is made of a present he received from Princess Ingegerd, of a long cloak of fine linen, richly embroidered with gold and with silk points.[3]

One of the most interesting portions of national British history relating to this period, is contained in Snorro's Sea-Kings of Norway, and as it gives a picture of the intestine discord of London at that time, and also of the city itself, it may not be ill-timed to introduce it here. King Olaf and others having joined Ethelred, the Chronicle proceeds to state that "they steered first to London, and sailed into the Thames with their fleet; but the Danes had a castle within. On the other side of the river is a great trading-place, which is called *Sudeviki*.[4] There the Danes raised a great work, dug large ditches, and within had built a bulwark of stone, timber, and turf, where they had stationed a strong army. King Ethelred ordered a great assault; but the Danes defended themselves bravely, and King Ethelred could make nothing of it. Between the castle and Southwark there was a bridge so broad that two wagons could pass each other upon it." On the bridge were raised barricades, both towers and wooden parapets, in the direction of the river, which were nearly breast high, and under the bridge were piles driven into the bottom of the river. Now, when the attack was made, the troops stood on the bridge everywhere, and defended themselves. King Ethelred was very anxious to get possession of the bridge, and he called together all the chiefs to consult how they should get the bridge broken down. Then said King Olaf, he would attempt to lay his fleet alongside of it, if the

[1] Anglo-Saxon Chronicle. [2] Ibid., Snorro.

[3] *Silki-ræmor* appear to have been silk tassels or ties on the cloak of fine linen (pelli), which was embroidered with gold.—Laing's Notes on Snorro.

[4] Or Southwark.

other ships would do the same. It was then determined in this council that they should lay their war forces under the bridge; and each made himself ready with ships and men.

"King Olaf ordered great platforms of floating wood to be tied together with hazel bands, and for this he took down old houses; and with these, as a roof, he covered over his ships so widely, that it reached over the ships' sides. Under this screen he set pillars so high and stout that there both was room for swinging their swords, and the roofs were strong enough to withstand the stones cast down upon them. Now when the fleet and men were ready, they rowed up along the river; but when they came near the bridge, there were cast down upon them so many stones and missile weapons, such as arrows and spears, that neither helmet nor shield could withstand it; and the ships themselves were so greatly damaged, that many retreated out of it. But King Olaf, and the Northmen's fleet with him, rowed quite up under the bridge, laid their cables around the piles which supported it, and then rowed off with all the ships as far as they could down the stream. The piles were thus shaken in bottom, and were loosened under the bridge. Now as the armed troops stood thick of men upon the bridge, and there were likewise many heaps of stones and other weapons upon it, and the piles under it being loosened and broken, the bridge gave way, and a great part of the men upon it fell into the river, and all the others fled, some into the castle, some into Southwark. Thereafter Southwark was stormed and taken. Now when the people in the castle saw that the river Thames was mastered, and that they could not hinder the passage of ships up into the country, they became afraid, surrendered the tower, and took Ethelred to be their king. So says Otta Swarte:—

'London Bridge is broken down,—
Gold is won, and bright renown,
Shields resounding,
War-horns sounding,
Hildur[1] shouting in the din!
Arrows singing,
Mail-coats ringing—
Odin makes our Olaf win!'

"And he also composed these:

King Ethelred has found a friend;
Brave Olaf will his throne defend—
In bloody fight
Maintain his right,
Win back his land
With blood-red hand,
And Edmund's son upon his throne replace—
Edmund, the star of every royal race!'

"Sigvat also relates as follows:—

'At London Bridge stout Olaf gave
Odin's law to his war-men brave—
'To win or die!'
And their foemen fly;

[1] The Scandinavian Bellona.

Some by the dyke-side refuge gain,
Some in their tents on Southwark plain!
This sixth attack
Brought victory back.'"

Olaf passed that winter with Ethelred, to whom all the country far around was brought into subjection; but the Thingmen[1] and the Danes held many castles, besides a great part of the country. Olaf was commander of the King's forces when they took Canterbury, where many were killed and the castle burnt: this is reckoned his eighth battle: he was also entrusted with the whole land defence of England, according to the Chronicle of Snorro, and sailed round the coast with his ships of war. After another battle against the Danes at Newport, in the Isle of Wight, Olaf scoured the country, "taking scott of the people, and plundering where it was refused. So says Ottar:—

'The English race could not resist thee,
With money thou madest them assist thee;
Unsparingly thou madest them pay
A scott to thee in every way:
Money, if money could be got—
Goods, cattle, household gear, if not.
Thy gathered spoil, borne to the strand,
Was the best wealth of English land.'

So that the friends of Ethelred were no more the friends of the English people than his enemies, and a woful season was his reign for them all."

Olaf remained in England for three years. The country was in a most pitiable condition, and if men could hardly feel themselves safe upon even a throne, how much more unprotected was the position of the other sex. It is hard to say what kind of court was that of Queen Emma at this troubled period of her life. With her young children forced from place to place, she still braved her fate with fortitude, and generously strove to animate the drooping spirits of her too desponding husband. It must have been to her a bitter and painful season, to behold the fierce strife maintained between the party of a husband such as Ethelred, and the countrymen of her mother, to whom she felt a preference; and had she been placed at the helm, probably the destiny of England had been very different to what it was. Ethelred's cowardice and extortions ruined his cause, and involved both himself and his family in ruin. There was, however, one of the sons of Ethelred whose bravery redeemed his father's character, though not his fortunes; and this was Edmund "Ironside," who comes into notice in a remarkable transaction about this period, A. D. 1015.

In those times of civil strife and warfare, the gift of female beauty was too often dangerous to its possessor, and many a high-born damsel and lofty princess was glad to enshrine herself from public gaze, in the quiet and safe seclusion of a monastery, preferring rather to forsake the world,

[1] Thingmen were hired men-at-arms, employed at the Danish court as a body-guard for their sovereigns. They formed bodies of standing troops over levies of peasantry, and to their superiority the victories of Sweyn and Canute have been ascribed. — Laing's Notes on Snorro's Sea-Kings.

than to risk the dangers she would inevitably be exposed to on every side, whether Saxon or Danish. Such, though frequently the case, was not the reason of the beautiful Algitha having become the inmate of the Abbey of Malmesbury. She had been sent there as a prisoner, by orders of Ethelred.

Algitha, a lady of noble parentage and great beauty, was the wife of Sigeferth, a nobleman of Danish extraction, who enjoyed extensive territories in Northumberland. The avaricious Ethelred coveted these rich possessions, and for the purpose of seizing on the Earl's estates, resolved to accomplish his death. Accordingly, the King convened a council at Oxford, A. D. 1015, in which Sigeferth, and another noble Danish lord, were accused of a conspiracy by Edric Streone, the King's favourite counsellor, the assembly being composed of Danes as well as English; yet was the motive of the King in the matter very evident. The unfortunate nobles were betrayed into confidence, and put to death in the King's own chamber. Their servants were so exasperated, that they would have revenged their murder, had they not been overpowered, and compelled to retreat to the Church of St. Frideswide, where they took refuge in the steeple, and defended themselves, until that being set on fire, they perished in the flames.[1]

On this melancholy occasion Algitha had been her husband's companion to Oxford, and on his death was seized and forcibly conveyed to Malmesbury under the royal mandate. The beauty of the widow of Sigeferth was, however, so noted, and the nobleness of her disposition so well known, that Prince Edmund was induced, from curiosity to become acquainted with her, to feign business in the neighbourhood of Malmesbury. In an interview with Algitha he fell deeply in love, and resolved to make her his wife. The match, as might have been expected, was strongly opposed by Ethelred, the lady being in his own power, and her rich possessions under his control; but the paternal prohibition did not deter Edmund from carrying off and espousing the lady of his choice, an event of great importance to the after-history of England. On his marriage, Edmund required his father to cede the territories of Sigeferth, in Northumberland, which amounted to the living of an earl. On the King's refusal, Edmund, without his authority, went into Northumberland, where the farmers and tenants of Sigeferth's estates willingly received him as their lord, influenced by his union with Algitha. This event embittered the close of Ethelred's career. The King survived his son's marriage scarcely twelve months, during which he not only beheld his eldest son and destined heir thus rebel against him, but his enemies triumphant. After frequently feigning illness as one excuse among many to evade his foes, domestic trouble and vexation at repeated losses caused the King to fall dangerously sick in earnest, and he died at the age of fifty, after a reign of thirty-seven years. His last remains were interred in St. Paul's, London, where they were seen by Speed before the destruction of the church, who says "his bones yet remain in the north

---

[1] Holinshed.

wall of the chancel, in a chest of grey marble, reared on four small pillars, and covered with a coped stone of the same."

Ethelred had a numerous family: Edmund "Ironside" and Edwy, with their three sisters, all born by this King's first marriage, survived him; and Alfred, Edward, and Goda, the children of Emma.

Popular consent, and the late King's will, accorded the crown to Edmund Ironside, who was accordingly crowned with the usual honours at St. Paul's, the ceremony being performed by the Archbishop of York. Canute, notwithstanding, caused himself to be proclaimed at Southampton, and not long after besieged Edmund in London.

Within the city at this critical moment were Edmund and his brother, the Queen-Dowager Emma, two bishops, and several distinguished thanes. An army of 27,000 men and a fleet of 340 sail had been collected in the mouth of the Thames. Canute found it easy to cut off the communication by land, but to prevent ingress and egress by water was more difficult. As the fortifications of the bridge impeded the navigation of the river, by dint of labour a channel was dug on the right bank. Through it was dragged a considerable number of ships, and the Northmen became masters of the Thames above as well as below the city.[1] While thus situated every means was tried to gain over the besieged. Canute demanded that Edmund and his brother should be given up, that 15,000*l.* should be paid for the ransom of the Queen, 12,000*l.* for that of the bishops, and that 300 hostages should be given for the fidelity of the citizens. If these terms were accepted, he would take them under his protection; if they were refused, the city should be abandoned to pillage and the flames.[2] But the brave Londoners held out, and the Danes were forced to retire. The royal brothers had escaped in a boat through the Danish fleet. Several encounters followed, and also a second siege of the city, which was relieved by Edmund, who entered London in triumph. The war was, after a truce, terminated by a friendly compact. The two kings had agreed to meet each other in single combat in the isle of Olney, near Gloucester, where after a few blows the rival monarchs shook hands and agreed to divide the kingdom, Canute receiving from Edmund the northern half of England.[3]

On the death of Ethelred Queen Emma had recalled King Olaf to England to assist her against Canute, but on a peace concluded between Edmund and the Danish monarch, Olaf soon withdrew, and was created King of Norway by the voice of the people. Queen Emma also, who was stepmother of "Ironside," fled for the second time into Normandy, taking with her the young princes Alfred and Edward.[4]

The Danish chronicler says that the murder of Edmund took place about a month after his agreement with Canute, who thus became master of the remaining half of the island, and took care to render permanent a power he had obtained only by repeated efforts.

Olaf, after the battle of London Bridge, spent two summers and a winter in France, and after the death of King Edmund in 1016 came to

---

[1] Chronicles of London Bridge.

[2] Holinshed.

[3] Lingard.

[4] Turner, Gaillard.

Rouen, where he met the sons of Ethelred, and entered into an engagement to assist them the following year in the recovery of their kingdom, for which he was to be rewarded with Northumberland if the enterprise was successful. This invasion was attempted, but was a failure, and the Princes were compelled to return to Rouen. There is no doubt that Emma not only sanctioned these efforts made by her sons to recover their rights, but also assisted them as far as was in her power.

Sigvat the Scald writes thus:—

> "Now all the sons of Ethelred
> Were either fallen or had fled;
> Some slain by Canute, — some, they say,
> To save their lives had run away."

Canute rightly deemed an alliance with their mother herself would most effectually silence the future claims of Ethelred's heirs. His own wife was just dead, and he determined to offer himself to the widow of Ethelred. As Emma was of Danish descent he supposed she would naturally prefer a Dane to an Anglo-Saxon for a husband, and he desired to secure the alliance of the Duke in his own favour, who had up to this time befriended the sons of his sister, the Queen of England. The young Princes having heard of the death of Edmund, and Canute's cruelty to their two young cousins, the sons of that King had resolved to remain at the court of Normandy; but Richard had fitted out a fleet in support of their claims. However, Canute despatched his embassy to the Norman Duke. Messengers, with right royal gifts and earnest supplications, proceeded to the Court of Richard, with instructions to demand Emma of her brother, and at the same time to offer one of Canute's own sisters, named Estrech, or Estritha,[1] to the Duke.[2]

It occasioned great wonder among many persons that Emma should agree to marry the mortal enemy of her first husband and of her young sons. Not long before, Canute himself had besiged London while Emma was within its walls, and now she accorded him her hand in marriage; yet not only did the Duke, her brother, consent, but took for his own wife the Lady Estritha. Some writers estimate Emma's conduct in this instance as very politic, for not only did she insure the succession to her own children, but effectually silenced the Danes. Had Emma been indifferent to the future welfare of her sons Alfred and Edward, she would have brought them over with her to England; but her anxiety for their safety caused her to prevent their leaving the Norman court; for she dreaded the jealousy of Canute, which had been excited by the vain endeavours of Duke Richard to place those princes on the throne of their ancestors; added to this, Edwy, brother of Edmund, had fallen a victim, and the young sons of Ironside had been sent to a foreign land.

By the agreement made with Canute, Emma did not take away her son's right, but removed it to a greater distance by interposing her own issue by Canute; so that after the death of the usurper Harold Harefoot, Hardicanute succeeded as rightful heir by virtue of Emma's agreement, and being established on the throne, ordained his brother Edward his suc-

[1] Sometimes written Ostrich.

[2] Lingard.

cessor. By Emma's policy the Danes were thus wholly excluded, and the English line restored, through a match beneficial both to herself and her family. In making this alliance she would appear to have acted as guardian of the young princes, and to have considered expediency with a view to the ultimate result. Such is the view taken in the work entitled "Encomium Emmæ," which was written by a monk contemporary with Emma, and as the title imports, in commendation of the Norman Princess.

The two marriages of Emma to Canute, and of Canute's sister, Estreth, to Duke Richard, were solemnized at the same time (in the month of July, 1018),[1] with vast magnificence. The two years of Emma's widowhood must have about expired when she became a second time a bride; for Edmund's reign had lasted eighteen months, and a few months had elapsed after the accession of Canute before the ceremony took place. According to Jumièges, Emma was married to Canute "Christiano more," in the Christian form, so that, prior to that marriage, he appears to have been a Pagan following the Danish rites. That this was really the case appears from Ordericus Vitalis, one of the most accurate and valuable of the Norman historians. We know that Emma was a Christian herself, and from Ordericus learn that "Canute was made a Christian, and married Emma to preserve peace." The ceremony seems to have taken place at London a few days after her arrival, and on the occasion the Danish King, fearing she would be carried away by the Saxon soldiery, presented to the whole army "her weight in gold and silver."[2] By this marriage Canute gained the alliance of Duke Richard, though for a short time only, for he did not long survive his union with Estritha, and at the death of this prince his duchy devolved on his eldest son, who died in another year, childless, and after him to Robert, his brother, a man of valour and abilities.

The English were pleased to find at court a sovereign to whom they were accustomed; they greatly loved Emma, and as the widow of Ethelred she had naturally a claim upon them. Harding writes:—

"Kyng Knowt reigned in Englâd the anon,
And wedded had Queen Eme of England,
Ethelrede wife, which gate him loue anon
In Englande of all the estates of the londe,
Of cōmons also that were both fre and bonde."

"Acting as mediatrix between Canute and the English nation, Emma counselled her husband to send back his fleet[3] and his stipendiary soldiers

[1] Turner, Gaillard, Higden, Fabian, Roger of Wendover. [2] Jamièges.

[3] In dismissing the Danish army and navy by request of his Queen, the King reserved for his own use forty vessels only, the crew or Thingmanen of which were intended for his body-guard. Edgar the Peaceable is thought to have kept his foes at a distance by the display of a fleet of 3,600 vessels, which each summer he employed to sail round the provinces he ruled. Before Canute's time the Danes had open barques with twelve oars; they afterwards enlarged these so that they contained more than 100 men. Canute's ships were covered over with gold and silver. They had one mast, on the top of which was a gilt vane, exhibiting some bird, to show which way the wind blew. Sometimes a man, a fish, a dragon, or a lion ornamented the stern of the vessel.—William of Malmesbury.

to their own country.[1] Accordingly after distributing among them 82,000 pounds of silver, he dismissed them to their native land."[2] This was an important concession, and betokened how great was the influence the Queen had already obtained over the heart of Canute.

The King of Norway and Denmark from the earliest period kept a "herd" or "court." "The herdmen were paid men-at-arms," who mounted guard at stated hours, posted sentries round the King's quarters, and had patrols on horseback, night and day, at some distance, to bring notice of any hostile advance. They were of two classes, udal-born to land, and called thingmen, from their being privileged to sit in *Things* at home, and those of a commoner class, *not* udal-born to land, and therefore unqualified, such as ordinary seamen, soldiers, and followers, but yet not of the class called slaves in England. The victories of Canute and his father are chiefly ascribed "to the superiority of the hired bands of thingmen in their pay. The massacre of the Danes in 1002, by Ethelred, appears to have been of the regular bands of thingmen, who were quartered in the towns, and who were attacked while unarmed and attending a church festival. The herdmen appear not only to have been disciplined and paid troops, but to have been clothed uniformly. Red was always the national colour of the Northmen, and continues still in Denmark and England the distinctive colour of their military dress. It was so of the herdmen and people of distinction in Norway, as appears from several parts of the Sagas, in the eleventh century."[3]

The dresses of the Danish kings were grand and magnificent, though not much unlike those of the Saxons, embroidered and worked with broad gold trimming. They had either a cloak or a robe, also resembling the Saxons, sometimes buckled over the right shoulder, and hanging on the left, and sometimes buckling on the middle of the breast; the cloak hung over the left shoulder of the King, without being buckled on the right at all, by way of distinction. They wore shoes, and also a kind of buskin, the toe of which was turned somewhat downward.

As early as the time of Edgar, the Danes who had settled in England were great beaux, constantly combing their hair, of which they were very fond.[4]

Canute himself is described as "large in stature and very powerful, fair, and distinguished for his beauty; his nose was thin, prominent and aquiline; his hair was profuse, his eyes bright and fierce."[5] His many

[1] The presence of the Danish army was a constant source of uneasiness and animosity to the English; but gratitude as well as policy forbade Canute to dismiss it without a liberal donation.—Lingard.

[2] Roger of Wendover, Turner.

[3] Laing; Preliminary Dissertation to Snorro, Chron. of the Kings of Norway.

[4] "The Danish mercenaries in England combed their hair once a day, bathed once a week, and changed their clothes frequently. A young warrior, going to be beheaded, begged of his executioner that his hair might not be touched by a slave, or stained with his blood; and Harold, surnamed Harfager, or 'Fair Locks,' made a vow to his mistress to neglect his fine hair until he had completed the conquest of Norway to gain her love."—Lingard.

[5] Saga.

great and good qualities obtained for him various surnames, such as the Brave, the Great, the Rich, and the Pious.[1]

The Danish manners and customs had been common in England long before, so that a Danish court would not occasion much astonishment among the Anglo-Saxons. Among the Danes themselves some court ceremonies, unknown before, had been introduced by Olaf Kyrre, or "the Quiet." "For each guest at the royal table he appointed a torchbearer, to hold a candle. The butler stood in front of the King's table to fill the cups, which, we are told, before his time were of deer's horn. The court-marshal had a table opposite to the King's, for entertaining guests of inferior dignity. The drinking was either by measure or without measure; that is, in each horn or cup there was a perpendicular row of studs at equal distances, and each guest, when the cup or horn was passed to him, drank down to the stud or mark below. At night, and on particular occasions, the drinking was without measure, each taking what he pleased; and to be drunk at night appears to have been common even for the kings. Such cups, with studs, are still preserved in museums, and in families on the Borders.[2]

"The kings appear to have wanted no external ceremonial belonging to their dignity: they were addressed in forms, still preserved in the northern languages, of peculiar respect; their personal attendants were of the highest people, and were considered as holding places of great honour. Earl Magnus, the saint, was in his youth, one of those who carried in the dishes to the royal table; and torch-bearers, herdmen, and all who belonged to the court, were in great consideration; and it appears to have been held of importance and of great advantage to be enrolled among the king's herdmen."[3]

There were many sorts of amusements in the Dano-English court: chess and dice are named among the rest. Bishop Ethern coming to Canute the Great about midnight, upon urgent business, found the king and his courtiers engaged at play, some at dice and others at chess.[4] Back-

---

[1] Turner.

[2] Until a few years since, the manor of Pusey, in Berkshire, has belonged to a family of the same name, their ancestor having received it from that king by the medium of a HORN, which bears the following inscription: —

"Kynge Knowd geve Wyilyam Pewse
Hys Horn to holde by the Londe."

This curious relic of antiquity is of a dark-brown tortoise-shell colour, mounted at each end with rings of silver, and a third round the middle, on which the inscription is written in characters of much later date than those of the time of Canute. The horn is of an ox or buffalo; two feet are fixed to the middle ring, and the stopper is shapped like a dog's head. The length of the horn is two feet and half an inch; its greatest circumference one foot. The person to whom the horn was originally given is said, by tradition, to have been an officer in Canute's army, who had informed his sovereign of an ambuscade formed by the Saxons to intercept him, and received the manor in reward for his intelligence. — Britton and Brayley.

This interesting heirloom was produced at the recent anniversary of Alfred's birth.

[3] Introductory Dissertation on Snorro, Laing.

[4] Turner.

gammon is reported to have been invented about this period in Wales, and derives its name from *bach* (little) and *cammon* (battle).

Canute patronised men of literary merit, being liberal to the clergy and the Scalds: of the latter class the names and verses of many have been preserved, who are quoted by Snorro. An amusing anecdote is on record of Thorarin, who had made a short poem on Canute, and went to recite it in his presence. On approaching the throne, he received a salute, and respectfully inquired if he might repeat what he had composed. The king was at table at the close of a repast; but a crowd of petitioners were occupying their sovereign's ear by a statement of their grievances. The impatient poet may have thought them unusually loquacious; he bore the tedious querulousness of injury with less patience than the King, and at last, presuming on his general favour with the great, exclaimed, 'Let me request again, Sire, that you would listen to my song; it will not consume much of your time, for it is very short.' The king, angry at the petulant urgency of the salutation, answered with a stern look, 'Are you not ashamed to do what none but yourself has dared, to write a *short* poem upon me! Unless by to-morrow's dinner you produce above thirty strophes, on the same subject, your head shall pay the penalty.' The poet retired, not with alarm, for his genius disdained that, but with some mortification at the public rebuke. He invoked the Scandinavian muses, his mind became fluent, verses crowded on it; and before the allotted time, he stood before the king with the exacted poem, and received fifty marks of pure silver as his reward."[1]

The beautiful manuscripts of the Anglo-Saxons have already been alluded to. Fosbrooke assigns two motives for the extraordinary pains taken in their illustrations: "one that perusal might be thus invited, the other that they might be presents of value. Ervenius, an Anglo-Saxon, was very skilful in writing and illumination. He committed two books, the Sacramental and the Psalter, in which he had decorated the principal letters with gold, to the care of Wulstan when a boy. Admiration of the workmanship invited Wulstan to a studious perusal. But Ervenius consulting the advantage of the age, as affirmed, with the hope of greater reward, presented the Sacramental to Canute, and the Psalter to Emma, his Queen."[2]

One of the royal residences[3] of Canute and Emma, was a house or palace in Westminster, which was burnt down in the reign of the Confessor,[4] but their principal abode was the palace, which at that time adjoined St. Paul's, and Canute endowed the office of its Dean with the plot of ground contiguous to the Cathedral, now called the Deanery, and also a valuable estate at Chadwell. The chronicler Knyghton relates that it was in the gardens of this city-palace, declining, with a gentle slope,

[1] Turner's Anglo-Saxon. [2] British Monachism.

[3] Raby Castle, the seat of the Earl of Darlington, about a mile to the north of Stamdrop, is supposed to occupy the site of a former mansion of Canute, given by him to the Church of Stamdrop. It stands on an eminence, founded on a rock, and is surrounded with a parapet and embrasured wall, together with a deep fosse.—Hutchinson.

[4] Fenn's Letters.

towards the banks of the river, that the well-known incident occurred of the king's reproof to his impious and scarcely half-Christianized courtiers. But Milner considers this to be a mistake, and says that Rudborne, who quotes more ancient authors, places this scene near the ancient Southampton, now the port of Northam.[1] The identical spot where the transaction took place, is still pointed out at Bittern, in Northam harbour, by the tradition of the inhabitants; the legend though well-known, is here given. "King Canute having walked one day to the sea-shore, attended by a train of courtiers, some sycophants began to address him in the courtly language of adulation, exalted his dominion, and pronounced him the most powerful and most happy of human beings; nay, they even had the boldness to add:—'Sire! nothing can resist you, nothing is impossible to your greatness.'

"Canute, disgusted with this fulsome flattery, ordered a chair to be brought, which he placed on the beach at low water. He then seated himself and exclaimed,—'Sea, thou art mine! and these sands acknowledge my sovereignty. I charge thee, therefore, rise no farther, nor presume to wet the feet of thy master.' The waves, however, obeying no laws but those of the Almighty, pursued their course, and dashed against the King, upon which he rose from his chair, exclaiming, 'Let all the inhabitants of the earth know, that the power of man is vain and contemptible, and that He only is a monarch at whose nod the heavens, the earth, and the sea, are ever obedient.'"[2]

This reproof sufficiently disconcerted the parasites, but Canute embraced another and more solemn occasion to acknowledge his sincere submission to the Almighty God, his Lord and Sovereign: he deposited the golden crown which he had been accustomed to wear, in the church at Winchester, and never afterwards placed it on his own head.

There yet exist coins of this King,[3] which were struck at Dublin,

[1] Milner's Hist. of Winchester. [2] Great and Good Deeds of the Danes.

[3] While this work is going through the press the newspapers of the day describe the finding by workmen of no less than one hundred and twenty coins of Canute and some of his predecessors, in a perfect state of preservation, at Wedmore, in Somersetshire. The labourers who found the earthen vessel in which they were contained, were digging for gravel in the churchyard.

"No king," says Gough, in his Catalogue, "ever coined in so many places as Canute." He mentions no less than thirty-seven.

A Danish medalist has observed that no coins of Canute are to be met with of any other than English mints; notwithstanding he reigned two years longer in his own country than over England, which he governed nineteen years. This observation seems to be confirmed by the discovery of some of this Prince's coins of English mintage, with others of our King Ethelred, in a barrow in Ireland, mentioned by Olaus Wormius. England might be his favourite residence, as he had made it so considerable an accession to his paternal territory by compact and succession; and he affected to court the good-will of his new subjects, by taking the title of "Rex Anglorum," and sinking his other title.

Keder has noted four varieties of this Prince's coins.

The first exhibits his bust in armour, with a helmet or diadem; in his left hand the sceptre surmounted by a lily. The cross is a quatrefoil with pellets at the corners, or with another kind of cross laid upon it.

2. The bust has the diadem or sceptre, which on some is surmounted by four pellets in form of a cross. The cross issues from a circle in the centre.

probably in acknowledgment of his power by the Danish settlers in that country. The portraits of Canute and Emma, were prefixed to a Saxon MS. register of Hyde Abbey, written during that monarch's reign. This antique and valuable document is now in the possession of Thomas Astell, Esq., by whose permission portraits alluded to were copied by Mr. Strutt for his work on Saxon Antiquities.[1]

Canute has been celebrated for his justice and equity, and doubtless his religious feelings, which prompted both, may be really attributed to the influence of Emma.

The following letter, written from Rome, attests the beneficial influence of awakened piety over the heart of the King. He wrote in these terms to some of the great men of his kingdom:—"Be it known to you that I have humbly made a vow to Almighty God, to conduct myself hereafter, as shall become me; to govern my kingdom as a religious and just monarch, and to distribute equal justice among my subjects. I have prepared to correct whatever errors I may have been led into by the impetuosity of youth or want of reflection. I therefore desire and command my counsellors, to whom the affairs of the kingdom are entrusted, on no pretence to be guilty in themselves, or suffer others to be guilty of any acts of injustice, either through fear of me, or with a view to favour any person high in power. The laws shall be equally distributed among my nobles and my commoners. Let him beware who either values my friendship or his own welfare."[2]

Canute and Emma are said to have, for several years, regularly attended together the Festival of the Purification. Emma was a great benefactress to the Saxon church, and the extraordinary liberality displayed by Canute towards the Abbeys of Winchester, Ramsey, and Ely, is to be ascribed to the interest Emma exerted in their favour; in especial Ramsey was beloved by the Queen, and received many splendid gifts from Canute on that account. The King and Queen, say the chroniclers, visited Croyland and Ely in person, and piously offered their regal donations. On Croyland, besides other and more valuable presents, the King bestowed "twelve beautiful white bears' skins, for the altars on festival days," and also a "vestment of silk embroidered with eagles of gold." These rich gifts were as rare as costly, for though the skin of the brown bear was then common in England, the white was scarce and uncommon.

Queen Emma's offering to the monks of Ely is worthy of remark, as showing how excellent the art of needlework was in her time, and how she excelled in embroidery, "and with her own hands wrought a beautiful

3. The bust in a quatrefoil, with a crown of fleurs-de-lis; the cross terminating in crescents, in a quatrefoil, with three pellets on the points.

4. The bust wearing a high pointed cap or helmet; the sceptre surmounted with three pellets. The cross in a circle, in the angles four rings enclosing a less.

A fifth sort has an arm to the bust.

A sixth has the bust helmeted in a quatrefoil.—[Catalogue of the Coins of Canute, by Richard Gough.]

[1] Plate 28. Strutt's Saxon Antiquities.

[2] Great and Good Deeds of the Danes.

altar-cloth," which she presented to the priests. This costly piece of ornamental industry is thus described:—"it was of a green colour, and beautified with plates of gold, that appeared raised: if viewed lengthways along the altar, it seemed of a blood-red colour, and it was finished at the corners with rich gold ornaments, which reached to the ground."[1] These gold ornaments were of a kind of gold thread and bullion-work termed "orfrays."

Canute liberally endowed St. Swithin's Abbey, Winchester: besides other rich jewels, the King bestowed on it a cross worth as much as the revenue of England amounted to in one year.[2] Roger, of Wendover, relates that "Canute decorated the Old Minster, Winchester, with such magnificence that the minds of strangers were confounded at the sight of the gold and silver and the splendour of the jewels. This too, was done at the instigation of Queen Emma, whose profuse liberality consumed whole treasuries on such objects." Upon the destruction of monasteries many of the costly presents of Canute and Emma to the church must have been rifled and cast into the melting-pot, for the mere value of the metals of which they were composed.

A pall is named, as presented by the King and Queen, probably of her work, to Glastonbury "of various colours woven with the figures of peacocks." This was on the occasion of the visit to the tomb of Edmund Ironside, whom Canute was accustomed to style "his brother." A rich cloth, embroidered with "apples of gold and pearls," was given at the same time the charter was granted to the Abbey of St. Edmunsbury, in signing which Emma writes "Ego Alfgifa Regina," and the King names her as "Myne Queen Elfgifa," who, he says, gave the church a revenue of "four thousand Eels, in Lakinghithe."[3]

It was on the occasion of Canute's visit to Ely, accompanied by Queen Emma and the nobles of the court, when they were gliding along the river in their barge, that the King himself composed that little Saxon ballad of which, unfortunately, one single stanza alone has been preserved. As the royal party approached the church the monks were at their devotions, and the sweetness of their melody was so attractive to the King, that he ordered his rowers to pause near the spot whence the sounds proceeded, and to move gently while he listened to the harmony of the voices which came floating from the summit of the high rock before him. So great was his delight that it broke forth in the following poem.

"Merie sungen the muneches binnen Ely,
Tha Cnut ching reuther by:
Roweth cnites nœr the land,
And here we thes muneches sœng.

[1] Resembling a short silk (such as is frequently seen in early miniatures); Gale, vol. ii., p. 505.

[2] Howel.

[3] Fisheries were one of the sources of rent noticed in the Domesday Survey, where the produce in kind is mentioned, it seems chiefly to have consisted in eels, herrings, and salmons; sometimes they were paid by stitches or sticks, each stick having twenty-five. This was commonly the case in payment from mills. — Sir H. Ellis.

"Merry sang the monks in Ely
When King Canute sailed by:
Row, Knights, near the land,
And let us hear the monks' song."

Probably Canute sang these lines to some musical instrument, like the minstrels.[1] It is much to be regretted that the rest is lost. It has been thought that this poem is not so early as the time of Canute, and Lappenberg's learned editor, Dr. Thorpe, considers it no older than the thirteenth century. However this may be, as regards the language of the songs as handed down to us, there is no reason to doubt that the King might actually have composed such a poem, if indeed it did not proceed from the cultivated mind of Queen Emma herself, which is by no means impossible. When the barbarous deeds of the personages of those times are considered, it is a fact which creates extreme surprise that the ideas expressed in ballads and poems by the minstrels of that very period should be so full of delicacy and refined feeling. In the sagas there is an occasional gentleness and tenderness, where love and beauty are the themes, which contrast singularly with the records of burning, slaying, and outrages of all kinds perpetrated by the heroes. The charms of nature and the beauties of scenery appear to be fully appreciated by the "barbarians," who, if they acted like savages in some respects, seem to have the less excuse, as their songs prove, that though they "pursued the wrong," they knew "the right."

The skill, so insisted on in all accounts of presents made to the church, both in the arts of needlework and in the chasing and carving of metals, cannot be denied them; and that they understood the degrees of perfection to which such arts might attain, is shown by their earliest traditions. For instance, the sacred histories of the Scandinavians relate the marvels wrought by Vaulund the Forger, the Vulcan of the North. The Icelandic Saga thus describes his skill: "Vaulund was so renowned throughout the north that by one consent all the smiths acknowledged him their superior. To denote the excellent property of any forged weapon it was usual to say the artist must have been a Vaulund. A rivalry having ensued between him and King Nigundur's former smith, it was agreed that Vaulund should forge a sword, and his rival a helm, which the latter was to put on, and if it were found proof against the sword, Vaulund's head should be forfeited. Accordingly the King's former smith put on the helm, and sitting on a bench, bid Vaulund, in defiance, use all his strength. The latter, who stood behind him, then raised his arm, and, at a single stroke clove the armour and armourer down to the girdle; and inquiring what he felt, was answered by the smith that he had an internal sensation, as if from a stream of cold

[1] The ancient musical instruments were the *viele*, the flute, the pipe, the harp, and the *rotæ* This last, a species of harp, occurs in Chaucer and all our early poets. The *viele* was not the instrument now called by that name, but shaped like a fiddle, and played with a bow. The early music was written with square notes, ranged on four lines; the fifth was not introduced till late in the reign of St. Louis. — M. Le Grand's Notes to Fabliaux.

water. 'Shake thyself,' said Vaulund: the smith immediately did so, his body separated, and either half fell on opposite sides of the bench."[1]

Canute and Emma were great encouragers of church building; and to them may be attributed some of the most celebrated in England, as well as several in Normandy, which "time, war, flood, and fire" have spared to the present time, to prove the wondrous powers of architects and carvers in the early ages, never to be even approached in excellence by later and more enlightened artists.

In 1020, the Cathedral of Chartres, still one of the most magnificent in France, which had been destroyed by lightning, was rebuilt by its bishop, Fulbert. The names of Canute and Richard II., Duke of Normandy, are recorded as among those who assisted the work by their contributions. In the same year, the second of his marriage with Emma, Canute built the Monastery at Edmundsbury, "where the body of King Edmond lies, and by the advice of Queen Emma and the bishops and barons, established monks in it under Guy, a man, humble, modest, and pious."[2] The Abbey of St. Bennet's in the parish of Sudham, county of Norfolk,[3] was another foundation of Canute, between the years 1020 and 1030, as well as a church at Ashdone, in Essex, at the dedication of which all the English and Danish lords assisted.[4]

Emma had only two children by Canute; they were named Hardicanute and Gunilda, the former was surnamed "the Hardy or Robust," from his personal accomplishments;[5] the latter was reckoned one of the loveliest of her sex, and in her father's lifetime was contracted to the Emperor of Germany, whom she afterwards married.

Hardicanute, who by Emma's agreement, prior to her union with Canute, was destined to inherit the crown of England, was quite a child when the ceremony of translating the body of Bishop St. Elphege took place, of which the Saxon Chronicle gives the following account:—

"This year, 1023, King Canute within London, in St. Paul's minster, gave full leave to Archbishop Ethelnoth and Bishop Brithwine, and to all the servants of God who were with them, that they might take up from the tomb the Archbishop St. Elphege; and they then did so, on the sixth before the ides of June. And the illustrious King, and the archbishop and suffragan bishops, and earls, and very many clergy, and also laity, carried in a ship, his holy body over the Thames to Southwark, and there delivered the holy martyr to the archbishop and his companions; and they then with a worshipful hand and sprightly joy, bore him to Rochester. Then, on the third day, came Emma the lady, with her royal child Hardicanute; and then they all, with much state and bliss, and songs of praise, bore the holy archbishop into Canterbury; and then worshipfully brought him into Christ's Church, on the third before the ides of June. Again, after that, on the eighth day, the seventeenth before the kalends of July, Archbishop Ethelnoth, and Bishop Elfsy, and Bishop Brithwine, and all those who were with them, deposited St.

[1] Notes to Frithiof's Saga, translated by Oscar Baker.

[2] Roger of Wendover.

[3] Seven miles from Norwich.

[4] Holinshed.

[5] Hume.

Elphege's holy body on the north side of Christ's altar, to the glory of God, and the honour of the holy archbishop, and to the eternal health of all who there daily seek his holy body with a devout heart and with all humility. God Almighty have mercy upon all Christian men, through St. Elphege's holy merits."[1]

Canute resided chiefly in England, yet he occasionally visited Denmark, attended by an English fleet. The year after his marriage with Queen Emma he went there, and in all probability was accompanied by his royal consort, A. D. 1019.[2]

It appears that Earl Ulf Sprakalegsson had been left protector of Denmark by Canute when he went to England, his son "Hardicanute" being in his hands. The summer after this arrangement had been made by the English King, the Earl gave it out that King Canute had at parting made known to him his will and desire, that the Danes should take his son Hardicanute as King over the Danish dominions. He said Canute had done this on it being represented to him that the nation suffered many disadvantages from the absence of its King. "Hitherto," said Earl Ulf, "we have been so fortunate as to live without disturbance, but now we hear that the King of Norway is going to attack us, to which is added the fear of the people, that the Swedish King will join him, and now King Canute is in England." The Earl then produced King Canute's letter and seal confirming all that he asserted. Many other chiefs supported this business, and in consequence of all these persuasions the people resolved to take Hardicanute as King, which was done at the same time.[3] This circumstance, passed over in our English histories, throws light on the procedings of Queen Emma: the Danish historian proceeds to say, "that Queen Emma had been principal promoter of this determination, for she had got the letter to be written and provided with the seal, having cunningly got hold of the King's signet; but from him it was all concealed."

By this account it would seem, that Emma was intriguing to advance her son before his father's death, and had not shrunk from forgery to accomplish her end. The story, whether true or false, is thus continued:—

"When Hardicanute and Earl Ulf heard for certain that King Olaf was come from Norway with a large army, they went to Jutland, where the greatest strength of the Danish Kingdom lies, sent out message-tokens, and summoned to them a great force: but when they heard that the Swedish King was also come with his army, they thought they would not have strength enough to give battle to both, and therefore kept their army together in Jutland, and resolved to defend that country against the Kings. The whole of their ships they assembled together at Lynnfiord, and waited there for King Canute."[4]

The Dano-English King, in the meantime, had sailed with a vast force from England, and arrived in safety at Denmark, where he went to

[1] Anglo-Saxon Chronicle.

[2] Lingard.

[3] Snorro's Kings of Norway.

[4] Snorro.

Lynnfiord, and there he found gathered besides, a large army of the men of the country.

When the Danes "heard that King Canute had come from the west to Lynnfiord, they sent men to him, and to Queen Emma, and begged her to find out if the King were angry or not, and to let them know. Your son Hardicanute will pay the full mulct the King may demand, if he has done anything which is thought to be against the King." He replies, "that Hardicanute has not done this of his own judgment, and, therefore," says he "it has turned out as might be expected, that when he, a child, and without understanding, wanted to be called King, the country when any evil came and an enemy appeared must be conquered by foreign princes, if our might had not come to his aid. If he will have any reconciliation with me, let him come to me and lay down the mock title of King he has given himself."

The Queen sent these very words to Hardicanute, and at the same time she begged him not to decline coming, for as she truly observed, he had no force to stand against his father. When this message came to Hardicanute, he asked the advice of the Earl and other chief people who were with him; but it was soon found that when the people heard King *Canute the Old* was arrived, they all streamed to him, and seemed to have no confidence but in him alone. Then Earl Ulf and his fellows saw that they had but two roads to take, either to go to the King and leave all to his mercy, or to fly the country. All pressed Hardicanute to go to his father, which advice he followed. When they met he fell at his father's feet, and laid his seal, which accompanied the kingly title, on his knee. King Canute took Hardicanute by the hand and placed him in as high a seat as he used to sit in before. Earl Ulf[1] sent his son Swend, who was a sister's son of King Canute, and the same age as Hardicanute, to the King. He prayed for grace and reconciliation for the Earl his father, and offered himself as hostage for the Earl. King Canute ordered him to tell the Earl to assemble his men and ships and come to him, and then they would talk of reconciliation. The Earl did so."[2]

Canute's happiness was not unfrequently clouded. Besides the annoyance caused him by the rebellion in the name of Hardicanute, directed by Earl Ulf, he was obliged to make war on his wife's brother, Duke Richard, in consequence of his having repudiated Estritha his duchess, on a very trifling pretence.[3] To avenge the affront, Canute sailed at the head of a large

---

[1] Wolf or Ulf was brother-in-law to Canute, and Earl Godwin was married to Gyda, sister of Ulf. He was afterwards assassinated by Canute's orders, after the battle of Helge, 1025–7.

[2] Snorro's Kings of Norway.

[3] Duke Richard, the second, or, as Holinshed calls him, third of that name, brother of Queen Emma, married first Judith, sister of the Earl of Bretagne, by whom he had three sons, Richard, Robert, and William, and three daughters, of whom one died young; Alix, another, married Reignold, Earl of Burgoyne; a third, *Eleanor, to the Earl of Flanders.* After a ten years' union Judith died, and Duke Richard married Estrida, sister of Canute. He purchased a divorce from her, and then married a lady called Pavia, by whom he had two sons, William, Earl of Arques, and Mauger, Archbishop of Rouen. Duke Richard died in 1022, fifteen years before Canute, and was succeeded by Richard III., who reigned only

fleet to Normandy, and landed at Rouen; but scarcely had he arrived, when he learnt the sad tidings of the death of his favourite son Sweyn,[1] governor of Norway. Some accounts relate that Canute was so deeply affected by this event, that it brought on an ague of which he died at Rouen.[2]

The Saxon Chronicle differs in the statement of Canute's death, and declares that event to have taken place at Shaftesbury, in England, on the second day before the Ides of November, 1035, and that he was interred at Winchester, the epitaph on his tomb being—

"HERE LIES CANUTE, CELEBRATED FOR HIS PIETY."

He was only forty years of age at the time of his death, and he had been eighteen years united to Queen Emma.

At the time of Canute's death, not one of the Queen's sons was in England; Hardicanute, on whom, by virtue of her marriage contract, and his father's dying wishes, the crown should have devolved, was in Denmark, where he had been crowned the preceding year, and made no haste to assert his claims in England. Harold Harefoot, the only surviving son of Canute's first marriage,[3] knowing how superior England was to the crown of Denmark, allotted to him by his father's will, hurried over to endeavour to secure it for himself. The Queen also, if she had not, as some say, returned with Canute prior to that monarch's death into England, lost no time in doing so; but before anything could be done in the behalf either of herself or her son, Harold had contrived to secure the kingdom for himself. The reason of this was that the cities north of the Thames durst not oppose the Danes, who ruled over them, and were forced to acknowledge him; but Wessex declared boldly for Hardicanute. This part of England was very populous, being a place of refuge for all those whom the Danish cruelty and oppression expelled from the more northern districts; it was chiefly inhabited by Saxons, who maintained their freedom,

---

one year, and then Robert became Duke A. D. 1023. After a vigorous reign of seven years, Robert departed on a pilgrimage to the Holy Land, leaving the dukedom to his son William, afterwards the Conqueror, then seven years of age (A. D. 1030). Richard having been so long dead, the expedition made in 1035 must have been grounded on some other cause. Edward and Alfred were at the Norman court, and Robert before his departure had, by an embassy, requested Canute to give his cousins a share of England; but that being refused, Richard had prepared a fleet, intending to assert their claims by force of arms. That was, however, prevented by the ships being destroyed in a storm. Afterwards Canute promised Wessex to the sons of Emma; but the pilgrimage of Robert, and his own subsequent death, put off the execution of this promise, had it ever been intended to perform it.—Rapin and Holinshed, Roger of Wendover.

[1] Rapin says that Sweyn, brother of Harefoot, survived Hardicanute.

[2] Saxo-Grammaticus, Grafton, and Polydore.

[3] Harold is said to have been surnamed "Harefoot," from having one foot covered with hair. Hume says, "from his agility in running and walking;" he was fond of hunting, and being averse to riding on horseback, pursued the amusement on foot.—Lingard.

"Harold would choose the time of prayer, when the people were going to church, to go out with his dogs."—Thierry.

and were attached to the persons of their royal family.[1] Emma herself was a great favourite with the West Saxons, who determined to uphold the rights of her children.

Winchester was the capital of Wessex, and royal residence, and thither Emma repaired; the palace contained not only her own private property, but the royal treasures which Canute had entrusted to her keeping for his son Hardicanute.[2] But a powerful combination was speedily formed against the widowed Queen, who, at this moment, though the mother of three sons and of two daughters, seems to have been left to support her sorrow alone. While Emma fixed herself at Winchester, a witenagemote was hastily assembled at Oxford,[3] which was to bring much more grief to her than she had yet experienced. Leofric, Consul of Chester; Godwin, Earl of Kent; and others were present,[4] the object being to discuss the claims of the rival princes, Harold and Hardicunate. The nobles of Wessex supported Hardicanute, in spite of his absence,[5] and were seconded by Earl Godwin, who objected to Harold on account of the rumoured illegitimacy of his birth; but this appears to have been considered no objection in the eyes of his own countrymen, the Danes. Leofric, "the trusty friend of Canute," overruled his remonstrance, and the Londoners and other lords north of the Thames, favouring Harold's claim, appointed him ruler of the kingdom, "not only for himself, but for Hardicanute who was then in Denmark." [6] The treachery of Godwin mainly brought about this conclusion, he having on Harold's arrival secretly placed in his hands the will of the late King, which had been entrusted to his care, and covenanted to establish him on the throne, provided only that he would espouse his daughter Editha. This understanding not being generally known, Godwin, in the council, craftily appeared to support the cause of Hardicanute. Ambition was the ruling feature of Godwin's character, and while thus through his connivance the council was called, which gave a crown to the future husband of his daughter, it was arranged by the same meeting that Emma and Godwin should jointly rule over the dependant territory of Wessex, until the arrival of Hardicanute;[7] the Queen was to maintain her royal state in Winchester, having with her "the household of the King her son," and Godwin was to be general of her forces. The royal treasures and furniture at Winchester were to belong to Emma and her son;[8] but scarcely had Harold been crowned at Oxford, an office performed with his own hands,[9] then he hastened in

[1] Rapin. [2] Simeon of Durham; Brompton.

[3] Oxford was often the seat of the English court; and Canute had held one great council there. The same city witnessed the murder of Sigeferth, husband of Algitha, who became the Queen of Edmund Ironside; on the present occasion, the accession of Harold was settled there, and it was not only the spot on which that King was crowned, but the one in which he ended his short career.

[4] Grafton, Saxon Chronicle. [5] Caradoc of Llancarvan.

[6] Ranulf Higden; Saxon Chronicle; Grafton.

[7] Lingard; Gaillard; Rapin. [8] Milner.

[9] Egelnoth, who had been seventeen years Archbishop, refused to crown Harold, saying that Canute had enjoined him to set the crown upon none but the issue of Emma. Then laying the crown on the altar, he denounced an imprecation against any bishop that should venture to perform the ceremony.

person to Winchester, whither indeed his emissaries had already preceded him, and seized on all the most precious articles at the royal palace, even "before Emma could take possession of them." In spite, however, of this violent treatment, Emma remained at Winchester, "as long as she was able to do so." Finding that Godwin engrossed all the power in Wessex in his own hands, and that her children were effectually shut out from the government, the Queen affected indifference from motives of policy, and devoted her whole time to the occupation of visiting the churches, as though her thoughts had been entirely bestowed on a future state and the salvation of her soul. In this, much also of sincerity was combined; for Emma was naturally pious, and deeply mourned the loss of a beloved and affectionate husband.

The affection of Emma for the sons of Ethelred did not appear as great as that she felt for the heir of Canute. Hardicanute came not, however, to her wishes, to assert his rights and reinstate her in her royal authority. Conceiving that the King and Godwin, deceived by her affected neutrality, had no fear of her interposing in affairs of state, Emma at length determined to recall her two sons by Ethelred to England, expressing the natural desire of a mother to behold the Princes who had been some time separated from her; but, in reality, her aim in sending for them was to awaken the love and affection of the Saxons for the race of their ancient kings, should Hardicanute fail to arrive; and Godwin's penetration having discovered this, he artfully applauded her scheme, and even aided her in the execution of it, but only with the view of delivering the Princes to Harold. The King informed, through Godwin, of Emma's wish, consented that her sons should be sent for. Edward, indeed, had early in Harold's reign come over with a considerable fleet, but not finding any countenance from his mother, who desired Hardicanute to succeed to the throne, and was, therefore, averse to his claim at that time, and probably unable to assist him without danger to both, had contented himself with burning a few villages, and then went back to Normandy.

Harold, aware that the Queen naturally aimed at placing her sons on the throne, had striven by many devices to get them into his power, and on Emma's determination to invite them to England, wrote them the following letter in their mother's name:—

"Emma, in name only Queen, to her sons Alfred and Edward, imparts motherly salutation. While we severally bewail the death of our lord the King, most dear sons, and while daily ye are deprived more and more of the kingdom your inheritance, I admire what counsel ye take, knowing that your intermitted delay is a daily strengthening to the reign of your usurper, who incessantly goes about from town to city, gaining the chief nobles to his party either by gifts, prayers, or threats. But they had much rather one of you should reign over them, than be held under the power of him who now overrules them. I entreat, therefore, that one of you come to me speedily and privately, to receive from me wholesome counsel, and to know how the business which I intend shall be accomplished. By this messenger present, send back what you determine. Farewell, as dear both as mine own heart." [1]

[1] Encomium Emmæ.

This letter, which, by what followed, might as well have been written by their mother, as it was what she wished, was delivered into the hands of the princes, together with presents really sent to them from Emma, and, as such, both were received with joy, and a glad message returned, appointing a time and place for the desired meeting.[1] That Godwin himself was the bearer of these tidings to Emma is not impossible, as some say he was employed as ambassador.[2] Fifty vessels of chosen men of Normandy and Flanders had accompanied the Saxon princes, one or both, who landed at Sandwich, and from thence proceeded to Canterbury. According to some authorities Emma, mistrusting Godwin, from some intelligence received by her sons on their arrival, permitted one only at a time to visit him, retaining the other with herself. Alfred, whether after having seen the Queen or not is uncertain, was about to pay a visit to Harold, when he was arrested by Earl Godwin. The Saxon Chronicle says, Godwin prevented Alfred going to his mother, "knowing it would be displeasing to King Harold." As Guildford was on the road to Winchester, it may be that Alfred had not yet seen Emma, and that he had but rested in his way to the court of Wessex, to partake of the sumptuous entertainment provided by the Earl. On this occasion it is said by some, that, in a private intercourse, Godwin offered the Prince the throne, with the hand of his daughter, which he refused.[3] The alternative was immediately had recourse to by the irritable noble, and the fate of Alfred was from that moment sealed. Guildford, the scene of the carousal of the Saxon and Norman lords on that eventful night, was a town belonging to Godwin. Alfred was under his protection, and he betrayed his trust. According to custom, the guests of the Earl drank deep, and, as the hour advanced, became overpowered with sleep. Then the work of death began, which the cowardly Harold had planned, and Godwin connived at as an ally. The attendants of Alfred were disarmed, and put to the sword; every tenth man only being spared. As for "the ill-fated Prince, who was every way worthy to be a king,"[4] the child of exile and misfortune, he found himself hurried away, first to the presence of Harold, in London, and afterwards to the Isle of Ely. The noble to whom the royal youth was consigned, aggravated his situation by every insult which could be offered. A sorry horse was provided, he was stripped of his royal attire, and his feet tied beneath the saddle, exposed to the mockery and derision of every ordinary beholder in the towns and villages through which he had to pass. Thus pitiable was the fate of the son of Emma, herself the Queen, and at the very moment ruling over some not inconsiderable portion of the land. A court was convened of persons suited to their office, at Ely, by whom Alfred was sentenced to lose his eyes; and the unfortunate youth, on whom this cruel decree was executed by force alone, expired after a few days of lingering torment, either from his suffering, or the hand of a secret assassin.[5]

Harold and Godwin stand charged to this day, in the face of posterity,

---

[1] Milton, Roger of Wendover. [2] Milner, Grafton, Scott.
[3] Gaillard, Grafton, Milner. [4] Roger of Wendover. [5] Lingard

with this inhuman murder.[1] Though the monk of St. Omer, who might be supposed well acquainted with the facts, represents the Earl as ignorant of Alfred's danger;[2] nevertheless, so convinced were his contemporaries in general of his guilt, that he was twice arraigned for the murder: four years after, in Hardicanute's reign, by the Archbishop of York, and after that by Robert, Archbishop of Canterbury, when Edward the Confessor was on the throne. On both those occasions he was acquitted; but Edward himself never really believed him innocent, though Godwin died in the very moment of defending himself from the renewed charge. There is too much reason to think self-interest blinded both Godwin and Harold to the enormity of the crime: one common in those times, where might was for ever struggling with right. The Queen herself has been charged with consenting and aiding in the crime, by sending the letter, which brought her sons to England; but this, of course, was the intention of the senders; and, that she was perfectly innocent is plain by the consternation she exhibited when the fatal tidings reached her, and her adopting the instant precaution of sending her remaining son, Edward, who is thought to have been with her at the time, to her Norman relatives; a step attended with no trifling difficulty, and which gave great mortification to the King and Earl by disappointing them of one of their intended victims. It was, perhaps, this act which brought fresh wrath from Godwin on Emma; for the Earl next accused her of treason, and Harold had formerly not only despoiled her of all the royal treasures,[3] but now seized on her private goods and treasures, left for her own use by Canute, and banished her from the kingdom.

Emma's friends, indeed, desired that she should quit England at this juncture, but where should she seek an asylum? It might have been expected that she would have taken shelter among her own relatives in Normandy, whither she had sent her son, Prince Edward;[4] but Duke William, being very young, was, while a minor, under the government of others,[5] and the Queen feared to awaken Harold's jealousy of her Norman connections. Emma preferred the asylum offered her by her cousin Baldwin, Earl of Flanders, who, finding the invitation he had sent to her was accepted, received her with all the respect due to misfortune, and treated her with the greatest courtesy and kindness.[6] He not only gave her the castle of Bruges for her residence, but assigned her a handsome provision for her support during her abode in Flanders. There the Queen remained for three years, attended by the few faithful adherents who had

---

[1] Turner.
[2] Lingard.
[3] Encomium Emmæ, Caradoc.
[4] Harding.
[5] Ibid.
[6] A. D. 1037. The Saxon Chronicle says, "This year was Harold chosen King of all, and Hardicanute forsaken, because he staid too long in Denmark; and then they drove out his mother Elfgiva, the Queen, *without any kind of mercy, against the stormy winter;* and she came then to Bruges beyond sea: and Baldwin, tne Earl there, well received her, and there kept her the while she had need." The Earl of Flanders was married to a princess of the ducal family of Normandy [Eleanor, Emma's niece: see p. 304 (note)]; but one of his daughters was wife of Tosti, son of Godwin, Emma's enemy, which makes his conduct only appear the more generous on this occasion towards Emma.

accompanied her in her exile. Emma informed the good Earl how hardly she had been treated by Harold, and how Alfred, her son, had been put to death, and Edward forced to fly from the kingdom.

> "Wherefore therle to Kyng Hardknowt then wrote
> All hir compleynt, and of his succour prayed
> And he should help with all his might, God wote,
> It were amended of that she was affrayed,
> He came anone in warre full well arrayed
> Into Flaundres, his mother for to please,
> Hir for to socour and sette hir hert in ease."[1]

A. D. 1039. After repeated messages from the Earl and Emma, and the lapse of two years from his father's death, Hardicanute, who was more "the Unready" than the sons of Ethelred, sailed for Flanders, and spent a year there with his mother, consulting as to their future plans.[2] Under the cover of this visit, the Danish King had assembled a fleet of sixty sail, and he was actually on the point of making a descent upon England, when the news of Harold Harefoot's death was forwarded to him,[3] on which he sailed for London, and was received with much triumph; his claim being at once acknowledged by the whole nation, 1040. He was shortly after crowned at London by Egelnoth, Archbishop of Canterbury, who had so resolutely refused to crown another than Canute's son. The favour which Hardicanute received is attributed to the regard entertained by the people, especially those of Wessex, for his mother, Queen Emma.

Emma, to her great joy, recalled by her son, after a three years' exile, returned to England. Hardicanute received her with much honour, and placed the administration of the affairs of government in her hands and those of Godwin,—a singular coincidence by which the second time Emma found herself on close terms of alliance with her old enemy. Godwin had been one of the first to do homage to Hardicanute, but the King, doubtless, feared his professions of regard even more than the open enmity he had before experienced. Having first sent for his half-brother, Edward, from Normandy, the Prince, under sanction of Hardicanute, raised against the Earl a charge of having murdered Prince Alfred, and loudly demanded justice. Living, Bishop of Worcester, was likewise accused of participation in the crime. Elfric, Archbishop of York, was the person who was employed with Godwin, by the King, to disinter Harold Harefoot's body, for the gratification of his revenge for the murder. In this painful task the Earl and prelate disagreed, and Elfric accused Godwin. Godwin denied the charge against him, making out, on oath, that the part he had in the putting out the eyes of Alfred, he was constrained to by order of Harold. He, in fact, legally acquitted himself "by his own oath, and the oaths of a jury of his peers, the principal noblemen of England." Whether innocent or not he was restored to favour, and shared with Emma in the administration of the kingdom. In all likelihood Hardicanute but carried out the wishes of his mother in this endeavour to bring Godwin to justice; if this was the case, and that

[1] Saxon Chron. [2] Lingard. [3] Hume, Roger of Wendover, &c.

a churchman was his accuser seems to render it likely, it may account for the vindictive feelings Godwin afterwards exhibited against Emma, upon the accession of Edward to the throne.[1]

The policy of Godwin had led him, in the hope of inducing the King to forgiveness, to offer him a very sumptuous present. His peace-offering, which was accepted, was a galley, finely rigged and manned. As for Living, he was deprived of his bishopric, which was given to his accuser, Elfric, but purchased his pardon by a round sum of money, when he was reinstated.

Godwin's ship had a stern of gold, and eighty soldiers uniformly and richly suited: on their heads they all wore gilt burgonets, and on their bodies a triple gilt habergeon: swords with gilt hilts girded to their waists; a battle-axe, according to the Danish fashion, on their left shoulder; a target with gilt bosses borne in their left hand, a dart in the right hand, and their arms bound about with two bracelets of gold. The gift of Godwin is quite in accord with the manners of the day, and seems an adroit imitation of the celebrated ship of the Viking Frithiof, the swift-sailing Ellida, thus beautifully described in the Saga of Bishop Tegner:[2]

"The bark Ellida next was Frithiof's own
Viking, 'tis said, from war returning home,
Sail'd by the strand, and on a wreck he spied
A man, who seemed to revel with the tide,
Of noble stature, and of face serene,
Joyful and glad, though changeful was his mien:
Like the sea basking in the solar sheen:
A cloak of blue and belt of gold he wore,
Bedecked with corals from a distant shore.
White, as the foam on billows, was his beard,
And, as the ocean, green his hair appeared.
Then, thither, Viking steered his floating shell,
And saved the Being from the billow's swell.

. . . . .

But he, while smiling, to his saviour said:
'My bark is staunch, the breezes will not fail;
This very night a hundred miles I sail.
Long shall thy kindness in my mem'ry dwell,
And soon some gift my gratitude shall tell.

. . . . .

Yes, when to-morrow thou shalt wander o'er
Thy lands, some gift shall wait thee on the shore.'
Next day, when Viking wandered by the sea,
Lo! as an eagle rushes at its prey,
A stately Dragon swept into the bay.
The rudder moved, untouched by human hand,
And none, save spirits, steered that bark to land.
But mid the reefs and shoals it held its way,
And scatheless flew amidst the driving spray.

. . . . .

The gift was kingly; for each oaken beam
Was grown together without joint or seam.

---

[1] Lingard. [2] Translated by Oscar Baker.

High in the stem the Dragon's head arose,
His gilded jaws a fiery gape disclose;
His breast was speckled o'er with blue and gold,
Whilst, in the stern, his tail in many a fold,
Bright as a mail of silver, upward flew,
Shining resplendent towards the heavens of blue:
When his jet pinions, edged with brilliant red,
High in the air, to catch the breeze were spread:
His speed outstripped the headlong raving wind,
And left the eagle in his flight behind.
When that brave bark was filled with steel-clad men,
It seemed a fortress floating on the main."

That Queen Emma was particularly attached to the city of Winchester,[1] is evident from her returning to dwell there after the death of Harold; even during her temporary absence also, she had continued to bestow her royal presents on the Cathedral.[2] The Queen's name is joined to that of her son Hardicanute, in his charters to her favourite monasteries,[3] and however authors may differ in their accounts of the character of that King himself, they unite in praising the kindness which he showed to his mother Queen Emma; in this he was at least much superior to his brother, the sainted and vaunted Edward.[4]

In another point, the character of Hardicanute also deserves admiration, that of fraternal affection. Edward, the son of Ethelred, was invited to his court, A. D. 1041, and not only came there without fear, but remained an honoured guest during this king's short reign.[5] Hardicanute also carried out the plan of his father, as regarded Gunilda, daughter of Emma, whom Canute contracted to the Emperor Henry. This lovely young Princess is designated as the King of England's "fairest sister," to distinguish her from her half-sister Goda, daughter of Ethelred, and sister of Prince Edward, who had been united first to Walter, Earl of Mantes, and afterwards to Eustace, Earl of Boulogne, of whom we shall have to speak hereafter. Gunilda was bestowed with much solemnity and magnificence on the Emperor. After some time, the young Empress was accused of infidelity to her husband, but was cleared by a judicial combat: a dwarf in her service named Mimicon, who had attended her from England, fought with the champion appointed by her accusers, who was named Rodingar, a man of gigantic frame: the dwarf obtaining the victory, the fair fame of his mistress was considered established. Gunilda, though vindicated by this happy event, could never be persuaded to live again with her husband. Forsaking the world, she assumed the holy veil of a nun, in which she ended her days,[6] five years only after the death of her father, King Canute. The Chronicle exclaims that she died "as the noble morning star sinks at early dawn."[7]

---

[1] Milner's History of Winchester.
[2] Howel.
[3] Roger of Wendover, Marianus, Higden.
[4] Personally, Hardicanute was mild, and of a generous nature. His table was spread at four different hours in the day for his guests. Perhaps to the conviviality of living acquired among the Danes, may be attributed his feeble health and constant attacks of illness.
[5] Roger of Wendover, Marianus, Higden.
[6] Ranulf, Higden.
[7] Norman Traditions, Malmesbury

Hardicanute's death was very sudden, in 1042, in the midst of the festivities of a wedding dinner, the nuptials celebrated being those of a noble Dane called Tovi and Gyda, the daughter of Osgod Clapa. Some say the King was poisoned; but it is more generally thought his death was the result of intemperance, for "he died as he stood at his drink." The scene of this event was the royal palace or mansion of the Saxon Kings, which formerly stood in that part of the parish of Lambeth,[1] now known by the name of Kennington, and which constituted part of the dower or estate of the Princess Goda, daughter of Ethelred and Emma.

The death of Hardicanute was a great blow to Emma: and the Saxon Chronicle states that his mother, who tenderly loved him, "for his soul gave to the New Minster the head of St. Valentine the Martyr." The English hailed the event as a signal of deliverance from the Danish yoke, and the festival called "Hog's Tide," or "Hock Wednesday," was for centuries after kept by them in commemoration of the circumstance.

At the time of Hardicanute's death, Prince Edward was in Normandy, The Queen, Godwin, and Living, Bishop of Worcester, in the emergency, united their interest in his favour, and on this occasion were upheld by Leofric, the powerful Earl of Chester:[2] by their combined exertions, Edward was recalled to assume the sovereignty, the English being persuaded easily to take this step, having never forgotten the fact that they had formerly sworn allegiance to him "while yet in his mother's womb."[3] Accordingly, Edward, after having given pledges that he would bring but few Normans with him,[4] came over to England, and ascended the throne, being consecrated on Easter Day, 1043, at Winchester, Queen Emma assisting at the ceremony.

Edward was thus restored to his rights, after having been excluded from them during a long succession of disappointments; for, twenty-five years before, Emma had, by her marriage contract with Canute, excluded the children of Ethelred, and since then Edward had dwelt at the court of his maternal relatives, a dependant and an exile.[5] The Queen had on

---

[1] MS. History of Lambeth Palace.

[2] Higden. [3] Brit. Sancta. [4] Higden.

[5] Edward testified much gratitude, on coming to the throne, to the Normans, who had befriended his adverse fortunes. He owed nothing, as he thought, to Godwin, his mother, or the Saxons; but surrounded his person with Norman favourites, while Emma still preserved a Saxon court at Winchester. Edward plainly showed his dislike to the Anglo-Saxon manners, and patronised foreign tastes. The Saxon nobles perceiving this, gave up their own fashions and imitated those of the French, together with their character and mode of writing, "speaking French in their halls, as though it were a more gentle tongue." The Normans, under Ethelred, Canute, and Edward, were in such favour, and enjoyed so much power at court, that their clerks, or clergy, obtained the best benefices in the land. Robert, "a jolly, ambitious priest," first got to be Bishop of London, and, at a later period, Archbishop of Canterbury, leaving for his successor, in that of London, a countryman named William. Ulfo, another Norman, was preferred to Lincoln, and others to different places, as the King, the benefactor of the church, pleased. These Norman clerks, on being promoted, mocked, abused, and despised the English; and the Saxon nobles were still more irritated to find them increasing so fast in royal favour, as to be called to the secret council of the King. The advancement of Robert, in particular, elated the French and irritated the Saxon nobles.—Ingulphus, Gale, Holinshed.

many occasions shown that her conduct towards him was guided by convenience rather than affection; but Edward, esteemed one of the most holy among those whose names have been recorded in the saintly calendar, was certainly not gifted with the Christian virtue of forgiveness of injuries, at least, as regarded his mother. Of his feelings towards Ethelred we know nothing, and, certainly, Edmund "Ironside," as an elder brother, had set a dangerous example; yet Edward the Confessor was still less filial in his behaviour towards his mother, Queen Emma. It was plain he could not forgive the past, and that although Emma, Godwin, and Living had united to place him on the throne when no other heir remained who had the power to dispute his claim, he remembered that in an earlier period when they might have upheld his right, it had been overlooked and permitted to sink into oblivion. He had no regard for any of them: from his mother he had been almost always separated, but to his murdered brother Alfred he was deeply attached, and, as he conceived both Emma and Godwin to have been implicated in his cruel death, an impression remained on his mind, never to be effaced.[1] It was not, however, at first that Edward testified the feelings which he harboured in his breast against his only remaining parent; for we find Emma's great spirit and enterprise had so far got the better of the king's naturally weak and indolent character, that she engrossed a large share of the administration. This awakened the jealousy of Godwin, her old enemy, though present ally, who was too ambitious to permit himself to be superseded. The Earl had stipulated as one of the conditions for Edward's being placed on the throne, that he should espouse his daughter Editha, which he hoped would be a new source of influence. Edward, on many pretences, delayed the performance of this engagement; and it is not impossible the Earl suspected Emma of intriguing against him in this matter, more especially as he knew the aversion Edward himself secretly entertained to a union with the daughter of one whom he suspected of his brother's murder.[2] Godwin determined to remove any such obstacle to his own ambition, and hoping to ruin Emma in the king's favour, accused her of several crimes. In this he was seconded by a person scarcely less powerful or ambitious than himself, Robert, Bishop of London,[3] the king's spiritual adviser, a prelate of Norman birth, and formerly monk of Jumièges, but whose fortunes had been advanced with those of his royal master. This priest, who warmly seconded Godwin in his charges against Emma, made the following accusations jointly with the Earl:—

---

[1] Biog. Brit., Higden.

[2] Whether Emma interfered in the matter of Edward's marriage is doubtful, for it took place in 1044, and in the year after that, the Queen-mother was present at the council when the first charter was granted for the monastery of St. Peter's, Westminster, 1045. Godwin and his sons, after the marriage of Editha, continued to contest for power with the Normans "in the very palace of which his daughter and their sister was lady and mistress;" and the insults they offered, "in turning their exotic modes into derision;" and blaming the King for his weakness in placing his confidence in them, were remembered and resented afterwards, when the favourable opportunity presented itself.

[3] Anglo-Saxon Chronicle.

First, that the Queen had consented to the death of her son Alfred: secondly, that she endeavored to prevent Edward's succession to the crown: thirdly, that she kept up an impure intercourse with Alwyn, Bishop of Winchester,[1] her relative, who had been her protector on her leaving Normandy, at the period of her union with Ethelred, having at that time been retained in the royal household, and created Earl of Southampton. On more than one occasion he had aided Ethelred against the Danes, and even opposed Canute the future sovereign. On the peace being made between Edmund Ironside and Canute, Alwyn ceased to oppose the Danes, and following his inclination for a life of retirement and devotion, assumed the monastic cowl of St. Benedict, in the monastery of St. Swithin, Winchester. In honour of his rank Bishop Ethelwold himself invested him with his holy garb, and soon after, Alwyn was appointed to the monastic office of sacristan. From the time of Emma's second marriage he became the firm friend of Canute, a friendship reciprocated by the monarch. As a monk, Alwyn could not receive presents for his own personal use; therefore, the only means of offering a compliment to him was, by a donation to the church of which he had the care. Many marks of favour were shown to Alwyn by Canute and Emma, who bestowed those rich gifts already described on Winchester Cathedral. In the nineteenth year of Alwyn's profession, A. D. 1032, the see of Winchester becoming vacant, he was promoted to it by Canute, at the Queen's especial request, which fact marks the unity of sentiment existing between the royal pair: this was retained by Alwyn through the reigns of Harold, Hardicanute, and Edward the Confessor.[2] It was the frequent visits of Emma to Alwyn which afforded one pretext of accusation against her. Robert, Archbishop of Canterbury, is said to have hated, with no common hatred, the Bishop of Winchester, and united with Godwin in machinations against him and the Queen. Edward, unfortunately, was but too easily imposed upon, and too many unfavourable circumstances had already transpired to warp his mind against his mother. Instigated by these bad advisers, Edward called a council at Gloucester. After this he proceeded to Winchester, accompanied by Godwin, Leofric and Siward, three nobles, who are said to have possessed so much individual power, that the King's safety consisted principally in their disunion, for, if united, they might easily have dethroned him. On arriving at the royal city where Emma dwelt, they seized her treasures, and swept away the cattle and corn from the lands which she possessed as her dower, "a sort of military execution," as the historian calls it;[3] while the unhappy Queen herself was committed to prison. The King's visit was so unexpected, and this treatment so unlooked for, that Emma was unable to secure the smallest part of her most private property; so that all her jewels, gold, silver, and other valuables were taken with the rest.[4] There was an order given that she should be supplied with every necessary, yet only a mean pension was left for her subsistence, and not the least respect shown towards her. It is said that in this season she was reduced to the greatest necessity and ex-

[1] Polydore Vergil, &c.

[2] Milner's History of Winchester.

[3] Lingard.

[4] Roger of Wendover.

posed even to the risk of dying of famine.[1] After this the Queen was obliged to retire to the neighbouring Abbey of Wherwell, until the crimes alleged against her were properly investigated. Edward's own charge against Emma was that "she had accumulated money by every method, regardless of the poor, to whom she would give nothing; therefore it was taken away, that it might aid the poor and replenish the King's exchequer." Malmesbury adds to this that Edward took his mother's estates from her "because she had for a long time mocked at the needy state of her son: nor did she ever assist him: transferring her hatred from the father to the child; for she loved Canute, both living and dead, *better than her first husband.*" Here was an allusion to the differences which had, at one time, existed between Emma and Ethelred, and it is easy to perceive with what jealous feelings Canute's children had been ever regarded by their disinherited elder brother.[2]

That Edward considered one of the three charges, made by her enemies, which respected himself, to be correct, is obvious[3] by his own conduct, and the excuses alleged for it: severe as it was in the case of a son to a parent, the sanction of his council made it appear not to be without cause. Accordingly, Emma was kept in close confinement in the Abbey of Wherwell, though some say both the Queen and Alwyn were placed in ward in Winchester. The Bishop was committed to the examination and correction of the clergy. Emma is said to have sorrowed more for the defamation of Alwyn, than her own state of degradation.

Soon after Emma's disgrace, "Stigand was deposed from his Bishopric, and all that he possessed was seized into the King's hands, *because he was nearest to his Mother's counsel, and she went just as he advised her, as people thought.*"[4] Stigand was a Prelate noted for covetousness; he had been Canute's Chaplain, and, as such was patronized and regarded with esteem by Emma, who seems to have delighted to reverence those whom Canute had loved. It was the Normans who prevented Edward's coffers from overflowing, and they not only detested Canute and all he had favoured, but disliked his widow for her half-Danish descent, and were glad of Godwin's accusation against Emma respecting Alfred's murder, though the Earl's chief object was evidently to throw off the odium of that crime from himself.

---

[1] Bethune.

[2] The reason why King Edward and the English so little respected "this great lady, whose many years had made her an actor of divers fortunes, was her never having affected King Ethelred nor the children she had by him, and for her marriage with Canute, the great enemy and subduer of the kingdom, whom she ever much more loved living, and commended dead."—Daniel's Coll. of the History of England, London, 1626.

[3] "Edward himself, in two of his charters, attributes the death of his brother to Harold and (which is more singular) to Hardicanute. Now, Hardicanute was in Denmark, and the accusation, if it mean anything, must allude to those who governed in the name of Hardicanute, and, in that hypothesis, may reach Emma or Godwin, or both. Yet, would Harold, who was then all powerful, have subscribed to these charters, if they had cast so foul a stain on the memory of his father?" — Lingard.

[4] Saxon Chronicle, anno 1043.

Far from being overcome by the sudden reverse in her fortune, and the serious accusations made by her enemies, Emma demanded justice, and wrote from her prison, at Wherwell, to different Archbishops and Prelates, asserting her innocence, and desiring to be put to the proof, professing herself willing to encounter any trial, even that of the fiery ordeal.[1] A Synod was accordingly convened by the Archbishop of Canterbury to examine into the charges against Queen Emma; on this occasion, the Bishops interceded in her behalf with the King, when Robert, the Archbishop, addressed them in the following terms, more forcible than delicate: "My brethren Bishops, how dare ye defend her, that is *a vile beast* and *not a woman;* who hath defamed her own son, the King; and called her leman, the Bishop, Christ her God. But, be it so, that the woman would purge the Priest, who shall then purge the woman, that is accused to consent to the death of her son, Alfred, and procured venom to the empoysoning of her son Edward?[2] But, how so it be, that she be guilty or guiltless, if she will go barefooted for herself over four ploughshares, and for the Bishop over five ploughshares, burning and fire-hot, then, if she escape harmless, he shall be assoiled of this challenge, and she also." This savage proposal was accordingly agreed to, and the day straightway appointed for Emma's purgation.

In those days, if a person was accused or suspected of crime, which could not be fully proved, he was put to his ordeal or trial, either by fire or water. The ordeal by fire was chiefly used for persons of rank. There were several kinds: the one which Emma underwent was, as follows:—Nine red-hot ploughshares were brought forth, and laid at unequal distances, and then the accused person having bare feet and eyes close blinded had to walk over them. If this was performed without touching the shares, the accused was instantly declared innocent; if not, GUILTY.

A woman might avoid being put to this proof, if she could find a champion to combat in her favour. Gunilda appointed her dwarf when accused. Few could fail to find a protector, when their honour was thus questioned; but Emma's was a rare case, and she herself seems to have felt so confident in her innocence, as to challenge being put to the most extreme proof in her own person.

Emma passed the night previous to her fiery trial in the Cathedral Church, where, at the tomb of St. Swithin, she remained in fervent prayer; she implored the aid of the Saint, and falling asleep was comforted by a dream, or vision, in which that Holy Prelate appeared to her, saying, "Be thou firm, daughter, I am Swithin, whom thou hast enriched; fear not, when thou passest through the fire, it shall not hurt thee, for thy son hath done evil in this." Emma arose refreshed and comforted, and all the preparations being completed, was led into the Church, and thus addressed the King:—"O Lord and Son, I, that Emma, who bore and brought thee forth, and Alfred my son, I invoke God to bear witness in my person this day, may I perish, if what has been charged against me,

---

[1] Polydore Vergil, Fabian, Grafton, Stowe, Milner, Boyle.

[2] This is a new charge, of having attempted the life of Edward himself, and Brompton also names it as such.

ever even entered my mind." The King, the Bishops, and an immense multitude of persons of all descriptions were assembled in the Cathedral to be spectators of the event. The pavement of the nave having been swept, nine ploughshares, red with heat, were placed in a line upon it; "and now Emma," say the Chroniclers, "having again invoked the Almighty to deal with her accordingly, as she is innocent, or guilty, of the crimes laid to her charge, prepares herself for the trial, by laying aside her robes, and baring her feet. She is then conducted by two Bishops, one having hold of each of her hands, to the glowing metal. In the meantime, the vaults of the Church thunder with the voices of the assembled multitude, who, in loud shouts, call upon the Almighty to save the royal sufferer, and their cries are echoed through the whole city, by the crowds who were unable to gain admittance into the Church. She, herself, raising up her eyes to Heaven, and slowly walking on, thus makes her prayer:—'O God, who didst save Susannah from the malice of the wicked elders, and the three children from the furnace of fire, save me for the sake of thy holy servant Swithin, from the fire prepared for me.' In a word, she is seen to tread upon each of the burning irons, and is not even sensible that she had touched them, but addressing herself to the Bishops, 'when shall I come to the ploughshares?' They turn round and show her that she has already passed them. The lamentations of the multitude then ceasing, the air resounds with acclamations of joy and thanksgiving, still louder than their former prayers had been. The King alone is found overwhelmed with grief and bathed in tears, lying upon the ground beside his chair, to whom Emma being conducted, he begs her forgiveness, in terms of the utmost humility and sorrow, for the injurious suspicions he had entertained concerning her, and the rigour with which he had treated her. Not content with this, he requires of her, and the Bishops then present, to strike him with a wand, which he presents to them. She accordingly gave her son three blows; when having embraced him, both she and Bishop Alwyn were put into full possession of their former rights and property, and ever after enjoyed the royal favor and respect, in the degree they merited."[1]

[1] Circumstantial as this strange narrative is, modern authors have endeavoured to refute the story altogether, stating that Emma's accuser, Robert, to blacken whose character it was invented, did not become Archbishop of Canterbury till 1050; others have pronounced it an invention of later times, resting on suspicious evidence, because the historians nearest the time do not name the circumstance. The "Encomium Emmæ," written by a monk of Emma's own times, would have been in this matter a valuable authority; but his record unluckily leaves off at the accession of Hardicanute. The Saxon Chronicle, regarding Emma as a private individual, neglects to name the fact, and the Latin historians are silent on a tale prejudicial to Edward. Brompton, Knyghton, Rudborne, and Harpsfield, relate the circumstance; and Robert of Gloucester, regarding it as a well-known fact, gives it a place with much minuteness in his Chronicle. Ranulf Higden, also a most accurate historian, related it at length in his Polychronicon, in the middle of the fourteenth century. In 1338, nearly the same date, it was sung amongst other popular songs relating to the history of Winchester, in the Prior's Hall there, at the translation of Orleton to that see. Everything considered, the annals of the church where the event occurred were most likely to contain the record, as in this instance was the case; and though Malmesbury does not mention the

The ploughshares over which Queen Emma had walked were, in memory of her extraordinary deliverance, buried in the west cloister of the Cathedral of Winchester.

The Queen and Alwyn, in gratitude for their acquittal of crime, each made a donation to the same church. Emma bestowed on it nine manors in her own behalf.

Alwyn likewise bestowed nine manors for himself.

King Edward made a donation to Winchester Cathedral at the same time, consisting of three manors.[1]

Emma, more fortunate even than her daughter Gunilda, thus triumphed completely over her enemies. But where was Robert the Archbishop, her accuser, when Emma returned thanks to God for her deliverance? The Archbishop "was absent," it is said, "from pity, or some other reason,"—most probably from shame for the defeat of his conspiracy against Emma, and mortification at the triumphant position she would obtain by her acquittal.[2]

Emma was, soon after this great event in her life, witness to the quarrels which ensued between the powerful personages who had been so violent in their enmity to her. Earl Godwin and Robert, the Norman archbishop, embroiled the country in their furious contentions; and the banishment of the first was followed by the expulsion of the second: on which Godwin, more than ever potent, returned to revenge his injuries, after a brief banishment.

During these occurrences, the Queen seems to have preferred a safe retirement, in the possession of her wealth, to again entering the lists with the view of obtaining a mastery for which so many ambitious spirits were contending.

The indignity of her trial seems to have weighed heavily on her mind, and she buried her grief in the retreat of the cloister of St. Mary of Winchester, where, in March, 1052, the year after her triumph,[3] she died. Her death is thus mentioned in the Saxon Chronicle: "This year, in the second day before the nones of March, died the aged lady, Elfgiva Emma, the mother of King Edward and King Hardicanute, the relict of King Etheldred and of King Canut; and her body lies at Winchester, in the Old Minster, with King Canut."

Emma was, most probably by her own request, buried beside her Danish husband; in this particular King Edward testifying a respect he had failed to show to his mother when living; thus the church that witnessed her trial, contained her remains. Her son Hardicanute also rested in Winchester Cathedral, by the side of his parents. The tomb of Emma

---

trial, he states that Emma was deprived of her lands by the King. The documents in Winchester Cathedral, moreover, prove that the Queen had given several manors to that Church, which certainly she could not have done if they were not in her possession.—Milner.

[1] Dugdale.

[2] Bale says, "I do not find what became of the accusers of Queen Emma."—Historical Dictionary.

[3] Lingard.

bore an inscription in rude Latin lines, setting forth that the Queen who reposed there was wife to two, and mother to two English monarchs.[1]

Emma was great-aunt to William the Conqueror, that King being second cousin to her two sons, Edward the Confessor and Hardicanute; and, as such, entitled far more justly to the English crown than Harold, the son of Godwin, who built his claim on his own power, and being brother of the Confessor's childless queen, the fair and harshly-treated Edith![2]

---

[1] Echard.

[2] At the disastrous siege of Winchester, during the reign of Stephen, the tomb of Queen Emma was destroyed, together with the "Abbey of St. Mary, twenty churches, the royal palace, lately erected in that quarter, the monastery of St. Grimbald, the suburbs of Hyde, and, in fact, nearly all the northern part of the city. The remains of the Queen were, however, preserved, and still rest within the walls of the Abbey, to which she was so great a benefactress. The screen which divides the sanctuary from the side aisles, Bishop Fox erected in 1525, and "on the top of the partition walls, and under the centre of each arch above are six mortuary chests, of carved wood, painted and gilt, and surmounted with crowns. These chests contain the remains of Saxon kings, prelates, and other distinguished personages interred in the cathedral, and are the work of Bishop Fox, who collected the bones from ancient lead coffins, which are supposed to have stood formerly in a similar situation.

The first chest from the altar-screen contains the bones of King Edred, and the second those of Edmund, son of Alfred; the third contains the mingled bones of King Canute, of Queen Emma, of King William Rufus, and of Bishops Wina and Alwyn. This chest has two inscriptions in Latin to this effect. On one side is the following:—

"In this, and in the other chest opposite, are the remaining bones of Canute and Rufus, Kings; of Emma, Queen; and of Wina and Alwin, Bishops."

And on the other side of this chest is the inscription:—

"In this chest, in the year of our Lord, 1661, were promiscuously laid together the bones of princes and prelates, which had been scattered about, with sacrilegious barbarity, in the year of our Lord, 1642."

So that nineteen years from the second spoliation of Emma's resting-place had passed away before the last mortal relics of the former fair "Pearl of Normandy" were restored to a consecrated and fitting position. The parliamentary soldiers, by whom the outrage had been committed of ravaging the cathedral in 1642, committed terrible depredations. "They broke in pieces the carved work of the choir, containing the story of the Old and New Testament, which was admirably executed. They totally destroyed the ancient organ; seized the rich tapestry, cushions, and vestments, in the choir, with the vessels of the altar; threw down the communion-table, and carrying off the rails which encompassed it, they burnt them in their quarters. They found a great number of Popish books, pictures, and crucifixes, in the prebendal houses, which, after a mock procession, were burnt, together with the organ-pipes, in the street. They defaced many of the monuments by tearing off their ancient brass inscriptions and other ornaments. They pulled down the mortuary chests containing the remains of Saxon kings, prelates, and other distinguished personages, and threw the bones at the stained glass, which they destroyed throughout the church, with the exception of that at the eastern window which had previously been taken out."

The first and second chests on the south side contain, as before-noticed, the bones of Kings Edred and Edmund. The former, who was the youngest son of Edward the Elder, was interred in the cathedral by direction of his friend St Dunstan, and the chest has an inscription in Latin, thus rendered:—

The struggles and vicissitudes of Queen Emma were many; and her character is one, which cannot be contemplated without exciting reflec-

---

"King Edred died 955. In this tomb rests pious King Edred, who nobly governed this country of the Britons."

Edmund, eldest son of Alfred the Great, who was crowned and died during his father's life, was buried in the second chest. The Latin inscription runs thus in English: —

"King Edmund died A. D. . . . . Edmund, whom this chest contains, and who swayed the regal sceptre while his father was living, do thou, O Christ, receive."

The third chest, on the south side, appropriated to Queen Emma, has been described already more particularly; and the first chest from the pulpit, on the north side, with its inscriptions, bones, &c., is similar to it. The second chest on the north side contains the remains of Kenewalch, who, with his father Kinegils, rebuilt the cathedral; and those of Egbert, founder of our English monarchy. One side has a Latin inscription, translated thus: "King Kenulph died A. D. 714." And the other side has this inscription: "King Egbert died A. D. 837. Here King Egbert rests, with King Kenulph. Each of them bestowed upon us munificent gifts."

The third chest, containing the remains of Kinegils, father of Kenewalch, the first Christian King of Wessex, and of St. Ethelwolf, father of Alfred the Great is thus inscribed: — "King Kinegils died A.D. 641;" and on the other side, "King Adulphus died 857." In this chest lie together the bones of Kinegils and Adulphus. The first was the founder, the latter the benefactor, of this church."

The contents of these mortuary chests were examined a few years ago by Henry Howard, Esq., of Corby Castle, and other talented and learned gentlemen, from whose account the following was written by the late Dr. Milner, to whom the particulars of that investigation were forwarded; —

"The first chest from the altar-screen, on the south side, inscribed Edred, contains many thigh bones and two skulls. The second chest, inscribed Edmund, contains five skulls, and three or four thigh-bones. One of the skulls, appears to have belonged to a very old man; another, also, belonged to a very old person. These, therefore, might have belonged to Wina and Alwin. The third chest on the south side, and the first chest from the pulpit, on the north side, bear the names of Canute, Rufus, Emma, Wina, Alwin, and Stigand. Neither of these contains any skulls; but they are full of thigh and leg bones; one set of which, in the third chest, is much smaller and weaker than the rest. This, with the supernumerary skull in the chest inscribed Egbert and Kenulph, might possibly have belonged to Queen Emma. The chest just referred to is the second from the pulpit, and contains three skulls, one of which is very small. One thigh-bone, wanting a fellow, is very stout, and measures nearly twenty inches long. But the two leg-bones, one of which is rather deformed, and the two hip-bones belonging to this body, are in the chest, and answer exactly. There are also two other thigh-bones and two leg-bones that pair; so that, with the exception of the third skull, these may be the bones of the aforesaid kings. The third chest from the pulpit, inscribed Kinegils and Adulphus, contains two skulls and two sets of thigh and leg-bones. From a measurement of the skulls and thighs, it appeared that they were about the ordinary size. It should be observed that the skulls actually at present in the chests are twelve in number, which is also the number of the names inscribed on the same chests.

"On the fine screen at the back of the capitular chapel in Winchester Cathedral, and opposite to the Chapel of the Virgin, is seen a range of canopied niches, in which formerly stood statues of the most eminent Saxon kings, from Kinegils to St. Edward, together with Canute, Hardicanute, Queen Emma, and, with them, Christ and the Virgin Mary."

Thus, huddled together, were the bones of friends and enemies, as if to show

tion. By turns triumphant and persecuted, she offers a remarkable instance of perseverance, courage, and ambition. Of human failing she had her share: her virtues were obscured by her too great desire of power, and she sacrificed much to obtain the end to which all her aspirations were directed. The most pleasing feature in her disposition is, her attachment to her husband Canute; with whose interests she identified herself, and for whose son she exerted all the energies of her powerful and active mind. She was less just to her children by her first marriage, but the circumstances of the time are a strong excuse for her conduct to them, as, of course, the suspicion of her causing the death of one must be at once dismissed.

That Emma was amongst the most remarkable personages of her period will be allowed by all, and her influence on the country over which she reigned, renders her biography one of the most interesting of any of the British Queens. The name of Queen Emma has been kept alive by tradition, and has more than once "adorned a tale."

As late as the year 1338, when Adam de Orleton, Bishop of Winchester, visited his cathedral priory of St. Swithin, in that city, a minstrel, named Herbert, was introduced, who sung the song of Colbrond, a Danish giant, and the tale of "Queen Emma delivered from the Ploughshares," in the hall of the Prior, Alexander de Herriard.[1]

---

how useless and how full of folly are human contentions, which all have the same close, and, after a few years, are a mere matter of transient wonder and curiosity.

[1] Warton's History of English Poetry, vol. i., p. 81.

EDITHA "THE GOOD."

"Rose among thorns"—Earl Godwin's romantic and eventful story—The Jarl Ulf in the forest—The peasant-boy—King Canute's new soldier—His advancement—Marries Githa; made Earl—Thora and the slave trade—Bristol the mart—Godwin's connexion with royalty—Editha's beauty and meekness—The compact of Earl Godwin—Delays of King Edward—His dislike to the match with Editha—Their marriage—Edward's coldness—Dress and manners of the time—Splendour of priests—Wulstan's reproof—Long hair—Editha's humility—Her coronation—King Edward's vows—Unkindness to his Queen—The Queen's spiritual friends—Westminster Abbey founded—Editha's pious donations—Leofrina's will—Curious stone picture on the screen at Westminster Abbey—Quarrel of Tostig and Harold, when boys, represented—Installation of Leofric, Bishop of Exeter—Famine—Edward remits the tax of Danegelt—Rupture with Earl Godwin—Flight of Godwin and his family to Flanders—His banishment—Triumph of the Normans—Imprisonment of Queen Editha—Bishop Robert's accusation—A year of seclusion at Wherwell—Weakness of Edward—Godwin's triumphal return—Restoration of his party—The Queen returns to Court—Her triumph—Earl Godwin's sudden death—Edward sends for the son of Edmund Ironside—His arrival and death—Editha accused of cruelty—Royal chaplains—Dedication of Waltham Abbey—Bore-stall—Havering Bower—The pilgrim and the ring—Dedication of St. Peter's, Westminster—The King's death—Harold succeeds—Battle of Hastings—William the Conqueror—Editha's epitaph.

AMIDST the scenes of strife and bloodshed which marked the eleventh century, the amiable and gentle-minded Queen Editha appears indeed, as one of our historians has observed, like "a rose among thorns." The placid and meek sport of party—her pious soul centred itself on that better world where strife entereth not, and discordant passions cannot dwell. Happy was it for this fair English flower, that, for the sake of others, she could dwell resigned in the midst of false splendour, and close the portals of her heart against those affections, which, in too many cases, make us lose the thoughts of hereafter, in the brief and passing joys of an earthly lot.

Editha was the daughter of that celebrated "King-maker," Earl Godwin, who played so distinguished a part in the violent contentions of the Danes and English which desolated the land for so many years. Her father's history is one of those which fill the pages of the past with romantic incident. From a humble position, he rose, first by accident, and afterwards by his genius and valour, to an equality with monarchs, to whom he became allied, and his enormous power swayed the destinies of nations, while kings were playthings in his hands.

After one of the five famous battles fought against the Danes by Edmund Ironside, in which that warlike prince had rescued London, and retrieved the wavering fortunes of his country,[1] a Danish jarl, named Ulf, who had escaped from the scene of contest to a distance from his followers, lost his way in a wood, where, after wandering about through the whole night, he encountered at break of day, a young peasant with a drove of oxen :—"Ulf, having saluted him," says the chronicler, "inquired his name. 'I am called Godwin, son of Ulfnoth,' answered the shepherd, 'and thou, if I mistake not, art of the Danish army?' Thus forced to confess who he was, the Dane entreated the young man to inform him of his distance from the vessels which were stationed in the Severn, or neighbouring rivers, and the road he ought to pursue to gain them. 'Foolish indeed,' replied Godwin, 'is the Dane who expects his safety from a Saxon.' Ulf besought the shepherd, nevertheless, to leave his cattle and guide him, making him those promises of reward which would be likely to influence a poor and simple-minded man. 'The way is not long,' returned the Saxon, 'but it would be dangerous for me to lead thee into it. The peasants, encouraged by our victory of yesterday, are armed throughout the country, and would show no favour, neither to thee, nor to thy guide.'

"On this, the chief took a gold ring from his finger, and offered it to the peasant, who took it, and after contemplating it for a few moments, gave it back to him, saying, 'I will take nothing from thee, but I will try to conduct thee.'

"They passed the day in the cottage of Ulfnoth, Godwin's father; at night, when they were departing, the old man said to the Dane, 'Know, that it is my only son who trusts himself to thy honour: there will be no safety for him amongst his countrymen when he has served thee as a guide; present him, therefore, to thy King, that he may receive him into his service.'

"Ulf promised this and much more for Godwin, and he kept his word. When they arrived at the Danish camp, he made the peasant's son sit in his tent, on a seat as elevated as his own, and treated him in every respect as his son. He obtained a military command for him from King Canute, and in process of time, this identical Saxon shepherd rose to the rank of governor of a province in England, which was occupied by the Danes, and was afterwards destined twice to destroy the foreign power by which he had risen.

"Godwin, from the first, by his promptitude and boldness, rendered service to Canute, and one of his early services was rewarded by the rank of Earl. This was on the occasion of Canute, then in Denmark, undertaking a campaign against the Vends. A battle was fixed for a certain day, with these barbarians, but Godwin, seeing that it was dangerous to lose time, ventured without the King's knowledge, to attack the enemy the night before, whom he entirely routed and put to flight, thereby rendering an essential benefit to the cause of his commander, whose gratitude knew no bounds.

"On Canute's return to England the following spring, the counties of

[1] Knytlinga Saga.

Kent, Sussex, and Surrey were given to the new Earl; and his services were, shortly after, further rewarded by the hand of Gyda, sister of Earl Ulphon,[1] who afterwards became mother of a numerous and promising family, and of these, one daughter, bearing the maternal name of Gyda or Editha, was destined to become the Queen-Consort of Edward the Confessor."

Godwin had previously been married to a Danish princess, named Thora, by whom he had an only son afterwards drowned in the river Thames, into which he was thrown by an unruly horse. Thora is said to have been nearly related to Canute; she was not, however, the mother of Editha, nor is it desirable to know more of her, as she is described as "a woman of much infamy, for the trade she drove of buying up English youths and maids to sell in Denmark, whereof she made great gain, but ere long was struck with thunder and died."[2]

The laws of Ethelred prove the horrible state of barbarity and cruelty existing in the country at this period; and the sermon extant of Lupus, (Bishop Wulfstan) written against the atrocities committed, is another evidence of the fearful consequence of the unsettled state of society. A traffic in slaves was carried on to an enormous extent. Bristol being one of the great marts, gaining at that early time a remarkable celebrity which the city kept to a late period, deserving the reproach of "her stones being cemented with blood." Greater cruelties were practised in England than amongst negro tribes, "brother sold brother, the father his son, the son his mother."[3]

Both Godwin's wives are spoken of as related to Sweyn, King of Denmark. According to Snorro, Ulf and his sister Gyda, were children of Thorkel Sprakalegg; Ulf had been placed over Denmark by Canute during his absence in England, he being the husband of Estrida, Canute's sister, the repudiated Duchess of Normandy, who at the time of Queen Emma's espousals had been united to her brother. The hand of Ulf's sister, Gyda, was, therefore, likely to be the coveted prize of many a Saxon and Danish chief. By this alliance, Godwin beheld himself a second time closely united to both the English and Danish royal families, and with the children of Ethelred and Canute: and Sweyn Ulfson, afterwards King of Denmark, nephew of his wife Gyda, connected him still further with that country.

Queen Editha is universally represented as possessing great beauty and accomplishments. The ambitious views, as well as affection of her parents, had induced them to bestow on her an education surpassing that of her sex in general.[4] She had been brought up in the Monastery of Wilton, distinguished for its learning, and afterwards noted as the spot selected for the education of "Good Queen Maude," wife of King Henry the First. While still at Wilton, Editha became remarkable for her acquirements, having a knowledge of books rarely attained in any age. As an instance of her taste for literature, Ingulphus relates that when he was a boy, his father being at King Edward's court, he had many interviews

[1] Snorro. [2] Milton. [3] Lappenberg.

[4] Burke's English History, Holinshed and others.

with the Queen, who would often stop him as he came from school, make him repeat his lesson, ask him questions in grammar and logic, and as a reward give him "a few pieces of silver, and send him to the larder."[1] Brompton tells us that "her breast was a storehouse of all liberal science," in which she differed greatly from the other members of her family, for neither Godwin nor his sons had any pretensions to literature. All our writers concur in praising her mental acquirements. Malmesbury calls her "a woman whose bosom was the school of every liberal art, though little skilled in earthly matters: on seeing her, if you were amazed at her erudition, you must absolutely languish for the purity of her mind and the beauty of her person."

Editha had been instructed in the popular art of needlework, in which she became quite a proficient. With her own hands the Queen is said to have wrought the magnificent robes[2] in which King Edward was accustomed to array himself on his collar-days or other great occasions; these were embroidered with gold in the most sumptuous manner. This King is described as being tall and well made in person, and possessing a white skin, fair hair, and a rosy complexion. Edward, in spite of his sanctity, delighted in the pomp of dress, in which he was not superior to the young men of his day. The age was one of singular taste for finery, even the clergy studying dress as much as the laity, and seeking to adorn their robes with richer furs than those worn by their neighbours. For this these prelates were reproved by Bishop Wulstan in these words: "Believe me, I never heard chanted *Cattus Dei*, but Agnus Dei."[3] Wulstan also boldly inveighed against the effeminate practice, then fashionable, of wearing long hair. When any one came to him to receive a blessing, and bowed down his head for that purpose, Wulstan, before he gave it, cut off a lock of his hair with a little sharp knife that he carried about him, and commanded him, by way of penance, to cut the remainder in a similar manner, denouncing heavy judgments against those who neglected to attend to his injunction.[4] The Saxon method of cutting and arranging the hair in the fourth century had the effect of enlarging the appearance of the face and diminishing the head. At a later period it was worn

[1] Lingard.

[2] The Domesday Book records that Leivede, a Wiltshire maiden, wrought in the time of King Edward *aurifrisium* for the King and Queen. This was a species of gold work, so much valued, that this same person held half a hide of land in Bucks, the grant of Godrei, the sheriff, that she might teach his daughter to make *orfrays*, for many centuries it was in fashion. The exquisite work of Editha has been noticed, and the garments of the Saxon hostages were a subject of surprise to the Normans, as the Conqueror's chaplain tells us: some of these specimens of needlework were left by Queen Matilda in her will to the Abbey of the Holy Trinity of Caen.

[3] Green's Worcester, p. 7.

[4] Pictures of Edward the Confessor and his Queen Editha, may be seen in Ducarel's Anglo-Norman Antiquities, in Strutt's Regal and Ecclesiastical Antiquities, and also in Caxton's Golden Legend. Harold's picture may also be seen in both these works. Edward the Confessor, as appears by his seal in Speed, wore very short cropped hair, but whiskers and beard exceedingly long.—Peck's Desiderata Curiosa.

diffused upon the shoulders, and the man who seized another by the hair was punishable by law. In France great value was attached to the ornament of hair; it was even necessary to any prince to enable him to ascend the throne, in which the Franks and Saxons differed from the ancient Britons, whose princes cropped their hair like the monks. Great pains were lavished on the cultivation of the hair by the French, so that if any one could boast of a peculiarity in this respect, he obtained a suitable surname, as among the Danes Sweyn was called Forked-beard, and a whole nation was called Longobardi or Lombards.[1]

The kings and nobles, when in their state dress, were habited in a loose coat, which reached down to their ankles, and over that a long robe, fastened on both shoulders, and on the middle of the breast, with a clasp or buckle. The edges and bottoms of their coats, as well as of their robes, were often trimmed with a broad gold edging, or else flowered with different colours.

The soldiers and common people wore close cloaks reaching only to the knee, and a short cloak over the left shoulder, which buckled on the right; this cloak was often trimmed with an edging of gold. The kings and nobles, also, in common were habited in a dress very similar to this, only richer and more elegant.[2]

Editha, notwithstanding her great elevation, is said to have been "very humble, and at variance with no one." This "very beautiful, virtuous, and chaste princess was wholly exempt from the savage pride which distinguished her whole family,[3] and in a court filled with strife and contention behaved with mildness and benevolence to all around her; so that, however hostile the ancient writers have shown themselves to Godwin and his sons, they have done justice to Editha."

She deserved a better fate than to be united to a man who did not appreciate her virtues and who never could dissociate her from her father, whom he hated, suspecting or affecting to suspect him, to the last, of the murder of his brother, Prince Alfred. Edward was almost forced into his union with Editha, and was perfectly aware of Godwin's ambitious motives in raising his daughter to the throne of England. It was only on the condition of his promise of marriage with her, that the powerful Earl restored him.

Edward resembled his father in disposition, having a weak constitution by nature, and a narrow genius, so that it was not difficult for those who had their own private ends to promote, to obtain an ascendency over his mind. As for Godwin, he had so much power at court, that as much deference was paid to him as to the King himself, although no real friendship existed between the Earl and his royal master. On one point the King was quite resolved, and that was to put off his marriage with Editha as long as possible, probably with a hope of evading it altogether. Pretext after pretext was devised as an excuse for this delay; but at length, at the expiration of two years, he was obliged to redeem the pledge he had given.

[1] Turner's Anglo-Saxons. [2] Strutt. [3] Lingard.

The nuptials were solemnized "ten days before Candlemas,"[1] A.D. 1044, Edward being then in the forty-fourth year of his age, much older than his bride. Although the fact is not exactly stated, it may be presumed that all the proud Godwin family were present at these triumphant espousals, including Githa and the many brothers of Editha, who are said afterwards to have obtained favour in the eyes of the King their brother-in-law, or, at least, to have appeared to do so.

The coronation of Editha soon followed, another triumph to the ambitious aspirations of Earl Godwin, whose aim was thus completely attained. A curious commentary on the deceptive glory of human successes is afforded in an account of the crown worn by Queen Editha on this and other state occasions: it is described in an inventory of that part of the regalia now removed from Westminster to the Tower Jewel House:—

"Queen Editha's crowne, formerly thought to be of massy gould, but upon triall found to be of silver gilt, enriched with garnetts, foule pearle, saphires, and some odd stones, p. oz. 50½, valued at £16."

If this account be true, it would almost seem as if Edward had intended thus early to affront the pride of the Godwin family, but it is more likely that there was another crown used on the occasion, and that this was not the only one possessed by the Queen; or it might be, that the jewels had been changed. It is interesting to trace back to this epoch those different portions of the modern regalia which are used at the coronation of our English sovereigns:[2] the Sword, the Sceptre, the Orb, the Ring, &c., are all derived from Anglo-Saxon customs, at the ceremony of coronation. The investiture by the ring was one of the most ancient ways of conferring dignity, and the ancient Coronation Ring is called also "The Wedding Ring of England." The queen consort had also a ring provided for her coronation, which is of gold, with a large table ruby set therein, and sixteen other small rubies set round about the ring, of which those next to the setting are the largest, the rest diminishing in proportion. That the sword was carried at Arthur's Coronation has been already mentioned, and not one only, but four several swords, each borne by a separate person. There are still four swords used in the coronation of a British sovereign: 1st. The Sword of State; 2d. The Curtana, or pointless Sword of Mercy; 3d. The Sword of Spiritual Justice; 4th. The Sword of Justice of the Temporality.

At Queen Guenever's Coronation, four queens bore each in their hand a white pigeon, having, probably, an allusion to the feast of Pentecost. Whether the dove which surmounts the sceptre of the monarchs of Britain has the same allusion it is difficult to say. The first House of French Kings always bore for a staff a golden rod, being crooked at one end, to resemble the crosier or pastoral staff, and was the same height as the King who bore it. The Queen-Consort of England has a Virga or Ivory Rod, garnished with gold, rather more than a yard long, surmounted by a dove enamelled white.

St. Edward's Staff, so named from the husband of Editha, is still carried before the English sovereigns in the coronation procession. It is a

[1] Saxon Chronicle.

[2] Lingard.

golden sceptre or staff, four feet eleven inches long, having a foot of steel, about four inches in length, with a mound and a cross at the top. It is about three quarters of an inch in diameter, and the ornaments are of gold.

From Edward the Confessor's time also, every English sovereign has been represented on coins or seals as bearing a globe in the left hand. The orb or globe was assumed by Augustus, the Roman Emperor, and friend of Cymbeline, and implied universal dominion. Constantine, the first Christian Emperor, added a cross to the globe. The statue of Justinian is thus described: "In his left hand he held a globe, in which a cross was fixed, which showed that by faith in the cross, he was emperor of the earth. For the globe denotes the earth, which is of like form; and the cross denotes faith, because God in the flesh was nailed to it."

It might have been expected that Edward's union with a princess possessed of so many attractions, and such sweetness of disposition as Editha, would have softened his feelings towards the Godwin family, and by degrees overcome his resentment: on the contrary, it proved but the cause of fresh strife with the Earl, and the hatred of the King towards him seemed transferred but the more bitterly to his daughter, because it could only be shown in that way. Editha could never acquire either the affections or confidence of her husband, and, his tardy nuptials solemnized, the King, far from evincing any love for Editha, did not treat her as his wife; so that, although fear of the powerful Earl, her father, deterred Edward from discarding Editha from his throne, the marriage was a mere matter of form: though attributing his conduct to an excess of self-negation, the titles of Saint and Confessor were afterwards accorded to him by the monkish chroniclers, and the most extravagant praises lavished on the virtuous example set by him, an example which, in those ages, called forth unqualified admiration.[1] It is indeed recorded, that at the time when Edward was importuned by his council to marry, he himself disclosed to Editha that he had bound himself to a life of celibacy, and should merely place her by his side on the throne:[2] William of Malmesbury declares he never could discover whether, in this instance, Edward acted from dislike to her family, which he prudently dissembled from the exigency of the times, or from motives of a pious nature;[3] but authors generally attribute his conduct rather to the first cause.[4] The smothered aversion he entertained for the Earl, was repeatedly exhibited in his treatment of Editha, his union with her being a daily recurring sting, showing the fear and forced submission under which he writhed. The gentle Queen resigned herself without a murmur to her husband's ill-treatment; and when she found all her endeavours to win the affections of Edward proved fruitless, she turned her thoughts solely to religion, and consoled herself by performing acts of devotion. Some, indeed, go so far as to say that Editha was perfectly agreeable to King Edward, but that her feelings being the same as his own, they mutually agreed to live on these distant terms. Edward was popular with the whole nation, and he is represented by his friends, the monks, as possessed of such great

[1] Hume, William of Malmesbury. [2] Lingard. [3] Holinshed. [4] Grafton.

patience, that he could scarcely ever be put in a passion.[1] He was, besides, the "father of the poor, and protector of the weak, more willing to give than to receive, and better pleased to pardon than to punish." The Queen is said also to have distinguished herself by her generosity.

In one point, certainly, Edward and his Queen were agreed, the patronage of the church and its holy prelates. Leofstan, Abbot of St. Alban's, is spoken of as the friend, confessor, and counsellor of both Edward and Editha:[2] to the former he filled the office of chaplain, and between this prelate and Queen Editha was a strict friendship.[3]

An old register of the Church of Worcester testifies how "Agelwin Dean of Worcester, and his brother Ordric, gave three lassats of land *in Cundicotan* to the monks there, which grant is confirmed by Edward,[4] and then Queen Editha."[5]

One of the earliest undertakings of King Edward after his marriage, was the foundation of that noble structure, the Abbey of Westminster. While yet an exile in Normandy, the son of Ethelred had vowed, in case of his obtaining the crown of his ancestors, that he would undertake a pilgrimage to Rome; and now that he was firmly seated on the throne, he did not forget this vow. It had been a subject of meditation until the year 1043, when he summoned his nobles and clergy, and informed them of his intentions. It was suggested that to go to Rome in person, would be dangerous both to himself and to his kingdom, but that ambassadors should be sent to the Pope to obtain a dispensation. This advice was adopted by Edward, and the dispensation granted, on condition that the money intended to be spent on the journey should be given to the poor, and that the King should either erect a new monastery, or repair some old one to the honour of St. Peter. On this King Edward caused his whole estates and possessions to be decimated, and appropriated to the pulling down the ruined Saxon Church which King Sigebert had built, and erecting in the same place a stately fabric, instead of the money being expended, as he had purposed, in a pilgrimage to Rome.

The earliest charter to the monastery is dated A. D. 1045, and signed first by the King, then by his mother "Alfgitha," and thirdly by Editha, his Queen. It would, therefore, seem that both ladies were present at the donation of the charter, and that the proud Norman widow of Ethelred and Canute took precedence in this instance, as perhaps in others, of her gentle daughter-in-law, the child of her old rival, Godwin.

Edward likewise founded that Church of St. Margaret, which now stands without the Abbey. The old church of St. Margaret standing in the way of the cloisters which were to be erected for the Abbey of St. Peter, the King caused it to be pulled down, and the present building erected."[6]

The erection of the Church of St. Peter was certainly the great event of Edward's reign: it occupied a space of twenty years, and was only finished at the close of his career. While the King was occupied in directing the new building at Westminster, an object zealously seconded

---

[1] Hallam. [2] Dugdale. [3] Weever.
[4] Lingard. [5] Carter and Dugdale, Selden. [6] Dart's Westminster.

by his amiable consort, Editha began and completed an Abbey of stone at Wilton, in lieu of the wooden one in which she had been educated; most of the early Saxon buildings being constructed of wood;[1] this circumstance marks the Queen's attachment to the spot in which her earlier years, probably the happiest portion of her life, had been passed.[2]

Editha appears to have had considerable property in England for her own private use, so that she was able to indulge her wishes in respect to pious donations and charities.

Her estates were very numerous, and situated in almost every county in England. In Somersetshire alone, she held Milverton, Twiverton, Crewkerne, Luckham, Bruiton, and Chewton Mendip, manors which yielded an annual sum of 100*l.*[3] Martock likewise, also in the same county, and Camel-Queens, so named from being vested in the queens of this realm. This place, at the Norman Survey, yielded 23*l.* of white money. Rivenhall, in Essex, also formed part of Editha's estates; so also was Bath (called Bade in Domesday Book). Wycombe, in Bucks, which was worth 12*l.* per annum, belonged to Editha; and Buthric held that manor, as her tenant,[4] during Edward's reign.

Notwithstanding she was the possessor of all these rich territories, Editha, on one occasion, manifests something of the acquisitive spirit of the Godwin race in laying claim to the town of Fisherton, which Leofrina, "a London Lady," had bequeathed by her will to the Abbey of Peterborough. Editha disputed this donation, and laid claim to the village in question, which she pretended Leofrina had decreed to her. A contest ensued, which terminated in the Abbey paying forty marks of gold to the Queen, and forty marks more in the ornaments of the church.[5] Leofrina was on a pilgrimage to Jerusalem, at the time of her death, about A. D. 1060. She is noticed by Stowe among his "Worthy Acts of Women."[6]

"The royal duty or revenue, known by the name of Queen Gold, and which belongs to every queen of England during her marriage to the king, was first paid to Queen Editha. This money is due and payable by persons in this kingdom and Ireland, on divers grants of the king, by way of fine or oblation, &c., and is one full tenth part above the entire fines on pardons, contracts, or agreements, which becomes a real debt to the queen, by the name of AURUM REGINÆ, upon the party's bare agreement with the king for his fine, and recording the same."[7]

---

[1] Wilton nunnery was first built by St. Alburg, sister of Egbert, for an abbess and twelve nuns; the number of the latter was increased by Alfred the Great to twenty-six.

[2] Domesday Book, Britton and Brayley, Collinson.

[3] Camden relates this on the authority of Mr. Douce in his account of Wilton. That author says he found it in a Life of Edward the Confessor.—Dugdale.

[4] Langley's History and Antiquities of Desborough.

[5] Stowe's London.

[6] Ency. Brit.

[7] Selden, who names the duty called "Aurum Reginæ," mentioning the following privileges attached to the queenly dignities in England:—"Divers prerogatives also are allowed in our laws to the Queen-wife, as those of making gifts or contracts, or suing without the King, and receiving by gift from her husband (which

For some time after the marriage of Edward, peace was preserved between him and Earl Godwin, whose family were admitted to familiar communion with him and the Queen. During this interval, an incident occurred considered so worthy of note at the time as to be recorded in imperishable stone. It is represented in the eighth compartment of the screen of King Edward the Confessor, in Westminster Abbey,[1] and presents to the eye, as well as to the mind, a picture of manners very remarkable. Tosti and Harold, the sons of Godwin, had a quarrel at the King's table; and, in the sculpture, "the contending brothers are shown in the foreground of the design, whilst Earl Godwin and the King and Queen are on the opposite side of a table, on which is a covered cup, with several articles of food." The quarrel between the sons of Godwin, who were yet boys, arose in consequence of the envious jealousy of Tosti at the King's drinking to Harold, his younger brother, in preference to himself. Harold, by superior strength, after Tosti had caught him by the hair and pulled him violently to the ground, recovered his feet, "and layed mightie blowes upon his brother, so that the King himself was fayne to put his hand and to separate them."[2] He then foretold the calamities which would befall the realm through the contention of the brothers, when arrived at manhood, and intimated their untimely and respective fates. The outline of this relation is corroborated by different historians. The designs for the singular sculptures upon the screen in Westminster Abbey have been chiefly deduced from Ailred's account of the Life and Miracles of King Edward, which was written in the time of Henry II., and presented to that monarch by Abbot Lawrance, on the very day, A. D. 1163, when, in honour of his recent canonization, the Confessor's remains were removed into a new shrine."

One of the remarkable and interesting records left of Queen Editha is that which concerns the Installation of Leofric, as first Bishop of Exeter. King Edward removed the Bishop's See from St. Germanus, at Crediton, to Exeter; and Editha, with her husband, assisted to instal Leofric, already Lord Chancellor of England and a member of the King's Privy

no other *femme coverte* may do), having her courts and officers, as if she were a sole person; that if the King or she be plaintiff, the summons in the process need not have the solemnity of fifteen days, which is extended also to their children, brothers, sisters, and *à ses parens*, as Bracton says, and such like. It is also treason to plot against her life."—Selden's Titles of Honour.

The duty was suspended during the reign of Edward VI., Mary and Elizabeth, there being no Queen-consort for sixty years: it was claimed by the Queens of James the First and Charles the First.—Sir H. Ellis's Introduction to Domesday Book.

[1] Lambard's Topographical Dictionary, article "Wynsore." That the Queen was present when Harold and Tosti quarrelled is confirmed by Caxton. Holinshed says it happened at Windsor the last year of Edward's reign. A MS. written in the time of Edward the First, and illuminated with great care, represents this famous quarrel, and has been copied in Strutt's Regal and Ecclesiastical Antiquities, where may be seen the picture of Queen Editha. Snorro tells us that Harold, Godwin's youngest son, "was brought up at Edward's court, and was his foster-son. The King loved him very much, and kept him as his own son, for he had no son."

[2] Neale's Westminster Abbey.

Council, as the first abbot of that church. The installation took place on the 27th of May, A. D. 1049, in the sixth year of the reign of Edward. As an instance of the great favour and honour which the bishop received from both the King and Queen at his instalment, we may quote the words of King Edward's Charter, viz.: "I, King Edward, taking Bishop Leofric by the right hand, and Edith, my Queen, by the left, do install him the first and most famous Bishop of Exeter, with a great desire of abundance of blessings to all such as should further and increase the same; but with a fearful and execrable curse upon all such as should diminish or take anything from it;" and within the choir, adjoining the high altar, is a monument, fairly arched, and under the same arch are three seats with side pillars of brass, erected in memory of the said King Edward, Edith his Queen, and Leofric, the first Bishop of Exeter; the middle of them being the seat of the said bishop, sitting in his pontificals between the King and the Queen.[1]

The year 1051[2] was signalized by one of the most dreadful famines ever known in England. A quarter of wheat rose to sixty pennies, a sum equal to fifteen shillings of our present money; consequently it was as dear if it now cost 7*l.* 10*s.*, and far exceeded that great dearth in the reign of Queen Elizabeth, when a quarter of wheat was sold for 4*l.*[3] Thousands were perishing for want, and it was the sight of the misery of the people on this occasion that led the King to repeal the heavy and odious tax called the Danegelt.[4] The mind of Edward was first attracted to the circumstance by his Queen Editha; who, one day, accompanied by her brother Harold, conducted him into the royal treasury, where the vast amount of this collected tax had been deposited. Edward was so affected by the sight of this large sum at such a moment of national affliction, that he immediately ordered the money to be restored to its former owners, and no more to be raised on such an assessment. Few incidents in the life of Editha show her character in a more humane and amiable light than this instance of blessed pity.

In the year previous to the famine, an open rupture took place between Earl Godwin and the King, on the occasion of Eustace, Earl of Boulogne, the husband of Goda, King Edward's sister, having landed at Dover, and unjustly and tyrannously treating the inhabitants—forcing them to provide dwellings for himself and his men—a fray with the townsmen ensuing, in which many were killed. The foreigners, being overcome by the people of the country after a loss of eighty men, fled to Gloucester to the King, complaining of their wrongs. Earl Godwin, who took the part of the English, but could not convince King Edward, assembled a large army and marched into Gloucestershire, threatening to make war on his sovereign unless Eustace and all his men were delivered into his

[1] Dugdale, Weever, Isaacke's Antiquities of Exeter, Speed.

[2] A snow-storm fell this year, in January, so deep that it covered the ground to the middle of March, causing cattle and fowls in abundance to perish; and the next year was remarkable for an earthquake, and lightnings which burnt up the cornfields and produced a dearth.—Howel, Med. Hist. Angl.

[3] Hume.

[4] Hoveden and Ingulphus, Sharon Turner.

hands. The King refused, and commanded Godwin to repair to court and account for his conduct. The royal order not being obeyed, Edward, by sentence of his court, banished Godwin and his five sons from England. Accordingly, the Earl and his wife, their son Tosti and his wife Judith, daughter of Baldwin Earl of Flanders, with Sweyn and Gurth, also sons of Godwin, took shipping, with immense treasures, and went to Flanders, to Earl Baldwin. Harold and Leofwin went to Bristol, and crossed the sea into Ireland: there they took refuge with King Donough, who is said to have espoused Driella, their sister. The Irish King received his English relatives with much honour, and they remained in Ireland all that winter, "on the King's security." The following year, Donough assisted them with a squadron of nine ships, or, as some say, a considerable body of land forces, with which they made a successful landing in Britain.[1] Of Donough, it is related that he either introduced first into Ireland, or encouraged, the custom of celebrating games or athletic sports on the Sabbath-day; the cœstus, or gloves used by the pugilists, being distributed, as it is said, in the King's own mansion,[2] perhaps, by the hand of the fair Driella. This was plainly done in honour of the day, and not a desecration of its duties; for, another author tells us that this king was a scrupulous observer of the Sabbath, and forbade any one to carry burdens, or hold hunting-matches or fairs on that day. Some have thought that the marriage of Driella, and flight of many English nobles to Ireland, in consequence of William the Conqueror's tyranny, where the Saxon protection, through her influence, was to be found, occasioned an improved knowledge of architecture in that country.[3]

The King had not only banished Godwin and his sons, but caused their estates to be confiscated. These were enormous,[4] and spread over numerous counties.

As might have been expected, the disgrace of her family involved also that of Editha; but it was necessary to have some form of accusation against her, which was not long wanting to her enemies. The usual pretence of infidelity to the King, a common resource against a defenceless woman, was set up, the accuser chosen being Robert, Archbishop of Canterbury. This man was a native of Normandy and monk of Jumièges, who had been known to King Edward during his exile abroad, and whom he had invited to England. After his arrival he was made Bishop of London, and subsequently Archbishop of Canterbury.[5] Of this prelate Speed remarks, "I am fully persuaded that the accusation with which Editha was charged by Robert, the Archbishop, was more upon envy to her father than truth of so foul a fact in her whose virtues were so many and so memorable, by report of authors that were eye-witnesses." The charge would be unworthy of notice but for the consequences to the innocent Queen, who on her death-bed, as well as at the time, protested that it was entirely false; her whole course of life was sufficient to prove this, even if the motives of Edward had not been as transparent as they

[1] Moore, O'Halloran.
[2] Ibid.
[3] Grose's Antiquities.
[4] Roger of Wendover.
[5] William of Malmesbury.

were. His vengeance against Earl Godwin, whether merited or not,—and in this instance it was ill-directed,—could not be complete without his daughter sharing his punishment.

Infamous and unjust as this accusation of the Archbishop was, Editha was treated most rigorously by the King her husband, who not only expelled her from his court, but subjected her to every possible disgrace. All her goods were taken from her, and, stripped of her lands, furniture and money, in which she shared the fate of the whole Godwin family, Editha was committed a prisoner to the Monastery of Wherwell, in Hampshire. The sister of King Edward presided over this establishment, and that abbess was appointed to keep her prisoner "very strictly;" one solitary female alone of all her train being permitted to attend on the deposed Queen. The King's Norman favourites indulged in scoffs and jeers at her expense, remarking, "that it was not fit that at the time when her family were suffering banishment, she herself should sleep on down." So many contradictions occur in early history, that, although some writers have recorded the severe treatment experienced by Editha, a contemporary historian affirms that on this distressing occasion the poor Queen was conducted with royal pomp to Wherwell, and informed that her confinement there was only a measure of temporary precaution.[1] As the author of this statement dedicated his work, which was the Life of King Edward, to Queen Editha, it deserves to have some weight. The circumstance would show Edward's own conviction of the Queen's innocence, and how little the merited harsh treatment. There is a clear proof also in his abandoning himself to the rule of Archbishop Robert at this epoch, as he had formally resigned himself to that of Godwin, that he required the direction of some master-mind, and was "steered by each pilot according as the rudder of his destiny was turned." Under the influence of the Archbishop's faction, it seemed by this sudden stroke on the fortune of Editha, that Edward's intention really was never again to receive back his wife, and that, although till now he had preserved fair terms with the daughter of his enemy's hated house, he had parted from her at the very first moment that he could do so with safety to himself.[2]

Editha's accusation and punishment were similar to those of Queen Emma, who received at the hands of her son no better treatment than his wife, and the same convent received both. However gratified Queen Emma might have been to have seen the ruin of the man who had alternately been her bitterest enemy and her ally, she could scarcely help sympathizing with her innocent daughter-in-law, the victim of the enmity of the same Robert, Archbishop of Canterbury, who had been instrumental in her own degradation, signal as the victory she obtained over him had been.

Editha bore her wrongs more meekly, and made no appeal to the fiery ordeal which Queen Emma had passed through; perhaps, aware of her father's real power, and the love borne to him by the English, as well as their hatred of the Norman favourites, she looked forward to his return

---

Quoted by Stowe, p. 96, and alluded to by Dr. Lingard. [2] Rapin.

and her own restoration; and these hopes supported her through a whole year, in spite of the natural tears which she shed during the forced retreat to which her husband's weakness and cruelty had condemned her.

But though Godwin, taken unawares, had submitted for a time to the force of circumstances, it was not to be expected that so powerful a leader, and one so popular in the country, would be content to abandon his possessions and his sway to the Norman favourites of the irresolute and priest-governed Edward. The struggle was soon renewed, and this time conducted with so much skill and vigour that, after a series of defeats and mortifications, Edward was obliged to succumb. The strong feeling of the nation was in favour of Earl Godwin, whose disgrace was felt to have taken place in consequence of his having defended the rights of the people against the oppression of the insolent Normans, and the King found himself unable to stand against the pressure. The Anglo-Danish yoke had, by this time, become light to the English. Canute had been admired and esteemed; but the foreign notions of Edward, which condemned everything English, habits, customs, and language, had disgusted the people with his court. The ill-treatment of Editha, the daughter of their popular chief, rankled in their minds; so far from molesting him, they declared for Godwin, from every part of the coast along which his fleet paused to ask for supplies, and when they found that a powerful fleet from Ireland, under the conduct of one of his sons, had reinforced his army, the whole country rushed to his side. The Welsh, glad of an opportunity to revenge old feuds, joined with the strongest party, and England was once more in the control of Godwin.

Then commenced a headlong flight on the other side; "there was mounting in hot haste"—the Norman favourites, seized with panic, rushed for their lives to their ships, got on board at any sacrifice, and left the King and his capital to the successful Earl. Edward was forced to appear content after having stood stiffly out as long as it was possible; and the end of all this confusion, bloodshed, and devastation, was Godwin's entire restoration to all his honours and possessions, the expulsion of Robert the Archbishop, and all the Normans in power, and the return, with suitable pomp and circumstance, of the disgraced Queen Editha.[1]

All now seemed prosperous with the family of Godwin, and Editha's heart was relieved of the burthen of sorrow which had lately nearly crushed her. Nothing was now to be heard but rejoicing; and festivals, both courtly and religious, filled up the time of the triumphant party. It was at one of these, which took place at Easter, at Winchester, that while sitting at table with the King, the Queen and all the court, in the midst of conviviality,[2] Earl Godwin was suddenly seized with a fit of apoplexy and fell speechless to the ground. He was borne from the chamber by his sons Tostig and Harold, and after a few days' extreme agony, expired.

By Norman writers, whose enmity to his house of course induced misrepresentation, and who delight in striking scenes, the story of Earl Godwin's death has been differently related. According to them one of the royal cupbearers, when presenting wine, happened to stumble with one

[1] Saxon Chronicle, William of Malmesbury, &c. [2] Saxon Chronicle

foot and saved himself from falling with the aid of the other, on which Godwin exclaimed: "Thus brother helps brother." Edward, from whose mind no asseverations, public or private, could efface the impression of Godwin's guilt, looked sternly at him and said: "Yes—and had Alfred lived, so might he have helped me." Godwin, indignant at the imputed charge, replied: "I know that you still suspect me of your brother's murder, but may God, who is true and just, not permit this morsel of bread to enter my throat without choking me if he suffered death or injury from me or by my counsel."

Having said this, the King blessed the bread, but the instant the Earl put it in his mouth, it choked him.[1] "Thus," adds the chronicler, "did Providence expose and punish the traitor and murderer."

If such a scene really took place, no doubt the passion of Godwin on finding that, under whatever circumstances they met, Edward persisted in casting the same crime in his teeth, was the cause of the apoplexy which seized him on the instant. Such events have been frequent when persons are violently excited, particularly after being heated at an entertainment in times when conviviality was carried to excess.

Godwin was so little a friend to the Church, and Edward was so completely the tool of Churchmen, that it naturally follows that the former should suffer in the report of those historians who look upon Edward as a saint. The death of the Earl happened at an unfortunate juncture, and great was the lamentation throughout England for the great "Child of Sussex," as he was called.[2]

Probably, if Edward had dared to do so, the family of the man he detested would again have suffered from his violence; but the times were altered, and all he could do was now to secure himself and endeavour to settle the succession on those nearest him in blood. He sent, therefore, to the Emperor, Henry III., at Cologne, requesting that the son of Edmund Ironside, whom he protected, and who had married his niece, might come over to him in England. After some delay, the Prince accordingly arrived with his wife Agatha and his children, Edgar Atheling, Margareta, and Christina, but he died almost directly after, suddenly, in London.

Meantime, Harold, the son of Godwin, was fighting against the usurper Macbeth, of famous memory, in the North, and succeeded to the Earldom of Siward of Northumberland, in whose cause he had drawn the

---

[1] Saxon Chronicle, 1053, 15th April.

[2] The famous Godwin, or Goodwin, Sands, formerly part of the Earl's domain, off the coast of Kent, lie between the North and South Foreland; and, as they run parallel with the coast for three leagues together, at about two leagues and a half distant from it, they add to the security of that spacious road, the Downs; for, while the land shelters ships with the wind from south-west to north-west only, these sands break all the force of the sea, when the wind is at east-south-east. The most dangerous wind, when blowing hard off the Downs, is the south-south-west. — Ency. Brit.

The lands were given to the Monastery of St. Augustine at Canterbury, and the Abbot, neglecting to keep in repair the wall that defended them from the sea, the whole tract was drowned in the year 1100, leaving these sands so great, yet so fatal a safeguard to the coast.

sword. A long series of contentions occupied him till after tranquillity was temporarily restored, he set out for Normandy on the errand which threw him into the intimacy of Duke William, so fraught with consequences to himself and England.

Whether any change came over the spirit of Queen Editha, after the calamity of losing her father, and whether she conceived it necessary to exercise a rigour and vigilance which appeared hitherto foreign to her nature,[1] it is difficult to determine; but she has been accused of abandoning her accustomed mildness, and acting with cruelty about this time. Most probably the acts of which she is accused should rather be attributed to her brothers, Tosti or Harold, who then swayed Northumberland. It appears that certain retainers of a Northumbrian chief were murdered in the court of Edward, and "the Queen's orders" are cited as giving sanction to the fact. "Even this fair rose was stained with blood,"[2] says an annalist; but it does not follow that she is guilty of more than severity, dictated by the representations of her brothers. The alleged treachery of Tostig has not been confuted, and this act was, doubtless, but a feature of the tragedy in which he performed.

Tosti having allured some Northumbrian nobles to his own chamber, in his palace at York, under pretence of concluding a peace, had caused them to be assassinated. These atrocities, and the imposition of a severe tax, caused the Northumbrians to arm against the Government. Tostig was surprised at York, and escaped by flight: his treasures and armory were pillaged, and two hundred Danish and English guards, with their leaders, Amund and Ravensworth, being made prisoners, were led out of the city and massacred in cold blood on the north bank of the Ouse. Morcar and Edwin were placed by the insurgents at their head; they were met by Harold, who, having inquired into their demands, obtained the King's assent to them. These were to confirm the laws of Canute, and appoint Morcar Earl of Northumberland. Tostig, dissatisfied at this peace, repaired to Bruges, the usual asylum of his family.[3]

The establishment of chaplains in the royal household is of very ancient date, and even in the Pagan times we find priests attendant on their regal patrons. Editha and her brother Harold had their chaplains. Walther, afterwards Bishop of Hereford, filled this office with the Queen; he was appointed to that see, and an instrument issued for the temporalities of Hereford in the year 1060, having previously been consecrated at Rome, together with Aldred, Archbishop of York, and Gisa, Bishop of Wells, the King's chaplain (April 4th, 1059).

Gisa was, as well as Walther, a native of Lorraine, and is said to have been treated with the utmost consideration by Queen Editha. It appears that, when Harold, Earl of Wessex, was banished by Edward, the King bestowed his possessions on the Church of Wells. Harold afterwards made a piratical descent in those parts, and having raised contributions among his former tenants, despoiled the church of its ornaments, drove away the canons, invaded their possessions, and converted them to his own

[1] Rapin. [2] Turner, Holinshed. [3] Holinshed, Lingard, &c.

use.[1] In vain had Gisa, who, on entering into his new diocese, found the church estates in a sad condition, expostulated with his royal patron on this outrageous usage, but the more generous and considerate Editha, bestowed on Gisa the manors of Mark and Mudgley as in part compensation for the injuries his bishopric had sustained through her brother's depredations. Harold,[2] on being restored to favour, procured Gisa's banishment, and still later, when on the throne, he resumed the estates of which he had formerly been deprived. That William the Conqueror recalled Gisa from exile, and with some trivial exceptions, restored to the Church of Wells all Harold's estates, was one of the many proofs he gave of his respect for Queen Editha, that prelate's generous benefactress.

Of the King's Chamberlain, or Thane of the Bower, "Bar-Theyn," an incident is on record, which gives a trait of Edward's character, more simple than just, and more good-natured than prudent; this officer was the appointed Keeper of the King's purse, and bore the name of Hugoline. "It chanced that Edward was lying in bed, and, as it appears, in the daytime, when the chamberlain came in and busied himself about the chest which held the King's money, either putting somewhat in, or taking somewhat out; and then he quitted the room, forgetting to lock the chest. The King saw him, and so did the little scullion-boy, who, fully persuaded that the Confessor was asleep, crept softly to the tempting hoard, and filling his bosom with the gold, he softly stole away. The King saw him, but said naught. Having safely deposited his acquisition, he ventured a second time into the King's chamber, made a second attempt, and was equally successful. The King saw him, but said naught. A third time he approached the hoard, and then Edward, alarmed, not for the safety of the money, but for the safety of the thief, exclaimed, 'Have a care, boy, and be off with what thou hast; for if Hugoline finds thee out, not a penny will he leave thee!'"

The lord chamberlain still displays the "key," as the token of the office.[3]

In 1062, Editha assisted at the dedication of Waltham Abbey. The estate of Waltham, which had devolved on the crown, had been bestowed by Edward the Confessor on his brother-in-law Harold, with a considerable grant of land. Harold rebuilt or enlarged the monastery, for the purpose of keeping a holy cross, said to have been miraculously brought thither, and richly endowed it as a college for a dean and eleven secular black canons. In King Edward's Charter of Confirmation, dated 1062, it is stated that Harold having founded a monastery to the holy faith, the King caused it to be honourably dedicated according to the due form and order of a holy church of God, "in the remembrance," so it is expressed, "of me and my wife, named Editha," for the founder himself, his father and mother, and for all related to him in consanguinity, whether living

[1] Collinson's Somersetshire.

[2] Leofgar, chaplain of Harold, preceded Walther in the see of Hereford, and had scarcely become a bishop when he forsook his chrism and rood, his spiritual weapons, and took to his spear and sword, and so going to the field against Griffith, the Welsh King, was slain, together with many of his priests.

[3] Palgrave.

or dead; and Harold bestowed seventeen lordships on this foundation, all which King Edward, to redeem his own and his predecessor's sins, confirmed to the Abbey, free of all suit and service, and with ample privileges, which he signed and sealed with the holy cross himself, together with his Queen Editha, and fifty-six of his great men. An immense number of rich and precious gifts were also bestowed by the noble founder on the Abbey.[1] In the Royal Charter appear the names of Stigand, Archbishop of Dover, and Harold, to which are added those of the King and Queen.[2]

The leisure of King Edward was divided between prayer and the chase; the latter always a favourite pastime with our Saxon monarchs. At Brill, in Buckinghamshire, was a palace to which King Edward would frequently resort that he might have the pleasure of hunting in Bernwood Forest. At that time the forest was much infested by a wild boar, which at length was fortunately slain by a huntsman of the name of Nigel. This person the King rewarded for his service by a grant of some lands, which he was to hold by a horn, a mode of livery common in those days, and of which an instance has already been given in this volume. "On the land thus given Nigel built a large manor-house, called *Borestall*, or Borstall, in memory of the event through which he obtained possession." This estate has descended in uninterrupted succession, by several heirs female, from the family of Nigel to that of Aubrey, and the original horn by which it was conveyed to the former is in the possession of Sir John Aubrey, Bart, as well as a folio volume, composed about the reign of Henry the Third, containing transcripts of papers relating to the manor, with a rude delineation of the site of Borstall House and its contiguous lands, beneath which is the figure of a man on one knee, presenting a boar's head on the point of a sword to the King, who is returning him a coat of arms. The horn is of a dark brown colour, variegated and veined like tortoise-shell; the ends are tipped with silver, and fitted with wreaths of leather to hang round the neck."[3]

Edward the Confessor built also for himself, in Essex, in a well-wooded locality, which from its solitude was suited to devotion, a goodly residence, or hunting-seat, known by the name of Have-he-Ring, or Take-the-Ring, as it would be rendered in modern English; at the time he resided there —whether alone or with the Queen, is not recorded—being, as it is said, troubled in his devotions by the sound of the nightingales, he humbly besought from God their absence, from which time forward "the song of the bird" was never more heard, except beyond the pales of his park, where, as in other places, they would abundantly resort.[4] Of Havering this legend is on record:—An aged pilgrim, from Jerusalem, solicited alms from King Edward, who, his almoner not being present, drew a ring from his finger, and presented it to the mendicant. This ring was after-

[1] Ogborne's Essex.

[2] Fuller's History of Waltham.

[3] Britton and Brayley. This curious plan and a representation of the horn have been engraved in the third volume of the Archæologia, whence many of the above particulars were derived.

[4] Camden.

wards returned by the pilgrim to certain Englishmen, in the East, to be restored to King Edward, with this message, that he had given it to St. John the Evangelist, who sent it back to him to inform him of the day on which it was appointed that he should die: the day named was January 5th, 1062. Accordingly, in passing through Westminster Cloisters into the Dean's Yard, you may see the King and Pilgrim cut in stone over the gate.[1] It is said that when the King received the pilgrim's message, he was taken ill, that he distributed his wealth to the poor, and prepared himself for the close of his earthly career. One subject, however, had for a long time pressed on the mind of the monarch; the completion of that grand undertaking, the Abbey of St. Peter's, Westminster. Edward had determined that the church should be dedicated in the most solemn and impressive manner, and for that purpose had convened a general assembly of all the bishops and great men in the kingdom, to be witnesses of the ceremony. It was the last Christmas festival which the pious monarch was destined to celebrate, memorable to his own and succeeding ages by the fact of this consecration and opening of an edifice, the building of which had occupied his entire reign. A splendid festival was to be held in the adjoining palace, to which all the nobles were invited.

On the vigil of Christmas the King was attacked by the fever, which ultimately proved fatal.[2] For the three following days he combatted the violence of the disease by a firmness and affected cheerfulness, which were shown in his holding his court as usual, and presiding at the royal banquet.[3]

The festival of the Innocents[4] was that which had been fixed on for the dedication of the new church, that edifice which had been so long and anxiously superintended during its progress by the monarch. When the day arrived, Edward was unable to quit his chamber, but would not delay the ceremony on that account. In the absence of her husband, it was the delegated office of Queen Editha to take charge of the decorations, and become his representative;—"providing all, arranging all, superintending all, she acted for both King and Queen."[5] On the same day the grand Convention was held, in the chamber of the doomed King, for the purpose of signing his great charter of donations, the third which had been bestowed.[6] The King, Queen, two archbishops, ten bishops, and many of the abbots and nobility, were present on the occasion. The earliest charter bears the date of 1045, and has the signatures of the King, the Queen, and the King's mother, Emma of Normandy, whose name, as before, precedes that of the Queen.

Some have asserted that Edward really was present at the solemn pageant of the dedication of the new abbey, and that he was taken ill immediately after it was over, and removed from the abbey to his bed; but others maintain a contrary opinion, and say that the fact of the King's absence, and the idea of danger in his condition of health, neces-

[1] Hearne, Caxton. [2] Lingard. [3] Dart's Westminster.
[4] December 28. [5] Twysden [6] Dart's Westminster.

sarily suggested in consequence, threw a deep gloom over the thousands who had assembled to witness the spectacle.

Edward lingered for a week longer in his sufferings. His death took place on the 5th of January, 1066, at Westminster, and the chamber in which he expired still remained in Camden's time, "close to Sir Thomas Cotton's House." The following account of the deathbed of the saintly monarch is from Caxton's Golden Legende:—

"Among the persons who surrounded the death-bed of Edward, were the Queen, Duke Harold, Robert, keeper of the palace, and Stigand. This last gave no credence to the prophetic words uttered by Edward, concerning the approaching disasters of the country, and, ascribing it to the King's age and feebleness, made it out to be a phantasy; but others present wept, sorrowed, and wrung their hands. Edward, perceiving his hour drew nigh, spoke to them that stood weeping about him, and in comforting them, said, 'Forsooth, if ye loved me ye would pray that I should pass from this world to the Father of Heaven, there to receive the joy which is promised to all true Christian men: put ye away your weeping, and speed forth my journey with prayers and holy psalms, and with alms-deeds. For though my enemy, the Fiend, may not overcome me in my faith, yet there is none found so perfect but he will assay, and tempt to let or to fear him.' When he beheld the Queen, and saw her weep and sigh, he said to her oftentimes, 'My daughter, weep not, for I shall not die, but I shall live, and shall depart from the land of death, I believe, to see the goodness of God in the land of life.' And then he set his mind all on God, and gave himself wholly to the faith of the Church, in the hope and promises of Christ, under the sacraments of the Church. He commended the Queen to her brother in praising her goodness and virtue unto his lords, and declared to them their mode of life. 'For she was to him in open places as his wife, and in secret places as his sister.'[1] And he commanded, also, that her dowry should be made sure to her; and that they that came with him out of Normandy should be put to their choice, whether they would abide still in England, and be endowed with livelihood after their degree, or else return again into Normandy with a sufficient reward; and he chose his place for his own sepulture in the Church of St. Peter, which he had newly builded. And among words of praising, he yielded up his spirit to God in the year of our Lord 1066."

The last wishes of the Confessor were strictly observed, and his remains deposited before the high altar in the Church of St. Peter's, Westminster, the funeral obsequies being attended by those very nobles he had himself invited to the solemn dedication of that sacred edifice:[2] the royal inter-

[1] Ailred.

[2] Robert of Gloucester, who says he died on the 4th and was buried on the 12th, thus notices the obsequies of Edward: — "With Edward the happiness of the English expired, liberty perished, and all vigour was inhumed. At his exequies, bishops and a multitude of priests and ecclesiastics, with dukes, earls, and governors, assembled together. A crowd of monks went thither, and innumerable bodies of people flew hastily to his funeral. Here psalms resound, there sighs and tears burst out; everywhere joy and grief commixed, are carried to the

ment took place on Twelfth Day, as some say, the day following that of the dedication of the abbey. As soon as Edward's mortal remains were placed in the tomb, "the same Witan which had met to consecrate the abbey,[1] proceeded to elect their new king. In this crisis, Harold, Earl of Wessex, the Queen's brother, took possession of the crown, which King Edward is said to have, previously to his death, granted him, and he was now consecrated King, "on the Twelfth Day," the day of the royal funeral, putting on his own head the insignia of his new dignity, at Lambeth. While this powerful noble maintained his authority as King, Editha's position as Queen Dowager was doubtless respected.

Editha's estates were very numerous, and scattered about in nearly every county of England, so that her generous mind had many opportunities of exercising private as well as public beneficence. Even after the Conquest, Queen Editha appears to have possessed, in some instances, the right of transferring her property: she is mentioned in Domesday, as having bestowed several parcels of land, in dower, upon one Ailsi, who had married the daughter of Wluard, probably one of her attendants, and also as having granted eight hides of land at Firle, in Sussex, to the foreign abbey of Greystein. Editha was, in general a great benefactress to the Church, and especially to Sarum; a grant was made by her, after she became a widow, to the Church of St. Mary. The following extract is copied from the records in the Bodleian Collection, of that act of royal munificence: "I, Editha, relict of King Edward, give to the support of the canons of St. Mary's Church, in Sarum, the lands of Sceorstan, in Wiltshire, and those of Forinanburn, to the Monastery of Wherwell, for the support of the nuns serving God there, with the rights thereto belonging, for the soul of King Edward."[2]

It has been asserted by some, that Editha was permitted by the Norman Conqueror to retain peaceably all her possessions for life, and that on her decease they reverted to the Crown. This is not, however, a correct statement, as some years before the death of Editha, King William despoiled her of all her rich territories, and amongst the number Martock and Chewton Mendip, which were in the King's hands at the time of the Norman survey.[3] When the survey was taken, the Earl of Brittany had also seventy-eight hides of land in his own possession, and ninety hides held under him, all of which had belonged to the widowed Editha.[4] Among other possessions, of which the Queen was deprived by William, was the Manor of Richmond, in the parish of Cambridge, which had formed a part of her large dowry, the whole of which was given by the Norman King to Alan, Earl of Brittany and Richmond.[5] Martock, in Somersetshire, which had been taken by King William from Queen Editha, was given to Eustace, Earl of Boulogne, who had married Goda, Edward the Confessor's sister. Twiverton, in Somersetshire, is thus

church, and that temple of chastity, that dwelling of virtue (the King) is honourably interred in the place appointed by himself."

[1] Dart's Westminster Abbey. [2] Philipp's Account of Old Sarum.

[3] Collinson. [4] Lysons's Cambridge. [5] Idem.

named in Domesday Book: "This land Alfred held of Queen Eddid. Now the Bishop holds it of the King, as he says."

The supposed generosity of William, if at all shewn towards Editha, does not appear to have extended to her mother Githa, Godwin's widow, who, through fear of so powerful an enemy, quitted England in 1068, an affliction, doubtless, deeply felt by her daughter. Githa, who was immensely rich, and at this time much advanced in years, had survived the deaths of her five gallant sons, all slain in the battle-field; she had before that been, as it would appear, a spectator of the catastrophe which deprived her husband of life; and after beholding Editha, her daughter, during eighteen years a queen in dignity, but a melancholy and unloved wife, witnessed her contented retirement to the condition of private life. The ambition of Harold, and his subsequent defeat and death, were her crowning sorrows; and after living two years in continual fear of King William, Githa retired to St. Omers, where her daughter Gunilda had assumed the religious veil, or to Bruges, where, it appears, that lady died in 1087; a fact ascertained by an epitaph discovered some years since, in the church in which Gunilda's remains were deposited. No sooner had the widow of Godwin departed from England than William the Conqueror seized on her immense landed possessions, amounting to 39,600 acres,[1] and distributed them among his Norman followers.

Queen Editha survived her husband nine years, spent principally at Winchester. During her residence there, she is said to have been a spectator of the procession to the Cathedral, when Walker was about to be consecrated Bishop of Durham, which drew from her the remark, "We have here a noble martyr!" So affected was she by the sight of that excellent prelate's appearance, with his snow-white hair, rosy countenance, and extraordinary stature; for her previous experience of the mutinous disposition of the people over whom he was about to preside, led her to fear his fate; so literally was this reflection of the Queen fulfilled that it was looked upon, by those who were acquainted with her piety, as a miraculous prediction, for, in 1080, six years after the death of Editha, Walker was severely maltreated by the Northumbrians, and, at length, put to death by them.[2]

Editha expired at Winchester, as is supposed, in the Abbey of St. Mary, about a week before Christmas, in the year 1074;[3] in her last moments, she solemnly affirmed, she had lived during the eighteen years of

---

[1] Some few years before the invasion of this country by the Normans, Gueda, wife of Godwin, Earl of Kent, in expiation of her husband's treacherous abuses of divers monastic institutions, had bestowed the Manor of Crowcombe, in Somersetshire, on the church of St. Swithin, at Winchester, in pure and perpetual alms; but amongst other depredations which took place at the coming in of the Conqueror, this manor was seized, and fell a sacrifice to private property, King William presenting it to his favourite, the Earl of Morton. — Collinson's Somersetshire.

[2] William of Malmesbury.

[3] Neale says 1073 was the date of this Queen's death, and that it took place on the 15th of the Calends of January, eight years after that of her husband. Roger of Wendover says the date was 1074.

her union, as though no such tie had existed;[1] in consequence of which asseveration, the following epitaph was composed in Latin for this Queen. "She sprung of an ancient house, lived godly, entered into marriage a chaste virgin, and into heaven a chaste spouse."[2]

If William the Conqueror did not spare Queen Editha's possessions in her lifetime, he showed much honour to that Queen after death, and the title of *Regina* was assigned to her in almost every entry of her name in the Domesday Book. William took care that the funeral obsequies of Editha should be performed in a manner befitting her royal dignity:[3] by his orders the Queen's remains were removed with every royal honour from Winchester to Westminster, having been previously placed in a coffin covered with plates of silver and gold; on their arrival they were deposited by the side of St. Edward the Confessor.

A splendid tomb or shrine "of delicately wrought gold and silver, and of admirable beauty," was soon afterwards erected at the express command of William over the remains of the royal pair. That they had one common tomb appears from the charter granted on this occasion, in which King William, after bestowing one hundred pounds of silver to complete the building of the abbey, adds: "From respect of the great love which I had for the renowed King Edward himself, I have caused the tomb of him, and his queen placed beside him, to be marvellously overlaid with smith's work of artificial beauty in gold and silver."

Not long after the offering made by King William at the tomb of St. Edward, miracles were said to be wrought there, of which the first was when Wulstan, bishop of Worcester, was required by the Conqueror to resign his see. The prelate answered that he had received his staff from St. Edward, and would resign it to him alone. Going to his tomb, Wulstan struck it with his staff, which adhered to it; nor could it be separated by any prayers or hands than those of the prelate, its owner.

Edward the Confessor was canonized by Pope Alexander the Third, A. D. 1161, at the solicitation of King Henry the Second, who was induced to request this by his favourite, Thomas à Becket; and it was appointed that St. Edward's festival should be kept throughout England on the 5th of January, and his translation on the 13th of October; this last being to commemorate the solemn translation of the King's body on that day, about two years from the date of his canonization, and its removal into a higher tomb, which had been prepared for it by the English monarch's directions, a new shrine being also made on the occasion at the request of Becket.[4] Upon opening the coffin, which was then done with much solemnity at midnight, the body of the King was found incorrupt, and his dress was taken off as a precious relic, and made into three embroidered copes by Abbot Lawrence; also the ring that had been given to St. John the Evangelist was taken off and given to the abbey. The royal corpse was afterwards re-wrapped up and deposited in its new tomb, October 13th, 1163, in presence of King Henry the Second, St. Thomas à Becket, Archbishop of Canterbury, and many bishops, abbots, and

[1] Holinshed, William of Malmesbury, Neale.
[2] Gough.
[3] Malmesbury.
[4] Brit. Sancta.

persons of distinction, who attest the incorrupt state in which the royal remains and the garments in which they rested were found.[1] On that same day a book of St. Edward's life and miracles, written by Ailred, Abbot of Rievaulx, in Yorkshire, was dedicated and presented to King Henry the Second, and at the same time a bull was issued by Pope Innocent the Fourth to settle the ceremonial of the anniversary of the festival of St. Edward.[2]

When the church was rebuilt the remains of the Queen of Edward the Confessor were transferred from the north to the south side of St. Edward's shrine, and Henry the Third ordered that a lamp should be kept burning perpetually over the tomb of Queen Editha "the Good."

---

[1] The surname of Confessor was given to St. Edward from the bull of his canonization issued by Pope Alexander, about a century after his death. — Lingard.

[2] In 1247, King Henry III. received a present from the Knights Templars in the Holy Land (attested by the Patriarch of Jerusalem and other bishops of that country) of a small portion of the blood of our Saviour shed at the Crucifixion. On the anniversary of King Edward's translation, October 13th, King Henry went in person, on foot, in solemn procession, from St. Paul's to Westminster Abbey, carrying this gift in a crystal vessel, elevated above his head, under a canopy, his arms supported by priests, attended by his nobility, who had been summoned on this occasion, with bishops, abbots, monks, and an innumerable multitude of persons, and offered it to God, St. Peter, and Edward the Confessor. The Bishop of Norwich celebrated high mass on this occasion, and pronounced on all attending the solemnity one hundred and forty days' indulgence. A sumptuous feast was also given at the adjoining palace. In 1297, King Edward I., to show his respect for his namesake-saint, offered at his shrine in Westminster, the chair, sceptre, and crown of gold of the Scottish kings.—Brit. Sanc.

After the coronation of King James II. the tomb of Edward the Confessor received some damage by an accident. The coffin, being of wood, bound with iron, was broken into a hole about six inches by four, near the right breast of the corpse, which was examined by Mr. Taylor on St. Barnabas's Day, 1685, by putting his hand into the chasm and drawing from under the shoulder-bones a crucifix, richly enamelled and gilt, on it the figure of Christ crucified, and an eye above casting a ray on him. On the reverse, a Benedictine monk, and on each side of him these Roman capitals: — on the right limb,
  A
Z A X;
  A
on the left,
  P
A   C.
  H
The cross was hollow, as if to enclose some relic; the upright part four inches, the transverse three. This was attached to a chain of pure gold, twenty-four inches long, the links oblong and curiously wrought, the upper joined by a locket composed of massy knobs of gold, and on each side were set two large red stones, supposed rubies. The examiner drew the head to the hole, and found it sound and firm, as were also the teeth and a list of gold, about an inch broad, surrounding the temples. There were also white linen and gold-coloured flowered silk, that fell to pieces on being touched. These were shown to the Dean of Westminster, Dr. Dolben, Archbishop of York, and Dr. Sancroft, Archbishop of Canterbury, and at length deposited with the King, and the coffin secured with a new one bound in iron.

EDITHA "THE FAIR."

The father of Editha—Godiva, wife of Leofric—Wealth and power of the Earl of Coventry—The famous legend considered—Leofric's munificence to the Church—The lines in the painted window—Godiva's donation of gems and goldsmith's work to Coventry Abbey—Algar, the father of Editha the Fair, flies to Wales—Marries his daughter to the Welsh Prince, Griffith ap Llewellyn — Nest, his first wife—Her sons—Griffith ap Conan and his wife Angharaud—Violent contentions of the Welsh and English—Restoration of Algar—Harold pursues the Welsh—Defeats them — Lays siege to and burns Ruddlan Castle — Editha the Fair taken prisoner — Death of Griffith — Harold marries his widow — Hereford destroyed and re-fortified — Harold's pillars — His breach of promise to Adeliza — Harold becomes King — The battle of Hastings — The search for the body — Editha the Swan-necked — The Recluse of Chester — Eddeva Dives — Her possessions seized by the Conqueror — Stortford in Hertfordshire — The tomb discovered.

EDITHA the Fair was the daughter of Algar, the third Earl of Chester and Coventry, and grand-daughter of Leofric the Third, husband of Godiva, so famous in traditional story. The title of Earl of Warwick and Earl of Leicester were more than once borne by the noble representatives of this family, but they are more commonly spoken of as Earls of Mercia.

Godiva, the grandmother of Editha, appears to have been sister of the first Queen of Ethelred the Unready; both were daughters of Earl Thorold, Sheriff of Lincolnshire, the founder of Spalding Abbey. Leofric was a warlike and powerful chief, who, in 1057, led an army in defence of Ethelred against the Danish King, Sweyn.[1]

The great wealth and power of Leofric, and the liberality of both himself and his wife Godiva to the Church, secured them the good repute of the monkish chroniclers. Perhaps the legendary tale of Godiva's ride through the silent streets of Coventry is not altogether a poet's fiction: the manners of the time were still rude and coarse, and a penance of any sort for the good of the Church was considered a worthy act. That Leofric granted many advantages to the city of Coventry, to his benevolent consort's prayers, is very probable; and in memory of the

[1] Some years ago the seal of the Earl of Mercia, Alfric or Leofric, was discovered in digging a bank near Winchester, and was found to bear the following inscription: — "+ Sigillum Alfric Al." The figure exhibited on the seal holds the sword with which the earls were installed in their new dignity. The head of Alfric is also encircled with a diadem similar to that borne by King Ethelred on his coins, — a proof of his high dignity. This noble was among the first to assent to the tribute called the Danegelt.

delivery of the citizens from oppressive enactments, the effigies of Leofric and Godiva were long to be seen in a window in the old church of Trinity, at Coventry, in which the Earl holds in his hand a charter, inscribed with lines which might have given rise to the legend—

"I, Leurich, for love of thee
Doe make Coventry toll free."

Godiva, on her own account, was a great benefactress to the city, and bestowed much wealth on the monastery there, which had been founded by Leofric and Godwin jointly. She showered on the monks jewels and ornaments, "having sent for skilful goldsmiths, who, with all the gold and silver she had, made crosses, images of saints, and other decorations." The value of the jewels bestowed on Coventry Abbey are said to be inestimable; and on her death-bed the Countess bequeathed a precious circlet of gems, which she wore round her neck, valued at one hundred marks of silver (about 2000*l.* of our money), to the image of the Virgin in Coventry Abbey, praying that all who come thither would say as many prayers as there were gems in it![1]

Leofric died in 1057, and was succeeded in the Earldom of Mercia by his son Algar, whose family consisted of two sons, Edwin and Morcar—names which occur frequently in the history of the continued struggles of the times—and of two daughters, Editha, sometimes called Edgifa, and Lucia.

The year after his accession to the paternal inheritance, Algar was outlawed by King Edward, the Confessor, but soon afterwards he recovered his earldom by the help of Griffith ap Llewelyn, King of Wales, and the Northmen. To return this well-timed favour, the hand of Editha, the beautiful daughter of Algar, was afterwards bestowed by the Earl on the Welsh king.

Ranulf, or Nest, as she is more frequently called, was the first Queen of Griffith ap Llewelyn, and had borne to him three children, Meredith, Ithel, and Agnes. She was daughter of Alfred King of Man, and the Isles, and after the death of her first husband, a King of Ulster, had married Conan, king of North Wales, son of Jago ap Edwal. Her son by these second nuptials is known in history as Griffith ap Conan, and was born and educated at Dublin. This prince was a remarkable person in his times, and has been thus quaintly described:—"Griffith in his person was of moderate stature, having yellow hair, a round face, and a fair and agreeable complexion, eyes rather large, light eyebrows, a comely beard, a round neck, white skin, strong limbs, long fingers, straight legs, and handsome feet. He was, moreover, skilful in divers languages, courteous and civil to his friends, fierce to his enemies, and resolute in battle; of a passionate temper, and fertile imagination." To him the Welsh people were indebted for a reform in their minstrels and national music. The mother and grandmother of Griffith being natives of Ireland, "the land of harps and harmony," they derived from them some of the best tunes, better performers, and a higher order of instruments. This King also built castles and churches, planted trees, orchards and

[1] Saxon Chronicle, Fl. Wigorn, R. Wendover.

gardens, and cultivated the soil. Maintaining peace with his neighbours, he appointed his sons guardians of the frontiers, and the petty princes repaired to his court for protection.[1]

The Welsh monk, to whom we are indebted for the Life of Griffith ap Conan, thus describes his Queen Angharaud, whose name is even at the present day held in honour in Wales:—"She was an accomplished person. Her hair was long and of a flaxen colour, her eyes large and rolling, and her features brilliant and beautiful. She was tall and well-proportioned, her leg and foot handsome, her fingers long, and her nails thin and transparent. She was good-tempered, cheerful, discreet, and witty; gave advice, as well as alms, to her needy dependents, and never transgressed the laws of duty."[2]

Overtaken by blindness in his old age, Griffith devoted himself to religion. Perceiving he was approaching the hour of dissolution, he sent for his sons, and gave his last directions, his Queen Angharaud being present. After a variety of bequests to the place of his birth and the churches he desired to advance, with those religious men who officiated in them, he bestowed his blessing on his sons,[3] foretelling the various fortunes of each, and the character he should support, enjoining them to combat their enemies with resolution and constancy, as he had himself done to show them an example. To Angharaud he bequeathed one-half of his personal estates, with two portions in land, and the customs at Aber-menai. To his daughters and nephews, who were also present, he appointed a sufficient legacy for their maintenance.[4] At the time when Griffith ap Conan died, A. D. 1136, he had attained his eighty-second year: he was interred on the left side of the great altar at Bangor.[5]

At the period of Editha's marriage with the step-father of this Griffith he was very young; he was about fourteen when she was married to Harold, and with his half-brothers and sisters lived in state at the castle of Griffith ap Llewelyn, at Rhuddlan.

---

[1] Yorke's Royal Tribes of Wales; Sebright MSS. Life of Griffith ap Conan.

[2] Angharaud's father was Owen ap Edwyn, Lord of Englefield: her great-grandfather Grono was founder of the tribe which bore his name. The tribe which derived its origin from Griffith ap Conan was ranked the first of the *five royal tribes of Wales.* The fifteen common tribes were all of North Wales, and their respective representatives, forming the nobility, were lords of distinct districts, and always bore some hereditary office in the palace; it being one of the laws of King Howel Dha that the Court of Wales should possess twenty-four great officers.

[3] Angharaud had a numerous family. Three sons bore the names of Owen, Cadwallader, and Cadwallo; and five daughters, of whom one was married to Griffith ap Rhys, King of South Wales, one of the ancestors of Owen Tudor. This high-spirited princess, who was called "Gwenlian," a term equivalent to "white linen," heading an army in her husband's favour, was taken prisoner in the battle and put to death. Her sister Susanna married Madog ap Maredudd; and Maryed, the offspring of their union, espoused Jorwerth Drwyndurn, by whom she had Llewelyn the Great. — Yorke's Royal Tribes of Wales.

[4] Rhys, brother of Griffith, having been taken prisoner by the English in 1053, was, by Edward's orders, put to death at Balandune, and his head sent to the King, then holding his court at Gloucester.

[5] Yorke's Royal Tribes of Wales.

When Algar sought assistance from Griffith ap Llewelyn, the commander sent by King Edward against their united forces was Harold, who, destined afterwards to become the husband of the young bride of the Welsh king, was to the end of his career his most mortal foe. He pursued the Welsh into their mountain fastnesses, inured his soldiers to similar hardships as that hardy people, and spared no pains to conquer so resolute and so dangerous a foe to the English.

Throughout Griffith's life, even after Algar had recovered his earldom by the tame acquiescence of King Edward, that prince never ceased attacking and annoying the country, out of which every precaution was taken in vain to keep him. Ruthless and savage, and glad of any excuse to contend against England, Griffith was still fighting for Algar when they laid waste together the English borders, and approaching within two miles of Hereford, encountered Ranulf, Earl of Hereford, whom, with his forces, they put to flight. Having entered the city, they burnt the minster, and slew seven of the canons in their attempt to defend it, levelled the walls, and fired the city. Many noble persons were put to death by the combined armies, and others carried off captive, the conquerors returning into Wales laden with their spoils. Harold's orders at this time were to assemble all the forces of the kingdom at Gloucester. At the head of the army the son of Godwin advanced as far as Snowdon; but hearing that Griffith and Algar had retreated into North Wales, he returned to Hereford, leaving a part of his army to keep the country in awe. He took this opportunity to rebuild the walls of Hereford and fortify the city. Meantime he negotiated a peace with Griffith, which has been esteemed dishonourable to that prince. It stipulated that Algar should be freely pardoned, without making any compensation for the damages done or expenses caused by the war. On this the Earl returned to Chester, and afterwards repaired to the court of Edward, from whom he obtained a confirmation of his pardon and dignity, A. D. 1058.

Griffith, husband of Editha, afterwards openly violated the peace he had made with the King, by an inroad into Herefordshire, when the Bishop of Hereford was slain at Glastonbury, as well as the viscompte or sheriff of the county, and many other persons. Again, however, peace was restored by the mediation of Harold and the Earl of Mercia.

In 1063, Algar, who had again forfeited, once more recovered his earldom.

The patience of the Confessor having been at length exhausted by these repeated incursions, he determined to utterly subdue the rebellious Welsh; and once more employed the son of Godwin as his general. At the head of a large army, Harold arrived in North Wales, having taken his measures with such expedition and good order, as nearly to surprise Griffith in his palace at Rhuddlan. Scarcely had the Welsh king effected his escape, with a few attendants, to one of his own ships, which set sail instantly and placed him beyond the reach of his enemies, when Harold and the English appeared before his castle gates; and such was the mortification of Harold at his escape, that he burnt the royal residence, and set fire to every ship and vessel left in the harbour. If Editha, at this disastrous epoch, was the companion of Griffith's flight, she must soon after have fallen into the hands of Harold. That chieftain returned to Bristol, where he fitted out a new fleet, and sailed round the Welsh coast. His brother Tostig, meanwhile, had marched into North Wales, where Harold landed, and they joined their forces for the final destruction of the unfortunate Welsh. These were driven out of their last retreats, and forced to sue for peace. Without their King, having no means of defence, and destitute of provisions, they could hold out no longer; they renounced their oath of allegiance to Griffith, and gave hostages to Harold for the secure payment of their ancient tribute. The triumphant Harold commemorated this occasion by erecting several stone pillars, each of which bore the pompous inscription, "HIC FUIT VICTOR HAROLDUS!"[1]

A. D. 1064. Griffith returned, the summer afterwards, to North Wales, where he landed, and endeavoured to raise a violent opposition to Harold, who was then in South Wales, part of which he had subdued. Some disaffection, however, had sprung up among the people, who, though fear had influenced them when they renounced their fealty in favour of the English, did not now welcome their King as he expected. Far from rallying under his standard, they listened to the instigations of Harold, and put their brave monarch to death, whose head, with the prow of the vessel in which he had returned, they sent to the son of Godwin.[2] "The idol of his people and terror of his enemies," as Griffith has been termed, fell thus ignominiously at the close of a thirty-four years' reign. He was renowned for his skill in government, ability in war, and those amiable manners which had commanded the affection of all who knew him.

After Griffith's death, Harold married Editha the Fair; their nuptials took place A. D. 1065,[3] and on the chief quitting Wales, Editha accompanied him as his wife.

Harold had been married before, but the name of his first wife is unknown. On her death, he had contracted to marry Adeliza, one of the daughters of William the Conqueror, who had aimed thus to unite his family to one whom Edward, who was childless, designed as his successor. Harold, when he married Editha, and broke through his promise to William, did it in the hope of strengthening his interest at home; for by this match he bound the two powerful Earls, Edwin and Morcar, the brothers of Editha, and with them the English, their adherents, to espouse his cause, and from this time the son of Godwin openly aspired to the succession. Tostig, Harold's brother, had been so tyrannical in his rule over the Northumbrians, that they rebelled, and he was forced to fly. Edwin and Morcar had taken part in the insurrection, and the former had been elected in the place of Tostig. Before the engagement, Morcar, knowing the generous temper of Harold, endeavoured to justify his own conduct, representing how unworthily Tostig had acted, and even urging that such conduct could not be supported even by a brother, without sharing in the infamy attached to it; that the Northumbrians were willing to submit to Edward, but only under a leader who would respect their rights; "that they had been taught by their ancestors, that death

[1] "William of Jumièges gives an account of Harold's victory in Wales.

[2] Yorke's Royal Tribes of Wales, Warrington. [3] Ordericus Vitalis.

was preferable to servitude, and had taken the field determined to perish rather than suffer a renewal of those indignities to which they had so long been exposed; and they trusted that Harold, on reflection, would not defend in a brother that violent conduct from which he himself, in his own government, had always kept at so great a distance." This vigorous remonstrance was accompanied with such a detail of facts, and so well supported, that Harold found it prudent to abandon his brother's cause; and returning to Edward, he persuaded him to pardon the Northumbrians, and to confirm Morcar in the government.[1] This moderation gained the affections of the people.

On the death of Algar, in 1065, Edwin succeeded, through Harold's interest, to the earldom, and thus the two brothers had considerable authority in the country.

Edward the Confessor, soon after dying, Harold, without any formality, snatched the crown of the realm, which he is said, like his predecessor, Harold Harefoot, to have put on his head with his own hands, at Lambeth: he was afterwards crowned at St. Paul's. The ceremony[2] of Harold's coronation is one of the subjects represented on the Bayeux tapestry. In this celebrated specimen of female art, one man offers him the crown, another a battle-axe. Harold appears on his throne, with the globe and cross in his left hand, and a sceptre in his right. On his right hand stand two men who are presenting to him a sword, and Stigand, the Archbishop, is standing on his left. The inscriptions are: "Here they gave the crown to King Harold: here sits Harold, King of the English, Stigand Archbishop.' There is no mention made of Editha, but most likely she shared in the coronation honours. Harold, on some of his coins, is represented with a diadem of pearls which he bears on a helmet. Although Editha is not styled "*Regina*" in Domesday Book, her regal rank is proved not only by her immense possessions, but by her having a chaplain, and by her also having for a tenant "a man of noble birth."[3]

Editha must have been more than ordinarily remarkable for personal beauty. She is always termed "the most beautiful Editha:"[4] the Domesday Book calls her Eddeva "Pulchra," and Eddeva "Faera:" even the Normans attest her remarkable beauty. Throughout the Domesday Survey, Harold is never mentioned as king; his wife, therefore, would not be likely to be designated as a queen. Another reason for this omission is obvious. Harold had been contracted to the daughter of William, and had broken his faith. The Conqueror could not forgive the insult, and would not acknowledge Harold or his wife to be legitimate heirs of the throne. Some writers say that William bitterly reproached Harold for his perfidy; others state that the young Princess

[1] Turner, Hume. [2] History of Lambeth Palace, Turner, Selden.

[3] Sir Henry Ellis, who says truly, that there was so short a time "between the battle of Hastings and the Conqueror's distribution of forfeited lands, that we cannot wonder to find every mention of a wife of Harold omitted in the Domesday returns."

[4] Jumiège. Saxon Chronicle.

of Normandy was dead at the time when Harold espoused Editha the Fair.

Under whatever circumstances Editha had become Queen of Harold, whether with or without her consent, after the death of her turbulent husband Griffith, to whom she was united by her father's policy, and who was much older than herself, she did not enjoy the regal honours of the English sway for more than a few months. Harold fell at Hastings within a year after his becoming king, and of all his glory and his valour nothing remained but a mangled corpse, sought for on the battle-field by two monks, who, unable to identify it, besought the aid of Editha the Fair, or the Swan-necked,—a personage about whom historians differ so widely, that it is impossible to pronounce positively whether she was the beautiful Queen herself, or a favourite of Harold's, whose beauty had gained her the same title as distinguished the consort of the monarch.

The mother of Harold is said to have offered its weight in gold for her son's body, and every possible effort was made to discover it amongst the slain. If it had really been found, the legend could scarcely have existed of the unfortunate King having been borne by secret friends from the field, his wounds healed by their care, and becoming afterwards a solitary hermit in a cave on the banks of the Dee, near the Abbey of St. John's at Chester, disclosing at length, on his death-bed, the fact of his identity. Equally uncertain must be the story of Editha the Swan-necked finding his body.

Queen Editha the Fair was at all events in London after the fatal battle, whither her brothers marched in great haste, to persuade the Londoners to advance them to the kingdom. Dreading the treatment their sister might receive from the hands of the Norman Conqueror, these Earls sent her from London to Chester,[1] which was a part of their own territories. Some say she was sent to West-Chester or Winchester. She resigned her regal rank from that time, and passed the rest of her life in obscurity. This prudent conduct did not, however, disarm the vengeance of William. "Eddeva Pulchra" was also known as "Eddeva Dives," from the great amount of her property; and the broad lands of the widowed Queen were seized by the successful Norman. These amounted to 27,600 acres.[2] Her fee in Cambridgeshire alone[3] was considered of sufficient value to form part of the noble reward bestowed by William upon Alan, first Earl of Richmond; and thus deprived of her rich inheritance and possessions, the widow of Griffith and Harold was compelled to seek the cloister as an asylum for her closing existence, not only as a place of safety, but a means of securing even a subsistence. A talented authoress of our own times,[4] in writing of Queen Editha, states that "the convent to which she retired, the date of her death, her place of burial, are alike unknown; and the record of her broad lands, and the fame of her beauty,

---

[1] Holinshed, Domesday Book.

[2] Holinshed, Florence of Worcester.

[3] Among these estates was the house and lands known by the name of Harold's Park. Harold received from his property in the manor of Waltham 36*l.*, in the time of King Edward the Confessor. — Ogborne.

[4] Miss Lawrence.

are all that now remain to us of Editha the Fair." One single line, however, preserved in Leland, informs us that the widow of Harold, after having lived through the greater part of the reign of William the Conqueror, deprived of regal dignity, stripped of lands and estates, the survivor of her parents, of two husbands and brothers, and of her namesake, Editha the Good, the widow of Edward closed a life of vicissitude and trial, in piety and peace, and was buried *and worshipped as a saint*, at Stortford, in Hertfordshire.[1] About twelve years ago, some workmen of that town, being employed in making preparations for an interment near the font of the church, came upon an ancient vault, exactly underneath it, constructed of rubble, and supposed to be as old as the Saxon times. This vault is considered the repository of the last remains of Editha the Fair, wife of the Saxon King Harold.

[1] "S. Aldgytha sepulta est in Storteford." (St. Algitha was buried at Stortford.) — Leland.

THE END.

www.ingramcontent.com/pod-product-compliance
Lightning Source LLC
LaVergne TN
LVHW020936110826
845150LV00004B/883